MIDDLE CHILDHOOD *to* MIDDLE ADOLESCENCE

DEVELOPMENT FROM AGES 8 TO 18

Libby Balter Blume
University of Detroit Mercy

Mary Jo Zembar
Wittenberg University

Upper Saddle River, New Jersey
Columbus, Ohio

Library of Congress Cataloging-in-Publication Data
Blume, Libby Balter.
Middle childhood to middle adolescence: development from ages 8 to 18/Libby Balter Blume, Mary Jo Zembar.
p. cm.
Includes bibliographical references and indexes.
ISBN 0-13-049490-9
1. Child development – Textbooks. 2. Adolescence – Textbooks.

HQ772.B55127 2007
305.231–dc22 2006041303

Vice President and Executive Publisher: Jeffery W. Johnston
Publisher: Kevin M. Davis
Development Editor: Autumn Crisp Benson
Editorial Assistant: Sarah N. Kenoyer
Production Editor: Mary Harlan
Production Coordinator: Rebecca K. Giusti, GGS Book Services
Design Coordinator: Diane C. Lorenzo
Photo Coordinator: Lori Whitley
Text Design and Illustrations: GGS Book Services
Cover Design: Candace Rowley
Cover Image: Workbook Stock
Production Manager: Laura Messerly
Director of Marketing: David Gesell
Marketing Manager: Autumn Purdy
Marketing Coordinator: Brian Mounts

This book was set in Garamond by GGS Book Services. It was printed and bound by Bind-Rite Graphics. The cover was printed by Phoenix Color Corp.

Photo Credits: Adamsmith/Getty Images, Inc.-Taxi: p. 193; Brady/PH College: p. 292; Michelle D. Bridwell/PhotoEdit Inc.: p. 223; Russell D. Curtis/Photo Researchers, Inc.: p. 127; Laima Druskis/PH College: pp. 324, 336; EyeWire Collection/Getty Images, Inc.-Photodisc: p. 96; © Randy Faris/Corbis: p. 130; © Tim Farrell/Star Ledger/Corbis: p. 58; Tony Freeman/PhotoEdit Inc.: p. 240; Eugene Gordon/PH College: pp. 308, 316; Steve Gorton © Dorling Kindersley: p. 81; Krista Greco/Merrill: pp. 43, 53, 263; Jeff Greenberg/PhotoEdit Inc.: p. 162; Ken Karp/PH College: p. 217; © Karen Kasmauski/Corbis: p. 88; Barnabas Kindersley © Dorling Kindersley: p. 109; Anthony Magnacca/Merrill: pp. 12, 107, 182, 203, 296; Tom McCarthy/PhotoEdit Inc.: p. 32; Pearson Learning Photo Studio: p. 274; Robert Pham/PH College: p. 340; Photolibrary.Com: p. 200; © Royalty-Free/Corbis: pp. 61, 232; Valerie Schultz/Merrill: p. 168; Silver Burdett Ginn: pp. 152, 372; Stockbyte: pp. 255, 270, 357; Vincent P. Walter/PH College: p. 379; Patrick White/Merrill: p. 20; Lori Whitley/Merrill: p. 348; David Young-Wolff/PhotoEdit Inc.: pp. 2, 147, 300; Shirley Zeiberg/PH College: pp. 52, 138, 391.

Pearson Education Ltd.
Pearson Education Singapore Pte. Ltd.
Pearson Education Canada, Ltd.
Pearson Education–Japan
Pearson Education Australia Pty. Limited
Pearson Education North Asia Ltd.
Pearson Educación de Mexico, S.A. de C.V.
Pearson Education Malaysia Pte. Ltd.

10 9 8 7 6 5 4 3 2 1
ISBN: 0-13-049490-9

FOREWORD

All readers of this book care about children and adolescents. Certainly, as students studying theory and research about human development during these periods of life, or as professors using this text as a resource in teaching about developmental science, readers have an investment in understanding the facts of childhood and adolescence. However, I believe that readers and instructors regard the subject matter of this book as more than matters of academic or intellectual interest. Children and adolescents—young people—are valued in and of themselves. We have all been young, many of us have or will have children of our own, and we all live in social networks, as family members, neighbors, friends, and community members, with children and adolescents. We are emotionally as well as intellectually invested in young people, and this is why we care deeply about the subject matter of this book.

We want to not just understand the facts of child and adolescent development. We want to know how, through the developmental science produced by the scholars whose work you will read about in this book, we can improve the lives of young people. We want to know how we can foster well-being and thriving among children and adolescents. Readers expect, then, more from a textbook about children and adolescents than a recounting of theory and the results of research. They want to be given tools for action. They want to learn what they can do—as scholars, educators, parents, practitioners, or citizens—to promote the positive and healthy development of young people.

Readers of *Middle Childhood to Middle Adolescence: Development from Ages 8 to 18* will not be disappointed. Their expectations for gaining cutting-edge understanding of childhood and adolescence, and for being given resources to use in enhancing the lives of youth, will be fulfilled in every chapter of this book. Professors Blume and Zembar have masterfully integrated the best of theory and research about development during the childhood and adolescent years with sage counsel about how to apply developmental science to improve the lives of the diverse children of our communities, nation, and world.

I want to underscore that the importance of this text extends beyond the superb and insightful integration of theory, research, and application that fills its pages. This text is also a model for how developmental science should be structured and enacted in the 21st century. Kurt Lewin, the renowned Gestalt psychologist, once said that there is nothing as practical as a good theory. Today, this insight has been extended by scholars of child and adolescent development. Through the integrations of science and application presented by Professors Blume and Zembar, contemporary developmental scientists demonstrate that there is nothing more important for the promotion of healthy children and strong families than sound scientific information used in collaborations among people from all sectors of communities, including academics, policy makers, practitioners, and youth and parents themselves.

Readers of this book will be treated to excellent and erudite writing as well as to an important and exciting vision for how we all, as citizens who care about the future of our youth and of the nation they will lead when they move into adulthood, may apply developmental science in actions that will promote positive development among diverse young people. After reading *Middle Childhood to Middle Adolescence: Development from Ages 8 to 18*, I know you will share with me gratitude toward Professors Blume and Zembar for the excellence of their effort. I believe you will also share with me great enthusiasm for pursuing the vision they convey about how we may all act to use knowledge about children and adolescents to make their lives and our world better.

Richard M. Lerner
Bergstrom Chair in
Applied Developmental Science
Director, Institute for Applied Research
in Youth Development
Tufts University
Medford, MA

Why We Wrote This Book

When we first discussed writing a textbook on middle childhood and adolescence three years ago, it was because no developmental text existed that focused specifically on the school years. That is still true as we go to press. School-age children are typically discussed by authors of life-span texts in only three brief chapters on middle childhood, or not addressed at all by authors of textbooks on adolescence. As a result, one of us has been using no text at all for her course on middle childhood and adolescence for several years. We heard many similar complaints from instructors who were teaching courses in psychology, teacher education, and child development across the country.

To prepare for this exciting project, we had many lively discussions with professors, researchers, and practitioners at the meetings of the Society for Research on Child Development, the Society for Research on Adolescence, the American Educational Research Association Special Interest Group on Middle Level Education, the MacArthur Research Network on Middle Childhood, the National Middle School Association, and the National Council on Family Relations. It became immediately clear that teaching resources on the middle childhood years were in short supply.

Middle Childhood to Middle Adolescence is written for advanced undergraduate courses that focus on the period from ages 8 to 18. By beginning with the period after early childhood and following children's development through middle adolescence, we intend this text to be a new and integrative resource for practitioners who work with school-age children from late elementary through high school. A major contribution of the text is to clarify what we mean by middle childhood, early and middle adolescence, and youth studies. All too often, many textbooks simply ignore the overlaps and ambiguities of this developmental period.

Special features of this text include:

- **A Focus on Developmental Pathways.** We explore the ways in which middle childhood and adolescence are considered both stages of development and transitional periods in three overview chapters called "Perspectives on Middle Childhood," "Perspectives on Middle Adolescence," and "Beyond Middle Adolescence: Emerging Adulthood."
- **A Developmental-Contextual Orientation.** Each chapter includes key research on the ecologies of home, school, and community highlighted in separate sections called "Contexts of Development" situating the study of middle childhood and adolescence in a historical and cultural context.
- **An Applied Developmental Perspective.** Throughout the text, current research is translated into practical applications for educators, parents, and other professionals in the special feature "Guideposts for Working with School-Age Children or Adolescents."
- **Integrated Discussion of Theories.** Rather than one abstract introductory chapter, psychological theories of development are applied throughout the text to address particular chapter content in integrated sections called "Theoretical Viewpoints."
- **Roadmaps to Understanding.** In each chapter, pedagogical boxes called "Roadmaps to Understanding Theory and Research" and "Roadmaps to Successful Practice" are included that alert students to key illustrations of chapter content.
- **Reflection Questions.** Throughout each chapter, students are presented with "Stop and Reflect" questions to encourage continuing integration of the chapter content with their own life experiences.
- **Suggested Activities, Readings, and Electronic Resources.** Included at the end of each chapter are up-to-date suggestions for instructors and students that extend the chapter content with opportunities for further learning.

In *Middle Childhood to Middle Adolescence*, we have utilized an applied "lens" to examine middle childhood (and in later chapters, middle adolescence) in order to facilitate several important student objectives:

1. To illustrate the *role of theory* in guiding research and practice
2. To *integrate basic and applied* research findings on middle childhood and adolescent development
3. To provide practitioners and educators with examples of research-based *prevention and intervention strategies*

4. To position the study of middle childhood and adolescence as a *reflexive* activity, or one in which readers reflect on their own experiences as valid sources of information
5. To help readers translate their own research questions into meaningful *action and results*
6. To promote *praxis*, or the dynamic interaction between action and critical reflection

As with the study of middle childhood and adolescence, writing this textbook has created both risks and opportunities. The risks, of course, lie in our hope that instructors and students will find the book useful and stimulating. The opportunities, however, reside in the process itself. Writing this text, we have learned from each other as we applied current literature to the exciting period from middle childhood to middle adolescence.

Online Test Bank

The Test Bank that accompanies this text contains 25–30 multiple-choice questions and 3–5 essay questions for each chapter. To access the online test bank, go to **www.prenhall.com**, click on the Instructor Support button, and then go to the Download Supplements section. Here you will be able to login or complete a one-time registration for a user name and password.

Acknowledgments

We thank our generous and loving families for patiently supporting our seemingly endless writing; the faculty, administrators, and students of our respective institutions, University of Detroit Mercy and Wittenberg University, for the faculty leaves so necessary for completing this project; Richard Lerner for writing an inspirational foreword; our development editor, Autumn Benson, for teaching us the myriad details of publication; and our publisher, Kevin Davis, for trusting us with this project from the initial proposal to its successful completion.

We would also like to thank the following reviewers for providing helpful suggestions on each chapter: Mary Abouzeid, University of Virginia; Lori Beasley, University of Central Oklahoma; Jacki Booth, San Diego State University; Margaret Z. Booth, Bowling Green State University; Eugene Folden, Ohio State University; Deborah Lewis Fravel, Indiana University; Albert H. Gardner, University of Maryland; Kimberly J. Hartman, University of North Carolina, Charlotte; Kathryn Herr, Montclair State University; Joan D. Ladderbush, California State University, San Bernardino–Palm Desert Campus; Ronald L. Mullis, Florida State University; Nancy Nordmann, National-Louis University; Sharon Seidman, California State University, Fullerton; Holly Thornton, University of North Carolina, Greensboro; and Manfred Van Dulmen, University of Minnesota.

Libby Balter Blume
Detroit, Michigan

Mary Jo Zembar
Springfield, Ohio

How to Use This Book

This text is about middle childhood and adolescence. It is also about the interplay between basic research and the applied questions that are often asked by parents, teachers, and other practitioners who work with school-age children and teenagers. Lastly, it is about the real world contexts of growing up. These three goals are illustrated in Figure 1, envisioned as a road to acquiring competence in working with children from ages 8 to 18.

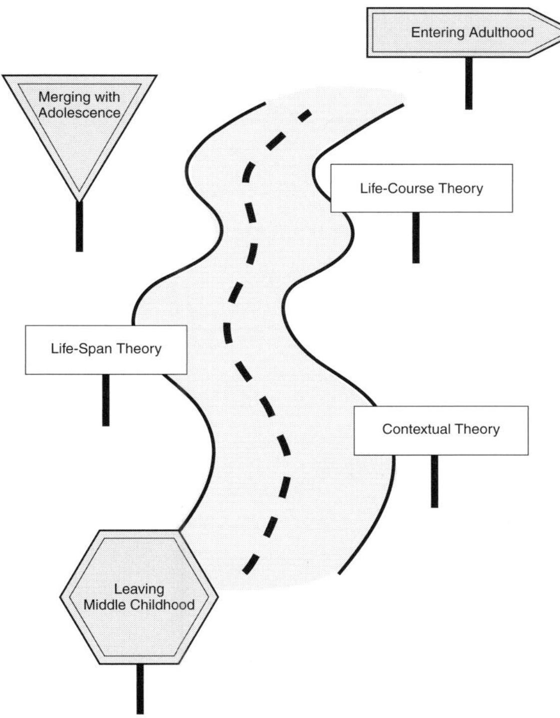

FIGURE 1 Goals of This Book
The goals of this book can be seen as a road to acquiring competence in working with school-age children and adolescents.

Goal 1: To Recognize Developmental Changes in Middle Childhood and Adolescence

This textbook is divided into two main parts. Part One focuses on the middle childhood years, from 8 to 12. In chapter 2, we describe the multiple ways that this age period has been defined by the people who work with and care for school-age children. Then in chapters 3 to 6, the four basic areas of middle childhood development are covered—including physical, cognitive, affective, and social development. In Part Two, chapter 7 provides an overview of the teenage years. Then in chapters 8 to 11, the same four areas of development are discussed for middle adolescence. Chapter 12 concludes the book with a brief view into development beyond high school. Throughout these chapters, current research is translated into practical applications for people working with school-age children, adolescents, or emerging adults.

Goal 2: To Understand Theories of Middle Childhood and Adolescent Development

Specific theories of development are integrated throughout the text in order to better address the particular content presented in each chapter. In chapter 1, we begin with the purpose of theories and the methods of doing research on middle childhood and adolescent development. In the overview chapters on middle childhood and middle adolescence (2 and 7), we present major theories that provide important perspectives on overall development, such as developmental-contextual theory. But in the content chapters, we selected specific theories to illustrate a particular developmental area, such as Piaget's theory of cognitive development or Bowlby's theory of emotional attachment. Finally, in chapter 12, we discuss how these theories work together to explain middle childhood and adolescent development. At the end of each chapter, a table summarizes the theory or theories presented in the chapter to help you review what you have read.

Goal 3: To Appreciate the Diverse Contexts of Middle Childhood and Adolescence

Each chapter concludes with a discussion of research in the cultural contexts of home, school, and community. The purpose of these sections is to locate the study of middle childhood and adolescence in diverse contexts. We discuss family, peer, and neighborhood influences on middle childhood and middle adolescent development, focusing on the each chapter's specific area of development.

A METAPHOR FOR LEARNING

Throughout the text, we have utilized the metaphor of *travel* to characterize your journey as a student. The boxes labeled "Roadmaps to Understanding" provide detailed extensions of the chapters' content. Interspersed through each chapter are "Guideposts for Working with School-Age Children or Adolescents" to stimulate your application of the basic research that you just read about. Throughout the text, you will find "Stop and Reflect" questions that ask you to think about your own pathways and life experiences.

We wish you a successful trip through *Middle Childhood to Middle Adolescence*!

Libby Balter Blume
Mary Jo Zembar

ABOUT THE AUTHORS

Libby Balter Blume earned a Ph.D. in human development from Texas Tech University. Professor and certified family life educator at the University of Detroit Mercy, she directs the developmental psychology and family life education program. Blume teaches undergraduate and graduate courses in child, adolescent, and lifespan human development; family relations; community development; visual communications; and women's studies. She has extensive experience as an art educator, preschool teacher, child development center director, and consultant to Head Start programs and to schools for gifted children from elementary to high school. Her research focuses on peer and family co-constructions of identity, ethnicity, and gender in middle childhood and adolescence. Blume has published articles in such journals as *Sex Education, Journal of Marriage and Family, Journal of Family Issues, Journal of Teaching in Marriage and Family*, and *Identity: An International Journal of Theory and Research* and is founding editor of the *Michigan Family Review*. When she is not teaching, writing, or editing, Blume enjoys spending time with her adult children and cooking gourmet meals with her husband for their friends and family.

Mary Jo Zembar earned a Ph.D. in developmental psychology from the University of Houston. Professor and chair of psychology at Wittenberg University, she directs the department's internship program. Zembar teaches undergraduate courses in child and adolescent development, adult development and aging, and childhood psychopathology. She has served several school systems and preschools as an assessment consultant. Her research focuses on memory development and function in childhood and old age, and she has more recently carried out research on contexts of socialization in middle childhood and rejection sensitivity in adolescent dating relationships. Zembar has published articles in such journals as *Personality and Individual Differences, Psychological Bulletin*, and *Journal of Experimental Child Psychology*. She has two children in the throes of middle childhood and enjoys eating the gourmet meals her husband prepares for the family.

BRIEF CONTENTS

PART ONE: TRANSITION FROM EARLY CHILDHOOD

1 Studying Middle Childhood and Adolescence 2

2 Perspectives on Middle Childhood 32

3 Physical Development in Middle Childhood 58

4 Cognitive Development in Middle Childhood 96

5 Affective Development in Middle Childhood 130

6 Social Development in Middle Childhood 162

PART TWO: TRANSITION TO ADOLESCENCE

7 Perspectives on Middle Adolescence 200

8 Physical Development in Middle Adolescence 232

9 Cognitive Development in Middle Adolescence 270

10 Affective Development in Middle Adolescence 300

11 Social Development in Middle Adolescence 336

12 Beyond Middle Adolescence: Emerging Adulthood 372

Appendix: A Primer in Research Design 397
References 401
Author Index 455
Subject Index 469

CONTENTS

PART ONE Transition from Early Childhood

CHAPTER 1
Studying Middle Childhood and Adolescence 2

Understanding Development 4
Theoretical Questions About Human Development 4
Linking Theory and Research 6
Linking Research with Practice 6
Studying Change over Time 6
Cross-Sectional Research Designs 6
Longitudinal Research Designs 7
Longitudinal-Sequential Research Designs 9
Variable-Centered Versus Person-Centered Approaches 9
Methods of Collecting Data 11
Quantitative Data Collection 11
Evaluating Quantitative Data 17
Qualitative Data Collection 18
Evaluating Qualitative Data 22
Conducting Your Own Research 23
Action Research 24
Program Evaluation 25
Ethical Guidelines 26
Chapter Review 27

CHAPTER 2
Perspectives on Middle Childhood 32

Defining the Middle Childhood Years 34
Reasons to Study Middle Childhood 35
Historical Views of Middle Childhood 36
Modern Contributions to Understanding Middle Childhood 37
Meanings of Childhood in Postmodern Societies 40
Developmental Milestones in Middle Childhood 44
Theoretical Viewpoints 45
The Ecology of Human Development 45
Developmental-Contextual Theory 47
Contexts of Middle Childhood 50
Families as Context 50
School as Context 51
Communities as Context 52
Chapter Review 56

CHAPTER 3
Physical Development in Middle Childhood 58

Middle Childhood Biological Development 60
Theoretical Viewpoints 60
Genetic Perspectives 60
Biological Perspectives 62
The Interaction of Nature and Nurture 62
Physical Development 63
Changes in Body Size 63
Changes in Body Proportions 67
Skeletal Development 68
Body Fat Levels and Muscle Mass 69
Contributions of Genetics, Biology, and Environment 70
Brain Development 71
Neuronal Development 72
Related Changes in Function 75
Contributions of Genetics, Biology, and Environment 75
Motor Skill Development 80
Gross and Fine Motor Skills 80
Perceptual-Motor Skills 81
Health and Well-Being 82
Functions of Physical Activity 82
Exercise 84
Sports Participation 84
Nutrition and Body Status 85
Development in Context 89
Family Contexts 89
School Contexts 90
Community Contexts 90
Chapter Review 92

CHAPTER 4
Cognitive Development in Middle Childhood 96

Cognition in Middle Childhood 98
Theoretical Viewpoints 98
Piaget's Cognitive Developmental Theory 98
The Concrete Operational Child 99
Basis of Cognitive Development 104
The Role of Culture 105
Sociocultural Perspective 107
Developmental Components of the Theory 107
Basis of Cognitive Development 109
The Role of Culture 109

Information-Processing Perspective in Middle Childhood 110
Developmental Components of the Theory 112
Basis of Cognitive Development 116
The Role of Culture 118
Language, Literacy, and Academic Learning 118
Language Development 118
Mathematical Operations 123
Cognitive Development in Context 124
Family Contexts 124
School Contexts 125
Community Contexts 126
Chapter Review 127

CHAPTER 5
Affective Development in Middle Childhood 130

Middle Childhood Affective Development 132
Theoretical Viewpoints 132
Personality Perspectives 132
Humanistic Perspectives 133
Development of Self-Understanding in Middle Childhood 136
Self-Concept 138
Self-Esteem 140
Self-Efficacy 144
Emotional Development and Temperament 151
Emotional Intelligence 151
Temperament 154
Contexts for Affective Development 156
Family Contexts 156
School Contexts 157
Community Contexts 158
Chapter Review 159

CHAPTER 6
Social Development in Middle Childhood 162

Middle Childhood Social Development 164
Theoretical Viewpoints 164
Social Learning 164
Social Information Processing 165
Social Theories of Mind 166
Social and Moral Understanding in Middle Childhood 167
Interpersonal Understanding 167
Moral Development 169
Peer Relations in Middle Childhood 178
Friendship 178
Social Skills and Social Behavior in Middle Childhood 183
Prosocial Behavior 184
Antisocial Behavior 185
Social Development in Context 192
Family Contexts 193
School Contexts 194
Community Contexts 195
Chapter Review 196

PART TWO TRANSITION TO ADOLESCENCE

CHAPTER 7
Perspectives on Middle Adolescence 200

Defining Middle Adolescence 202
Historical Views of Adolescence 202
Modern Contributions to the Construction of Adolescence 203
Meanings of Adolescence in Postmodern Societies 208
Developmental Milestones in Adolescence 211
Theoretical Viewpoints 212
Life-Span Theory 212
Life-Course Theory 213
Research on Risk and Opportunity in Adolescence 217
Perspectives on Teen Risks 217
Perspectives on Teen Opportunities 219
Social Policy Implications 223
Contexts of Middle Adolescence 225
Family Contexts 225
School Contexts 226
Community Contexts 227
Chapter Review 228

CHAPTER 8
Physical Development in Middle Adolescence 232

Adolescent Physical Development and Health Behaviors 234
Theoretical Viewpoint 234
Biological Maturation 234
The Pubertal Process 234
Secondary Sex Characteristics 236
Somatic Growth 237
Factors Influencing Pubertal Growth 239
Psychosocial Consequences of Pubertal Timing 240
Relationships Between Puberty and Function 241
Brain Development 243
Structural and Functional Change 243
The Role of the Environment in Brain Development 245
Motor Skills and Performance 247
Related Health and Development Issues 248
Nutritional Needs and Dietary Behavior 249
Disordered Eating Behavior 249
Sleep 250
Substance Use and Abuse 252
Adolescent Sexuality 257
Puberty and Sexuality 257
Noncoital Sexual Behavior 257

Sexual Intercourse 258
Gay, Lesbian, and Bisexual Orientations 258
Contraceptive Use 259
Sexually Transmitted Diseases (STDs) and HIV/AIDS 261
Adolescent Pregnancy 261
Development in Context 265
Family Contexts 265
School Contexts 265
Community Contexts 266
Chapter Review 266

CHAPTER 9
Cognitive Development in Middle Adolescence 270

Cognitive Development in Adolescence 272
Theoretical Viewpoints 272
Piaget's Formal Operational Stage 272
Limitations of Formal Operational Thought 275
Information Processing in Adolescents 277
Reasoning and Decision Making 281
Scientific Reasoning 281
Decision Making 282
Psychometric Approach to Intelligence 282
Theories of Intelligence 284
Measures of Intelligence 285
The Relationship of Intelligence to Academic Achievement and Occupation 288
Factors That Influence Intelligence Scores 289
Alternative Views of Intelligence 290
Cognitive Development in Context 293
Family Contexts 293
School Contexts 293
Community Contexts 296
Chapter Review 297

CHAPTER 10
Affective Development in Middle Adolescence 300

Affective Development in Adolescence 302
Theoretical Viewpoints 303
Psychoanalytic Perspectives 304
Social-Psychological Perspectives 306
Research on Identity in Middle Adolescence 307
Identity Status 308
Racial/Ethnic Identity 312
Spiritual/Religious Identity 315
Vocational/Political Identity 319
Emotion and Self-Esteem in Middle Adolescence 326
Emotion and Mood 326
Adolescent Self-Esteem 327
Contexts for Affective Development 331
Family Contexts 332
School Contexts 332
Community Contexts 332
Chapter Review 333

CHAPTER 11
Social Development in Middle Adolescence 336

Social Development in Adolescence 338
Theoretical Viewpoints 338
Attachment Perspectives 338
Family Systems Perspectives 341
Gender and Sexuality in Middle Adolescence 341
Gender-Role Orientation 343
Stages of Gender Development 344
Social Constructions of Sexuality 346
Close Relationships in Middle Adolescence 351
Middle Adolescent Friendships 351
Family Relationships 360
Contexts of Adolescent Social Development 366
Family Contexts 366
School Contexts 367
Community Contexts 367
Chapter Review 369

CHAPTER 12
Beyond Middle Adolescence: Emerging Adulthood 372

Defining Emerging Adulthood 374
Historical Views of Adulthood 378
Early History of Adulthood 378
Modern Contributions to the Construction of Adulthood 379
The Meaning of Adulthood in Postmodern Societies 382
Developmental Milestones in Emerging Adulthood 385
Integration of Theoretical Viewpoints 387
Diverse Contexts of Emerging Adulthood 389
Family Context 389
School/Workplace Context 391
Community Context 393
Concluding Remarks 394
Chapter Review 394

APPENDIX
A Primer in Research Design 397

References 401

Author Index 455

Subject Index 469

PART 1

Transition from Early Childhood

CHAPTER 1 Studying Middle Childhood and Adolescence

CHAPTER 2 Perspectives on Middle Childhood

CHAPTER 3 Physical Development in Middle Childhood

CHAPTER 4 Cognitive Development in Middle Childhood

CHAPTER 5 Affective Development in Middle Childhood

CHAPTER 6 Social Development in Middle Childhood

CHAPTER

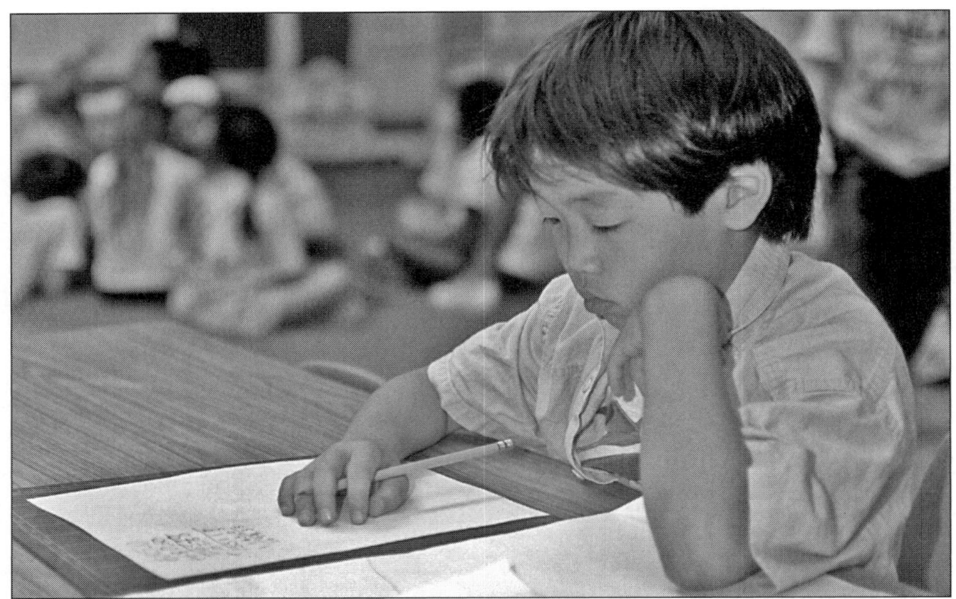

Studying Middle Childhood and Adolescence

CHAPTER OBJECTIVES

After reading this chapter, students will be able to:

- Understand the role that theory plays in generating research on middle childhood and adolescence
- Describe three theoretical issues that are debated in the study of human development
- Identify developmental research designs and the purpose, strengths, and limitations of each method
- Summarize quantitative and qualitative data collection techniques
- Communicate their own basic or applied research questions and related ethical concerns associated with studying middle childhood and adolescence

Ten-year-old Takuya sits in his fifth-grade classroom anxiously watching the clock. He has only 5 minutes before the bell rings and releases him for lunch. Takuya and his family have just moved to this city, and he has had to make his way in a new community, neighborhood, and school. Takuya has had no problem adjusting to the academic challenges of his new school. As a matter of fact, he finds the demands of his teachers to be less rigorous than those at his old school. However, Takuya has had a tough time making friends and fitting into the cliques in school. It has been especially hard for him because he is more quiet and shy than most boys his age. Takuya has a difficult time approaching boys he doesn't know and making conversation. His 16-year-old brother, Naoki, is more outgoing and has made friends already with some boys he met working at his part-time job. The bell rings, Takuya gathers up his books and makes his way to the lunchroom, where he will probably eat lunch alone, again.

Understanding Development

As you observe the lunchroom scene, you have a number of thoughts about Takuya's behavior: *"I wonder if some children are born to be more shy than others?"* or *"Takuya seems to be so quiet. Be has probably been encouraged to act this way at home, in the classroom, or in his neighborhood."* All of us have observations about school-age children and adolescents that encourage us to think and speculate about the nature of children, how they develop, and what variables influence their behavior. These thoughts reflect our personal philosophy of human nature and child development (Kagan, 1980, 1983; Lerner, 2002). If you think that Takuya is shy because of inborn tendencies and that the environment has little influence on this trait, you are making an assumption that most human behavior and development are shaped by innate tendencies at birth and remain relatively stable across the life span. If, however, you walk away from the lunchroom thinking, *"I wonder who taught him to be so quiet and well behaved?"* then you are suggesting that he has been encouraged to be so by his family or peers—an assumption that behavior is shaped largely by the environment in which children are raised. Each of these thoughts represents a general philosophy about the origins of human behavior and growth that you may not realize you hold. These implicit personal philosophies help us organize observations and make sense of the wide range of data we collect in our daily interactions with children. They also represent a specific theoretical viewpoint.

In developmental psychology, human development, and education, researchers studying middle childhood and adolescence—as well as the practitioners who work with school-age and teenage children—rely on scientific **theories** to interpret children's development and behavior. A theory is a formal or informal attempt to describe or explain real phenomena, such as growth and change. A **developmental theory** describes changes within or among developmental domains or explains the course of development over time. Theories play a vital role in any scientific discipline. They give meaning to and provide a framework for facts, help us organize research questions and the information gathered from them, and help guide and direct future research (Miller, 2002).

 **Do you often wonder what causes children to behave the way they do?**

Theoretical Questions About Human Development

All developmental theories possess underlying assumptions about the nature of development (similar to thoughts you may have had about Takuya and Naoki as you read this chapter's case study). These assumptions can vary widely from one theory to another. Specific developmental theories are presented throughout the subsequent chapters of this book. This chapter introduces three theoretical issues that form the foundation for all developmental theories and continue to be prominent questions in most child development research (Lerner, 2002; Miller, 2002). The study of human development raises questions about the progression of change over time (continuity–discontinuity), the influences of biology and the environment (nature–nurture), and the consistency of characteristics and behavior over one's lifetime (stability–instability).

Continuity or discontinuity? This question asks whether development proceeds in a gradual, cumulative fashion (**continuity**) or in fits and starts, with periods of rapid development followed by periods of slower development (**discontinuity**). In developmental theories, the meaning of *continuity* is not unlike its common meaning: "something that has uninterrupted duration or continuation, especially without essential change" (Merriam-Webster, 2002). Therefore, if a developmental ability or behavior has continuity, we would expect it to gradually increase across developmental periods—the acquisition of motor skills, for example. Continuity may also represent the relationship between earlier forms of development and later ones. For example, the continuity of shyness during childhood does not mean that shyness increases per se, but rather that earlier levels of shyness are related to later ones.

Takuya's wariness of all adults in toddlerhood may manifest itself in his unwillingness to raise his hand in class in middle childhood.

Other aspects of development, however, may be discontinuous, or emerge in *stages*. For example, school-age children typically show changes in problem-solving ability as they move from the logical reasoning stage of middle childhood to the abstract reasoning stage of adolescence. What all developmental *stage theories* have in common is an assumption of discontinuity, or changes in development that are not simply gradual but sudden leaps in level of performance. Figure 1.1 is a visual illustration of the different rates of development represented by these two viewpoints.

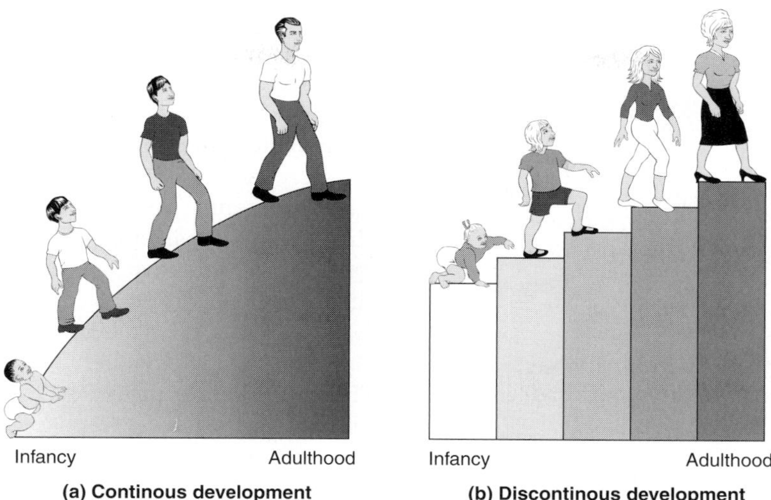

FIGURE 1.1 Continuity vs. Discontinuity
Panel 1 illustrates continuous development; panel 2 illustrates discontinuous development.

Source: From Berk, L. (2006), *Child Development* (7th ed.) (p. 7). Published by Allyn and Bacon, Boston, MA. Copyright © 2006 by Pearson Education. Reprinted by permission of the publisher.

The best answer to this question is that *some* aspects of development, such as the increase in the size of our short-term memory, reflect more continuous change. Other aspects of development, such as problem solving, appear to develop in a more stagelike progression.

Nature or nurture? This question asks whether development is influenced primarily by biological inheritance (**nature**) or environmental experiences (**nurture**) (Anastasi, 1958; Bronfenbrenner & Ceci, 1994). Those proposing that nature or biology dominates development point to genetic blueprints and biological predispositions (e.g., shy or outgoing) to explain children's development. Others argue that although genetic and biological predispositions may be important, children's environments and experiences (e.g., parenting styles, educational opportunities, sociocultural surroundings) play a greater role in shaping who a child becomes.

Using the case study, you could ask whether Takuya was born with shy tendencies or whether his family and peers encourage this reticent behavior.

Developmental scholars today agree that it is probably a combination of both biological and social factors that determine development (Sameroff, 1983; Lerner, 1985; Lerner, 1998; Bronfenbrenner & Morris, 1998). For example, researchers (Graber, Brooks-Gunn, & Warren, 1995) have found that the timing of puberty is influenced by both heredity (e.g., the onset of menstruation in mothers predicts onset in daughters) and environment (e.g., low levels of body fat delay menarche in female athletes).

Stability or instability? This issue focuses on whether developmental characteristics are consistent over time and predictive of later development (**stability**) or subject to change over time and context (**instability**). Theorists who suggest that certain aspects of development, such as shyness, are stable would predict children to exhibit the same shy characteristics in adulthood. *They would argue that Takuya would grow up to be a shy and quiet man.* An alternative suggestion is that whether shy children will become shy adults is dependent upon the experiences that they undergo during development. *Takuya may be required to take assertiveness training courses in his first job and may become less shy in adolescence.*

Evidence of stability in the personality of an individual across the years from early to middle childhood would be observed if a shy preschooler were to remain cautious of others in elementary school and still socially reserved in middle school. Furthermore, if personality traits were stable, it would *not* be developmentally appropriate to think that children who have always seemed shy and reserved will ever be very outgoing. On the other hand, children's specific behaviors, such as aggression or withdrawal, may show instability over time as they try out varying strategies of coping with the demands of the ever-widening contexts of childhood—from home to school and community.

Do you think that your personality has changed since you were a young child?

Linking Theory and Research

Theories and the research undertaken to investigate them are connected through either **deductive** or **inductive reasoning**. Using deductive reasoning, a researcher begins with a theory and then collects data to support or refute it. The majority of research studies are based on questions generated through deductive reasoning (Lerner, 2002). One common deductive reasoning model is hypothesis testing. A **hypothesis** is a theoretical prediction, or statement, that has yet to be tested or supported. In hypothesis testing, if a theory suggests that environment largely influences behavior, then you might hypothesize that school-age children and adolescents who watch violent sports on television (e.g., football, boxing) would behave more aggressively than children who do not watch violent sports on television. If the theory is accurate, then the findings of the study will support the hypothesis that environment influences behavior.

A second way that research and theory are linked is through inductive reasoning. Using inductive reasoning, a researcher begins with a research question or a general observation and collects data to gain an answer for immediate application or to generate a new theory, not necessarily to test the tenets of an existing theory. This reasoning style is more typical of practitioners and teachers who work with children on a day-to-day basis and who generate research questions out of necessity rather than for theoretical hypothesis testing. For example, a counselor in an after-school program observes fifth graders segregating into same-sex peer groups. She wants to know if this is "normal" or if she should try to intervene. Her research approach and her findings have immediate application to her question but are not related directly to a specific developmental theory about gender identity or peer affiliation.

Linking Research with Practice

Researchers, program providers, parents, policy makers, teachers, and students have in common the need to translate research into practice. **Basic research** in middle childhood development and adolescence begins with the study of normative development. However, **applied research** asks how this basic information is relevant to solving particular problems of practical significance. The integration of these two approaches—basic and applied—has been deemed a new model for the 21st century (Schwebel, Plumert, & Pick, 2000). This integrative model has three goals that are addressed in successive chapters of this book. First are the implications of basic research for applied issues. But a second, more challenging, goal is to examine how applied research studies are grounded in basic developmental theories. A third goal is to explore how you may conduct research of your own in the context of an applied problem facing you in the real world of the family, school, or community (Schwebel, Plumert, & Pick, 2000).

Do you have a question you want answered about development in middle childhood or adolescence?

This text focuses on middle childhood to middle adolescence. In chapter 2, middle childhood is defined as the years between 8 and 12. Development during this period—also called the school-age years—is covered in the first half of the book. Middle adolescence, defined in chapter 7, describes youth from ages 13 to 18 and is presented in the second half. Throughout the book, we integrate theory, research, and practice to help you understand the fascinating changes that occur during these periods of the life span.

STUDYING CHANGE OVER TIME

The study of development involves understanding change over time. Three developmental approaches are designed specifically to assess age-related differences and change over time. (For a primer on other types of research designs, refer to the appendix.)

Cross-Sectional Research Designs

The first approach, **cross-sectional studies**, assesses different age groups of children at the same point in time. For example, if you were interested in how strategies used in a memory task may change as

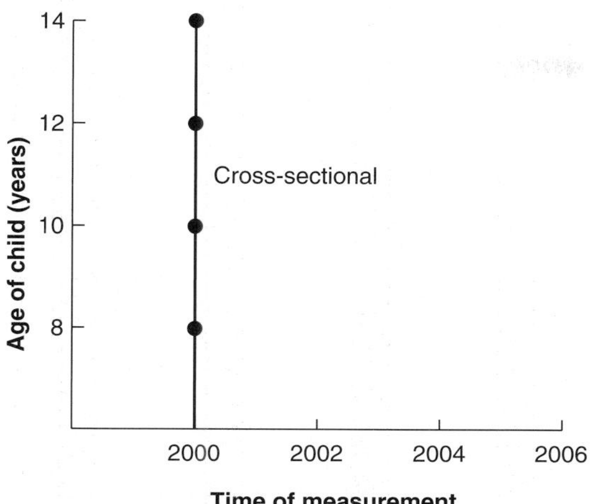

FIGURE 1.2 Cross-sectional Design
Cross-sectional designs assess different-aged children at the same point in time.

children get older, you could administer a recall task to children who are 8, 10, 12, and 14 years old and ask them to rehearse aloud. By averaging the number of words rehearsed for each age group, you may find that as children get older, they rehearse more words together. Therefore, as children age, memory strategies become more complex. Figure 1.2 illustrates how this type of study is configured.

Cross-sectional studies are used frequently in developmental research because they are time- and cost-efficient. In addition, a well-designed cross-sectional study that includes an appropriate level and number of different age groups can accentuate developmental differences among cognitive and behavioral skills and, more specifically, identify *when* a skill emerges.

Limitations of cross-sectional research. Cross-sectional designs are less able to identify *how* the change occurs (e.g., how does an individual child move from simple to complex rehearsal?) and the variables that may influence that change (e.g., practice at home or at school). In addition, because different age cohorts are used, it is difficult to rule out the possibility that the unique experiences of one age group have biased the results, called **cohort bias**. For example, all of the 10-year-olds in the study may have had a student teacher last year who specialized in teaching memory strategies to children. In such a case, the results might look as if rehearsal strategies are very sophisticated at 10 years of age and then become less so at 12! This finding would not be a reflection of the true pattern of memory strategy development, but rather an atypical developmental pattern due to a cohort effect.

Longitudinal Research Designs

The second approach to studying change over time is a **longitudinal study**. In a longitudinal study, one group of same-aged participants is studied at several different points in time. This design is illustrated in Figure 1.3.

These studies can take place over the course of several weeks or over many years. Since longitudinal studies follow the same child over time, changes in individual children can also be assessed. For example, if your research question asks *both* "To what extent are the memory strategies used by 8-year-olds different from those of 12-year-olds?" *and* "How and when do they change?" a longitudinal design will best answer these questions. You could assess the memory strategies of a group of 8-year-olds, followed by similar assessments of the same group at 10, 12, and 14 years of age. Not only could you observe potential differences between the memory strategies of the 8- and the 12-year-olds but you can also identify the evolution of memory strategies.

Longitudinal studies also allow for connections to be made between early experience and later development. For example, Emmy Werner (1989, 1993; Werner & Smith, 2001) was interested in how children's health status at birth and their early home environments affected later social and cognitive development. The findings of this landmark longitudinal study are described in Box 1.1.

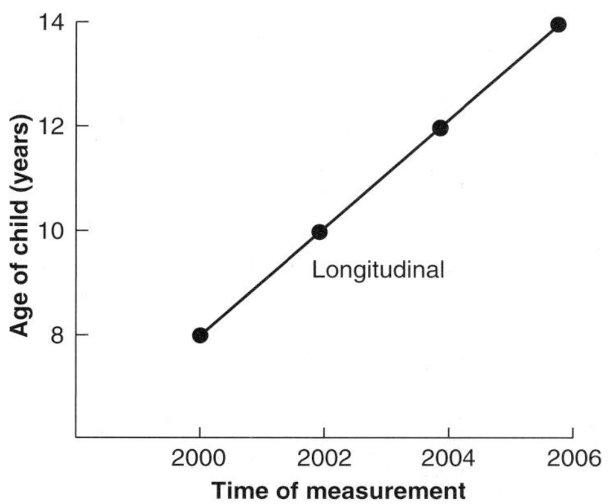

FIGURE 1.3 Longitudinal Design
Longitudinal designs assess the same children over time to document developmental change.

BOX 1.1 ROADMAP TO UNDERSTANDING THEORY AND RESEARCH

Longitudinal Designs

The Kauai Longitudinal Study conducted by Emmy Werner and colleagues is considered a classic in longitudinal investigations for both its design features and research findings (Werner, 1989, 1993; Werner & Smith, 2001). The study had two principal goals: (1) to assess the long-term consequences of prenatal and perinatal stress and (2) to document the effects of adverse early rearing conditions on children's physical, cognitive, and psychosocial development. In order to accomplish these goals, Werner chose to study all children born in 1955 on the Hawaiian island of Kauai. Werner explained that Kauai was chosen because its medical, public health, educational, and social services were comparable to a community of the same size on the U.S. mainland. (The island population was 45,000.) In addition, the population was known for its low mobility, its diversity of cultural influences, and its receptiveness to the goals of the research study.

In 1955, 698 infants were born on Kauai (i.e., they were considered a birth cohort). Their development was followed at ages 1, 2, 10, 18, and 31 or 32, and 40 years. Physicians and public health nurses recorded complications during the prenatal period, labor, and the neonatal period. Nurses and social workers interviewed the mothers in the postpartum period and when the children were 1 and 10 years old; observations of parent-child interactions also were made at this time. Pediatricians and psychologists examined the children at 2 and 10 years of age and assessed their physical, intellectual, and social development. Any developmental delays, handicaps, or behavior problems were noted. Teachers evaluated the children's academic progress and school behavior. A research team administered a variety of aptitude, achievement, and personality tests in elementary grades and high school.

Information about the material, intellectual, and emotional aspects of family life was recorded, with special attention paid to stressful life events that disrupted the family unit (e.g., divorce, imprisonment, mental illness, drug and alcohol abuse). Interviews were conducted with the children when they were ages 18 and 31 or 32. The comprehensiveness of this database was nearly unprecedented!

Of the 698 children included in the study at birth, the majority, or two thirds, were born without complications and grew up in supportive home environments. Approximately one third of the children (n = 201) were identified as high risk because they suffered some degree of perinatal stress, were born into poverty, and experienced some form of family distress. Two thirds of *these* children went on to develop serious learning or behavior problems by age 10 and had mental health problems, delinquency records, and/or teenage pregnancies by age 18.

One third of these high-risk children, however, *did not* develop learning or behavior problems and by age 18 appeared to have developed into competent and caring young adults. Werner was able to identify some of the factors that protected these children from developmental risk and supported their attempts to thrive in less-than-optimal home environments. She called them *resilient*.

As infants, these resilient children seemed to share an "easy" temperament, which made them easier to care for and thus more likely to elicit positive attention from family members and others. As toddlers, they were described as alert and autonomous and exhibited advanced communication, locomotion, and self-help skills. In elementary school, teachers reported that these children got along well with their classmates, and by high school they exhibited a positive self-concept. All had the opportunity to establish a close bond with at least one caregiver during infancy, although for some of the children this relationship took place with someone other than a parent, such as a grandparent, older sibling, or baby-sitter. The resilient children sought further emotional support outside the home in the form of close friendships, extracurricular activities, and church involvement; during the interviews at 18, they believed that their lives had meaning.

Because the design of the study allowed Werner to follow the same children forward through time, she was able to identify early those children "at risk" and follow their developmental outcomes. From this continuity she determined that the negative impact of birth complications diminished over time and were overshadowed and mediated by child-rearing conditions. In addition, she identified protective factors that made some children resilient and develop into competent and caring young adults despite their biological and environmental risk factors.

Longitudinal studies can assist us in examining the stability of a characteristic or behavior. Does an inhibited toddler remain cautious into middle childhood and adolescence? By employing a longitudinal design, Kagan and Saudino (2001) studied temperamental qualities in children from birth and suggested that if infants were "avoidant, affectively subdued, and remained proximal to a caregiver during initial encounters with an unfamiliar event [essentially shy]" (p. 111), they typically would show similar characteristics throughout the first decade of life.

Finally, a longitudinal design allows us to explore how different factors may be related to one another over time. For example, what if we were to observe Takuya over the school year and find that he exhibits less shy behavior and has made friends with several boys who are more outgoing then he is. What we might ask is, "What factors influenced this change and in what way? Did his new friends encourage him to be more outgoing?" (i.e., friends mediate the change in behavior). Or, "Did his involvement in extracurricular activities give him the confidence he needed to become more outgoing towards others?" (i.e., individual characteristics lead to behavior change). By following groups of children like Takuya over time, a longitudinal design will allow you to examine the relationships among different variables and to identify which variables may predict change more reliably than others.

Limitations of longitudinal research. Despite the many benefits of this research approach in the study of human development, not many longitudinal studies are conducted. They are costly and can take many years to complete. Research participants may also drop out of longitudinal studies, for a variety of reasons (e.g., moving away from the area, transferring to a different school, or disinterest). A loss of participants over time is referred to as **attrition**. Attrition can affect the results of a longitudinal study by reducing the total number of participants and thereby limiting the types of statistical analyses that can be performed. In addition, it may be precisely those characteristics that you had hoped to study that cause some participants to discontinue their participation!

Perhaps even more problematic is the often *selective* nature of attrition, meaning that certain types of participants may remain (e.g., people interested in learning about themselves or who appreciate the value of research) or may drop out of the study (e.g., people with low socioeconomic status or who are highly mobile). To conduct her longitudinal study, Werner (1989, 1993) chose the Hawaiian island of Kauai in part because of the population's low mobility; despite the common problem of attrition in longitudinal research, at the 18-year follow-up the researchers were able to locate 88% of the original cohort.

A final difficulty with longitudinal research involving tests (e.g., intelligence or personality assessments) is that the participants may become "test wise" after repeated exposures to the same measures. They might show improvement over time—not because of developmental change, but because of practice.

Longitudinal-Sequential Research Designs

The third approach, the **longitudinal-sequential study**, is a combination of cross-sectional and longitudinal approaches (Baltes, 1968; Nesselroade & Baltes, 1974). In a longitudinal-sequential study, several different-aged groups of children are studied over a multiyear period (see Figure 1.4).

A longitudinal-sequential design capitalizes on the strengths of both cross-sectional and longitudinal studies while eliminating many of the disadvantages. For example, if the memory strategies of 8-, 10-, and 12-year-olds were measured in a cross-sectional study, you could observe age-related differences. If these same children were also assessed once a year over several years, this component of the research design would resemble a longitudinal study that could determine whether the rehearsal strategies of individual children changed over time. In this way, the effects of age and generation can be examined simultaneously.

Variable-Centered Versus Person-Centered Approaches

The research designs we have presented have been used for many years to study how one or more **variables**, or factors that vary across individuals in a study, may *cause* change to occur in another variable or group of variables, an approach referred to as the **variable-centered approach**. For example, to understand Takuya's shyness, research using a variable-centered approach would focus on which variables, such as late maturation or peer rejection, might contribute to or *cause* his shyness. More complex developmental theories, such as those presented in chapter 2, have moved away from

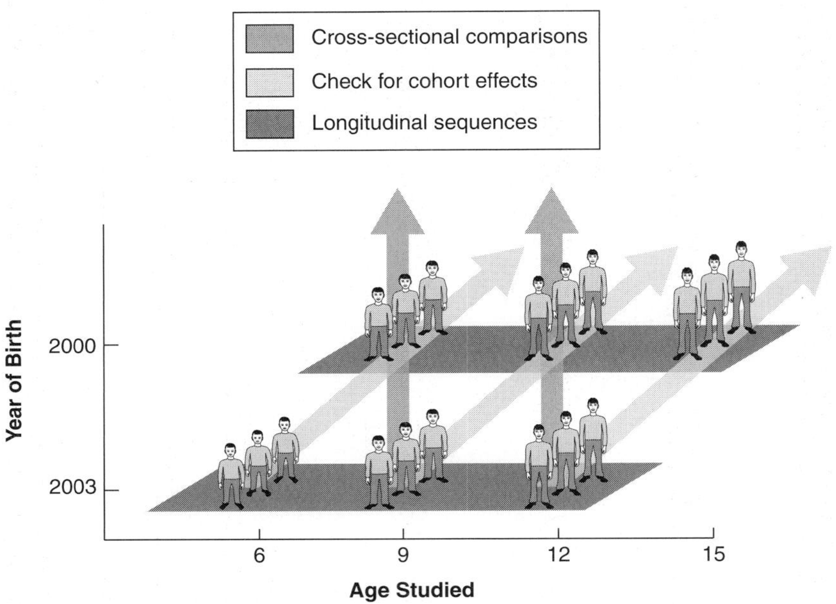

FIGURE 1.4 Longitudinal-Sequential Design
A longitudinal-sequential design involves the study of different age groups of children over several different points in time.

Source: From Berk, L. (2004), Child Development (3rd ed.) (p. 63). Published by Allyn and Bacon, Boston, MA. Copyright © 2004 by Pearson Education. Reprinted by permission of the publisher.

variable-oriented models because they do not capture the complexity of development in all of its forms. The discipline of child development encourages the use of many of the same developmental research designs described in this chapter, but with the additional goal of describing *patterns* of individual development within multiple changing contexts.

In recent years, the study of development across the life span has become more person-centered (Magnusson, 2000). Researchers are increasingly studying the ways in which individuals contribute to their own development in the various contexts in which they find themselves (Lerner, 2002). This **person-centered** approach permits the researcher to cluster together individuals who are functioning in similar ways and to follow their development over time (Cairns, 1979; Magnusson & Stattin, 1998; Overton, 1998). For example, the person-centered approach would allow you to group Takuya with other children who have similar characteristics (e.g., Profile 1: minority ethnicity, English as a second language, late physical maturation, high shyness, poor peer relationships) compared to a group unlike him (e.g., Profile 2: majority ethnicity, native English speaker, on-time physical maturation, low shyness, good peer relationships). Then you could follow their development as they transition to high school, begin to date, make new friends, or engage in extracurricular activities in many changing contexts.

This approach may better answer the questions of (a) how these early characteristics (i.e., high shyness and poor peer status) might be related to later characteristics (i.e., compliance and loneliness) and (b) what variables might intercede to play a mediational role in development (e.g., involvement in extracurricular activities) (Mahoney, 2000). The person-centered approach allows for the assessment of multiple aspects of functioning simultaneously, takes a nonlinear approach to data analysis, and formulates the research in person terms. Person-centered research represents a theoretical shift in the study of human development that will likely affect not only the

TABLE 1–1

A Summary of the Strengths and Limitations of Three Developmental Designs
Developmental researchers most often use these designs in developmental research.

Design	Strengths	Limitations
Cross-sectional	• Assesses different age groups of children at the same time • Time- and cost-efficient • Can help identify norms for *when* a skill emerges	• Cannot identify *how* change occurs or which variables most influence change and in what ways • Cohort effects
Longitudinal	• Assesses same-aged participants over several data points • Identifies *when* and *how* change occurs • Connections can be made between early experience and later development • Studies how variables are related to one another	• Long and costly • Attrition • Participants may become "test wise" • Cohort effects
Longitudinal-sequential	• Assesses different-aged groups of participants over several different points in time	• Not widely used or understood

ways that research designs, data collection methods, and analytical techniques are selected but also the way research findings are reported in the future.

What are the personal characteristics that set you apart from your peers?

Methods of Collecting Data

To answer research questions about middle childhood and adolescence or to test hypotheses regarding school-age and teenage children, information needs to be collected systematically. The strategies used in this process are called *data collection techniques*. These techniques are not reserved for professional researchers only. A child care worker can utilize them in a day care facility, a nurse in a pediatrician's office, a supervisor at a playground, or a counselor in high school. The challenge of data collection is to employ an appropriate assessment tool, which depends on a number of factors:

- Number of children to be studied
- Ages of children
- If siblings, parents, teachers, or peers will be assessed
- Whether the variables of interest are personal characteristics or behavioral indices
- The setting in which the study will take place
- The purpose of the research

For example, identifying factors that may precipitate violent outbursts by a single child in the classroom requires a data collection approach different from that used to survey a large group of school-aged children about the loss of extracurricular activities in their school district. Data collection techniques are generally divided into two distinct approaches: quantitative and qualitative.

Quantitative Data Collection

Quantitative data collection techniques collect data and information about the child in a way that allows the assigning of numbers to target behaviors. A score on a self-esteem questionnaire, the number of aggressive behaviors observed, or an intelligence quotient from an intelligence test are all examples of quantitative data.

Although using quantitative data makes traditional statistical analyses of the data easier, the original research question should dictate which technique is best suited to your research. For example, if the purpose of a research project is to understand the reading level of a group of fourth graders, or the memory capacities of 9-year-olds, or the number of hours middle-schoolers in the United States spend on homework compared to middle-schoolers in Japan, then it would make sense to use a quantitative data collection technique.

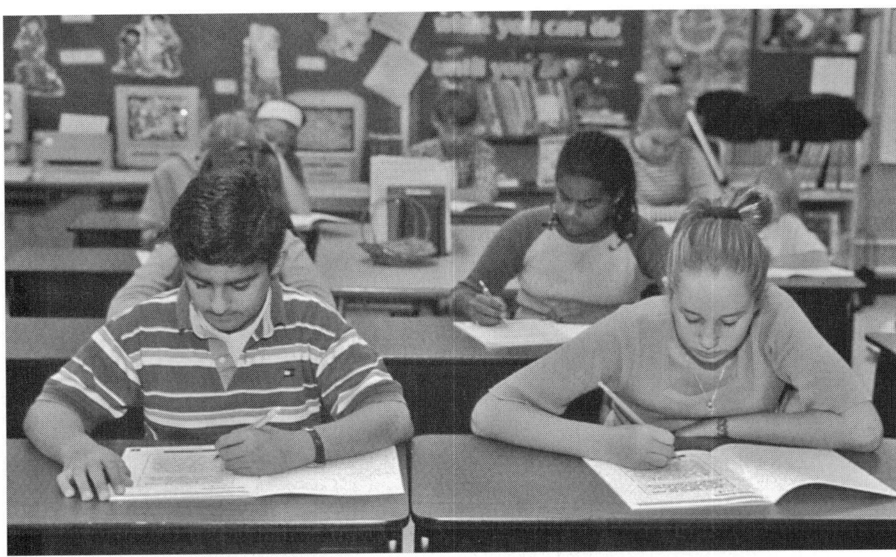

Standardized tests follow a uniform set of rules for administration, scoring, and interpretation.

Standardized measures. The easiest way to collect quantitative information about a child or group of children is to use scores from **standardized tests**. These tests are called *standardized* because the administration, scoring, and interpretation of the tests follow uniform procedures. Standardized tests have been shown to consistently evaluate individual abilities in specific domains. Examples of this type of data include an intelligence test, such as the *Wechsler Scale of Intelligence for Children, Fourth Edition* (Wechsler, 2003), or an achievement test, such as the *IOWA Test for Basic Skills* (Hoover, Dunbar, & Frisbie, 2001). Such tests follow specific rules for test taking, scoring, and interpreting scores.

All standardized tests produce a summary numeric score, which may provide useful comparative information about the child's social, emotional, or cognitive status. When standardized tests have been administered to hundreds or thousands of children to establish **norms**, or average performance standards for different-aged groups, they are called **norm-referenced tests**. Norm-referenced tests are useful because they provide a comparison, or "normative," group for your developmental data. **Criterion-referenced tests** are used often in educational settings and assess the performance of the student against some standard or set of standards.

There are different types of standardized measures, each assessing different competencies. For example, **aptitude tests** are used to *predict* performance, and **achievement tests** measure the skills the child has mastered. Standardized tests may provide us with information that is not easily observable, such as decision-making or hypothesis-testing abilities. Psychological tests that assess constructs such as self-esteem, social dissatisfaction, and peer relationships are often used in research to tell us something about the internal world of the child. It is important to understand the differences between the purposes of these tests so that the information can be used appropriately (Johnson & Johnson, 2002).

The primary advantage of using standardized tests is that measurement experts have previously examined and confirmed their **validity** (i.e., the test measures what it is supposed to measure) and **reliability** (i.e., the test performs consistently). When faced with a choice between using a published standardized test or creating your own, most experts recommend using an existing test. However, because of the proliferation of tests in the educational and mental health fields, many of these scores may already be noted in the school or medical records of the children you wish to study. The availability of such information may be helpful in understanding the hypothetical question you have posed.

The disadvantages of standardized tests are that many people may not have access to them and may lack training in administering them. An additional concern is that multiple-choice tests may not be a valid assessment of a child's skills. Therefore, **performance measures**, which measure children's ability to perform a given skill, should be used in conjunction with standardized paper-and-pencil tests. Performance measures typically assess motor and cognitive skills. They might require a child to walk a straight line with one foot in front of the other (motor skills) or put small blocks together to match a pattern (visual-spatial skills). However, performance measures only allow researchers to *infer* the cognitive steps taken to solve a performance task correctly. Finally, many researchers caution against relying too heavily on the use of a single score to make generalizations about a child's development. They recommend that test scores be used as only one piece of the total picture of a child's developmental profile.

Using a score from an introversion-extroversion scale may not capture the complexity of Takuya's social interactions during the first year in his new school.

Systematic observation. There may be times when a hypothesis is best tested by observation—simply watching and listening to people. **Observational techniques** that involve the systematic collection and documentation of overt behavior are useful when the topic of study involves complex actions or interactions among a number of people (e.g., behavior of adolescents between classes in high school), behavior of which the participant may be unaware (e.g., reasons for self-consciousness), or transgressions (e.g., bullying). Observations can vary in structure and in information obtained. Again, the method chosen is based on the research question that needs to be answered.

Observing children in their natural environment requires **naturalistic** observational techniques. Many researchers feel that these techniques present the most accurate portrayal of the variables that influence development (Bronfenbrenner, 1979). The obvious advantage of these techniques is they allow the researcher to observe the child's behavior in a realistic setting, such as the playground. It is, however, problematic in that it is difficult for the observer to remain unobtrusive, and it is critical to do so to avoid biasing the child's behavior. Children and adolescents may change their behavior if they feel they are being watched (especially by a strange adult!). Additionally, since the researcher has no control over the setting, the child of interest could disappear and there would be large blocks of time in which the target child is unobservable.

A potential solution to this problem is a **structured observation** of a child in a controlled setting, such as a laboratory classroom, school classroom, or home. A good example of how development can be studied using a structured observational technique is researchers' observations of the conversational styles of mothers in their homes with their 8- to 10-year-old daughters and with their 14- to 16-year-old daughters (Beaumont, 2000). The observers also coded the conversational styles of these same mothers at home in conversation with a friend. By observing these interactions in a structured situation in which they gave the participants a topic to discuss, the researchers were able to determine that mothers used a very different style when communicating with their friends than with their daughters. In addition, they found that daughters' and mothers' conversational styles differed depending on the age of the daughter (e.g., number of interruptions, amount of overlap). The researchers suggested that these differences explain some of the dissatisfaction and conflict that late school-agers and early adolescent girls have with their mothers (Beaumont, 2000).

Regardless of which observation technique is chosen, keeping a record of behavior is necessary. Record-keeping techniques require little or no training to use and are easy to employ in a variety of settings. The most inclusive type of record is a **specimen record**, in which the researcher records all observed behaviors over a specified period of time. This type of technique should be used if your research question is largely exploratory or if it's important to record the precursors and antecedents of the target behavior.

A specimen record would allow you to observe and record the series of events that led up to Takuya eating lunch alone (e.g., does he choose a seat away from others or avoid others' invitations to join them?), as well as how others responded to Takuya's lack of lunchroom companionship (e.g., does anyone approach him?).

Time sampling is the recording of observable behaviors every time they occur during a designated time period (e.g., for 15 minutes) or at designated time intervals (e.g., every 30 seconds for 15 minutes). The behavior and interval for observation are agreed upon prior to the start of the observation. For example, a group of researchers may create a list of social play behaviors that include both physical and verbal acts of friendship. Child A is observed for 15 minutes, and every time he engages in positive behavior its frequency and duration are recorded; child B is observed for the next 15 minutes and his positive behavior is recorded; child C's positive behavior is observed for the next 15 minutes; and then the order may be repeated. This technique records both the frequency *and* duration of a target behavior (or set of behaviors), thereby allowing a researcher (a) to see if the frequency of the behavior increases or decreases during a certain activity or time of day, and (b) to observe differences in the behavior's frequency and duration among the different children. The sample sheet in Figure 1.5 shows how time sampling can be applied to this chapter's case study.

Event sampling records how often a specific behavior occurs; it is used in research when a behavior is relatively infrequent. For example, a school counselor might notice Takuya sitting alone. Event sampling, where the frequency of his time spent alone is recorded over several weeks or months, could determine whether the behavior should be of concern and require intervention. A recording sheet for event sampling is included in Figure 1.6.

Regardless of which of the various record-keeping methods is employed, the disadvantage of observational techniques is that the target behavior may occur infrequently, thus resulting in large amounts of time and energy spent by the observer with very little payoff by way of observation. In addition, all researchers are subject to bias in their observations. What one researcher may code as shyness, another may not. Typically, more than one observer should be used and some training given regarding the targeted behavior. For example, some discussion and consensus on what constitutes shyness might help decrease observer bias. Perhaps the greatest limitation of observational techniques is that a researcher can only infer the thought processes that led to the observable behavior.

Self-report. Self-report techniques are defined as any method used to collect data in which the research participants report on their own feelings, abilities, attitudes, and behaviors or those of their siblings, parents, teachers, and peers. Questionnaires are a common self-report technique. Questionnaires may consist of structured items that may require a yes or no response, a response on a rating scale, or open-ended responses. The major advantage of questionnaires is that they allow for the collection of information from large groups of research participants in a relatively short period of time. They also tap into a person's attitudes and feelings, something not easily observed or reported by someone other than the respondent.

FIGURE 1.5 An Example of a Time-Sampling Observation Form
Time sampling allows the observer to record behavior in segments of time and track patterns of behavior over time.

Observer: **Grade:** **Date:**

Participant	10:00	10:15	10:30	11:00	TOTAL

FIGURE 1.6 Event-Sampling Observation Form
Event sampling allows the observer to record the frequency of a targeted behavior or group of behaviors.

Observer: **Grade:** **Date:**

Participant	Raises Hand	Talks to other Children	Interacts with Others	Talks to Adults	TOTAL

Questionnaires are used often in research on middle childhood and adolescence. For example, researchers used a homework questionnaire to find out whether student, family, and parenting style differences were related to the homework process and student outcomes (Cooper, Lindsay, & Nye, 2000). By using a questionnaire, they found that parents with students in higher grade levels reported giving students more homework autonomy, which in turn was found to be highly associated with higher standardized test scores, higher class grades, and more homework completed. Parental responses that reflected low homework autonomy (e.g., doing the assignment for their child, or helping so that it could get done faster) and poor elimination of distractions for their children (e.g., TV was always on) were related to their children's poorer school performance. A creative approach to collecting self-report data is presented in Box 1.2.

Despite the widespread use of questionnaires as a self-report technique, there are limitations to their usefulness when studying school-age children and adolescents. Answers on questionnaires may be susceptible to a number of biases. An **honesty bias** is the tendency for children to present themselves in the best possible light. Children will be more honest if the responses make them look good, compared to those that make them look bad. For example, children would be less likely to answer honestly questions about theft or cheating than questions about friendships. Children between the ages of 8 and 18 also are vulnerable to **social desirability bias**, which is the need to please and seek approval from adults. This phenomenon may result in children's answering questions in the way they think you want them to respond, rather than in a way that provides a more accurate record of their own feelings and behaviors.

Siblings, parents, teachers, and peers can report on the targeted child as a way of checking the accuracy of the child's responses. However, if questions are retrospective, relying on a parent's or teacher's memory of the past, answers may reflect a **memory bias**, which is the tendency to underestimate or overestimate the abilities of a child (Henry, Moffitt, Caspi, Langley, & Silva, 1994).

Finally, the most challenging aspect of using questionnaires with this age group is the reading ability and comprehension required, which may affect participants' ability to understand and follow directions, to read and understand questionnaire items, or to interpret the questions correctly. If open-ended questions are used, then a child's writing skills may add an additional complication to

BOX 1.2 ROADMAP TO UNDERSTANDING THEORY AND RESEARCH

Cultural Influences on Family Relationships as Reflected in Self-Reports

From middle childhood to early adolescence, American children shift from spending more time with families to spending more time with peers, and increased conflict with parents parallels this shift (Richards, Crowe, Larson, & Swarr, 1998). This pattern has been described as a normative developmental task of Western adolescents as they attempt to establish a sense of autonomy and independence.

Reed Larson and colleagues (Larson, Verma, & Dworkin, 2000) wondered if the same shifts occurred in middle-class eighth graders living in Chandigarh, a northern Indian city. In India, adolescents are encouraged to value family relationships, and autonomy and independence are viewed as disobedience (Bharat, 1997).

To study the settings in which these children spent their days, Larson employed the Experience Sampling Method (ESM). Participants carried alarm watches, and each time they received a random signal they recorded (a) where they were, (b) with whom, and (c) what they were doing (i.e., self-reports). In addition, participants reported on their emotional state, the social climate they were experiencing, and who they perceived to be the leader of the current interaction.

The results from this ingenious self-report technique were compared to those from a sample of eighth graders in the United States studied with exactly the same procedures. As shown in Figure 1.7, Indian eighth graders spent significantly more time with families. Larson et al. (2000) also found that this time was spent mostly with nuclear family members (e.g., mothers and siblings) at home watching TV, doing homework, or in conversation. Indian middle-schoolers reported feeling happier during this time with family than American middle-schoolers and rated the social climate more positively than Americans. Lastly, Indian eighth graders reported there was no leader 72% of the time (compared to 62% reported by American eighth graders), which reflected a more authoritative household rather than an authoritarian one.

The self-report technique provided interesting insight into the role that culture plays in influencing the social settings within which Indian middle-schoolers spend their time as well as the emotional experience associated with the interactions that take place within these settings.

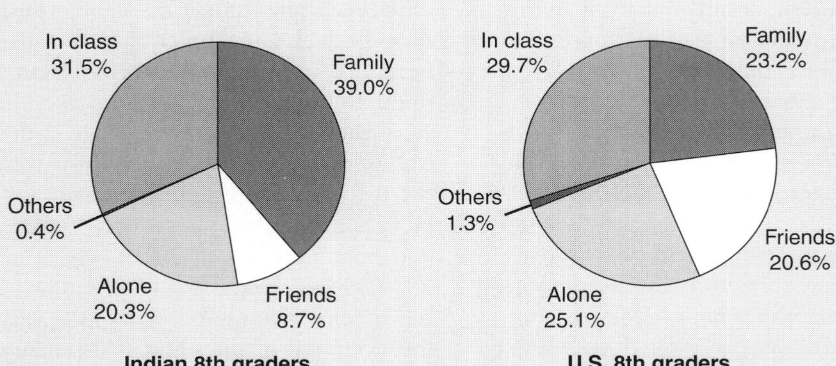

FIGURE 1.7 With Whom Adolescents Spend Time
Eighth graders in India spend more time with family members than U.S. eighth graders; U.S. eighth graders spend significantly more time with peers than Indian eighth graders.

Source: From "Adolescents' family relationship in India: The daily lives of Indian middle-class teenagers" by R. Larson, S. Verma, & J. Dworkin (2000). Unpublished paper presented at the biennial meeting of the Society for Research on Adolescence, Chicago. Reprinted by permission.

the data collection technique. Since children's reading and writing skills can vary greatly, their responses may not be an accurate reflection of thought or feeling, but rather a reflection of what the child was capable of reading, understanding, or writing. For children aged 8 to 12, and for many groups of adolescents, it is best to avoid these potential complications by either reading the questionnaire items to them or by changing the data collection procedure to an interview, which will be discussed in the following section on qualitative techniques. Observation methods and self-report techniques can yield more than quantitative information; however, data from these methods are typically numeric.

Evaluating Quantitative Data

In order to draw conclusions from the quantitative data collected and apply it in an appropriate context, a number of questions may be asked to assess the quality of the data collection approach.

- Is the data collection technique reliable?
- Is the data collection technique valid?
- Is the data collection technique generalizable?

These questions should be asked not only of your own collection method but also of others' quantitative research findings. If the answers to these questions are affirmative, then you can feel *more* confident about the conclusions drawn. However, if the answer to any one of these questions is negative, then you have to acknowledge the limitations of the study.

Reliability. Is the data collection technique you use reliable? In other words, does the measure consistently yield similar results when given to the same research participants under similar circumstances? If a study is reliable, the measure used in a study will reflect similar scores from the same child over time and testing situation. One way to assess reliability is to readminister the same test to the same child after a short time interval (several months). This assessment of consistency is called **test-retest reliability**. Repeated performance on a test has been shown to vary as a function of time of day the test is administered or the gender of the test administrator, but performance should not vary so much that the findings for that child change significantly (Murphy & Davidshofer, 2001). For example, under normal circumstances, a child would not be categorized as having "normal" intelligence and then 6 months later receive a score on the same intelligence test that categorizes him as "educable mentally impaired."

If you are using an interview or observational technique, your observers should be recording and coding the same behavior in similar ways. A statistical check can be performed on the coding scores of the observers to see if they are coding similarly. The assessment of agreement is called **interrater reliability**. A researcher should report these reliabilities along with the results of the study so that others can evaluate the dependability of the findings. If, however, a readministered test were to yield a test score vastly different from the first, or two observers vary widely in how they are coding behavior, then the results of these data collection techniques would be regarded as unreliable and therefore suspect.

Validity. Is the technique valid? Validity is the extent to which the technique measures what it claims to measure. For example, if you are using a measure of rejection sensitivity, the instrument should assess sensitivity to rejection, not social avoidance or neuroticism. Likewise, a measure of tolerance for aggression should not measure dislike for the experimenter or experimental situation. The **predictive validity** of a measure refers to how accurately it predicts children's behaviors in the future or, perhaps, in other contexts. This type of validity is often of particular interest to developmentalists. For example, a finding that early aptitude in mathematics predicts good grades in math classes in middle school demonstrates predictive validity. A published test should report this information in its instruction booklet or manual. Also, if an interview or observational technique is used, the behavior being observed should meet the definitions for the construct in the research. For example, acts that count as physical and verbal aggression are clearly described in several published research articles and can be used in your own research (Crick, 1996; Tremblay, 2000). Even if the criteria or definitions of a certain set of behaviors are unclear, decisions about what you are interested in studying within your own research agenda need to be made prior to the commencement of your study (Johnson & Johnson, 2002).

Generalizability. One final question regarding the quality of the data collection approach is how **generalizable** the results are. Generalizability is the extent the findings of the study are applicable to other children or groups of children. This issue is common to several of the data collection techniques. If only a single child or group is tested, interviewed, or observed, the results cannot be applied beyond the research participants used in the study. If, however, the group of participants tested, interviewed, or observed includes a large number of persons with diverse racial, ethnic, economic, religious, and sexual-orientation backgrounds, then the results could be generalized to others. However, the goal of research is not always to generalize the results to others; it depends on the original research questions asked. It may be that the original hypothesis is best tested by a clinical interview with a small group of families, thereby limiting generalizability. However, if the results of a study are meant to apply to *all* 10-year-olds, then the participant population should be large and diverse. Information about the number and type of research participants in the study is typically included in the method section of a published study to allow the reader to draw conclusions about the generalizability of the findings.

A summary of the various quantitative data collection techniques can be found in Table 1–2.

The quantitative data collection techniques discussed in this section describe how researchers have collected information about the abilities and behaviors of school-age children. Recent textbooks on research methodology focus on these traditional methods exclusively (e.g., Greer & Mulhern, 2002; Vadum & Rankin, 1998). A reliance on quantitative data-gathering strategies has a long history within the social sciences, which have mimicked the natural sciences in reducing human behavior to quantifiable unit of analysis (Fox, Porter, & Wokler, 1995). However, the complexity of human behavior does not lend itself easily to this type of reductionism (as might a chemical or biological phenomenon), and some researchers argue the overuse of these techniques is restricting our view of developing children in all of their complexities and contexts for growth (Overton, 1998). For this reason, a movement is taking place within the field of child development toward the increased use of qualitative data collection strategies (Camic, Rhodes, & Yardley, 2003; Hayes, 2000; Magee, 2002).

Qualitative Data Collection

Qualitative methods typically yield nonnumeric data that lead to a greater understanding of the participant. The data are summaries or descriptions of the development, and/or the factors that influence development, of an individual or groups of individuals. Such data are not ready for statistical analysis,

TABLE 1–2

Summary of Quantitative Data Collection Techniques

Data collection techniques that typically yield numerical data, their suggested uses, and limitations.

Technique	Uses	Limitations
Self-report questionnaires	• Used with large number of participants • Assesses attitudes and feelings • Much data collected in a short period of time	• Subject to honesty bias, memory bias, and social desirability bias • Requires reading and writing competency
Systematic observations	• Used with a small number of participants • Yields information about overt behavior in the child's natural environment • Useful to understand complex actions and interactions	• Behaviors may be influenced by observer presence • No control over experimental setting • Time-consuming and effortful • Subject to observer bias • Can only infer cognitions
Standardized measures	• Used with large groups • Participants' scores can be compared to established norms • Reliability and validity can be established • Useful information in specific domains	• Limited test availability • Must be trained to administer • Cannot generalize from a single score • May not reflect developmental change

but need some processing by the researcher. Qualitative researchers rely on the human researcher as instrument (rather than a pencil-and-paper test), respect the cultural and sociohistorical "truths" told by their participants, and recognize their bias as "outsiders" and "interpreters" of experience (Merrick, 1999). Qualitative research may be conducted in many ways, but there are recurring features in the variety of approaches used (Miles & Huberman, 1994):

- Qualitative research is conducted through an intense and/or prolonged contact with a "field" or life situation.
- The researcher's role is to gain a "holistic" overview of the context under study.
- The researcher attempts to capture data "from the inside" and suspend preconceptions about the subject of interest.
- Researchers allow original responses to be maintained throughout the study.
- Most analysis is done with words.

Qualitative data collection techniques bring to a research question a rich analytical perspective that can be viewed as complementary to the more traditional quantitative techniques (Denzin & Lincoln, 2000; Ponterotto, 2005).

Interview studies. An interview allows the researcher to pose questions to a person face-to-face. An advantage of this method is that it eliminates reading and writing skill requirements for the research participant, and the interviewer can answer any questions the interviewee may have about directions or specific items. An interview technique is particularly useful when researching populations in which English is a second language or when the researcher anticipates a need for flexibility in the generation of questions. Interviews can be conducted in different ways and can vary in structure and in the generalizability of the information obtained.

A **clinical interview method** is a flexible interview procedure that allows the interviewer to shape the order and type of questions asked to obtain the best reflection of the child's or parent's thinking. This technique involves modifications to questions based on the responses as well as multiple follow-up probes. Jean Piaget (1896–1980) was well known for using this technique to study cognitive development. After a child responded "yes" or "no" to a problem-solving question, Piaget proceeded to ask a series of questions that revealed the child's approach to his answer. The following conversation between Piaget and an 8-year-old illustrates the child's developing concept of age:

> Question: Have you siblings?
> *Answer*: *I have two small brothers, Charles and Jean.*
> Question: Who was born first?
> *Answer*: *Me, then Charlie, and finally Jean.*
> Question: When you are grown up, how old will you all be?
> *Answer*: *I'll be the oldest, then Charlie and then Jean.*
> Question: How much older will you be?
> *Answer*: *The same as now.*
> Question: Why?
> *Answer*: *It's always the same. It all depends on when one was born.*

For Piaget, the child's approach to the problem, not his final response, identified developmental differences in cognitive processing.

This flexible method allows an interviewer to gather in-depth information on a wide range of topics from a single interviewee. However, the questions developed during the interview are unlikely to be the same questions generated in an interview with another child, or by another interviewer, thereby making it difficult to generalize the findings to any other participant or population. Given the purposes of your research, this may not be a major concern. Another consideration is that most interviews will need to be transcribed and coded from audio or audiovisual tapes, which might be very time-consuming if you have interviewed large numbers of children. One way to solve this problem is to use a more structured interview.

A **structured interview** asks the same questions of every person in the same way. This format assures that all interviewees are treated the same way and eliminates any researcher bias that may influence the direction of the interview. The design of the questions in a structured interview can also limit the length of response, thereby reducing the time spent transcribing the interview. Much valuable information and insight can be gathered by asking children and adolescents, parents, and teachers to comment on their lives and experiences. In one study, for example, researchers used a structured interview to determine which variables influenced girls to choose careers in science. Interviewers asked girls in grades 2, 5, 8, and 11 their feelings about science, science careers, peer and parental support, and how science is taught (Baker & Leary, 1995). Through this structured

A structured interview asks the same questions of all participants in the same way.

interview method, the researchers found that girls thought that women can and should do science and that they liked learning science in an interactive social context rather than in activities that encouraged independence and isolation, like reading, writing, and note-taking. Also, girls who chose science careers were attracted by the careers' potential to help others (e.g., medicine).

Structured interviews are also an integral part of focus groups, which generate and process qualitative data. Box 1.3 describes how focus groups operate.

Some researchers have concerns about the suitability of this research methodology with school-age children and young adolescents (Morgan, 1996, 1997). However, others have argued that the format is well suited for young participants (Graue & Walsh, 1998; Horner, 2000) (for a review, see Morgan, Gibbs, Maxwell, & Britten, 2002).

BOX 1.3 ROADMAP TO UNDERSTANDING THEORY AND RESEARCH

Using Focus Groups in Developmental Research

Focus groups are a data collection technique that yields qualitative data. When a researcher is interested in learning about participants' perspectives, beliefs, and attitudes, focus groups are particularly fruitful. Focus groups involve children and adolescents in the research process by inviting everyone in a target group to respond to a set of semistructured discussion questions. Observing the dynamics of the group interaction is as interesting and important a part of the process as the responses given. Focus groups typically are used in applied settings, such as health-related fields, psychological counseling, and education (Heary & Hennessy, 2002; Kennedy, Kools, & Krueger, 2001; Krueger & Casey, 2000).

A focus group approach was used to study how middle-school children experience and manage their asthma (Penza-Clyve, Mansell, & McQuaid, 2004). Thirty-six students (age range 9–15) participated in a series of interviews to discuss their health experiences with the interviewer and each other. Semistructured interview questions included:

- What are some of the annoying things about having asthma?
- What gets in the way of taking your regular inhalers?
- What advice would you give a kid with asthma who was having a hard time taking his or her medications regularly?

Analysis of the qualitative responses showed that most participants mentioned lack of motivation, remembering difficulties, and social barriers as reasons for not taking their medication.

> You can't just stop what you are doing with your friends, go home and take your inhalers and then go back to where your friends were, because they are not there anymore. (p. 193)

With the guidance of the interviewer, participants were also able to generate strategies to combat these problems. They suggested reward systems to increase motivation, enhancing memory by using more effective strategies such as notes and setting watches, and taking one's medication in private to avoid social embarrassment. One paradoxical finding was that although this age group complained that parental reminders to take their medication were annoying, they also reported that parental prompts helped them adhere to their medication schedule.

Focus group methodology allows the participants to generate responses that are then used in a feedback loop to structure further questions. Responses to these questions are then used to assist in the identification of and potential solution to a problem, as was done in this study.

Arguments Against Using Focus Groups	Arguments for Using Focus Groups
• Middle-school children may lack the cognitive competency to analyze and hypothesize about health issues.	• Research has shown this age group to be cognitively competent to utilize this format.
• Middle-school children may be unable to formulate responses to open-ended interview questions.	• When asked to describe specific events or activities, young persons give complete, descriptive responses.
• Not all topics of study are suitable for this discussion format.	• The format encourages children and adolescents to talk to peers when they feel they cannot talk to adults.
• Peer hierarchies can dominate the flow of the discussion despite the best attempts of the interviewer to intervene.	• Participants feel empowered using the focus group format.
• Consensus building by can majority mute the voices of the minority.	• The group provides a safe haven for personal responses.
	• Middle-schoolers can gain support from peers who share their experiences.
	• Participants can learn from peers how they handle health issues.

Narrative studies. Many researchers recognize the limitations of traditional quantitative research methods, especially when studying experiences that are extremely difficult to speak about, such as difficult life transitions and trauma (Roth, 1993). At times, the best data collection method may be having the person tell a story about what transpired. **Narrative analysis**, or the analysis of stories, examines not only the content of the story but the *way* the story is told. This data collection technique focuses on how a person imposes order on experiences, the language that is used to tell the story, and the cultural influences that are reflected in the story (Muller, 1999; Flick, 2002).

For example, Lyn Mikel Brown, Carol Gilligan, and their research team (1992) were engaged in a longitudinal study of girls (ages 7–18) to assess how their relational worlds and "voices" changed as they navigated through adolescence. After 3 years of structured interviews—asking carefully developed questions consistently and using standard procedures for analyzing interview data—the research team decided to abandon their research strategy. They felt that their well-designed questions no longer "seemed right" and "seemed to be cutting off girls' voices" (Brown & Gilligan, 1992, p. 18). Instead, they adopted a narrative approach to allow the girls to tell stories about when they felt "in relationship" and when they did not.

Here is a story told by Noura about her anger when a teacher asked her to leave class for making a laughing noise:

> *He could have just tried to ignore [my laughter], because we have to ignore a lot of things that a lot of our teachers do . . . like when they are really mean . . . not necessarily mean, but like we think of it as unfair, but I guess it really is fair in a way . . . . It's his class and he can, or any teacher can just assign whatever they want, but I mean it seems unfair to us . . . I hate it . . . . It makes me mad when they make you do like, I mean I guess it's good in the long run, but I don't know.* (p. 121)

Consistent with the narrative format, Noura's story was analyzed for four components as she speaks of relationships: (a) Who is speaking? (b) In what body? (c) Telling what story about relationships—from whose perspective or from what vantage point? and (d) In what societal and cultural frameworks? Her telling of the story is noted for "speaking her feelings and then retracting them," for being "sure of her feelings and then uncertain" (p. 121). Her mixed response to what she perceives as unfair is compared to her ability to openly and confidently express anger 3 years previously at age 11.

Narratives were a rich source of data for this longitudinal study (Brown & Gilligan, 1992) that yielded important results about adolescent girls and their struggle to maintain their "voices" and sense of self. Narrative analysis has also been used to analyze stories about decisions to smoke (Baillie, Lovato, Johnson, & Kalaw, 2005), menarche (Teitelman, 2004), and gender and socioeconomic experiences of minorities (Mainess, Champion, & McCabe,

2002). It has provided another dimension to understanding these phenomena, but narrative analysis also has limitations (Riessman, 1993). It may not be useful with large numbers of participants, given the labor-intensiveness of the data collection, transcription, and analysis. And because of the importance of embedding the narrative in context, it is difficult to generalize the results from one participant's story to others', even from the same small sample.

Do you have a story that captures or defines some aspect of your development?

Ethnography. The increasing need to understand the role that culture plays in the development of school-age children and adolescents encourages us to look for techniques that disciplines like sociology and anthropology may use to study other societies and cultures. If your research question were to ask the extent to which cultural differences mediate adolescents' views towards work, then **ethnography**, a technique borrowed from anthropology, might be useful. Ethnography is the study of a culture or social group, rather than of individuals, in order to understand the unique characteristics and values of the group and how they may influence the development of their children and adolescents (Creswell & Maietta, 2002; McCurdy, Spradley, & Shandy, 2002). Using a method called *participant observation*, the researcher lives with a group for several months or years and participates in their daily lives. Extensive field notes are taken and combined with observational data and interviews to present a detailed account of the unique values, attitudes, and behaviors of a culture or societal group.

For example, ethnographic data collection was used to explore what makes students in middle school popular or unpopular (Eder, 1995). By spending a great deal of time at the middle school, eating lunch in the cafeteria with the students, and attending extracurricular events, the research team amassed extensive observations and field notes about the social world of these middle-schoolers. In the sixth grade, they found that the social hierarchy was not well established and that popularity was defined as "most visible" rather than "best liked." But because the sixth graders had few opportunities to become "more visible," there was a greater sense of equality among students. However, in the seventh grade, when students were able to join cheerleading and athletic clubs, a few chosen ones attained greater visibility. A hierarchy was quickly established, with the male athletes and female cheerleaders becoming the "most visible" and, therefore, members of an elite peer group. This hierarchy appeared to be accepted and supported not only by the students themselves but also by the parents, teachers, coaches, and community members.

The greatest advantage to using ethnography to study development is its ability to immerse observers in the culture so they can record the role that culture plays in the targeted area of development. A limitation is the bias an ethnographer's presence may introduce into the group. However, a clinical interview method or observational technique may also introduce bias. The cultural perspective of the researcher may inadvertently influence the questions asked, the observations made, and the conclusions drawn. Finally, the findings from one culture or social group cannot be generalized (Hammersley, 1992).

Perhaps an ethnographic study of Takuya with his family, peers, and larger cultural community might yield interesting insights into his social skills, ability to deal with social exclusion, interactions with authority figures, and minority status within a majority culture.

Evaluating Qualitative Data

Qualitative data-gathering strategies have expanded our knowledge of how children develop within complex social networks and settings. They are not, however, immune to criticism. Some view qualitative research as too "relativistic," "loose," and subjective. Critics claim that there is no way to establish the validity or "truth value" of scientific claims or observations based on qualitative work (e.g., Jessor, 1996). Those researchers who employ qualitative data collection techniques argue that the criteria by which we judge quantitative data do not, and *should* not, apply to qualitative research findings. So how should we judge the quality of this research process and its findings?

It is debatable whether the terms *validity* and *reliability* have a place in the evaluation of qualitative data (Becker, 1996; Lather, 1994). Typically, statistical analyses measure these criteria for various quantitative scores. If, however, your data collection methods provide no numbers, how can we be sure that you are measuring what you say you are (i.e., validity) and that your results will be consistent (i.e., reliability)? Because many researchers are trained to evaluate research findings using these criteria, qualitative researchers have provided the following comparable criteria or questions to employ with qualitative data (Lincoln & Guba, 2000; Morrow, 2005; Patton, 2002):

- Can I *depend* upon the research process as well as the findings? (i.e., reliability)
- Was the research process and interpretation of data *credible?* (i.e., validity)
- Are the findings *transferable* to another individual, group, or context? (i.e., generalizability)

Dependability. This term refers to the rigor of the methodology used to collect data as well as takes into account the researcher's characteristics. Asking the following questions can assess the dependability of qualitative research:

- What types of data collection techniques were used? With whom? Under what arrangements?
- Who conducted this research and interpreted the data?
- What biases or preconceptions might the researchers have brought with them to the study?

The "dependability" of the study can be established by the researcher (a) disclosing his or her orientation, (b) engaging the material in an intensive and prolonged manner, (c) carrying out repeated observations, (d) checking the accuracy of specific items of data by using multiple sources (called **triangulation**), and (e) discussing the findings and process with colleagues and the participants in the study. If the data are collected and recorded in a careful and systematic manner and in a way that acknowledges the researcher's biases, then the findings of the study are dependable and likely to be found again in a similar research context.

Credibility. This criterion refers to the accuracy of the data collected and conclusions drawn. Readers of qualitative research can assess credibility by determining the adequacy of the researcher's understanding, interpretation, and representation of people's meanings (Altheide & Johnson, 1994; Banister, Burman, Parker, Taylor, & Tindall, 1994). **Credibility** can be established by **referential adequacy**, which means comparing interpreted findings with the data and using consensus or peer agreement to achieve interpretive conclusions.

Transferability. Transferability is the ability to apply the findings of one qualitative research study to another. Qualitative researchers should provide a complete description of the process of their study, the data, and the interpretation of those data to enable the reader to make a decision about the transferability of findings from one individual or group to another. However, qualitative researchers believe that the strength of the qualitative method is its recognition of the subjectivity and reflexivity of the researchers and of the unique time and place associated with each study.

Conducting Your Own Research

After reading this chapter you might feel overwhelmed by the many choices researchers must make in order to study school-age children and adolescents. However, becoming familiar with these data collection techniques allows you to link theoretical questions with practical application. Tables 1.2 and 1.3 can be used as guides to remind you of the common use, strengths, and limitations of each technique. Remember, it is the theoretical question or hypothesis that best determines which data collection method should be used.

By presenting these data collection techniques one-by-one, we may have given the impression that choosing one excludes the others. Not so. Many researchers rely on a combination of these techniques to reach the best conclusions about development. For example, **case studies** are an accumulated record of a single child or group over time. Researchers using case studies may organize and summarize information obtained from a variety of measures, such as questionnaires, interviews, observations, and standardized or performance measures. For example, researchers followed a group of academically successful, low-income African American sixth graders as they made the transition from ninth grade into high school (Newman, Myers, Newman, Lohman, & Smith, 2000). In order to investigate which youth navigated the transition

TABLE 1–3

Summary of Qualitative Data Collection Techniques

Data collection techniques that typically yield verbal responses or descriptions and their suggested uses and limitations.

Technique	Uses	Limitations
Interviews	• Used with a small number of participants • Yields in-depth information • Requires no reading or writing competency	• Questions may vary • Difficult to generalize results • Relies on verbal ability • Subject to interviewer bias
Narrative studies	• Used with a small number of participants • Useful for studying developmental transitions or trauma • Useful to understand the content of stories and *how* they are told	• Behavior may be influenced by observer • Data collection, transcription, and analysis is time-consuming and effortful • Researcher bias
Ethnography	• Used with large or small groups • Can observe the role of culture in development	• Ethnographer may influence group dynamics • Subject to observer bias • Difficult to generalize results

successfully and why, they used the following data collection strategies:

- Tape-recorded, in-depth interviews with students
- Student responses to standardized measures of academic motivation, self-esteem, and academic self-efficacy
- Taped interviews with coordinators of the youth program
- Paper-and-pencil questionnaires completed by persons identified by the students as academically supportive

Case narratives for each student were then generated from these four sources of information. The researchers found that mothers' support, difficulty of the ninth-grade curriculum, and adjustment to a bigger and more complex school were related to students' academic performance after the transition to high school.

Action Research

The desire of social scientists to conduct research with greater social relevance has resulted in the increased use of **action research** (Small, 1995). Action research is a methodological approach in which the researcher uses research findings to solve a practical problem or concern while, at the same time, generating critical knowledge about the issue. Action research has been practiced since the 1920s as a general strategy for institutional change. More recently, action research has been conducted in both educational and family practice settings and has informed social policy makers about human development (Brydon-Miller, 1997, 2001; Greenwood & Levin, 1998).

Action research does not have any prescribed methodology; its unique feature is that a study's focus and method may change as the research process unfolds. Most important, action researchers work collaboratively with research participants to shape the focus of the inquiry and to craft a solution to a mutually identified problem based on the study's findings.

Action research typically includes the following four steps, as illustrated in Figure 1.8:

1. Selecting an area of focus or inquiry
2. Collecting data and information
3. Analyzing and interpreting the data
4. Developing and implementing a plan for action

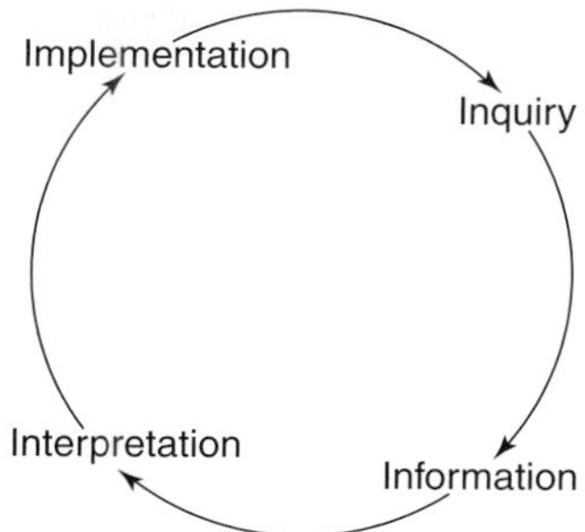

FIGURE 1.8 The Interactive Components of Action Research
This figure shows how the outcomes of action research influence the research process in a continuous feedback loop.

To apply the action research steps, you would begin with the identification of a question. For example, you might want to find out why a majority of your seventh-grade algebra students are not completing their homework. You construct a brief survey with items that ask the students to rate their level of agreement with a variety of possible explanations (e.g., not enough time due to extracurricular activities, not enough time due to part-time job, don't understand the problems, not motivated). You also ask the students to answer open-ended questions that give them the opportunity to explain why their homework was not completed. Much to your surprise, you learn from your students that the book required for completing their homework was too heavy to take home on a regular basis. As a result, many students planned to finish their algebra assignment at school the next day, often unsuccessfully. You can now interpret the responses with your students and try several plans of action to increase the probability that homework is finished in the future.

The preceding example followed the four suggested steps for action research. You identified a practical problem (unfinished homework) and collected data not only to identify the source of the problem but also to generate solutions with the participants in the study (the students). One of the advantages of action research is that it empowers practitioners working closely with school-age children and youth to identify, explore, and "solve" their own specific research questions. However, it shares with many research methods vulnerability to experimenter bias. Remember that the biases of the person or persons asking the questions, collecting the information, performing analysis or interpretation, and planning a course of action may alter the direction and success of an action research project.

Based on your personal experiences with school-age children, how would you involve them in asking a research question?

Program Evaluation

Many of you may be involved, currently or in the future, with a program that is designed to protect, help, and/or enhance the development of school-age children and adolescents. At some point, either your own agency or program or an external funding source may want to know if your efforts are successful. The process of identifying the goals of your organization and assessing your success in meeting those objectives is **program evaluation**. The type of evaluation you undertake to assess your program depends on what you want to learn about the program. For example, if you are involved in a community recreation center and one of the center's goals is to provide a safe environment for teenagers in the evening and on the weekends in order to reduce victimization rates, then your program evaluation should assess this component.

There are many ways to evaluate a program and many resources available to help you do so (Chen, 2005; Royse, Thyer, Padgett, & Logan, 2006). Asking the following questions is a good way to begin:

- Why is the evaluation being done?
- Who will receive the information from the evaluation?
- What kinds of information are needed to make the decision you or others need to make?
- From what sources should the information be collected?
- How can that information be collected? (For this step, you can use any number of the data collection techniques presented in this chapter.)
- What resources are available to collect the information?
- How should the outcome information be presented?

A thorough program evaluation can help you identify the strengths and weaknesses of your organization or program, assist you in increasing the efficiency and effectiveness of your services, and verify that you are doing what you think you are doing (McNamara, 1998).

TABLE 1–4

Ethical Standards for Research

Fuller explanations of each guideline can be found at http://www.srcd.org/about.html#standards.

1. *Non-harmful Procedures*: The investigator should use no research procedure that may harm the child either physically or psychologically.
2. *Informed Consent*: The investigator should inform the child of all features of the research that may affect his or her willingness to participate and should answer the child's questions in terms appropriate to the child's comprehension.
3. *Parental Consent*: The informed consent of parents or legal guardians should be obtained, preferably in writing.
4. *Additional Consent*: The informed consent of any persons, such as teachers, for example, whose interaction with the child as the participant in the study, should also be obtained.
5. *Incentives*: Incentives to participate in a research project must be fair and must not unduly exceed the range of incentives that the child normally experiences.
6. *Deception*: If withholding information or deception is practiced, and there is reason to believe that the research participants have been negatively affected by it, adequate measures should be taken after the study to ensure the participants' understanding of the reasons for the deception.
7. *Anonymity*: To gain access to institutional records, the investigator should obtain permission from responsible authorities in charge of records. Anonymity of the information should be preserved and no information used other than that for which permission was obtained.
8. *Mutual Responsibilities*: From the beginning of each research investigation, there should be clear agreement between the investigator and the parents, guardians or those who act *in loco parentis*, and the child, when appropriate, that defines the responsibilities of each.
9. *Jeopardy*: When, in the course of research, information comes to the investigator's attention that may jeopardize the child's well-being, the investigator has a responsibility to discuss the information with the parents or guardians and with those expert in the field in order that they may arrange the necessary assistance for the child.
10. *Unforeseen Consequences*: When research procedures result in undesirable consequences for the participant that were previously unforeseen, the investigator should immediately employ appropriate measures to correct these consequences.
11. *Confidentiality*: The investigator should keep in confidence all information obtained about research participants.
12. *Informing Participants*: Immediately after the data are collected, the investigator should clarify for the research participant any misconceptions that may have arisen and report general findings in terms appropriate to their understanding.
13. *Reporting Results*: Because the investigator's words may carry unintended weight with parents and children, caution should be exercised in reporting results, making evaluative statements, or giving advice.
14. *Implications of Findings*: Investigators should be mindful of the social, political and human implications of their research and should be especially careful in the presentation of findings from the research.
15. *Scientific Misconduct*: Misconduct is defined as the fabrication or falsification of data, plagiarism, misrepresentation, or other practices that seriously deviate from those that are commonly accepted within the scientific community.
16. *Personal Misconduct*: Personal misconduct that results in a criminal conviction of a felony may be sufficient grounds for a member's expulsion from the Society.

Source: From "Ethical Standards for Research with Children" by the Society for Research in Child Development, 1990–1991. Retrieved from: http://www.srcd.org/about.html#standards (October 20, 2002).

Ethical Guidelines

When initiating research or evaluation with children and adolescents, ethical standards need to be followed. In any study, the needs of the children, their parents, and their families must take priority over the advancement of science. It is imperative that you, as a potential researcher, know and adhere to ethical principles in your research. Ethical guidelines to protect the rights of children and parents who participate in research studies, listed in Table 1–4, have been adopted by the Society for Research in Child Development.

This chapter has provided you with an introduction to research designs and methods of collecting information about school-age children and adolescents. Our hope is that as you develop questions about children with whom you work or the setting within which you work, you can employ some of these techniques to find answers. Even more important—regardless of whether you are a student, day care provider, or future teacher—this information may assist you in assessing the research methods used by others and thereby recognizing the strengths and limitations of developmental research.

CHAPTER REVIEW

Theoretical Issues

- Developmental theories describe change and the variables that affect that change. They also help organize our observations and guide our everyday interactions with school-age children and adolescents.
- A number of theoretical issues distinguish developmental theories from one another. Differences are based on whether children's skills develop in a continuous (i.e., gradual) or discontinuous (i.e., stagelike) pattern, how much nature (e.g., biology) or nurture (e.g., environment) influences development, and whether characteristics of children remain stable or unstable across time and contexts.
- Theories are linked to research through either deductive or inductive reasoning. Research is linked to practice through both basic and applied research. Basic research informs professional practice with school-age children and adolescents. Applied research is used to solve real-world problems facing children, their families, and teachers.

Developmental Research

- Cross-sectional studies assess children of different ages at the same point in time. These designs identify differences in a skill or ability between different-aged children and *when* a skill emerges or changes. They are less able to identify how change occurs, and cohort effects may influence the developmental differences found in such studies.
- Longitudinal studies assess the same children over time. Because these designs follow the same children, *how* a skill or ability develops and *which* variables most influence the developmental process can be identified. Longitudinal studies also tell us something about how early experiences influence development later in life and the stability or instability of certain characteristics. Cohort effects, attrition, and research participants becoming "test wise" need to be taken into consideration.
- Longitudinal-sequential studies combine cross-sectional and longitudinal designs by including several different cohorts and then following these groups over several years. These designs avoid many of the limitations of cross-sectional and longitudinal studies; however, not many sequential studies are conducted because of the time and costs involved.

Data Collection Techniques

- The type of data collection technique that researchers use depends upon the question that needs answering. Quantitative data collection techniques include standardized measures, observations, and self-reports. Each of these data-gathering strategies has its strengths and limitations. Assessing the reliability, validity, and generalizability of each technique helps to determine the best use of the results.
- Qualitative data collection techniques typically yield nonnumeric data. Interviews, case studies, narrative studies, and ethnographies collect verbal information from the participants, and their content and "voice" are interpreted to understand development. Assessing the dependability, credibility, and transferability of each technique aids in understanding how and to what extent the information from one particular study can be used.

Conducting Your Own Research

- One can make use of multiple data collection techniques when conducting research. Case studies are often derived by using several different methods.
- Action research combines data collection with a feedback loop so that the participants are continuously influencing the research question(s) being asked and the way the data are being collected.
- Program evaluation is a systematic process through which the goals of a program are identified and assessed. The outcomes of program evaluation can be used to improve the program by identifying its areas of strength and weakness.
- Researchers need to acquire informed consent, protect the identity of the participant, and treat any information obtained from the participant with confidentiality.

TABLE 1–5

Summary Table of Developmental Theories

Chapter	Theories	Focus
1: Studying Middle Childhood and Adolescence	Purpose of theories	Generating research questions and a framework for organizing facts, interpreting data, and drawing conclusions.
2: Perspectives on Middle Childhood	Ecological	The many embedded environments in which children develop over time—from the more immediate, such as family, school, and community, to the more remote, such as the broader society and culture.
	Developmental-contextual	Dynamic developmental and reciprocal relationship processes that occur between parents, children, and their social networks within the embedded contexts of ecological theory.
3: Physical Development in Middle Childhood	Behavior-genetic	Influence of genes and the environment on development through the analysis of shared and nonshared environments.
	Biological	The study of such fields as behavioral neuroscience of how brain structure, function, and chemistry influence behavior.
4: Cognitive Development in Middle Childhood	Cognitive-developmental	How children develop thought and problem-solving skills in direct interaction with the environment through the processes of assimilation and accommodation.
	Sociocultural	Development of thought through language development and interacting with elders from one's culture.
	Information processing	How children process information through perception, memory, and knowledge and the factors that influence their development.
5: Affective Development in Middle Childhood	Psychoanalytic	The process of individuation as the basis for personality development and establishing a sense of self.
	Psychosocial	Period of industry vs. inferiority in which a major task is the acquisition of competence and the avoidance of failure.
	Humanistic	Self-actualization and personal growth as well as the importance of positive regard from others in "being human."
6: Social Development in Middle Childhood	Social learning	Learning by observing models and by examining the consequences of their own and others' behaviors in the social environment.
	Social information processing	Cognitive steps that children take when making sense of social cues and deciding how to respond to others.
	Social theories of mind	Ways that children themselves create theories to explain and predict other people's motivations and behaviors.
7: Perspectives on Middle Adolescence	Life span	Development in relation to preceding and subsequent stages with a focus on both individual differences and developmental changes over time.

TABLE 1–5
Summary Table of Developmental Theories (Continued)

Chapter	Theories	Focus
	Life course	Normative and nonnormative life events that are shaped by both historical events and adolescents' personal life histories.
8: Physical Development in Middle Adolescence	Evolutionary	How selected genes helped our ancestors survive and reproduce, and how these same genes may influence our behavior and thinking.
9: Cognitive Development in Middle Adolescence	Cognitive-developmental	Series of stages in which adolescents struggle to make sense of the world. Through active construction of schemata, they become abstract reasoners.
	Information processing	How information is stored and operated on internally. Adolescents process information more quickly, use more effective strategies, and have a greater knowledge base upon which to build.
10: Affective Development in Middle Adolescence	Ego development	Gradual changes in self-definition during adolescence that involve increasing autonomy and self-reliance.
	Identity	Exploring ideological and interpersonal commitments as well as group identities, such as ethnicity, religion, and gender.
	Symbolic interaction	Relationships take place in a social context and are subject to socially constructed meanings.
11: Social Development in Middle Adolescence	Attachment	Internal working models of early relationships in families as the basis of later close relationships, such as peer relations, friendships, and romantic partnerships.
	Family systems	Equilibrium among simultaneous interdependent subsystems, such as the parent-child, marital, or sibling systems.
12: Beyond Middle Adolescence: Emerging Adulthood	Applied developmental psychology	Health and well-being across the life span taking into account cultural and ethnic background, economic and social opportunity, physical and cognitive ability, and family, neighborhood, and community.
	Developmental science	Complex interactions between persons and environments using interdisciplinary frameworks, holistic models, and policy applications.

KEY TERMS

Achievement tests
Action research
Applied research
Aptitude tests
Attrition
Basic research
Case study
Clinical interview method
Cohort bias
Continuity
Credibility
Criterion-referenced tests
Cross-sectional study
Deductive reasoning
Dependability
Developmental theory
Discontinuity
Discontinuous
Ethnography
Event sampling
Generalizable
Honesty bias
Hypothesis
Inductive reasoning

Instability
Interrater reliability
Longitudinal study
Longitudinal-sequential study
Memory bias
Narrative analysis
Naturalistic
Nature
Norm-referenced tests
Norms
Nurture
Observational techniques
Performance measures
Person-centered approach
Person-environment centered
Predictive validity
Program evaluation
Qualitative methods
Reliability
Self-report techniques
Social desirability bias
Specimen record
Stability
Standardized tests
Structured interview
Structured observation
Test-retest reliability
Theories
Time sampling
Transferability
Triangulation
Validity
Variables
Variable-centered approach

SUGGESTED ACTIVITIES

1. Observe any group of children between 8 to 18 years of age playing or interacting in their natural environment (e.g., playground, park, school, team practice). Record behaviors or characteristics you find interesting on the left side of the paper, and on the right, write down your assumptions about the origins of those behaviors or characteristics. After you have recorded eight to ten observations, examine the list of assumptions on the right. Where do you think the majority of behaviors originate? Why? Do you have any information to support your assumptions?
2. Observing the same group of children/adolescents, use the time sampling and event sampling sheets from this chapter (Figures 1.5 and 1.6) to record information about a target behavior (e.g., helping behavior, aggressive behavior, conflict resolution tactics). Which sampling sheet provided the best information about your target behavior? Why? What were the strengths and limitations of using observational techniques to understand the target behavior? Which data collection technique would you prefer to use?
3. Locate three recently published journal articles that use a cross-sectional, longitudinal, or longitudinal-sequential design. Ask yourself what research question was asked originally and if the question was answered by using the specific design. What design limitations did the authors of the article identify?
4. Ask several friends to share with you a story about their childhood that includes a common theme, such as getting into trouble at school, or their first romantic encounter, or an argument with their best friend. After collecting several stories, try to analyze components of the stories that may reflect something about the developmental status of the storyteller. Were common themes shared, and what can these themes tell us about how children develop in different contexts?

RECOMMENDED RESOURCES

Suggested Readings

Camic, P. M., Rhodes, J. E., & Yardley, L. (Eds.). (2003). *Qualitative research in psychology: Expanding perspectives in methodology and design*. Washington, DC: American Psychological Association.

Haladyna, T. M. (2002). *Essentials of standardized achievement testing: Validity and accountability*. Boston: Allyn and Bacon.

Hartmann, D. P., & George, T. P. (1999). Design, measurement, and analysis in developmental research. In M. H. Bornstein & M. E. Lamb (Eds.), *Developmental psychology: An advanced textbook* (4th ed.). Hillsdale, NJ: Erlbaum.

Sagor, R. (2005). *The action research guidebook: A four-step process for educators and school teams*. Thousand Oaks, CA: Corwin Press, Inc.

Suggested Online Resources

Action Research (2005).
http://carbon.cudenver.edu/~mryder/itc/act_res.html

Analyzing Qualitative Data (1997).
http://www.ehr.nsf.gov/EHR/REC/pubs/NSF97-153/CHAP_4.HTM

Basic Guide to Program Evaluation (1999).
http://www.mapnp.org/library/evaluatn/fnl_eval.htm

Suggested Web Sites

Ethical Standards for Research with Children (1990–1991). http://www.srcd.org/about.html#standards

Research: Nonexperimental Methods (2001). http://psyl.clarion.edu/mm/General/Methods/Methods.html

User-Friendly Handbook for Mixed Method Evaluations (1997). http://www.ehr.nsf.gov/EHR/REC/pubs/NSF97-153/START.HTM#TOC

Suggested Films and Videos

Learning to observe. (2003). Insight Media, Inc. (Windows or Mac CD-ROM)

Observing child development. (2003). Prentice-Hall, Inc. (Windows or Mac CD-ROM)

Research methods for the social sciences. (1995). Insight Media, Inc. (33 minutes)

Survey savvy: Planning and conducting a successful survey. (2002). Insight Media, Inc. (24 minutes)

CHAPTER 

Perspectives on Middle Childhood

CHAPTER OBJECTIVES

After reading this chapter, students will be able to:

- Define the period of middle childhood
- Explain the reasons students, researchers, educators, and service providers should study middle childhood
- Discuss historical and contemporary portrayals of middle childhood
- Name the developmental achievements of middle childhood
- Identify the assumptions of ecological and contextual theories of human development
- Describe the diverse contexts in which middle childhood development occurs

Robyn, aged 8, arrives late to breakfast and plops down at the kitchen table with a thud, quickly pouring milk onto her cold cereal. Her 12-year-old sister Rachel and her 5-year-old sister Emily are almost finished eating. Hurrying to pack the girls' lunches before she is late for work again, their mother looks up, "How are you today, Robyn?" Robyn shrugs and replies, "I'd be lots better if I didn't have to go to that boring after-school program with Emily!" Rachel asks, "Why, don't you like it?" Robyn frowns. "None of my friends go there. They all say it's for little kids." "I'm not little!" chimes in Emily. "Little enough!" snaps Robyn. "Why can't I go to swimming practice or dance classes like Rachel? I want to do something IMPORTANT after school, not just play!"

Defining the Middle Childhood Years

Middle childhood is the developmental period between early childhood and adolescence, from approximately ages 8 to 12. Age 8 is typically thought of as the end of early childhood and the beginning of middle childhood. This period of development thus follows what developmental psychologists have described as a "5- to 7-year-old shift" in thinking ability (Davis-Kean & Sandler, 2001; White, 1996; Sameroff & Haith, 1996) but precedes the onset of puberty. As child developmentalists, we usually define middle childhood using indicators of child growth and development, such as cognitive or social maturation, rather than chronological age. School-age children, for example, are likely to be developing new skills and making new friends.

In this book, we are treating middle childhood as a developmental stage in its own right as well as a transitional period leading to adolescence. Because new developmental abilities emerge that cause school-age children to appear qualitatively different from children who are either younger or older than they are—either physically (e.g., the growth spurt), cognitively (e.g., the shift to concrete logic), affectively (e.g., feelings of self-competence), or socially (e.g., increased importance of peers)—we consider middle childhood to be an important and unique developmental stage in the life span. Developmental scholars have summarized the nature of middle childhood as follows:

- Around ages 6 or 7, new cognitive capacities emerge that enable school-age children to handle more complex intellectual problem solving and more intimate friendships than in early childhood.
- By around age 12, greater self-regulation and the consolidation of problem-solving skills allow school-age children to extend their abilities to tasks requiring flexible, abstract thinking and the maintenance of social relationships.
- Middle childhood development, although characterized by individual differences in the rates of growth, more powerfully predicts adolescent behaviors and success than does early childhood development (Collins, 1984).

These statements address, respectively, how school-age children typically appear when they *begin* this period and when they *end* the period and what can be predicted about their *futures*. For example, research suggests that Robyn's involvement in extracurricular activities in middle childhood will lead to her positive adjustment in early adolescence (McHale, Crouter, & Tucker, 2001).

Studies of middle childhood development come from many different sources—from medicine, psychology, education, anthropology, and sociology, to name just a few. Many of these fields define middle childhood *developmentally*. Health care providers, for example, describe middle childhood as the period after early childhood growth and development but before puberty. In fact, many clinical psychologists characterize middle childhood as a latency period that precedes the intense sexual interest of adolescence. And many educators believe that middle-school students are developmentally "in between" elementary and high school students, as humorously depicted by the "betweenagers" in the chapter's opening cartoon (see Figure 2.1).

Other disciplines define middle childhood *culturally*. Sociologists and anthropologists, for example, believe that society or culture determines the timing of both middle childhood and adolescence, whereas historians are likely to think that *all* of childhood is a modern invention. From today's perspective, for example, after-school child care is necessary because we believe that school-age children are not yet mature enough to be left unsupervised, as in the case study of Emily and Robyn. Similarly, juvenile justice programs have been established because we believe that most children are not legally competent to stand trial as adults until age 16 (Steinberg & Cauffman, 2001).

In Part I of this text, we have adopted the following underlying assumptions about middle childhood development (see Collins, 1984; Wyn & White, 1997):

- The period of middle childhood is not defined by biological age but by culture.
- The school-age child is an individual worthy of our attention, rather than a person to be marginalized as someone who is merely on a path to adolescence.
- The study of middle childhood requires understanding the contexts in which normal development occurs and the dynamic interactions between persons and environments.
- The concept of transitions is useful to understanding changes in the lived experiences of school-age children, brought about by developmental tasks, such as puberty, or by social practices, such as changing from elementary to middle school.
- Scholarship on middle childhood development relies on research from diverse disciplines,

FIGURE 2.1 Betweenagers
Luann and her best friend Bernice describe a common frustration of middle childhood.
Source: From "Luann" by G. Evans, January 14, 1990. Copyright 1990 by GEC Inc. Adapted by permission of United Features Syndicate, Inc.

traditionally organized under rubrics other than *middle childhood,* such as *school-age children* or *early adolescents.*

What other labels or descriptions have you heard to describe this age group?

Reasons to Study Middle Childhood

Developmental researchers from the related disciplines of psychology, child development, applied developmental science, family studies, and the health fields have emphasized the importance of the preadolescent period as a time of rapid growth and change. Understanding the developmental processes and contextual factors influencing middle childhood may provide answers to important basic questions about how children develop between ages 8 and 12. For example, as we learn more about the importance of protective factors—such as close relationships with significant adults—we find that youth who have a role model, teacher, or mentor are less likely to use drugs and alcohol, attempt suicide, engage in violence, or become sexually active at an early age (Werner & Smith, 1992; Resnick et al., 1997).

Many professionals who work with children between ages 8 and 12—whether in after-school child care centers, out-of-school recreation centers, or extramural athletic programs—need information on normative development, that is, on what to expect from children this age. We know, for example, that they are industrious workers, engaged learners, and loyal friends. But as we learn even more about middle childhood development and the factors that affect resiliency to risks such as poor neighborhoods, poverty, or family dysfunction, we will be able to design better programs to meet these group's developmental needs. For example, we have learned from researchers who evaluate prevention and intervention programs that to be successful, community-based programs for at-risk youth should be long-term and intensive rather than short-term and less engaging (Roth, Brooks-Gunn, Murray, & Foster, 1998). Applying the findings of basic developmental science may help practitioners design better services for 8- to 12-year-olds.

Adults raising children also want to know how best to enhance their children's success and development. For example, since families remain an important developmental influence even as school-age children expand their interest in peers, we know it is important for parents to remain connected with maturing early adolescents as they begin to seek more autonomy (Roth & Brooks-Gunn, 2000). Most research on middle-childhood parenting informs us that although a parenting style that is democratic, firm, and loving is beneficial for both children and adolescents (Baumrind, 1971), more strict limit setting may be necessary for youth living in dangerous neighborhoods (Sampson & Morenoff, 1997). Understanding the development of their school-age children and seeking ways to enhance their family and peer relationships may help parents and other caregivers improve the daily lives of children and families.

Legislators and policy makers often look for information on the effectiveness of youth intervention programs or prevention policies. Many public policy makers rely on findings from multidisciplinary middle childhood studies regarding the different developmental pathways of low-risk and high-risk youth and the factors that may alter healthy and risky behaviors (Roth & Brooks-Gunn, 2000). For example, researchers in pediatrics, psychiatry, psychology, public health, family studies, sociology, and education contribute to an overall understanding of such issues as substance abuse or school violence (McCall & Groark, 2000). Increasingly, public policy recommendations recognize middle childhood and early adolescence as important periods in which youth are seen as assets rather than as liabilities to the communities in which they live (Roth & Brooks-Gunn, 2000). Broadening their awareness of developmental outcomes in middle childhood may help policy makers and government agencies make better use of research findings in funding youth programs.

Teachers, principals, and school board members frequently use research findings on the middle childhood years to create developmentally appropriate curricula for the middle-level grades. Teachers who work with late-elementary or middle-school children need to identify developmental transitions between middle childhood and adolescence, such as signs of early puberty or hypothetical thinking. In view of research indicating substantial declines in academic achievement and motivation between elementary and middle school (Eccles & Buchanan, 1996), many scholars believe that the middle grades are "the last, best time" to reach vulnerable youth before educational problems become chronic (*Growing Up,* 2001). More important, researchers studying middle-level education believe that the developmental needs of the learner should dictate the curricular, instructional, and structural practices of a school (Anfara, 2001).

Historical Views of Middle Childhood

Our current view of middle childhood is based on the emergence over time of the idea of childhood as a period of development that is somehow distinct from adulthood. According to histories of childhood, Western cultural views of childhood began in the Middle Ages, when children's lives were first seen as separate from the world of adults (Aries, 1960/1962; deMause, 1995). Medieval European cultures divided childhood into *infancy, puerility*, and *adolescence* (Aries, 1960/1962). In this sequence, infancy (*in fans* means "without language" in Latin) preceded childhood (*pueritia* means "childhood or boyhood" in Latin), which was followed by adolescence (*adolescere* means "to grow into maturity" in Latin). This concept of developmental stages persisted throughout the European Renaissance and Enlightenment periods of the 17th and 18th centuries. Nevertheless, few Western children were protected from harsh treatment by adults or guaranteed the right to an education (deMause, 1995).

By the 19th century, however, an emerging middle class in both Europe and America allowed children time to prepare for a productive adult life. Childhood was viewed as a period worthy of nurture and protection. However, in both Europe and America, poor children and children from underrepresented groups did not enjoy the same privileges as the rest of the population (Trawick-Smith, 2003). For example, many children were required to work on farms or in factories as slaves or for extremely low wages rather than attend school. Although African American and American Indian children often did not have the social and economic advantages of most European American children, those cultures also regarded middle childhood as an important and cherished developmental period (Horn, 1993).

Today, in non-Western cultures childhood is often more highly valued than in European societies. For example, in Far Eastern cultures, Confucian teachings to value and respect children underlie a traditional emphasis on childhood education in countries such as China and Japan. In traditional African cultures, adults—especially mothers—exhibit a high degree of caring and concern for children. Historically, Latino cultures have stressed a commitment to sharing childrearing among all community members. And most American Indians emphasize teaching children and adolescents to be competent and skillful in the ways of their tribe (Trawick-Smith, 2006).

Most early practices in America, however, expressed ambiguity about childhood and adolescence on the one hand, and the following stage, known as *youth,* on the other (Aries, 1960/1962). Economic arrangements, such as apprenticeships

TABLE 2–1

Definitions of Middle Childhood

Definitions of middle childhood vary by discipline.

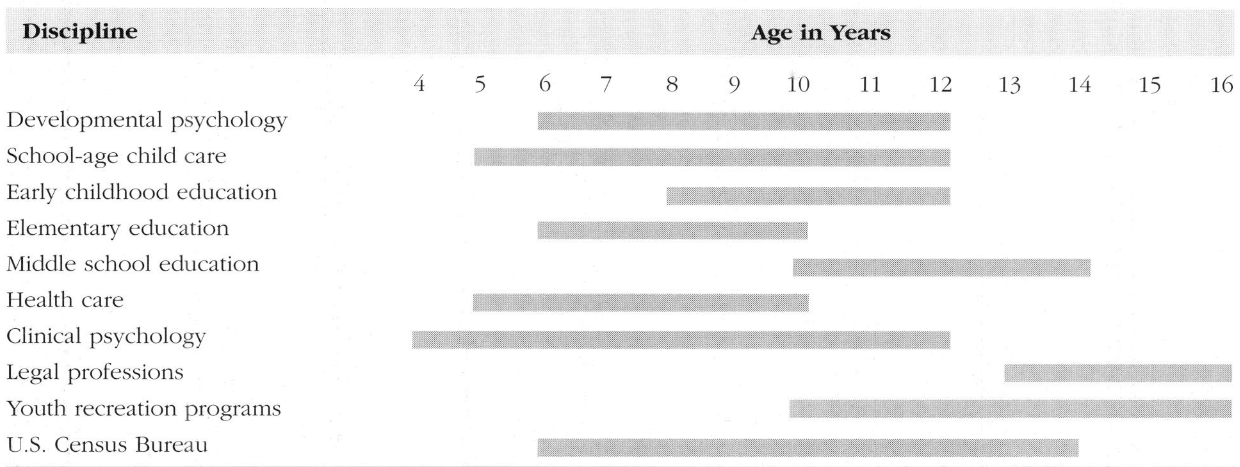

that often began at age 7 or 8, often obscured the boundary between childhood and adulthood. To a great extent, this confusion persists today, as demonstrated by the overlapping or conflicting age parameters used by different disciplines for the period of middle childhood (refer to Table 2–1). Inconsistent use of terms such as *school-age children, early adolescents, preteens*, and *youth* also makes it very difficult for educators, researchers, parents, or service providers to know when they are referring to the same children. This problem is exacerbated when parents try to find suitable programs: Should they look at "youth" services if their child is only 10 years old?

How would you have felt as a 10-year-old attending a youth program for teenagers?

Robyn, the middle child in her family, feels out of place in the after-school child care program attended by her younger sister Emily. She seems eager to engage in more varied out-of-school activities that could challenge her cognitive and physical skills beyond the classroom and would allow opportunities for more focused social interaction with friends.

Modern Contributions to Understanding Middle Childhood

At the turn of the 20th century, G. Stanley Hall, considered the first developmental psychologist by many scholars, reviewed the theoretical evidence for the concept that development extended beyond childhood into adolescence (Hall, 1904). Many developmental researchers, often Hall's students, carried out empirical studies of American children at different ages in an attempt to document the interaction of biological maturation, such as neurological development, and environmental experience, such as learning to read (Gesell & Ilg, 1943, 1946; Gesell, Ilg, & Ames, 1956). They accomplished this groundbreaking work by painstakingly assessing, interviewing, and observing children from infancy through adolescence. As a result, the first half of the 20th century was notable for the documentation of **normative**, or average, developmental abilities based on age across the years from birth through adolescence. By mid-century, the psychologist Arnold Gesell (1956) and his colleagues at the Yale Child Study Center had written a series of three books that fulfilled their goal of tracing "the course of development of normal youths in the concrete setting of their home, school, and community" (p. xii).

Middle childhood as a developmental period. Gesell documented the periods of infancy (birth to 2 years), preschool age (2 to 5 years), childhood (5 to 12 years), and adolescence (12 to 24 years) in three popular books published in the 1940s and 1950s. The first volume, *Infant and Child in the Culture of Today* (Gesell & Ilg, 1943), focused on early childhood (birth through age 5). The second and third volumes overlap the period presently called *middle childhood: The Child from Five to Ten* (Gesell & Ilg, 1946) and *Youth: The Years from Ten to Sixteen* (Gesell, Ilg, & Ames, 1956).

Gesell emphasized middle childhood as a distinct phase in the life span, in between early childhood and adolescence. He also believed that middle childhood is intermediate in both a maturational and a cultural sense. For example, cutting the first permanent tooth, a biological event, occurs around the time of school entrance, a sociological event. In fact, Gesell thought that middle childhood had been "slighted" by the educational system of his day, in which the curriculum was determined more by the institutional pressures of school and society than by the "psychology of development" (Gesell & Ilg, 1946). To understand how middle childhood came to be accepted as a stage of development, it is necessary to briefly examine what was occurring in American education in the early half of the 20th century.

In 1909, partly influenced by Hall's (1904) influential writings on development and partly as a response to overcrowding in the high schools of the era, the first junior high school was established to serve children in the seventh, eighth, and ninth grades. These "intermediate-school" models slowly began to replace the more common configuration of primary schools for grades 1 to 8 followed by secondary schools for grades 9 to 12. By the 1920s there were over 400 intermediate schools, and by the mid-1950s there were approximately 6,500 junior high schools in the United States (Wiles & Bondi, 2001). By this time, there also was an extensive educational literature on school-age children that described middle childhood as a unique developmental period called "preadolescence."

In the 1960s, a reform movement led by the humanistic educator William M. Alexander that focused on the needs of the student rather than the content of the curriculum resulted in the emergence of the modern middle school. These new schools started at even earlier ages than junior highs—at grade 5 or 6 (Manning & Bucher, 2000). The emergence of both junior high schools and middle schools was attributable to a desire to have high school academic subjects taught in earlier grades while emphasizing developmental differences in the ways that subject matter should be taught to less cognitively and socially mature students (Eichhorn, 1980; Wiles & Bondi, 2001).

In the 1970s, when most U.S. school systems were changing from junior highs to middle schools, the National Society for the Study of Education created a Committee on the Middle School Years to focus on ages 10 to 14 (Johnson, 1980). Noting the importance of the middle-school years, this committee recognized that the "pre-adolescent of eleven or twelve years is neither the ideal typical child of nine nor the archetypal adolescent of sixteen" (Lipsitz, 1980, p. 12). Its major concern was the "fit" or "lack of fit" between social institutions, especially schools, and the developmental needs of school-age children (Lipsitz, 1980).

In the 1980s, a panel of experts—assembled by the U.S. Committee on Child Development Research and Public Policy, the U.S. Commission on Behavioral and Social Sciences and Education, and the National Research Council—reviewed research on middle childhood and made recommendations for future research and public policy (Collins, 1984). The first task was to identify the age period commonly referred to as middle childhood. The panel sought to understand not only the development of children in middle childhood but also the **secular trends**, or variations across history, in the average age when a given phenomenon occurs. It soon realized that secular trends towards earlier puberty (than age 12) required more workable age groupings (e.g., preteens) for children whose physical, cognitive, and social characteristics were in transition (Collins, 1984). (Secular trends are discussed in detail in chapter 3.) Although any segmentation into age periods was viewed as somewhat arbitrary, the panel also observed that scholars had previously not been much concerned about the significance of changes in middle childhood. The members thought that recognizing middle childhood as a separate developmental period was important because it focused attention on the developmental characteristics of children and on the potential implications for teaching school-age children (Collins, 1984).

How many children comprise this group? In the United States, elementary school enrollment is estimated at 16.8 million in grades 1 through 4, and 16.1 million in grades 5 through 8, comprising about 40 percent of the total population (U.S. Census Bureau, 2001a, 2001b).

Middle childhood as a transition. During the 1990s, scholars from many disciplines (including developmental psychology, human development, family science, education, social work, and others) began to reconceptualize middle childhood as a transitional period between early childhood and adolescence. Developmental researchers reviewed the scientific evidence for considering (a) childhood and adolescence as different stages of the life span and (b) the onset of early adolescence as a transitional period (Montemayor, Adams, & Gulotta, 1990). Their work was summarized in a book called *From Childhood to Adolescence: A Transitional Period?* After examining the similarities and differences between children and adolescents, most scholars have concluded that many developmental abilities emerge gradually rather than suddenly (Montemayor & Flannery, 1990). For example, the onset of puberty—as measured by hormone levels—begins earlier (around age 9 or 10!) than previously thought based on the appearance of observable secondary sexual characteristics, such as girls' breast development (Brooks-Gunn & Warren, 1989).

Today, many researchers identify developmental or social transitions, such as puberty, as events that bring about long-term psychological change (Graber, Brooks-Gunn, & Petersen, 1996). Other scholars, however, consider the study of transitions as a way to focus on how institutions, such as families or schools, structure the process of growing up (Wyn & White, 1997). Still others view transitions as opportunities to study how children may change their behaviors to fit a particular context, such as changing from elementary to middle school (Graber et al., 1996; Simmons & Blyth, 1987). Middle childhood transitions, however, depend on *both* age and generation; for example, children who are in the same grade level may experience similar educational and cultural trends. A few scholars have used a unique, though not popular, term to characterize the transitional nature of middle childhood: **tranescence**, defined as the stage of development that begins prior to the onset of puberty and extends through the early stages of adolescence (Eichhorn, 1966).

In considering the conditions necessary for successful navigation through the middle childhood years, psychologists, educators, and social policy experts increasingly have focused on predictors of adolescent outcomes. In 1994, building on the work of a previous research network on early childhood transitions, the MacArthur Foundation established a Task Force on Middle Childhood as well as an ongoing national research network. From the time children entered school until the early years of adolescence, the MacArthur Network on Successful Pathways through Middle Childhood (1997) attempted to capture children's individual differences as well as the diversity of influences and experiences of people of different ethnic, cultural, and economic backgrounds. In addition to school, the network's investigators examined other contexts important to children, including family, community, economic resources, and culture, to address the following questions:

- What influences and experiences contribute to different outcomes for children during their first school years?
- How can the likelihood of successful outcomes be increased? (MacArthur Network on Successful Pathways through Middle Childhood, 2002).

See Table 2–2 for examples of current research trends in middle childhood.

Today, when contemporary scholars meet to discuss research and share findings and methods of studying middle childhood, they often consider the implications of defining middle childhood as a period of preparation for adolescence along a path with many choices or "forks in the road." These alternative pathways may result in either risks or opportunities for school-age children. As summarized by one researcher, development "is about motion and momentum, about growing 'into' something, about making a transition, and about getting from one point to another" (Steinberg, 1995, p. 246). Thus, the current conceptualization of middle childhood development as a pathway, or developmental *trajectory,* reflects a movement away from describing developmental *periods* and toward explaining developmental *transitions.*

When you were in middle childhood, what did you, your family, or your friends think that you were likely to "grow into"?

Guideposts for Working with School-Age Children

- Children in middle childhood are often referred to as *school-age children, early adolescents, preteens,* or *youth.* Ask them which term best describes them and what they would like to be called.
- Familiarize yourself with developmental norms for the school-agers for whom you are responsible and carefully observe individual children to determine whether they are developing faster or slower than their age-mates.
- Determine what developmental transitions are facing the school-age children you work with by speaking with their parents or teachers.
- Talk with children to prepare them for what to expect as they face transitions, such as changing schools.

TABLE 2–2

Research Initiatives on Middle Childhood

The MacArthur Network on Successful Transitions through Middle Childhood has conducted cutting-edge research on middle childhood. Detailed information on each project is available on the web site: http://childhood.isr.umich.edu/index.html

Project	Focus
MacArthur School Transition Study	Early intervention effects on school entry
The New Hope Child and Family Study	Work and family economics study
California Childhoods Project	Institutions, contexts, and pathways of development
Empirical Explorations of Pathways Through Middle Childhood	National longitudinal study of youth
Authority, Discipline, Compliance, and Autonomy in Middle Childhood	Historical essays on children's participation in institutions
Children of Immigrants	Ethnic identity and prejudice study
Task Force on "Race" and Ethnicity	Effects on developmental pathways
Ecocultural Interview Development	Daily routines and activities of middle childhood
Engagement With Institutions	How schools and communities engage children

Meanings of Childhood in Postmodern Societies

The idea that children's development in middle childhood represents a unique pattern of biological, social, and historical factors reflects an increasing emphasis on cultural relativism seen in many fields of study beginning in the late 20th century. You may have encountered this perspective in literature, philosophy, or the arts under the label of *postmodernism.* In historical terms, **postmodernity** refers to the idea that knowledge achieved through scientific research, sometimes called *logical positivism,* can no longer be regarded as universal and objective. A concept is **universal** when it has the same meaning, or exists in the same form, across different cultures. Postmodernists believe instead that all knowledge is partial and subjective. In this view, the meanings of childhood will vary from situation to situation and from culture to culture. Many postmodern academic approaches **deconstruct** the social discourse, or "read between the lines" of commonly held but often unconscious beliefs expressed in everyday conversations or routine actions. For example, understanding more fully contemporary usage of such terms as *middle childhood, the school-age years, early or preadolescence,* and *youth* requires deconstructing their meanings in the varied contexts of family, school, and community.

Do parents think there are unique challenges in middle childhood parenting? Do teachers believe that school-age children have special abilities, roles, and status in society? Do youth think of themselves as different from other age groups? Often, as we see in television portrayals of middle childhood, such as *Malcolm in the Middle* (Boomer, 2000), school-age children may feel powerless and dependent on others, whether in the family or the school context. However, if we instead view middle childhood, youth, and adolescence as *social constructions* designed to control and limit children's access to power in society (Foucault, 1976/1978), the social function of childhood would become apparent.

The **social construction** of childhood refers to the ways in which the understandings of and expectations about children (and, later, adolescents) are passed on through society. For example, legally restricting child labor and mandating school attendance function together to limit youth's economic independence (Polakow Suransky, 1982). Families may also impose distance or curfew restrictions on children that limit their social interactions (O'Neil, 2002). In other words, the focus is not "on the inherent characteristics of young people themselves, but on the construction of youth through social processes (e.g., schooling, families or the labour market)" (Wyn & White, 1997, p. 9). In this view, the position individuals occupy in their social world (e.g., their age, gender, ethnicity, or social class) may interact with their exposure to material conditions (e.g., media, music, school environments, and youth subcultures) to socially construct the cultural life of middle childhood (Wyn & White, 1997).

Cultural influences. Central to both positivist and postmodernist perspectives on development is the influence of culture: "Cultures make sense of the way people grow up" (Modell & Elder, 2002, p. 174). This view, called the **cultural ecology** of childhood, argues that children's participation in cultural activities is the major experience shaping development (Weisner, 1996). Through various social practices carried out in family, peer, and school contexts, children in middle childhood construct a sense of identity in relation to their families, their peer group, and the school culture.

In cultures whose primary goals for their children are other than individual achievement, children may be more often expected to assist with family and community survival (Weisner, 1998). For example, in some cultures, family life is often dependent on older children as important caregivers for younger siblings (Whiting & Edwards, 1992). When children are an important source of unpaid child care or family labor, the arbitrary separations between childhood, adolescence, and adulthood as unique developmental periods begin to blur (Montemayor, 2000).

Some cultures emphasize the difference between childhood and adulthood while others perceive development as continuous. In a classic ethnographic study, *Coming of Age in Samoa,* Margaret Mead (1928) found that the transition to adulthood was relatively smooth for Samoan adolescents because of their culture's structuring of adolescence as continuous with childhood, as compared to Western societies (Côté, 2000a). Similarly, compared to the majority culture in the United States, many American Indian tribes do not expect children to be submissive to adults any more than adults are required to be submissive to each other (Broude, 1995).

Across ethnic groups in the United States, cultural constructions of middle childhood differ by family **ethnicity**, the sum total of ancestry and culture (McAdoo, 1999). Ethnicity is not so much a group characteristic as it is an encounter with a cultural difference that is perceived to influence social relations (Gjerde & Onishi, 2000). For example, African American and Hispanic children are often expected to take care of younger siblings. In fact, children of color frequently take on adult roles at an earlier age than do White children. In addition, youth who live on farms take on adult roles and responsibilities at an earlier age than do urban children; for example, Native American boys take on adult responsibilities of caring for family livestock (Montemayor, 2000). As a result, most scholars acknowledge that there are wide ethnic variations in individuals' behaviors that are based on the symbolic meanings attached to developmental processes in their societies (Cunningham & Spencer, 2000).

Anthropologists generally agree, however, that all cultures around the world draw some distinction among people on the basis of age, a phenomenon called **age grading**. At a minimum, most societies recognize differences between immature, mature, and elderly people (Broude, 1994). Although some form of age grouping is found in virtually all cultures, various ethnic groups may define middle childhood differently from others. As we have discussed in this chapter, Europeans and Americans commonly distinguish between infants, toddlers, schoolchildren, adolescents, young adults, middle-aged adults, and senior citizens. In many African cultures, males are classified into the categories of newly born infants, children on the lap, uninitiated boys, initiated bachelors, married men, elders, and retired elders (Broude, 1994).

When considering middle childhood as socially constructed, the idea that these age breakdowns may not be universal is important. A common fallacy is to think that children's development looks the same in different cultures (Chatterjee, Bailey, & Aronoff, 2001; Cole, 1996). Although humans, like most species, must necessarily experience biological immaturity, *childhood* is the manner in which a society understands and assigns a role to that physical reality (Woodson, 1999). Anthropologists refer to taking an **emic** approach, one that acknowledges culturally specific variations, as contrasted with an **etic** approach, one that assumes similarity across cultures (Liddell, 2002). For example, cultural anthropologists have suggested that the concept of a middle childhood developmental transition toward more complex cognitive capacities and social skills may be more cultural (emic) than universal (etic) because it promotes the Western concept of individualized achievement in school (Weisner, 1998). The United Nations has stated (1986), that if "youth" is understood as an extension of childhood in some cultures but as the beginning of adulthood in others, then the concept is not universal. In the United

States, for example, there are child labor laws to protect children from economic exploitation or developmentally inappropriate experiences. However, if we consider that—worldwide—50 million children under age 15 are required to work in fields and factories (or fight in armed conflicts), childhood cannot be considered a protected status in all cultures (Wyn & White, 1997).

The meaning of being a school-age child depends on your experiences in a specific historical time and place (Närvänen & Näsman, 2004). For example, some authors have referred to children born in or after 1982 as the "millennial" generation, because the first of this **cohort** (a group born in the same year) will have graduated from high school in or after the year 2000 (Howe & Strauss, 2000). Yet there are many ways in which the experiences of a school-age child in the early 21st century may differ from those of "millennials," who were in middle childhood during the late 20th century—such as experiencing the 2001 terrorist attacks on the United States as an infant rather than as a young adult (see Gershoff & Aber, 2004a, 2004b). And although a generational event may affect all children, the experience of American children in immigrant families from Islamic countries may be quite different from the that of nonimmigrants. Muslim American children, for example, may encounter prejudice and discrimination despite having been born in the United States.

Social position, racism, and segregation may also interact to create unique contexts and pathways for children of color and of immigrant families. Segregated school or neighborhood environments with limited resources may, at the same time, be supportive if they promote children's emotional and academic adjustment, helping them to manage the societal demands imposed by discrimination. Such environments have been termed *adaptive* because they help children to navigate successful pathways through middle childhood (Garcia Coll & Szalacha, 2004; Garcia Coll et al., 1996).

Demographic influences. Of the 32.9 million U.S. students in the grades below high school, 61% are identified as White (non-Hispanic), 19% as Hispanic, 16% as Black, and 4% as Asian and Pacific Islander and other races. Twenty percent have at least one foreign-born parent, and 5% were born outside the United States. By 2020, the numbers of children of color are expected to increase dramatically, as seen in Figure 2.2. Between 2000 and 2004, the percentage of children who are non-Hispanic White declined slightly, to 59%, and is

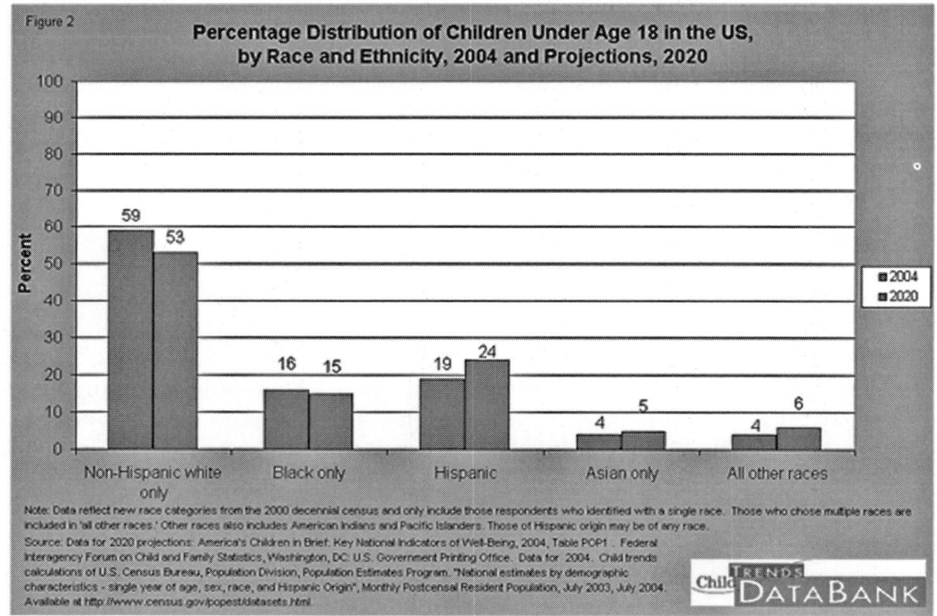

FIGURE 2.2 U.S. Ethnic Population of Children
The population of children of color in the United States is projected to increase dramatically by 2020.

Source: Child Trends. Child Trends Data Bank Indicator: Racial and Ethnic Composition of the Child Population. Retrieved from http://www.childtrendsdatabank.org/figures/60-Figure-2.gif Copyright © 2005 by Child Trends, Inc. Reprinted by permission.

projected to decline to 53% by 2020. The percentage of the child population that is Hispanic increased from 9% to 19% between 1980 and 2004 and is expected to increase further, to 24%, by 2020. Non-Hispanic Asian and Pacific Islander children increased from 2 to 4% of the child population between 1980 and 2001; Asian-only children made up 4% of the child population in 2004 and are expected to increase to 5% of the population by 2020. The percentage of the child population that is non-Hispanic Black has stayed relatively constant, at about 15%, since 1980, where it is expected to remain in 2020 (Child Trends, 2005).

In 2000, the United States had only 3.3% of the world's children under age 15 but ranked sixth among the world's countries in contributing to the under-15 population. By contrast, the developing countries of India, Nigeria, Pakistan, Ethiopia, and Congo (Kinshasa) contributed approximately 60% of the growth in the world's population of children under age 15 during the last decade. By 2025, the United States is expected to have 15% more children, while the number of children globally will be just 3% larger than in 2000 (U.S. Census Bureau, 2002).

These trends are important for understanding school-age children as a diverse group and for creating successful middle childhood programs. Increasingly, educators recognize that schools have the opportunity to structure the teaching and learning environment to allow for the emergence of multiple perspectives (Slattery, 1999).

A majority of today's school-age children have access to computers, either at home or school.

Technological influences. Diversity is also connected to technological innovations, particularly in terms of global media and communications technologies (Luke, 1999). Our discussion of postmodern influences on the social construction of youth would therefore, be incomplete without considering **new media**, such as instant messaging, web logs (blogs), and chat rooms; pagers, personal digital assistants (PDAs), and cell phones; video streaming, digital cameras, and high-definition television (HDTV); and digital video discs (DVDs), compact discs (CDs), and digital music players (MP3s, iPODs). Researchers know much about children's use of computers, video games, and the Internet but relatively little about their use of PDAs, cell phones, and wireless technologies (Wartella, Caplovitz, & Lee, 2004).

Through the influence of the Internet and global communications, world youth culture is growing in importance (Weisner, 2001). The contemporary school-age child from a middle-class family is more connected to global cultures than youth from previous generations (Howe & Strauss, 2000). In the year 2000, nearly two thirds (64.1%) of children aged 6 to 11 years had access to a computer at home, and nearly one quarter (25%) had access to the Internet at home. Of all school-age children (6 to 17 years), 22% had access only at school, and only 10.4% had no access at all (U.S. Census Bureau, 2001c). Among 8- to 16-year-olds, 20% had a computer in their bedroom (of whom 54% had Internet access) (Wartella, Caplovitz, & Lee, 2004).

By around age 10, school-age children show increased understanding of the technical and social complexities of the Internet, regardless of experience (Yan, 2005). Children are not only aware of historical change, such as new technologies, but they are also often part of that change (Modell & Elder, 2002). Newer, nonsequential ways of accessing information, such as hypertext, have caused theorists to question developmental stage approaches to children's construction of knowledge (Luke, 1999). Let's see what that means in terms of our case study child, Robyn:

When Robyn expresses interest in dance, what does she do? She doesn't want to go to the same dance studio as her older sister. In her after-school program that day, Robyn sits down at the computer, clicks on the icon for a web browser, and logs on to

Guideposts for Working with School-Age Children

- Because middle childhood is a social construction, talk with teachers, parents, and school-agers themselves to determine how they think about the "rules" of childhood.
- Conduct home visits or parent conferences to learn about cultural or ethnic values among diverse families when addressing their children's developmental, psychological, or educational needs.
- Consider the pervasive influence of new media on school-age children by making sure that you design or select curricula that make effective use of information and communications technology.

the Internet. Robyn types "dance studios" into the search engine and finds four in her hometown!

In what ways do you think your middle childhood was socially constructed?

Developmental Milestones in Middle Childhood

Now that we have defined middle childhood, you may be wondering "*What* is it that develops?" Recall that in this chapter we have described middle childhood both as a *stage* and as a *pathway* to future development. The metaphor of transition (i.e., the pathway) involves looking at markers (i.e., milestones) along the way in order to measure developmental progress. Developmental milestones in middle childhood can be classified into one of four broad **domains**, which provides the organizational framework for the remainder of this text. A developmental *domain* is an area of child or human development, such as physical, cognitive, affective, or social development. Each of these domains is the focus of a separate chapter in Part I: Middle Childhood and in Part II: Adolescence. Refer to Figure 2.3 for a depiction of the four domains in middle childhood.

1. **Physical Development.** In middle childhood, this domain includes biological and neurophysiological development, the refinement of perceptual and motor skills, and physical health, including nutrition and exercise. School-age children undergo rapid spurts in height and weight as well as improvement in athletic abilities. They begin the onset of puberty at varied ages, with 11 years the average age for girls and 13 years for boys, marked first by hormonal changes followed by observable changes in physical appearance and behavior.

2. **Cognitive Development.** This domain includes intellectual and language development, reasoning abilities, and memory capacities. The middle years of childhood are characterized by a gradual increase in logical reasoning using concrete examples, increased awareness of memory and learning strategies, and the achievement and consolidation of important academic skills, such as reading, writing, and computing.

3. **Affective Development.** This domain includes personality, emotional development, motivation, and self-esteem. School-age children acquire personal competencies through participation in academic, athletic, or artistic activities; emotional attachments to family members and others; and a deepening sense of who they are and what they can achieve through serious effort and commitment.

4. **Social Development.** This domain includes social skills and interpersonal understanding, moral and ethical development, and maintaining close relationships. Youth develop reciprocal understandings of others through family and peer interactions, deepening same-sex friendships, and seeking fairness in their family, school, and peer groups.

Individual children, however, are whole persons, living in the real world and developing as a totality rather than in separate functional domains of development (physical, cognitive, affective, social). Although a great deal of our knowledge about middle childhood comes from studies conducted on specific areas of development, our study of middle childhood takes a **holistic approach** to human development (Cairns, 2000; Magnusson, 1995, 2000). From a holistic point of view, biological, psychological, and social factors operate together to produce growth and change through reciprocal interaction with the environment, a process that starts at

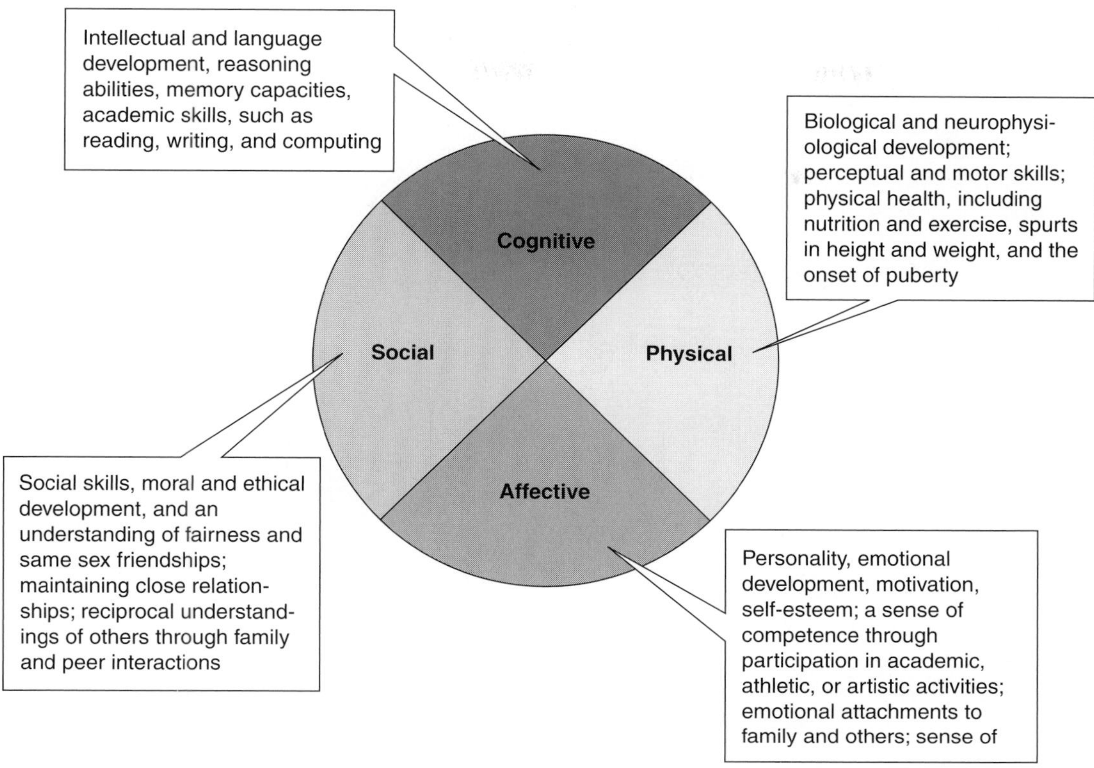

FIGURE 2.3 Developmental Domains of Middle Childhood
Middle childhood is a distinct developmental period with normative changes occurring simultaneously in all domains.

conception and goes on throughout the life span (Magnusson, 1995).

THEORETICAL VIEWPOINTS

In this text, theories of development are integrated throughout the topical discussions of middle childhood to middle adolescents, as illustrated by Table 1–5 in the previous chapter. In each chapter, you will read about the specific theories that exemplify particular domains of study, such as physical, cognitive, affective, or social development. Because this text presents a contextual view of development, we first must examine two theories that are overarching in their scope: ecological theory and developmental-contextual theory. These two major theoretical perspectives have guided a holistic approach to middle childhood. They do not focus on any one developmental domain, but rather describe and explain the interrelationships across time among many areas of development in the real world.

The Ecology of Human Development

The concept of interrelated systems in human development is epitomized by Urie Bronfenbrenner's ecological theory, which describes the complexity of human development, as well as the idea that the developing person is a biological system interacting with other systems that are external to the individual. **Ecological theory** is important because it demonstrates the systemic interaction between the person and the environment, or ecology, at four different levels: the **microsystem**, the **mesosystem**, the **exosystem**, and the **macrosystem** (Bronfenbrenner, 1979; Bronfenbrenner & Crouter, 1983).

- The first of these levels, the *microsystem,* consists of interaction between the developing person and

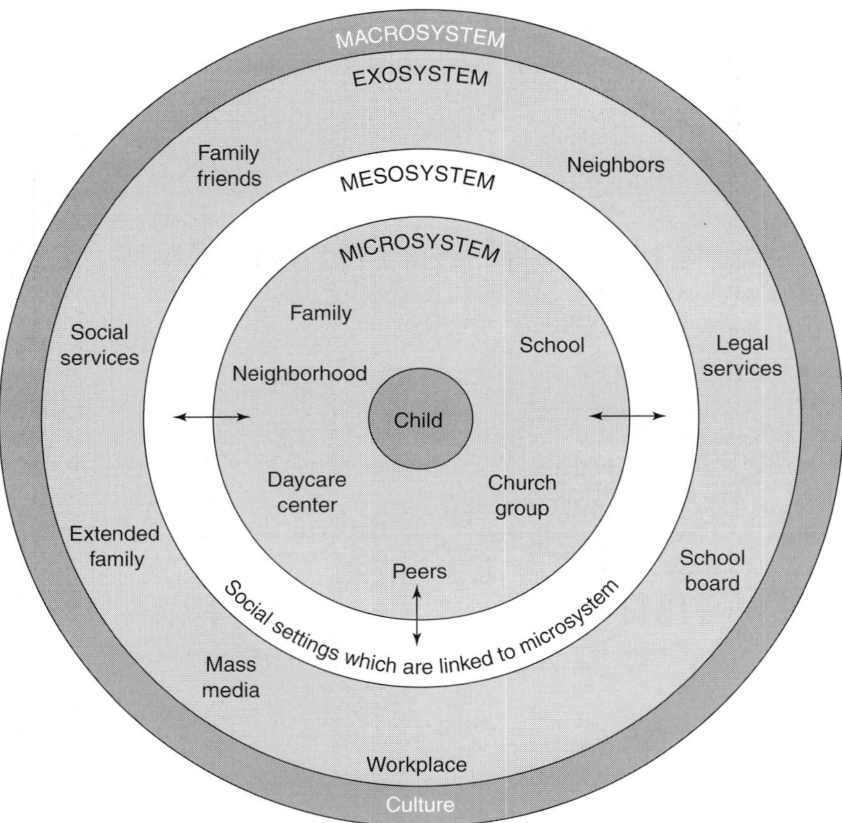

FIGURE 2.4 Bronfenbrenner's Ecological Model
School-age children develop in the embedded contexts of families, communities, societies, and cultures.
Source: From Lerner, Richard. Adolescence: Development, diversity, context, and application (1st ed.) (p.50). Copyright © 2002 by Pearson Education, Inc., Upper Saddle River, NJ. Adapted by permission of the publisher.

other individuals, such as parents. Thus, we may speak of the parent-child or the teacher-child systems, for example, as operating as *microsystems*.

- When two or more microsystems interact either indirectly, such as a parent-teacher conference in which parents and teachers interact together, or directly, such as when schoolchildren enter a new ecological setting like middle school, a *mesosystem* is operating.
- An *exosystem* refers to influences that are external to an individual child—such as the effect of parental employment—but which nevertheless affect children's development either directly, such as through school-age children's need for out-of-school supervision, or indirectly, such as through family income.
- Lastly, the *macrosystem* includes the broader cultural influences on development, such as ethnic or religious values.

Bronfenbrenner's (1979) ecological model is illustrated in Figure 2.4 using ever-widening circles of influences surrounding the child, who is pictured at the center. Recently, ecological theory has been reconceptualized using *time* as a defining feature:

- **Microtime** is used to analyze continuity within immediate episodes of children's behavior.
- **Mesotime** is used to examine stability over longer periods of time—even years.
- **Macrotime** is used to interpret historical influences in the society over the life span of a person or a generation. (Bronfenbrenner & Morris, 1998)

In addition to emphasizing ecological contexts (the **bioecological model**, as it is now called), Bronfenbrenner and his colleagues have attempted to create a model that can be used to empirically test **proximal processes**, or mechanisms that mediate the interaction *over time* between genetics and the environment. Examples of such processes are parent-child activities, group or solitary play, reading, learning new skills, problem solving, performing complex tasks, and acquiring new knowledge (Bronfenbrenner & Ceci, 1994). These processes are a function of the characteristics of the developing person (e.g., middle childhood dispositions or abilities), the immediate or remote environmental context (e.g., home, school, or neighborhood), and the time periods in which the activity takes place (e.g., immediately, across days and weeks, or within and across generations) (Bronfenbrenner & Morris, 1998).

Developmental-Contextual Theory

Like bioecological theory, **developmental-contextual theory** also describes dynamic interactions between people and environments that occur simultaneously on many levels—biological, psychological, sociocultural, and historical (Riegel, 1976). In addition, developmental-contextual theory translates bioecological theory into a framework for applied research and practice (Ford & Lerner, 1992; Lerner, 2002). For example, changes within one level of organization, such as developmental changes in the individual (e.g., *Robyn's interest in developing competence in swimming or dance*), are related to reciprocal changes in other levels, such as changes in patterns of family interaction (e.g., *she will no longer attend after-school care with her younger sister*) (Lerner, 1996). The case study of Robyn illustrates an important assumption of this theory: Stability or change in human development is dependent on person–context interactions (Lerner, 2002; Magnusson & Stattin, 1998).

A key to understanding developmental-contextual theory is knowing that it describes a *dynamic* system (Lewis, 2000), from the micro level of the individual person (e.g., Robyn) to the macro level of the environment (e.g., her family, her friends, her after-school activities) (Magnusson & Stattin, 1998). In a developmental-contextual system, people are "fused" with their contexts across the life span such that "children function within and as part of, not just in relationship to, their contexts" (Ford & Lerner, 1992, p. 76). Developmental-contextual theory goes a step further than ecological theory by enumerating varied contexts, specific people, and the relationships among them.

Developing individuals are embedded in a broader social network of school, work, or family relationships. In the developmental-contextual model depicted in Figure 2.5, both parent and child are whole persons, each developing in all domains of human development (represented as slices of a pie) while interacting in multiple environments. And, finally, all of these relations are continually changing across time. For example, families change from being made up of infants and young children to being made up of teenagers. Similarly, communities, societies, and cultures can also change over the course of time. Also, individuals and groups exist in a physical world that, of course, changes as well. Changes in any of these levels, therefore, may produce transformations in the other levels (Lerner, 2002).

How have you changed since middle childhood, and how are these changes interrelated?

Another way to understand this dynamic process is to recognize that any developmental outcome is **probabilistic**—it will *probably* occur due to variations in the context or the timing of an interaction (Lerner, 2002). Given that human development is the outcome of these ongoing exchanges between individual and environment, the essential process of development, called **probabilistic epigenesis**, involves *changing relations* between developing persons and changing contexts, whether the family studied over its life cycle, the classroom studied over the school year, or the community studied over several weeks, months, or years (Lerner, 1996). Box 2.1 provides an example of longitudinal research on the benefits of extracurricular activities in middle childhood for adjustment in adolescence.

Take Robyn, for example: If she enrolls in dance classes instead of the after-school program, she will probably meet new friends, gain physical skills, and develop an appreciation of the arts—but only if she and her family choose dance over swim classes. For her to achieve a future dance career depends not only on her body type and talent but also on her persistence over time and on continued family, teacher, and peer support throughout her middle childhood and adolescence.

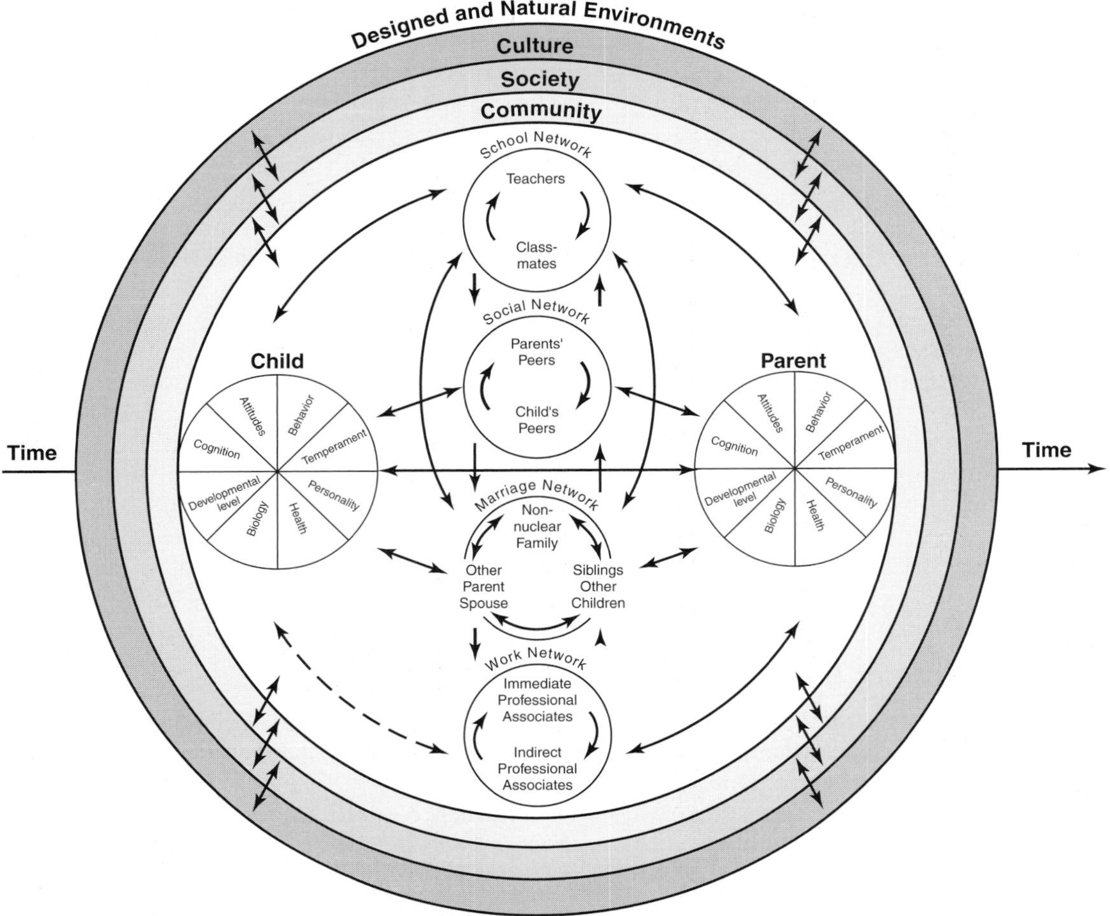

FIGURE 2.5 Lerner's Developmental-Contextual Model
The developmental-contextual model illustrates how children's and parents' development are comprised of multiple, ongoing interactions among various social networks.

Source: From *Developmental Systems Theory: An Integrative Approach* (p. 77) by D. H. Ford and R. M. Lerner, 1992, Newbury Park, CA: Sage. Copyright 1992 by Sage Publications, Inc. Adapted by permission of the publisher.

Guideposts for Working with School-Age Children

- Because middle childhood is not only an important developmental stage but also a transition to adolescence, use children's current abilities as a foundation for teaching future skills.
- Since home, school, and community are the primary contexts in which middle childhood development occurs, become familiar with these settings for the children you work with.
- Evaluate the ways that diverse contexts may affect children's performance, for example, comparing their success on classroom tasks to their completion of homework assignments.
- Take a long view of growth and change over time by comparing children's current achievement of developmental or educational milestones to their performance over longer periods, such as the school year.
- Keep in mind how historical events, such as school desegregation, have shaped the contexts of middle childhood development over time.

BOX 2.1 ROADMAP TO UNDERSTANDING THEORY AND RESEARCH

Free-Time Activities in Middle Childhood

The study *Free Time Activities in Middle Childhood: Links with Adjustment in Early Adolescence* (McHale, Crouter, & Tucker, 2001) used ecological theory to guide an investigation of the developmental significance of children's activities. Researchers assessed the links between how children spent their free time (in sports, hobbies, playing with toys and games, outdoor play, reading, television viewing, and hanging out) and their adjustment as they moved through middle childhood. As suggested by Bronfenbrenner's (1979) theory, across diverse ecologies the demands of children's daily activities offer important developmental opportunities. Researchers Susan McHale, Nan Crouter, and Corinna Tucker (2001) hypothesized that the different social contexts of children's free-time activities—whether children spend time with parents or in unsupervised settings with peers—would influence their later adjustment in early adolescence. The researchers (2001) cited several reasons why "middle childhood may be an important developmental period in which to study free-time use":

- Important individual and group differences may emerge in middle childhood. Although time use varies less in early childhood, by adolescence social class differences are more pronounced.
- Middle childhood is described by Erikson (1968) as a time of "industry," when children's attention is on becoming competent in a range of important skills.
- How children spend their time in middle childhood may have important implications for opportunities and choices later in adolescence, when they have more chances to select their own "niches."
- American children spend more time than children from other countries on leisure activities—up to 50% of their waking hours. In addition, school-age children from lower socioeconomic backgrounds watch more television and spend more time playing outdoors (riding bikes, playing on playgrounds) than middle-class children, who spend more time reading or in organized sports.
- Studies of gender differences indicate that in the United States, boys and girls with similar amounts of free time spend it in different ways. Boys are more often involved in television viewing or sports, while girls spend more time reading or doing hobbies.

According to the authors,

> Free-time activities may bring children into contact with peers and adults who share their interests; spending time in mutually enjoyable activities, in turn, may foster feelings of closeness and affiliation, with positive implications for psychological well-being. From a sociological perspective, time use matters because of both the nature *and* the social contexts of individuals' activities. (McHale, Crouter, & Tucker, 2001, p. 1766)

A second goal of the study was to explore whether the social contexts of activities (either with parents, unrelated adults, unsupervised peers, or alone) made a difference in later adjustment.

Method

Families with first-born boys (102) and first-born girls (96) were recruited for the study from rural and small school districts in a northeastern state. At the beginning of the study, the average age of the children was almost 11 years old, all but two adopted Asian children were White, and their families ranged from working- to upper-middle class. Ninety percent of mothers and all of the fathers were employed.

Two procedures were used for data collection in the study. First, an initial home interview and seven follow-up evening telephone interviews were conducted in which children and parents reported on (a) their daily activities outside of school and work (*hobbies, sports, reading, playing with toys and games, outdoor play, watching television, or hanging out);* (b) how long each activity lasted (*in minutes*); and (c) with whom they had engaged in that activity (*time with mother, time with father, time with peers with no adult present, time with nonparental adults, and time alone).* Second, several measures of the children's adjustment also were collected: (a) mothers rated their children's *conduct,* (b) children reported on their symptoms of *depression,* and (c) report cards were examined to determine school *grades.*

Results

The study revealed positive links between school-age children's free-time activities and their adjustment, suggesting that structured activities, such as hobbies and sports, are constructive ways for children to spend their time. In contrast to the positive implications of sports and hobbies, time spent playing outdoors and hanging out were linked to less-adaptive functioning, including both poorer grades and more behavior problems. Although reading was positively related to academic achievement, it was

(*Continued*)

BOX 2.1 (CONTINUED)

also associated with depression, perhaps because it is a solitary activity.

The researchers also demonstrated that the nature of activities in middle childhood is related to differing opportunities for social ties. Some activities were done alone (e.g., *reading* and sometimes *hobbies*), some with unrelated adults (e.g., *hobbies* and *sports*), some with parents (e.g., *sports* and *TV*), and some with peers unsupervised by adults (e.g., *hanging out, playing outdoors*). Beyond these direct links between activities and social contexts, time spent with parents and adults was related to positive adjustment, whereas time spent alone and in unsupervised peer activities predicted adjustment problems. In the case of outdoor play and school grades, the results suggested that effects were different for girls and boys. Girls' adjustment was linked to time in particular social contexts, whereas boys' adjustment was explained by the nature of their activities (McHale, Crouter, & Tucker, 2001).

Conclusion

This study by McHale, Crouter, and Tucker (2001) exemplifies research conducted from an ecological perspective. In addition to examining factors at the *micro* level of analysis (e.g., children's grades, depression, and conduct), the authors also analyzed *mesosystem* relationships between the nature of the child's activities and differing social contexts (e.g., with parents, peers, unrelated adults, or alone). *Exosystem* considerations were reflected in controlling for such influences as parent employment, education, and socioeconomic status. Finally, while not explicitly addressed, the fact that the families in the study represented a very narrow sample of the rural northeastern United States, may have underestimated *macrosystem* influences, such as ethnic or cultural differences, which might have been more significant if the study had included a more diverse group.

CONTEXTS OF MIDDLE CHILDHOOD

Now that we have identified the age groupings, the developmental domains, and the theoretical assumptions that have been used to study school-age children, it is necessary to more closely examine the specific contexts of middle childhood, or *where* their development occurs. The multiple contexts that school-age children experience across middle childhood influence their development, and, like development, contexts are dynamic and changing (Crockett & Crouter, 1995; Sarampote, Bassett, & Winsler, 2004). In this chapter, our discussion of contexts describes the nature of developmental interactions between children and the people in the immediate setting (Silbereisen & Todt, 1994) rather than the diversity of family, school, or community contexts themselves. Specific findings related to these three contexts are discussed in more detail in the later chapters on the developmental domains.

Developmental researchers studying this period have found that key contexts, such as family, school, peer group, and local neighborhood, help to shape both the opportunities and the risks to which children may be exposed (Crockett & Crouter, 1995). For example, feeling unsafe on the way to and from school is a problem for children in rural as well as urban areas, for school-age children just starting their growth period, and for boys (Middle Start Initiative, 2002). One of the most difficult challenges for parents and teachers is to know when an individual child is developmentally ready for a given experience, such as walking home alone or attending after-school classes. Age alone does not tell us. Box 2.2 provides recommendations for practitioners on the design of developmentally appropriate after-school programs.

While Robyn is ready to join her older sister Rachel in attending dance classes, other girls of her same age may be too physically immature or emotionally undisciplined and need a less structured activity in which to demonstrate their competencies—such as swimming or arts and crafts.

Families as Context

In middle childhood, families are an important developmental context for continuity and change; however, some aspects of family contexts may be more likely to change than others (Collins, 1990). For example, the family socioeconomic context—barring sudden unemployment or a winning

BOX 2.2 ROADMAP TO SUCCESSFUL PRACTICE

After-School Programs Promote Children's Development

In 1999, the National Research Council Board for Children, Youth, and Families and the Forum on Adolescence held a workshop for policy makers, researchers, and practitioners to examine research on (a) the developmental needs of children aged 5 to 14 and (b) the types of after-school programs that they need. The workshop participants discussed ways that after-school programs can be designed to provide school-age children with opportunities:

- To develop competence in a number of developmental domains
- To develop cross-cultural skills
- To learn from older youth and to mentor younger children
- To interact successfully with peers
- To establish close bonds with caring adults
- To contribute to their communities

The experts agreed that school-age children need a variety of skills to move successfully from middle childhood to adolescence. They also recognized that after-school programs may help children explore different areas of interest in which they can exercise their talents and achieve competence. Finally, they concluded that successful experiences in a wide range of out-of-school programs can give school-agers a positive sense of themselves and a healthy appreciation of others (Gootman, 2000).

In the past several years, there has been a dramatic increase in the level of state and federal funding for after-school programs. For example, the U.S. Department of Education funds the 21st Century Community Learning Center Program. The focus of this school-based program, authorized under Title X, Part I, of the Elementary and Secondary Education Act, is to provide learning opportunities for school-age children in supervised, drug-free environments in public school buildings. Other sources of funding for after-school programs have also been increasing, including the Safe Schools/Healthy Students Initiative (Gootman, 2000).

The National Research Council established the following recommendations to guide new after-school programming:

- Programs need to be designed to address age-related stages of development.
- Programs need to incorporate the kinds of activities that will build physical, cognitive, emotional, and social competencies.
- Programs need to incorporate academic experiences that will encourage a positive attitude toward learning.
- Programs need to address the challenges faced by school-age children in their daily lives.

lottery ticket—is more likely to stay stable across the childhood years from 4 to 13 than the school context, in which a normative transition to middle school is expected to occur around fifth or sixth grade (Crockett & Crouter, 1995). On the other hand, nonnormative events, such as family relocation, divorce, or remarriage, may also cause changes in context, such as moving to a new neighborhood or school district, which—taken together with expected transitions, such as puberty—may be particularly stressful in middle childhood or early adolescence (Crockett & Crouter, 1995).

Families are also an important context for socialization (e.g., Hofferth & Sandberg, 2001). Despite recent claims that peers overshadow parents in middle childhood (Harris, 1998), researchers have consistently documented that parents, as supportive adults, continue to be important in encouraging school-age children to engage in activities within safe boundaries (Middle Start Initiative, 2002). In addition, parents and siblings provide opportunities for understanding relationships (Collins, 1990). Through family relationships, school-age children learn to negotiate with others and adapt to others' individual differences and developmental needs (Baenen, 2002; Blume & Blume, 1997).

Schools as Context

Many schools in the 21st century, like the rest of U.S. society, are becoming increasingly diverse in terms of ethnicity, race, religion, and sexual preference, allowing school-age children more opportunities to enhance their cultural sensitivity and tolerance in the

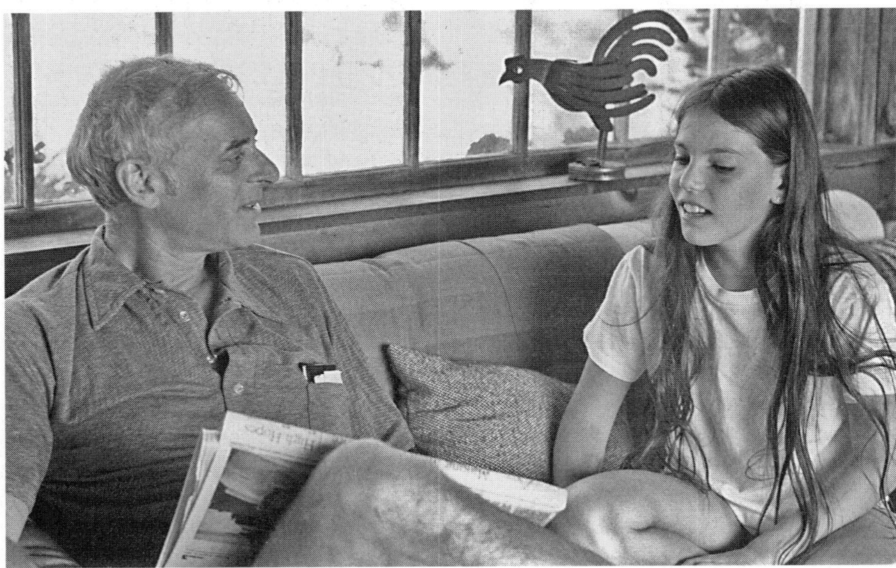

Parent and child communication is an important component of family socialization.

school context (Civil Rights Project, 2002). A wide range of facilities, varied enrollments, and class sizes also characterizes school environments. Despite this diversity, however, most schools are age-segregated environments, especially when contrasted with mixed-age settings like families and neighborhoods (MacKinnon, Volling, & Lamb, 1994; McCarthy, 1972).

Across middle childhood, most American children are likely to move from a primary to a secondary school, whether from a K–6 primary school to a junior high for grades 7 to 9, or from a K–5 elementary school to a middle school for grades 6 to 8. This transition usually means a change from a small, neighborhood school with one group of classmates and only one teacher per grade to a larger school, farther from home, with many different classes and teachers (Jackson & Davis, 2000). In Michigan, for example, average enrollment per school more than doubles between the fifth and ninth grades (Middle Start Initiative, 2002).

Researchers studying school contexts have found that elementary and middle schools also differ in terms of both teacher-child and teacher-parent involvement (Eccles & Harold, 1993). Because they often have different teachers for each subject, children in middle schools have many more daily contacts with teachers than they did in elementary settings, but their parents are typically less involved. In *Turning Points 2000,* the most recent Task Force on the Education of Young Adolescents recommended not only involving families but also communities, recognizing that families and community contexts are inextricably linked (Davis, 2001).

Communities as Context

In middle childhood, school-age children increase their interactions with peers, usually with same-age and same-sex friends. Peer interactions in neighborhoods or nearby playgrounds are often school-age children's first community experiences. Although school-age children spend increasing amounts of time in out-of-school leisure activities, gender and social class distinctions shape their content (e.g., Posner & Vandell, 1999). For example, middle-class 7- to 10-year-old boys typically spend more time in activities that enhance skill development while working-class boys spend more time in informal play, visiting relatives, or just "hanging out" (Lareau, 2000).

Parents also tend to supervise school-age children more closely if they judge their neighborhood quality to be poor, thus limiting children's opportunities to develop social skills with peers (O'Neil, Parke, & McDowell, 2001). However, as children move through middle childhood and become increasingly involved in contexts outside the family, it becomes harder for parents to know all the details of their activities in the community (Crouter, Helms-Erikson, Updegraff, & McHale, 1999).

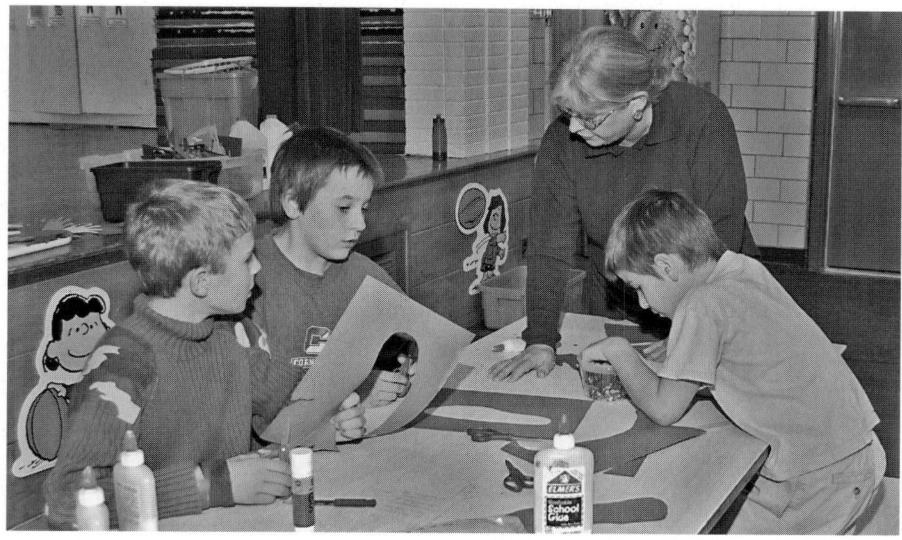

After-school programs for school-aged children are usually based on activities.

In the middle childhood period, many children also increase their familiarity with community organizations, such as Boys and Girls Clubs, Scouts, 4H, the YWCA or YMCA, Little League, and recreational programs. For example, Boys and Girls Clubs of America operates over 2,850 neighborhood clubs serving 2,800,000 children, 71% of whom live in low-income areas (Anderson-Butcher, Newsome, & Ferrari, 2003; Roffman, Pagano, & Hirsch, 2001). Youth organizations, hobbies, and arts programs effectively encourage middle- and working-class school-agers to resist delinquent behaviors (Larson, 1994). In addition, as their social context expands, school-age children acquire a sense of belonging to a wider community than their immediate neighborhoods—called **social integration**—and develop positive relationships with peers and adults outside the family (Larson, 1994). See Box 2.3 for a model community effort to assess and provide after-school programs.

As many as 6 million students participate in middle childhood after-school programs (U.S. Department of Education, 2000). Researchers suggest that children who attend such programs have increased achievement, better school attendance, and lower dropout rates (Fashola, 1998). Results of a study of seventh and eighth graders who attended an after-school program at least 3 days per week showed that they were happier, enjoyed activities more, and were less bored than when they were not attending (Dadisman, Vandell, & Pierce, 2002). Structured time is also related to a pattern of less risky behavior in middle school and high school (Mancini & Huebner, 2004). Other researchers studying out-of-school involvement, such as taking dance classes, playing sports, or doing handicrafts, found that children's free-time choices influenced positive social development (Blume, 2001; McHale, Crouter, & Tucker, 1999). Lastly, person-centered research has revealed substantial variation in patterns over time of participation in out-of-school activities such as sports. Key factors limiting involvement were parental under- and unemployment and timing of the transition to middle school or junior high, with a later transition being less likely to disrupt activity continuation (Pederson, 2005).

At age 8, Robyn is already expressing to her mother an abiding interest in joining such activities to enhance her newly acquired sense of industriousness and her budding relationships with peers. As Robyn progresses from ages 8 to 12, she may be protected from risk by involvement in out-of-school activities—whether an after-school program, a sports program, a recreation center, or instruction in the performing or visual arts.

What out-of-school contexts did you experience during middle childhood and how did they change across ages 8 to 12?

BOX 2.3 ROADMAP TO SUCCESSFUL PRACTICE

Moving an Out-of-School Agenda: The GRASP Project

Recognizing the critical role of community-level change in moving an out-of-school agenda, the Forum for Youth Investment began the Greater Resources for After-School Programming (GRASP) Project, with support from the Charles Stewart Mott Foundation. Through GRASP, the Forum partnered with four cities—Chicago, Kansas City, Little Rock, and Sacramento—to assess their current work in, and deepen community discussions about, out-of-school time. They addressed the following concerns:

- Opportunities are uneven across communities so that some young people have remarkably few choices.
- Programming drops off dramatically during the evening hours; weekend programs are in remarkably short supply.
- Only a small percentage of young people are enrolled in consistent, daily programs.
- Many providers are striving to provide well-balanced programming, focusing on a range of outcomes, but many of the largest programs take on a much narrower focus.
- Civic outcomes are consistently neglected, and the programs that do support them tend to be smaller and focused on older age groups.

A Case Study: Kansas City, Missouri

In keeping with national trends, 28 school-based programs are the primary providers of school-age child care in Kansas City. The overwhelming majority of children enrolled in school-based programs are elementary school age. Although nearly 27,000 children are being served, these programs are reaching less than 9% of the target population of 6- to 18-year-olds and less than 15% of the elementary children. Approximately 6% of school-age children and youth participate in voluntary, activity-based programs, such as Boys and Girls Clubs, Camp Fire, Boy Scouts, Girl Scouts, and city Parks and Recreation. The rest are served in smaller programs provided by child care centers, community-based groups, and faith-based organizations.

Among the school-based programs, all but one serve children aged 6 to 11; slightly less than half serve middle-schoolers aged 12 to 15; and only 7% serve youth over age 16. Although the activity-based programs enrolled only 8% of the population of school-age children in Kansas City, many families reported that they rely on such programs to create a network of out-of-school supervision for older children (Tolman, Pittman, Yohalem, Thomases, & Trammel, 2002).

Over 80% of all out-of-school programs in Kansas City identified care and supervision, socialization and recreation, and academics as primary outcomes. When asked to name the primary activities available to children and youth, Kansas City agencies named five areas with about equal priority: hobbies (52%), tutoring (51%), physical exercise (48%), academic enrichment (46%), and unstructured time (44%).

GRASP Project Conclusions

The following lessons and challenges emerged from the GRASP projects in all four cities:

- Opportunities for learning and engagement happen in multiple places and programs found in communities (e.g., youth organizations, libraries, parks, homes, schools, faith institutions, city halls, community organizations, dance studios, workplaces)—places that are not only open and active in the hours immediately after school but also in the evenings, on weekends, and in the summers.
- Schools should be the anchor learning institution in a young person's life, but schools occupy less than a quarter of students' waking hours each year. In addition, they focus heavily on building strong academic skills—skills that are critical but not sufficient.

Developmentally, gaps exist that schools do not fill. Children and youth are looking for learning experiences across a range of areas from academic to social to civic (e.g., things to do, places to go, people to talk to). Many young people cannot find suitable experiences in or out of school.

Moving an Out-of-School Agenda (2002) concluded that creating the quality, quantity, and continuity of opportunities for young people from early childhood through the beginning of adulthood will require engaging in the following tasks:

1. Ensuring adequate coordination, collaboration, and networking among those working with young people—within sectors, across sectors, and between organizations and community/family stakeholders

2. Building a stable, high-quality workforce through credentials, staff development, training, and compensation
3. Creating quality standards, assessments, and supports that result in effective organizations and programs
4. Developing the physical infrastructure (e.g., the transportation and physical space) that is the necessary context for accessible and quality out-of-school opportunities
5. Marshalling adequate funding streams (e.g., local, state and national, public and private) to guarantee stable and sufficient resources for programming
6. Building leadership and political will by engaging champions in the public and private sectors, and at the highest levels of city government, to create and move an agenda
7. Ensuring consistent, meaningful youth engagement in decision making at the program, organization, and city levels
8. Building public will and constituency engagement in order to support stakeholder involvement, promote public commitment and awareness, and leverage meaningful action
9. Developing planning and visioning processes, structures, and products to build alignment, intentionality, and comprehensiveness within out-of-school programming
10. Strengthening mapping, monitoring, and research systems to collect, analyze, and disseminate information about programs, providers, funding, and young people

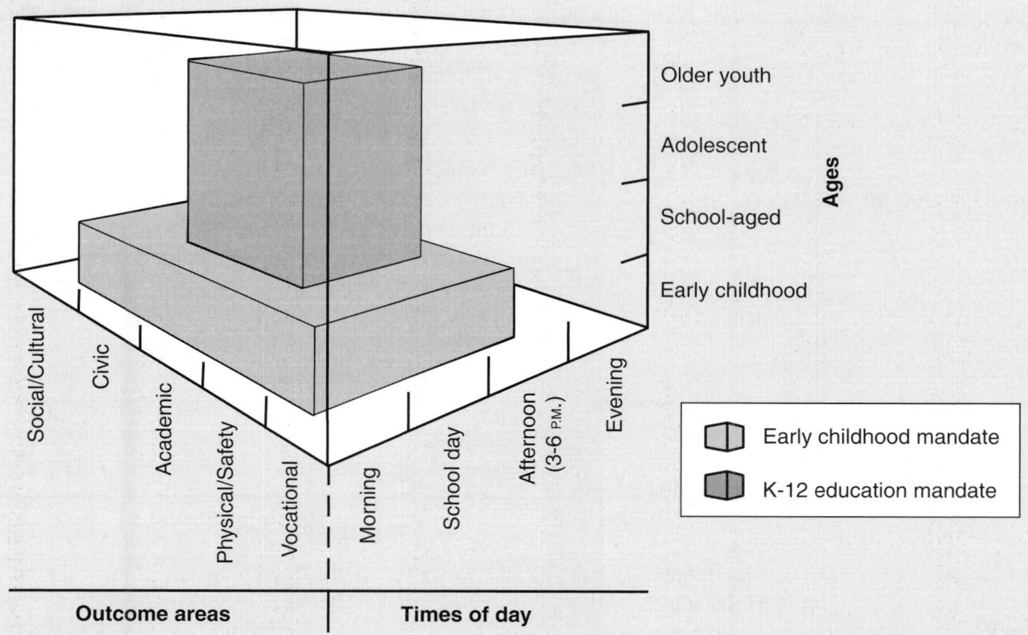

FIGURE 2.6 What Fills the Space?
Imagine the empty space. How is it filled in your community?

Source: From Tolman, J., Pitman, K., Thomases, J., & Trammel, M. (2002). *Moving an Out-of-School Agenda: Lessons and Challenges Across Cities*. Washington, DC: The Forum for Youth Investment. http://www.forumfyi.org/Files/GRASPpaper.pdf

CHAPTER REVIEW

History of Middle Childhood

- Middle childhood is defined as ages 8 to 12, although different terms may be used to describe the middle childhood period and age groupings may vary by field.
- The history of childhood reveals that childhood as a distinct stage in the life span dates from medieval times, but the concept of childhood as a protected status is much more recent, beginning in the early 20th century. Only recently has society considered middle childhood to be a transitional pathway to adolescence.
- Middle childhood is socially constructed in several ways. In different generations, in diverse cultures and ethnicities, and in various socioeconomic groups, the meaning of middle childhood may vary widely.

Developmental Perspectives

- Middle childhood can be thought of as a distinct stage with its own developmental characteristics and abilities.
- Middle childhood can also be thought of as a transitional pathway to adolescence.
- Research on middle childhood is divided into four broad developmental domains: physical, cognitive, affective, and social.

Theoretical Perspectives

- The ecological theory of human development describes the multiple, overlapping environments in which children develop over time.
- Developmental-contextual theory describes multiple interrelationships among developmental domains, as well as dynamic interactions with the contexts in which children develop.

Contexts of Middle Childhood

- Family, school, and community contexts are linked.
- Families, schools, peer groups, and communities help to shape both the opportunities and risks to which children may be exposed.
- Moving from an elementary to a middle-school environment may signal changes in peer group interactions, teacher-child relationships, and parent-teacher communication.

TABLE 2–3

Summary of Developmental Theories

Chapter 2 presented two broad theoretical frameworks for examining school-age children in their social and cultural context.

Chapter	Theories	Focus
2: Perspectives on Middle Childhood	Ecological	The many embedded environments in which children develop over time—from the more immediate, such as family, school, and community, to the more remote, such as the broader society and culture.
	Developmental-contextual	Dynamic developmental and reciprocal relationship processes that occur between parents, children, and their social networks within the embedded contexts of ecological theory.

KEY TERMS

Age grade
Applied research
Basic research
Bioecological model
Cohort
Cultural ecology
Deconstruct
Developmental-contextual
Domains
Ecological theory
Emic
Epigenesis
Ethnicity
Etic
Exosystem
Holistic approach
Logical positivist
Macrosystem
Microsystem
Microtime
Middle childhood
Mesosystem
Mesotime
Middle childhood
New media
Normative
Postmodernist
Praxis
Probabilistic
Proximal processes
Reflexive
Secular trends
Social constructions
Social integration
Theoretical models
Tranescence
Universal

SUGGESTED ACTIVITIES

1. Watch television programs, look at magazines, or read fiction that is directed at school-age children. How is this age group portrayed? Note the development of the characters or the subjects of articles. Compare what you find to the developmental domains described in the chapter. Are some developmental domains addressed more than others? How do the authors view middle childhood?
2. Talk with two or three school-age children about what they do before and after school. How long have they been involved in these activities? Are their siblings or friends also involved? What developmental contexts do they inhabit? Do you think that their experiences are typical of the out-of-school activities of middle childhood? Why or why not? What else could the community do to provide developmentally appropriate out-of-school activities for 8- to 12-year-olds?
3. Meet with the parent(s) of a school-age child. What are their developmental expectations for their child? How do they judge when their child is ready for a new experience? Do you think that their expectations are developmentally appropriate? Why or why not? Have they ever read advice books or attended classes for parents? If not, how did they learn about children's development? How do they think children in middle childhood are different from young children or adolescents? What do they want for their children in the future?
4. Interview an elementary teacher and a middle-school teacher about the age groupings or grade levels in their schools. Describe their schools' organization or model (e.g., primary, middle, or junior high school). How are children grouped (e.g., by grade, by age, by ability)? When do children change schools (i.e., after what grade do they move from elementary to middle school or junior high)? How satisfied are the teachers with the current structure? How, if at all, would they change it? How has the educational system changed from when they went to school? Which model do they prefer? Why?

RECOMMENDED RESOURCES

Suggested Readings

Campbell, P. (2000). Middle muddle. *The Horn Book, 76,* 4, 483–487.

Gesell, A., & Ilg, F. L. (1946). *The child from five to ten.* New York: Harper.

Howe, N., & Strauss, W. (2000). *Millennials rising: The next great generation.* New York: Vintage.

West, E. (1996). *Growing up in twentieth century America: A history and reference guide.* Westport, CT: Greenwood.

Suggested Online Resources

Growing up: W. K. Kellogg Foundation 2001 annual report
http://www.wkkf.org/pubs/Pub3363.pdf

Out-of-school time resources
http://www.forumforyouthinvestment.org/portalcat.cfm?LID=B7F8C ACE-5A57-42F2-85C12AA02E13E438

The future of children: When school is out
http://www.futureofchildren.org/information2826/information_show.htm?doc_id=71875

When schools stay open late: National evaluation of the 21st century community learning centers
http://www.ed.gov/rschstat/eval/other/cclcfinalreport/index.html

From Baby Einstein to Leapfrog, from Doom to the Sims, from instant messaging to Internet chat rooms: Public interest in the role of interactive media in children's lives.
http://www.srcd.org/Documents/Publications/SPR/spr18-4.pdf

Suggested Web Sites

After School Alliance
http://www.afterschoolalliance.org

National Middle School Association
http://www.nmsa.org

National Institute on Out-of-School Time
http://www.niost.org

Successful Pathways through Middle Childhood
http://childhood.isr.umich.edu/index.html

Turning Points
http://www.turningpts.org/

Suggested Films and Videos

Best of the wonder years (1999). Delta Entertainment (70 minutes)

Billy Elliot (2000). Universal Pictures (1 hour, 51 minutes)

Mad hot ballroom (2005). Paramount Classics (1 hour, 50 minutes)

Setting the stage for school-age child care (2005). Magna Systems, Inc. (30 minutes)

Program activities: Fostering the development of the school-age child (2005). Magna Systems, Inc. (30 minutes)

School days (2003). Insight Media, Inc. (30 minutes)

The child from seven to twelve (2001). Insight Media, Inc. (20 minutes)

CHAPTER 

Physical Development in Middle Childhood

CHAPTER OBJECTIVES

After reading this chapter, students will be able to:

- Define the theoretical assumptions and predictions of biological theories of development
- Outline the developmental patterns of physical and brain maturation in middle childhood
- Describe the general phases of motor skill acquisition in school-age children
- Explain the importance of healthy levels of physical activity, exercise, sports participation, and nutrition in middle childhood
- Discuss the complexity of multiple contexts and their influence on physical well-being in middle childhood

To complete the requirements for a class, you visit an after-school recreation program to determine what types of activities are appropriate and desirable for children in elementary through middle school. You notice that the younger children in grades K to 2 are running, tumbling, singing, and coloring. The slightly older children in grades 3 to 5 are skipping, playing hopscotch and basketball, tossing beanbags, and playing card games. Children in grades 6 to 8 are bouncing on pogo sticks, playing air hockey and chess, and making braided friendship bracelets. You begin to reach some conclusions about age-appropriate activity, but you wonder, "Why these activities at these ages?"

Middle Childhood Biological Development

A casual observer of this case study might notice several developmental trends—or patterns—among the different-aged children. The younger children are engaged in activities that involve high levels of energy and gross motor movement. The slightly older group is engaged in activities that require finer motor skills, better coordination, and sustained attention. The oldest group is engaged in skills that require balance, quick responses, and thoughtful or careful planning. These group differences reflect the changes that occur in physical, motor, and brain development in school-age children. The many physical changes taking place during the middle childhood years require parents, educators, practitioners, and coaches to provide children with environmental support for optimal physical growth.

Theoretical Viewpoints

In chapter 1, the *nature versus nurture* controversy was presented as one of several critical issues in developmental psychology. The general question raised was, "To what extent do genetics and biology shape who we become, compared to the contributions made by our environment?" A more specific question elicited by the case study in this chapter might be, "To what extent are the physical, cognitive, and motor skill differences of the children in the after-school program a product of genetic or environmental opportunities?" It is a difficult question to answer in theory; it is equally difficult to answer when applied to a specific domain. Because many experts believe that physical, brain, and motor development may be influenced more by "nature," a review of several of these theoretical viewpoints is warranted. Although other theoretical perspectives will be presented throughout the textbook, additional genetic/biological perspectives are presented in chapter 8 to explain physical development in adolescents.

Genetic Perspectives

A genetic theoretical viewpoint proposes that most development is determined by a child's genetic blueprint. In this view, children's height and bone length, motor milestones, and brain characteristics are largely determined by genetic codes passed down through the chromosomes of their parents, grandparents, great-grandparents, and so on. Although this theoretical viewpoint acknowledges the influence of the environment on development, the environmental role is small.

Theories espousing this view are supported by studies that have found many physical and cognitive similarities among individuals who are genetically similar, such as siblings (Plomin & Petrill, 1997; Scarr, 1997). Physical, intellectual, and personality characteristics that are similar among the most genetically related family members (e.g., identical twins) are thought to be genetically determined (Betancur, Leboyer, & Gillberg, 2002). Using this theoretical perspective, geneticists would explain size and motor skill differences between children in the case study as largely determined by a preprogrammed genetic plan. This supposition is supported, for example, by the finding that height is more similar in identical twins—differing by only about one third of an inch—than in fraternal twins who differ by 1½ inches on average (Mange & Mange, 1994).

A theoretical approach that emphasizes the role of genetic information is **behavioral genetics**. Behavioral genetics explains the observable variation in children's behavior and development by examining the relative contributions of genes and environmental factors (Plomin, 2000). Behavioral geneticists use twin and adoption studies to demonstrate that *all* behavioral, intellectual, and personality traits are to some extent influenced by genetic predispositions (Turkheimer, 2000). The general methodology is to look for similarities and differences between identical and fraternal twins in order to determine which characteristics have a higher **heritability estimate**, or an estimate of the degree to which variation of a specific characteristic in a population is due to genetic factors (Plomin, 2000). The estimate can range from 0.00 to 1.00, with higher heritability estimates indicating greater genetic influence. For example, height has been found to have an 80 to 95% heritability estimate. This means that 80 to 95% of the differences in height that exist among people can be explained by a programmed genetic code. Only 5 to 20% of the variation in height that you see among people today is influenced by environmental factors known to affect growth, such as diet, chronic illness, or early maturation.

Behavioral geneticists emphasize the role of genetics but do not ignore the role of the environment. They are interested in teasing out the effects of each on differences in development (Pike, 2002; Plomin, 2000). For example, they recognize that genetically related children are typically raised in the same home by the same parents. Behavior geneticists acknowledge this influence, labeling this component **shared environments**. It is the environmental component (e.g., parenting, socioeconomic status, and schooling opportunities) that children share. Behavioral geneticists argue, however—and correctly so—that related siblings growing up in the same home may develop quite differently from one another (Pike, Manke, Reiss, & Plomin, 2000). They attribute this difference to **nonshared environments**. Nonshared environments include differential parental treatment due to birth order or gender, different teachers, different peer relationships, or extracurricular activities. Behavior geneticists argue that the effects of nonshared environments appear to be *greater* than those of shared environments (Plomin, Chipuer, & Neiderhiser, 1994). In other words, biological siblings growing up in the same home are more likely to be *different* than they are similar. What makes them similar is largely genetic, followed by a smaller contribution of shared environmental experiences. What contributes to their differences is their nonshared experiences.

Behavior geneticists would predict that siblings in the after-school program are more likely to be similar in height than nonrelated peers. This height similarity would be attributed to genetic inheritance. Differences in height among siblings are not only due to genetics but also to nonshared environmental factors, such as one sibling who eats very poorly when the other does not.

Critics of behavioral genetics say that in most of the studies cited as support for a *nature* position, genetics and environment are correlated (Maccoby, 2000). For example, athletic parents not only contribute their genes to their offspring but also typically provide a very active and stimulating environment for their children. Other critics cite the documented effectiveness of intervention programs. Children from disadvantaged backgrounds can be provided with improved nutrition and safe, structured opportunities to exercise, and an improvement in skeletal and muscular health is realized (Stone, McKenzie, Welk, & Booth, 1998).

Nonshared environments contribute to the differences between siblings raised in the same home.

Biological Perspectives

Biological theories, like genetic theories, also recognize the important role that heredity may play in determining development. Biological perspectives, however, place greater emphasis on biological structures and children's functioning. In biologically based theories, developmental patterns are studied and explained by examining hormonal functioning, brain maturation, the chemical makeup of the brain, and other physiological measures.

For example, a biological psychologist might explain the differences in size among same-aged children in the after-school program by differences in growth hormone levels or body metabolism.

A specific example of an area within psychology that uses this biological perspective is **behavioral neuroscience**. Behavioral neuroscience is the study of the relationship between brain and behavior. Due to recent breakthroughs in biomedical technology, researchers can watch the brain function as a child engages in a variety of tasks. Using this technique, a direct connection may be observed between brain activity and overt behavior. This perspective emphasizes the role that biological growth and brain functioning may play in determining the behavioral differences or similarities observed among children.

The Interaction of Nature and Nurture

Although both the genetic and biological theoretical perspectives described above emphasize the role of nature in development, they also recognize the role of the environment, or nurture. All developmental theories tend to vary in the degree to which contributions are attributed to nature and to nurture. The most contemporary approach to understanding the nature-nurture debate is that *both* genetic predispositions *and* environmental experiences shape the development of children. The question posed now is "How?" (Gottesman, 2005). There are several ways that genetic information may interact with the environment to influence development.

Maturation. The process whereby genes largely guide development over time is called **maturation**. A child's increase in height from birth to early adulthood is an example of a maturational process. This pattern of development is relatively universal for all children, driven by a biologically controlled release of growth hormones and interrupted only by extreme environmental interference, such as malnutrition or chronic illness.

Reaction range. Reaction ranges explain how children differ in their responses to either the same environment or different environments (Goldsmith & Gottesman, 1996). How children respond depends both on their genetic makeup and on the quality of the environment. Figure 3.1 illustrates the genetically determined ranges of height for two different children and how the environment (e.g., prenatal exposure to alcohol or a healthy diet) may influence *where* each child may fall within the range of reaction.

Reaction ranges help us to understand how genetically similar children can differ in the way their genetic makeup responds to different life circumstances. It also accounts for how two children with extremely different genetic backgrounds can respond differently to the same environment. Remember the resilient children from the island of Kauai described in chapter 1?

Niche-picking. The tendency for children to choose environments that are consistent with their inherited tendencies is referred to as **niche-picking** (Scarr & McCartney, 1983; Crosnoe & Muller, 2004). For example, shy children may gravitate toward activities or hobbies, such as chess or reading, that are solitary or quiet. Their choice of environment may encourage, or reinforce, the innately shy tendencies of children that—in turn—may reinforce their choice of activity, and so on. This concept suggests not only how intricately woven genetics and socialization processes are in the development of children but also how genetic predispositions may actually influence the types of environments to which children are exposed.

Niche-picking also suggests that the *way* nature interacts with nurture may change across time. Genes interact with the environment to shape development in a variety of ways. As we discuss the research on physical, brain, and motor skill development in this chapter, we will continue to focus on the ways in which a child's genetic makeup—together with unique experiences—influence physical development.

Do you resemble your biological parents in height? If not, what factors might have contributed to this difference?

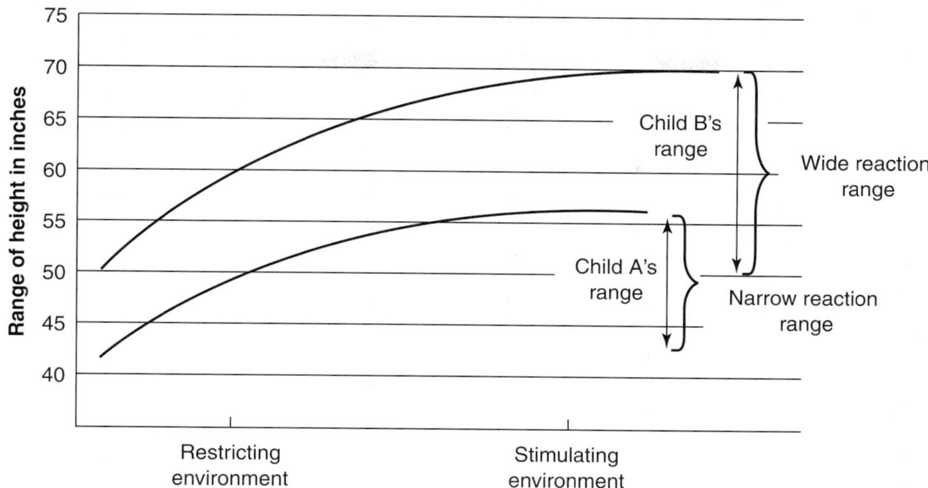

FIGURE 3.1 Reaction Ranges for Physical Growth
Each child's genetic inheritance determines the upper and lower limits of physical growth. The quality of the environment influences their growth within this range.

Source: From *Child and Adolescent Development for Educators* (p. 67), by J. L. Meece, 2002, New York: McGraw-Hill. Copyright 2002 by McGraw-Hill. Adapted by permission of the publisher.

PHYSICAL DEVELOPMENT

Physical development most often refers to gains in height and weight. During middle childhood physical transformations also occur in facial structure, body proportion, bone growth, and fat and muscle tissue distribution. These physical changes that are driven by genetic, biological, and environmental factors transform childlike body shapes into more mature physical forms.

Changes in Body Size

The most notable difference among the children from the case study at the beginning of this chapter is the variation in their size. The general pattern of physical development between the ages of 8 and 12 is one of steady **growth**. Growth refers specifically to proportional changes in size. Children in middle childhood typically gain 2 to 3 inches in height and 4 to 6 pounds in weight per year (Tanner, 1990). This steady increase in body size is illustrated in Figure 3.2, where growth data are represented as **distance curves**.

Distance curves plot cumulative height and weight for a sample of children over time. The curve compares children's progress toward eventual adult maturity. Notice the similarity in patterns of growth from birth for boys and girls. In the height curve, note that the girls' curve crosses the boys' at age 10 and, for the next three years, girls are, on average, taller than boys. Similarly, the girls' weight curve crosses the boys' curve at 11 years and the girls are, on average, heavier than boys for the next several years. This change documents girls' earlier entry into pubertal maturation by approximately two years. After age 13, when boys begin pubertal maturation, they surpass girls in both height and weight.

Parents and health care providers typically pay the closest attention to an individual child's growth patterns. Many of us can visit the house in which we grew up and identify a marker showing that our height increased over time. Parents and health care providers are also often first to detect that children may be beginning to fall above or below the norms for their height or weight. In the majority of cases, there is no cause for alarm. Experts emphasize the need to treat these normative data as just that: an *average* height or weight for a given chronological age. Many children grow at different rates and follow different growth trajectories. Growth rates can vary based on genetic histories, ethnic background, illness, and other factors. For example, children from North America, northern Europe, and Africa tend to be taller than children from Asia and South America. Within the United States, African American children are on average taller than Caucasian, Asian, and Hispanic children.

Typically, pediatricians create a growth chart for an individual child and plots his or her

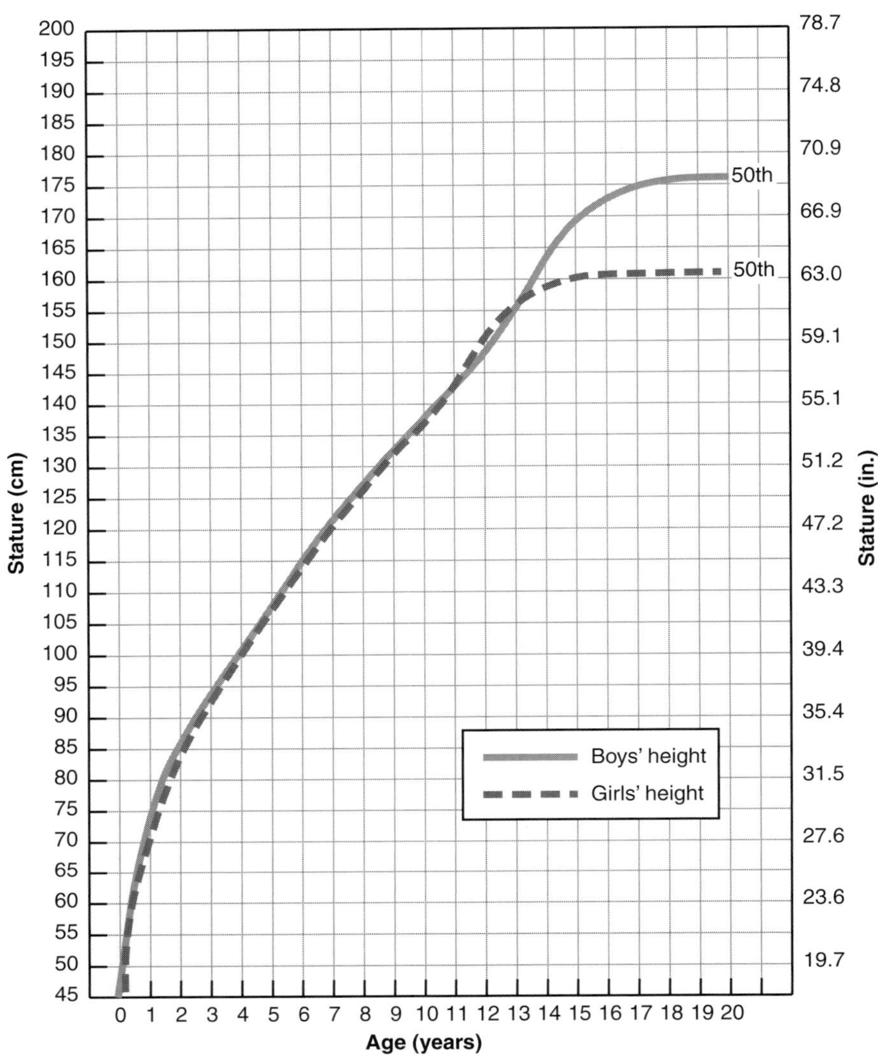

FIGURE 3.2 Distance Curves for Height and Weight
These growth curves show the gradual increase in height and weight that takes place over middle childhood.

Source: Based on data from the National Center for Health Statistics in collaboration with the National Center for Chronic Disease Prevention and Health Promotion 2000. http://www.cdc.gov/nchs/about/major/nhanes/growthcharts/clinicalcharts.htm.

increases or decreases in height and weight over time. Comparisons are then made not only to the national averages but, more importantly, also to the child's growth history. Although it may have been correct for the observer in the chapter case study to assume that the larger children were the oldest, such an observation may not prove to be true for all children.

Recognizing that growth may occur at different rates, when might there be a cause for concern? A generally accepted rule of thumb is that if a child's height or weight falls below the 10th percentile, the cause should be investigated. When, based on national averages, 90% of same-aged children in a sample weigh more than a targeted child, or if height falls above the 90th percentile, further

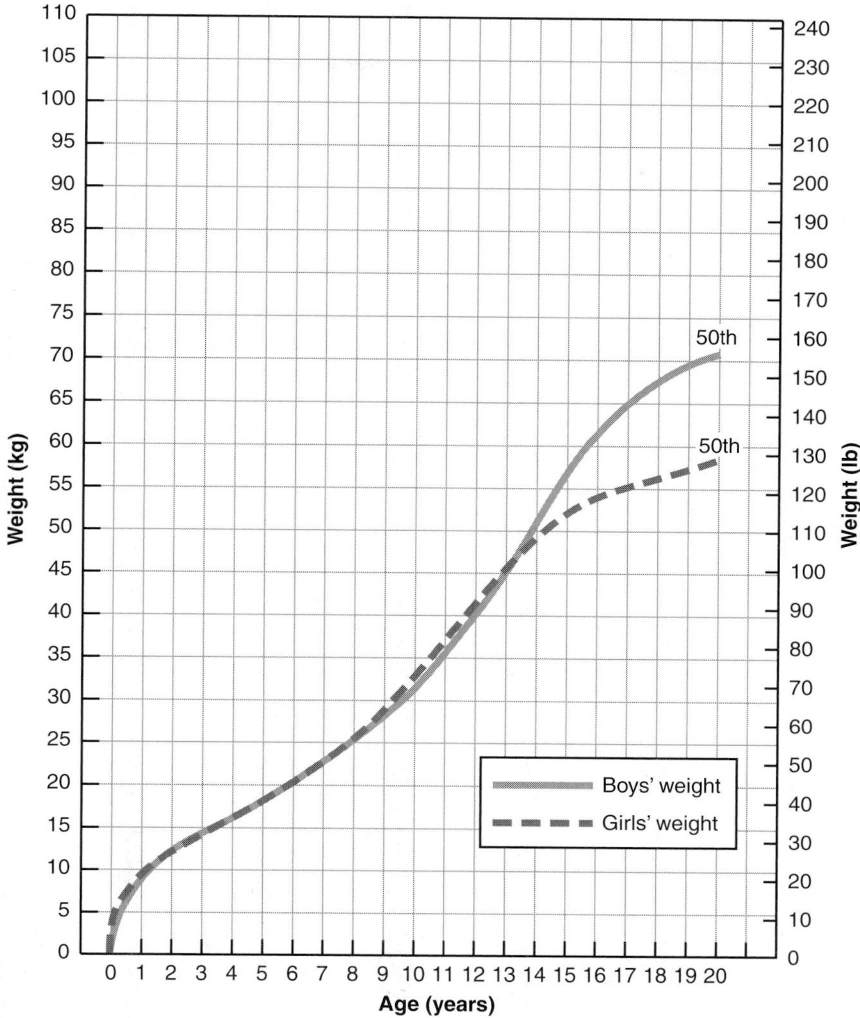

FIGURE 3.2 (Continued)

examination is warranted. Box 3.1 examines the health and psychosocial consequences to children who are short in stature.

Height and weight data collected from children in the late 1800s has shown that children today—in almost all regions of the world—are taller and heavier. This pattern is referred to as a **secular trend** in growth (Tanner, 1990). Children raised in average economic conditions have increased in height approximately 2 centimeters (cm) each decade since the beginning of the 20th century. Evidence of this secular trend may be noted immediately after birth. Today's newborns have been found to be larger, on average, than their counterparts who were measured decades earlier. Reasons offered for this trend are multiple, complex, and include both genetic and environmental components. An evolutionary explanation for the secular change asserts that "tallness" genes are being selected over "shortness" genes (Tanner, 1978). Alternatively, environmental explanations may include improved prenatal care, immunizations, hygiene and sanitation, better nutrition, and less illness.

A related outcome to this growth trend is that girls and boys appear to be entering their second

BOX 3.1 ROADMAP TO UNDERSTANDING THEORY AND RESEARCH

The Psychosocial and Cognitive Consequences of Being Short

Children who are considered **short of stature (SS)** are at or below the third percentile in height compared to the height of same-aged peers. An additional characteristic of SS children is that there is no known organic cause for their shortness. They are not deficient in growth hormones, nor do they have a history of severe malnutrition or **failure to thrive**, a condition whereby infants show delays in growth due to a lack of attention or stimulation.

For many years, parents and physicians assumed that SS children would experience poor psychosocial functioning. Studies showed that SS children experienced poorer self-concepts and low self-esteem, exhibited fewer prosocial behaviors, exhibited more behavior problems, had difficulty with peer relationships, and generally felt uncomfortable about themselves, especially in social settings (for a review see Voss, 1999).

These were appropriate conclusions to draw given the populations that were studied. Children in these studies had more difficulty with parents and peers or performed more poorly in school and, as a result, sought the advice of physicians and psychologists for a remedy. Using participants from this clinical sample created a psychological profile of SS children that may not have applied to *all* SS children—just to those seeking professional help. In addition, there was no information to suggest that their height was the source of their problems! Even studies that used clinical samples did not show consistent or pervasive psychosocial problems in SS children when compared to normal-height children (Skuse, Gilmour, Tian, & Hindmarsh, 1994; von Busschbach, Hinten, Rikken, et al., 1999; Zimet, Cutler, Litvene, Dahms, Owens, & Cutler, 1995).

Using a clinical population, Sandberg and colleagues (1999) asked parents and SS children to report on social competencies (e.g., issues related to growth problems and height), internalizing behaviors (e.g., anxiety, depression), and externalizing behaviors (e.g., aggressive, uncontrolled behavior). Parents reported that their children experienced more teasing about their height, but there was little evidence that the teasing manifested itself in any significant internalizing behavior. Parents also reported that SS children were treated as younger than their chronological age, and this "juvenilized" treatment corresponded to reports of increased externalizing behavior. For SS children who had a younger sibling who was taller, the disparity produced enough stress to be related to lower feelings of self-competency and increased behavior problems; however, no other psychosocial factors showed a significant difference between SS and normal-height children. The most telling finding of the study was that parental reports about their children's psychosocial factors and behaviors were significantly more pessimistic than reports by the SS children. In other words, parents *thought* that their children were more affected by their height than the children themselves reported.

In a more recent study, children from a general population were asked to cast their peers in various roles for a class play (Sandberg, Bukowski, Fung, & Noll, 2004). The roles were accompanied by descriptions such as "good leader," and "has many friends" as well as "is very shy" and "doesn't join in." SS children were just as likely to be cast in a leadership role and fit the description "has many friends" as their taller peers.

More consistent findings emerge, however, when cognitive and academic outcomes are measured. Short-stature children have significantly poorer reading and math skills and poorer overall cognitive functioning and display underachievement in school (Sandberg et al., 1998), and these deficiencies are exacerbated by socioeconomically disadvantaged backgrounds (Dowdney, Skuse, Morris, & Pickles, 1998). These studies confirm the long-term cognitive outcomes for these children but have not yet begun to address the causal links between factors that cause short stature and cognitive deficits.

growth spurt associated with puberty earlier than ever before. Recent public health research indicates that some girls between 8 and 10 years of age are displaying early stages of pubertal maturation (Herman-Giddens et al., 1997). Earlier maturation has critical implications for social and emotional development as well as for how peers, parents, and teachers react to the maturing youth. Although these growth trends should be recognized as potentially occurring in the middle childhood years, we will present these research findings in chapter 8, since most of the research that examines the adjustment to puberty includes early adolescents.

Changes in Body Proportions

Although the most common childhood assessments of physical growth are height and weight, other parts of the body change in proportion. Ten-year-olds are not simply "bigger infants"; they have increased in size *and* changed in proportion. The child does not grow "all of a piece" but rather "differentially in all of his parts and systems" (Krogman, 1972, p. 60). **Stature**, or total height, is made up of head and neck length, trunk length, and leg length. The changing linear contributions of each body part can be seen in Figure 3.3, which shows that as children move through middle childhood, all three areas increase in their contributions to total stature. Boys' and girls' growth patterns are similar until puberty, when girls surpass boys, showing slightly greater growth in all three areas. After puberty, boys catch up and may even surpass girls' growth patterns.

The pattern of change in these separate body components illustrates two growth principles: *cephalocaudal* and *proximodistal* development. **Cephalocaudal** development is growth that proceeds from head to toe. For example, during prenatal and (most of) postnatal development, the head and neck areas develop first and more quickly than the trunk, followed by the legs and feet. In contrast, **proximodistal** development proceeds from the inside out, with internal organs developing before the third layer of skin, limbs, hands, feet, fingers, and toes. For example, in infancy, the head accounts for a greater proportion of total body stature than in middle childhood or adolescence, when the trunk and limbs begin to grow proportionately (see Figure 3.4).

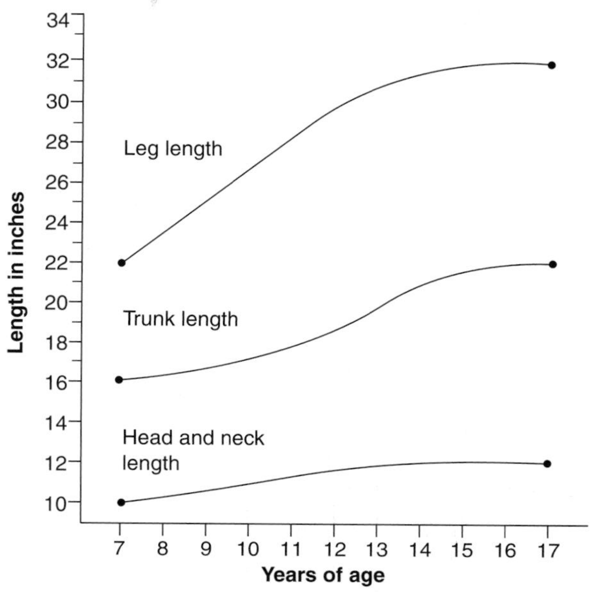

FIGURE 3.3 Changes Over Time in the Head and Neck, Trunk, and Legs

During middle childhood, leg length increases more rapidly followed by the trunk and then the head and neck.

Based on data from "Length of Head and Neck, Trunk, and Lower Extremities of Iowa City Children, Aged 7–17 Years," by H. V. Meredith, 1939, *Child Development, 10*, pp. 129–144.

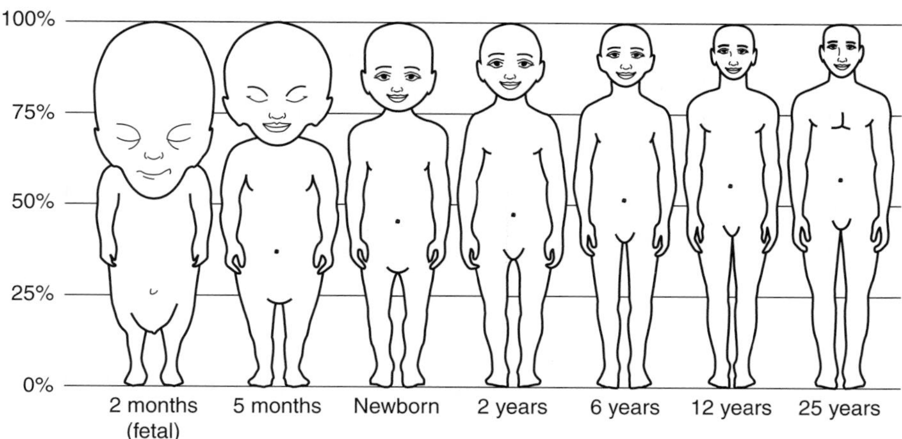

FIGURE 3.4 Changes in Body Proportions from the Prenatal Period to Adulthood

At birth, the head accounts for approximately 25% of an infant's total stature. This proportion changes as the child grows.

In addition, as girls and boys begin their pubertal growth spurts, proximodistal development reverses, so that hands and feet, followed by arms and legs, develop more quickly than trunk, head, and neck areas (Wheeler, 1991)! This explains the long-legged, gangly look of prepubescent children who are often described as "all arms and legs." For example, an average 10-year-old girl's foot size is 90% of its eventual adult size. So it is possible for a mother to have a 12-year-old daughter with the *same* shoe size. The daughter's feet, however, will not continue to grow. After the peak growth spurt, proximodistal development reverses again, and the trunk and head areas will catch up. This rapid growth of hands, feet, and limbs not only contributes to a disproportioned body in the latter years of middle childhood but also causes more tripping, dropping of objects, and general all-around clumsiness as prepubescent children grow accustomed to functioning with their quickly growing appendages.

Finally, the jaws, teeth, and face also grow throughout middle childhood into adolescence. The first set of teeth, commonly known as "baby teeth," begins to fall out at 6 or 7 years of age. These 20 baby teeth are replaced by 32 permanent teeth that begin to "erupt" around 6 to 7 years of age, with some of the molars coming in as late as 10 to 12 years of age. The emergence of new teeth has implications for jaw growth, as the jawbone must grow to accommodate more and larger teeth. In fact, the correspondence between jawbone growth and tooth eruption may determine who will need braces to align their permanent teeth and who will not.

A larger and more angular jaw line characterizes facial growth as children move from early childhood to adolescence. Although the face grows wider from cheekbone to cheekbone, it grows even longer from lengthening forehead to angular chin. Lastly and most dramatically, the face increases in depth, literally growing forward in relation to the skull. This pattern of facial growth may explain the loss of the round faces that characterize most young children, giving way to a sharper, more defined, and distinctive facial profile.

The oldest children in the after-school program have longer legs and trunks in relationship to their heads. Their faces are more angular, and they have all their permanent teeth.

Think about your school pictures from kindergarten and sixth grade. What were the most notable changes that took place in your face?

Skeletal Development

The bones of the body start out as soft, cartilage tissue but harden over time, a process called **ossification**. This hardening process continues until late adolescence; however, the onset and rate of ossification are different for various bones as well as for individuals. Because many of the bones in school-age children have only partially ossified, they are more pliable and less susceptible to breaks—an advantage considering the strain highly active children place on their bones.

Bones grow from special areas called **epiphyses**, or growth plates. A long bone, such as those in the limbs, will develop epiphyses at both ends, and over time the cartilage cells in the growth plates will harden, thus fusing the main bone shaft with the epiphysis at each end (see Figure 3.5). When this fusion takes place, further growth is no longer possible (Tanner, 1978).

Infancy and puberty are the two periods of greatest bone growth, with girls experiencing a steeper rise in bone density compared to boys as they enter puberty (McKay, Bailey, Mirwald, Davison, & Faulkner, 1998). Boys catch up as they enter puberty, with up to 90% of adult bone

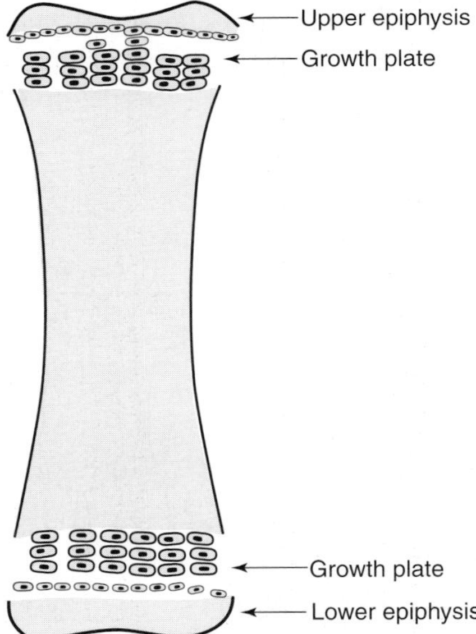

FIGURE 3.5 Limb Bone with Upper and Lower Epiphyses and Growth Plates
This diagram of a bone limb with underdeveloped growth plates at the top and bottom characterizes bone growth in middle childhood.

deposited by the end of adolescence for both boys and girls (Lypaczewski, Lappe, & Stubby, 2002).

Calcium is important for the growth of bones. A deficiency of calcium, usually due to poor diet, may cause **demineralization**. Demineralized bones are weaker, more brittle, and susceptible to breaks. Poor calcium intake during the growing years has been associated with a higher incidence of stress fractures in late adolescence and with osteoporosis later in life (Fassler & Bonjour, 1995).

The high phosphorus content in soft drinks affects the retention of calcium and the formation of new bone by reducing the concentration of calcium in the blood, which in turn causes a release of calcium from bone. In addition, anabolic steroid use may—among many other potential side effects—cause the epiphyses to close prematurely, thus stunting bone growth and affecting eventual adult height (Jenkins & Reaburn, 2000).

The greatest threat to bone mineralization, however, is inactivity (Janz, 2002). Exercise increases bone width and mineralization, producing stronger bones and lessening susceptibility to injury (Bass et al., 1998; Bailey et al., 1999; Barr & McKay, 1998). Intervention programs that attempt to increase the physical activity of children aged 6 to 14 or that supplement the diets of children with calcium do indeed increase bone mass in children and adolescents (French, Fulkerson, & Story, 2000).

Body Fat Levels and Muscle Mass

Height and weight measures provide us with several important indices of growth. Measuring body fat and muscle mass provides additional indicators of a child's health and nutritional background. A heavy child may be large-boned, heavily muscled, or overweight.

Body fat levels. The amount of body fat, or **adipose tissue**, can be measured in *skinfolds*, a pinch of skin and fat measured to the nearest millimeter (mm) by a **skinfold caliper**. Skinfold measurements are usually taken at several different sites on the body. Figure 3.6 shows that there is a slight decrease in adipose tissue after age 4. At approximately age 7 for girls and age 8 for boys, there is a gradual increase in fat tissue, referred to as the **adiposity rebound**, which continues at a slightly higher rate throughout adolescence.

Another method used to measure body fat is the **body mass index** or **BMI**. BMI is a number that shows body weight adjusted for height. BMI is both gender and age specific and shows a pattern of development similar to skinfolds. BMI decreases during the preschool years and then increases into adulthood.

Before puberty, fat content is highly correlated with weight in both girls and boys. After puberty, muscle mass is more highly correlated with weight in boys. Girls consistently have greater skinfold totals than boys, and after age 12 this difference becomes more pronounced. By the end of the growth spurt in adolescence, fat accounts for 16% of total body weight in boys and 27% of total body weight in girls. As a result of the increase in adipose tissue after age 7, we find that physical activity and a balanced diet are important in maintaining body weight for both sexes, but particularly for girls. The number of children in middle childhood who are overweight or obese has increased in the United States over the past several decades (National Center for Health Statistics, 2001). The health and psychological consequences of this trend are discussed later in the chapter.

In the after-school recreational program, differences in body fat among children were readily observable. Some children were overweight and others were quite thin.

Muscle mass. We are born with most of the muscle fibers we are ever going to have. During the course of normal development, there is a large increase in muscle length and breadth with age. An increase in muscle size, called **hypertrophy**, results from both genetic and environmental factors. Muscle development appears to proceed along a normal maturational course consistent with bone growth and is a prerequisite to certain motor abilities. Systematic physical activity, however, enhances muscle composition. Physically active children have a higher proportion of muscle mass to body fat.

Boys and girls appear to be equal in tasks that require muscle movement until puberty. As boys enter puberty, the release of the hormone testosterone promotes the growth of muscle and subsequently widens the gender difference in muscle mass between males and females. Since muscle mass is harder to measure than body fat levels, measures of strength are often used to reflect muscle growth. Figure 3.7 shows age increases and gender differences in leg and arm strength.

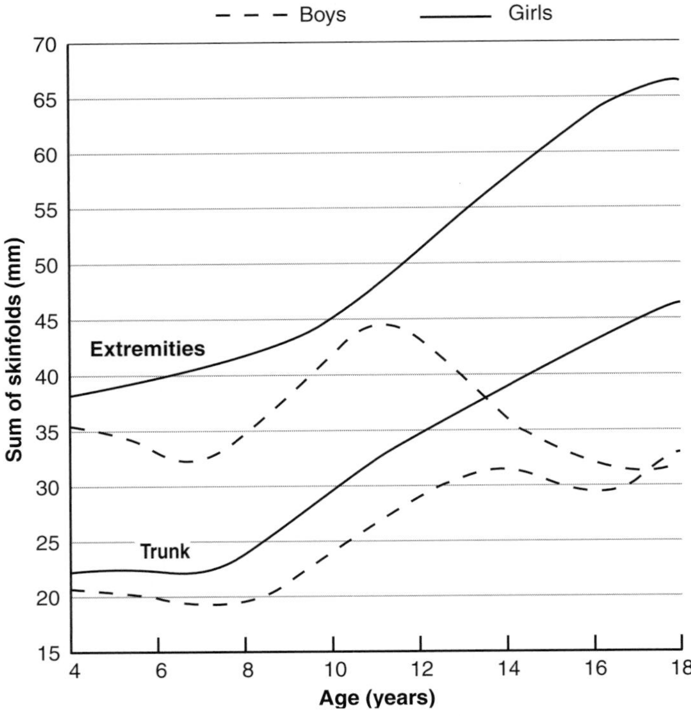

FIGURE 3.6 Developmental Changes in Fat Distribution for Boys and Girls

Trunk and extremity skinfold measures show an increase in subcutaneous fat for girls and a decrease for boys, particularly following puberty.

Source: From "Subcutaneous Fat Distribution During Growth" (p. 70) by R. Malina and C. Bouchard (1988) in C. Bouchard and F. E. Johnston (Eds.), *Fat Distribution During Growth and Later Health Outcomes*. New York: Liss. Copyright 1988 by Alan R. Liss. Reprinted with permission of Wiley-Liss, Inc., a subsidiary of John Wiley & Sons, Inc.

A popular myth is that weight training should not begin until puberty since testosterone production is responsible for the increase in muscle mass in boys. This myth includes the warning that not only will premature weight lifting fail to produce any muscle gain but also may interfere with normal growth. This myth is only partially supported by research. Lifting *maximum* weights in middle childhood will not produce the significant muscle gain that is typically sought. In addition, using incorrect lifting techniques to lift maximum weights can cause serious and sometimes permanent injury to immature tendons, ligaments, and bones (American Academy of Pediatrics, 1983). However, other research shows that resistance training (i.e., *low* weight at high repetitions) in prepubescent boys and girls can produce increases in muscle mass and strength (Faigenbaum, Westcott, Michell, Outerbridge, & Long et al., 1996; Guy & Michell, 2001).

Contributions of Genetics, Biology, and Environment

Physical and skeletal growth is a maturational process that reflects a strong genetic component. Growth hormones are released according to a genetically encoded timetable, and only dramatic differences in environments will influence this development. Both body fat and muscle mass have some genetic predispositions as well (Guillame, Lapidus, Beckers, Lambert, & Bjorntop, 1995). However, these areas of growth also can be shaped by pubertal maturation, diet, sedentary or active lifestyles, and activity opportunities. Despite the parameters set by genetics, parents, teachers, and practitioners play an important role in physical maturation.

The children in the case study display the developmental differences outlined in this section. The

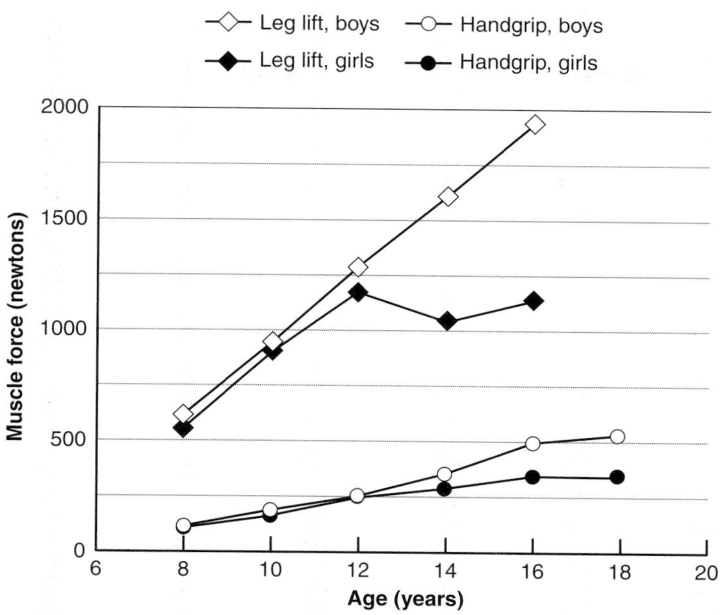

FIGURE 3.7 Strength Differences Between Males and Females
Boys show a steady increase in leg and arm strength throughout middle childhood and adolescence. Girls tend to plateau after puberty.

Source: From *Physical Activity and Growth* (p. 80), by R. J. Shepard, 1982, Chicago: Year Book Medical. Copyright 1982 by C. V. Mosby. Adapted by permission of Elsevier.

Guideposts for Working with School-Age Children

- Because children grow at different rates and proportions, have children track their growth by keeping personal height charts. Calculate the average height of the group or different subgroups to emphasize this point.
- Since there may be psychosocial consequences to extreme statuses in height and weight, encourage children to be tolerant of those different in size.
- Provide ample opportunities for physical activity to promote bone growth and to regulate weight gain.
- Design activities so that children of all sizes can feel physically competent by varying the skills required.
- Try to make physical activity fun!

older children are typically larger, better proportioned, and stronger than the younger children. This difference in size and strength is reflected in the activities in which they engage. The older children, for example, are able to shoot a heavy basketball over their heads while the younger children do not engage in play activities that require size or strength.

BRAIN DEVELOPMENT

Over the past decade, studies documenting developmental changes in brain structure and function have proliferated. An increase in our understanding of brain development is due largely to technological improvements in assessment. Modern brain-imaging techniques allow closer examination of brain tissue as well as identification of which parts of the brain are called into action during various cognitive, emotional, and motor tasks. The majority of this research has focused on brain development during the prenatal and infancy periods because of the presumption that these periods are ones of tremendous growth and change. Neurological developmental phenomena begin before birth and continue to change during middle childhood. This early childhood research has direct implications for understanding brain maturation between the ages of 8 and 12.

Neuronal Development

One of the most significant developments in the brain during prenatal and early postnatal development is an increase in **neurons**. Neurons are nerve cells in the brain and spinal cord that transmit and receive information throughout the nervous system. Each neuron has a rounded body, called the **soma**, and two types of branched fibers: **dendrites**, which receive impulses, and an **axon**, which sends impulses through its terminals. Neurons are not physically connected to one another; instead, a tiny gap, or **synapse**, exists between neurons.

As illustrated in Figure 3.8, chemicals called **neurotransmitters** are released into the gap, thus completing the transmission of a neural impulse from one neuron to another. Sending and receiving neural impulses are the means by which communication takes place in the brain. This communication occurs between individual neurons, groups of neurons, and ultimately, brain structures.

The rate at which neurons develop prenatally is astounding. Before birth neurons are being generated in the brain at a rate of more than 250,000 per minute! This calculation contributes to current estimates that at birth the human brain possesses approximately 10 billion neurons. One particularly interesting aspect of neural development is that

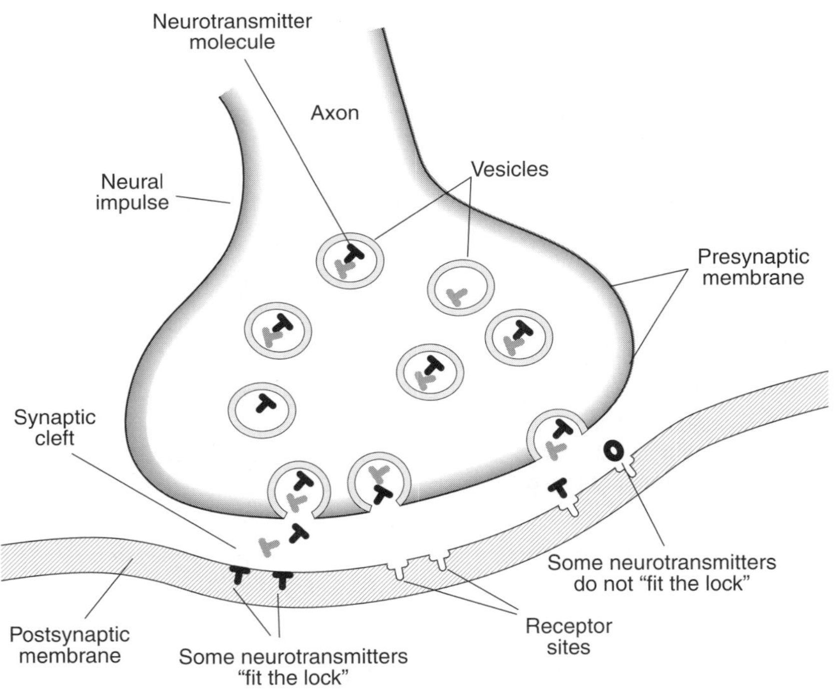

FIGURE 3.8 Synaptic Transmission
A neurotransmitter is released and floats across the "synaptic cleft," where it binds to the receptor sites on the receiving dendrite and the process begins anew.

Source: From *Psychology: Core Concepts* (p. 54), by P. G. Zimbardo, A. L. Weber, & R. L. Johnson, 2003. Boston: Allyn & Bacon. Copyright 2003 by Pearson Education. Reprinted by permission of the publisher.

during the prenatal period, the brain *overproduces* neurons, possibly by a factor of 2 (Kolb, 1989). A process called **programmed cell death**, however, eliminates the extra cells. Recent research shows that the postnatal cell loss is a function of an infant's experiences (Klintsova & Greenough, 1999). In infancy, if neural pathways are stimulated, such as in the visual cortex from visual stimulation, these neurons are more likely to entrench themselves and to survive within the neuronal network. Neurons that are not stimulated die off at high rates.

Neurons in the **cerebral cortex** are commonly referred to as "gray matter" because the tissue from the cerebral cortex turns a gray color when placed in alcohol or other preservatives. The cerebral cortex is a layer of nerve cells 1/32 to 1/8 inch thick at the outer edge of the brain. The growth of gray matter has been shown to increase after birth until approximately early adolescence, followed by a gradual decrease (Gogate, Giedd, Janson, & Rapoport, 2001). However, increases in gray matter differ regionally, with peak volumes in the frontal and parietal areas around age 12 and peak volumes of gray matter in the temporal area at age 18. These areas are identified in Figure 3.9.

Synaptogenesis. The second most significant aspect of brain development is an increase in the number of dendritic branches per neuron, a process called **synaptogenesis**. This dendritic branching results in complex "webs" or "networks of neurons" that represent an increase in connections between neurons and, consequently, greater communication among different and more distant structures of the brain.

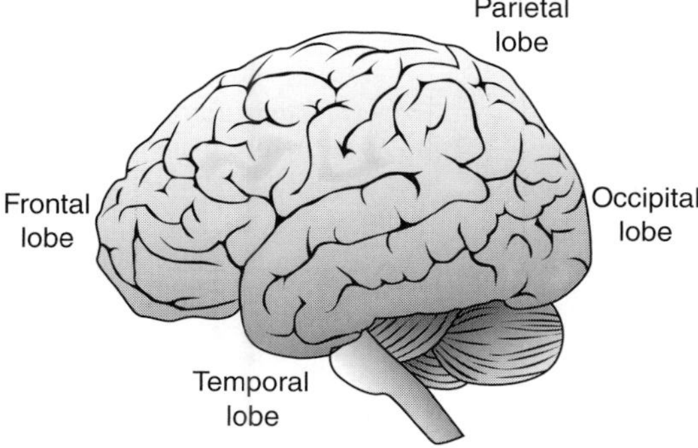

FIGURE 3.9 The Four Lobes of the Brain
Neuronal connections develop first in the occipital lobe, followed by the parietal, frontal, and then the temporal lobes.

As in neuronal production, there appears to be an overproduction of synaptic connections as well. This synaptic overproduction occurs in two waves: right before birth and during early adolescence (Andersen, 2003). The role of postnatal experience in enhancing dendritic branching is similar in enhancing neuronal growth. Neurons in networks receiving stimulation from the environment have been shown to maintain and increase their connections. However, neurons that are not stimulated lose their connective fibers, a process known as **synaptic pruning**. A slight decrease in gray matter reported during middle childhood and middle adolescence most likely reflects evidence of severe pruning of neuronal networks following the waves of overproduction. Evidence of this pruning can be seen in Figure 3.10, where the adolescent brain shows fewer dendritic branches than that of the younger child. This pattern suggests that children during middle childhood and adolescence have fewer neurons and dendritic connections with which to work. Technically this is true, but what actually results from cell loss and pruning is a more integrated and differentiated brain. In other words, during middle childhood and adolescence, the brain becomes a leaner, meaner, learning machine! Synaptic pruning is also reflected in the finding that *overall brain size* shows little change between the ages of 4 and 18 (Giedd et al., 1999). The cognitive advantages school-age children show over infants are a result of a more refined, specialized, and connected brain—not simply one with more neurons.

Myelination. The third significant aspect of brain development is an increase in the **myelination** of axons. Myelination is the process whereby **glial cells** form an insulating sheath around the axons of neurons (Li & Noseworthy, 2002). Half of the brain's volume is made up of glial cells, which do not carry messages but rather serve to support and nourish neurons. Glial cells coat the axons of neurons with a fatty substance called **myelin**. The process of myelination serves to speed up neural impulses, as shown in Figure 3.11.

Studies show that myelination increases steadily with age (Giedd et al., 1999). An even more interesting finding is that some structures in the brain show earlier myelination than others (Gogate et al., 2001). For example, axons in the brain stem as well as axons in the major nerves running to the face, limbs, trunk, and organs all receive their myelin sheaths before birth or during infancy. Brain structures such as these are

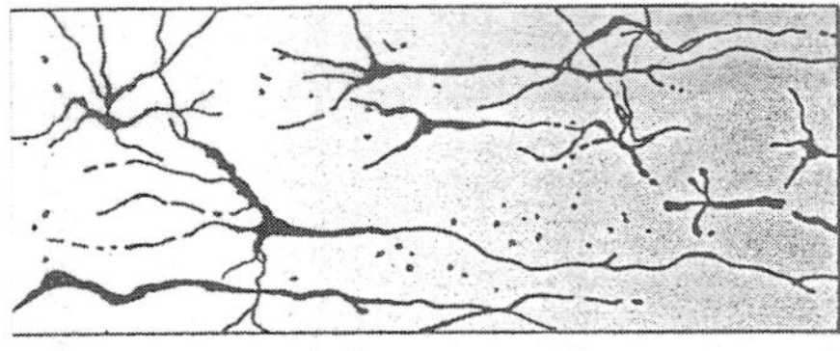

At birth
(A)

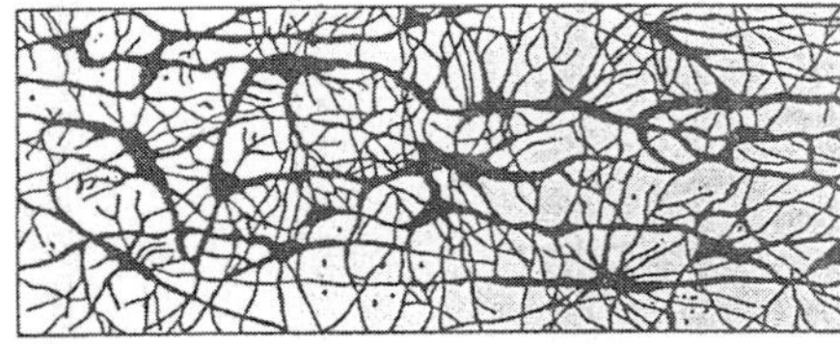

Six years old
(B)

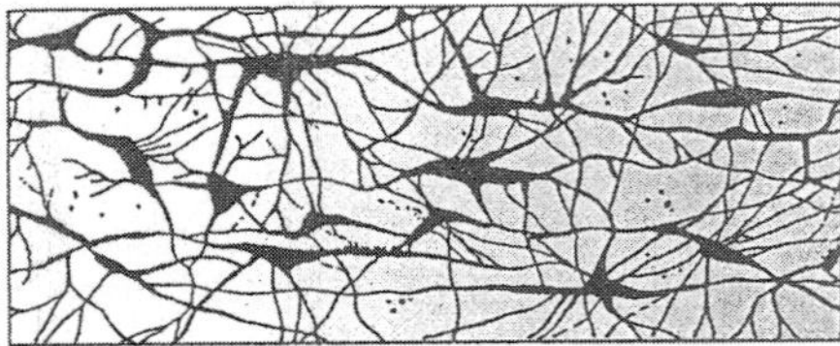

Fourteen years old
(C)

FIGURE 3.10 Changes in Dendritic Branching in the Cerebral Cortex
The brain of a 6-year-old shows increased "weblike" neuronal connections. However, the 14-year-old's brain shows less webbing as a result of synaptic pruning.

Source: From *The Postnatal Development of the Human Cerebral Cortex* by J. L. Conel, 1975, Cambridge, MA: Harvard University Press. Copyright 1975 by the President and Fellows of Harvard College. Reprinted by permission of the publisher.

critical for survival and thus myelinate very soon after birth, whereas other structures—such as the **corpus callosum**, **limbic system**, and **frontal cortex** that are responsible for more complex human functioning—continue to myelinate through middle childhood into adolescence and early adulthood (see Figure 3.12 for the location of these structures).

Fiber tracts. The last significant change that characterizes brain development in middle childhood is the maturation of **fiber tracts**. Fiber tracts are bundles of axons largely responsible for passing neural impulses from one region of the brain to the other. Over time, the axons in these pathways become myelinated and, because of the density of the fatty covered axons, this tissue is referred to as "white matter." White matter shows a linear increase over childhood and adolescence and serves as connections between various areas of the brain (Giedd et al., 1999; Watts, Liston, Niogi, & Ulug, 2003).

Neuronal production, synaptic pruning, myelinated axons, and better communication between distant regions of the brain as a result of fiber tract maturation characterize the middle childhood years. These changes in brain structure appear to be

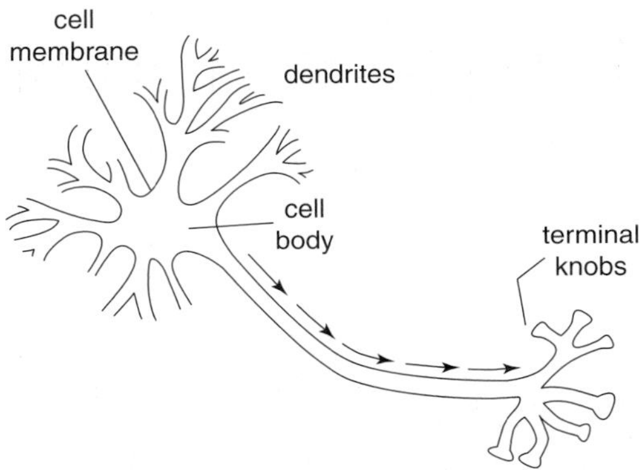

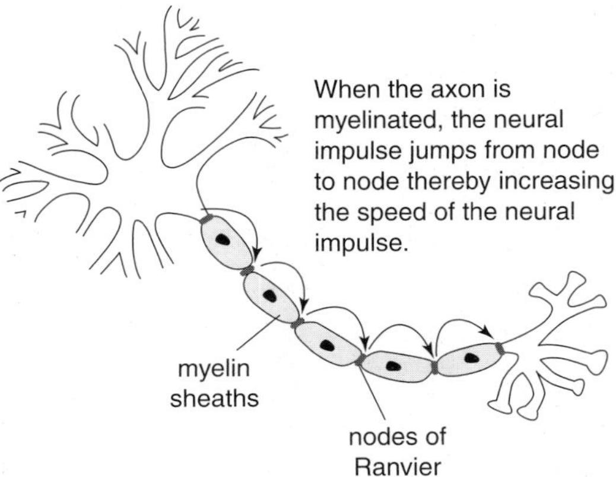

FIGURE 3.11 Effect of Myelination on Neural Impulses

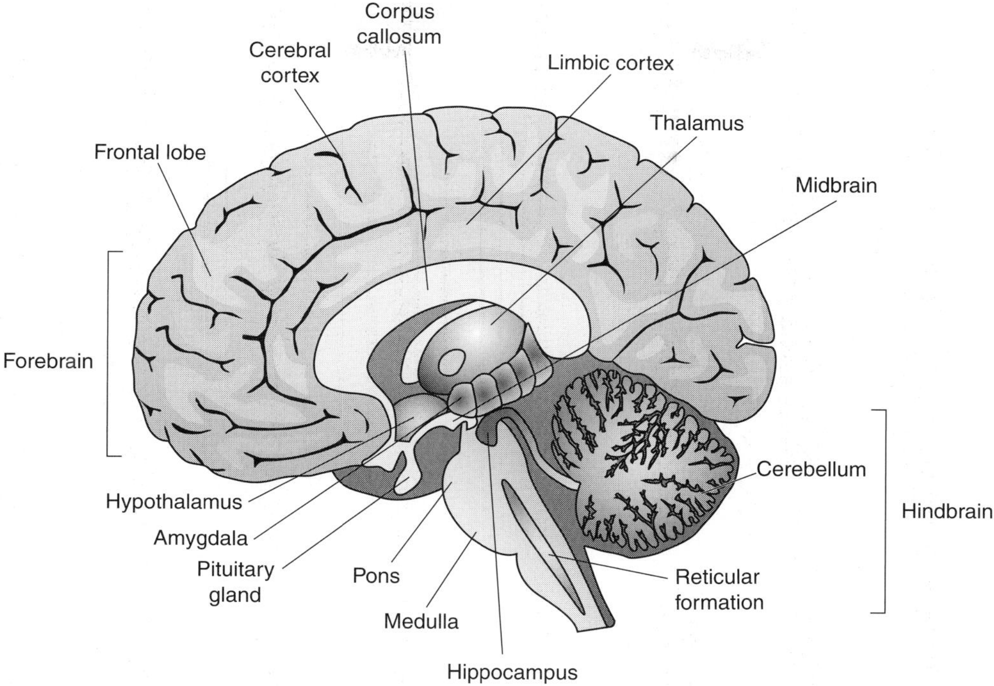

FIGURE 3.12 Brain Structures That Myelinate and Are Related to Changes in Function and Behavior
Structures of the brain myelinate at different times throughout early development.

related to changes in how 8- to 12-year-old children think, feel, and act.

Related Changes in Function

Some recent studies have shown that rather than a steady increase of myelination with age, there are growth spurts or periods within brain development. These growth spurts have documented high rates of programmed cell death and synaptic pruning in conjunction with higher levels of brain metabolism and myelination (Chugani, 1994). They appear to correspond in time to significant shifts in the perceptual-motor, cognitive, and emotional functioning of school-age children (Casey, Giedd, & Thomas, 2000; van Baal, Boomsma, & de Geus, 2001). For example, researchers have shown a growth spurt in the cerebellum between ages 4 and 6 that corresponds to improved coordination and balance in school-age children (Paus et al., 2001). Table 3–1 provides a more extensive list of how the heavily pruned and myelinated structures of the brain may coincide with patterns of pronounced perceptual, cognitive, and motor development during the same time period.

These neurological advancements are reflected in the tasks that engage children in the after-school program. The older children exhibit better coordination (e.g., skipping, hopscotch, and balancing on the pogo stick). They are able to concentrate on games that require focus and attention (e.g., card playing), and they exhibit more planful and purposeful behavior (e.g., chess).

Contributions of Genetics, Biology, and Environment

Just what are the contributions of genetics and the environment to the development of the brain? Emerging consensus from research is that genetic effects may largely determine synaptic growth (Changeux & Dehaene, 1989; Chen & Tonegawa, 1997). During synaptic pruning, however, genetic

TABLE 3–1

Myelinated Brain Structures and Parallel Cognitive and Behavioral Functioning

This table shows the progress of myelination with age and the relationship between myelinated brain structures and function.

Brain Structure	Age of Myelination	Related Function
Brain stem, thalamus, cerebellum	First several months of life	The control of vital signs, sensations, reflexes
Visual cortex	2 to 4 months	Vision, forming three-dimensional images
Some areas of the cerebellum and cerebral cortex	3 months	Seeing, hearing, and sensing touch, certain reflexes disappear, involuntary jerking subsides
Some areas of the cerebellum and midbrain region	2 years	More complex motor control, such as walking, running, and manipulating objects; improved balance
Auditory cortex	5 to 11 years	Late stages of speech development and sensory-motor integration
Reticular formation	Around 10 years	Improved attention
Left temporal lobe	4 to 10 years	Increased proficiency in speaking, understanding, reading and writing language; multiple languages are learned most easily during this time
Right parietal lobe	6 to 12 years	Spatial perception, right-left orientation, spatial cognition
Corpus callosum	5 to 18 years	Increased speed of neural transmission between hemispheres, motor coordination, selective attention, skills that require holistic processing, such as reading; some aspects of creativity and difficult cognitive tasks
Frontal lobe	Throughout early adulthood	Logic, planning, reasoning, motivation, organizing, self-reflection
Hippocampus	Throughout life	Memorizing and recalling information

effects interact with environmental effects to determine which connections will be maintained or eliminated (Klintsova & Greenough, 1999). For example, a child who wears a patch over one eye beyond age 10 may never regain vision in that eye because the visual cortex will prune away the synapses necessary to process information from the eye. In this example, the child's *genetic predisposition* called for neuronal production and dendritic branching in the visual cortex, which is responsible for the sense of sight. However, the child's restrictive *environment* (i.e., the eye patch) resulted in the pruning of these unstimulated synaptic connections during middle childhood, and hence, the permanent loss of sight in one eye (Lewis & Maurer, 2005).

It appears that although human genetics provide the foundation for neuronal production, dendritic branching, and pruning, stimulation from a child's environment has an effect on how the brain continues to develop into early adulthood. Box 3.2 provides research findings on how child abuse and neglect affect the development of the brain. The effects of abuse are worse if they occur prior to adolescence (Teicher et al., 2003). This finding and others suggest that brain development may possess "**critical periods**," or periods of vulnerability, during which development may be interfered with and permanent changes result (Maurer, 2005).

Other researchers, however, argue that very few critical periods can be identified in brain development (Thompson & Nelson, 2001). One explanation for the lack of critical periods is that children's

BOX 3.2 ROADMAP TO UNDERSTANDING THEORY AND RESEARCH

The Effects of Child Abuse and Neglect on Brain Development

In this chapter you have learned that brain growth and maturation are influenced by the interaction of genes and experience. You've also learned about changes that take place in the brain under "normal" developmental conditions. What happens to the brain when a child is deprived of sufficient amounts of sensory and cognitive stimulation as well as nurturance and care taking? In 2003, 3 million cases of child abuse were reported to authorities; fewer than 1 million were substantiated, but the real incidence number is probably higher than either of these figures (Children's Bureau, 2005). How do child abuse and neglect affect brain development?

The answers to these questions are being investigated in a new subfield of child psychiatry called **developmental traumatology**, the systematic study of the psychobiological impact of chronic interpersonal violence on the child (De Bellis, Keshavan et al., 1999). It merges information from developmental psychopathology, developmental neuroscience, and stress and trauma research.

Child maltreatment affects the brain either *indirectly* through the stress response system elicited by the abuse or more *directly* through **experience-expectant processes** (Greenough & Black, 1992). Experience-expected processes are those that are genetically programmed to receive stimulation necessary for survival (e.g., neurons in the visual cortex of a human *expect* to receive stimulation in order that vision sensory areas can develop).

Indirect Effects

Stress is defined as an experience that produces a negative emotional reaction, including fear and a sense of loss of control. When an animal or human experiences stress, a physiological coping response is triggered. This response involves the hormonal system, the sympathetic nervous system, the neurotransmitter system, and the immune system. Physiological changes, such as increased heart rate, blood pressure, and the secretion of adrenaline, generally prepare your body to fight or flee impending danger. This response is very adaptive and serves humans, and other animals, well when threatened. Deleterious effects of the stress response system emerge when the system is called into action too often and for long durations.

Children who have been abused or neglected experience physiological stress responses at much greater frequencies and levels than nonabused children (Glaser, 2000). Specifically, elevated levels of **catecholamines** and **cortisol**, hormones that are released in response to stress, may alter brain development by

1. Accelerating the loss of neurons (i.e., higher-than-normal programmed cell death) (De Bellis, Keshaven, & Harenski, 2001)
2. Delaying myelination (Dunlop et al., 1997)
3. Interfering with normal synaptic pruning (Todd, 1992)

Direct Effects

Based on assumptions from the experience-expectant model (Greenough & Black, 1992), some brain researchers have proposed that, during sensitive periods of brain development, maltreated children may be denied the stimulation or input necessary for neuronal proliferation and/or dendritic pruning. This lack of input thus results in the delay or absence of certain skills.

Whether the brain is affected indirectly through the stress response system or more directly by understimulation, studies have shown that maltreated children differ from nonmaltreated children in brain structure (DeBellis, & Keshavan, 2003; DeBellis, Keshavan et al., 1999; Teicher et al., 2003). Maltreated children have

- Smaller intracranial and cerebral volumes
- A smaller corpus callosum

(*Continued*)

BOX 3.2 (CONTINUED)

- Limbic system dysfunction
- Larger ventricles

Maltreated children show different cognitive and emotional functioning (Bolger & Patterson, 2001; Margolin & Gordis, 2000), such as

- Poor planning and organizational skills
- More attention to distraction
- Low IQ and reading ability
- Poor grades in school
- Language deficits
- Poor emotional self-regulation
- Low levels of empathy and sympathy
- Poor self-concept and low self-esteem
- Poor peer relationships

Maltreated children also are at higher risk of developing psychopathology (Cicchetti & Toth, 1998; Kaplan, Pelcovitz, & Labruna, 1999; Teicher et al., 2003).

Although children who have been abused and neglected share many of the characteristics mentioned here, it is difficult to draw causal links among abuse, changes in brain morphology, and functional or behavioral deficits. The lists of cognitive, emotional, and mental health outcomes for abused children can also result from living in a chronically stressful and impoverished environment with little stimulation or proper nutrition. The outcomes can also be linked to prenatal exposure to **teratogens** (i.e., factors that cause malformations in the fetus, such as postnatal exposure to lead) or to mental illness. More research needs to be carried out in order to distinguish between the different types of abuse (e.g., physical, sexual, emotional, and neglect), their specific effects on the brain, and later cognitive, emotional, and pathological outcomes that may be traced to abuse.

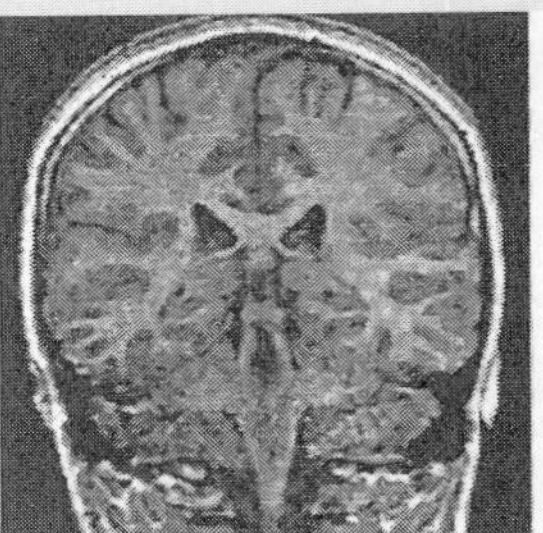

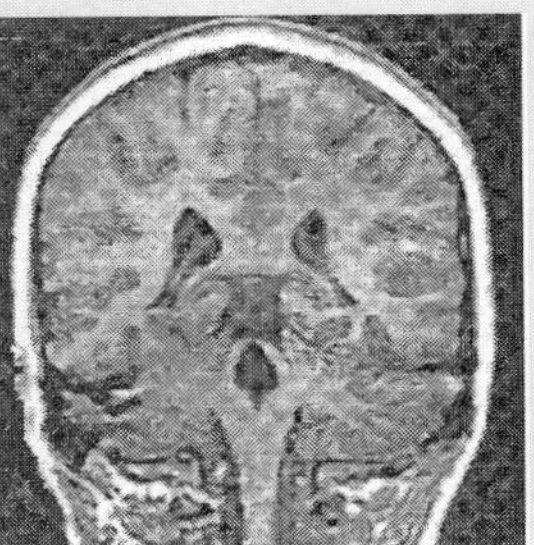

FIGURE 3.13 Effects of Traumatic Stress on the Brain

The brain on the right is that of a maltreated 11-year-old male. Larger "spaces" or ventricles in the middle of the brain translates into less brain tissue.

Source: From "Developmental Traumatology Part II: Brain Development," (p. 1277), by M. D. DeBellis, M. S. Keshavan, D. B. Clark, B. J. Casey, J. N. Giedd, A. M. Boring, K. Frustaci, & N. D. Ryan, 1999, *Biological Psychiatry, 45,* pp. 1271–1284. Copyright 1999 by the Society of Biological Psychiatry. Reprinted by permission.

brains possess **plasticity**. Plasticity is defined as the ability of neurons adjacent to damaged tissue to change their structure in order to support new and different tasks (Kolb & Whishaw, 1998; Kolb, Gibb, & Robinson, 2003). Research shows that if brain injury occurs early in life, many of the capabilities are recovered fully. If, however, damage occurs after adolescence when most of the pruning has taken place, recovery is often partial at best.

Another explanation is that much of brain development occurs over long periods of time, which eliminates the possibility of specific critical periods. One example of a critical period, given earlier, involving the visual system demonstrates that lack of visual stimulation to a patched eye will permanently change the neurological structures that control vision in that eye. However, the visual cortex develops very early and early interference in this system tends to show more long-term effects (Huttenlocher & Dabholkar, 1997). Most of the other areas of the brain take a much longer time to mature and therefore do not seem to possess such narrow developmental windows. For example, recent research shows that in the hippocampus, which is responsible for memory functioning, the formation of new neurons continues throughout one's lifetime (Tanapat, Hastings, & Gould, 2001). This extended developmental period, illustrated in Figure 3.14, argues against specific critical periods in brain development.

Some researchers refer to vulnerable periods of development as **sensitive periods** rather than

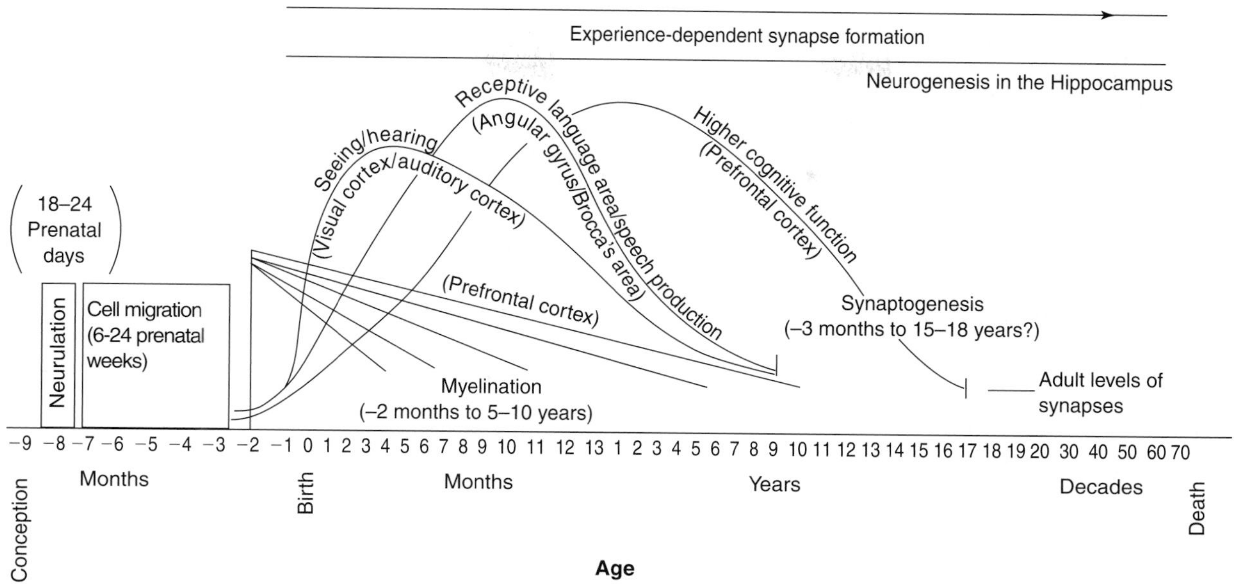

FIGURE 3.14 Developmental Course of Human Brain Development
This graph illustrates the waves of neuronal production followed by synaptic pruning and myelination that occur in brain structures throughout development.

Source: From "Developmental Science and the Media," by R. A. Thompson & C. A. Nelson, 2001, *American Psychologist, 56*, p. 8. Copyright 2001 by the American Psychological Association, Inc. Reprinted by permission of the author.

as critical periods (Johnson, 2005). Sensitive periods represent points during development in which certain kinds of experiences are *especially important* to optimal development. In this chapter, we have identified several periods during brain development after synaptogenesis occurs when environmental stimulation is critical for the maintenance of synapses and dendritic branching. Poor stimulation does not *prevent* synaptic connections or dendritic branching from occurring, but high levels of stimulation during these sensitive periods optimize neuronal growth that enhances brain development.

Both genetic inheritance and environmental experience play a critical role in brain development. Parents, teachers, and practitioners can exert a positive influence both directly and indirectly on the neuronal development of children.

Guideposts for Working with School-Age Children

- Provide safe, healthy, and stimulating environments for children of all ages.
- To encourage growth in different parts of the brain, expose children to a variety of experiences, such as music, visual and performing arts, languages, verbal information, literature, oral histories, tactile experiences, and symbol manipulation, such as mathematics.
- Expose children to new material at their own pace and according to individual progress since neurological functioning may dictate different rates of learning among children.
- Because environmental conditions that introduce stress, malnutrition, abuse, neglect, and poverty into children's lives can have sustained effects on brain development, support local, state, and federal initiatives that attempt to eliminate these risk factors from children's lives.

MOTOR SKILL DEVELOPMENT

The development of children's motor behavior begins with simple reflexes and ends with very complex coordinated motor skills. Keep in mind that the motor behaviors we discuss in this section are based upon the physical developmental patterns presented in earlier sections. These skills also adhere to the principle of cephalocaudal and proximodistal development, with motor control of the head and neck area developing earlier than that of trunk and limbs. Figure 3.15 displays four stages of motor development that proceed from very rudimentary movements to those that are much more specialized.

The children in the chapter case study display developmental differences in motor skills similar to the ones presented in the table. The older children are using skills that are more refined and require greater dexterity, such as striking the puck in air hockey and braiding bracelets. Many of the younger children find these skills quite challenging.

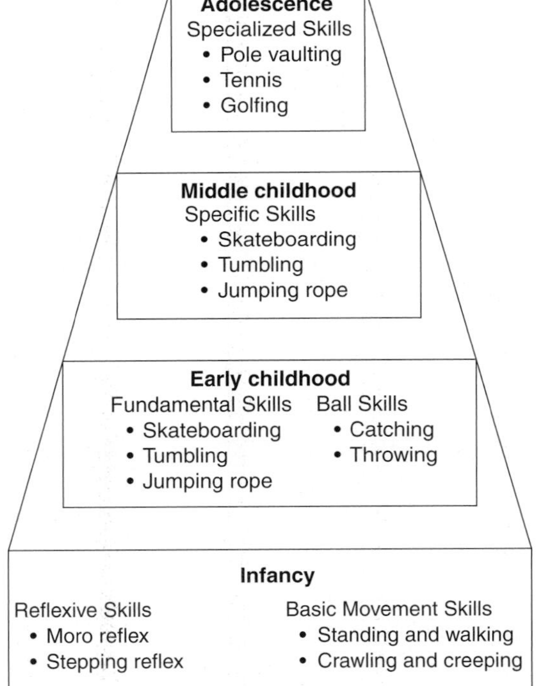

FIGURE 3.15 Phases of Motor Skill Development
This pyramid suggests that children build on earlier foundations of rudimentary motor skills to develop more specific and specialized skills over time.

Source: Based on *Growth and Development: The Child and Physical Activity* (p. 32), by L. D. Zaichkowsky, L. B. Zaichkowsky, & T. J. Martinek, 1980. St Louis: C. V. Mosby. Copyright 1980 by the C. V. Mosby Company. Adapted by permission of Elsevier.

What physical activities did you engage in during your school-age years?

Gross and Fine Motor Skills

Although the rate of physical growth slows somewhat during this period, **gross motor skills** continue to improve. Gross motor skills use large muscle groups and include movements such as running, jumping, throwing, and balancing.

Developmental patterns of specific motor movements emerge during the school years:

1. **Running.** As children mature motorically they develop into more proficient runners. Their trunk rotation increases to allow for a longer stride and better arm-leg opposition. The longer stride encourages greater push-off from the back leg and thus increases running speed (Haywood & Getchell, 2001).

2. **Jumping.** Children's vertical jumping ability increases linearly between the ages of 7 and 11. Boys and girls also increase standing broad jump performance by 3 to 5 inches per year. Children accomplish this by engaging in a deeper preparatory crouch, extending both legs at liftoff, extending arms overhead in midjump, and flexing knees and torso forward for a two-footed landing.

3. **Throwing.** Boys and girls improve more than 100% in throwing accuracy and distance between the ages of 7 and 11 (Roberton & Konczak, 2001; Yan & Jevas, 2004). This skill is accomplished by shifting one's weight to the back foot, rotating the trunk back, stepping forward while extending the throwing arm fully, and rotating the trunk forward. In general, boys throw harder and more accurately than girls. This gender difference persists even with increased throwing practice and experience for girls (Runion, Langendorfer, & Roberton, 2003).

4. **Balancing.** This ability is measured by asking children to stand on one foot or walk a narrow beam. Because children's center of gravity moves lower in the body as a function of the physical development of trunk and limbs, their balance improves after ages 6 or 7. At 5 years of age, the center of gravity is near the belly button, while at 13, it is horizontal to the top of the hip. This development makes it easier for older children to balance in an upright position and facilitates the

A lower center of gravity in school-age children improves balance.

refinement of other skills (Loovis & Butterfield, 2000).

Because school-age children have increasing opportunities to participate in different activities, their motor skills become more *specific* and *integrated*. For example, during middle childhood, children convert their running and jumping skills to basketball playing and jumping rope; strength and flexibility, to gymnastics; throwing and catching skills, to baseball; and balance, strength, and coordination, to skating and hockey.

Recall from our chapter case study that an increasing specificity of motor skills is observed in the children enrolled in the after-school program. The older children engage in tasks that require greater accuracy (e.g., bean bag tossing), balance (e.g., hopscotch) and coordination (e.g., air hockey).

In addition to gross motor skill development, children show improvement in **fine motor skills**. Fine motor skills usually involve controlled and precise use of the hands and fingers and, with age, produce better coordination and dexterity. Skills using fine motor movements, such as piano playing, sewing, braiding, and handwriting, all show improvement during middle childhood. Studies show that girls tend to have more advanced fine motor skills, but it is difficult to know if this is a true difference in skill or a preference for or practice of the activity.

Perceptual-Motor Skills

Perceptual-motor skills are abilities that require extensive integration between the sensory system (e.g., vision, hearing, taste, touch, smell) and the motor system. Although perceptual processes may develop somewhat independently of motor abilities, we cannot perform most motor skills without sensory perception (Cratty, 1986). As children get older, they are better able to process complex sensory information, which, in turn, allows them to have better motor control over skills such as catching, throwing, and hitting. Four major changes typically occur in perceptual-motor abilities between early childhood and middle childhood:

1. **A Shift in the Dominant Sensory System Occurs.** Young children's predominant reliance on touch and taste shifts to a reliance on visual information and influences school-age children's motor abilities.
2. **Intrasensory Communication Increases.** School-age children use information coming in from multiple senses, rather than just one, to regulate their motor behavior. For example, using information from eyes, ears, and hands makes older children better ball hitters.
3. **Discrimination Among the Senses Improves.** Older children achieve finer distinctions among sensory information. For example, as school-age children are running to catch a pop-up ball, they make a distinction between visual information and tactile cues and choose the one that provides them with the most accurate information—thus catching the ball.
4. **Perception of Body Awareness Develops.** The development of **laterality**, the ability to distinguish between two sides of the body, develops quite early in most children. However, **lateral awareness**, the correct labeling of the two sides of the body, is not well developed until age 7. **Lateral dominance** is a developed preference for the use of the left or right hand, the left or right foot, and the left or right eye. Studies show that 90% of children have an established hand preference by age 5 (Ozturk et al., 1999). However, the data also show that hand preference may take longer to develop in some children than in others, resulting in a debate over the origins of handedness (i.e., genetic or learned) (Annett, 1999; Provins, 1997).

Such changes reflect the relationship between improved perception and better-coordinated motor skills. For example, between ages 6 and 11, children exhibit more accurate perceptions of moving

Guideposts for Working with School-Age Children

- Because children of the same age may differ widely in their skill and coordination ability, make a variety of activities available that require different skill levels.
- Provide a variety of motor activities for children to try. This broad exposure may encourage the development of different interests in the future.
- Allow children in middle childhood opportunities to practice and refine skills such as throwing, catching, balancing, and kicking.
- Since boys' and girls' interests and ability to learn the same skills are highest during middle childhood, encourage both sexes to try a range of activities.
- Try to minimize competition by finding creative ways to choose teams and by encouraging teamwork so that children of all motor skill levels can feel good about their abilities.

objects and thus can more accurately judge the flight path of a ball (Lefebvre & Reid, 1998).

Do the physical activities you recall from your middle childhood reflect development of your motor abilities?

Health and Well-Being

Most school-age children engage in high levels of physical activity, as seen in the opening case study. **Physical activity** is usually defined as taking place any time the child is not asleep or completely sedentary (Steinbeck, 2001). This definition includes lower-level movement activities (e.g., eating, attending school, completing homework, or playing a musical instrument) and higher-level movement activities (e.g., playing on the playground or at a park, as well as participating in organized sports practices or competitions). Research findings show that levels of physical activity increase from infancy, peak in middle childhood, and begin to decrease during middle adolescence (Eaton, McKeen, & Campbell, 2001). This pattern of activity may surprise you since most people assume that 2- or 3-year-olds are the most active. However, when researchers strapped motion recorders on the wrists and ankles of participants aged 6 weeks to 52 years, they found that children between the ages of 7 and 9 were the most active, as seen in Figure 3.16 (Eaton et al., 2001). This peak of activity occurred later in childhood than others have suggested (Pellegrini & Smith, 1998) and consequently elicits several interesting questions about the function of physical activity. These findings also have direct implications for how we parent and teach these highly active youth as well as how we may diagnose psychopathology, such as attention deficit hyperactivity disorder (ADHD).

Functions of Physical Activity

Researchers have found an inverted U-curved distribution for physical activity, indicating that activity is highest in middle childhood. This curve suggests a sensitive period in development during which motor activity alters brain development. Children's motor activity peaks at exactly the same

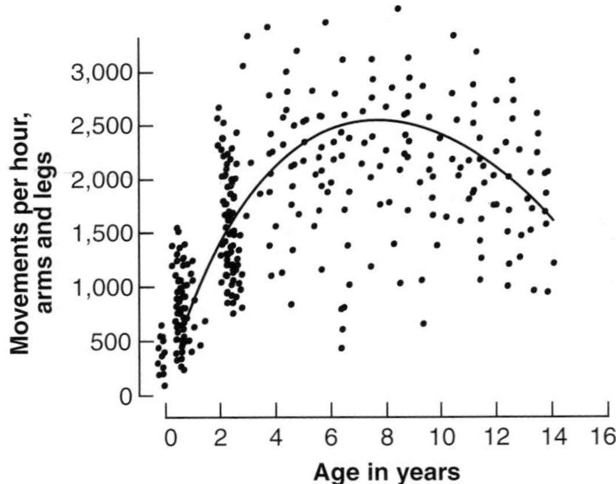

FIGURE 3.16 Arm and Leg Movements per Hour by Age

Children appear to be most active during the middle childhood years.

Source: From "The Waxing and Waning of Movement: Implications for Psychological Development," by W. O. Eaton, N. A. McKeen, & D. W. Campbell, 2001, *Developmental Review, 21*, p. 205. Copyright 2001 by Academic Press. Reprinted by permission of Elsevier.

time the cerebellum, which is responsible for the control of gross and fine motor movement, is pruning unstimulated synapses and dendrites (Byers, 1998). Researchers have proposed that since most children obtain rudimentary gross motor skills in early childhood, middle childhood is the period in which they seek practice and subsequent refinement of motor skills. In addition, in middle childhood, children may ultimately show mastery of a skill, thus contributing to their sense of self-competency and self-esteem. In other words, being physically active may be one domain in which a child excels (Rose, Larkin, & Berger, 1997).

Physical activity also increases bone mineralization, lowers blood pressure, and may help regulate weight (Suter & Hawes, 1993; Saris, 1996; Heelan et al., 2005). Finally, researchers believe that high levels of physical play behavior, such as **rough-and-tumble play**, encourage social competency—especially among boys—and support the formation of hierarchical peer groups (Pellegrini & Smith, 1998). Rough-and-tumble play looks like fighting but involves chasing, wrestling, and restraining moves where no real conflict is involved. It is a form of play that assists boys in developing a leadership "pecking order" and, once established, may lead to *less* aggression and group conflict.

You notice gender differences in the types of activities in which boys and girls engage in the after-school program. In their game of chase, the boys have to be reminded to lower their voices and not play "so rough." The girls play separately from the boys and play games in which they take turns and accommodate each other's skill levels.

Relationship between physical activity and other developmental domains. Children's high activity levels may reflect a more concrete and experiential way of learning about the world (Bjorklund, 1997). For example, children in middle childhood may be capable of some abstract thought but may still be relying on interactions with tangible objects to facilitate their thinking.

High levels of movement in children may be their way of exploring the world in a physical way. Other researchers have suggested that physical movement may be involved in emotional expression. School-age children are more reliant upon physical means of expressing emotions, such as arm-flailing temper tantrums, fighting, or running away from a scolding parent, than are adolescents. A decline in overall physical activity after middle childhood is often paralleled by an increase in sophisticated means of emotional expression (e.g., arguing) and regulation (Eaton et al., 2001).

Factors that influence levels of physical activity. Research clearly shows that physical activity level is influenced by gender: Boys are more active than girls (Eaton et. al., 2001). In addition, a decline in physical activity during adolescence is more pronounced for females than males (Goran, Gower, Nagy, & Johnson, 1998; Thompson, Baxter-Jones, & Mirwald, 2003). Children who are overweight or obese are less likely to be physically active, with parental activity a major influence on children's activity level (Hancox, Milne, & Poulton, 2004). Children of active mothers are twice as likely to be active compared to children of inactive mothers. This level increases threefold if fathers are active. If both parents are active, children are six times more likely to be active (Aarnio, Winter, Kujala & Kaprio, 1997). Socioeconomic status is also moderately associated with activity level (Frenn & Malin, 2003; Guillaume, Lapidus, Bjorntorp, & Lambert, 1997). This relationship manifests itself in the safety of and opportunity to engage in physical activity outside of school.

Implications of these findings for parents, educators, and practitioners. A peak in movement at 8 years does not correspond well with the expectations often placed on children by parents and teachers. Parents typically expect children of this age to be "old enough to control their behavior," especially if child care experts have given parents the impression that things will improve after the "terrible twos." Adults need to be discouraged from criticizing their school-age children for too high levels of activity and need to provide for them appropriate outlets for this normal expenditure of energy. Teachers need to be made aware of the normative activity levels of this age group and of research findings that recess breaks during elementary school seem to produce more on-task behavior and less fidgeting (Pellegrini & Bohn, 2005). Recess or other outlets for high levels of motor activity may facilitate school performance (Pelligrini & Bjorklund, 1997). Therefore, teachers should find ways to incorporate movement in many of their lesson plans for children throughout the middle childhood years. Finally, practitioners should be aware that middle childhood is the developmental period in which the greatest number of diagnoses is made for attention deficit hyperactivity disorder (ADHD) (Brownwell & Yogendran, 2001). Two of the symptoms of this disorder are rapid shifts in attention and high activity level, both of which are in evidence in "normal" groups of 7- to 9-year-olds. Although many diagnoses are valid, researchers have found that childhood hyperactivity is not a predictor of any other pathology in childhood or beyond, suggesting that high levels of activity are more normative than pathological (Nagin & Tremblay, 1999).

Exercise

A subcategory of physical activity is **exercise**. The most distinguishable characteristics of exercise are that it is planned, structured, repetitive, purposeful, and requires moderate to high levels of activity (Livingstone, Robson, Wallace, & McKinley, 2003). The National Association for Sport and Physical Education (NASPE) has issued specific activity guidelines for elementary school-age children. NASPE recommends that children engage in some form of moderate to high physical activity (i.e., exercise) for 30 to 60 minutes almost every day of the week (Corbin & Pangrazi, 2000). Children who meet or exceed these minimums have stronger and healthier cardiovascular systems, lower blood pressure, more favorable blood lipid profiles, stronger bones, and less body fat (Witzke & Snow, 2000).

Despite these well-supported health benefits, less than 50% of children and adolescents meet these minimal standards (NASPE, 1998). In addition, a significantly smaller proportion of girls than boys exercise sufficiently (Stone et al., 1998). School-age children who do not meet the minimum activity goals are at higher risk for becoming overweight, experiencing elevated blood pressure, being diagnosed with type 2 diabetes (i.e., diabetes mellitus), or having one or more risk factors for cardiovascular disease or osteoporosis. Studies have also shown that when these health risk factors are identified in middle childhood they tend to carry over into adolescence and adulthood (Li et al., 2003; McGill & McMahan, 2003).

Clearly, finding ways to increase children's daily and weekly exercise opportunities should become a priority for parents, teachers, and practitioners. Recent conferences such as the one sponsored by the Centers for Disease Control and Prevention, *Guidelines for School and Community Programs to Promote Lifelong Physical Activity Among Young People* (1998), suggest focusing on the infrastructures in schools and communities to promote healthy physical activity patterns. Intervention programs that target children, their schools, and communities have been successful in increasing children's level of exercise in school but have been less successful with influencing exercise outside of school (Sallis et al., 1997).

You observed that the children in the after-school program who are most overweight are also the least physically active.

Sports Participation

As children enter middle childhood, they spend less time in unstructured free play and more time in structured activities, such as school- or church-sponsored activities and organized sports practices or competitions (Hofferth & Sandberg, 2001). In the last decade, the United States has seen a dramatic rise in the number of children involved in organized sports, especially girls. Approximately 46 million children and adolescents participate in some type of organized sport (Griffin, 1998). Despite the increase in the number of children involved, not all children participate to the same extent. For example, as girls move into adolescence, their participation typically declines. Low-income children spend less time in organized sports than middle-class children, often due to the expenses involved.

A variety of physical and psychological benefits may result from sports participation. The multiple physical benefits of systematic exercise outlined in the previous section of this chapter also apply to children who participate in organized sports. In addition, individual athletes (e.g., swimmers, runners, or skiers) learn the value of practice, self-discipline, and time and effort commitments. They also may gain feelings of competency and self-worth, have higher levels of self-esteem, and report enjoying themselves (Pugh, Wolff, DeFrancesco, Gilley, & Heitman, 2000). Participating in a sport increases skill building and, in many peer groups, is a characteristic of popularity and status among peers. As a member of a team (e.g., soccer, baseball, football)—in addition to the advantages gained from individual participation—children learn about cooperation, perspective taking, and the benefits of teamwork. They also have opportunities to spend time with friends or to make new friends (Ewing, Gano-Overway, Branta, & Seefeldt, 2002). Studies show that if children enjoy their participation, they are much more likely to stay involved and to continue this activity for longer periods of time—sometimes into adulthood (Perkins, Jacobs, Barber, & Eccles, 2004; Thompson, Humbert, & Mirwald, 2003).

Disadvantages of participating in organized sports include acute injuries or—less often—permanent injuries to vulnerable bones and joints (Maffulli, Baxter-Jones, & Grieve, 2005). Also, children may be encouraged to continue to play or compete in less-than-favorable weather conditions. Box 3.3 describes how children's bodies heat and cool themselves differently from adults' and, if not properly monitored, how children could experience stress resulting in illness or death.

Some developmentalists worry that time spent in organized sports may reduce the amount of time spent in unstructured free play, which encourages imagination and self-motivation. Others suggest that participation in organized sports encourages a mindset of competition and winning. A survey of 10,000 youth athletes found that children stopped playing a sport due to lack of interest, lack of fun, poor coaching, and an overemphasis on winning. Their main sources of stress were criticisms (i.e., "being yelled at") from coaches, parents, fans, and teammates as well as performing poorly in competition (Ewing & Seefeldt, 1990).

If you participated in an organized sport growing up, did you experience any positive or negative outcomes? What were the costs and benefits?

Nutrition and Body Status

Because school-age children are still growing, their nutritional intake is important. During middle childhood, energy intake (i.e., calories) must be sufficiently high to meet both growth *and* physical activity demands. Active children should aim to consume between 55 and 60% of their energy intake in the form of carbohydrates, less than 30% in the form of fats, and between 12 and 15% in the form of proteins. Protein is necessary for body growth, and thus protein requirements for children and adolescents are higher than for adults.

It is often difficult for active children to reach minimum nutritional goals by consuming three large meals a day. Consequently, it is suggested that children be provided four or five smaller meals a day with healthy snacks in between to provide sufficient energy.

Small amounts of vitamins and minerals are needed as well to maintain health. To ensure that children are receiving the necessary vitamins and minerals, it is best to encourage a well-balanced diet, rather than vitamin supplementation. Table 3–2 shows the food sources of essential nutrients for children in middle childhood.

In 2001, just under half a million children in the United States reported living in a household with repeated hunger and insecure food sources, although this number is much higher in developing countries (Federal Interagency Forum on Child and Family Statistics, 2003). Nutritional deficiencies have direct implications for children's learning and behavior in school (Lozoff, Jimenez, Hagen, & Wolf, 2000). Early nutritional deficiencies in infancy can inhibit critical growth in the brain and can impact long-term cognitive abilities (Brown & Pollitt, 1996). Daily deficiencies in school-age children can cause lethargy, poor concentration, greater susceptibility to illness, moodiness, and poor psychomotor skills. Supplemental breakfast and lunch programs provided to children from low socioeconomic households have been shown to improve overall health, energy levels, attendance, and subsequent academic performance (Grantham-McGregor, Ani, & Fernald, 2001; Shemilt et al., 2004).

Obesity, dieting, and body satisfaction. When the intake of calories exceeds total energy expenditure, weight gain results. Excessive weight gain can lead to **obesity**, which is defined as weighing more than 20% over one's ideal weight based on height, sex, and body composition. Several decades ago, a section on obesity, dieting, and body image would probably not have been included in this textbook—most certainly not in a section describing the development of school-age children. Unfortunately, the prevalence of obesity among young children has increased significantly in recent years (Heinberg, Thompson, & Mateson, 2001). Approximately 25% of children and adolescents are obese or at risk of becoming obese (Troiano & Flegal, 1998). The prevalence rates are higher for Blacks and Hispanics than they are for Whites and Asians and are inextricably tied to socioeconomic status. Figure 3.17 shows the increase in obesity over the past few decades and illustrates gender and race differences. The origins of obesity have been traced to genetics, sedentary lifestyles, increased television viewing, and high-fat diets as well as socioeconomic status (Beunen et al., 1998; Drewnowski, 2004).

Obesity has a strong developmental component, with obesity in childhood predictive of obesity later in life. Both physical and psychological consequences may result from being overweight or obese. Children who are obese are at risk for

BOX 3.3 ROADMAP TO SUCCESSFUL PRACTICE

The Effects of Exercise on Children in Hot and Cold Weather

Children in middle childhood are highly active in both free play and organized sports and exercise programs. They differ from adults, however, in how their bodies react physiologically to rigorous physical activity in hot or cold climate conditions. Their bodies respond to an increase or loss of heat or cold in relatively inefficient ways, putting them at greater risk for heat- or cold-related injuries or illness (Jenkins & Reaburn, 2000). It is imperative for adults who are monitoring children during active play, sports training, or competitive events to be aware of these differences and to know how to identify early warning signs so that serious or permanent illness can be avoided.

Hot and Humid Weather

Because of the following physiological differences between children and adults, children fare less well when exercising in the hot and humid conditions that exist in most places during the summer months. Children have

- A reduced ability to sweat
- A greater body surface area-to-weight ratio, meaning that they have more skin surface-area to gain or lose heat
- A lower sweat rate
- The commencement of sweating at a higher temperature
- A reduced thirst mechanism
- A reduced ability to acclimatize

Based on these physiological responses, children react to heat differently than adults. For example, once the air or water temperature gets above skin temperature (about 32 to 33 degrees Celsius), children's high surface area-to-weight ratio causes them to gain heat from the environment. This factor, combined with their reduced ability to sweat and to sweat only at higher temperatures, puts them at higher risk of suffering heat-related illness. This risk factor applies particularly to children with heavy or solid builds who have a large muscle mass that generates a lot of heat. Body fat serves as an added layer of insulation, so children with high levels of body fat also are at higher risk for heat injury. In addition, large bandages or tape wrappings, sweatbands, bandanas, or gloves serve to trap heat and to increase the body temperature of children.

Because heat-related illness can be very serious, it is essential that coaches, parents, and teachers be able to identify the following early warning signs:

- Tiredness
- Weakness
- Headache
- Muscle or stomach cramping
- Nausea
- Bright red skin
- Excessive sweating
- Fainting

To prevent heat-related illness or injury, adults should make sure that children are wearing sunscreen, hats, cotton fabrics (not nylons or rayons, which hold heat) and that they drink plenty of fluids—before, during, and after physical activity.

Cold Weather

Children are more susceptible than adults to illness and injury in cold climates based on the same physiological differences described above. Children's large body-to-weight ratio means that they will also lose heat faster than adults. If the temperature is lower than 20 to 25 degrees Celsius, children can lose heat quickly in cold air or water. This risk applies most specifically to children who are thin or have low levels of body fat. Children also have a less well-developed perception of when they are cold and may keep playing or exercising longer than they should. Early warning signs of cold illness in children are

- Weak pulse
- Slurred speech
- Cold skin temperatures
- Blueness of the lips
- Irrational thinking
- Decreased performance

Adults need to monitor children closely when they are playing, training, or exercising in cold temperatures. To prevent cold-related illness or injury, children need to wear appropriate clothing such as hats and gloves, stay dry, and drink plenty of fluids.

Source: Based on *Guiding the Young Athlete*, by D. Jenkins & P. Reaburn, 2000, St. Leonards, NSW: Allen & Unwin Book Publishers. Copyright 2000 by David Jenkins and Peter Reaburn. Adapted by permission of the publisher.

TABLE 3–2

Major Vitamin and Mineral Sources

A well-balanced diet that consists of a variety of these foods will ensure proper nutrition.

Vitamin A	Yellow and orange fruit and vegetables, eggs, dairy products, margarine and oils
B vitamins	Whole grain bread and cereals, brown rice and pastas, lean meats, dairy products, green leafy vegetables
Vitamin C	Citrus, tropical and berry fruits, and tomatoes
Vitamin E	Whole grain bread and cereals, wheat germ, nuts and seeds, unsaturated oils
Iron	Organ meats (e.g., liver), beef and other meats, turkey, chicken, fish and seafood; eggs, green leafy vegetables, dried fruits, and legumes
Calcium	Dairy products and fortified soy milk; fish, dark green vegetables, nuts, seeds, and whole grains

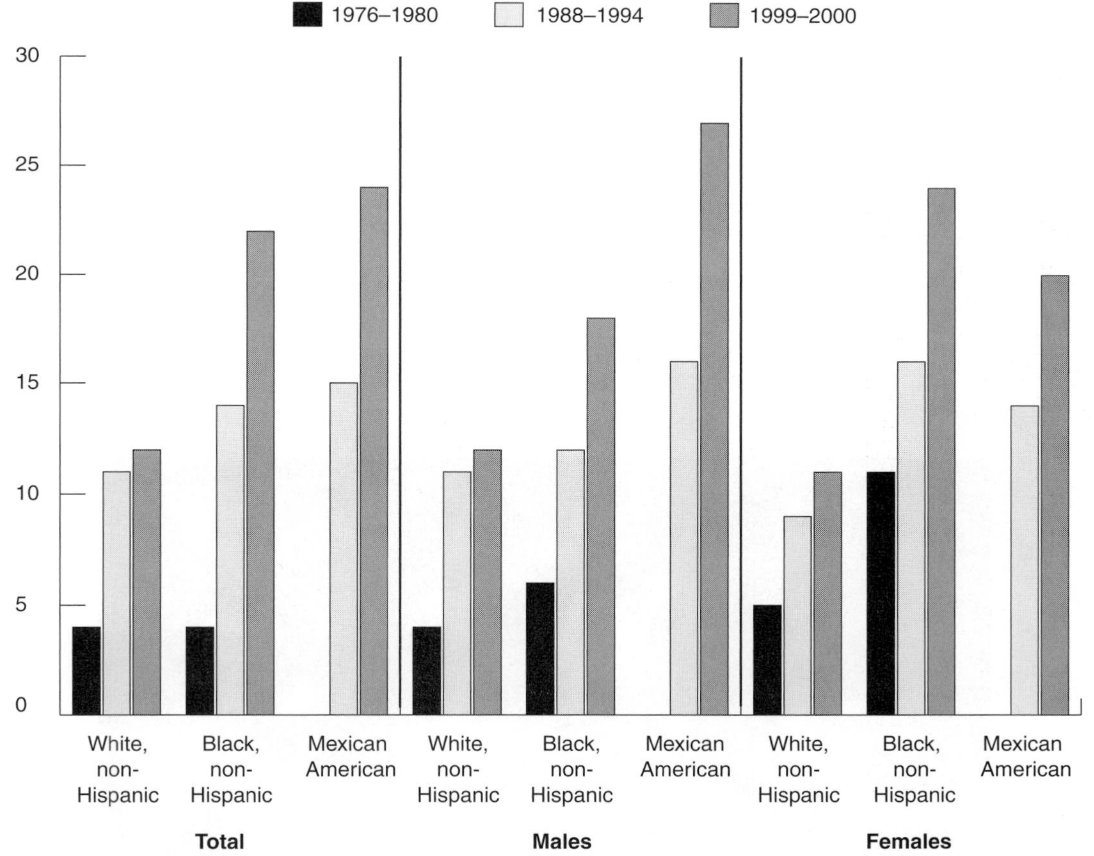

FIGURE 3.17 Percentage of Children Who Are Overweight by Gender, Race, and Hispanic Origin

Since 1976 there has been an increase in the percentage of children who are overweight in every category of race and gender.

Source: Data from Centers for Disease Control and Prevention, National Center for Health Statistics, National Health and Nutrition Examination Survey. Reprinted from Federal Interagency Forum on Child and Family Statistics (2003). *America's Children: Key National Indicators of Well-Being, 2003*. Federal Interagency Forum on Child and Family Statistics, Washington, DC: U.S. Government Printing Office.

hypertension, respiratory disease, type 2 diabetes, and orthopedic disorders (Hill & Pomeroy, 2001). Heavier weight has also been associated with lower self-esteem and exclusion from peer groups (Miller & Downey, 1999). Psychosocial problems may include persistent teasing, which may produce body-image problems and eating disturbances (Gardner, Stark, Friedman, & Jackson, 2000; Heinberg, 1996).

The most overweight children in the program often are not included in group games and are the target of teasing.

Obesity may also increase body dissatisfaction. For example, researchers surveyed 8- to 10-year-olds and found that 55% of the girls and 35% of the boys were dissatisfied with their size (Wood, Becker, & Thompson, 1996). Girls typically want to be thinner, while boys desire to be larger and more muscular (Smolak, Levine, & Thompson, 2001). In addition, European American girls generally have greater body dissatisfaction than African American girls. Body dissatisfaction can lead school-age children (and adolescents) to engage in caloric-reducing behavior such as dieting or hyperexercise.

Researchers surveyed more than 16,000 9- to 14-year-old boys and girls and found that only 20% of the 9-year-old girls were trying to lose weight compared to 44% of the 14-year-old girls (Field et al., 1999). In the study, girls were more likely to exercise than to diet, but the information on body fat, muscle, and physical activity in this chapter would suggest that a reduced balanced diet in addition to increased exercise is critical for weight loss in girls. Of the 9-year-old boys in this study, 17% were trying to lose weight while 19% of the 14-year-olds were. They also were more likely to use exercise to control their weight. Information from this chapter would predict that increased exercise is sufficient for weight loss in boys.

Body dissatisfaction and dieting may be influenced by factors such as comparing oneself to media standards, peers, parents' weight attitudes and behaviors, sexual abuse, and early puberty maturation (Muir, Wertheim, & Paxton, 1999; Vander Wal & Thelen, 2001).

While observing in the recreation program, you are surprised to overhear a group of 10-year-old girls talking about who has the best shape.

Research findings have indicated that many school-age children are struggling with a weight problem that may affect their health as well as how they feel about themselves. Even when children

There are long-term health risks associated with obesity in middle childhood..

Guideposts for Working with School-Age Children

- Incorporate many opportunities for physical movement in your interactions with school-age children.
- Provide opportunities for all children to experience exercise and/or participation in sports.
- Offer school-age children more frequent, smaller, and healthier meals.
- Teach school-age children about the determinants of weight and body shape and the importance of exercise and how these are related to their current and future health.
- Provide children with opportunities to develop healthy cooking and eating habits and to view adults as positive role models for healthy diet and exercise.

are not obese, they often desire their bodies to be different. Parents, educators, and practitioners need to be aware that body dissatisfaction, dieting, and obesity are no longer problems that are relegated to developing adolescents. We need to be knowledgeable about the determinants of weight and body size and the importance of physical activity and exercise, and we need to impart this knowledge to school-age children.

Were you satisfied with your body shape in middle childhood?

Development in Context

Chapter 2 emphasized the importance of examining the development of children within multiple contexts: family, school, and community. How children influence—and are influenced by—these contexts often produces variations in physical development and behavior.

School-age children in the after-school recreation program differ in physical appearance and skill level, in part as a result of differences among familial and cultural eating patterns, opportunities to be physically active, and environmental stimulation that influences brain development.

Family Contexts

Children's physical growth may be affected by the genetic history of their parents as well as by how well families provide proper nutrition, medical care, and safe and stable homes for their children. Homeless children, for example, have been found to suffer from high levels of stress that ultimately affect their health and school performance (Parrish, 2004).

Similarly, the motor coordination and skill level of children may be a result of the opportunities provided by parents. For example, children who are White, from the Northeast and Midwest, from intact families, and whose parents have higher educational levels are more likely to participate in organized sports. Children who come from families with an older brother also participate in sports more, presumably because they are influenced by the participation of their older siblings (Hofferth & Sandberg, 2001; Videon, 2002).

Parents can influence the health of their children by making healthy foods available, modeling good eating habits, or possessing positive attitudes and behaviors about eating. Research that examined household, parent, and child contributions to obesity showed that parents of obese children did not recognize the importance of their role in shaping their children's nutritional patterns. Parents of obese children were more likely to agree with statements such as "It doesn't matter which foods my child eats. As long as they eat enough, they will grow properly"; and "[My child] is old enough to take care of feeding him/herself." They also seemed less cognizant of the relationship between physical activity and related health and weight issues. The results of the study suggested that any effort to curb childhood obesity should include improving parent knowledge of child nutrition (Gable & Lutz, 2000).

Since parents are responsible for monitoring the amount of time children spend watching television, they can reduce the time spent on this activity and encourage children to engage in more cognitively stimulating activities such as reading. An enriched environment is necessary for optimal brain development.

School Contexts

Schools should play a major role in facilitating the physical and motor growth of children. Teachers can provide children with the opportunity to experience new and different ways to move and use their bodies. Teachers also should recognize the different physical and motor competencies of children and provide opportunities so that children at all skill levels can experience success. Recess and physical activity during the school day is essential for optimal learning and fitness. Opportunities within the school day are especially important for children who may not be active outside of school due to financial constraints, limited parental involvement or supervision, or poor play area availability or safety. However, schools vary in the types and quality of play areas they offer students. As shown in Box 3.4, different types of playgrounds facilitate different skills in school-age children (Barbour, 1999).

Several school districts are trying to encourage greater physical activity among their students by encouraging students who live less than one mile from school to walk, rather than be driven. To increase safety for children who walk, schools have developed partnerships with surrounding neighborhood associations to ensure that walkways exist and are kept safe and clear, in addition to creating "safe homes" where children can go if they feel threatened. For example, in a high-crime neighborhood in Chicago, a "walking school bus" program was initiated. Parents walked with their children to school and picked up additional children along the route (Chicago Department of Transportation, 1999). This program not only increased activity for both children and parents but also decreased crime in the neighborhoods (Kennedy, Washburn, & Martinez, 1998).

Intervention programs designed to increase physical activity in school-age children have found that the groups who show the greatest increase in physical activity were provided an educational component along with the physical activity opportunities (Economos, 2001). Teachers should continue to teach children about the value of eating well and the benefits of life-long exercise. Schools can also provide supplemental meals for children who need them, as well as try to provide more nutritious lunches and vending machine options (Bauer, Yang, & Austin, 2004).

Community Contexts

Communities vary in the support they provide for optimal physical, brain, and motor development in children. The most direct influence that communities have on development is through the resources made available to children and families. Resources vary in quantity and quality based on the earning power of the people who live in a given community. Children who are raised in low-income communities typically have access to fewer or poorer-quality resources. For example, school-age children who live in low-income neighborhoods may be less likely to have access to proper medical care, proper nutrition, quality after-school care, parks, and playgrounds (Brooks-Gunn, Duncan, & Aber, 1997; Leventhal & Brooks-Gunn, 2003). All of these features could adversely affect the physical and motor development of the child, as well as general health.

In addition, poor neighborhoods are often characterized by social disorganization and violence. Children who grow up in self-perceived dangerous neighborhoods may experience more stress and more stress-related symptomology (Xue, Leventhal, Brooks-Gunn, & Earls, 2005). Researchers have found that these children have a much more pessimistic view of life, report a lessened ability to control their well-being, and tend to do more poorly in school (Garbarino, Hammond, Mercy, & Yung, 2004).

Researchers have also found that children from some low-income families may be exposed to inside (e.g., reading books) and outside (e.g., trips to the library, museums, nature centers) learning opportunities less often (Brooks-Gunn, Klebanov, & Liaw, 1995). Children from low-income families also tend to go to poorer-quality schools that have fewer resources to offer to both low- and high-competency children. Researchers have reported that poor children were more likely to repeat a grade in school or to drop out, have a learning disability, or obtain lower grades in school (Duncan & Brooks-Gunn, 2000; McLoyd, 1998).

Homes, schools, and neighborhoods influence the physical growth and biological maturation of children. These different contexts, in turn, elicit and support different development at varying rates for each child. We need to continue to study children's growth within these multiple settings so that we might understand the multiple pathways that lead to eventual adult health and well-being.

BOX 3.4 ROADMAP TO SUCCESSFUL PRACTICE

Playground Design and Children's Play Behavior

Barbour (1999) carried out an observational study that showed how different play equipment and configurations on school playgrounds can encourage different types of physical activity among children. The type and placement of equipment are listed in Figure 3.18. This study compared the play behavior of children who attended Schools A and B. The researchers found that children who played at School A's playground demonstrated less variety in their play, exhibited less extensive sand play of shorter duration, played soccer as the only game with rules, and played hide-and-seek less often because of fewer places to hide. In School A there was much less **cooperative play**, or play in which children orient toward a common goal, and less **sociodramatic play**, or pretend play with other children. Children also were more likely to run into one another as a result of cramped space, and there was greater competition for the equipment because it had to be shared with all other kindergarten through grade 8 children at the school.

In contrast, children who played at School B showed a greater variety of play. They showed more extensive and longer sand play that involved construction (e.g., buildings and bridges); engaged in more cooperative and sociodramatic play; played soccer, football, Frisbee, and hide-and-seek; and also engaged in playground maintenance (e.g., raked the sand beneath the swings). They were less likely to run into one another, and there was less competition for equipment and toys because the older children in the school had their own playground with more age-appropriate equipment. This study illustrated that one group of children was afforded greater play options than the other. The type of play encouraged by the configuration of School B facilitated cognition and enhanced social skills, and the benefits translated into the classroom (Bergen & Mauer, 2000).

School A	School B
Equipment	
playstructure (built of wood)	playstructure (built of various materials)
narrow platforms	wide platforms
fireman's pole	fireman's pole
clatter bridge	clatter bridge
3 steel jungle gyms	2 tunnels
8-foot double slide	chain ladder
6 strap-seat swings	tire raft
2 seesaws	overhead ladder
overhead ladder	rings
uneven bars	parallel bars
soccer ball (on occasion)	2 slides
	spiral climber
	tic-tac-toe board
	dramatic play features (e.g., steering wheel, window)
	wheeled vehicle path
	storage shed
	tricycles, wagons
	various loose parts (e.g., building blocks, wooden planks, tires, plastic spools, pails, tools, containers, chairs, dramatic play props, sports equipment)
	canopied sand play area surrounded by benches
	2 play houses
	car (built of tires and posts)
	water play table
	4 raised, open-ended barrels
	3 strap-seat swings
	2 tire swings
	seesaw
	garden area
	picnic table

BOX 3.4 (CONTINUED)

School A	School B
	Spatial Configuration
equipment scattered	equipment clustered
mainly isolated pieces of equipment (except wooden superstructure)	linkages of equipment
space crowded	space not crowded
adjacent field for group games	central open area for group games

FIGURE 3.18 Playground Design and Physical Competence
School A provides less equipment in a nonoptimal play space. School B provides a greater variety of equipment in a better-planned and larger play space that facilitates the quality of play interactions among children.
Source: From "The Impact of Playground Design on the Play Behaviors of Children with Differing Levels of Physical Competence," by A. C. Barbour, 1999, *Early Childhood Research Quarterly, 14,* p. 79. Copyright 1999 by Elsevier Science, Inc. Reprinted by permission of the publisher.

CHAPTER REVIEW

Theoretical Perspectives

- Theoretical perspectives vary widely in their emphasis on the genetic or biological origins of development.
- The contribution of genetics is emphasized by the viewpoint of behavioral genetics.
- Behavior neuroscience is an example of a biologically based approach to understanding the relationship between brain and behavior.
- Reaction ranges and niche-picking are ways in which genetic predispositions and biological processes interact with the environment to influence physical, cognitive, and motor development.

Physical Development

- Physical growth, typically measured by height and weight, increases gradually in middle childhood until the growth spurt associated with puberty in early adolescence.
- Girls begin to grow sooner and more quickly than boys. Once boys begin pubertal growth, they catch up and surpass girls in height and weight.
- Skeletal growth and a gradual increase in body fat and muscle tissue continue throughout middle childhood.
- Gender differences emerge and increase significantly during puberty. Females possess more body fat during middle childhood than males, who have slightly greater muscle mass.
- Although much of this development is maturational, environmental factors such as diet and physical activity can influence the dimensions of this growth.

Brain Maturation

- Brain development in middle childhood is characterized by neuronal loss, dendritic pruning, increased myelination, and increased communication among the brain regions.
- Structural changes correspond to motoric and cognitive changes in middle childhood, such as improved gross and fine motor coordination; improved speaking, writing, and reading skills; increased attentional capacity; more logical and abstract thought; and the appearance of planning and reasoning skills.
- A well-coordinated interaction between genetically based neuronal change and environmental influence shapes brain growth and function during middle childhood.

Motor Skill Acquisition

- Between the ages of 8 and 12, motor skills become more integrated, specialized, and refined, encouraged by both brain development and opportunities presented to the child for motor movement.
- Gender differences in motor skill and coordination are minimal during this developmental period, with those skills that show differences (e.g., throwing) tending to originate more from cultural biases than physical capabilities.

- Perceptual-motor skills that require an integration of perceptual skills and motor abilities result from better brain integration and practice.
- Improvements in perceptual-motor skills are reflected in the child's increased ability to hit or catch a ball, dodge a ball, jump rope, or throw darts.

Health and Well-Being

- Children's opportunities to be involved in physical activity, structured exercise, or organized sports as well as their nutritional intake, have a significant impact on physical, skeletal, motor, and cognitive development.
- Weight, body fat levels, and body image are determined in part by children's level of involvement in various types of physical activity.
- Families, schools, and communities play a role in the type and degree of physical activity opportunities afforded to children.

Contexts for Development

- Multiple contexts within which a child grows can influence and be influenced by the child.
- Families make genetic contributions to physical growth and brain maturation and influence development by providing opportunities for children to practice motor skills, engage in physical activity, and shape their dietary habits and exercise levels.
- Playgrounds, recess periods, physical education classes, extracurricular athletic programs, and after-school programs serve as valuable venues for the development of skills and as a safe, structured environment for physical activity.
- Schools can capitalize on the cognitive windows of opportunity provided by brain growth as well as provide constant exposure to materials and instruction to enhance brain development through middle childhood.
- Communities differ in their abilities to provide resources for optimal physical and cognitive growth, such as the quality and quantity of early health care and nutrition; enrichment opportunities, such as museums and libraries; and activity environs, such as safe parks, playgrounds, athletic facilities, and community centers.

TABLE 3–3
Summary of Developmental Theories

Chapter	Theories	Focus
3: Physical Development in Middle Childhood	Behavior-Genetic	Influence of genes and the environment on development through the analysis of shared and nonshared environments.
	Biological	How brain structure, function, and chemistry influence behavior in such fields as behavioral neuroscience.

KEY TERMS

Adipose rebound
Adipose tissue
Axon
Behavioral genetics
Behavioral neuroscience
Body mass index
Catecholamines
Cephalocaudal
Cerebral cortex
Cooperative play
Corpus callosum
Cortisol
Critical period
Demineralization
Dendrites
Developmental traumatology
Distance curve
Epiphyses
Exercise
Experience-expectant processes
Failure to thrive
Fiber tracts
Fine motor skills
Frontal cortex
Glial cells
Gross motor skills
Growth
Heritability estimates
Hypertrophy
Lateral awareness
Lateral dominance
Laterality
Limbic system
Maturation
Myelin
Myelination
Neurons
Neurotransmitters
Niche-picking
Nonshared environments
Obesity
Ossification
Physical activity
Plasticity
Programmed cell death
Proximodistal
Reaction ranges
Rough-and-tumble play

Secular trend
Sensitive period
Shared environments
Short of stature
Skinfold caliper
Sociodramatic play
Soma
Stature
Stress
Synapse
Synaptic pruning
Synaptogenesis
Teratogens

SUGGESTED ACTIVITIES

1. Collect pictures of children from birth to age 2, around age 6 or 7, and between 10 to 12 years of age. Identify the similarities among facial features in the infant pictures. Mix up the pictures and have everyone try to match the pictures with their adult classmates. At 6 or 7, the pictures should show increased facial structure, tooth loss, and hair color that is closer to adult coloring. At 10 or 12, the jawline should be more defined; nose, ears, and forehead are disproportionately large; and eyeglasses may be needed. The photographs at this age can be more easily matched with classmates.
2. Observe a group of children between the ages of 8 and 12 and identify differences and similarities in their physical appearance (e.g., height and weight, body shape). How does their appearance relate to their motoric abilities? Does their physical size enhance or detract from their ability to engage in both gross and fine motor skills? How so?
3. Survey parents of children between the ages of 8 and 12. Ask them about the number of hours per day their school-age child spends in stationary activities versus physical activities. Identify specifically the number of hours they spend in school, on homework, watching television, and practicing or playing a sport. Average the hours across a week or month and create a pie chart that represents different physical and sedentary activity segments of school-age children's lives. Are there age or gender differences?

RECOMMENDED RESOURCES

Suggested Readings

Biehl, M.C., Park, M. J., Brindis, C. D., Pantell, R. H., & Irwin, C. E., Jr. (2002). *Building a strong foundation: Creating a health agenda for the middle childhood years*. San Francisco, CA: University of California, San Francisco School of Medicine, Public Policy and Education Center for Middle Childhood and Adolescent Health.

Cheatum, B. A., & Hammond, A. A. (2000). *Physical activities for improving children's learning and behavior: A guide to sensory motor development*. Champaign, IL: Human Kinetics.

Diamond, M., & Hopson, J. (1998). *Magic trees of the mind: How to nurture your child's intelligence, creativity, and healthy emotions from birth through adolescence*. New York: Penguin Putnam.

Jenkins, D., & Reaburn, P. (2000). *Guiding the young athlete: All you need to know*. St Leonards, NSW: Allen & Unwin.

Suggested Online Resources

2000 CDC Growth Charts: United States.
http://www.cdc.gov/growthcharts/

Brain Development from the Neuroscience for Kids Web site at the University of Washington.
http://faculty.Washington.edu/chudler/introb.html

Exercise and Physical Activity Recommendations from the American Heart Association.
http://www.americanheart.org/presenter.jhtml?identifier=4596

The Health of America's Middle Childhood Population (2002).
http://policy.ucsf.edu/pubpdfs/PC%20MC%20Mono.pdf

Poinsett, Alex. (1996). The role of sports in youth development.
http://www.carnegie.org/sub/pubs/reports/poinst1.htm

Suggested Web Sites

American Academy of Pediatrics
http://www.aap.org

Children's Nutrition Research Center
http://www.bcm. tmc.edu/cnrc/

Guidelines for School and Community Programs to Promote Lifelong Physical Activity among Young People
http://www.phppo.cdc.gov/cdcRecommends/showarticle.asp?aartid=M0046823&TopNum=50&CallPg=Adv

National Health and Nutrition Examination Survey
http://www.cdc.gov/nchs/nhanes.htm

Teaching Youngsters How to Be Good Sports
http://www.youth-sports.com/related.html

Suggested Films and Videos

The brain: Effects of childhood trauma. (2002). Magna Systems, Inc. (29 minutes)

Middle childhood: Physical growth and development. (1997). Magna Systems, Inc. (28 minutes)

Mystery of twins. (1997). Insight Media (26 minutes)

Nature and nurture: Heredity and environment. (2003). Insight Media (30 minutes)

Physical growth and motor development. (1991). Concept Media, Inc. (19 minutes)

Right from birth: The wonders of the brain. (2001). Insight Media (15 minutes)

The secret life of the brain. (2002). Insight Media (Series of five 60-minute programs)

CHAPTER

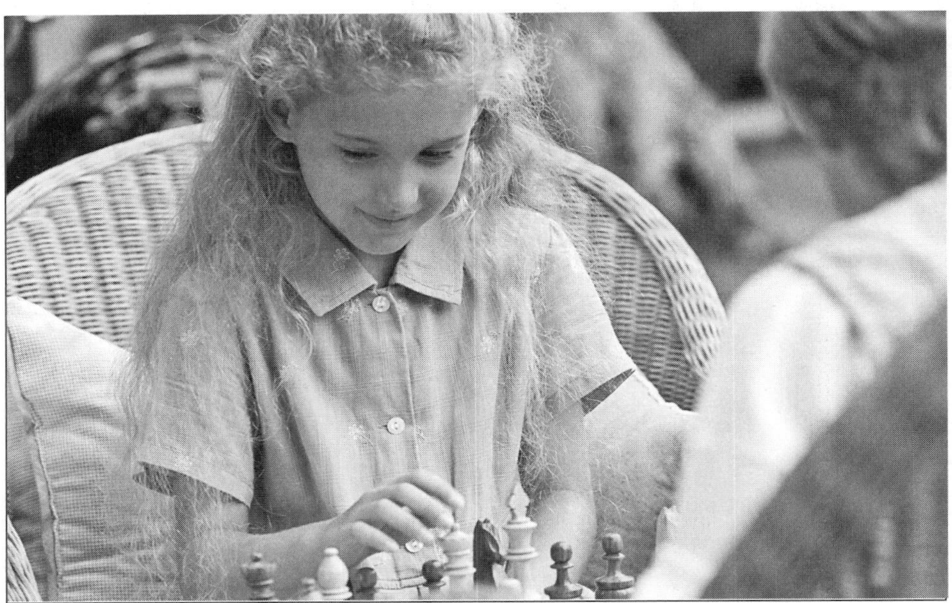

Cognitive Development in Middle Childhood

CHAPTER OBJECTIVES

After reading this chapter, students will be able to:

- Define cognitive development in middle childhood
- Identify three theoretical approaches to cognitive development
- Understand how each theoretical perspective explains the cognitive development of school-age children
- Translate how changes in cognition throughout middle childhood are reflected in language development, reading, writing, mathematical skills, and scientific reasoning
- Appreciate the diverse contexts of cognitive development in middle childhood

Nine-year-old Anya's older brother Alexandr, age 13, wants her to play chess with him. He participates in an informal chess club at the local high school and is always looking for ways to practice his game. "Anya, wanna play chess?" "No," she responds, "I'm not very good. You always beat me." Alexandr asks, "How do you expect to get better if you don't practice? Come on, I'll help you." Alexandr is true to his word. He reminds Anya what the names of all the pieces are and how they move. He also reminds her of the rules and how someone wins. Anya tries her best, but it takes her a long time to decide how to move her pieces; sometimes she does so incorrectly and she forgets to play defensively. Alexandr, on the other hand, is able to see the game as it unfolds across the entire board. He ascertains what the pros and cons of a move might be very quickly, and then he decides on the best move. He is able to think several moves ahead and plays both defensively and offensively.

COGNITION IN MIDDLE CHILDHOOD

Cognition is a categorical term that represents thinking, reasoning abilities, memory skills, decision making, problem solving, and other aspects of intellectual functioning. The middle years of childhood are characterized by a gradual increase in logical thought, an improvement in memory and learning strategies, and the ability to learn through dialogue with others. The case study of Anya and Alexandr, for example, illustrates cognitive differences among different-aged youth. Cognitive changes occurring in middle childhood, as well as practice and familiarity with both formal and informal experiences, moderate the development of cognitive skills. In addition, changes in basic cognitive processing influence the development of reading, writing, and mathematical skills. Finally, family, school, community, and culture play important roles in the development of school-age children's intellectual lives.

THEORETICAL VIEWPOINTS

In this chapter three different theoretical perspectives are presented to explain the cognitive competencies that emerge in middle childhood, how they are different from the cognitive competencies of preschool children and adolescents, and how they develop over time. They are Piaget's cognitive developmental theory, Vygotsky's sociocultural theory, and the information-processing perspective. Although each theoretical perspective is presented separately, they should be viewed as complementary to one another. Together, all three theories provide us with a better understanding of how 8- to 12-year-old children think.

These theories also are offered as contemporary alternatives to a theoretical viewpoint that dominated psychology through the better part of the 20th century: **behaviorism**. Behaviorists argued that the environment influenced developmental change and that development occurred through principles of learning. From a behaviorist's perspective, children's learning is largely determined by paired associations with environmental events (i.e., **classical conditioning**) and/or influenced by the rewards and punishment that followed behavior (i.e., **operant conditioning**). Observation supports the notion that children develop paired associations (e.g., a child may wince after the appearance of lightning because of previous experience with the thunder that follows). There is also research evidence that external rewards and punishments influence children's behavior (e.g., *verbal praise after making a good move in chess may encourage Anya to continue this behavior in the future*).

Much of what we learned from this theoretical perspective is still widely applied in the fields of education and clinical and counseling psychology. For example, a system of rewards that is used to change children's study habits employs principles of learning theory. But learning theorists could offer insight into the internal mechanisms that promote cognitive advancement or explain the cognitive connections children make on their own without influence from the outside world. The field needed theoretical perspectives that better reflect the rich and complex inner worlds of school-age children and adolescents. The following theoretical frameworks meet those needs.

Piaget's Cognitive Developmental Theory

Jean Piaget (1896–1980) created a theory that explains how children come to understand the world and create internal cognitive concepts about the world through their direct experiences and interactions with the environment. Piaget thought that children constructed knowledge through their interactions with the environment (e.g., running their fingers through water) that resulted in internal cognitive change. Therefore, his theory is referred to as a **constructivist view** of cognitive development.

Developmental components of the theory. A fundamental concept in Piaget's theory is a **schema**, or a mental structure by which children organize their world. A schema can be simplistically thought of as a concept or category. Another helpful analogy might be a file folder that helps children organize and differentiate incoming information. **Adaptation** is the process by which children build schemata (the plural of *schema*) through direct interaction with the environment. Piaget called the mechanisms by which schemata increase and change *assimilation* and *accommodation*.

Assimilation represents the process by which an already existing schema is applied to the external world and helps the child to incorporate new information. For example, when confronted with a new version of checkers (e.g., Chinese checkers), Anya assimilates by playing the game according to the old rules of checkers with some minor modifications.

The existing schema of how to play checkers provides her with the fundamental knowledge of or experience necessary for playing this new version and thus assimilation occurs with a successful outcome. However, this existing file folder (i.e., schema) would **not** be useful to adapt to playing the game of chess. The existing schema would need to be drastically modified.

Changing or creating a new schema to better fit new information or experience is called **accommodation**. Learning to play chess would require accommodation of game-playing strategies. Learning the difference between the rules of checkers and chess reflects accommodation. Accommodation has occurred by either changing the existing file folder of "games" to include checkers *and* chess or creating a new file folder for chess. By constantly assimilating and accommodating schemata, the child grows and develops cognitively.

The rates at which assimilation and accommodation are used vary over the course of development. When a child is not changing much, assimilation is predominantly used because the existing schemata are sufficient to make sense of the world. If, however, a child is going through a rapid period of development, assimilation may not be enough, and *cognitive disequilibrium* occurs. **Cognitive disequilibrium** represents an imbalance of developmental mechanisms, and accommodation is necessary for new schemata to be created to handle the new information. The constant cycles between cognitive equilibrium (when the information is assimilated easily) and cognitive disequilibrium (when accommodation is required) is called **equilibration** and, simply put, is Piaget's theoretical explanation for *how* and *why* a child learns.

Piaget's stages of cognitive development. The method Piaget used to learn about children's thinking is called the clinical interview process, which was explained in chapter 1. He watched how children solved a problem or asked them questions about what caused things to happen (e.g., "How does the sun rise?"). Then, he followed up their original answers with a series of probe questions so that he could understand the nature and process of their thinking (Gardner, Kornhaber, & Wake, 1996).

As Piaget interviewed more children of all ages and as his own children grew older, he began to see distinct and qualitative differences in the ways in which different-aged children interacted with and learned about the world. From these observations he proposed four stages through which children progress as they develop cognitively (Piaget, 1963; 1977).

- **Sensorimotor Stage** (ages 0–2). Children predominantly learn and act upon the world through their senses and motor abilities.
- **Preoperational Stage** (ages 2–7). Children learn about and act upon the world through symbols and language. They rely on their perceptions and how things appear to them.
- **Concrete Operational Stage** (ages 7–11). Children develop the ability to apply logical thought to concrete problems.
- **Formal Operational Stage** (ages 11–15 years or older). Preadolescents and adolescents are able to apply logic to all types of problems including abstract ones.

Piaget suggested that these stages are **universal** and **invariant**: They apply to children everywhere, and cognitive development proceeds through these stages in order. No stage can be skipped or missed, since each follows the previous one in a specific order. Although there are many interesting dimensions to both the sensorimotor and preoperational stages, this chapter will focus only on the school-age child in the concrete operational stage. We will give more emphasis to adolescents in the formal operational stage in chapter 9.

The Concrete Operational Child

The period of middle childhood defined in this textbook (8 to 12 years of age) consists of school-age children transitioning from preoperational thought to concrete thought and then preparing to move on to formal operational thinking. This pattern of development reflects the change from a dependency in early childhood on rigid, self-centered thought that relies heavily on how things appear at that moment to a dependency on *operations*. The term **operation** refers to an internalized mental action that follows logical rules. School-age children tend to develop internalized representations about *concrete* objects, such as things that can be seen, felt, or experienced. Thus, concrete operational thinkers are usually characterized by the tangible logic of their thinking. During formal operational thinking, on the other hand, internal representations are based upon more abstract concepts.

Conservation. One of the major accomplishments of the concrete operational period is the ability to *conserve*. **Conservation** is the ability to understand that the amount or quantity of an object remains the same despite an outward change in appearance. For example, if you were to take a ball of clay and roll it into a long, thin shape, a 10-year-old child would understand that it is still the same amount of clay. Likewise, if you took two glasses with equal amounts of water, poured one in a tall cylinder and the other in a low, flat dish, an 11-year-old child would claim that the amount of water is equivalent—despite the difference in appearance. Table 4.1 provides a series of tasks that Piaget developed to illustrate the progression through which school-age children develop conservation.

One interesting note is that children do not seem to grasp the concept of conservation uniformly. The application of conservation principles to different types of problems usually follows a sequence (Piaget & Inhelder, 1969):

Conservation of number	Ages 5–6
Substance (mass)	Ages 7–8
Area	Ages 7–8
Liquid	Ages 7–8
Weight	Ages 9–10
Volume	Ages 11–12

The ability to conserve is promoted by the development of several separate abilities. The first is **decentration**, or the ability to consider more than one feature of an object at a time. Most 5-year-olds have difficulty taking more than one dimension into consideration when approaching a problem. For example, in a water conservation task, preoperational children will typically answer that the *taller* cylinder has more water. They are taking into account only one dimension (i.e., height) and ignoring others (e.g., width or depth). A concrete operational child, however, will typically be able to take more than one dimension into account at the same time.

Notice that Alexandr is much better at thinking about offensive ***and*** *defensive moves when moving his chess pieces than Anya, who is exhibiting decentration, but not as expertly as her older brother.*

Decentration contributes not only to the development of conservation but also to a child's social competence. When a child recognizes that there are multiple sides to an argument, or multiple viewpoints to an issue, a greater sense of one's role in relationship to others results (Bonino & Cattelino, 1999). Decentration also can be observed in children's emerging comprehension that words can have more than one meaning, as explained in Box 4.1.

Another concept that contributes to the development of conservation is **reversibility**. Children capable of reversible thought can follow a line of reasoning back to where it started. In the event of a water conservation task, a concrete operational child might follow the line of reasoning that if you poured the water back into the original glasses the amount of liquid would be the same. Her answer would be correct based upon reversible thinking.

Finally, understanding **transformation**, or paying attention to the means by which one state is changed to another, allows conservation to develop. Concrete operational thinkers are capable of integrating a series of events into a whole with a beginning and endpoint compared to preoperational thinkers who tend to focus on a single point in time. A good illustration of this thinking is reflected in the following task. Take a pencil and hold it upright. Now let it fall. Ask a child to choose between the figures (illustrated in Figure 4.1) that represent what just happened.

Preoperational thinkers will focus on the beginning and end states and consistently choose Panel A; concrete operational thinkers will attend to the transformation of the pencil from its vertical to horizontal position and most likely choose Panel B. The choice of Panel B represents an understanding that a relationship exists between the beginning and end states and the successive steps in between.

The gradual development of decentration, reversibility, and transformation contribute to the development of conservation, the precursor to logical thought in school-age children. Piaget thought that conservation gave a certain stability to the physical world and also made it possible for children to learn and understand mathematical operations such as multiplying, dividing, ordering (i.e., greater than, less than), and substituting (i.e., one thing equals another).

Classification. To classify is the ability to place objects that are alike in the same class or category. A simple classification task would present a child with the following array of objects: one large red triangle, one large blue circle, one small red circle, and one small blue triangle. The child is asked to sort the objects into groups or to "put the objects together that belong together." A preoperational thinker might focus on a single dimension (an example of centration) and put the triangles together and the circles together. This is one way in which these objects "fit together." When asked if there is another way to group them, many young

TABLE 4–1

Examples of Piagetian Conservation Tasks

Piagetian conservation tasks assess children's problem-solving approaches. The understanding of conservation typically follows this sequence of tasks.

Conservation Task	Original Presentation	Transformation
Number	 Are there the same number of pennies in each row?	 Now are there the same number of pennies in each row, or does one row have more?
Length	Is each of these sticks just as long as the other?	 Now are the two sticks each equally as long, or is one longer?
Liquid	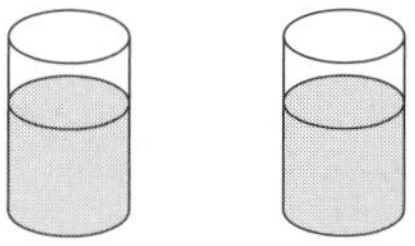 Is there the same amount of water in each glass?	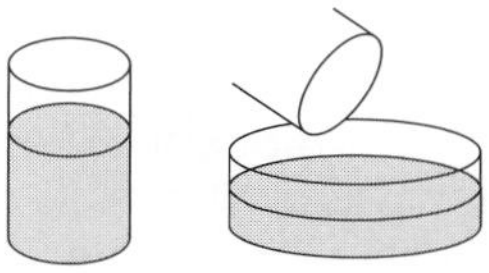 Now, Is there the same amount of water in each glass, or does one have more?
Mass	Is there the same amount of clay in each ball?	 Now does each piece have the same amount of clay, or does one have more?
Area	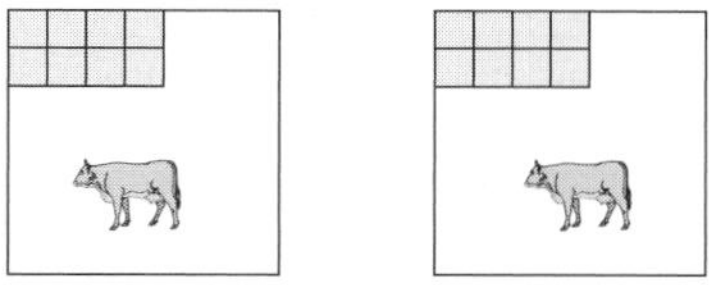 Do each of these two cows have the same amount of grass to eat?	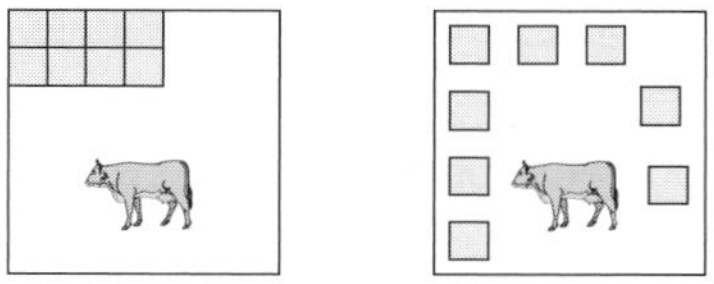 Now does each cow have the same amount of grass to eat, or does one cow have more?
Weight	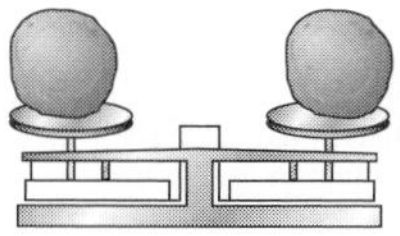 Do each of these two balls of clay weigh the same amount?	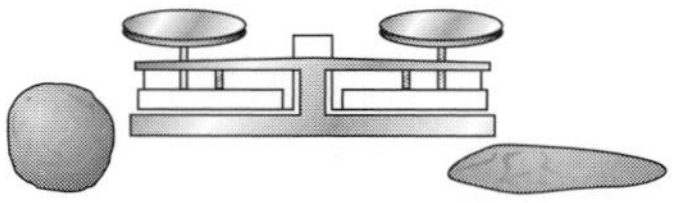 Now (without placing them back on the scale to confirm what is correct for the child) do the two pieces of clay weigh the same, or does one weigh more?
Volume	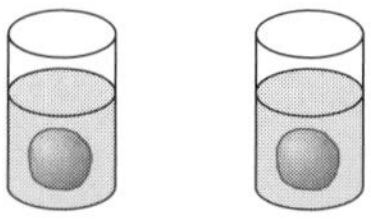 Does the water level rise equally in each glass when the two balls of clay are dropped in the water?	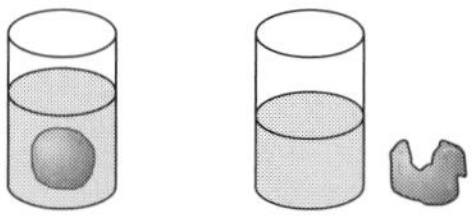 Now (after one piece of clay is removed from the water and reshaped) will the water levels rise equally, or will one rise more?

Source: From *Child Development* (3rd ed.) (p. 236), by Laura E. Berk, 1994, Boston: Allyn & Bacon. Copyright 1994 by Pearson Education. Reprinted by permission of the publisher.

BOX 4.1 ROADMAP TO UNDERSTANDING THEORY AND RESEARCH

A Developing Sense of Humor

In middle childhood, advances in cognition are reflected and influenced by children's use and understanding of language. As school-age children begin to utilize multiple perspectives to solve conservation tasks, so too do they use and understand language in multiple ways. For example, learning homonyms requires children to comprehend that words that sound the same, *pair* and *pear*, may be spelled differently and have different meanings. They also learn to appreciate that the same word may have multiple meanings, such as the words *cool* or *neat*. *Cool* can be used to express a temperature, "It's cool outside," or satisfaction, "That bike is so cool!" (Berk, 2003). This more sophisticated understanding of double meanings allows 8- to 10-year-olds to comprehend metaphors, such as "thin as a rail" or "cute as a button" (Nippold, Taylor, & Baker, 1996). Children as young as 8 are also able to recognize some forms of irony as well as exaggerated forms of sarcasm (Creusere, 2000; Cappelli, Nakagawa, & Madden, 1990).

Advanced uses and comprehension of language are also reflected in a child's changing sense of humor. Preschoolers and early elementary schoolchildren laugh at incongruencies such as a male calling a female "a boy," or a donkey wearing a lion's mane (McGhee, 1976). Children from ages 8 to 12 are delighted by jokes, puns, and riddles that play off the double meaning of words such as:

> "Is your refrigerator running?
>
> "Yes."
>
> "Then you better catch it!"

or,

> "Knock, knock"
>
> "Who's there?"
>
> "Boo."
>
> "Boo who?"
>
> "Why ya cryin'?"

This recognition and appreciation for multiple interpretations of word meaning in middle childhood might also explain the popularity of particular children's literature such as the stories of Amelia Bedelia, the scatterbrained housekeeper who misinterprets most of her housekeeping instructions (Parish, 1963). When told to draw the drapes when the sun comes in, she sits down and draws a picture of them rather than closing them. When told to dress the chicken for dinner, she dresses the chicken in suspenders and booties rather than herbs and spices.

Consider this passage from *Charlie and the Chocolate Factory*, another favorite story of this age group:

> Grandpa Joe lifted Charlie up so that he could get a better view, and looking in, Charlie saw a long table, and on the table there were rows and rows of small white square-shaped candies. The candies looked very much like square sugar lumps—except that each of them had a funny little pink face painted on one side. . .
>
> "There you are!" cried Mr. Wonka. "Square candies that look round!" "They don't look round to me," said Mike Teavee. "They look square," said Veruca Salt. "They look completely square." "But they are square," said Mr. Wonka. "I never said they weren't." "You said they were round!" said Veruca Salt. "I never said anything of the sort," said Mr. Wonka. "I said they looked round." "But they don't look round!" said Veruca Salt. "They look square!". . .
>
> [Mr. Wonka] took a key from his pocket, and unlocked the door, and flung it open. . . and suddenly. . . at the sound of the door opening, all the rows and rows of little square candies looked quickly round to see who was coming in. The tiny faces actually turned toward the door and stared at Mr. Wonka. "There you are!" he cried triumphantly. "They're looking round! There's no argument about it! They are square candies that look round!"

Source: Excerpt from *Charlie and the Chocolate Factory* by Roald Dahl. Text and illustrations copyright 1964, renewed 1992 by Roald Dahl Nominee Limited. Used by permission of Alfred A. Knopf, an imprint of Random House Children's Books, a division of Random House, Inc.

preoperational children would respond, "No." A concrete operational thinker, however, would group according to shape, then size, and then color.

In addition to understanding that objects possess multiple attributes that fit together with other objects, Piaget described concrete operational thinkers as being able to comprehend that there can be a hierarchy of groupings, which he called **hierarchical classification**. Children in the concrete operational stage begin to understand that

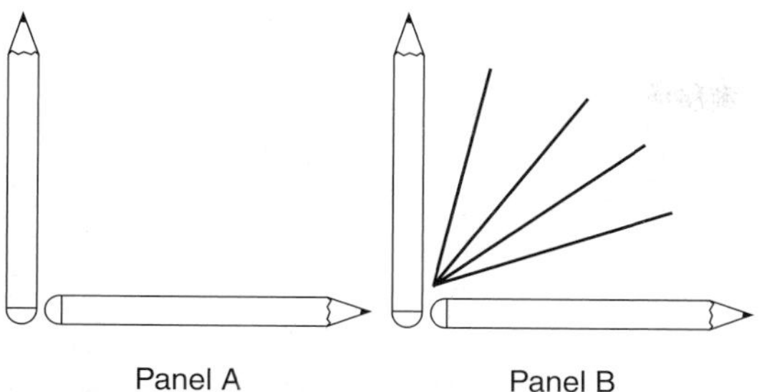

FIGURE 4.1 A Transformation Task
Children younger than 7 tend to pay most attention to static states, or what the object looks like at the beginning or end of a task. Children in concrete operations begin to attend to the transformations an object undergoes.

smaller groups can be subsets of larger groups. For example, in a **class inclusion** task that assesses classification skills, Piaget would present a child with 18 brown wooden beads and 2 white wooden beads and ask the child, "are there more brown wooden beads or wooden beads?" Concrete operational thinkers seem to recognize that brown wooden beads *and* white wooden beads belong to the larger class of wooden beads. Younger preoperational thinkers usually focus on the larger number and respond (incorrectly), "brown wooden beads."

Understanding hierarchical classification assists in the understanding of numerical and mathematical concepts (e.g., subsets) as well as phenomena in the natural sciences where classifying plants and animals, natural elements, and types of rocks helps us organize and make sense of our physical world.

Finally, the tendency of school-age children to collect things is both a reflection of as well as practice in classification schemes. Collecting stamps, baseball cards, rocks, autographs, and American Girl dolls, for example, provides the school-age child with many opportunities to sort, group, and reorganize objects that share common attributes.

Seriation. Another logical operation of concrete thought is **seriation**, or the ability to mentally arrange elements according to increasing or decreasing size. When provided with different-sized sticks and asked to put them in order from the tallest to the shortest, preoperational thinkers usually can correctly identify the tallest and shortest, but have difficulty ordering the sticks in between. Correct ordering of the sticks in a seriation task requires an understanding that stick A has a relationship to stick B (i.e., taller) *but also* and *at the same time* a relationship to stick C (i.e., taller or shorter).

The schema to understand seriation is created during the concrete operational period. The acquisition of decentration promotes comprehension of a series. Learning about seriation is similar to learning about conservation in that it emerges at different ages in the following sequence:

Seriation of length	Ages 7–8
Seriation of weight	Ages 9–10
Seriation of volume	Ages 11–12

Seriation is also demonstrated in school-age children's ability to order a series of events, such as the four seasons, or the order of holidays throughout the year.

Causality. Preschool children tend to believe that if two events occur together, one caused the other. During one of Piaget's interviews, for example, a young child reported that she causes the sun to rise by waking up in the morning

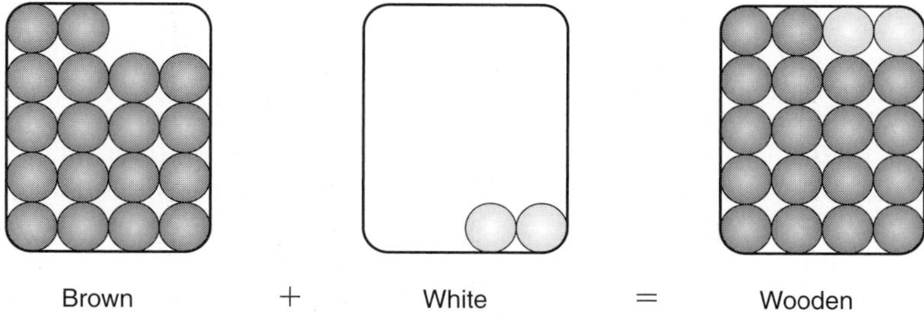

FIGURE 4.2 A Class Inclusion (Classification) Task
Successful completion of a classification task requires an understanding that both brown and white wooden beads belong to the larger group, wooden beads.

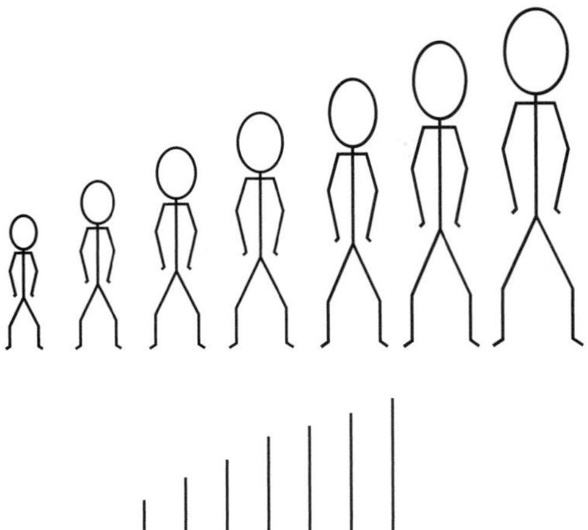

FIGURE 4.3 A Seriation Task Using Dolls or Sticks
In a seriation task a child is asked to put the dolls or sticks in order from the shortest to the tallest

(Piaget & Inhelder, 1969). These two events are paired together in her mind in a causal relationship. Children aged 7 to 11 tend to understand cause and effect more accurately. The implications of this cognitive development are that school-aged children are more curious about the origins of physical phenomena and may ask many questions that begin with "Why?" and "How come?" The science curriculum for this age group can be broadened to include experimentation (e.g., science-fair projects) because experiments are of interest to this age group, and multiple causal connections can be explored and better understood.

In addition, more accurate reasoning about causality promotes social interactions. Concrete operational thinkers can now make the distinction between accidental versus intentional behavior and its consequences. This differentiation may influence the nature of a relationship between friends and peers, discussed further in chapter 6.

Seven- to eight-year-old children begin to accommodate their schemata so that logical or practical thought begins to dominate over perception of how things appear. They show gradual mastery over conservation tasks by employing decentration and reversible thought and by taking transformations into account. Their ability to understand hierarchical classification, seriation, and causality promotes a more realistic understanding of mathematics, history, and social studies. These cognitive advancements also apply to their view of themselves in the world and their relationships with others. Children in middle childhood, however, learn best when concepts are made more concrete or embedded within concrete contexts. Box 4.2 illustrates how teachers can make assignments more concrete.

If you ever participated in a science fair, how old were you and what types of cognitive skills did you employ?

Basis of Cognitive Development

Piaget proposed that the basis upon which one develops cognitively is influenced by *both* biological maturation *and* environmental stimulation. Normal physical maturation of the brain and central nervous system as well as motor development are essential for cognitive development to occur. Healthy neurological development, development of the senses, and the progression of motor skills are necessary for children to act upon their environment, thereby making changes to their internal schemata. Equally influential, however, are the opportunities presented by one's surroundings. Children need to have the opportunity to experience and interact with their world and, as they mature, to explore and experiment with objects and people in their environment. Optimal cognitive development results from healthy brain and motor development coupled with opportunities to explore the world.

Think about how Anya's chess-playing experiences with her brother may influence the development of the cognitive skills required to play this game.

Piaget did not think that children should be pushed academically before they are cognitively ready to master concepts on their own. Attempts to teach preoperational children conservation skills, or concrete operational children formal operational skills, have not been successful (for a review, see Wadsworth, 1996). Piaget suggested that changes in schemata necessary for higher-order thinking come about only after considerable assimilation and accommodation of experiences and that premature direct instruction has little long-lasting effect. He also did not think that children need expensive or elaborate toys to facilitate learning. Rather, children learn through interacting with common objects found in their world, such as arranging sticks or shells or collecting dried leaves and reeds.

BOX 4.2 ROADMAP TO SUCCESSFUL PRACTICE

Making School Assignments More Concrete

Piaget proposed that children during the middle childhood years learned more easily if concepts were presented more concretely (Piaget & Inhelder, 1958). What does it mean to make concepts more concrete? The following ideas were taken from a list compiled by a middle-school teacher under the heading of "active learning." Incorporating movement into his pedagogy and content, he has made the learning process more tangible, sensory-based, easily linked to past experience and memorable—in other words, more concrete.

- With colored chalk, draw a huge interior diagram of the heart on the school parking lot or a sidewalk. Let the students walk through the diagram as you demonstrate how blood flows from the body into the heart through the chambers and valves, to the lungs, back to the heart, then out to the body again. They can narrate the process while walking or race to different sections by traveling the way the blood does. They can hold different-colored cards to represent oxygenated and unoxygenated blood. They can do crazy dances in the lung area to simulate the oxygen–carbon dioxide exchange.
- Encourage students to represent concepts and terms artistically. They can draw science cycles, dramatically portray atomic interaction, and sculpt with clay while describing the stages of the writing process.
- In science you can ask students to portray the earth, the moon, and the sun in a darkened room with a single light source, watching the changing shadow patterns on the students' bodies as they rotate and revolve.
- In English classes, adopt Victor Borge's idea of each punctuation mark representing a particular noise. A whistle, clap, or howl can substitute for commas, question marks, and quotation marks, respectively. Ask students to read dialogue between two characters aloud and, every time they come to a punctuation mark, to make the representative noises.

Source: From *Meet Me in the Middle: Becoming an Accomplished Middle-Level Teacher* (pp. 44–48), Rick Wormeli, 2001, Portland, ME: Stenhouse.

The Role of Culture

What role might culture play in the development of schemata, and how might it affect progress through the four stages of Piaget's theory? Research carried out with children from different cultural backgrounds shows differential progress through these stages (for a review, see Rogoff, 2003). Participation in formal schooling, for example, seems to facilitate logical problem-solving skills (Morrison, McMahon, Griffith, & Frazier, 1996). Studies have found that children who do not attend school, such as the Hausa of Nigeria, show delayed conservation skills and do not show mastery of conservation (e.g., number, length, and liquid) until age 11 or 12 (Fahrmeier, 1978). Others, such as Mongolian nomads, never demonstrate mastery of tasks from Piaget's final formal operational stage (Cole, 1990). Practice using reversible and transformational thought may account for these differences. For example, school activities and curricula appear to encourage the ordering of objects and learning about multiple ways that objects are related to one another. Children not exposed to these structured tasks may show delayed or absent reasoning skills on traditional conservation tasks.

However, cross-cultural research also has identified the nature of the task as equally predictive of children's performance. Children with little or no formal schooling did less well than schooled peers on Piaget's tasks *when they were presented in a traditional format*. On the other hand, when the tasks were embedded in a more familiar context, operational skills appeared *even in children with little formal education*. Six- to nine-year-old Brazilian street vendors who spent most of their time selling candy on the streets were presented with the following class inclusion task:

> For you to get more money, is it better to sell me the mint chewing gum or [all] the chewing gum? Why?

Using this more familiar and practical class inclusion task, the street vendors showed *greater* classification skills than more formally educated middle-class Brazilian children their same age (Ceci & Roazzi, 1994). Formal educational opportunities as well as familiarity and practice with the task may explain the variability children show in their cognitive skills throughout their middle childhood years.

Culture influences cognitive development in the opportunities it affords children in their everyday lives. For example, high-speed mathematical calculations are exhibited by young Brazilian street vendors. Mexican children who participate with their families in the making of pottery show conservation of quantity skills at a very young age (Price, Williams, Gordan, & Ramirez, 1969). Advanced spatial maps are developed by aboriginal youth in Australia, and Mayan children remember complex weaving patterns (Serpell, 1979; Levinson, 1997). These findings suggest that culture influences the everyday tasks in which children engage and consequently manifest its influence in the *types* of cognitive skills that emerge first and develop more quickly.

Anya and Alexandr's parents are immigrants from Russia, a country with a rich tradition in chess playing. Both parents are skilled players and play with their children often. Their cultural background influences Anya and Alexandr by giving them more opportunities to play this particular game and, for Anya, by having an older brother to tutor her.

Piaget's theory has its critics. Some researchers believe that the clinical interview method is too flexible and does not provide consistency in the probe questions asked and, therefore, in the children's responses. Others argue that the problem-solving tasks he created are too unfamiliar to children and thus underestimate their cognitive abilities. Critics also point out that the proposed mechanisms of cognitive development such as equilibration, assimilation, and accommodation cannot be measured (for a review, see Feldman, 2003). Perhaps the most important criticism of all is that the problem-solving skills Piaget assessed should not be used as the standard of cognitive achievement. Children from immigrant cultures within the United States and from other countries may excel at other cognitive skills that are more adaptive to their environment (Mistry & Saraswathi, 2003).

Despite these criticisms, Piaget has provided us with a unique way of looking at cognitive development and a comprehensive theory that accurately describes differences in the ways that Western-schooled children think and learn about the world. His assessment about how cognition develops has direct implications for educational practice and has been incorporated into classrooms all over the world (Vergnaud, 1996). For example, Piagetian educators present material to children when they are "cognitively ready." In doing so, they allow students' current level of thinking to let them know when school-age children are ready to assimilate new material into their present cognitive structures. In other words, children's learning should never be rushed or hurried just to move on to a new unit. Practitioners who are sensitive to individual differences in rates of learning are also applying Piagetian theory. Since building on earlier schemata is essential to successful later learning, individualized instruction for each child or instruction in small groups with same-skilled children is optimal.

Guideposts for Working with School-Age Children

- Develop as many "hands-on" and experiential learning opportunities as possible, since children learn best when they are active participants in the process.
- Spend more time on one theme or unit as opposed to introducing a new theme often to allow for optimal exploration and self-discovery by the students.
- Because children's cognitive skills may be influenced by their cultural experiences, try to capitalize on those experiences and make them part of the instruction.
- Evaluate children's learning and educational progress against their own performance.

Sociocultural Perspective

Although Piaget's theory of cognitive development is taught widely and is perhaps more well known, there are alternative and complementary ways to think about how children learn and the factors that facilitate this development. Lev Vygotsky (1896–1934), a Russian psychologist, offered a different view of cognitive development. Whereas Piaget observed children constructing knowledge independently, Vygotsky believed that cognitive development was inextricably tied to the child's social and contextual environment. In other words, children's cognitive growth is constructed out of their interactions with others as well as the roles and expectations that are assigned to them in a given context.

For example, a 9-year-old girl like Anya who is taught to play chess through the mentoring of siblings, peers, and parents learns that this is an age-appropriate expectation of her culture and a desirable skill for her to develop.

This sociocultural perspective would "observe the changing participation of children in sociocultural activity rather than aim to understand what pieces of knowledge or skill they have already 'acquired'" (Rogoff, 1996, p. 284). The units of analysis in this perspective are what the child says and does, how others respond to the child, and how these dynamics may change over time.

Developmental Components of the Theory

Vygotsky proposed that children's interactions with others in a social setting and their developing use of language or numbers create thought (Blanck, 1990). He suggested several ways that both the social context and others in that context specifically contribute to the development of knowledge.

Zone of proximal development. First, he defined the **zone of proximal development (ZPD)** as a range of skills or tasks that include on one end what a child can do easily alone and at the other what a child can do with assistance from another. Each child approaches a task with her own "zone of readiness" and learns from her interactions with others. Consider the following example from the chess-playing case study at the beginning of the chapter:

Alexandr watches Anya move her bishop incorrectly. "No, Anya," he says, "the bishop can only move diagonally," and he physically shows her the directions this piece can move. Later in the game, Anya puts her hand on her bishop and repeats to herself what Alexandr has told her, "only diagonally," and proceeds to move the piece correctly.

Vygotsky's theory proposes that children take the dialogue from these interactions and convert it

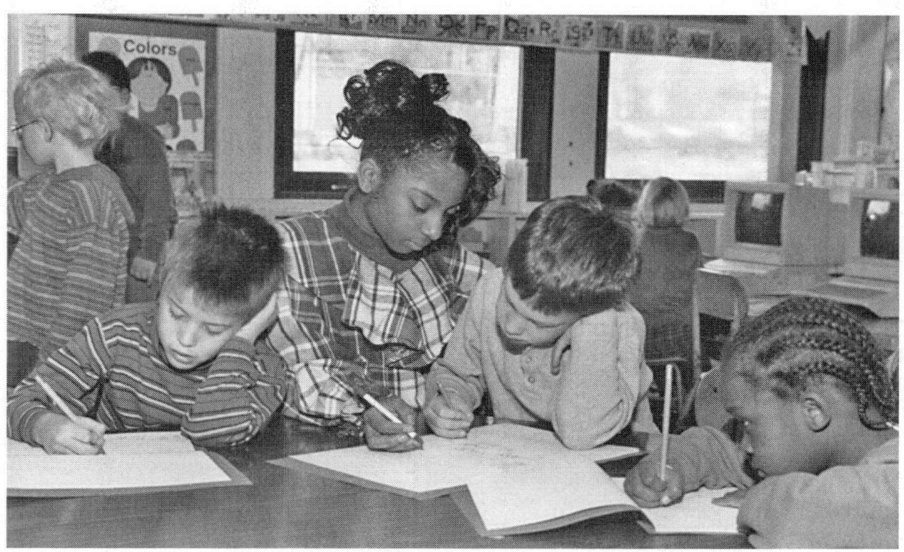

According to Vygotsky, guidance from an older peer facilitates learning.

into **private speech**, or self-guiding speech, and use this speech to organize their own thoughts and behaviors (Vygotsky, 1987).

Under what circumstances (e.g., a difficult task, an embarrassing situation) are you helped by using private speech (i.e., talking to yourself)?

A zone of proximal development requires guidance or collaboration with a peer, an older sibling, a parent, teacher, or elder. These others can facilitate cognitive development by prompting, providing clues, modeling, explaining, questioning, discussing, encouraging, and holding the child's attention. Cognitive development occurs when a child is provided with a challenge just beyond her current competency level and then is assisted in her success by another. That assistance is internalized and becomes a part of the competency with which the child approaches another task. For example, research with Mexican American and African American children shows that students learn more in school when involved in group projects and cooperative learning assignments than when working alone (Landrine, 1995).

Scaffolding. Another method that is used intuitively by parents and teachers to assist children in their zones of proximal development is called *scaffolding*. **Scaffolding** refers to decreasing the amount of direct instruction provided to the child over the course of a single learning session.

In the chapter case study, as the game advances, Alexandr reduces the number of verbal corrections he gives Anya and eventually stops showing her how the pieces move. (Alexandr sensed that Anya needed more explicit intervention at the beginning of the game and less as the game progressed).

Research has shown that children who are exposed to effective scaffolding are more successful when asked to master the task on their own (Berk & Spuhl, 1995; Conner, Knight, & Cross, 1997). Box 4.3 illustrates how scaffolding can be used in reading instruction.

Scaffolding tends to rely on verbal as well as physical instruction and describes well the transmission of knowledge that occurs when a child is

BOX 4.3 ROADMAP TO SUCCESSFUL PRACTICE

Enhancing Reading Comprehension with Reciprocal Teaching

Reciprocal teaching is an interactive teaching technique designed to improve reading comprehension in children (Palinscar & Brown, 1984; Latendresse, 2004). It is based upon the Vygotskian principles of zones of proximal development and scaffolding and requires the teacher and a small group of students (e.g., between two and four) to engage in a cooperative dialogue to enhance the understanding of a passage of text using four strategies:

1. Questioning
2. Summarizing
3. Clarifying
4. Predicting

Once the group has read a passage, the dialogue leader (at first the teacher, later a student) begins by asking questions about it. Students offer answers, raise additional questions, and in case of disagreement about content, reread the text. Next, the leader summarizes the passage, and students discuss the summary and clarify ideas that are unfamiliar to any group members. Finally, the leader encourages students to predict future content based on prior knowledge and clues in the text narrative. The four strategies ensure that students will link new information to previously acquired knowledge, explain their ideas, use what they have learned to acquire new knowledge, and keep their interaction goal oriented.

This exercise creates a zone of proximal development by providing the students with a passage of text that is just above their comprehension level. With the teacher's guidance, the students gain access to the necessary information to facilitate understanding. The teacher also exhibits scaffolding by first asking, explaining, and modeling the four strategies listed above and then gradually decreasing involvement and thereby making the students assume more responsibility for their learning.

Research shows that children from the primary through middle-school grades who experience reciprocal teaching show impressive gains in reading comprehension (Hashey & Connors, 2003; Lederer, 2000).

performing a task or solving a problem. However, it also has been demonstrated that many children learn within informal contexts, such as when they observe a skilled adult perform a task without direct instruction. This type of learning is more accurately referred to as **guided participation**. Early observation gives way to guided participation until mastery of an everyday task is complete. A Mayan girl begins to learn to weave by watching her mother and other adult women weave on a loom. At age 5 she weaves leaves on a play loom, at age 7 she weaves with help from her mother, and by age 9 she weaves alone (Rogoff, 1990). Guided participation extends Vygotsky's notion of learning from structured and explicit learning situations (e.g., schools) to informal everyday contexts.

Sociocultural expectations influence what is learned.

Basis of Cognitive Development

Vygotsky and other socioculturalists see biology and environment as intertwined and as forces that coconstruct development. Vygotsky suggested that one's biological predisposition—gender, temperament, or mental retardation—may be viewed and valued by one's culture differentially. For example, being a boy or girl, having a difficult or easy temperament, or having special needs influences how you interact with the world and how others respond to that interaction. Although socioculturalists acknowledge the role of biology in development, they tend to focus more on articulating and assessing the cultural forces that shape cognition.

The Role of Culture

Vygotsky's theory did not propose stages of cognitive development, nor did it summarize what 8- to 12-year-olds can or cannot cognitively accomplish. The absence of both universal stages and a summary of competencies reflects the very focus of this theory. There *are no* universal stages and competencies because children's learning is created by their individual sociocultural histories and interactional contexts. One's culture does not merely contribute *to* development. Rather, it *is* the context that is necessary for development to take place.

For example, in the United States, it is not until around age 10 that parents report feeling comfortable leaving their children to take care of themselves or younger children (Rogoff, 1996). By contrast, in San Pedro, located in the highlands of Guatemala, 3- to 5-year-old children are responsible for taking care of 1-year-old siblings. The difference in caretaking abilities between U.S. and Guatemalan children seems to emerge from differential sociocultural experiences and expectations. These 3- to 5-year-olds have grown up observing other children caring for younger siblings (i.e., guided participation) and most likely experiencing care by an older sibling themselves (i.e., scaffolding).

In addition, it is against Mayan cultural norms to force someone to cooperate against their will. San Pedro children treat their infant siblings with respect and autonomy and willingly subordinate their wishes to those of the infant. The result of this cultural experience is that children who care for younger children show less cognitive egocentrism and learn to become a cooperative and interdependent member of the community (Rogoff, 1996; Gaskins, 1999). This theoretical perspective places great emphasis on the role of culture as it is transmitted and embodied by siblings, parents, teachers, and elders in the community.

Critics of Vygotsky's theoretical perspective point to the vagueness of some of his developmental concepts. For example, the zone of proximal development, defined broadly, focuses our attention on the "readiness" of children to learn certain tasks with or without the assistance of

Guideposts for Working with School-Age Children

- Because siblings, parents, and teachers play an important role in children's cognitive development, involve them and others in all levels of instruction whenever possible.
- Include same-age or older peers in the learning process through peer tutoring or collaborative learning environments.
- Try to present tasks to children that are just above their competency level and that they can accomplish with help to increase children's joy and excitement in a challenge.
- Utilize scaffolding by providing children with modeling or clues so that you can gradually withdraw your support and they may begin to carry out the activity independently.
- Contextualize learning skills so that children see the connection between the skill and how it applies to their everyday lives.
- Focus assessments not on what children have learned but on what they can do with help to determine their readiness, or zone of proximal development.

others. But Vygotsky never suggests *what types* of mental representations are formed by these social interactions and *how* they are formed.

We also do not get a sense of how cognitive development influences the way children progress through the zone of proximal development. How do children's newly developed cognitions influence the way they interact with their environment? Finally, unlike Piaget, Vygotsky did not leave a legacy of tasks that allow us to see development clearly in children.

Vygotsky did, however, redirect our focus to several critical aspects of cognitive development. His proposal that language and social interaction are tools that help develop thought has spurred much research in this area. His emphasis on culture and context helps us understand the cultural variation we see in cognitive skills and correctly predicts multiple pathways of cognitive development (Guberman, 1999; Miller, 2002; Rogoff, 2003).

What role did older siblings, friends, relatives, and other adults play in your learning and what did you learn from them?

Many of these practical suggestions are incorporated in the pedagogical philosophy of Maria Montessori. Although Maria Montessori's writings preceded the published works of both Piaget and Vygotsky, many of their theoretical assumptions about cognitive development are reflected in her teaching methods and educational philosophy, as presented in Box 4.4.

Information-Processing Perspective in Middle Childhood

This theoretical perspective has emerged as a result of the rise of modern technology, most specifically the computer. When computer scientists began to create computer programs that took in information, matched it with existing information, analyzed, manipulated, transformed, and stored information, it appeared to some cognitive psychologists that this might be how humans process information as well. In the late 1960s a model was designed to simulate how humans think and learn (Shiffrin & Atkinson, 1969).

In the first stage, called the **sensory register**, individuals take in information from the outside world and hold it for a very short period of time (e.g., milliseconds). For example, your experience of reading this page might register in this first stage as black words on a white page, the weight of the book in your hands, the movement of your eyes across the page and the sound of music in another room. The purpose of this phase of processing is to hold information in storage until attention is paid to certain elements of the experience. If attention is directed to the words on the page, for example, then this information is **encoded**, or transformed into a representation, and transferred to the second stage, called your **short-term memory**.

In the second stage, the new information is held for a longer period of time (e.g., 20–30 seconds) so that decisions about what to do with it can be made. You have to work quickly, though,

BOX 4.4 ROADMAP TO SUCCESSFUL PRACTICE

The Montessori Approach

There are more than 4,000 Montessori schools throughout the United States. Each Montessori school builds upon the educational legacy of Dr. Maria Montessori, who founded the first school in 1907. In Montessori schools throughout the world, children develop the habits and skills of lifelong learning. Guided by teachers trained to observe and identify children's unique learning capabilities, children learn in educational partnership with their teachers. Try to identify the components of the "Montessori Way" that reflect the theoretical ideas and suggestions of either Piaget, Vygotsky, or both.

1. **A Child-Centered Environment.** The focus of activity in the Montessori setting is on children learning, not on teachers teaching. Generally, student will work individually or in small, self-selected groups. There will be very few whole-group lessons.
2. **A Responsive Prepared Environment.** The environment should be designed to meet the needs, interests, abilities, and development of the children in the class. The educators should design and adapt the environment with this community of children in mind, rapidly modifying the selection of educational materials available, the physical layout, and the tone of the class to best fit the ever-changing needs of the children.
3. **A Focus on Individual Progress and Development.** Within a Montessori environment, children progress at their own pace, moving on to the next step in each area of learning as they are each ready to do so. While the child lives within a larger community of children, each student is viewed as a universe of one.
4. **Hands-on Learning.** In a Montessori learning environment, students rarely learn from texts or workbooks. In all cases, direct, personal, hands-on contact with either real things under study or with concrete learning materials that bring abstract concepts to life allow children to learn with much deeper understanding.
5. **Spontaneous Activity.** It is natural for children to talk, move, touch things, and explore the world around them. Any true Montessori environment encourages children to move about freely, within reasonable limits of appropriate behavior. Much of the time the children select work that has been presented to them individually and that captures their interest and attention, although the Montessori educator also strives to draw their attention and capture their interest in new challenges and areas of inquiry. And even within this atmosphere of spontaneous activity, students do eventually have to master the basic skills of their culture, even if initially they would prefer to avoid them.
6. **Active Learning.** In Montessori learning environments, children not only select their own work from the choices presented to them but also continue to work with tasks, returning to continue their work over many weeks or months, until finally the work is so easy for them that they can demonstrate it to younger children. This is one of many ways that Montessori educators use to confirm that students have reached mastery of each skill.
7. **Self-motivated Activity.** One of Montessori's key concepts is the idea that children are driven by their desire to become independent and competent beings in the world, to learn new things and master new skills. For this reason, outside rewards to create external motivation are both unnecessary and can potentially lead to passive adults who are dependent on others for everything from their self-image to permission to follow their dreams. In the process of making independent choices and exploring concepts largely on their own, Montessori children construct their own sense of individual identity and personal judgment of right and wrong.
8. **Freedom within Limits.** Montessori children enjoy considerable freedom of movement and choice; however, their freedom always exists within carefully defined limits on the range of their behavior. They are free to do anything appropriate to the ground rules of the community but are redirected promptly and firmly if they cross over the line.
9. **Self-disciplined Learning.** In Montessori programs, children do not work for grades or external rewards, nor do they simply complete assignments given them by their Montessori educators. Children learn because they are interested in things and because all children share a desire to become competent and independent human beings.

Source: From *The 20 Best Practices of an Authentic Montessori School* by Tim Seldin & Paul Epstein, 2003. Retrieved from http//www.montessori.org. Copyright 2004 by The Montessori Foundation. Adapted by permission of the author.

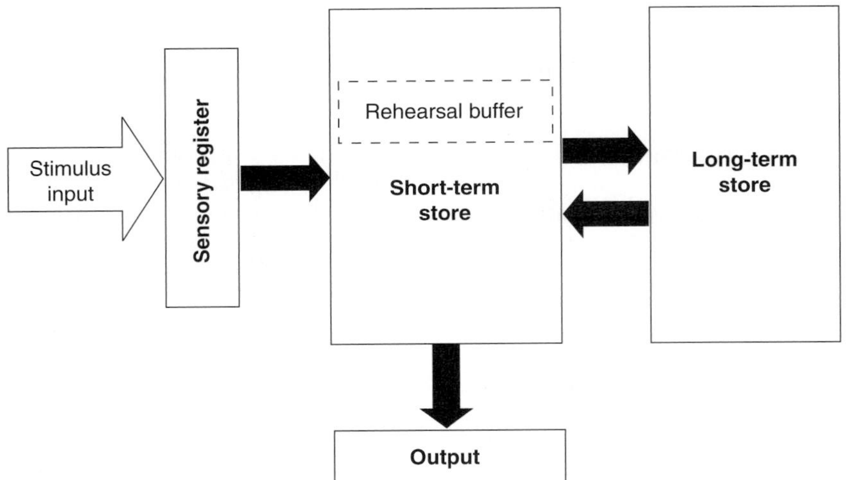

FIGURE 4.4 Information-Processing Model
A flowchart of the memory system.

Source: Based on "Storage and Retrieval Processes in Long-Term Memory," by Richard M. Shiffrin & Richard C. Atkinson, 1969, *Psychological Review, 76*, pp. 179–193. Copyright 1969 by the American Psychological Association. Adapted by permission of the author.

because this store is very limited in capacity and information is very vulnerable to loss or interference. If you are motivated to retain the information from the page, then more processing of the information should occur (e.g., you might reread some parts of a paragraph or take notes on a section or practice memorizing an italicized word). As a result of processing this information more deeply, it will be transferred to **long-term store** (LTS).

Long-term store, the third stage in information processing, is unlimited in capacity, and the information stored lasts for a very long time. Information in long-term store, like the words on this page, gets stored along with similar information and is permanently ready for you to retrieve at a later date. When you are ready to use the information, it is called back to the short-term memory and is displayed as output in the form of a correct answer, idea, or behavior.

The focus of this perspective is on how information is encoded, manipulated, transformed, memorized, retrieved, and used in cognitive processing. It uses the computer as a metaphor for the human mind to help reduce, compartmentalize, and analyze the cognitive components that contribute to the process of learning.

Developmental Components of the Theory

The model shown in Figure 4.4 is based on how adults might process information. It does not suggest how cognitive processes develop over time or what influences their development or how children might process information differently from adults. Over the past few decades, developmental psychologists have focused their research on these developmental questions and have identified the following seven components as responsible for the increased cognitive processing exhibited by school-age children, adolescents, and adults (Schneider & Bjorklund, 2003):

1. Increased short-term store capacity
2. Faster speed of processing
3. Improved attentional focus
4. Improved mnemonic strategies
5. Increase in knowledge base
6. Greater automaticity
7. More metacognition

Short-term store (STS) capacity. You read in the previous section that the short-term store is limited in capacity, or in the amount of information that it can hold. Capacity is usually measured by a **digit**

span task, where a child must repeat, in exact order, a series of rapidly presented digits that increases in number of digits at every trial. Studies have shown that capacity increases with age. The memory span of 2-year-olds is about two items, 5-year-olds about four items, 7-year-olds about five items, 9-year-olds about six items, and the average span of adults is about seven items (Dempster, 1981). The greater the capacity of the STS, the more information it can hold to be manipulated and transferred to long-term store (LTS).

Speed of processing. The amount of time it takes for children to encode the information that comes into their STS, transfer it to LTS and retrieve information from LTS decreases with age (Dempster, 1981; Hitch & Towse, 1995; Gathercole, 1998). This means that as most children get older they process information faster. The advantage of greater speed of processing is that it gets information from STS to LTS faster, thus clearing space for more information to enter STS, increasing processing capacity (for a review, see Kail, 1995). These age differences are in part explained by maturational factors, such as myelination of neuronal axons (see chapter 3), and in part by experience with the tasks and material (Schneider & Bjorklund, 2003).

Notice how quickly Alexandr moves his chess pieces and how much longer it takes Anya to evaluate the board, calculate the consequences of her next move, and make her decision.

Attention. Selective attention is the ability to ignore irrelevant stimuli or distractions and focus on just those aspects of a situation that are relevant to achieving the goals of the task. Researchers presented different-aged children with a stream of numbers on a computer screen and asked them to push a button whenever they saw a particular sequence of numbers (e.g., 1, 3, 9). Older children between 6 and 9 years of age showed markedly superior selective attention when compared to younger children (Lin, Hsiao, & Chen, 1999).

Selective attention develops as a result of **cognitive inhibition**, or the ability to ignore both internal and external distraction (e.g., irrelevant thought, behaviors, impulses). Gains in cognitive inhibition occur from early to middle childhood and into adolescence. The development of the frontal lobes is responsible for controlling irrelevant information and unwanted impulses (see chapter 8). Studies have also found that damage to the frontal lobes increases distractibility in both children and adults (Dempster, 1995). By clearing the STS of irrelevant information, cognitive inhibition increases cognitive capacity in the same way as speed of processing does by freeing up more STS to apply to the task at hand.

Mnemonic strategies. Mnemonic strategies are any strategies that aid in remembering. The most common mnemonic techniques used by school-aged children are **rehearsal** (repeating the to-be-remembered items) and **organization** (putting together words or objects that go together).

Rehearsal is typically studied by presenting the child with a list of related or unrelated items, one at a time, and asking them to "say aloud anything that is going on in your head to help you remember them." Children 5 years of age or younger tend not to rehearse at all. Six- to seven-year-olds engage in **passive rehearsal**, or single-item rehearsal (e.g., dog, dog, dog), and children in middle childhood begin to transition between passive and **active rehearsal**, or multiitem rehearsal (e.g., dog, cat, fish, dog, cat, fish) also known as **cumulative rehearsal** (Ornstein, Naus, & Liberty, 1975; Guttentag, Ornstein, & Siemens, 1987).

To study mnemonic organization, children are presented with a randomly ordered list of categorizable pictures or words printed on cards (e.g., animals, fruits, pieces of clothing, body parts). They are told to "sort the cards in any way that will help you remember them later." Children 5 years of age and younger tend to sort the cards randomly or in the order the cards were handed to them. Around ages 6 and 7, children begin to sort together items that are highly associated with one another (e.g., dog, cat, fish and apple, pear, orange). Eight- to eleven-year-old children consistently cluster highly associated items together and also less closely associated items together (e.g., dog, cat, goat, deer) (Bjorklund & de Marchena, 1984; Schneider, 1986). The developmental progression of these and other mnemonic strategies are in Table 4.2.

Research has shown a link between the effective use of a strategy and improved memory performance. Those children who use more active rehearsal or categorical sorting remember more words than those children who use passive rehearsal or very little grouping in their organizational strategies (Cox et al., 1989; Carr & Schneider, 1991).

A recent model of strategy development suggests that strategies do not develop one at a time in a unilinear way. Rather, as children develop they generate a variety of strategies, make a decision to use one or several strategies, and then modify their

TABLE 4–2

Approximate Ages by Which Most Children Spontaneously Display Various Memory Strategies Effectively for Children in Schooled Cultures[1]

Children develop better organizational and retrieval strategies during middle childhood as well the ability to apply more focused attention to a task.

	6–7 years	8–10 years	11–14 years
Single-item rehearsal	X		
Cumulative rehearsal			X
Organization with highly associated items	X		
Organization with less highly associated items		X	
Effective allocation of study time		X	
Retrieval strategies		X	
Elaboration[2]			X
Strategies for remembering complex text[2]			X

[1] Younger children than listed often display effective strategies when prompted.

[2] These strategies may not be displayed until later and many adults fail to use these strategies effectively.

Source: From "Memory and Knowledge Development," by W. Schneider & D. Bjorklund, 2003, in J. Valsiner & K. Connolly (Eds.), *Handbook of Developmental Psychology* (p. 378). Thousand Oaks, CA: Sage. Copyright 2003 by Jaan Valsiner and Kevin Connolly. Reprinted by permission of Sage Publications, Inc.

strategy choice the next time. Sometimes the strategy improves their performance, but sometimes—especially the first few times they try out a new strategy—it does not. Gradually the strategy that results in the best performance over time wins out (Siegler, 1996).

It appears that effective spontaneous strategy use develops from a number of different factors. An increase in STS capacity frees up space for more items to be rehearsed or grouped together, and increased speed of processing frees up cognitive capacity to be applied to more complex strategy use (Case, Kurland, & Goldberg, 1982). In addition, research has shown that both parents and teachers play a critical role in the development and use of mnemonic strategies. Parents and teachers are both explicit (e.g., they provide the phrase "**E**very **G**ood **B**oy **D**oes **F**ine" to remember a musical scale) and implicit (e.g., the parent organizes her grocery list by store aisle) in their memory instruction (Bjorklund, 2000; Fivush, 1997; Moely et al., 1985).

Children who receive mnemonic advice tend to use strategies more and are better memorizers compared to those who receive little guidance. Practice with a task and familiarity with the materials also aids in strategy use. For example, children who memorize a list of spelling words every week during the school year have more strategy practice than children who do not engage in this academic exercise. They also may be more successful in their memory performance if they practice spelling words in familiar English (for English-speaking children) than if the words were presented in an unfamiliar language.

When was the last time you had to remember something and what did you do to remember it?

Knowledge base. A **knowledge base** is what children have stored in their long-term memory (LTS). It is their representation of world knowledge that is usually highly organized, with strong connections among items that are related. As children reach middle childhood, they have more experiences than younger children, gain more knowledge about the world, and increase the amount and richness of their knowledge bases. Research has shown that children who are more familiar with the to-be-remembered information (i.e., those who have richer and more extensive knowledge bases) recall that information better and typically implement mnemonic strategies faster and more effectively, producing better memory performance (i.e., better test scores). This developmental difference is not all that surprising, but what happens on memory tasks when the tables are turned and the *younger* child is the one who knows *more?* In a study, children who were advanced chess players (i.e., chess experts) were asked to memorize a series of chess positions on a chessboard. Their memory performance was compared to college-age chess novices (i.e., college students who knew very little about the game of chess). The younger children remembered more chess positions than the college students (Chi, 1978)! This and other studies point to the important role that knowledge base plays in improving cognitive performance by increasing the speed and ease with which information is moved and retrieved from LTS (Schneider, Bjorklund, & Maier-Bruckner, 1996; Bjorklund & Schneider, 1996).

Alexandr has a full repertoire of opening and closing moves from past playing experience from which to draw. He relies automatically on his past knowledge. Most of the positions on the chessboard are new to Anya and she is just beginning to add to her knowledge base of chess positions and movements. Comparing new moves to what she knows takes effort, as does committing new moves to memory.

Cognitive efficiency. When children are confronted with a new learning task, such as memorizing the capitals of the 50 states, they may spend considerable effort simply coming up with memory strategies to learn so much information. Consequently, their strategies may take so much mental effort that they have little attentional capacity left over to apply to remembering many of the capitals. As children gain practice on cognitive tasks, their performance becomes more **automatic**, or requires less attentional capacity, and therefore more attention can be applied to the to-be-learned material. This *automaticity*, or increased cognitive efficiency, takes place over time, with both practice and sufficient motivation (Guttentag, 1995). This is another explanation for why older children perform better on cognitive tasks than younger children. School-age children are able to implement cognitive strategies more automatically, thus leaving more room in STS for performing the learning task (i.e., transferring information into LTS) (Case, 1992).

With practice, the effort it takes Anya to recall moves and strategies will become more automatic, allowing her to focus on other aspects of the game.

Metacognition. As children approach middle childhood they show improved **metacognitive skills**, or a more sophisticated understanding of how their mind and the minds of others works. They are more likely to describe the mind as an active, constructive agent that selects and transforms information (Flavell, 2000). This more mature understanding of the mind reflects an increase in **metamemory**, or a specific knowledge about what memory is, how it works, and what factors influence its functioning (Flavell, Miller, & Miller, 2002). Research has shown that older children are more aware that the type of cognitive task and the difficulty of the to-be-learned materials determines how much effort they need to put into the task as well as what their predicted success might be. For example, when compared to 6- to 7-year olds, 11-year-olds were more likely to report that memorizing pairs of opposites (e.g., boy, girl) would be easier than memorizing pairs of unrelated words (e.g. Mary, walk) (Kreutzer, Leonard, & Flavell, 1975).

Older children also more accurately estimate their memory abilities (e.g., how many words out of 100 could you remember if you were able to study them only once?). They allocate their study time appropriately (e.g., more study time needed for more difficult material) and realize that recall of gist is easier than verbatim memory and that sets of categorized items are easier to recall than sets of noncategorized items (Schneider, 1998; O'Sullivan, 1993; O'Sullivan, 1996). They are also much better at monitoring their cognitive progress, referred to as **self-monitoring**, and determining when the material has been learned sufficiently (Ringel & Springer, 1980; Flavell et al., 1970).

In general, children's metamemory knowledge increases with age and is correlated with age-related improvements in memory behavior (Schneider, 1999; Schneider & Pressley, 1997). Metamemorial knowledge may in part develop from a child's successes and failures in remembering but also from direct encouragement from parents and teachers. For example, a parent may ask a child to help create a way to remember a permission slip that is due the next day and then discuss why the method worked or didn't work. Contemporary memory strategy training programs usually include some metamemory component that teaches children to assess their performance when using different types of cognitive strategies and to attribute their relative performance to these various strategies (Schneider & Pressley, 1997).

Were you taught explicitly how to remember? If so, what suggestions were provided to you?

Basis of Cognitive Development

The information-processing perspective recognizes the contributions of both nature and nurture. Biological brain maturation increases brain capacity, myelination of neuronal axons increases the speed of processing, and frontal lobe development may influence the development of selective attention and cognitive inhibition that improve the child's ability to focus on the task at hand and ignore distracting stimuli. Equally important are the practice opportunities provided by a child's home and educational environments. Explicit and implicit memory instruction from peers, parents, and teachers facilitates mnemonic strategy development and increases metamemorial knowledge. Informal practice, such as playing memory games, may encourage the automatization of strategies, and knowledge acquisition from a child's environment may improve cognitive performance. Box 4.5 provides an example of how neurological and environmental factors interact in children who have attentional processing disorders.

BOX 4.5 A ROADMAP TO UNDERSTANDING THEORY AND RESEARCH

The Relationship between ADHD, School Performance, and Reading Comprehension

ADHD is **attention deficit disorder** with **hyperactivity** (American Psychiatric Association, 2000). It is estimated that approximately 1–5% of children have ADHD, with boys diagnosed three to nine times more often than girls. The main characteristic of this disorder is the inability of children to inhibit their behavior. This inability manifests itself in impulsivity, poor attention, an inability to complete a task or adhere to rules of social conduct, and, for many children, overactivity (Barkley, 2000).

It should come as no surprise that in a school setting that requires children to sit still, attend, listen, obey, inhibit impulsive behavior, cooperate, organize actions, and follow through on instructions, children with ADHD do poorly. They seem to have at least two main problems with academic work: (1) They are not getting as much done as non-ADHD children, and so have lower grades and are retained more often. Approximately one third of these children will be retained in at least one grade before reaching high school, and ADHD children are more likely than their classmates to drop out of school or be suspended. (2) Their ability levels are also somewhat below those of children without ADHD and may decline over time. Children with ADHD are more likely to have learning disabilities (LDs), with 20 to 25% of them having a reading disorder (Barkley, 2000).

How, specifically, does ADHD affect children's information-processing capabilities and therefore academic performance? Research has found that ADHD is associated with deficits in sustained attention and "executive functioning," which enables a school-age child to engage successfully in independent, purposive, self-serving behavior. Executive functioning includes nonverbal working memory, internalization of speech, self-monitoring, and self-regulation (Barkley, 1998; Perugini, Harvey, Lovejoy, Sandstrom, & Webb, 2000). Researchers have also found that when asked to generate a list of words all beginning with the same letter, children with ADHD show a delay in the first 15 seconds of the task. This delay reflects insufficient automating skills for processing verbal information (Hurks, Hendriksen, Vles, Kalff, Feron, et al., 2004). Children with ADHD also show poorer story recall (Lorch, O'Neil, Bertiaume, Milich, Eastham, et al., 2004).

Interventions at home and in the classroom tend to focus on space and time management. For example, parents might ensure that their child has a quiet place to study with minimal distraction. Teachers might provide the child with shorter blocks of instruction and frequent opportunities to engage in physical activity. These modifications in the learning environment are helpful, but recent research suggests that parents and teachers could play a more critical role in the learning process.

A series of studies examined children's story comprehension (Lorch et al., 2004; Lorch, Diener, Sanchez, Milich, Welsh, & van den Broek, 1999; Lorch, Eastham, Milich, & Lemberger, 2004; Lorch, Milich, & Sanchez, 1998). A story comprehension task was chosen because successful comprehension requires multiple cognitive skills: the strategic allocation of attention; the selection, encoding, and interpretation of important information; the retrieval of relevant background information; the generation of inferences; and the monitoring of comprehension. In one study, 7- to 11-year-old children listened to one of two folktales on audiotape and

BOX 4.5 (CONTINUED)

recalled the story both before and after studying a written version for up to 10 minutes. Non-ADHD children recalled more causal connectors, or themes that moved the story along, than ADHD children. In addition, there was no difference in studying time between the two groups. These findings showed that study time alone does not improve story comprehension for children with ADHD. These children experience difficulty extracting and encoding the main events and then constructing a coherent story from memory, not simply slower processing.

Based on these findings, one practical intervention strategy would be to assist the child in pulling out the connected or causal events of a story and putting them into a more memorable form. For example, parents or teachers might ask why certain events occurred in the story or have the children predict what might come next based on prior events. The researchers suggest that the story comprehension task they used approximates some of the academic requirements of a classroom, such as listening to directions, stories, or lectures. This connecting ability is critical when children in grade 4 and higher are required to read chapters of texts or lengthy books, extract the main ideas, and connect the information together to be remembered at a later time. More direct intervention techniques like the one suggested here might prove to be more beneficial for children with ADHD.

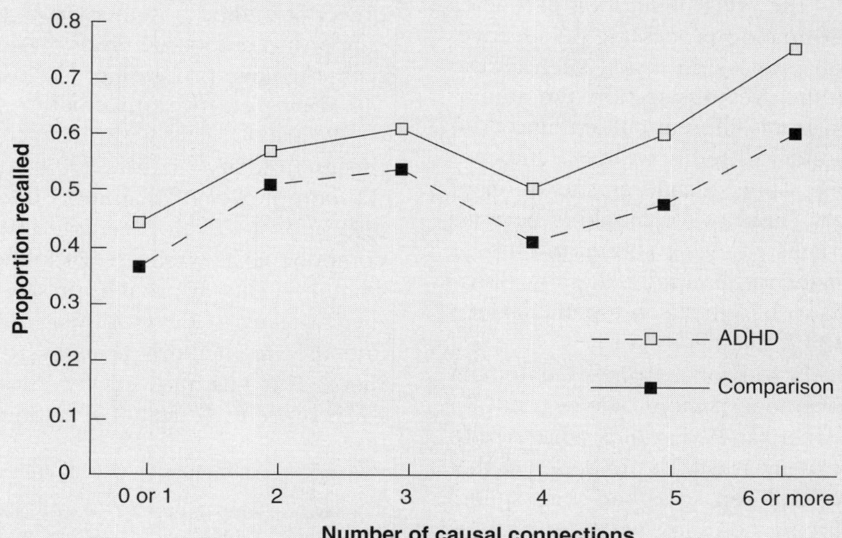

FIGURE 4.5 Proportion of Events Recalled as a Function of Diagnostic Group and Number of Causal Connections

Children with ADHD recall fewer causal connections when listening to a story, compared to non-ADHD children.

Source: From "Story Comprehension and the Impact of Studying or Recall in Children with Attention Deficit Hyperactivity Disorder," by E. P. Lorch et al. 2004, *Journal of Clinical Child and Adolescent Psychology, 33*, p. 511. Copyright 2004 by Lawrence Erlbaum Associates, Inc. Reprinted by permission of the publisher.

Guideposts for Working with School-Age Children

- Because selective attention improves with age, help younger school-age children avoid distractions by providing them with quiet work and study environments at home and school.
- Help children focus attention on the relevant information by asking questions about the main ideas of a story or having them outline the steps of their solution to a math problem.
- Use instructional activities that will capture and hold children's interest by incorporating physical activity into the lesson or by using examples or materials that are currently popular (e.g., movies, video games).
- Discuss with children how one might remember better and let them share their strategies with one another. Be explicit about what mnemonic strategies are and how and why they work.
- Help children to set their learning goals and monitor their progress toward those goals.

The Role of Culture

Children educated in an American school system typically exhibit the cognitive competencies defined by the information-processing perspective. When information-processing tasks, such as the ones described in the previous section, are administered to children from different cultural and educational backgrounds, differences in abilities are noted. For example, Chinese children show greater short-term memory capacity for numbers because the terms for the digits 1 to 9 are shorter in Chinese and can be articulated more rapidly, thereby allowing more numbers to be rehearsed together (Chen & Stevenson, 1988).

Nine-year-old children from Guatemala remember the placement of more objects (out of a total of 40) than American 9-year-olds who tried to rehearse the objects in a list. The experience that these Guatemalan children have had with spatial memory in producing complex weaving designs proved useful in this memory task (Rogoff & Waddell, 1982). The mathematical calculating abilities of 6- to 9-year-old Brazilian candy vendors based on need and practical experience exceed the calculating ability of their American counterparts (Saxe, 1988). The experience and expectations of one's culture have a significant influence on the types of memory and problem-solving skills required and produced by children of all ages.

The computer metaphor provides the information-processing perspective with some of its strengths, but this model fails to communicate the different ways children may learn in different contexts. For example, although information processors acknowledge the contributions of the environment, the model fails to articulate how that give-and-take interaction occurs. The model also does not explain well the development of creativity and imagination, or thinking "outside the box," and it does not outline how human factors such as motivation and emotional arousal enhance or interfere with cognitive processing.

However, the information-processing approach provides us with an accurate portrayal of the complexity of thought. It also breaks down the complexity of cognition into its components and shows developmental differences in these components as well as what influences their development. The approach proposes very specific mechanisms of development and offers rigorous and precise methods to assess cognitive development. This has allowed very specific applications to be made to educational settings.

Language, Literacy, and Academic Learning

Although theories provide us with explanations of how cognition develops, it is less clear how this development is related to language acquisition or to learning a specific skill in an academic setting. Cognitive changes in school-aged children contribute to, and are reflected by, change in children's language, literacy, and mathematical skills during middle childhood.

Language Development

The foundation of language development is established during the preschool and early elementary school years. However, children of middle childhood age continue to refine their language skills in several domains. For example, their understanding of word meaning, or **semantic** development, continues throughout middle childhood. A first grader may know the meaning of 8,000 to 14,000 words, but a high-schooler knows 80,000 words (Owens, 1996). These numbers are equivalent to the acquisition of 6,200 words a year between first grade and graduating from high school. The understanding that words have multiple meanings also increases. This more complex understanding of word use may be attributed, in part, to cognitive development.

With the advancement of cognition children become better communicators and possess a more sophisticated sense of humor. A related advancement is that school-age children also begin to comprehend the use of idioms such as "Who let the cat out of the bag?" Research shows that the comprehension of multiple word use, idioms, and forms of sarcasm may not occur until adolescence (Bloom, 1998). Semantic development in middle childhood seems to rely heavily on the context of the conversation and children's ability to figure out the meaning of a word or phrase by what another person *intended* to say, rather than a literal interpretation of word choice (Baumann, Font, Edwards, & Boland, 2005; Cain, Oakhill, & Elbro, 2003).

Syntax development, or grammatical understanding and construction, expands during middle childhood. Children begin to understand the difference between active and passive voice (O'Grady, 1997). If given a toy car and truck and asked to show the experimenter "the car hit the truck" and "the car was hit by the truck," a 10-year-old is more likely than a 6-year-old to play out the scene of both statements correctly. The older child will listen to the meaning of the statements rather than automatically link the action of the verb to the nearest noun. They also begin to understand and use more sophisticated syntactical rules, such as the correct use of subject-verb and noun-pronoun agreement, correct uses of *that* and *which* to introduce subordinate clauses, and the proper use of punctuation such as colons and semicolons. Children during middle childhood also begin to learn how to use the articles *a* and *the* correctly as well as understand connectives such as *but, although, yet, however*, and *unless* (Nippold, 1988; Vion & Colas, 2004).

Middle childhood is also the period in which children improve upon the **pragmatics** of language, or the social etiquette of language. For example, school-age children become better at maintaining and contributing to a conversation by asking questions and adding information. Between ages 5 and 9, children become better at **shading**, or changing the topic during a conversation. They do so more gradually and tactfully than younger children. This results from an increasing awareness of the needs of the listener. As children move through middle childhood they become more aware of when they are misunderstood and do a better job of clarifying their meaning by changing or adding words to their sentences (Ninio & Snow, 1996).

Compared to preschool and early elementary schoolchildren, children from 8 to 12 years of age are more effective communicators, use more complex grammatical constructions, and are more aware of their role as a listener and communicator within multiple contexts. Greater diversity among language skills in older children results largely from environmental factors. Children with larger vocabularies, more complex grammar, and social language manners have been shown to come from homes with two parents and parents with higher educational backgrounds and income levels. They also converse with their parents more often and have more positive speech interactions with them (Hoff & Tian, 2005; Weigel, Martin, & Bennett, 2005). The differences in language development influenced by these factors are evident by kindergarten and remain stable through adolescence (Farkas & Beron, 2004).

One's cultural background has been shown to influence language development as well. In the development of pragmatics; for example, American children argue with their older siblings and sometimes speak to them with disrespect. Children from Japan are expected to speak to elders, which includes older siblings, with respect at all times. In Western societies children are expected to speak up and ask questions when they have them. But Mexican American and Southeast Asian communities, as well as some African American communities from the Southeast, have been taught to engage in conversation with an adult only when the adult initiates the conversation (Grant & Gomez, 2001). This means that much of vocabulary, grammar use, and pragmatics is influenced by the language culture that surrounds the child. Children's language development will impact their ability to learn in school and converse with others (Craig & Washington, 2004; Gonzalez, 2005). Likewise, their cognitive development will impact their language development.

Reading. Just as in language development, much of the foundation for reading has been laid prior to preschool, during preschool, and in the early elementary grades (K–3). The identification of letters and the matching of letters with individual sounds, knowing what a word is, and the interpretation of spaces and punctuation are the earliest building blocks for reading skills. By third grade, children are engaging in rapid word recognition (made easier by increased vocabularies) and are capable of self-monitoring reading comprehension (Howes, 2003).

In the United States, fourth grade is considered a critical point in the elementary school experience. Grade 4 is the year in which the linguistic, cognitive, and conceptual demands of reading increase substantially. These greater demands emerge largely as a result of the increased reliance on textbooks as the main instructional tool. There are also greater expectations for independent reading and writing; more unfamiliar, specialized, and technical vocabulary; more complex syntax in textbooks; increased requirements for **inferencing**, or drawing conclusions from existing information; and using prior knowledge to "figure things out." It is also the point at which children who had been previously successful begin to experience reading difficulties, perhaps because of these increased demands (Allington & Johnston, 2002). Fourth grade has been described as a transitional year in which reading shifts from learning to read to reading to learn (Chall, 1983; Ely, 1997).

For some children, their developing cognition prepares them to deal with increased demands on their intellectual competencies. For example, increases in selective attention and speed of processing, which occurs with age and practice, allow for more rapid decoding and word recognition (Beers, 2003). These two processes are critical for the development of reading skills and comprehension, and problems with decoding and/or word recognition is a possible source of poor reading ability, as suggested in Box 4.6.

Increases in short-term capacity allow for greater verbal memory. Increases in knowledge base, or available schemata, facilitate the use of old or familiar knowledge to make sense of new knowledge. For example, children who exhibit good reading comprehension skills display extensive background knowledge of the world, a wide vocabulary, and a familiarity with the semantic and syntactic structure of the English language (Snow, Burns, & Griffin, 1998). Practice in strategy use comes in handy as children initially use conscious strategies to understand and use text, which then become more automatic (Burns, Griffin, & Snow, 1999). An increase in metacognitive skills is reflected in children's increased awareness of what they know and don't know, or what they comprehend or don't comprehend, from their reading.

The shift from preoperational thought to concrete operational thought results in children being less **egocentric** (i.e., focusing on one's own perspective) and therefore more capable of understanding the viewpoint of the author, which might be different from their own or one with which they disagree. School-age children also demonstrate the ability to recognize different writing conventions that are used to achieve different purposes via text (e.g., humor, explanation, dialogue) (Lyon, 1999). They can incorporate this understanding into their writing as well.

Changes in cognitive development between the ages of 8 and 12 allow for the average reader to do the following:

- Read and learn from all variety of texts, including both fiction and nonfiction
- Monitor their own comprehension, summarize main points, and discuss details of text
- Expand their understanding of concepts and ideas by making inferences and using additional print resources
- Build a connection between existing knowledge and learn something new from material presented in print

Writing. The skill of writing develops in a very similar way to reading and within the same developmental time frame. Young children (ages 2 and 3) in the early phases of the preoperational stage of cognitive development begin to recognize and use a letter to represent a sound, a string of sounds to represent words, and words to represent people, objects, and ideas. They begin to write, as well as their fine motor skills allow, somewhere between the ages of 3 and 5. Parents and preschool programs should not be concerned with teaching children how to write but rather with providing young children with the opportunities to write and use writing implements.

With time, practice, encouragement, and opportunity, children in the early elementary school grades (ages 5–7) are able to hold the writing implements more correctly, which gives them better control over the mechanics of writing. They tend to write more often and construct longer pieces of written work. At this developmental

BOX 4.6 ROADMAP TO UNDERSTANDING THEORY AND RESEARCH

The Acquisition of Reading and Its Relationship to Later Reading Disabilities

Skilled readers are able to derive meaning from printed text accurately and efficiently. Research has shown that in doing so, they fluidly coordinate many component skills, each of which has been sharpened through instruction and experience over many years. Figure 4.6 illustrates the major "strands" that are woven together during the course of becoming a skilled reader. It is customary to consider separately the strands involved in recognizing individual printed words from those involved in comprehending the meaning of the string of words that have been identified, even though those two processes operate (and develop) interactively rather than independently (Committee on the Prevention of Reading Difficulties in Young Children, 1998).

There are a number of hypotheses as to what is responsible for poor reading skills; however, many children who have trouble learning to read in the early school years stumble in mastering the "word recognition" strands. They need to understand that a printed letter represents the smallest meaningful speech element, or **phoneme**. Grasping this alphabetic principle will be difficult if a child does not yet appreciate that spoken words consist of phonemes. Without this "phonemic awareness" the child cannot truly understand what letters stand for (Liberman, 1973).

Recognizing printed words further requires that one learn and apply the many correspondences between particular letters and phonemes, so that

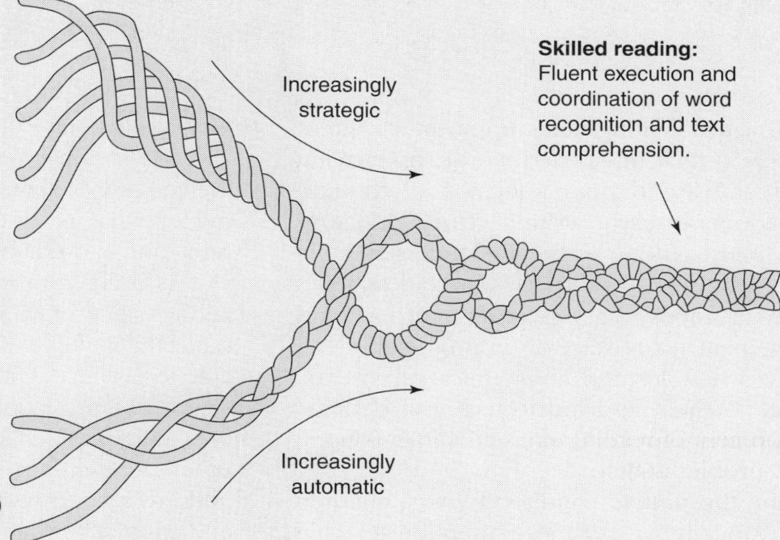

FIGURE 4.6 Illustration of the Many Strands That Are Woven Together in Skilled Reading
The ability to read requires the mastery of word recognition and language comprehension. Poor reading skills can result in difficulty with any number of strands.

Source: From "Connecting Early Language and Literacy to Later Reading (Dis)Abilities: Evidence, Theory, and Practice," by Hollis S. Scarborough, in Susan B. Neuman & David K. Dickinson (Eds.), 2001, *Handbook of Early Literacy Research,* Vol. 1 (p. 98). New York: Guilford. Copyright 2001 by The Guilford Press. Reprinted by permission of the publisher.

BOX 4.6 (CONTINUED)

the pronunciation of a printed word can be figured out (i.e., decoded) and then matched to stored information about spoken words in one's mental lexicon to enable the identity of the printed word to be recognized. Phonological decoding is the most reliable guide to word recognition.

Finally, skilled reading requires that the processes involved in word recognition become so well practiced that they can proceed extremely quickly and almost effortlessly, freeing up the reader's cognitive resources for comprehension processes.

Although most reading disabilities are associated with deficits in phonemic awareness, decoding, and sight recognition of printed words, reading skill can also be seriously impeded by weaknesses in the "comprehension" strands, particularly beyond second grade when reading materials become more complex. Even if the pronunciations of all the letter strings in a passage are correctly decoded, the text will not be well comprehended if the child (1) does not know the words in their spoken form, (2) cannot parse the syntactic and semantic relationships among the words, or (3) lacks critical background knowledge or inferential skills to interpret the text appropriately and "read between the lines." Note that in such instances, "reading comprehension" deficits are essentially oral language limitations.

A daunting fact about reading (dis)abilities is that differences among schoolchildren in their levels of reading achievement show strong stability over time, despite remedial efforts usually undertaken to strengthen the skills of lower achievers (Scarborough, 1998). Only about 5–10% of children who read satisfactorily in the primary grades ever stumble later, and 65–75% of children designated as reading disabled early on continue to read poorly throughout their school careers (and beyond).

Source: From "Connecting Early Language and Literacy to Later Reading (Dis)Abilities: Evidence, Theory, and Practice," Hollis S. Scarborough, in Susan B. Neuman & David K. Dickinson (Eds.), 2001, *Handbook of Early Literacy Research,* Vol. 1, (pp. 97–98). New York: Guilford. Copyright 2001 by The Guilford Press. Reprinted by permission of the publisher.

level, the act of writing takes up so much attentional capacity that misspelled words, no spacing or punctuation, and poor cohesion of thought often accompany early writing efforts. Because these technical writing errors are understandable from a developmental perspective, avoid criticism and instead focus on providing support and encouragement for the act of writing itself as an attempt at a new form of communication in early childhood. Greater attention to technical errors is more appropriate for children in middle childhood (Puckett & Black, 2001).

During the middle childhood years, children gain the capacity to pay more attention to what they are writing and how they are writing, so technical features such as spelling, spacing, punctuation, and coherence improve. Greater attentional capacity also allows them to focus a piece of writing, maintain a constant point of view, and carry a story through to the middle and the end. Constructing a complete and coherent story makes cognitive demands on long-term memory and sequencing abilities, which children in middle childhood are better able to meet. Their more complex and expansive knowledge base enables them to generate more ideas from which to write and access larger vocabularies. In addition, greater metacognitive skills encourage constant monitoring of what is written, as exemplified by more rereading and editing.

As children progress toward the concrete operational stage of thought, they begin to decentrate (i.e., take multiple dimensions into account) and are able to produce written work in both print and cursive letters (around ages 6 and 7). As concrete operational thinkers, children understand and appreciate other perspectives (i.e., become less egocentric) and are able to modify their writing for particular audiences. They can also take multiple perspectives into consideration. Writing assignments that encourage them to compare and contrast several viewpoints or critique a single perspective or provide an alternative viewpoint are appropriate for this age group. The multiple topics about which children write also reflect a move away from stories written about themselves (e.g., egocentrism) or events that have occurred (i.e., concrete experiences) to more abstract or imaginary stories (e.g., formal operational thought). During middle childhood some children begin to show preferences for writing compared to other academic skills as well as specific strengths in certain genres, such as poetry or science fiction. In addition, children in this age group begin to recognize and appreciate writing as a process. Varied writing opportunities that may encourage and support writing in middle childhood include autobiographies, fortunes, songs, bumper stickers, scripts, cereal boxes, epithets, and travel brochures (for a more extensive list, see Wormelli, 2001, p. 120).

Mathematical Operations

In the preschool years, children begin counting by reciting the number words in sequence (e.g., one, two, three, four, five). This **rote counting** helps them develop number sense. They learn that numbers come before or after each other and that numbers are smaller or larger than one another. They learn that one counting word corresponds with each object they count (i.e., one-to-one correspondence), and they also develop a sense of sequence and pattern (Franke, 2003). Counting, sequencing, and detecting patterns are often considered the basis of the elementary school curriculum. Comprehension of these concepts is necessary to support students in developing the skills and understanding necessary to operate on numbers and solve a variety of mathematical problems that are introduced in the early elementary school grades, such as addition and subtraction.

Multiplication, division, fractions, decimals, ratios, and geometry are some of the mathematical concepts and operations typically introduced during middle childhood. A number of developmental changes described in the previous sections may help explain why children in middle childhood might be cognitively "ready" to address these mathematical skills and concepts. For example, Piaget researched extensively how children develop the concept of number. A developmental pattern he observed was that as children exhibit decentration they can begin to generate multiple ways to solve a mathematical problem. For example, $9 \times 2 = 18$, but so does 3×6; and you can solve the addition problem $9 + 4$ by adding 4 units to 9 or knowing that $10 + 4$ is 14 and taking away 1.

Children who showed an understanding of seriation demonstrated a more sophisticated understanding of mathematical concepts. They were able to assimilate not only that one number can be larger than another but that it can also, and at the same time, be smaller than another number. Seriation allows for a comprehension of number lines as well as greater- and/or less than problems. Understanding reversibility allows a child to appreciate the relationship between addition and subtraction. Taking two apples out of a basket after adding two reverses or "undoes" the first operation. The same understanding of reversibility can be applied to multiplication and division.

Perhaps the most significant cognitive advancement toward understanding mathematical concepts is the ability to conserve number. If children begin with two equivalent quantities (i.e., numbers) and can comprehend that the quantity of 5 does not change when one group is spread out or bunched together, then they have begun to understand the invariance of numbers in the environment. With such knowledge, school-age children can better predict relationships between numbers and quantities.

Learning more demanding mathematical concepts also requires some memorization. Even though math educators argue that understanding is more important than rote memorization, students still need to memorize rules that can be applied to a variety of problems. Usually, school-age children either intentionally or unintentionally memorize their multiplication tables, as well as other mathematical "facts" or "rules." Over time and with practice, children also tend to invent their own strategies to facilitate the learning of mathematical concepts and operations (Ernst, 2000). Once certain operations become *automatized*, attentional capacity becomes available to apply to the remainder of the problem. Learning how to identify the greatest common factor in the numerator and denominator of a fraction, for example, would be much easier if you could focus your attention on what those common factors are, rather than struggle to determine which factors go into either the numerator or the denominator.

Finally, mathematical concepts are learned best if they can be linked to something that is familiar or known to the child. In other words, if the concepts can be linked to previously learned math concepts or embedded in practical problems that make sense to children, they will be able to assimilate the information more easily. Using other terms, one's knowledge base can and will facilitate the decoding and storage of this new information.

While the developmental progressions described in this chapter are relatively universal, there are individual differences in learning rates and styles among school-aged children. During the past decade in particular, researchers have determined that if the task is made more familiar, children will typically exhibit cognitive abilities, such as

Guideposts for Working with School-Age Children

- Engage children in conversation often. Ask them questions, answer their questions, and correct improper grammar and vocabulary use by repeating what was said correctly.
- Encourage reading in all forms. Read to children and have them read to you and to each other. Provide them access to appropriate reading-level materials.
- Provide opportunities for children to write, about anything! Help them to appreciate writing as one form of communication by encouraging them to write letters to loved ones or long-distance pen pals.
- Show children that mathematics is an integral part of their lives by having them count change, calculate discounts at the grocery store, tell time, or engage in any number of common everyday tasks that involve numerical understanding and calculation.

decentration, multiple-perspective taking, strategy generation, and even mathematical skills, at a much earlier age than Piaget predicted (Siegler, 1996). Despite the appearance of these skills in highly supportive environments, however, there is a tendency for children to approach the world in the patterns outlined earlier.

The patterns of skill development portrayed in this chapter describe "average" learners who share a common cultural background with their teacher, class, school, and curriculum material. Much of how children learn and what they learn can also be traced to their parents' educational values, the pedagogical practices of their teachers, their classroom environments, and the support they receive from their schools and communities.

Cognitive Development in Context

All three theoretical perspectives presented in this chapter recognize, to varying degrees, the role that the environment plays in the intellectual functioning and growth of children. Research shows that cognitive development can be enhanced or inhibited by the educational opportunities—or lack thereof—provided by parents, teachers, schools, neighborhoods, and communities. In return, the child's cognitive status influences how that child is responded to or treated by others.

Family Contexts

How well children may perform in school is based, in part, on their cognitive abilities. Decades of research show, however, that parental interest and involvement in their children's school life is also related to school achievement (Van Voorhis, 2000). Studies have illustrated that parental involvement is most effective when parents support their children's academic achievement *at home* in the following ways (Finn, 1998):

- **Managing and Organizing Time.** Parents of successful students actively help them organize their daily and weekly schedules and check to see if they are following their routines. Regular routines at home are also related to better school performance (Taylor, 1996).
- **Involvement with Homework.** Making certain that homework is completed, discussing the specifics of assignments and papers, explaining the assignments, checking accuracy, and actively helping children complete assignments are all related to children's academic performance (Cooper, Jackson, & Nye, 2001).
- **Discussing School Matters.** Children whose parents converse regularly with them about school experiences, both good and bad, perform better academically (Ho & Willms, 1996; Steinberg, 1996).
- **Literacy and Reading at Home.** There is a strong relationship between literacy activities and opportunities in the home (e.g., silent reading time, numerous printed materials) and school performance (Gauvain, McCollum, & Savage, 2000).

Unfortunately, parental involvement in children's schooling occurs less often in working-class families and families in which mothers work full-time (Muller & Kerbow, 1993). Also, parents with more formal education are more likely to be involved in their children's schooling than parents with less education (Useem, 1992). Box 4.7 provides examples of ways that parents and students can get more help with homework.

More important than family demographics, however, is parents' and teachers' perceptions of the roles they should play in their children's education. If they believe that their involvement can affect their children's education, parents tend to be more engaged in schools and at home (Hoover-Dempsey, Walker, Jones, & Reed, 2000; Sheldon, 2002). Research also shows that when teachers and schools reach out to families and make them feel comfortable and capable of promoting their children's education, parents are likely to become more involved in helping their children succeed in school (Giles, 2005; Simon, 2000; Van Voorhis, 2000). Improved reading and math achievement, student attendance, and perceptions of the school climate by students and parents reflect this greater success (Haynes, Emmons, & Woodruff, 1998; Sheldon, 2003).

School Contexts

The transition from elementary school to middle school, discussed in chapter 2, is an important developmental context. Students experience a dramatic shift in context as they move from an educational environment that is reportedly more familiar, friendly, safe, and secure to one that is larger, more unfamiliar, and aloof. The following list describes six ways in which elementary schools typically differ from middle schools (Eccles, Midgley, Wigfield, Miller Buchanan, Rueman, et al., 1993). Middle schools are characterized by

1. A greater emphasis on teacher control and discipline and fewer opportunities for student decision making, choice, and self-management
2. Less personal and positive teacher-student relationships
3. An increase in practices such as whole-class task organization, between-classroom ability

BOX 4.7 ROADMAP TO SUCCESSFUL PRACTICE

Homework Help for Students and Parents

For the student who can't remember a homework assignment or is having difficulty with geometry, and for parents who may not be confident that their child does not have homework for the second week in a row, help is here. **Schoolnotes.com** is a free online service that, if adopted by the teacher, offers multiple services to students and their parents. Students can

- Email their teacher to seek clarification
- Get a list of suggested web sites for student research
- Utilize electronic flashcards
- Review their homework assignments
- Finish copying notes and other material from the chalkboard
- Receive recognition from teachers for their effort and success

Parents can

- Email the teacher with questions
- Review the homework assignments posted for their child
- Understand better the goals and expectations of the teacher

There are several advantages to this three-way communication system. First, it allows parents to more directly understand the academic expectations, thereby providing them with more information with which to assist their child. Second, teachers and parents can hold students more accountable for their learning. Third, if students miss school, this service provides an immediate opportunity for them to learn what they have missed and need to make up. The greatest disadvantage of this service is the need for Internet access and computer skills, neither of which is distributed equally across the population.

Source: Excerpted from *Meet Me in the Middle: Becoming an Accomplished Middle-Level Teacher* (pp. 172–173), by Rick Wormeli, 2001, Portland, ME: Stenhouse Publishers.

grouping, and public evaluation of the correctness of work

4. Teachers who feel less effective as teachers, especially with low-ability students
5. Classwork that requires lower-level cognitive skills than does classwork at the elementary level
6. Teachers who appear to use a higher standard in judging students' competence and in grading students' performance

Unfortunately, the structural, curricula, pedagogical, and personnel changes that take place in middle school do not match well with the developmental needs of a middle-school child. This mismatch may well lead to decreased motivation, interest in curricula, and self-esteem (Eccles et al., 1993; Pianta, Stuhlman, & Hamre, 2002; Erkut, Marx, Fields, & Sing, 1999).

In their report. *Turning Points: Preparing American Youth for the Twenty-First Century*, the Carnegie Council on Adolescent Development (1989) recognized the mismatch and made several recommendations for middle schools:

- Develop smaller "communities" or "houses" to lessen the impersonal nature of large middle schools.
- Lower student-to-counselor ratios from several hundred-to-1 to 10-to-1.
- Involve parents and community leaders in schools.
- Develop curricula that produce students who are literate, understand the sciences, and have a sense of health, ethics, and citizenship.
- Have teachers team-teach in more flexibly designed curriculum blocks that integrate several disciplines, instead of presenting students with disconnected, rigidly separated, 50-minute segments.
- Boost students' health and fitness with more in-school programs and help students who need public health care get it.

These recommendations have begun to be implemented in nearly 100 schools and 15 states. Results show significant improvements in reading, math, and language arts achievement (Carnegie Council on Adolescent Development, 1995).

Community Contexts

That the role of parents, teachers, and schools directly impact the cognitive development of children in middle childhood may be more obvious than how one's culture does so. An example of how culture may influence cognitive development—both directly and indirectly—is reflected in differences in science and mathematics performances on international skills tests among children in the United States, Japan, and China (Stevenson, Lee, & Stigler, 1986; Mathematics Achievement, 1996). The best-performing U.S. fifth graders (from Minnesota) scored lower on the mathematics test than the worst-performing Japanese classrooms and all but one of the Chinese classrooms.

Studies that have attempted to identify the cultural influences that contribute to these differences have isolated factors in both the home and school environments. For example, American children spend about half as much classroom time in academic activities as children in Japan and China. Teachers in the United States spend a much smaller proportion of their time imparting information than do Japanese or Chinese teachers (e.g., American teachers spend more time giving directions). Teachers in the United States also focus more of their instruction on skills and basic computation and less on higher-order conceptual thinking and problem solving. This emphasis is reflected as well in the textbooks used (Brenner, Herman, Hsiu-Zu, & Zimmer, 1999; Mayer, Sims, & Tajika, 1995). In addition, both the school day and year is much shorter in the United States, and American children spend less time on homework than Japanese or Chinese students (Chen, Lee, & Stevenson, 1996).

Researchers have also found differences in the values and communities that surround academic achievement and group relations, particularly in Japan (Lewis, 1995). Japanese attitudes toward achievement emphasize that success comes from hard work. In class, Japanese teachers focus on the children's engagement in their work rather than on discipline. Japanese teachers also delegate more classroom responsibility to children and support the development of peer groups as part of the learning environment. For example, classmates serve as resources in examining mathematical concepts. Teachers typically examine a few problems in depth rather than cover many problems superficially. Often, children's errors are used as learning tools for the entire class (Stevenson & Lee, 1990).

What makes the achievement of Japanese children so surprising to educators in the United States is that during early childhood, Japanese parents and teachers emphasize social development much more than cognitive development (Abe & Izard, 1999; Lewis, 1995). For example, Japanese parents emphasize empathy for others, and Japanese kindergartners spend four times as much time in free play as kindergartners in the United States. Japanese elementary schools also emphasize

Japanese students show academic superiority over Chinese and American students.

children's supporting each other and working together, not grades or test scores. Perhaps this attention to sociability allows children in elementary school to develop a sense of community in the classroom and encourages them to focus their attention on the subjects being taught (Lewis, 1995).

CHAPTER REVIEW

Piaget's Theoretical Perspective

- According to Piaget's theory of cognitive development, children learn by experiencing cognitive disequilibrium. Through the processes of assimilation and accommodation children add to schemata to enhance their understanding of the world.
- Children in middle childhood are in Piaget's stage of concrete operational thought that spans ages 7 to 11.
- Concrete operational thinkers are able to conserve because they can decentrate and can engage in reversible and transformational thinking. They can also understand hierarchical classification, seriation, time and space, and causality. Their thought is logical and based on concrete objects and experiences.
- Piaget's theory of cognitive development recognizes the equal contribution of biology and environment to the development of cognition. Piaget's theory best describes the development of problem-solving skills in a Western educational setting.

Sociocultural Perspective

- Vygotsky's theory of cognitive development proposes that cognition arises out of children's interactions with their environments and the expectations of their cultural contexts.
- Through zones of proximal development, scaffolding, and guided participation children are active participants in the learning process.
- Vygotsky's theory places much greater emphasis on the role of culture in a child's learning and is particularly useful as we gain more knowledge about the diversity of development.

Information-Processing Perspective

- The information-processing model uses the computer as a metaphor for learning and examines the role of attention and memory in how children process information.
- Children in middle childhood have increased short-term memory capacity, process information more quickly, exhibit improved attention, and use more sophisticated mnemonic strategies. Their knowledge base is more extensive, their skills become more automatic, and they have greater metacognitive understanding. All of these components add together for a more efficient, quicker, and sophisticated learner.
- The information-processing approach recognizes equal contributions from nature and nurture, with children's cultural experiences influencing the type and rate of skill development.

Language, Literacy, and Academic Learning

- Language development in middle childhood involves semantic, syntactic, and pragmatic usage.
- The three theoretical approaches presented in this chapter have direct application to the development of language, basic literacy skills, and mathematical understanding.

Cognitive Development in Context

- Parents can play a unique role in the academic lives of their children. Their contributions are most effective when they help their children organize their time and schedules, assist them in their homework, and discuss school-related matters with their children on a regular basis.
- The perceived academic and personal support of a school in middle childhood can affect the motivation and ability of children to succeed at the middle-school level.
- There are cultural differences in the expectations and support some cultures provide for their youth that can be realized in the home and classroom environment.

TABLE 4–3
Summary of Developmental Theories

Chapter	Theories	Focus
4: Cognitive Development in Middle Childhood	Cognitive-Developmental	How children develop thought and problem-solving skills through the processes of assimilation and accommodation that result in direct interaction with the environment
	Sociocultural	Development of thought through language development and the interaction with elders from one's culture
	Information Processing	How children process information by studying perception, memory, and knowledge and the factors that influence their development

KEY TERMS

Accommodation
Active rehearsal
Adaptation
ADHD
Assimilation
Attention deficit disorder
Automatic
Behaviorism
Classical conditioning
Class inclusion
Cognitive disequilibrium
Cognitive inhibition
Concrete operational stage
Conservation
Constructivist view
Cumulative rehearsal
Decentration
Digit span task
Egocentric
Encoded
Equilibration
Formal operational stage
Guided participation
Hierarchical classification
Hyperactivity
Inferencing
Invariant
Knowledge base
Long-term store
Metacognitive skills
Metamemory
Mnemonic strategies
Operant conditioning
Operation
Organization
Passive rehearsal
Phoneme
Pragmatics
Preoperational stage
Private speech
Reciprocal teaching
Rehearsal
Reversibility
Rote counting
Scaffolding
Schema
Selective attention
Self-monitoring
Semantic
Sensorimotor stage
Sensory register
Seriation
Shading
Short-term memory
Syntax
Transformation
Universal
Zone of proximal development

SUGGESTED ACTIVITIES

1. Conduct several conservation tasks with children of different ages. Table 4.1 provides you with an outline of several conservation tasks.
2. Observe children in a classroom, social gathering (e.g., Girl Scouts or Boy Scouts), after-school activity, athletic practice or event, a church service or church-related event, or at home. Record examples of scaffolding and guided participation. What is being learned? Who is teaching, who is learning, and what is the interactive process, if any?
3. On a set of index cards make two lists. One list should consist of the picture and printed word of 16 common items (e.g., ball, cup, shoe). The other list should consist of the picture and printed word of 16 common items that belong to four separate groups (e.g., four fruits, four pieces of clothing, four modes of transportation, and four tools). Using these two lists, monitor the types of rehearsal and organizational strategies different-aged children use as they try to remember the lists of unassociated and then associated items.
4. Ask different-aged children the following metamemory questions:

   "How many words out of 100 could you remember if you could study them only once?"

   "How would you remember to bring your skates to school tomorrow?"

   These questions assess a child's metacognitive skills.

RECOMMENDED RESOURCES

Suggested Readings

Beers, K. (2003). *When kids can't read, what teachers can do: A guide for teachers, 6–12.* Portsmouth, NH: Heineman.

Berk, L. E. (2001). *Awakening children's minds: How parents and teachers can make a difference.* New York: Oxford University Press.

DuPaul, G. J., & Stoner, G. (2003). *ADHD in the schools: Assessment and intervention strategies* (2nd ed.). New York: Guilford.

Rogoff, B. (2003). *The cultural nature of human development.* New York: Oxford University Press.

Wadsworth, B. J. (1996). *Piaget's theory of cognitive and affective development: Foundations of constructivism* (5th ed.). White Plains, NY: Longman.

Suggested Online Resources

Attention Deficit Hyperactivity Disorder. (2003).
http://www.nimh.nih.gov/publicat/adhd.cfm

Before it's too late: A Report to the Nation from the National Commission on Mathematics and Science Teaching for the 21st Century.
http://www.ed.gov/inits/Math/glenn/report.pdf

Bergen, D. (2004). *Play's Role in Brain Development.*
http://www.acei.org/brainspeaks.pdf

Children's Literature
http://www.scils.rutgers.edu/~kvander/ChildrenLit/index.html

Streaming Video of Piagetian Tasks
http://www.soe.jcu.edu.au/subjects/edl481/movies/

Suggested Web Sites

International Children's Digital Library
http://www.icdlbooks.org/

International Reading Association
http://www.reading.org/

The Montessori Foundation
http://www.montessori.org

National Commission on Mathematics and Science Teaching
http://www.ed.gov/inits/Math/glenn/index.html

National Forum to Accelerate Middle Grades Reform
http://www.mgforum.org

Suggested Films and Videos

Concrete operations. With David Elkind, Ph.D. (1993). Davidson Films (25 minutes)

Maria Montessori: Her life and legacy. (2004). Davidson Films (35 minutes)

Piaget's developmental theory: An overview. (1989). Davidson Films (25 minutes)

Scaffolding self-regulated learning in primary classrooms. With Elena Bodrova, Ph.D. and Deborah Leong, Ph.D. (1996). Davidson Films (35 minutes)

Vygotsky's developmental theory: An introduction. (1994). Davidson Films (28 minutes)

The wonder years, episode 25: "Math class" (1989). New World Entertainment

CHAPTER 

Affective Development in Middle Childhood

CHAPTER OBJECTIVES

After reading this chapter, students will be able to:

- Define affective development in middle childhood
- Summarize theories of middle childhood personality development
- Describe school-age children's achievement of self-competence, self-esteem, and self-efficacy
- Discuss current research on emotional understanding, temperament, and coping in school-age children
- Explain the contributions of family, school, and community contexts to affective development in middle childhood

Justin is the best video game player in the fifth grade. He plays every spare moment, even when he is supposed to be doing his homework. In fact, his mother is concerned that he spends too much time playing computer games. When he and his friends get together at the neighborhood arcade, the group of boys take turns, trying hard to beat Justin's best score. While they are playing, they talk about their day, their activities, and their accomplishments. "I scored three points more'n you!" "I got to the next level of the game!" No matter where they are—at the arcade, at school, or at each others' houses—Justin and his friends try to outperform each other.

Middle Childhood Affective Development

Affective development in middle childhood includes personality, emotional development, motivation, and self-esteem. School-age children acquire personal competencies through participation in academic, athletic, or artistic activities; emotional self-regulation; and a deepening sense of who they are and what they can achieve through serious effort and commitment. Middle childhood is a period of intense acquisition of physical and cognitive abilities and the application of these newly learned skills to concrete problems school-age children encounter in the real world.

In this chapter, we explore more deeply the nature of school-age children's competencies, motivations, and commitments. Children between ages 8 and 12 often may seem obsessed with one task while never completing another. They may seem unfeeling or uncaring when interacting with friends or family, yet show immeasurable empathy when thinking about feelings or emotions in particular situations. Often, they act like young children. At other times, they may seem emotionally mature beyond their years. Why are school-age children so self-absorbed, so intense, and usually so confident? To answer these questions, we must turn to theories of personality and motivation.

Our case study child Justin's perceptual-motor skills are exceptional. He could be great at sports like soccer or hockey. Justin just doesn't seem to care about anything except video games!

Theoretical Viewpoints

Personality psychology is the study of individual differences among people. Theories of personality offer us several alternative explanations for differences in personal characteristics, such as temperament, motivation, or self-esteem—to name just a few. Because the overarching perspective of this text is contextual, however, our task is to ask how personality differences in middle childhood interact with the demands of the school-age child's environment to result in dynamic and adaptive development.

For example, Justin's personal desire to build his skills on computer games bumps up against his family's demands for emotional availability. His sisters always seem to bother him when he's trying to concentrate. When he tells his sisters to go away, they complain to his father that he's being mean. How do personality theorists explain such interactions?

Two compatible theoretical approaches to the study of personality are **psychodynamic theories** and **humanistic theories**. What these two approaches have in common is a focus on the individual person—that is, on the *self*.

Personality Perspectives

Personality psychology has its origin in the psychoanalytic theory of Sigmund Freud. Freud (1959) developed a theory of human personality development based on biological drives and instincts—specifically, *pleasure*. In Freudian theory, the "self" resides in three major personality systems: the *id, ego*, and *superego*. The **id** represents the inner world of subjective experience (e.g., *Justin's enjoyment of video games*). The **ego**, or rational mind, represents the part of the personality that interacts with objective reality and struggles against the pleasure-seeking drives of the id to maintain self-control (e.g., *Justin's need to balance video-gaming with other activities*). The self is also constantly reminded by the **superego**, or conscience, to resist the pleasure-seeking drives of the id and to strive towards an **ego ideal**, or perfect self (e.g., *Justin's drive to record the highest score*). Through clinical work with adult patients over many years, Freud constructed a developmental stage theory, shown in Figure 5.1, that describes the gradual unfolding of personality from infancy through adolescence, driven by the gratification of pleasure.

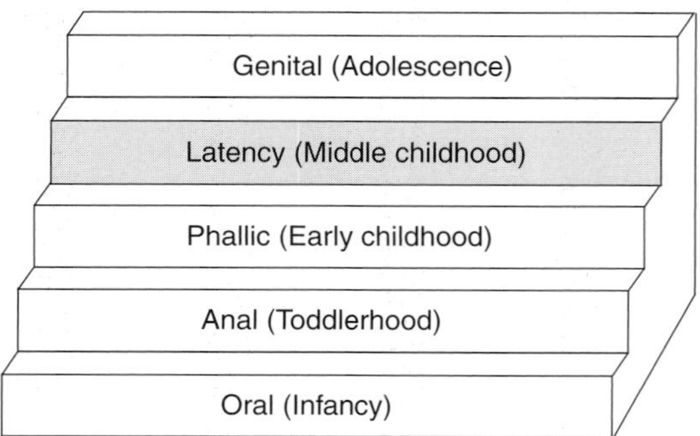

FIGURE 5.1 Freud's Psychosexual Stages
Freud's developmental stage theory characterizes middle childhood as a calm period when children show little or no sexual interest.

In Freud's (1959) developmental approach, infants fulfill their pleasure-seeking needs by nursing or sucking (oral stage); toddlers achieve emotional satisfaction by acquiring control over biological functions, such as toileting (anal stage); and preschoolers enjoy discovering and exploring their own bodies, often sexually through masturbation, or using scatological (i.e., bathroom) humor (phallic stage). In middle childhood, however, Freud believed that the child's sexual jealousy becomes dormant (**latency stage**). According to Freudian theory, the latency-age child does not show sexual interest again until puberty. Recently, however, researchers of school-age children's curiosity about sexuality and attention to sexualized content in society and the media have refuted Freud's proposed period of latency (see Strasburger & Wilson, 2002).

Many contemporary scholars have criticized Freud's psychosexual approach. For example, Freud described a period in early childhood in which young children "fall in love" with their opposite-sex parent to the point of jealousy or fear of the other (same-sex) parent, called the Oedipal complex, named for Oedipus, a character from Greek mythology who killed his father and married his mother (for girls, this is called the Electra complex after Agamemnon's daughter who revenged her father's murder by killing her mother). Cognitive developmental psychologists have offered an alternative explanation for the child's resolution of the Oedipal crisis by citing the preoperational child's emerging conservation abilities (described in chapter 3). The post-Oedipal child can now reason that since age and social roles (such as mother/son) are related, a little boy will never grow old enough to marry his mother (Watson & Fischer, 1980)! In addition, feminist psychoanalytic theorists have questioned the validity of the Oedipal/Electra crisis, claiming that girls as well as boys must develop and maintain a close emotional attachment to a nurturing parent (usually female) in order to assure the "reproduction of mothering" in successive generations (see Chodorow, 1999). (Attachment theory will be fully discussed in chapter 6.)

Psychosocial theory. Erik Erikson, a child psychoanalyst, revised and expanded Freud's theory to better account for the influence of society and culture on personality. In Erikson's (1950, 1968) *psychosocial* approach, the support and guidance of significant others influence the possible outcomes of normative developmental crises that occur at each of eight stages of the life span (see Figure 5.2). Erikson considered the primary psychosocial task of infancy to be the development of *basic trust*, or the belief that others will care for you. For toddlers, the normative task is to develop *autonomy*, or a sense of yourself as a separate individual, as in learning to walk without assistance. And in early childhood, the psychosocial challenge is to develop *initiative*, or a sense of curiosity, typically through play and experimentation with toys and other common materials.

In each of the psychosocial stages, if the individual is not provided adequate support for the appropriate tasks, a crisis may occur. For example, infants may develop a *mistrust* of others if they are ignored when crying, fearful, or hungry. Toddlers may experience *shame or doubt* in their ability to act independently of their caregivers, especially if they are criticized during their immature attempts at self-care (e.g., using the toilet). Preschoolers may experience *guilt* if their initiatives are criticized for not meeting adult standards (e.g., drawing a picture or dressing themselves).

In middle childhood, the school-age child's primary psychosocial task is to acquire a **sense of industry**, or the ability to work on a skill or project and to follow through over an extended period of time (e.g., art or science projects). However, school-age children who are not provided adequate encouragement for their "industriousness" may develop a sense of inferiority—especially if they were to try new skills or plans without adequate instruction or support, or if they were ridiculed for their failures (Erikson, 1950). A sense of industry *and* appropriate guidance from others are required to acquire the basic skills needed both in the wider culture in school settings, such as reading, writing, and computing. In fact, most school-age children seem to focus the majority of their time and attention on the acquisition of skills and the development of competence.

Recall our case study child, Justin. He really enjoys playing computer games. And he knows that he is good at it!

The industry stage in middle childhood contributes to the development of adolescents' emergent sense of identity. But first, we need to understand the development of the school-age child's sense of self.

Humanistic Perspectives

Personality theories that focus on the development of a positive sense of self are often termed ***humanistic***. Humanistic theorists draw our attention

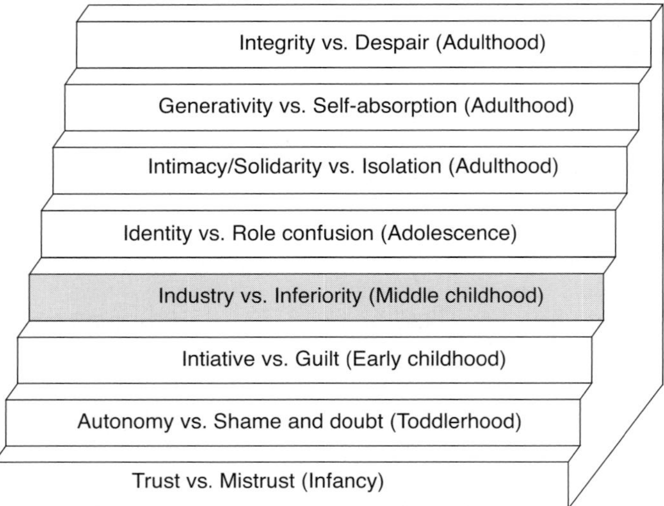

FIGURE 5.2 Erikson's Psychosocial Stages
Erikson's developmental stage theory characterizes middle childhood as a time of industriousness.

Source: From *The Young Child: Development from Prebirth through Age Eight* (4th ed.) (p. 256), by Margaret B. Puckett & Janet K. Black, 2005, Upper Saddle River, NJ: Merrill/Prentice Hall. Copyright 2005 by Pearson Education, Inc. Adapted by permission of the publisher.

to the basic human needs of individuals and to their emotional well-being. In contrast to psychodynamic theories that explain connections between the past and present (e.g., Freud) or the person and others (e.g., Erikson), humanistic theories focus on the person's current inner experiences. Among many other approaches, humanistic psychology includes theories of **self-actualization** and **person-centered experience**.

Self-actualization theory. Abraham Maslow (e.g., 1962, 1971) is often considered the founder of humanistic psychology. His book *Toward a Psychology of Being* (1962) outlined self-actualization theory. He proposed that all people try to satisfy five basic human needs:

1. Physiological needs
2. Needs for safety and security
3. Needs for love and belonging
4. Need for self-esteem
5. Need for self-actualization

Maslow (1962) theorized that these requirements form a **hierarchy of needs**, from physiological and safety needs that are essential for physical survival to those needs that are essential for psychological health, such as love, belonging, and self-esteem. Figure 5.3 depicts Maslow's hierarchy as a pyramid. This hierarchy of needs, according to Maslow, leads ultimately to **self-actualization**, or the drive to be your best and fulfill your potential.

Because they focus primarily on the individual, self-actualization approaches have been criticized for ignoring the social context of the larger environment or community (see Prochaska & Norcross, 2002). In his later writings, however, Maslow (1971) revised the hierarchy by adding a higher need beyond self-actualization: **self-transcendence**, or a drive toward life experiences that go beyond your personal goals and connect you with others or with universal human experience. Maslow (1971) called these transcendent "ways of being" **peak experiences**. During peak experiences, the person is totally absorbed—emotionally and intellectually—in an activity. Maslow believed that children are naturally capable of peak experiences, which occur frequently in the school-age years.

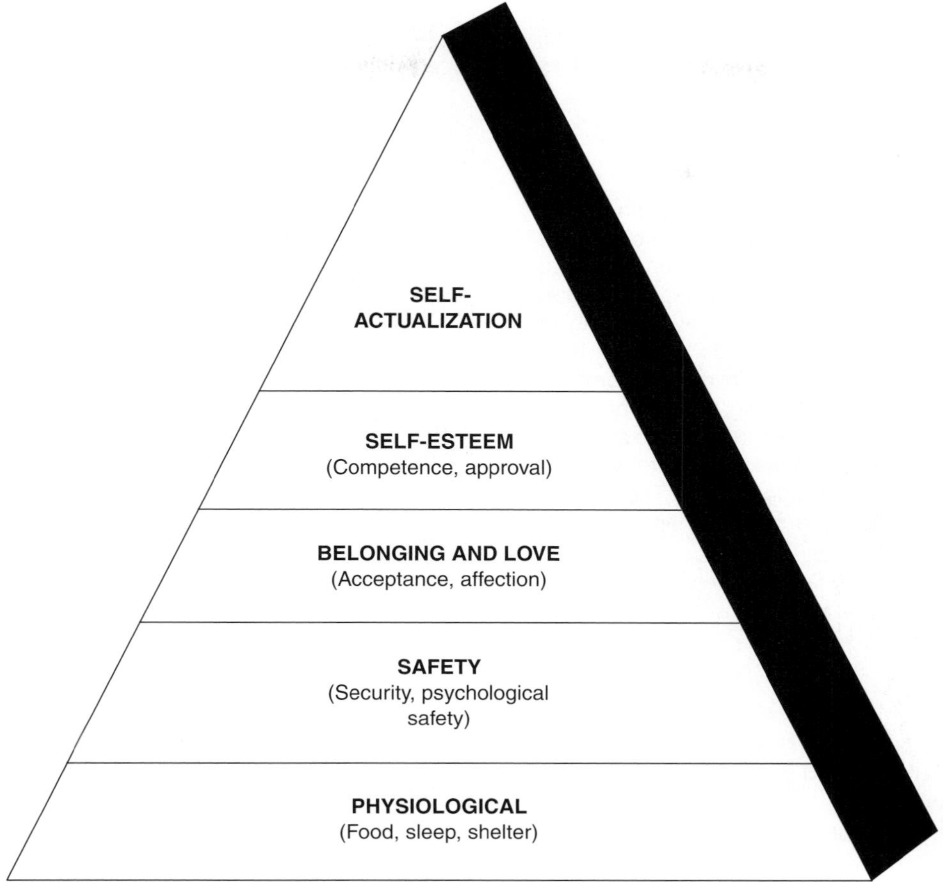

FIGURE 5.3 Maslow's Hierarchy of Needs
A sense of self-esteem, competence, and belonging are basic human needs according to Maslow.

Justin's computer gaming is an example of just such a peak experience. When Justin is "in the zone" he sometimes forgets to eat and doesn't even hear his mother calling him to the table for dinner!

The task of education, according to Maslow, is to cultivate self-actualization: "Even the difficult tasks of learning to read and subtract and multiply, which are necessary in an industrialized society, can be enhanced and made joyful" (1971, p. 188). These activities then become self-validating. Self-actualization theory was applied to education by Carl Rogers in his book *Freedom to Learn* (1969) (see Box 5.1).

Person-centered theory. According to Maslow's contemporary Carl Rogers (e.g., 1961, 1980), children are born with an innate capacity to experience the world. Although their reality is shaped in part by the environment (*in Justin's case by the virtual world of his game!*), Rogers (1961) believed that individuals respond not to an "objective" reality, but to the world as they *experience* it, an approach also called **phenomenological**. Person-centered psychologists, like Maslow and Rogers, assert that individuals positively value those experiences which they perceive as life-enhancing and negatively value those experiences which may limit personal

BOX 5.1 ROADMAP TO SUCCESSFUL PRACTICE

Freedom to Learn

In the beginning of his book on education, Carl Rogers (1969) quoted a diary sent to him by an elementary teacher. The sixth-grade teacher had decided to try a new, unstructured approach. She began by telling the class that they were going to experiment: The students could do anything they wanted, or nothing at all! Most children became so interested in what they were doing, they did not even go out to recess. By the end of the term, the students were described as having developed their own standards of behavior and living up to them. The teacher wrote, "I cannot explain exactly what happened, but it seems to me, that when their self-concept changed, when they discovered they can, they did!" (p. 22).

Rogers (1969) compared this teacher's classroom experiment to the tenets of a therapeutic encounter group: relatively unstructured and providing a climate of maximum freedom for personal expression, exploration of feelings, and interpersonal communication. Rogers's therapeutic goal was to promote optimal personal growth. In *Freedom to Learn*, he proposed a humanistic model for education, stressing that schools should encourage children to be dependable, realistic, self-enhancing, socialized, creative, unpredictable, and ever-developing.

Source: Based on *Freedom to Learn*, by C. R. Rogers, 1969, Columbus, OH: Merrill. Copyright 1969 by Charles E. Merrill Publishing Co.

growth (Prochaska & Norcross, 2002). These opportunities are called *self*-experiences in Rogerian theory.

In middle childhood, growth-enhancing opportunities often involve the development of skills and abilities that allow school-agers to succeed in a particular culture, what Erikson (1968) called *a sense of industry*. As school-age children acquire (or "own" in Rogerian terms) positive self-experiences, they begin to develop what Rogers called **positive self-regard**, or acceptance of themselves. School-age children also come to value those experiences that afford them opportunities for positive regard from others, such as parents, teachers, or peers. Taken together, these internalized notions of what is valued by self and others are called **conditions of worth**. (*Certainly, Justin's peers admire his computer skills.*)

Developmental psychologists have examined various aspects of self-worth in middle childhood as well as the motivation of school-age children toward self-actualization and competence. Practitioners have also applied Rogerian techniques to support children's affective development, using techniques described in Box 5.2.

When you were in middle childhood, who regarded you highly? Why? How did you know?

Development of Self-Understanding in Middle Childhood

Many related terms have been used by developmental, clinical, and personality psychologists to describe individuals' understanding and evaluation of themselves (for a recent review, see Jacobs, Bleeker, & Constantino, 2003). *Self-concept, self-competence, self-worth*, and *self-esteem* are the psychological constructs most typically employed in research and practice with school-age children—but they are not interchangeable! *Self-concept* and *self-competence* are cognitive constructions. **Self-concept** comprises your *knowledge* of who you are, and **self-competence** refers to what you can do. On the other hand, *self-worth* and *self-esteem* are affective terms. **Self-worth** is the *feeling* that you are valued for yourself as an individual person, reflecting the Rogerian notion of positive regard discussed in the previous section. More often, in educational or counseling settings, such self-evaluations are referred to as **self-esteem**.

These two approaches to describing the *self* (i.e., cognitive and affective) are derived from a distinction originally made by the psychologist and philosopher William James in 1890 (for a review of self-representations in children, see Harter, 1998). James (1890) distinguished between two fundamental aspects of the self: **the "I"** and **the "me."**

BOX 5.2 ROADMAP TO SUCCESSFUL PRACTICE

Rogerian Techniques

Rogerians believe that children internalize positive regard from significant others when they receive support, acceptance, and approval (Marion, 1999). In 1962, Thomas Gordon, a Rogerian therapist, developed a program of child guidance based on Carl Rogers's theory, called *Parent Effectiveness Training* (PET) and, later, a variation called *Teacher Effectiveness Training* (TET). Other, similar guidance programs include *Systematic Training for Effective Parenting* (STEP), developed by Don Dinkmeyer and Gary McKay (1989).

These programs are designed to teach adults to identify the owner of a problem before deciding how to deal with it. If the child, rather than the adult, owns the problem, the adult may ask, "You seem to have a problem. Do you need my help?" Active listening is a strategy that an adult trained in the Rogerian framework would use. For example, if a child were to say, "I hate school!" an active listener would say, "It sounds like you are upset about going to school. . . ." With this kind of feedback, the listener can be sure of what the child meant to say. Active listening involves simply reflecting the child's message and communicating acceptance of the child's feelings without judging or offering advice.

On the other hand, sending "I messages" is a communication strategy that one can use when the adult (not the child), owns a problem. "I messages" are clear declarative statements that do not accuse the child of causing the adult's feeling: "I feel frustrated when you play video games instead of doing your homework" or "I'm really proud of your hard work on this science project" (Marion, 1999, p. 265). Table 5.1 provides a list of terms that can be used to express a wide range of positive and negative feelings.

Table 5–1
Semantic Differential of Emotions
These opposing emotion terms can be useful to help school-age children identify their feelings in an "I" message.

Negative	"I feel . . . "	Positive
Sad		Happy
Angry		Glad
Scared		Brave
Ashamed		Proud
Anxious		Relaxed
Distrustful		Trusting
Worried		Confident
Disappointed		Satisfied
Calm		Excited
Confused		Sure
Hated		Loved
Disliked		Liked
Rejected		Accepted

Source: Based on *Guidance of Young Children* (pp. 260–265), by M. Marion, 1999, Upper Saddle River, NJ: Prentice Hall/Merrill. Copyright © 1999 by Charles E. Merrill Publishing Co.

The "*I*" refers to a subjective awareness of yourself as a person, sometimes referred to as the *self as subject or agent*. The "*me*" refers to facts that are objectively known about you, sometimes called the *self as object*. For James, a person must first construct an "I-self" in infancy, who then, throughout childhood and adulthood, constructs the "me-self" (for historical reviews, see Harter, 1992, 1999). These dual aspects of the self were subsequently elaborated by sociologists like Charles Cooley

(1902) and George Herbert Mead (1934), who described a "looking-glass self," the idea that you see yourself as others see you (cf. Harter, Stocker, & Robinson, 1996). Thus, the middle childhood period involves both the cognitive construction of self-concept, based on knowledge of your own skills and abilities (i.e., self-competence), and the affective construction of self-esteem, based on the internalization of positive regard from others (i.e., self-worth). See Figure 5.4 for a graphic example of how *competence* and *worthiness* intersect to form a matrix of meaning for individuals.

Justin, for example, knows he's skilled at video games and receives admiration from his friends, leading to his positive sense of self-worth.

Self-Worth

Self-Competence	Low self-worth (Self-Worth: Low)	High self-worth (Self-Worth: High)
High	Low self-competence/ High self-worth	High self-competence/ High self-worth
Low	Low self-competence/ Low self-worth	High self-competence/ Low self-worth

FIGURE 5.4 Self-Esteem Matrix
Self-esteem is based on school-age children's self-evaluations of their competencies and worthiness to significant others.

Self-Concept

Developmentally, self-concept progresses from the recognition in early childhood of concrete, observable characteristics (e.g., "I have red shoes") and overt abilities or activities (e.g., "I'm a good runner") to more of a focus in middle childhood on inner, psychological characteristics (e.g., "I'm a competitive person") and comparisons to others (e.g., "I scored more than you") (Harter, 1998). A common approach to the study of person concepts is to ask children for open-ended descriptions of themselves or others (Ruble & Dweck, 1995). In these studies, researchers have found that at age 8, there seems to be a change in school-age children's evaluation of enduring personal features rather than immediate behaviors (e.g., Livesly & Bromley, 1973; Peevers & Secord, 1973). Studies using hypothetical stories about target children who are, for example, *generous* or *athletic* have also found that children over age 7 were more likely to predict future behavior based on stable personality traits than were younger children, who more often based their evaluations on whether or not they liked the person or valued their behavior in the immediate context (Alvarez, Ruble, & Bolger, 2001; Ruble & Dweck, 1995).

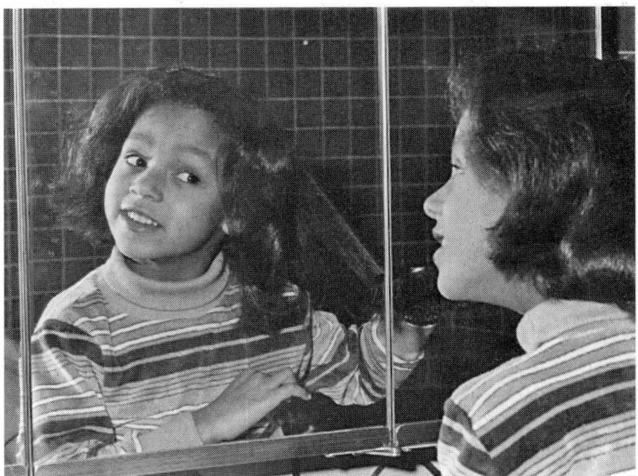

School-age children begin to reflect on how they are distinct from others.

Self-competence. The school-age years, beginning around ages 7 or 8, seem to be a "sensitive period" in self-concepts about competence (Ruble, 1987). A popular measure of self-perception is called the "What I am Like" scale that includes the following components of self-concept (Harter, 1982, 1985):

- Physical appearance
- Social acceptance
- Scholastic competence
- Athletic competence
- Behavioral conduct

Refer to Table 5.2 for sample items from this measure of self-competence. Researchers have consistently found that school-age children can successfully differentiate among these five areas.

Recent results of a longitudinal-sequential study of two cohorts of children from elementary school through high school revealed strong, positive increases in self-competence ratings between grades 3 and 6 for both girls and boys in the domains of scholastic competence, social acceptance, and athletic competence (Cole et al., 2001). However, in the domains of physical appearance (for both sexes, but especially for girls) and behavioral conduct (for both sexes, but more so for boys), self-ratings declined during middle childhood (Cole et al., 2001). In addition, behavior genetic researchers studying children from 10 to 18 have suggested that the stability of perceived scholastic and athletic competence as well as physical appearance and general self-worth may be genetically influenced (McGuire et al., 1999). (Behavior genetics was discussed in chapter 3.)

TABLE 5–2

Sample Items from the "What I am Like" Scale

This self-report instrument is used to assess school-age children's sense of self-competence.

Really True for Me	Sort of True for Me				Sort of True for Me	Really True for Me
		Some students feel that they are good at their school work	**BUT**	Other students worry about whether they can do the school work assigned them		
		Some students find it hard to make friends	**BUT**	For other students it's pretty easy		
		Some students do very well at all kinds of sports	**BUT**	Others don't feel that they are very good when it comes to sports		
		Some students aren't sure their teacher likes them	**BUT**	Other students are pretty sure their teacher likes them		
		Some students wish their physical appearance was different	**BUT**	Other students like their physical appearance the way it is		
		Some students feel that they are just as smart as other students their age	**BUT**	Other students aren't so sure and wonder if they are as smart		
		Some students have a lot of friends	**BUT**	Other students don't have very many friends		
		Some students wish they could be a lot better at sports	**BUT**	Other students feel they are good enough at sports		
		Some students feel that there are a lot of things about themselves that they would change if they could	**BUT**	Other students would like to stay pretty much the same		
		Some students are pretty sure of themselves	**BUT**	Other students are not very sure of themselves		
		Some students feel good about the way they act	**BUT**	Other students wish they acted differently		
		Some students think that maybe they are not a very good person	**BUT**	Other students are pretty sure that they are a good person		
		Some students are very happy being the way they are	**BUT**	Other students wish they were different		
		Some students aren't very happy with the way they do a lot of things	**BUT**	Other students think the way they do things is fine		
		Some students are usually sure that what they are doing is the right thing	**BUT**	Other students aren't so sure whether or not what they are doing is the right thing		

Source: From *The Self-Perception Profile for Children*, by S. Harter. Unpublished manual, Denver, CO. Copyright 1985 by Susan Harter. Reprinted by permission.

In middle childhood, a major advance in thinking about one's own skills is the ability to generalize across the competency domains. Note that school-age children's understanding of *multidimensional* self-concepts (i.e., constructed across several competency domains) can be explained by the shift to concrete operations, as was described by Piaget (and discussed in chapter 4). During middle childhood, school-age children acquire the cognitive conservation abilities that allow them to recognize a stable self despite differing self-presentations (i.e., transformations) in varied academic or social contexts. Neo-Piagetians (e.g., Fischer, Shaver, & Carnochan, 1990) and information-processing theorists (e.g., Case, 1991) have similarly explained the acquisition of other, higher-order generalizations, such as emotional dispositions and personality traits.

In the chapter case, for example, Justin is confident and self-assured, whether he is playing video games, doing classroom assignments, or just talking to his friends.

In these cognitive conceptualizations, a second major advance of middle childhood is the coordination of self-concept features into a representational *system* of the self. For example, the school-age child may construct the self-concept "smart" based on successful performance in both English and math or, conversely, "dumb" based on poor performance. The school-age child also has increasing tolerance for contradictory self-representations, sometimes called "bidimensional thought" (Case, 1991; Jacobs, Bleeker, & Constantino, 2003). For instance, a child who does well in language and social studies but receives low grades in math and science could construct a self-concept of "good at some things, bad at others," leading to both positive *and* negative self-evaluations (Harter, 1998). The extent to which these labels may become internalized as **personality *traits***, that is, as stable characteristics of the person, depends in part on the support and feedback provided by others. A balanced view of self, in which both positive and negative attributes are acknowledged, is fostered by comparing one's skills and abilities to those of others.

A third major advance in middle childhood is the ability of school-age children to compare themselves to others, called **social comparison** (Harter, 1998; for a review, see Frey & Ruble, 1990). In middle childhood, comparisons to peers become particularly salient as a means for the self-assessment of personal competence, compared to *temporal* comparisons (i.e., "how I am performing now compared to when I was younger") or to age norms (i.e., "what kids my age should be able to do") (Damon & Hart, 1988; Harter, 1998; Jacobs, Bleeker, & Constantino, 2003). Often, school-age children boast to others about their accomplishments (*remember Justin?*) with social comparisons leading to the "positive self-evaluations that typically persist at this age level" (Harter, 1998, p. 570). Consistent with Rogers's (1961) humanistic theory of positive regard from others, school-age children—like all humans—value affirming feedback from others.

By about 7 or 8, children spontaneously compare peers' performance to their own, although at first their perceptions may seem unrelated to normative judgments of competence by adults! As school-age children mature, the accuracy of their self-evaluations increases due to their increasing ability to incorporate environmental information and to make realistic social comparisons (Novick, Cauce, & Grove, 1998). For example, agreement between children's self-evaluations and teacher evaluations of their cognitive competencies, such as reading or math ability, increases between the third and sixth grades (Shirk & Renouf, 1992). Overall, self-competence ratings become increasingly correlated with the appraisals of others (Phillips & Zimmerman, 1990).

By the end of middle childhood, however, children are keenly aware of both the positive *and* negative consequences of overtly comparing themselves to others; older children are more likely than younger children to perceive such behavior as "showing off." Nevertheless, researchers have found that older children do not abandon their use of social comparison; they simply become more covert, using visual attention, such as watching or glancing, rather than direct questioning. This finding suggests that "children may learn that subtle comparison yields positive [affective] consequences while avoiding negative [social] consequences produced by more detectable forms of comparison" (Pomerantz, Ruble, Frey, & Greulich, 1995, p. 736).

What areas of competence did you excel in as a child? Did you compare yourself to your friends?

Self-Esteem

During middle childhood, school-age children readily construct affective judgments about their competencies, which is made possible by their ability to form a multidimensional self-concept and

Guideposts for Working with School-Age Children

- Help children to identify their skills in a variety of competence domains by talking about what they're good at.
- Because school-age children may hold both positive and negative self-concepts at the same time, support children by accepting their strengths and their limitations.
- Help children to realize that overt social comparisons may lead to negative interactions with peers by suggesting strategies that may help them to be more subtle, such as complimenting others' achievements.
- Encourage children to strive for self-competence rather than always comparing themselves to others.

to engage in social comparisons. Taken together, these self-evaluations contribute to a sense of **self-esteem**, or how they feel about themselves. By around age 8, children experience an important developmental shift in the relation between self-perceptions and behavior (Davis-Kean & Sandler, 2001). Assessing feelings of self-esteem is the most common way for researchers to measure positive or negative affect in school-age children (Anderson, 1992).

Self-worth. In research with both late-elementary and middle-school children, looking good (i.e., physical appearance) and being well liked (i.e., social acceptance) were most highly related to **self-worth**, or liking oneself (Harter, 1987). In addition, when researchers examined the relationship between peer approval and self-worth in sixth to eighth graders, they found support for the idea that peer approval may *precede* self-worth (Harter, Stocker, & Robinson, 1996). Despite their increasing self-competence, *how* school-age children think others see them and *how much* they are accepted are still important. (Peer relations in middle childhood are discussed in chapter 6.)

By middle childhood, most children have established a sense of their own *global* self-worth, or how much they are valued *as a person* (Harter, 1998). When researchers compared the degree to which self-worth is related to the five competency areas rated by elementary-age and middle-grades students on the "What I Am Like" scale, physical appearance was the area most highly related to self-worth for both age groups. Social acceptance, however, was more highly related for children in grades 6 to 8 than for elementary-age children. By comparison, preschool children can discriminate among four domains of competence (physical competence, cognitive competence, maternal acceptance, and social acceptance) but perceptions of their competencies do *not* include an overall sense of self-worth (Harter & Pike, 1984; Harter, 1996a).

These findings generally support Erikson's (1950) psychosocial theory that in middle childhood developing a sense of industry (vs. inferiority) is related to the development of competence. However, "the salience of competence as a developmental issue is at once both a source of self-esteem and a potential threat to one's self-worth. Thus, a . . . task in middle childhood involves coordination of one's sense of self-worth with one's emerging sense of competence" (Shirk & Renouf, 1992, p. 56). For example, when researchers compared school-age children's perceptions of their *competence* in different domains with their ratings of the *importance* of these factors, they found that all of the competency domains contributed to children's overall evaluation of their self-worth, but to differing degrees. Figure 5.5 illustrates how the discrepancies between competency ratings and importance ratings predicted self-esteem for two children with similar domain-specific self-competence profiles *but very different levels of global self-worth* (Harter, 1992).

Overall, researchers on self-competence have found considerable support for a hierarchical model (not unlike Maslow's hierarchy of needs) in which general self-concept is placed at the apex of an organizational chart with the competence domains nested underneath according to the importance an individual child may place on particular domains, as shown in Figure 5.6 (Harter, 1996b; see also Marsh & Hattie, 1996, and Eccles-Parsons et al., 1983). Because individual acts of competence occur in a socially constructed world, children—like adults—evaluate their accomplishments in terms of

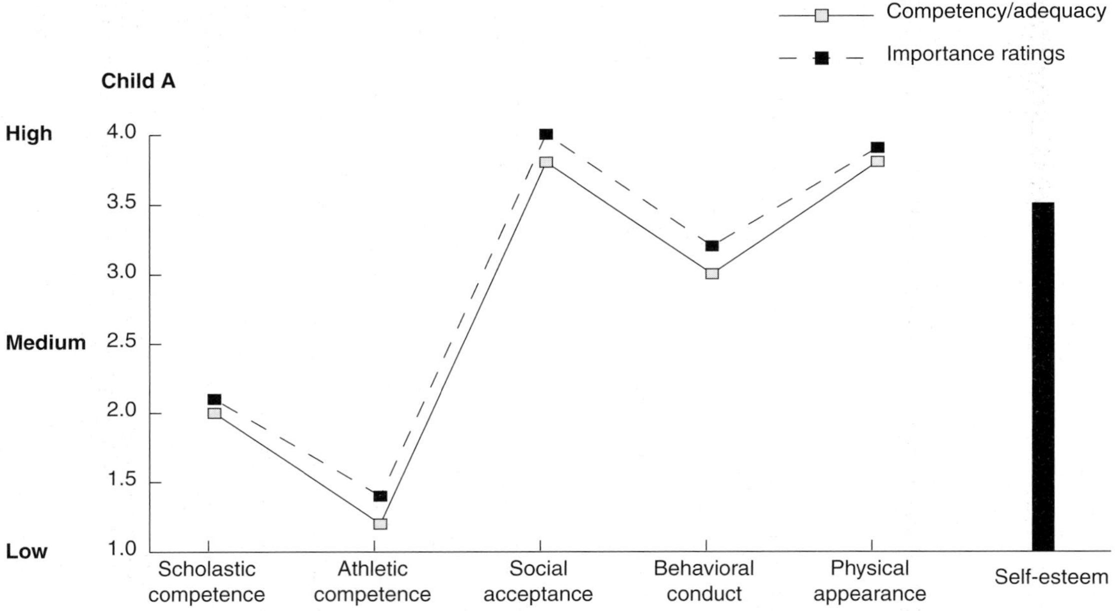

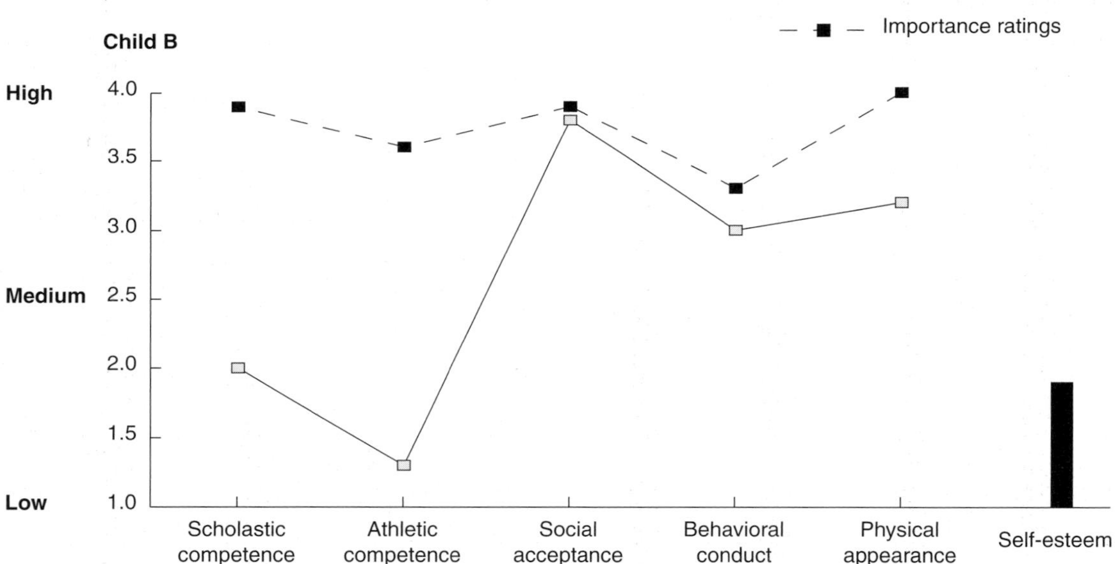

FIGURE 5.5 Importance Ratings of Competence as Predictors of Self-Esteem
Self-esteem is higher in a child (top graph) for whom competency judgments and importance ratings are closely related than a child for whom there is a greater discrepancy (bottom graph).

Source: From "Visions of Self: Beyond the Me in the Mirror," by S. Harter, 1992, in S. Harter, J. S. Eccles, & L. L. Carstensen (Eds.), *Nebraska Symposium on Motivation: Vol. 40. Developmental Perspectives on Motivation* (p. 108). Lincoln, NE: University of Nebraska Press. Copyright 1992 University of Nebraska Press. Reprinted by permission of the publisher.

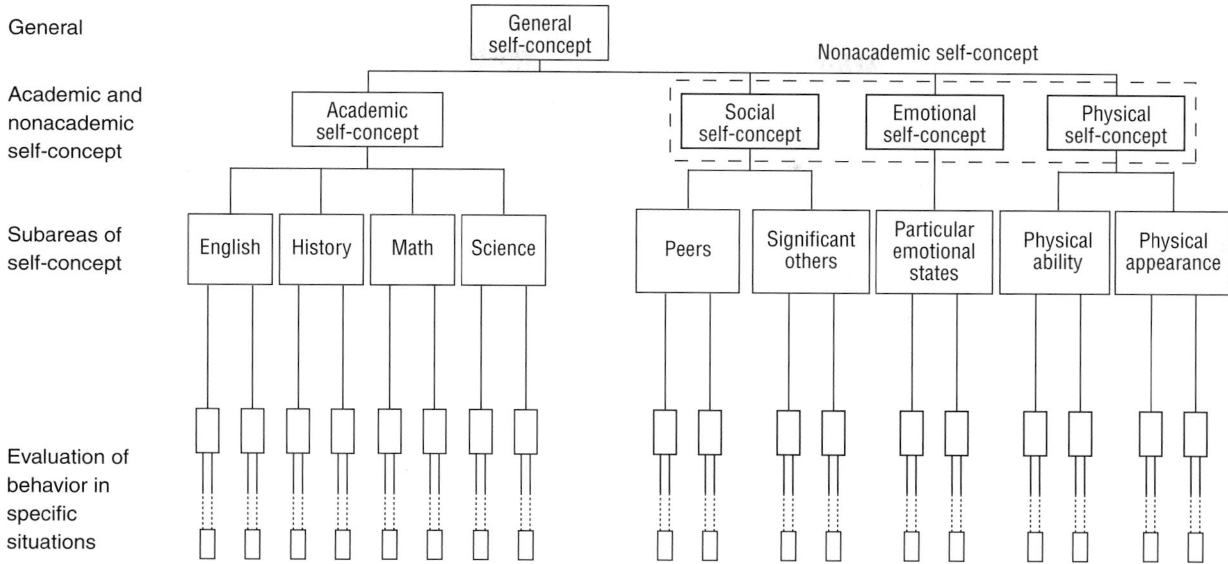

FIGURE 5.6 Self-Worth Hierarchy

Overall self-concept is composed of separate areas in a hierarchy from general to specific.

Source: From "Theoretical Perspectives on the Self-Concept," by H. W. Marsh & J. Hattie, 1996, in B. A. Bracken (Ed.), *Handbook of Self-Concept: Developmental, Social, and Clinical Considerations* (p. 54). New York: Wiley. Copyright 1996 by John Wiley and Sons. Reprinted by permission of the publisher.

social standards for what is valued or "worthy" (Mruk, 1995).

Did your parents, teachers, or friends value your performance in certain school subjects or extracurricular activities more than in others?

While some researchers have found that domain-specific ratings, such as academic competence, drop sharply during the transition between elementary and junior high or middle school (e.g., Simmons & Blyth, 1987), other researchers have found that the high self-esteem typically found in early childhood levels off in middle childhood. Still others have found that domain-specific self-evaluations may yet change as individual children change interests and activities during the school-age years (Jacobs, Bleeker, & Constantino, 2003). For example, in a study of individual differences in sixth-, seventh-, and eighth-grade children's ratings of perceived competence *after* the middle school transition, researchers found that about 50% of the children were stable over seven months in their self-competency ratings in the academic domain, while the other 50% of students either increased or decreased in their self-evaluations of academic competence (Harter, Whitesell, & Kowalski, 1992)!

The focus of most middle childhood school transition research has been on the systematic effects that changes in the educational environment have on school-age children (Harter, Whitesell, & Kowalski, 1992). In most school districts, a shift to junior high or middle school is associated with an increase in whole-group instruction, between-classroom ability grouping, and public evaluation of the correctness of work; changes such as these are likely to increase social comparison, concerns about evaluation, and competitiveness (Eccles, 1992). Researchers have found that the strain associated with both changes in the peer group and the demands of school work during the transition to middle school—although moderated by support from close friends, parents, and teachers—was related to lower feelings of competence and self-worth (Fenzel, 2000).

In addition, a large-scale longitudinal study of school-age children in family and school contexts found that junior high teachers also felt less effective, especially for low-ability students (Eccles, 1992). Figure 5.7 illustrates the effects on low-ability students' self-ratings of math competence. "High-to-high" students had a teacher who was rated as highly effective in both sixth and seventh grades; "high-to-low" students had a highly effective teacher in sixth grade but a teacher rated as less effective in seventh; "low-to-high" students had a less effective teacher in sixth but a highly effective teacher in seventh

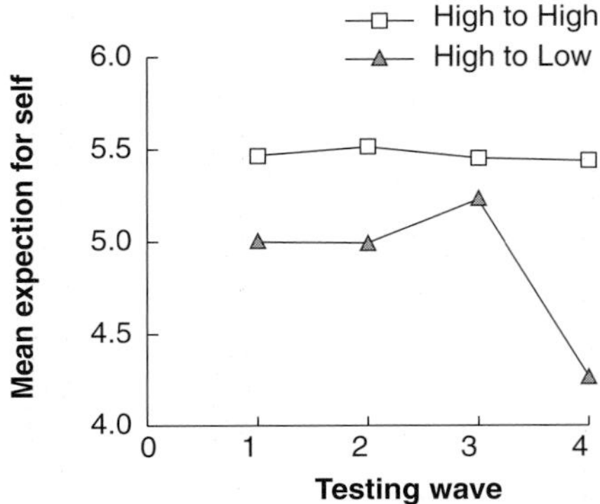

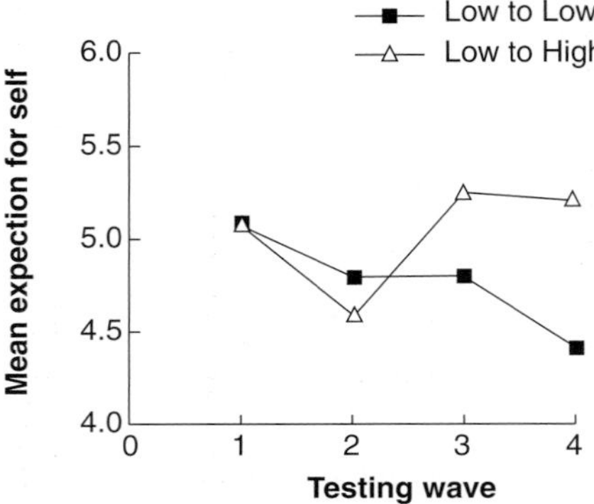

FIGURE 5.7 Expectations for Math Performance
Low-ability students expect to do worse across the transition to junior high school when they rate their teachers as less effective.

Source: From "School and Family Effects on the Ontogeny of Children's Interests, Self-Perceptions, and Activity Choices," by J. Eccles, 1992, in S. Harter, J. S. Eccles, & L. L. Carstensen (Eds.), *Developmental Perspectives on Motivation* (pp. 188–189). Lincoln, NE: University of Nebraska. Copyright 1992 University of Nebraska. Reprinted by permission.

grade; and "low-to-low" students had teachers rated as less effective in both grades.

Ideal self. One plausible explanation for such differing perceptions of their competence is that most school-agers can also create representations of what they may *want* to be, or feel that they *should* be, comprising an **ideal self** (Harter, 1998). The contrast between children's **real self** (i.e., how they perceive themselves to be, in actuality) and their ideal self (likely fostered by social comparisons) may lead to negative self-evaluations, especially if children experience repeated social or academic failures (Harter, 1998; see also Pomerantz & Ruble, 1997; Pomerantz & Saxon, 2001). The disparity between children's real and ideal selves is lower in middle childhood than in adolescence, however, presumably because school-age children are not yet abstract, hypothetical thinkers (Higgins, 1991; see also chapter 10 for a discussion of "possible selves" and "true vs. false selves" in adolescence).

Box 5.3 describes classroom strategies that teachers can use to support school-age children's sense of self-competence and self-worth. Interestingly, when sixth and seventh graders were asked (in small focus groups) to invent a program to enhance self-esteem for other students, they described activity-based (rather than didactic) programs individualized to the developmental level of the participants. They also stressed using locations and resources in the surrounding community that included older students, role models, and teachers (DuBois, Lockerd, Reach, & Parra, 2003).

Self-Efficacy

According to personality psychologists, all people have an innate drive toward mastery over the environment, referred to as **effectance motivation** (White, 1959) or **self-efficacy**, the belief in your own ability to solve a problem or accomplish a task (Bandura, 1981, 1990, 1994). Self-efficacy includes perceived abilities that are demonstrated in achievement behaviors in various school subjects (Schunk & Pajares, 2002). Self-efficacy has been linked to choice of tasks, effort and persistence, and achievement. Individuals' perceived self-efficacy is related to four determinants:

1. **Previous Performance.** Succeeding leads to a stronger sense of personal efficacy.
2. **Vicarious Learning.** Watching models succeed or fail on similar tasks teaches the task.
3. **Verbal Encouragement by Others.** Parents, teachers, or peers are the primary influences in middle childhood.
4. **Emotional Reactions.** Anxiety or worry may lead to a lower sense of self-efficacy (Bandura, 1994; see also Eccles, Wigfield, & Scheifele, 1998).

Much prior research has suggested that children's conception of their own ability tends to be more predictive of their achievement than are their conceptions of *others*' abilities (Pomerantz & Saxon, 2001). Recall that older children are able to make comparisons based on *ability*, such as "I'm

BOX 5.3 ROADMAP TO SUCCESSFUL PRACTICE

Teachers' Support for Competence

Teachers establish an overall context for competence by

1. **Employing Different Activity Structures in the Classroom.** Students working in small groups, in contrast to those working individually or in a whole-class activity, are more likely to seek assistance from other students as well as the teacher. During small-group activities, students work collaboratively with others, reducing the potential for social comparison.

2. **Fostering Help-Seeking Behaviors.** In classrooms that foster conversation, discussion, and inquiry, students feel free to seek help for tasks. With increased competence, children become more accurate in monitoring their knowledge states, more attuned to when help is necessary, and better at formulating questions when they encounter difficulties.

3. **Establishing Patterns of Discourse That Facilitate Intrinsic Motivation.** Teachers who provide feedback that focuses on specific strengths and weaknesses in performance rather than global assessments or normative grading tend to maximize intrinsic motivation and, as a result, support students' continued effort following failure.

4. **Helping to Socialize Students' Expectancies for Success.** Teachers who respond to requests for help with hints and contingent instruction, rather than direct and controlling answers, help students learn that problems and uncertainties can be tolerated—and perhaps even shared and transformed into intellectual challenges. Demonstrating to children that they deserve answers to their questions arguably helps children with a personal sense of empowerment.

Source: Based on "What Do I Need to Do to Succeed . . . when I Don't Understand What I'm Doing!?: Developmental Influences on Students' Adaptive Help-Seeking," by R. S. Newman, 2002, in A. Wigfield & J. S. Eccles (Eds.), *The Development of Achievement Motivation* (pp. 293–295), San Diego, CA: Academic. Copyright 2002 by Academic Press.

Guideposts for Working with School-Age Children

- Support their need to look good and be well liked because these are the most important contributors to school-age children's self-esteem.
- Compliment children's efforts because a competency domain that is highly valued by parents, teachers, or peers contributes more to overall self-worth than other skills.
- School-age children may need emotional support from parents and teachers since their positive self-evaluations often weaken across school transitions, especially to middle school or junior high school.
- Support children's changing goals by fostering the acquisition of new skills.
- Provide performance feedback to individual children rather than group evaluations or ability comparisons.

smart"; younger children make comparisons based on a specific performance, such as "I won" (e.g., Ruble, Eisenberg, & Higgins, 1994). In several studies designed to distinguish the multiple dimensions of school-age children's conceptions of their own competence, researchers have found that whether or not ability is thought of as stable over time may affect self-evaluations in middle childhood. Thinking of ability as stable is typically associated with placing importance on being *competent* (Pomerantz & Ruble, 1997; Pomerantz & Saxon, 2001). In addition, stability may be thought of in two ways:

1. **Stable to External Forces.** (e.g., teacher evaluations or peer comparisons).
2. **Stable to Internal Forces.** (e.g., trying hard or feeling competent) (Pomerantz & Saxon, 2001).

From fourth to sixth grades, children increasingly view ability as stable to external forces but decreasingly view it as stable to internal forces, meaning that their own abilities are more often defined by others. In addition, these school-agers are likely to perceive their failures as a negative predictor of their future performance and to experience lower feelings of self-efficacy (Pomerantz & Saxon, 2001).

Although children think of ability as stable at about 7 to 9 years of age, conceptions of ability as *capacity* do not emerge until about 11 to 13 years (Pomerantz & Ruble, 1997). Not surprisingly, children who think of ability as capacity seem to incorporate external feedback more readily, such as teacher evaluations, probably because they believe that they can acquire new abilities; they have *capacity*.

Consider Justin, a fourth-grader. He clearly thinks of his ability as constant, and that translates into a high level of perceived competence. Justin also receives positive regard from peers for his skill at progressing through the levels of the game easily. But at age 10, he is just beginning to conceive of his computer ability as capacity. What would this newly emergent understanding afford? If Justin were to believe in his own capacity, he may be more likely to incorporate suggestions from others or to utilize the embedded hints that were programmed into the game because he would believe that he could improve his score!

Research on academic achievement in middle childhood has demonstrated that when children believe that their ability is due to a fixed trait (e.g., intelligence) they tend to be more vulnerable in the face of difficulty or challenge because they may see failures as an indictment of their intelligence. In contrast, children who think that their ability is due to a capacity for learning tend to persevere despite failure experiences because they believe that the goal of learning is to increase their mastery (see Henderson & Dweck, 1990). In this manner, children's expectancies regarding their future performance may mediate their level of motivation for certain tasks, as shown in Table 5–3.

Achievement motivation. Heightened feelings of self-efficacy occur when an activity or task is seen as *intrinsically motivating*. **Intrinsic motivation** concerns the performance of activities for their own sake, in contrast to **extrinsic motivation**, in which activities are performed for an external reward. *Academic* instrinsic motivation involves enjoyment of school learning characterized by the following criteria:

- Mastery orientation
- Curiosity
- Persistence
- Task autonomy
- Seeking of challenge
- Desire for novelty (adapted from Gottfried, Fleming, & Gottfried, 2001)

Providing choices in curriculum assignments and projects, encouraging greater autonomy in classroom activities and homework, and decreasing extrinsic motivational practices, such as working for a grade rather than for the fun of learning,

TABLE 5–3

The Motivational Process Model

Whether school-age children think that their ability is fixed or changing has been shown to influence their goal orientation, confidence, and achievement.

Theory of Intelligence	Goal Orientation	Confidence in Ability	Achievement Behavior
Stable	Performance		Mastery oriented
• Intelligence is fixed	• To gain positive evaluation of competence	If high →	• Seek challenge • High persistence
			Helpless
		If low →	• Avoid challenge • Low persistence
Capacity	Learning		Mastery oriented
• Intelligence is malleable	• To increase competence	If low or high →	• Seek challenge • High persistence

Source: Based on "Motivation and Achievement," by V. L. Henderson & C. S. Dweck, in S. Feldman & G. R. Elliott (Eds.), *At the Threshold: The Developing Adolescent* (p. 310). 1990, Cambridge, MA: Harvard University Press. Copyright 1990 by Carol S. Dweck and Valanne Henderson. Adapted by permission.

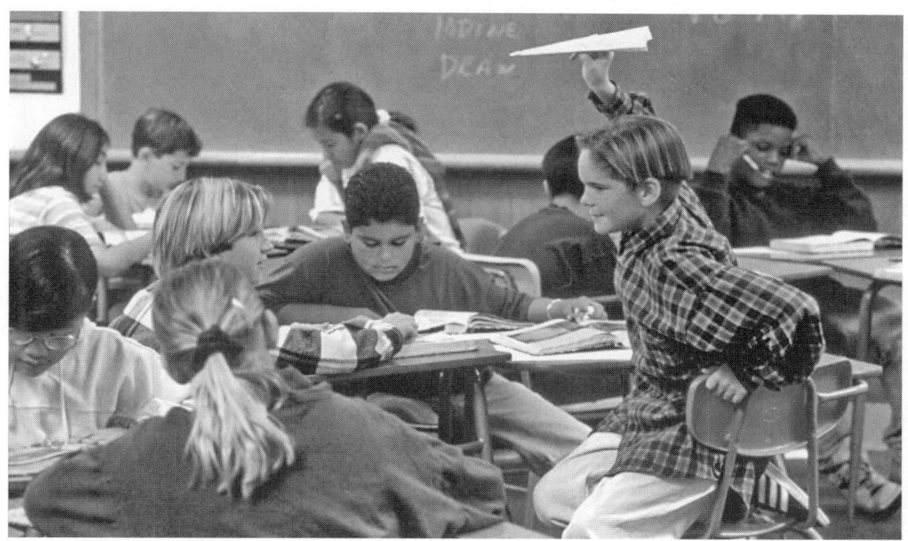

Children who are intrinsically motivated are often immersed in challenging activities.

have been suggested as ways to increase school-agers' intrinsic motivation (Gottfried, Fleming, & Gottfried, 2001). Examples of such teaching strategies are provided in Figure 5.8. In a longitudinal study of reading, math, science, and social studies, researchers found that academic intrinsic motivation at ages 9, 10, 13, and 16 predicted school-age children's academic motivation at subsequent ages in all domains (Eccles, Wigfield, & Schiefele, 1998).

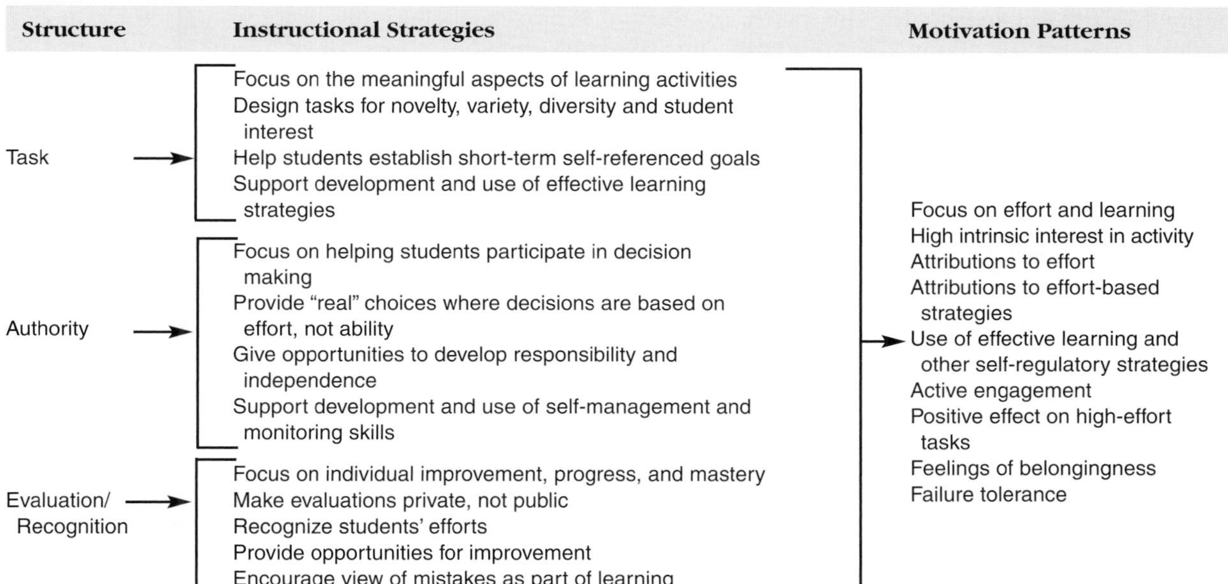

FIGURE 5.8 Instructional Strategies and Student Motivation

The instructional strategies teachers employ to teach a task, provide support, or evaluate students' work can influence school-age children's motivation.

Source: From "Motivation to Succeed," by J. Eccles, A. Wigfield, & U. Schiefele, in N. Eisenberg (Ed.), *Handbook of Child Psychology, Vol. 3: Social, Emotional, and Personality Development*, 1998 (p. 1065). New York: Wiley. Copyright 1998 by John Wiley & Sons Inc. Reprinted by permission of the publisher.

Intrinsically motivated activities are inherently pleasurable and offer the school-age child opportunities for what Rogers (1980) called "self-experiences" or Maslow (1987) called "peak experiences." Researchers who have studied school-age children's engagement in such activities have called them *"flow experiences"* (Csikszentmihalyi & Rathunde, 1992). **Flow** is characterized by

- Being immersed in an activity
- Merging actions and awareness (nothing else matters!)
- Focusing attention on a limited stimulus field
- Lack of self-consciousness
- Feeling in control of the environment and one's actions

Have you ever become so engaged in what you were doing that you lost track of time and place?

Box 5.4 illustrates the nature of a flow activity. Flow researchers have stressed that such activities must occur in a context of *self*-evaluation, rather than be driven by a concern with evaluation by others. For example, the discovery of problems that have the potential for creative solutions, such as a scientific question, is partly driven by an interest in the subject matter and partly by the intrinsic reward of finding a solution! These two factors have been integrated into a theory of motivation called **self-determination** (Deci & Ryan, 1985). Self-determination involves the degree to which school-age children experience themselves as autonomous, that is, as having choices as opposed to feeling pressured (Grolnick et al., 2002). Self-determination theory also suggests that a basic need for competence is the major reason why people seek out optimal stimulation and challenging experiences (Eccles, Wigfield, & Schiefele, 1998).

Self-determination theory may help to explain why Justin seeks out computer games to challenge his personal sense of efficacy. When he is playing, Justin appears to be in a state of "flow." He doesn't hear his mother calling. He doesn't care if his sister is waiting. Why? Flow happens because the video game provides a perfect opportunity for action that matches Justin's abilities.

Sometimes, however, *synergistic* extrinsic motivators, or extrinsic motivation "in the service of intrinsic motivation" may help to support a sense of competence or involvement with a particular task (e.g., teaching the skills necessary for solving a problem in a specific domain, or daily charting of a child's progress) (Collins & Amabile, 1999; see also Deci & Ryan, 1985). For example, helping children to develop short-term goals has been found to promote self-efficacy and intrinsic interest (Schunk & Pajares, 2002). A study of school-age children's interest in self-evaluative information about their math performance is described in Box 5.5.

BOX 5.4 ROADMAP TO UNDERSTANDING THEORY AND RESEARCH

The Psychology of Flow

In research conducted by Mihalyi Csikszentmihalyi (1990), flow experiences provided participants with a sense of discovery and creativity, pushed them to higher levels of performance, and led to altered states of consciousness. According to Csikszentmihalyi, flow transforms the self by making it more complex. Using the example of a tennis match, Figure 5.9 illustrates two theoretically important dimensions of flow experiences: challenges and skills, represented on the two axes of the diagram. The letter A represents a boy who is learning to play tennis. The diagram shows him at four different points in time:

A_1 When he starts playing and has practically no skills, he will probably be in flow if he just hits the ball over the net.

A_2 After a while, if he keeps practicing and his skills improve, he will grow bored just batting the ball over the net and will no longer feel in flow.

A_3 If he meets a more practiced opponent, he may feel anxiety concerning his poor performance and be out of flow.

A_4 If he improves his skills as a way to regain flow, he will have achieved a more complex experience than A_1 because it involves greater challenges and demands greater skill.

BOX 5.4 (CONTINUED)

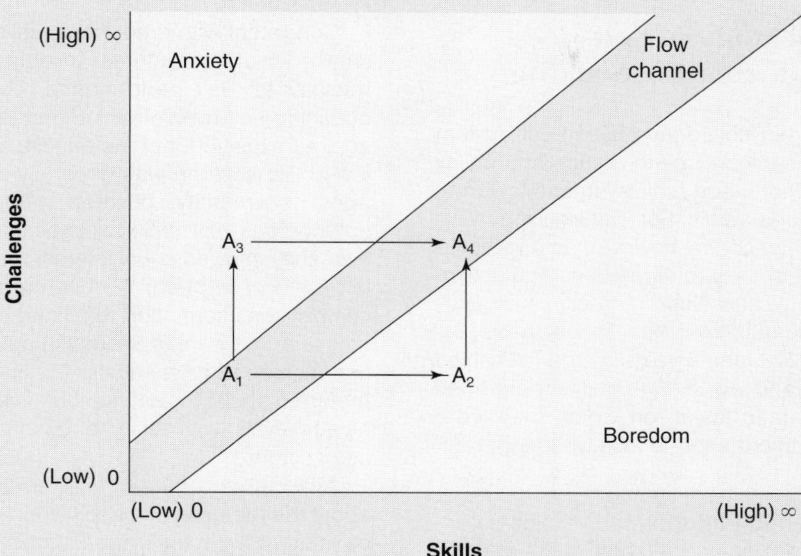

FIGURE 5.9 Creative Flow
Flow experiences intensify as optimal challenges and the skills to meet those challenges increase.
Source: From *Flow: The Psychology of Optimal Experience* (p. 74), by M. Csikszentmihalyi, 1990, New York: Harper & Row. Copyright 1990 by Mihalyi Csikszentmihalyi. Reprinted by permission of HarperCollins Publishers.

This final state (A_4), although complex and enjoyable, does not represent a stable situation. As he keeps playing at that level, either he will become bored by a lack of challenge or he will become anxious and frustrated by his relatively low ability. Flow theory predicts that the motivation to enjoy himself again will push him to get back into the flow channel, but now at a level of complexity even higher than A_4. According to Csikszentmihalyi (1990), this dynamic feature explains why flow activities lead to growth and discovery.

Not accidentally, video games are designed to keep track of players' progress and chart the highest scores.

Longitudinal research with children from grades 6 to 8 has also shown that increases in students' self-evaluations of their academic competence predicts increases in intrinsic motivation, while decreases in perceived competence predicts *declines* in intrinsic motivation. Students who show no change in perceived academic competence also show little change in their motivational orientation (Harter, Whitesell, & Kowalski, 1992). In addition, feeling positive toward school is associated with intrinsic motivation *but not with extrinsic motivation*.

Specific anxiety about school performance, on the other hand, is related to extrinsic motivation but not to intrinsic motivation. These findings suggest that an extrinsic orientation may be accompanied by pressure to perform and thus lead to feelings of anxiety, whereas an intrinsic orientation may lead to liking school (see Harter, Whitesell, & Kowalski, 1992; Isen, 2000). Generally, academic intrinsic motivation decreases slightly across the years from middle to high school. Similar findings have been reported for both American and European students, especially in the curriculum areas of science and math (Eccles, Wigfield, & Schiefele, 1998).

BOX 5.5 ROADMAP TO UNDERSTANDING THEORY AND RESEARCH

A Laboratory Study of Self-Evaluative Information Seeking

Diane Ruble and her colleagues hypothesized that changes in the meaning of performance and ability should lead to increased self-evaluation during the early school-age years. For children receiving relatively negative feedback, however, an approach-avoidance conflict is likely to emerge, such that low-ability children would show less interest in evaluative feedback than high-ability children. To test these predictions, children 7, 8, and 9 years of age (classified as high, medium, and low in math ability) performed a series of arithmetic tasks, on which they were given ambiguous information to look at during "rest" periods:

1. **Social Comparison Information.** Folders containing the outcomes on the same tasks of other children their age.
2. **Autonomous Evaluation Information.** Folders containing information on their own performance on previous tests and the answer keys.
3. **Control Condition.** The room also contained age-appropriate toys.

Consistent with predictions, children low in ability showed the *least* interest in obtaining information relevant to their performance. Overall, interest in obtaining self-evaluative information increased with age, as expected, but the relative "avoidance" of the low-ability children was generally consistent across ages. Low-ability children preferred social to autonomous information at ages 9 and 11. At 7, however, they showed equal interest (or lack of interest?) in both. For high-ability children, interest in social comparison information remained relatively constant across age, whereas interest in autonomous evaluation increased dramatically. Medium-ability children preferred social to autonomous evaluation folders at all age levels, with little change in evaluation interest across age.

Although the researchers could only speculate about the meaning of these trends, the findings were consistent with their predictions that information seeking would increase with age and that high- and low-ability children would show differential interest. A self-evaluation of high ability apparently allowed older children to shift toward emphasizing mastery rather than self-assessment goals, a shift with major implications for subsequent performance and self-esteem.

Source: Based on "The Acquisition of Self-Knowledge: A Self-Socialization Perspective," by D. Ruble, in N. Eisenberg (Ed.), *Contemporary Topics in Developmental Psychology*, 1987 (pp. 255–256), New York: Wiley. Copyright 1987 by John Wiley & Sons.

Guideposts for Working with School-Age Children

- Help children to recall their previous performance of a task when attempting it again and to analyze what they might do differently next time.
- Encourage children to think about their capacity for learning rather than about their ability as unchanging by reminding them of a past success.
- Since children's expectations of success or failure affect their motivation for the task, praise the effort rather than the outcome.
- Provide activities that are intrinsically motivating, such as art and music, and discourage working only for extrinsic rewards, such as grades.
- Stimulate flow experiences by allowing school-age children to work independently and to become immersed in activities that are engaging and challenging.

Emotional Development and Temperament

How do feelings, such as anxiety or pleasure, either hinder or support school-age children's growing sense of self-competence and self-worth? Emotion theorists have defined the concept of **emotional competence** as "readiness to establish, maintain, or change the relation between the person and the environment on matters of significance to that person" (Saarni, 1998, p. 238). This action-oriented definition varies from most definitions of emotional development because it does not refer to inner feelings (e.g., happy or sad), outer emotional expressions (e.g., laughing or crying), internal affective states (e.g., calm or nervous), or cognitive abilities (e.g., emotional intelligence). Instead, *emotion is described as a person-environment transaction* whereby emotional meaning is socially constructed in each interaction. Such an approach fits best with the contextual framework of this text.

Emotional competence refers to how children and adults understand emotions in the context of the social demands placed on them (Saarni, 1990, 2000, 2001a; Halberstadt, Dunsmore, & Denham, 2001). This approach to emotional development has been termed a *functionalist approach* to emotion in that it focuses on the function of emotion in human experience (Campos et al., 1994). As an example of functionalism, it also relates to our previous discussion of self-efficacy (see Saarni, 2001b); school-age children need to have the capacity and skills to regulate their own emotional experience as well as to respond to others.

In middle childhood, emotional competence involves the ability of school-age children to understand their own emotional states, to correctly interpret their affective experiences with others, and to control their emotions. This complex task of emotional self-regulation involves managing negative feelings, such as anxiety or frustration, and focusing on positive goals. For example, emotion-regulating skills allow school-age children to manage their emotions by seeking out rewarding experiences and avoiding unpleasant ones (Salovey, Bedell, Detweiler, & Mayer, 2000). In self-psychology, such self-control behaviors are commonly referred to as successful coping skills. In the school-age years, a variety of emotional coping strategies emerge:

- **Redefining a Situation.** Thinking "it's just a story" when listening to a sad account
- **Altering an Emotional Reaction.** Thinking happy thoughts in a sad situation
- **Dissociating Emotional Expression from Emotional Experience.** Expressing an emotion to others that is different from how you really feel
- **Relating Self-Regulation to Goals.** Thinking about the potential benefits of self-control versus the potential costs of losing control
- **Attributing Intent to Emotion.** Thinking "I shouldn't be mad at my little brother; he didn't mean it" (adapted from Thompson, 1998)

Emotional Intelligence

Emotion has been studied from a variety of theoretical frameworks (e.g., Fox, 1994). Psychoanalytic theorists have viewed emotions as instinctual physiological drives, such as fear, pleasure, or anger. Developmental psychologists have described emotion based on human infants' ability to discriminate among facial expressions of emotion, such as frowning or smiling. Cognitive psychologists have described emotion as the interpretation of affective experiences, such as feeling upset and deciding whether you are experiencing anger or sadness. Evolutionary psychologists have theorized that emotional behavior is an adaptive mechanism that serves to motivate all action, as in "fight-or-flight" decisions. Neuropsychological researchers have identified the areas of the brain that control emotions, such as the amygdala, and have proposed that emotions are neural events. Recently, social psychologists have proposed that individuals differ in how skilled they are at perceiving, understanding, and utilizing emotion information, called "emotional intelligence." The emotional intelligence framework is specified in Table 5.4.

Emotional intelligence is "the ability to perceive and express emotions, to understand and use them, and to manage emotions so as to foster personal growth" (Salovey, Bedell, Detweiler, & Mayer, 2000, p. 504). Researchers have operationally defined emotional intelligence by the specific competencies it encompasses, including:

- Ability to perceive, appraise, and express emotions accurately
- Ability to access and generate feelings when they facilitate understanding
- Ability to understand affect-laden information and make use of emotional knowledge
- Ability to regulate emotions to promote intellectual growth and well-being

How many of these competencies are present by middle childhood? To answer this question

TABLE 5–4

The Emotional Intelligence Framework

Emotional intelligence in middle childhood develops gradually as school-age children begin to understand and manage complex and conflicting emotions.

Perception, appraisal, and expression of emotion

- Ability to identify emotion in one's physical and psychological states.
- Ability to identify emotion in other people and objects.
- Ability to express emotions accurately, and to express needs related to those feelings.
- Ability to discriminate between accurate and inaccurate, or honest and dishonest, expressions of feelings.

Emotional facilitation of thinking

- Ability to redirect and prioritize one's thinking based on the feelings associated with objects, events, and other people.
- Ability to generate or emulate vivid emotions to facilitate judgments and memories concerning feelings.
- Ability to capitalize on mood swings to take multiple points of view; ability to integrate these mood-induced perspectives.
- Ability to use emotional states to facilitate problem solving and creativity.

Understanding and analyzing emotional information; employing emotional knowledge

- Ability to understand how different emotions are related.
- Ability to perceive the causes and consequences of feelings.
- Ability to interpret complex feelings, such as emotional blends and contradictory feeling states.
- Ability to understand and predict likely transitions between emotions.

Regulation of emotion

- Ability to be open to feelings, both those that are pleasant and those that are unpleasant.
- Ability to monitor and reflect on emotions.
- Ability to engage, prolong, or detach from an emotional state, depending upon its judged informativeness or utility.
- Ability to manage emotion in oneself and others.

Source: From *Emotional Development, Emotional Intelligence* by P. Salovey, 1997, New York: Basic Books. Copyright 1997 by Peter Salovey and David J. Sluyter. Reprinted by permission of Basic Books, a member of Perseus Books, LLC.

requires a description of the development of emotional understanding in the school-age years.

By middle childhood, children are able to reflect on their own emotional experiences and those of others. They readily understand that their cognitive appraisal of emotional states is important in determining how they feel about people or events. For example, although children under age 7 can describe how their parents might be proud or ashamed of their actions, not until about age 8 can children understand that they can be proud or ashamed of *themselves*, even in the absence of adult observation or feedback (Harter & Whitesell, 1989). They also believe that emotions are strongest immediately after an emotion-eliciting situation, and that they become weaker with time (Saarni, Mumme, & Campos, 1998).

School-age children are able to reflect on their own emotional experiences.

In addition, several studies have shown that school-age children understand that they can conceal their genuine feelings and instead display false emotional reactions, for example, pretending you like a gift so as not to hurt your grandfather's feelings (Saarni, Mumme, & Campos, 1998). Researchers have consistently found that schoolagers between ages 9 and 12, compared to younger children, can understand multiple, sometimes conflicting, emotions. For example, school-age children can be *happy* and *sad* at the same time when thinking about a divorce situation ("I'm glad I get to live with my dad, but I'm sad about not being able to live with my mom too"). However, not until age 12 can children think simultaneously about opposing emotions towards the same target ("I love my dad, even though I'm mad at him right now") (Whitesell & Harter, 1989). Children's book authors routinely focus on such middle childhood emotional conflict, as discussed in Box 5.6.

If the conflicting emotions are not equally *intense* or if the emotions are very *dissimilar*, children may experience conflict (Whitesell & Harter, 1989). For example, depression has been described by early adolescents as a mixture of sadness and anger. Researchers have found that emotions produce the greatest conflict (a) when a negative emotion is either equal to or more intense than a positive emotion *and* (b) when the two emotions are quite different, or even opposites (Harter & Whitesell, 1989).

For example, imagine that our case study child Justin is proud of himself for winning his game and simultaneously angry with his best friend for not congratulating him.

By the end of middle childhood, children are also better able to appreciate the psychological complexity of emotional experiences. For example, by age 11 they are more likely to attribute emotional arousal to internal causes rather than to external events. This emergent emotional understanding allows school-age children to predict the emotions of others without needing to observe facial or verbal cues, such as inferring how others may feel in competitive or conflictual situations even if they were not present (Thompson, 1998; see also Lightfoot & Bullock, 1990).

Consider that even if he had not seen Justin reach a difficult level of the video game, his friend could have inferred that Justin is pleased with himself.

BOX 5.6 ROADMAP TO SUCCESSFUL PRACTICE

Ramona and Her Father by Beverly Cleary

In an intriguing essay, Carolyn Saarni (1990) discusses a favorite children's book for middle childhood readers, *Ramona and Her Father* by Beverly Cleary (1975). When 8-year-old Ramona came home from school, no one was waiting for her. She pounded on the back door, and no one answered. She rang the front doorbell, but still no one came. The book's narrative describes her mixed emotions when her father finally arrived:

- Maybe her father was angry with her.
- Maybe he had gone away because she tried to make him stop smoking.
- Maybe he was worried about being out of work.
- Maybe she had made him so angry he did not love her anymore.

In her essay, Saarni points out Ramona's own emotional state (fear), the attributions she makes about her father's emotional condition (anger), personal information (unemployment), and her own relationship with him (love). When Mr. Quimby finally appeared, Ramona was simultaneously relieved, glad to see him, and angry. Saarni suggests that books such as the *Ramona* series can assist young readers to comprehend the emotional roller coaster that school-age children often experience by mirroring the internal processes they go through as they develop emotional competence.

Source: Based on "Emotional Competence: How Emotions and Relationships Become Integrated," by C. Saarni, in R. A. Thompson (Ed.), *Socioemotional Development: Nebraska Symposium on Motivation* (pp. 115–182). 1990, Lincoln, NE: University of Nebraska Press. Copyright 1990 by the University of Nebraska.

Guideposts for Working with School-Age Children

- Notice when children experience intense feelings of pride or shame about their own behavior or performance and be supportive.
- Accept that children may not wish to reveal their true feelings to you or to others, and do not pressure them.
- Help children recognize when they are experiencing simultaneous, conflicting emotions by using reflective listening.
- Model emotional competence by talking with children about your feelings using "I-messages."

Temperament

As children mature during middle childhood, they are better able to discern the emotional experience of others by combining situational cues with information about the target person's past experiences or their characteristic emotional reactions, often called *temperament* (Saarni, Mumme, & Campos, 1998). **Temperament** refers to a person's characteristic behavioral style based on individual differences in personality. People differ in the ways that they respond to people, tasks, and events. These predispositions in how they react to outside stimuli are usually quite stable across the life span and are generally considered a personality influence on the ability for self-regulation (Goldsmith, 1993; Bates, 2000). In middle childhood, temperament characteristics may include:

- Activity level
- Approach/extraversion
- Attention
- Fear
- Flexibility/adaptability
- High intensity pleasure
- Irritability
- Negative emotionality
- Positive mood
- Regularity of daily habits
- Shyness
- Task orientation/persistence (adapted from Capaldi & Rothbart, 1992 and Rothbart & Bates, 1998).

Temperament researchers have found that African American and European American 10- to 14-year-old boys were rated higher than girls on positive mood and activity level. On the other hand, girls were rated higher than boys on attention (Kim, Brody, & Murry, 2003). Other researchers have reported positive relationships between specific temperament characteristics (e.g., positive mood, approach, flexibility, task orientation, persistence, and regularity) and school-age children's self-reported competence (Windle et al., 1986). Figure 5.10 illustrates how individual temperament characteristics form three behavioral

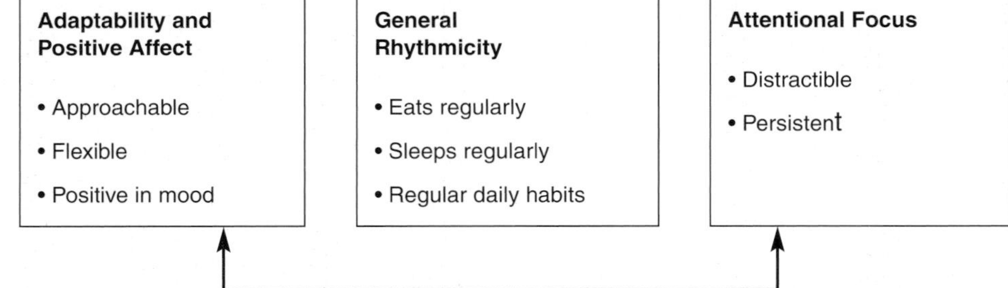

FIGURE 5.10 Dimensions of Temperament
Adolescents vary from high to low on these three interrelated dimensions that compose temperament.

Source: Based on "Revised Dimensions of Temperament Survey (DOTS-R): Simultaneous Group Confirmatory Factor Analysis for Adolescent Gender Groups," by M. Windle, 1992, *Psychological Assessment*, 4(2), 231. Copyright © 1992 by the American Psychological Association.

tendencies in adolescence. These categories of temperament have been used to assess (a) how adaptable and positive teens are, (b) how regular they are in their habits, and (c) how focused they are (Windle, 1992).

Temperament and emotions. Affective temperamental dispositions, such as a tendency to be easily angered, constitute individual differences in **emotionality** (Bates, 2000). Although school-age children may vary somewhat their reactions in various social contexts, such as the home or the classroom, researchers have found that overall they may possess a particular adjustment style that is predictable from certain aspects of temperament. For example, positive emotionality predicts higher well-being and social competence (Lengua, 2003). In addition, temperament traits measured in early childhood, such as negative emotionality, predicted more behavior problems in the school-age years (Bates, 2000; see also Menzulis, Hyde, & Abramson, 2003). Figure 5.11 illustrates a conceptual model of how temperament is related to emotion: The environment affects motivation and self-regulation, which in turn influence the child's emotions and subsequent actions.

Justin's temperamental characteristics of low distractibility and high task persistence positively influence his motivation to play video games and his ability to regulate his emotional reactions while he is engaged. In turn, he experiences emotional satisfaction or pleasure, which then leads to the action of pursuing his goal of mastery over the game.

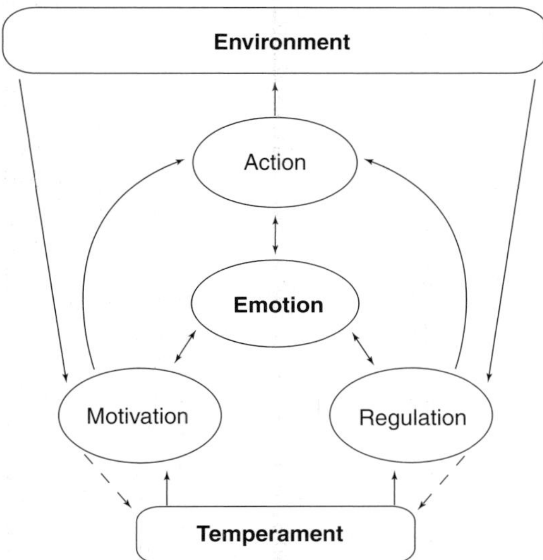

FIGURE 5.11 A Conceptual Model of Temperament as Related to Emotion
Differences in temperament influence school-age children's motivations, self-regulation, and actions in the real-world environment.

Source: From "Temperament as an Emotion Construct: Theoretical and Practical Issues," by J. E. Bates, in M. Lewis & J. M. Haviland-Jones (Eds.), *Handbook of Emotions*, 2nd ed. (p. 386). 2000, New York: Guilford. Copyright 2000 by The Guilford Press. Reprinted by permission of the publisher.

Temperament and self-regulation. Temperament is a useful construct for thinking about how school-age children develop different styles of coping with environmental demands (Saarni, Mumme, & Campos, 1998). When researchers examine *how* children respond emotionally to other people or events, they usually measure the intensity of their response, the level of their emotional arousal, the duration of their response, and their overall emotional tone. These measures comprise an estimate of emotionality, which is often used to infer temperament's influence on emotional experience (Saarni, Mumme, & Campos, 1998). For example, if a child typically responds with *high* emotionality, we can then examine how this temperamental trait may influence coping ability in different social situations. Individual differences in children's emotional competence, however, may influence their perceptions of emotional experiences or interactions with others. For example, a 10-year-old said about the loss of her allowance, "I wouldn't let my anger show, because my father doesn't like that and he would yell at me. That would only make things worse" (Meerum Terwogt & Olthof, 1992, p. 228).

How is your typical emotional response today similar to the coping style you remember using in middle childhood?

Although temperamental traits are sometimes seen as innate characteristics that are stable across childhood, successful outcomes also depend on developmental processes, such as increasing self-control, in varying social contexts

Guideposts for Working with School-Age Children

- Notice children's characteristic ways of responding to other people or events and provide them with the space and time they need to adjust.
- Provide suggestions to children for coping strategies that minimize negative emotions and avoid behavior problems, such as giving them choices of activities, work schedules, and partners.
- Encourage self-control by helping children think through the outcomes of their past responses to stressful situations.

(Rothbart & Bates, 1998). The benefits of self-control are most evident in studies of individual differences, which have found that higher self-control is related to better grades and greater social acceptance (Twenge & Baumeister, 2002). For example, in a study of children in grades 3 to 5, self-regulation predicted more active coping and lower adjustment problems (Lengua & Long, 2002).

Contexts for Affective Development

By middle childhood, most school-age children have formed beliefs about their own self-efficacy and self-control, in part based on their developing self-competence and on positive regard from others. Family, school, and community contexts, therefore, are important influences on affective development in middle childhood, especially on school-age children's emotional competence.

Family Contexts

School-age children's emotional competence is related to parents' feelings of self-efficacy (Coleman & Karraker, 2000; Grusec & Mammone, 1995). If parents think that their children are behaving appropriately, the adults are more likely to experience feelings of success in child-rearing, or high *parenting* self-efficacy. On the other hand, if parents think that their children's behavior is "out of control," they are more likely to feel unsuccessful as parents. Low self-efficacy parents often give difficult children inconsistent affective messages, for example, negative messages delivered in a teasing or joking style (Grusec & Mammone, 1995).

In addition, parents may make inferences, called **attributions**, about the causes of children's misbehavior, such as whether a behavior was intentional or accidental. The more intentional a negative behavior is seen to be, the more angry parents become. Such negative attributions may, in turn, influence parents' expectations about school-age children's future coping behaviors. If they view their children's behavior as intentional, parents are more likely to view problem behaviors as influenced by personality traits (internal attribution) than by environmental circumstances (external attribution) (for a review of parental attribution, see Grusec & Mammone, 1995).

Children's resistance to parental control has been shown to directly predict middle childhood behavior problems (Bates, 2000). When researchers examined the effects of family factors on fifth- and sixth-graders' self-control, they found that the quality of mother-child interactions and mothers' self-control were related to the self-control of the school-age children themselves, regardless of the number of parents or number of siblings in the home (Zauszneiwski, Chung, Chang, & Krafcik, 2002).

Many studies have demonstrated school-age children's self-esteem is enhanced by **authoritative parenting**, or parental practices that

- Offer acceptance, approval, affection, and involvement
- Treat the child's interests and problems as meaningful

- Give the child reasons for rules and enforce limits fairly
- Encourage children to uphold high standards of behavior
- Use noncoercive forms of discipline, such as denial of privileges
- Take into account the child's opinions in decision making (Baumrind, 1978; Coopersmith, 1967; Harter, 1996a)

Researchers have found that open communication between parents and children between ages 5 and 10 is related to lower levels of harsh discipline and higher levels of positive child adjustment in middle childhood (Criss, Shaw, & Ingoldsby, 2003). In addition, authoritative parenting that involves the granting of autonomy along with high levels of involvement and modest levels of structure from parents has also been associated with academic competence, general conduct, and positive psychosocial development in adolescence (Gray & Steinberg, 1999a). For African American, Asian American, and Latino American students, however, authoritative parenting is not as strong a predictor of academic success and other positive outcomes as it is for European Americans (Chao, 2001; Steinberg, Dornbusch, & Brown, 1992). (Diversity in parenting styles is addressed in more detail in chapter 11.)

School Contexts

In middle childhood, school environments exert demands on children that make self-evaluation more salient and peer comparison more likely, especially during the transition from elementary to middle school or junior high. Because they become much better at understanding, evaluating, and integrating the feedback that they receive from teachers and peers, older school-age children become more accurate in their self-assessments, which may cause some to become more negative (Wigfield & Eccles, 2002). In addition, gender differences in competency beliefs are common in school contexts, particularly in gender-stereotyped domains, such as math and science. For example, even after controlling for differences in actual skills, researchers reported that boys held higher competency beliefs for math and sports than did girls, whereas girls rated themselves higher in reading, English, and social studies than did boys (Wigfield & Eccles, 2002). In the Michigan Study of Middle Childhood, mothers who believed that males are better at math than girls also rated sons as having more math talent than daughters compared to those mothers who thought that boys and girls were equally likely to be talented in math (Eccles, 1992).

When social and economic conditions are prejudicial, even students with confidence in their competence may find that no level of effort will bring about desired results (Schunk & Pajares, 2002). For example, studies of the academic achievement of African American students in the United States often focus on achievement differences with the majority population of European American children. Most studies, however, have not adequately separated differences due to racial/ethnic culture and those due to social class, despite the fact that approximately one third of African American and Latino youth, compared to one quarter of Asian youth and only 5% of European American youth, are enrolled in the 47 largest urban school districts in the country. In these schools, 28% of families live at the poverty level, and 58% are eligible for free or reduced-cost lunches (Eccles & Wigfield, 2002).

Many minority students are vulnerable to social stereotypes of low achievement to the extent that mixed messages about their academic potential may undermine their achievement motivation and school success (Eccles & Wigfield, 2002; see also Graham & Taylor, 2002). Given these statistics, many comparative studies may really be assessing differences in school context, not student ability. In a recent study of seventh- and eighth-grade African American students, the percentage of middle-class neighbors and perceived academic abilities were linked to children's educational values, which in turn were linked to school effort (Ceballo, McLoyd, & Toyokawa, 2004).

More recently, research has included new immigrant populations, who are often doing better than both white middle-class children and third- or fourth-generation members of the same national heritage. In schools where students are successful, teachers establish *contextual* learning goals, such as mastery-oriented learning, autonomy of students, and feedback individualized to each child's intellectual development. In these environments, students are energized by challenges, persevere when facing difficulties, and request task-relevant information when they need help. In contrast, in schools that emphasize *performance* goals, students more often stress getting good grades, get feedback based on comparisons with classmates, and ask for the correct answers—if they ask for help at all (Newman, 2002).

Effective teachers are those who promote the best "fit" between a student's personal learning goals and the classroom environment, such as individual, whole-class, and small-group activities that allow for different types of student-teacher interaction. Patterns of classroom discourse that potentially facilitate help-seeking skills, such as fostering discussion, conversation, and inquiry, have been found to maximize students' expectancies for success (Newman, 2002). For example, if girls were to refrain from asking questions in math class so as not to appear "dumb," they would put themselves at a disadvantage consistent with gender stereotypes!

In a large cross-cultural study of German, Russian, Swiss, Czech, and American children between ages 7 and 13, girls who outperformed boys had stronger beliefs than did boys in their own effort, in being lucky, and in getting their teacher's help—although they tended to discount their own talent (Stetsenko, Little, Gordeeva, Grasshof, & Oettingen, 2000). In terms of academic achievement, late-elementary and middle-school girls in mixed-sex schools may often feel caught between a desire to achieve and concern about appearing too competitive or unattractive by gender-stereotypic standards of femininity. Ideally, single-sex classes may improve girls' achievement in math and science, a topic we discuss further in chapter 9 (AAUW, 1992; Orenstein, 1994).

How did the expectations between your school and home differ? Were your teachers from the same cultural, language, or ethnic group as you?

Community Contexts

From a contextual perspective, cultures influence affective development and the interpretation of the meaning of emotion in particular settings. To examine the cultural context of affective development we must ask four important questions:

1. Are emotions universal?
2. Does emotional development look different in diverse cultural contexts?
3. What role do cultural beliefs play in understanding emotional expression?
4. How do societies construct meaning from emotional experience? (adapted from Saarni, 1998)

Although basic human emotional experiences remain very similar across cultures, cultural variation in terms of how emotions are *valued* is best illustrated by cross-cultural research. For example, Utku Eskimos teach that anger is *always* inappropriate and immature (Nussbaum, 2000). Cultural beliefs and norms may also help us to interpret the acceptability of individual characteristics, such as temperament, and the behaviors that are permissible or expected in a given culture. For example, shyness, defined as an anxious reaction to novel or stressful situations, has different meanings in American and Asian cultures (recall the case study of Takuya from chapter 1). Because assertiveness and competitiveness are often endorsed in our individualistic American culture, a shy child in the United States may be more disadvantaged than a shy child in China or Japan, where inhibited behavior is seen by the more collectivistic culture as supporting group efforts (Rubin, 1998).

Cross-cultural studies also provide pertinent information about how children may develop emotionally in response to adults' repetition of the cultural discourse on child-rearing. For example, the appropriateness of emotional arousal (e.g., "we don't laugh out loud in church"), the degree of caregiver responsiveness to emotional distress (e.g., "you'll go to your room if you don't stop crying"), and norms for the regulation of emotion (e.g., "big kids don't have temper tantrums") may all affect children's opportunities to learn to cope successfully with emotion (Thompson, 1990).

Cultural competence is defined as respecting and responding positively to differences between groups and individuals of diverse backgrounds and traditions (Huebner, 2003). People from diverse cultures are likely to respond affectively in different ways both to the world around them and to their own feelings since they must ultimately make use of the vocabulary of emotions that the culture makes available (Hewitt, 1998). Cultural competence can be fostered by providing school-age children with opportunities for interracial and intercultural interactions. When youth do not live in culturally diverse neighborhoods, cultural competence may be encouraged by identifying the following resources (see Huebner, 2003):

- Community-based activities or volunteer projects in other parts of the community
- Church services in ethnically diverse neighborhoods
- Exchange programs with youth from other countries
- Pen pals or Internet buddies from other places

CHAPTER REVIEW

Affective Development

- Affective development is a domain of middle childhood development that includes self-understanding, emotional development, self-control, and motivation.
- School-age children acquire personal competencies through participation in academic, athletic, or artistic activities.
- School-agers apply their skills to concrete problems they encounter in the real world.

Theoretical Viewpoints

- Erikson believed that in middle childhood, the school-age child's primary psychosocial task is to acquire a sense of industry, or the ability to work on a skill or project and to follow through over an extended period of time. The opposite of a sense of industry is a sense of inferiority.
- Maslow believed that school-age children have an innate need to feel *self-actualized*, to do their best and fulfill their potential.
- Rogers believed that school-age children come to value those experiences that afford them opportunities for positive regard from others, such as parents, teachers, or peers. Taken together, these internalized notions of what is valued are called *conditions of worth*.

Self-Understanding

- Developmentally, self-concept progresses from a focus on concrete, observable characteristics, overt abilities, or activities to more of a focus on inner, psychological characteristics.
- School-age children can successfully differentiate among multidimensional components of *self-competence* (e.g., athletic, academic, social, behavioral, and physical appearance).
- During middle childhood, school-age children readily construct affective judgments about their competencies, made possible by the ability to conceive of a multidimensional self-concept and to engage in social comparisons. Taken together, these self-evaluations contribute to their sense of *self-esteem*, or how they feel about themselves.
- Most school-agers can also create representations of what they may *want* to be, or feel that they *should* be, comprising their *ideal selves*.
- Positive self-evaluations of academic competence in middle childhood predicts *increases* in school-age children's intrinsic motivation, which, in turn, may positively influence their academic achievement.

Emotion and Temperament

- Emotional competence refers to how school-age children understand emotions in the context of the social demands placed on them.
- In middle childhood, emotional competence involves the ability of school-age children to understand their own emotional states, to correctly interpret their affective experiences with others, and to control their emotions.
- By the end of middle childhood, school-age children are also better able to appreciate the psychological complexity of emotional experiences, such as having two conflicting feelings or purposely displaying false emotions.
- *Temperament*, or a person's characteristic behavioral style based on individual differences in personality, is sometimes seen as stable across childhood but may also be affected by development in middle childhood, such as increases in self-control.

Affective Development in Context

- Parents can enhance school-age children's academic motivation by providing them with an intellectually stimulating home environment and offering support for homework and school projects.
- Effective teachers promote the best "fit" between a student's temperament and the classroom environment.
- Cultural competence can be fostered by providing school-age children with opportunities for interracial and intercultural interactions.

TABLE 5–5

Summary of Developmental Theories

Chapter 5 presented three theoretical approaches for examining school-age children's self-understanding, sense of competence and self-worth, and emotional development.

Chapter	Theory	Focus
5: Affective Development in Middle Childhood	Psychoanalytic	Process of individuation as the basis for personality development and establishing a sense of self
	Psychosocial	Period of industry vs. inferiority in which a major task is the acquisition of competence and the avoidance of failure
	Humanistic	Self-actualization and personal growth as well as the importance of positive regard from others in "being human"

KEY TERMS

Achievement motivation
Authoritative parenting
Conditions of worth
Cultural competence
Effectance motivation
Ego
Ego ideal
Emotional competence
Emotional intelligence
Emotionality
Extrinsic motivation
Flow experiences
Hierarchy of needs
Humanistic theories
I, Me
Id
Ideal self
Intrinsic motivation
Latency stage
Peak experiences
Personality traits
Person-centered theory
Phenomenological
Positive self-regard
Psychodynamic theories
Real self
Self-actualization
Self-competence
Self-concept
Self-determination theory
Self-efficacy
Self-esteem
Self-evaluation
Self-transcendence
Self-worth
Sense of industry
Social comparison
Superego
Temperament

SUGGESTED ACTIVITIES

1. Visit a recreation center or playground and observe a group of school-age children. Describe the activities you see that could be characterized as helping to develop their sense of competence.
2. Interview a middle-school teacher about the school curriculum. How does he or she evaluate the students? Do students usually work alone or in groups? Ask about possible effects of social comparison on academic motivation. What does the teacher do to enhance students' intrinsic motivation?
3. Interview a school-age child about his or her sense of self-competence. In what domains (e.g., athletic, academic, social, emotional, cultural) does the child feel most effective? Ask if those areas are important to significant others, such as parents, teachers, or peers.
4. Analyze your own family-of-origin experiences. What cultural messages did you receive from family members or significant others that increased or diminished your sense of self-worth?

RECOMMENDED RESOURCES

Suggested Readings

Csikszentmihalyi, M. (1990). *Flow: The psychology of optimal experience.* New York: Harper and Row.

Goleman, D. (1995). *Emotional intelligence: Why it can matter more than IQ.* New York: Bantam.

Hewitt, J. P. (1998). *The myth of self-esteem: Finding happiness and solving problems in America.* New York: St. Martin's.

Orenstein, P. (1994). *SchoolGirls: Young women, self-esteem and the confidence gap.* New York: Anchor.

Rogers, C. R. (1969). *Freedom to learn*. Columbus, OH: Merrill.

Suggested Online Resources

Bright Futures Family Tip Sheets: Middle Childhood (2001). http://www.brightfutures.org/TipSheets/pdf/mc_color.pdf

The Effects of Reward Systems on Academic Performance (2001). http://www.nmsa.org/research/res_articles_sept2001.htm

The Importance of Emotional Intelligence during Transition into Middle School (2002). http://www.nmsa.org/research/res_articles_jan2002a.htm

Promoting Involvement of Recent Immigrant Families in their Children's Education. http://www.gse.harvard.edu/hfrp/projects/fine/resources/research/golan.html

Suggested Web Sites

Active Listening: A Communication Tool http://edis.ifas.ufl.edu/BODY_HE361

Family Involvement Network of Educators http://www.gse.harvard.edu/hfrp/projects/fine.html

Media Awareness Network http://www.media-awareness.ca/english/parents/video_games/concerns/violence_videogames.cfm

Succeeding in School http://genesislight.com/web%20files/index.html

Suggested Films and Videos

The development of self (1991). Insight Media, Inc.

Emotional intelligence (1997). Insight Media, Inc.

Boys, girls, and games (2001). Insight Media, Inc.

Erik H. Erikson: A life's work (1991). Davidson Films

Flow (2003). Insight Media, Inc.

Middle childhood social and emotional development (1997). Magna Systems, Inc.

The wonder years, episode 13: "Coda" (1989). New World Entertainment.

CHAPTER 

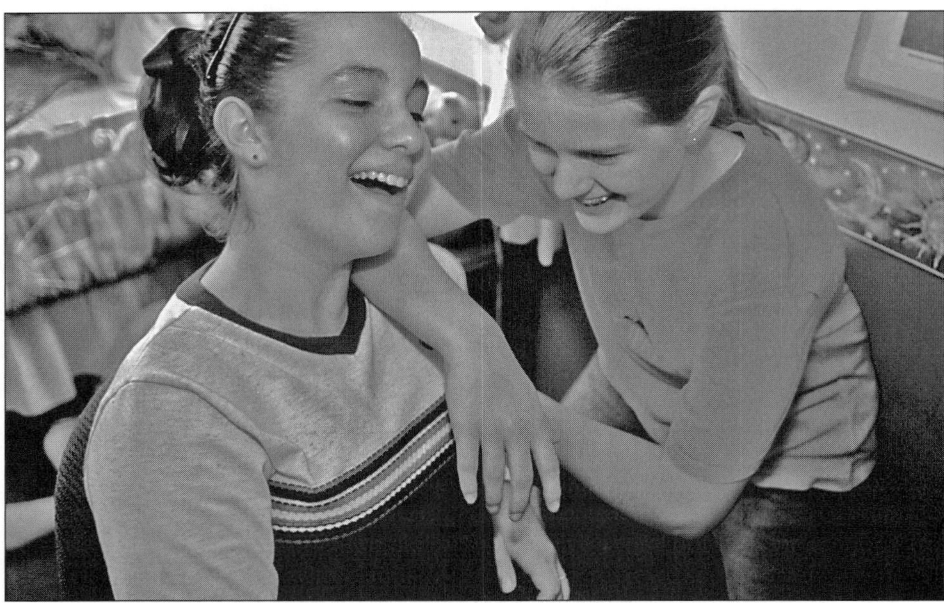

Social Development in Middle Childhood

CHAPTER OBJECTIVES

After reading this chapter, students will be able to:

- Define social competence in middle childhood
- Summarize theories of social cognition
- Describe the development of social perspective taking and moral reasoning in school-age children
- Examine the influences of friendship and popularity on school-age peer relations
- Discuss current research on school-age children's prosocial and aggressive behavior
- Explain the contributions of family, school, and community contexts to social development in middle childhood

Alesha, age 11, is just settling into her new middle school. The first two months have been stressful—learning the new building, meeting new people, changing classes five times a day—but she has survived with the help of her two closest friends from elementary school. She has just started to feel adventurous enough to meet some new people. Choir, last hour of the day, is one of the few places she goes without her best friends, Jennifer and Kelly. There is one nice girl, Mandy, and within a few days they seem like old friends—they know about each others' secrets and most embarrassing moments—and Mandy invites Alesha over after school.

MIDDLE CHILDHOOD SOCIAL DEVELOPMENT

Building on an understanding of *self* (discussed in chapter 5), school-age children can move beyond themselves and on to relations with others. **Social development** in middle childhood includes acquiring social skills, increasing interpersonal understanding, refining concepts of friendship, and using moral reasoning to guide social interactions with family and peers. **Social competence** is defined as the ability to interact effectively with others, based in large part on school-agers' maturing emotional understanding and self-control.

School-age children's social and moral development allows relationships built during middle childhood to pave the way for adolescent dating experiences and social identity (discussed in chapter 11). How do children make friends and influence other people? Do school-age children really disregard their parents in favor of peers? Does peer pressure influence children's moral reasoning? Understanding these complex social interactions requires that we examine theories of social cognitive development and social learning.

THEORETICAL VIEWPOINTS

The study of social development in middle childhood involves **social cognition**, or the understanding of others, such as friends or family. Social cognitive development also influences school-age behaviors, such as the imitation of peers. Social cognitive theories provide explanations of how social interactions (behaviors) help to construct our understandings of social relationships (cognitions). Specifically, the study of middle childhood social development utilizes three related theories: social learning theory, social information-processing theory, and social theories of mind.

Social Learning

Bandura's (1971) **social learning theory** states that we learn social skills and behaviors by observing the behavior of others. Also called "observational" learning, social learning offers a straightforward way to understand school-age children's readiness to copy the attitudes and actions of highly respected peers and positive (or sometimes negative) role models. Social learning theory draws heavily on the principles of behaviorist theory, especially reinforcement. However, in *social* learning theory, **vicarious reinforcement** is the cognitive process through which people of all ages formulate expectations about the desirability of certain behaviors by seeing the results of others' behaviors—even before any direct action is taken (Crain, 2000).

When Mandy invites Alesha over after school, the girls go upstairs to Mandy's bedroom. Alesha is completely surprised when Mandy pulls an aerosol can out of her dresser drawer. Alesha and her friends have always been antidrug, and she tries to stay away from the obvious drug users in the school. But Mandy seems like a really normal person, someone Alesha liked!

Social learning theory takes into account a person's perceptions and cognitions of their own and others' behaviors and their positive or negative consequences. Social learning, therefore, goes far beyond a direct, linear connection between an environmental model (stimulus) and a person's behavior (response) as described by classical learning theory (Muuss, 1996). Social, or observational, learning is divided into four sequential processes:

- **Attention.** To imitate a model, individuals first have to pay attention to it. Models are attractive because they have status, power, or influence, such as media celebrities or older peers.
- **Retention.** Because individuals often imitate models some time after they have observed them, retention abilities allow them to remember the model's features and behaviors.
- **Motor Reproduction.** From observation alone, individuals can learn a behavior pattern, but to successfully copy it may require skill acquisition and practice.
- **Reinforcement.** If individuals successfully perform according to a model that they have observed, the behavior may be self-reinforcing. They may also be vicariously reinforced if the model's behavior has been positively rewarded by others.

In a more recent revision of his original theory, Bandura (1987) proposed a contextual model called **reciprocal determinism** that includes a bidirectional relationship among three interacting factors, as shown in Figure 6.1. In the revised theory, now known as **social *cognitive* theory**, to reflect the influence of people's own thoughts on

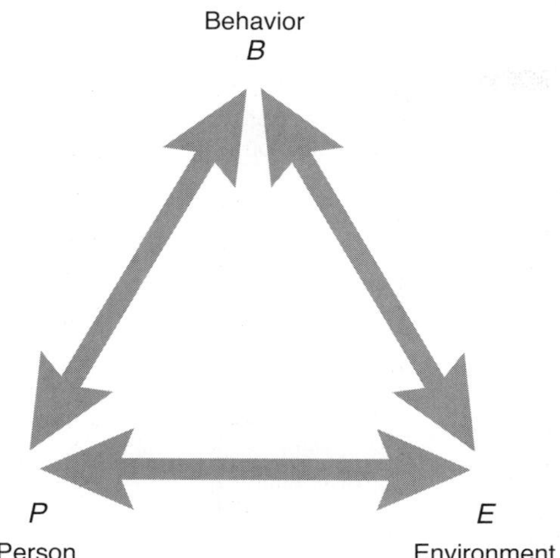

FIGURE 6.1 Reciprocal Determinism in Social Cognition
Social understanding in middle childhood is determined by mutual, ongoing interactions between school-age children, their social environment, and their interpretation of their own and others' behaviors.

their behavior, three determinants reciprocally affect each other:

- **E = Environment.** The external, social environment that provides the stimulus for learning
- **B = Behavior.** The learner's response to the environmental stimulus
- **P = Person.** The personality, cognitive ability, motivation, and beliefs of the person

In recent explanations of social cognitive theory, Bandura (2001) has called attention to **agency**, or a person's ability to choose among several alternative courses of action: "Agency refers to acts done intentionally" (p. 6). In addition, people evaluate the effects of their actions on others.

Alesha, for example, ponders the possible result of rejecting Mandy's offer: losing a new friend; or of rejecting her parents' values: disappointing them.

This agentic perspective on social cognition, therefore, requires a further understanding of precisely how school-age children may make decisions about the appropriateness and desirability of certain social behaviors.

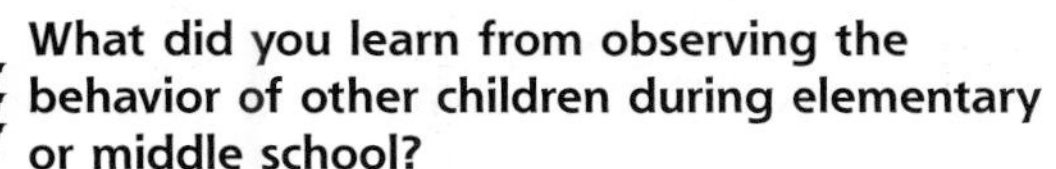
What did you learn from observing the behavior of other children during elementary or middle school?

Social Information Processing

In recent years, **social information-processing** models of children's social behavior have emerged to describe the specific cognitive mechanisms school-age children use to process social information (for a review, see Crick & Dodge, 1994). From this perspective, when children are faced with a social situation, they engage in six mental steps as they make a decision how to act:

1. **Encoding of Internal and External Cues.** Selectively attending to filtered, personalized memories of similar situations (e.g., *the intent of a peer with whom the child is interacting, for example, Mandy*).
2. **Interpretation and Mental Representation of Cues.** Analyzing the events that have occurred in the interaction and making an inference about the perspectives or intentions of others (e.g., *"She is lowering her voice; she seems secretive"*).
3. **Clarification of Goals.** Selecting a desired outcome for the current situation (e.g., *"I want to be her friend"*).
4. **Construction of a Response.** Accessing possible responses from memory or constructing novel ones and evaluating possible outcomes (e.g., *"I could ask her what's wrong so she'll see that I want to be her friend, or I could just wait and see what she does next"*).
5. **Response Decision.** Selecting the response with the most positive outcome based on the degree of confidence (i.e., self-efficacy) they have in their own ability to enact the response (e.g., *"I don't want to embarrass her; I'll wait until she shares her secret with me"*).
6. **Behavior Enactment.** Evaluating the peer's response and reenacting steps 1–5, if necessary, with different strategies (e.g., *"I'll continue playing as if nothing is wrong"*).

Often children engage in multiple social information-processing steps at the same time. For example, they may interpret cues while encoding them or consider the meaning of their partner's behavior while accessing other possible responses. Overall, however, the information-processing components, or six mental steps, of this problem-solving process have been predictive of children's social adjustment (Crick & Dodge, 1994). The model has also been used to teach school-age children successful ways to work together to influence social situations.

Describing the ways in which school-age children's mental processes are influenced by their

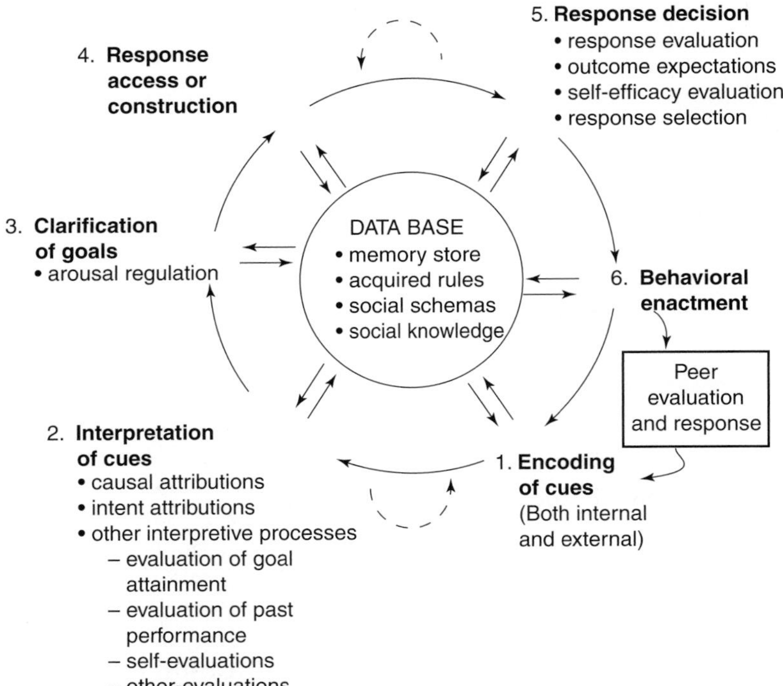

FIGURE 6.2 Social Information-Processing Model
School-age children go through six steps of information processing to make sense of peer interactions.

Source: From "A Review and Reformulation of Social Information-Processing Mechanisms in Children's Social Adjustment," N. R. Crick & K. A. Dodge, 1994, *Psychological Bulletin*, 115, p. 76. Copyright 1994 by the American Psychological Association. Reprinted by permission of the author.

interactions with others is a major contribution of social information-processing research. Social information-processing theorists have proposed that social experiences may lead to the generation of mental structures that are remembered in the form of social knowledge. These stored memories form a "database" that influences children's future processing of social cues, as diagrammed in Figure 6.2. In other words, children mentally represent social behavior and its outcomes, store these representations in memory as part of their general social knowledge, and use this information to guide their future actions with others (Crick & Dodge, 1994).

This theoretical perspective on social cognition is also likely to lead to a better understanding of *how* children learn about themselves and others in a social context. During middle childhood, most children become increasingly capable of representing, organizing, and interpreting social information.

Alesha thinks to herself, "Only losers use drugs." In essence, children create their *own* theories about people and how they may be likely to act in social situations, called *theories* of mind.

Social Theories of Mind

Recall that social cognition means knowing about people and how they act (Flavell & Miller, 1998; see also Shantz, 1983). Even very young children can "theorize" about others' mental states to predict and explain behavior, a process called **social theories of mind**. For example, beginning around age 4, a child may start to perceive that two people's conflicting representations of the same event caused them to behave differently (Flavell & Miller, 1998). Children's theories of mind help them to understand not only simple links between a psychological cause and a behavior but also a larger system of interconnections among the environment, behavior, and the person (recall Bandura's reciprocal determinism: $E \times B \times P$).

A theories-of-mind perspective contributes the idea that *children themselves* construct theories as they interact with others. For example, during middle childhood, children come to understand the reciprocal nature of friendship based on an emerging understanding that their friends can "think about each other's beliefs about each other." By adolescence, most children will come to understand that all such social knowledge is *situated* in the personal and sociocultural context of relationships (Flavell & Miller, 1998). This evidence has implications for both basic research (i.e., understanding how peers influence social development) and for applied research (i.e., helping children with poor peer relations) (Ladd, 1999). School-age children's development of social knowledge about others is also central to studies of social perspective-taking and moral reasoning.

Social and Moral Understanding in Middle Childhood

School-age children's social interactions are an important developmental context for the growth of interpersonal understanding and of moral reasoning. Although these research foci each provide a slightly different "lens" to use in examining school-age social-cognitive understanding, together they can provide a clearer picture of middle childhood than when viewed separately. For example, how do developmental psychologists explain school-age children's struggles to understand the nature of interpersonal relationships and to recognize the perspective of others? How might such mental representations affect their ongoing moral conduct?

Why does Mandy believe that she can predict what Alesha will think (e.g., "getting high is cool") or do (e.g., agree to huff)? Mandy's theory could be based on social interactions with Alesha and memories of her past behavior, or it may be Mandy's own vicarious desire. Mandy decides to share her secret with Alesha.

Interpersonal Understanding

Because understanding others is necessary for success in social interactions, the study of children's *social perspective-taking ability* has been a major focus in research on social development (Cillessen & Bellmore, 2002). **Social perspective-taking** involves a gradual, qualitative progression from egocentric thinking to an eventual understanding of mutual perspectives within a social system, such as a family or peer group (Durkin, 1995).

In research on social perspective-taking, children are typically asked to respond to a series of social dilemmas in which conflicting feelings may occur (Selman, 1980). For example, one dilemma involves a hypothetical child, Holly, who is confronted with an urgent choice between climbing a tree to save her friend's kitten and honoring a promise to her father not to climb trees. The children in the study were asked a series of social perspective-taking questions, such as "Does Holly know how her friend feels about the kitten?" and "How will Holly's father feel if he finds out that she climbed the tree?"

In early childhood, most interviewees focused on saving the kitten by climbing the tree and assumed that everyone would feel the same way; however, by middle childhood, most children could take other people's perspectives into account (i.e., the father's concern for Holly's safety as well as her friend's distress) and considered other solutions to the dilemma, such as calling the fire department (Selman, 1980).

Recall from chapter 4 that in early childhood the majority of children are *egocentric*, failing to distinguish between their own perspective and that of others. Between ages 6 and 8, however, most children begin to engage in *social informational role-taking*. For example, researchers have found that 6- and 7-year-olds may not take into account others' perspectives, relying instead on their own subjective experiences (i.e., a first-person perspective). These children are aware that other people may have a view of events that differs from their own, but still can focus on only one perspective at a time.

By age 8, children begin to understand others' feelings and intentions—not just their own. Between ages 8 and 11, most children can put themselves in another's place and reflect on another's intentions and behaviors, called *reciprocal role-taking* (i.e., a second-person perspective). By around age 12, most school-agers can appreciate the fact that people often differ in their views of the same experience. Between ages 12 and 14, however, children can also view themselves from the perspective of a third person, called *mutual role-taking*. Nevertheless, until adolescence most children do not take into account the social conventions that govern behavior regardless of the partners' viewpoints in a particular situation, called

TABLE 6–1

Stages of Social Perspective-Taking

School-age children can understand how they are seen by a friend but are just beginning to develop an understanding of how others might view their friendship.

Developmental Levels (Approximate Age of Emergence in Reflective Social Thought)	Levels of Social Perspective-Taking Used to Analyze the Understanding of Interpersonal Issues
0: Preschool (ages 3 to 5)	To understand my own perspective (first-person [egocentric] and physicalistic level)
1: Early elementary (ages 6 to 7)	To understand your perspective, distinct from mine (first-person and subjective level)
2: Upper elementary (ages 8 to 11)	To understand your view of my (subjective) perspective (second-person and reciprocal level)
3: Middle school (ages 12 to 14)	To understand her or his view of us (our perspective) (third-person and mutual level)
4: High school (ages 15 to 18)	To understand my own perspective in the context of multiple perspectives (third-person and generalized other level)

Source: Table 2–1 "Overview of Social Perspective-Taking: A Developmental Analysis." In *The Promotion of Social Awareness: Powerful Lessons from the Partnership of Developmental Theory and Classroom Practice* (p. 21) by Robert L. Selman, 2003, New York: Russell Sage Foundation.

generalized other role-taking (Selman, 1980, 2003). Refer to Table 6–1 for a chart of the levels of social perspective-taking used to understand interpersonal issues.

This developmental sequence also influences social behavior. Most researchers have found that children with more advanced role-taking skills are more socially skilled with peers and play more cooperatively. Others have found that training children in perspective-taking does not always lead to improved social relations (Durkin, 1995; Selman, 2003). In addition, researchers report that children may use role-taking in some situations but not in others (Damon, 1983a; Selman, 2003). As a result, some developmental theorists have suggested that social perspective-taking may not be a general "ability" that children acquire but rather an "activity" they increasingly engage in as they mature (see Damon, 1983a).

For example, in the case study, there may have been other discussions of shared intentions, negotiation of each other's perspectives, or evaluations of alternatives that led Mandy to predict Alesha's attitude toward using drugs.

In social situations, children's perspective-taking must also be *coordinated* with the perspectives of others. In this context, successive levels of interpersonal understanding are applied to social interactions through a process that researchers have called **interpersonal negotiation** (Selman, 2003).

School-age children still need help from adults to negotiate successfully with other.

Table 6–2 illustrates the conceptual relationships among interpersonal understanding, coordination, and negotiation, called the *interpersonal action framework*. In this developmental sequence, each step in the development of children's social perspective coordination broadens their social understanding as well as their strategies for negotiating interpersonal conflicts (Selman, 2003).

The interpersonal conflict that Alesha faces involves not only resolving the dilemma of accepting

TABLE 6–2

Stages of Interpersonal Action

School-age children's interpersonal negotiation strategies are linked to their level of social perspective-taking.

Levels of Social Perspective-Taking	Interpersonal Negotiation Strategies
0: Egocentric, undifferentiated	Physical force
1: Subjective, differentiated	Unilateral power
2: Reciprocal, self-reflective	Cooperative exchange
3: Mutual, third-person	Mutual compromise
4: Intimate, societal	Collaboration

Source: Based on *The Promotion of Social Awareness: Powerful Lessons from the Partnership of Developmental Theory and Classroom Practice* (p. 31) by R. L. Selman, 2003, New York: Russell Sage Foundation. Copyright 2003 Russell Sage Foundation.

or rejecting an offer of inhalants at that moment but also of facing Mandy at school afterwards.

In interpersonal negotiation research, children are asked to respond to hypothetical dilemmas called "risky incidents." For example, one incident involved Kathy, a 10-year-old girl, and her best friend, Becky. When Jeanette, a new girl in town, invited Kathy to go to a show on the same afternoon that she had a date with Becky, Kathy was not sure what to do. Compared to the previously described "Holly dilemma," this story requires children to coordinate the differing perspectives in a social interaction and then to negotiate *with others* to avoid a conflict. In solving such a dilemma, children could negotiate solutions in which they might either

- Change their own goal
- Change the goal of the other person
- Find a mutually acceptable goal

Possible actions at the lowest level of interpersonal negotiation, called *impulsive*, would include Kathy accepting Jeanette's invitation without thinking, or Becky breaking off her friendship with Kathy in an unreflective reaction. At the next level, called *unilateral*, Becky could order Kathy to "never do it again" or Kathy could simply comply: "I'll never do it again." In either case, the girls have not negotiated but rather given orders or obeyed orders unilaterally. At the next two levels, called *cooperative* and *compromise*, the girls could agree to take turns: "I'll go with Jeanette this Saturday, but next week I'll get my mom to take you and me to the movies" (Selman, 2003, p. 35). At the highest level, called *collaborative*, children together focus on what it may take to maintain their friendship in the future.

By middle childhood, most children can consider the "we-ness" of an interpersonal dilemma—in this case, the ongoing friendship between Kathy and Becky. Research on interpersonal negotiation strategies when children are engaged in actual social interaction, however, has revealed that school-age children's choice of one strategy over another is fluid and context-dependent (Selman, 2003). For example, Kathy may know that she *should* talk to Becky before deciding what to do, *but she may not.* Researchers have suggested that the choice of a strategy may be based on a personality factor, called **interpersonal orientation**: the characteristic tendency either to transform one's own behavior or to try to change the other person. Nevertheless, interpersonal orientation may depend, in part, on children's level of negotiation skill (Selman, 2003). Therefore, action researchers have developed intervention programs and classroom-based curricula to foster negotiation skills in school-age children, as described in Box 6.1 (Nakkula & Nikitopoulos, 2001).

How did you and your friends arrive at a mutually acceptable solution to situations in which you had to negotiate a conflict?

Moral Development

As school-age children mature, they become increasingly able to think about moral issues that may occur during social interactions. Not infrequently, social dilemmas—such as, whether to rescue Holly's cat, whether to go out with Jeanette and leave Becky alone, or whether to use inhalants with Mandy—invoke choices between behaviors that could be considered either "right" or "wrong." Researchers on moral reasoning pioneered the use of hypothetical stories (like those used to assess

BOX 6.1 ROADMAP TO SUCCESSFUL PRACTICE

Program for Young Negotiators

Young Negotiators is a middle-school problem-solving and conflict-resolution curriculum of the *Program on Negotiation* at Harvard Law School designed to train middle-school students in principled negotiation. The curriculum guides its participants through 10 sequentially ordered modules. Each of the modules uses a combination of games, role plays, and class discussions to teach particular negotiation concepts, such as perceptions, empathy, negotiation interests versus positions, and collaboration versus competition. The overall program goal is to teach a "win-win" approach. In the beginning levels, students learn what negotiation is and why it is important. Then they learn to use specific negotiation techniques. In the final levels, students apply their negotiation skills to situations from their own lives (Nakkula & Nikitopoulos, 2001).

In an evaluation study of the *Young Negotiators* curriculum in Argentina, early adolescents' negotiation scores improved by almost 5% on a measure of overall negotiation. These results exceeded changes we have found with the same measure in studies of the *Young Negotiators* curriculum when taught in other contexts, possibly because teachers in Argentina expressed a strong interest in being trained in the model and using it with their students. In addition, many of the school administrators stated that *Young Negotiators*' focus on problem solving and perspective-taking was consistent with the core mission of their schools (Nakkula & Nikitopoulos, 2001).

Participants in the study also showed increases in their developmental level of interpersonal competence (Selman, 2003) that exceeded the degree of developmental growth that would be expected over a five-month period. In this social cognitive approach, the transition from late elementary school to middle and high school is marked by changes in perspective-taking, collaboration, and interpersonal negotiation skills.

Although the *Young Negotiators* curriculum offers both perspective-taking and action-strategy exercises, students seem to prefer interactive role plays over reflective discussions. Based on these findings, teachers should think about balancing the curricular activities. In addition, teachers who incorporate the negotiation approach into their everyday instruction are likely to reinforce the messages presented through the formal training modules. In this sense, the *Program for Young Negotiators* can be considered an effective comprehensive approach to conflict resolution (Nakkula & Nikitopoulos, 2001).

Guideposts for Working with School-Age Children

- Discuss youth fiction or feature films that present social perspectives that may be different from those of the children in your care.
- Foster discussion of conflicts that allows school-age children to disagree but still listen to each others' perspectives.
- Have students role-play social dilemmas in pairs or small groups to encourage the awareness of others' perspectives on issues.
- Help them think through the short-term and long-term consequences of their own social behaviors by reviewing what happened in prior social interactions.
- Minimize the stating of arbitrary rules for social behavior in favor of discussing particular social negotiation strategies in specific situations.

social perspective-taking) that present children with questions about what course of action a fictional character should take (see Colby & Kohlberg, 1987a, 1987b). For example, one story recounts the moral dilemma of Heinz, who cannot afford to buy a drug that could save his wife's life. Should he steal it? How do school-age children resolve such moral or ethical dilemmas? To answer this important question, we must look again at the influential developmental theory of Jean Piaget.

According to Piaget's (1932/1965) cognitive developmental theory (introduced in chapter 4), preoperational children are **moral realists**. In early childhood, they consider the *consequences* of an action over and above the consideration of a person's *intentions*. For example, accidentally breaking 10 cups is usually seen by younger children as worse than intentionally breaking just 1. Young children may only understand a morality of "constraint" in which their moral behavior is controlled by the unilateral authority of adults or of powerful peers, such as bullies, rather than by mutual respect (Lapsley, 1996).

By the time children reach the concrete reasoning stage of middle childhood, however, most have become **moral relativists**. They now think that an intentional action is worse than an accidental behavior, regardless of the result. In addition, contemporary theorists claim that school-age children do not just shift from one type of reasoning to another (Lapsley, 1996). Rather there is a gradual developmental trend toward increasing integration of consequences and intentions with age (see Grueneich, 1982) such that by the end of middle childhood, school-agers have achieved what Piaget referred to as the morality of "cooperation."

In Piaget's view, the fundamental understanding of morality is transformed as children gain greater experience with peers (Lapsley, 1996; Youniss, 1980). Through cooperative exchanges with others, children learn that the rules guiding social life are not just arbitrary but rather are socially constructed, flexible arrangements with others. Some researchers have called this developmental domain an understanding of social conventions rather than of *morality* (Rest, Narvaez, Bebeau, & Thoma, 1999; Turiel, 1998). **Social conventions** are behaviors that are agreed upon by society but are not necessarily guided by moral obligations to others. Can school-age children *really* make moral decisions? In defining the moral domain, researchers have described four interrelated psychological processes (Rest et al., 1999):

1. **Moral Judgment.** Judging which action would be justifiable as moral.
2. **Moral Sensitivity.** Being aware there is a moral problem when it exists, interpreting the situation, role-playing how various actions would affect others.
3. **Moral Motivation.** Committing to a moral course of action, valuing moral actions over other values, taking personal responsibility for moral outcomes.
4. **Moral Character.** Having courage; persisting in a moral task.

Alesha thinks about making up an excuse so she can decline Mandy's offer without taking a moral stand on drug use. She could claim she had asthma or something, but she is afraid that it will end the new friendship. And if Mandy gets high, and still is a good student, maybe it isn't so bad after all?

Stages of moral judgment. Based on Piaget's stage approach to cognitive development as the acquisition of increasingly mature problem-solving strategies, Lawrence Kohlberg described six stages of **moral reasoning**, as seen in Table 6–3 (Colby, Kohlberg, & Gibbs, 1983). In the first stage, called *heteronomous* morality, children use a punishment and obedience orientation to make moral judgments based on adult rules for appropriate behavior and comply with social norms imposed

TABLE 6–3

Moral Reasoning

Six stages of moral reasoning were proposed by Lawrence Kohlberg. By the end of middle childhood, most children can use conventional thinking that is based on conforming to others' expectations.

Ages	Level	Stage
5–8 years	I. Preconventional	1. Heteronomous morality
8–10 years		2. Instrumental morality
10–12 years	II. Conventional	3. Interpersonal morality
12–18 years		4. Social system morality
18–26 years	III. Postconventional	5. Social welfare morality
26+ years		6. Principled morality

by adults (e.g., avoiding punishment [*getting caught with drugs*]), similar to Piaget's morality of constraint. In the second stage, called *instrumental* morality, they use an individualistic orientation to satisfy their own needs by engaging in concrete exchanges with others (e.g., sharing [*drugs*] to get something in return [*friendship*]). Both of these stages together comprise the **preconventional** level of moral reasoning, typical of early childhood, in which many children are still egocentric.

By middle childhood, however, most children have moved into the second level of moral reasoning ability, called **conventional**, composed of stages 3 and 4. School-age children in the third stage of moral reasoning, called *interpersonal* morality, can understand the perspectives of others (as described by social role-taking) and make moral judgments based on shared expectations in a relationship or on obligations to others (e.g., pleasing an authority figure [*or peer*]), similar to Piaget's morality of cooperation. In the fourth stage, called *social system* morality, children are able to adopt the perspective of society and make judgments based on the good of the group (e.g., following the rules [*or social norms*]).

The final level of moral reasoning is called **postconventional** morality, comprised of stages 5 and 6. In the fifth stage, called *social welfare* morality, school-age children and adolescents begin to understand abstract moral values and the importance of human rights (e.g., treating people equally). The sixth stage—which researchers have rarely observed, even in adults—is called *principled* morality and requires that individuals use universal ethical principles to guide everyday decision making (e.g., promoting social justice).

Kohlberg's moral reasoning stages have been widely criticized for several reasons. First, it is not clear whether they are based on a process of coordinating conflicting perspectives (as suggested by the social role-taking sequence discussed earlier) or by an increasing ability to generate solutions to moral dilemmas by applying universal moral principles (Carpendale, 2000). Why is this distinction important? Our concern—and that of Kohlberg's critics—involves his belief that there is a moral ideal against which all people should be evaluated. From our developmental-contextual viewpoint, however, a universal approach to morality runs counter to the idea that in differing cultures there may be different norms for moral behavior, often called **ethical relativism** (Shweder, 1991).

A second major criticism of Kohlberg's moral reasoning stages is that both children and adults often perform better on the hypothetical moral dilemmas than they do in real life (referred to in chapter 1 as the *competence-performance distinction*).

Alesha knows that inhalant use is dangerous and that her parents would not approve of any involvement with peers who abuse drugs. But when faced with a situation in which drugs are offered by a familiar and trusted friend, she nevertheless may choose to try them.

Piaget believed that a stage approach does not necessarily imply consistency in reasoning across widely varying content (Carpendale, 2000). The empirical fact that an individual uses more than one stage to think about various moral issues may depend more on the *personal relevance* of the particular situation under discussion and on *caring about* the people involved. A third criticism of Kohlberg's moral reasoning stages is that they were developed based on research *only* with men and boys. To remedy this significant limitation, Carol Gilligan (1997), a student of Kohlberg, conducted a study of women and girls.

Ethics of care. Gilligan (1977, 1982) argued that Kohlberg's emphasis on justice ignored a uniquely feminine approach to moral reasoning: caring for others. She claimed that girls and women approach moral problems from the perspective of interpersonal ideals, whereas boys and men more often rely on a commitment to ideals of justice. Her research with girls and women did, in fact, demonstrate a gender bias in the scoring of moral dilemmas: Females were more likely than males to be scored at Kohlberg's stage 3 (interpersonal morality). However, Gilligan claimed that these scores did not mean that females are less mature than males in moral reasoning ability but rather that they more often base their moral decision making on a concern for others.

From this perspective, Alesha might inhale because she doesn't want to insult Mandy.

Based on her research with girls and women, Gilligan (1977) described three levels in females' moral reasoning, referred to as the **ethics of care**:

1. Being responsive to others and appreciating the importance of relationships
2. Caring for others, even if it may mean self-sacrifice
3. A sense of universal obligation for all people

TABLE 6–4

Comparing Moral Orientations

Carol Gilligan proposed the ethics of care as an alternative to Kohlberg's focus on moral justice reasoning.

Moral Orientation	What Becomes a Problem	Resolution of a Conflict
Care	A morality of care rests on an understanding of relationships and a response to another in terms of that person's terms and contexts (e.g., not breaking trusts or severing ties between people).	Resolutions are sought that restore relationships or connections between people (e.g., ensuring the care of others or stopping hurt and suffering).
Justice	A morality of justice or fairness rests on understanding relationships as reciprocity between separate individuals (e.g., mediating conflicting claims with fairness as the goal).	Resolutions are sought that consider duties and obligations and adherence to one's values and principles (e.g., using an impartial, objective measure of choice that ensures fairness in arriving at a decision).

Source: Based on "Listening to Voices We Have Not Heard," by N. P. Lyons, in C. Gilligan, N. P. Lyons, & T. J. Hanmer (Eds.), *Making Connections: The Relational Worlds of Adolescent Girls at the Emma Willard School* (pp. 42–44), 1990, Cambridge, MA: Harvard University Press. Copyright 1990 by the President and Fellows of Harvard College.

Table 6–4 compares the ethics of care to a moral orientation based on justice, such as Kohlberg's stages of moral reasoning.

Not all moral reasoning research unequivocally supports the ethics of care, however (see Turiel, 1998). In research using stories about friendship considerations versus self-interests with 7- to 15-year-olds, both justice and care orientations became more interconnected (Keller & Edelstein, 1990). For example, researchers interviewed 10 boys and 10 girls from grades 1, 4, 7, and 10 in a study designed to compare "care" versus "justice" orientations (Walker, de Vries, & Trevethan, 1987). In thinking about real-life dilemmas, compared to hypothetical dilemmas, children who used a care orientation or a split orientation (care/justice) showed higher levels of moral reasoning. Neither girls nor boys used one orientation more than the other, however. In a similar test of the care orientation, no differences between boys and girls were reported for African American adolescents who were asked a hypothetical dilemma about leaving their grandmother's home to move with their mother to a northern city (Stack, 1990). Therefore, many researchers have concluded that the two moral orientations may not be gender typed (Lapsley, 1996). Furthermore, feminist ethicists have questioned the distinction between care and justice, claiming that it reinforces feminine stereotyping and creates a false dichotomy between a concern for justice and the well-being of others (Turiel, 1998; see Okin, 1989).

Developmental researchers and educators recommend school-based programs to help students think about their relationships and the kinds of moral dilemmas they may face in school, such as being angry with friends, struggling for independence, and experiencing unfairness (Gilligan, Lyons, & Hanmer, 1990). In most secondary schools, successful educational interventions have involved minimizing competition, redefining responsibilities, listening to others, and making fair decisions (Gilligan, Lyons, & Hanmer, 1990; see also Gilligan & Brown, 1992, and Pipher, 1994).

Fairness. In middle childhood, concern about fairness—whether in the family, the classroom, or the peer group—is a common moral issue. Often the focus of such research is on **distributive justice** reasoning, or how children decide what is "fair." As in the other moral domains we have discussed, studies of children's thinking about distributive justice have utilized hypothetical stories about sharing to assess fairness decisions. One such sharing dilemma describes students who sold the drawings and paintings they made in class at the local fair and made a lot of money. The "fairness" dilemma asked how the students should split up the money (Damon, 1975). Children's responses were rated according to the following criteria:

- **Equality.** Everyone gets the same.
- **Merit.** Whoever makes the most or the best gets the most.

- **Equity.** The poorer or youngest child gets more than the others.
- **Self-interest.** Whoever wants the most should get it.
- **Behavioral or Physical.** The best-behaved, the biggest child, or girls should get more (adapted from Lapsley, 1996).

Their responses were then categorized into levels of distributive justice (fairness) reasoning (Damon, 1975).

By middle childhood, fairness reasoning is positively related to Piaget's stage of concrete operational thought: Most 8-year-olds can coordinate claims based on equality and merit (Damon, 1975). For example, in order to coordinate sharing with the idea that some people may deserve more, children need to be able to use conservation skills (i.e., compensate claims for equality with claims of merit). In addition, in order to assess each person's claim, children need perspective-taking skills. For example, self-reflective role-taking is necessary for Level 2-B positive justice reasoning when children consider claims for equality and reciprocity, such as "We can't give him more just because he's older!" (Lapsley, 1996).

By age 10, notions about reciprocity are usually consolidated into what some theorists call "moral necessity," resulting from moral reasoning that requires equal treatment (Nucci, 2001). However, between 10 and 12 years of age, children typically realize that fairness doesn't always mean equality. For example, children begin to realize that the "fairness" inherent in unequal treatment of older and younger siblings by parents may be based on a system of "equity" that often requires taking into account others' special needs or status (Nucci, 2001). Positive justice reasoning is therefore, not surprisingly, often associated with more successful social interactions. Using naturalistic observations, researchers have found that children with higher levels of positive justice reasoning not only are more socially competent *themselves* but also receive more positive interactions from their peers (for a review, see Lapsley, 1996). Table 6–5 provides a comparison of Kohlberg's stages of moral reasoning with school-age children's understanding of fairness.

As we discussed in chapter 5, teachers can encourage a social context where differences in ability or status are accepted, thereby modeling a sense of fairness based on equity rather than

TABLE 6–5

Comparing Justice and Fairness Reasoning

In middle childhood, justice *means* fairness, as shown in this comparison of Kohlberg's and Damon's sequences of moral reasoning.

Ages	Moral Justice Domain (Kohlberg)	Fairness Domain (Damon)
5–8	Stage 1: Rules are to be obeyed. One should avoid physical damage to persons and property. Inability to coordinate perspectives of self and others; thus, favoring the self is seen as right.	Recognition of prima facie obligations (e.g., not to hit and hurt others). However, beyond those basic requirements, fairness is prioritized in terms of self-interest.
8–10	Stage 2: Morality as instrumental exchange—"You scratch my back, I'll scratch yours." Act to meet one's own interests and needs and let others do the same. Rules followed only when in someone's interest.	Fairness is now coordinated with conceptions of "just" reciprocity defined primarily in terms of strict equality, with some beginning concerns for equity.
10–12	Stage 3: Being good means living up to what is expected by people around you and by one's role (e.g., good brother or sister). Fairness is the golden rule. One should be caring of others.	Fairness is seen as requiring more than strict equality. Concerns for equity (taking into account the special needs, situations, or contributions of others) are now coordinated with reciprocity in structuring moral decisions.

Source: Based on *Education in the Moral Domain* (pp. 83–85), by L. P. Nucci 2001, Cambridge, UK: Cambridge University Press. Copyright 2001 by Cambridge University Press. Adapted by permission of the publisher.

equality. For example, teachers who offer classroom help to less advanced children in a social climate free from ridicule also encourage respect among their peers. In addition, researchers on moral education recommend that teachers should refrain from creating and enforcing arbitrary or needless rules, especially in middle childhood and adolescence. For example, in one research focus group, fifth graders objected to "the need to raise one's hand to say something in class. . . . As one girl put it, "'We manage to be polite and talk at home without raising our hands, why can't we be expected to do that here?'" (Nucci, 2001, p. 164).

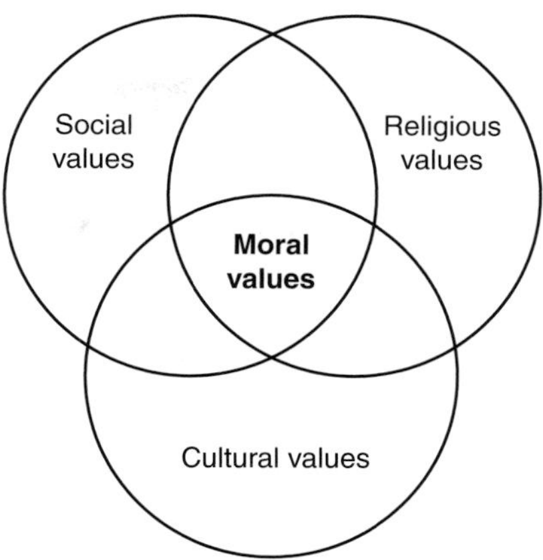

FIGURE 6.3 Domains of Moral Values
Moral values representing the overlap among social, religious, and cultural values are taught in character education programs.

Source: From "Can Good Character Be Taught?" by M. Murphy, in *Character Education in America's Blue Ribbon Schools: Best Practices for Meeting the Challenge* (p. 12), 2002, Lanham, MD: Scarecrow Press. Copyright 2002 by Madonna M. Murphy. Reprinted by permission.

Character education. Many schools have developed **character education** programs consisting of techniques for enhancing moral behavior (e.g., Huffman, 1994; Lickona, 1991; Murphy, 2002; Nucci, 2001). In general, such school-based programs have demonstrated decreases in disciplinary problems and absenteeism (Huffman, 1994). One character-building program for 8- to 12-year-olds, for example, stresses school-agers' industriousness and perseverance as well as the moral values of generosity, companionship, and social responsibility (Isaacs, 2001). **Moral values** are those values that all people "ought to" uphold no matter what their culture, society, or religion, such as kindness (Murphy, 2002), as illustrated by the Venn diagram in Figure 6.3. In this respect, then, character education programs are consistent with Kohlberg's belief in universal moral principles, discussed earlier. However, like Kohlberg's stages of moral reasoning, these programs have been criticized for ignoring differences in values among multiethnic children and their families.

What family or school experiences taught you the values of your community?

Nevertheless, if parents and teachers are involved in developing the content of character education in their local areas, these programs can be effective in promoting a schoolwide focus on ethical behavior (Murphy, 2002). Figure 6.4 depicts a comprehensive model of character education used in the U.S. Department of Education's Elementary School Recognition Program, also called "Blue Ribbon Schools."

Researchers (Murphy, 2002) who have evaluated character education in the Blue Ribbon Schools determined that successful programs include:

- **A Strong School Mission.** Committing to developing students' sense of moral values
- **Participation by the Entire Community.** Collaborative decision making by principals, teachers, staff, students, and parents to determine the desired character qualities and the activities to foster them
- **High Standards for Academic Performance.** Encouraging cooperative learning and interdisciplinary character-building themes across the curriculum
- **High Standards for Student Behavior.** Creating a caring school climate that is safe, nurturing, drug-free, and involved in community and global affairs
- **A Student Recognition Program.** Communicating, encouraging, and reinforcing the character qualities, attitudes, and behaviors that are valued by the school and community
- **Comprehensive Character Education.** Integrating character education into all subject areas

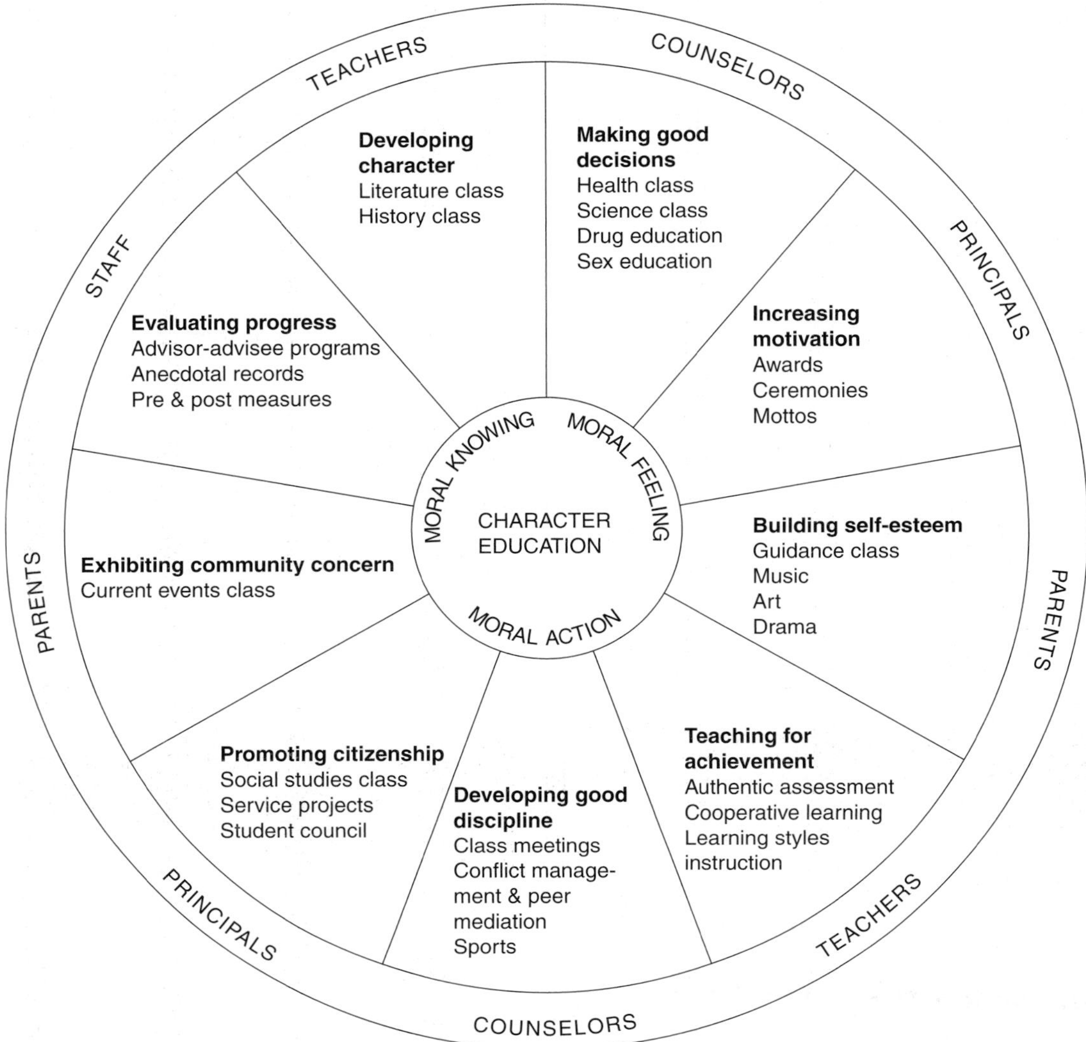

FIGURE 6.4 A Model for Character Education
This comprehensive model for character education developed for the U.S. Department of Education's Blue Ribbon Schools promotes moral knowing, moral feeling, and moral action.

Source: From "Can Good Character Be Taught?" by M. Murphy, In *Character Education in America's Blue Ribbon Schools: Best Practices for Meeting the Challenge* (p. 22), 2002, Lanham, MD: Scarecrow Press. Copyright 2002 by Madonna M. Murphy. Reprinted by permission.

(e.g., math, science, literature, social studies, health) and service areas (e.g., counseling, cafeteria, administration)

- **Schoolwide Evaluation.** Assessing the success of character education in the school

The objectives of character education, however, can often be met by a wide variety of programs, as seen in Table 6–6. One popular example, a service learning approach, is more fully elaborated in Box 6.2.

TABLE 6–6

Types of Character Education

Character education programs take many different forms.

Type of Program	Content
Moral reasoning/cognitive development	Discussion of moral dilemmas facilitates student development of moral reasoning.
Moral education/virtue	Academic content (literature, history) used to teach about moral traditions in order to facilitate moral habits and internal moral qualities (virtues).
Life skills education	Practical skills, communication, and positive social attitudes (self-esteem) stressed.
Service learning	"Hands-on" experiences of community service integrated into curriculum.
Citizenship training/civics education	American civic values taught as a preparation for future citizenship.
Caring community	Caring relationships fostered in the class and school.
Health education/drug, pregnancy, and violence prevention	Program-oriented approach used to prevent unhealthy/antisocial behaviors.
Conflict resolution/peer mediation	Students trained to mediate peer conflicts as a means of developing constructive conflict resolution skills.
Ethics/moral philosophy	Ethics or moral philosophy, explicitly taught.
Religious education	Character education taught in the context of a faith tradition justifying morality from a transcendent source.

Source: From *A Primer for Evaluating A Character Education Initiative* (p. 3) by Martin W. Berkowitz, 1998, Washington, DC, The Character Education Partnership. Copyright 1998, Character Education Partnership. Reprinted by permission.

BOX 6.2 ROADMAP TO SUCCESSFUL PRACTICE

Moral Action Through Service Learning

In a book titled *Education in the Moral Domain*, Larry Nucci describes service learning as an organized effort designed to give students opportunities to engage in helpful behavior. He assumes that the formation of moral identity is enhanced when children and adolescents explore forms of moral action, such as service to others. Through service-learning programs, youth are supported in their explorations by people they trust and admire and feel that their actions genuinely contribute to the welfare of others. For service learning to have meaning for the young person, however, the activities must also be voluntary or have a significant element of choice (Nucci, 2001).

Children and adolescents benefit from opportunities to engage in community-service activities if they are provided a range of volunteer options. Such choices, according to Nucci, fit with their own sense of personal autonomy as well as their developing moral identities. For example, elementary schools may require service hours for graduation from the eighth grade but allow students a large choice of options through which to meet such community service. Service learning also need not be limited to extracurricular activities, such as a "buddy system" in which upper-grade students serve as tutors for lower-grade students.

Research examining service-learning programs has reported that students who have been involved in volunteer experiences, such as serving as a referee or coach for youth sports, helping with a community food-distribution program, or tutoring, were less likely than other adolescents to be involved in problem behaviors. Studies have also reported that early engagement in social organizations is associated with long-term engagement in positive social activities and can have a positive impact on inner-city youth whose daily lives may not provide environmental support for the construction or enactment of positive moral identities (Nucci, 2001).

Guideposts for Working with School-Age Children

- Implement character education approaches that help children develop an understanding of moral values.
- Foster discussion of values that allows school-age children the opportunity to listen to the moral reasoning of others.
- Discuss the fairness of parental or teacher rules.
- Encourage cooperation and caring rather than winning or losing by implementing cooperative learning and team activities.

Peer Relations in Middle Childhood

A positive climate for social and moral growth is one that fosters peer interaction (Nucci, 2001). In middle childhood, 30% of a child's social interactions involve peers, compared to 10% in early childhood (Rubin, Bukowski, & Parker, 1998). Children's behavior in the peer group has proven to be a stable indicator of their social competence (Hartup, 1996; Zeller, Vannatta, Schaffer, & Noll, 2003). School-agers not only construct understandings of others but must also interact competently with their peers and sustain friendships over time. In addition, children's concerns about acceptance in the peer group often rise during middle childhood. Many peer relations researchers, not surprisingly, have focused on the study of friendships among school-age children (for a review, see Rubin, Bukowski, & Parker, 1998).

Friendships are important for social development. Friendship processes are linked to social developmental outcomes, also called **social provisions**. In a classic text called *The Interpersonal Theory of Psychiatry*, Harry Stack Sullivan (1953/1981) argued that friends fulfill social needs, called **communal needs**, such as companionship, acceptance, and intimacy (Buhrmester, 1996). In many ways, this formulation is similar to Maslow's need for belonging (described in chapter 5). Furthermore, communal needs can be distinguished from other human needs:

- **Communal Needs.** Interpersonal needs for affection, nurturance, enjoyment, support, companionship, intimacy, and sexual fulfillment
- **Survival Needs.** Physical needs for safety, food, shelter, and health
- **Agentic Needs.** Individual needs for competency, achievement, status, power, approval, autonomy, identity and self-esteem (see Buhrmester, 1996)

The social concerns of school-age children often focus on the communal needs of acceptance by peers and avoidance of rejection.

Alesha's need for continued acceptance by her best friends from elementary school—Jennifer and Kelly—may prove stronger than her need for Mandy's companionship. When confronted with Mandy's offer to get high, Alesha seems genuinely fearful of rejection by her peer group. Will they still like her if she started hanging out with Mandy? Why should they continue to be friends if she's becoming one of the "druggies"?

Friendship

Middle childhood brings about marked changes in the understanding of friendship. In early childhood, friendship is usually associated with sharing a current activity, whereas in middle childhood children begin to recognize that friendships can last over time (Parker & Seal, 1996). Sullivan (1953/1981) referred to friends in the preadolescent years between ages 8 and 10 as **chums**. School-age children usually indicate an increasing appreciation of each others' feelings and intentions, brought about by advances in their social perspective-taking ability (Rubin, Bukowski, & Parker, 1998).

Contemporary researchers have typically investigated school-age children's friendship concepts by asking them what they expect from a best friend. **Friendship stages** in middle childhood have been found to parallel the stages of social understanding (discussed earlier). Children who are *social-informational* perspective takers and *unilateral* negotiators will likely think of friendships as *one-way*, that is, they may think about what a friend could do for them, or vice versa, but not what they reciprocally could do for each other (Selman, 1980). For example, in the hypothetical friendship story told previously, it is likely that a child at this level would suggest that Kathy take the "better" offer. Some researchers have termed this period a "reward-cost" stage, in which children around 7 or 8 believe that friends are rewarding to be with compared to nonfriends (Bigelow, 1977; see also Robin, Bukowski, & Parker, 1998). Many school-age children have best friends and are satisfied with those friendships (Parker & Asher, 1993).

By ages 10 or 11, however, most school-age children demonstrate "normative" friendships, in which they recognize that friends are supposed to be loyal to each other (Bigelow, 1977). Recall that these children are likely to be *self-reflective* perspective takers and *cooperative* or *compromising* negotiators. They conceptualize friendships as *reciprocal*, although it is still highly unlikely that these relationships will survive difficult arguments or negative events (Selman, 1980). For this reason, school-agers have often been called "fairweather" friends because their relationships may not weather stormy periods (Rubin, Bukowski, & Parker, 1998). In addition, when boys in one study terminated a friendship because of conflict, the typical length of time for working it through and renewing the friendship was one day, but for girls it took about two weeks. One explanation for this sex difference is that triads (*like Alesha, Jennifer, and Kelly*) are more common in the friendships of school-age girls than boys, causing one member of the group to feel left out (Azmitia, Kamprath, & Linnet, 1998).

By the end of middle childhood, most children are capable of *mutual* role-taking and *collaborative* negotiation, as we have discussed. Friends at this stage expect each other to provide companionship, help, protection, and support (Azmitia, Kamprath, & Linnet, 1998). For them, friendships are becoming *intimate*, characterized by an enduring sense of trust in each other. For example, between third and sixth grades, the expectation that friends would keep secrets rose from 25% to 72% among girls, although boys had no such similar expectation until the end of sixth grade (Azmitia, Kamprath, & Linnet, 1998). These maturing notions of friendship translate into social interaction with peers during middle childhood. In addition, peer acceptance influences school-age friendship dynamics, as seen in Table 6–7. Overall, the ability to form close, intimate friendships becomes increasingly important during early adolescence (Buhrmester, 1990).

Popularity. During middle childhood, some children seem to have many friends and others only a few. However, a central concern of many—if not all—school-agers is *popularity*. **Popularity** (also called *social status*) has been operationally defined by a majority of peer interaction researchers as the number of individuals who name an individual target child as "liked" or "disliked" or as a "friend" or "best friend" (Newcomb, Bukowski, & Pattee, 1993). Children with the most "liked" nominations are considered *popular*, whereas those with the most "disliked" nominations are considered *rejected*. Children with few or no nominations are often termed *neglected*. Children are considered *controversial* if they are both nominated frequently by some *and* actively disliked by others.

Boys' social status tends to be based on social dominance, athletic ability, coolness, and tough-

TABLE 6–7

Comparing Friendship and Peer Relations

In middle childhood, maturing peer relations are dependent on children's developing understanding of friendship.

Stage	Peer Relations	Friendship
Stage 0	Physical connections	Momentary physical interaction
Stage 1	Unilateral relations	One-way assistance
Stage 2	Bilateral partnerships	Fairweather cooperation
Stage 3	Homogenous community	Intimate and mutual sharing
Stage 4	Pluralistic organization	Autonomous interdependence

Source: Based on "Four Domains, Five Stages: A Summary Portrait of Interpersonal Understanding," by R. S. Selman, in *The Growth of Interpersonal Understanding: Developmental and Clinical Implications* (pp. 136–147), 1980, New York: Academic.

ness, whereas girls' status depends more on family background, socioeconomic status, and physical appearance (McHale, Dariotis, & Kauh, 2003). Generally, school-age children with diverse social status classifications differ in behavior and characteristics (Newcomb, Bukowski, & Patee, 1993; Wentzel, 2003):

- **Popular Children.** Tend to exhibit higher levels of positive social behavior and cognitive ability and lower levels of aggression and withdrawal than average children
- **Rejected Children.** Tend to exhibit just the opposite pattern—more aggressive and withdrawn and less sociable and cognitively skilled than average children
- **Neglected Children.** Tend to exhibit less social interaction and disruptive behavior but more withdrawal than average children
- **Controversial Children.** Tend to be less compliant and more aggressive than average children

In addition to totaling the number of friendship nominations a particular child may receive, researchers may examine the nominations to see if they are reciprocal. Peer relations researchers often distinguish **peer acceptance** (i.e., the number of "liked" ratings children receive) from friendship (i.e., the number of reciprocated "friend" choices) (Asher, Parker, & Walker, 1996). The concept of peer acceptance differs from friendship because it refers to children's relationships within a *group* rather than the quality of children's *dyadic* relationships with individual peers. For example, peer relations researchers sometimes observe classroom or playground social interactions and chart peer relationships based on frequencies of actual contacts between acquaintances (i.e., peers children "know" but with whom they have no close reciprocated ties) (Ladd & Kochenderfer, 1996). Either method (i.e., ratings or observations) is called a **sociometric** classification of group acceptance and can be summarized in a visual diagram called a *sociogram*, shown in Figure 6.5.

Peer acceptance may influence friendships by determining the amount of choice that children have in friends (Azmitia, Kamprath, & Linnet, 1998). Recall that in the transition to middle

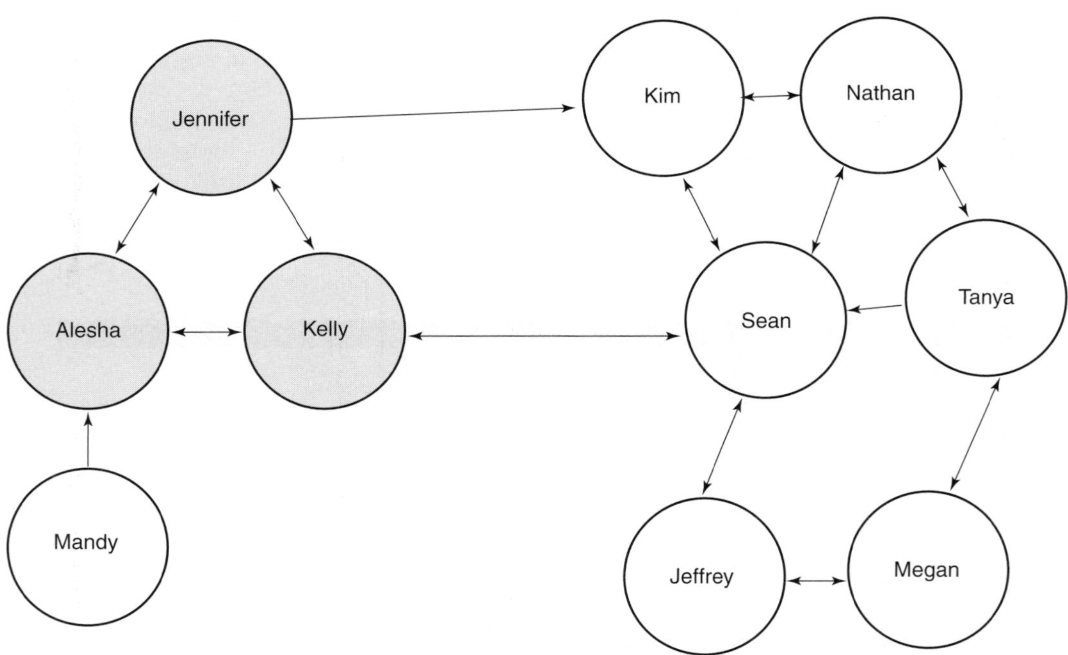

FIGURE 6.5 Sociogram
This sociogram of best-friend choices in a middle childhood classroom models the reciprocal best-friend choices of the girls from the chapter case (shaded circles) as well as a mixed-sex peer network with a popular boy named Sean at the center.

school, peer group sizes may increase as children attend several different classes in a typical day. For both boys and girls, the anticipated transition produced feelings of anxiety (Pratt & George, 2005). When patterns of attraction to peers were examined across the transition to middle school, researchers found that attractions to aggressive peers and to children who stand out in the peer group increase with age, especially attraction to aggressive boys among girls (Bukowski, Sippola, & Newcomb, 2000).

Girls experience less stability in the number of reciprocated friendships across the school transition than do boys, although they have similar numbers of friends overall. Girls also are more likely than boys to form new reciprocated friendships with previously unfamiliar peers, especially if they had attended relatively small elementary schools (Hardy, Bukowski, & Sippola, 2002). In other words, girls may experience more *changes* in friends than boys after the middle school transition.

Did you keep the same friends across the transition to middle school or junior high? What did it mean to be "popular"?

Recall that Alesha and Mandy had just met in middle-school choir and quickly formed a new friendship, as is typical of many middle-school girls.

In a recent study, sixth-grade sociometric status ("liked-most" and "liked-least" scores) predicted eighth-grade school adjustment (Wentzel, 2003). Although the number and stability of friendships do not always contribute to adjustment in the transition to middle school, having supportive friends predicts increasing popularity (Berndt, 1989). A classroom activity called the "Class Play" is described in Box 6.3. This technique has proven useful for determining school-agers' reputations in their peer groups.

Peer groups, like other organizations, have distinctive structures. In a peer group's organization, some members are central while others are marginal, for example. In a study of fourth, fifth, and sixth graders, peers' positions in the organization of same-sex peer groups were significantly related to their social status. Peer group members who were marginal in the peer group organization were more likely to be rejected and friendless, whereas those in a central position were likely to be popular and have at least one friend (Lease & Axelrod, 2001). Furthermore, rejected children on the margins of the group were perceived by their peers as "different" in their social behavior (i.e., more odd, inattentive, excluded, shy, or anxious) compared to rejected peers who were less marginal in the peer group organization (Lease, McFall, & Viken, 2003).

Peer networks. Researchers studying the formation of peer networks define a **clique** as a small group of close friends (for an ethnographic study of peer networks, see Adler & Adler, 1998). Generally, girls' friendship networks are smaller (i.e., more *intensive*) than boys' networks (i.e., more *extensive*). Longitudinal research, however, has shown that boys' friendship networks are more likely to become interconnected over time compared to girls' (Ladd, 1999). Interestingly, the size and density of adolescents' networks has been

BOX 6.3 ROADMAP TO UNDERSTANDING THEORY AND RESEARCH

The Revised Class Play

Using a procedure called the *Revised Class Play*, designed to measure peers' behavioral reputation ("*What is this child like*?"), elementary, middle, and high school students were asked to cast their classmates into 30 roles (half reflecting positive attributes, half negative) in a hypothetical play. Both boys and girls categorized their peers according to four types of behaviors:

- Leadership behaviors
- Prosocial behaviors
- Aggressive-disruptive behaviors
- Sensitive-isolated behaviors

Middle-school children and adolescents perceived leadership and prosocial behaviors as positive, and aggressive-disruptive and sensitive-isolated behaviors as negative. However, compared to elementary-age children, they also saw aggressive-disruptive behaviors as positively related to *leadership*. In middle school, the researchers suggested, a peer with a "bad reputation" would be likely to become a leader in the peer group (Zeller, Vannatta, Schaffer, & Noll, 2003).

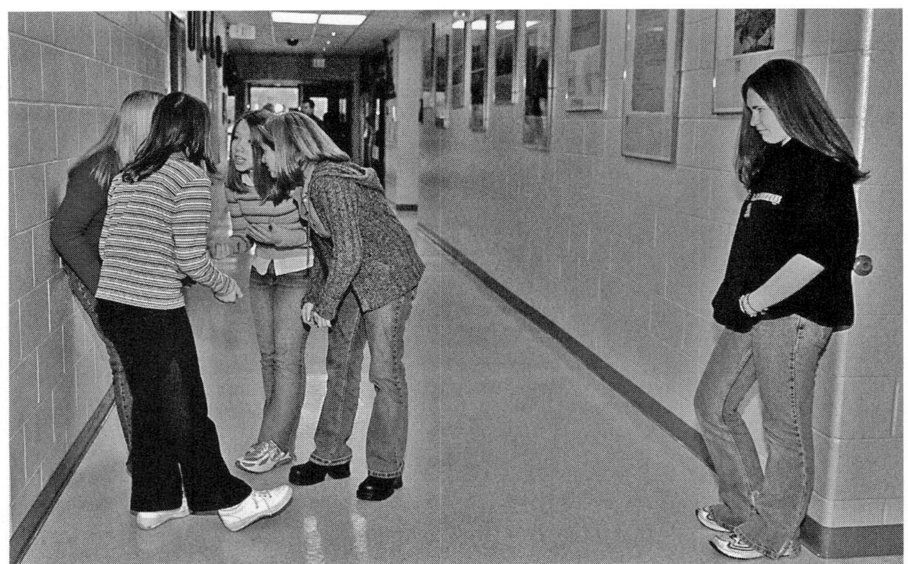

A small group of friends that deliberately excludes nonmembers is called a clique.

related to parents' friendship networks—especially mothers'—perhaps due to the influence of social learning (Parke & Buriel, 1998).

Unlike interaction-based cliques that are composed of friendship networks, **crowds** are reputation-based groups of children who are not necessarily friends but who share similar values, attitudes, and behaviors, such as "jocks" or "brains" (Prinstein & La Greca, 2002; see also Brown, Eicher, & Petrie, 1986). Peer crowds serve an important relational function when children enter a new school and interact with increasing numbers of peers. The crowd system may act as a social guide to help school-age children maintain peer relationships, meet possible friends, and—eventually—choose romantic partners. In adolescence, students who are more central in their peer networks feel more positively about school (Crosnoe, 2000). On the other hand, adolescents who affiliate with deviant crowds (e.g., "burnouts") report higher levels of illegal behavior, alcohol and marijuana use, aggression, and risky sexual behavior (Prinstein & La Greca, 2002).

Will Alesha be able to build connections between her "clique" of friends from elementary school and a new "crowd" in middle school?

Peer and friendship networks are likely to form because of three factors, based on the principles of social learning theory discussed earlier (Hartup, 1996):

1. **Sociodemographics.** Children are likely to come into proximity because of age, socioeconomic status, ethnicity, etc.
2. **Social Selection.** Children construct relationships with others who are similar to themselves or to whom they are attracted.
3. **Mutual Socialization.** Children become increasingly similar to their friends as they interact.

Typically, the peer groups of school-age children are segregated by sex, although socially unskilled children who are rejected by their peers may be more likely to seek opposite-sex friends. Girls usually place a priority on interpersonal connections (i.e., communal needs), whereas boys place a higher priority on status concerns (i.e., agentic needs) (see Maccoby, 1990, 1998). For example, in a study of friendship quality, girls reported more frequent intimate and supportive interactions with female friends than boys did with male friends (Buhrmester, 1996). In other studies, boys were more likely than girls to express anger towards well-liked peers, perhaps due to concerns about competition. Girls were more likely to judge a friend's misdeeds in terms of how these behaviors would affect their relationship (see Ladd, 1999).

Such sex differences are likely due to differential gender socialization experiences in family, school, and community contexts (discussed later in this chapter). For example, in a study of school-age children's social networks on a school playground, ethnographic observers found that sex-typed play (i.e., all-boy or all-girl) interacted with stereotypical behaviors related to other social categories, such as

Guideposts for Working with School-Age Children

- Provide opportunities for school-agers to reflect on the nature of friendship by reading youth literature and discussing themes such as support, loyalty, and trust.
- Frequently reassign students to different groups for classroom projects so that they can become better acquainted with less familiar peers.
- Praise children for befriending students who may differ from themselves or who interact on the margins of their friendship network or peer group.
- Encourage boys and girls to appreciate the social provisions of cross-sex peer groups by pointing out the strengths of fulfilling their needs both for individual agency and for communion with others.

age, race, and social class. Girls' and boys' hairstyles and clothing, for instance, amplified differences between male and female peer groups (Thorne, 1993, 1997a). In addition, the greater social prestige of early pubertal maturation for boys versus girls reproduced the dynamics of male dominance on the playground (Thorne, 1997b).

Another typical cross-sex interaction, heterosexual dating (or "going together"), is often an extension of peer networks in middle childhood rather than the intimate dating relationship characteristic of adolescents. For example, middle-school dating usually consists of groups going out together, often a combination of male and female cliques (Pellegrini, 2001).

Social Skills and Social Behavior in Middle Childhood

In the chapter introduction, we defined *social competence* as the ability to interact effectively with others. Refer to Figure 6.6 for a model of social competence in school-age children. In studying children's social competence, researchers have increasingly focused on how positive social relationships are linked to acquiring the skills necessary for effective social interaction, such as maintaining friendships (Chan, Ramey, Ramey, & Schmitt, 2000). In particular, the study of social behavior in middle childhood often involves identifying how children who differ in social skills respond when they encounter conflicts (Cillessen & Belmore, 2002).

Social skills are usually assessed using parent or teacher rating scales (see Demaray, Ruffalo, Carlson, & Busse, 1995, for a review of six measures). For example, the *Social Skills Rating System* (Gresham & Elliott, 1990) includes items such as

- Makes friends easily
- Cooperates with peers without prompting
- Gets along with people who are different

Many researchers have found that socially skilled children are more often nominated by their peers as popular (Chan, Ramey, Ramey, & Schmitt, 2000). Level of peer acceptance or rejection is also related to the ability of school-age children to resolve interpersonal conflicts with peers and to the causal attributions they make about disagreements between friends (Joshi & Ferris, 2002). For example, in a study of 9- to 12-year-olds, children ascribed conflicts between friends to one of four causes:

1. **Human or Relationship Characteristics.** Conflict is attributable to an inevitable characteristic of the relationship or to human nature in general (e.g., *"Friends have a lot in common but not everything"* or *"Because people are different"*).
2. **Interactional Condition.** Conflict is the result of a specific situation, such as conflicting goals (e.g., *"One person wants something the other has"*).
3. **Person Characteristics.** Conflict is caused by the characteristics, attributes, or actions of a specific person—either self or other (e.g., *"Because someone is in a bad mood"*).
4. **Extraneous Characteristics.** Conflict is the result of factors unrelated to the friendship (e.g., *"God thinks you need to fight in your life"*) (adapted from Joshi & Ferris, 2002, pp. 68–69).

Most children attributed the causes of conflicts with friends to features of the relationship or interaction rather than to individual personality characteristics of themselves and their friends (Joshi & Ferris, 2002).

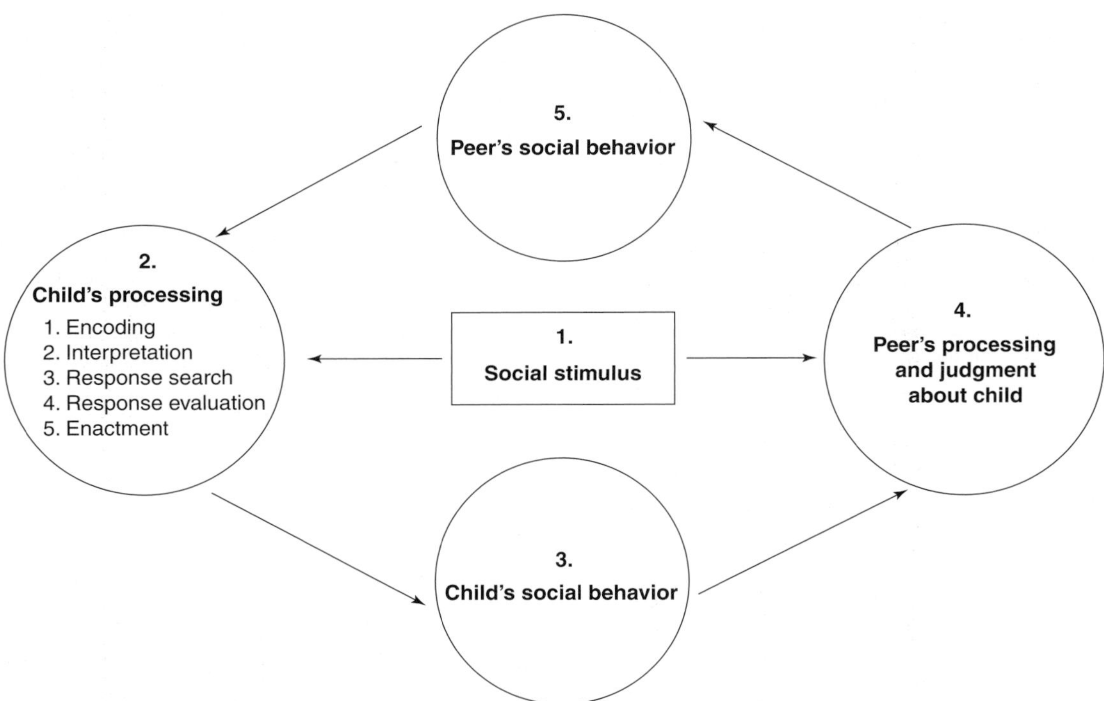

FIGURE 6.6 Social Competence Model
In middle childhood peer interaction, a social stimulus, such as an argument, causes social information processing on the part of both children, resulting in both peers making judgments about each other and then acting accordingly.

Source: From "Social Competence in Children," by K. A. Dodge, G. S. Petit, C. I. McClasky, & M. M. Brown, 1986, *Monographs of the Society for Research in Child Development, 51* (2 Serial No. 213), 2. Copyright 1986 by the Society for Research in Child Development. Reprinted by permission of the society.

If Alesha has a fight with Mandy over "huffing," she would likely attribute the cause of their disagreement to conflicting goals in that specific situation.

Considerable evidence exists for considering friendships as important contexts for developing social skills (Berndt, 2002; Ladd & Kochenderfer, 1996; Hartup 1996). For example, the quality of children's friendships may influence social skill acquisition because friends

- Communicate with each other more effectively than nonfriends
- Provide more support and assistance than nonfriends
- Problem-solve together in a "climate of agreement" compared to nonfriends
- Seek ways of resolving disagreements that support continued interaction (adapted from Hartup, 1996)

A high-quality friendship is characterized by high levels of positive behaviors and low levels of conflicts (Berndt, 2002). In studying the development of social skills, most middle childhood researchers have focused on two opposing types of social interactions, *prosocial* (e.g., helping, protecting) and *antisocial* (e.g., aggression, bullying). Children who are similar in levels of prosocial and antisocial behavior are more likely to become friends than those who are not (Haselager, Hartup, van Lieshout, & Rilke-Walraven, 1998). In addition, prosocial friends may serve as a protective factor against antisocial behavior (see Berndt, 2002, for a review).

Prosocial Behavior

Prosocial behavior is defined in most studies of children's social development as "voluntary behavior intended to benefit another person" (Eisenberg & Fabes, 1998, p. 701). A related term is **altruism**, or prosocial acts that are motivated by internal rewards, such as concern for others, rather than by the expectation of external rewards, such as parental or teacher approval. Like the other social-cognitive and moral reasoning abilities discussed in this chapter, prosocial reasoning is commonly assessed using hypothetical stories, and children are asked whether or not the protagonist should help the person in need (see Carlo, Hausmann, Christiansen, & Randall, 2003).

School-age children with prosocial tendencies differ from nonprosocial children. Prosocial behavior has been linked to stable individual differences in emotionality and self-regulation (Eisenberg et al., 1999). Prosocial children are typically **empathic** (i.e., they respond to others' emotional states). Specifically, prosocial children tend to be high in social skills (i.e., socially appropriate behavior and constructive coping behavior) and low in negative emotionality (discussed in chapter 5). A theoretical model of the relationship between emotion and self-regulation is provided in Table 6–8.

The empathy skills of school-age children can be enhanced by classroom activities such as role-playing and discussing alternative solutions to conflicts. For example, compared to control groups, children given empathy training subsequently showed significantly more cooperation, helping, and generosity (Mussen & Eisenberg, 2001; see Feshbach & Feshbach, 1982, 1983). Both school and peer success may also be enhanced by associations with prosocial models, as suggested by Bandura's social cognitive theory. Prosocial behavior (i.e., cooperating, helping, sharing, and consoling) assessed in third grade predicted academic achievement and social preferences in eighth grade, with adolescents preferring to study or play with peers who share, console, and help others (Caprara, Barbaranelli, Pastorelli, Bandura, & Zimbardo, 2000).

Although many social behaviors fall under the general heading of "*prosocial*," when third- to sixth-grade children were asked what *they* thought was normative in their own peer groups (e.g., "*What do boys/girls do when they want to be nice to someone*"), they responded with behaviors other than sharing, comforting, or acting altruistically, such as "*be friends*" or "*include them in our group*" (Greener & Crick, 1999; see also Thompson, Arora, & Sharp, 2002). For example, "*being included*" was the most frequent prosocial behavior cited by both boys and girls, especially for grades 3 and 4, probably because same-sex peer relationships and friendships become particularly important during the school-age years.

On the other hand, cross-sex interactions included more *sharing* and *caring*, especially for grade 6 when the prospect of dating became more salient. When the children were asked about prosocial behaviors toward the opposite sex (e.g., "*What do boys do when they want to be nice to girls?*"), two additional categories of responses were found: romantic behaviors (e.g., "*flirt,*" "*ask them out on a date,*" "*send love letters*") and negative behaviors (e.g., "*push,*" "*pretend they hate them,*" "*tease*") (Greener & Crick, 1999). Interestingly, many researchers have found that pushing, poking, and teasing are actually common courtship behaviors in middle childhood, rather than indicators of males' cross-sex aggression or sexual harassment (see Pellegrini, 2001).

Antisocial Behavior

Antisocial behavior is defined as actions "that inflict physical or mental harm or property loss or damage on others, and which may or may not constitute the breaking of criminal laws" (Coie & Dodge, 1998, p. 781). They typically include **aggressive behaviors**, or behaviors aimed at harming or injuring another person. In addition, it is helpful to our understanding of antisocial behaviors to consider aggression as distinct from other kinds of antisocial behavior, such as substance abuse or lying, based on the fact that aggressive behaviors (e.g., bullying or fighting) are usually both destructive and overt acts, as illustrated in Figure 6.7.

As early as middle childhood, antisocial children tend to associate with other antisocial or rejected peers. For example, the friends of antisocial boys tend to live in the same neighborhood block and to have met in unsupervised activities (Dishion, Andrews, & Crosby, 1995). According to the **differential-association hypothesis** of delinquent behavior, youth who spend time with delinquent friends are expected to commit delinquent acts themselves. Furthermore, delinquent friends are assumed to have greater influence if they have more positive relationships with their friends (Berndt, 2002; see also Fuligni, Eccles, Barber, & Clements, 2001). The influence of antisocial peers has been termed "deviancy training" (i.e., contingent positive reactions to rule-breaking discussions) and is associated with higher levels of adolescent violence (Dishion, McCord, & Poulin, 1999).

Not all studies have supported this social learning hypothesis, however (Agnew, 1991). For

TABLE 6–8

Dispositions for Prosocial Behavior

School-agers who engage in prosocial behaviors tend to be high in self-regulation and low in negative emotionality.

Emotional Intensity	Style of Regulation		
	Highly Inhibited	**Optimal Regulation**	**Under-Regulation**
Moderately High	Inhibited Expressive at a young age but learns to inhibit overt expressions of emotion Shy Low to average social skills Prone to reactive (emotion-induced) withdrawal Lack of flexibility in coping Prone to anxiety, fear, and personal distress	Expressive Interpersonally engaging Sociable Socially competent and popular Constructive coping behaviors Resilient Prone to sympathy and spontaneous prosocial behavior Prone to high levels of positive emotion	Uncontrolled, active behavior Social or extroverted Frequently controversial or rejected children (particularly boys) Nonconstructive ways of coping with emotion Prone to reactive aggressions Low in prosocial behavior Prone to personal distress, frustration, and negative affectivity
Moderately Low	Inhibited and passive Highly controlled Nonexpressive Unsociable or introverted Prone to proactive withdrawal Low to average social skills and popularity Lack of flexibility in coping Somewhat flat affect	Placid Average expressiveness Sociable Socially competent and popular Constructive coping behaviors Resilient Moderately high in prosocial behavior and sympathy Prone to positive emotion	Erratic behavior Extroverted and sensation-seeking Low to average popularity Often nonconstructive coping Prone to proactive aggression and manipulative behavior Low in prosocial behavior and vicarious emotional responding

Source: From "The Relations of Children's Dispositional Prosocial Behavior to Emotionality, Regulation, and Social Functioning," N. Eisenberg et al., *Child Development, 67*, 975.

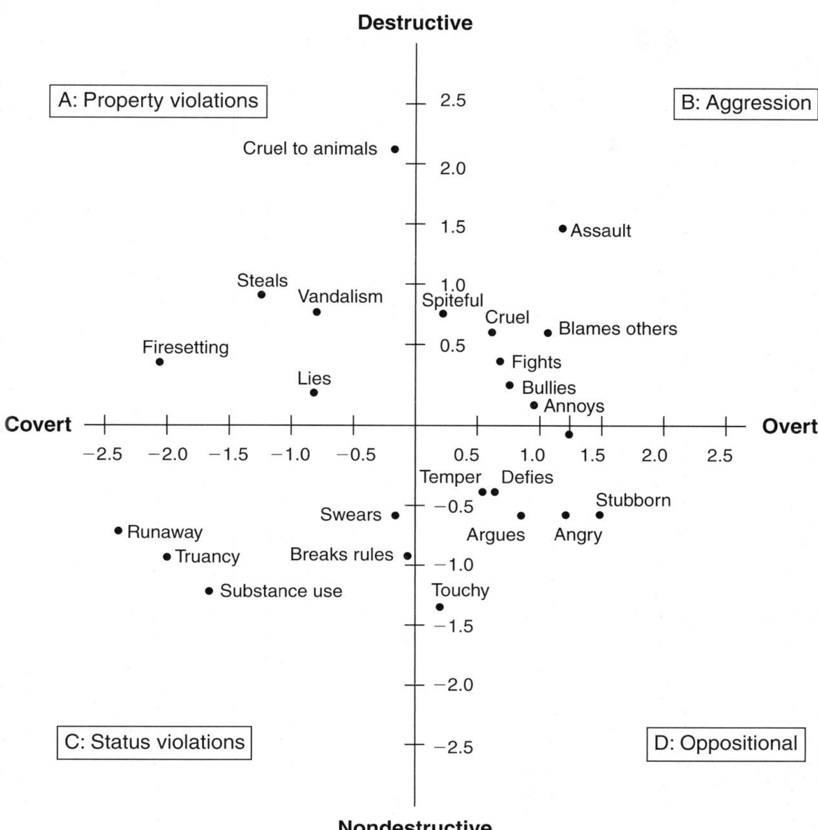

FIGURE 6.7 Dimensions of Antisocial Behavior
Antisocial behaviors can be classified into four categories based on parent and teacher ratings.

Source: From "Aggression and Antisocial Behavior," by J. D. Coie & K. A. Dodge, in W. Damon & N. Eisenberg (Eds.), *Handbook of Child Psychology*, Vol. 3 (p. 782), 1998, New York: Wiley, 1998. Copyright 1998 by John Wiley and Sons, Inc. Reprinted by permission of the publisher.

example, it does *not* appear that antisocial children have deficits in interacting with their friends (Dishion, Andrews, & Crosby, 1995). In fact, having just one close friend may have a moderating effect on antisocial behavior.

Kelly, Jennifer, and Alesha have a long-standing friendship based on shared prosocial activities. For example, last year they tutored elementary school students after school, which helped them overcome the temptation to hang out with an antisocial crowd.

Aggression. In middle childhood, aggressive behaviors typically involve fighting, threats of harm, bullying, gossiping, or teasing (Underwood, Galen, & Paquette, 2001; Underwood, 2003). Most middle childhood developmental researchers distinguish among three types of aggression (e.g., Crick, 1996):

1. **Physical Aggression.** Using violence to hurt someone physically (e.g., hitting, pushing, assaulting)
2. **Verbal Aggression.** Using words to hurt someone psychologically (e.g., insulting, teasing, name-calling)
3. **Relational Aggression.** Using exclusion to ostracize someone socially (e.g., shunning, spreading rumors, gossiping)

As a group, boys appear to be significantly more aggressive than girls, especially in using physical aggression, whereas girls appear to be higher in verbal and relational aggression. However, many of these findings are based on peer or teacher self-reports and may reflect gender stereotyping rather than actual sex differences. In addition, when girls do engage in physical aggression, their behavior is often seen as more deviant by their peers and teachers than boys' aggression (see Underwood, Galen, & Paquette, 2001). For example, in a Canadian study of playground behavior, aggression was negatively related to likeability for girls but not for boys (Serbin et al., 1993).

In a person-centered study of popular boys in grades 4 to 6 (refer to chapter 1 for a discussion of person- vs. variable-centered approaches), peers saw *prosocial* boys as "models" (i.e., "cool, athletic, leaders, cooperative, studious, not shy, and nonaggressive"). On the other hand, they perceived the popular *antisocial* boys as "tough" (i.e., "cool, athletic, and aggressive"). "These findings suggest that highly aggressive boys can be among the most popular and socially connected in elementary classrooms" (Rodkin, Farmer, Pearl, & Van Acker, 2000, p. 14). In longitudinal research, both physical and verbal aggression (e.g., fighting, insulting, and hurting others) were related to third-graders' low school achievement and peer preferences, but they did not predict these outcomes in eighth grade (Caprara, Barbaranelli, Pastorelli, Bandura, & Zimbardo, 2000).

By middle childhood, most children refrain from physical aggression. Instead, they may use relational aggression to maintain a sense of belonging to their peer group or to test out various social norms (Underwood, Galen, & Paquette, 2001). As we saw in chapter 5, most school-agers can understand the nature of deception and false statements. For example, in a study of third to sixth graders, both boys and girls questioned the veracity of gossip (i.e., references to the personal qualities, behaviors, or affairs of others), although girls were more likely to attribute false gossip to jealousy than were boys (Kuttler, Parker, & LaGreca, 2002). Middle childhood girls are also significantly more likely than boys to recruit other girls to retaliate or "freeze out" their friends (Azmitia, Kamprath, & Linnet, 1998). Therefore, it should be no surprise that relationally aggressive children (often girls) also report significantly higher levels of loneliness, depression, and isolation compared to their nonaggressive peers (Crick & Grotpeter, 1995). Relationally aggressive dominant girls, however, are often perceived as popular by their peers, suggesting that leadership also may serve as a risk factor for antisocial behavior (Sippola, 2004; see also Underwood, 2003).

Bullying. An all-too-commmon form of aggression during middle childhood is **bullying**, or long-standing acts of physical, verbal, or relational aggression that are directed at a *particular* peer (Rubin, Bukowski, & Parker, 1998; Sharp & Smith, 1994). Estimated numbers of bullying victims range from 10 to 27% of the school-age population (Hawkins, Pepler, & Craig, 2001; Ma, Stewin, & Hah, 2001; Sutton, Smith, & Swettenham, 1999a). Bullying may include *racial harassment*, based on membership in an ethnic or racial minority group, or *sexual harassment*, based on gender or sexual orientation. Although *homophobic* bullying (i.e., calling someone "gay") may be a way of labeling a heterosexual child "weak," when it is used against a sexual minority adolescent it is particularly hurtful and damaging (Thompson, Arora, & Sharp, 2002). Definitions of bullying also have recently been expanded to include "*cyber*bullying," or using the Internet to stalk or humiliate a peer by sending email or posting online journals (also called weblogs, or "blogs" for short) to circulate rumors, photographs, or other slanderous material) (Simmons, 2003).

When middle-school students were asked in individual interviews about bullying and victimization they described a wide range of behaviors—from physical aggression to verbal teasing to social exclusion. Sixth graders were most often the targets of name-calling and teasing, which usually decreased by eighth grade. While age and ethnicity were frequently cited as risk factors for victimization by bullies, having less money, fewer fashionable clothes, wearing glasses, and being overweight also led to harassment (Espelage & Asidao, 2002). During middle childhood, the ability to infer stereotypes increases dramatically (Abrams, Rutland, & Cameron, 2003; McKown, 2004). In addition, school-age children's awareness of the widely held stereotypes of others also increases, especially among stigmatized groups, such as African Americans and Latinos (McKown & Weinstein, 2003).

Were you ever bullied? How did your parents, teachers, and peers respond to bullies or victims?

Whether bullies are motivated by a lack of social perspective-taking ability, low self-esteem, deficits in information-processing ability, or a faulty theory-of-mind about others is a matter of continuing theoretical debate (Arsenio & Lemerise, 2001; Crick & Dodge, 1999; O'Moore & Kirkham, 2001; Sutton, Smith, & Swettenham, 1999a, 1999b; Toblin, Schwartz, Gorman, & Aboudezzeddine, 2005). Each

BOX 6.4 ROADMAP TO UNDERSTANDING THEORY AND RESEARCH

An Experiment in Emotion Regulation

In a laboratory study, children were made angry by losing at a computer game while being taunted by a peer who was a "confederate" in the research (Underwood & Hurley, 1999). After the provocation but before a debriefing, the researchers asked the children a series of questions about what they felt like doing to the peer and why they did not show their true feelings. Responses reflected the extreme variability in strategies for emotion regulation during middle childhood:

- *"Keeping my mouth shut, and smiling back at him."*
- *"Teaching him a lesson, telling him how to do things to make people like him," but did not because he "didn't feel like it."*
- *"I felt like hitting her," but did not because "I knew it wouldn't help me win the game or anything."*
- *"I felt like I wanted to smack her," but did not "because I am not here to fight." This same girl told us that she usually hits people who provoke her.*
- *"Just killing myself—I hate my sister when she is being sassy and naughty, that's when I feel like killing myself," but that he did not do this because "I usually hit myself in the head or stop thinking about it or stop the game."*
- *"I felt like saying 'I am trying as hard as I can and please don't tease me,'" but did not because "I thought I would be hurting her feelings."*

The researchers questioned why some children are able to be very strategic about controlling their emotions in a manner consistent with their social goals and why others are so disregulated. They acknowledged that emotion researchers and peer relations experts alike have agreed that emotions influence all aspects of social information processing and that emotions are regulated at many different levels. But they concluded that emotion regulation is complicated by the fact that emotional arousal is determined not only by various types of regulatory processes but also by individual differences in temperament, such as emotional intensity, as shown in the previous examples. The researchers suggest that given that children's interactions with peers can generate everything from extreme happiness to intense pain, examining children's developing emotion scripts for managing emotions with peers might provide insight into how and why emotions can energize or overwhelm us.

Source: Based on "Emotion Regulation in Peer Relationships During Middle Childhood," by M. K. Underwood & J. C. Hurley, in L. Balter & C. S. Tamis-LaMonda (Eds.), *Child Psychology: A Handbook of Contemporary Issues* (p. 255), 1999, Philadelphia: Psychology Press. Copyright 1999 by Psychology Press.

of these explanations has some empirical support. For example, among fourth-grade boys, better perspective-taking ability was related to more severe antisocial behavior—perhaps because the bully knows what will "get" the other person (e.g., Sutton, Smith, & Swettenham, 1999a).

In other studies, the processing of social information has successfully discriminated ***proactive* aggression**, which is similar to bullying, from ***reactive* aggression**, which occurs in the heat of the moment (e.g., Crick & Dodge, 1999). The model of proactive aggression assumes that there is usually an ulterior motive for aggressive behavior, such as appearing powerful to your peers. Such socially reinforced aggression does not need a precipitating event for it to occur, but may be prompted by temperamental dispositions of the bully (Thompson, Arora, & Sharp, 2002). For example, individual differences in empathy and emotional regulation have been suggested as an alternative explanation for bullying (Arsenio & Lemerise, 2001), as described in Box 6.4. Research on bullying suggests that bullies are characterized by weak impulse control, strong aggressive tendencies, and a high tolerance for aggression. Not surprisingly, affiliating with an aggressive crowd decreases the likelihood that children will be victims of overt aggression (Prinstein & La Greca, 2002).

Frequently, bullies do not experience much resistance to their aggression (Rubin, Bukowski, & Parker, 1998). Reluctance to intervene begins with children over the age of 8 or 9, possibly because younger children are less aware of peer group pressure (Thompson, Arora, & Sharp, 2002). See Box 6.5 for a sample checklist to screen for bullying victimization. Victims of bullies often have difficulty

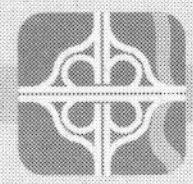

BOX 6.5 ROADMAP TO SUCCESSFUL PRACTICE

Life in School Checklist

The *Life in School Checklist* can provide the following:

- A bullying index
- A comprehensive picture of "life in school"
- A means of identifying individuals who are likely to be victims of bullying
- Extra information of your own choice can be obtained by putting your own questions on the back page

TABLE 6–9

Life in School Checklist

This checklist can be used to determine if school-age children were bullied in the past week.

I am a boy ☐ **I am a girl** ☐ **Age** ☐ **Year** ☐

During this week another child	No	Once	More than once
1. Helped me with my homework			
2. Called me names			
3. Said something nice to me			
4. Teased me about my family			
5. Tried to kick me			
6. Was very nice to me			
7. Teased me because I am different			
8. Gave me a present			
9. Threatened to hurt me			
10. Gave me some money			
11. Demanded money from me			
12. Tried to frighten me			
13. Asked me a stupid question			
14. Lent me something			
15. Told me off			
16. Teased me			
17. Talked about clothes with me			
18. Told me a joke			
19. Told me a lie			
20. Ganged up on me			
21. Tried to aspire me hurt other people			
22. Smiled at me			
23. Tried to get me into trouble			
24. Helped me carry something			
25. Tried to hurt me			
26. Helped me with my classwork			
27. Made me do something I didn't want to			
28. Talked about T.V. with me			
29. Took something off me			
30. Shared something with me			
31. Was rude about the colour of my skin			
32. Shouted at me			
33. Played a game with me			
34. Tried to trip me up			
35. Talked about interests with me			
36. Laughed at me			
37. Threatened to tell on me			
38. Tried to break something of mine			
39. Told a lie about me			
40. Tried to hit me			

Source: From "Measuring Bullying with the 'Life in School' Checklist," by T. Arora, in D. Thompson, T. Arora, & S. Sharp, *Bullying: Effective Strategies for Long-Term Improvement* (pp. 184–189), 2002, London: Routledge Falmer. Copyright 2002 by David Thompson, Tiny Arora, & Sonia Sharp. Reprinted by permission.

Children are asked to report only on those events that happened during the past week because people's recall of events that happened more than a week ago is fairly poor, and estimates based on looking further back in time are therefore more unreliable. The index can be used for groups of students of around 40 or more, so it will also be possible to assess the effects that the strategies are having on different groups in the school. For groups smaller than 40, the index will not be sufficiently reliable to allow valid comparisons.

Based on the checklist designed for secondary schools, over half of both students and teachers see the following items as instances of bullying:

- ***Item 5.*** Tried to kick me
- ***Item 9.*** Threatened to hurt me
- ***Item 11.*** Demanded money from me
- ***Item 25.*** Tried to hurt me
- ***Item 38.*** Tried to break something of mine
- ***Item 40.*** Tried to hit me

Children who check these items under the "*more than once*" category are likely to see themselves as victims of bullying. If limited time is available for analysis and if the main interest is in bullying, then the responses to these items alone will give a quick impression of the extent of this occurring in a school.

Scoring the Bullying Index

- ***Step 1.*** For each of the six items, count the number of times that a check was placed under the category "more than once." Do this separately for each item (Items 5, 9, 11, 25, 38, and 40).
- ***Step 2.*** Divide the scores for each separate item by the number of checklists completed. Multiply by 100 to obtain the percentage of student responses under each item.
- ***Step 3.*** Add all six percentages.
- ***Step 4.*** Divide this number by 6.

The figure thus obtained is the Bullying Index (e.g., 7.12 or 8.03). The range of the index can vary a great deal from school to school.

The entire checklist can be used to obtain a more all-around picture of what happens in school during a period of one week. This is also useful for looking at a small group or for assessing how an individual student experiences contacts with other students in the school. In the case of groups, it will be possible to work out the percentages of the responses to each item on the checklist under the two different categories of "*once*" and "*more than once*." The main purpose of the index is to use it like a dipstick, at the beginning of an intervention and at later intervals in order to find out whether the antibullying strategies are having an effect.

managing conflicts and lack self-confidence, self-esteem, and prosocial skills (Champion, Vernberg, & Shipman, 2003).

A recent naturalistic study of bullying in grades 1 to 6 examined what happens when peers *did* intervene (about half the time) on behalf of the victim (Hawkins, Pepler, & Craig, 2001). Interventions directed toward the bully were likely to be aggressive, whereas interventions directed toward the victim or the dyad were nonaggressive. In addition, girls were more likely to intervene when the bully and victim were female and used mostly verbal assertions. Boys were more likely to intervene when the bully and victim were male and used verbal, physical, and a combination of the two types about equally. The majority of all peer interventions were effective in stopping the bullying (Hawkins, Pepler, & Craig, 2001).

Antibullying programs may be individual, family, or systems focused (Kerns & Prinz, 2002). Such programs in schools recommend teaching children conflict resolution skills, how to help victims, and when to seek adult help (Garrity et al., 1995; Swearer & Doll, 2002). Other recommendations include promoting relationships between students and playground or lunchroom supervisors, raising teachers' awareness of bullying, and providing training for all the adults in identifying bullying incidents (Sharp & Smith, 1994). For example, one successful violence prevention provided workshops for teachers, administrators, hall monitors, teaching assistants, the school secretary, nurse, and police officer on a curriculum in teaching prosocial skills and anger management (Casella & Burstyn, 2002). See Box 6.6 for a list of bullying prevention strategies.

Guideposts for Working with School-Age Children

- Encourage prosocial reasoning by doing activities such as role-playing and discussing alternative ways of helping others in need.
- Help children to identify the various crowds in their school or neighborhood and to think about with whom they may feel either comfortable or challenged.
- Discuss the hurtfulness of stereotyping others based on their social group membership (e.g., ethnicity, race, gender, nationality, religion, or sexual orientation).
- Discourage gossiping, peer exclusion, and other forms of relational aggression.
- Suggest to children ways of identifying and responding to bullying.

BOX 6.6 PREVENTION OF BULLYING

Prevention Strategies

- Patrol "bullying hot spots."
- Find out who is often involved in bullying.
- Avoid labeling children.
- Watch out for lone students.
- Talk to students who are directly involved.
- Make it known that bullying won't be tolerated.

Responding to Aggression and Resolving Conflict

- Try to keep calm.
- Avoid rushing.
- Do not be seen to jump to conclusions.
- Listen well.
- Don't be sidetracked.
- Avoid sarcasm and direct personal criticism.
- Label the behavior and not the child.
- Don't make threats that can't or won't be carried out.
- Don't use severe threats at the very beginning.
- Avoid using teachers as a means of controlling children.
- Consider using a "time-out" tactic.
- Look for a "win-win" solution.
- Develop a hierarchy of sanctions.

Encourage Positive Behavior

- Adopt a "catch them being good" philosophy.
- Small rewards can be effective.
- Have the same reward system in the classroom as on the school grounds.
- Pass on information about good behavior.
- Remember individual differences.
- Respond to children's self-reports of good behavior.
- Introduce a student "things I am proud of" book.
- Set up student self-monitoring using a charting system.

Source: Based on "How to Prevent and Respond to Bullying Behavior in the Junior/Middle School Playground," by M. Boulton, in S. Sharp & P. K. Smith (Eds.), *Tackling Bullying in Your School: A Practical Handbook for Teachers (pp. 122–130), 1994,* London: Routledge. Copyright 1994 by Sonia Sharp and Peter K. Smith.

Social Development in Context

The contexts for peer interaction in middle childhood have changed since early childhood, from home and child care settings to a wider variety of social settings, such as being together at school, talking on the telephone, "hanging out" in the neighborhood, watching videos or listening to music, and sports (see Zarbatany, Hartmann, & Rankin, 1990). Each of these social contexts provides school-age children frequent opportunities to develop deeper understandings of others, increased moral and prosocial reasoning, and effective social skills. For example, the quality of parents' friendships is related to the quality of children's friendships (Simpkins & Parke, 2001).

Family Contexts

A great deal of debate has centered around the relative impact of parents and peers in middle childhood, but despite the claims of peer socialization theorists (see Harris, 1999), most scholars maintain that parents have an important influence on middle childhood (and adolescent) values, attitudes, and behaviors. For example, when fifth- to ninth-grade students reported to whom they talked over the course of a week, time spent talking to friends increased dramatically with age, as expected, but *did not* replace talk with family members (Raffaelli & Duckett, 1989). In addition, when children trust parents not to overreact or ridicule their behaviors, future positive communication is promoted (Kerr, Stattin, Biesecker, & Ferrer-Wreder, 2003). In a study of seventh graders, for example, parents' supportive behaviors promoted their children's positive behaviors towards their siblings and friends, which, in turn, predicted the quality of teenagers' friendships four years later. (Cui, Conger, Bryant, & Elder, 2002).

Although in some ways siblings are like peers, the nature and level of negativity between siblings is likely to differ from that of friends for two reasons (McHale, Dariotis, & Kauh, 2003, for a review of sibling relationships in middle childhood):

- **Siblings Are Not Usually the Same Age.** (unless they are twins) Children more often assume a leader or follower role with siblings than their friends, who are more often age peers.
- **Sibling Relationships Are Not Voluntary.** Children are more likely to invest in maintaining harmony with their peers because they could lose their friendship.

Parents not only influence their children through direct interaction but also function as managers of their children's lives (Parke & Buriel, 1998). For example, see Figure 6.8 for ways parents can influence children's choice of friends. Some family theorists have recently proposed models that integrate parent and peer contexts through the mechanisms of children's disclosure of their daily activities to parents (e.g., Kerr et al., 2003) or parental monitoring of their children's activities and whereabouts (e.g., Dishion & McMahon, 1998). Much research now supports a link between parents' monitoring of their children's lives and less antisocial behavior (Amato & Fowler, 2002). For example, children in grades 6 to 9 (especially girls

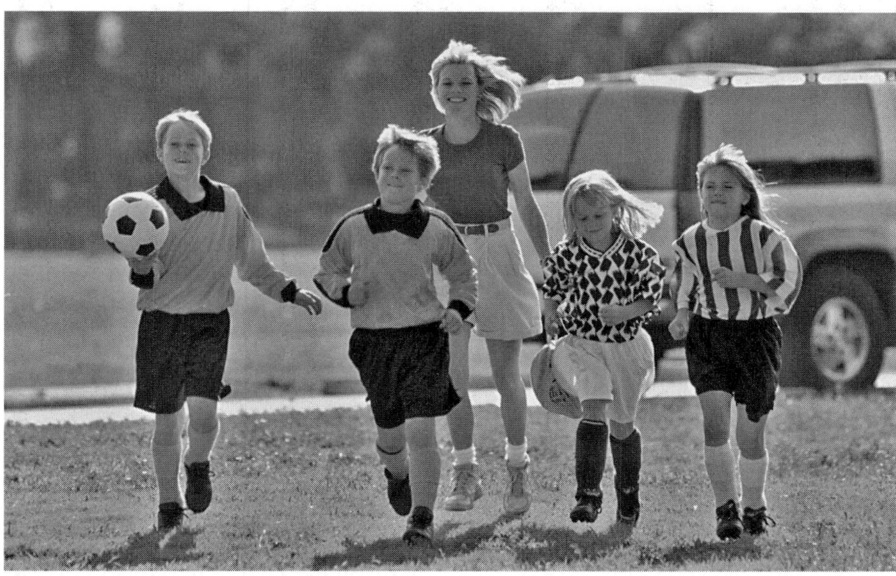

By supporting their children's extracurricular activities, parents can structure and influence children's friendships.

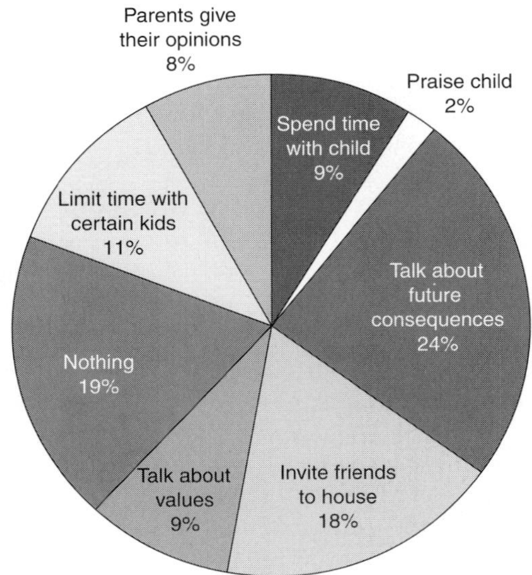

FIGURE 6.8 Parenting Strategies
Parents use a variety of strategies to influence their children's choices of friends.

Source: From "Parental Management of Adolescent Peer Relationships," by N. S. Mounts, in K. A. Kerns, J. M. Contreras, & A. M. Neal-Barnett (Eds.), *Family and Peers: Linking Two Social Worlds*, (p. 174), 2000, Westport, CT: Praeger. Copyright 2000 by Katherine A. Kerns, Josefina M. Contreras & Angela M. Neal-Barnett. Reprinted by permission of Greenwood Publishing Group, Inc.

who are on their own after school) are more susceptible to peer pressure after school to engage in antisocial activity, such as stealing or vandalism (Steinberg, 1986). In addition, ineffective parenting predicted middle childhood boys' antisocial behavior and association with deviant peers at ages 12 to 16 (Bank, Burraston, & Snyder, 2004).

Mandy and Alesha are unsupervised after coming home from school, giving them an opportunity for drug use.

Discussions of parenting and family contexts inevitably raise the issue of values (Cowan, Powell, & Cowan, 1998). For example, there is little agreement on whether children should fight back when bullied or try to avoid aggression or retaliation. To think about how children acquire values or standards of behavior in social contexts, such as family or peer contexts, requires "a more explicit interest in the agency of parents and children, that is, in the meanings they construct of each others' behavior, in their capacity for strategic action, and in their ability to behave 'as if' the other is also an agent" (Grusec, Goodnow, & Kuczynski, 2000, p. 205). Such approaches may include alerting school-age children to competing ways to view the world and helping them to hold "internal dialogues" with others—their parents, for example—as they face moral or social dilemmas (Grusec, Goodnow, & Kuczynski, 2000).

Let's return to our chapter case one last time. As Alesha is thinking about Mandy's offer to get high and contemplating the dilemma of doing inhalants or risking the new friendship, she engages in an "internal" conversation with her parents. She can hear her parents say, "Only losers do drugs" and thinks to herself, "But I'm not one of those kids!"

School Contexts

The two contexts that are most frequently cited in the study of social development in middle childhood and adolescence are peer networks and schools. Past research has shown that characteristics of schools (e.g., structure, composition, climate) predict friendships and peer interaction. For example, curriculum tracking and extracurricular activities are key organizers of friendships (Crosnoe, 2000). In a study of fifth- and sixth-grade girls, students kept week-long diaries of important peer activities and liked and disliked peer behaviors in those activities (Zarbatany, Hartmann, & Rankin, 1990). Students preferred school activities that provided

- A context for sociability
- Concern for achievements
- Integrity of the self
- Opportunities for instruction and learning

As we saw in chapter 5, students report higher social and affective competence in schools that present them with appropriate challenges, help them to see value in participation, and make them feel safe and cared for by others (Roesner, Eccles, & Sameroff, 2000).

Recent research has also demonstrated that academic achievement, substance use, and delinquency are moderated by school climate (Crosnoe & Needham, 2004). In a person-centered study of friendship in grades 7 to 12 (again, see chapter 2), researchers obtained four friendship group profiles comprised of friends' drinking behavior, academic achievement, extracurricular participation, and emotional distress (see Figure 6.9). In schools where there was more closeness between students and teachers, there were fewer behavioral problems across all four types of friendship networks. These results suggest that a school climate promoting closeness, caring, and mentoring may be a

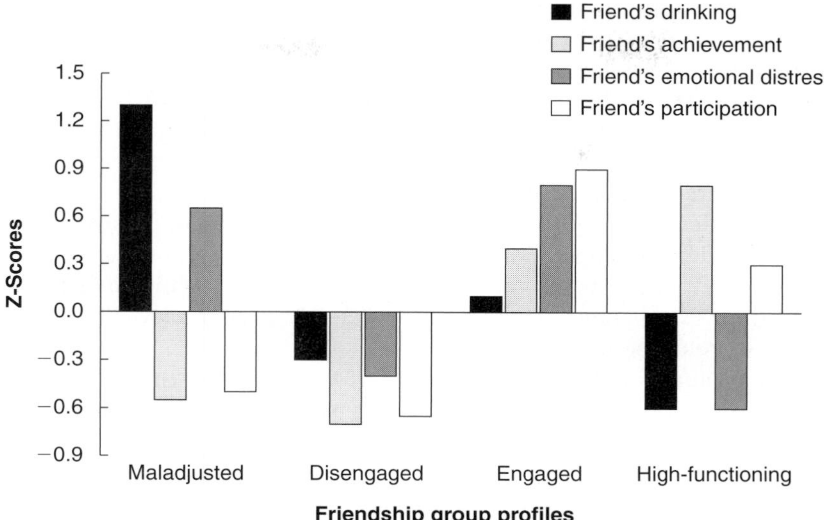

FIGURE 6.9 Adolescent Friendship Group Profiles
For all four types of friendship groups, a positive school climate counteracted problem behaviors.

Source: From "Holism, Contextual Variability, and the Study of Friendships in Adolescent Development," by R. Crosnoe & B. Needham, 2004, *Child Development, 75*, p. 271. Copyright 2004 by the Society for Research in Child Development. Reprinted by permission of the society.

protective factor against risk of problem behaviors in adolescence (Crosnoe & Needham, 2004).

The prevention of violence is a concern in most present-day schools, and the last decade in particular has seen a burgeoning of violence prevention programs in schools. Researchers have recently examined the effects of school-based interventions on developmental trajectories toward violence in grades 1 to 6. In general, boys, lower-income students, and racial minority children demonstrated higher initial levels of risk and increases in violence from ages 6 to 12, but lower-risk children (i.e., girls, higher-income students, and White children) caught up to the high-risk group by age 12. All of the children, however, were deflected from paths toward aggression and violence when their teachers taught a conflict resolution curriculum (Aber, Brown, & Jones, 2003).

Other violence prevention programs are addressing the whole school, meaning that they attempt to alter the school climate. For example, middle-school students who have engaged in violent behavior also experience disconnection from the school and teachers. Therefore, a starting place for violence prevention may be to enhance students' sense of belonging (Karcher, 2002).

Community Contexts

School-age children tend to draw their friends from their communities (Crosnoe, 2000). An ecological perspective (refer to chapter 1) considers peer and family relationships in the context of the larger cultural community in which they are embedded (e.g., McHale, Dariotis, & Kauh, 2003). Does community disadvantage tend to affect peer relationships? In an investigation of the social networks of parents and children, adolescents who had a high degree of contact among their parents, their friends, their friends' parents, and other adults in the community (termed **social integration**) had lower levels of deviancy but only in neighborhoods that were "*positive*." In poor neighborhoods with less social integration, effects were negative (see Parke & Buriel, 1998).

Efforts to capture variation in children's life circumstances have often relied on global indexes, such as social class or ethnic background, called *social address* variables. However, cultural anthropologists have described children's social ecologies, called **niches** (McHale, Dariotis, & Kauh, 2003; see also Weisner, 2001). Ecological niches have direct implications for social development in middle childhood. Examples of niches include how and where school-age children spend their time, their companions in everyday activities, and accompanying cultural scripts (McHale, Dariotis, & Kauh, 2003), *such as "just say no to drugs."*

Despite developmental psychologists' use of ecological theory, however, they often focus on individual child outcomes rather than the paths that children must travel during development (Crosnoe, 2000). Sociologists and social psychologists, on the other hand, have utilized life-course theory (described in detail in the next chapter). The life-course study of social development emphasizes history as an important context for development. For example, changes in growth, technology, schooling, family patterns, community organization, and the rights and responsibilities of youth could affect their orientation to friends, the influences exerted by friends, and the control of friendship by adults (Crosnoe, 2000). A life-course perspective operates on the premise that social behavior depends on carefully analyzing the potential role of community-level agents of socialization, including friends, social clubs, youth organizations, religious groups, informal peer associations, and even gangs (Mussen & Eisenberg, 2001).

What family, school, or community groups did you belong to as a child?

CHAPTER REVIEW

Social Development

- Social development in middle childhood includes increasing interpersonal understanding, refining concepts of friendship, using moral reasoning to guide social interactions, and acquiring social skills.
- Social competence is defined as the ability to interact effectively with others.

Theoretical Viewpoints

- Social learning theory states that we learn social skills by observing others, using the processes of attention, retention, motor reproduction, and reinforcement.
- Social cognitive theory accounts for the reciprocal influences of the environment, the person, and his or her own behaviors on subsequent actions.
- Social information-processing theory describes the cognitive steps used to process social information, from initially encoding internal and external cues to finally enacting a behavior.
- Social theories of mind claim that we construct predictions about others' behaviors based on our understandings of their mental states.

Social and Moral Understanding

- Social role-taking involves a gradual increase in understanding the perspectives of others in social interactions.
- Interpersonal negotiation strategies for resolving social conflicts increase across middle childhood.
- Moral reasoning changes from compliance with authority to an increasing ability to reflect on social conventions, fairness, and the needs of others.

Peer Relations

- Peer acceptance fulfills school-agers' communal needs for support and companionship with others.
- Friendships during middle childhood change from occasional interactions into enduring reciprocal relationships involving trust and mutual support.
- Popularity, or social status, becomes a central concern in middle childhood and predicts school-agers' social skills and school adjustment.
- Friendship networks in middle childhood are usually composed of same-sex, same-age peers.

Social Skills and Behavior

- Prosocial behavior in middle childhood often involves supporting friends and including others in peer groups, as well as the more common sharing and helping behaviors seen in early childhood.
- Antisocial behaviors of school-age children often include peer aggression and bullying, as well as acts of delinquency, such as substance abuse, stealing, or lying.
- Aggression may be physical, verbal, or relational (the social exclusion of others).

Social Development in Context

- Peer relations supplement, but do not replace, family relations and the importance of parenting during middle childhood.
- Schools with a positive social climate among students, staff, and teachers are less prone to school violence and bullying.
- Neighborhoods with high levels of social integration (frequent contact among adults and children) and many culturally relevant models provide opportunities for positive social and moral development.

TABLE 6–10

Summary of Developmental Theories

Chapter 6 presented three social-cognitive theories to explain social development in middle childhood.

Chapter	Theory	Focus
6: Social Development in Middle Childhood	Social Learning	Learning by observing models and by examining the consequences of their own and others' behaviors in the social environment
	Social Information Processing	Cognitive steps that children take when making sense of social cues and deciding how to respond to others
	Social Theories of Mind	Ways that children themselves create theories to explain and predict other people's motivations and behaviors

KEY TERMS

Acquaintances
Agency
Aggressive behavior
Altruism
Antisocial behavior
Bullying
Character education
Chums
Clique
Communal needs
Controversial status
Conventional level
Crowd
Differential-association
Distributive justice
Empathic
Ethical relativism
Ethics of care
Friendship stages
Interpersonal orientation
Interpersonal negotiation
Moral realists
Moral reasoning levels
Moral relativists
Moral values
Peer acceptance
Popularity/popular status
Proactive aggression
Prosocial behavior
Reactive aggression
Reciprocal determinism
Social cognition
Social cognitive theory
Social competence
Social conventions
Social information processing
Social learning theory
Social perspective-taking
Social provisions
Sociometric
Theories of mind
Vicarious reinforcement

SUGGESTED ACTIVITIES

1. Select a novel for young readers from the youth literature section of a library or bookstore. Describe the nature of the peer interactions, friendships, and moral dilemmas portrayed in the story.
2. Interview a school-age child about his or her friendships. Ask about the child's best friend, peer network (clique), and social group (crowd).
3. Read an early adolescent online diary (web log, or "blog") at http://diaryland.com, http://livejournal.com, http://freeopendiary.com, http://blurty.com, http://xanga.com, or http://deadjournal.com. Analyze the blog's content and related peer commentary for evidence of antisocial behavior (e.g., relational aggression, gossip) or prosocial behavior (e.g., support, friendship).
4. Play a card game, such as "Scruples for Children," that presents moral dilemmas for discussion or make up some ethical issues of your own. How would school-age children typically answer if they were conventional thinkers? How would they apply the positive justice principles of fairness to the situation?

RECOMMENDED RESOURCES

Suggested Readings

Blume, L. B., & Isbey, J. A. (2002). Youth fiction: Using chapter books and novels for young readers to teach about middle childhood. *Journal of Teaching in Marriage and Family: Innovations in Family Science Education, 2*(4), 454–474.

Gilligan, C. (1982). *In a different voice: Psychological theory and women's development.* Cambridge, MA: Harvard University Press.

Nucci, L. P. (2001). *Education in the moral domain.* Cambridge, UK: Cambridge University Press.

Selman, R. L. (2003). *The promotion of social awareness: Powerful lessons from the partnership of developmental theory and classroom practice.* New York: Russell Sage Foundation.

Simmons, R. (2002). *Odd girl out: The hidden culture of aggression in girls.* New York: Harcourt.

Suggested Online Resources

Bullying Resources: California Department of Education. http://www.cde.ca.gov/ls/ss/se/bullyres.asp

Olweus Bullying Prevention Program. http://modelprograms.samhsa.gov/pdfs/FactSheets/Olweus%20Bully.pdf

Stop Bullying Now. http://www.stopbullyingnow.hrsa.gov/index.asp?area=main

Overlap Between Peer Networks and Friends and Its Implications. http://www.sonet.pdx.edu/PeerNetworks/GroupID/Overlap-Net&Frnds.htm

Teaching Social Awareness: An Interview with Robert Selman. http://gseweb.harvard.edu/news/features/selman02012003.html

Young people in Canada: Their health and well-being. Chapter 4: The peer group. http://www.phac-aspc.gc.ca/dca-dea/publications/hbsc-2004/chapter_4_e.html

Suggested Web Sites

Association for Moral Education http://www.amenetwork.org

Character Education Partnership http://www.character.org

Office for Studies in Moral Development and Education http://MoralEd.org

Social Networks Research Group: Peer Networks http://www.sonet.pdx.edu/PeerNetworks/index.htm

Sociometry in the Classroom: How to Do It http://www.users.muohio.edu/shermalw/sociometryfiles/sociointroduction.htmlx

Suggested Films and Videos

Bandura's social cognitive theory: An introduction (2003). Insight Media, Inc. (30 minutes)

Moral development I & II (1989). Magna Systems, Inc. (29 minutes each)

Peer pressure: Why are all my friends staring at me? (1991). Insight Media, Inc. (15 minutes)

How to develop values (2001). Magna Systems, Inc. (19 minutes)

A Society of children: Psychosocial development during the School Years (2003). Insight Media, Inc. (30 minutes)

Understanding and coping with bullies (2001). Magna Systems, Inc. (20 minutes)

The wonder years, episode 29: "*Odd man out*" (1989). New World Entertainment (25 minutes)

PART 2

Transition to Adolescence

CHAPTER 7 Perspectives on Middle Adolescence

CHAPTER 8 Physical Development in Middle Adolescence

CHAPTER 9 Cognitive Development in Middle Adolescence

CHAPTER 10 Affective Development in Middle Adolescence

CHAPTER 11 Social Development in Middle Adolescence

CHAPTER 12 Beyond Middle Adolescence: Emerging Adulthood

CHAPTER 

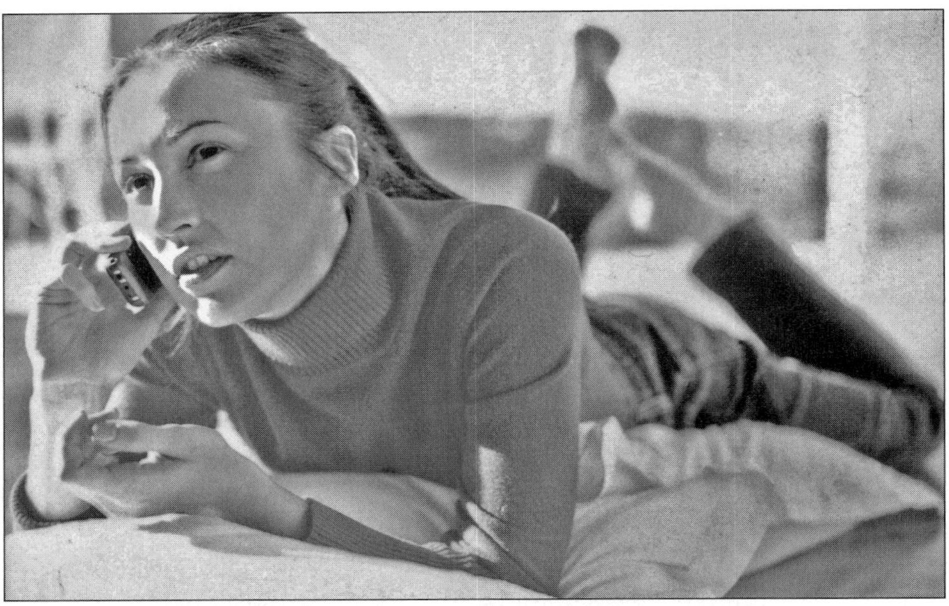

Perspectives on Middle Adolescence

CHAPTER OBJECTIVES

After reading this chapter, students will be able to:

- Define middle adolescence and the timing of adolescent transitions
- Discuss historical and contemporary portrayals of adolescence as a distinct period of development
- Name the developmental achievements of middle adolescence
- Describe the diverse ecological contexts of middle adolescence
- Compare research perspectives on risk and opportunity in the teen years
- Explain the goals of an applied focus that translates practice into policy

Leticia is worried. She's 15, and she hasn't yet been on a real date. She frequently goes to movies or parties on the weekends, but always in a group. Leticia looks grown up. She is tall for her age, has a great figure, and wears the latest styles. Fitting in and having lots of friends is becoming more important to Leticia than getting good grades. But her mother insists that Leticia pick up her younger brother Raúl from elementary school and come right home, so she can't hang out like the other kids. She fixes Raúl a snack, does her homework, and then calls her girlfriend Marina on the phone. Leticia complains, "Now if I can just convince my mother to let me go to the mall on school nights! After all, I'm almost 16!"

DEFINING MIDDLE ADOLESCENCE

Middle adolescence is the developmental period between puberty and young adulthood, roughly ages 13 to 18. The problems faced by Leticia are part of a normative dilemma experienced by many adolescents. Caught between childhood and adulthood, their struggle is to find a place in family, school, society, and peer cultures consistent with the ways in which adolescence is defined in each of these developmental contexts. Problems arise, however, because—as with middle childhood—our society defines adolescence differently depending on your perspective as a parent, teacher, program provider, employer, or policy maker. Teens themselves, whether just 13 or almost 18, may think that their lives are "on hold," as illustrated in Figure 7.1. In addition, teen self-help books, such as *What Teens Need to Succeed: Proven, Practical Ways to Shape Your Own Future* (Benson, Espeland, & Galbraith, 1998) often characterize teens as future adults.

What self-help books or teen magazines did you read as an adolescent? How did they portray adolescents?

A recurring question frequently asked by adolescents is "*Am I old enough now [to drive, to work, to date . . .]*?" A corresponding question asked by many parents and teachers is "*How do I know when adolescence begins, and when it ends?*" Still a third question often asked by community leaders is "*How will adolescents fit into the adult world?*" These three questions correspond to three underlying assumptions that will guide our study of middle adolescent development in the remaining chapters of this text:

- The primary developmental achievement of adolescents is maturing into adults—whether in the physical, cognitive, affective, or social domains of development.
- Adolescence is a cultural construction that may be differently defined across cultures, ethnic groups, or nationalities, or perhaps not exist at all in some societies.
- A society's ultimate goal for adolescents is to prepare for adulthood, by minimizing possible risks and maximizing potential opportunities for youth development.

Therefore, we view adolescence as *both* a stage of development and as a developmental transition, echoing the approach to middle childhood used in the first half of this textbook. For example, when we examine whether the socially constructed meanings of "being adolescent" have changed historically or are essentially unchanged from G. Stanley Hall's (1904) turn-of-the-20th-century description, we find that current developmental researchers often conceptualize adolescence as affording either opportunities or risks to teens in transition. For example, a book called *Youth Crisis: Growing Up in a High Risk Society* (Davis, 1999) portrays the social conditions of adolescence at the end of the 20th century as affording many *risks*, such as homelessness, addiction, and violence, but little *protection* by society.

The contemporary perspective (i.e., that youth-in-crisis occurs in the context of a high-risk environment) contrasts with Hall's earlier idea that a crisis in adolescence is developmental (i.e., that all adolescents experience a normative crisis). Hall's hypothesis was that adolescence is a normative period of ***sturm und drang*** ("storm and stress") that must be endured on the pathway to adulthood. This viewpoint has affected not only today's popular notion of the teen years as troubled but also the scientific study of adolescents in crisis in such fields as psychology, psychiatry, education, criminal justice, sociology, and social work.

HISTORICAL VIEWS OF ADOLESCENCE

The English word **adolescent** is derived from a Latin root meaning "to nourish or to grow." Western societies saw adolescence as a time for education, training in practical arts, or apprenticeship. This formative view of adolescence persisted in Europe throughout the Middle Ages and the Enlightenment and was subsequently brought to the United States by the early colonists. Apprenticeship, however, was seen as more important than formal schooling for most adolescents in colonial America, as we discussed in chapter 2.

Most children did not stay in school beyond the primary grades, except for wealthy boys (and a few privileged girls) who attended private academies intended to prepare them for elite colleges. Most adolescents worked on farms, in mines, or in factories as soon as they could legally leave school (i.e., at age 16, or at age 14 if their labor was needed to support their families). Native American and African American children often could not attend school at all (Hine, 1999).

FIGURE 7.1 Teenagers
Teenagers are often impatient when it comes to acquiring the privileges that accompany increasing maturity.
Source: From G. Evans, "Luann," February 20, 1994. Copyright 1994 by GEC Inc. Reprinted by permission of United Features Syndicate, Inc.

Modern Contributions to the Construction of Adolescence

The first public high school, in Boston, opened in 1821, partly as a result of a national committee called the Committee on Secondary School Studies (Hine, 1999). Also known as the "Committee of Ten," this group directed the work of 90 subcommittee members from all parts of the United States (National Education Association, 1969). They identified three major problems with secondary education:

- Wide divergence in courses of study
- Uncertain standards of admission
- Minimal requirements for graduation

In their final report to the U.S. Bureau of Education in 1893, the committee concluded that secondary schools were the most "defective" part of education in the United States.

Ten years later, in 1913, the National Education Association appointed a commission to reorganize secondary education. Their report, called *The Cardinal Principles of Secondary Education*, stated broad social goals for schools and for society, such as education for living in a democracy and preparation for the workplace (Boyer, 1983). But despite the best efforts of educators, secondary schools were not prevalent in all U.S. communities until the 1930s. Even then, high schools served only

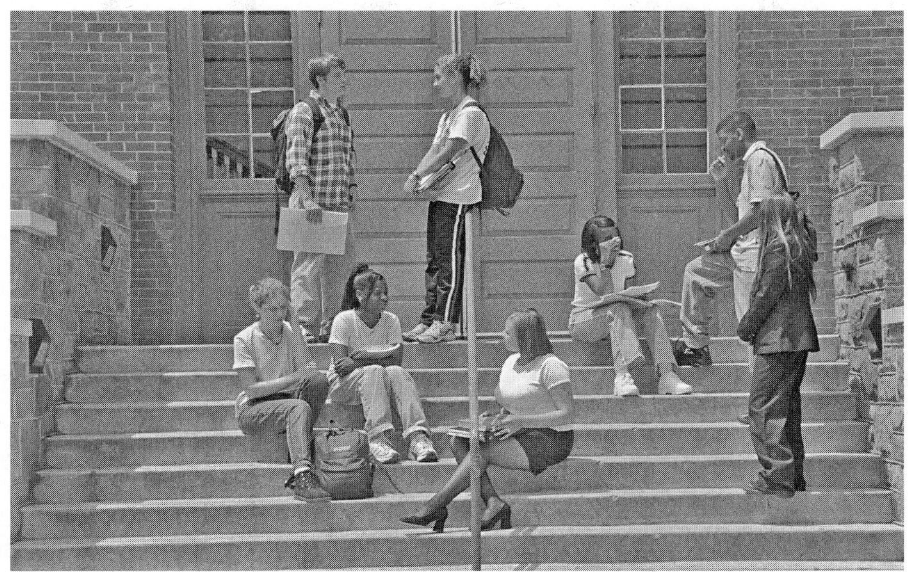

Modern high schools are an important context for adolescent development.

47% of the adolescent age group, with separate schools for Black students (Hine, 1999).

By the 1950s, a majority of White American teenagers completed high school. Box 7.1 highlights a now-classic study that describes the segregated education of adolescents in Elmtown, a prototypical Midwestern town (Hollingshead, 1949). However, in 1954, the U.S. Supreme Court mandated equal access to education for racial minorities with the Brown vs. Board of Education decision (Boyer, 1983). America struggled to improve secondary education—not only as a response to the civil rights movement but also to satisfy a popular desire for scientific superiority during the Cold War of the 1950s and 1960s. For example, a Carnegie-funded study of American high schools urging a more comprehensive academic curriculum called *The American High School Today* (Conant, 1959/1967) became a best seller.

During the 1960s and 1970s, concerns about the academic preparedness of adolescents were replaced by an even more democratic concern. An emphasis on community service and youth leadership arose from a focus on disadvantaged students during the federal "War on Poverty" (Boyer, 1983; Tucker, 1999). By the early 1980s, the Carnegie Foundation for the Advancement of Teaching issued a comprehensive report on secondary education in the United States, affirming two goals for improving public education:

- To recognize that all students must be prepared for a lifetime of both work and further education, and
- To give students more opportunities for service in anticipation of their growing civic and social responsibilities as they become adults (Boyer, 1983).

Box 7.2 outlines five items from the agenda developed by the Carnegie Commission. These recommendations are significant because they focused the nation's attention on the importance of educational opportunity for all adolescents.

At about the same time, the Commission on Work, Family, and Citizenship was formed by the William T. Grant Foundation to study the economic conditions affecting adolescents and young adults in the United States who did *not* attend college after completing high school (Youth and America's Future, 1988). In their report, called *The Forgotten Half*, they cited factors that inordinately affected teenagers from working-class families:

- High unemployment
- A 27% decrease in the median income levels of American families
- Greater numbers of single-parent households

BOX 7.1 ROADMAP TO UNDERSTANDING THEORY AND RESEARCH

Elmtown's Youth

August B. Hollingshead's ethnographic research of the 1940s was one of the first studies to highlight the impact of social class on youth development. A professor at Yale University, he studied a typical Midwestern U.S. town he called Elmtown (pop. 6,200). According to Hollingshead, Elmtown teenagers knew more about the family, the school, the church, the grocery, and the butcher than they did about the county government or banking institutions, as would be expected. Nevertheless, although there were not *supposed* to be class differences in America, most high-schoolers knew that their families' economic status would subtly affect them as they faced the transition from child to adult.

Hollingshead also found that adolescents, no matter what their class position, who could not obtain money from their families to participate in their peer group's activities faced the dilemma of entering the workforce or staying in school. "If he takes the school road, he will move into an entirely different social world from the one he will traverse if he takes the work road. A middle road between the two is traveled by those who combine school with part-time work out of school hours" (p. 148). Hollingshead concluded that sometime between ages 14 and 18, Elmtown's teens made this choice, a decision that affected their social relations with practically every institution in the community throughout the adolescent years and into adult life.

Source: Based on "The Adolescent in the Community," by A. E. Hollingshead, 1949 Elmtown Youth (pp. 148–159), New York: Wiley. Copyright 1949 by John Wiley & Sons, Inc.

BOX 7.2 ROADMAP TO SUCCESSFUL PRACTICE

High School: Five Items from "An Agenda for Action"

1. **Clarifying Goals.** A high school, to be effective, must have a clear and vital mission. Educators must have a shared vision of what, together, they are trying to accomplish. That vision should go beyond keeping students in school and out of trouble, and be more significant than adding up the Carnegie course units the student has completed.

2. **The Centrality of Language.** The next priority is language. Formal schooling has a special obligation to help all students become skilled in the written and oral use of English. Those who do not become proficient in the primary language of the culture are enormously disadvantaged in school and out of school as well.

3. **The Curriculum Has a Core.** A core of common learning is essential. The basic curriculum should be a study of those consequential ideas, experiences, and traditions common to all of us by virtue of our membership in the human family at a particular moment in history. The content of the core curriculum must extend beyond the specialties, and focus on more transcendent issues, moving from courses to coherence.

4. **Transition to Work and Learning.** The high school should help all students move with confidence from school to work and further education. Today, we track students into programs for those who "think" and those who "work," when, in fact, life for all of us is a blend of both. Looking to the future, we conclude that, for most students, twelve years of schooling will be insufficient. Today's graduates will change jobs several times. New skills will be required, new citizenship obligations will be confronted. Of necessity, education will be lifelong.

5. **Service: The New Carnegie Unit.** Beyond the formal academic program the high school should help all students meet their social and civic obligations. During high school young people should be given opportunities to reach beyond themselves and feel more responsibly engaged. They should be encouraged to participate in the communities of which they are a part.

Source: From "High School: An Agenda for Action," by E. L. Boyer, 1983 in *High School: A Report on Secondary Education in America* (pp. 301–319), New York: Harper & Row. Copyright 2005 by the Carnegie Foundation for the Advancement of Teaching. Reprinted by permission.

As the 1990s began, high school students felt an unrelenting pressure, not for real academic accomplishment, but "to get their tickets punched so that they could get to the next stage in an increasingly competitive economy" (Tucker, 1999, p. 21).

Did you feel prepared for college or a job when you left high school?

Adolescence as a transition. The dominant view of adolescence during the 20th century was that the teenage years constituted *a developmental transition* between childhood and adulthood. (This view is similar to the assertion of current researchers discussed in chapter 1 that middle childhood falls in between early childhood and adolescence.) For example, during the social upheaval of the 1960s, many sociologists considered adolescents to be "characterized by the confusion and uncertainty of not knowing exactly what [their] role expectations are during the period of transition from childhood to adulthood. It is this vague no man's land that is defined as *adolescence*" (Sebold, 1968, p. vii). Many developmental scholars who described adolescence as a transition did not focus on the developmental achievements of this age group (i.e., from 13 to 18), but rather emphasized their progress toward becoming adults (Offer, Ostrow, & Howard, 1981). Adulthood scholars have recently used the term *adultification* to refer to an acceleration of adult responsibilities in childhood, particularly among high-risk teens (Burton, 2002). However, as with both middle childhood and adolescence, the study of adults has also been stymied by a lack of clear definitions (Côté, 2000b). *When does adolescence end and adulthood begin?*

Some developmental researchers have suggested that the term **adultoid** be used to describe adolescents who have assumed adult behaviors, such as working, but do not have the psychological maturity of adults (Greenberger & Steinberg, 1986). In a person-centered study of adolescents from ages 10 to 18 who were classified as either immature, adultoid, or mature on the basis of personal profiles, researchers found that "adultoid" adolescents had more advanced physical maturity, earlier expectations for attaining privileges, and higher social involvement than adolescents who were either more or less mature (Galambos & Tilton-Weaver, 2000). (For an explanation of person-centered research, refer to chapter 1.) These results suggest that a successful adolescent transition to adulthood may vary from person to person depending on the fit between an individual's maturity level and the demands of the environment.

In late modern societies, the average transition to "adulthood" has became more prolonged and difficult, partly because of economic factors, such as unemployment trends, or because of social trends, such as delaying marriage or parenthood. Popular books, such as *Grownups: A Generation in Search of Adulthood* (Merser, 1987), underscores the social construction of both adolescence and adulthood and emphasizes our society's cultural idealization of "youth" in both age groups.

Today, many developmental psychologists see the functional significance of adolescence (i.e., as a transition to adulthood) as equal in significance to the formal maturational changes that occur in adolescents' reproductive status or appearance brought about by puberty. For example, by the 1990s, three simultaneous and equally significant research efforts were documented in the adolescent literature:

- *At the Threshold* (Feldman & Elliott, 1990), supported by the Carnegie Council on Adolescent Development, published by a collaborative group of researchers
- *Pathways through Adolescence* (Crockett & Crouter, 1995), supported in part by the Reproductive Transition Group of the MacArthur Foundation
- *Transition through Adolescence* (Graber, Brooks-Gunn, & Petersen, 1996), the report of a conference held by the Policy, Research, and Intervention for Development in Early Adolescence (PRIDE) project and supported by the Carnegie Corporation

Most research on adolescence as a transitional period has focused on the educational pathways available to teenagers as they journey from middle childhood to adolescence, such as the transition from middle to high school (e.g., Barber & Olsen, 2004).

Leticia has just started high school. As a ninth grader, she has expectations that her life should change somehow! She wants to start dating and to be given new privileges in recognition of this important transition.

To clarify the *developmental* transitions of adolescents for their families, and often for the wider community, many U.S. ethnic or religious subcultures mark entrance into "maturity" by observing formal **rites of passage**, or ritual ceremonies marking a person's movement from one stage to another (Delaney, 1995; Markstrom & Iborra, 2003). For example, rites of passage may be used to facilitate family members' understanding of the *transitional* function of adolescence:

- African American boys may participate in a church- or school-based program modeled after African rites-of-passage traditions.
- American Indian boys may fast and stay in a "sweat lodge" to be purified by heat and prayer. Girls may participate in a formal ritual celebrating their first menstrual cycles.
- Jewish boys and girls may celebrate their *Bar* or *Bat Mitzvah* at age 13 by reading aloud a portion of the Old Testament in the synagogue or temple.
- Latina girls may celebrate their 15th birthday, or *quinceañera*, with a religious mass and family party.

In contemporary U.S. society, however, many adolescent rites of passage are often informal, such as getting keys to the family car on your 16th birthday. Family therapists have recommended instead that more formalized rituals, such as graduation parties or changes in living arrangements (e.g., moving from a room shared with younger siblings to a private bedroom), be used to identify *structural* changes in an adolescent's developmental status (Quinn, Newfield, & Protinsky, 1985).

Adolescence as a stage. An alternative to the view of adolescence as a *transition* is that the teen years constitute a *distinct* developmental *stage*, characterized by unique developmental achievements and stresses. More importantly, stage approaches theorize adolescence as a **structural period** that begins with a biological event (i.e., puberty) and typically ends with a sociological event (i.e., graduating from high school or college, marrying, or joining the workforce). If these structural markers occur out of the normative order, such as bearing a child before graduating from high school, then the onset or termination of adolescence may seem ambiguous.

Biological or behavioral changes associated with puberty, in combination with structural conditions (e.g., compulsory secondary schooling, laws prohibiting child labor, a juvenile justice system that operates on the basis of age), may also lead to increasing stress in the relationship between the adolescent and others (Quinn, Newfield, & Protinsky, 1985). For example, in a classic portrait of an adolescent, Rousseau (1762/1970) described the interaction with his student Emile as suddenly troubling at the age of puberty, "He no longer listens to his schoolmaster's voice. He is a lion in a fever. He mistrusts his teacher and is averse to control" (p. 96).

Reflecting Rousseau's 18th-century case study description of Emile as a youth overcome by adolescent drives, G. Stanley Hall (1904) theorized that adolescence was a maturational period in individual human growth and development, or **ontogeny**, echoing the evolution of the entire human species, or **phylogeny**. Hall proposed this process, known as **recapitulation theory**, to account for adolescents' immaturity compared to "fully evolved" adults! Hall saw adolescents as primitives, prone to disruptive emotions and impulsive behaviors, who would eventually—like the species as a whole—grow out of their savagery. As humorously written by the author of a popular book called *The Rise and Fall of the American Teenager*, "If your teenager is a Neanderthal, you can take heart. It's only a phase he's going through" (Hine, 1999, p. 36).

Recall also the influential work of Arnold Gesell (discussed in chapter 2), who carefully documented the normative stages of child and adolescent development in the early 20th century. Gesell, Ilg, and Ames (1956) wrote the following description of an "average" adolescent: "He glimpsed the future and what he wanted to become . . . but all too often he became discouraged, lost his incentive, and expressed himself more in rebellion than in cooperation" (p. 262).

Leticia thinks, "Maybe I should stop studying so hard. Then I'd have more time to spend with my friends, and the boys wouldn't think I'm so smart."

Even as late as the 1980s, David Elkind, a well-known child development expert, described children who are physically mature but have no "place" in society (Elkind, 1984). He claimed that adolescents have lost adults' support for their struggle to achieve a sense of personal identity. According to psychologists, the popular phrase *identity crisis* that is so commonly associated with teenagers is a normal experience. Normative adolescence involves a **moratorium**, or delay, in making commitments during the years between childhood and adulthood; instead, it is a time for testing and discovery (Erikson, 1968).

Leticia's older brother Lorenzo, a junior, just wants to have fun in high school. These are the best years of their life, right? Why waste them on studying, anyway. "Pretty soon," he plans, "I'll turn 18, graduate, and get a full-time job."

In advanced industrial societies like the United States, formally structured institutional settings, such as schools, often provide adolescents with a time-out before taking on adult responsibilities (Côté & Allahar, 1996). In theory, these adolescent contexts (e.g., high schools; youth programs; music, arts, or sports subcultures) can provide teenagers with opportunities to experiment with roles, ideas, beliefs, and lifestyles that they might follow in later life (Côté & Allahar, 1996). (Identity development in adolescence will be discussed in detail in chapter 10.)

To the present day, social discourse on the storm and stress of adolescence has endured, despite the fact that there is little, if any, scientific evidence to support the culturally constructed myth of rebellion. Empirical research on adolescence from the 1950s to 1990s has indicated that most teens share their parents' values and attitudes and progress through early, middle, and late adolescence with few serious problems (Offer, 1969; Barnes & Olsen, 1985; Laursen, Coy, & Collins, 1998; Lerner & Knapp, 1975). For example, researchers studying American adolescents' responses to national events from 1966 (in early 10th grade) to 1970 (one year after high school graduation) reported that adolescent boys' dissent over military involvement in Vietnam increased along with that of many adults who also became increasingly frustrated with the war (Bachman & Van Duinen, 1971), as is true with respect to the war in Iraq. Even in the turbulent 1970s, a large cross-cultural study of adolescent self-image revealed that American teenagers—like teens from Israel, Ireland, and Australia—held very positive feelings toward their families and tended to be only slightly more rebellious than adolescents from other cultures (Offer, Ostrow, & Howard, 1981). Then, as today, in the great majority of families, parents and adolescents actually hold similar attitudes about sexuality, drug use, war and peace, and human rights (Lerner, 2002a).

Guideposts for Working with Adolescents

- Because teens may not know exactly what role expectations will accompany the transition to adulthood, be specific in articulating your expectations for their behavior.
- Avoid stereotyping all teens as rebellious, especially when they are exploring new or controversial ideas.
- Mark teens' normative rites of passage, such as getting a driver's license, finding a first job, or taking the SAT exam as a special occasion.
- Talk with adolescents about their future options, whether furthering their education, entering the military, or getting a job.

Meanings of Adolescence in Postmodern Societies

In 2002, the Society for Research on Adolescence issued a groundbreaking report by the Study Group on Adolescence in the 21st Century that examined how the demands of the new millennium are reshaping adolescents' experiences and their preparation for adulthood (Larson, Brown, & Mortimer, 2002). Because global communication, increased emigration, and a shared geopolitical climate have made an international perspective on adolescence seem necessary, the study group went beyond a strictly Western conception of adolescence. "What is emerging across the world are postmodern assemblages of local and global elements combined in different and challenging ways. It is important to ask whether the assemblages shape pathways that are secure or precarious" (Larson et al., 2002, p. 2).

As we discussed in chapter 2 with respect to middle childhood, postmodern scholars often emphasize diversity in the study of adolescence. At the turn of the 21st century, adolescent researchers have increasingly emphasized the importance of differences in context on developmental processes (Silbereisen & Todt, 1994). For example, the meaning of being an adolescent in a working-class, single-mother family where a teenager is expected to assume responsibilities for household chores or for the child care of younger siblings may be quite different from its meaning in an upper-income, two-parent family where the primary household and child care chores are the responsibilities of either a stay-at-home parent or a paid household employee.

After school, Leticia has to watch Raúl until their mother gets off work. Sometimes, when her mother is going to be late, she even cooks dinner for the whole family.

Diverse ecological contexts. In varied cultural, social, or economic contexts, divergent pathways, or what scholars have termed the "new adolescences," result from factors such as increased education, delayed employment, and later marriage and parenthood (Larson, 2002). In most industrialized cultures, adolescence as a transitional period has been lengthened over the past half century. For example, the average age of marriage has changed from 12 to 16 in rural India and from 22 to 26 in Europe (Larson, Brown, & Mortimer, 2002). According to sociologists, adolescence is longer in societies with greater technological complexity, with urban adolescents requiring a longer time to reach adulthood than adolescents from rural communities or agrarian societies (Chatterjee, Bailey, & Aronoff, 2001).

In developing countries, high birthrates also mean that the numbers of adolescents will grow over the next several decades, straining employment and educational resources and possibly limiting adolescents' opportunities and transition into adult roles (Larson, 2002). For example, 56% of Saudis are under age 20 (Saudi Arabia Information Resource, 2005). Similarly, the United States also has both high immigration rates and an expected 18% increase in the numbers of 15- to 25-year-olds by 2010 (U.S. Census Bureau, 2001).

But there are also many differences in adolescent experiences across nations (Larson, 2002). Trends in Japan, Europe, and the former Soviet states are just the opposite! In Japan, for instance, many 21st-century youth are postponing or forgoing marriage in favor of a prolonged and self-focused single life—they are referred to by Japanese adults as "single parasites."

Psychologists studying later adolescence have termed this period of the life span *emerging adulthood* (to be discussed in chapter 12) (Arnett, 2002). Thus, the length of adolescence may be very different throughout the world, depending on diverse cultural responses to increased socioeconomic opportunities caused by globalization.

Effects of globalization. **Globalization** refers to increases in communication, shared economic influences, and political alliances among the nations of the world. Globalization has existed for many centuries as cultures became more alike through trade, immigration, and the exchange of ideas; however, recent advances in telecommunications and increases in financial interdependence have accelerated globalization in the 21st century (Arnett, 2002). For example, current trends in **economic globalization** have increased the stratification between rich and poor, in which adolescents in successful global markets see improved educational and job opportunities while adolescents in poorer countries may see fewer.

Economic globalization also has disrupted **social reproduction**, or the ways that adolescents receive the knowledge and skills necessary for the world in which they will come of age as workers. In Third-World countries like Sudan, for example, agricultural development has displaced rural populations to its cities, resulting in "street children" in the towns of Sudan as an unwanted outcome of economic globalization. Similarly, in the so-called First-World cities of the United States, disinvestments in manufacturing have dimmed the prospects for well-paying, stable, and meaningful jobs for many working-class adolescents while deteriorating school budgets have diminished their access to quality education (Katz, 1998).

At the same time, adolescents living in global economies may experience **cultural globalization**, or the effects of material culture on societies, such as the spread of brand-named products or music and film icons, thus increasing their commonalities (Larson, 2002). Although fundamental differences in cultural values are likely to persist, adolescents in the future may know more about each other than in past centuries because of satellite communication, cable news networks, and the Internet (see Lim & Renshaw, 2001). A simultaneous trend toward economic and cultural globalization may mean that differences in adolescence could be minimized across cultures, as seen in Box 7.3. In fact, a 1998 United Nations report identified a market for brand-name music, videos, T-shirts, and soft drinks among "global teens" (Arnett, 2002).

But despite the trends toward globalization, many world cultures resist its influence. Orthodox Islam, for example, has organized opposition to globalization in the Middle East among its youth by promoting traditional religious values (Larson, 2002). In Samoa, postmodern adolescents have revived an ancient rite-of-passage custom of tattooing as an overt sign of maintaining their indigenous culture in the face of increasing globalization (Arnett, 2002). If adolescents are in the forefront of these religious and political movements, what is the current cultural construction of adolescence in these nations?

Poststructural ideas. Most scholars in the 20th century subscribed to the structural view of adolescence as a distinct stage of development, bounded by puberty on one side and by adulthood on the other. **Structuralism** implies that adolescence is a defined stage. On the other hand, **poststructuralism** rejects physical metaphors (i.e., that adolescence has distinct age boundaries).

Cross-cultural research supports a *poststructural* view of adolescence, which has increasingly influenced developmental scholars in the 21st century (see Maira & Soep, 2004). Sociologists and anthropologists, in particular, have explained that the cultural construction of adolescence—like that of middle childhood—does not exist in some cultures. For example, Islamic youth are generally regarded as interchangeable with adults. Also recall (from chapter 1) that Mead (1928) described the transition to adulthood for Samoan adolescents as smooth because their culture did not structure adolescence as a separate stage. Mead's hypothesis was that the "storm and stress" of adolescence—postulated by Hall (1904) as biologically universal—was, in fact, not universal at all.

Was your adolescence "stormy" or "stressful" and, if so, how?

Such conclusions regarding the cultural diversity of adolescence have been carefully examined and are supported by a majority of contemporary scholars (Côté, 2000b). For example, in India most adolescents and young adults—even though they often participate in a global high-tech culture—prefer to have an arranged marriage in accordance with Indian tradition (Arnett, 2002). Variations in the social construction of adolescence suggest that the meanings of adolescence are not universal in either their structure (e.g., timing or duration) or in their function (e.g., preparation for adulthood).

BOX 7.3 ROADMAP TO UNDERSTANDING THEORY AND RESEARCH

The Construction of Youth Cultures

While filming in Mexico, Doreen Massey interviewed a group of women in their Yucatán homes. With light from an open fire, they sat on stones on the earth floor in an adobe house with a thatched roof. While they talked, the women were making tortillas "by hand, as it had always been done" and talking about their lives. Massey recorded what she called a truly indigenous culture intent on preserving its customs, clothing, food, and beliefs.

When the interview was over, the filmmakers walked back to their jeep. As they approached the road, they heard electronic sounds, American slang, and Western music. From another building—this one wired for electricity—a dozen or so youth were playing computer games. Machines were lined up around the walls of the shack, and every one was surrounded by players. Of course, they filmed the adolescents, too.

The filmmakers later suggested that the youth culture of the Yucatán countryside may serve as an entry point for external influences on, and maybe the eventual breakup of, inherited Mayan culture. Because the cultures of the young seemed more internationalized than those of older generations, Massey asked, "Was this a local culture, or were these youngsters part of the emerging global culture of youth?"

The answer depended on how she conceptualized culture: Was it *global* in the full sense that everyone, everywhere, has access to it? Massey saw the roomful of computer games as a link between this small cluster of houses in eastern Mexico and something that might be characterized as global (or American) culture—for example, the T-shirts with slogans in English, the baseball caps, the athletic shoes, the litter of cola cans. Nevertheless, the filmmakers suggested that the youth culture here was quite different from that of San Francisco, or a small American town, or England, or Tokyo, for example.

In each place, T-shirts and computer games are mixed in with locally distinct cultures that have their own histories. For example, the meaning of what is and what is not a status symbol, or of how particular slogans or music are interpreted, changes. In Mexico, global elements were embedded in Mayan family relations, in the culture's unique understanding of ancient cosmology, or in Mexico's particular Latin American consciousness. Massey concluded that local variations in youth cultures can be constantly reinvented even while international influences are accepted and incorporated.

Source: Based on "The Spatial Construction of Youth Cultures," by Doreen Massey, in T. Skelton and G. Valentine (Eds.), *Cool Places: Geographies of Youth Cultures* (pp. 121–129), 1988, London: Routledge.

Guideposts for Working with Adolescents

- Remember that adolescence has different meanings in diverse cultures.
- Ask teens to keep a log of comments they hear in the media or in the community about teenagers.
- Talk with teens about the social construction of adolescence in contemporary culture.
- Help teenagers understand parental, educational, and societal expectations for adolescents by reading and discussing youth fiction from around the world.
- Encourage today's global teens to learn about their similarities to adolescents from other countries by using email, Internet chat rooms, or web logs (blogs).

DEVELOPMENTAL MILESTONES IN ADOLESCENCE

In adolescence, as in middle childhood and in all other periods of the life span, biological maturation (e.g., physiological or genetic factors) and environmental influences (e.g., social or cultural influences) interact to produce change over time, or *development*. Recall from chapter 1 that a developmental interaction is a dynamic exchange of reciprocal influences between maturation and experience. For example, a given 13- or 14-year-old might not have developed the abstract reasoning ability to engage in moral reasoning about ethical dilemmas sometimes facing adolescents (e.g., abortion vs. adoption decisions in pregnant teens), whereas at age 16 or 17 the same adolescent may be able to think hypothetically about possible alternatives. Developmental educators refer to this phenomenon as **readiness**.

Marina just started going out with a boy from church named Jaime. Leticia certainly doesn't want to feel like a "third wheel." More to the point, when will she meet someone?

Developmental theories are useful because they concentrate our attention on "time-dependent *phenomena of becoming* or emergence of a new structural order of the phenomena from their previous state" (Valsiner, 1997, p. 3). The developmental milestones along the road to maturity can be summarized using normative expectations for adolescent development in the same four domains we discussed in part 1 of the text, as depicted in Figure 7.2:

1. **Physical Development.** As in middle childhood, this domain includes biological and physiological development. In adolescence, children experience changes associated with puberty. Onset of puberty occurs at varied ages, with 11 years the average age for girls and 13 years for boys, marked by hormonal and reproductive changes (i.e., primary sexual characteristics) and by observable changes in physical appearance (i.e., secondary sexual characteristics).

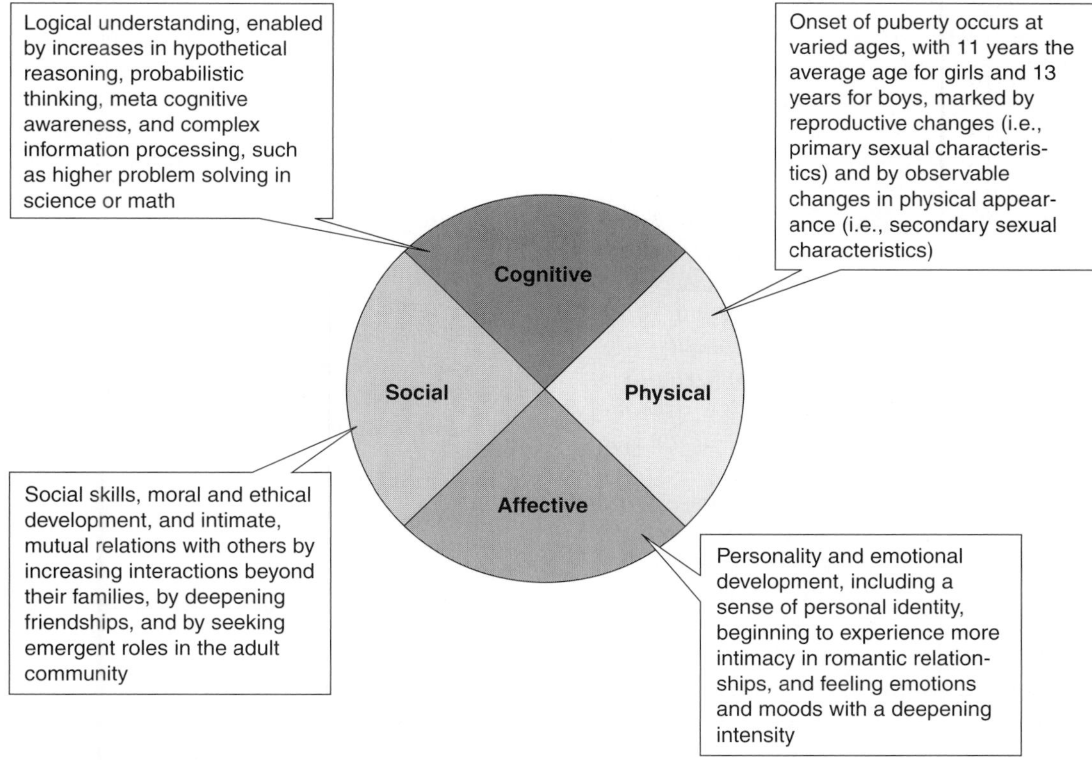

FIGURE 7.2 Developmental Domains of Adolescence
The developmental milestones of adolescence correspond to the domains of middle childhood development.

2. **Cognitive Development.** As in younger children, this domain includes intellectual and language skills, reasoning abilities, and memory capacities. Adolescence is characterized by a qualitative change in logical understanding involving hypothetical reasoning, probabilistic thinking, and complex information processing, such as higher problem solving in science or math.

3. **Affective Development.** As seen previously, this developmental domain includes personality, emotional development, motivation, and self-esteem. During the adolescent years, teens are developing a sense of personal identity, are beginning to experience more intimacy in romantic relationships, and are feeling emotions and moods with a deepening intensity.

4. **Social Development.** As in middle childhood, this domain includes social skills and interpersonal understanding, moral and ethical development, and maintaining close relationships. Adolescents develop intimate, mutual relations with others by increasing interactions beyond their families, by deepening friendships, and by seeking emergent roles in the adult community.

Let's think about Leticia. Her physical appearance (i.e., tall, with enlarged breasts and hips) indicates that she has probably undergone menarche and is now reproductively mature. Cognitively, Leticia demonstrates the hypothetical thinking about her future that typically distinguishes adolescents from school-age children (e.g., she anticipates the challenges of adolescence). Emotionally, Leticia appears quite mature. She keeps up a "B" average and is active in her church. Socially, however, Leticia could be considered preoccupied with "silly" concerns that—from an adult's perspective—are just "growing pains," such as making friends or getting a date. But Leticia's experience is typical of most adolescents who ask impatiently, "If not now, when?"

Anticipation of major life transitions, such as graduating, getting a job, or leaving home, is called **life-course development**. Social historians have successfully employed this concept to analyze changing patterns in individual development across a generation, a culture, or a particular historical context (Mintz, 1993). Since the 20th century, life-course decisions have increasingly reflected individualized choices or social norms (Mintz, 1993). (Recall that a developmental norm is the average age at which a particular behavior typically occurs in the adolescent population.) In the case of legally sanctioned activities, however, such as getting a driver's license or a work permit, age norms have been institutionalized by society. Other social norms may be particular to families or communities, such as the age at which a teenager is allowed to date.

THEORETICAL VIEWPOINTS

Two complementary theoretical perspectives provide a developmental framework for the study of middle adolescence: (1) life-span theory, and (2) life-course theory. Life-span approaches examine adolescence in relation to other developmental *stages* in the life span. On the other hand, life-course approaches examine major life *transitions* over a lifetime. These complementary approaches allow us to see how adolescence is *at once* a developmental stage and a transition to adulthood.

Life-Span Theory

Life-span psychology is the study of development from conception to death. Life-span theorists and researchers expect each period in the life span (e.g., infancy, childhood, adolescence, adulthood, old age) to have its own developmental agenda and to contribute to continuity and change across the life course (Baltes, Reese, & Lipsett, 1980; Baltes, Lindenberger, & Staudinger, 1998). The three major goals of life-span theorizing (Baltes, 1987) are to obtain knowledge about:

1. General principles of development across the life course, called **ontogenesis**;
2. Differences *between* people, called **interindividual differences**; and
3. Changes *within* a person, called **intraindividual change**.

Although adulthood and aging have been the primary interest of many life-span researchers, they have contributed several important theoretical propositions to a general view of development that will assist us in examining adolescence as a stage in the life span:

- **Development is multidirectional, or comprised of the capacity both for gains and for losses.** For example, in adolescence, as teenagers move towards new levels of abstract logical reasoning and probabilistic thinking, their peer conformity may decline, and they may start to think for themselves.

- **Development can vary substantially with history, called historical embeddedness.** How age-related development proceeds is markedly influenced by sociocultural conditions in a given historical period. For example, adolescents born after 1980 may be much more likely than previous generations to practice "safe sex" because of the threat of HIV/AIDS.
- **Any particular individual's development can be understood as the outcome of developmental influences that are age-graded (e.g., the onset of puberty); history-graded (e.g., beginning middle school); and nonnormative (e.g., moving to a new community).** Much like developmental-contextual and bioecological theories (described in chapter 1), life-span psychology uses contextualism as its **metatheoretical paradigm**, or world view, and thus considers development to be highly dependent on life experiences in a specific time and place.
- **Life-span theory is multidisciplinary.** Life-span researchers often employ many diverse disciplinary perspectives on adolescence (e.g., social history, sociology, or anthropology).

Figure 7.3 illustrates the interplay of age-graded, history-graded, and nonnormative influences as taking place throughout our lives. The life span unfolds in *ontogenetic time*, during which the forces of biology and the environment continuously interact.

Recently, life-span theory has been discussed in terms of **evolutionary psychology** (Baltes, 1997). Evolutionary developmental psychology is the study of the genetic and ecological mechanisms that govern development and adaptation of the species (Geary & Bjorkland, 2000). A long developmental period, such as human childhood and adolescence, is thus seen as allowing enough time to refine the physical, social, and cognitive competencies that support survival and reproduction of the species. Seen from this perspective, life-span theory asserts that adolescence provides **selective optimization**, or movement toward increased efficiency and higher levels of functioning, such as increasing autonomy in adolescence, and **compensation**, or making up for a level of functioning no longer present, such as spending more time with friends than family (Baltes, 1997). (Evolutionary theory is discussed more fully in chapter 8.)

Life-Course Theory

Like life-span theory, **life-course theory** also focuses on systematic changes experienced by individuals as they move through their lives. But instead focusing on developmental changes as does life-span theory, life-course theory focuses on life *events*, such as starting school, graduating, entering the workforce, getting married, or having children. According to its major proponent, Glen

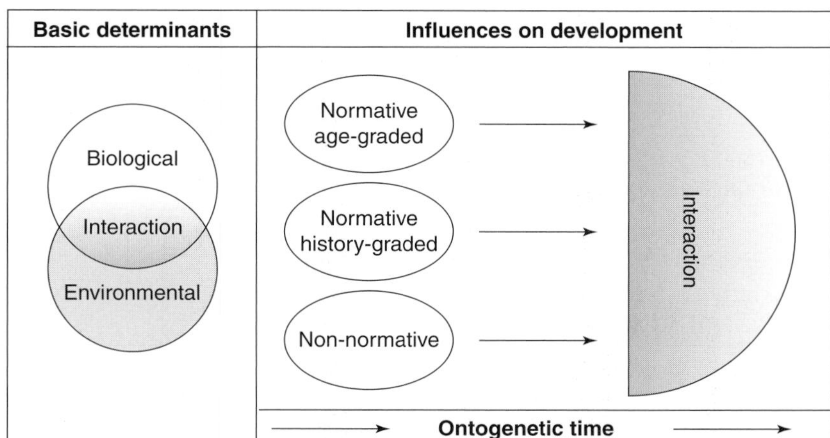

FIGURE 7.3 Theoretical Model of Life-Span Development

Source: From "Life-Span Theory in Developmental Psychology," by P. B. Baltes, U. Lindenberger, & U. M. Staudinger, in W. Damon (Series Ed.) & R. M. Lerner (Vol. Ed.), *Handbook of Child Psychology, Vol. 1: Theoretical Models of Human Development* (5th ed., p. 1049), 1998, New York: Wiley. Copyright 1998 by John Wiley & Sons, Inc. Reprinted by permission of the publisher.

Elder (1998), the life-course perspective includes four central principles:

1. The life-course of individuals is embedded in and shaped by the historical times and places they experience over their lifetime.
2. The developmental impact of a life transition or event is contingent on when it occurs in a person's life.
3. Lives are lived interdependently, and social and historical influences are expressed through a network of shared relationships.
4. Individuals construct their own life course through the choices and actions they take within the constraints and opportunities of history and social circumstances. (Elder, 1998, p. 961)

The significance of life-course theory for studying adolescence is its ability to weave the development of *individuals* into the social fabric of developmental *contexts*, that is, to explain how lives are socially organized. Life-course theorists view the ontogeny of individuals and the development of history as one system (Lerner, 2002b). This emphasis on the simultaneous contributions of individual and historical development leads life-course researchers to use the following methods:

- Analysis of **life histories**, or the examination of the transitions between major life events;
- Investigation of the timing and sequencing of **life events**, or major milestones within any individual's life history; and
- Emphasis on accepted variations in individuals' life histories as a way to investigate the strength of norms in any given cohort or historical period.

What life events signaled to you that you were becoming an adolescent?

According to life-course methodology, your birth year is your point of entry into the social system, and your life course is constructed by your location along three temporal dimensions, including

- **Developmental time** (i.e., birth to death)
- **Family time** (i.e., your location relative to preceding or successive generations)
- **Historical time** (i.e., the social and cultural system that exists during your lifetime)

Refer to Figure 7.4 for an illustration of developmental, family, and historical time portraying our lives as existing in a three-dimensional space created by successive generations born at different points in history. According to Elder (1998), life-course theory

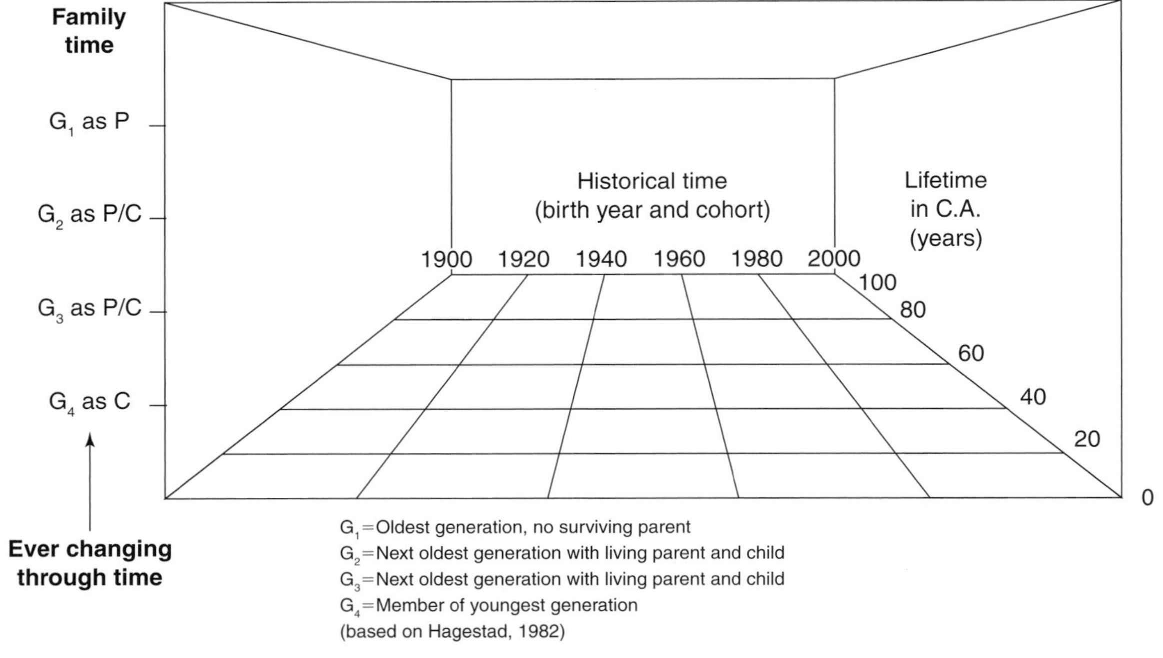

FIGURE 7.4 Theoretical Model of Life-Course Development

Source: From "The Life Course and Human Development," by G. E. Elder, Jr., in W. Damon (Series Ed.) & R. M. Lerner (Vol. Ed.), *Handbook of Child Psychology, Vol. 1: Theoretical Models of Human Development* (5th ed., p. 949), 1998, New York: Wiley. Copyright 1998 by John Wiley & Sons, Inc. Reprinted by permission of the publisher.

investigates changing environments, social relationships, and historical influences in terms of their developmental implications for individuals, who are active participants in shaping the course of their lives.

Recently, family theorists have proposed a variation of life-course theory called **family development theory** (White, 1991; White & Klein, 2002). The emphasis in family development theory is on the concept of transitions through what was traditionally called the **family life cycle**, depicted in Figure 7.5 (Duvall, 1957; White, 1991). For example, like biological organisms, families may go through developmental stages: formation, growth, maintenance, shrinkage, and dissolution (White & Klein, 2002). Family members may also be seen as progressing through **family careers** (Aldous, 1996), such as the sibling career in childhood and adolescence (assuming you have brothers and/or sisters); the marital career (if you are married); and the parental career (provided you have children).

For most developmentalists, the newer concept of the family life course has replaced the earlier concept of the family life cycle because it better reflects variations in norms across cultures and societies (White & Klein, 2002). For example, not all families progress through similar stages at the same rate (e.g., adolescents whose youngest sibling is born after they leave home) or sequence (e.g., a teenage mother who becomes a parent before marrying). In this view, the deviation of a large number of individuals

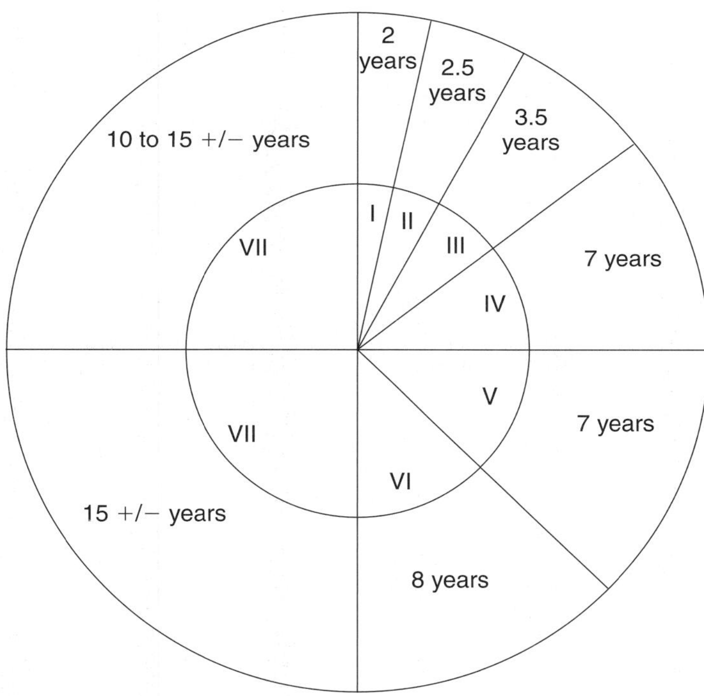

I. Married couples (without children).
II. Childbearing families (oldest child, birth–30 months).
III. Families with preschool children (oldest child 30 months–6 years).
IV. Families with school children (oldest child 6–13 years).
V. Families with teenagers (oldest child 13–20 years).
VI. Families with launching centers (first child gone to last leaving home).
VII. Middle-aged parents (empty nest to retirement).

FIGURE 7.5 Traditional Model of Family Development
In the 1950s, family scholars diagrammed an idealized family life cycle.

Source: From "The Family Life Cycle," by E. M. Duvall, in *Marriage and Family Development* (5th ed.), 1977, Boston, MA: Allyn & Bacon. Copyright 1977 by Pearson Education, Inc. Reprinted by permission of the publisher.

or families from a normative path would be seen as an indication of social change (White & Klein, 2002). A recent revision of the family developmental model, illustrated in Figure 7.6, accommodates the variations in timing and structure common to diverse families in contemporary society, such as single parents, gay or lesbian families, or intergenerational households (Richman & Cook, 2004).

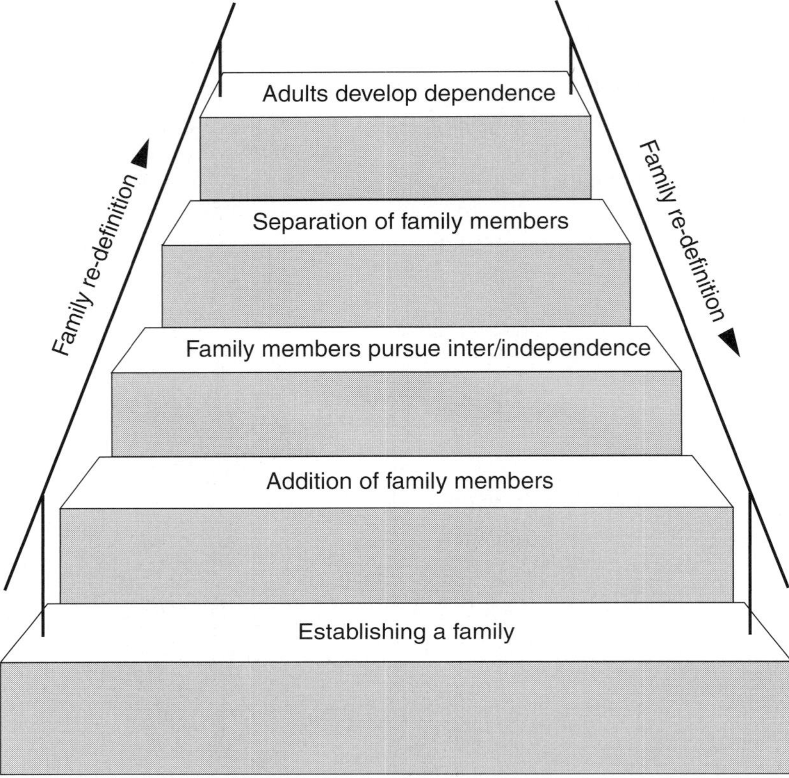

FIGURE 7.6 A New Family Development Framework
Today, family scholars recognize that diverse families vary in the ways they are established, develop, and change.

Source: From "A Framework for Teaching Family Development for the Changing Family," by Jack M. Richman & Patricia G. Cook, 2004, *Journal of Teaching in Social Work, 24*(1/2), pp. 1–18. Copyright 2004 by The Haworth Press. Reprinted by permission.

Guideposts for Working with Adolescents

- Remember that there is often wide variation in the norms for individual development across domains, and expect adolescents to be more mature in some areas than others.
- When considering teens' readiness for new experiences, discuss their fears and expectations as well as their individual development.
- Have teens diagram their family life course, creating a family tree or a historical timeline across the generations.
- Engage teens in group discussions with other adults and adolescents to help them see how their lives may be socially organized by family, school, or community norms.

Research on Risk and Opportunity in Adolescence

During adolescence, teens may be learning to deal with their own and others' potentially risky behaviors (e.g., abusing substances like tobacco, alcohol, and other drugs; engaging in sexual activity; dropping out of school) as well as potentially risky environments (e.g., poor neighborhoods, violent schools, stressful families) (Furstenberg, 2001). In the last decade, researchers have focused on the relative influences of risk and opportunity in adolescence. This abiding concern for adolescents' well-being has also reflected the debate (discussed earlier) over whether the teen years are (a) stormy and inherently stressful or (b) relatively calm and normal.

Conceptually, **risk factors** are conditions or variables associated with a higher likelihood of negative outcomes in a variety of areas—from health and well-being to socially desirable behaviors. Risk factors operate by instigating or supporting problem behaviors that promote actions inconsistent with, for example, staying in school or avoiding substance abuse. On the other hand, **protective factors** have the reverse effect—they lessen the likelihood of negative consequences from exposure to risks (Jessor, Turbin, & Costa, 1998). For example, the Kauai study described in chapter 1 conceived of high-risk individuals who demonstrated successful outcomes in adulthood as *resilient* (Werner, 1993). Although some child development researchers have criticized the construct of resilience as too broad, most scholars agree that it commonly refers to a dynamic process of adapting positively in the context of significant adversity (Benson, Scales, & Mannes, 2003; Luthar, Cicchetti, & Becker, 2000; Masten & Curtis, 2000; Perkins & Borden, 2003). Box 7.4 describes a study of risk and protective factors in adolescence.

Many psychologists and sociologists have attempted to predict adolescents' risk behaviors. Yet there is a second, increasingly strong view, grounded in developmental theory, that is closer to "risk-taking as opportunity." In this view, adolescent problem behaviors are seen as normative, involving typical teenage experimentation, autonomy, and identity development (Lightfoot, 1997). Whether you are a high school teacher, social service provider, youth program specialist, or child development student, it is important to review the research on adolescent behavior from each of these two perspectives: risks and opportunities.

Perspectives on Teen Risks

Researchers examining teen risks have attempted to identify overlapping problem behaviors (e.g., delinquency, substance use, teenage pregnancy, and school failure). Six common characteristics

Teens living in high-risk environments can be protected from negative outcomes by a sense of competence, family support, and constructive involvement in activities and youth programs.

BOX 7.4 ROADMAP TO UNDERSTANDING THEORY AND RESEARCH

Risk and Protection in Successful Outcomes Among Disadvantaged Adolescents

In a study of 1,638 socioeconomically disadvantaged middle school and high school students (40% Hispanic, 37% White, and 23% Black) from a large suburban school district, Richard Jessor and his colleagues Mark Turbin and Frances Costa assessed the role of risk and protective factors in promoting successful adolescent development. Despite adverse circumstances—such as poverty, dilapidated neighborhoods, inadequate resources, and exposure to dangers—many, if not most, teenagers "make it."

Conceptually, risk factors were defined as conditions associated with a lower likelihood of positive outcomes; protective factors were defined as the opposite, that is, as lessening the likelihood of negative consequences from exposure to risk. This study used the theoretical perspective of life-course development, in which successful outcomes are defined by the developmental stage of the person's life course—in this case, adolescence. Success was measured by two important tasks of adolescence, engaging in school and avoiding problem behavior.

Five risk factors and seven protective factors were examined in this study, as follows:

- **Risk Factors** Low expectations for success
- Low self-esteem
- Sense of hopelessness
- Greater orientation to friends than parents
- Friends as models for problem behavior
- **Protective Factors** Intolerance of deviance
- Positive orientation to health
- Religiosity
- Positive relations with adults
- Perception of social controls
- Friends as models for conventional behavior
- Involvement in prosocial activities

Socioeconomic disadvantage and risk factors were found to have significant negative effects on success, whereas protective factors had significant positive effects. In addition, protection moderated the effects of risk, especially for more disadvantaged youth. Key risk factors were low expectation for success, low self-esteem, hopelessness, and having friends as models for problem behavior. Key protective factors were intolerance of deviance, positive orientation to health, and having friends as models for conventional behavior.

The authors concluded that strengthening protective factors, as well as reducing risks, may enhance successful development:

> Overall the findings from this study begin to tell a story about how adolescents manage to make it despite the risk, the adversity, and the disadvantage that may have characterized their lives. A large part of that story, a part that is emerging more insistently in recent years, has to do with protection. The direct and the moderator effects of protection would seem to warrant further attention from researchers and interventionists alike. (p. 207)

Source: Based on "Risk and Protection in Successful Outcomes among Disadvantaged Adolescents," by R. Jessor, M. S. Turbin, & F. M. Costa, 1998. *Applied Developmental Science 2*, pp. 194–208. Copyright 1998 by Lawrence Erlbaum Associates, Inc.

have predicted high-risk involvement (Dryfoos, 1990):

1. **Age.** Early initiation or occurrence of any problem behavior predicts heavy involvement and more negative consequences.
2. **Expectations for Education and School Grades.** Doing poorly in school, and expecting to do poorly, are associated with more problem behaviors, such as delinquency.
3. **General Behavior.** Acting out, truancy, antisocial behavior, and other conduct disorders are related to high-risk behaviors, like substance abuse.
4. **Peer Influence.** Having low resistance to peer pressure and having friends who participate in the same behaviors are common to high-risk adolescents.
5. **Parental Role.** Having parents who do not monitor, supervise, offer guidance, or communicate with their children, or who are too authoritarian or too permissive, is related to being at high risk for problem behaviors.

6. **Neighborhood Quality.** Living in a poverty area or in an urban, high-density community predicts high-risk behavior in adolescents.

Researchers have estimated that as many as one in four adolescents between ages 10 and 17 are in need of assistance because they are at high risk of engaging in multiple problem behaviors. Although ethnic-minority youth seem to have higher prevalence rates (i.e., because they may more often live in poorer, urban environments), the majority of multiproblem youth are White and male (Dryfoos, 1997). Researchers have compared inner-city youth to suburban adolescents and found that both groups experienced emotional distress and substance abuse, with higher levels among the more affluent teens (Luthar & Latendresse, 2002). In addition, so-called "normative risks," such as depression, may have different outcomes for sexual-minority youth who simultaneously experience peer harassment and discrimination (Russell, 2005). Unique risk factors for sexual-minority adolescents include (adapted from Russell, 2005)

- **Coming out at a young age** (e.g., associated with increased suicide)
- **Coming out at school** (e.g., related to peer harassment)
- **Conflict with parents over coming out** (e.g., linked to running away)

In defining who is *at risk*, adolescents needing prevention services should include not only those teenagers who may not yet have initiated a problem behavior (e.g., smoking or drinking) that can have negative outcomes (i.e., lung cancer or drunk driving) but also those whose demographic, social, or personal characteristics predict that they are vulnerable (Dryfoos, 1997). Recent research on adolescents' judgments of "what is risky" has found that teenagers were likely to perceive themselves as vulnerable to personal risks, such as getting drunk, injured, or pregnant—even when controlling for experience and age differences (Millstein & Halpern-Felsher, 2002).

Perspectives on Teen Opportunities

Psychologists have suggested that an important developmental capacity of adolescence is **initiative**, or the motivation and ability to direct attention and effort toward a challenging goal (Larson, 2000). Much of the research on the normal developmental tasks of adolescence minimizes problem behaviors and instead considers adolescent risk-taking as a potential growth experience, associated with feelings of maturity and independence (Lightfoot, 1997; see also Jessor, Turbin, & Costa, 1998). Although some teen behaviors may be seen by parents as rebellious (e.g., spiking your hair or dressing "goth"), in fact they may be no more risky than many acceptable expressions of adolescent autonomy, such as learning to drive or beginning to date.

Research on teen opportunities emphasizes positive youth development despite the presence of risks in the environment. This area of study is known as **developmental strengths**, an approach to conducting adolescent research and preventive interventions with teens that focuses on three major elements (Benson, Scales, & Mannes, 2003):

1. **Competence.** Competence refers to successfully completing the developmental tasks expected at a given age in a particular cultural and historical and context (Masten & Curtis, 2000). Research with adolescents has found that areas of competence may include academic, social, athletic, romantic, and job competencies.
2. **Protective Factors.** Protective factors refer to factors that play a role in protecting adolescents from risk, including intelligence, parenting, high commitment to school, positive orientation to health, having friends as models for conventional behavior, high self-efficacy, and a support system that encourages coping and positive values.
3. **Connectedness.** Connectedness refers to the quality and stability of the emotional bonds of support and caring that exist between teens and families, peers, and other adults. The National Longitudinal Study of Adolescent Health (Resnick et al., 1997) found that young people who experienced closer connections to their families and schools were less likely than other adolescents to engage in a variety of risk-taking behaviors, such as violence and substance abuse.

Some researchers have called these "the five C's of positive youth development: *Competence, Confidence, Character, Connection, and Caring*" (Lerner, Brentano, Dowling, & Anderson, 2002, p. 23). Researchers studying developmental strengths have also identified sets of **developmental assets**, or strengths that serve a protective function in adolescence, listed in Table 7–1.

TABLE 7–1

Developmental Assets

Developmental assets help adolescents grow up healthy, caring, and responsible.

	Category	Asset Name and Definition
External Assets	**Support**	**1. Family Support.** Family life provides high levels of love and support. **2. Positive Family Communication.** Young person and her or his parent(s) communicate positively, and young person is willing to seek advice and counsel from parents. **3. Other Adult Relationships.** Young person receives support from three or more non-parent adults. **4. Caring Neighborhood.** Young person experiences caring neighbors. **5. Caring School Climate.** School provides a caring encouraging environment. **6. Parent Involvement in Schooling.** Parent(s) are actively involved in helping young person succeed in school.
	Empowerment	**7. Community Values Youth.** Young person perceives that adults in the community value youth. **8. Youth as Resources.** Young people are given useful roles in the community. **9. Service to Others.** Young person serves in the community one hour or more per week. **10. Safety.** Young person feels safe at home, school, and in the neighborhood.
	Boundaries & Expectations	**11. Family Boundaries.** Family has clear rules and consequences and monitors the young person's whereabouts. **12. School Boundaries.** School provides clear rules and consequences. **13. Neighborhood Boundaries.** Neighbors take responsibility for monitoring young people's behavior. **14. Adult Role Models.** Parent(s) and other adults model positive, responsible behavior. **15. Positive Peer Influence.** Young person's best friends model responsible behavior. **16. High Expectations.** Both parent(s) and teachers encourage the young person to do well.
	Constructive Use of Time	**17. Creative Activities.** Young person spends three or more hours per week in lessons or practice in music, theater, or other arts. **18. Youth Programs.** Young person spends three or more hours per week in sports, clubs, or organizations at school and/or in the community. **19. Religious Community.** Young person spends one or more hours per week in activities in a religious institution. **20. Time at Home.** Young person is out with friends "with nothing special to do" two or fewer nights per week.
Internal Assets	**Commitment to Learning**	**21. Achievement Motivation.** Young person is motivated to do well in school. **22. School Engagement.** Young person is actively engaged in learning. **23. Homework.** Young person reports doing at least one hour of homework every school day. **24. Bonding to School.** Young person cares about her or his school. **25. Reading for Pleasure.** Young person reads for pleasure three or more hours per week.
	Positive Values	**26. Caring.** Young person places high value on helping other people. **27. Equality and Social Justice.** Young person places high value on promoting equality and reducing hunger and poverty. **28. Integrity.** Young person acts on convictions and stands up for her or his beliefs. **29. Honesty.** Young person "tells the truth even when it is not easy." **30. Responsibility.** Young person accepts and takes personal responsibility. **31. Restraint.** Young person believes it is important not to be sexually active or to use alcohol or other drugs.
	Social Competencies	**32. Planning and Decision Making.** Young person knows how to plan ahead and make choices. **33. Interpersonal Competence.** Young person has empathy, sensitivity, and friendship skills.

TABLE 7–1
Continued

	Category	Asset Name and Definition
Internal Assets		**34. Cultural Competence.** Young person has knowledge of and comfort with people of different cultural/racial/ethnic backgrounds. **35. Resistance Skills.** Young person can resist negative peer pressure and dangerous situations. **36. Peaceful Conflict Resolution.** Young person seeks to resolve conflict nonviolently.
	Positive Identity	**37. Personal Power.** Young person feels he or she has control over "things that happen to me." **38. Self-Esteem.** Young person reports having a high self-esteem. **39. Sense of Purpose.** Young person reports that "my life has a purpose." **40. Positive View of Personal Future.** Young person is optimistic about her or his personal future.

Source: From *"40 Developmental Assets"* by P. L. Benson, 2004, Minneapolis, MN: Search Institute. Copyright 2004 by Search Institute, 615 First Ave. NE Suite 125, Minneapolis, MN 55413, 800-888-7828, www.search-institute.org.

The average number of assets decreases from 23 in sixth grade to 18 in twelfth grade, with boys averaging fewer assets than girls overall despite variations across communities (Benson, 2002). However, as assets rise in number, risk behavior patterns are reduced: alcohol, tobacco, and illicit drug use; antisocial behavior; violence; school failure; sexual activity; attempted suicide; and gambling. The cumulative effect is equally predictive of increases in positive behaviors: academic achievement; school grades; leadership; prosocial behavior; delay of gratification; and affirmation of diversity (Benson, 2002).

Leticia and her youth group at church are highly motivated to raise money for a good cause. They will work hard, hoping to raise $1,000 to buy new shoes for the children at the homeless shelter.

Built into the developmental asset model are external, **ecological assets**: support, empowerment, boundaries and expectations, and structured time use (Benson, 2002, Mancini & Huebner, 2004). Of course, what is protective may not be the same across differing contexts or cultures (Benson, Scales, & Mannes, 2003). For example, African American or Latino adolescents living in urban and/or high-risk environments may benefit from stricter parenting than teens whose parents think their neighborhoods are high in quality and safety (see reviews in Furstenberg, 2001; and O'Neil, Parke, & McDowell, 2001).

Developmental scholars, in particular, have reexamined risk and resilience concepts as they apply to adolescence and have incorporated culture and diversity (Arrington & Wilson, 2000). For example, in revising risk and opportunity models for studying ethnic minority youth, who comprise one in three American adolescents (U.S. Census, 2000), researchers have asserted that several major factors affect the development of youth of color (Garcia Coll et al., 1996):

- **Social position** (e.g., social class, gender, or race)
- **Racism and discrimination** (e.g., residential and psychological segregation)
- **Promoting/ inhibiting environments** (e.g., schools and health care)
- **Adaptive culture** (e.g., traditions and legacies)
- **Children's characteristics and developmental competencies** (e.g., age or temperament)
- **Family values and beliefs** (e.g., ethics and religion)

The display of developmental competence despite possible adversity constitutes *resilience*, or successful adaptation. For example, new immigrants who settle in the downtown areas of large U.S. cities often achieve success despite being surrounded by poverty (Arrington & Wilson, 2000; Coatsworth, Pantin, & Szapocznik, 2002).

Sometimes, families may need supportive community programs to help them reduce the risks to adolescents that are too often associated with poor, urban environments. For example, Box 7.5 describes Familias Unidas, a community program designed to help Hispanic families build a strong parent support network and strengthen

BOX 7.5 ROADMAP TO SUCCESSFUL PRACTICE

Familias Unidas

Familias Unidas is a family-centered, multilevel prevention program designed to link together groups of recently immigrated Hispanic parents and to empower them to take leadership in structuring their adolescents' social ecology. The intervention aims to accomplish this goal by enhancing parents' knowledge about adolescent development in a multicultural urban environment and by assisting parents in developing the kinds of skills that will help them reduce risks and enhance protection in important developmental domains.

The program's philosophy is a blend of cognitive change strategies, behavioral skills training, and empowerment. The goal is the creation of a social ecology that is rich with positive, supportive interconnections, including a parenting network. The intervention goals and activities are pictured in Figure 7.7.

In Familias Unidas, all intervention activities are organized around strengthening the family and placing it in charge of enhancing protective processes and decreasing risk within and across social systems. There are four phases: engagement, skill-building, restructuring, and evaluation.

Results from analysis of the effectiveness of Familias Unidas showed more improvement in parental investment and more consistent declines in behavior problems of adolescents than those of control groups. In addition, families who participated in more intervention sessions showed significantly greater investment by parents, especially for higher socioeconomic and more acculturated families.

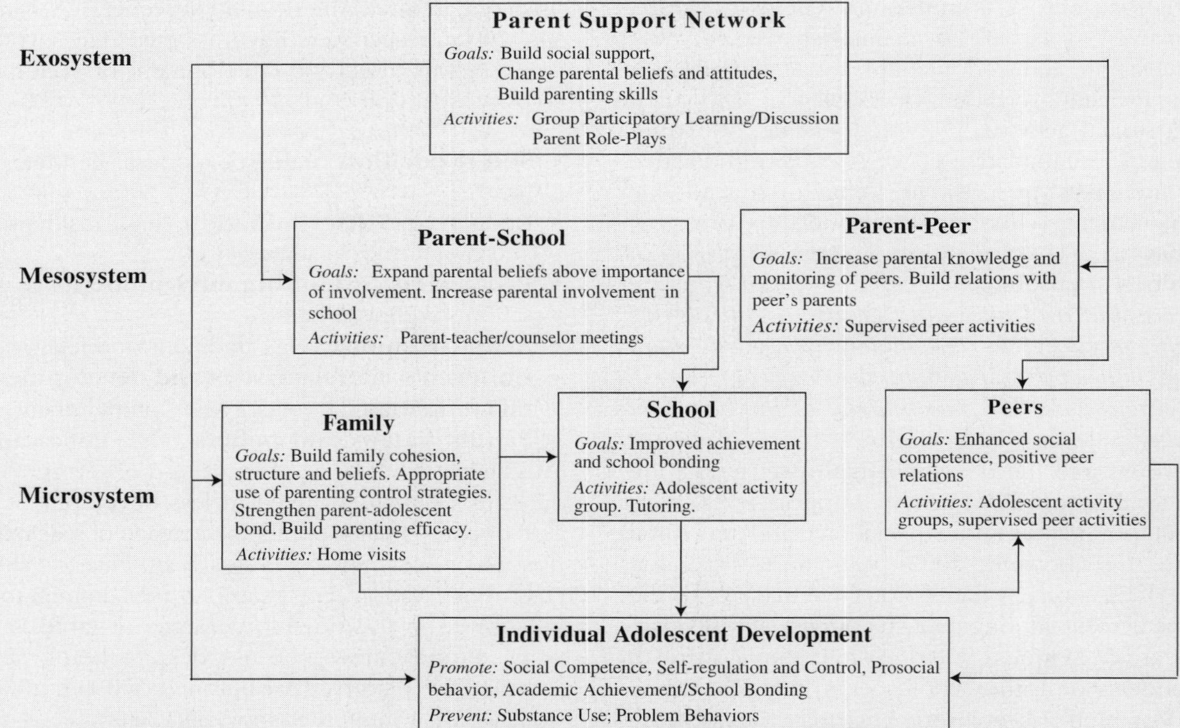

FIGURE 7.7 The program goals of Familias Unidas are conceptualized at three different levels of Bronfrenbrenner's ecological model: the microsystem, the mesosystem, and the exosystem.

Source: From "Familias Unidas: A Family Centered Ecodevelopmental Intervention to Reduce Risk for Problem Behavior Among Hispanic Adolescents" by J. D. Coatsworth, H. Pantin, & J. Szapocznik, 2002, *Clinical Child and Family Psychology Review*, 5, p. 116. Copyright 2002 by Plenum Publishing Corporation. Reprinted by kind permission of Springer Science and Business Media.

A supportive and involved family life is a developmental asset for adolescents.

their culturally relevant parenting strategies (Coatsworth, Pantin, & Szapocznik, 2002).

What risks and what opportunities did you face as a teenager?

Developmental scholars have found that "youth development programs seek to enhance not only adolescents' skills but also their confidence in themselves and their futures, their character, and their connections to other people and institutions by creating environments, both at and away from the programs, where youth can feel supported and empowered" (Roth & Brooks-Gunn, 2003, p. 219). In studies of sixth to twelfth graders in over 200 U.S. communities, asset-building strategies that went beyond "village rhetoric" (i.e., it takes a village to raise a child) created healthy communities through economic development, neighborhood revitalization, and civic engagement (Scales et al., 2000; Lerner, Taylor, & von Eye, 2002). Developmental assets, such as school success, leadership, valuing diversity, physical health, helping others, delaying gratification, and overcoming adversity have predicted thriving among adolescents across six ethnic groups. Furthermore, these developmental assets contribute significantly to positive adolescent outcomes over and above the influence of demographic variables, such as social class and geography (Scales, Benson, Leffert, & Blyth, 2000).

To support and foster positive youth development, we need to examine the key features of youth programs in schools, in communities, and in youth organizations (Oden, 1995).

- To learn how and why programs are effective.
- To expand knowledge of outcomes for the youth who participate.
- To guide policy or program replications from place to place.

Refer to Table 7–2 for a description of effective youth development programs as they are currently being implemented in both community-based and school settings.

Social Policy Implications

As we have seen, the social construction of adolescence has changed from the earlier notion of a *problem* stage to the current conceptualization of the teen years as a *positive* developmental transition toward adulthood. Researchers have found that even if youths were vulnerable (i.e., had fewer developmental strengths or lived in less developmentally attentive communities), the percentage of vulnerable adolescents who successfully avoided problem behavior was higher in healthy communities (19% vs. 35%) (Blyth & Leffert, 1995). This finding means that vulnerable youth with fewer personal assets, in particular, may benefit from living in healthier communities. The policy implication is to improve neighborhood quality and community environment rather than to focus exclusively on adolescent problem behaviors.

Today, applied developmental researchers are attempting to reframe adolescence to policy makers. Public opinion of adolescents is too often framed by negative media reports. For example,

TABLE 7–2

Characteristics of Youth Development Programs

Effective programs for youth development involve improving adolescent outcomes, creating a positive atmosphere, and offering activities to teens.

Outcomes	Definition
Competence	Interpersonal skills, cognitive abilities, school performance, work habits, and career choice
Confidence	Self-esteem, self-concept, self-efficacy, identity, and belief in the future
Connections	Building and strengthening relationships with other people and institutions, such as school
Character	Increased self-control, decreasing problem behaviors, respect for culture and society, morality, and spirituality
Caring	Improved empathy, compassion, and identification with others
Atmosphere	
Supportive	Encourage supportive relationships with adults and/or peer mentors
Empowering	Encourage useful roles, self-determination, and develop or clarify goals for the future
Expecting	Communicate expectations for positive behavior, clear rules, consequences; foster prosocial norms and healthy behaviors
Rewarding	Reward positive behaviors or structure opportunities for public recognition of skills
Lasting	Offer enduring support and opportunities for meaningful relationships that are ongoing
Activities	
Build skills	Engage in real and challenging activities, such as life-skills training or academic instruction
Authentic activities	Employment, leadership opportunities, such as peer mentoring or tutoring, and community service
Broaden horizons	Field trips, cultural activities, exposure to new people, places, or opportunities
Other contexts	Improve at least one other context: family, school, or community, e.g., parent activities or teacher training

Source: Based on "What Is a Youth Development Program? Identification of Defining Principles," by J. L. Roth & J. Brooks-Gunn, in R. M. Lerner, F. Jacobs, & D. Wertleib (Eds.), *Handbook of Applied Developmental Science, Vol. 2: Enhancing the Life Chances of Youth and Families: Contributions of Programs, Policies, and Service Systems* (p. 218), 2003, Thousand Oaks, CA: Sage. Copyright 2003 by Sage Publications, Inc.

public opinion polls have shown that 71% of Americans (and 74% of parents) believe that teenagers are disrespectful, irresponsible, and wild and that only 15% (and 12% of parents) think teens are smart, curious, or helpful (Public Agenda, cited in Roth & Brooks-Gunn, 2000). To counter these perceptions, youth policy advocates suggest four remedies (Roth & Brooks-Gunn, 2000):

1. Conduct positive media campaigns, legislative briefings, and liaisons with journalists and politicians.
2. Publish research reports that focus on the positive, not just on preventing problems, such as the percentage of youth who are engaged in volunteer activities, after-school programs, and school clubs.
3. Stress the intersections among the different settings influencing adolescents, such as schools, families, and peer groups.
4. Initiate community mobilization efforts, such as the Search Institute's *Healthy Communities—Healthy Youth Initiative* or the Social Development Research Group's *Communities That Care*.

A common framework emphasizing positive youth development has recently been developed to guide worldwide social policy makers using a broad set of principles applicable to wide-ranging contexts. Social policies should (adapted from Pittman, Diversi, & Ferber, 2002)

Guideposts for Working with Adolescents

- Acknowledge adolescents' positive development in multiple contexts—home, school, and neighborhood—by attending local sporting events or extracurricular activities.
- Visit the communities in which teens live, work, and play and meet their families and friends.
- Remember that even if teens face numerous risk factors, such as poverty, they may be resilient due to protective factors in their environment, such as parental support.
- Make a list with teenagers of their "developmental assets" and design activities or create opportunities that build on their strengths.

- Aim not only at preventing youth problems but also at promoting youth development and youth engagement in their communities.
- Be written in a way that presents clear pathways and trajectories of support from birth through adulthood.
- Reach across a range of settings, providing a full range of services, supports, and opportunities.
- Feature the voices and actions of young people themselves as agents of positive change.

If you were a policy maker or legislator, what youth policies or laws would you work to change?

Developing social policy for adolescents in the 21st century has become more challenging as societies become increasingly diverse, global, and postmodern. The changing view of adolescence has influenced youth policies in most American communities. Instead of the earlier focus on reducing problem behaviors, most policy makers now emphasize creating healthy communities as contexts for positive youth development.

Contexts of Middle Adolescence

From the perspective of positive youth development, adolescents' social contexts are central to understanding dynamic developmental change. In a fascinating experiment, low-income youth who moved from economically and racially segregated neighborhoods to middle-class, primarily White neighborhoods responded to surveys two years after relocating. Compared to demographically similar youth who did not relocate, 8- to 9-year-olds experienced less victimization, fewer family and peer problems, and lower delinquency. However, 16- to 18-year-olds who moved to a "low-risk" neighborhood experienced *more* problems than youth who stayed in "high-risk" communities! Few effects were found for 10- to 15-year-olds (Fauth, Leventhal, & Brooks-Gunn, 2005). These results suggest that residential moves can have complex implications for developmental outcomes, especially in adolescence.

In adolescence, as in middle childhood, three contexts are salient: family, school, and community. Although developmental contexts are often viewed as separate environments, they are, in fact, overlapping. From a life-course perspective, studying context-context interactions also presents a changing picture over time, as adolescents move through normative developmental transitions, like getting a job or beginning to date. Most studies of the impact of context on adolescent behaviors have shown that the effects of families, schools, and neighborhoods are independent but, when added together, may exert a powerful influence on adolescent development (Furstenberg, 2001; see also Silbereisen, 2003).

Family Contexts

Researchers studying the interplay of family, schools, peers, and work in adolescence have found that the parent-adolescent relationship seems to be a major mediating link between experiences in various contexts outside the family and adolescents' psychosocial development (Silbereisen & Todt, 1994). Recent surveys also indicate that many Americans believe that most parents provide too little supervision of their teenagers (Furstenberg, 2001). Several recent studies of family relations during adolescence have demonstrated that parenting influences many areas of adolescent development, such as temperament, autonomy, school achievement, and problem behavior (Borkowski, Ramey, & Bristol-Power, 2002). For example, in a recent study, parents' prior stereotypes about adolescence and their specific beliefs about their own children were related to their teens' social behaviors and relationships with deviant peers three years later (Jacobs, Chin, & Shaver, 2005).

In addition, interrelationships between the family context and other environments change as a function of adolescent development. Parents, for example, typically relax their rules for older adolescents. Adolescence is a time of major developmental transitions and of significant realignments in family relations as parenting demands change (Small & Eastman, 1995). Contextual sources of support for parenting, such as informal support networks through the child's school, need to change as adolescents develop relationships in the wider community. Leticia illustrates a central issue in understanding the importance of context in the study of adolescence:

Leticia is still worried. Her parents and older brother Lorenzo still see her as a child and won't accept the fact that she is responsible. "Why won't they let me grow up?" she asks Marina in frustration. At school, no one questions her judgment. Even her youth minister thinks that she is a good leader. If only her family could see her at school or volunteering at the homeless shelter! Leticia's involvement in youth ministry increases the likelihood that her mother will see her as able to make more of her own decisions in the near future.

Children become more active in the selection of contexts when they reach adolescence. Time spent outside the home in adolescence generally increases at the expense of family time, although parents may choose neighborhoods, schools, churches, and other voluntary organizations in order to situate their adolescents in communities that are consistent with their own values (Furstenberg, 2001).

Studies of adolescent work have consistently demonstrated important linkages between contexts (Mortimer & Finch, 1996). For example, farming traditions in rural communities contribute to higher levels of prosocial behaviors, such as helping the family, among rural youth than among adolescents who leave the farm (Elder & Conger, 2000). In addition, researchers studying the relationships between work and family contexts have suggested that, due to gender-specific role expectations, females see home and work as conflictual, whereas male adolescents see these two contexts as compatible (Bowlby, Evans, & Mohammad, 1998; Camarena, Stemmler, & Petersen, 1994).

Some researchers have also pointed out harmful effects for both sexes of working during adolescence on school performance and educational commitment, such as getting good grades and staying in school (Greenberger & Steinberg, 1986). Other researchers have pointed out potential benefits of employment for gaining skills, psychological maturity, and social contacts (Mortimer & Finch, 1996). Most researchers studying adolescents with jobs agree that the consequences of working depend on the quality and safety of the context in which it occurs, the amount of adult supervision provided, and the limiting of long hours (Furstenberg, 2001).

Lorenzo works at the public library after school and on weekends. He wanted to work at an all-night diner, but his mother said no, emphatically. The library is well supervised, safe, and educational.

School Contexts

Recently, community schools have emerged as a framework within which schools and many different community agencies, or partners, can come together to improve learning and development while strengthening families and communities (Blank, Shah, Johnson, Blackwell, & Ganley, 2003). In a summary report called *Learning Together*, the Institute for Educational Leadership described four major strategies of community schools: (a) service reform, (b) youth development, (c) community development, and (d) education reform (Melaville, 1998), as summarized in Table 7–3.

A significant shift in thinking about what adolescents need to become successful adults has been behind these recent efforts of the federal government to fund community-based schools, called *21st Century Learning Centers* (Roth & Brooks-Gunn, 2003). Twenty-first-century schools

TABLE 7–3
Strategies of Community Schools

Strategy	Goal	Objectives
Service reform	Remove the nonacademic barriers to school performance by providing access to improved health and human services to young people and families	Create family support centers, health clinics, mental health services, crisis intervention programs, and other supports for students and their families, and sometimes residents, in the school
Youth development	Help students develop their talents and abilities to participate fully in adolescence and adult life by increasing young people's opportunities to be involved in learning, decision making, service, and supportive relationships with others	Provide after-school mentoring, community service, service learning, recreation, leadership development, and career development programs
Community development	Enhance the social, economic, and physical capital of the community by focusing on economic development	Create jobs, engage in community organizing, advocacy, and leadership development among community members, students, and parents
Education reform	Improve educational quality and academic performance by improving the management, curriculum, instruction, and general culture within schools and classrooms	Engage parents, families, and teachers in school-based decision making; engage the private sector in a range of activities described in the previous objectives

Source: From *Learning Together: The Developing Field of School-Community Initiatives* by A. I. Melaville, 1998, pp. 14–15, Washington, DC: Mott Foundation. Available from http://www.mott.org/publications/pdf/SPECIALlearningtogether.pdf. Copyright 1998 by the Charles Stewart Mott Foundation. Adapted by permission.

were originally a response to a 1983 report of the National Commission on Excellence in Education, called *A Nation at Risk*. Complex studies of peer groups, especially in classroom and school contexts, have demonstrated how factors such as learning communities have shaped the course of adolescents' social and academic development (Furstenberg, 2001; Wigfield, Eccles, & Rodriguez, 1998). Researchers studying community schools have found significant improvements in the following areas (Dryfoos, 2000):

- **Achievement.** Academic gains in the areas of math and reading over a two- or three-year period
- **Attendance.** Lower drop-out rates, including the rate for pregnant teens
- **Suspensions.** Reductions in suspensions, suggesting improved school climate
- **High-Risk Behaviors.** Lower rates of substance abuse, teen pregnancy, and disruptive behavior
- **Parent Involvement.** Heightened sense of adult support and parent involvement
- **Neighborhood.** Less violence and safer streets in their communities

A 21st-century school would provide Leticia's younger brother Raúl with an after-school program while she participates in a school youth group. It could even provide career counseling and job placement for their older brother Lorenzo.

Community Contexts

Youth development programs focus on communities to build the developmental strengths of adolescents and to promote their health and well-being (Benson, Scales, & Marines, 2003). A **developmentally attentive community** is an environment that encourages the strength-building capacity of both youth and adults (as in Familias Unidas). In order to sustain a developmentally attentive community, adult engagement with adolescents is encouraged through the application of financial resources, social norms, and policies. Five types of community capacity have been described by researchers (Benson, et al., 2003):

1. **Adult Engagement.** Community adults build sustained, strength-building relationships with youth, both within and beyond family.
2. **Child, and Especially Youth, Engagement.** Adolescents use their asset-building capacities with peers and younger children and in activities that enhance the quality of their communities.
3. **Community Engagement.** Families, neighborhoods, schools, congregations, and youth organizations activate strength-building potentials.
4. **Programs.** A community infrastructure of quality after-school, weekend, and summer programs is available and used by children and youth.
5. **Community Supports.** Financial, leadership, media, and policy resources are mobilized to sustain youth development.

The intersection of adolescent and community development has recently been termed **community-based human development** (Benson, Scales, & Mannes, 2003). This approach involves the social construction of adolescence as a *positive* period in human development and stresses the interplay of action and reflection, or *praxis*, in which teens and adults together engage in contemplating their own experiences as change agents in their communities. Participation in community service activities provides a context for youth civic participation (Youniss et al., 2002). More importantly, these experiences may provide adolescents with reflective opportunities at a critical juncture in the development of their adult identity (Larson, 2000). Ideally, a community-based human development approach would allow youth to become adults who contribute to their own self-development *and* to their communities in a way that advances social justice and a civil society (Lerner et al., 2002).

Leticia is able to reflect on the needs of homeless children and on how to raise money for the local shelter. As a result, Leticia not only sees herself as a change agent but also has enhanced her future identity as a socially responsible citizen.

Studies have consistently demonstrated the influence of the community context on individual outcomes and positive adolescent development, but not on risky individual behaviors (Gilliam & Bales, 2001; Pittman, Diversi, & Ferber, 2002). For example, "overcoming the odds" against positive development, African American male adolescents in urban gangs demonstrate developmental assets remarkably similar to those of youth living in the same communities but belonging to community-based organizations instead of gangs (Taylor et al., 2002). Acknowledging the resilience of ethnic minority adolescents, applied developmental researchers have recognized the multiple contexts of school, family, neighborhoods, and religious institutions as a framework for the positive development of African American youth (Swanson et al., 2002). Thus, community-based researchers have integrated developmental scholarship with the promotion of positive youth development (Lerner, Fisher, & Weinberg, 2000; Lerner, Taylor, & von Eye, 2002).

CHAPTER REVIEW

History of Adolescence

- Adolescence is defined as the developmental period between puberty and young adulthood, roughly ages 13 to 18, although some researchers divide adolescence into early (10 to 14), middle (15 to 18), and late (18 to 24) adolescence.
- Adolescence has historically been viewed as a period of storm and stress, although current empirical research does not support this negative view. Recently, adolescence is more often viewed as a positive transition to adulthood.
- Rapid globalization has influenced adolescents across diverse societies, but due to variations in the social construction of adolescence, the meanings of adolescence are not universal in either their structure (e.g., timing or duration) or in their function (e.g., preparation for adulthood).

Developmental Perspectives

- Adolescent research is commonly divided into physical, cognitive, affective, and social domains of development.

- Life-span theory suggests that adolescence is a stage in the life span characterized by intraindividual change, interindividual differences, and historical embeddedness.
- Life-course theory suggests that adolescence can be studied by examining the timing, sequencing, and transitions between major life events in any given cohort or historical period.

Risk and Opportunity

- Researchers examining teen risks have attempted to identify overlapping problem behaviors that predict vulnerability during adolescence.
- Researchers examining teen opportunities have attempted to identify developmental assets or strengths that predict resilience to adversity during adolescence.
- Youth policies reflect a changing focus from preventing problem behaviors to enhancing developmental and ecological assets and positive youth development.

Contexts of Middle Adolescence

- The interrelated contexts of positive development in adolescence include families, schools, and communities.
- Policy makers are increasingly involving community members and adolescents themselves in formulating youth policies.

TABLE 7–4

Summary of Developmental Theories

Chapter 7 discussed two theories that position adolescence in relation to earlier and later stages and milestones of development.

Chapter	Theory	Focus
7: Perspectives on Middle Adolescence	Life Span	Development in relation to preceding and subsequent stages with a focus on both individual differences and developmental changes over time
	Life Course	Normative and nonnormative life events that are shaped by both historical events and adolescents' personal life histories

KEY TERMS

Adolescence
Adultoid
Age-graded
Compensation
Competence
Community-based development
Connectedness
Contextualism
Cultural globalization
Developmental assets
Developmental strengths
Developmental time
Developmentally attentive communities
Ecological assets
Economic globalization
Evolutionary psychology
Family careers
Family development theory
Family life cycle
Family time
Globalization
Historical embeddedness
Historical time
History-graded
Initiative
Interindividual change
Intraindividual differences
Life events
Life histories
Life-course theory
Life-span psychology
Metatheoretical paradigm
Moratorium
Multidirectional
Multidisciplinary
Nonnormative
Ontogenesis
Ontogeny
Phylogeny
Poststructuralism
Protective factors
Readiness
Recapitulation theory
Risk factors
Rites of passage
Selective optimization
Social reproduction
Structural period
Structuralism
Sturm und drang

SUGGESTED ACTIVITIES

1. Talk with adolescents about the daily ups and downs in their lives. How supportive do they think their parents, siblings, and peers are of their concerns? Do you think these are typical concerns of most adolescents? Do they face any unusual stress? Do they show any unusual strengths?
2. Interview the parent(s) of a teenager. How has being the parent of an adolescent differed from what they expected? How do other people react when told the age of their teenager? Is their adolescent typical of teenagers today? How?
3. Look through a teen magazine of your choice. What is the magazine's general attitude about adolescence? Are the articles, advertisements, and photographs consistent with a positive image of adolescence, or do they reinforce negative stereotypes and problem behaviors?
4. Modify the traditional family development cycle pictured in Figure 7.5 so that it accurately represents your family of origin by enlarging or decreasing time spent in each stage, or changing the order of life-course events. Note how your family differs from Duvall's (1957) model family!
5. Ask an adolescent and/or a young adult to examine the list of personal risks and protective factors provided in Box 7.4. Ask them to imagine the various situations described and to make risk judgments for themselves in similar situations. Which risks were judged more likely to occur? How protected do they seem overall? How might personal experience and context have influenced their ratings?
6. Analyze an existing policy in youth in your state or local area. Who were the framers of the policy? Were youth involved in the establishment of the policy? Does the policy conform to the framework described in this chapter emphasizing positive youth development? If not, how could it be modified?

RECOMMENDED RESOURCES

Suggested Readings

Brown, B. B., Larson, R. W., & Saraswathi, T. S. (2002). *The world's youth: Adolescence in eight regions of the globe*. Cambridge, UK: Cambridge University Press.

Elkind, D. (1997). *All grown up and no place to go: Teenagers in crisis* (rev. ed.). New York: Perseus.

Gesell, A., Ilg, F. L., & Ames, L. B. (1956). *Youth: The years from ten to sixteen*. New York: Harper & Row.

Hersch, P. (1998). *A tribe apart: A journey into the heart of American adolescence*. New York: Ballantine.

Nichols, S. L., & Good, T. L. (2004). *America's teenagers—myths and realities: Media images, schooling, and the social costs of indifference*. Mahwah, NJ: Erlbaum.

Turning points: Preparing American youth for the 21st century (1989). Available from the Carnegie Council on Adolescent Development, P.O. Box 753, Waldorf, MD 20604.

Villarruel, F. A., et al. (2003). *Community youth development: Programs, policies, and practices*. Thousand Oaks, CA: Sage.

Suggested Online Resources

Adolescents' Preparation for the Future: Perils and Promise (2002). Available from the Society for Research on Adolescence.
http://www.s-r-a.org/studygroup.html

Building a Better Teenager: A Summary of "What Works" in Adolescent Development (2002).
http://12.109.133.224/Files/K7Brief.pdf

Community Programs to Promote Youth Development (2002).
http://books.nap.edu/books/0309072751/html/index.html

Forum for Youth Investment: Youth Development Resources.
http://forumforyouthinvestment.org/portalcat.cfm?LID=D662C83D-BEEE-4E8E-A926F89515009A78

Great Transitions: Preparing Adolescents for a New Century (1995).
Available online from
http://www.carnegie.org/sub/pubs/reports/great transitions/grintro.html

Suggested Web Sites

ADOL: Adolescence Directory Online
http://education.indiana.edu/cas/adol/adol.html

Advocates for Youth
http://www.advocatesforyouth.org/

Carnegie Council on Adolescent Development
http://www.carnegie.org/sub/research/#adol

Center for Youth Development and Policy Research
http://www.aed.org/Youth/

Communication with Your Adolescent
http://www.aap.org/pubed/ZZZGP4ZUR7C.htm?&sub_cat=106

Society for Research on Adolescence
http://www.s-r-a.org/sra_intro.html

Suggested Films and Videos

Adolescence: Current issues I and II (1995). Magna Systems, Inc.

A kind of childhood (2003). Insight Media, Inc.

My so-called life (2002). Ventura Distribution.

Sixteen candles (2003). Universal Studios.

Thirteen (2003). Fox Searchlight.

The teen years (Ages 13 to 18). Films for the Humanities & Social Sciences.

Tough times, resilient kids: The documentary (2002). Insight Media, Inc.

CHAPTER

Physical Development in Middle Adolescence

CHAPTER OBJECTIVES

After reading this chapter, students will be able to:

- Understand the process of puberty and the variables that influence pubertal development in adolescence
- Summarize changes in physical, brain, and motor development in middle adolescence
- Recognize the important roles played by diet, sleep, and health-related lifestyle choices in middle adolescence
- Define the changes occurring in adolescent sexuality and how they relate to contraceptive use and pregnancy
- Explain the contributions of family, school, and community contexts to physical development and maturation in middle adolescence

As you arrive at the local pool one summer day, you notice that a group of middle- and high-school students is enjoying a day of swimming. As you continue to observe these students, you notice that they come in all shapes and sizes. Some of the males are tall and lanky with apparent muscles and body hair, other males are shorter and smaller muscled with no outward signs of maturity, and some are overweight. Several of the females are tall with developing breasts while others are considerably shorter with no figure and some look too thin and unhealthy.

In addition to the different body types among the group you notice differences in their coordination, strength, and speed as they move both in and out of the water. Some of them are playing sophisticated card games at poolside, and others are playing a game in the water that, based upon your observations, consists of elaborate rules and a complicated scoring system. Everyone, however, seems to know and understand this game. Several youth have paired off as couples, but most stay in same-sex groups with varying degrees of flirting between the sexes.

Adolescent Physical Development and Health Behaviors

The case study introducing this chapter depicts the physical, neurological, and motor changes that take place from middle childhood to middle adolescence. Dramatic changes in physical growth are accompanied by changes in strength and speed. Significant gender differences in these areas emerge as well. Brain development, related to corresponding changes in thinking and motor coordination, also takes place during this developmental period. Emerging sexuality and health-related behaviors such as diet, sleep patterns, and substance use accompany the transition to adolescence. Theoretical perspectives that help explain how and why these changes occur describe the patterns of physical, brain, and motor changes that take place during adolescence.

Theoretical Viewpoint

Chapter 3 presented a brief introduction to genetics-based theoretical perspectives (e.g., behavioral genetics) and how they emphasize the role of inherited traits in the development of children and adolescents. **Evolutionary developmental theory**, another genetics-based perspective, provides a different explanation of development and is highlighted in this chapter (Geary, 2000; Geary & Bjorklund, 2000). This theory is based upon Darwin's influential theory of evolution (Darwin, 1859). Darwin observed that animal and plant species appeared to be marvelously adapted to their environments. He hypothesized that this adaptation was a result of **natural selection**, a process whereby, over time, animals or plants that possess those characteristics or traits that best ensure the survival of the species pass them down to future generations. Which traits survive is genetically determined, but they also shape—and are shaped by—the organisms' immediate ecology. Evolutionary developmental theory studies current human development as a product of the evolutionary history of our species.

This theoretical perspective posits current predispositions or behaviors as having been adaptive for our ancestors millions of years ago. For example, the length of our current developmental period, or the time from infancy to reproduction, has increased considerably over time. Comparative studies suggest that this longer period before reproduction allows for humans to develop the physical, cognitive, and social competencies necessary to survive into adulthood and reproduce (Geary, 1998).

This lengthy developmental period is highlighted in the opening case study. The young people are clearly experiencing physical, social, and cognitive growth but many are years away from reproductive status.

Evolutionary developmental psychology has been used more recently to explain the phenomenon of early sexual maturation in girls (see Box 8.1).

This perspective emphasizes genetic contributions and focuses our attention on the competencies of our ancestors that are currently shared by all humans (e.g., a propensity to create emotional attachments, communicate, and explore our environments). Critics claim that this theoretical perspective places too much emphasis on genetics and pays too little attention to environmental influences. Other critics argue that there is no way to test evolutionary hypotheses. Evolutionary developmental theory, however, provides us with provocative ideas about how our biological inheritance may influence our physical, social, and cognitive growth.

Biological Maturation

One of the major developmental tasks that children in middle childhood and adolescents face is **puberty**, or the transition from infertility to fertility. Puberty involves biological and physiological changes that have social and cognitive consequences for young people. The first of several major physical changes is sexual maturation, or the development of **secondary sex characteristics** (e.g., pubic hair, body hair, genital and breast development). The second is somatic growth, or changes in the size, shape, and composition of the body. Researchers are still uncertain about the factors that trigger pubertal change, but we know a fair amount about the process once it begins.

The Pubertal Process

Between the ages of 6 (for girls) and 9 (for boys) there is an increase in adrenal androgens, hormones produced by the adrenal gland. The rise in androgens is referred to as "**adrenarche**" and occurs prior to any outward signs of pubertal change. Several years later, gonadal hormones begin to increase around age 8 for girls and age 11 for boys. This

BOX 8.1 ROADMAP TO UNDERSTANDING THEORY AND RESEARCH

Application of Evolutionary Developmental Theory to Pubertal Timing

The evolutionary developmental model has been used to explain early pubertal development in girls (Belsky, Steinberg, & Draper, 1991; Ellis, 2005). The theory suggests that early child-rearing contexts influence the individual's reproductive strategy in a way that resembles what would have been adaptive as the human species evolved: That over the course of human history, females growing up in adverse environments (e.g., instability, scarce resources, stressful living arrangements) would increase the survival of the species more by reproducing early. The application of evolutionary developmental theory to contemporary adolescent developmental patterns would suggest that family composition (e.g., who lives in the home) and family processes (e.g., how well they get along) may influence the physiological mechanisms that initiate and control pubertal development and thus reproductive capabilities. Specifically, the theory would predict that girls who are exposed to unstable resources, father absence in the first seven years, negative, coercive, and nonsupportive family relationships will show accelerated pubertal maturation, early sexual activity, and unstable adult romantic relationships.

This prediction was examined in a longitudinal study to see if mood disorders in mothers, biological father absence, and stressful family relationships led to earlier maturation in girls (Ellis & Garber, 2000). Researchers found that a history of mood disorders in mothers predicted earlier pubertal timing in daughters and this was mediated by biological father absence. These results support the evolutionary developmental model of pubertal timing by linking stressful early family environments to early puberty.

But what is the mechanism by which family environments prompt biological maturation? One possibility is that girls reared in homes without their biological fathers have an increased chance of being exposed to unrelated male figures such as stepfathers or mothers' boyfriends (Manning, 2002). Exposure to *pheromones*, or chemical molecules emitted by humans and other animals, from unrelated males can accelerate female pubertal development (Izard, 1990). The evolutionary developmental model would predict that girls who are exposed to stepfathers and mothers' dating partners should mature earlier than those who live with biological fathers only. This pattern was found in the same longitudinal study. The greater the duration of exposure to the unrelated father figures, the earlier the pubertal timing (Ellis & Garber, 2000).

Another study found that the quality of the father-daughter relationship was highly associated with age of menarche. Absence of a warm and positive father-daughter relationship rather than the presence of a negative, coercive relationship was associated with early puberty (Ellis, Bates, Dodge, Fergusson, Horwood, et al. 2003; Ellis, McFayden-Ketchum, Dodge, Pettit, & Bates, 1999).

A more recent study provides an alternative explanation for early puberty (Comings, Muhleman, Johnson, & MacMurray, 2002). The results of this study suggest that an X-linked gene predisposes the father to behaviors that include family abandonment, which is passed to their daughters, causing early puberty, precocious sexuality, and behavior problems. These findings support a genetic explanation of the evolutionary developmental hypothesis regarding the association of early environmental stressors and later reproductive strategies.

Whether it is exposure to pheromones or a recessive gene, both explanations rely on the premise that early puberty in females is adaptive behavior and is an evolving response to the increasing exposure children have to cohabiting parents and unstable and stressful family environments and relationships.

hormonal increase is referred to as "**gonadarche**," which is the increased hormonal production by the pituitary gland. Adrenarche, in conjunction with gonadarche, begins the process of sexual maturation. Gonadarche involves a brain structure (e.g., the hypothalamus), a glandular system (e.g., the pituitary gland), and the gonadal system (e.g., the ovaries in females and testes in males). Together, this system is called the hypothalamic-pituitary-gonadal axis (illustrated in Figure 8.1). Figure 8.1 shows the components within the axis and how each contributes to the process of puberty.

Beginning around age 8 in girls, the hypothalamus, which is located in the limbic system, or the midbrain (see Figure 3.9 in Chapter 3), signals for the release of gonadotropin-releasing hormone (GnRH). GnRH encourages the pituitary gland, which is part of the endocrine system, to release **gonadotropins**, which stimulate the growth of the sex organs (the testicles in boys and the ovaries in

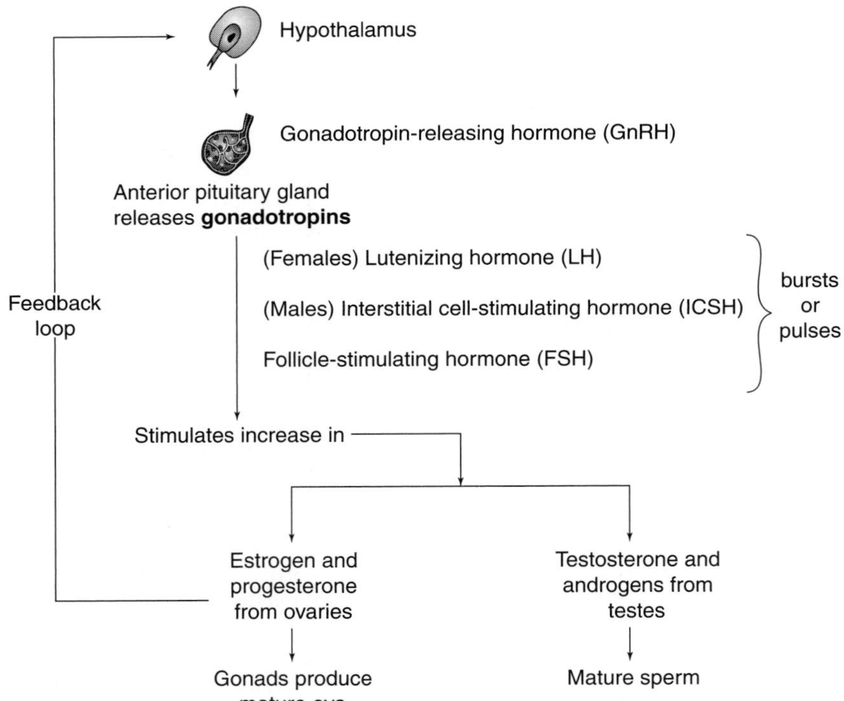

FIGURE 8.1 Hypothalamic-Pituitary-Gonadal System
The neurological and hormonal mechanisms that trigger the onset of puberty as well as the feedback loop that determines hormone production.

girls). The most prevalent gonadotropins are follicle-stimulating hormone (FSH), which is produced in both males and females, and either lutenizing hormone (LH), produced by females, or interstitial cell-stimulating hormone (ICSH), produced by males. Released in pulsating patterns or bursts and at higher levels during sleep, these gonadotropins elicit an increase of estrogen production from the ovaries in females and androgens, specifically testosterone, from the testes in males. The increased production of these sex steroids causes the ova and sperm to mature in females and males, respectively. The now-mature sperm can fertilize a mature egg to result in a viable pregnancy (Wilson, 2003).

This maturational process involves a feedback loop whereby the levels of sex steroids are monitored by the hypothalamus (illustrated in Figure 8.1). During puberty, the hypothalamus becomes deaf to the signals being sent regarding the high levels of sex steroid production. An appropriate example would be a malfunctioning thermostat. If the thermostat kept registering the temperature in your house as too cold, your furnace would run longer and far more often than it should. This "deafness" or insensitivity of the hypothalamus during puberty contributes to the consistently high levels of sex steroid production during early adolescence. High hormone production is largely responsible for the somatic and maturational changes that result in the development of secondary sex characteristics.

Secondary Sex Characteristics

Hormonal changes take place several years before there are any visible signs of physical maturation. Although there is large variation among individuals in regard to the onset and course of development, there is a "typical" age of onset and set sequence for secondary sex characteristics (Brooks-Gunn & Reiter, 1990). Around age 8 in African-American girls and 9 to 10 years of age in Caucasian girls breast budding occurs almost simultaneously with an acceleration in height (Herman-Giddens, Slora, Wasserman, et al., 1997).

Approximately 6 months later, pubic hair appears, and approximately 1 to 2 years after the onset of breast development, **menarche**, or the onset of menstruation, occurs. Table 8–1 shows the developmental sequences with variations in timing among subsets of girls, as we now understand it. Of note is that breast and height development as well as the emergence of pubic hair follows a stagelike progression (Marshall & Tanner, 1990). In females, the duration of pubertal development is 3 to 3.5 years but may be completed in as little as 2 years or take up to 5 to 6 years (Rogol, Roemmich, & Clark, 2002).

Boys typically begin pubertal development 1 to 2 years later than girls. The sequence of sexual maturation for boys begins at 11 to 12 years of age with testicular growth that in its third stage includes an increase in penis size. Testicular growth is generally followed by a growth spurt that is followed approximately 3 months later by the first appearance of pubic hair. The peak growth spurt for boys occurs between the ages of 13 and 14 years and corresponds with the occurrence of **semenarche**, or the first ejaculation.

Other changes for boys include voice deepening, a result of rapid vocal chord growth, which occurs around ages 14 to 15, and the growth of facial hair that begins on the upper lip and cheeks and then proceeds to the chin and neck. A complete list of pubertal changes for both boys and girls is provided in Table 8–1.

The middle- and high-schoolers at the pool reflect different maturation rates for secondary sex characteristics in same-aged youth. Some of the girls exhibit breast development and tallness and some of the boys show body hair and height.

Somatic Growth

In addition to being responsible for sexual maturation, puberty also contributes to dramatic changes in body height, size, and proportion. Increased secretion of growth hormone, thyroid hormone, and sex steroids (e.g., estrogen and testosterone) is most responsible for these increases in growth.

Linear growth (height). The rate of linear growth slows during middle childhood and "dips" just before the growth spurt in early adolescence (Tanner, 1990). Girls and boys differ in the timing and magnitude of their growth spurts. Girls grow an average of 9.75 inches with a gain of 3.5 inches per

TABLE 8–1

A Typical Sequence of Pubertal Development

A list of secondary sex characteristics that represent biological changes undergone during puberty.

In Females	Age Range of Appearance
Breast development	8–13
Pubic hair development	8–14
Growth spurt	9.5–14.5
Menarche	10–16.5
Underarm hair	Approximately 2 years after the appearance of pubic hair
Increased oil- and sweat-gland output	Simultaneous with underarm hair
In Males	**Age Range of Appearance**
Growth of testes, scrotum	10–13.5
Pubic hair development	10–15
Growth spurt	10.5–16
Increase in size of penis	11–14.5
Change in voice	11–14.5 (same as growth of penis)
First ejaculation	Approximately 1 year after penis growth
Facial and underarm hair	Approximately 2 years after the appearance of pubic hair
Increased oil- and sweat-gland output	Simultaneous with underarm hair

year during their peak growth spurt at about age 12 (Marshall & Tanner, 1969). These patterns of growth can be seen in Figure 8.2. Skeletal maturity in African American girls is more advanced and the age of peak growth is earlier (Birom, McMahon, Striegel-Moore, et al., 2001).

Boys grow an average of 10.92 inches with a peak growth spurt of 4 inches per year around age 14. The greater growth rate in males is largely accounted for by a greater increase in trunk length compared to girls (Tanner, 1990).

Body weight and composition. Body weight also increases dramatically during puberty. Girls' average weight gain peaks at 18.26 pounds per year around 12.5 years of age. By the end of the pubertal process, girls have gained an average of 24 pounds (Warren, 1983). Boys' peak weight gain is 19.8 pounds per year and occurs at 14 years of age (Barnes, 1975).

In addition to weight gain there is a change in the distribution of fat and muscle tissue in girls and boys (Grumbach & Styne, 1998). Before puberty begins, girls and boys have similar fat/muscle tissue ratios. During puberty, however, girls show an increase in fat tissue particularly in the breast, abdominal, and hip areas. Since this increase in fat tissue corresponds with menarche, it is believed that a certain amount of body fat is necessary for the onset and maintenance of menstruation in girls (Berkey, Gardner, Frazier, & Colditz, 2000).

During puberty, boys gain bone and muscle tissue while simultaneously losing fat tissue. As adults, males have 150% of the lean body mass of the average female and twice the number of muscle

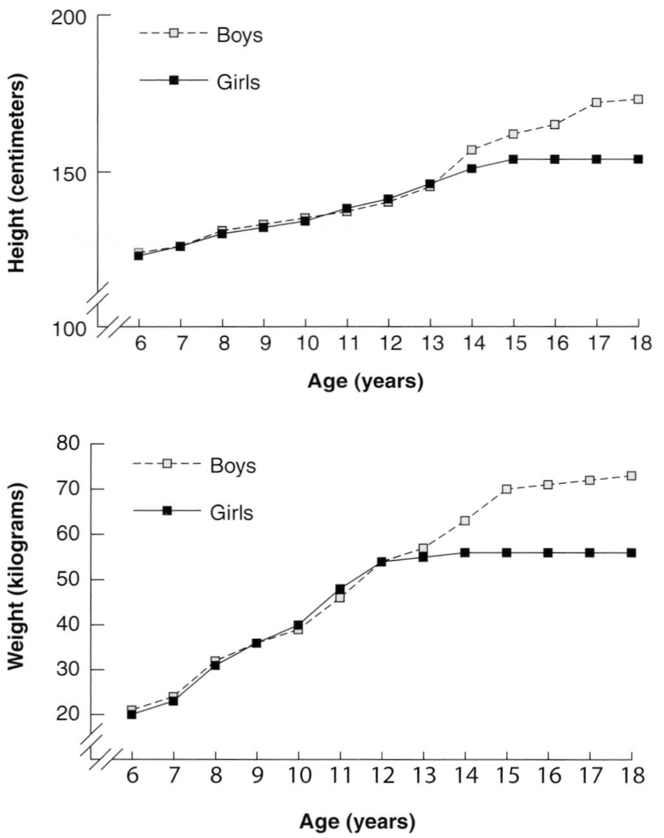

FIGURE 8.2 Average Heights and Weights from Ages 6 to 18
Patterns of height and weight gain for adolescent males and females.

Source: From *Guiding the Young Athlete: All You Need to Know* (pp. 2–3), by D. Jenkins & P. Reaburn, 2000, St. Leonards, Australia: Allen & Unwin. Copyright 2000 by Allen & Unwin. Reprinted by permission.

cells (Cheek, Grumbach, Grave et al., 1974). This increase in muscle mass results in greater average strength in males compared to females in late adolescence. Boys also develop larger hearts and lungs relative to their size, a higher systolic blood pressure, a lower resting heart rate, and a greater capacity for carrying oxygen in the blood. These physiological changes probably contribute to the superior performance of males in athletic endeavors that require such capacities (e.g., weight-lifting, cross-country running).

Skeletal size. The production of both estrogens and androgens promotes the deposition of bone mineral so that 90% percent of skeletal mass is present by age 18 in adolescents. In girls, bone mineral density increases significantly in the 3- to 4-year period after the onset of puberty. In boys, mineral density accrues over a longer period of time, 5 to 6 years.

Factors that may influence bone mineralization during puberty include adequate calcium intake, physical activity, and ethnic background. African American children, for example, have greater bone mineral density than do Caucasian and Hispanic children after age 5 (Rogol et al., 2002). In addition, adolescents with delayed puberty or those who are **amenorrheic** (i.e., without a menstrual cycle) fail to accumulate normal bone mineral density and may show reduced density, putting them at risk as adults for osteoporosis (Finkelstein, Neer, Biller, et al., 1992).

Some of the girls at the pool are taller, heavier, and exhibit a more curvaceous figure (e.g., wider hips, narrow waist, larger breasts) while some of the boys are heavier and more muscular with broader chests and more narrow waists.

Factors Influencing Pubertal Growth

Individual adolescents vary in the timing of pubertal onset, its duration or "tempo," and its termination. In fact, very little is known about the "offset" mechanisms of puberty. There are a number of variables that may influence directly or indirectly when and how quickly one moves through puberty:

Genetics	Nutrition
Health and well-being	Metabolism
Physical activity and fitness	Gender
Socioeconomic conditions	Ethnicity
Exposure to environmental toxins	Hormonal levels
Family constellations	Social stressors

It is unlikely that any one of these variables alone will delay or accelerate pubertal growth. Rather, it is the interaction among several of these variables that may affect maturation in complex ways. For example, since the turn of the 20th century, children in average economic conditions have increased in height approximately 1 to 2 cm per decade, a growth trend first discussed in chapter 3. Many sources report that this trend stabilized in industrialized countries in the mid-1900s. However, several recent comprehensive studies in the United States suggest that this secular growth trend is reoccurring (Freedman, Kahn, Serdula, Srinivasan, & Berenson, 2000; Herman-Giddens, Wang, & Koch, 2001). More specifically, in studies done on several U.S. populations, height gains were found to be significantly greater in 9- to 12-year-old children, with the largest height increases among African Americans and boys. The height gain was greater among younger adolescents compared to older adolescents, so the pattern points to earlier maturation rather than a difference in overall eventual adult height.

A similar secular trend has been observed in the onset of menstruation (Blythe & Rosenthal, 2000). Figure 8.3 shows a marked decrease in the age of menses as well as breast and pubic hair development in industrialized countries over the last several decades. Most recently, a growth study in the Netherlands showed a 6-month decline in the age at menarche between 1955 and 1997 (Fredriks et al., 2000). Similarly, a U.S. study including both African American and Caucasian females showed that twice as many girls (in a 1992–1994 cohort) reached menarche before age 12 compared to girls from a 1978 to 1979 cohort (Wattigney, Srinivasan, Chen, Greenlund, & Berenson, 1999). Many explanations have been offered for these historical trends, including the reduction of growth-retarding illnesses and family size and changes in child labor, diets, housing, personal hygiene, health habits, medical care, exposure to sex steroids, and/or environmental estrogens (Susman, Dorn, & Schiefelbein, 2003).

Overnutrition or obesity, which is on the rise in this country, has been linked consistently to the precocious development of secondary sex characteristics (Wattigney et al., 1999; Adair, Gordon-Larsen, 2001). Recent findings suggest that obese children show higher levels of the hormone **leptin**, which is responsible for signaling to the brain information about sufficient fat stores (Clayton & Trueman, 2000). Leptin may spark the brain-hormone cycle; however, it is unclear whether

Pubertal changes, such as sexual maturation and somatic growth, may take place at different rates among individual adolescents.

leptin *causes* puberty or is merely present at higher levels when puberty begins. To further complicate matters, obesity is linked to early maturation in *females only* and early-maturing males in fact are skinnier (Wang, 2002)! More research is needed to understand how increased storage fat prompts early puberty.

At the pool, you observe that many of the girls who show the greatest evidence of breast development are also the ones who possess the greatest amounts of body fat.

• Tanner Stage 2 of pubic hair development
□ Tanner Stage 2 breast development
△ Menarche
Average age in years
13.5
13.0
12.5
12.0
11.5
11.0
10.5
10.0
9.5
9.0
8.5
8.0
*1969
**1997

FIGURE 8.3 Secular Trend in Pubertal Maturation
The mean age of pubertal maturation including breast, public hair development, and menarche has decreased over the last several decades.

*Marshell & Tanner (1969) studied 192 British Caucasian girls.
**Herman-Giddens et al. (1997) studied 17,000 American girls (data reported for Caucasian girls only).

Psychosocial Consequences of Pubertal Timing

Once the process of puberty begins, how do young adolescents adjust psychologically to the rapid development of their bodies? The answer to this question is, "it depends." Research tells us that, among other individual and environmental factors, adolescent adjustment depends on

- The timing of puberty
- Gender
- Ethnicity
- Simultaneous occurrence of other stressors
- Adjustment in middle childhood (Weichold, Silbereisen, & Schmitt-Rodermund, 2003).

The *early-maturation* or *early-timing* hypothesis identifies early maturation as the best predictor of adjustment to puberty (Brooks-Gunn, Petersen, & Eichorn, 1985; Caspi & Moffitt, 1991). Specifically, girls who mature *early* have the most difficulty adjusting to pubertal change because early physical changes are not accompanied by similar cognitive, social, and emotional changes. Thus early-maturing females are ill equipped to cope with the different expectations placed upon them.

Researchers have found that when compared to same-aged peers, early-maturing girls experience significantly higher levels of psychological distress and are more vulnerable to prior psychological problems, deviant peer pressures, and fathers' hostile feelings (Ge, Conger, & Elder, 1996). Early-maturing girls are least satisfied with their height and weight, have poorer body image, and reported eating problems (Stice, Presnell, & Bearman, 2001). Early-maturing girls also engage more in drinking, smoking, and sexual activity (Magnusson, Stattin, & Allen, 1985; Wilson et al., 1994). These patterns of behavior apply to African American females as well as early-maturing female adolescents in many other countries (see Table 8–2).

It had long been thought that there was very little psychosocial risk associated with being an early-maturing male (Jones & Bayley, 1950; Mussen & Jones, 1957). In fact, the thinking was that it was advantageous for males to mature early because they were viewed as more desirable by females and were more admired by their peers. Recent research, however, shows psychosocial adjustment problems similar to those of females (Ge, Conger, & Elder, 2001). Early-maturing males manifest more hostile feelings and internalizing symptomology (e.g., anxiety) than on-time and late-maturing males. In addition, early-maturing males are more likely to engage in delinquent behavior, drug and alcohol use, and sexual activity and to experience greater depression (for a review, see Huddleston & Ge, 2003). These findings hold true for African Americans, Mexican American adolescents, and many others from around the world (see Table 8–2) (Cota-Robles, Neiss, & Rowe, 2002).

Although there appears to be less psychosocial risk for girls associated with maturing later, in part because they are better prepared for puberty (Brooks-Gunn & Warren, 1989), this is less true for boys. Late-maturing boys have higher incidences of psychopathology and depressed mood, poorer body image, and lower self-esteem (Graber, Lewisohn, Seeley, & Brooks-Gunn, 1997; Siegel, Yancy, Aneshensel, & Schuler, 1999). These findings support an alternative hypothesis called the *maturational-deviance* hypothesis, which posits that adolescents who are off-time (either early *or* late) will show greater adjustment problems.

Research findings support *both* hypotheses, and studies continue to be carried out to clarify whether early maturers or both early *and* late maturers exhibit higher risk behavior and emotional distress. As consistent as some of these patterns of adjustment are, researchers recognize that they do not hold true for *all* adolescents and that there are likely to be complex interactions of factors that determine the specific pathway an adolescent will travel.

Did you experience pubertal development at the same time as your peers?

Relationships Between Puberty and Function

The implicit assumption of the previous section is that pubertal change *causes* distress in adolescents or encourages them to engage in more high-risk behavior. The direct link between puberty and behavior is, unfortunately, not as simple as it might appear. The driving force behind puberty seems to be hormone production, and hormones often get blamed for the stress and unpredictability of adolescent behavior. Hormones are both directly *and* indirectly responsible for some of the psychosocial consequences presented in Table 8–2.

Two models explain how adolescents may be affected by biological change (Petersen & Taylor, 1980). The **direct-effects model** proposes a direct connection between physiological change and psychological adaptation. For example, research shows a relatively direct link between higher levels of testosterone and an increased readiness to respond with aggression to provocation (Olweus, Matison, Schalling, & Low, 1988).

In the **indirect-effects model**, on the other hand, the link between biological change and psychological adjustment or behavior is influenced by both **mediator** and/or **moderator** variables. Mediating variables could be internalized psychological factors, such as fantasies, beliefs, attitudes, or concerns. For example, an adolescent male may act aggressively because he has a fantasy about maintaining a masculine image. The fantasy is the mediating variable that contributes to the aggressive behavior. Moderator variables are outside of the individual. They could be such things as sociocultural contexts or socialization practices. A cultural expectation of masculinity that includes aggression would be a moderator variable that

TABLE 8–2

Summary of Pubertal Maturation Status and Associated Outcomes in Diverse Populations

Country	Gender	Maturational Status	Outcomes
Hong Kong	Females and males	Early	• Earlier reported dating and sexual intercourse in males (Lam, Shi, Ho, Stewart, & Fan, 2002)
Finland	Females and males	Early	• More substance use • More friends who also engage in substance use (Dick, Rose, Pulkkinen, & Kaprio, 2001)
Germany	Females and males	Early	• Higher frequency of cigarette smoking and alcohol use (Wiesner & Ittel, 2002)
Jamaica	Females	Early	• Earlier sexual intercourse (Wyatt, Durvasula, Guthrie, LeFrance, & Forge, 1999)
Mexico	Females and males	Early	• Increased depressive symptoms in females (Benjet & Hernandez-Guzman, 2002)
The Netherlands	Females and males	Early and late	• Early-maturing females showed an increase in withdrawn and delinquent behavior • Late females showed increased social problems • Early-maturing males showed a decrease in social and attention problems • Late males showed increased attention problems (Laitinen-Krispijn, Van der Ende, Hazebroek-Kampschreur, & Verhulst, 1999)
Norway	Females and males	Early and late	• Early-maturing females showed poorer body image and negative self-evaluations • Late-maturing males showed greater negative self-evaluations (Alsaker, 1992)
Scotland	Females	Early	• Lower ratings of body image • Lower self-esteem (Williams & Currie, 2000)
Slovakia	Females	Early	• Greater adjustment problems with parents and teachers • More externalizing problems (Ruiselova, 1998)
Sweden	Females	Early	• Earlier sexual intercourse (Andersson-Ellstrom, Forssman, & Milsom, 1996)
	Males	Early and late	• Higher alcohol use • Greater alcoholism for late maturers (Andersson & Magnusson, 1990)
United States Caucasian	Females	Early	• Higher levels of psychological distress • More vulnerable to prior psychological problems, deviant peers, fathers' hostile feelings (Ge, Conger, & Elder, 1996)
	Males	Early	• More externalized hostile feelings • More internalized distress symptoms (Ge, Conger, & Elder, 2001)
	Females and males	Early	• More substance abuse (Tschann et al., 1994)
Caucasian African American Mexican American	Males	Early	• Higher levels of both violent and nonviolent delinquent behavior (Cota-Robles, Neiss, & Rowe, 2002)
African American	Females and males	Early	• Early-maturing boys and girls showed greater depressive symptomology • No difference in male depression (Ge et al., 2003)

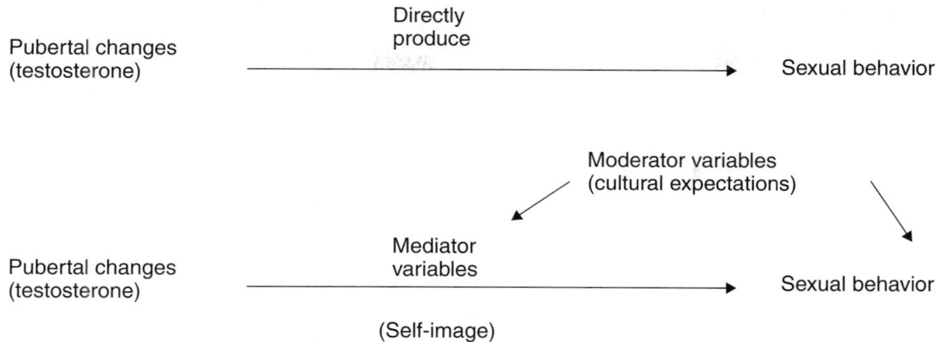

FIGURE 8.4 Two Models of the Relationship Between Pubertal Maturation and Psychological Development

The top figure represents a direct-effects model; the bottom figure, an indirect-effects model.

Source: Based on "The Biological Approach to Adolescence: Biological Change and Psychological Adaptation" (pp. 133–134), by Anne C. Peterson & Brandon Taylor, in J. Adelson (Ed.), 1980, *Handbook of Adolescent Psychology* (pp. 117–155). New York: Wiley. Copyright 1980 by John Wiley and Sons. Reprinted by permission of the publisher.

could contribute to the young adolescent's self-image, and consequently, behavior.

Each model, shown in Figure 8.4, provides a framework to understand the relationship between biological changes and psychosocial adjustment in this rapid period of development.

BRAIN DEVELOPMENT

Chapter 3 outlined the development of brain structure and function from the prenatal period to middle childhood. Brain researchers have recently discovered that the period of adolescence is accompanied by growth spurts in specific regions of the brain. These growth spurts may be linked either directly or indirectly to changes in function, such as higher-order thinking, as well as to improved emotional regulation.

Structural and Functional Change

Recent advances in technology have provided a more accurate picture of development and function in the adolescent brain. Although, as stated in chapter 3, grey matter in the brain begins to decrease during adolescence, there continue to

Guideposts for Working with Adolescents

- Remember that a growth spurt will mark the beginning of puberty for girls and occurs later in the sequence for boys.
- Recognize the role that environmental factors such as poverty, diet, and stress may play in the timing and adjustment to biological change.
- Help middle-schoolers and young adolescents understand the various rates of development and what is "within the norm."
- Adjust your expectations of adolescent behavior because their cognitive, social, and emotional development may not be commensurate with their physical development.
- Be aware that some adolescents may have more difficulty adjusting to these biological changes and may be in need of professional help.

be periods of **dendritic branching**. So even though the actual number of neurons is not increasing, the number of dendritic branches—and therefore synaptic connections—are. This means that there is more opportunity for the neurons to "talk" to one another and therefore greater opportunity for structures to communicate within the brain.

Peak periods of synaptic growth do not occur throughout the entire brain at the same time. As described in chapter 3, increases in synaptic connections progress from within the most inner structures of the brain (during prenatal development) to the most outward structures (during adolescence) and from the back to the front of the brain (Huttenlocher & Dabholkar, 1997). This pattern of development is best illustrated by research that shows growth spurts in neuronal connections between ages 10 to 12, 14 to 16, and 18 to 20 years of age in the prefrontal cortex, which is the outermost and frontmost structure of the brain (see Figure 8.5) (Fischer & Rose, 1994).

At the same time as synaptic connections are peaking, there is evidence of increased synaptic pruning. As chapter 3 explained, connections that are not activated and reinforced are "pruned away," leaving fewer but more solid neuronal connections to carry out functioning. At no other time is the phrase "use it or lose it" (Landau, 2000) more appropriate than during periods of peak synaptic pruning, which appear to occur between 10 and 16 years of age (Huttenlocher, 1979).

This pattern of synaptic pruning does not mean that learning capacities are decreasing; rather, they are becoming more efficient. However, research does suggest that nature makes it easier to learn a second language or a musical instrument before the drastic pruning in adolescence begins. It is not impossible to learn these skills later; it will just be more difficult (Thompson et al., 2000). But just as the sensitive period for learning a language begins to gradually draw to a close after age 15, research has shown that neural pathways involving visuospatial processing have not yet begun to be pruned (Passarotti et al., 2003). This development means that some parts of the adolescent brain are very open to experience that will help shape and sculpt the neuronal pathways that activate visuospatial skills, such as those required to detect and interpret patterns and shapes (Brecelj, Strucl, Zidar, & Tekavcic-Pompe, 2002).

There are other patterns of brain development that show constant development throughout adolescence. For example, myelination of axons, the development of myelin sheaths around the axons of neurons, continues to increase in the following brain structures during adolescence:

- The corpus callosum, which connects the two hemispheres of the brain and is related to perceptual functioning, comprehension, and

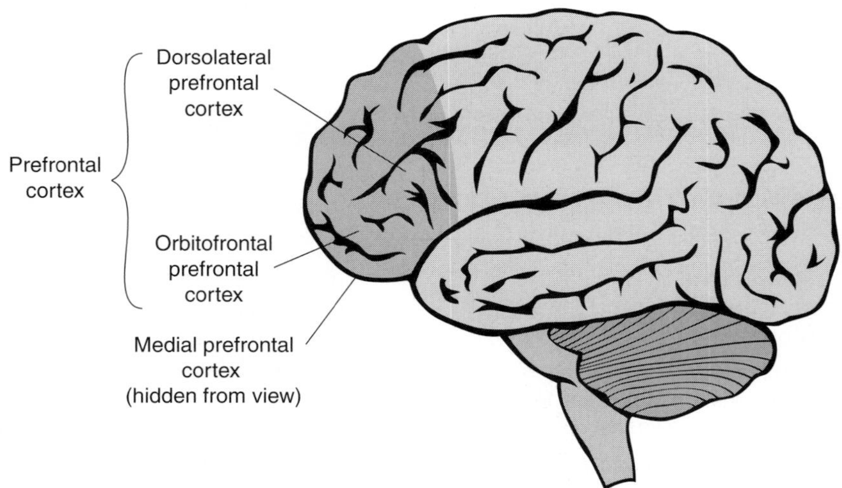

FIGURE 8.5 Prefrontal Cortex with Prefrontal Lobes
The prefrontal lobes show dramatic development during adolescence.

response time (Giedd et al., 1999; Mukherjee, Miller, Shimony, Philip, & Nehra, et al. 2002).
- Neural pathways responsible for motor and speech functions (Paus et al., 1999; Conturo, Lori, Cull, Akbudak, & Shimony, et al., 1999).
- The hippocampus, which is linked to memory functioning (Suzuki, Hagino, Nohara, et al., 2005).
- The prefrontal cortex, which houses executive functions such as planning, decision making, and the inhibition of emotional impulses (Kanemura, Aihara, Aoki, Araki, & Nakazawa, 2003).

Increased myelination has been associated with faster processing, resulting in quicker thinking and responding in adolescents.

The **prefrontal lobes** of the prefrontal cortex undergo significant maturation during the adolescent period. The lobes show high synaptic density in early adolescence and myelination late into adolescence. This part of the brain is what makes us most uniquely human. It controls our executive functions, such as planning, decision making, transforming action into thought, controlling impulses, and using rational thought to control our emotions. Studies show that the development of higher cortical processes parallels very nicely the appearance of more sophisticated cognitive functions. Skills such as abstract reasoning, the use of propositional logic, and being able to see multiple dimensions of an object or situation at the same time appear in adolescents as the prefrontal lobes mature (Fischer & Rose, 1994).

The prefrontal lobes not only control higher cognitive functioning but also appear to assist in emotional regulation. Prior to the maturation of the prefrontal lobes, young adolescents confronted with a situation that provokes strong emotions tend to respond with "gut instincts." Research shows that these immediate emotional responses activate the **amygdala**, a part of the brain located in the limbic system that is responsible for processing emotional responses (refer to Figure 3.9). This finding may explain why some adolescents "fly off the handle" or misread the facial expressions of others (Dahl, 2001; Baird et al., 1999). When adults are faced with the same situation, their prefrontal lobes are activated more than the amygdala. The development of the inhibitory component of the prefrontal lobes may help older adolescents use cognitive reasoning when faced with strong emotions and may contribute to reducing risky behavior.

Advanced cognitive functioning can be seen in the adolescents at the pool who are playing complicated card and water games. They are able to engage in games that have complex rule systems and require sophisticated strategies. More complex thinking is also reflected in the calculations they make about whom to flirt with and how to negotiate social relationships.

The Role of the Environment in Brain Development

Since many cortical areas of the adolescent brain are at their peak synaptic density and have yet to be pruned, it is possible that environmental experience may have an even greater influence during this developmental period. For instance, if a young adolescent is exposed to multiple languages, a musical instrument, or a creative hobby or practices a motor skill frequently, these will be the neuronal pathways that are going to continue to solidify. If, however, a young adolescent is disengaged in school and is denied cognitive or motoric opportunities, more dendrites are likely to be pruned away. Watching television, for example, stimulates the visual cortex, but the prefrontal lobes show very little activation during this activity (Diamond & Hopson, 1998). An adolescent's experiences may influence which neurons get pruned and which neuronal pathways sprout more dendritic branches.

Exposing adolescents to different and stimulating experiences can change the makeup of the brain significantly. Box 8.2 provides suggestions for an adolescent enrichment program (Diamond & Hopson, 1998).

Figure 8.6 is a model of human enrichment that illustrates various ways the environment "gets into the brain" (Curtis & Nelson, 2003, p. 476). The model consists of two phases:

- **Phase 1.** Experience causes changes in the chemical and structural makeup of the brain.
- **Phase 2.** These result in changes in behavior.

If enrichment activities can enhance the adolescent brain, so can nonoptimal environmental circumstances and behavior damage it. Research shows that cigarette smoking, the use of alcohol, marijuana, and cocaine, physical and/or sexual victimization, and highly stressful environments that may include poverty and violence all have long-term effects on the structure and functioning of the brain (Tarter, Mezzrich, Hsieh, & Parker, 1995).

BOX 8.2 ROADMAP TO SUCCESSFUL PRACTICE

Magic Trees of the Mind

Marian Diamond has spent her professional life unraveling the mysteries of the development of the brain. It was in her lab at Berkeley in the 1960s that the critical role of the environment on brain development was discovered. When her research team exposed laboratory rats to an enriched environment (e.g., toys and companion rats) they found that the brains of these rats were better developed. When compared to the brains of rats who were not exposed to a stimulating environment (e.g., alone with no toys), the brains of the "enriched" rats had more dendritic branches and thicker cerebral cortexes (Diamond, Krech, & Rosenzweig, 1964). Apparently, an enriched environment not only provides stimulation but also changes the neurological makeup of the brain! Since that time, more research has been done with noninvasive techniques that suggests human infants, children, and adolescents can also reap neurological benefits when exposed to enriched environments.

In 1998, Marian Diamond wrote a book with coauthor Janet Hopson to share in a comprehensible format the results of decades of brain research. In *Magic Trees of the Mind*, she makes specific suggestions about ways in which the adolescent brain may be stimulated:

- *Teens can exercise their imaginations, as well as build self-expression, and self-confidence, by taking speech, poetry, or writing classes, or joining a theater group. Even a non-joiner can get the same effect by following Robert Alexander's Daily Recipe for the Imagination: Make up and say aloud three stories and three poems each day for the rest of your life!*
- *Teens can continue developing language skills by*
  - *Taking school courses that assign frequent writing assignments*
  - *Keeping a daily journal*
  - *Reading fiction, plays, literature, biographies of successful people, mysteries, history, and science fiction*
  - *Using a daily vocabulary-building calendar*
  - *Writing to a pen pal or e-mailing friends on the Internet*
  - *Continuing foreign language study*
  - *Working on the school newspaper or yearbook*
- *Teens can build math and science skills through:*
  - *School classes and special projects*
  - *Enrichment classes after school or at science centers in subjects like higher math, animal conservation, astronomy, ecology, robotics, or physics*
  - *Tutoring younger students in basic math skills*
  - *Learning applied math such as beginning statistics and beginning computer programming*
  - *Using math- and science-oriented CD-ROMs*
- *Teens can continue expanding their music appreciation and performance skills through:*
  - *Musical instrument lessons and/or choral singing*
  - *Writing music or lyrics for rock, rap, or other music groups*
  - *Classes sponsored by local symphonies*
  - *Deliberately expanding musical interests beyond rock and rap to classical, bluegrass, jazz, New Age, musicals, gospel, and others*
- *Teens can develop existing physical skills through lessons or team participation, and learn new ones such as tennis, golf, skiing, snorkeling, dancing, football, basketball, aikido, soccer, dressage, karate, surfing, boogie boarding, skating, gymnastics, or swimming.*
- *Volunteer work, hometown environmental efforts, and part-time jobs can help adolescents expand relationship skills, social responsibility, and practical skills.*
- *Teenagers can reinforce artistic skills or learn new ones with materials, books, and classes on caricature and animation, photography, video, drawing, watercolor, landscape, pottery, ceramics, costume design, and art appreciation classes at local museums and galleries.*
- *A motivated teen can turn off the television or computer games after a limited time per day.*
- *Traveling with family and organized groups can be enlightening and stimulating.*

Source: From *Magic Trees of the Mind: How to Nurture Your Child's Intelligence, Creativity, and Healthy Emotions from Birth through Adolescence* (pp. 260–262), by M. Diamond & J. Hopson, 1998, New York: Dutton.

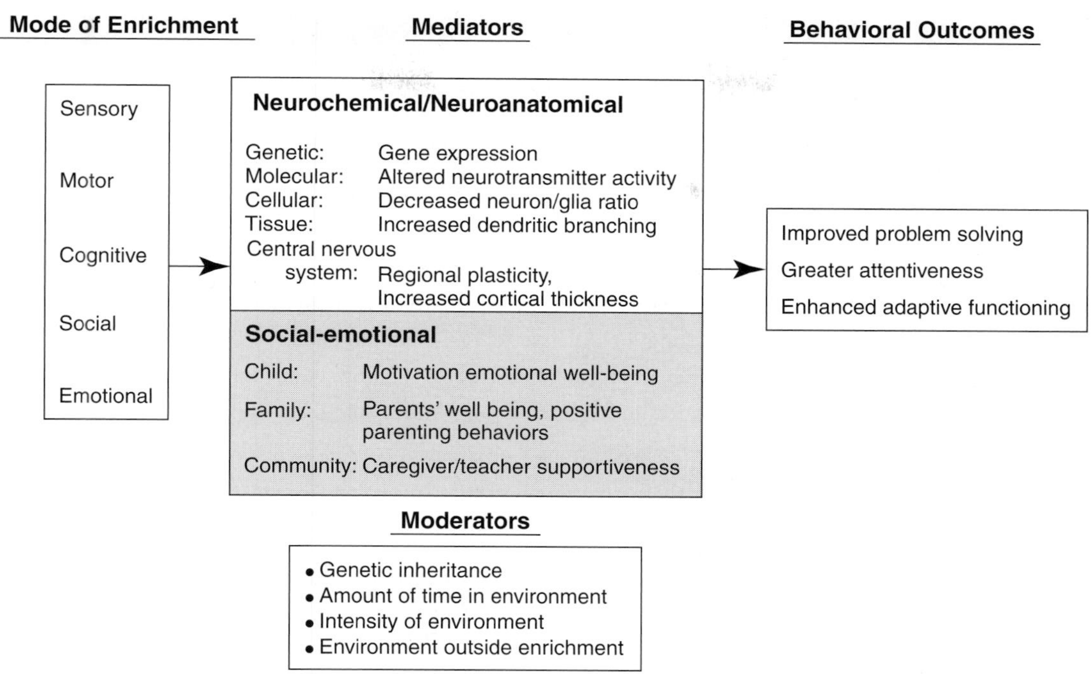

FIGURE 8.6 A Model of Effective Human Enrichment
A model that shows multiple ways in which stimulation from the environment might impact brain development and, ultimately, behavior.

Source: From "Toward Building a Better Brain: Neurobehavioral Outcomes, Mechanisms, and Processes of Environmental Enrichment" (p. 479), by W. John Curtis & Charles A. Nelson, in Suniya S. Luthar (Ed.), 2003, *Resilience and Vulnerability: Adaptation in the Context of Childhood Adversities*, New York: Cambridge University Press. Copyright 2003 by Cambridge University.

Guideposts for Working with Adolescents

- Expose adolescents to a variety of cognitive and motor opportunities with as much hands-on learning as possible.
- Design enrichment activities that are intense and comprehensive.
- Because the ability to take advantage of enrichment opportunities will be based, in part, on adolescents' socioemotional status, support their social and emotional development.
- Be aware of and try to educate teens about the effects drugs and alcohol have on the brain.

Motor Skills and Performance

Gross and fine motor skills exhibit the most significant improvement over the middle childhood years (Haywood & Getchell, 2001). Chapter 3 stated that by 10 or 11 years of age, children have developed the balance and coordination necessary to carry out most motor tasks correctly and competently. By the end of elementary school, children are exhibiting proficient jumping, skipping, sliding, kicking, and punting skills. *Proficient* means that the children are using their arms and legs correctly and are at an advanced stage in the developmental sequence of the skill. One study showed that 80% of 11- to 12-year-olds successfully adjusted their bodies to catch a ball. Another study showed that

TABLE 8–3

Maturation and Improvements in Motor Activity

Pubertal and brain maturation can result in improved adolescent motoric activities.

Increases in	Related Improved Performance
Size, strength	Weight lifting, football, shotput and discus throw, rugby, pitching a ball
Speed	Soccer, sprints, swimming
Endurance	Cross-country running, long-distance swimming, cross-country skiing, basketball
Balance	Gymnastics, skate- or surfboarding, cycling, karate, diving, skating
Hand-eye coordination	Catching a ball, table tennis, juggling, darts
Interskill coordination	Tennis serve, jumping hurdles, driving, volleyball, batting a baseball
Steadiness (ability to block out distractions and inhibit impulsive motoric movements)	Billiards, archery, shooting skills, fishing, shooting and free throw in basketball

by seventh grade, 80% of boys and 29% of girls had achieved the most advanced level of overarm throwing (Strohmeyer, Williams, & Schaub-George, 1991; Halverson, Roberton, & Langendorfer, 1982). The latter study illustrates that early adolescence is the developmental period where males begin to outperform females in many motor activities. The period of adolescence itself appears to be one of motor skill refinement rather than one of distinct qualitative changes in movement.

Despite general patterns of motor skill improvement, the onset of puberty has been documented as a period of "awkwardness" or "clumsiness" for some boys. A longitudinal study found that as boys were going through their peak growth spurt (around 13–14 years of age) their performance in some motor tasks declined. The researchers hypothesized that rapid leg growth in the early part of the spurt, and rapid trunk growth in the later part of the spurt, might account for temporary problems in balance, coordination, and speed (Beunen & Malina, 1988). A more recent study showed a similar pattern of high velocities in growth associated with poorer motor competency in boys. This disruption appears to be temporary (6–12 months) and high levels of activity and practice were shown to improve motor performance over time (Visser, Geuze, & Kalverboer, 1998).

Pubertal maturation and changes in the brain may contribute to the most significant differences between elementary school-aged children's and adolescents' motor skills. For example, the puberty-induced changes in body size and composition outlined earlier in the chapter contribute largely to increases in skills that require speed, strength, and endurance. On average, older adolescents are better at physical activities that capitalize on these size differences. In addition to increases in physical size, the center of gravity is lower in adolescents' bodies, thus improving their balance in all types of activities.

Myelination of certain cortical areas in the adolescent brain will also produce faster reaction times and improve communication between different association areas in the brain necessary for intermodal coordination. For example, motor skills that require hand-eye coordination or the coordination of multiple skills such as those required in a tennis serve will show marked improvement during the adolescent years. Frontal lobe development may also help an adolescent block out distractions and focus more attention on the task at hand. Table 8–3 shows how physical and brain maturation might translate into enhanced performance in various sports and activities.

The teens are moving quickly and competently in and out of the water. Physical and motor development makes them stronger swimmers—especially in strokes that require strength, like the butterfly—and more competent divers. Some adolescents are able to sustain a card game despite the noisy activity around them.

 **In what motor activities did you excel during adolescence and in what specific ways?**

Related Health and Development Issues

Research presented in chapter 3 emphasized the important role that a healthy diet and regular exercise play in optimal physical development in middle childhood. These factors are equally important in a growing adolescent.

Nutritional Needs and Dietary Behavior

Adolescents actually have *greater* nutritional needs than younger children due to rapid growth, sexual maturation, changes in body composition, skeletal mineralization, and physical activity. These changes result in an increase in total energy needs due to the maintenance of a larger body size. For example, during their peak growth years (11–14 years of age) girls require approximately 2200 kcal/day to sustain growth, whereas boys during ages 15 to 18 require 2500–3000 kcal/day (Mascarenhas, Zemel, Tershakovec, & Stallings, 2001).

In addition to the need for increased calories, adolescents also require more protein, calcium, iron, and zinc in their diet. Although these additional vitamins and nutrients are required for optimal physical growth and development, rarely does the average adolescent consume a diet that consists of these recommended levels. One national study (see Table 8–4) found that adolescents, particularly girls, demonstrated an insufficient intake of calcium, iron, and vitamins A and C (NHANES III, 1988–1994). When 12,500 children aged 11 to 18 years were surveyed, researchers found that vegetable intake was lower in all age groups than the recommended five servings per day (remember, new guidelines recommend nine servings per day). In fact, french-fried potatoes made up 25% of all vegetables consumed! Intake of simple sugars (like those found in soda and noncitrus juices) exceeded the intake of complex carbohydrates, and more than one-third of the dietary fat was saturated (Gavadini, Sieja-Riz, & Popkin, 2000). Diets poor in essential vitamins and minerals can result in slowed or retarded maturation (zinc deficiency), nonoptimal bone mass accrual or bone mineral density (poor calcium intake), or anemia (iron deficiency).

Adolescents differ from children and adults in that they are more likely to skip meals, eat more meals outside their homes, eat unhealthy snacks that include soda and candy, diet, or consume fast foods. Excessive consumption of simple sugars and saturated fats can contribute to weight gain or obesity in some adolescents (Neumark-Sztainer, Story, Hannan, & Croll, 2002).

Recent findings show that more teens are overweight than ever before (CDC, 2003a). In 1991 the prevalence of overweight adolescents was 11%; by 1999 this had increased to 14%. Recent surveys indicate that the greatest increases in the prevalence of obesity are in minority groups (especially African Americans) and in the proportion of adolescents in the highest percentile of obesity (BMIs > 95th percentile) (Neumark-Sztainer et al., 2002). Health risks associated with obesity in adolescence include increased risk for obesity in adulthood, coronary heart disease in adulthood, and type 2 diabetes. The long-term health care consequences and costs of obesity in adolescents are enormous. Prevention programs encourage not only healthier eating styles but also an increase in regular exercise (U.S. Department of Health and Human Services, 2005).

Disordered Eating Behavior

Adolescence is a developmental period in which individuals experience increased awareness of **body image**, or how they think and feel about their bodies. A preoccupation with body image and size may be further exacerbated by school transitions and the simultaneous occurrence of puberty, dating, and associated social and academic pressures (Levine, Smolak, Moodey, Shuman, & Hessen,

TABLE 8–4

Actual (and Recommended) Calcium Intake (mg/day) in Adolescents by Race/Ethnicity and Sex

	Males		Females	
	6–11 years	12–15 years	6–11 years	12–15 years
Non-Hispanic White	994 (800)	822 (1200)	822 (800)	744 (1200)
Non-Hispanic Black	761 (800)	688 (1200)	688 (800)	613 (1200)
Mexican American	986 (800)	890 (1200)	890 (800)	790 (1200)

Actual data source: From Third National Health and Nutrition Examination Survey, by K. Alaimo, M. A. McDowell, R. R. Breifel, et al., 1994. *Dietary intake of vitamins, minerals, and fiber of persons ages 2 months and over in the United States: Third National Health and Nutrition Examination Survey, Phase 1, 1988–1991.* Advance Data from Vital and Health Statistics, no. 258. U.S. Department of Health and Human Services. Hyattsville, MD: National Center for Health Statistics.

1994). Research illustrates that body and weight dissatisfaction occurs as early as third grade; is greater in European American than in African American children, females than males, and those with a heterosexual orientation; and increases over time, peaking around eighth or ninth grade (Thompson, Rafiroiu, & Sargent, 2003). These patterns of body dissatisfaction also tend to occur in other affluent countries, such as Hong Kong, Australia, and Sweden (Lam et al., 2002; Lunner et al., 2000).

Body dissatisfaction and weight concerns can lead to unhealthy dieting behaviors, which in turn may promote the development of disordered eating in adolescents (Killen et al., 1996). Studies of middle-school students have reported that between 30 and 55% have dieted at some time (Shisslack et al., 1998) and that, among females, about one-third of normal dieters progress to other problem dieting behaviors (Shisslack, Crago, & Estes, 1995). Problem dieting behavior includes fasting or skipping meals, the use of diet pills, vomiting or using laxatives, smoking cigarettes, or binge eating (Neumark-Sztainer, Story, Falkner, Beuhring, & Resnick, 1999; Croll, Neumark-Sztainer, Story, & Ireland, 2002). These unhealthy dieting behaviors are far more prevalent among adolescents than among children in middle childhood and often go unaddressed because of the varied unmonitored settings within which teenagers consume food. In addition, most unhealthy dieting patterns fall below the criteria for diagnosable eating disorders and may not be viewed as problematic.

Health consequences result from both disturbed eating patterns and eating disorders. Health problems associated with disturbed eating patterns are delayed sexual maturation, menstrual irregularity, constipation, weakness, irritability, sleep problems, and poor concentration (Story & Alton, 1996). Health consequences for eating disorders, however, presented in Box 8.3, are much more severe.

Different body weights are evident at the pool. There are several girls who look very, very thin and you don't see them eat anything all day. There are also several boys who have excess weight around their midsection and snack continuously on junk food.

Sleep

While the majority of this chapter deals with adolescent behavior during the waking hours, adolescent sleep patterns and their relationship to adolescent health are equally important. Research shows that sleep and waking behaviors change significantly during the adolescent years (for a review, see Carskadon, 2002). More specifically, adolescents go to sleep later than preadolescents and, if allowed, sleep later in the morning. This delayed onset of sleep has both a physiological and a sociocultural explanation.

First, researchers have identified that the **circadian cycle**, which is responsible for sleep/wake cycles in humans and other animals, shifts during adolescence. The shift involves releasing **melatonin**, a sleep-inducing hormone, approximately one hour later (10:30 P.M.) than in middle childhood (9:30 P.M.). This is why adolescents report "not feeling sleepy" until much later at night. In addition, studies show that adolescents also stay up later voluntarily as a result of late-night jobs, extracurricular activities, academic pressures (e.g., homework), and social activities (Wolfson et al., 1995). So later sleep onsets for adolescents are a function of both biological and psychosocial change.

During the school year, a later sleep onset paired with an earlier wake time results in insufficient amounts of sleep for many adolescents. Adolescents *need* 9.5 hours of sleep per night to report feeling "rested." But most are getting on average 7.5–8 hours of sleep per night, and those adolescents who work more than 20 hours a week are getting even less (Vinha, Cavalcante, & Andrade, 2002). One consequence of this sleep deprivation is that adolescents play catch-up on the weekends, sleeping approximately 2 hours longer a night than preadolescents. Other consequences that are a source of concern for parents, teachers, practitioners, and health care workers are

- Increased daytime sleepiness
- Increased daytime naps (even during school!)
- Poorer concentration and ability to focus attention
- Poorer school performance
- Increased moodiness and mood disorders
- Higher accident rates
- Higher rates of substance abuse
- Higher use of products with caffeine and tobacco (adapted from Dahl & Lewin, 2002; Wolfson & Carskadon, 1998).

These sleep/wake trends and similar outcomes have also been found in adolescent populations in other countries (Andrade & Menna-Barreto, 2002; Gau & Soong, 1995; Giannotti & Cortesi, 2002; Park, Matsumoto, Seo, Kang, & Nagashima, 2002; Strauch & Meier, 1988).

BOX 8.3 ROADMAP TO UNDERSTANDING THEORY AND RESEARCH

The Symptomology and Health Consequences of Eating Disorders

It has been said that eating disorders are better understood as dieting disorders and that the emergence of eating disorders in early adolescence is closely related to poor body image and weight dissatisfaction in young teens (Thompson & Smolak, 2001). The most prevalent eating disorders are **anorexia nervosa (AN), bulimia nervosa (BN)**, and **binge-eating disorder (BED)**.

The prevalence rate of AN in adolescents ranges from 0.1% to 1%, with a greater incidence among girls than boys (a gender ratio of 10 to 1; Bulik, 2002). The mean age of onset for AN is 17, with peaks at 14 and 18 (American Psychiatric Association, 2000). The following are the DSM-IV diagnostic criteria for AN:

- Refusal to maintain a body weight at or above a minimally normal weight for age and height.
- Intense fear of gaining weight or becoming fat even though underweight.
- Disturbance in the way in which one's body weight or shape is experienced, undue influence of body weight or shape on self-evaluation, or denial of the seriousness of the current low body weight.
- In postmenarcheal females, amenorrhea (i.e., the absence of at least three consecutive menstrual cycles) (p. 589).

Related health consequences for those diagnosed with AN are

- Thinning hair
- Dry, flaking skin
- Constipation
- Downy growth of body hair (**lanugo**)
- Low blood pressure
- Passing out, dizziness, weakness
- Heightened sensory experiences
- High cholesterol levels
- Low chloride levels
- Severe electrolyte imbalances leading to heart attacks
- Kidney failure
- Low body temperature (hypothermia)
- Delayed bone growth and future osteoporosis

Bulimia nervosa is found in approximately 1% of the population. Like anorexia, BN is more common in females, with a female-to-male gender ratio of 33:1. The peak onset for BN is between 15 and 19 years of age. DSM-IV diagnostic criteria are

- Recurrent episodes of binge eating. An episode of binge eating is characterized by the following:
  - Eating within any two-hour period an amount of food that is definitely larger than most people would eat during a similar period of time.
  - A sense of lack of control over eating during the episode.
- Recurrent inappropriate compensatory behavior to prevent weight gain, such as self-induced vomiting, misuse of laxatives, diuretics, enemas, or other medications; fasting; or excessive exercise.
- The binge eating and inappropriate compensatory behaviors both occur, on average, at least twice a week for three months.
- Self-evaluation is unduly influenced by body shape and weight.
- The disturbance does not occur exclusively during episodes of AN (APA, 2000, p. 594).

Health-related consequences resulting from prolonged BN are

- Gastrointestinal disorders
- Anemia
- Tooth damage and gum disease
- Chronic sore throat
- Difficulties in breathing/swallowing
- **Hypokalemia** (abnormally low potassium concentration)
- Electrolyte imbalance
- General ill health/constant physical problems
- Possible rupture of heart or esophagus
- Dehydration
- Irregular heart rhythms

A more recently proposed diagnostic category is binge-eating disorder, differentiated from BN by its lack of a purging component. Population-based studies suggest that between 0.7% and 3% of individuals report binge eating at least once per month. Binge eating is relatively equivalent between genders, and there are few differences across races and ethnic groups, with a slightly higher incidence in lower socioeconomic groups. One major health risk for this disorder is obesity and all its health-related consequences (see this chapter and chapter 3).

(*Continued*)

BOX 8.3 (CONTINUED)

Although eating disorders occur most often in Caucasian female populations, recent research suggests that adolescent males are experiencing increasing pressure to adhere to an ideal muscular body type that may lead to purging as well as dietary supplement abuse and steroid use (Cohane & Pope, 2001; McCabe & Ricciardelli, 2003; Garry, Morrissey, & Whetstone, 2003; Dunn et al., 2001). In addition, recent studies that include large numbers of minority females are finding that in some subsamples, minority females are manifesting disordered eating and eating disorders at rates similar to those found in Caucasian populations (Striegel-Moore, Schreiber, Crawford, Obarzanek, & Rodin, 2000; Walcott, Pratt, & Patel, 2003).

Eating disorders may be caused by a variety of influences, including such factors as comparing one's self to media ideals or peers, internalizing unrealistic media images of attractiveness, being teased about one's appearance, modeling peers' or parents' weight practices or attitudes, sexual abuse or harassment, and early pubertal maturation (Vander Wal & Thelen, 2001; Shisslak & Crago, 2001).

The research on sleep patterns and subsequent effects in adolescence has prompted a reevaluation of high school starting times in cities across the United States. When researchers examined the transition that adolescents made from a ninth-grade start time of 8:25 A.M. to a tenth-grade start time of 7:20 A.M., they found that compared to the previous year students in the tenth grade showed less sleep, earlier rising times, and greater morning sleepiness (Carskadon et al., 1998). Conversely, school districts that have moved to a later high school starting time have shown improved school performance, graduation rates, attendance, and continuous enrollment (Wahlstrom, 2002).

Substance Use and Abuse

Researchers who have examined the health status of adolescents conclude that the main threats to adolescents' health are the health-risk behaviors in which they engage and choices they make. Deciding to experiment with drugs or to engage in their continuous use compromises the health of adolescents. Although the reasons why adolescents use substances are numerous and diverse, there exists a prevalent perception that adolescent recreational drug use is normative (MacDonald & Marsh, 2000). In some countries (e.g., the United States, England, and Finland) there is a greater societal tolerance of drug use among youth and a proliferation of references to drugs and drug use within the youth culture. In addition, drug use in adolescence is often dictated by social contexts such as dance clubs and "raves." Drug use in the club cultural context is a means of maintaining social categories and distinctions and promoting peer inclusion (Salasuo & Seppala, 2004). Therefore, the societal and social contexts that support recreational drug use must be considered when identifying the variables that predispose teens to use or abuse illegal substances.

Alcohol. There has been an overall decline in alcohol use among adolescents over the past decade (see Figure 8.7) (CDC, 2003b). However, 83% of high school seniors reported having drunk alcohol at least once, 55.9% had at least one drink in the past 30 days, and—of more concern—37.2% reported having five or more drinks in a row within a couple of hours. In other words, over one-third admit to **binge drinking**. In 2003, females had more experiences with alcohol than males, at all grade levels, but males reported more binge drinking at all grade levels. In 2003, Hispanic high-schoolers showed higher lifetime drinking experience (79.5%) compared to Caucasians (75.4%), African Americans (71.4%), and other groups (68.4%) (CDC, 2003b).

Alcohol use has also been implicated in adolescent sexual activity and injurious behavior to self and others (Sindelar, Barnett, & Spirito, 2004). For example, approximately one quarter of high school students (grades 9–12) said they used drugs or drank alcohol before their last sexual intercourse. And 41% of all deaths from motor vehicle crashes involved alcohol (U.S. Department of Transportation, 2004).

The health consequences of long-term alcohol misuse are liver disease, cancer, cardiovascular

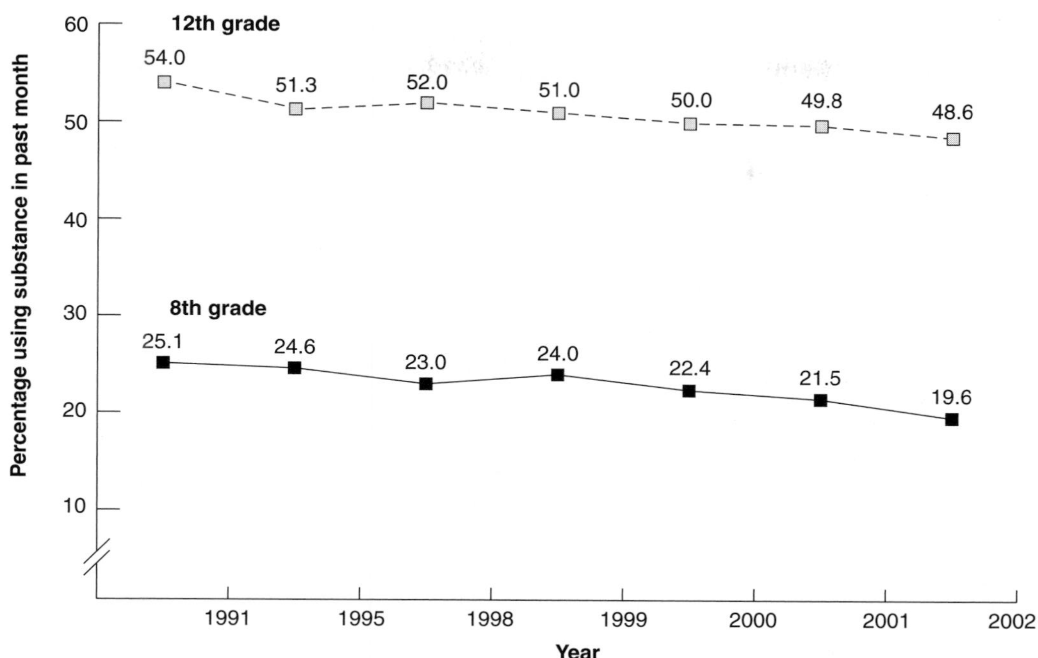

FIGURE 8.7 Use of Alcohol by High School Seniors and Eighth Graders, Selected Years 1991–2002 There has been a decline in alcohol use in the past decade; however, almost half of high school seniors still report alcohol use in the past month.

Source: Data are from the "Monitoring the Future" Study, 2003, National Institute on Drug Abuse (NIDA), Annual Surveys. Available from http://www.drugabusestatistics.samhsa.gov/

disease, and neurological damage as well as psychiatric problems such as depression, anxiety, and antisocial personality disorder (Naimi, Brewer, Mokdad, Serdula, Marks, & Binge, 2003). Box 8.4 discusses the effects of alcohol consumption on the developing brain.

Factors associated with alcohol use are low grades in school, low educational aspirations, and engagement in antisocial behavior/delinquency (Lerner, 2002; Perkins & Borden, 2003). Frequent use of alcohol is also associated with accidental deaths (e.g., drowning; Mitic & Greschner, 2002). In addition, poor parental monitoring and discipline and having one or more alcoholic parents or an alcohol-addicted sibling predict alcohol use in adolescents (Masten & Coatsworth, 1998). Finally, one of the most powerful predictors of adolescent alcohol use is the alcohol use of a teen's best friend (Borden, Donnermeyer, & Scheer, 2001). This last finding might suggest that peer use "influences" an adolescent's drinking behavior. But when researchers followed 755 6-year-old boys for 7 years to determine whether individual characteristics (e.g., fighting, hyperactivity, likability) or peer influences were linked to subsequent substance abuse, they found that individual characteristics are *more* predictive of later substance abuse than having deviant peers (Dobkin et al., 1995). In other words, a given adolescent with certain behavioral characteristics is attracted to peers who like the same involvement in high-risk behavior rather than being "turned bad" by deviant friends.

Cigarette smoking. The initiation of smoking appears to occur between grades 7 and 9, and nearly all first use occurs by age 18 (U.S. Department of Health and Human Services [USDHHS], 1994). A consistent finding among national surveys is that the younger the age at which teens begin to smoke regularly, the more regular and heavier the use and the more likely they are to be nicotine dependent in adulthood (Chassin, Presson, Pitts, & Sherman, 2000).

BOX 8.4 ROADMAP TO UNDERSTANDING THEORY AND RESEARCH

The Effects of Alcohol Use on Brain Functioning and Development

The American Medical Association (AMA) has recently announced that adolescent drinkers are at a higher risk of brain damage than adult drinkers. The findings are contrary to the myth that a young brain is more resilient and can recover from drug and alcohol abuse better than that of an adult. The AMA's report also suggests that even low-level drinking can be harmful to the development of the brain.

Adverse Effects of Alcohol on the Brain: Research Findings

Teen alcohol users are most susceptible to damaging two key brain areas that are undergoing dramatic changes in adolescence:

- The hippocampus, which handles many types of memory and learning, suffers the worst alcohol-related brain damage in teens. Research shows that those who had been drinking more and for longer had significantly smaller (by 10%) hippocampi (DeBellis, Clark, Beers, Soloff, & Boring, et al., 2000).
- The prefrontal area (behind the forehead), which plays an important role in personality formation, executive planning, and emotional inhibition and undergoes the most change during adolescence. Researchers found that adolescent drinking caused severe changes in this area of the brain (Crews, Braun, Hoplight, Switzer, & Knapp, 2000).

Consequences Related to Underage Drinking

- Adolescent drinkers scored worse than nonusers on vocabulary, general information, memory, memory retrieval, and at least three other tests (Brown, Tapert, Granholm, & Delis, 2000).
- Verbal and nonverbal information recall was most heavily affected, with a 10% performance decrease in alcohol users (Brown et al., 2000).
- Significant neuropsychological deficits exist in early to middle adolescents (ages 15 and 16) with histories of extensive alcohol use (Tapert & Brown, 1999).
- Adolescent drinkers perform worse in school, are more likely to fall behind, and have an increased risk of social problems, depression, suicidal thoughts and violence (Substance Abuse and Mental Health Services Administration, 1999; Naimi et al., 2003).
- Alcohol affects the sleep cycle, resulting in impaired learning and memory as well as disrupted release of hormones necessary for growth and maturation (National Institute on Alcohol Abuse and Alcoholism, 1998).
- Alcohol use increases risk of stroke among young drinkers (Seppa & Sillanaukee, 1999).

In addition, short-term or moderate drinking impairs learning and memory far more in youth than in adults. Adolescents need only drink half as much to suffer the same negative effects (Pyapali, Turner, Wilson, & Swartzwelder, 1999).

Lasting Implications

Compared to students who drink moderately or not at all, frequent drinkers may never be able to catch up in adulthood, since alcohol inhibits systems crucial for storing new information as long-term memories and makes it difficult to immediately remember what was just learned. Additionally, those who binge once a week or increase their drinking from age 18 to 24 may have problems attaining the goals of young adulthood—marriage, educational success, employment, and financial independence (Schulenberg, O'Malley, Bachman, Wadsworth, & Johnston, 1996).

Source: Based on Underage Drinking Is a D.U.M.B. Decision (Drinking Underage Maims the Brain), by the American Medical Association, Fact Sheet, retrieved December 13, 2002. Available from http://www.edc.org.hec.thisweek.

The prevalence of smoking cigarettes over time can be seen in Table 8–5. These data come from the Center for Disease Control's online Youth Risk Behavior Survey (2003c) and show that smoking *increased* at all grade levels from 1997 to 1999 and then *decreased* for all grade levels between 1999 and 2003. Declines in smoking rates in adolescence have been attributed to the increased cost of cigarettes, the prohibition of adolescent-targeted advertising, more prevalent antismoking messages, and increased negative public images of tobacco companies (Johnston, Terry-McElrath, O'Malley, & Wakefield, 2005; Myers & MacPherson, 2004). Despite recent trends that show a decline in use,

Having friends and peers who drink is a significant predictor of a teen's drinking behavior.

23% of high school seniors still report daily smoking, with 8.9% of seniors smoking more than 10 cigarettes per day (CDC, 2000c).

The health risks of smoking include increased respiratory infections, lessened lung capacity, and permanent lung damage (USDHHS, 1994). Perhaps the greater health risks occur over a longer period of time. Nearly one-third of young people who take up smoking in adolescence will eventually die of a smoking-related illness (Gilpin, Choi, Berry, & Pierce, 1999).

Research shows that the time interval between first use (experimentation) and regular use is quite variable, with an average length of several years (USDHHS, 1994). This finding suggests that there is a small window following first use in which smoking can be either encouraged or discouraged. Factors associated with the increased likelihood of regular cigarette use are accessibility, affordability, peer and parental smoking, academic difficulty, school misbehavior (e.g., skipped classes, truancy, suspensions), and peer encouragement of such misbehaviors (Alexander et al., 2001; Bryant et al., 2000; Bryant, Schulenberg, O'Malley, Bachman, & Johnston, 2003; Robinson, Klesges, Zbikowski, & Glaser, 1997). Early experience with nonusing peers, parents who convey nonuse messages and monitor time spent with deviant peers, successful school achievement, high levels of motivation, and commitment to school are protective factors against increased cigarette use over time (Bryant et al., 2003).

At one point you notice a small group of boys and girls gathered around a lounge chair at the pool, smoking cigarettes. Most of the teens in the group were smoking, but several were merely observing.

Adolescents resemble adults in that they report frequent attempts to quit smoking and experience nicotine withdrawal when nicotine abstinent (Colby, Tiffany, Shiffman, & Niaura, 2000). In a review of 17 cessation programs for adolescents, 10 were found to be effective—but with only a 12% success rate. This finding means that it is as difficult for adolescents who are regular smokers to quit smoking as it is for adults (Sussman et al., 1999). The key lies in prevention, although the most successful prevention programs begin early (grade 6) and are interactive. They teach young teens refusal skills (i.e., how to say "no"), use peer leaders, and emphasize that fewer adolescents actually smoke than teens frequently believe (Tobler et al., 2000). It also appears that recent antitobacco media campaigns may be

TABLE 8–5

Adolescent Smoking

Since 1999 there has been an overall decline in cigarette smoking for adolescents in grades 9 through 12.

	Percentage of Students Who Smoked Cigarettes on 20 or More of the Past 30 Days						
Grade / Year	2003	2001	1999	1997	1995	1993	1991
Total	9.7 (0.7)	13.8 (0.8)	16.8 (1.3)	16.7 (1.0)	16.1 (1.4)	13.8 (0.8)	12.7 (1.2)
9	6.3 (0.8)	8.9 (1.1)	11.2 (1.3)	13.1 (1.9)	9.6 (1.3)	8.8 (0.8)	8.4 (1.3)
10	9.2 (1.0)	12.3 (0.9)	15.2 (1.8)	15.0 (0.9)	13.3 (1.5)	12.5 (1.4)	11.3 (1.3)
11	11.2 (1.3)	15.2 (1.3)	18.7 (1.4)	18.9 (1.4)	19.1 (1.6)	15.3 (1.4)	15.6 (1.5)
12	13.1 (1.2)	21.0 (1.8)	23.1 (3.5)	19.4 (1.6)	20.9 (2.1)	17.8 (1.7)	15.6 (1.7)

Source: Data from the Youth Risk Behavior Survey, 2003, Healthy Youth web site, National Center for Chronic Disease Prevention and Health Promotion. Available from http://www.cdc.gov/healthyyouth/index.htm.

effective when paired with the prevention components mentioned above (Pechman, 1997).

Other drugs. Table 8–6 displays the use of other drugs such as marijuana and cocaine. Note the inclusion of inhalants in this table. These drugs appear to be more accessible and affordable to young adolescents and therefore are used and abused with more frequency in this age group.

What factors influenced your decision to use or not use substances?

Guideposts for Working with Adolescents

- Encourage adolescents to get as much sleep as possible within the parameters of their academic, social, and working lives. Limit the number of hours worked during the week to less than 20.
- Since a well-balanced diet is important, teach teens about proper nutrition and eating habits, model good eating habits, and provide nutritious snacks and meals.
- Try to send constant messages about the value of a "normal" body shape because adolescents may be hypercritical of their bodies. Along with other factors, a poor body image may manifest itself in eating disturbances or disorders.
- Be aware that most adolescents will try smoking cigarettes and drinking alcohol at least once; encourage good parental monitoring with strong nonuse messages.
- Remember that there is a short period between first use and regular use (approximately 2 years) when comprehensive prevention is the most effective.

TABLE 8–6

Use of Substances by High School Seniors, Eighth, and Tenth Graders, Selected Years: 1995–2002

Substance and Grade in School	Percent Using Substance in the Past Month 1995	2000	2002
MARIJUANA			
All seniors	21.2	21.6	21.5
10th graders	17.2	19.7	17.8
8th graders	9.1	9.1	8.3
COCAINE			
All seniors	1.8	2.1	2.3
10th graders	1.7	1.8	1.6
8th graders	1.2	1.2	1.1
INHALANTS			
All seniors	3.2	2.2	1.5
10th graders	3.5	2.6	2.4
8th graders	6.1	4.5	3.8
MDMA (Ecstasy)			
All seniors	—	3.6	2.4
10th graders	—	2.6	1.8
8th graders	—	1.4	1.4

Source: Data taken from the Monitoring the Future Study, 2003, National Institutes of Health, National Institute on Drug Abuse (NIDA), Annual Surveys. Available from http://www.drugabusestatistics.samhsa.gov/

ADOLESCENT SEXUALITY

Aspects of children's sexuality may develop during early and middle childhood, but during adolescence their sexuality is brought into sharper focus. Sexual desires and arousal, sexual experimentation, and the formation of a sexual identity are more pronounced in adolescence. These events may occur as a result of puberty, how one's friends and family respond to a more adultlike appearance, social mores regarding time and place spent with romantic partners, and cultural messages that shape one's view of oneself as a sexual being (Graber & Brooks-Gunn, 2002).

Puberty and Sexuality

At the beginning of this chapter we discussed how the process of puberty encourages the release of specific hormones that are primarily responsible for the development of secondary sex characteristics and for the emergence of reproductive capabilities. The relationship between pubertal change and adolescent sexuality may not only be hormonal but may also include how the teen and others respond to changes in secondary sex characteristics. For example, researchers have found that adolescent boys who demonstrated higher levels of testosterone also reported higher levels of sexual activity (i.e., coitus) (Udry, 1985; Halpern, Udry, & Suchindran, 1998; Finkelstein et al., 1998).

Researchers have also linked hormonal changes at puberty and increased sexual/emotional arousal (Brooks-Gunn et al., 1994). However, higher levels of androgens in adolescent females were *not* related to higher rates of sexual behavior, but rather were predictive of their anticipation of future sexual involvement. The best predictor of coital behavior in these girls was whether their friends were sexually active or at least supportive of sexual experimentation (Udry, Talbert, & Morris, 1986). More recent research continues to support a mediated model between puberty and sexual behavior (Udry & Campbell, 1994; Halpern et al., 1997). In other words, hormones may enhance feelings of sexual arousal in adolescents but how they act on those feelings is very much determined by multiple internal and external variables (see Figure 8.4 earlier in the chapter).

The more mature-looking boys and girls at the pool are constantly flirting with one another and trying to get the attention of the opposite sex. There are a number of identifiable "couples" who engage in varying degrees of physical contact with one another.

Noncoital Sexual Behavior

These increased "feelings of arousal" or "desire" manifest themselves in a variety of noncoital and coital thoughts and behaviors (Halpern et al., 1993).

Fantasy. Having erotic fantasies was acknowledged by 72% of 13- to 18-year-olds (Coles & Stokes, 1985). Sexual fantasies may allow for a safe and nonthreatening way to experience sexual arousal and provide insight into sexual desires and preferences (Katchadourian, 1990).

Masturbation. When surveyed, 81% of males and 45% of females report **masturbating**, or bringing themselves to orgasm, by age 18. Adolescent males masturbate three times as often as females, and it is usually their earliest sexual experience. Females usually experience sexual contact with another person before they masturbate. The high prevalence rate suggests that it is a "normative" adolescent sexual experience. However, masturbation is still perceived as "taboo" in the United States and other countries, such as Finland, Sweden, Estonia, and Russia (Kontula & Haavio-Mannila, 2002). It appears that parents rarely talk to their teens about masturbation as a normal sexual outlet and that it is perceived by teens to be less desirable than sex with a partner. As the result of a study comparing young adult males' reports of their own adolescent masturbation practices to self-reports collected when they were teens, researchers suggested that most studies underestimate the percentage who masturbate by as much as one-third (Halpern et al., 2000).

Petting and oral sex. When asked about sexual activity, most White adolescents report a continuum of noncoital activity that begins with kissing and French kissing and proceeds to fondling genitalia over and then under clothing, followed by oral sex, and then intercourse (Boyce, Doherty, Fortin, & MacKinnon, 2003). This sexual continuum may not represent the noncoital sexual experiences of all adolescents (Smith & Udry, 1985).

Survey data suggest that overall rates of reported oral sex have increased over the past decade. In a study of over 11,000 students in grades 7, 9, and 11, 32% of grade 9 males and 28% of grade 9 females, as well as 53% of grade 11 males and 52% of Grade 11 females reported that they had engaged in oral sex at least once (Boyce et al., 2003). Another study found that girls are more likely to give rather than to receive from their partner (Gates & Sonenstein, 2000). Adolescents report that oral sex has become a more "normative" aspect of their sexuality and is perceived as a "safe" method of sexual pleasure (McKay, 2004).

Sexual Intercourse

Sexual intercourse is the behavior used most often to report on the status of adolescents' sexual behavior. It is only one behavior along the sexual continuum, but because of the potential long-term consequences of intercourse it is the most often-reported index. The latest figures show that more than one-half of high school seniors (61.1%) have had sexual intercourse at least once, an approximately 5% decrease since 1991 (CDC, 2003d). These data vary according to gender, race, and ethnicity (see Table 8–7). Approximately 7.4% of young adolescents had sex prior to age 13 (a figure which is on the decline). This percentage is significantly different from the 19% reported by young Black adolescent males, who, as a whole, engage in intercourse at a much higher rate at a significantly younger age. Also, 28.8% of young African American males report intercourse with a greater number of partners (four or more) than Caucasian (10.8%), Hispanic (15.7%), or other (16.0%) males report (CDC, 2003).

Why do some adolescents initiate sexual intercourse earlier than others? Who delays their **sexual debut**, or first-time intercourse, and who abstains? These questions are of interest to parents, teachers, practitioners, and health care professionals who want to understand the individual and contextual variables that promote sexual debuts. The answer is determined by the complex interaction of biological, psychological, and sociocultural factors that exert both direct and indirect pressure on the adolescent (Crockett, Raffaelli, & Moilanen, date). Variables such as early maturation, substance use, having a history of sexual abuse, and having friends who view sexual behavior as acceptable are linked to the initiation of sexual intercourse. Having educational plans, good grades, high religiosity, family support, and parental supervision are linked to the delay of sexual intercourse (Kirby, 2001; Miller et al. 2001). It is unlikely, however, that any single variable can be identified as the sole cause of sexual behavior. Rather, these variables are most likely to aggregate into a profile that is predictive of sexual debut or delay.

When was your sexual debut and what were the circumstances surrounding the event?

Gay, Lesbian, and Bisexual Orientations

The incidence rates discussed in the previous section assumed heterosexual behavior. What is not known is how many same-sex experiences were included in the data. In fact, very little is known about the sexual experiences of lesbian, gay, and bisexual youth. Recent research has helped shape our understanding of how *sexual orientation* and *sexual identity* provide a context of development for adolescents (D'Augelli & Patterson, 2001; Savin-Williams, 2001).

This section will focus on same-sex **sexual orientation**, defined as "a consistent pattern of sexual arousal toward persons of the same gender encompassing fantasy, conscious attractions, emotional and romantic feelings, and sexual behaviors" (Remafedi, 1987, p. 331). **Sexual identity**, to be elaborated upon in chapter 11, is an "organized set of self-perceptions and attached feelings that an individual holds about self with regard to some social category" (Cass, 1984, p. 110). Although some scholars are concerned that this distinction is too simplistic, it clarifies some of the following survey results. For example, when the sexual

TABLE 8–7
Percentage of Students Who Had Sexual Intercourse by Race/Ethnicity and Sex in 2003

	Males	Females
Non-Hispanic White	40.5 (1.8)	43.0 (1.6)
Non-Hispanic Black	73.8 (1.8)	60.9 (2.0)
Hispanic	56.8 (2.2)	46.4 (1.8)
Other	35.3 (3.8)	47.1 (4.7)

Source: Data from Youth Risk Behavior Survey, 2003, National Center for Chronic Disease Prevention and Health Promotion. Available from http://apps.nccd.cdc.gov/yrbss/QuestYearTable.

orientation of 35,000 students in grades 7 through 12 was assessed, only a very small percentage of students defined themselves as lesbian/gay (1.1%) or bisexual (0.9%). However, 11% admitted to being "unsure" of their sexual orientation; this percentage was highest in the lower grades.

In the higher grades, adolescents reported more homosexual activity. The number who self-defined themselves as exclusively gay, lesbian, or bisexual increased from 1 to 3% by age 18, although a larger percentage reported same-sex attractions: 2% at age 12, and 6% at age 18, while 3% reported same-sex fantasies (Remafedi et al., 1992). Consistent with these findings, in a study carried out in Australia, a significant minority of adolescents, between 8 and 11%, did not define themselves as exclusively heterosexual (Hillier, Warr, & Haste, 1996).

Most of this research has been carried out in high schools and most likely has underrepresented sexual-minority youth because they do not always identify themselves. It has been suggested that researchers may be missing at least half if not three-quarters of youth with same-sex attractions (Savin-Williams, 2001).

You cannot identify a single same-sex romantic couple at the pool.

It may also be the case that youth who self-identify early in adolescence as lesbian, gay, or bisexual are significantly different from those who self-identify in late adolescence or early adulthood. Taking into account the limitations of the methodology and sampling techniques, the following is a summary of research findings on sexual-minority youth:

- Gay adolescents experience the same pubertal transitions as heterosexual adolescents at approximately the same time (Savin-Williams, 1994a).
- Gay adolescents experience similar physiological arousal and seem to be aroused by the same tactile stimulations (Savin-Williams, 1995).
- Studies show a range in the age of initiation of sexual behavior by bisexual and gay males, 12.5 to 16 years, and a higher number of sexual partners than heterosexual adolescents (median age = 8) at age 15 (Remafedi, 1994; Rotheram-Boris et al., 1992).
- When heterosexual, bisexual, and gay males are recruited from similar settings, such as homeless shelters, the number of high-risk sexual acts is *similar* across groups (Rotheram-Borus et al., 1999).
- Sexual-minority youth are more likely to engage in heterosexual sex than heterosexual teens (Meininger, Cohen, Neinstein, & Remafedi, 2002).

Some research shows that sexual-minority youth have higher incidences of homelessness, substance abuse, eating disorders, isolation, runaway behaviors, domestic violence, risky sexual behaviors, depression, suicide attempts, and pregnancy (Garofalo & Katz, 2001). Although this profile suggests that bisexual, gay, and lesbian youth engage in more high-risk behavior than heterosexual youth, it is inappropriate and inaccurate to overgeneralize this negative trajectory to all sexual-minority youth (Savin-Williams, 2001). Recent longitudinal research shows that the incidence rates of substance abuse, progress at school, feelings of anxiety and depression, conduct problems, and delinquency match the rates of adolescent ethnic minorities and adolescent females, thereby making their experiences far more "normative" than thought previously (Rotheram-Borus & Langabeer, 2001). The focus of future research should be on the identification of moderator variables (e.g., supportive parents) that make some gay, lesbian, and bisexual youth more resilient and on comprehending the diverse developmental pathways *within* sexual minority groups.

Contraceptive Use

Adolescents' understanding of contraception as well as their motivation to use it is determined not only by individual characteristics (e.g., gender, race, cognitive level) but also by how their friends, families, teachers, and society at large perceive its use and effectiveness (Lagana, 1999). Condoms and birth control pills are the two most commonly used methods of contraception. The Youth Risk Behavior Survey (CDC, 2003) reports that 63% of adolescents said they used condoms during their last sexual intercourse, up from 46.2% who reported condom use in 1991. The reported use of condoms, however, is highest in the 9th and 10th grades (69%) and then drops to 57.4% in 12th grade. In addition, males report higher use (68.8%) than females (57.4%), and 81.2% of African American males reported condom use during their most recent sexual intercourse experience.

When asked about using birth control pills during last intercourse, 22.6% of all adolescents responded affirmatively. Such use increases from 9th to 12th grade, and females report higher use

(27.2%) than males (17.5%). White American females report the highest use of birth control pills (26.5%), with African American females reporting the lowest use (11.7%). Other contraceptive methods used included injectable contraception (10%), withdrawal (4%), and implants (3%) (Alan Guttmacher Institute (AGI), 1998).

Although the use of contraceptives is increasing, many adolescents (37%) do not use any, use them inconsistently, or do not use them during first-time intercourse. An adolescent who does not use effective contraception consistently has a 90% chance of pregnancy within a year (AGI, 1998). Because unsafe sexual practices, such as not using a condom, may result in an unplanned pregnancy or a life-threatening sexually transmitted disease, researchers have tried to understand which adolescents are least likely to use contraceptives and why. Adolescents under 13 are less likely to use contraceptives or use them consistently (Kirby, 2001). Adolescent females are particularly vulnerable to the contraceptive preferences of a partner with whom they would like to stay emotionally connected (Tschann, Adler, Millstein, Gurvey, & Ellen, 2002). Adolescents who have a positive and warm relationship with their parents and are able to talk about sexual behavior and contraceptive use are more likely to use protection (Kirby, 2002a, 2002b).

Focus groups with Latina and African American youth ages 14 to 19 were conducted to try to understand their knowledge of and attitudes toward contraception. The most frequently mentioned barrier to consistent and effective use of contraception was misinformation provided by friends, relatives, and neighbors about current contraceptive practices (Aaron & Jenkins, 2002).

> AFRICAN AMERICAN PARTICIPANT 1: This girl, she got Norplant in her arm. And some other girls told me it don't work, but she got pregnant when she had hers.
>
> MODERATOR: Somebody got pregnant with Norplant?
>
> AFRICAN AMERICAN PARTICIPANT 1: That's what she told me.
>
> AFRICAN AMERICAN PARTICIPANT 2: They say it's not for everybody to get Norplant.
>
> AFRICAN AMERICAN PARTICIPANT 1: Well, it won't be for me.
>
> MODERATOR: And what do you think is the best [contraceptive] method?
>
> LATINA PARTICIPANT 1: None.
>
> MODERATOR: No method?
>
> LATINA PARTICIPANT 1: Maybe condoms or injections, and the pill.
>
> LATINA PARTICIPANT 2: But they say that condoms break sometimes.
>
> LATINA PARTICIPANT 1: Yes they break. (from Aarons & Jenkins, 2002, pp. 17–18)

The teens in this study conveyed a sense that no single contraceptive was infallible and might even cause side effects (e.g., cancer from implants). Therefore, using contraceptives was perceived as equally risky as not using them and pregnancy was perceived as somewhat inevitable. Other reasons for noncontraceptive use are

- Unavailability (i.e., they were unprepared)
- Being prepared (i.e., carrying a condom) might send the wrong message (e.g., slut versus good girl)
- Too costly
- Uncomfortable (i.e., condoms reduced sensation and feelings of pleasure)
- No use of contraception is a sign of trust and fidelity in a sexual relationship
- Teens feel ambivalent or positively predisposed towards pregnancy

Aspects of contraceptive education programs that successfully increase use include

- Increased contraceptive availability and affordability
- The building of psychosocial skills that teach proactive contraceptive practices and conversational strategies
- The changing of the subculture so that contraceptive use becomes the norm rather than the exception

Contraceptive education programs are usually incorporated into sex education classes of school- or community-based pregnancy prevention programs. Several consistent findings among studies that evaluate components of contraceptive education are that making condoms more available to adolescents does *not* increase sexual activity but *does* increase the percentage of youth who report using condoms (Schuster, Bell, Berry, & Kanouse, 1998; Sellers, McGraw, & McKinlay, 1994). Another finding is that education/prevention programs are more effective with those adolescents who have not yet had intercourse. For some populations (e.g., Black urban youth), this means providing contraceptive information or making condoms available sooner (fifth or sixth grade) rather than later (Johnson, 2002).

Sexually Transmitted Diseases (STDs) and HIV/AIDS

A possible consequence of not using effective contraception is contracting a **sexually transmitted disease (STD)**. STDs are bacterial or viral infections that are passed from one person to another through sexual contact. Approximately 25%, or 3 out of 12 million, of sexually active youth (ages 15–19) contract an STD each year (CDC, 2003e). Sexually active adolescents are at high risk for STDs because they are more likely to have multiple sex partners in shorter-term relationships, engage in unprotected sex, and have partners who are also at higher risk for STDs.

Chlamydia and gonorrhea are the most common bacterial, and therefore curable, STDs among teens, and genital herpes is the most common viral STD contracted by adolescents.

Human immunodeficiency virus, or **HIV**, is the virus that causes **AIDS**. AIDS stands for **A**cquired **I**mmuno**d**eficiency **S**yndrome. Adolescents are disproportionately affected by the HIV/AIDS epidemic—they have higher infection rates than any other population group in the United States. The group with the highest infection rates is 20- to 24-year-olds. Given the 10-year incubation period for HIV, these young adults were most likely infected during adolescence. Reported rates for adolescents in other countries, particularly sub-Saharan Africa, are alarmingly high (UNAIDS/WHO, 2002). Adolescent subgroups in the United States are not equally at risk for contracting HIV/AIDS. African American youth, other minorities, and females are particularly susceptible (see Figure 8.8). Homosexual male youth, urban youth, pregnant adolescents, and adolescent mothers are also at higher risk (Koniak-Griffin, Lesser, Uman, & Nyamathi, 2003). Although there is a decline in the national incidence of HIV/AIDS, it has not been accompanied by a decline in the number of new HIV cases among adolescents (CDC, 2003e).

Information about STDs is usually incorporated into sex education programs and, more recently, AIDS awareness programs. However, a recent study showed that being more knowledgeable about STDs or contracting an STD does not necessarily lead to an increase in condom use (AGI, 2003).

Adolescent Pregnancy

Another possible outcome from not using contraceptives is pregnancy. A total of 4.2% of adolescents reported being pregnant or had gotten someone pregnant one or more times (CDC, 2003d). This percent age marks a significant decline in pregnancy rates over the last decade (see Figure 8.9), but the United States still has the third-highest adolescent pregnancy rate in the world, behind only the Russian Federation and Bulgaria (Singh & Darroch, 2000). The pregnancy rate of African American teens in 2003 (9.1%) was almost four times higher than that of Caucasians who reported pregnancy during the same year (2.3%) (CDC, 2003d). The proportion of older adolescent females who become pregnant is twice as high (15.3% for ages 18–19) as

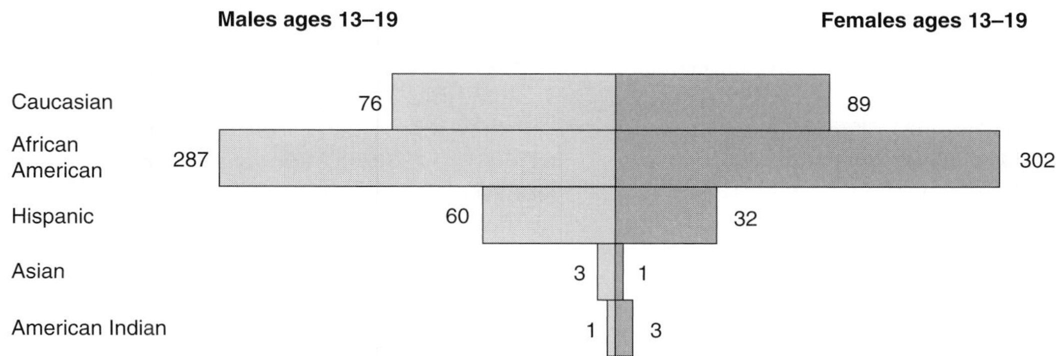

FIGURE 8.8 Estimated Numbers of Diagnoses of HIV/AIDS by Race/Ethnicity in 2002 with Confidential Name-Based HIV Infection Reporting

There are significant ethnic and gender differences in the reported incidence rates of HIV/AIDS in adolescents.

Note: These numbers do not represent actual cases in persons with a diagnosis of HIV/AIDS. Rather, they are point estimates of cases diagnosed that have been adjusted for reporting delays. The estimates have not been adjusted for incomplete reporting.

Source: Data from the *HIV/AIDS Surveillance Supplemental Report* (Vol. 10, No. 1), 2004, by the Centers for Disease Control and Prevention, Department of Health and Human Services, Washington, DC.

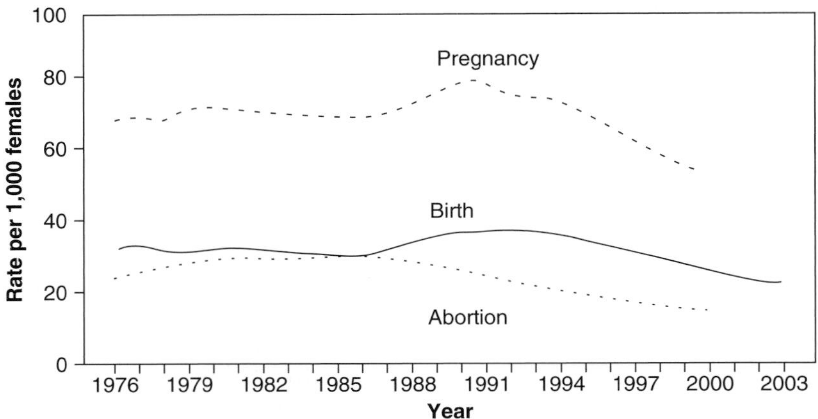

FIGURE 8.9 Pregnancy, Birth, and Abortion Rates Among Females Aged 15 to 17 in the U.S, 1976–2003

Pregnancy, birthrate, and abortion rates have declined since 1992.

Source: Data from Estimated Pregnancy Rates for the United States, 1990–2000: An Update by S. Ventura, J. Abma, W. Mosher, and S. Henshaw, 2003, *Morbidity and Mortality Weekly Report, 54*, p. 1. Published by the Centers for Disease Control and Prevention. Washington, DC: United States Government Printing Office.

the proportion of middle adolescents (6.2% for ages 15–17) (AGI, 1999).

An adolescent pregnancy may have several outcomes. The first is **miscarriage**, or a **spontaneous abortion**, in which the nonviable embryo or fetus is naturally expelled from the body. Approximately 14% of teen pregnancies end in miscarriage. A second outcome of pregnancy may be an **induced abortion**, in which the pregnancy is deliberately terminated. Abortion terminates approximately 30% of all adolescent pregnancies and involves a disproportionate number of Caucasian and higher-income teens (Donovan, 1995). Rates of adolescent abortion appear to be heavily underreported in national surveys, especially for non-White females (Jones & Forest, 1992). The number of reported adolescent abortions also has declined over the past decade (refer to Figure 8.9).

A third pregnancy outcome is giving birth. The 2000 teen birthrate of 48.7 births per 1,000 15- to 19-year-old females is at a historic low for all racial/ethnic groups (Moore, Papillo, Williams, Jager, & Jones, 1999) (again refer to Figure 8.9). Approximately one quarter of these births are to females under 15 years, and about three quarters are to 18- and 19-year-olds.

What you don't know is that one of the girls who is sitting in a pool chair and not dressed in a bathing suit is three months pregnant. She has not told anyone but her best friend and is afraid that her classmates might see that she has gained weight. She has not yet decided what she is going to do about the pregnancy.

The recent trends in reduced adolescent pregnancies and births have been attributed to a decline in sexual activity and an increase in contraceptive use. The decline in sexual activity has been linked to greater HIV/AIDS awareness, more cautious attitudes towards casual sex, the heightened impact of abstinence education programs, and increased communication between parents and youth about sex. The increase in contraceptive use has also been attributed to HIV/AIDS awareness and to increased parent-teen communication. In addition, the higher availability of effective contraceptives and their correct use may have contributed to the reduction in pregnancies. From an analysis of available data the Alan Guttmacher Institute (2001) estimated that one quarter of the decline in teen pregnancies was due to delayed onset of sexual activity (abstinence) and three quarters to improved contraceptive use. A more recent study estimated that among single 15- to 19-year-old females, the delay of sexual activity (abstinence) accounts for 67% of the decline in pregnancy rates and 100% of the decline in birthrates (Mohn, Tingle, & Finger, 2003).

Consequences of adolescent pregnancy. Despite these recent declines in adolescent pregnancies and birthrates, approximately 900,000 adolescent females give birth each year in the United States. Our society believes that teenage mothers put themselves and their offspring "at risk." Past research has shown that mothers under 19 exhibit poorer educational achievement and are more likely to drop out of school (Hotz, McElroy, & Sanders, 1997; Woodward & Fergusson, 2002). They are also more likely to experience high stress and to suffer from depression (O'Callaghan, 2001), are less involved with peers and families, less effective in problem solving, and less cognitively prepared to assume parenting roles (Sommer, Whitman, Borkowski, Schellenbach, Maxwell, & Keogh, 1993). Adolescent mothers followed 3 to 5 years after the birth of their first child by the Notre Dame Parenting Project still tended to be undereducated, underemployed, and give birth to additional children (Whitman, Borkowski, Keogh, & Weed, 2001). Adolescent fathers typically complete less schooling, earn less income, and appear to engage in more delinquent behaviors and drug use than older fathers (Brien & Willis, 1997; Thornberry, Smith, & Howard, 1997; Thornberry et al., 2000).

Children of adolescent mothers weigh less at birth, have more health problems, suffer more physical abuse and neglect, and perform at a lower level in school (Wolfe & Perozek, 1997; Maynard, 1997; Moore, Morrison, & Greene, 1997). Children of adolescent mothers are also more likely to drop out of high school, run away from home, spend time in prison, and have their own children before the age of 19 (Haveman, Wolfe, & Peterson, 1997; Grogger, 1997).

In addition to the less-than-desirable individual outcomes associated with teenage parenting, Maynard (1997) estimated the financial cost to society of adolescent childbearing to be approximately $21 billion per year. As a result of a range of negative and costly consequences, countless pregnancy prevention programs have been designed and implemented, as illustrated in Box 8.5 (Kirby, 2001). The following recommendations for middle and high school pregnancy prevention programs are based on existing programs that have had proven success:

- Use instructional techniques that encourage youth engagement in and attachment to school
- Address both pregnancy and STDs/HIV in sex education programs
- Develop service-learning programs that incorporate community service and ongoing small group discussions
- Have school-based or school-linked clinics that focus upon reproductive health and give clear messages about abstinence and use of contraception
- Make condoms available through school programs

Although teenage pregnancy is viewed in the United States largely as a "problem" with negative short- and long-term outcomes for mothers, fathers, and children, recent research based on comprehensive and longitudinal data suggests that this profile does not apply to all adolescent families (Whitman, Borkowski, Keogh, & Weed, 2001). For some adolescent girls, becoming mothers makes them vulnerable to the stress associated with single parenting, including higher rates of depression, child abuse, unemployment, and poverty. However, there are teen mothers who, with sufficient cognitive skills and educational and economic support, show a resiliency that encourages competent parenting and more favorable developmental outcomes for themselves and their children. By examining individual trajectories, we get a better and more accurate sense of the complexity of the factors that determine the outcomes of teenage pregnancy. In addition, we see more clearly how the "interwoven lives" of mothers and children influence the direction of these trajectories.

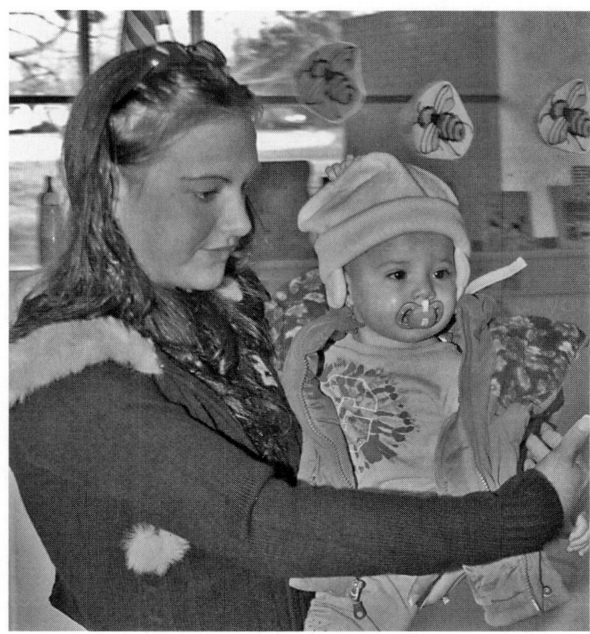

Some teen mothers are very resilient, develop into warm and attentive mothers, and achieve positive outcomes in young adulthood.

BOX 8.5 ROADMAP TO SUCCESSFUL PRACTICE

Integrating Diversity Issues into Sex Education and Pregnancy Prevention Programs

Reviews of successful sex education and pregnancy prevention programs often include checklists of effective components accumulated from many different programs (see Kirby, 2001, 2002a, 2002b). This chapter has done the same. A disadvantage of summarizing this information, however, is that effective features of individual programs are grouped together and the uniqueness of an individual program is lost. Also, checklists don't convey the sensitivity to the needs of a specific ethnic, cultural and/or socioeconomic adolescent group necessary to the success of many of these programs. For example, the focus of a pregnancy prevention program for middle- to upper-class Caucasian youth would be different in some ways from the focus of a program for low-income African American urban youth. These two groups of adolescents come from different racial, cultural, and socioeconomic backgrounds and as a result have different motivations, hopes, experiences, and aspirations for sexual activity.

But discussion of racial/ethnic and cultural differences regarding sexual activity and its consequences is becoming more prevalent in the literature and they have subsequently been addressed in many sex education, prevention, and intervention programs. For example, research has revealed that Latino male youth are particularly resistant to using condoms during intercourse because they believe it reflects poorly on their masculinity. The concept of "machismo" in the male Latino culture predisposes these youth to high rates of STDs and HIV/AIDS. Sex education programs directed towards a Hispanic population would therefore need to address this cultural issue and promote and maintain masculine standards that incorporate the use of contraceptives (Aarons & Jenkins, 2002).

Studies of Asian youth from Japan and Taiwan describe a culture that discourages open discussion of sexual issues. The Japanese phrase is "*Nemureru ko wo okosu mono dearu*," which literally means an issue that wakes up sleeping children; a comparable expression in English is "let sleeping dogs lie." Because sexual issues are a "forbidden" topic for most Asian youth, a direct, risk-related sexual behavior prevention program might not be effective. The emphasis should be on creating a safe environment within which to present information about sexuality and related behaviors, followed by a focus on teaching these youth how to communicate with their sexual partners without violating the sense of privacy about sex and interrupting what Asian youth refer to as "naturally occurring sex" (Castro-Vazquez & Kishi, 2002; Yeh, 2002).

Educational programs sensitive to the needs of African American youth often employ an "Afrocentric approach," which may include a focus on African heritage and racial identity formation, the teaching of successful life skills, and encouraging a future orientation (Jemmott, Jemmott, & Gong, 1998; Stanton, Ricardo, Galbraith, Feigelman, & Kaljee, 1996). A Journey Toward Womanhood is an Afrocentric pregnancy prevention program for adolescent females developed by Sisterhood Agenda in Durham, North Carolina. A 13-week program in which small groups (no more than 10) meet for 4 hours once a week, it has four components:

- **Reaching for Success.** Explores self-definition and the importance of seeing oneself as a unique individual.
- **Developing Inner Health for Outer Beauty.** Explores diet and nutrition, exercise and fitness, holistic well-being, peer pressure, sexual health, and healthy relationships.
- **Progressing with Finesse, Dignity, and Pride.** Uses role-playing and affirmations to help participants develop skills in public speaking, job interviewing, and interpersonal communication.
- **Knowing the Tools for Survival.** Encourages self-sufficiency. Entrepreneurship and economic stability are encouraged, and teen pregnancy is discouraged.

The program has been successful in delaying the initiation of sexual intercourse, increasing contraceptive use among those who were having intercourse, and reducing the incidence of teen pregnancy (Coleman Dixon, Schoonmaker, & Philliber, 2000).

Effective sex education and HIV/AIDS and pregnancy prevention programs are not "one size fits all." Each program must be designed to focus on adolescents from diverse backgrounds, who possess a range of needs unique to their ethnic, cultural, and socioeconomic circumstances.

Guideposts for Working with Adolescents

- Because the majority of teens will have had intercourse at least once by age 18, engage in honest communication with them about abstinence, sexual behavior, and contraception.
- Teach adolescents how to negotiate sexual encounters and how to openly communicate with sexual partners about contraceptive use, STDs, and HIV/AIDS.
- Encourage parents to talk to their teens about sex, which may delay the sexual debut of their adolescents.
- Try to engage teens in academic and extracurricular activities, because teens who are engaged in school delay sexual activity longer than those who are not.
- Involve adolescents in service learning and encourage them to think about careers and education. These variables are protective factors for healthy sexual behavior.

Development in Contexts

The physical, neurological, and motor development of adolescents is in large part a function of the contexts within which they live. Health-related behaviors also are influenced by and consequently influence ecological niches. The familial, educational, and community contexts of adolescents help shape the developmental trajectories of their biological maturation and health.

Family Contexts

Puberty may appear to be a phenomenon largely determined by genetics and biology, but as Box 8.1 illustrated, the family environment may affect the timing of pubertal maturation in girls. Research has shown that the absence of a biological father and the presence of an unrelated male, in addition to the absence of a warm and positive family connection, may accelerate girls' pubertal development. Early maturation and greater levels of family conflict have been associated with earlier sexual debut in African American youth as well (McBride, Paikoff, & Holmbeck, 2003).

Familial variables are also very closely linked with health-related behaviors in adolescents. For example, living with both parents protects against early sexual debut, as does having good teen-parent communication, close parental monitoring, and strong parental attachment—particularly for African American and Hispanic youth (Crosby & Miller, 2002; Karofsky, Zeng, & Kosorock, 2001).

Research shows that mothers are more likely than fathers to communicate with their adolescents about sex-related topics (Miller, Kotchick, Dorsey, Forehand, & Ham, 1998). Mothers have more influence on the age of sexual debut of their daughters than their sons and have greater impact on age of sexual debut than condom use (Averett, Rees, & Argys, 2002; McNeely et al., 2002).

Were you able to talk to adults about contraceptive use; how did it influence your sexual behavior?

School Contexts

School transitions may influence how well adolescent females adjust to puberty. One study found that when girls experienced multiple stressors, such as puberty and dating, while they were transitioning to a middle school, their self-esteem declined precipitously (Simmons & Blyth, 1987). School was no longer an "arena of comfort" and they were particularly vulnerable to stress and its related outcomes. **Arenas of comfort** are contexts in which individuals can relax and rejuvenate so that stressful changes in another arena can be managed. Supportive schools can serve that role or, in the case of early-maturing girls, add to the stress (Call & Mortimer, 2001). Doing poorly in school and being disengaged from the academic environment *precedes* substance abuse, delinquency, and dropping out (Bryant et al., 2003). However, research shows that engagement in school as well as achievement is a protective factor against substance abuse and delinquency.

Schools also educate youth about pubertal changes, sexuality, STDs, HIV/AIDS, contraceptive use, and pregnancy. Forty-three of the 50 states now mandate that schools provide students with information about HIV/AIDS and its prevention. Approximately 88% of all high school students report being taught about HIV/AIDS infection in school (CDC, 2003). The most effective school-based programs combine information with condom access, the teaching of social skills, and increased self-efficacy, or the teens' perception that they can control outcomes (Coyle et al., 1999).

Community Contexts

The effects of the surrounding neighborhood on adolescent development often manifest themselves in socioeconomic opportunities or in the traditions of racial/ethnic groups. For example, one study assessed the neighborhood context in which adolescents lived to help explain why members of racial/ethnic minorities or teens of lower SES were more likely to develop high-risk cardiovascular behaviors. The researchers found that youth (ages 15–19) who resided in neighborhoods characterized by low income, high levels of poverty, low education, low housing values, and more blue-collar workers were more likely to have poorer dietary habits. This was particularly true for females and African Americans. Lower SES also predicted higher smoking rates in Caucasian adolescent males and reduced physical activity for Hispanic teens. Neighborhood characteristics such as the unavailability of nutritious and low-cost foods, access to cigarettes, and lack of opportunities to exercise in safe locations put minority and poor youth at risk for cardiovascular disease (Lee & Cubbin, 2002).

Similarly, another studied examined adolescent sexual behavior within the neighborhood context, specifically how having more family planning clinics available influenced sexual behavior. Researchers found that having more than one family planning clinic per 10,000 females increases the use of contraceptives but does not increase the level of sexual activity or number of abortions. Adolescent females who live in environments with more access to family planning services are at lower risk for STDs and pregnancy than those who live in neighborhoods with less availability (Averett, Rees, & Argys, 2002).

CHAPTER REVIEW

Adolescent Physical Development and Health Behaviors

- The physical development of adolescents includes changes in height and weight, pubertal maturation, brain development, and motor skill refinement.
- Physical changes elicit accompanying changes in nutritional needs, exercise requirements, and sleep patterns.
- Adolescents' cognitive and social contexts may encourage disturbed eating patterns and substance use/abuse.
- Physical maturation prompts the development of adolescents' sexual orientation and preferences.
- Individual, familial, school, and community variables influence healthy and high-risk sexual practices.

Theoretical Viewpoint

- Evolutionary developmental theory is a genetics-based theoretical perspective that emphasizes the adaptive features of our ancestors.
- Current genetic traits may have originated in previous eras while simultaneously adapting to present environmental demands.

Biological Maturation

- Puberty is a maturational process prompted by neurological and hormonal changes.
- Pubertal change includes the development of secondary sex characteristics and somatic growth (e.g., height and weight).
- Numerous factors such as genetics, nutrition, and health influence pubertal growth.
- Pubertal change requires psychosocial adjustment. Some adolescents (e.g., early-maturing girls and boys and late-maturing boys) have more difficulty adapting to pubertal change than those who mature on time or girls who mature later.
- Pubertal maturation may have both direct and indirect effects on how adolescents think, feel, and act.

Brain Development

- The adolescent brain undergoes tremendous dendritic branching and synaptic pruning.
- The association between brain structures and speed of processing improves.

- The prefrontal lobes develop rapidly during adolescence and seem to be responsible for increased planning, complex thinking, and emotional control.
- The environment continues to have both direct and indirect effects on the brain during this developmental period.

Motor Skills and Performance

- Motor skills attain a higher level of refinement during adolescence.
- Increases in size and strength translate into superior performance in some motor tasks for some adolescents. Sex differences in motor tasks that rely on size and strength begin to emerge.
- Brain maturation prompts increased intermodal coordination and increased reaction times that manifest themselves in improved complex motoric skills, such as swinging a golf club or serving a tennis ball.

Related Health and Development Issues

- Because of their rapid physical maturation, adolescents require greater caloric intake and specific vitamins and nutrients, such as calcium and iron.
- Adolescents do not typically follow healthy diet recommendations. Heightened sensitivity to body shape may be a precursor to eating disturbances or disorders that are maladaptive and dangerous to the health of the adolescent.
- Adolescents require more sleep, not less, to promote healthy emotional and cognitive functioning. Adolescents grow tired later in the evening and need to sleep later in the morning. Early school start times disrupt this pattern, and sleep deficits result.
- National trends indicate a decline since the late 1990s in alcohol and other drug use as well as in smoking cigarettes.
- Drug use usually follows difficulty in school and exists concurrently with other high-risk behaviors, such as juvenile delinquency and unsafe sex practices.

Adolescent Sexuality

- Hormonal secretions that promote puberty are associated with increased sexual arousal. Sexual behavior may be influenced by hormones in boys but is mediated by social norms in girls.
- A sexual continuum exists in adolescence that ranges from kissing to petting to intercourse to oral sex. By age 18, the majority of adolescents have had intercourse at least once.
- Gay, lesbian, and bisexual youth are probably underrepresented in surveys of sexual experience. Teens experience homosexual as well as heterosexual encounters as they form their sexual orientation and identity during adolescence.
- Contraceptive use has increased in the last decade; however, many adolescents still use contraceptives inconsistently or ineffectively.
- Ineffective or nonuse of contraception puts adolescents at high risk for STDs and HIV/AIDS. Adolescents with STDs are five times more likely to contract HIV/AIDS.
- Adolescent pregnancy rates have declined in the United States but are still much higher than in most industrialized countries. Race/ethnicity, socioeconomic status, family, and peer relationships are variables associated with adolescent pregnancy and should be addressed in prevention programs.

Adolescents in Context

- Families pass along genetic information that may influence puberty. In addition, familial configurations and dynamics may influence the timing and tempo of maturation.
- Having open communication and warm and positive relationships with families serve as protective factors against drug use, high-risk sexual behavior, and unplanned pregnancies.
- The transition between and structure of schools may act as an additional stressor for adolescents who are experiencing puberty, especially girls. Schools also play a vital role in educating young adolescents about abstinence, sexual behavior, and contraceptive use.
- Communities provide adolescents with differential opportunities to engage in healthy or unhealthy behaviors. The prospects of succeeding in a community are powerful predictors of abstinence, delayed sexual activity, and nonuse of drugs.

TABLE 8–8

Summary of Developmental Theories

Chapter	Theories	Focus
8. Physical Development in Middle Adolescence	Evolutionary	How selected genes helped our ancestors survive and reproduce, and how these same genes may influence our behavior and thinking

KEY TERMS

Acquired Immunodeficiency Syndrome (AIDS)
Adrenarche
Amenorrheic
Amygdala
Anorexia nervosa
Arenas of comfort
Binge drinking
Binge-eating disorder
Body image
Bulimia nervosa
Circadian cycle
Dendritic branching
Direct-effects model
Evolutionary developmental theory
Gonadotropins
Gonardarche
Human Immunodeficiency Virus (HIV)
Hypokalemia
Indirect-effects model
Induced abortion
Lanugo
Leptin
Masturbating
Mediator variables
Melatonin
Menarche
Miscarriage
Moderator variables
Natural selection
Prefrontal lobes
Puberty
Secondary sex characteristics
Semenarche
Sexual debut
Sexual identity
Sexual orientation
Sexually transmitted disease (STD)
Spontaneous abortion

SUGGESTED ACTIVITIES

1. Visit a school, recreational facility, or mall where you can observe the different maturation rates of young adolescents. How do they differ in height, weight, body shape, and observable secondary sex characteristics? What gender and/or racial/ethnic differences do you see? How does the level of maturation seem to affect how they behave and how others behave towards them?
2. Watch several contemporary movies about teenagers and chart the types of "problem behaviors" (e.g., drinking, smoking, disordered eating, sexual activity) that are represented. Is the portrayal of the behavior consistent with the material presented in the chapter? If not, how might the movies distort the engagement in these behaviors and how might this distortion be helpful or hurtful to adolescent moviegoers?
3. Using the information from the chapter, design an effective sex education program for middle- or high-school students. What content would be included? What teaching techniques might be most effective? How might gender, race/ethnicity, or socioeconomic status influence the design of the program? What other components should be included or addressed? You could also design an HIV/AIDS or pregnancy prevention program addressing the same questions.

RECOMMENDED RESOURCES

Suggested Readings

Berninger, V. W., & Richards, T. L. (2002). *Brain literacy for educators and psychologists.* Boston: Academic Press.

Diamond, M., & Hopson, J. (1998). *Magic trees of the mind: How to nurture your child's intelligence, creativity, and healthy emotions from birth through adolescence.* New York: Penguin Putnam.

Johnson, N. G., Roberts, M. C., & Worell, J. (Eds.). (1999). *Beyond appearance: A new look at adolescent girls.* Washington, DC: American Psychological Association.

Maine, M. (2000). *Body wars: Making peace with women's bodies: An activist's guide.* Carlsbad, CA: Gurze.

Rew, L. (2004). *Adolescent health: A multidisciplinary approach to theory, research, and intervention.* Thousand Oaks, CA: Sage.

Savin-Williams, R. C. (2005). *The new gay teenager.* Cambridge, MA: Harvard University Press.

Suggested Online Resources

Adolescence: Change and Continuity—Biological Transitions/Sexuality
http://inside.bard.edu/academic/specialproj/darling/adolesce.htm

Family and Community Influences on Adolescent Sexuality (1999)
http://www.advocatesforyouth.org/publications/european/influences.htm

Gay, Lesbian & Straight Education Network Library
http://www.glsen.org/cgi-bin/iowa/all/library/index.html

Investing in Clinical Preventive Services for Adolescents (2001)
http://policy.ucsf.edu/pubpdfs/Prevention.pdf
Sex Education and Teenage Sexuality Fact Sheet
http://newmedia.colorado.edu/~socwomen/socactivis/TeenSexFact.pdf

Suggested Web Sites

Dietary Guidelines for Americans 2005
http://www.healtheirus.gov/dietaryguidelines/
Girls, Incorporated
http://www.girlsinc.org
Healthy People 2010
http://www.cdc.gov/nchs/hphome.htm
National Clearinghouse for Alcohol and Drug Information
http://www.health.org
Sexuality Information and Education Council of the United States
http://www.siecus.org

Suggested Films and Videos

Adolescence: Physical growth and development (1995). Magna Systems, Inc. (25 minutes)
Animated neuroscience and the action of nicotine, cocaine, and marijuana in the brain (1998). Films for the Humanities & Sciences (25 minutes)
Biology of sex and gender (2003). Insight Media, Inc. (30 minutes)
Eating disorders: Causes, symptoms, and treatment (2002). Insight Media (22 minutes)
Inside the teenage brain (2002). Insight Media (40 minutes)
Teen sexuality in a culture of confusion (1998). Media, Inc. (40 minutes)

CHAPTER 

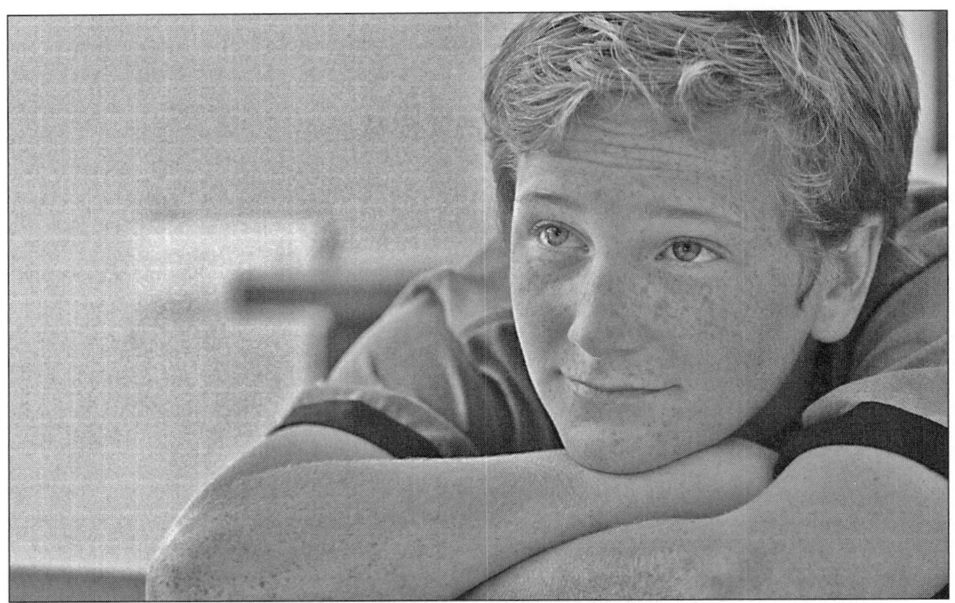

Cognitive Development in Middle Adolescence

CHAPTER OBJECTIVES

After reading this chapter, students will be able to:

- Define cognitive development in middle adolescence
- Analyze adolescent cognition using cognitive developmental and information-processing theories
- Apply the cognitive advances (and limitations) of middle adolescence to learning and decision making
- Define a psychometric approach to intellectual functioning in middle adolescence
- Discuss the contributions of family, school, community, and cultural contexts to cognitive development in middle adolescence

It is 11:00 A.M. Saturday morning and 16-year-old Kevin is lying in bed wondering how he did on his preliminary SAT (PSAT). He felt pretty good about his performance on the math items, but he thought the reading comprehension sections were really difficult. He knows that good SAT scores are his ticket to a good college. His sister interrupts his daydreaming to tell him that his basketball coach is on the phone and wants to speak with him. He begins to worry because yesterday he made an impulsive decision to skip school and spend the day with Gina, a girl he has started dating and is just getting to know. He had faked a note from his mother that asked for him to be released from school for a doctor's appointment. But now, with his coach on the phone, Kevin thinks quickly about how his plan may have gone awry. He also generates a series of excuses and lies he can tell his coach as well as several versions of the truth. He runs through his possible stories and evaluates their believability and potential consequences. As he gets out of bed he decides on what he is going to tell his coach and heads for the phone.

Cognitive Development in Adolescence

Kevin's dilemma offers us the opportunity to see the many ways an adolescent's thinking and ability to process information changes with age and experience. Adolescents' thinking is characterized as logical, systematic, hypothesis-generating, and abstract. Adolescents have larger memory capacities, quicker processing, more elaborate knowledge bases, and mnemonic strategies as well as more advanced metacognitive skills. However, adolescents' thinking is also more susceptible to peer influence and less future-oriented and places more emphasis on reward than on risk. These cognitive changes influence decision making and risk-taking during adolescence.

Theoretical Viewpoints

Numerous theories can help us understand cognitive development during adolescence. Our goal is to extend the earlier discussion of reasoning ability in middle childhood to an examination of the emergent changes occurring during adolescence. In this chapter, we return to two of the more prominent theoretical perspectives that were presented in chapter 4: cognitive developmental theory and information-processing theory.

Piaget's Formal Operational Stage

Piaget proposed that preadolescents, around ages 11 or 12, begin to demonstrate characteristics of formal operational thinking that continue to develop through the adolescent period (Inhelder & Piaget, 1958; Piaget, 1972). These characteristics include the ability to

- Think about abstract concepts
- Think about possibilities
- Generate and evaluate hypotheses
- Think about thought

Thinking about abstract concepts. The ability to form pure abstract ideas (i.e., those that have no direct basis in the perceivable world) is one of the distinct advances of the adolescent over the concrete thinker. Consider this question (adapted and modified from Inhelder & Piaget, 1958):

There are three girls: Mary, Jennie, and Sally. Mary is taller than Sally; Mary is shorter than Jennie. Who is shortest of all?

Concrete thinkers could solve this seriation task if the three girls were there in person or if they were able to write things down. Formal operational thinkers, however, could solve this seriation problem at a purely verbal level.

Another dimension of abstract thought is revealed in the following problem where two participants, one concrete and one formal operational, are asked, "What do you think about this statement?"

"I am glad that I do not like liver, because if I liked it, I would always be eating it, and I hate eating things I dislike."

Consider their responses:

- **Opal, age 10.** "I don't like liver either. It's awful tasting."
- **Pat, age 14.** "You can't say that. If you disliked it, you wouldn't be eating it."

Opal centers on the content of the statement and then expresses her preference. Pat, a formal operational thinker, is able to differentiate form from content and analyze or evaluate the form of reasoning involved in a statement regardless of his like or dislike of liver. Piaget referred to the ability to distinguish the form of an argument or statement from its content as **propositional thought**.

A final characteristic of abstract thought is the ability to understand a relation between relations. This ability is what is required to solve analogies successfully, such as *"15 is to 3 as 40 is to what?* The correct answer, 8, demonstrates the ability to understand the relationship between two ratios or relations. In other words, formal thinkers can combine two relations into a law. Although concrete thinkers can grasp relationships, only formal operational thinkers can handle the higher-order operation of relating relations into laws and applying them across content.

The ability to operate on a purely verbal level also allows adolescents to think about and comprehend abstract concepts, such as fidelity, loyalty, existentialism, and infinity, as well as unseen phenomena, such as light-years. The ability to comprehend and interact with more abstract concepts may be reflected in the older adolescent's more sophisticated classroom discussions, deeper analyses of literature and art, and more carefully crafted arguments and debates.

Think about the craftiness of Kevin's deceit. Faking the note from his mother to skip school reflects a higher level of thinking and ability than if he were still a concrete thinker.

Thinking about possibilities. When adolescents think about what is possible, they are not bound to the here and now or to a concrete experience. They are able to consider reality as but a subset of what is possible. For example, consider the variety of responses that are generated when we drive by a traffic accident that has just occurred. We tend to speculate on what might have happened. Concrete thinkers would speculate on what they had just observed (e.g., which direction the cars were facing, the position of the cars, the nature of the damage). Formal operational thinkers would speculate based on the same concrete information but could also generate possibilities beyond factual observable information (e.g., the cars were traveling at such high speeds that they flipped over and ended up facing the opposite direction). Formal operations open up the hypothetical world for adolescents, such that reality becomes "secondary to possibility" (Inhelder & Piaget, 1958, p. 51).

For example, Kevin thinks of all the possible ways he could have been caught. Some of them are based on what has happened to him or his friends in the past—"A jealous teammate told on me"; other possibilities could be purely hypothetical—"Maybe a teacher saw us."

The ability to think about what is possible often promotes idealism in teens because it predisposes them to ask "What if?" "What if world hunger were eradicated?" or "What if you woke up one morning and you were the only person alive?" This idealism manifests itself in stories teens write, their appreciation for science fiction and fantasy literature, and also a dedication to social, political, or religious causes that was not well developed in middle childhood. Teens in middle adolescence can develop strong passions for social justice, conservation, and prolife or prochoice viewpoints. But they may also feel frustration because their distinctions between what is real and what is ideal are much less complex than the actual solutions to the problems about which they care so deeply.

The cognitive capacity of thinking about what is possible can also be applied to themselves and others. They may develop ideal standards regarding appearance, behavior, and personality characteristics that are unrealistic and difficult to meet. It may also explain the intensity with which some adolescents pursue their goals. Thinking about what is possible also encourages teens to be oriented to the future. The questions "What will I become as an adult?" as well as "What might happen at the football game Friday night?" dominate their daydreams.

Kevin is thinking about his PSAT scores and how they might enhance or hurt his future.

How did thinking about possibilities influence your adolescence?

Generating and evaluating hypotheses. When presented with a physics or chemistry problem to solve, formal operational thinkers generate a series of hypotheses and then systematically evaluate each one before deciding or deducing a single solution. Piaget referred to this as **hypothetico-deductive reasoning**. This approach is in contrast to that of a concrete operational thinker, who can generate hypotheses but does so in a "trial-and-error" manner. Both approaches are illustrated in the following experiment:

> The subject is provided with four bottles of transparent, odorless liquids:
> 1. Water
> 2. Oxygenated water
> 3. Diluted sulphuric acid
> 4. Thiosulphate
> 5. A smaller bottle with a dropper containing potassium iodide
>
> The participant is told that some combination that includes the liquid in the smaller bottle (5) will result in a yellow color. The task is to find that combination.

Now consider these responses:

- **Carl, Age 9.** He mixes 5 with 1, 5 with 2, 5 with 3, and 5 with 4. "*Nothing happens.*" Are there other ways to mix them? "*Perhaps all together.*" He mixes 1 and 2, then adds a drop or two of 5, adds 3—"*It's starting to turn yellow!*"—and finally pours some of 4 in. "*It's gone away.*"
- **Doris, Age 13.** She tries 1 and 5, 2 and 5, 3 and 5, 4 and 5 with no result. "*I guess you have to mix them.*" She tries 1, 2, and 5; 1, 3, and 5; 1, 4, and 5; 2, 3, and 5. "*There it is!*" Are there any other ways? "*I'll see.*" She mixes 2, 4, and 5; and then 3, 4, and 5. "*No.*" Are there any other combinations? "*By fours.*" She proceeds to combine 1, 2, 3, and 5. "*There's yellow again. This [1] is probably water since it doesn't make any difference [from 2, 3, and 5].*" She continues with other combinations—

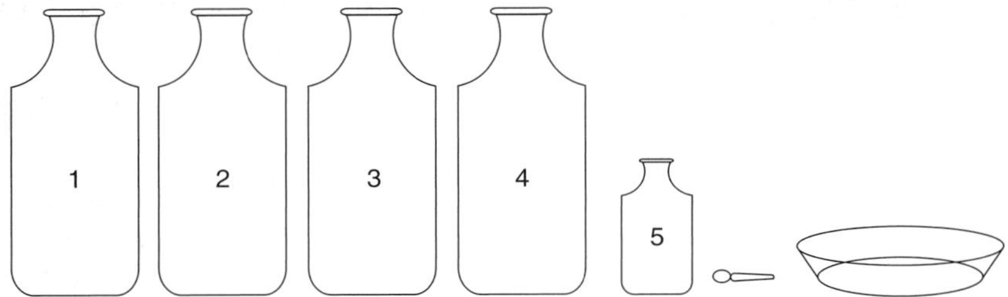

FIGURE 9.1 Formal Operational Problem Using Liquids in Bottles
Participants are asked to find which combination of bottles, when mixed together, make yellow.

> 1, 3, 4, and 5; 2, 3, 4, and 5; and finally 1, 2, 3, 4, and 5—with no success. *"No, somehow it's only the second and third combined with the smaller bottle—or the first, second and third—that make yellow."* (Gorman, 1972, p. 34)

Doris not only generates more combinations, or hypotheses, but does so in a more systematic way than Carl. She uses a **combinatorial system**, or a structured whole of all possible combinations, that is characteristic of formal operational thinking.

Another dimension of a formal operational approach is learning to hold all variables but one constant to assess the outcome of the experiment. Notice how Doris changes only one substance at a time, unlike Carl, who changes several substances simultaneously. By holding one variable constant, Doris can see more clearly the outcome of her manipulation and is able to pinpoint more correctly the substance responsible for turning the liquid yellow. The approach that Doris used in solving this chemistry problem is the basis of the scientific method—taught in high school science labs all over the world. Though it may be easier to comprehend the generation and evaluation of hypotheses to solve a chemistry problem, notice how Kevin (in the chapter case study) demonstrated some of the same abilities as he attempted to solve his personal dilemma:

Kevin believes that he has been found out. He begins to generate a series of excuses, lies, and half-truths (i.e., hypotheses) that will help him solve his problem. He also evaluates each one of these in terms of how believable it sounds as well as its predicted outcome. Through systematic reasoning, he decides on his best solution.

Formal operational thought includes hypothesis generation, which is an integral step in the scientific method.

Thinking about thought. Adolescents are also able to think about thought and about the process of thinking, referred to as **reflective thinking**. Piaget suggested that reflective thinking is an essential aspect of formal operations since many of the cognitive abilities we have described require adolescents to evaluate and monitor their thoughts.

Reflective thinking not only allows for better problem solving but also for recognition of one's self as thinker. For example, the beginning of the formal operational stage often corresponds to a period during which preadolescents begin to record their thoughts and ideas in journals and diaries, poems, short stories, and songs. Reflective thinking can also be the source of interpersonal difficulties of the "But I thought that you thought that I thought . . . " variety.

Based on the findings of Piaget and others, early adolescents can think about abstract concepts and other possibilities, both real and imagined; generate and evaluate hypotheses when confronted with a problem to solve; and systematically deduce the best solution. They also can think about thought and about thinking itself.

Limitations of Formal Operational Thought

Piaget recognized that 11- to 13-year-olds usually exhibit the beginnings of formal operational thinking, but it is not until mid- to late adolescence that consistent formal operational thinking occurs (Piaget, 1972). Other studies have shown that anywhere from 30 to 50% of any random sample of adults are not consistently formal operational thinkers (Blasi & Hoeffel, 1974; Shayer, 1980). This finding raises a potential problem if the design of high-school curricula is based on the presumption that the majority of adolescents engage in formal operational thinking. If, as the data suggest, less than 50% of high-school students meet formal operational criteria, then there is a mismatch between high-school instruction and the students' ability to interact effectively with the material (Collings, 1994).

Although Piaget claimed that his stages and the structures necessary for formal operational thinking were universal, subsequent studies have shown that practice, quality, and years of education are also positively related to levels of formal operational problem solving (Mwamwenda & Mwamwenda, 1991). College-educated adults show more formal thinking than non-college-educated adults, and graduate students show higher levels of formal operational functioning than undergraduates (Mwamwenda, 1999). The implications of these findings are that formal operational skills may develop with the structured support provided by a Western educational system. Depending upon one's cultural experience, formal thinking may be delayed or nonexistent in traditional Piagetian testing situations (Cole, 1990).

Research also suggests that formal operational thinking may not be applied under all circumstances. This **asynchrony** is demonstrated by the phenomena that adolescents may exhibit formal thinking in social domains, such as interpersonal relationships, but not in intellectual domains, such as a physics lab, or vice versa (Gordon, 1988). How teens' cognitive abilities affect their emotional and interpersonal lives is explored further in Box 9.1.

Although the cognitive changes that result in formal operational thinking may promote better problem-solving skills in some adolescents, researchers believe that formal operational thinking may also give rise to a form of egocentrism that distorts thinking and explains poor decision making in adolescents (e.g., Weinstein, 1980; 1984; Hudson & Gray, 1986). This egocentrism is described as the failure to differentiate between the cognitive concerns of others and those of the self (Elkind, 1967; 1978). Despite having the ability to take multiple perspectives, adolescents tend to be preoccupied with their own point of view. This preoccupation is reflected in two constructs: the imaginary audience and the personal fable. Each reflects different aspects of adolescent egocentrism.

An **imaginary audience** represents adolescents' presumption that everyone is looking at and judging them, when in fact they are not. This construct may help explain the extreme self-consciousness that adolescents experience regarding their appearance, behavior, personality characteristics, and abilities (Muuss, 1982). It may also explain the embarrassment that adolescents experience when something trivial happens to them in public (e.g., tripping over the curb). Some researchers have suggested that imaginary audience behavior declines with age. However, other studies have shown a different pattern. At least one study has shown that first-year college females exhibit an *increase* in imaginary audience behavior in their new environment (Peterson & Roscoe, 1991).

Personal fables are created when adolescents become preoccupied with their own thoughts, view their thoughts and themselves as unique, and therefore see themselves as invulnerable to events that happen to others. It is an intriguing explanation for why teenagers engage in high-risk behaviors such as drinking and driving, unprotected sexual activity, and frequent use of drugs (Gardner & Herman, 1990). Although familiar with the risks, they underestimate the risks *to themselves* or deny the possibility that anything will happen *to them* (Moore & Rosenthal, 1991; Halpern-Felsher, et al., 2001).

Kevin didn't think he would get caught. And even if he did, he's the star of the basketball team! Surely his coach won't impose the "no school, no play," rule on him. Kevin's disbelief illustrates his personal fable.

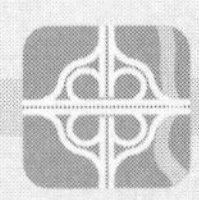

BOX 9.1 ROADMAP TO UNDERSTANDING THEORY AND RESEARCH

Formal Operational Thought and Its Implications for Affective and Interpersonal Development

Studies have found that not all adolescents reach the stage of formal operational thinking between the ages of 11 and 14 (Kuhn, Langer, Kohlberg, & Haan, 1977). Failure to achieve formal operational thought has clear educational implications, but formal operational dysfunction may also impact adolescents' affective (i.e., emotional) and interpersonal growth (Gordon, 1988). Limited cognitive functioning may influence adolescents' abilities to manage their emotions and interact effectively with others. Research on the relationship between adolescent psychopathology and formal operational functioning shows that inadequate formal operational processing is related to depression, impulsive and conduct-disordered behavior, delinquency, and teenage pregnancy (Black & DeBlassie, 1985; Hains & Ryan, 1983; Moilanen, 1993).

The ways in which limitations in formal operation thinking relate to pathology or high-risk behavior and subsequent therapeutic intervention can be illustrated through the following interactions of two adolescent therapy groups. The therapy groups were made up of students who were reported by teachers and administrators to have a wide range of affective and interpersonal difficulties. Some of the students had difficulty completing class work and homework, others were disruptive and aggressive towards teachers and peers, and still others were reported as socially withdrawn. The group therapy setting provided an excellent context for observing the formal operational skills, or lack thereof, of these students and the impact of their thinking on decision making in everyday life.

1. **Formal Operational Function: Envisioning Alternatives**
   - In the group therapy sessions, many of the group members expressed frustration about their school situations (e.g., inflexible teachers, repeated reprimands) and felt little hope for changes in their school situation. They could not envision alternative ways to respond to challenging situations.
   - During one group discussion, Andrea relayed how her English teacher's continual reprimands finally got to her and how she lost her temper in response. Cynthia reported that she continues to get in trouble for putting makeup on during class.
   - The therapist asked the group members to envision other possibilities for each of these students. Suggestions included Andrea telling her teacher how she feels, avoiding the teacher, transferring to another class, or behaving in a non-aggressive way. Peers suggested to Cynthia that she apply makeup outside of class and others things that she can do to avoid boredom in the class.
2. **Formal Operational Function: Evaluating Alternatives**
   - Many of the adolescent group members did not regularly consider the consequences of their actions or reason about how their behavior affected future events.
   - As a therapeutic intervention, the group members were asked to generate not only alternative courses of action but what a direct consequence of each alternative might be. The therapist further guided the students by posing hypothetical propositions such as "If Andrea apologizes to her teacher then . . . " or "If Cynthia puts makeup on tomorrow in class then . . . ."
3. **Formal Operational Function: Perspective-Taking Abilities**
   - Students in the group frequently had difficulty adopting the viewpoint of others. Robert, for example, had trouble controlling his angry outbursts at school.
   - Therapeutic intervention involved having Robert role-play himself (with his peers as the teacher) and then his teacher. After talking about his thoughts and feelings after each role-play, Robert was able to articulate how he felt as the teacher and how his teacher might feel scared or angry or have the sense that he was losing control of the entire class.
4. **Formal Operational Function: Reasoning About Chance and Probability**
   - These adolescents seemed to have difficulty estimating the odds or probability of an event occurring.
   - Andrea discussed plans for approaching her teacher about their relationship.
   - The therapist asked Andrea to consider how her teacher was likely to respond. Group members generated several possibilities using the teacher's response to other students as well as the history of the relationship between Andrea and her teacher. The therapist also asked Robert to evaluate the response of his peers to his aggressive behavior.

This cognitive-developmental approach to affective and interpersonal dysfunction highlights the role that features of formal thinking play in shaping not only the intellectual problem-solving skills of teens but also their decision-making abilities in the context of emotional and personal relationships.

Although the constructs of imaginary audience and personal fable provide a colorful characterization of adolescents and hold an intuitive explanatory appeal, they are not well supported by research (for a review, see Vartanian & Powlishta, 1996). The constructs are difficult to measure and are not consistently related to high-risk behavior (Quadrel, Fischhoff, & Davis, 1993; Frankenberger, 2004). A recent study examined the perception of invulnerability in fifth, seventh, and ninth graders and its relationship to their alcohol and tobacco use. The results showed that, indeed, all students underestimated the risks of alcohol and tobacco use, supporting the notion of a personal fable. However, the study also assessed the perceived *benefits* of alcohol and tobacco use. Perceived benefits were found to increase with age and were better predictors of adolescents' actual drinking and smoking behavior 6 months later compared to perceived risks (Goldberg, Halpern-Felsher, & Millstein, 2002). In other words, a sense of invulnerability plays only a minor role in adolescent decision making. There are many other components, such as perceived benefits, that are more powerful predictors of risk-taking behavior.

Some critics of adolescent egocentrism suggest that too much emphasis has been placed on the role of cognition and formal operational thinking. They propose that these constructs are better reflected by developmental changes in adolescents' social perspective-taking skills and interpersonal understanding as outlined by Selman (1980) and presented in chapter 6 (Jahnke & Blanchard-Fields, 1993). These critics also suggest that imaginary audience and personal fable behavior operate as protective factors for the adolescent's ego in the process of separating from parents and striving for autonomy (Aalsma & Lapsley, 1999). These ideas are explored further in chapter 10.

Did you take risks as a young adolescent? How did you perceive the benefits compared to the risks? What factors went into your decisions?

Information Processing in Adolescents

Using the computer as a metaphor to describe how adolescents process information, the information-processing perspective focuses on individual components of cognition, how they change over time, and how each contributes to the cognitive abilities present in middle adolescence. In sum, adolescents have a greater capacity for temporary storage and quicker processing. They have more knowledge to build and draw upon, and they use more sophisticated strategies and metacognitive skills.

Capacity increases. It used to be thought that short-term memory capacity, or the ability to temporarily hold something in memory, changed very little after middle childhood. But several recent studies suggest that short-term memory capacity does increase during adolescence to approach that of adults (Cowan, Nugent, Elliott, Ponomarev, & Saults, 1999; Zald & Iacono, 1998). For example, one study found increases in both verbal and spatial working memory between the ages of 6 and 35 (Swanson, 1999). These increases make it possible for adolescents to hold

Guideposts for Working with Adolescents

- Mix hands-on experiential learning and verbal lecture to assess adolescents' understanding of verbally presented material.
- Encourage students to design and conduct experiments in all academic subjects using natural phenomena.
- Assess adolescents' problem-solving skills and stages of reasoning in addition to their final answers. Engage in dialogues with adolescents as you attempt to understand how they are approaching a problem.
- Capitalize on teens' egocentrism by providing creative opportunities for self-reflection, such as journal writing.
- Let adolescents demonstrate to you where they are in their thinking and what they are ready for rather than rely on Piaget's proposed age ranges.

BOX 9.2 ROADMAP TO SUCCESSFUL PRACTICE

Problem-Based Learning from a Sociocultural Perspective

Chapter 4 presented in detail Vygotsky's sociocultural theory of cognitive development. Several constructs of this theory—zones of proximal development, scaffolding, and teacher as guide—can be found in the **problem-based learning (PBL)** technique. PBL is a pedagogical method in which students learn through facilitated problem solving (Barrows & Kelson, 1995), based on the premise that by having students solve real problems, they learn both content *and* thinking strategies. PBL fits into a larger category of experiential learning techniques that have been emphasized in recent reviews of middle- and high-school reform efforts (Bransford, Brown, & Cocking, 2000; Greeno, Collins, & Resnick, 1996).

In the problem-based learning cycle, students are presented with a complex problem that has multiple solutions. Students work in collaborative groups to identify what they need to learn in order to solve the problem. They engage in self-directed learning with the help of the teacher and then apply their new knowledge to the problem. PBL also requires students to reflect on what they learned was well as the effectiveness of their problem-solving approach (Hmelo-Silver, 2004).

The PBL process incorporates many features of Vygotsky's theory of how students learn, as illustrated in the following example. Middle-school students were asked to design a pair of artificial lungs (Hmelo, Holton, & Kolodner, 2000). The problem, designing lungs, was identified by the teacher as a topic that was within the "readiness zone of learning" for this age group. With the help of the teacher, the students created a structured whiteboard that listed facts, ideas (e.g., hypotheses), learning issues, and action plans related to designing artificial lungs. Through constructing the whiteboard, the students realized, for example, that they needed to find out how much air the lungs had to displace. The whiteboard operated as a scaffold or learning support that guided the problem solving at the beginning of the project and was relied upon less as the process moved towards completion.

Most of the learning in this project was collaborative, with students generating information, hypotheses, resources, and action plans in small groups. Collaborative learning reflects the premise of Vygotskian psychology that knowledge is constructed through social interactions. In PBL, the teacher does not act as a repository of knowledge, but rather as a facilitator of collaborative learning. The teacher helps guide the learning process through open-ended questioning designed to get students to clarify their thinking and to keep all the students involved in the problem-solving process.

After students designed the lungs using the PBL approach, their knowledge was compared to that of students in classrooms who did not engage in PBL. The PBL students showed greater gains on both short-answer tests and a drawing task than non-PBL students. These results suggest that experiential problem-solving pedagogical approaches, which utilize many components of Vygotskian cognitive developmental theory, are effective ways to help students develop flexible understanding and life-long learning skills.

and consider more information simultaneously when making a decision.

Efficiency increase. There is abundant evidence that the speed of processing increases with age (Kail, 1991; 2000). Reaction times—or the time it takes to respond during a motor, perceptual, or memory task—decrease with age, leveling off at around 17 to 18 years of age. Increased speed allows relevant past and present information to be used during a cognitive task (Salthouse, 1996).

In the case study, Kevin shifts from his thoughts about PSAT scores to his potential problem with his coach. He also generates multiple hypothetical responses in the time it takes him to roll over and get out of bed!

Increases in knowledge base. There are three kinds of knowledge structures stored in long-term memory:

1. **Declarative knowledge**. A compilation of all of the facts an adolescent knows (e.g., "knowing that")
2. **Procedural knowledge**. A compilation of all of the skills an adolescent knows (e.g., "knowing how to")
3. **Conceptual knowledge**. Understanding when and how to use declarative and procedural knowledge (e.g., "knowing why")

All three of these types of knowledge increase with age (Byrnes, 2001a). This developmental finding is best demonstrated by the results of the National Assessments of Educational Progress (NAEPs). The NAEP test assesses the declarative, procedural, and conceptual knowledge of fourth, eighth, and twelfth graders in reading, writing, math, science, history, geography, and civics. Students show an increase in knowledge in all domains from the fourth to the twelfth grade (Beatty, Reese, Persky, & Carr, 1996). When comparisons are made among the three types of knowledge, however, conceptual knowledge shows the lowest gains in all domains at grade 12 (Byrnes, 2001a, 2001b). Although there is a steady increase in knowledge from childhood to adolescence, conceptual understanding may not develop as quickly. Studies also show that many adolescents (as well as adults) possess faulty information and misconceptions about a range of topics (Byrnes, 2001a, 2001b).

Kevin is able to draw on his procedural knowledge to forge a note from his mother. His declarative knowledge provides him with multiple courses of action.

Effective use of mnemonic strategies. Studies show that by adolescence, most teens utilize the more sophisticated and effective forms of rehearsal and organizational mnemonic strategies (Ornstein, Naus, & Liberty, 1975; Ornstein & Naus, 1985). However, one mnemonic strategy that is typically not used successfully until adolescence is elaboration (refer to Table 4.3 in chapter 4). **Elaboration** is a mnemonic device in which a person generates a detailed verbal or visual relationship between pairs of items (Schneider & Pressley, 1997).

To assess this ability, children are presented with a **paired-association task**. In this task, pairs of words are presented to the participant for memorization (e.g., fish-tree). At recall, only one word from the pair is presented, and the participant must remember the other. Verbal elaboration might include generating a sentence that includes the two words, "The fish is hiding beneath the fallen tree in the pond." Visual elaboration could involve creating an image of fish hanging from trees. Children in elementary school rarely use elaboration; perhaps because the strategy itself takes so much processing, there is little attentional capacity left to apply to memorization. With increased capacity, speed, and a larger knowledge base, adolescents are more capable of utilizing this strategy and reaping memorial benefits (Schneider & Bjorklund, 2003).

Other mnemonic strategies that do not emerge until adolescence are strategies for comprehending complex texts. These strategies involve identifying main ideas, synthesizing, and summarizing related points (see Table 4.3). These strategies are usually explicitly taught in school, require prolonged practice, and do not appear spontaneously or consistently until adolescence (Pressley, Forrest-Pressley, Elliot-Faust, & Miller, 1985).

Advanced metacognitive skills. The ability to monitor one's own cognitive activity, or **metacognition**, develops over time. It has been suggested that the status of metacognitive development helps to explain how and why cognitive development both occurs and fails to occur in adolescence (Kuhn, 2000). Adolescents are better able to monitor their comprehension, understand when they have failed to learn, and articulate what strategies they need to employ to improve retention (Schneider, 1999).

Metamemory is a metacognitive skill that refers specifically to the knowledge one has of the working and contents of one's memory. Adolescents know what their memory limitations are, allocate their study time better, and understand that some tasks are harder to remember and that some study strategies are more effective than others (Schneider, 1999; Schneider & Pressley, 1997). This increased awareness of how one's memory works has been linked to improved memory performance.

Because research findings have linked metacognitive skills to more advanced cognition, efforts have been made to train adolescents in the use of metacognitive skills. Early attempts showed only short-term gains in cognitive performance and a failure to generalize across tasks and domains. More recent attempts, however, that have embedded metacognitive instruction within the school curriculum have met with greater success (Rosenshine & Meister, 1997). An example of effective metacognitive training is presented in Box 9.3.

The study of metacognition also includes how adolescents come to understand the origins, nature, and legitimacy of knowledge (Kuhn, Cheney, & Weinstock, 2000). This is referred to as **epistemological understanding**, which changes as the child develops.

- **Preschoolers are *realists*.** What one knows is a reflection of reality. There are no inaccuracies in the interpretation of an event, or conflicting beliefs, because everyone has the same view of reality.

BOX 9.3 ROADMAP TO SUCCESSFUL PRACTICE

Prompting that Promotes Productive Thinking and Learning

One method of promoting metacognitive skills is to encourage students to reflect upon the material to be learned. Reflection is thought to promote multiple and complementary ways of integrating and processing knowledge as well as identifying lack of knowledge or understanding. The purpose of this classroom study was to determine if students merely need to be prompted to reflect or if they need guidance in reflecting productively (Davis, 2003).

One hundred and seventy-eight middle-school science students were assigned a complex science project on thermodynamics and light and given one of two types of reflection prompts. The first group was given "generic prompts." These prompts encouraged students to stop and think at various points during the problem-solving process without providing instruction in what to think about, for example, "Right now I'm thinking . . . " or "My thoughts right now are . . . ."

The second group received "directed prompts" that provided hints of potential directions for their reflection, for example, "When I critique evidence I . . . " or "Pieces of evidence I don't understand are . . . " or "In thinking about how these ideas all fit together, I'm confused about . . . . "

When the final projects were compared, results surprisingly showed that students in the *generic* prompt condition developed more coherent understanding of the material and were more successful on the science project than those students who received more directed prompts. Further analyses revealed that students who received generic prompts cited more ideas, multiple principles, and multiple pieces of evidence in response to prompting. In contrast, students who received directed prompts exhibited more unproductive reflections, such as "I'm having no problems," and were less successful on the project.

The authors of this study suggest that those students who responded to a generic prompt had to come up with more concrete responses on their own and thereby made the material more concrete and easier to learn. The generic prompts may also have matched the students' own thinking at the time and served as thinking supports rather than distracters. In this study, generic prompts seemed to have elicited deeper self-reflection and allowed the students to identify what they knew well and less well. Generic prompts encouraged students to "fill in the gaps" of their knowledge better. Genetic prompts seem more useful when asking students to engage in written reflection or in a problem-solving task that has multiple solutions, and directed prompts are more helpful when an unfamiliar concept is being taught.

- **Around age 4, children become *absolutists* and remain so throughout middle childhood**. They become aware that mental representations do not duplicate reality. If you and I disagree, one of us is right and one is wrong. The resolution is simply finding out which is which. They believe that knowledge is an accumulation of facts and objectivity dominates.
- **Adolescents are described as *multiplists* (or *relativists*)**. They demonstrate a growing awareness of the subjectivity of knowledge and consequently reject the notion that knowledge is fact and accept that knowledge is opinion. The assumptions that follow from this are that opinions are freely chosen by their holder and not open to challenge. In other words, "everyone is right." This belief that all knowledge is subjective is dangerous because it eclipses recognition of an objective standard. It obscures the reality of fact and therefore makes adolescents' judgments of information and knowledge indiscriminatory.
- **Many adolescents and adults remain *absolutists* or *multiplists* for life**. Some adolescents begin to reintegrate objectivity into knowing. Although everyone may have an opinion, some opinions are more fact-based than others.
- **Adolescents who make judgments about knowledge based on evidence and argument are called *evaluativists***. They rely on an intellectual basis for judging one idea better than another, rather than mere personal preference.

The implications of the evolution of epistemological understanding are that adolescents who never move beyond an absolutist belief about religion, for example, or adolescents who equate knowledge with personal preferences (i.e., multiplists) lack a reason to engage in further intellectual inquiry. It is the

BOX 9.4 ROADMAP TO UNDERSTANDING THEORY AND RESEARCH

The Developmental Competency of Adolescents to Be Tried as Adults

Beginning in the 1990s, the trend in the criminal justice system has been to impose harsher penalties on youth who commit violent crimes. This trend, grounded in providing protection for the public, reflects abandonment of hope for the rehabilitation of youthful offenders (Steinberg & Scott, 2003). For example, in the 1990s, states lowered the age at which youths could be tried in adult criminal courts, thus expanding the age range that could be subject to adult adjudication and punishment. Currently, 21 states in the United States allow offenders under 18 to be executed; in many of these states, those as young as 16 can be put to death (Streib, 2002).

During this same time period, however, researchers within the MacArthur Foundation's Research Network on Adolescent Development and Juvenile Justice began to show that adolescent defenders exhibit developmental immaturity in their participation and decision making within the criminal court system. As a result, the Network argued that adolescents should be dealt with in a separate justice system (Grisso et al., 2003; Grisso & Schwartz, 2000; Fagan & Zimring, 2000). This argument is consistent with a recent Supreme Court ruling that protects the mentally retarded from receiving the death penalty. In *Atkins v. Virginia* (2002) the Supreme Court ruled that the execution of mentally retarded offenders was unconstitutional because they were unable to

- comprehend the purpose and nature of the trial process,
- provide relevant information to counsel and process information, and
- apply information to their own situation in an unbiased or rational manner (Bonnie, 1992; 1993).

The justification for this legal decision could be applied to the majority of juvenile offenders under the age of 18. Recent research supports this argument.

In one study, youth from juvenile detention facilities (detained), ages 11 to 17, were compared to youth from the community as well as to both detained and nondetained young adults (ages 18–24). All participants were administered an assessment tool designed to assess criminals' abilities to participate in their defense (*MacCAT-CA*, Poythress et al., 1999). The items on this measure can be grouped into three subscales:

- **Understanding.** Assesses comprehension of courtroom procedures, the roles of court personnel, and the defendant's rights at trial.
- **Reasoning.** Assesses the recognition of information relevant to a legal defense and the ability to process that information.
- **Appreciation.** Assesses the recognition of the relevance of information for one's own situation.

Results, illustrated in Figure 9.2, show a significant age difference on the *Understanding and Reasoning* subscales of the *MacCat-CA*. A significantly greater percentage of younger adolescents (ages 11 to 13) showed significant impairment on the *Understanding*

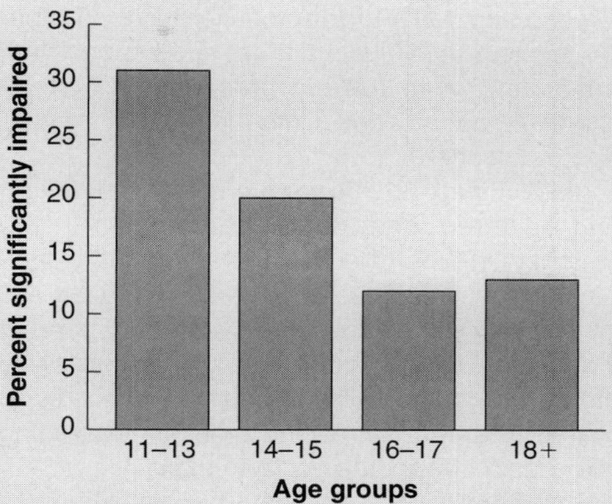

FIGURE 9.2 Proportion of Individuals at Different Ages Who Are Significantly Impaired with Respect to Either or Both MacCAT-CA Understanding and Reasoning
The younger the defendants, the more they demonstrate impaired understanding of courtroom procedure, their rights, or information relevant to their defense.

Source: From "Juveniles' Competence to Stand Trial", by L. Steinberg, T. Grisso, J. Woolard, E. Cauffman, E. Scott, et al., 2003, *Social Policy Report, XVII* (IV), p. 10. Copyright 2003 by the Society for Research in Child Development. Reprinted by permission of the society.

(*Continued*)

BOX 9.4 (CONTINUED)

and Reasoning items of the questionnaire. In other words, younger individuals did not show a sufficient understanding of courtroom proceedings or their rights and did not recognize information that was relevant to a defense.

In addition, participants were given an instrument that posed three legal decisions common in the delinquency/criminal process to assess their decision-making skills. Results shown in Figure 9.3 reveal that younger adolescents, when compared to older adolescents and young adults, are more likely to comply with authority by choosing confessing to the police rather than remaining silent and accepting a plea bargain rather than going to trial.

Examination of their decision-making rationales further reveal that younger adolescents less often recognize the risks inherent in some decision options, less often think the risks apply to them, and do not consider the risks serious if they are present. To complicate matters, intelligence or IQ level also significantly predicted an individual's performance on the *Understanding and Reasoning* subscales and decision-making task. The lower the IQ, the more likely the youth was to qualify as cognitively incompetent to stand trial (Steinberg et al., 2003).

It is the contention of the researchers from the MacArthur Network that youth under the age of 18 are not developmentally competent to be tried as adults. More specifically, those under the age of 14 exhibit the same cognitive, psychosocial, and neurobiological deficits as the mentally incompetent, who are legally shielded from the death penalty.

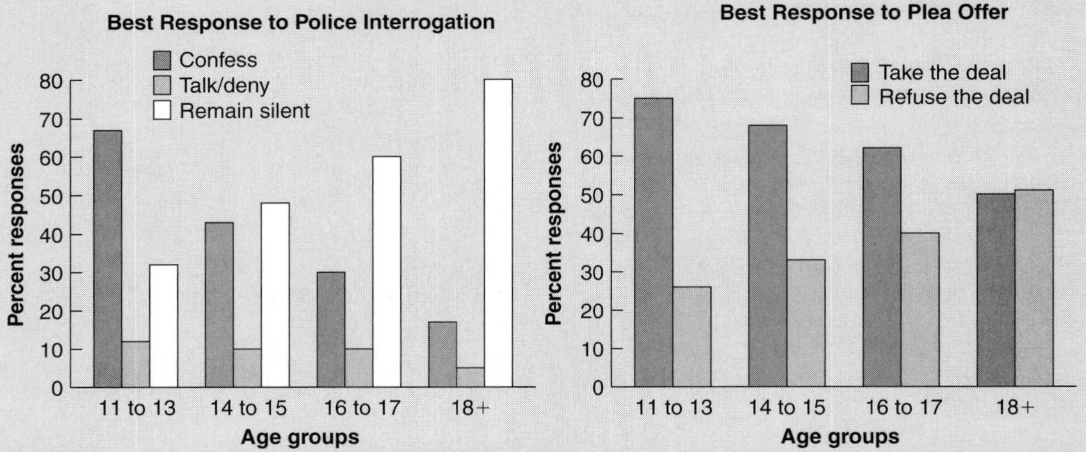

FIGURE 9.3 Decision Choices for Police Interrogation and Plea Agreement Vignettes as a Function of Age

Younger defendants are more likely to confess and accept a plea bargain although neither might be in their best interest.

Source: From "Juveniles' Competence to Stand Trial" by L. Steinberg, T. Grisso, J. Woolard, E. Cauffman, E. Scott, et al., 2003, *Social Policy Report, XVII* (IV), p. 10. Copyright 2003 by the Society for Research in Child Development. Reprinted by permission of the society.

intellectual skills and uses the results to make predictions about adolescents' future performance potential. Perhaps the most well-known contribution of psychometrics is the development and widespread use of intelligence tests. However, there is a long and controversial history in this country about what constitutes intelligence, how it should be measured, and how the scores from intelligence tests should be used. A brief summary of this history will be helpful in providing a context for understanding where we are today in the testing movement.

Theories of Intelligence

Charles Spearman was responsible for developing one of the earliest theories of intelligence, in

1904. He proposed a two-factor theory of intelligence that included a global mental ability called *g* that represented general intelligence and was highly correlated with academic achievement. He also identified *s* as an ability specific to the particular test. One conclusion derived from this model was that since specific factors (*s*) were unique to individual tests, any individual test differences were due solely to individual differences in general intelligence, or *g*. Spearman's concept of *g* is traditionally associated with the representation of intelligence as a single global factor.

E. L. Thorndike, and later L. L. Thurstone, argued that although most cognitive tests of *g* correlated positively with one another (which supported the concept of a global *g*), there were individual factors within the tests that were more highly related to one another. For example, items that assessed reading comprehension and verbal analogies were more highly related to each other than reading comprehension and adding fractions. Using a statistical technique called **factor analysis** that identifies groups of items in a test which are highly correlated with one another, Thurstone (1938) proposed seven group factors, or **primary mental abilities**, that make up intelligence:

1. **Verbal Comprehension.** Vocabulary, reading comprehension, and verbal analogies
2. **Word Fluency.** Ability to quickly generate and manipulate a large number of words with specific characteristics, as in anagrams or rhyming tests
3. **Number.** Ability to quickly and accurately carry out mathematical operations
4. **Space.** Spatial visualizations as well as ability to mentally transform spatial figures
5. **Associative Memory.** Rote memory
6. **Perceptual Speed.** Quickness in perceiving visual details, anomalies, and similarities
7. **Reasoning.** Skill in a variety of inductive, deductive, and arithmetic reasoning tasks

The foundation of this theory is that intelligence is made up of multiple, independent dimensions. The implication is that two adolescents with similar *g* could actually differ dramatically in their cognitive strengths and weaknesses. Thurstone thought, therefore, that any intelligence test should include assessment of all seven primary abilities. There have been additional theories of intelligence put forth in the ensuing years, but most contemporary theories derive from the Spearman/Thorndike-Thurstone traditions (e.g., Jensen, 1998; Garlick, 2002).

In your opinion, what are the characteristics of someone who demonstrates intelligence?

Measures of Intelligence

Alfred Binet and Theodore Simon, commissioned by the French government to devise a test that would differentiate between children who could not learn because of low ability and those who would not learn because of poor motivation, created the first intelligence test in 1905 (Thorndike, 2005). Binet did not really have a theory of mental ability, but he thought that intelligence could be best expressed in and assessed by complex cognitive tasks. The first intelligence test consisted of items that assessed memory, knowledge, and reasoning skills arranged in a sequence of increasing difficulty and grouped into age levels, or when the "average" child could accomplish them. This first test has undergone numerous revisions and is now known as the *Stanford-Binet Intelligence Scale, Fifth Edition* (Roid, 2003).

Currently, the most widely-used intelligence tests are the Wechsler Scales. Designed by David Wechsler (1939), a clinical psychologist who used the test to help identify cognitive strengths and weaknesses in his clients and assist in diagnoses, the tests were based on his definition of intelligence as "the aggregate or global capacity of the individual to act purposefully, to think rationally, and to deal effectively with his environment" (p. 3). Because the test seemed to be a valid measure of general intelligence, its use expanded to other populations.

There are three separate Wechsler scales:

- ***Wechsler Preschool and Primary Scale of Intelligence, 3rd ed.*** (*WPPSI-III*) (Wechsler, 2002)
- ***Wechsler Intelligence Scale for Children, 4th ed.*** (*WISC-IV*) (Wechsler, 2003)
- ***Wechsler Adult Intelligence Scale, 3rd ed.*** (*WAIS-III*) (Weschler, 1997)

The WISC-IV is designed for use with children and adolescents ages 6 to 16 years 11 months and will be the focus of this section. Sample items from several of the 10 core subtests are presented below:

- **Similarities.** In what way are wool and cotton alike?
- **Vocabulary.** What does corrupt mean?

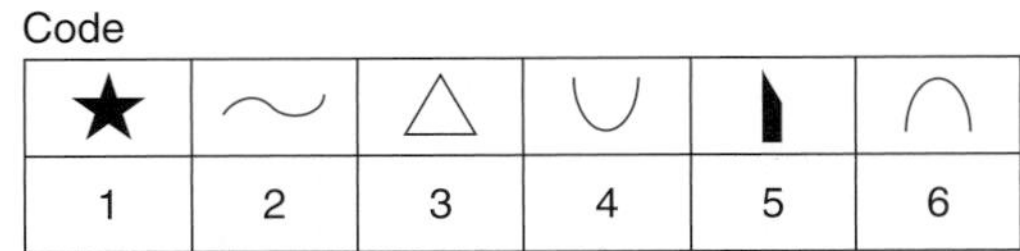

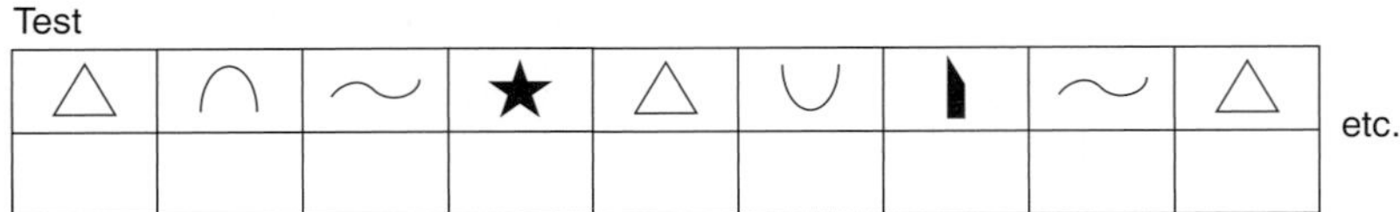

FIGURE 9.4 Sample Coding Task
This sample task, similar to items on the WISC, requires test takers to fill in the bottom row with the appropriate numbers deduced from the code.

- **Comprehension.** Why do people buy fire insurance?
- **Digit Span.** I am going to say some numbers. Listen carefully and when I am through, say the numbers right after me: 7 3 4 1 8 6
- **Coding.** In the top row, each figure is shown with a number. Fill in the number that goes with each figure in the second row.
- **Matrix Reasoning.** For each item the child looks at an incomplete matrix and selects the missing portion from five response options.
- **Picture Concepts.** The child identifies objects that share some common property.

Some of the items in this test require children and adolescents to arrange materials rather than talk with the test administrator. This procedure allows non-English-speaking children, as well as youth with speech or language disorders, to demonstrate their intellectual capabilities. Some professionals find the division between verbal and performance items very useful for assessment purposes (Hildebrand & Ledbetter, 2001). The items make up four index scores—*Verbal Comprehension, Perceptual Organization, Freedom from Distractability,* and *Processing Speed*—that are combined to give an overall ability score. When the four index scores are added together, they produce a total ability score, or **intelligence quotient (IQ)**. On the Wechsler scales, the mean total IQ is set at 100 with a standard deviation of 15. Most other major intelligence tests have set the same mean so it is easy to compare the IQ score from one intelligence test to another.

How to interpret an IQ score. An IQ score represents how far the adolescent's raw score (number of items answered correctly) differs from the typical performance of same-aged individuals. To develop the norms for the WISC-IV (for more on norm-based tests, see chapter 1), thousands of children and adolescents were given the test; their performance created a bell-shaped curve, as shown in Figure 9.5. The highest point of the curve represents the aver-

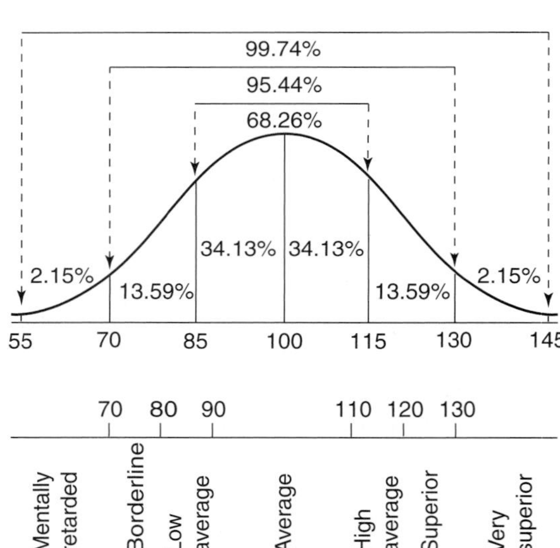

FIGURE 9.5 Percentage of Individuals and Intelligence Classifications at Different Points from the Mean IQ of 100
The normal curve shows that the majority of people fall within 1 standard deviation of the mean. Most people achieve an IQ between 85 and 115.

Source: From *Psychological Testing and Assessment* (4th ed.), by R. J. Cohen & M. E. Swerdik, 1999, Mountain View, CA: Mayfield. Copyright 1999 by the McGraw-Hill Companies. Reprinted by permission.

age performance of a particular age group and accounts for the scores of the largest number of adolescents. Adolescents who are represented to the right of the highest point answered more items correctly, and adolescents who are represented to the left of the highest point answered fewer items correctly. The bell-shaped, or **normal, curve** has at its center the mean, or average, score on this intelligence test (100) and a **standard deviation** of 15, which shows how spread out the scores are from the mean. Figure 9.5 also displays the intellectual labels that are applied to the various ranges of scores. An IQ of 100 can be interpreted to mean that an adolescent scored higher than 50% percent of adolescents who took this test and is in the "average" range.

The stability of IQ. Stability refers to the consistency of performance over time. In other words, is an IQ score achieved at age 10 related to IQ at age 20? Research on the stability of IQ shows that the older the individual is at the first test-taking session, the better that score predicts IQ at later points in time. Correlations between IQ scores achieved after age 6 and those taken later are quite high (e.g., .70s–.80s). IQ scores obtained during preschool are less predictive of later scores (Humphreys & Davey, 1988). In addition, the less time between test-taking sessions produces stronger relationships between IQ scores. IQ tests taken several years apart yield IQ scores that are more similar than those from tests taken 20 years apart.

The Relationship of Intelligence to Academic Achievement and Occupation

Researchers have found that IQ scores are related to a number of variables that we value highly in our society. For example, a high score on an intelligence test is related to higher academic achievement (Jensen, 1998). Research also shows that IQ is positively correlated with achievement test scores, higher grade point averages (GPAs), and adult education attainment (McCall, Evahn, & Kratzer, 1992). Box 9.5 provides more information on the aptitude and achievement tests for adolescents most widely used in the United States.

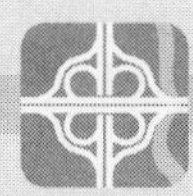

BOX 9.5 ROADMAP TO UNDERSTANDING THEORY AND RESEARCH

Aptitude and Achievement Tests for Adolescents

Chapter 1 differentiated between aptitude tests, defined as those that predict performance, and achievement tests, which purport to measure mastered facts or skills. The two most widely used tests administered to adolescents assess both aptitude *and* achievement.

The SAT, formerly called the Scholastic Aptitude Test and Scholastic Assessment Test, was revised in March of 2005 and consists of two tests. The first, the SAT Reasoning Test (formerly the SAT I), measures verbal, mathematical, and writing skills, while the second, SAT Subject Tests (formerly SAT II), assesses knowledge of particular subject areas such as biology and world history. Some suggest the SAT Reasoning Test measures reasoning aptitude and the SAT Subject Tests measure achievement.

The new SAT Reasoning Test consists of ten sections divided into three math, three reading, and three writing sections, with an additional equating section that may be any one of the three types. Separate verbal, writing, and mathematical scores are reported with a range of 200–800 for each. A perfect score on this new three-part version of the SAT is 2400.

SAT Subject Tests are one-hour multiple-choice tests given in individual subjects such as English, history and social studies, mathematics, science, and languages. Each individual test is scored on the same scale of 200 to 800.

The SAT is administered to approximately a million high-school seniors every year and used by a majority of colleges and universities in the admissions process. Scores from the old SAT appear to be

BOX 9.5 (CONTINUED)

good predictors of college grades across a wide range of majors and areas of concentration. Old SAT scores also are predictive of college graduation rates and were found to be related to *g* or intelligence (Frey & Detterman, 2004; Stumpf & Stanley, 2002).

The *American College Testing* (ACT) *Assessment Program* (1995) is another widely used assessment instrument. The ACT consists of three parts: the *Academic Tests*, the *Student Profile Section*, and the *ACT Interest Inventory*. The *Academic Tests* assess four content areas: English, mathematics, reading, and science reasoning. The *Student Profile Section* collects demographic data, high-school activities, and academic plans for college. The *ACT Interest Inventory* surveys students' vocational interests. The ACT yields scores of 1 to 36, which are averaged to create the ACT Composite. The ACT differs from the SAT in two distinct ways. First, the ACT measures basic competencies that are necessary for success in college in addition to vocationally relevant interests. This makes the ACT more useful than the SAT for counseling students in their educational and career decisions. The second difference is that the ACT is more closely tied to secondary school curricula and therefore functions as a truer achievement test than the SAT.

The main advantage for colleges in using these test scores is that tests like the SAT and ACT make it easier to compare students from different educational backgrounds and grading systems. However, critics of the SAT and the ACT argue that they are not immune to the race/ethnicity, socioeconomic, and gender biases discussed in regard to intelligence tests. In addition, high-school grades are almost equally predictive of success in college. Finally, both tests claim to measure innate ability; however, special classes and coaching can significantly influence the scores on either of these tests. For these reasons, the College Entrance Examination Board has long since encouraged colleges to rely on other admissions information.

In addition, numerous studies have demonstrated that IQ is significantly related to job performance and job complexity (Gottfredson, 1997). Figure 9.6 depicts the mean *g* scores (comparable to IQ) for different occupations. The bars represent the range of *g* scores for approximately two thirds of persons in that occupation (Ree & Earles, 1992). There is also a relationship between *g* and both income and job prestige (Nyborg & Jensen, 2001). Clearly, high scores on intelligence tests are related to greater success in academics and job-related performance.

Factors That Influence Intelligence Scores

The originators of intelligence tests believed that they were assessing general intellectual competency that predicted success in life. Research has revealed, however, there are other factors not related to ability that may influence adolescents' performance on intelligence tests.

Socioeconomic status (SES). Children who are raised in poverty are severely limited in their intellectual potential by their environment (Turkheimer, Haley, Waldron, D'Onofrio, & Gottesman, 2003). Adolescents who come from low-income homes score as much as 15 to 20 points below their middle-class peers (Neisser et al., 1996). The reasons suggested are that poor children and adolescents may lack the material (e.g., books, music lessons, computers) and familial support (e.g., help from parents on homework, engagement in school-related activities) that promote intellectual development. Low-income adolescents are also more likely to live in neighborhoods that lack extracurricular opportunities (e.g., parks, recreational facilities) and contain poor-quality schools. Furthermore, adoption studies using a behavior-genetic framework have shown that when low-income children are adopted into middle-class families, their IQ scores rise.

Ethnicity. African American youth score, on average, 15 points below Caucasian youth. Hispanic youth fall midway between these two groups, and Asian Americans score slightly higher than Caucasians (Ceci, Rosenblum, & Kumpf, 1998). Part of this pattern may be explained by the large per-

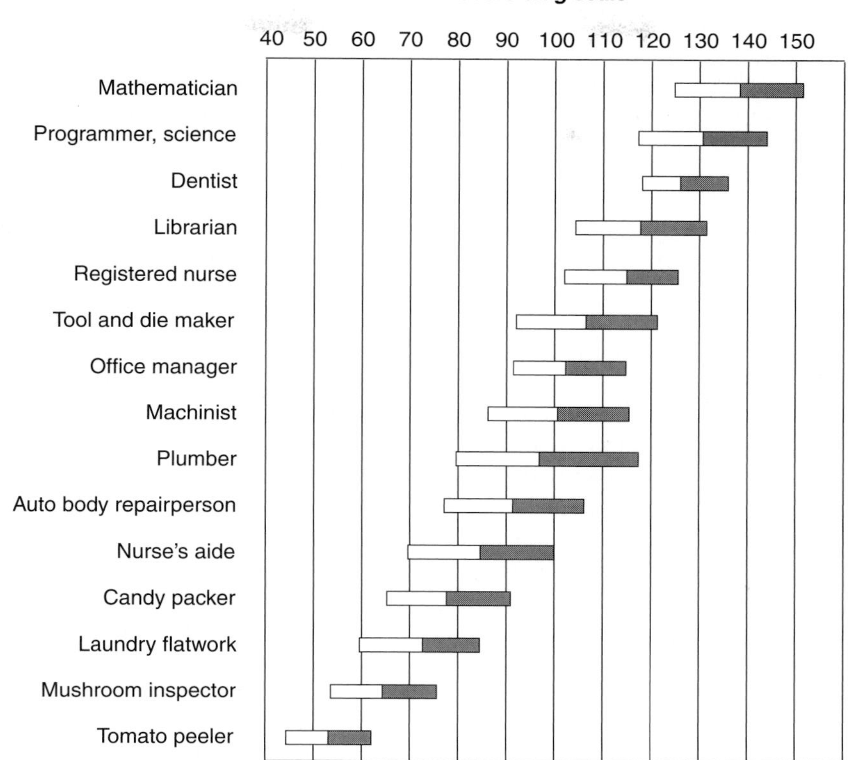

FIGURE 9.6 Mean General Intelligence Scores (g scores) on the General Aptitude Test Battery for Selected Occupations

The bars represent the range of *g* scores for different occupations.

Source: From *Measurement and Evaluation in Psychology and Education* (7th ed., p. 282) by R. M. Thorndike, 2005, Upper Saddle River, NJ: Pearson Education, Inc. Copyright 2005 by Pearson Education, Inc. Reprinted by permission of Pearson Education, Inc., Upper Saddle River, NJ.

centage of African American youth who live in poverty—42%, compared to 22% of all American children. Studies that equalize SES show differences in IQ scores, with Caucasians scoring higher than African Americans (Jensen & Reynolds, 1982).

These findings are not controversial in themselves; it is how they have been interpreted that has raised the concern of many social scientists. Controversies have stemmed from the claims some researchers have made about the origins of intelligence. They have suggested that intelligence is largely biologically determined and therefore not amenable to improvement (Jensen, 2001). Opponents of this view argue that scores on intelligence tests can be influenced by many nonintellectual factors, such as years of schooling, SES, and familiarity with the culture for whom the test was written. Researchers have in fact shown that when any one of these factors is manipulated, IQ changes (Grissmer, Williamson, Kirby, & Berends, 1998).

Alternative Views of Intelligence

Some researchers are dissatisfied with our nation's heavy reliance on intelligence tests and the subsequent use of these tests for educational and occupational prognoses. Consequently, several alternatives to the traditional views of intelligence and assessment have been introduced.

Multiple intelligences. Howard Gardner (1993b, 1995, 1999) proposed a theory of multiple intelligences that takes into account more than just the higher-order cognitive abilities that make up *g*. He believed that people can be "intelligent" in many different ways and consequently proposed nine basic forms of intelligence:

1. **Linguistic.** The ability to use language well (e.g., journalists and lawyers)
2. **Spatial.** The ability to reason well about spatial relations (e.g., architects and surgeons)
3. **Musical.** The ability to compose and understand music (e.g., audio engineers and musicians)
4. **Logical-Mathematical.** The ability to manipulate abstract symbols (e.g., scientists and computer programmers)
5. **Bodily-Kinesthtic.** The ability to plan and understand sequences of movements (e.g., dancers and athletes)
6. **Intrapersonal.** The ability to understand oneself (e.g., clergy)
7. **Interpersonal.** The ability to understand other people and social interactions (e.g., politicians and teachers)
8. **Naturalist.** The ability to observe carefully (e.g., forest rangers)
9. **Existential.** The ability to address "the big questions" about existence (e.g., philosophers and theologians) (Gardner, 1999)

These separate classifications are not meant to suggest that individuals excel in only one domain, but rather that these abilities work together to allow people to solve a range of problems and learn what they need to adapt to their environment.

Gardner's theory holds wide appeal because it resonates with people who may know someone who is not "book-smart" but "street-wise." It values the talents of someone who may have dropped out of high school but can reconstruct a car engine in very little time. It lends equal weight to a form of practical intelligence that guides people to act purposefully, think rationally, and deal effectively with their environment—ideas not dissimilar from Wechsler's definition of intelligence.

Triarchic model of intelligence. Sternberg (1985, 2003) has also developed a theory of multiple intelligences. His theory is labeled the **triarchic model of intelligence** because he proposes three distinct types of intelligence:

- **Componential.** The ability to learn to write clearly, calculate and reason about math, and understand literature
- **Experiential.** The ability to formulate novel solutions to problems
- **Contextual.** Involves knowing how to do things related to your sociocultural background

Componential or analytical intelligence is what is tested with traditional intelligence tests. Experiential or creative intelligence facilitates creative solutions to problems or the development of novel product. Contextual or practical intelligence is largely distinct from analytical intelligence but also highly correlated to job performance (Sternberg et al., 2000). Box 9.6 illustrates how these three types of intelligences can be integrated into the instructional and assessment techniques of a high-school curriculum.

Sternberg defined successful intelligence as the "ability to succeed according to what one values in life, within one's sociocultural context" (Sternberg, 2003a, p. 400). This definition broadens the scope of what it means to be intelligent and opens the door to the possibility that there is more to intelligence than *g*. His argument was based on studies that explored what is considered "intelligent" in other countries. Cross-cultural studies have shown that those individuals who score high in practical intelligence are usually considered most intelligent. In rural Kenya, for example, practical knowledge regarding use of natural herbal medicines is valued highly and correlates negatively with tests of intelligence as well as math achievement (Sternberg et al., 2001). In another study, 261 adolescents who lived in rural and semiurban Yup'ik Alaskan communities were administered tests that assessed academic intelligence and practical intelligence (e.g., knowledge of fish preparation, weather, hunting, and herb and berry gathering). Urban Yup'ik youth outperformed rural Yup'ik on tests of componential intelligence. But rural Yup'ik scored higher than their urban counterparts on tests of practical intelligence, and both Yup'ik youth and adults rated the value of practical skills more highly (Grigorenko, Meier, Lipka, Mohatt, Yanez, & Sternberg, 2004). Results such as these strengthen the argument for multiple means of assessing intelligence with sensitivity to cultural experience. The advantage of this approach is that we learn more about the role intelligence plays in the everyday lives of diverse adolescents.

Creativity. The theories of Gardner and Sternberg challenge the long-held unidimensional view of

BOX 9.6 ROADMAP TO SUCCESSFUL PRACTICE

The Triarchic Model of Intelligence Goes to School

Most initiatives to improve student's achievement in school are not based upon psychological theories of intelligence. However, recent attempts have been made to infuse the triarchic theory of intelligence into the curricula so as to improve both school achievement and the cognitive skills that contribute to it (Sternberg, Grigorenko, Ferrari, & Clinkenbeard, 1999; Williams, Blythe, White, Li, Gardner, & Sternberg, 2002).

Sternberg and his colleagues (Grigorenko, Jarvin, & Sternberg, 2002) invited 432 public high-school students in grades 10 through 12 to participate in a 6-week study in which half of the students were taught curricula (e.g., mathematics, history, physical sciences, foreign languages, and the arts) with standard techniques and half were taught with triarchic-infused instruction. Those who were taught with standard pedagogical techniques were encouraged to use conventional, memory-based instruction that involves memorizing, recalling, recognizing, and repeating to achieve learning. Those in the triarchic instruction group were exposed to analytical, creative, and practical exercises.

In the triarchic instruction group, students were given a paragraph to read on Alan Stocker's paintings and tested on their analytical vocabulary skills. Students also were presented with an analytical comprehension question that asked them to "Compare and contrast the distinct features of Stocker's paintings with the distinct features of any other painter you know" (Grigorenko et al., 2002, p. 195). Creative tasks encouraged them to imagine, invent, discover, and explore. For example, in addition to assessing students' understanding of a word that taps into their analytical knowledge, they would also be asked to take a vocabulary word from the same paragraph and invent a sentence containing the given word. Practical techniques required the students to apply, use, implement, and put into practice what they were learning. In a history unit on *The Heritage of Latin America*, students were asked to apply their new vocabulary knowledge in the following exercise:

> Using the enclosed map of Central and South America, design a trip you would like to take. Draw lines on the map showing how you would travel, and describe your trip using the following words: *Colombia, disembark, expedition, isthmus, Jamaica, Mexico, Panama, Peru, voyage* (Grigorenko et al., 2002, p. 198).

After the 6-week session, students who were exposed to the triarchic condition excelled on all three types of tasks: analytical, creative, and practical. They showed greater gains in reading and comprehension skills in all subjects. The analyses showed that even in a relatively short time period students taught through triarchic methodologies benefited more from instruction that did students who were taught in more conventional ways.

Sternberg's explanation of these results is that by implementing triarchic exercises that tap into all three components of intelligence, teachers increase their likelihood of matching at least one, if not two or three, intellectual strengths of the student. Greater learning takes place when there is a match between how one processes information and the means by which the material is presented for learning.

Note: All instructional and assessment materials are available at http://www.yale.edu/pace/resources under the heading "Educational Resources."

intelligence. Analytical thinking, which is what is largely measured by intelligence tests, represents only one aspect of thinking and predicts success in life in a very narrow way. Possessing practical or creative ways of thinking may make you equally successful in life; however, these abilities are not regularly assessed by tests or valued very highly by schools. **Creativity** is defined as thinking that is novel and that produces ideas or outcomes that are of value (Sternberg, 1999). A distinction made between intelligence and creativity is that analytical intelligence is associated with **convergent thinking**. Convergent thinking is called for when individuals are presented with novel problems that have a single best answer. Creativity, however, is associated with **divergent thinking**. Divergent thinking is called for when individuals have to produce multiple responses and no one answer is correct. Creativity is

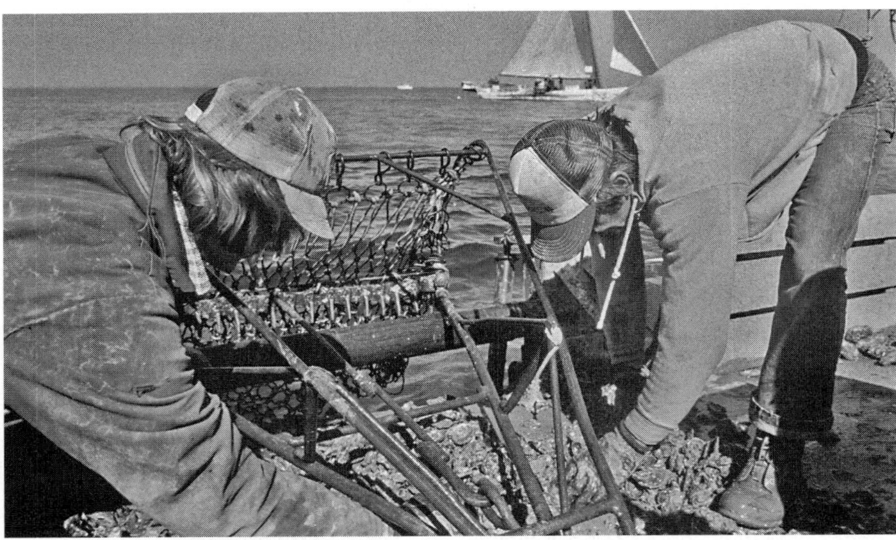

Practical intelligence is highly valued in many cultures.

distinctly different from practical and analytical intelligence and the ability in one cannot be predicted from the others (Sternberg, 2003b). In addition, the conception of creativity, the domains of the creative process (e.g., art, music, science, literature), and the extent to which creativity is nurtured varies across cultures (Lubart, 1999).

Creative thinking can be taught, however, or at least encouraged, and should be rewarded by teachers (Niu & Sternberg, 2003). For example, students can be asked to create novel products, such as a new type of doorknob; to write stories from a choice of titles; or to produce artwork to illustrate a concept (Sternberg, 2003b). Teaching creative thinking skills to middle- and high-school students has improved not only their creative thinking but their overall academic performance as well (Sternberg & Williams, 1996).

Cognitive Development in Context

Each of the theoretical approaches discussed in this chapter incorporates the role of context in the development of adolescent cognition. In some respects, external contextual support for cognitive development becomes even more critical in adolescence; research shows that different contextual experiences lead adolescents down divergent academic pathways. For example, during early adolescence gender differences in mathematical ability

Guideposts for Working with Adolescents

- To help put the adolescent's score in context, make sure you understand what information is being reported (e.g., general ability score, IQ).
- Help parents, educators, practitioners, and adolescents understand what is being measured and what the limitations of the tests are.
- Limit your reliance on intelligence tests since factors such as socioeconomic status and ethnicity can influence performance on any test of cognitive abilities.
- Encourage adolescents to develop their intelligence in as many different areas as possible, such as music or athletics.
- Value practical intellectual skills and recognize their relationship to future job success.

emerge. In addition, the cognitive abilities of adolescents who choose to drop out of school begin to diverge from those of their in-school classmates. Also, the learning and academic challenges low-income children face in elementary and middle school may grow into major obstacles by high school.

Family Contexts

In 1996, 20,000 high-school students and their families participated in a study that explored adolescents' disengagement from their school experience (Steinberg, 1996). For example, a high proportion of the students reported not taking school, or their studies, seriously.

- Over one third of the students said that they get through the day in school primarily by "goofing off with their friends."
- Two thirds of the students said they cheated on a school test during the past school year. Nearly nine out of ten students said they copied someone else's homework sometime during the last year.

A unique feature of this study was its revelation of the emphasis placed on extracurricular activities, peers, and parents and their contributions to these feelings of disengagement. The students reported that their extracurricular activities competed with their studies and that their peer culture discouraged trying to do well in school. Perhaps most serious was the reported disengagement of the parents from their teen's education.

- More than half of the students said they could bring home grades of C or worse without their parents getting upset. One quarter said they could bring home grades of D or worse without upsetting their parents.
- Nearly one third said their parents have no idea how they are doing in school. About one sixth of all students reported that their parents don't care whether they earn good grades in school or not.
- Only one fifth of parents consistently attended school programs. More than 40% *never* did.

What makes these data so disturbing is that research consistently finds that students who have involved parents do better in school academically than those whose parents are uninvolved (Grolnick & Slowiaczek, 1994; Gregory & Weinstein, 2004). This is true even at the high-school level, and therein lies the irony. When interviewed, parents listed a number of reasons why their involvement was low (e.g., work schedule, childcare issues, not welcomed by the school); but they also admitted that they thought because their child was older, they didn't need to be as involved. This is supported by other research that shows a significant drop-off in parental involvement as the child makes the transition from elementary to middle school (Chira, 1994). However, contrary to parental beliefs, high-school students benefit from parental involvement as much as younger children do.

This study also found that high-school students benefit from parental involvement *differently* than children in middle childhood do. In chapter 4 we discussed how parents could best influence their children's academic success by providing a home environment that supported their academic work (e.g., checking over homework, monitoring their children's time spent on schoolwork). Findings from this study showed that the type of parental involvement that made a real difference was activities that drew the parents into the school. Parents who attended school programs, extracurricular activities, teacher conferences, and "back-to-school" nights sent strong messages about how important school was to them and, by extension, how important it should be to their teen.

These research findings and others emphasize the important and necessary role that parents play in the cognitive lives of their adolescents.

School Contexts

During the past decade there has been a concerted effort to find out why there is a shortage of women in the science, math, engineering, and technical fields (AAUW, 1992). In 1995, 22% of America's scientists and engineers were women, compared to half of the social scientists. Women who do pursue careers in science, engineering, and mathematics most often choose fields in the biological sciences, where they represent 40% of the workforce, with smaller percentages found in mathematics or computer science (33%), the physical sciences (22%), and engineering (9%) (National Science Board, 1998).

Part of the answer to this question can be traced to gender differences in cognitive abilities in middle-school students. In early adolescence, females outperform males on several verbal skills tasks: verbal reasoning, verbal fluency, comprehension, and understanding logical relations (Hedges & Nowell, 1995). Males, on the other hand, outperform females on spatial skills tasks such as mental rotation, spatial perception, and spatial visualization (Voyer, Voyer, & Bryden, 1995) (see Figure 9.7). Adolescent males also perform better on mathematical achievement tests than females. However, gender differences do not apply to all aspects of mathematical skill. Males and females do equally well in basic math knowledge, and girls actually have better computational skills. It is performance in mathematical reasoning and geometry that shows the greatest difference (Fennema, Sowder, & Carpenter, 1999). Males also display greater confidence in their math skills, which is a strong predictor of math performance (Casey, Nuttall, & Pezaris, 2001). Table 9–1 provides a more extensive list of gender differences in cognitive abilities.

The poorer mathematical reasoning skills exhibited by many female adolescents have several educational implications. Beginning at age 12, girls begin to like math and science less and to like language arts and social studies more than boys do (Kahle & Lakes, 2003; Sadker & Sadker, 1994). They also do not expect to do as well in these subjects and attribute their failures to lack of ability (Eccles, Barber, Jozefowicz, Malenchuk, & Vida, 1999). By high school, girls self-select out of higher-level, "academic track" math and science courses, such as calculus and chemistry. One of the long-term consequences of these choices is that girls lack the prerequisite high-school math and science courses necessary to pursue certain majors in college (e.g., engineering, computer science). Consequently, the number of women who pursue advanced degrees in these fields is significantly reduced (Halpern, 2004).

Some researchers argue that the gender gap in mathematics is biologically driven. Select research shows that prenatal hormones circulating in the brain encourage differential development in the hemispheres of male and female fetuses (Berenbaum, Korman, & Leveroni, 1995). Others believe intelligence has its roots in genetics (Plomin, 2000; see chapter 3 for a review of behavioral genetics).

There is evidence, however, that sociocultural factors may influence girls' attitudes towards math and science. For example, parents tend to view math as more important for sons and language arts and social studies as more important for daughters (Andre, Whigham, Hendrickson, & Chambers, 1999). Parents are more likely to encourage their sons to take advanced high-school courses in chemistry, mathematics, and physics and have higher expectations for their success (Wigfield, Battle, Keller, & Eccles, 2002).

TABLE 9–1

Cognitive Tasks That Usually Show Sex Differences

Women Score Higher	Men Score Higher
Tasks that require rapid access to and use of phonological, semantic, and other information in long-term memory	Tasks that require transformations to visual working memory
Knowledge areas of literature and foreign languages	General knowledge
Production and comprehension of complex prose	Tests of fluid reasoning (especially in math and science)
Fine motor tasks	Motor tasks that involve aiming
Perceptual speed	Tasks that involve moving objects
Decoding nonverbal communication	
Perceptual thresholds (in multiple modalities)	
Higher grades in school (all or most subjects)	
Speech articulation	

Source: Based on "Sex Differences in Intelligence: Implications for Education" (p. 1102) by D. F. Halpern, *American Psychologist, 52* (10), pp. 1091–1102. Copyright by the American Psychological Association. Reprinted by permission of the author.

Mental rotation
Choose the responses that show the standard in a different orientation.

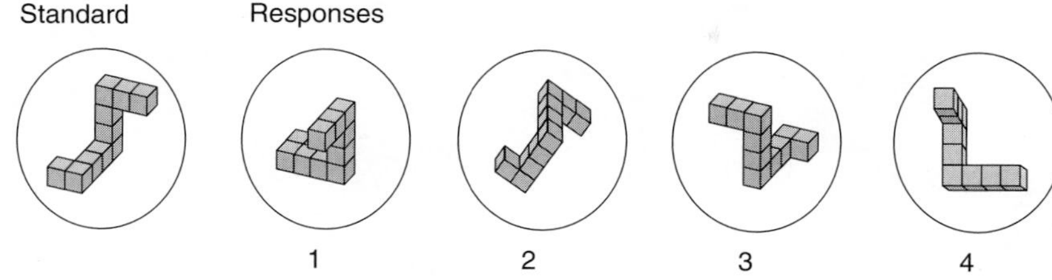

Spatial perception
Pick the tilted bottle that has a horizontal water line.

Spatial visualization
Find the figure embedded in the complex shape below.

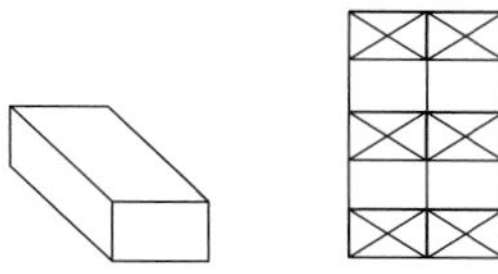

FIGURE 9.7 Types of Spatial Tasks
Examples of visual-spatial tasks on which adolescent boys typically outperform adolescent girls.

Source: From "Emergence and Characterization of Sex Differences in Spatial Ability: A Meta-analysis," by M. C. Linn & A. C. Petersen, 1985, *Child Development*, 56, pp. 1482, 1483, 1485. Copyright 1985 by the Society for Research in Child Development, Inc. Reprinted by permission of the society.

Teacher characteristics and the classroom environment also have been identified as contributors to this gender gap. Seventh and eighth graders attending math and science camps identified a math or science teacher as "a person who has made math, science, or engineering interesting" for them (Gilbert, 1996, p. 491). Unfortunately, many adolescent females report being passed over in classroom discussions, not encouraged by the teacher, and made to feel stupid (Sadker & Sadker, 1994). Classroom environments can be made to feel more "girl-friendly" by incorporating:

- Low levels of competition, public drill, and practice
- High levels of teacher attention
- Hands-on activities
- Female role models
- Same-sex cooperative learning communities
- Nonsexist books and materials (Evans, Whigham, & Wang, 1995)

Fortunately, sex differences in mathematical reasoning have begun to decline, and females' enrollments are up in math and science courses (Campbell, Hombo, & Mazzeo, 2000). Programs

Traditional science classes are intimidating and noninspiring for many girls. Small groups, a female teacher, and lessons about how science can be used to help people attract girls to science classes.

designed to interest girls in math and science and that demonstrate how this knowledge will allow them to help others appear to be working.

Community Contexts

Adolescents are coming of age today in an advanced technological society, described as the "knowledge society" or the "information society" as seen in Table 9-2 (Anderson, 2002, p. 177). Recall from chapter 7 that, globally, adolescents' everyday experiences include not only radio, television, and CDs but also computers, the Internet, cell phones, and MP3s. For example, an American survey of adolescent computer access and use revealed the following:

- Seventy-eight percent of youth ages 10 to 17 had a computer at home, and 98% of them said they used it. A majority of them said they used it "almost every day."
- Of those with a computer at home, 73% said they used their home computer for Internet access or email. Eighty-one percent said they had access to the Internet at school, and one third of them said they used it at school "almost every day." (Cole, 2004).

Adolescents 15 years of age and older report using this technology to play games, carry out school assignments, do word processing, utilize educational programs, email friends, and download graphics, in that order (U.S. Census Bureau, 2001c). How does this exposure to new methods of data gathering and information management influence the cognitive processes of adolescents?

A longitudinal study that followed seventh through twelfth graders showed that students who had computers at home had higher total grade point averages and higher grades in English and math and demonstrated more advanced scientific reasoning (Subrahmanyam, Kraut, Greenfield, & Gross, 2000). The greatest cognitive gains seem to come from highly interactive software that encourages students to use higher-order thinking skills and to gain conceptual knowledge (Weglinsky, 1998). While access to a computer may be an advantage to some students, the lack of access disadvantages others. Low-income adolescents tend to have less access to computers both at home and at the schools they attend. When they have access, they are more likely to use computers for remediation or practicing skills. Middle-class adolescents are more likely to use computers for research, analyses, and written expression (Becker, 2000).

A cautionary note offered by educators and practitioners is that technology alone does not make a process better. The computer may improve the learning skills of adolescents only when it is paired with supportive and pedagogically meaningful instruction.

TABLE 9–2

Implications of the Demands of the Global Knowledge Economy for Youth in Terms of Required Skills and Learning Strategies

The globalization of technology offers new contexts within which adolescents need to learn and work. As societies' needs change (e.g., demands of society), they require new and different skills from adolescents that must be shaped by their learning environments.

Demands of Society	Required Skills	Learning Strategies
Knowledge as commodity	Knowledge construction	Inquiry, project learning, constructivism
Rapid change, renewal	Adaptability	Learning to relearn, on-demand learning
Information explosion	Finding, organizing, retrieving	Multidatabase browsing exercises
Poorly organized information	Information management	Database construction
Poorly evaluated information	Critical thinking	Evaluation problem solving
Collective knowledge	Teamwork	Collaborative learning

Source: From "Youth and Information Technology," by R. E. Anderson, in J. T. Mortimer & R. W. Larson (Eds.), 2002, *The Changing Adolescent Experience: Societal Trends and the Transition to Adulthood* (p. 178). New York: Cambridge University Press. Reprinted by permission.

CHAPTER REVIEW

Cognitive Development in Adolescence

- The study of cognitive development in adolescence focuses on the growth in problem-solving skills and in the speed and efficiency of working with and retaining information.
- Cognitive advances in adolescence have an influence on decision-making skills and risk-taking behavior.
- One's general cognitive abilities can be assessed by intelligence and/or achievement tests.

Theoretical Viewpoints

- According to Piaget's theory of cognitive development, teenagers develop formal operational thought. They become capable of thinking about abstract concepts and about possibilities. They can systematically generate and test hypotheses and engage in reflective thought.
- Asynchrony, and the egocentrism of adolescence that emerges in the imaginary audience and personal fable, may limit the decision-making skills of adolescents.
- According to the information-processing perspective, adolescents show an increase in working memory capacity, quicker processing, and increases in knowledge base. They also have more sophisticated mnemonic strategies and advanced metacognitive skills at their disposal.
- Most adolescents operate at the multiplist level of epistemological understanding. They equate opinion with fact and view all information, opinion and fact, as equally legitimate.

Reasoning and Decision Making

- Adolescents develop scientific reasoning by identifying variables, holding all variables constant but one, and testing their hypotheses. Sometimes adolescents' misconceptions about scientific principles interfere with rational reasoning.
- Adolescents can engage in analytical thinking, but when they are presented with information that runs counter to a deeply held belief system, they use heuristic reasoning.
- Decision-making skills require setting a goal, generating and evaluating options to attain that goal, and then implementing the best option. When adolescents make decisions in their personal lives, they often overemphasize the benefits of a behavior compared to the risks involved.

Psychometric Approach to Intelligence

- The psychometric approach to intelligence focuses on individual and group differences in cognitive abilities. The emphasis is on creating tests that measure an outcome of intelligence.
- The first intelligence test, created by Binet and Simon in 1905, discriminated among low-achieving students in the French educational system. The current intelligence tests, *Stanford-Binet—V* and the WISC-IV, produce an IQ score that compares an adolescent's cognitive performance with same-aged peers.

- Adolescents' intelligence remains relatively stable over their lifetime, is highly related to achievement test scores, and is predictive of job performance and success.
- One major criticism of the use of intelligence tests is their cultural bias, in that both socioeconomic status and ethnicity can influence test performance.
- Two alternative views of intelligence are Gardner's theory of multiple intelligences and Sternberg's triarchic model of intelligence.

Cognitive Development in Context

- The involvement of parents in the school lives of adolescents increases their level of engagement in school and their achievement.
- A supportive school environment can enhance adolescent girls' interest and performance in math and science.
- The increasing availability of technology may change the way that adolescents process information.

TABLE 9–3
Summary of Developmental Theories

Chapter	Theories	Focus
9: Cognitive Development in Middle Adolescence	Cognitive-Developmental	Series of stages in which adolescents struggle to make sense of the world. Through active construction of schemata, they become abstract reasoners.
	Information Processing	How information is stored and operated on internally. Adolescents process information more quickly, use more effective strategies, and have a greater knowledge base upon which to build.

KEY TERMS

Absolutist
Analytical reasoning
Asynchrony
Combinatorial system
Conceptual knowledge
Convergent thinking
Creativity
Declarative knowledge
Desynchrony
Divergent thinking
Elaboration
Epistemological understanding
Evaluativists
Factor analysis
Heuristic reasoning
Hypothetico-deductive reasoning
Imaginary audience
Intelligence quotient
Metacognition
Metamemory
Multiple intelligences
Multiplists
Normal curve
Paired-association task
Personal fable
Primary mental abilities
Problem-based learning
Procedural knowledge
Propositional thought
Psychometric approach
Realists
Reflective thinking
Relativists
Stability
Standard deviation
Triarchic model

SUGGESTED ACTIVITIES

1. Carry out several of Piaget's formal operational tasks with children from 7 to 11 years of age and 12 or above. Study the approach different-aged children use in addition to the answers they give. Use probe questions to understand the adolescent's thought processes.
2. Discuss the concepts of imaginary audience and personal fable. Generate examples of each from your own experiences. How much did these concepts influence your decision making as an adolescent?
3. Observe adolescents playing video games in a video arcade. Identify the components an information-processing theorist would study. What can you conclude about the following: processing capacity (e.g., holding more than one variable in their heads),

speed of processing, game-strategy development, memory for rules and playing patterns, metacognitive skills (e.g., adjustments to poor game-playing)?

4. Write down on an index card a religious, political, or social issue you feel very strongly about. Find one article that opposes your position and write a one-page summary of that article. On the second page of the paper, write about your response to the article. Did this new information influence your position? Why or why not? Finally, identify where you are in Kuhn's stages of epistemological understanding and why you are at that stage.
5. Discuss whether several of Gardner's intelligences (e.g., interpersonal intelligence) or Sternberg's practical intelligence should be considered intelligence. Why or why not?

RECOMMENDED RESOURCES

Suggested Readings

Gardner, H. (1983). *Frames of mind: The theory of multiple intelligences.* New York: Basic Books.

Jessor, R. (Ed.) (1998). *New perspectives on adolescent risk behavior.* New York: Cambridge University Press.

O'Reilly, P., Penn, E. M., & deMarrais, K. (Eds.) (2001). *Educating young adolescent girls.* Mahwah, NJ: Erlbaum.

Steinberg, L. (1996). *Beyond the classroom: Why school reform has failed and what parents need to do.* New York: Touchstone.

Suggested Online Resources

Evaluating the National Outcomes: Youth—Social Competencies; Decision Making
http://ag.arizona.edu/fcs/cyfernet/nowg/sc_decision.html

Girls in Science, Girls in Research
http://www.uky.edu/PR/News/040305_girls_in_science.html

John D. and Catherine T. MacArthur Foundation Research Network on Adolescent Development and Juvenile Justice
http://www.adjj.org

Problem-Based Learning
http://ud-pbl@udel.edu

Suggested Web Sites

Cognitive Growth and Education
http://www.ncrel.org/sdrs/areas/at0cont.htm

Cognitive Changes in Adolescence
http://www.personal.psu.edu/faculty/n/x/nxd10/cognitiv.htm#top

Rubrics for the Triarchic Model of Intelligence in the Classroom
http://www.yale.edu/pace/resources

An Intelligence Test
http://iqtest.com

Suggested Films and Videos

Adolescent cognition: Thinking in a new key (1999). Insight Media, Inc. (30 minutes)

Intelligence (2001). RMI Media (30 minutes)

Teenage mind and body (1992). Insight Media, Inc. (30 minutes)

The 21st century classroom: Beyond standards and testing (2002). Insight Media, Inc. (80 minutes)

What if? Cognitive development in adolescence. (2003). Insight Media, Inc. (30 minutes)

CHAPTER 

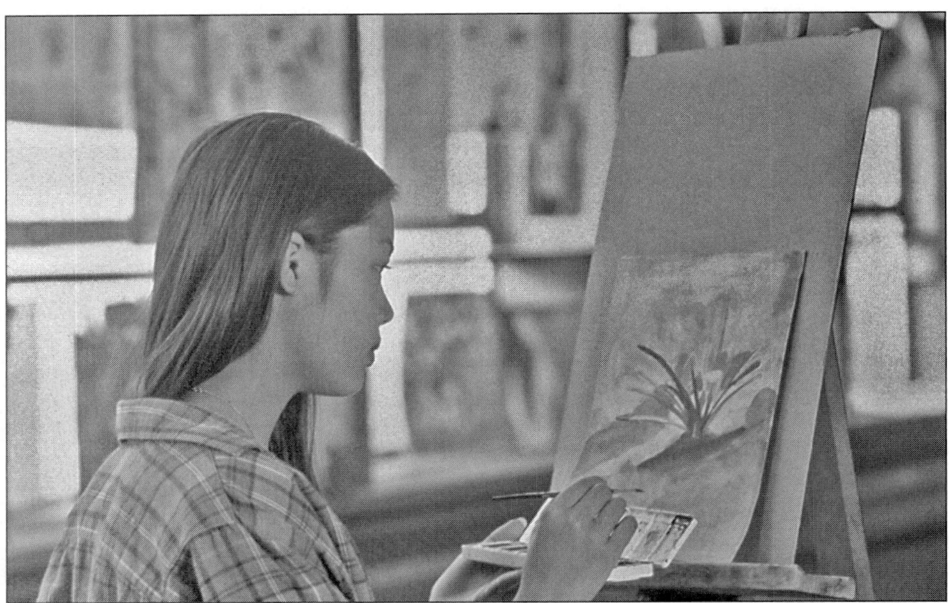

Affective Development in Middle Adolescence

CHAPTER OBJECTIVES

After reading this chapter, students will be able to:

- Define affective development in middle adolescence
- Summarize theories of adolescent individuation and autonomy
- Describe the development of identity in adolescence
- Discuss current research on emotion, self-esteem, and possible selves in adolescence
- Explain the contributions of family, school, and community contexts to affective development in middle adolescence

Sun is a 17-year-old Korean American with a strong desire to attend art school and become an artist. However, Sun's parents disapprove of her passion for art and think that her career choice should be about responsibility, not enjoyment. Her parents say that they will support her if she gets the necessary education to obtain a financially secure position. Her responsibility is to help others in her family, like her younger brother who plans to go to college and become a minister. But Sun really wants to be an artist and carries her sketchbook everywhere, drawing what she sees and how she feels despite her family's wishes.

Affective Development in Adolescence

The affective domain includes personality, self-understanding, and emotional development. During the teenage years, adolescents are beginning to experience autonomy, developing a sense of who they are, and feeling emotions and moods with a deepening intensity. A developmental model of self-understanding is illustrated in Figure 10.1. In early and middle adolescence, according to this model, the development of identity involves defining yourself (the "I") and imagining how others see you (the "Me"), which "provides the adolescent with the sense of self-continuity, as well as the experience of uniqueness or distinctness from others" (Damon, 1988, p. 74).

As we discussed in chapter 5, adolescents are able to consider their own beliefs and present a "false self" to others (Harter, 1998). Such a charade implies that adolescents must also have a sense of their "true self." But who is that person? Is it who you are (your actual self) or who you wish to

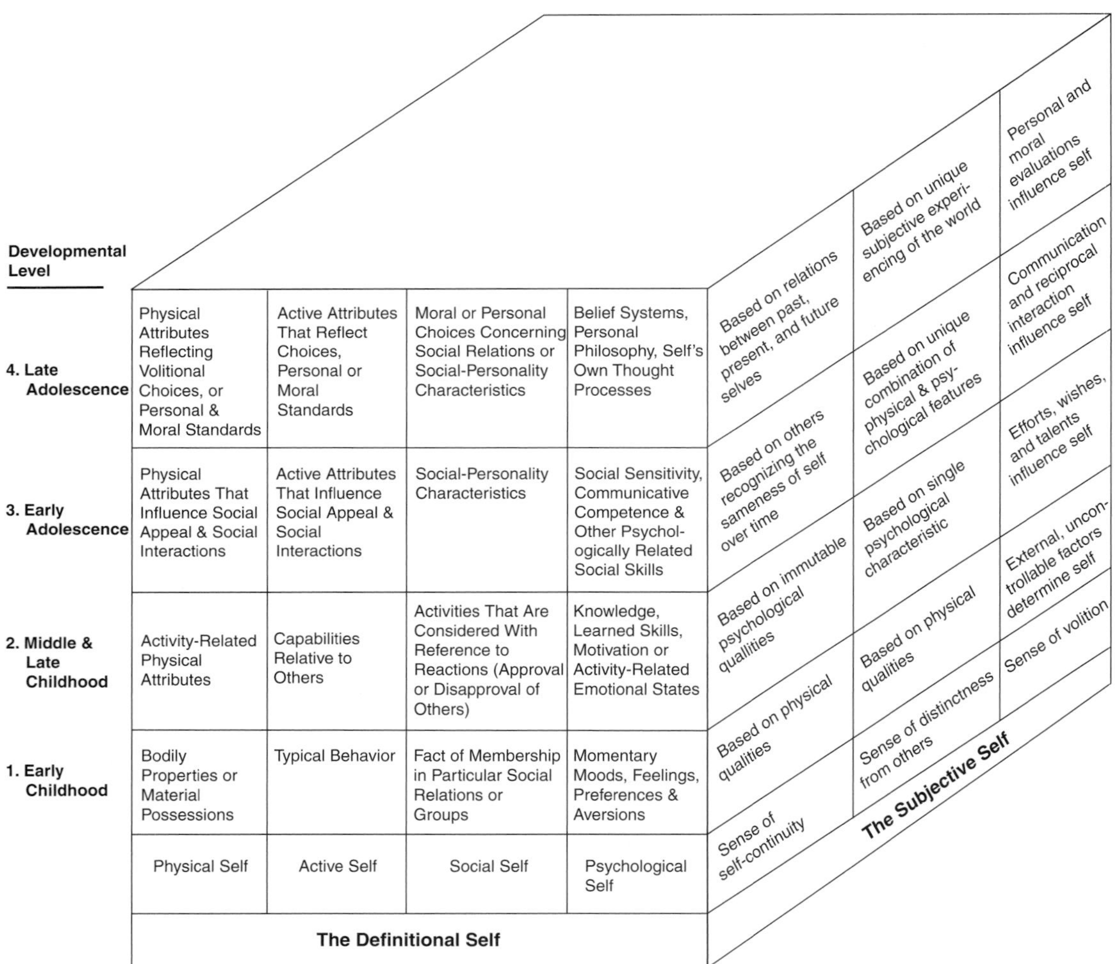

FIGURE 10.1 Developmental Model of Self-Understanding
In this three-dimensional model, the "I" is represented by the definitional self (front), and the "Me" is the subjective self (side).

Source: From "A Developmental Model of Self-Understanding" (p. 56) by W. Damon and D. Hart, in *Self-Understanding in Childhood and Adolescence*, 1988, New York: Cambridge University Press. Copyright 1988 by Cambridge University Press. Reprinted by permission.

become (your ideal self)? Contradictions between self-attributes in different contexts begin in midadolescence when cognitive development allows teens to detect—but not resolve—conflicting selves (Harter, Bresnick, Bouchey, & Whitesell, 1997; Harter, Waters, & Whitesell, 1998). Conflict is greatest when self-attributes oppose your true self, which may result in low self-esteem—especially if adolescents perceive little social support across the contexts in which they are constructing their "life story" (Harter et al., 1997). Figure 10.2, for example, depicts how an older adolescent described herself differently with a variety of people, such as peers, parents, or a potential boyfriend. The process of identity development requires that adolescents integrate various self-beliefs into a unified whole and perceive themselves as distinct individuals (Makros & McCabe, 2001). How middle adolescents negotiate the task of consolidating their self-understandings and others' perceptions into a personal ideology is the process of **identity** development (Harter, 1990).

Let's think about Sun. Is her true self a 17-year-old Korean American student or the artist she dreams of becoming? Does it matter how her family perceives her?

THEORETICAL VIEWPOINTS

Two theoretical perspectives inform the study of adolescent identity: psychoanalytic theory and social identity theory. According to psychoanalytic theory, teenagers' major psychological task involves becoming an increasingly autonomous individual—having a well-defined sense of who you are, what you believe in, and what you want to become. Whereas

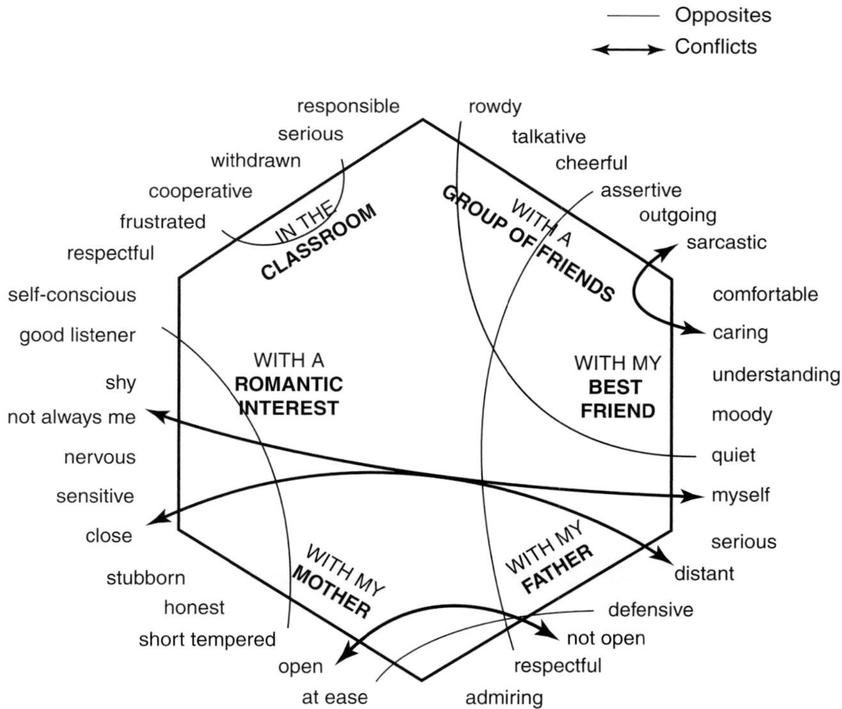

FIGURE 10.2 Multiple Selves in Adolescence
An adolescent girl filled in this hexagon with adjectives to describe her multiple selves with different people. Some terms are opposites (connecting lines); others are conflicts (arrows).

Source: From "The Development of Multiple Role-Related Selves During Adolescence" (p. 842), by S. Harter, S. Bresnick, H. A. Bouchey, and N. A. Whitesell, 1997, *Development and Psychopathology, 9*, pp. 835–853. Copyright 1997 by Cambridge University Press. Reprinted by permission.

a focus on the development of *self* is central to psychoanalytic views, social identity perspectives stress the importance of the social context in developing a sense of self that integrates multiple, intersecting identities, such as your gender, sexuality, race/ethnicity, and religion. First, however, teens must differentiate themselves from others, particularly their parents and other family members.

Psychoanalytic Perspectives

In psychoanalytic theories, the loosening of ties to parents is essential to becoming an individual capable of independent functioning (Zimmer-Gembeck & Collins, 2003). In his influential book *On Adolescence*, psychoanalyst Peter Blos (1962) asserted that achieving independence involves a process of **individuation**, or psychological separation, from parents. Individuation first occurs in early childhood (recall Erikson's autonomy stage described in chapter 5) and then is recapitulated in adolescence as teens seek greater independence from parents or other adults (Blos, 1962). Individuation is composed of two interrelated processes (Lapsley, 1993):

- **Intrapsychic.** Reviewing your sense of yourself (e.g., thinking about your likes and dislikes)
- **Interpersonal.** Renegotiating your family relationships (e.g., beginning to date)

In healthy families, individuation is encouraged within a context that maintains a balance between connection and separateness (Sabatelli & Mazor, 1985; Grotevant & Cooper, 1985), a process called *ego development* in psychoanalytic theory.

Ego development. Building on personality theory, **ego development** theory describes changes in self-definition that involve increasingly complex ways of becoming a separate individual (Muuss, 1996; Loevinger, 1976; Loevinger & Knoll, 1983; Westenberg, van Strien, & Drewes, 2001). As seen in Table 10–1, the stages reflect gradually maturing levels of autonomy (Broughton & Zahakevich, 1988). During early adolescence, *conformists* still depend on others for feedback. But by middle adolescence, most teens become more *self-aware*. Self-awareness, in turn, allows late adolescents to become *conscientious, or* responsible to others and to society. As *individualistic* emerging adults, most people increasingly become tolerant of others' differences and conflicting feelings. Finally, according to ego development theory, young adults eventually achieve *autonomy*, or the ability to maintain a distinct identity or role (Loevinger, 1990).

Seeking autonomy is seen as one of the key psychosocial tasks of normal adolescence (Zimmer-Gembeck & Collins, 2003). To define **autonomy**, developmental theorists usually refer to three related dimensions:

- **Behavioral Autonomy.** Active, independent functioning (e.g., self-regulation and decision making)
- **Cognitive Autonomy.** Believing that you have control over your life (e.g., being able to make decisions without excessive input or validation)
- **Affective Autonomy.** Gaining a sense of individuation from parents (e.g., becoming less emotionally dependent)

In adolescence, autonomy is associated with a general feeling of confidence and trust in one's own choices (Noom, Dekovic, & Meeus, 2001). Developmental researchers have found, however, that achieving a sense of autonomy does not necessarily imply severing connections with parents, but rather results in an increase in adolescents' self-reliance

TABLE 10–1
Loevinger's Stages of Ego Development

Age Range	Ego Level	Characteristic
2 to 7	Impulsive	Dependent
8 to 10	Self-protective	Wary
10 to 14	Conformist	Loyal
14 to 18	Self-aware	Helpful
18 to 21	Conscientious	Responsible
21 to 25	Individualistic	Tolerant
25 and up	Autonomous	Interdependent

(Cooper, Grotevant, & Condon, 1983; see also Collins, Gleason, & Sesma, 1997; Meeus, Iedema, Maassen, & Engels, 2005). They cite the fact that most teens maintain harmonious relationships with their families throughout adolescence. In fact, adolescents who score higher on measures of autonomy also rate their parents as more supportive than teens with lower degrees of autonomy (Lamborn & Steinberg, 1993). Feminist theorists have questioned the very notion of psychological autonomy—especially in the contexts of adolescent female identity. Psychologists studying women's development have demonstrated that girls define themselves more often through their interpersonal relationships than through separation and individuation (Gilligan, 1982; Josselson, 1988). Loevinger's ego development theory, however, is not necessarily incompatible with women's development. In fact, the instrument used to measure ego development stages includes items that assess compassion and caring for parents, children, and others (Thorne, 1993).

Think about what Sun is going through as she tries to achieve behavioral, cognitive, and emotional autonomy. She wants to become an art student but still maintain a close relationship with her family. When Sun wins a statewide art award, it is not something she can keep secret. Her family will hear about it. Besides, what her parents think still does matter to her.

Adolescent egocentrism. According to Blos (1969), adolescents must maintain a firm grasp on "who they are" while—at the same time—imagining "who they want to become." Psychoanalytic theorists have termed adolescents who focus excessively on themselves as *narcissistic*. According to social-cognitive theorists, however, a normal part of adolescent ego development is *adolescent egocentrism*. Discussed in chapter 9 from a cognitive perspective, *personal fables* and *imaginary audiences* also provide evidence of teens' ego development (Elkind, 1967, 1985). Recently, developmental theorists have integrated psychoanalytic and social-cognitive perspectives into a framework for adolescent ego development (Lapsley, 1993). In this synthesis, a "self-observing ego" is the result of the social-cognitive understanding of early adolescents (i.e., Selman's Level 3), who can see themselves as others see them and imagine an "admiring audience" (Laspley & Rice, 1988).

In Sun's case, her personal fable is that no one else could be going through what she is as an aspiring but misunderstood artist. Sun imagines that "everyone" will see her award-winning drawing in the statewide exhibition—an obvious exaggeration and evidence of her imaginary audience.

Researchers have suggested that personal fables may have an important role in the separation-individuation process, for example, in believing that you are unique (Goossens, Beyers, Emmen, & van Aken, 2002). In most cross-sectional studies of adolescents' personal fables, however, boys score higher than girls on uniqueness, omnipotence, and invulnerability (Goossens, Beyers, Emmen, & van Aken, 2002). But longitudinal research with adolescents also suggests that with age and social experience, personal fables seem to decline for both sexes, as discussed in chapter 9 (Vartanian & Powlishta, 1996). In support of this developmental hypothesis, a study compared adolescents aged 14 to 18 and adults aged 19 to 89 on adolescent egocentrism. Teenagers scored significantly higher than adults. However, when the adults were divided into younger, middle, and older adult subgroups, adolescents and young adults (ages 19–30) were not different. These results suggest that imaginary audiences and personal fables may not be confined to adolescence (Frankenberger, 2000).

Adolescent egocentrism, as part of a normative process of adolescent individuation, may protect teens from undue anxiety about separation and may impart a sense of mastery, coping, and self-worth (Lapsley, Flannery, Gottschalk, & Raney, 1996). Developmental psychologists have generally supported the idea that adolescents call upon fantasy (i.e., an imaginary audience) as a way of trying on new roles—as would be required by individuation. However, they also acknowledge that the feeling that you are unique (i.e., a personal fable) may be more characteristic of Western cultures, which emphasize individualism, than non-Western cultures, which are more communal (Vartanian, 2001).

Identity formation. In an influential work entitled *Identity: Youth and Crisis* (1968), Erikson applied a psychosocial approach to understanding identity formation. He theorized about the interaction between individuals' ego development and their social contexts, such as culture, family, and society, and defined **ego identity** as persons' awareness of their own uniqueness and of the continuity of their identity over time (Kroger, 2003). According to psychosocial theory (first discussed in chapter 5), identity formation in adolescence involves the ego's ability to synthesize aspects of self discovered during adolescence into a new identity that involves "feeling at home in one's body, a sense of 'knowing where one is going,' and an inner assuredness of anticipating recognition from those who count" (Erikson, 1968, p. 165).

Erikson also stressed the importance of providing adolescents with a psychological **moratorium**, or the time and space to experiment with different roles and beliefs. Although Erikson applied his theory of identity to diverse cultures, societies with an extended period of adolescence (discussed in chapter 7) are more likely to encourage such explorations of identity during the teen years. Perhaps because Erikson's (1968) theory of identity was published in the United States during the turbulent 1960s, his most widely adopted concept has been the **identity *crisis***, defined as a critical turning point in the life of an individual. Teenagers who have a crisis of identity commonly face "role confusion" as they explore alternative beliefs and commitments. Today, contemporary adolescents often express their search for identity in personal web pages or Internet journals, also called "blogs" (see chapter 6) (Stern, 1999).

As a high school student, did you experience feelings of identity confusion?

Identity versus identity confusion, the fifth stage in Erikson's lifespan theory, constitutes the primary developmental task of adolescence (refer to Figure 10.3). For Erikson, the identity-formation process involved exploration of various roles (e.g., occupational or family roles) followed by commitment to a particular identity. In adolescence, the task of consolidating one's self-concept and integrating it into a sense of personal identity becomes central. For example, adolescents typically struggle with existential questions such as "Who am I?" and epistemological questions such as "What do I believe?"

Sun questions not only her career and family roles but also her ethnic identity as an obedient Korean daughter.

Social-Psychological Perspectives

Social-psychological theory, a second important theoretical perspective on the development of adolescent identity, comes from the fields of social psychology and sociology. In this view, individuals construct personal meaning through interaction with others, called ***symbolic interaction***.

Sun, for example, is trying to figure out who she is in terms of how her teacher and her family

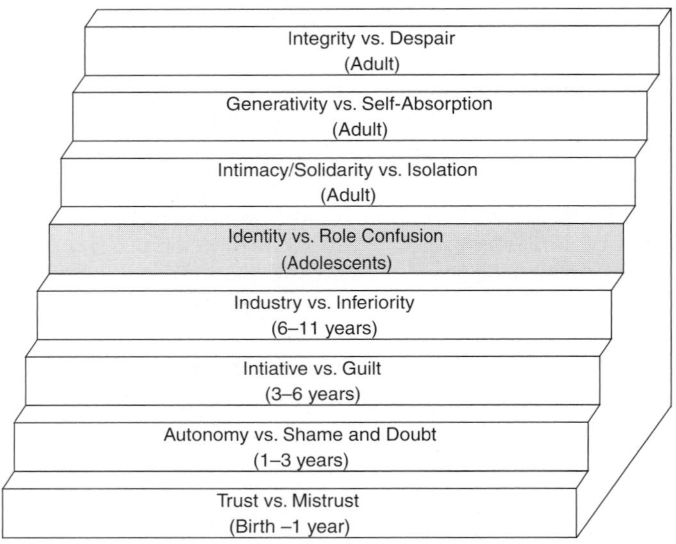

FIGURE 10.3 Adolescent Psychosocial Development
Erikson's developmental stage theory characterizes adolescence as a time of identity exploration.

Source: From *The Young Child: Development from Prebirth through Age Eight* (4th ed., p. 458) by M. B. Puckett & J. K. Black, 2005, Upper Saddle River, NJ: Merrill/Prentice Hall. Copyright 2005 by Prentice Hall Publishing Co. Adapted by permission of Pearson Education, Inc., Upper Saddle River, NJ.

view her, referred to in chapter 5 as her "looking-glass self."

Symbolic interaction theory. According to this view, individuals construct their identities through interactions with others. Symbolic interactions take place in a social context. This perspective, derived from the ideas of Mead and Cooley regarding the "I" and the "Me," asks questions, such as:

- What is the relationship between the self as "knower" and the self as "known"?
- Is there such a thing as a "unified" self or is it more appropriate to think of multiple selves, depending on the situation? (Côté & Levine, 2002)

Symbolic interactionists place the origins and functions of personal identity in the context of a person's enactment of social roles (Côté & Levine, 2002). In this sense, symbolic interaction theory complements Erikson's theory of identity. Some symbolic interaction theorists focus more on constructing an identity through social interaction, while others focus more on the roles available in the social structure (Côté & Levine, 2002). What all symbolic interactionists share, however, is an emphasis on the importance of the social context in figuring out "who you are."

Social-identity theory. Group identities that are collectively based—such as ethnicity, race, class, gender, or sexual orientation—are called ***social identities*** (e.g., Tajfel, 1981; Turner, 1987). Social-identity theory states that identity develops not only from an individual's sense of belonging to a particular group but also from an affective component in which self-esteem is based on positive feelings about your group membership (Umaña-Taylor, Yazedjian, & Bámaca-Gomez, 2004). For example, adolescents often derive a sense of belonging and connection from their peer group identity (Newman & Newman, 2001; Tarrant, 2002; Tarrant, North, Edridge, Kirk, Smith, & Turner, 2001). However, if society does not value the group to which one belongs (e.g., ethnic group), the individual will likely experience prejudice or discrimination and may exhibit lowered self-esteem (Phinney, Cantu, & Kurtz, 1997).

Feminist theorists also have described the *intersection* of multiple identities (Collins, 1991). **Intersectionality** refers to the ways that social identities (e.g., race, ethnicity, class, gender, sexuality, nationality, ability, and religion) mutually construct one another. The concept of intersectionality requires us to examine how social institutions, patterns of social interactions, and other social practices may influence the choices, opportunities, and identities that individuals and groups make and claim as their own (DeReus, Few, & Blume, 2005). For example, given the prevalence of gender-linked racial stereotypes, African American adolescents must understand not just what it means to be Black, but what it means to be a Black American male or female (Swanson, Spencer, Dell'Angelo, Harpalani, & Spencer, 2002).

Let's reflect again on the case study. Exploring her desire to study art, Sun must consider her emergent identity as an artist in interaction with her religious and ethnic identities. She is pretty sure that she knows what is coming: Her mother will say to put herself in God's hands.

Postmodern identities. Recall from chapter 7 that postmodern views of adolescence emphasize the fluidity and changing nature of identity. Contemporary psychologists often view identity as a series of narratives or autobiographical stories (e.g., Gergen, 1991; Thorne, 2004). Such a postmodern view contrasts with Erikson's emphasis on the adolescent task of establishing the continuity of identity over time, even under varying conditions (Côté & Levine, 2002). Contemporary researchers, however, are also studying how people configure an integrated identity when presented with potentially conflicting identifications, such as religion and sexual identity (Schachter, 2004).

To theorize adolescent identity from a postmodern perspective is to capture the fluidity of identities by examining socially constructed differences. For example, adolescent identity exploration might involve experimenting with piercing, tattooing, or hair dyeing, reflecting changing images in popular culture (Blume & Blume, 2003). In this approach to identity, adolescents are thinking, feeling social agents who reflect on the prevailing cultural discourse and on the options available to them (DeReus, Few, & Blume, 2005; Schachter, 2005).

Sun experiments with her identity as an aspiring artist. She dresses like the downtown art students: white shirts and black jeans.

Research on Identity in Middle Adolescence

One of the most popular research approaches to studying identity has been to explore the relationship between Erikson's notions of *exploration* and *commitment* (Berzonsky & Adams, 1999; Kroger, 2003). **Exploration** refers to the examination of alternatives with the intent of establishing a firm commitment in the near future; **commitment** refers to a stable investment in one's goals as evidenced by actions (Archer, 1993). Why should we be interested in helping adolescents explore their options and make commitments? Identity researchers have established five critical functions of identity development, described in Table 10–2 (Adams & Marshall, 1996; Serafini & Adams, 2002).

Dress is one way that teens experiment with their identities.

Identity Status

Identity research typically examines how adolescents differ in their approach to exploring identity issues and making commitments in a variety of identity domains originally proposed by Erikson, such as vocational, sex-role, and religious values

TABLE 10–2

Functions of Identity

In adolescence, identity functions in five important ways to enhance self-understanding.

Functions of Identity	Definition
Function 1	
To provide the structure for understanding who one is	Identity provides an awareness of the self as an independent and unique individual. It is most apparent when it is about to transform or change, in which change is accompanied by extreme identity consciousness. A sense of understanding who one is provides the structure for (a) self-certainty and self-esteem and (b) a foundation for an emerging and unfolding self.
Function 2	
To provide meaning and direction through commitments, values, and goals	Identity is based on the capacity for faith that commitments or chosen values or goals will receive institutional confirmation. The commitments or goals of identity direct or channel behaviors and actions.
Function 3	
To provide a sense of personal control and free will	Identity is based on the distinctions between passivity or compliance and an active or willful nature. Passive forms of identity are based on compliance, imitation, and identification. Active forms of identity are based on self-expression, independent construction, and a sense of free will and autonomy.
Function 4	
To provide consistency, coherence, and harmony between values, beliefs, and commitments	Identity formation is based on the organizing agency of synthesis or integration at one point and across time. Identity in its best state offers a sense of coherence between values, beliefs, and commitments. This sense of coherence is accompanied with harmony or low anxiety and a sense of peace with one's self.
Function 5	
To provide the ability to recognize potential in the form of future possibilities and alternative choices	A sense of identity is, in part, based on self-initiative and on a sense of purpose that offers the promise of fulfilling one's range of capacities. Thus, self-initiative, purpose, and capacities offer the promise of a tangible future.

Source: "Functions of Identity: Scale Construction and Validation" (p. 367), by T. E. Serafini & G. R. Adams, 2002, *Identity: An International Journal of Theory and Research, 2* (4), pp. 361–389. Copyright © 2002 by Lawrence Erlbaum Associates, Inc. Reprinted by permission of the authors.

(Waterman, 1999). Researchers have created various interviews and questionnaires to assess identity. See Box 10.1 for sample items from a widely used paper-and-pencil questionnaire on identity (Adams, Bennion, & Huh, 1989). This measure is especially helpful for evaluating *ideological identity*, such as religious or political values, and *interpersonal identity*, such as family and sex roles. Based on the degree of individuals' exploration and commitment in many of these domains, four categories of identity resolution, called **identity statuses**, have been identified (Marcia, 1966):

- **Achieved.** Exploring meaningful life directions prior to making commitments (e.g., successfully considering your identity choices)
- **Foreclosed.** Making commitments without meaningful exploration of alternatives (e.g., doing what your parents want without questioning)
- **Moratorium.** Actively searching for meaningful roles but not yet making commitments (e.g., exploring your options)
- **Diffused.** Not yet interested in exploring or making commitments (e.g., not yet experiencing a crisis)

These four statuses can vary from high to low levels of exploration and commitment, as shown in Table 10–3.

Although there is *not* a fixed developmental sequence to the identity statuses, identity-status transitions usually occur from diffusion, through foreclosure and moratorium, in the direction of achievement (Waterman, 1985, 1993). However, many adolescents in the foreclosure status often have a positive sense of well-being (Archer, 1993; Meeus et al., 1999). In other words, both identity statuses with a high level of commitment (i.e., foreclosed and achieved) appear to be related to

BOX 10.1 ROADMAP TO UNDERSTANDING THEORY AND RESEARCH

Revised Objective Measure of Ego Identity Status

This research instrument was designed by Gerald Adams and his colleagues to assess adolescents' ideological and interpersonal identity domains. Respondents are instructed to read each item in the statement and to indicate the degree the statement reflects their own thoughts and feelings on a scale of strongly agree to strongly disagree. Sample items from different domains follow for each identity status:

Ideological Scale

- **Diffused.** I haven't chosen the occupation I really want to get into, and I'm just working at whatever is available until something better comes along. (Occupation)
- **Foreclosed.** I guess I'm pretty much like my folks when it comes to politics. I follow what they do in terms of voting and such. (Politics)
- **Moratorium.** I'm not so sure what religion means to me. I'd like to make up my mind but I'm not done looking yet. (Religion)
- **Achieved.** After a lot of self-examination I have established a very definite view on what my own lifestyle will be. (Philosophy of Life)

Interpersonal Scale

- **Diffused.** I've never really seriously considered men's and women's roles in marriage. It just doesn't seem to concern me. (Family)
- **Foreclosed.** I only pick friends my parents would approve of. (Friendship)
- **Moratorium.** I'm trying out different types of dating relationships. I just haven't decided what is best for me. (Sex Roles)
- **Achieved.** I've chosen one or more recreational activities to engage in regularly from lots of things and I'm satisfied with those choices. (Recreation)

Items from the full scale are then combined to result in scores for each of the four identity statuses (diffused, foreclosed, moratorium, achieved) across the two types of domains: ideological and interpersonal.

Source: Based on *An Objective Measure of Ego Identity Status: A Reference Manual* (pp. 105–111), by G.R. Adams, L. Bennion, & K. Huh, University of Guelph, Canada, 1989. Copyright 1989 by Gerald R. Adams.

TABLE 10–3

Matrix of Identity Statuses

Adolescents' identity status depends on varying levels of exploration and commitment.

	Commitment	
Exploration	**High**	**Low**
High	Achieved	Moratorium
Low	Foreclosed	Diffused

positive adjustment, On the other hand, in most identity-status research, teens in diffusions or moratoriums are more likely to be either unfocused or anxious compared to foreclosed or achieved teens who have already made commitments, for example, to college or to a job. Highest in self-esteem are those individuals who have achieved identity, followed by those in moratorium (Damon, 1983b). In addition, for many ethnic-minority adolescents—including African American, Asian American, Latino American, and Eastern European—ethnic identity achievement is positively related to self-esteem (Bracey, Bámaca, & Umaña-Taylor, 2004; Umaña-Taylor, Diversi, & Fine, 2002; Valk, 2000).

In studies of early or middle adolescents (i.e., under age 18), researchers have found that *most* teens are in either the diffused or foreclosed statuses (Archer, 1982, 1993). *But not all teens experience a crisis of identity during the high-school years* (see Waterman, 1985). In longitudinal research with late adolescents (ages 18 to 22), over half were *still* either diffused or foreclosed across all content domains, suggesting that considerable identity development may take place in early adulthood (Kroger, 2000). Moreover, when adolescent identity exploration characteristic of the moratorium or achieved statuses does occur, it has been strongly linked to *moderate* levels of both separation and connection with parents (Kroger, 2000), suggesting that teens do not have to rebel to "find" themselves.

Erikson (1968) originally theorized that young men and women would follow different pathways to identity resolution because he believed that males are more concerned with occupational goals and that females are more concerned with interpersonal relationships. However, little or no support for gender differences in identity formation has been found *at any age* (Kroger, 1997). Although some researchers suggest that the identity domains of family and sexuality may hold more salience for adult women than men (e.g., Gilligan, 1982; Josselson, 1987, 1988), adolescent girls do not put aside identity concerns to focus on relationships (Kroger, 1997). In high school, for example, both boys and girls hold similar identity statuses in the domains of occupational choice, religious beliefs, and sex-role orientation (Archer, 1989). In terms of identity development trajectories, both sexes move from foreclosure and diffusion to moratorium and achievement. Some studies have found, however, that boys undergo this transition later than girls, perhaps due to differences in the timing of puberty (Kroger, 1997).

Identity processes. Identity researchers have recently suggested that particular information-processing styles may characterize the various identity statuses (Berzonsky, 2003; see also Krettenauer, 2005). According to this social-cognitive model (see Figure 10.4), individuals differ in the manner in which they construct and change their identities, using three distinct **identity styles**:

- **Information-oriented.** Seeking out information when solving problems and making decisions (e.g., searching the Internet for colleges or career options)
- **Normative.** Conforming to the prescriptions of significant others and peers (e.g., following the advice of a school counselor)
- **Diffuse/Avoidant.** Being reluctant to face up to problems and conflicts (e.g., refusing to think about life after graduation)

In studies of identity styles, college students who were in the moratorium or achieved identity statuses were more often information-oriented, foreclosures were more often normative, and diffusions used an avoidant approach more often (Berzonsky & Sullivan, 1992).

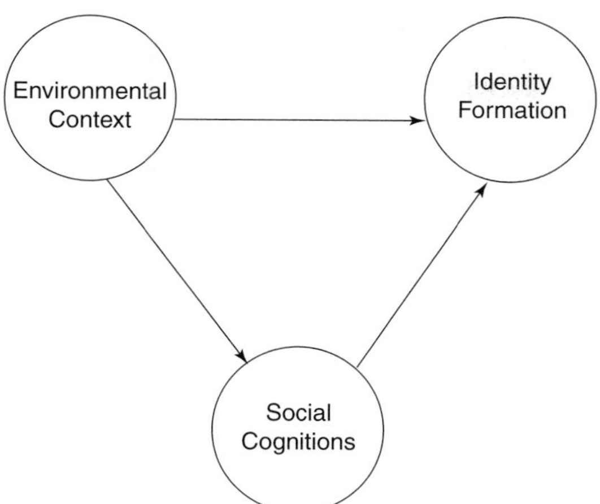

FIGURE 10.4 A Social-Cognitive Model of Identity

Identity formation is influenced directly by the environmental context in which it occurs and indirectly as adolescents think about themselves and others (social cognitions).

Source: From "Reevaluating the Identity Status Paradigm: Still Useful after 35 Years" (p. 582), by M. D. Berzonsky and G. R. Adams, 1999, *Developmental Review, 19*, pp. 557–590. Copyright 1999 by Academic Press. Reprinted by permission of Elsevier.

What are the implications for early or middle adolescents? It seems likely that high-school students' concerns with peer conformity would predispose teens to be overrepresented in the normative identity-processing style. As a result, helping high-school students to process relevant information pertaining to career or relationship decisions may enhance their identity exploration. For instance, school curricula could encourage critical discussions of how adolescents are limited in their attempts to explore certain roles (e.g., boys becoming nurses or elementary school teachers and girls becoming scientists or politicians) because of stereotyped gender discourse in the wider culture. Box 10.2 describes a program called *Life Choices* that was designed to help teens with identity exploration based on the three identity-processing styles (Ferrer-Wreder et al., 2002).

Although many identity researchers posit that adolescents (and adults) construct their identities from available alternatives, others claim that identity formation involves "finding yourself" through a process of discovering your unique talents and dispositions (Schwartz, 2002). Such a discovery model of identity also has clear implications for adolescent development. Recall from chapter 5 our discussion of Erikson's stage of middle childhood industry, in which the child develops a sense of self-competence. In adolescence, teachers and parents can enhance identity formation by reviewing with teens the areas in which they have specific skills, general competencies, or potential abilities.

In the chapter case study, the art teacher supports Sun's talent by submitting her drawing to the state art competition. Sun's winning an award may lead to her "discovery" of a possible future as an artist.

What if, however, an adolescent's actual attributes differ from those characteristics that the teen may wish to obtain? According to Erikson (1968), the more developed a person's sense of identity, the more congruity (or less discrepancy) there should be among the adolescent's self-beliefs, referred to as **self-discrepancy**. Self-discrepancies can exist between persons' actual and ideal selves (i.e., who they are versus who they want to become) or between persons' self-image and others' ideals (i.e., who they are or want to become versus what others want them to be). Self-discrepancies may also exist if there is a mismatch between who they actually are and what they (or others) think they *ought* to be (Makros & McCabe, 2001).

Here, Sun's struggle against her family's expectations indicates self-discrepancy with others' ideals.

In identity status research with high-school students aged 14 to 18, adolescents who were foreclosed and achieved had lower self-discrepancy ratings than the moratorium or diffused teens. These findings support the idea that foreclosed and achieved adolescents are fairly satisfied with the way they are (Makros & McCabe, 2001). Alternatively, these results may suggest that adolescents who have not yet found and made commitments to an ideological or interpersonal identity need support for exploration from teachers, parents, and other adults.

Several studies have found that ethnic-minority adolescents in the United States (e.g., African American, Asian American, Mexican American, and Native American) are more often foreclosed in both interpersonal and ideological identities than teenagers from the majority culture, suggesting that fewer options for exploration may be available to minorities, or that ethnic-minority teens may be less inclined to explore outside their own groups (Markstrom-Adams, 1992). An alternative identity framework that integrates social, historical, and cultural contexts with a developmental perspective

BOX 10.2 ROADMAP TO SUCCESSFUL PRACTICE

The *Making Life Choices Program*

The *Making Life Choices Program* (MLCP) is an intervention designed to provide opportunities for teens to develop the skills and competencies for making identity commitments by creating contexts in which adolescents themselves can discover their own ability to influence the direction of their lives. MLCP was originally designed for multiethnic adolescents in an alternative high school who were evaluated by their school system as being at risk for problem behaviors.

In the program, participants engage in learning activities to generate plans of action and to address the identified choices and challenges. By engaging in this reciprocal process, teens come to acquire greater critical understanding, transform their sense of control and responsibility, and increase their ability to define for themselves who they are and what they believe in. The MLCP intervention activities are designed to encourage change in four areas:

1. **Skills/Knowledge.** Promotion of critical problem solving and decision making
2. **Attitudes.** Increasing teens' sense of control over and responsibility for life choices and their consequences
3. **Identity Styles.** Increasing use of the informational style and reducing use of the normative and diffuse/avoidant styles
4. **Exploration and Commitment.** Defining a direction and purpose that is worthy of personal commitment

Both quantitative and qualitative evaluations of the *Making Life Choices Program* are positive overall. Participants in the intervention program showed significant gains in their skills, knowledge, and attitudes. Results for identity-style orientation and exploration/commitment also showed a trend towards positive gains. Narrative histories provided additional indications of the impact of intervention on the lives of these adolescents as well as barriers to implementation.

For example, one teen had a long history of school failure and involvement in the juvenile justice system. His behavior in the initial sessions was dominated by a "one-sided" and reactive approach to life. However, with time, he displayed a changing pattern of behavior by engaging the group in a dialogue on the problem and how to solve it. With a growing sense of mastery, he was able to deal with even the most difficult aspects of his life. The evaluation study concluded that the opportunity to engage in MLCP activities changed the pattern of participants' lives toward identity exploration and commitment.

Source: Based on "Promoting Identity Development in Marginalized Youth" by Laura Ferrer-Wreder et al., 2002, *Journal of Adolescent Research, 17*(2), pp. 168–187. Copyright © 2002 by Sage Publications.

was originally developed to describe identity formation in African American youth (Spencer, 1995; Swanson, Spencer, Dell'Angelo, Harpalani, & Spencer, 2002). From this perspective, as self-perceptions are gained by ethnic-minority adolescents in interaction with their environment (e.g., home, school, and church or mosque), racial/ethnic identity emerges.

Racial/Ethnic Identity

Identity development involves defining yourself both as an individual and as a social group member. **Racial identity** refers to your sense of self compared to other perceived racial groups (for a recent review, see Helms, 2003). This definition is based on the assumption that racial categories are socially constructed. For example, people are usually treated as if they belong to only one racial group (e.g., White or Black) even though such racial groupings have no biological basis. Racial categories are often based solely on physical appearance (i.e., skin color), an aspect of self-identity most salient for many adolescents (Helms, 2003). Consistent with social-identity theory, most studies of racial identity describe stages of identification: from low racial or ethnic awareness, often with a preference for the majority culture, to an appreciation and acceptance of your own racial/ethnic group (Phinney & Rosenthal, 1992; see also Vandiver, Cross, & Worrell, 2002).

How did your adolescent experiences create a sense of racial belonging and ethnic pride?

Four stages in the development of racial identity have been described (Table 10–4). From the

Guideposts for Working with Adolescents

- Support adolescent experimentation with dress, hairstyle, interests, and music without unnecessary criticism of their choices.
- Accept teenagers' expressions of unorthodox opinions as they explore different roles or ideologies and do not overreact.
- Talk with adolescents about their unique gifts and talents and support their creative expression or academic and athletic abilities.
- Since many teenagers have no idea what they want to do after high school (i.e., diffused identity), some are open to exploration (i.e., moratorium status), while others will be firmly set on their career or college goals (i.e., foreclosed or achieved), start from where they are.
- Encourage critical thinking about how the dominant cultural discourse may limit identity pathways for females, ethnic-minority adolescents, or different social-economic classes.

social-identity perspective, racial identity is influenced by direct interactions (e.g., parents, teachers) and indirect influences (e.g., media, peers) in the sociocultural environment, often called *racial socialization*. **Racial socialization** refers to the laws, customs, or traditions that teach individuals to value (or disparage) their own racial/ethnic groups or themselves as group members (Helms, 2003). In a study of African American parents, positive socialization messages were less frequent than were messages promoting mistrust or preparing their 9- to 14-year-olds for bias (Hughes & Chen, 1997). Compared to their peers, African American school-age children have more differentiated ideas about racism and negative evaluations of their own group. However, by age 10, 80% of African American and Latino children and 63% of White and Asian American children are aware of racism (McKown, 2004).

Ethnic identity. A closely related construct, **ethnic identity**, refers to a sense of belonging to an ethnic group, such as Latinos or African Americans (Phinney & Rosenthal, 1992; Rotheram & Phinney, 1987). Most, but not all, ethnic-identity research has been conducted with members of racial/ethnic minorities.

TABLE 10–4

Stages of Racial Identity

Positive racial identity develops gradually—from little or no identification with your racial/ethnic group to the eventual integration of your culture with your personal identity.

Stage	Description	Example
1. Pre-encounter	Preferring the dominant culture's values to your own culture	Perceiving your physical features as unattractive
2. Encounter	Wanting to identify with your racial/minority group, but not knowing how	Realizing you will never belong to the majority culture
3. Immersion/emersion	Immersing yourself in your minority culture and rejecting the dominant society	Participating in cultural explorations and discussions of racial issues
4. Internalization/ commitment	Experiencing a sense of fulfillment by integrating your personal and racial identities	Becoming socially active by fighting racial discrimination

Source: Based on "Racial Identity and Racial Socialization as Aspects of Adolescents' Identity Development," by J. E. Helms, in R. M. Lerner, F. Jacobs, and D. Wertleib (Eds.), 2003, *Handbook of Applied Developmental Science: Promoting Positive Child, Adolescent, and Family Development Through Research, Policies, and Programs, Vol. 1* (pp. 143–163), Thousand Oaks, CA: Sage.

Adolescents who belong to racial/ethnic minorities may differ with respect to their

- Self-identification as a group member
- Feelings of commitment to the group
- Positive or negative attitudes toward the group
- Sense of shared values, traditions, and customs (Phinney & Rosenthal, 1992)

A sense of ethnic identity and the ability to be **bicultural** (i.e., navigate between your ethnic-minority culture and the majority culture) have been found to be protective factors against such problem behaviors as youth violence, whereas **acculturation**, or assimilating into the majority culture, is a potential risk factor for adolescents (Soriano et al., 2004). For example, in a recent study of 12- to 15-year-olds from a Southeastern American Indian community, most adolescents were either self-protective or conformist on a measure of ego development and expressed positive feelings about their ethnic affiliation. However, postconformist Indian teens with greater needs for identity exploration had the highest levels of psychological distress and family conflict (Newman, 2005).

Ethnic-identity researchers have conducted numerous studies using identity status classifications that are consistent with Eriksonian theory (see Phinney, 1989). For example, in-depth interviews with Asian American, African American, and Latino high-school students revealed that about half of the adolescents had not explored their ethnicity (i.e., diffused or foreclosed), about one quarter were engaged in exploration (i.e., moratorium), and about one quarter had explored and were committed to an ethnic identity (i.e., achieved). As expected, ethnic-identity-achieved students also had the highest scores on a separate measure of ego identity (Phinney, 1989; see also Newman, 2005). See Table 10–5 for sample responses from each ethnic-identity status.

Recently, researchers examined a diverse sample of 11 graders from 88 different ethnic backgrounds (e.g., Polish, Vietnamese, Mexican, Native American) using a scale designed to assess three components of ethnic-identity formation (Umaña-Taylor, Yazedjian, & Bámaca-Gomez, 2004):

1. **Exploration.** The degree to which individuals have explored their ethnicity
2. **Resolution.** The degree to which they have resolved what their ethnicity means to them
3. **Affirmation.** The positive or negative feelings that come with resolution

Not surprisingly, higher levels of family ethnic socialization were associated with greater exploration and resolution of teenagers' ethnic identity (i.e., commitment). In addition, higher scores on resolution and affirmation were related to adolescents' self-esteem (Umaña-Taylor, Yazedjian, & Bámaca-Gomez, 2004).

Biracial/multiethnic identity. What if an adolescent is biracial or multiethnic? Some biracial adolescents may have difficulty integrating both racial heritages into a coherent identity (Collins, 2000). The *Multigroup Ethnic Identity Measure* was developed to examine similarities and differences in ethnic identity among adolescents from different racial/ethnic groups (Phinney, 1992). Using this measure, no differences in ethnic identity have been found between multiracial and monoracial Black and Asian high-school students, but multiracial adolescents with one White parent and one minority parent had higher ethnic-identity scores than monoracial White teenagers (Phinney & Alipuria, 1996). However, other researchers have found that early adolescents from monoracial minority groups and multiracial subgroups scored similarly on overall ethnic identity (Spencer et al., 2000), suggesting that ethnic identity may still be emerging in younger teens.

Overall, biracial adolescents from ages 13 to 20 scored higher on ethnic identity than Whites but lower than their Black, Asian, and Latino peers. These results suggest that when compared to their ethnic-minority peers, biracial adolescents may have less commitment or more inconsistent feelings about their ethnicity. However, for all racial/ethnic groups, including biracial adolescents, ethnic identity was related to positive self-esteem (Bracey, Bámaca, & Umaña-Taylor, 2004; see also Umaña-Taylor, Diversi, & Fine, 2002; Carson, Uppal, & Prosser, 2000).

Too often, researchers may assume that White adolescents do not develop an ethnic identity (Perry, 2001). However, ethnic-identity researchers studying Greek, Italian, and English adolescents living in Australia found that teens' feelings of being "ethnic" depend on the situation and the people they are with (Rosenthal & Hrynevich, 1985). Similarly, U.S. researchers have found that American Jewish teens (ages 11 to 13) had high levels of ethnic belonging compared to an older group (ages 15 to 18), possibly because they were more involved in religious activities preceding their Bar or Bat Mitzvahs (Davey, Eaker, Fish, & Klock, 2003).

TABLE 10–5

Ethnic-Identity Development

These quotations illustrate adolescents' ethnic-identity development.

Diffusion

"My past is back there; I have no reason to worry about it. I'm American now." (Mexican-American male)

"Why do I need to learn about who was the first Black woman to do this or that? I'm just not too interested." (Black female)

"My parents tell me . . . about where they lived, but what do I care? I've never lived there." (Mexican-American male)

Foreclosure

"I don't go looking for my culture. I just go by what my parents say and do, and what they tell me to do, the way they are." (Mexican-American male)

Foreclosure (Negative)

"If I could have chosen, I would choose to be American White, because it's America and I would then be in my country." (Asian-American male)

"I would choose to be White. They have more job opportunities and are more accepted." (Mexican-American male)

Moratorium

"I want to know what we do and how our culture is different from others. Going to festivals and cultural events helps me to learn more about my own culture and about myself." (Mexican-American female)

"I think people should know what Black people had to go through to get to where we are now." (Black female)

"There are a lot of non-Japanese people around me and it gets pretty confusing to try and decide who I am." (Asian-American male)

Achieved

"People put me down because I'm Mexican, but I don't care anymore. I can accept myself more." (Mexican-American female)

"I have been born Filipino and am born to be Filipino . . . I'm here in America, and people of many different cultures are here too. So I don't consider myself only Filipino, but also American." (Asian-American male)

"I used to want to be White, because I wanted long flowing hair. And I wanted to be real light. I used to think being light was prettier, but now I think there are pretty dark-skinned girls and pretty light-skinned girls. I don't want to be White now. I'm happy being Black." (Black female)

Source: From "Stages of Ethnic Identity Development" (p. 44), by J. S. Phinney, 1989, *Journal of Early Adolescence, 9*, pp. 34–49.

Recently, multicultural psychologists have called for relating ethnicity and gender in developmental research (Reid, 2002). In a Canadian study of ethnic identity, for example, immigrant Chinese mothers' ethnic-identity scores were correlated with their teenage daughters' scores but not with those of their teenage sons, suggesting the importance of examining the interaction of gender and ethnicity during adolescence (Kester & Marshall, 2003).

What does her Korean American ethnicity mean to Sun? Ethnic socialization is evidenced by her father's expectations of a sense of obligation to an intergenerational extended family and by her mother's strong faith. However, at her school or in the wider community context, it appears that Sun does not feel very Korean.

Spiritual/Religious Identity

Adolescents' search for identity is frequently described as a search for meaning. G. Stanley Hall called adolescence a stage of *conversion*, or a shift from concern with only oneself to a concern for others and a search for the meaning of life (Ream & Savin-Williams, 2003). The findings of contemporary researchers have supported this notion, discovering positive relationships between adolescents' religious identity, their concern for others, and their quest for personal meaning (e.g., Furrow, King, & White, 2004).

Faith, spirituality, and *religion* are related systems of meaning through which adolescents seek to understand their reason for being and their place in the universe. Developmental researchers, faith-based practitioners, and religious educators

Guideposts for Working with Adolescents

- Ask adolescents to name their racial/ethnic identities, avoiding racial categorization based on appearance.
- Encourage adolescents to explore their ethnicity through discussions of films, literature, music, poetry, and cultural celebrations.
- Recognize that adolescents' ethnic or racial identities may "feel" stronger or weaker depending on the context (e.g., home or school) and with whom they are interacting (e.g., parents or peers).
- Create a positive school climate for all ethnic-minority groups by avoiding comparisons to the majority culture.
- Since White students also belong to ethnic groups, help them explore their family histories of immigration.

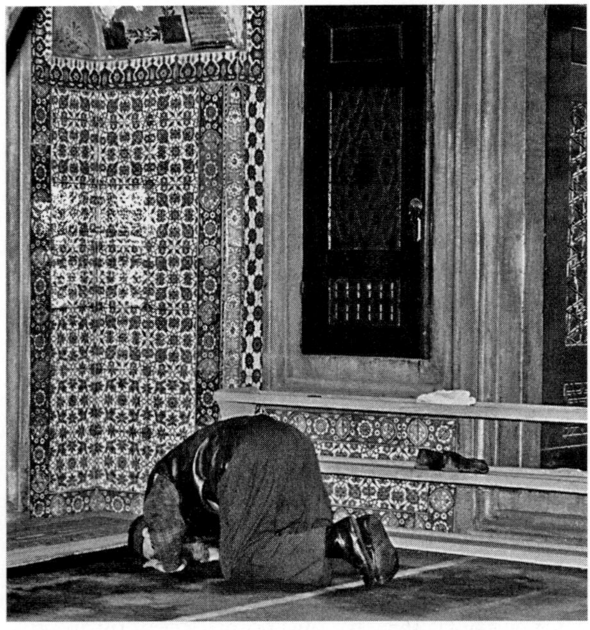

Religious practices give adolescents opportunities to feel connected to a higher power.

use different—but related—constructs to describe a person's process of self-discovery.

Faith is defined as a way of finding shared meaning and purpose in life, an orientation of the person toward values and beliefs, and a capacity to acknowledge and commit to a higher power in a quest for the universal (Fowler, 1981, 1991).

Similarly, **spirituality** is usually characterized as a personal and subjective feeling or experience of connectedness/relationship/oneness with a higher power or transcendent reality (e.g., God or Nature). Spirituality has also been described in terms of integrating one's values or beliefs with one's behavior in daily life; attaining a desirable inner affective state such as comfort, anxiety reduction, or security; and obtaining personal growth, actualization, mastery, or self-control (Zinnbauer, Pargament, & Cole, 1997).

On the other hand, definitions of **religiosity**, or religiousness, typically include organized religious practices or activities, such as attendance at religious services, performance of rituals, and membership in a church, temple, synagogue, or mosque; commitment to organizational beliefs or adherence to specific institutionally based belief systems; and integrating one's values or beliefs with behavior in daily life and personal worship or practices (e.g., prayer, scriptural reading, meditation) (Zinnbauer et al., 1997).

However, developmental theorists have cautioned against an artificial separation of constructs such as spirituality, faith, and religion, especially since worldwide data show that most people see themselves as both spiritual and religious (e.g., King & Boyatzis, 2004). In actual practice, and among both adolescents and adults, much overlap exists (Benson, 2004). For example, about 95% of American youth aged 13 to 17 believe in God; 75% agree "very much" or "somewhat" with the statement "I try to follow the teachings of my religion"; 42% of youth frequently pray; 36% regularly attend a church youth group; and 23% participate in faith-based service projects (King & Boyatzis, 2004). According to *Monitoring the Future*, a U.S. national survey collected annually since the 1970s, 47% of high-school seniors report that religion is important in their lives (Kerestes & Youniss, 2003). Nevertheless, faith, spirituality, and religion have all been relatively neglected areas in developmental research (Benson, 2004; King & Boyatzis, 2004).

Faith development. Although little empirical research has been conducted on the development of faith in adolescence, an influential theory of **faith development** outlines a six-stage sequence through which individuals mature into believers in a higher power (Fowler, 1981, 1991). In early childhood, during the stage called *intuitive-projective*, young children are becoming self-aware and experience intuitive understandings of their existence in the world. Later, as children attain concrete operational thinking during the school-age years, they begin to adopt the stories, beliefs, and observances that symbolize their belonging to a community. In this stage, called *mythic-literal faith*, beliefs, moral rules, and obligations are absolute (recall the discussion of moral reasoning in middle childhood in chapter 5).

In adolescence, however, teenagers begin to form a personal myth: "the myth of becoming one's own in identity and faith, incorporating one's past and anticipated future . . ." (Fowler, 1981, p. 173). This stage, called *synthetic-conventional faith*, is a conformist period in which teens are tuned in to the values and expectations of others. Although personal values and beliefs may be deeply felt, they are not fully examined until later adolescence when most people begin to develop an *individual-reflective faith* and take responsibility for their own commitments. In this stage, young adults can critically reflect on their identity (self) and outlook (ideology) (Fowler, 1981).

These stages describe a cognitive-developmental theory of the understanding of faith. However, the assumption that adolescents do not examine their religious beliefs until they reach young adulthood is unsupported. For example, the moral ideology of high-school seniors attending Catholic schools corresponded with the position of the Church on moral issues, such as killing or theft. However, students' opinions on abortion and homosexuality were arrived at independently of the Church's position (Turiel, Hildebrandt, & Wainryb, 1991).

How has your religiosity or spirituality changed since adolescence?

Religiosity. Most research on adolescent religious identity has been focused on the benefits of participation in organized religion rather than on the development of spirituality or faith. In addition, researchers only recently have begun to focus on the contribution of religious involvement to adolescent behavior, well-being, and identity (Kerestes & Youniss, 2003). For example, increasing or stable religious participation from 10th grade to 12th grade is positively related to involvement in social issues (e.g., working on a political campaign, demonstrating for a cause), participation in extracurricular activities, and performing volunteer service (Kerestes, Youniss, & Metz, 2004). Similarly, adolescents who reported that religion was important in their lives are almost three times more likely to engage in community service than teens who are not religious (Youniss, McLelland, & Yates, 1999).

Considerable evidence also demonstrates that religious involvement is associated with a decrease in adolescent risk behaviors, such as drug and alcohol use, smoking, sexual risk-taking, dropping out of school, and delinquency (Benson, 2004; Frank & Kendall, 2001; Smith, 2003; Wills, Yaeger, & Sandy, 2003). Many studies have also demonstrated that religious involvement serves as a protective factor against mental health problems, such as narcissism, depression, and suicide, and health-compromising behaviors, such as poor diet, exercise, dental hygiene, sleep habits, and seatbelt use (Smith, 2003a; Aalsma & Lapsley, 1999).

Most contemporary research on the relationship between adolescent identity formation and religiosity or spirituality supports the importance of religion in the lives of today's adolescents. Box 10.3 summarizes the conclusions from a recent review of the religious participation of American adolescents (Smith, Denton, Faris, & Regerus, 2002). Religious involvement may offer teens a distinct setting for identity exploration and commitment by providing an ideological context that transcends the self and promotes the common good (King, 2003). For example, in a multiethnic American sample of mostly Christian 9- to 15-year-olds, spirituality was positively related to an orientation to help others and negatively related to activities that promote self-interest (Dowling et al., 2004). Adolescents' prosocial concerns were also predicted by their religious identity in a study of multiethnic urban high-school students in the United States (Furrow, King, & White, 2004).

Many Black churches encourage positive youth development through outreach responsibilities, especially for adolescents. Tutoring, conferences, rites of passages, essay and rhetorical contests, concerts,

BOX 10.3 ROADMAP TO UNDERSTANDING THEORY AND RESEARCH

Mapping Adolescent Religious Participation

In a review of adolescents' participation in organized religious activities and organizations, Christian Smith and his colleagues (2003) drew the following eight conclusions about American teenagers and religion:

1. **The majority of American youth are religious.** Nearly one quarter of American youth are Catholic and one quarter are Baptist, with the remaining half spread thinly across a variety of different traditions and denominations (only 13% were not religious). Although the researchers expected the religious affiliations of youth to fairly closely track that of their parents, a majority of church-attending youth claimed that they go to religious services not only because their families make them but because they themselves want to. In addition, older adolescents sometimes explored religious traditions other than those in which they were raised.
2. **The number of Christian adolescents has been gradually declining.** The percent of American youth affiliating with a Protestant denomination declined by 10% and with the Catholic tradition by 1%. On the other hand, the number of youth reporting no religion increased by 5%. The number of teens practicing other religions also grew by 5% over 20 years—perhaps due to immigration from other countries. The reviewers concluded that American adolescents are gradually becoming more religiously pluralistic and tolerant.
3. **About half of American adolescents regularly participate in religious activities.** Youth who participate in services tend to be the same youth who participate in youth groups. Because religious involvements tend to group together, the reviewers concluded that teens who are religiously involved tend to engage in multiple forms of religious participation.
4. **About half of American youth are not religiously active.** About half of youth do not attend church services and are not involved in a religious youth group during their high-school years. Because regular church attendance among American high school seniors declined gradually between the mid-1970s and the mid-1990s, the reviewers suggest that the proportion of American youth who are not religiously active may be growing over time.
5. **The religious participation of American teens declines with age.** Older adolescents are less likely to report a religious affiliation, attend church services regularly, and be involved in a religious youth group. The reviewers concluded that this decline with age may reflect increased autonomy from the authority of parents, increased participation in jobs that may compete with religious activities for time, or an expansion of recreational activities because teens (or their friends) can drive.
6. **Adolescent girls tend to be more religiously active than boys.** Girls were more likely than boys to report a religious affiliation, to attend church regularly, and to be involved in a religious youth group. The reviewers note that this gender difference is similar in adult men and women in the United States and many other countries.
7. **The religious participation of American adolescents varies by race.** Race somewhat influences church attendance and youth group involvement, with African American youth being the most involved, followed by White youth and youth of other races. According to the reviewers, these differences probably derive in large measure from the cultural expectations for religious participation within racial/ethnic communities and the religious traditions in which African American, Hispanic, and Asian youth tend to participate rather than socioeconomic differences.
8. **The religious participation of American adolescents varies by region.** As with adults in the United States, adolescents living in the South are the most religiously involved, followed by teens in the Midwest and West. Youth who live in the Northeast participate in religion the least, although they are not the least likely to report having no religion.

Given this variation, Smith and colleagues (2003) concluded that more research is needed to sort out the relative importance of alternative factors in predicting variance in religious participation among American youth.

Source: Based on "Mapping American Adolescent Religious Participation" (pp. 609–610) by C. Smith, M. L. Denton, R. Faris, and M. Regerus, 2003, *Journal for the Scientific Study of Religion, 41*(4), pp. 597–612. Copyright 2003 by Blackwell Publishing.

Black college tours, childcare, health education, and employment preparation are just a few examples of outreach programs offered by Black churches (Williams, 2003). Not surprisingly, low-income African American adolescents who regularly attended religious services, Bible study groups, and church youth groups also scored high on ethnic identification (Markstrom, 1999).

Most researchers have found that as adolescents move towards identity achievement, teens who share a religious ideology are also more likely to report that they have a framework of meaning for their lives (Furrow, King, & White, 2004). For example, Mormon high-school students are more often foreclosed in religious identity than American adolescents from other Christian denominations. In addition, frequent church attendance is related to higher identity achievement for Mormon teenagers. For non-Mormon adolescents, however, *less* frequent attendance is related to higher identity achievement, attesting to the importance of religion in the lives of Mormon teens (Markstrom-Adams, Hofstra, & Dougher, 1994).

Although the majority of research on religious identity in adolescence has been conducted in North America and Europe, international and cross-cultural studies affirm the influence of religion on youths' psychosocial development across the globe. For example, researchers in Israel found that Arab adolescents are more often foreclosed and achieved (i.e., committed) in the religious domain than in the occupational and political domains, suggesting that context significantly influences religious identity formation (Dwairy, 2004). Similarly, religion plays a large role in the lives of immigrant youth and offers a strong connection to ethnic identity (Thompson & Gurney, 2003).

Postmodern spirituality. Over the course of adolescence, interest in *formal* religion, such as church attendance, typically declines. Many studies have found that religiosity and age are inversely related among 10- to 18-year-olds (Markstrom, 1999). This decline may reflect increases in autonomy, job participation, and competing leisure opportunities associated with teenage driving (Smith, Denton, Faris, & Regnerus, 2002). But does this decrease signal a decline in spirituality or in the personal expression of faith beliefs and values? Not necessarily. For example, compared to freshmen, predominantly Catholic and Protestant high-school seniors had a more integrated sense of religious identity, personal meaning, and social concern (Furrow, King, & White, 2004).

In a recent book called *Gen-X Religion* (Flory & Miller, 2000), the authors describe religious contexts created by adolescents and young adults themselves, such as a Korean American campus ministry at a major university (Kim, 2000), an evening worship service in a downtown nightclub (Walsh, 2000), or an evangelical youth culture in a Latino community (Prieto, 2000). "In the twenty-first century, youth may hold sacred any space, context, or medium, such as the Internet, where people share a genuine commitment to personally held values or can identify with others' beliefs" (Ream & Savin-Williams, 2003, p. 51). In Germany, for example, adolescents consider occult or "off-road" religions to be a lifestyle choice and an alternative to traditional religious socialization (Streib, 1999).

Adolescents usually convert to new religious groups because the congregation provides them with a sense of belonging, a social network, or a spiritual solution to their problems (Ream & Savin-Williams, 2003). In this manner, religious congregations that offer a connection to others can provide unique settings for adolescent identity formation (King, 2003). Developmental theorists also have suggested that a postmodern emphasis on self rather than on community may occasion adolescents to embark on a search for uniqueness as an adaptation to increasing freedom of choice and a loss of traditional values (Baumeister & Muraven, 1996).

When Sun's grandmother insists she wear a dress to church, Sun stops going. Sun begins to question the existence of God and what it means to be Korean American. Rather than manifesting evidence that she has lost her faith, however, Sun's behavior may express her desire to explore alternative ways of being a spiritual individual.

Vocational/Political Identity

Many developmental theorists and researchers consider work and civic responsibility to be at the center of what it means to be an adult (e.g., Vondracek & Porfeli, 2003; Yates & Youniss, 1998). From an individuation perspective, work provides adolescents with opportunities to achieve independence and responsibility. To many adolescents, having a "real job" and being paid for their work represents autonomy and individuation from their families. For instance, Dutch adolescents most frequently mention their future schooling or occupation as important to their identities (Vondracek & Porfeli, 2003).

Guideposts for Working with Adolescents

- Because religion may offer adolescents an ideological context for identity exploration and commitment, validate their religious involvement.
- Praise teens' faith-based or religiously affiliated activities since they often serve a protective function against problem behaviors.
- Point out to parents that across the high-school years, it is normal for participation in organized religion to decrease.
- Because spirituality may be expressed in many nontraditional ways by postmodern adolescents, expose them to other religions and worship experiences.

Vocational/political identity refers to both vocational development and to the political commitments that may guide adolescents' future career goals. From a social-identity perspective, jobs allow teens to identify with the world of work: "I'm a lifeguard." But what is the difference between a job and a career? In the 20th century, it was not uncommon for employees to spend their entire working life with one company. In the new century, a work career is likely to consist of a series of related (or perhaps unrelated) jobs over the course of a lifetime (Vondracek & Porfeli, 2003).

Adolescents' exploration of the world of work may lead smoothly to a career choice for some, while other teens may struggle to find an area of interest. Many adolescents gain their first work experience in part-time employment. However, research findings on whether or not working is always beneficial to high-school students are mixed (refer to chapter 7). For example, working teenagers are often more dependable, punctual, and responsible than teens who do not have jobs, provided that long working hours do not detract from the ability to maintain their grades, health, or social relationships (Blustein, 1997; Vondracek & Porfeli, 2003).

Did you do volunteer work or have a job as a teenager that was related to your career or political interests?

Studies comparing urban and rural adolescents suggest that rural youth are more likely to work in response to the economic needs of their families and to spend less of their earnings on themselves. More importantly, some researchers have found that farm boys' involvement in chores when they do not plan to become farmers may make individuation more difficult. Generally, however, the educational and career aspirations of rural youth are only slightly lower than those of urban youth. In several recent studies, about half of rural adolescents (compared to about 60% of urban youth) anticipated attending college or holding technical and professional jobs as adults (Crockett, Shanahan, & Jackson-Newsom, 2000).

Career development. Career development is defined as vocational knowledge and the acquisition of work experience. Fifty percent of American adolescents enter the labor market directly from high school and about half report earning a college degree as their goal (Vondracek & Portelli, 2003). Counselors generally agree that youth cope better with the school-to-work transition if they have career-planning information on the choices available (Savickas, 1999). For example, in Great Britain, a large-scale study found that having work-related skills and career role models was positively related to career development in 14- to 17-year-olds. On the other hand, adolescents who reported that they felt pressured by their families about their studies or work scored lower on measures of career maturity (Flouri & Buchanan, 2002). Committing prematurely to an academic or occupational career may actually limit teens' opportunities for career exploration and occupational identity development (Ireh, 2000).

The best predictors of job stability are a planning orientation to the work world and specific knowledge about preferred occupations (Savickas, 1999). In most high-school settings, the exploration of career choices is usually guided by one or more of the approaches to career development listed in Table 10–6 (Ireh, 2000; see also Beale, 2001). Consistent with the postmodern approach, researchers have noted that students in grades 7 to 12, representing all socioeconomic groups, did not make significant distinctions among work, leisure, and school activities. As a result, the National Career Development Guidelines for middle school and

TABLE 10–6

Approaches to Career Development

Career development approaches vary widely based on differing theoretical perspectives.

Approach	Example
Personality or Trait	
Matching adolescents' personal dispositions, aptitudes, or skills with a college curriculum or job, usually through a formal assessment	Taking the *Scholastic Aptitude Test* or SAT
Occupational Choice	
Helping teenagers become increasingly realistic about the match between their talents and opportunities in the real world	Compromising on a satisfying, but low-paying, job
Self-Concept	
Exploring, role-playing, and reality testing leading to development of a vocational self-concept	Selecting an occupation that is consistent with how you view yourself
Information Processing	
Using vocational information in career problem solving and decision making	Prioritizing your career alternatives, also called "valuing"
Lifespan Developmental	
Supporting career development through five stages: Growth (ages 4–13), Exploration (15–24), Establishment (25–44), Maintenance (45–64), and Disengagement (65 and up)	Experimenting with choices before choosing a career
Contextual Action	
Conceptualizing career development as a joint project in a relational context	Parents and adolescents talking about career possibilities
Postmodern	
Viewing work as an activity of everyday life from the perspective of persons *doing the work* rather than from the perspective of a career	Teenagers describing the meaning of work in their lives

Source: Based on "Career Development Theories and Their Implications for High School Career Guidance and Counseling" by M. Ireh, 2000, *The High School Journal, Dec/Jan*, pp. 28–40. Copyright 2000 by the University of North Carolina Press.

high school recommend the exploration of a wide range of activities (Vondracek & Skorikov, 1997).

Longitudinal research on career development supports the importance of adolescents exploring their identities via clearly delineated career choices. For example, a simulation that involved talking to an "imaginary friend" in a small group was effective in helping teens to clarify their personal values and career goals (Jepsen & Dickson, 2003). Family involvement has also proven important in the development of a vocational identity through talking about careers with adolescents (Young et al., 2001), by participating in the career counseling process alongside teens (Amundson & Penner, 1998), or by understanding teenagers' need for individuation and supporting their exploration of careers (Kracke, 1997). For example, adolescent-parent discussions of career choices revealed that choices appraised as "boring, scary or not fun or exciting" were considered undesirable; however, careers co-constructed as "exciting and challenging" were considered capable of sustaining adolescents' interest over time (Young, Paseluikho, & Valach, 1997). Parent-adolescent negotiation about identity during the process of career development is illustrated in Box 10.4.

Vocational researchers have noted that career development is predicted by adolescents' identity status (e.g., Blustein, 1994; Wallace-Broscious, Serafica, & Osipow, 1994). For example, measures of overall interest in work, occupational exploration, and self-efficacy of seventh- to twelfth-grade students were positively correlated with achieved ideological identity (i.e., work, politics, religion, lifestyle domains), whereas diffused ideological identity was negatively related, as expected (Vondracek & Skorikov, 1997). Furthermore, when compared by their identity status,

BOX 10.4 ROADMAP TO SUCCESSFUL PRACTICE

Negotiating Identity in Parent-Adolescent Relationships

Adolescence is a critical period for career development because identity-relevant feedback from others, previously mostly from the family, comes increasingly from nonfamily sources. Individuals are influenced by their contexts at the same time as they also revise their core self-perceptions and commitments. The question to be answered whenever changes are faced in any relationship is, "Who will you let me be?" In successful identity negotiations, all family members—not only the adolescent—are validated in their self-perceptions, and their identity explorations are supported. Unsuccessful career identity negotiations, on the other hand, may lead to a variety of coercive and self-destructive outcomes for both parent and adolescent.

Social role negotiation theory, an integrative approach to human behavior in interaction, is based on symbolic interaction theory and Selman's levels of interpersonal negotiation (described in chapter 6). Focused on conflict and change, it acknowledges both intrapersonal development and changing relationships and emphasizes the contextual nature of human behavior. Identity, from this perspective, is not fixed but rather is continually renegotiated in every context. A sense of self is constructed from the cumulative experience of these negotiations; consistent experiences lead to a clear sense of self—positive or negative—while inconsistent experiences lead to confusion.

Identity negotiation strategies may be thought of as having two kinds of goals. Some strategies seem to be intended to accomplish behavioral change in the other.

For example, the family of Sun might want her to quit drawing and focus on her education instead. They could complain of the mess, threaten to destroy her artwork, and otherwise make it uncomfortable for her to continue. To the extent that drawing has become a central identity element, giving up her sketchbook would mean giving up her authenticity and becoming another kind of person.

Other strategies seem designed instead to alter the other's view of self.

The family desiring less clutter in the house might pursue their goal by trying to convince Sun that she is without artistic talent or, alternatively, that her drawing has taken valuable time away from the development of her academic skills.

Cultural prescriptions for gender-related behavior often operate in this way.

If parent-adolescent relationships involve the negotiation of career identities, a constructive conflict process might, however, serve the interests of all participants. Parents and adolescents alike would see themselves as applying negotiation strategies in their interactions. The following review of Sun's story will illustrate both the use of low-level strategies and the potential for improving the negotiation process.

- **Low-Level, Self-Transforming Strategies.** This kind of extreme behavior typifies the individual who expects to lose in every dispute.

  Sun, as a child, did not have confidence in her ability to defy family rules. Choosing to accept the family goals without a struggle, she gives up the potential of creating her own kind of person. Now, as an adolescent, she resigns herself to give up her own dream of becoming an artist without defying the authority figures in the family.

- **Low-Level, Other-Transforming Strategies.** This type of behavior characterizes the individual who does not seem to consider the possibility of losing.

  Sun's mother would be operating at this level if she continues to pressure Sun to give up art in an attempt to defeat her daughter, and she single-mindedly pursues her goal that Sun attend college. Threats, bribes, and even physical violence are often seen in parent-adolescent relationships.

- **Medium-Level, Pseudo-Cooperative Strategies.** Individuals using these more sophisticated approaches attempt to resolve identity conflicts through persuasion or even more indirect means. Among the most subtle is the attribution of an identity based on some behavior.

  Sun was labeled as an honor student, a kind of person, based on the fact that she performed well in school. Honor students, according Sun's parents, did not pursue careers in art. Sun, on the other hand, presented herself as a artist who just happened to be a good student.

- **Higher-Level Problem-Solving Strategies.** The most mature negotiation strategies involve open sharing of feelings and beliefs, hopes and fears, and honest observations of self and other. These negotiations seek a resolution in which parents and adolescents alike are validated and their relationship is strengthened. For that reason, no individual is wedded to a particular solution; instead, there is an honest exploration of the basis for the identity conflict and an openness to all possible resolutions.

  This kind of conversation can still take place for Sun. Her parents can ask about her goals and her decision-making process, her views of herself, and her reasons for the things she has been doing. Even

BOX 10.4 (CONTINUED)

after a joint decision is made, there is continuing review of the process and the decision in hopes of improving future conflict management.

Social role negotiation theory points to a central dynamic in families: a negotiation process in which family members seek to promote or to resist identity change. This dynamic has special relevance for families with adolescent members, because identity formation assumes particular intensity during the adolescent years.

Source: From "Negotiating Identity in Parent-Adolescent Relationships," by T. W. Blume and L. B. Blume. Paper presented at the Theory Construction and Research Methodology Workshop, National Council on Family Relations. Copyright 1997 by Thomas W. Blume. Adapted by permission of the author.

a higher proportion of students in each grade were either in the moratorium or achieved status in vocational identity than in the other domains, suggesting the salience of work and career to most adolescents (Skorikov & Vondracek, 1998).

Although minority adolescents do not differ in their career development interests or aspirations, they tend to have lower expectations regarding their career attainment than White adolescents (Constantine, Erickson, Banks, & Timberlake, 1998). Vocational counselors and other professionals working with racial/ethnic minority youth can work to improve teens' vocational outcomes even though they may not be able to significantly affect socioeconomic barriers (Constantine, Erickson, Banks, & Timberlake, 1998). For recommendations to assist career counselors in meeting the vocational needs of minority youth, see Box 10.5.

BOX 10.5 ROADMAP TO SUCCESSFUL PRACTICE

Career Counseling with Ethnic-Minority Youth

In an article on career development with racial- and ethnic-minority youth, Michael Constantine and colleagues (1998) outlined almost 20 recommendations, including the following points:

1. Be aware of the ways that environmental stressors, such as violence and poverty, influence urban racial- and ethnic-minority youth and their ability to address career development issues.
2. Carefully attend to students' career aspirations and expectations to ensure that lowered expectations for success are not inhibiting urban racial- and ethnic-minority youth from achieving their potential.
3. Identify ways to involve parents or legal guardians in their children's career development process.
4. Help teachers to have realistic expectations of urban racial- and ethnic-minority youth by ensuring that the teachers are not underestimating these students' abilities.
5. Work with educators to help them incorporate vocational information and themes into existing curricula.
6. Teach racial- and ethnic-minority youth how to deal with and address issues such as prejudice, discrimination, and racism in their pursuit of career goals.
7. Involve local business leaders in identifying and instituting strategies (e.g., offering work apprenticeships or meaningful part-time jobs) that may positively and directly influence the career development of urban racial- and ethnic-minority youth.
8. Advocate for social change regarding the societal barriers to their career development that urban racial- and ethnic-minority youth face.

Source: Based on "Challenges to the Career Development of Urban Racial and Ethnic Minority Youth: Implications for Vocational Intervention," by M. G. Constantine, C. D. Erickson, R. W. Banks, and T. L. Timberlake, 1998, *Journal of Multicultural Counseling & Development, 26*(2), pp. 82–95. Copyright 1998 by the Association for Multicultural Counseling and Development.

Let's imagine what the art teacher could do to help Sun and her family realistically explore Sun's career choice. She could arrange for Sun to visit a local artist's studio and see what painters really do on a typical day. She could ask an arts business consultant to talk to Sun and her father about making a successful living as a practicing artist. She could suggest that Sun volunteer to teach an art class to children in her church to see if art education might interest her. Finally, she could invite Sun's parents to a guided tour of the art exhibit in the state capitol and describe art's value to the community.

Political development. As adolescents reflect on the possible roles they may have in adulthood, they engage the values, ideologies, and traditions of their communities and the larger society (Yates & Youniss, 1998). Political socialization theorists see adolescents as molded into a political orientation by social forces, such as the political attitudes of their families or local region (Haste & Torney-Purta, 1992). For instance, political identity in adolescence may include forming an unwavering ideological commitment to a political party. Often, affiliation with the party politics of parents indicates identity foreclosure. In other cases, teens in identity moratorium may explore ideologies that are purposely divergent from family members' political views as part of the normative individuation process.

Political development is the understanding of community action and the social processes through which political commitments and identities emerge (see Yates & Youniss, 1998). For example, adolescents who have been involved in political experiences are more likely to be tolerant of others. Perhaps because of the transition in adolescence from concrete to abstract thought, which also increases the likelihood of political involvement, older teens also tend to be more tolerant than younger teens (Avery, 1992).

Cognitive-developmental theorists have proposed stages of political development, similar to the stages of moral reasoning discussed in chapter 6, involving increasing levels of abstraction and understandings of social identities. From this perspective, teenagers construct their political understanding through interaction with their communities. The issues are less about party affiliation and more about understanding society and power (Haste & Torney-Purta, 1992).

An approach to studying political awareness that is consistent with our contextual approach is the study of teens' political identity as the range of civic and community activities youth engage in, often referred to as **civic engagement**. Researchers have identified three ways that adolescents are likely to learn about politics:

1. **Observation.** Observing how people relate to them as an individual or a member of a racial/ethnic minority (e.g., how Chicanos are treated by Anglo society)

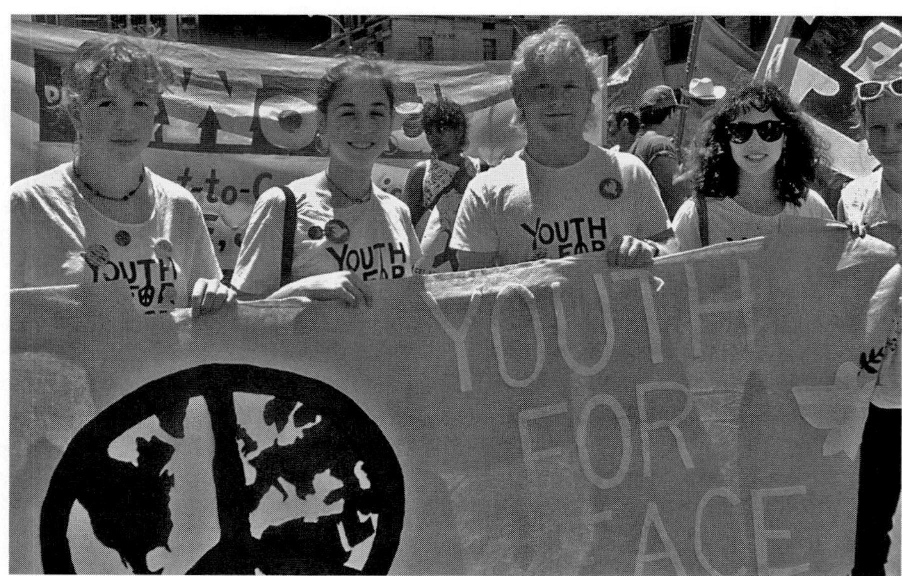

Social activism helps teens think about government and politics—not as distant institutions but as forces that affect people's lives.

2. **Listening.** Listening to what other people are saying about politics and relating it to what they see (e.g., hearing parental discussions or media analysis of political issues)
3. **Personal Action.** Learning about politics by participating in political activities (e.g., picketing, boycotts, protests, or volunteering for political candidates) (adapted from Jankowski, 1992)

Longitudinal research has clearly demonstrated that youth involvement in their communities is related to political identity and civic engagement in adulthood, especially when volunteerism is supported by their close friends and family. For example, adolescents' involvement in community service projects in an inner city sustained their social activism into adulthood (Yates & Youniss, 1998). High-school students who are engaged in service-learning projects increase their understanding of political issues and decisions, such as limits on individuals or on the spending of public funds (Yates & Youniss, 1998).

Civic engagement and service projects help adolescents to think about government and politics—not as distant institutions, but as forces that affect their own lives and communities. But is it ever appropriate to *require* volunteer service? Many high schools do so, especially private or religiously affiliated schools. Students were interviewed from two comparable high schools that required service. One school integrated volunteer service into the curriculum; the other school left the choice to individual students. Adolescents in the former school were more apt to do the kinds of service learning that engaged them cognitively and emotionally and involved them in reflection on politics and morals. These students were also more likely to have parents and best friends who volunteered and to belong to churches and civic organizations that sponsored or encouraged community service as part of an ideological commitment (McLellan & Youniss, 2003).

Recently, developmental theorists have described the importance of having a sense of purpose in adolescence. ***Purpose*** is defined as "a stable and generalized intention to accomplish something that is at once meaningful to the self and of consequence to the world beyond the self" (Damon, Menon, & Brunk, 2003, p. 121). A **sense of purpose** is different from personal meaning in the following ways:

- **Purpose Is a Goal.** Compared to low-level goals, such as "to find a parking space," purpose is more stable and far-reaching.
- **Purpose Has an External Component.** Purpose is part of one's personal search for meaning but also includes a desire to make a difference in the world and contribute to matters larger than oneself.
- **Purpose Is Always Directed at an Accomplishment.** Unlike meaning alone, which may or may not be oriented towards a specific purpose, one can make progress towards a goal. (adapted from Damon, Menon, & Brunk, 2003)

Researchers have linked having a sense of purpose to identity achievement and future orientation, goal-directedness, achievement, motivation, educational aspirations, healthy expectations, persistence, and hopefulness. In addition, adolescents who express a sense of purpose show higher degrees of religiosity, more integrated identities, and deeper senses of meaning than teens who do not experience purpose (for a review, see Damon, Menon, & Brunk, 2003).

Guideposts for Working with Adolescents

- Provide teens with opportunities to seek out accurate information about varied career choices through volunteering or by inviting guest speakers from differing occupations to the classroom.
- Encourage adolescent career exploration by identifying their strengths, providing realistic and accurate information about career choices, and pairing students with mentors from the community.
- Arrange for teens to engage in volunteer service through high schools, religious congregations, or community programs.
- Envision career and political awareness as a family project by supporting adolescents in talking with their parents and other adult role models, visiting colleges or potential employers, or participating in educational programs, such as "Take-Your-Son/Daughter-to Work-Day."

Emotion and Self-Esteem in Middle Adolescence

When many people hear the word *teenager*, they often think "emotional, moody, difficult. . . ." But we now know that G. Stanley Hall's view of adolescence as a period of "storm and stress" has been largely refuted (Larson & Ham, 1993). Hall's (1904) belief was that adolescence is filled with hormone-induced emotional turmoil. Some consistent associations have recently been found between specific hormones and feelings of aggression or depression; however, only a small proportion of variance in emotion (up to 6%) is attributable to hormones (Galambos & Costigan, 2003). As a result, complex models of the interactions among hormones, personality, and contextual characteristics have been proposed (Richards & Larson, 1993).

Although hormonal fluctuations related to puberty may play some part in the emotionality of adolescents (Brooks-Gunn, Graber, & Paikoff, 1994), our functional perspective on affective development (see chapter 5) requires us to examine how adolescents' emotional experiences influence—and are influenced by—the social context (Cummings, Braungart-Rieker, & du Rocher-Scudlich, 2003). For example, when researchers coded the family interaction of 14- to 16-year-old adolescents and their parents in a longitudinal study, results revealed that difficulties in establishing autonomy and relatedness with parents were linked to depression and problem behaviors at age 17 (Allen, Hauser, Eickholt, & Bell, 1994).

As she rides the bus home on the day the art awards were announced, Sun experiences varied emotions: pride in what she has accomplished, fear at what her parents will say, and hope that she can reconcile her new ambition with her parents' expectations. Her emotional experience is typical of a teenager who is actively seeking autonomy while maintaining a viable connection with her family.

Researchers have also found that adolescents make different connections between identity and their emotions than younger children. For example, children connected more positive and negative emotions (e.g., happy or angry) to the roles of son or daughter than teens (Haviland, Davidson, & Ruetsch, 1994). In contrast, adolescents are more likely to connect their emotional experiences to interactions with friends (see Rosenblum & Lewis, 2003). Why? A plausible explanation is that adolescents are in a period of reorganization prior to identity exploration (Haviland-Jones & Kahlbaugh, 2000). Recall that adolescence is a period of identity diffusion or foreclosure for the majority of teens. The adolescent search for individuation relates to two important areas of research on affective well-being in adolescence: emotional development and self-esteem.

Emotion and Mood

Although the terms *emotion* and *mood* are often used interchangeably, **emotions** are discrete affective states, usually felt in response to an external event, whereas **moods** are low-level generalized feelings generally rated on a continuum from positive to negative (Ganzel, 1999). Adolescents commonly report more negative moods than school-age children (Larson & Lampman-Petraitis, 1989) and wider and quicker mood swings than adults (Larson, Csikzsentmihalyi, & Graef, 1980). Emotion theorists and researchers, however, have moved away from conceptualizing emotions as sources of negative behavior and towards a view of emotions as adaptive (Galambos & Costigan, 2003).

How did your family and friends respond to your emotions and moods during your teen years?

Recall from chapter 5 that an **emotional competence** perspective examines how school-age children and adolescents effectively regulate their emotions and interact successfully with others. In a longitudinal study of high-school students and adults (Freeman et al., 1986), objective ratings of the quality of their moods across a 2-year period did not change, but as adolescents got older they learned to interpret their experiences in more positive ways (Ganzel, 1999).

Adolescents' reports of their own daily emotions indicate that they are not more likely to experience rapid mood swings than preadolescents. Recent longitudinal studies using experience sampling with middle-class and working-class students have demonstrated that teens' daily emotions were related to life stress across both early (grades 5 to 8) and middle adolescence (grades 9 to 12). Although adolescents' average emotional states became less positive and were less stable across early adolescence, the downward trend stopped in grade 10 (Larson, Moneta, Richards, & Wilson, 2002).

The popular misperception of adolescent moodiness may be due to the fact that older teens are less likely to report positive emotions and more likely to report mildly negative moods than younger

Guideposts for Working with Adolescents

- Since adolescents typically experience more emotional highs and lows than school-age children or adults, help teens recognize that their identity stays intact in the face of fluctuating emotions by giving them consistent feedback.
- Help adolescents, especially girls, manage their emotions by talking, drawing, or writing about their feelings because external life events are often related to teens' experience of negative emotions.
- Help teens negotiate interpersonal relationships in the face of strong feelings by distinguishing emotional reactions from facts.
- Identify adolescents who appear depressed by asking how they feel at various times during the day.
- When in doubt about a teen's emotional well-being, always make a referral for counseling.

teens. For example, in another experience-sampling study of early adolescents in grades 5 to 9, older students reported more negative affect related to school, peer, and family events than did the younger students (Larson & Lampman-Petraitis, 1989). Furthermore, the decision-making strategies used by junior-high girls in a career choice task of choosing a part-time job were less effective when they were in a negative mood (Ganzel, 1999).

Alternatively, researchers have suggested that higher levels of reported distress may be attributable to the fact that the older students *actually* encounter more negative life events (Larson & Ham, 1993). This possibility has been supported by longitudinal research in which stressful life events, such as pubertal changes and relationships with others, explained variations in teens' self-awareness and levels of depression (e.g., Chen, Mechanic, & Hansell, 1998). Adolescents who experience stress in meeting their everyday life demands may experience greater variations in their emotional well-being (Moneta, Schneider, & Csikzsentmihalyi, 2001). For example, in a recent experience-sampling study of emotion regulation and adjustment, seventh graders who reported more intense and varied emotions and less effective emotional regulation, such as denying their feelings or acting impulsively, also reported more depression and problem behaviors (Silk, Steinberg, & Morris, 2003).

While rates of depression and negative mood increase between ages 11 and 12 for both sexes, by age 13 girls often show significantly more symptoms of depression than boys. Girls also report more feelings of shame, guilt, sadness, and shyness, especially in interpersonal contexts than do boys—who often deny having feelings at all! Thus, the higher rates of negative affect in girls may reflect our socially constructed definition of depression, which is more closely related to the emotional experiences of women and girls than to men and boys (Rosenblum & Lewis, 2003).

Adolescent Self-Esteem

Recall from chapter 5 that **self-esteem** is defined as "how you feel about yourself." Contrary to popular and clinical portrayals of teenagers, self-esteem ratings of adolescents appear mostly stable across the high-school years (Demo & Savin-Williams, 1992; see also Block & Robins, 1993; O'Malley & Bachman, 1983). After a short-term drop just after the transition to middle school (Simmons, 1987; Simmons & Blyth, 1987), overall self-esteem (measured by traditional self-report scales) shows a gradual increase from about the ninth through eleventh grades (Demo & Savin-Williams, 1992). A recent study of African American, Latino American, and Asian American high-school students also revealed similar increases in self-esteem with age for both boys and girls, although, compared to their Latino peers, Black adolescents reported higher self-esteem and Asian American students reported lower self-esteem (Greene & Way, 2005). In a multiethnic longitudinal study of teens in grades 6 to 12 that used both traditional self-report and experience-sampling measures of self-worth (e.g., living up to your own expectations and to those of others, feeling successful, feeling in control), self-esteem declined until about grade 10 and then rose. Girls' self-esteem scores on traditional measures were lower than boys' overall, but no differences were found in experience samples of self-worth, such as feeling successful or feeling in control (Moneta et al., 2001).

Although researchers on adolescence have often reported lower self-esteem for girls than boys (e.g., Block & Robins, 1993; Marsh, 1989; Baldwin & Hoffman, 2002), when such gender effects on self-esteem have been found, they are often small. For example, extensive meta-analyses reveal that similar levels of self-esteem have been reported for males and females in most studies, with only *small* sex differences favoring boys through adolescence but then declining to zero by adulthood (Hyde & Linn, 1990; Kling, Hyde, Showers, & Buswell, 1999). (The timing of pubertal maturation and self-esteem was discussed in chapter 8.) Researchers also have not found gender differences in self-esteem in studies of ethnic minority adolescents. For example, no significant gender differences were found in overall self-esteem among Puerto Rican school-age children (Erkut, Szalacha, García Coll, & Alarcon, 2000).

When researchers have examined the influence of family, peer, and school contexts, family experiences were most strongly related to changes in self-esteem (Greene & Way, 2005). In this respect, self-esteem is significantly related to **affective experiences**, or feeling positive and negative emotion. For example, most middle-school students report that when they are depressed they think that others see them as less worthy. Others report that their feelings of low self-worth *preceded* feelings of depression, citing causes involving dissatisfaction with *themselves* (Harter & Jackson, 1993). Furthermore, identity researchers have related affective well-being to the degree of integration of adolescents' *here-and-now* identities with their contexts, called **spatial-temporal integration** (van Hoof & Raaumakers, 2002).

Sun struggles with how she sees herself at school (high-school student, aspiring artist) and how her family sees her at home (Korean American, dutiful daughter).

Beginning in middle childhood, preteens construct multiple selves in different contexts, causing internal conflicts between opposing roles (Harter, Bresnick, Bouchey, & Whitesell, 1997). For example, Figure 10.5 shows that early adolescents report fewer opposing attributes than those in middle or late adolescence across different roles (e.g., with mother, father, best friend, a group of friends, romantic interest). With increasing age and educational level, adolescents can consider more personally relevant contexts for exploring their identities and making personal commitments

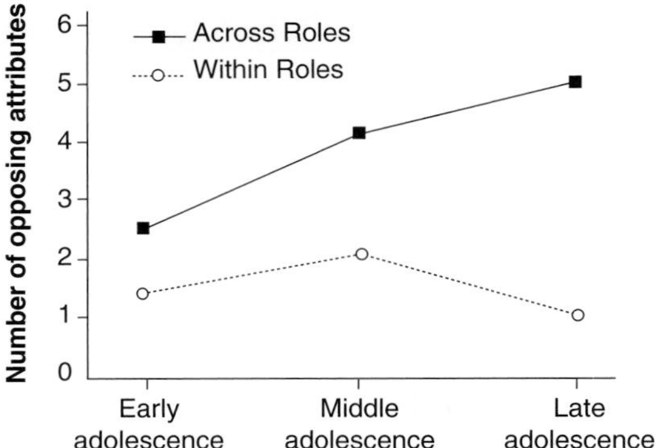

FIGURE 10.5 Opposing Attributes During Adolescence

Across adolescence, teens become increasingly likely to describe themselves using opposing attributes when engaged in different roles, such as "friend" versus "daughter." During middle adolescence, however, there is a slight increase in the use of opposites to describe themselves, even within a single role.

Source: From "The Development of Multiple Role-Related Selves During Adolescence" (p. 841), by S. Harter, S. Bresnick, H. A. Bouchey, and N. A. Whitesell, 1997, *Development and Psychopathology, 9*, pp. 835–853. Copyright 1997 by Cambridge University Press. Reprinted by permission.

(van Hoof & Raaumakers, 2003). When multiracial high-school students were asked to choose among racial identities, for example, more biracial teens chose their minority category rather than White, especially part-Black adolescents. In addition, many of the multiracial youth who had less-than-positive ethnic identities nonetheless had high self-esteem (Herman, 2004).

Similarly, research on the emotional struggles of adolescents who question their sexual orientation reveals that self-esteem is related to positive feelings about their gender and sexuality (e.g., Herschberger & D'Augelli, 1995). For example, in middle childhood feeling like a "typical" boy or girl is positively related to self-esteem, whereas pressure to conform to gender stereotypes is negatively related (Carver, Yunger, & Perry, 2003; Egan & Perry, 2001). In adolescence, sexual-minority youth often report feeling emotionally distant from their social networks, especially from their families, because they have to hide a part of their self-identity (Tharinger & Wells, 2000). (Sexual identity and "coming out" in adolescence will be discussed in chapter 11).

Possible selves. An identity perspective on affective development includes the role of **possible selves**, defined as the images or conceptions of what a person might become, or is afraid of becoming (Markus & Nurius, 1986). The number of possible selves a person can generate is related to identity exploration, whereas the consistency of hoped-for selves over time is related to identity commitment (e.g., Dunkel & Anthis, 2001). Refer to Table 10–7 for examples of possible selves organized by themes (Yowell, 2000). This perspective on the self involves **self-completion**, a process that focuses on the implementation of self-defining goals (Gollwitzer, Bayer, Scherer, & Seifert, 1999).

Research with early adolescents has demonstrated that possible selves evoke positive feelings and a sense of optimism about the future, particularly when they provide a "roadmap" to future goals (Oyserman, Bybee, Terry, & Hart-Johnson, 2004). For example, researchers noted the possible selves of an inner-city eighth grader, with strategies noted in parentheses: "Next year, I expect to be 13 years old, playing football (I am going to practice this year), in high school, playing basketball (I am coming to my games this year)" (Oyserman et al., 2004, p. 130).

In middle adolescence, a balance between hoped-for and dreaded possible selves has successfully differentiated nondelinquent from delinquent teens in an urban context, whereas global self-esteem did not (Oyserman & Markus, 1990; Oyersman & Saltz, 1993). In addition, the risk of dropping out of high school has been predicted by Latino early adolescents' *feared* possible selves, such as getting pregnant or becoming involved with gangs (Yowell, 2000, 2002). Even health-risk behaviors, such as smoking and alcohol use, are negatively related to having more possible selves in early adolescence and to a balance between feared and hoped-for selves (Aloise-Young, Hennigan, & Leong, 2001).

What were your hoped-for possible selves in high school?

In a study of 14- to 19-year-old, mostly White high-school students, girls reported more possible selves than did boys. In addition, consistent with gender stereotypes, adolescent girls' feared possible selves were more often about relationships,

TABLE 10–7

Possible Selves

These quotations illustrate adolescents' possible selves categorized by themes.

Themes	Examples
The good life	"Yeah, I'll go to college and I think my life will be good. Why wouldn't it be?" (girl)
Locus of control	"I can do anything I want if I try hard enough." (boy)
Role models	"My sister is my role model. She finished high school and went to college. . . I don't know how long she was there. . . I know she took a few courses, but then she had to go and work in my father's store." (girl)
Education/occupations	"I'm just hoping I'll graduate from the eighth grade, go to a good high school, go to college. But first I got to get my IGAP scores up or else I won't pass the eighth grade. . . . People that fail school work in factories and don't get paid that much. If you don't go to school you don't go nowhere." (boy)
Family	"First, I want to get a job when I'm 16 so I can help my family with the bills, then I want to be rich so I can buy my parents a nice house so they won't have to work anymore. I'll want them to come and live with me 'cause I want to take them wherever I go." (girl)
Risk taking	"I'm afraid I might start hanging out with the wrong people. . . I gotta stay away from people [gangs] that I'm not supposed to be with and just to like do my best that I can do." (boy)
Friendship	"You know, they're just friends. I'm not just saying, they're nobody, they're close to me, you know. But we're just friends. I can't explain it. . . but they don't have to go all out on me. I expect my family to do that, not my friends 'cause they have their own family and stuff. . . ." (girl)

Source: From "Possible Selves and Future Orientation: Exploring Hopes and Fears of Latino Boys and Girls," by C. M. Yowell, 2000, *Journal of Early Adolescence, 20*(3), pp. 265–266. Copyright 2000 by Sage Publications, Inc. Adapted by permission.

Guideposts for Working with Adolescents

- Because teenagers often construct multiple selves in different situations (e.g., with parents or with friends), talk with them about how they feel about themselves in each of these contexts.
- Since girls may experience lower feelings of self-worth than boys during high school, help them recognize areas in which they feel successful.
- Endorse identity exploration by asking teens to generate a list of possible selves (hoped-for and feared).
- Role-play how adolescents might explore their identities with their parents or friends by acting out their hoped-for possible selves.

whereas teenage boys generated more feared possible selves related to occupations (Knox, Funk, Elliott, & Bush, 2000). Similarly, secondary-school girls' in Northern Ireland more often included family roles among their possible selves than did boys (Curry & Trew, 1994). On the other hand, occupations were more of a priority for early adolescent boys than for girls among eighth-grade Latino students in the United States (Yowell, 2000, 2002). In recent comparison of American high-school and college females on masculine-stereotyped domains linked to powerful careers (e.g., math, science, business), high-school students endorsed more possibilities for themselves than did college students, suggesting that adolescence may be a critical time to support gender-balanced identity exploration (Lips, 2004). Box 10.6 provides examples of two innovative programs to enhance the exploration of possible selves with adolescents.

BOX 10.6 ROADMAP TO SUCCESSFUL PRACTICE

Enhancing Identity Exploration with Possible Selves

Many programs have developed possible-selves interventions to assist school-agers and adolescents with identity exploration. One such effort in an after-school setting focused on enhancing African American middle-schoolers' ability to imagine themselves as successful adults. After a 9-week program, students had more balanced possible selves and improved bonding to school, concern about doing well, and (for boys) attendance (Oyserman, Terry, & Bybee, 2002).

A creative writing project in which adolescents write autobiographical fiction, or "life writing," guided by the analysis of literary texts assumes that adolescent identity development is an inherently aesthetic process. These fictional narratives were examined for evidence of identity and self-transformation. High-school students typically produced narratives that were hero-myths and autobiographies (Lightfoot, 2001a). For example,

> *Giai loved the game of basketball. . . The team was going to the State Championships. . . When the game was over, Giai had 40 points, 10 steals, 20 assists and 9 blocks. Her team won. . . Everyone was happy and proud.*
>
> *About two weeks later Giai received a letter from Syracuse asking her to play basketball for them. They indicated they would offer a scholarship to assist with college tuition. Hard work and perseverance had paid off. Giai's dream finally came true.* (Lightfoot, 2001b, p. 2)

Another type of program related to possible selves, called personal projects analysis (Little, 1999), involves asking adolescents what kind of personal projects they engage in and the extent to which the projects are *self-prototypical*, or represent who they are. Those projects rated by adolescents as highest in self-prototypicality were community activities, spiritual activities, sex, and boyfriend/girlfriend relations, and the lowest were related to schoolwork. These self-analyses were then used for the exploration of adolescents' identity (Little, 1987). See Table 10–8 for a sample of adolescents' personal projects.

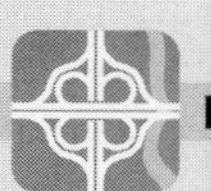

BOX 10.6 (CONTINUED)

TABLE 10–8
Adolescent Personal Projects
These personal projects are typical of many teens.

Riding my new windsurfer this summer
Trying to understand and help my family and friends
Learning to be a better marksman for next duck-hunting season
Picking up girls
Finish my computer assignment
Getting along with as many people as I can
What to do in the future
Try to get Susan to notice me
Going for a cigarette once in a while behind my parents' backs
Getting my ring from my boyfriend
Control my feeling of immense dislike for my friend's friend
Trying to increase my social life (which includes someone special)
Getting involved with a girl
Trying to understand quadratic equations
Working with mentally disturbed children
Finding the perfect girl
Stop smoking
Trying to keep gas tank full
Parties during break
Lose some weight
Quit smoking
Phoning up guys
Getting a driver's license
Party a lot
Trying to attract a guy
Make the dinners at home
Taking Tai Kwon Do
Party!

Source: Based on "Personal Projects and Fuzzy Selves: Aspects of Self-Identity in Adolescence" (p. 233), by B. R. Little in T. Honess and K. Yardley (Eds.), *Self and Identity: Perspectives Across the Lifespan* (pp. 230–245), New York: Routledge & Kegan Paul 1987. Copyright 1987 by Taylor & Francis Group, Ltd.

CONTEXTS FOR AFFECTIVE DEVELOPMENT

The term *context* has been used in two ways by identity researchers: "that which surrounds" and "that which weaves together" (Goossens & Phinney, 1996). Researchers studying contextual influences on adolescents' individuation, identity formation, and positive development have examined both adolescents' surroundings and the relationships among those contexts. For example, both mothers' and fathers' religiosity is associated with the authoritative parenting of adolescents (Gunnoe, Hetherington, & Reiss, 1999). Parents who do not regularly attend church or synagogue and whose children do not participate in a religious youth group were unlikely to know the names of their children's friends or their friends' parents or teachers or to have spoken with them (Smith, 2003b). In addition, in a recent test of the "channeling hypothesis" of parental influence on religious identity (i.e., that parents influence adolescents by selecting their religious congregation and a faith-oriented peer group), researchers found that *both* peer and parent influences remained stable across grades 7 to 12 (Martin, White, & Perlman, 2003). Family and peer contexts are both significant predictors of high school students' experiences of God and attitudes towards religion (King, Furrow, & Roth, 2002).

Family Contexts

As we discussed in this chapter, a key psychosocial task in adolescence is individuation from parents or other significant family members. Using this perspective, several influential studies of adolescent-parent relationships have clearly demonstrated that the interplay of individuality and connectedness in families is associated with the breadth and depth of adolescents' identity exploration (e.g., Cooper, Grotevant, & Condon, 1983; see also Cooper, 1999). Separation anxiety is also associated with the imaginary audience behavior of early adolescents and reflects a desire for maintaining closeness with parents. On the other hand, personal fables are related to separation-individuation and reflect a desire to establish a separate sense of self (Vartanian, 1997, 2000).

These studies demonstrate that a balance between parental behaviors, such as emotional support and parental authority, significantly influences adolescents' autonomy. For example, adolescents who score high in emotional autonomy (i.e., a subjective feeling of self-reliance) but low in parental support have more adjustment problems (Lamborn & Steinberg, 1993). Depression is more closely linked to difficulties establishing autonomy, whereas problem behaviors are more closely linked to difficulties maintaining relatedness (Allen, Hauser, Eickholt, & Bell, 1994).

Comparable findings emerge from studies of adolescents with depressed parents. For example, teens who scored high in emotional autonomy but were living with clinically depressed mothers had adjustment problems, whereas adolescents who scored high in autonomy but had psychologically healthy mothers did not (Garber & Little, 2001). Similarly, in an experience-sampling study, adolescents—especially girls—who had a depressed parent were more likely than other teens to report depression themselves (Sarigiani, Heath, & Camarena, 2003). Such findings demonstrate the importance of emotional support and availability from parents for the positive development of adolescent autonomy and emotional well-being.

The specific pattern of parenting behaviors or "parenting style" also impacts adolescents' affective experiences and interests. For example, when teens between grades 6 and 12 reported (through experience sampling) high levels of family support, they were more likely to report positive moods one year later. If parents provided high support but low challenge ("permissive parenting") or low support but high challenge ("authoritarian parenting"), adolescents' interests were more often conflicted and their emotions were more uneven. However, when parents provided interesting challenges along with supportiveness ("authoritative parenting"), teens were more positive about their goals two years later (Rathunde, 2001). Furthermore, identity researchers have found that patterns of parental authority contributed to identity commitments in later adolescence (Berzonsky, 2004).

School Contexts

As we discussed in chapter 6, *school climate* (i.e., the quality of interactions between adults and students in a school community) is a powerful influence on middle childhood attitudes and behaviors. For example, middle-school students' perceptions of school climate predict their self-esteem (e.g., Hoge, Smit, & Hanson, 1990). In a study of African American and White early adolescents, perceptions of school climate explained adolescent adjustment after controlling for teens' perceptions of family and peers (Eccles, Midgley, Wigfield, Miller Buchanan, Rueman, Flanagan, et al., 1997). Similarly, support from the school staff contributed to a decrease in psychological distress in African American and White early adolescents, over and above the support of family and friends (DuBois, Feiner, Brand, Adin, & Evans, 1992). In a longitudinal study of multiethnic high-school students from low-income families, both positive perceptions of school climate and increases in family support over time also contributed to adolescents' self-esteem (Way & Robinson, 2003). Finally, in a recent study of 9th- to 12th-grade students in seven ethnically diverse high schools, a sense of belonging, such as relationships with teachers and peers, accounted for student motivation and success (Faircloth & Hamm, 2005).

Developmental researchers have suggested that for teens who have not yet achieved a personal identity, "fitting in" with peers is particularly important (Dusek & McIntyre, 2003). Past research has demonstrated that support from their peers is positively associated with self-esteem and negatively related to depression. A few studies found that peer interactions were related to higher self-esteem in boys, but not in girls. Other studies have found that the relationship between self-esteem and peer support is weaker during early adolescence but becomes stronger during middle adolescence.

Community Contexts

Extensive research with ethnic-minority high-school students has linked developmental and ecocultural perspectives on identity (Cooper, 1999). An **ecocultural perspective** considers the everyday contexts in which individuals interact, such as school activities and everyday routines (e.g., Weisner, Gallimore, & Jordan, 1988). Also called a **multiple worlds model**, this approach considers the fact that ethnic-minority teens navigate diverse cultures, such as family, peer, and school contexts (e.g., Phelan, Davidson, & Yu, 1991). A central concern of researchers is how to understand the multiple worlds of diverse adolescents without fostering stereotypes based on race, ethnicity, gender, social class, and country of origin (Cooper, 1999; Cooper, Jackson, Azmitia, & Lopez, 1998).

In focus groups, African American and Latino adolescents talked about a wide array of worlds, including their families, countries of origin, friends' homes, churches, mosques, academic outreach programs, shopping malls, video arcades (mostly junior high boys), school clubs, and sports. They also discussed their "scripts" for communicating across these worlds, especially for responding to adults' "*gatekeeping*" (e.g., teachers who discouraged them from taking academics that would prepare them for college) and negative expectations (e.g., adults who thought they would fail, become pregnant, or engage in delinquent activities). On the other hand, students described how their families, friends, siblings, and teachers spoke up for them at school, at home, or in their neighborhoods, called "*brokering*" (Cooper, 1999). The challenges presented by *gatekeeping* and the support provided by *brokering* facilitated adolescents' identity formation and their motivation to succeed on behalf of their families and communities. For example, analyses that compared high and low achievers found that higher-achieving students were more likely to describe their parents as making them feel special, teachers as helping them stay on track to college, and sisters as helping them with homework and planning for the future (Cooper, 1999). The researchers concluded that the interplay of individuality and connectedness fosters identity development in adolescents.

CHAPTER REVIEW

Affective Development

- The affective domain of adolescent development includes personality, self-understanding, and emotional development.
- Adolescents negotiate the task of consolidating their self-understandings and others' perceptions into a personal ideology known as identity.
- The process of identity development requires that adolescents integrate various self-beliefs into a unified whole and perceive themselves as distinct individuals.

Theoretical Viewpoints

- According to psychoanalytic theory, teenagers' major psychological task involves becoming an increasingly autonomous individual, called individuation.
- Adolescent egocentrism, composed of two major thought patterns, an imaginary audience and a personal fable, is common in early adolescence.
- According to symbolic interaction theory, adolescents construct personal meaning and identity through their interactions with others.
- According to social identity theory, adolescents' identities are based on their positive or negative feelings about their group membership(s).

Identity Development

- Erikson believed that the primary task of adolescence is identity formation.
- Identity is accomplished through the processes of exploration and commitment. Most adolescents have either a foreclosed or diffused identity status.
- Identity style describes the different approaches that adolescents use to construct and change their identities.
- Self-discrepancy describes the congruity (or lack of congruity) among the adolescent's self-beliefs or identities.

Racial/Ethnic Identity

- Racial identity refers to adolescents' sense of self compared to other perceived racial groups.
- Ethnic identity refers to a sense of belonging to one's ethnic group.
- Multiethnic or biracial adolescents may have difficulty integrating both racial heritages into a coherent identity.
- Adolescents' feelings of being "ethnic" often depend on the situation and the people they are with.

Spiritual/Religious Identity

- Different but related constructs describe adolescents' discovery and practice of self-transcendence: faith, spirituality, and religion.

- Six stages of faith development describe a cognitive-developmental theory of understanding of religious beliefs.
- Contemporary research generally supports the importance of religion in the lives of today's adolescents, including nontraditional forms of worship.
- Religious participation serves as a protective factor against risky behavior in adolescence.

Vocational/Political Identity

- Vocational identity refers both to career development and to the political commitments that may guide adolescents' future goals.
- Career development in adolescence involves career exploration, volunteer opportunities, and paid work experiences.
- Political identity involves a range of civic and community activities, often referred to as civic engagement.
- A sense of purpose is defined as a stable and generalized intention to accomplish something that is both meaningful to adolescents and of consequence to the world beyond themselves.

Emotion and Mood

- Adolescents commonly report more negative moods than school-age children and wider and quicker mood swings than adults, but they are not more likely to experience rapid mood swings than preadolescents.
- As adolescents mature they learn to interpret their experiences and regulate their emotions in more positive ways.
- The myth of adolescent moodiness may be due to the fact that older teens are less likely to report positive emotions and more likely to report mildly negative moods than younger teens.
- While rates of depression and negative mood increase between ages 11 and 12 for both sexes, by age 13 girls often show significantly more symptoms of depression than boys.

Adolescent Self-Esteem

- Self-esteem is significantly related to the affective experience of feeling positive and negative emotions.
- Self-esteem ratings of adolescents appear mostly stable across the high-school years.
- Girls' scores on traditional measures of self-esteem are lower than boys' but the differences are small.
- A balance between hoped-for and dreaded possible selves is related to adolescent adjustment and positive self-esteem.

Affective Development in Context

- A balance between individuality and connectedness with parents and family members positively influences adolescents' development of autonomy.
- A positive school climate and emotional support from teachers and parents contribute to adolescents' high self-esteem.
- Ethnic-minority adolescents typically navigate diverse cultures, such as family, peer, and school contexts, called "multiple worlds."

TABLE 10–9
Developmental Theories

Chapter	Theory	Focus
10: Affective Development in Adolescence	Ego Development	Gradual changes in self-definition during adolescence that involve increasing autonomy and self-reliance.
	Identity	Exploring ideological and interpersonal commitments as well as group identities, such as ethnicity, religion, and gender.
	Symbolic Interaction	Relationships take place in a social context and are subject to socially constructed meanings.

KEY TERMS

Acculturation
Affective experiences
Autonomy
Bicultural
Career development
Civic engagement
Commitment
Conformist stage
Ecocultural perspective
Ego development
Ego identity
Emotional competence
Emotions
Ethnic identity
Experience sampling
Exploration
Faith
Faith development stages
Identity
Identity crisis
Identity statuses

Identity styles
Identity vs. role confusion
Individuation
Intersectionality
Moods
Moratorium
Multiple worlds model
Political development
Possible selves
Racial identity
Racial/ethnic socialization
Religiosity
Self-discrepancy
Self-esteem
Sense of purpose
Social identity theory
Spatial-temporal integration
Spirituality
Symbolic interaction
Synthetic-conventional faith
Vocational identities

SUGGESTED ACTIVITIES

1. Examine adolescents' personal home pages on the World Wide Web. Refer to this article: http://www.aber.ac.uk/media/Documents/short/strasbourg.html. Analyze a teenager's home page for evidence of identity diffusion, foreclosure, moratorium, or achievement.
2. Visit a church, temple, synagogue, or mosque youth group and talk with adolescents about what their religion means to them.
3. Talk to a career counselor at a local high school. Find out what activities and opportunities they make available to students. Ask particularly about the involvement of parents. Refer to Table 10–6. Can you determine what career development approach they are using?
4. Select a popular magazine with an ethnic minority or sexual minority target audience, such as *blackgirl* or *OUT*. Read the letters to the editor. What identity issues do you find to be salient in readers' responses?

RECOMMENDED RESOURCES

Suggested Readings

Csikzsentmihalyi, M., & Schneider, B. (2001). *Becoming adult: How teenagers prepare for the world of work.* New York: Basic Books.

Flory, R. W., & Miller, D. E. (Eds.) (2000). *Gen-X religion.* New York: Routledge.

Fowler, J. W. (1981). *Stages of faith: The psychology of human development and the quest for meaning.* San Francisco: Harper & Row.

Josselson, R. (1987). *Finding herself: Pathways to identity development in women.* San Francisco: Jossey-Bass.

McAdoo, H. P. (Ed.) (1999). *Family ethnicity: Strength in diversity.* Thousand Oaks, CA: Sage.

Suggested Online Resources

Chandler, D., & Roberts-Young, D. (1998). *The construction of identity in adolescent personal homepages.* http://www.aber.ac.uk/media/Documents/short/strasbourg.html

Ineffable: Fiction for teens about religion, God & spirituality
http://www.berkeleypubliclibrary.org/teen/ineff.html

National Study of Youth and Religion
http://www. youthandreligion.org/research/

Parenting and Career Development
http://career.ucsd.edu/parents/PACD.shtml

The Internet: A Resource for Religious Teens
http://www.youthandreligion.org/news/2003-1210.html

Suggested Web Sites

America's Career Resource Network
http://www.acrnetwork.org/

Child Trends: Racial and Ethnic Composition of the Child Population
http://www.childtrendsdatabank.org/indicators/60RaceandEthnicComposition.cfm

Life Works: Explore Health and Medical Science Careers
http://science.education.nih.gov/LifeWorks.nsf

The New Americans
http://www.pbs.org/independentlens/newamericans/

Parent's Guide: Your Teen in the Working World
http://inside.bard.edu/academic/specialproj/darling/transition/group27/career.htm

Safe Teens: A place for parents and teens to learn how to use the Internet safely
http://www.safeteens.com/

Suggested Films and Videos

Adolescence: Social and emotional development (1995). Magna Systems, Inc. (38 minutes)

Everybody's ethnic: Your invisible culture. Learning Seed, Inc. (21 minutes)

Ghost world (2001). MGM Home Entertainment (111 minutes)

My so-called life: Pilot. (2002). Ventura Distribution (47 minutes)

Reviving Ophelia (2003). Media Education Foundation (38 minutes)

Self, identity & sex role development (1993). Magna Systems, Inc. (29 minutes)

CHAPTER 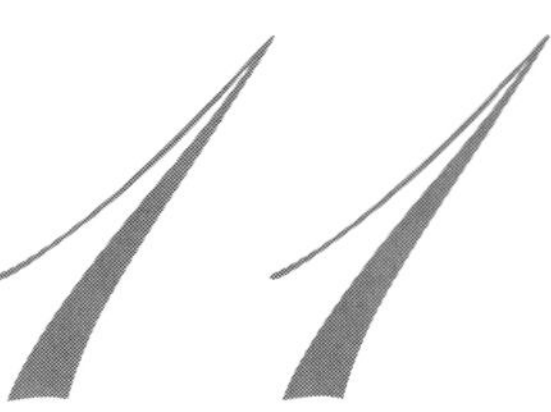

Social Development in Middle Adolescence

CHAPTER OBJECTIVES

After reading this chapter, students will be able to:

- Define social development in middle adolescence
- Summarize theories of adolescent attachment and family systems
- Describe adolescents' understanding of gender and sexuality
- Discuss current research on intimate friendships, romantic relationships, and family relationships in middle adolescence
- Explain the contributions of family, school, and community to social development in middle adolescence

They seem like a perfectly normal family. Richard Chasen, his wife Joan, 15-year-old Annie, and 18-year-old Rick are getting ready for the wedding of 20-year-old Beth. Mr. and Mrs. Chasen are relieved to be launching the first of their three children. And next fall, Rick goes off to college. That leaves Annie, who is just beginning to date. But Annie is worried about her brother. She suspects that if their parents find out that he's gay, they will be bitterly disappointed, maybe even angry. Besides Annie, only Matthew, his best friend, knows about Rick's romantic attraction to boys. He certainly can't talk to his parents about it—although he knows his mom suspects. Rick just hopes that he can make it through the summer without telling his parents about his sexual orientation.

Social Development in Adolescence

Adolescent social development describes the interactions of teens with their friends and families. Most of the research on adolescent social development is based on the study of same-sex and cross-sex friendships and on parent-adolescent relationships. Compared to social interactions in middle childhood, personal relationships with friends become more intimate while interactions with family members often become more distant (Collins & Repinski, 1994). In this chapter, close relationships are defined as enduring ties or connections between two people, composed of frequent interdependent action sequences that occur across diverse settings and tasks (Kelley et al., 1983).

Theoretical Viewpoints

Various theories have guided the existing research on close relationships in middle adolescence, primarily attachment theories and family systems theories. Both of these theoretical perspectives assume the dyadic relationship *itself* adds a new dimension to each interaction, whether it is between siblings, teenage friends, parents and children, or adolescent romantic partners. In this regard, our focus is not on the individual adolescent, as in chapter 10, but on the characteristics of close relationships, social networks, and family systems.

Attachment Perspectives

Theories of attachment have been important in the study of relationship development since the mid-20th century. Growing out of psychoanalytic theory's emphasis on the importance of early relationships—especially the mother-infant bond—attachment theories have been used to describe relationship histories across the life span, from infancy to adulthood (e.g., Ainsworth & Bell, 1969; Bartholomew & Horowitz, 1991; Bowlby, 1988; Elicker, Englund, & Sroufe, 1992; Hazan & Shaver, 1987; Lewis, Feiring, & Rosenthal, 2000; Main, Kaplan, & Cassidy, 1985; Thompson, 1999; Weinfeld, Sroufe, & Egeland, 2000). However, while psychoanalysis focused primarily on the development of *individuals*, attachment theory focuses on the development of *relationships* (Fonagy, 1999).

Stages of attachment. John Bowlby (1969, 1973) described a developmental sequence of attachment relationships in the first 3 years of life. These phases of early attachment are described in Table 11–1. For

TABLE 11–1
Phases of Attachment
Bowlby's phases of infant attachment are parallel to the phases of romantic attachment in adolescence.

Attachment Phase	Infancy and Childhood	Adolescence
1. Preattachment	8 to 12 weeks • Orienting to people • Crying, cooing, smiling • Reaching towards others	Attraction and flirting
2. Attachment-in-the-making	3 to 6–7 months • Discriminates primary caregivers • Social smiling • Babbling with familiar others	Falling in love
3. Clear-cut attachment	6 months to 2–3 years • Crawls, walks • Explores environment using attachment figure as a secure base • Stranger anxiety begins about 10 months	Loving relationship
4. Goal-corrected partnership	2–3 years and older • Communicates with words • Able to consider intentions of caregivers • Less distress at separation with secure attachment	Postromance phase (life-as-usual)

Source: Based on "Pair Bonds as Attachments" (pp. 349–351), by C. Hazan and D. Zeifman, in *Handbook of Attachment: Theory, Research, and Clinical Applications* (pp. 336–354), 1999, New York: Guilford. Copyright 1999 by the Guilford Press.

Bowlby and other psychoanalysts (e.g., Mahler, Pine, & Bergman, 1975) the goal of attachment is to move from a totally dependent relationship with an attachment figure in infancy to a more interdependent partnership. By age 3, young children are likely to have formed an enduring emotional attachment to at least one, if not more, caregivers. Recently, developmental theorists have described the phases as they apply to the development of romantic attachments in adolescence, also shown in Table 11–1.

Bowlby was influenced by **ethology**, or the study of animal behavior, such as research on imprinting, or following behavior, in goslings (e.g., Lorenz, 1970) and comfort-seeking behaviors in infant monkeys separated from their mothers at birth (e.g., Harlow & Harlow, 1962). Bowlby theorized that proximity-seeking behaviors in animals may serve a similar function in humans. For example, all children turn to their parents for security, but in middle childhood and adolescence, they also seek proximity to their peers for a safe haven (e.g., Nickerson & Nagle, 2005). Subsequent life-span research has documented that four types of attachment behaviors apply to childhood and adolescence as well as to infancy, as illustrated in Table 11–2 (Bowlby, 1988). From this perspective, the responsiveness of an adolescent's attachment figure can provide a sense of security that is highly adaptive, similar to Erikson's sense of "basic trust" in others (described in chapter 5). On the other hand, unresponsiveness may result in a sense of "mistrust" of others, described by attachment researchers as **anxious attachment**, or insecurity.

In the case of Rick, insecurity is demonstrated by a lack of trust that his parents will accept his sexual orientation.

Categories of attachment. Researchers who have studied infants in stressful situations have found that they may experience a range of attachment, from secure to insecure (Ainsworth, Bell, & Stayton, 1971). During a sequence of short-term separations and reunions alternating between their mother and a stranger in a laboratory playroom, called the *Strange Situation*, researchers classified children into four attachment groups (Ainsworth, Blehar, Waters, & Wall, 1978; Main & Solomon, 1990):

A. **Anxious-avoidant.** Explores readily; little visible distress when left alone; looks away and actively avoids parents upon reunion.
B. **Secure.** Uses mother as a secure base for exploration; shows signs of missing parent during separations; greets parent positively upon reunion.
C. **Anxious-resistant.** Visibly distressed upon entering playroom; fails to explore; is distressed during separation; shows angry rejection or ambivalence upon reunion.
D. **Disorganized.** Does not show a clear-cut attachment strategy; appears confused, disoriented.

With older children, adolescents, and adults, self-report methods of assessing attachment security have proven equally useful for determining attachment classifications (for reviews of measures, see Bartholomew & Horowitz, 1991; Kerns, Tomich, Aspelmeier, & Contreras, 2000; Solomon & George, 1999). For example, school-age children have successfully characterized their own sense of security or anxiety by using paper-and-pencil measures based on Harter's "How I See Myself" scale described in chapter 5: "Your family moves to a new neighborhood. Some kids would

TABLE 11–2

Goals of Attachment

Attachment behaviors may fulfill any of four functions in adolescence.

System	Description	Example
Attachment	Behaviors that maintain proximity to an attachment figure	Checking in with their parents; staying near to a boy/girlfriend
Affiliative	Behaviors that ensure social relatedness to an attachment figure	Smiling, hugging, flirting, or holding hands
Caretaking	Behaviors that elicit care from an attachment figure	Seeking comfort from family or friends when distressed
Reproductive	Behaviors that promote sexual attachments	Kissing, petting, or having sexual intercourse

want to explore their new neighborhood a little on their own, but other kids would stay home unless their mother could go with them. Which is more like you?" (Finnegan, Hodges, & Perry, 1996; Kerns, Klepac, & Cole, 1996, p. 1326). Other researchers have observed and coded children's doll play (Main, Kaplan, & Cassidy, 1885), asked children to complete stories about separation (Oppenheim & Waters, 1995), or asked children to draw pictures of their families and coded them for indications of the attachment categories (Fury, Carlson, & Sroufe, 1997).

Generally, researchers have found that the secure (group B) and insecure groups (groups A and C) are replicable with adolescents (group D is not classifiable, by definition) (Waters, Hamilton, & Weinfeld, 2000). In addition, secure attachment to caregivers measured at age 16 is related to identity achievement at age 18, whereas insecure attachment is related to identity diffusion (Zimmerman & Becker-Stoll, 2002). Recall, however, that attachment is not considered a personality *trait* that is stable across the life span, but rather is seen as a feature of a particular relationship.

For example, Rick's secure early attachment to his mother is likely to influence his disclosure first to her and then to his father.

Therefore, it is important to remember that a secure or insecure attachment classification applies *only* to the relationship being studied *at that time* (e.g., a parent-child relationship). If *every* relationship can potentially be classified as either *secure* or *insecure*, however, how can attachment theory contribute to our overall understanding of social development?

Teens who are securely attached to their parents are also likely to have positive relationships with friends and romantic partners.

Working models of attachment. Bowlby (1969) theorized that our early attachments to parents or other caregivers would form the basis of all future relationships through the mechanism of an **internal working model**, or the mental representation of *all* relationships. The working model formulation states that our earliest attachments may influence our social relationships—from early childhood peer interactions to middle childhood friendships to adolescent romantic partnerships (for a complete review, see Bretherton & Munholland, 1999). From this perspective, then, adolescents continue to be affected by early attachment relations to others, called "social objects."

Over the years since Bowlby first proposed attachment theory, many developmental researchers have tested the "working model" hypothesis through longitudinal studies (e.g., Bohlin, Hagekull, & Rydell, 2000; Elicker, Egelund, & Sroufe, 1992; Freitag, Belsky, Grossmann, Grossmann, & Scheuerer-Englisch, 1996; Lewis, Feiring, & Rosenthal, 2000; Weinfield, Sroufe, & Egeland, 2000; for a review, see Thompson, 1999). For example, children who are securely attached to parents during the middle childhood years have shown greater social skills, have more reciprocated friendships, and are more popular with their peers (Coleman, 2003; Granot & Mayseless, 2001; Kerns, Klepac, & Cole, 1996).

Similarly, in a study of 15- to 18-year-olds in the Netherlands, adolescents with high scores on a parent-adolescent attachment measure were more socially skilled with peers. Furthermore, their social skills were related to higher perceived competence in relationships with friends and romantic partners (Engels, Finkenauer, Meeus, & Dekovic, 2001). Among sexually active adolescents, attachment security has also been associated with becoming sexually active at later ages, having fewer sexual partners, and using contraception more often (Allen & Land, 1999). Taken together, these varied research studies lend strong support for Bowlby's hypothesis that an internal working model of relationships guides social interaction during adolescence.

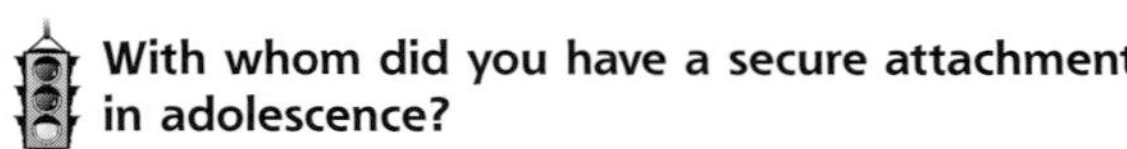
With whom did you have a secure attachment in adolescence?

Family Systems Perspectives

In the early 20th century, scholars in several disciplines (e.g., biology, mathematics, physics, computer engineering) began to theorize about the interrelationships among the components of living and nonliving systems, such as biological environments and electronic circuits (White & Klein, 2002). The basic principle of **systems theory** is that all of the components of a system are interrelated and cannot be understood as individual parts. Put another way, the whole is greater than the sum of its parts. By the 1960s, psychologists, anthropologists, and sociologists began to apply these concepts to the study of interpersonal relationships (White & Klein, 2002). In terms of a social system, such as a family or friendship network, each person influences—and is influenced by—everyone else in the group.

In the chapter case example, Rick imagines what he'll do and say at the wedding based on everyone else's reaction to him. He thinks that it's definitely going to be weird: all of the relatives asking if he has a girlfriend.

In a **family systems** approach, the unit of analysis is the *family* rather than the individual. Every person in a family affects the interactions and relationships among the other family members, even when they are not physically present! Family theorists and therapists have identified general principles of family systems (Blume, 2006), for example:

- **Levels.** Families are composed of many simultaneously operating subsystems (e.g., the marital system, the parent-child system, or the sibling system).
- **Boundaries.** Families can be more or less open to exchanges with their surroundings (e.g., the walls of the house serve as physical boundaries, but the Internet or cell phones can extend teens' relationships beyond the home).
- **Equilibrium.** Family systems ultimately strive for balance in their relationships (e.g., gay youth who don't want to upset their parents by sharing information about their romantic attractions).

Systems theory has significantly influenced family therapy interventions, such as working with troubled adolescents and their parents and/or siblings. But it is only beginning to be applied to the study of close relationships in adolescence, such as interactions between parent and peer systems. For example, a recent model of communication processes within families is pictured in Figure 11.1. This family systems model illustrates how adolescents' disclosure to parents about their activities with friends provides parents with knowledge, which creates trusting parents, who in turn do not react negatively to their teenagers' disclosures (Kerr, Stattin, Biesecker, & Ferrer-Wreder, 2003).

Think about Rick's reluctance to risk "coming out" as gay to his parents. Their reaction to his spending so much time with Matthew has already been pretty negative, so he is unlikely to say more.

How did your relationships with your friends influence other members of your family?

GENDER AND SEXUALITY IN MIDDLE ADOLESCENCE

Social interactions are influenced not only by the characteristics of a particular relationship (e.g., secure/insecure) but also by the social constructions of the relationship partners themselves (e.g., gender/sexuality). Extensive research on the development of childhood gender understanding and gendered behaviors has documented that, by middle adolescence, most teens have an elaborate self-construction of their gender identity. **Gender identity** refers to one's biological sex as well as to one's identification with **gender roles**, a set of attitudes and behaviors associated with the cultural conventions of being male or female (Bailey, 1996; O'Brien, 1992; Green, 1985). Adolescents show a range of behaviors from stereotypically male to stereotypically female (see Feiring, 1999a; Tolman, Spencer, Rosen-Reynoso, & Porche, 2003).

Let's examine Annie's social construction of gender in the chapter case. Annie sees the family wedding as a romantic occasion. Unlike Rick, Annie is excited and eager to attend her first wedding. Her mother has told her many romantic stories about her own wedding, and she hopes to catch the bouquet!

Gender identity is composed of five major components (Egan & Perry, 2001):

1. **Membership Knowledge.** Knowledge of membership in a gender category (e.g., "I am a girl")
2. **Gender Typicality.** The degree to which one feels like a typical member of a gender category (e.g., "I'm just like the other girls")
3. **Gender Contentedness.** How happy one is with one's gender assignment (e.g., "I like being a girl")

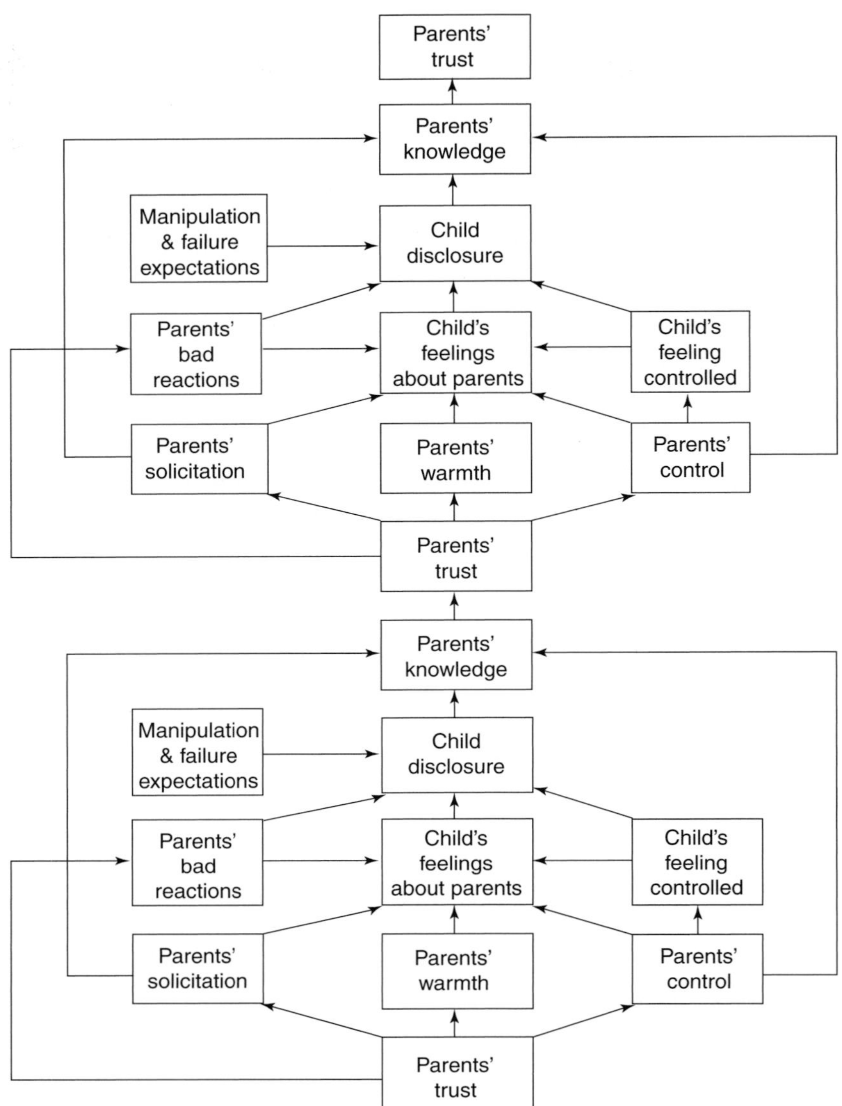

FIGURE 11.1 A Systems Model of Family Communication
This systems model applied to the Chasen family would suggest that Rick's feelings about his parents' likely reactions (e.g., support or control) are an important link in the chain of events leading to a possible disclosure of his sexual orientation and subsequently to their increased knowledge and trust.

Source: From "Relationships with Parents and Peers in Adolescence" (p. 409) by M. Kerr, H. Stattin, G. Biesecker, and L. Ferrer-Wreder, in R. M. Lerner and M. A. Easterbrook (Eds.), *Handbook of Psychology: Developmental Psychology, Vol. 6: Emotion and Personality Development in Childhood* (pp. 395–419), 2003, New York: Wiley. Copyright 2003 by John Wiley and Sons. Reprinted by permission.

4. **Pressure for Gender Conformity.** The degree to which one feels pressure from parents, peers, and oneself for conformity to gender stereotypes (e.g., "I ought to act like a girl")
5. **Intergroup Bias.** The extent to which one believes one's sex is superior to the other (e.g., "Girls are better than boys") (adapted from Carver, Yunger, & Perry, 2003)

For example, most children recognize that social expectations for the activities of boys and girls are stereotyped by sex (e.g., boys are football players, girls are cheerleaders). In addition, most school-age children conform to gender boundaries for self-presentation (e.g., dress, hairstyle) that are strictly enforced by peer culture (Martin, Ruble, & Szkrybalo, 2002; Thorne, 1993). By adolescence, most children can recognize that gender-role stereotypes are social conventions. However, most still choose the "safe" alternative of behaving in sex-stereotypic ways (O'Brien, 1992).

But how accurate are stereotypes about sex differences between males and females? Recall from chapter 9 that researchers have examined previous research findings using a technique called *meta-analysis*. In meta-analyses of social behaviors, sex differences in aggression appeared fairly reliably across different studies but tended to be smaller in more recent studies. Overall results of meta-analyses indicate that sex differences decrease with age and that only about 5% of the difference is due to gender (Hyde, 1984).

Gender-Role Orientation

Gender-role behaviors that are more or less stereotypic are called **sex-typed** (e.g., *masculine, feminine*) or **nonsex-typed** (e.g., *androgynous, undifferentiated*) (Bem, 1974, 1981; see also Spence & Helmreich, 1980):

- **Masculine.** Behaviors that are male-stereotypic (e.g., competitive, aggressive, interested in instrumental, or goal-oriented, activities)
- **Feminine.** Behaviors that are female-stereotypic (e.g., nurturing, expressive, interested in relationships)
- **Androgynous.** Behaviors that combine male and female characteristics (e.g., instrumental and expressive)
- **Undifferentiated.** Behaviors that are not typical of either sex-role stereotype (e.g., acts differently in varying contexts)

Box 11.1 provides an example of a measure for adolescents to rate themselves on sex-typed characteristics. This inventory was originally designed by Sandra Bem (1974) for adults and later revised for use with adolescents (Thomas & Robinson, 1981).

Some developmental theorists have argued that gendered behaviors intensify in adolescence as a result of the onset of puberty, called the **gender intensification hypothesis** (Hill & Lynch, 1983). As adolescents begin to adopt male or female roles in anticipation of dating and other adult behaviors, they are presumed to act in more sex-stereotyped ways. For example, early-maturing adolescents are more likely to become wives and mothers than attend college if they associated with older teens during adolescence (Stattin & Magnusson, 1990).

Research in support of gender intensification is mixed. One study found that sex differences in masculinity, but not femininity, increased from ages 11 to 13 years (Galambos, Almeida, & Petersen, 1990). **Masculinity ideology** is the belief that men and boys ought to adhere to culturally defined standards for male behavior. The girls may not have shown as dramatic a rise in femininity as boys did in masculinity because masculinity is more highly valued in society.

The form of masculinity that is culturally dominant in a given setting is called **hegemonic masculinity.** Furthermore, hegemonic masculinity is highly visible, as in school peer groups, where a small number of highly influential boys are admired by many others (Connell, 1996). For example, in a study of African American, White, and Latino boys from ages 15 to 19, masculinity ideology was related to boys' self-reported problem behaviors (e.g., sexual activity, substance use, delinquency, school problems), suggesting that traditional masculinity is a negative influence on adolescent boys (Pleck, Sonnenstein, & Ku, 1993).

Recently, scholars have criticized gender-role orientations as outdated since they are based on dichotomous sex categories (i.e., male is the opposite of female) that no longer reflect 21st-century constructions of gender as fluid and context dependent (Bailey, 1996; Bem, 1993; Hegarty, 2002). In addition, gay and lesbian adolescents may not feel as bound by gender roles as heterosexual teens (Turner, 2003). Because of their cognitive constructions of gender, called **gender schemas**, adolescents may either act in sex-typed ways or may transcend stereotypic gender roles (Eccles, 1987).

According to gender-schema theory, gender-role transcendence involves reducing dependence on gender-based stereotypes as a basis for

BOX 11.1 ROADMAP TO UNDERSTANDING THEORY AND RESEARCH

Adolescent Sex-Role Inventory

1. Stand up for your ideas†
2. Loving*
3. Care about the things you do
4. On your own†
5. Understanding*
6. Moods go up and down
7. Forceful†
8. Aware of other people's feelings*
9. Someone you can count on
10. Bold†
11. Can feel how another person feels*
12. Afraid someone is taking your place
13. Make people do what you want†
14. Caring*
15. Honest
16. Able to direct a group†
17. Want to help someone*
18. Keep to yourself
19. Willing to take risks†
20. Warm*
21. Able to adjust
22. Take charge†
23. Tender*
24. Think you are better than most people
25. Not afraid to speak out†
26. Love children*
27. Think before you talk
28. Go after what you want†
29. Gentle*
30. Do things the way others expect them done

†Masculinity Scale
*Femininity Scale

Each item is self-rated by the adolescent on a scale of 1 (low) to 7 (high). A higher masculinity score indicates a masculine gender-role orientation; a higher femininity score indicates a feminine gender-role orientation. High scores on both the masculinity and femininity scales indicate androgyny. Low scores on both indicate an undifferentiated orientation.

Source: Based on "Development of a Measure of Androgyny for Young Adolescents," by S. Thomas and M. Robinson, 1981, *Journal of Early Adolescence, 1* (2), pp. 195–209. Copyright 1981 by Sage Publications, Inc.

determining one's own actions and beliefs and for judging the behavior of others (O'Brien, 1992). For example, gender development researchers have studied the relationship between school-age children's attitudes about others and their self-characterizations in middle childhood. They found that girls who held fewer stereotypes of masculine activities for others showed greater acceptance of masculine attitudes in themselves. Boys, on the other hand, who endorsed more feminine traits in themselves in grade 6 held increasingly egalitarian gender attitudes by grade 7 (Liben & Bigler, 2002). From this perspective, an adolescent's ability to move past traditional concepts of male and female represents a processing of gender schemas that incorporates aspects of both masculine and feminine into an integrated identity (O'Brien, 1992).

Recall Annie from the chapter case. She confidently wears pink nail polish, and at the same time is considered the family athlete.

Stages of Gender Development

Based on gender-schema theory, developmental psychologists proposed a sequence of gender-role stages from undifferentiated gender identity in infancy to the transcending of gender roles in adolescence, as shown in Table 11–3 (Eccles & Bryan, 1994; Rebecca, Hefner, & Oleshansky, 1976). In this developmental sequence, early childhood understandings of gender are both descriptive (i.e., "she's a girl") and prescriptive (i.e., "only girls play with dolls"). By school age, children are cognitively able to separate external manifestations (e.g., appearance) from internal stable constructs like gender identity (e.g., boys can do many things girls do without altering their sex) (Eccles & Bryan, 1994).

In early adolescence (roughly ages 10 to 15), however, because of the appearance of the secondary sex characteristics associated with puberty

Guideposts for Working with Adolescents

- Be a model for nonsexist language and teach nonsexist usage in the language arts curriculum.
- Avoid labeling activities and interests as masculine or feminine.
- Help both boys and girls recognize male privilege in society by analyzing institutions in which hegemonic masculinity is common, such as politics.
- Ask teens to make a list of their own sexist attitudes as a way to reflect on the origin of such beliefs.

and the increasing social pressure to conform to traditional gender-role expectations, such as dating, many teens may "regress" to gender-role stereotypes (Eccles & Bryan, 1994). This process is consistent with the gender intensification hypothesis described earlier. In seventh grade, for example, physically mature boys spent more time playing sports, whereas physically mature girls spent less time on sports. More mature seventh graders of both sexes, however, spent more time socializing

TABLE 11–3

Stages of Gender-Role Identity

Adolescent gender roles are usually intensely stereotypical, but this rigidity often declines with identity formation during middle adolescence.

Stage	Age Period	Description
Stage I	0–2 years	**Undifferentiated Gender Role** The child is unaware of gender as a social category and has not yet learned gender-role stereotypic beliefs.
Stage II	2–7 years	**Hyper-Gender-Role Differentiation** Gender becomes a very important and salient social category. Children actively seek to learn their culture's gender-role system, and, in so doing, generate their own gender-role stereotypes that are consistent with the commonly held stereotypes in their culture.
Stage III	7–11 years	**Gender-Role Differentiation** Cognitively, the emergence of conventional moral thought and a growing awareness of social roles may lead the child to maintain a belief in the prescriptive nature of stereotypes, particularly if this view is reinforced by the social actors in a child's life.
Stage IV	12–16 years	**Transition Phase 1** Despite the cognitive capacity to transcend the prescriptive function of stereotypes, sociocultural forces may produce a rigidification of gender-role schema and a reemergence of confusion between gender identity and gender-role identity. **Transition Phase 2** If the sociocultural milieu provides the necessary stimuli and adolescents have not committed to traditional gender roles, they may transcend the gender-role identity as one element of the resolution of their identity crisis.
Stage V	16–22 years	**Identity and Gender-Role Transcendence** The ambivalent crises of Stage IV have been resolved into an integration of masculinity and femininity that transcends gender roles.

Source: Based on "Adolescence: Critical Crossroad in the Path of Gender-Role Development," by J. Eccles and J. Bryan, in M. R. Stevenson (Ed.), *Gender Roles through the Lifespan: A Multidisciplinary Perspective* (pp. 132–134), 1994, Muncie, IN: Ball State University Press.

with the opposite sex than did their less mature peers (Eccles & Bryan, 1994).

Although researchers have extensively documented the development of gender-role attitudes, gender schemas, and gendered behaviors during the early and middle childhood periods, much less research has been conducted on adolescence (for a review, see Ruble & Martin, 1998). In fact, the legacy of same-sex peer groups in middle childhood—when boys and girls acquire different experiences and therefore relational skills—may foster potential conflicts and relationship dissatisfaction for adolescents in romantic relationships (Leaper, 1994; Leaper & Anderson, 1997).

As middle and late adolescents (roughly ages 13 to 26 years) explore their gender identities, gender-role stereotyped behaviors may decrease. Growth towards gender-role transcendence means reducing the salience of biological sex as a defining property of one's identity (Eccles & Bryant, 1994). For example, children and adolescents exposed to an egalitarian child-rearing environment in which men and women, and boys and girls, are treated equally are more likely to transcend traditional gender roles (Risman, 1998; Risman & Johnson-Sumerford, 1998; Risman & Myers, 1997; see also Weisner & Wilson-Mitchell, 1990). When adolescents transgress gender categories, they are referred to as **gender nonconforming**.

This term could be used to describe Rick's early development. As a child, he avoided playing outside with the other boys in the neighborhood. Joan always thought to herself that her son was different from the others—more interested in playing with his sisters or helping around the house. Her husband always tried to get Rick interested in sports, but Annie was the athlete in the family, not Rick.

Generally, cross-gender behavior receives greater disapproval when done by boys than girls (Ruble & Martin, 1998). Girls are not often considered masculine if they play competitive sports, but boys may be seen as effeminate if they pursue creative arts or literature (Owens, 1998; Savin-Williams, 1996). For example, recalling his adolescence, a 19-year-old gay youth stated that, as far back as he could remember, he was always teased about not being very masculine and was called a "sissy" and a "fairy" (Savin-Williams, 1996). According to social-identity theory (discussed in chapter 10), males are the high-status group. Therefore, boys tend to emphasize sex-stereotypic behaviors more than girls in order to maintain their social advantage. A cross-cultural study of adolescents' perceptions of an "ideal" man and woman illustrates this nicely. Teens drew pictures that were clearly influenced by the gender roles in their cultures, as seen in Box 11.2.

When one's gender identity differs from one's biological or genetic sex, the descriptive term is ***transgender*** (i.e., feeling, looking, or acting like the other sex). Although many adolescents either seek counseling or try to "fit in" by wearing gender-neutral or gender-typical clothing, some adolescents may start high school as clearly transgendered, and their families may have made an arrangement with the school for them to be registered in the "new" sex and adopt an opposite-sex name (Cohen-Kettenis & Pflafflin, 2003). Some may eventually fall in love and have relationships with same-sex peers. However, *transgender* refers only to gender identity, not to sexuality.

What is known about the sexual orientation of children and adolescents with atypical gender identities? Studies of very feminine boys suggest that most will become gay or bisexual. On the other hand, studies of masculine girls suggest that they have a higher-than-average chance of becoming lesbians, although most will be heterosexual (Bailey, 1996). Fourth- to eighth-grade boys and girls who questioned their heterosexuality also viewed themselves as gender nonconforming (Egan & Perry, 2001; Carver, Yunger, & Perry, 2003; Carver, Egan, & Perry, 2004). An extensive review of studies of gender-atypical play in childhood revealed that both homosexual men and women recall substantially more cross-sex-typed play in childhood than do heterosexuals, although effects were strongest for gay men (Bailey & Zucker, 1995).

What were your favorite activities in childhood and adolescence? Were they gendered?

Social Constructions of Sexuality

The social pressure to conform to normative gender roles and to identify with heterosexuality is referred to by sociologists as **heteronormativity** (Oswald, Blume, & Marks, 2005). In fact, feminist theorists usually refer to this compelling cultural force as "compulsory heterosexuality" (e.g., Rich, 1980). From this perspective, the social discourse surrounding teenagers' experience of sexuality may compel teens to enact traditional gender roles (Raymond, 1994). For example, research with teenage girls has revealed that media images are critical vehicles for adolescent girls' normative constructions of their sexuality (Chapin, 2000; Durham, 2003; Fingerson, 1999; Hyde & Jaffee, 2000; Ward, 2003; Ward, Hansbrough, & Walker, 2005).

BOX 11.2 ROADMAP TO UNDERSTANDING THEORY AND RESEARCH

Cross-Cultural Drawings of Ideal Woman and Man in a Nontraditional Role

This bar graph represents the percentage of adolescent drawings of an ideal woman or man in a nontraditional role arranged by countries' masculinity scores (endorsement of earnings, recognition, advancement, challenge, and use of skills). In "masculine" countries, women were more likely to be drawn in nontraditional roles than were men. That is, women were depicted as successful business executives, presidents of companies, and managers. In "feminine" countries, men were more often drawn in nontraditional roles than women. That is, men were drawn caring for children or engaging in housework. These differences were significant in the United States and Mexico. Overall, cultural values appeared to interact with gender roles, in that persons were more likely to be shown in the opposite gender's traditional role when those roles were consistent with cultural values.

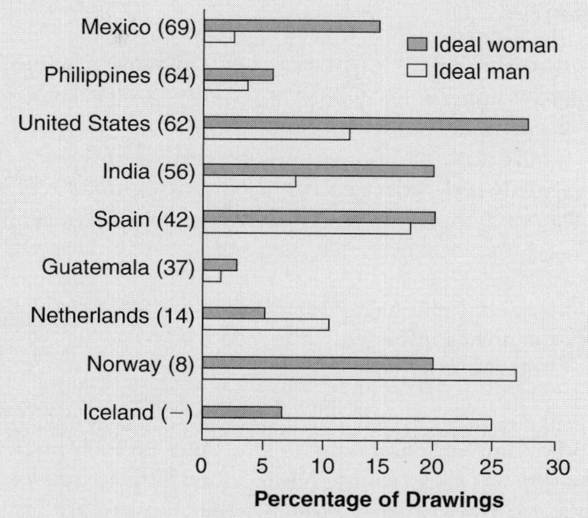

Drawings of idealized women and men by adolescents from nine countries reveal differences in cultural views of traditionality.

Source: From "Cultural Masculinity/Femininity and Adolescents' Drawings of the Ideal Man and Woman" by J. L. Gibbons, D.A. Stiles, Y. Wood, and E. Biekert, 1994, paper presented in G. Hofstede (Chair), Masculinity/Femininity as a Cultural Dimension: 12th Congress of the International Association of Cross-Cultural Psychology, Pamplona, Spain. Reprinted by permission of the author.

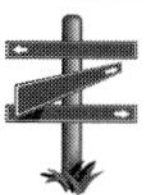

Guideposts for Working with Adolescents

- Praise teens' diverse interests, especially when they transcend gender stereotypes.
- Encourage adolescents to experiment with gender roles by assigning tasks without regard to sex, such as teaching car repair and cooking to both boys and girls.
- Support adolescents who cross gender boundaries in their friendships, interests, or appearance by stating your approval.
- Seek out positive role models of nonstereotypical gendering, such as female athletes or male dancers.

Sexuality pervades the media and popular culture, especially in advertising campaigns for teen fashion, music, and movies in which the pubescent body is glamorized (Durham, 1998). Media exposure in adolescence has been estimated at 40 to 45 hours per week (compared to about 35 to 50 hours of school and 55 to 75 hours of sleep) (Turner, 2003). Through magazines, television, movies, the Internet, and music, adolescent girls in most industrialized countries are encouraged to see themselves as sexualized (Durham, 1998; Jones, Vigfusdottir, & Lee, 2004;

L'Engle, Brown & Kenneavey, 2006; Strouse, Goodwin, & Roscoe, 1994; Ward, 2003). For example, in a study of popular teen magazines, several areas of cultural influence were apparent (Durham, 2003):

- **Bodies and Appearance.** Cosmetics and grooming, diet and weight, clothing and fashion
- **Love and Romance.** Dating and boyfriends, family and relationship advice, and weddings
- **Gendered Sexuality.** Feminine ideal of beauty, looking "sexy" and attractive to men, and compulsory heterosexuality

How did magazines, television, books, or movies influence your response to heteronormativity as a teenager?

Bodies and appearance. The ways in which cultural images are incorporated into our body image is called **embodiment**. Recall from chapter 8 that adolescent girls are more likely to think that they are overweight even when they are average or underweight. On the other hand, boys are as likely to think they are underweight as overweight. Most girls want to be thinner while most adolescent boys want to be more muscular, taller, and heavier. In a recent study of male and female adolescents in grades 7 and 10, three types of influences were examined as risk or protective factors of teenagers' body images (Barker & Galambos, 2003):

- **Physical Factors.** The teens' pubertal status, body weight, and weight management behaviors (e.g., dieting and exercise)
- **Contextual Factors.** The extent to which teens are teased about their appearance by family or peers and are involved in popular culture (e.g., TV, music, movies, magazines)
- **Resource Factors.** The degree to which the environment protects teenagers from being dissatisfied with their bodies (e.g., parental acceptance, sports involvement, attendance in church or religious activities)

The risk factors of weighing more, dieting more, and being teased predicted girls' dissatisfaction with their bodies compared to boys', for whom the only significant risk factor was teasing. Of the protective factors, parental acceptance was a significant predictor of body satisfaction for girls but not for boys. However, none of the protective resource factors moderated the effects of significant risk factors for either sex, such as teasing or media influences (Barker & Galambos, 2003). Taken together, these findings demonstrate that the cultural construction of adolescent bodies may be problematic for both girls and boys.

Annie hopes she looks okay in her new dress. On the other hand, Rick hopes no one from school will see him wearing that awful tuxedo he wore to the ridiculous junior prom.

Love and romance. As we discussed in chapter 8, girls' first experiences with sexual arousal are less likely than boys' to occur during masturbation and more likely to occur with a partner of the opposite sex. In addition, girls' motives for sexual intercourse more often involve relationship and romance

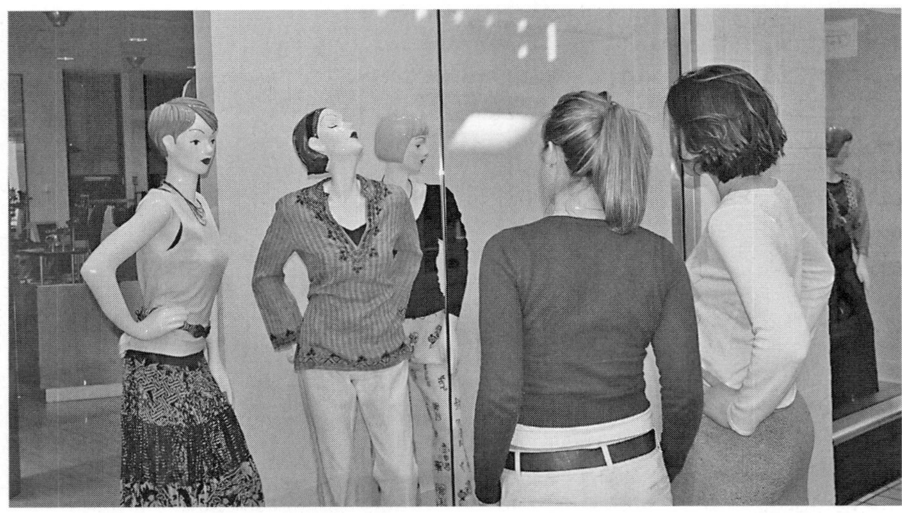

Teenagers are particularly susceptible to cultural constructions of femininity.

(Hyde & Jaffee, 2000). In interviews with both urban and suburban adolescent girls, researchers have documented the ways that girls speak about their sexual desire (Tolman & Szalacha, 1999). Heterosexual adolescent girls, for example, have been characterized as "daring to desire" (Tolman, 1994, 2002; Tolman & Brown, 2001). Even though adults often ignore the extent to which teenage sexual desire exists, schools are frequently a site of conversations about sexuality, as seen in Box 11.3 (Fine, 1997; Schwartz & Rutter, 2000). Two opposing discourses of sexuality were revealed in a recent study of adolescent girls (Schalet, Hunt, & Joe-Laidler, 2003):

- **Sexual Respectability.** "Good" girls versus "bad" girls based on their peer reputations, and
- **Sexual Autonomy.** The girls' own sexual needs, choices, and actions

In our chapter case, Annie's thinking about the wedding illustrates the influence of gendered constructions of sexuality. She wants to catch the bouquet, signifying her romantic fantasy of marriage. She wishes her boyfriend Josh could be there too, but they've only been "going together" for a week!

Sexual disclosure. Individual differences, such as gender, ethnicity, personality, confidence, sex drive, resilience, and attractiveness, as well as contextual factors, such as social class and living in a rural or urban community, may influence the developmental pathways of sexual disclosure (Diamond & Savin-Williams, 2003a; Floyd & Stein, 2002). **Sexual disclosure** refers to "coming out" as a gay person to your friends or family (Savin-Williams & Rodriguez, 1993). For example, when teenagers are asked to self-identify as gay, lesbian, or bisexual, only 1 to 3% say they are homosexual compared to about 1 to 4% of adult women and 2 to 8% of adult men. However, about 7% of both sexes admit having felt same-sex desire (Savin-Williams, 2001b). Many reasons have been asserted for this low percentage among teenagers (adapted from Savin-Williams, 2001b):

- **Adolescents are not "out" to themselves.** The average age for self-disclosure among sexual-minority youths is just prior to high-school graduation.
- **Adolescents have not come out to others.** The average age of disclosure to others, usually to a best friend, is just after high-school graduation.

BOX 11.3 ROADMAP TO SUCCESSFUL PRACTICE

Discourses of Sexuality in Schools

To understand how sexuality is managed within schools, Michelle Fine (1997) examined the major discourses of sexuality that characterize American public schools. "Official" sexuality education was present in social studies, biology, and sex education classes as well as the nurse's office. But she also found that talk of sexuality is *everywhere* within public high schools—in the halls, classrooms, bathrooms, lunchrooms, and the library. She called this "unofficial" conversation about sex a "discourse of desire" that is seldom explored in U.S. classrooms but which occurs in less structured school situations. Conversations among adolescent girls contained themes about their subjective experiences of bodily and sexual desire as well as critiques of marriage and sexual victimization.

Despite the fact that the political climate in schools tried to suppress such conversations, some teachers and community advocates struggled for an empowering sex education curriculum both within and outside of the high-school classroom. In the privacy of their classrooms, she found that teachers subverted the official curriculum and engaged students in critical discussion of issues. Other teachers advocated publicly for enriched curricula and training. For example, family life curricula and/or plans for a school-based health clinic were carefully generated in many communities.

Michelle Fine concluded that a discourse of desire in which young women have a voice is informed and generated out of their own socially constructed sexual meanings. In a context in which desire is not silenced but acknowledged and discussed, conversations with adolescent women can, according to Fine, speak fully to the sexual identities of both young women and men.

Source: Based on "Sexuality, Schooling, and Adolescent Females: The Missing Discourse of Desire," by M. Fine, in M. M. Gergen and S. N. Davis (Eds.), *Toward a New Psychology of Gender: A Reader* (pp. 379–381), 1997, New York: Routledge. Copyright 1997 by Routledge.

- **Adolescents are unlikely or unwilling to classify themselves as lesbian, bisexual, or gay.** Even adolescents with same-sex attractions, particularly females, may not believe that they fit the label, dislike the political or sexual associations with the label, or feel that labels are too simplistic.
- **Same-sex behavior is not the best criterion for identifying sexual-minority adolescents.** Not all youths with same-sex attractions engage in same-sex behavior during adolescence, and not all youths who *do* are gay, lesbian, or bisexual.

Most researchers studying sexual identity have used developmental models to understand the process by which people become aware of, acknowledge, and accept **sexual minority** (or nonheterosexual) identities (Dubé & Savin-Williams, 1999). A traditional stage model, as seen in Table 11–4, suggests that there is a developmental sequence of events to "coming out." Recent studies, however, suggest that this developmental sequence may not describe the experiences of younger generations, lesbian and bisexual women, or members of various ethnic groups (e.g., Diamond, 2003; Friedman et al. 2004; Maguen, Floyd, Bakeman, & Armistead, 2002).

Think about the chapter case again. Rick's emergent sexual orientation is based on his romantic attractions, not on same-sex behavior.

Gender differences. A meta-analysis of research on sexual attitudes and behaviors among adolescents found no gender differences in attitudes toward homosexuality (Oliver & Hyde, 1993). However, most gay and bisexual adolescent boys display considerable diversity in responses to feelings of sexual attraction (Diamond, 2003). For example, in retrospective accounts, about two thirds of boys seemed aware of their same-sex attractions from an early age. Others were cross-gendered in their interests and behaviors and associated mostly with girls. Only a few participated in masculine activities, such as all-male sports, while convincing their peers that they weren't gay (Savin-Williams, 1996; see also Egan & Perry, 2001).

In contrast, many sexual-minority women have no recollections of child or adolescent same-sex attractions and reveal a great variability in when they first became aware of their sexual orientation (sometimes as late as age 20). Complicating female sexual identity even further, about two thirds of *all* adult females (heterosexual *and* lesbian) have reported attractions to men, and about 84% of adult women who identify as heterosexual have had same-sex attractions (Diamond & Savin-Williams, 2000, 2003b).

What does this fluidity tell us about the development of sexual identity in adolescent girls? An intense, emotionally intimate relationship often characterizes same-sex attraction in adolescent girls, yet may or may not predict their future self-identification as a sexual minority (Diamond & Savin-Williams, 2000). On average, the time from first same-sex attractions at ages 8 or 9 to first disclosure at around age 18 is about 10 years for both sexes (Savin-Williams & Diamond, 2000).

For instance, even as a high-school senior, Rick has not yet disclosed to anyone except his best friend. And he has not yet used "gay" to refer to himself.

Ethnic differences. When college students were asked to recall their coming-out process, a majority of African American students recalled having engaged in sex before labeling their sexual

TABLE 11–4

Predicted Sequence of Sexual Identification

This sequence of sexual identification as a gay youth describes the experience of only some boys.

Stage	Ages
Awareness of same-sex attractions	8 to 11
Same-sex sexual behaviors	12 to 15
Identification as gay or lesbian	15 to 18
Disclosure to others	17 to 19
Same-sex romantic relationships	18 to 20

Source: Based on "Sexual Identity Development Among Ethnic Sexual-Minority Male Youths", by E. M. Dubé and R. C. Savin-Williams, 1999, *Developmental Psychology, 35*(6), pp. 1389–1398. Copyright 1999 by the American Psychological Association.

Guideposts for Working with Adolescents

- Keep in mind that cross-sex behavior or gender-atypical appearance does not necessarily correspond to sexual orientation.
- Be aware that not all adolescent sexual attractions may involve the opposite sex and that teens may be questioning their sexual identities.
- Whenever possible, engage teens in critically analyzing media images of men and women, gays and straights, and femininity and masculinity, and advocate not labeling people.
- Discuss with teenagers the culture's expectations regarding sexual disclosure or sexual behavior and how "coming out" may affect them or their families.

identities, but Asian Americans overwhelmingly labeled themselves as gay or bisexual *before* having sex (Dubé & Savin-Williams, 1999). These results are pictured in Figure 11.2 for African American, Latino, Asian American, and White students.

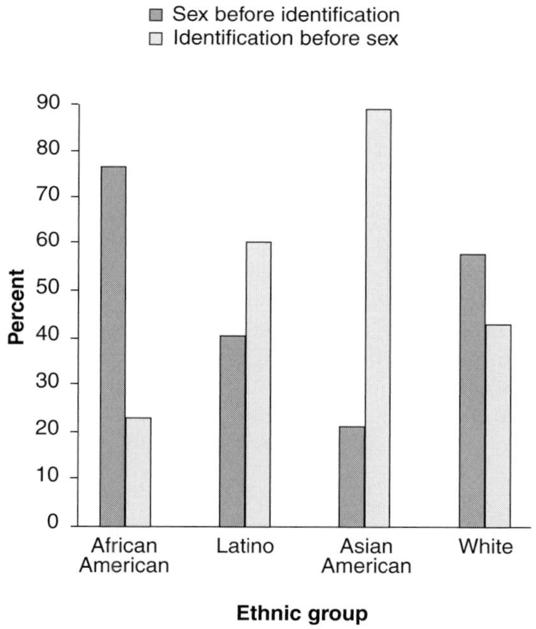

FIGURE 11.2 Sexual Identity among Ethnic Sexual-Minority Males
Latino and Asian American sexual-minority males self-identified as gay before becoming sexually active.

Source: From "Sexual Identity Development Among Ethnic Sexual-Minority Male Youths," (p. 1394) by E. M. Dubé and R. C. Savin-Williams, 1999, in *Developmental Psychology, 35*(6), pp. 1389–1398. Copyright by the American Psychological Association. Reprinted by permission of the author.

Other researchers have found no differences in the sexual orientation, sexual behavior, or sexual identity of lesbian, gay, and bisexual ethnic youth between ages 14 and 21. They did, however, find that Latino and African American gay youth had disclosed to fewer people than White gay youth. They also found that Black gay youth were involved in fewer gay-related social activities than White gay youth, possibly due to homophobia or heterosexism in the African American community (Rosario, Schrimshaw, & Hunter, 2004).

Close Relationships in Middle Adolescence

A relational view of adolescent social development requires an examination of three types of close relationships: with friends, with romantic partners, and with family members. Recall that a close relationship is an ongoing pattern of association and interaction between two individuals who acknowledge a connection with each other (Brown, Feiring, & Furman, 1999). Romantic partners are generally the highest in relationship closeness in adolescence, and siblings are usually the lowest (Laursen, 1996). Friendships often provide the context and opportunity for dating and the development of teens' romantic relationships (Wood, Senn, Desmarais, Park, & Verberg, 2002). Furthermore, successful relationships in adolescence will likely lead to Erikson's stage of intimacy versus isolation by early adulthood (discussed in chapter 12).

Middle Adolescent Friendships

In chapter 6, we characterized same-sex friendships as most typical of middle childhood. Those "chumships" are usually reciprocal relationships, with school-age children sharing secrets and trusting each other not to reveal them. Recall that in early adolescence, however, the ability to form close, intimate friendships becomes increasingly important (Buhrmester, 1990; see also Furman & Shaffer, 2003; Collins & Repinski, 1994). In middle adolescence, intimacy and loyalty are seen as the primary characteristics of teenage friendships (Savin-Williams & Berndt, 1990; Laursen, 1996). Table 11–5 provides examples of how teenagers conceptualize friendships. In addition, high-school students' working models of friendship are positively related to their ratings of support from friends (Furman, 2001).

Most researchers have found that closeness with best friends peaks in middle adolescence (Laursen, 1996). ***Closeness*** has been defined not only as emotional cohesion but also as the degree of mutual impact between friends (e.g., Berscheid, Snyder, & Omoto, 1989). "Relationship closeness" in adolescence is measured in this manner as the

- Frequency of social interactions
- Diversity of social interactions
- Influence of social interactions

In middle childhood and adolescence, however, intimacy is more important to girls than to boys. For example, when describing friendships, girls are more likely to mention mutual support and self-disclosure, whereas boys more often refer to joint activities and companionship (Feiring,

TABLE 11–5

Adolescent Working Models of Friendship

These quotations from teenagers illustrate some working models of friendship in adolescence.

Illustrations of Various Working Model Scales

Idealization

Participant: I guess, no matter what it is we tell each other stuff. So, I don't know. I guess we can communicate real good. So.

Interviewer: Again, is there an example that shows that?

Participant: An example. I don't know, like if I get a. Like one quarter or something. I got a bad grade or something. You know when you get a bad grade you don't want to tell nobody. So you know, but I told him and he kind of laughed at me and stuff, but it was better than telling somebody else cause I don't know. Cause I just feel better telling, telling him stuff, I guess.

Involving Anger

Participant: There were these girls, they were so mean and as I was going by she spit her gum out and she spit it into my hair and I cursed at her and [friend's name] heard me and she was just looking over at me just shaking her head [Participant's name] you know you're not supposed to cuss' and it just drove me up the wall I was like 'She spit gum in my hair what am I supposed to do? If I beat her up, you're going to tell me I shouldn't do it. If I cussed her out, you're gonna say I shouldn't do it, so what difference does it make? She spit gum in my hair.' You know so that was one time when it just errrrrr irked me. I just couldn't believe that she said, '[Interviewee's Name] you shouldn't' Oh man please I'll just spit gum in your hair.

Passivity (Vagueness in Discourse)

Participant: I'd probably say my friend was abusive. You know it was to a point that I lost my confidence in what I could do. So I wouldn't say anything to him about it. I wouldn't say blah, blah, blah, blah, blah, blah.

Valuing of Autonomy

Participant: When we're apart. It's like—like I don't feel lonely or like I need to talk to em right away. Like it's good to be apart from them sometimes.

Valuing of Intimacy

Participant: The relationship is] especially intimate in that um, we share a lot of information that you wouldn't normally share about the opposite sex, um . . . Um. she's very important to me, she, and and. It's just, it's just a espec, it's especially nice to have someone like that in life.

Note. These examples illustrate the kinds of statements that are scored on these scales. It is important to emphasize, however, that the interpretation of any statement is dependent on context, and the scale score is based on all the examples in the transcript.

Source: From "Working Models of Friendship" (p. 589), by W. Furman, 2001, *Journal of Social and Personal Relationships, 18*(5), pp. 583–602.

1993). Although girls become intimate with friends earlier in adolescence than boys, we also know that same-sex friendships are equally important to adolescent boys (Roy, Benenson, & Lilly, 2000).

Friendships among diverse youth. Overall, the development of friendships by ethnic-minority adolescents is similar to that of White teens (Way & Chen, 2000). However, from the few U.S. studies of racial/ethnic adolescents' friendships, several additional findings have emerged (for a review, see Way & Chen, 2000). Compared to European American teens, for example, African American adolescents have a larger network of neighborhood friends and more close relationships outside of school with children from another race. They also report more contact with their best friends outside of school compared to White students. With respect to gender, African American, Asian American, and Latino girls report more close friendship support than boys do. However, African American boys are more likely to reveal their thoughts and feelings to their same-sex friends than are Mexican American or European American boys (Way & Chen, 2000).

Cross-cultural research also suggests the importance of intimacy with friends. For example, an Israeli study found that securely attached adolescents highly valued affiliation with same-sex friends and perceived friends as sources of companionship and stimulation, compared to insecure adolescents (Mikulincer & Selinger, 2001). In another study, the relationship quality most often mentioned by adolescents included the elements of trust, loyalty, and closeness (Flum & Lavi-Yudelevitch, 2002). Furthermore, when Canadian teens were asked whether they "matter" to friends, *mattering* was positively associated with measures of satisfaction with friends' relatedness (Marshall, 2001). A questionnaire on mattering provided in Box 11.4 is useful for determining closeness in adolescent friendships.

Sexual-minority youth may fear developing close, same-sex, platonic relationships that may be jeopardized when their "true" sexual orientation is revealed (Savin-Williams, 1994a). They also may fear reprisals from larger peer groups. Name-calling, harassment, and other homophobic behavior is still as prevalent among adolescents as in middle childhood (Savin-Williams, 1994b). Prejudice against sexual minorities, for example, is reported to be twice as frequent as against ethnic minorities (High Achieving Students, 1994).

Recall Rick's fear of coming out. Only Matthew, his best friend, and Annie, his younger sister, know about his attractions to boys.

Dating. In adolescence, same-sex friendships are increasingly augmented by other-sex friendships or by mixed-sex peer groups (Connolly, Craig, Goldberg, & Pepler, 2004; Connolly & Goldberg, 1999). In fact, among heterosexual teens, having a large other-sex friend network predicts developing a romantic relationship with someone, as shown in Figure 11.3

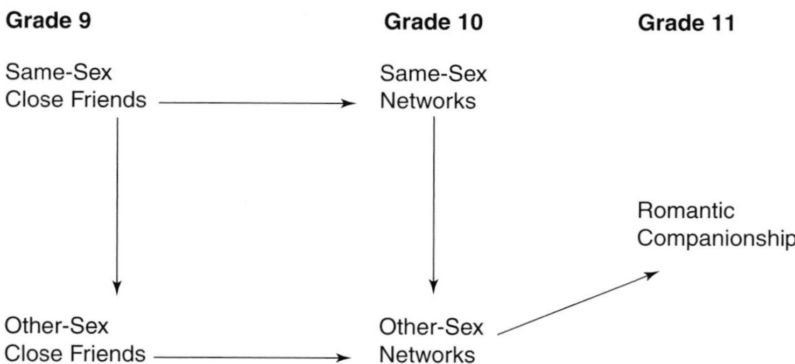

FIGURE 11.3 Predicting Heterosexual Relationships from Friendship Networks

Having close friends of both sexes in grade 9 leads to belonging to same- and other-sex friendship networks in grade 10, which in turn predicts romantic relationships in grade 11.

Source: From "The Role of Peers in the Emergence of Heterosexual Romantic Relationships in Adolescence" (p. 1402), by J. Connolly, W. Furman, and R. Konarski, 2000, *Child Development, 71*(1), pp. 1395–1408. Copyright 2000 by the Society for Research in Child Development. Adapted by permission.

BOX 11.4 ROADMAP TO UNDERSTANDING THEORY AND RESEARCH

Perceived Mattering Scale

Each person has ideas or feelings about how other people see them. I am interested in how you think people think about you. Choose the rating you feel is best for you and circle the number provided.

	Not much		Somewhat		A lot
1. I feel special to my ________.	1	2	3	4	5
2. I am needed by my ________.	1	2	3	4	5
3. I am missed by my ________when I am away.	1	2	3	4	5
4. When I talk, my ________tries to understand what I am saying.	1	2	3	4	5
5. I am interesting to my ________.	1	2	3	4	5
6. My ________notices my feelings.	1	2	3	4	5
7. My ________gives me credit when I do well .	1	2	3	4	5
8. My ________notices when I need help.	1	2	3	4	5
9. I matter to my ________.	1	2	3	4	5

10. People have many things to think about. If your ____________ made a list of all the things s/he thinks about, where do you think you would be on the list?

Top
5
4
3
2
1
Bottom

11. If your ________ made a list of all the things s/he cares about, where do you think you'd be on that list?

Top
5
4
3
2
1
Bottom

This instrument has been used to measure whether adolescents believe they matter to their parents and friends.

Source: From "Do I Matter? Construct Validation of Adolescents' Perceived Mattering to Parents and Friends" (pp. 489–490), by S. K. Marshall, 2001, *Journal of Adolescence, 24*, pp. 473–490. Copyright 2001 by the Association for Professionals in Services for Adolescents. Reprinted by permission of Elsevier.

(Connolly, Furman, & Konarski, 2000). In addition, heterosexual teenagers who have more other-sex friends in early adolescence are more likely to have supportive and longer-term romantic relationships in middle adolescence (Feiring, 1999b). On the other hand, among adolescents who are unpopular in their same-sex peer groups, those with heterosexual romantic partners report lower self-esteem and more antisocial behavior than those who do not have a boyfriend or girlfriend (Brendgen, Vitaro, & Doyle, 2002).

Keep in mind that, although adolescents are *beginning* to explore their own identities (as discussed in chapter 10), they still may belong to small friendship groups (called **cliques**) and larger social groups (called **crowds**), as in middle childhood. Crowds serve the function of defining those peers with whom adolescents share a group identity and a relational affiliation. Refer to Figure 11.4 for an illustration of how crowds typically change from middle school through high school. By providing a system for categorizing unknown peers, crowds allow adolescents to anticipate the type of relationship that might develop with a person in a particular crowd, such as "trendies" or "grits" (Brown, Mory, & Kinney, 1994). Often, potential dating partners will be members of a teenager's crowd.

In the chapter case, Annie's boyfriend Josh is likely a member of her crowd at school, and it is also likely that their "dates" consist of hanging out with mixed-sex groups of friends rather than going somewhere as a couple.

A developmental sequence of heterosexual dating includes the following four stages (Dunphy, 1963):

- **Affiliative Interchanges.** Interactions with opposite-sex peers, often in the context of the crowd (e.g., "group dating")
- **Casual Dating.** Short-term relationships that may include closeness and/or sexual experimentation (e.g., "hooking up")
- **Stable Relationships.** Exclusive, longer-term relationships with one person (e.g., "going together")
- **Committed Relationships.** A long-term relationship that is expected to result in a permanent commitment or marriage (e.g., "getting engaged" or "living together") (adapted from Furman & Wehner, 1994)

Most early adolescents are usually in one of the first two stages. As shown in Figure 11.5, only about 30% of teens under age 14 report that they have had a dating relationship, but this percentage rises to almost 50% by age 15, and to almost 75% by age 17 (Collins, 2003). The percentage of teens with relationships lasting over 11 months increases dramatically between ages 14 and 16.

However, just because younger teens are not dating does not imply that are not engaged in romantic activity, such as flirting or kissing (Connolly, Craig, Goldberg, & Pepler, 2004). For example, in a recent test of the dating stages previously outlined,

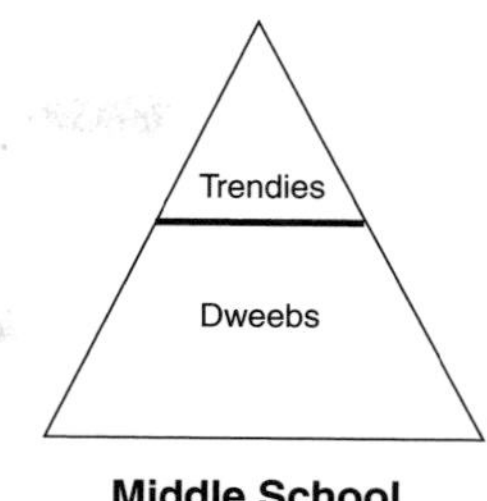

Middle School (Grades 6–8)

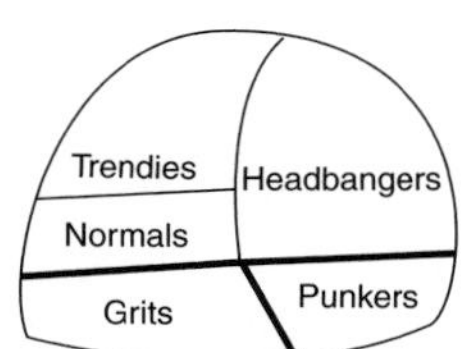

Early High School (Grades 9–10)

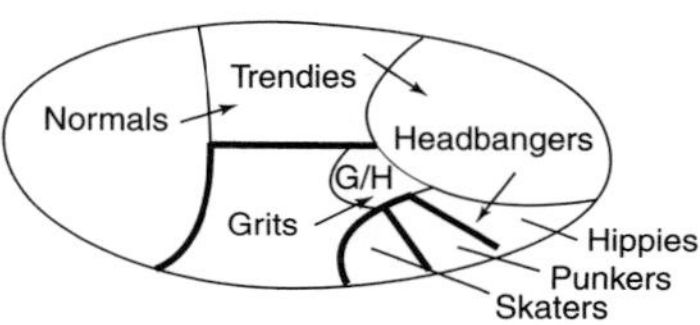

Later High School (Grades 11–12)

FIGURE 11.4 Developmental Changes in Adolescent Crowds

The structure of teenagers' crowds becomes more elaborate and less hierarchical from middle school to high school.

Source: From "Casting Adolescent Crowds in a Relational Perspective: Caricature, Channel, and Context" (p. 145), by B. B. Brown, M. S. Mory, and D. Kinney, in R. Montemayor, G. R. Adams, and T. P. Gulotta (Eds.), *Personal Relationships During Adolescence: Advances in Adolescent Development* (Vol. 3, pp. 125–167), 1994, Thousand Oaks, CA: Sage. Copyright 1994 by Sage Publications, Inc. Reprinted by permission.

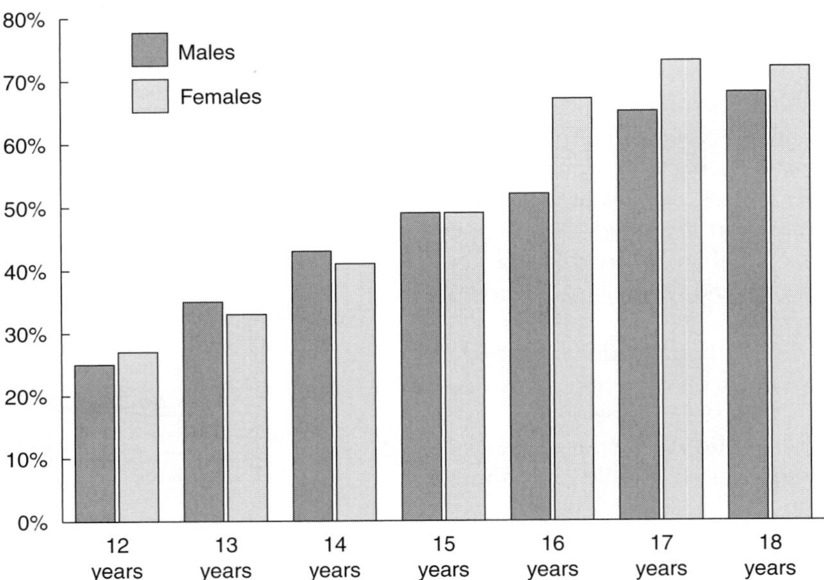

FIGURE 11.5 Percent of Adolescents with Romantic Relationships
Percentages of adolescents reporting romantic relationships in the past 18 months increase steadily from ages 12 to 18.

Source: From "More Than Myth: The Developmental Significance of Romantic Relationships During Adolescence" (p. 3), by W. A. Collins, 2003 *Journal of Research on Adolescence, 13*(1), pp. 1–24. Copyright 2003 by the Society for Research on Adolescence. Reprinted by permission.

researchers found that, in the transition from same-sex friendships to dating, heterosexual teenagers typically join mixed-sex groups in which they begin to pair off. In this sense, mixed-sex affiliative and dating stages may coexist rather than be sequential (Connolly, Craig, Goldberg, & Pepler, 2004). Table 11–6 provides percentages of teens' participation in various dating activities.

High-school dating has recently been characterized by students as "keeping your options open," whereas "relationships are about closing them" (Denizet-Lewis, 2004, p. 32). Increasingly, dating may mean hanging out at the mall, or at each others' houses, or—if they can't meet in person—meeting on the Internet. For some high-school students, "hooking up" (covering everything from kissing to oral sex to intercourse) has replaced dating altogether. These teens refer to friends they hook up with regularly as "friends with benefits" (Denizet-Lewis, 2004). However, teens between ages 12 and 16 who dated fewer *different* people also exhibited fewer problem behaviors (Zimmer-Gembeck, Siebenbruner, & Collins, 1991).

While heterosexual teens may use the convenience of dating to explore their sexuality, many sexual-minority youth are denied this supportive experimental context and often put their exploration on the "back burner" until a safer environment presents itself (e.g., college) or experiment in heterosexual relationships (Diamond, 1998; Meininger, Cohen, Neinstein, & Remafadi, 2002). Often, they are unable to date those to whom they are most attracted. In addition, our culture is far less tolerant of romantic relationships between gay teens than of homosexual exploration, frequently seen as "just a phase" (Savin-Williams, 1994a). Instead, gay and lesbian teens need the same opportunities for socializing at youth groups or dances as heterosexual teens (Turner, 2003).

Even though Rick feels pressure to hide his sexual orientation from everyone at school, he often feels erotic or romantic attractions but can't talk openly about them. Annie, on the other hand, who met her boyfriend in school, is always talking with her girlfriends about guys!

Among heterosexual youth, most—if not all—adolescents experience some form of dating before

TABLE 11–6

Participation in Romantic Activities in Adolescence

In early adolescence, a higher percentage of teens engage in group activities than in actual dating.

Type of Romantic Activity	Percent
Mixed-Gender Affiliative Activities	
• Hang around with boys and girls	80%
• Go to clubs, groups, or sports activities	76%
• Go to dances or parties with boys or girls	74%
Dating Activities	
• Go out with a boy (girl) and a couple of girls (boys)	31%
• Go out with a group of boys and girls at night	27%
• Girls and boys go on dates	26%
• Go on dates with a boy (girl) in a group	24%
• Have a boyfriend (girlfriend) now	21%
Same-Gender Activities Only	6%

Source: Based on "Mixed-Gender Groups, Dating, and Romantic Relationships in Early Adolescence" (p. 193), by J. Connolly, W. Craig, A. Goldberg, and D. Pepler, 2004, *Journal of Research on Adolescence, 14* (2), pp. 185–207. Copyright 2004 by the Society for Research on Adolescence.

Even today, it is rare for gay teens to receive enough peer, teacher, or family support to "come out" in high school.

graduating from high school (Savin-Williams & Berndt, 1990; see also Longmore, Manning, & Giordano, 2001). Early and middle adolescents may date as a form of recreation, to gain status with peers, or to establish a romantic relationship with someone (Collins & Sroufe, 1999). Like friendship, dating provides many opportunities for adolescent development, such as enhancing teens' sense of identity, prosocial skills, and empathy (Savin-Williams & Berndt, 1990). Dating also encourages a sense of relatedness to others and of belonging in the peer group (Collins, 2003).

Recent data from the National Survey of Adolescent Health (Add-Health) suggest that racial/ethnic groups differ in their willingness to engage in interracial dating (Carver, Joyner, & Udry, 2003). In most school contexts, African Americans were the least likely to identify romantic partners of a different race, Whites were in the middle, and Asian and Latino Americans were the most likely to do so. In addition, when schools afforded fewer opportunities to interact with other racial/ethnic groups, boys were more likely than girls to nominate other-race romantic partners. On the other hand, girls were more likely to do so when schools afforded greater opportunity. Overall, most adolescents prefer to date persons from the same racial/ethnic group (Carver, Joyner, & Udry, 2003). In addition, Add-Health data, graphed in Figure 11.6, show that Asian American teens are less likely than African American, Latino, Native American, and Caucasian adolescents to have had

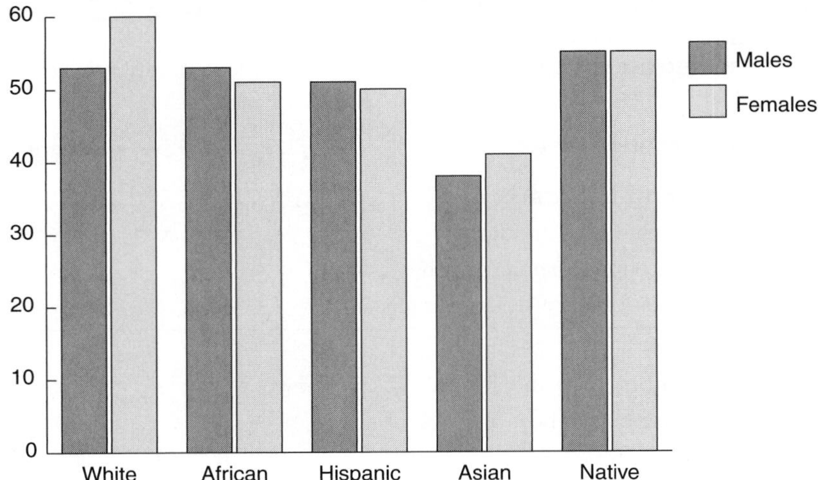

FIGURE 11.6 Romantic Relationships Among Racial/Ethnic Adolescents
Percentages of adolescents from five racial/ethnic groups reporting romantic relationships in the past 18 months.

Source: From "More Than Myth: The Developmental Significance of Romantic Relationships During Adolescence" (p. 13), by W. A. Collins, 2003, *Journal of Research on Adolescence, 13*(1), pp. 1–24. Copyright 2003 by the Society for Research on Adolescence. Reprinted by permission.

a romantic relationship in the past 18 months (Collins, 2003).

 **What was "dating" like in your high school? Did you have a romantic relationship?**

Romantic relationships. Unlike dating, **romantic relationships** are characterized by a close, intimate bond between the partners. Adolescent romantic relationships are often theorized by developmental psychologists from an attachment perspective (Furman & Wehner, 1994, 1997; Furman & Simon, 1999). Attachment theorists have suggested that four types of goals organize relationships: attachment, affiliation, caregiving, and sexual/reproductive (refer back to Table 11–2). For example, the primary goal of attachment behavior in infancy and early childhood is to maintain proximity to caregivers, usually parents. By middle childhood, however, affiliative goals are often met by peers and friends in a quest for social connections to others beyond their families (Furman & Wehner, 1994; see also Mikulincer & Selinger, 2001).

In adolescence, although all four goals may be met by teenagers' romantic partners, sexual and affiliative goals are more likely to be met by boyfriends or girlfriends than are attachment or caretaking goals (Furman & Simon, 1999). "Thus prior to adolescence, parents and peers are the key figures for the attachment, caregiving, and affiliative systems. As romantic relationships develop and become more central, however, romantic partners become key figures for these different systems as well as for the sexual/reproductive system with its emergence in adolescence" (Furman & Wehner, 1994, p. 177).

The attachment theory concept of *working models* has also influenced the study of adolescent romantic relationships. Relationship theorists have proposed that working models of romantic relationships, called ***romantic views***, are specific to different *types* of relationships, such as dating or romantic relationships (Furman & Wehner, 1994, 1997). For example, if you look to your parents for security or affiliation, you are likely to look to your romantic partner for similar provisions. This model of close relationships is illustrated in Figure 11.7. Essentially, romantic views are expectations regarding intimacy and closeness that are enacted in terms of attachment, affiliation, caregiving, and sexuality (Furman, Simon, Shaffer, & Bouchey, 2002).

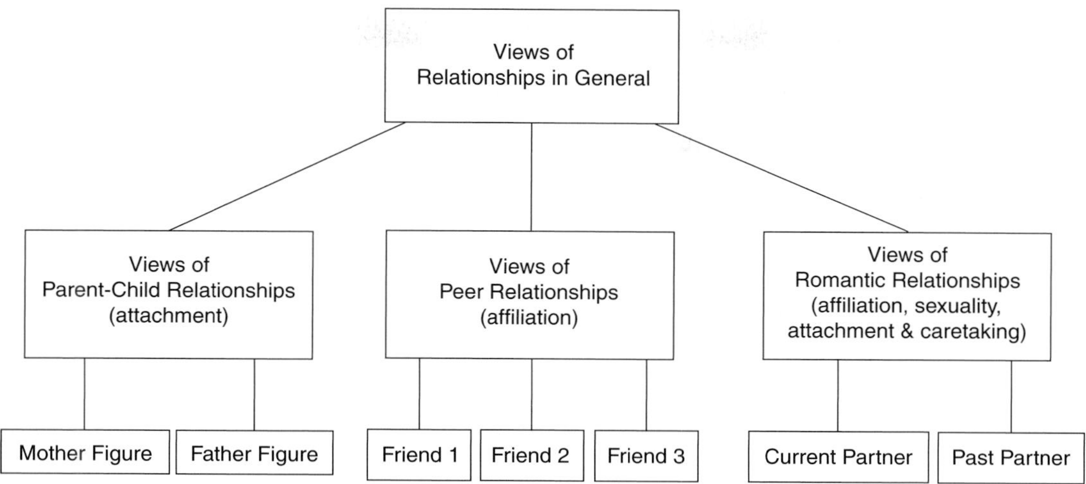

FIGURE 11.7 Cognitive Model of Relationships
Working models of attachment influence parent-child, peer, and romantic relationships.

Source: From "Cognitive Representations of Adolescent Romantic Relationships" (p. 81), by W. Furman and V. A. Simon, in W. Furman, B. B. Brown, and C. Feiring (Eds.), *The Development of Romantic Relationships in Adolescence* (pp. 75–98), 1999, Cambridge, UK: Cambridge University Press. Copyright 1999 by Cambridge University Press. Reprinted by permission.

Romantic views—like working models of attachment—can be categorized as secure, dismissing, or preoccupied. As adolescents' behavioral goals and their dating experiences change, the relative importance, or hierarchy, of their attachment figures and their views of their romantic partners may also change (Furman, Simon, Shaffer, & Bouchey, 2002). For example, teens may turn first to their boyfriend or girlfriend in times of distress because they view those figures as more supportive than their parents or siblings (Furman & Wehner, 1994, 1997). Increasingly, relationship theorists and researchers are focusing on the positive outcomes of committed romantic relationships for adolescents (Bouchey & Furman, 2003; Collins, 2003).

Romantic love. Adolescent notions of relationships are often idealized images of love (Bouchey & Furman, 2003). For example, adolescents frequently report "being in love" although they may not have even spoken to that person yet (Brown, Feiring, & Furman, 1999; Montgomery & Sorell, 1998)! In other cases, teenagers may be inseparable at school but never spend time with each other apart from members of their crowd. Still others may talk on the phone every night but never display any affection for each other in public (Brown, Feiring, & Furman, 1999). As a result of such extreme variation, different styles of experiencing love have been suggested, such as physical love or friendship (Hendrick & Hendrick, 2001). Table 11–7 illustrates six **love styles** that have been used to describe adult romantic experiences (Shulman & Scharf, 2000). When teenagers were asked about the advantages of having a boyfriend or girlfriend, they responded in ways that reflect the "love styles":

- **Companionship.** "You have somebody to go out with, to study together with before exams."
- **Intimacy.** "To share my personal stuff with someone."
- **Attachment.** "I feel that somebody, who is not family, really loves me."
- **Care.** "Somebody who spoils you and you spoil her."
- **Status.** "In my class, it makes me a *man*."
- **Sex.** "You can kiss him and do things you can't with a friend."
- **Excitement.** "It is just great to think that you are involved and to wait for the next time you meet" (adapted from Shulman & Scharf, 2000).

Because the love styles are not mutually exclusive, teens frequently experiment with different ways of relating to a current boyfriend or girlfriend as they explore dating and intimacy in successive relationships over the course of adolescence (Furman & Simon, 1999).

TABLE 11–7

Styles of Love

Teenagers, like adults, are likely to view romantic love in many different ways.

Style	Definition	Example
Eros	Physical love	"We were attracted to each other immediately when we first met."
Ludus	Game-playing love	"I try to keep him uncertain about my commitment to her."
Storge	Friendship, companionate love	"The best kind of love grows out of a long friendship."
Pragma	Practical, objective love	"An important objective in choosing a boyfriend is how he will be as a father."
Mania	Preoccupation with the relationship	"When I am in love, I have trouble concentrating on anything else."
Agape	Caregiving, self-sacrificing love	"I always try to help him through difficult times."

Source: Based on "Adolescent Romantic Behaviors and Perceptions: Age- and Gender-Related Differences, and Links with Family and Peer Relationships," by S. Shulman and M. Scharf, 2000, *Journal of Research on Adolescence, 10*, pp. 99–118. Copyright 2000 by Blackwell Publishing, Ltd.

Guideposts for Working with Adolescents

- Because both same-sex and cross-sex friendships become more intimate in adolescence, expect that romantic attractions may occur in the context of teenagers' crowds.
- Support teens who wish to cross gender, race, or class boundaries in forming friendships and close relationships.
- Encourage adolescents to resist sexual and romantic stereotypes as portrayed in movies and popular music.
- Help sexual-minority adolescents who may feel unable to express their romantic attractions gain parental or peer group acceptance by talking openly and positively about differences in sexual orientation.
- Refer gay teens to GLBT organizations and support groups in your community.
- Refrain from asking teens if they have a boyfriend or girlfriend. Instead ask, "Is there anyone special?"

Family Relationships

Our first relationships are usually family relationships. From an attachment theory perspective, recall that families—particularly parent and sibling interactions—influence adolescents' relationships with friends and romantic partners. From a family systems view, interpreting the quality of a relationship between any two people also requires examining the forces that contribute to and emerge from their interactions (Cowan, Powell, & Cowan, 1998). For example, to understand adolescent friendships or dating, we must also consider the quality of relationships among parents, siblings, and extended family. In addition, we need to think about interactions with groups outside the family, such as peers, schools, and communities (Cowan, Powell, & Cowan, 1998; see also Updegraff et al., 2002).

Person characteristics. The influences of biological or psychological characteristics of parents and adolescents on family relationships has been the focus of a recent major research project conducted jointly by a team of psychiatrists, family sociologists, and psychologists (Reiss, Neiderhiser,

Hetherington, & Plomin, 2000). This project combined developmental, family systems, and behavior-genetic approaches to studying family interaction (refer back to chapter 3 for a review of behavior-genetic theory). The sample included 720 pairs of same-sex adolescent siblings—including twins, half siblings, and genetically unrelated siblings—and their parents. The results, published in a book titled *The Relationship Code* (Reiss, Neiderhiser, Hetherington, & Plomin, 2000), revealed that overall, the genetic predispositions (e.g., temperament, sexual orientation) both of parents and adolescents made a major contribution to the association between family relationships and adolescent adjustment. Although the nonshared environment (e.g., differential treatment of siblings) was significantly related to adolescent adjustment, the researchers did not find that differences in parenting added any information beyond that which was accounted for by genetic differences between siblings (Reiss, Neiderhiser, Hetherington, & Plomin, 2000).

Behavior-genetic research has been harshly criticized for considering nonshared influences to be any family or parent factors that serve to make siblings different rather than similar (Maccoby, 2000). As a result, this study augmented behavioral-genetic measures with direct measures of potential environmental influences, such as observations of family interaction, in an effort to document environmental effects more precisely (Collins, Maccoby, Hetherington, Steinberg, & Bornstein, 2000). The researchers also acknowledged the influence of the adolescents themselves on their own development. For example, across all 3 years of the study, parents reported that they treated their children similarly in terms of knowledge of their activities, attempts to control their behavior, and successes in controlling them, whereas adolescents reported that parents treated them differently! "Indeed, at any point in time, measures of the nonshared environment reflect—in all likelihood—a bidirectional effect: the influences of parents, siblings, peers and others on the developing child and the continuing impact on that child of family and friends" (Reiss, Neiderhiser, Hetherington, & Plomin, 2000, p. 164).

In our chapter case study, for example, the Chasen parents treat Beth, Rick, and Annie differently, based on the different characteristics of their three children.

Quality of parenting. Developmental psychologists assert that it is not reasonable to expect that a given style or quality of parenting would have the same effect on every child. For example, different parenting strategies or degrees of effort may be required to bring about the same outcome in different children (Collins, Maccoby, Hetherington, Steinberg, & Bornstein, 2000; Conger & Conger, 1994). **Parenting styles** may vary from *authoritarian* (e.g., controlling but low in warmth) to *permissive* (e.g., warm but low in control), with most research demonstrating that *authoritative* parenting (e.g., high levels of control and warmth) is associated with positive psychosocial outcomes (Baumrind, 1971).

Generally, research on the influence of parenting styles in adolescence indicates that authoritative parents raise teenagers who achieve more in school, score higher on self-esteem, report less depression and anxiety, and are less likely to engage in problem behavior (Gray & Steinberg, 1999a; Steinberg, 2001). Despite findings that African American teens seem less negatively affected by authoritarian parenting than White teenagers, positive results have consistently been reported for authoritative parenting of adolescents from all racial/ethnic groups and nationalities (Steinberg, 2001). In addition, when researchers more closely examined which aspects of authoritative parenting may contribute to positive outcomes in adolescence, parental involvement and support were positively related to adolescents' psychosocial development, whereas behavioral control, although reducing behavior problems, was negatively related to emotional well-being (Gray & Steinberg, 1999a).

Developmental scholars have also suggested that authoritative parenting provides an emotional context for adolescent adjustment (Darling & Steinberg, 1993). For example, researchers who examined differences in parenting styles across teenagers' friendship networks have found that adolescents whose *friends* described their own parents as authoritative had higher academic competence and reported lower levels of delinquency and substance use. In addition, boys whose friends described their parents as authoritative reported lower levels of peer conformity and were less likely to engage in misbehavior at school. Among girls, higher levels of authoritative parenting by friends' parents was related to higher scores on measures of work orientation, self-reliance, and self-esteem and lower levels of depression or anxiety. These results suggest that the quality of parenting available in teenagers' friendship network is an important, although indirect, influence (Fletcher, Darling, Steinberg, & Dornbusch, 1995).

Generally, securely attached adolescents have working models of relationships that extend to their interactions with peers (e.g., Miller, Notaro, & Zimmerman, 2002). In a recent Canadian study, secure attachments to fathers were associated with less conflict in their 15- and 16-year-olds' peer interactions. Moreover, adolescents who had secure attachments to their parents rated themselves as more emotionally expressive and had more positive and fewer negative interactions with parents than did insecurely attached teens (Ducharme, Doyle, & Markiewicz, 2002). For example, in an Australian study of adolescent twins between ages 15 and 18, teenagers' reports of differential parental affection and control between twins were related to adolescents' attachment insecurity, anxiety, and lower self-esteem (Sheehan & Noller, 2002).

Parent-adolescent conflict. Parent-adolescent conflict is commonly reported by parents of teenagers, despite scholars' overall assertion that adolescent "storm and stress" is a myth (Steinberg, 2001). It appears that while teens themselves may not be "stressed out" by the everyday struggles that typically ensue in families around issues of adolescent autonomy and individuation, parents are!

The Chasens are relieved to see their children growing up. Richard, Sr. is glad that they've almost made it through adolescence . . . only one more teenager at home! His wife Joan thinks that their marriage has been challenging, but now she is glad they stayed together. They'll be a "couple" again in a few short years.

A qualitative study that investigated how parents who considered themselves "normally stressed" by their first child's transition to adolescence used family systems theory to model how families maintain equilibrium. "From the parents' perspective, the transition to parenting an adolescent began with a specific, noticeable change in their teenager, which led to a process of adjustment on their part" (Spring, Rosen, & Matheson, 2002, p. 411). The responses of these mostly Caucasian middle-class parents involved effectively reorienting to the needs of their teenagers in order to avoid conflicts. But how typical is parent-adolescent conflict in households with teenagers?

Meta-analyses of studies on parent-adolescent conflict during adolescence reveal little support for the commonly held view that parent-child conflict rises and then falls across early to late adolescence (Laursen, Coy, & Collins, 1998). Both rates of conflict and total amount of conflict declined from early adolescence to late adolescence. Only negative affect was slightly greater during middle adolescence (i.e., the high-school years) than during early adolescence. Such findings suggest that adolescent-parent conflict is less frequent but more intense in middle adolescence (Laursen, Coy, & Collins, 1998).

Gay, lesbian, and bisexual adolescents often experience intense conflicts with parents when they disclose their sexuality. Researchers have reported that only about 11% of adolescents receive positive parental responses after disclosing their sexual orientation (D'Augelli & Hershberger, 1993). Box 11.5 provides advice for parents whose adolescent "comes out" to them from Ritch Savin-Williams' (2001a) book titled *Mom, Dad. I'm Gay.* The guidelines effectively illustrate a family systems perspective on accepting a gay son or daughter.

In a telephone interview study of the nature of adolescents' conflicts with parents and friends, researchers asked teens to describe all the disagreements they had during the preceding day (Adams & Laursen, 2001). Compared to conflicts with friends, parent-adolescent conflicts more often involved arguments over "daily hassles" with win-lose outcomes and negative (or neutral) feelings afterwards. Compared to parental conflicts, however, arguments with friends involved more relationship issues with no resolution but friendly affect afterwards. Conflicts with parents and friends occurred at about the same rates, but parents usually reported more coercion, whereas friends reported more compromise (Adams & Laursen, 2001). Such results are consistent with the nature of interpersonal negotiation among friends (discussed in chapter 6). As one African American adolescent girl told an interviewer in an urban high school, "My friends and I always argue because that's what friends do." She also explained, "You know you always argue with your family and friends but that don't mean you don't care about them. So it's always, you gotta have disagreements in a relationship and then happiness comes along with it . . . " (Way, 1995, pp. 119–120).

Sibling interaction. Relationships with siblings are often models for friendships or peer interactions. Nevertheless, siblings are a relatively new focus in the study of adolescents' personal relationships. As with parenting research, sibling research has been guided primarily by attachment and family systems theories (see Hetherington, 1994). As a normative component of many family systems, the sibling

BOX 11.5 ROADMAP TO SUCCESSFUL PRACTICE

How to Move Toward Acceptance

In the book *Mom, Dad. I'm Gay* developmental clinical psychologist Ritch Savin-Williams offers advice to parents of lesbian and gay adolescents. Savin-Williams believes that parents have been given an honor, a gift—the opportunity to know their child better, more completely than previously. If parents want to show their acceptance of their gay son or daughter, they should first listen, ask questions, and then:

- Give unconditional love and reassure their child that they love and support her or him regardless of the child's sexuality.
- Continue to meet their child's basic needs, such as safety, structure, and affection.
- Refrain from pathologizing their child because of his or her sexuality.
- Help their child enjoy childhood and adolescence. Let their child be a kid and provide her or him space to be herself or himself.
- Give themselves some time to adjust to this new status: parent of a sexual-minority child.
- Seek educational information for parents (e.g., literature from P-FLAG, or Parents, Families and Friends of Lesbians and Gays). Modify previous beliefs regarding the consequences of a nonheterosexual identity.
- Talk with other parents in similar situations to gain information and support.
- Be aware that extended family members can play an integral role assisting parents to adapt to their new status.
- Encourage the child to share his or her history of same-sex attractions, the ways in which sexual orientation has influenced the child's life, who else knows and how they have reacted, and future expectations the youth has about his or her life as a gay person (Savin-Williams, 2001, p. 230).

Parents who adjust best give preeminence to the relationship they have with their child, preserve the child's integrity, and enhance family unity through unconditional love.

Source: Based on "*Mom, Dad. I'm Gay: How Families Negotiate Coming Out*" (pp. 229–231), by R. Savin-Williams, 2001, Washington, DC: APA Books. Copyright 2001 by the American Psychological Association.

subsystem has many features in common with other relationships. Like parent-child relations, interactions between older and younger siblings are usually hierarchical because of differences in age and status (Stoneman & Brody, 1993). Sibling relationships are also characterized by high levels of conflict, although—like parent-adolescent conflict—sibling conflict also seems to decrease across adolescence after a peak in middle childhood (Cole & Kerns, 2001).

During adolescence, what were areas of conflict with your parents? with your siblings?

Researchers have identified three **sibling interaction styles**, based on the degree of siblings' positivity or negativity:

- **Harmonious.** Compassionate or caring sibling relationships
- **Typical.** Relationships that are characterized by ambivalence among siblings
- **Conflicted.** Sibling relationships that are hostile and/or alienated (adapted from Brody, Stoneman & McCoy, 1994)

Reflect again on the family in our chapter case study. There are no hints of sibling conflict, suggesting that the sisters and brother are probably "typical."

In sibling studies using a family systems perspective, researchers have emphasized the interdependency among the marital relationship, the general emotional climate of the family, and sibling characteristics. Siblings with less difficult temperaments, whose parents perceived their family relationships to be close, and whose fathers were generally positive in their interactions with them are more likely than siblings from other families to have less conflicted sibling relationships in early adolescence (Brody, Stoneman, & McCoy, 1994). Similarly, ineffective parenting and sibling conflict measured in early adolescence interacted to predict boys' antisocial behavior and peer adjustment between ages 12 and 16 (Bank, Burraston, & Snyder, 2004).

When considering parental involvement in sibling relationships, mothers spent more time overall with siblings than fathers; however, parental roles were also related to the gender composition of the dyad, with fathers spending more time with male-male dyads. Parental reactions to sibling conflicts were either *noninvolvement* (e.g., tell them to work it out), or *intervention* (e.g., step in and solve the problem), or *coaching* (e.g., give advice).

Mothers and fathers differ in their reactions to sibling conflict, with mothers using noninvolvement and coaching more than fathers (McHale, Updegraff, Tucker, & Crouter, 2000). Behavior-genetic researchers who investigate the differential treatment of adolescent siblings have suggested that parenting directed at siblings is part of the shared environment of adolescents. Monitoring and control, as well as parental warmth, are related to siblings' social competence during adolescence (Anderson, Hetherington, Reiss, & Howe, 1994).

In middle childhood and early adolescence, children's perceptions of sibling relationships differ according to the gender composition of the sibling dyad (McHale, Crouter, & Tucker, 1999). Male sibling dyads report lower levels of intimacy, caring, and conflict resolution than either male/female or female sibling dyads (Cole & Kern, 2001). In a longitudinal study across middle childhood and early adolescence, older (first-born) siblings' gender-role attitudes, personality characteristics, and leisure activities predicted their younger (second-born) siblings' gender-role orientations 2 years later, independent of parental influences and children's own characteristics (McHale, Updegraff, Helms-Erikson, & Crouter, 2001).

On the other hand, with development, older siblings became *less* like their younger brothers or sisters, suggesting a process of individuation not unlike the process we discussed in chapter 10 with respect to parents. (*Beth, for example, has little in common with either Rick or Annie and is the first to leave home and get married.*) First-born siblings also became more gender stereotyped between ages 10 and 12, unlike second-borns, indicating that first-born children may be more susceptible to gender intensification in early adolescence than their younger siblings. Overall, however, most girls were less traditional in terms of sex roles than boys, especially boys with younger sisters (McHale, Updegraff, Helms-Erikson, & Crouter, 2001).

Moreover, having a brother or sister and belonging to a same- versus opposite-sex sibling dyad affected adolescents' friendship experiences. Although girls often learned control tactics from their brothers, which they applied to their friendships, boys were less likely to model the intimacy that characterized their sisters' friendships. Furthermore, adolescents from mixed-sex sibling dyads were more likely to have friends with instrumental (masculine) qualities and who engaged in masculine-stereotyped activities (Updegraff, McHale, & Crouter, 2000).

Parental relationships. The quality of the relationship between the parents in two-parent households is a significant influence on adolescents' romantic relationships, perhaps because teenagers observe adults' intimate behavior (Gray & Steinberg, 1999b). For example, adults who recalled a loving, affectionate relationship between their parents more often classified themselves as secure and comfortable in intimate relationships (Hazan & Shaver, 1987). On the other hand, exposure to parental conflict negatively influences teens' sensitivity to their romantic partners' perspective, their ability to listen, and their own conflict management in relationships (Gray & Steinberg, 1999b).

Marital dissatisfaction also seems to promote gender-stereotypical patterns in adolescence (e.g., compliance in teenage girls and assertiveness in teenage boys) that may influence future interactions with romantic partners (Feiring, 1999a). For example, a recent study examining dating and early adolescent adjustment found differences based on families' degree of marital discord. For families high in marital conflict, teens' steady dating was associated with lower self-esteem in girls, but not in boys. Boys who dated from high-conflict families also reported fewer feelings of depression than boys who did not date (Doyle, Brendgen, Markiewicz, & Kamkar, 2003). These results were not found in low-conflict families, suggesting that parental conflict may negatively impact adolescents' ability to engage successfully in intimate relationships, particularly for girls. Marital conflict is more traumatic to adolescents than the effects of divorce. Parental conflict has been linked to behavioral and emotional adjustment problems in both boys and girls (Amato, 2000; Amato & Booth, 1996;

Amato & Keith, 1991; Kelly & Emery, 2003). However, from a relationship standpoint, divorce may be particularly difficult for adolescents because they are just beginning to explore the meaning of dating and romantic commitments themselves (Hines, 1997). For example, when mothers disclosed their anger over divorce or their concerns about money, their daughters reported more depression and anxiety than sons, reflecting the importance of intimacy in girls' close relationships (Koerner, Jacobs, & Raymond, 2000).

Divorce may also indirectly impact the quality of parenting before, during, and after a divorce (Buehler & Gerard, 2002; Sun & Li, 2002). For example, in a large-scale study of ethnically diverse 9th, 10th, and 11th graders, adolescents in newly formed single-parent families experienced a drop in parental control and responsiveness compared to adolescents in stable nondivorced and stable mother-custody households (Freeman & Newland, 2002). Moreover, a majority of divorced parents will repartner and form stepfamilies within 5 years, adding new relationship stress to adolescents' lives as they adjust to stepparents and/or stepsiblings (Kelly & Emery, 2003). Potential protective factors for adolescents experiencing divorce are supportive relationships with same-sex parents prior to divorce (Videon, 2002) and continuing supportive relationships with their noncustodial parents (Amato & Gilbreth, 1999; Kelly & Emery, 2003). See Box 11.6 for a discussion of ways to assist teenagers' adjustment to divorce.

BOX 11.6 ROADMAP TO SUCCESSFUL PRACTICE

Intervention Programs for Adolescents' Divorce Adjustment

Joan Kelly and Robert Emery (2003) advocate a systems approach (including family systems and broader social and legal systems) to adolescent adjustment problems following divorce. They specifically recommend intervention programs that minimize parental conflict, promote authoritative and close relationships between children and both of their parents, enhance economic stability in the postdivorce family, and, when appropriate, help children have a voice in the interventions. Examples of program interventions currently available are parent education programs for parents and children, divorce mediation, collaborative lawyering, judicial settlement conferences, parenting coordinator or arbitration programs for chronically litigating parents, and family and group therapy for children and parents.

Of these types of programs, only mediation and divorce education have been consistently evaluated by researchers. For example, Emery has found that an average of 5 hours of custody mediation led to significant and positive effects on parent-child and parent-parent relationships 12 years later, including more sustained contact between fathers and children. Most divorce education programs for parents and children in the United States in the past decade, particularly those associated with family courts, are generally limited to one to two sessions in the court sector and four to six sessions in the community or schools. They are usually evaluated only through parent satisfaction questionnaires. However, evaluation studies of research-based programs designed to facilitate children's postdivorce adjustment have found them to be effective in educating parents and promoting changes in parenting behaviors associated with poor child outcomes.

Kelly and Emery encourage researchers to develop objective, reliable, and valid measures of the important struggles associated with divorce that might be apparent first in schools or clinical practice. They suggest, however, that practitioners and educators remember that many painful memories expressed by young people from divorced families are not evidence of pathology. They conclude that the majority of findings show that most children do well following divorce. Furthermore, Kelly and Emery believe that public policies need to acknowledge that when divorce occurs, parents and legal systems designed to assist families can utilize research knowledge and skills to reduce the risks associated with divorce.

Source: Based on "Children's Adjustment Following Divorce: Risk and Resilience Perspectives" (p. 360), by J. B. Kelly and R. E. Emery, 2003, *Family Relations, 52*(4), pp. 352–362. Copyright 2003 by the National Council on Family Relations.

Guideposts for Working with Adolescents

- Acknowledge diversity in the families of adolescents, such as intergenerational families, adoptive families, gay or lesbian families, never-married or cohabiting families, divorced or separated families, and stepfamilies.
- Be ready to listen when teens talk about parent-adolescent or sibling conflicts because they may affect teens' peer relationships and social behaviors.
- Provide information to parents on authoritative parenting, conflict resolution strategies, and, when appropriate, divorce adjustment in teenagers.
- Invite whole families to participate in school activities or events, not only teenagers' biological or custodial parent(s).

A growing number of adolescents are living with gay or lesbian parents who adopted, conceived through donor insemination, or had children from a previous heterosexual relationship. Like heterosexual families, gay and lesbian families vary in terms of the reasons for dissolution of previous relationships, children from previous marriages, and custody arrangements (Berger, 2001). For example, in a longitudinal British study of lesbian mother households, teenagers raised by lesbian mothers had more postseparation contact with their fathers than children raised by heterosexual mothers. In addition, teens often viewed their mother's female partner as an added member of their family constellation rather than as a competitor to their fathers (Tasker & Golombek, 1997). In contrast, teens raised by single-parent or divorced heterosexual mothers often resisted their mothers' new male partners becoming father figures, especially if their biological fathers were still in contact with them. But how adolescents felt about their mothers' relationships and their family identities did not differ between children raised by heterosexual and lesbian mothers (Tasker & Golombek, 1997). Overall, the picture emerging from over two decades of studies of children raised in lesbian and gay families confirms that the sexual orientation of parents is not a factor in adolescent outcomes (Stacey & Davenport, 2002).

Let's take a glimpse into the Chasen family's future. Next year, Beth will have a baby, Rick will come out to his mother, and Annie will start her first job. From a systems perspective, even though the family members do not all live together in the same household, their actions will continue to influence family dynamics.

Contexts of Adolescent Social Development

From the perspective of contextual influences on close adolescent relationships, the parent/family and peer/school systems are embedded in the community context. Contextual factors in families, schools, and communities can serve as a lens for examining in greater detail particular social issues in adolescence. For example, researchers have suggested that neighborhood quality and teens' degree of access to the wider community have a significant impact on adolescents' perceptions of life stresses, particularly in terms of peers (Allison et al., 1999).

Family Contexts

Families, as we have seen in this chapter, are an important context for the development of adolescents' friendships and close relationships. For example, the longitudinal study of friendship discussed in chapter 6 (refer to Figure 6.8) adopted a social-contextual model to examine the social context surrounding families, the intergenerational impact of family interactions, and the quality of adolescents' social ties outside their families (Cui, Conger, Bryant, & Elder, 2002). Data from self-report questionnaires, parent-child discussions, family problem-solving tasks, sibling interactions, and videotaped problem-solving tasks with friends support the contextual model. Recall that the researchers found parents' support (or hostility) during middle childhood promoted teenagers' supportive (or hostile) behavior towards a close friend during middle adolescence. Supportive relationships with siblings also carried over to friends, as predicted. The results revealed that higher income and levels of education were significantly related to parents' supportive behaviors and that there were gender differences in the quality of friendships, with girls' friendships more supportive than boys'. However, after controlling for the effects of socio-contextual factors (e.g., gender, income, education), family interaction processes still predicted teens' behavior and the quality of their friendships (Cui, Conger, Bryant, & Elder, 2002). Overall, the results confirmed the predictions of family systems theories regarding significant interrelationships between the parent, friend, and sibling subsystems of adolescents.

School Contexts

As we have discussed throughout this chapter, intimate friendships and romantic relations are central to high-school culture. The school context, therefore, is a potentially supportive system for adolescents' exploration of their views on close relationships. The sex education curriculum distributed by the Sexuality Information and Education Council of the United States (SIECUS) highlights the importance of sexuality in adolescent development (National Guidelines Task Force, 1996). The SIECUS Report (1998) also states that sexuality education is a lifelong process of acquiring information and forming attitudes, beliefs, and values about identity, relationships, intimacy, sexual development, reproductive health, interpersonal relationships, affection, intimacy, body image, and gender roles. According to SIECUS, parents, peers, schools, religion, the media, friends, and partners all influence the way people learn about sexuality.

Teachers who reflect on their own understandings of sexuality and how these have been socially constructed are better able to help teens comprehend what the sexual experiences undergone by young people mean (Diorio & Munro, 2003). Recent research has also shown that teachers' positive attitudes can help mediate the school difficulties often faced by sexual-minority adolescents because of heterosexism or homophobia (Barber & Eccles, 2003; Gilliam, 2002; see also Russell, Seif, & Truong, 2001). In one study, 50% of gay males reported having been victimized in junior high school because of their perceived sexual orientation. In high school, this figure rose to almost 60%. In another study, gay, lesbian, and bisexual students were five times as likely to miss school because of fears about safety (Rivers & Carragher, 2003). Yet teachers are often the least willing group in the school to discuss homosexuality with students (Tharinger & Wells, 2000). As a result, many sexual-minority teens are often isolated from each other and from many of their heterosexual peers (Owens, 1998).

Educational settings can contribute positively to the way both heterosexual and gay, lesbian, bisexual, or transgender (GLBT) youth interact when formal school policies define sexual harassment to include sexual orientation (D'Augelli, 1996). Although few school-based support services or groups are specifically designed for lesbian, gay, and bisexual teens (Owens, 1998), a growing number of studies suggest that attending schools characterized by gay-sensitive HIV instruction and by social support from GLBT peers is linked to positive self-esteem and less sexual risk-taking (Russell, 2005) For a history of gay youth programs, from counseling programs to Gay-Straight Alliances and online forums, see Cohen, 2005. Table 11–8 lists many different types of programs that can be successfully delivered in an educational context. Essential to almost all types of interventions is the provision of a safe and secure environment (Tharinger & Wells, 2000).

Community Contexts

Although parents may select the particular contexts in which their adolescents interact (e.g., families, schools, neighborhoods), parenting practices are given meaning by the culture (Granic, Dishion, & Hollenstein, 2003). For example, researchers observed parents' limit-setting in both European American and African American families. Teachers also rated the adolescents as either "successful" or "high-risk." *High* scores on limit-setting characterized the European American families with successful adolescents, as expected. However, *low* scores on limit-setting characterized

TABLE 11–8

GLBT Youth Development Programs

These examples of support programs for lesbian, gay, and bisexual teens vary from individual to large-group settings.

	Level of Operation			
Objectives	**Individual**	**Small Group**	**Organizational**	**Institutional/Community**
Remediation	Affirmative counseling	Groups on coping with parental rejection	Alternative protective programs for high-risk youths	Community-coalitions for service development
Enhancement	Life goals groups	Programs on dating skills	Awareness programs in schools	Cultural events related to GLBT youths
Competence	Assertiveness training	Problem-solving skills for relationship building	Methods for reporting discrimination	Sexual health promotion
Education	Brochures on stress management, etc.	Pamphlets for parents, siblings, teachers, etc.	Information on anti-discrimination/ violence in policies	Information about local and national sources of help
Prevention	Coping skills; training groups for coming out	Discussion groups for families with newly disclosed youths	Publication of procedures for discrimination/violence management	Safer sex campaigns for GLBT youths
Advocacy	Case management testimony in judicial hearings, etc.	Work for inclusion of same-sex dating and partnerships in classes	Advocacy for explicit equal protection clauses in educational settings	Advocacy for protective legislation and funds for services
Resource Provision	Telephone help lines; Internet materials	Monitor and buddy systems for youths	Funding youth outreach programs in human service settings	Help for homeless, poor, HIV+, and victimized youths
Social Protection and Control	Education on legal rights of GLBT youths	Seminar on partnership legal issues	Assurance of confidentiality of youth counselling	Protective legislation; penalties for violence and discrimination

Source: From "Enhancing the Development of Lesbian, Gay, and Bisexual Youths" (p. 144), by A. R. D'Augelli, in E. D. Rothblum and L. A. Bond (Eds.), 1996, *Preventing Heterosexism and Homophobia* (pp. 124–150), Thousand Oaks, CA: Sage. Copyright 1996 by Sage Publications Inc. Reprinted by permission.

African American families with successful adolescents, *not* with high-risk teens (Dishion & Bullock, 2002).

Research and practice with adolescents, therefore, requires knowledge and understanding of community values and relationships. In a New Zealand study, for example, high-school students from European, Maori, and Chinese cultural backgrounds were asked to define families. Over 80% included married and cohabiting families, single-parent households, and extended family members in their answer to the question "What is in a family?" Maori adolescents endorsed the most family forms. Few differences in family definitions were based on the adolescents' own family structures, implying that variations in their culture were a more important factor (Anyan & Pryor, 2002). In addition, in some cultures more than in others, teenagers may spend more time with extended family members, such as aunts, grandparents, or cousins (Granic, Dishion, & Hollenstein, 2003).

CHAPTER REVIEW

Social Development

- The study of adolescent social development includes personal relationships with family members, friends, and romantic partners.
- Close relationships are enduring ties or connections between people with frequent interdependent action sequences that occur across diverse settings and tasks.

Theoretical Viewpoints

- Attachment theory describes four behavioral systems that organize relationships (attachment, affiliation, caretaking, and sexual/reproductive systems).
- Attachments, which may be either secure or insecure, generate internal working models of relationships that guide future social interactions.
- Family systems theory asserts that families are composed of many simultaneously operating subsystems and can only be understood by viewing the entire system as a whole.
- Families can be open or closed systems that maintain their equilibrium through mechanisms such as system rules, system goals, and feedback loops.

Gender

- Gender identity refers to one's biological sex as well as to one's identification with gender roles.
- Gender roles are a set of attitudes and behaviors associated with the cultural conventions of being male or female. Gender-role orientation can be feminine, masculine, androgynous, or undifferentiated.
- Overall, males and females are more similar than different.
- Developmental psychologists have proposed a sequence of gender-role stages, moving from undifferentiated gender identity in infancy to gender identity that transcends gender roles in adolescence.
- Transgender is a gender identity that differs from a person's biological or genetic sex.

Sexuality

- Sexual identity refers to an enduring sense of oneself as a sexual person who fits into a culturally constructed category.
- Embodiment refers to the ways in which cultural images are incorporated into body image, or how individuals think or feel about their bodies.
- Heteronormativity, or compulsory heterosexuality, is the social pressure to be heterosexual.
- Most gay or lesbian adolescents do not disclose their sexual orientations until around age 20, although they are often aware of erotic attractions much earlier—around age 9 or 10.

Friendships, Dating, and Romantic Relationships

- Friendships become more intimate during adolescence across racial/ethnic groups, especially among girls.
- Although same-sex friendships are still important, adolescents increase their opposite-sex friendships, which—for heterosexual adolescents—may serve as a prelude to dating and romantic relationships.
- High-school crowds often serve as the context for dating and romantic relationships, which often occur in mixed-sex groups.
- Adolescents often have idealized or romanticized images of love or expectations based on hegemonic masculinity, the cultural belief that males have power over females.

Family Relationships

- Individual characteristics of adolescents, their parents, and siblings influence family interactions.
- Parent-adolescent and sibling conflicts are most intense in middle adolescence and decline in later adolescence.
- Authoritative parenting styles and secure attachments lead to positive psychosocial outcomes for adolescents.
- Ongoing conflict between parents is more distressing to adolescents than divorce or separation.
- Contemporary adolescents live in diverse types of families (e.g., gay or lesbian, single-parent, intergenerational, adoptive or stepfamilies).

Social Development in Context

- Families are an important context for the development of adolescents' friendships and close relationships.
- Because intimate friendships and romantic relationships are central to high-school culture, schools need to support adolescents of all sexual orientations through sexuality education, sexual harassment policies, and social programs.
- The meaning of authoritative parenting may vary from community to community.

TABLE 11–9

Summary of Developmental Theories

In chapter 11, adolescents' social development was explained by two influential theories of interpersonal relationships.

Chapter	Theory	Focus
11: Social Development in Middle Adolescence	Attachment	Internal working models of early relationships in families as the basis of later close relationships, such as peer relations, friendships, and romantic partnerships
	Family Systems	Equilibrium among simultaneous interdependent subsystems, such as the parent-child, marital, or sibling systems

KEY TERMS

Affiliative system
Androgynous
Anxious-avoidant
Anxious-resistant
Attachment system
Caretaking system
Cliques
Closeness
Crowds
Differential developmental trajectories
Embodiment
Entropy
Ethology
Family systems approach
Feminine
Gender identity
Gender nonconforming
Gender roles
Gender schemas
Hegemonic masculinity
Heteronormativity
Internal working model
Love styles
Masculine
Masculinity ideology
Meta-analysis
Romantic view
Secure attachment
Sex-typed
Sexual disclosure
Sibling interaction styles
Sexual minority
Sexual/reproductive system
Systems theory
Transgender
Undifferentiated

SUGGESTED ACTIVITIES

1. Interview a teenager who is dating and find out what a typical date might involve: who, what, when, and where? Does this teen fit into one of the dating stages?
2. Look through a magazine for girls, such as *YM* or *Seventeen*, or go to their web sites. Count the number of sexist or sexual images and topics. Overall, what influence do you think this media source has on teens—both boys and girls?
3. Go to dinner with a family that has a teenager(s). Observe the parent-to-parent, parent-child, and sibling interactions. How did the various subsystems affect the conversation? Did you see examples of feedback loops?

RECOMMENDED RESOURCES

Suggested Books

Edut, O. (1998). *Adios, Barbie: Young women write about body image and identity.* Seal Press.

Howey, N., & Samuels, E. (Eds.) (2000). *Out of the ordinary: Essays on growing up with gay, lesbian, and transgender parents.* New York: St. Martin's Press.

Savin-Williams, R. C. (2001). *Mom, dad. I'm gay: How families negotiate coming out.* Washington, DC: American Psychological Association.

Tolman, D. L. (2002). *Dilemmas of desire: Teenage girls talk about sexuality.* Cambridge, MA: Harvard University Press.

Way, N., & Chu, J. (Eds.) (2004). *Adolescent boys: Exploring diverse cultures of boyhood.* New York: New York University Press.

Suggested Online Resources

Be yourself: Questions and answers for gay, lesbian, and bisexual youth
http://www.pflag.org/fileadmin/user_upload/Be_Yourself_TT.pdf

LGBT Parents and their Children Fact Sheet
http://newmedia.colorado.edu/~socwomen/socactivism/lgbtparenting_kjoos.pdf

National Gay and Lesbian Family Study
http://www.mindfully.org/Reform/Gay-Lesbian-Family-Study.htm

Transgender Youth and the Role of Service Providers
http:// advocatesforyouth.org/publications/transitions/transitions1404.pdf

Voices of a Generation: Teenage Girls on Sex, School, and Self
http://www.aauw.org/research/voices.cfm

Suggested Web Sites

American Association for Marriage and Family Therapy
http://aamft.org/index_nm.asp

Council on Contemporary Families
http://www.contemporaryfamilies.org/public/links.php

Gay, Lesbian, and Straight Education Network
http://www.glsen.org/cgi-bin/iowa/home.html

National Council on Family Relations
http://www.ncfr.org

Parents and Families of Lesbians and Gays (PFLAG)
http://www.pflag.org

Suggested Films and Videos

Being gay: Coming out in the 21st century (2004). Films for the Humanities & Social Sciences (25 minutes)

Boys will be men (2001). Insight Media, Inc. (57 minutes)

Boys don't cry (1999). Fox Searchlight Video (118 minutes, R-rated

Diversity rules: The changing nature of families (2001). Insight Media, Inc. (25 minutes)

Talking gender (1999). Insight Media, Inc. (23 minutes)

Teenage relationships (1992). Insight Media, Inc. (30 minutes)

What a girl wants (2003). Media Education Foundation (33 minutes)

CHAPTER

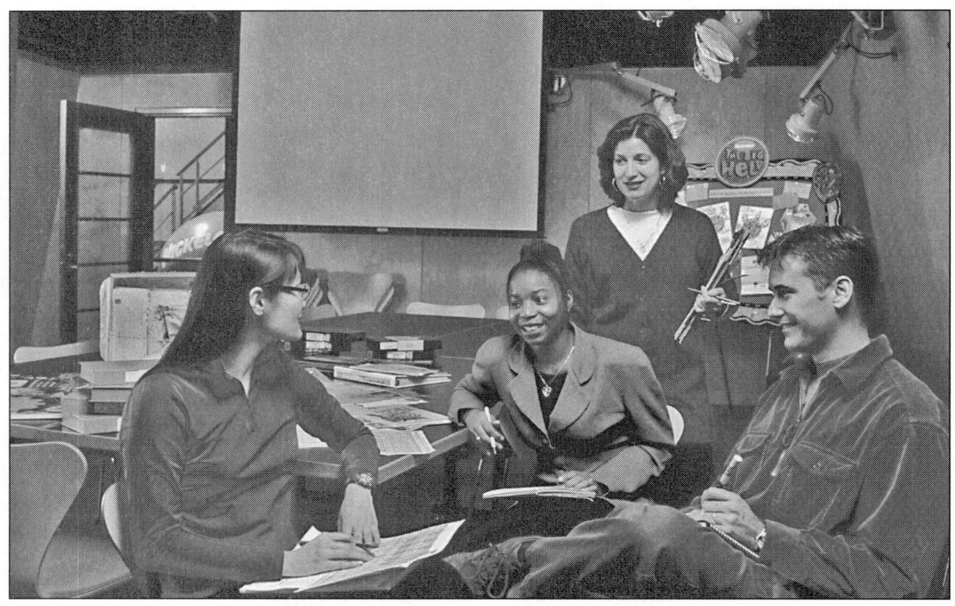

Beyond Middle Adolescence: Emerging Adulthood

CHAPTER OBJECTIVES

After reading this chapter, students will be able to:

- Define late adolescence and emerging adulthood
- Discuss historical and contemporary portrayals of adulthood as a developmental period
- Integrate theoretical perspectives on emerging adulthood
- Describe the developmental achievements of emerging adulthood
- Explain the contributions of diverse contexts to emerging adulthood

It's 5:40 P.M. and Devon, Kate, Maria, and Prasad are about to leave work. Devon, age 19, a part-time college student, has to rush off to the community college for an evening class. He says goodbye to his friends and heads for the bus. Meanwhile, Kate, age 23, calls her husband Keith on his cell phone to ask him to pick up their 3-year-old from the child care center because she's running late. Maria, age 22, who lives with her parents because she can't yet afford her own apartment, calls her mother to say she's eating out. Prasad, age 25, lives with an unemployed roommate who usually comes and goes at odd hours anyway, so Prasad is free to do as he pleases.

Defining Emerging Adulthood

In this textbook, we have explored middle childhood to middle adolescence—ages 8 to 18—not only as developmental *milestones* but also as *pathways* to the future. Our challenge now is to consider the *destination* sought after by adolescents as they leave high school: to enter the world of adulthood. **Emerging adulthood** is a relatively new concept that attempts to differentiate the developmental stages of adolescence and adulthood while recognizing that the ages from 18 to 25 are simultaneously a *transitional* period, as seen in Figure 12.1 (Arnett, 2000a). In this manner, the cultural construction of emerging adulthood is similar to constructions of middle childhood and adolescence as *both* a developmental stage *and* a transitional period.

Late adolescence, typically defined as ages 18 to 21, has often been described as the developmental period in which postformal thinking (described in chapter 9) is possible and socialization into adult society is accomplished (Arnett & Taber, 1994). **Young adulthood**, on the other hand, is a sociological term commonly used to refer to ages 21 to 30, depending on the age of legal majority in a particular society, and is often used interchangeably with the developmental period of **early adulthood** (for reviews, see Arnett & Tabor, 1997; Arnett & Galambos, 2003).

When researchers asked 18- to 23-year-old college students and 21- to 28-year-old young people (not in college) what characteristics were necessary for a person to be considered an "adult," the most often endorsed criteria for both groups were related to individual behaviors of persons at that stage (Arnett, 1997):

- "Accept responsibility for the consequences of your own actions."
- "Decide on your own beliefs and values independently of parents or other influences."
- "Establish a relationship with parents as an equal adult."

In contrast, adult social-role transitions that are often studied by sociologists—such as finishing your education, entering the workforce, getting married, or becoming a parent—were rejected by both college students and by other young adults as indicators of adulthood. Nevertheless, on the question "Do you think that you have reached adulthood?" the two groups differed: The majority (63%) of college students chose the ambiguous response "in some respects yes, in some respects no" compared to noncollege young adults, who most often responded "yes." In addition, the proportion of people in their 20s indicating "yes" increased with age, from 53% among the 21- to 24-year-olds to 71% among the 25- to 28-year-olds (Arnett, 1997, 2001a).

FIGURE 12.1 Emerging Adults
Relationships between parents and children need to change even if emerging adults live at home.
Source: From "Luann," by G. Evans, November 5, 2000. Copyright 2000 by GEC, Inc. Reprinted by permission of United Features Syndicate, Inc.

In postmodern industrialized societies, the stage of emerging adulthood is seen as a developmental period that is somehow distinct from late adolescence and young adulthood. Conceptions of the transition to adulthood were compared across adolescents (ages 13–19), young adults (ages 20–29), and midlife adults (ages 30–55). As seen in Figure 12.2, the same three criteria previously cited were once again judged most important, but with the additional criterion of "becoming financially independent." However, adolescents (not surprisingly) believed that biological transitions, such as puberty, were more important than did the adults. In addition, midlife adults were more likely than either adolescents or young adults to view compliance with social norms, such as not driving under the influence of alcohol, as a necessary characteristic of adulthood. As in previous studies, role transitions, such as finishing school, finding employment, getting married, and becoming a parent, were ranked lowest in importance by all three age groups (Arnett, 2001b). See Table 12–1 for a complete list of the rankings.

When young adults in their mid-20s were asked to rate how they usually feel in 10 different situations (e.g., home, school, work, family, recreation) with response options ranging from "not at all like an adult" to "entirely like an adult" as well as a global measure ("most of the time"), some interesting results emerged. Most respondents were likely to feel like an adult at work (70%) or in their private lives (78% at home, 75% with their child, and 70% with their romantic partner). They were least likely to feel like an adult with friends (37%) or parents (43%). Overall, only 60% of these 25- and 26-year-olds felt like an adult most of the time. However, youth who had already experienced family transitions, such as establishing an independent household, getting married or cohabiting, or having children, were twice as likely to feel like an adult than those who had not. These results suggest that adulthood is a subjective and context-dependent experience (Shanahan, Porfeli, Mortimer, & Erickson, 2005).

During emerging adulthood most young people are in the process of completing the transition to adulthood. For example, person-centered research has revealed six paths to adulthood: fast starters, parents without careers, educated partners, educated singles, working singles, and slow starters (Osgood, Ruth, Eccles, Jacobs, & Barber, 2005). In addition, diverse cultures may differ in the criteria they use to mark the transition to adulthood (Arnett, 2003). For example, chronological markers or events such as marriage hold differing importance among families from various nationalities, religions,

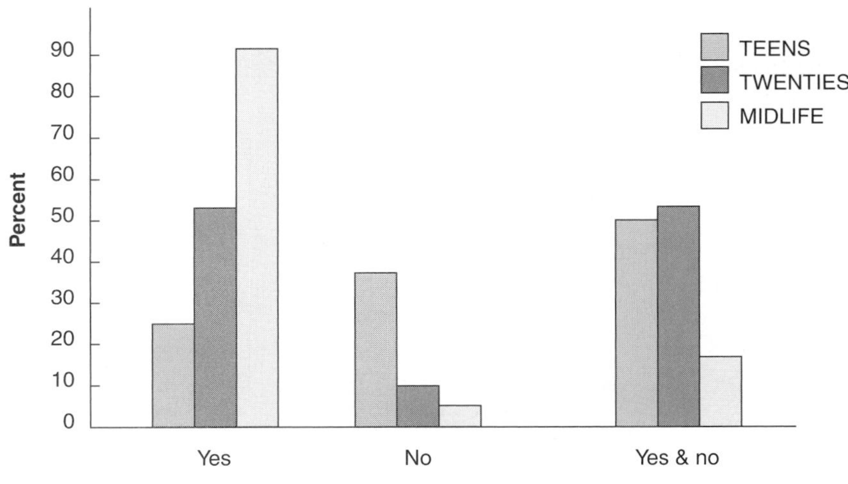

FIGURE 12.2 "Have You Reached Adulthood?"
About half of emerging adults (dark bars) feel that they have reached adulthood.

Source: From "Conceptions of the Transition to Adulthood: Perspectives from Adolescence Through Midlife" (p. 140), by J. J. Arnett, 2001, *Journal of Adult Development*, *8*, pp. 133–143. Copyright 2001 by Plenum Publishing Corporation. Reprinted with kind permission from Springer Science and Business Media.

TABLE 12–1

Criteria for Adulthood

For each item, participants were asked to 'Indicate whether you think each of the following must be achieved before a person can be considered an adult', and they responded by indicating yes or no.

Necessary for Adulthood?	% Indicating 'Yes'
1. Accept responsibility for the consequences of your actions	94
2. Decide on personal beliefs and values independently of parents or other influences	78
3. Financially independent from parents	73
4. Capable of running a household (man)	72
5. Establish a relationship with parents as an equal adult	69
6. Avoid committing petty crimes like shoplifting and vandalism	66
7. Capable of running a household (woman)	67
8. Use contraception if sexually active and not trying to conceive a child	65
9. No longer living in parents' household	60
10. Avoid drunk driving	55
11. Capable of keeping family physically safe (man)	52
12. Learn always to have good control of your emotions	50
13. Capable of supporting a family financially (man)	50
14. Capable of caring for children (woman)	50
15. Capable of caring for children (man)	50
16. Capable of keeping family physically safe (woman)	47
17. Capable of supporting a family financially (woman)	42
18. Avoid using illegal drugs	41
19. Reached age 18	39
20. Make lifelong commitments to others	36
21. Drive an automobile safely and close to the speed limit	32
22. Reached age 21	31
23. Avoid becoming drunk	30
24. Capable of fathering children (man)	30
25. Capable of bearing children (woman)	29
26. Have no more than one sexual partner	29
27. Obtained driver's license	24
28. Settle into a long-term career	21
29. Not deeply tied to parents emotionally	19
30. Avoid using profanity/vulgar language	18
31. Married	17
32. Employed full-time	17
33. Purchased a house	17
34. Committed to a long-term love relationship	16
35. Have at least one child	14
36. Grow to full height	13
37. Finished with education	10
38. Have had sexual intercourse	9

Source: From "Learning to Stand Alone: The Contemporary American Transition to Adulthood in Cultural and Historical Context" (p. 303), by J. J. Arnett, 1998, *Human Development, 41* (5–6), pp. 295–315. Copyright 1998 by S. Karger AG, Basel. Reprinted by permission.

or racial/ethnic groups (Barry & Nelson, 2005). In most Western cultures, the most important task is becoming an independent, self-sufficient individual. This requires the qualities of accepting responsibility, making independent decisions, being considerate of others, and achieving financial independence (Arnett, 1998). Although most Americans name individualistic criteria, ethnic minority groups in the United States (e.g., African Americans, Latino Americans, and Native Americans) are more likely than the majority culture to favor criteria that reflect obligations to community (Arnett, 2003; see also Cooper, Jackson, Azmitia, & Lopez, 1998).

For example, of the characters in the chapter case study, Devon, an African American student, is the first in his family to attend college and is working to earn money for tuition and books; Kate is married to her high-school sweetheart and has worked as a secretary at ABC Corporation for 5 years already; Maria is a brand-new professional with a bachelor's degree in marketing; and Prasad is the newly hired manager of the department they all work in! Devon, Kate, Maria, and Prasad have differing developmental trajectories and social locations. But despite their different pathways to adulthood, they are all still just in their early to mid-20s.

In this chapter, as we explore *emerging* adulthood, remember that age is only a rough indicator of transitions between developmental periods. Only a small percentage of 18- to 25-year-olds consider themselves to have met the criteria for adulthood (Nelson & Barry, 2005). "There are 19-year-olds who have reached adulthood—demographically, subjectively, and in terms of identity formation—and 29-year-olds who have not. Nevertheless for most people, the transition from emerging adulthood to young adulthood intensifies in the late 20s and is reached by age 30 in all of these respects" (Arnett, 2000a, p. 477). See Table 12–2.

Do you consider yourself an adult? When do you think adulthood begins?

TABLE 12–2

Transitions to Adulthood

This table shows the percent of emerging adults (first column) who have experienced various transitions compared to older age groups.

Number and Types of Adult Transitions

Selected Characteristics		Age Groups in Young Adult Transitions: (18–24 yrs) Early transition	(25–29 yrs) Middle transition	(30–34 yrs) Late transition	Total (18–34 yrs)
Total young adults:	N	27,117,388	19,178,062	20,325,174	66,620,624
Number of adult transitions:					
None or 1	%	40.7	6.6	2.5	19.2
2 or 3	%	43.0	41.7	28.0	38.0
4 or 5	%	16.3	51.7	69.5	42.7
Mean number of adult transitions		1.98	3.42	3.90	2.98
Types of adult transitions:					
Not living with parents	%	55.7	84.1	91.4	74.8
Not attending school	%	55.4	85.5	91.2	75.0
Working full-time	%	48.1	73.7	74.0	63.4
Married or ever married	%	24.6	60.4	76.7	50.8
Has one or more children*	%	13.8	38.5	56.4	33.9

Note: 5% PUMS, 2000 Census

*Refers to respondents' children living in the household.

Source: From "Young Adults in the United States" (p. 5), by R. G. Rumbaut, Working Paper No. 4, Network on Transitions to Adulthood, available from: http://www.pop.upenn.edu/transad/news/Young%20Adults%20in%20the%20United%20States%20-%20A%20Profile.pdf Copyright by Rubén G. Rumbaut. Reprinted by permission of the author.

Historical Views of Adulthood

As with middle childhood and adolescence, the history of developmental periods and age groupings also informs contemporary conceptualizations of adulthood. In chapters 1 and 7, we emphasized that *adulthood* itself is a social construction that has been defined differently in diverse contexts and historical periods. For example, Western cultures, such as the postindustrial nations in Europe and North America, have defined adulthood differently from most nonindustrialized societies. Although adolescence and adulthood are prevalent social constructions in non-Western cultures, emerging adulthood exists primarily in societies where adult status is not attained until the mid- to late 20s. In this respect, emerging adulthood is seen as the period of the life span bridging adolescence and adulthood during which young people are no longer adolescents but have not yet attained full adult status (Arnett, 1998). However, more traditional cultures typically define the beginning of adulthood at marriage, which is usually between ages 16 and 18 for women and between ages 18 and 20 for men (Arnett, 2000a).

An intermediate period (sometimes also called youth) exists in only about 20 to 25% of some 186 traditional cultures (Arnett, 2000a; see Schlegel & Barry, 1991). For example, Moroccan youth who were interviewed between ages 9 and 20 said that they are "grown up" on the basis of physical development, chronological age, or character qualities rather than marriage; Moroccan adults emphasized *'aql*, an Arabic word implying rationality and impulse control (Arnett, 1998; see Davis & Davis, 1989). Similarly, the Inuit first-nation people of Canada see establishing a household with a prospective spouse as important even before marriage and emphasize spending more time at home with your partner rather than "running around" as in adolescence (Arnett, 1998; see Condon, 1987). In the Marquesas Islands of Polynesia, 14-year-olds work alongside adults but are not considered adults themselves because they lack *taure'are'*, or the character qualities necessary for the fulfillment of adult responsibilities (Arnett, 1998; see Kirkpatrick, 1987). Taken together, these anthropological studies suggest that emerging adulthood is a distinct period of life.

Early History of Adulthood

The term *adulthood* did not appear in the *Oxford English Dictionary* until 1870, although the word *adult* appeared in 1656. It was derived from ***adultus*** ("grown"), the past participle of the Latin ***adolescere*** ("to grow up or mature"). Note that the term *adolescent*, as we saw in chapter 7, appeared in the 1400s, but the term *adult* did not come into English usage for another half century. Many European languages that have a word for adolescence do not have a separate term for adulthood (Côté, 2000b). This disparity suggests that the meaning of social or psychological adulthood varies by culture and historical time. For example, recall from chapter 1 that many young people in early English society moved out of their family home during middle childhood or early adolescence but were not granted independence. Boys and girls commonly lived as apprentices to tradespeople or in household service to wealthy families until such time as they married and had children of their own (Arnett, 1998; see also Ben-Amos, 1994).

In North America, the early settlers were more likely to define adult social roles according to gender than age. Women were seen to have more in common with girls than with men or boys (Côté, 2000b). After the American Revolution, however, when education for citizenship was increasingly viewed as important, children began to be differentiated from adults because they attended school (Côté, 2000b), as discussed in chapter 2. Nevertheless, even after the abolition of slavery in the mid-1800s, many racists continued to call African American adult men by the pejorative term *boy*!

In the 17th through 19th centuries, when America gained independence from Britain and sovereignty over lands formerly held by Spain and France, the qualities of individualism, self-control and self-determination became important as criteria for adulthood, at least among European Americans (Arnett, 1998). In addition, political practices, such as the denial of voting rights, implied that legal adulthood was seen as a social privilege rather than a civil right well into the middle of the 20th century. For example, the Fifteenth Amendment to the U.S. Constitution granted all male citizens, regardless of race, color, or previous condition of servitude, the right to vote in 1870. Until the Voting Rights Act of 1965, however, many African, Asian, and Latino Americans were still disenfranchised. Women were not granted the vote until passage of the Nineteenth Amendment in 1920. Similarly, until the Citizenship Act of 1924, American Indians were not granted citizenship rights under the Fifteenth Amendment (Jackson, 2004).

Modern Contributions to the Construction of Adulthood

During the first half of the 20th century, marriage became the definitive sign of the transition to adulthood, with the median age of marriage in the United States declining steadily for both women and men through the 1950s. In the 1960s, however, the average age of first marriage began to rise. By the end of the century, the average marriage age was 24.5 years for American women and 26.7 for American men (Arnett, 1998). Changes in the timing of marriage reflected the increasing freedom, prosperity, and social upheaval of the 1960s that permitted young people to choose the timing of their own life course (Modell, 1989).

In the 1970s, the American sociologist Kenneth Keniston (1971) suggested using the term ***youth*** to describe a period of the life span between adolescence and adulthood. His book *Youth and Dissent: The Rise of a New Opposition* reflected changes in the United States during the second half of the 20th century brought about by young people's participation in civil rights, opposition to the war in Vietnam, and the sexual revolution. At about the same time, developmental psychologists studying adulthood used the term ***novice*** to describe a period of transition to adulthood (Levinson, 1978, 1986). During the novice phase, lasting about 15 years, young people were seen to be establishing themselves interpersonally (e.g., through marriage or cohabitation) and economically (e.g., through education or employment) (Arnett, 2000a).

Devon, Maria, and Prasad are all single, reflecting the later normative ages of first marriages for their generation. Kate, however, is married and has one child. Only Maria and Prasad have completed college degrees. Nevertheless, they are all considered "emerging" adults, according to our definition.

In the second half of the 20th century, macroeconomic factors also reshaped the Western definition of adulthood. For example, both the aging of the workforce and the need for technical training to perform skilled labor influenced American society to become increasingly age-differentiated (Mortimer & Larson, 2002). Scholars studying this demographic change have concluded: "In general, the economically active, adult population is shrinking relative to those who are economically dependent, including both younger and older generations. Therefore, investment in youth who will become the adults of the future deserves special attention" (Mortimer & Larson, 2002, p. 3).

In 1987, the Devon T. Grant Foundation assembled a panel of scholars and policy makers, called the Commission on Work, Family and Citizenship, to address the social and economic concerns of American young adults who do not attend college after high school. They found that approximately 48% of young adults (or about half) did not complete high school or did not continue their education after high-school graduation. (For historical perspective, note that a century ago fewer than 5% of young adults in the United States attended college, compared to over 60% today (Arnett, 2000a).) In their 1988 report, called *The Forgotten Half: Non-College-Bound Youth in America*, the commission concluded that adults who did not attend college earned about 28% less than college graduates of the same age (Youth and America's Future, 1988).

A decade later, in 1998, the commission reexamined national trends for non-college-bound youth aged 18 to 24. They reported in *The Forgotten Half Revisited* that educational attainment increased overall between 1988 and 1998, with more young adults entering 2- or 4-year colleges (Halperin, 1998). However, youth who continued their education tended to come from upper-income families (83.4%), whereas only 34% of students from low-income families went to college. Although overall unemployment rates declined by 4.5% in from 1989 to 1998, youth from minority

Young people without a college degree often find themselves in low-wage jobs.

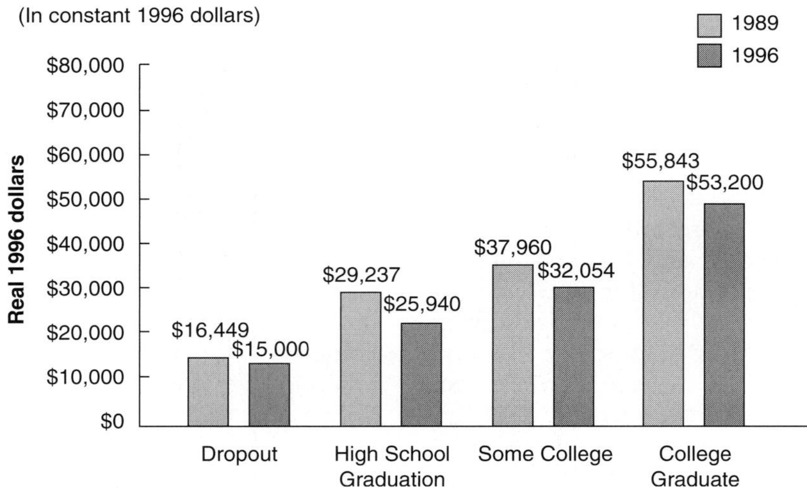

FIGURE 12.3 Median Family Income by Education in 1989 and 1996
Regardless of education, real incomes of young families are down.

Note: CLMS tabulations from March 1990 and March 1997 CPS surveys. Note that those with 1–3 years of college suffered proportionately larger declines in real income than high school graduates.

Source: From *The Forgotten Half Revisited: American Youth and Young Families, 1988–2008* (p. 13), by S. Halperin (Ed.), 1998. Copyright 1998 by the American Youth Policy Forum. Reprinted by permission of the author.

groups continued to experience unemployment rates as high as 30%. In addition, youth earned one third less than their counterparts earned 24 years before, adjusted for inflation (Halperin, 1998). Refer to Figure 12.3 for a comparison of median family incomes by highest level of education from *The Forgotten Half Revisited* report. Today, emerging adults who do not finish college still find themselves in low-paying and unstable jobs (Kerchoff, 2002). Between 2000 and 2003, unemployment rose by 8% among 16- to 24-year-old high-school graduates not in college. Overall, women and ethnic minorities have had the greatest declines in employment (Sum & Khatiwada, 2004).

In the 1990s, a group of interdisciplinary scholars formed the MacArthur Network on Transitions to Adulthood and Public Policy to examine research on emerging adulthood and determine how social institutions could enhance this period of the life span. Box 12.1 provides a description of the network. Using a strict sociological definition of adulthood (i.e., completing the transitions of leaving home, finishing school, becoming financially independent, getting married, and having a child), network demographers found that "adulthood" begins later than it did just three or four decades before. Figure 12.4 illustrates this historical change in the age of transition to adulthood. Only 46% of women and 31% of men aged 30 in 2000 had reached the criteria for adulthood, compared to 77 and 65%, respectively, aged 30 in 1960 (Furstenberg et al., 2003).

Continuing trends expected to affect the timing of the transition to adulthood in the 21st century include:

- **Changing Demographics.** Large increases in the numbers of adolescents and emerging adults are expected for the next several decades.
- **Ethnic Diversity.** The children of immigrants who came to the United States between 1970 and 2000 will reach adolescence and young adulthood.
- **Work and the Economy.** The economy is shifting from an industrial to an information technology (IT) economy.
- **Lifelong Learning.** Education for the future requires people to learn new skills throughout the life course.

BOX 12.1 ROADMAP TO UNDERSTANDING THEORY AND RESEARCH

The Network on Transitions to Adulthood

The Network on Transitions to Adulthood is a group of researchers who examine the experiences of adults that are rarely examined from a developmental perspective. They believe that during the early years of adulthood—approximately age 18 to 30—many individuals acquire the skills needed for jobs and careers, establish positive interpersonal relationships, prepare for parenthood, and begin to contribute to their community. They also recognize that early adulthood can be particularly difficult for non-college-bound youth who lack the structure of school to organize their time and facilitate their development. Network researchers examine the multiple transitions of young adulthood—leaving home, entering or leaving school, finding employment, marriage, cohabitation, childbearing—and explore how one transition relates to the others and how societal institutions may facilitate the transition from adolescence to adulthood. They focus on four areas:

- **Education.** The transition from school to work, community colleges, and linking high schools and employers
- **Labor economics.** Labor markets, job development efforts, and linking training programs with real-world employment
- **Social history.** Delay of marriage, cohabitation, trends for childbearing, and examining policies and programs that support the development of children and young families
- **Ethnography.** Ethnic minority youth, immigrant populations, and understanding how they negotiate the transitions of young adulthood

The Network on Transitions to Adulthood includes experts in the field of sociology, criminology, pediatrics and public health, developmental psychology, policy/program evaluation, and economics. They use existing data sets on young adults and develop collaborations with ongoing studies to develop a descriptive, demographic picture of young people during the transition to adulthood. Their research initiatives include

- *On the Frontier of Adulthood: Theory, Research, and Public Policy*
- *On Your Own Without a Net: The Transition to Adulthood for Vulnerable Populations*
- *Opening Doors: Students' Perspectives on Juggling Work, Family, and College*
- America's Promise: Civic Engagement in Early Adulthood
- National Guard Challenge
- Youth Development Study
- The Michigan Study of Life Transitions
- Economics of the Transition to Adulthood
- Coming of Age in America

Source: Based on "About the Network" by The Network on Transitions to Adulthood. Available from http://www.pop.upenn.edu/transad/about/index.htm. Copyright 2003 by the University of Pennsylvania.

- **Role of Parents.** Instead of being keepers of tradition, parents provide guidance and access to resources.
- **Global Community.** Information and financial capital are increasingly connected across the world's societies.
- **Government Resources.** Competition for limited resources for youth programs will increase.
- **Multidisciplinarity.** Because no single discipline can solve the problems of youth, we need to form collaborative endeavors.
- **Ethics.** Equal access for youth to resources and education in an increasingly competitive job market has become an ethical concern (adapted from Youniss & Ruth, 2002).

Increasingly, the various transitions marking adulthood—such as leaving home, finishing education, getting full-time jobs, marrying, and having children—occur at older ages, have become more variable, or do not occur in the traditional order (Mortimer & Larson, 2002).

What historical, economic, or social influences do you think most affect the emerging adults you know?

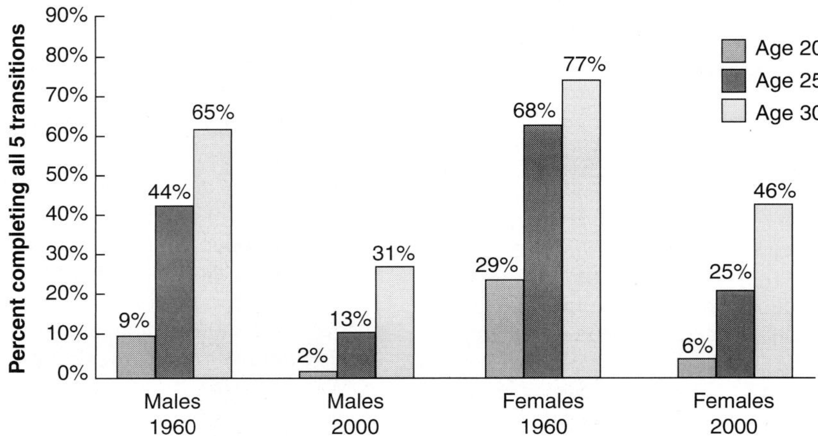

FIGURE 12.4 Completing Adult Transitions in 1960 and 2000
In the year 2000, fewer emerging adult men and women completed the transitions of leaving home, finishing school, becoming financially independent, getting married, and having a child than in 1960.

Notes: Data are from the Integrated Public Use Microdata Series extracts (IPUMS) of the 1960 and 2000 U.S. Censuses. Men are defined as financially independent if they are in the labor force; women are defined as financially independent if they have completed all transitions except employment in the labor force.

Source: From *Between Adolescence and Adulthood: Expectations about the Timing of Adulthood, Working Paper No. 1*, Network on Transitions to Adulthood, by F. F. Furstenberg et al., 2003. Available from: http://www.pop.upenn.edu/transad/news/between.pdf Copyright 2003 by Frank F. Furstenberg. Reprinted by permission of the author.

THE MEANING OF ADULTHOOD IN POSTMODERN SOCIETIES

Perhaps the most important theoretical influence on contemporary scholarship on emerging adulthood is postmodernism. Postmodern social theory has contributed several important ideas to our understanding of what it means to "grow up" in a postmodern society:

- Emerging adults are often faced with rapid social change.
- Emerging adults may live in a chaotic, complex, and relativist society.
- Emerging adults may face multiple contexts and multiple realities over time.

Although some scholars have criticized postmodernism as a nonscientific perspective unsupported by empirical research (e.g., Côté, 2000b), postmodern theory is, in our view, compatible with the contextual approach adopted in this text. For example, individuals in diverse contexts also differ in their constructions of the meaning of risk and resilience in a particular setting or neighborhood (Ungar, 2004). Refer to Box 12.2 for a summary of research on factors affecting young adult retention in college.

Return for a moment to the chapter case study. Devon, first in his family to attend college—an opportunity not available to his parents or grandparents—sees working full-time while going to school as a challenge rather than a limitation.

Recall from chapter 7 that risks are those individual or environmental factors that predict vulnerability. On the other hand, protective factors are those factors that predict resilience. These two

BOX 12.2 ROADMAP TO UNDERSTANDING THEORY AND RESEARCH

Opening Doors: Students' Perspectives on Juggling Work, Family, and College

Opening Doors: Students' Perspectives on Juggling Work, Family, and College gathered information from focus groups at six community colleges. Researchers talked to current, former, and potential students (most of them single parents) who sought a workable balance of college, work, and family responsibilities. The focus group participants identified stable child care, personal support from family members, peers, and college faculty and staff, and accommodating employers as major factors influencing their ability to stay in college, complete their programs of study within expected time frames, or enroll in the first place.

Although the direct costs of tuition and books were also significant factors in the ability of low-income students to attend community colleges, the focus group participants emphasized that lost wages from having to reduce work hours strongly influenced their ability to afford college. They also had difficulty accessing safety-net programs such as Food Stamps, Medicaid, Earned Income Credits, Section 8 housing vouchers, and child care subsidies.

The focus group findings had important implications for the community colleges, employers, and policy makers who work with these nontraditional students. For example, community colleges could offer low-wage workers opportunities to increase their earnings and improve their family's overall economic well-being by enhancing their marketable job skills with advanced education and training. However, many adults who could benefit from community college programs either do not enroll or drop out before completing their coursework. The study concluded that community colleges could improve student access by developing partnerships with public agencies and community-based organizations.

Source: Based on *Opening Doors: Students' Perspectives on Juggling Work, Family, and College* (online), by S. Gooden, L. Matus-Grossman, M. Wavelet, M. Diaz, and R. Seupersad, 2003. Copyright 2004 by MDRC. Available from http://www.mdrc.org/publications/260/overview.html.

constructs are influenced by the prevailing social discourse on what constitutes illness and what constitutes health, or what constitutes risk and what constitutes resilience. In other words, risk and resilience can be considered opposing discourses.

A postmodern perspective on resilience can account for cultural and contextual variations in how resilience is expressed by diverse individuals, families, and communities. For example, in a qualitative study (Klevens & Roca, 1999), researchers found that the common predictors of violence were insufficient to explain young men's violent behavior in Colombia, where the use of violence was a coping strategy rather than an indication of vulnerability (Ungar, 2004). Similar explanations of urban youth violence in the United States have also been suggested (e.g., Cunningham, 1999; Spencer, Dupree, & Cunningham, 2003; Taylor et al., 2002). Male attitudes, such as exaggerated masculinity, or *machismo*, may be coping strategies for survival in high-risk environments (Cunningham, 1999).

Compared to an approach that defines resilience as "health despite adversity" and emphasizes predictable relationships between risk and protective factors, a postmodern approach defines resilience as the outcome of negotiations between individuals and their environments to define *themselves* as healthy despite conditions viewed as adverse (Ungar, 2004). Researchers using postmodern perspectives see opportunities for alternative explanations of behavior and novel avenues for interventions in particular contexts (Russell, 2005; Ungar, 2004). For example, Box 12.3 describes the exploration of virtual reality as a positive coping strategy. Even emerging adults' increased risky behaviors, such as binge drinking (as shown in Figure 12.5), can also be seen as exploratory, that is, reflecting their desire to engage in a wide range of experiences before settling into adult roles and responsibilities (Arnett, 2000a).

BOX 12.3 ROADMAP TO UNDERSTANDING THEORY AND RESEARCH

Parallel Lives

"In a recent New Yorker cartoon, one dog, paw on keyboard, explains to another: 'On the Internet, nobody knows you're a dog.' " (Turkle, 1996, p. 156). Studying virtual communities on the Internet, researcher Sherry Turkle believes that people are acting as authors not only of text but of themselves. She studies computer environments known as multi-user domains (MUDs). MUDs are social virtual realities in which players are logged on from all over the world, each at his or her individual computer. Users join communities that exist only "in" the computer and find themselves in the same "space." They communicate with each other either in large groups or privately.

Turkle described the case of a young person who MUDded over 80 hours a week when at college and away from his high-school friends and family, and over 120 hours a week during a time of particular stress. Eventually, he became the administrator of a new MUD, which involved responsibilities in cyberspace equivalent to those of someone with a full-time job. Initially, the MUD provided him with what Erikson would have called a psychosocial moratorium, a time of intense interaction with people and ideas, but eventually it afforded him an opportunity to use his considerable skills.

Turkle concluded that a virtual community, like any society, allows people to create a sense of self through their interaction. Through such intensive exploration, young adults can work on their identities in virtual space. According to Turkle, cultural theorists routinely use postmodern philosophy to think about constructing multiple selves in emerging adulthood. Furthermore, she relates these positive experiences in cyberspace to psychological theories about the self as socially constructed through interaction.

Source: Based on "Parallel Lives: Working on Identity in Virtual Space" (pp. 156, 169–172), by S. Turkle, in D. Grodin & T. R. Lindlof (Eds.), *Constructing the Self in a Mediated World* (pp. 156–175), 1996, Thousand Oaks, CA: Sage. Copyright 1996 by Sage Publications, Inc.

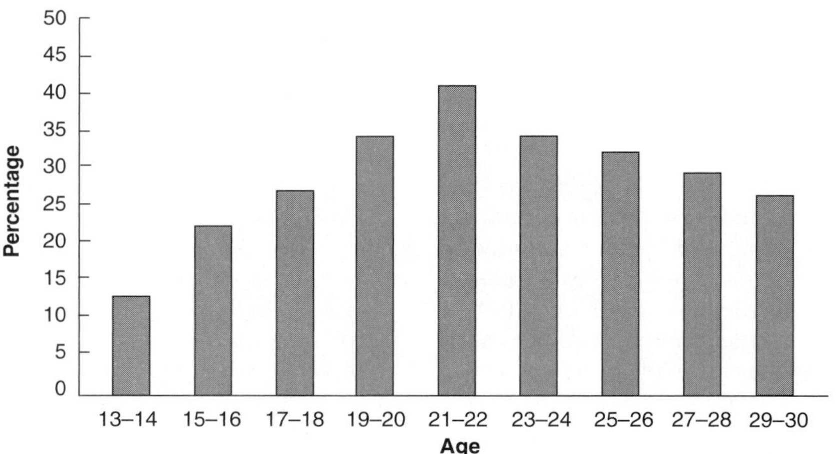

FIGURE 12.5 Rates of Binge Drinking from Ages 13 to 30
Binge drinking peaks during emerging adulthood.

Source: From "Emerging Adulthood: A Theory of Development from the Late Teens Through the Twenties" (p. 475), by J. J. Arnett, 2000 *American Psychologist, 55,* pp. 469–480. Copyright 2000 by the American Psychological Association. Reprinted by permission of the author.

Guideposts for Working with Emerging Adults

- Discuss with emerging adults popular novels, films, and television programs that characterize their struggles to achieve adult status.
- Familiarize yourself with the government programs in your state designed to assist young people in finding jobs, housing, or other social services.
- Try to accommodate the wide variations in transitions to adulthood by involving emerging adults in the design of programs and services.
- Take into account the ways in which emerging adults themselves are interpreting social realities in diverse settings by talking with them about their lives.
- Reflect continuously on your own attitudes about risk and resilience in emerging adulthood.

DEVELOPMENTAL MILESTONES IN EMERGING ADULTHOOD

In emerging adulthood, as in all other periods of the life span, biological maturation (e.g., physiological or genetic factors) and environmental influences (e.g., social or cultural influences) interact to produce growth and development. As seen in Figure 12.6, developmental milestones along the road to maturity can be summarized using normative expectations for emerging adult development in the same four domains that we applied to middle childhood and adolescence:

1. **Physical Development.** The final four molars, euphemistically called *wisdom teeth*, emerge during early adulthood, signaling skeletal maturation. The growth platelets of the long bones (described in chapter 3) also begin to fuse in emerging adulthood, resulting in individuals reaching their eventual height by age 19 for females and 21 for males. This process has implications for broken bones during early adulthood: longer healing times and, depending on the break, possible long-term implications for movement and athleticism. Maximum performance in most sports (e.g., swimming, track and field, tennis, baseball, and golf) is reached in early adulthood, especially skills that require control or strategy (Schultz & Curnow, 1988).

With respect to brain development, another neuronal spurt occurs in emerging adulthood, as well as evidence of synaptogenesis throughout adulthood, especially in the hippocampus, which results in memory improvement. Emerging adults (ages 17 to 21) demonstrate advanced frontal lobe functions compared to children and adolescents, such as the ability to organize and reorganize attention (Hudspeth & Pribram, 1992). These changes may mean that emerging adults are uniquely ready for intellectual challenges, such as higher education or advanced skills training.

Compared to adolescence, health risks for sexually transmitted diseases increase (among emerging adults who are sexually active), as does the risk of disordered eating. For example, bulimia nervosa has two incidence peaks, one during early adolescence and one around 18 to 20 years of age (Neumark-Sztainer, Story, Falkner, Beuhring, & Resnick, 1999). As previously discussed, binge drinking also typically increases, often even before emerging adults reach legal drinking age (refer again to Figure 12.5).

2. **Cognitive Development.** Emerging adulthood brings a qualitative change in cognitive abilities. Some researchers have proposed adding a fifth stage of cognitive development to Piaget's four-stage structural sequence (discussed in chapters 4 and 9). Adulthood's *postformal* stage is characterized by a newly emergent relativism, or an understanding that different points of view may be equally relevant depending on the situation (Sinnott, 1998). Problem solving in emerging adulthood has been described among college students as moving from dualistic thinking (i.e., "it's true or false") to multiple solutions (e.g., "it could be both") to relative judgments (i.e., "it depends") (e.g., Kitchener, Lynch, Fischer, & Wood, 1989; Perry, 1970/1999). Such thinking has also been described as **dialectical** in that adults are able to see and appreciate unresolvable tensions between competing viewpoints when there is no absolute "truth" to be known (Basseches, 1984).

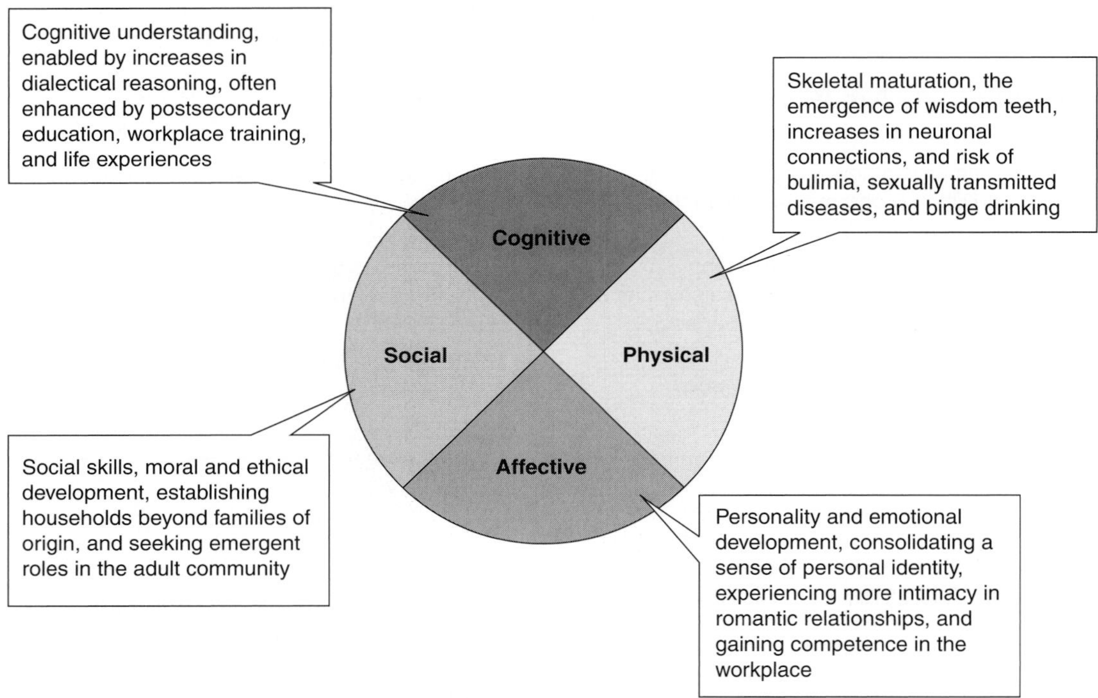

FIGURE 12.6 Developmental Domains of Emerging Adulthood
In emerging adulthood, continued growth and change occur in each of the developmental domains.

Other cognitive researchers have argued that rather than a new *kind* of thinking, adults are able to use their skills to solve different kinds of problems as they adapt to the new environmental pressures of adulthood (Schaie, 1994). Emerging adults are typically in an *achieving* stage of cognitive development when applying their intellectual skills to long-term goals, such as establishing their careers and becoming financially secure (e.g., Schaie & Willis, 2000). Research has shown that advanced reasoning abilities are enhanced by postsecondary education, workplace training, and life experiences that often occur in emerging adulthood.

3. **Affective Development.** During the emerging adult years, late adolescents typically consolidate their personal identities, experience intimacy in romantic relationships, and gain a sense of self-competence in the workplace. As we discussed in chapter 10, ideological and interpersonal identity issues are present throughout the life span, especially in emerging adulthood when many young people are committing to careers and to partners. As young adults make vocational or educational choices, often following an intense exploratory period (often involving jobs, college, and/or travel), they move towards identity achievement (e.g., Josselson, 1987; Waterman, 1993). Emerging adults also may engage in a process of self-reflecting, or productive thinking about their lives, their feelings, and their own development (Bell, Wieling, & Watson, 2004).

Many emerging adults often begin new educational experiences, new friendships or romantic relationships, and/or new jobs during the years from 18 to 25. Adult developmental researchers have described emerging adulthood as a "novice" phase, as previously discussed. In this phase, young adults begin to construct a **life structure**, or the patterns that will guide their life. Tasks involved in this process—for both men and women—involve defining goals, finding mentors, developing careers, and establishing intimacy (Levinson, 1986).

Recall that in Erikson's (1968) psychosocial stage theory, the stage of **intimacy versus isolation** follows identity resolution. In many cases, however, intimacy is likely to be explored simultaneously with identity—especially by young women, who frequently make personal decisions based on an ethic of care (i.e., a concern for others), as discussed in chapter 10. In the intimacy stage, close relationships with friends, family, or romantic partners result in emerging adults' feelings of stability and trust.

4. **Social Development.** Interpersonal relationships in emerging adulthood involve deepening friendships, establishing romantic partnerships, and seeking social roles in the adult community. For example, recall that research on romantic relationships has revealed that the same attachment classifications (i.e., secure, anxious-ambivalent, or avoidant) described by Ainsworth are seen in emerging adulthood (e.g., Hazan & Shaver, 1987; Bartholomew & Horowitz, 1991). Secure adults are often more interdependent and more committed in relationships than anxious and avoidant adults.

With respect to family relations, emerging adults typically gain independence from their parents as they establish their own residences, careers, and families. Most young adults, however, still use their families of origin as a secure base during this relatively unstable period. Because the age of first marriage has increased in most industrialized nations, many emerging adults will not begin a long-term relationship until their mid- to late 20s.

In your own development, what significant changes do you remember from your late adolescence or emerging adulthood?

Now let's reflect on the developmental status of our emerging adult group. All are reproductively mature, but not all are sexually active. Kate and Keith are trying to get pregnant with their second child. The others are not in intimate relationships right now. Prasad, for one, is too focused on his career to worry about it, even though his roommate's girlfriend frequently stays overnight at their apartment. Socially, Maria feels more isolated than her friends, probably because she lives with her parents in a suburban neighborhood instead of in town. Cognitively, they have all reached the stage of formal thought, but Devon and Kate still struggle to see both sides of dialectical issues when the friends get together for lunch and discuss relationships or politics.

Integration of Theoretical Viewpoints

Theories are essential to guiding the research and practice of those working to enhance the lives of school-age children, adolescents, and emerging adults. Throughout the chapters of this text, we have integrated those theories of human development that are related to specific domains of middle childhood and adolescent development. Figure 12.7 illustrates the text's recurring metaphor that the numerous theories described in previous chapters serve as possible directions along the roads (or pathways) leading from middle childhood to adolescence to emerging adulthood. Research on emerging adulthood has been guided by many of these theoretical perspectives, such as life-span developmental theory, life-course theory, ecological theory, and developmental-contextual theory. In addition, a relatively new approach, called applied developmental psychology, has been especially useful over the past two decades for studying emerging adulthood.

In the 1980s, American scholars from several disciplines organized a National Task Force on Applied Developmental Science (Lerner, 2002b). Members included professionals associated with the American Psychological Association, the National Council on Family Relations, The International Society for Infant Studies, the Society for Research in Child Development, The Black Child Development Institute, the Society for Research on Adolescence, and the Gerontological Association of America. The task force acknowledged that in order to address the development of individuals who vary with respect to culture and ethnic background, economic and social opportunity, physical and cognitive abilities, and family, neighborhood, and community settings, the field needed an integrated perspective to address development across the life span (Lerner, 2002b). The focus of **applied developmental psychology** is on promoting the health and welfare of individuals and families (Fisher & Lerner, 1994) through the following five principles:

1. **Temporality of Change.** Individual functioning is the product of person-environment interactions that continuously emerge and change over time.
2. **Individual Differences and Within-Person Change.** An individual's actions at any one point in development is a function of prior development as well as current historical, social, cognitive, and situational factors.

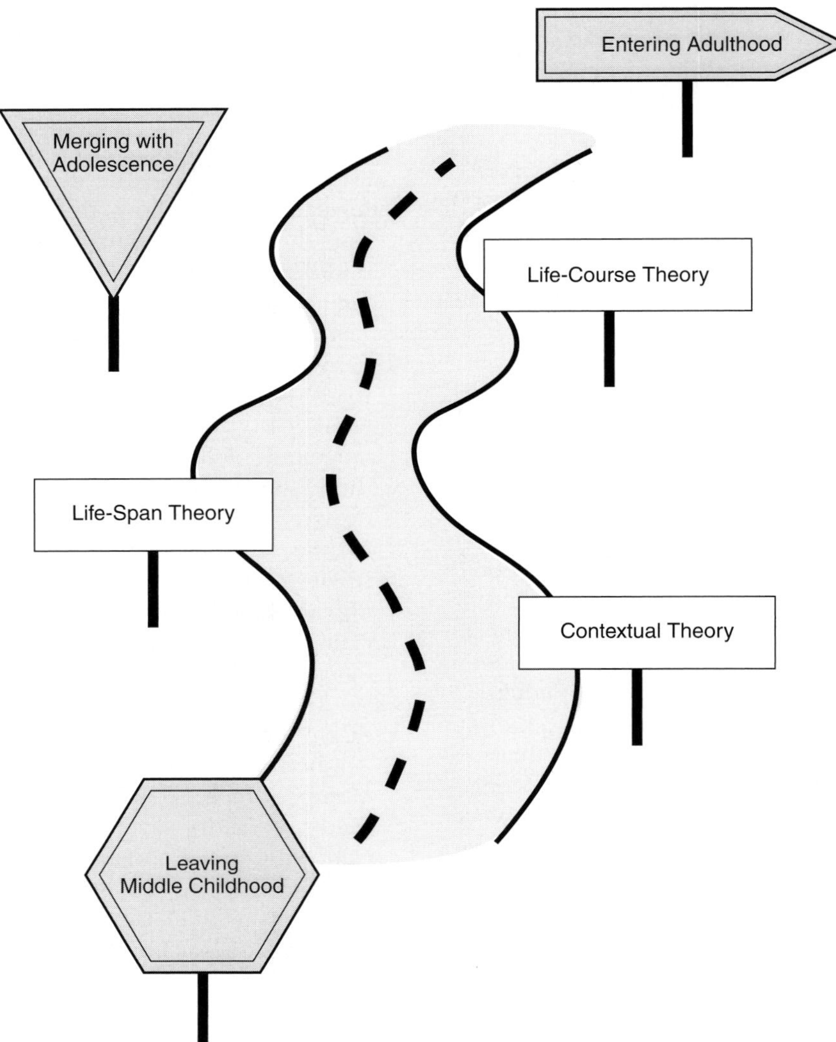

FIGURE 12.7 Pathways to Adulthood
The journey from childhood through adulthood is described and explained by applied developmental science.

3. **Centrality of Context.** Knowledge of persons' biological, physical, interpersonal, cultural, and historical contexts is necessary to understand their development.
4. **Normative Developmental Processes.** Understanding normative and atypical development is essential to designing intervention strategies at all points along the life span for individuals embedded in contexts with varying levels of risk.
5. **Bidirectional Relationship Between Knowledge Generation and Knowledge Application.** Interventions or policies affecting individuals and families depend on scientific research and theory to guide their application.

Many developmental researchers now advocate using this holistic approach to studying human development, often referred to as **developmental science** (Cairns, 2000; Magnusson, 2000). In developmental science, holistic models emphasize:

- **The integration of complex processes** (e.g., biological, cognitive, and social systems)

Guideposts for Working with Emerging Adults

- Keep in mind that adult development is complex, bidirectional, and multifaceted.
- Look for evidence that emerging adults are continuing to mature in each of the four domains and try to meet their developmental needs accordingly.
- Work with professionals across human service disciplines to create multidisciplinary efforts to improve the lives of emerging adults.
- Consider not only emerging adults' individual development but also their diverse social contexts, such as dorms, workplaces, or clubs.

- **Continuous bidirectional interactions between persons and environments** (e.g., children, adolescents, and emerging adults in diverse contexts)
- **Interdisciplinary frameworks** (e.g., biology, psychology, sociology, education, human development, and family studies)

Each of these tenets is often reflected in developmental research on emerging adulthood.

In your own study of development, how many courses have you taken from faculty in different disciplines, such as education, psychology, child or human development, family studies, sociology, anthropology, biology?

Diverse Contexts of Emerging Adulthood

As of 2000, there were about 67 million adults in the United States between the ages of 18 and 34, with 27 million between 18 and 24. In addition, one in five 18- to 34-year-olds, and one in seven 18- to 24-year-olds, are immigrants to the United States (Rumbaut, 2004). Emerging adulthood differs from adolescence and young adulthood in its heterogeneity of diverse contexts and experiences (Arnett, 2000a). For example, exploration and experimentation is not possible for all people in their late teens and early 20s due to differing economic and social constraints, such as having to work to support one's family. Family, school or workplace, and community factors all are influences on development in emerging adulthood (see Larson, Wilson, Brown, Furstenberg, & Verma, 2002).

Family Context

Emerging adults are likely to have more independence from their families than adolescents, often living in separate residences. In fact, emerging adulthood is the period when many American young people change residences most often, as seen in Figure 12.8. Some researchers have suggested that it may be difficult for emerging adults to feel "grown-up" before they have established a stable residence of their own (Arnett, 2000a). Today, most contemporary adolescents leave home at age 18 or 19 and do not marry until age 25 or older (Arnett, 2000a). (See Table 12–3 for data on recent trends in the age of marriage in selected countries.) These trends mean that many emerging adults may spend at least half of their 20s "on the move."

Living away from home during emerging adulthood has implications for family relations. As part of a large cohort-sequential study (Petersen, 1984), young adults were interviewed by phone at age 21 and asked where they currently lived. About 16% lived at home, 13% lived within an hour's drive of their parents, 41% lived within a weekend's drive, and 30% lived in another part of the country. Approximately 60% of those living at home or nearby were college students, whereas 97% of those living farther away were students. Four percent had finished college and were living at home. Only 15% of the sample was employed full-time, but 39% worked part-time (Dubas & Petersen, 1996). The results revealed that the farther adult children lived from their parents, the better the quality of family relations! Students living farthest away or within a weekend's drive reported close relations with both mothers and fathers and valued their parents' opinions. Emerging adults who lived within an hour's drive had the poorest overall family relations, the lowest level of intimacy with their mothers, the least financial support, and valued their parents' opinions least, despite the finding that living closer was related to more frequent contact. Young adults living at home reported low levels of family closeness but

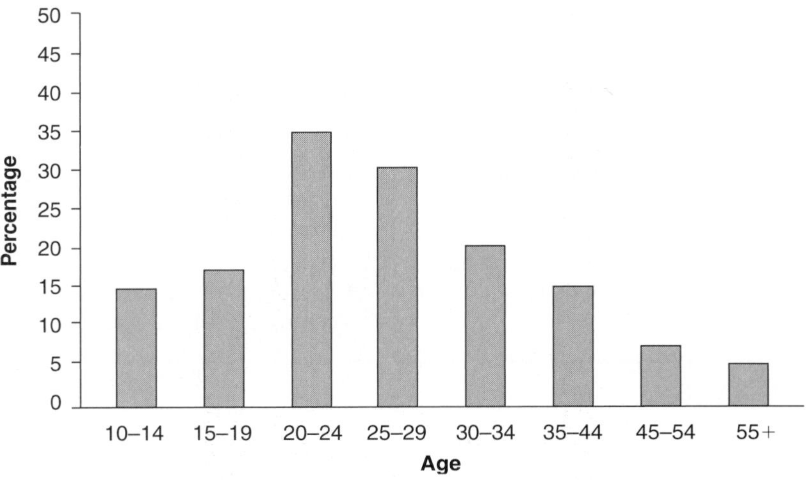

FIGURE 12.8 Residential Change by Age
Emerging adults change residences most often during their 20s.

Note: Data are from "Geographic Mobility: March 1997 to March 1998," by the U.S. Bureau of the Census, 2000. *Current Population Reports* (Series P-20, No. 520). Washington, DC: U.S. Government Printing Office.

Source: From "Emerging Adulthood: A Theory of Development from the Late Teens Through the Twenties" (p. 472), by J. J. Arnett, 2000 *American Psychologist, 55,* pp. 469–480. Copyright 2000 by the American Psychological Association. Reprinted by permission of the author.

also lower levels of problem behaviors, such as drug use, compared to students living away from home (Dubas & Petersen, 1996).

What are the implications for family relationships of living at home during emerging adulthood? Research has shown that young adults remain at home longer when living at home provides support, security, and company—as well as financial benefits (White, 2002). When emerging adults continue to live with their parents, they often have greater autonomy within the household (Arnett, 1998). As we discussed in chapters 10 and 11, increases in autonomy and self-reliance do not necessarily preclude close relationships to parents. In fact, in many

TABLE 12–3

Age Trends in Marriage

The median age of marriage differs in various cultures.

Median Marriage Age of Women in Selected Countries

Industrialized countries	Age	Developing countries	Age
United States	25.2	Egypt	21.9
Canada	26.0	Morocco	22.3
Germany	26.2	Ghana	21.1
France	26.1	Nigeria	18.7
Italy	25.8	India	20.0
Japan	26.9	Indonesia	21.1
Australia	26.0	Brazil	22.6

Source: From "Emerging Adulthood: A Theory of Development from the Late Teens Through the Twenties" (p. 478), by J. J. Arnett, 2000, *American Psychologist, 55,* pp. 469–480. Copyright 2000 by the American Psychological Association. Reprinted by permission of the author.

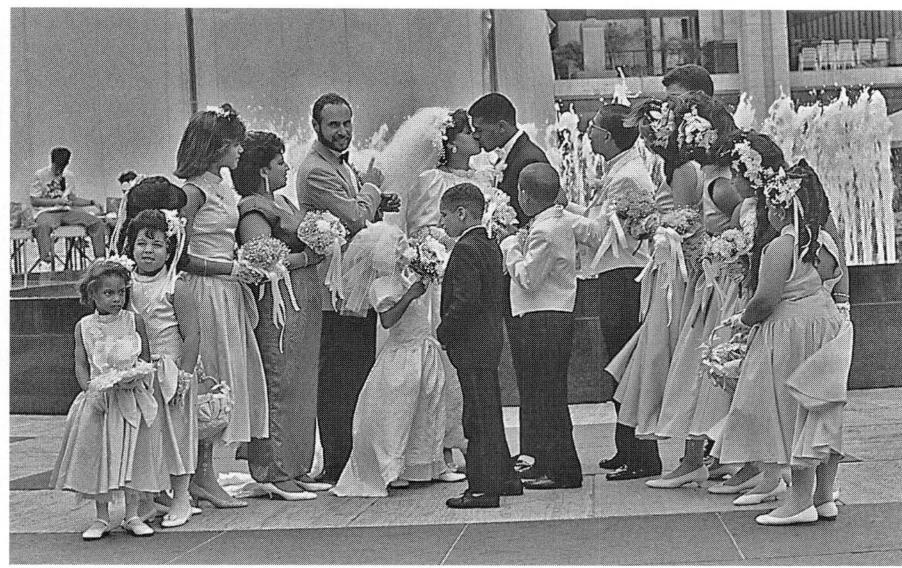

The average age of marriage in the United States is 25 years or older.

non-Western cultures, such as Japanese and Chinese, as well as many American ethnic-minority groups, such as Latinos and Native Americans, adult interdependence with parents is the norm.

Maria and her parents came to the United States from Mexico when she was 17. She spent just a year in an American high school before moving into a dorm at the university. But now that she has graduated and is working, she again lives at home.

Like the meaning of adulthood, the meaning of *home* is socially constructed. For example, for most adults, home is a place of relative autonomy, whereas for adolescents it is a place where adults have more authority (White, 2002). In emerging adulthood, however, these boundaries are not as clear. Are grown offspring in their 20s seen as adults or as children by their families? As discussed in chapter 11, the rate of conflict between parents and children is highest during early adolescence and declines by late adolescence. Degree of conflict with parents depends more on cultural beliefs, reasons for living at home, or personalities and family dynamics than on chronological age! An Australian study of emerging adults in their 20s demonstrated that the meaning of living with their parents was intimately connected to the following:

- Perceived rights to make decisions about how the household operates
- Division of household labor
- Emotional relationships among family members
- Issues of privacy and autonomy

When control resided with parents, the words *house* or *household* were used more often than *home* by the young adults who were interviewed. A **house** refers to a physical dwelling, a **household** is a socioeconomic unit, but **home** symbolizes a place for emotional attachment, self-definition, and identity formation (White, 2002). These results suggest that family conflicts (e.g., disagreements about contributing to household duties or finances; views about smoking, alcohol, or drug use; or permissibility of sexual relations) may be negatively related to the meaning of home as a place for identity exploration in emerging adulthood.

Recall that Maria phoned home to tell her parents she would not be home for dinner. Such autonomous behavior is typical of a young person who has lived away (e.g., at college) and has returned to reside with her parents just until she has enough money to get her own place.

School/Workplace Context

Adolescent employment often affects the transition to adulthood (Leventhal, Graber, & Brooks-Gunn, 2001). Recall from chapter 10 that a majority of high-school students work at some point during high school but that the impact of work experiences on adolescent development remains controversial. From a developmental-contextual perspective, however, we would assume that stable teenage employment might vary for youth in differing social contexts. For example, working may benefit low-income urban youth by increasing financial resources and adult supervision that, in turn, may increase school engagement and decrease problem behavior (Leventhal, Graber, & Brooks-Gunn, 2001).

As part of a three-decade longitudinal study in Baltimore in the late 1960s (Furstenberg, 1976), African American teenage mothers' first-born children were followed during childhood, adolescence, and early adulthood. Researchers assessed family context variables (e.g., parental employment), school context variables (e.g., academic performance), and problem behaviors (e.g., substance use) as predictors of adolescent employment, education in emerging adulthood, and adult employment (Leventhal, Graber, & Brooks-Gunn, 2001). See Figure 12.9 for an illustration of the theoretical model.

Results indicated that low-income African American youth who did not repeat a grade in middle childhood were more likely to enter the workforce at earlier ages than their peers who repeated a grade. Mothers' employment status and adolescents' problem behaviors were unrelated to teenage employment. At the transition to adulthood, however, adolescents who had started to work earlier were more likely to have completed high school. In addition, especially for young men, stable employment during the teen years positively affected their chances of attending college (Leventhal, Graber, & Brooks-Gunn, 2001). The few teens in this study who never worked had poorer school

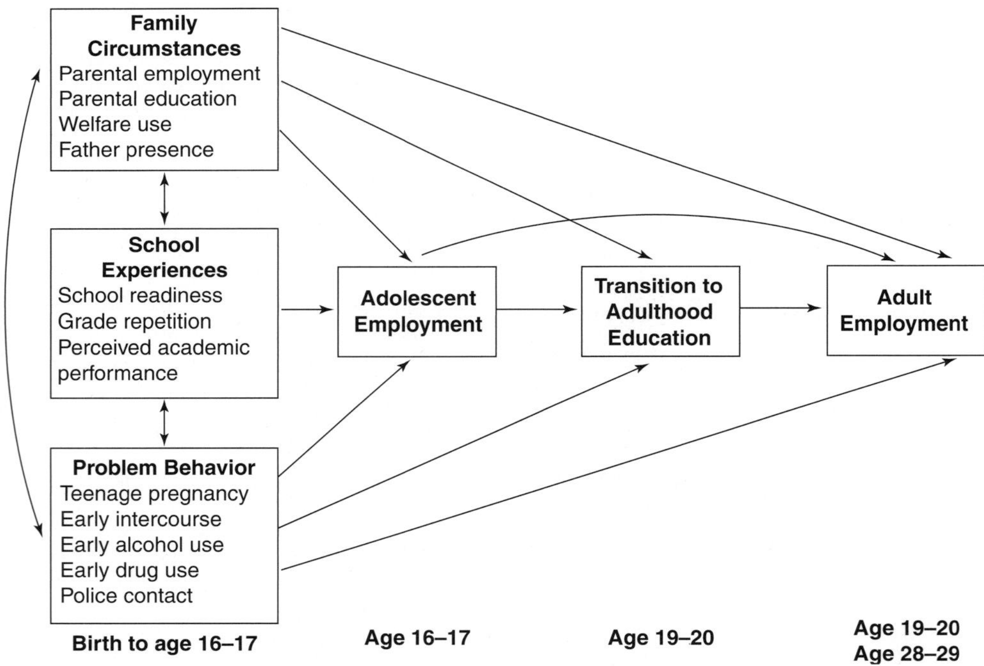

FIGURE 12.9 Theoretical Model of Adolescent Employment
Working during high school may influence the transition to education in emerging adulthood as well as current and future employment opportunities.

Source: From "Adolescent Transitions to Young Adulthood: Antecedents, Correlates, and Consequences of Adolescent Employment" (p. 299), by Tama Leventhal, J. A. Graber and J. Brooks-Gunn, 2001, *Journal of Research on Adolescence*, 11, pp. 297–323. Copyright 2001 by the Society for Research on Adolescence. Reprinted by permission of Black well Publishing, Ltd.

achievement, more family experience of unemployment and welfare, and increased problem behavior. The study's overall finding that educational and work trajectories are connected—particularly for low-income males—suggests that informal workplace networks, mentoring relationships formed through adolescents' work experiences, and the acquisition of work-related skills may be important for educational attainment in emerging adulthood (Leventhal, Graber, & Brooks-Gunn, 2001; see also Sum & Khatiwada, 2005; Sum, Khatiwada, McLaughlin, & Palma, 2004).

Take Prasad, for example. He worked at a local computer company during high school and college. When he applied to business school, his supervisor was an important personal reference. Now he tries to do the same for other youth in his community.

Community Context

The meaning of community in emerging adulthood has been examined by researchers who asked adults in their 20s, "When you get toward the end of your life, what would you like to be able to say about your life, looking back on it?" and "What values or beliefs do you think are the most important to pass on to the next generation?" This ethical examination of emerging adults' social ideology also tapped their psychosocial and spiritual development. Studies of emerging adulthood (described earlier) have shown that most people define adulthood in terms of individualistic over community-oriented criteria, such as "decide on your own beliefs and values." In fact, based on previous studies (e.g., Jensen, 1997), researchers predicted that emerging adults would use concepts of autonomy more than of community, and concepts of community more than of spirituality, to answer these questions (Arnett, Ramos, & Jensen, 2001).

This qualitative interview study included mostly White socioeconomically diverse adults aged 20 to 29 from a medium-sized city in the midwestern United States. The participants were evenly divided between men and women, 60% were married, and about one fourth had one or more children. Interviews lasting about an hour were recorded, transcribed, and coded for the use of autonomy, community, or spirituality themes:

- **Autonomy.** Responses that focused on the person's own needs desires, and interests (e.g., "I'd like to be able to say that I achieved all I set out to do")
- **Community.** Responses that focused on the needs, desires, and interests of others (e.g., "That I was a good father to my kids")
- **Divinity.** Responses that focused on religious authorities, religious texts, or religious beliefs (e.g., "Just to believe in God")

Themes were not coded as mutually exclusive (Arnett, Ramos, & Jensen, 2001). About 75% gave autonomy responses to the first question and about 50% to the second. Divinity responses were relatively infrequent (6% to the first question, and 21% to the second). In addition, autonomy and community were compatible for some emerging adults but not for others. For example, a 26-year-old woman combined the two ethics, "Just that they value themselves first of all and then they value the other people around them . . . " (Arnett, Ramos, & Jensen, 2001, p. 77). In contrast, a 24-year-old man, for example, thought that autonomy and community were in opposition, "I think we've become so egocentric that caring for others and responsibility for others deteriorates, and so does society" (Arnett, Ramos, & Jensen, 2001, p. 77).

Compare and contrast the case of Devon. He hurriedly sends his little sister a text message as he leaves work to say he can't make it home before class, but he'll help her with her homework later.

Other researchers have shown that although the communal value of "becoming a parent" is endorsed by only 14% of emerging adults as a necessary marker of adulthood, parenthood ranks sixth highest in criteria considered important in their *own* transition to adulthood (Arnett, 1998)! In addition, many parents see children as lessening their egocentrism and directing their attention to others: "Children can definitely make you feel like an adult because you have responsibilities, and it's not so much myself anymore, because you have to raise someone else" (Arnett, 1998, p. 309). These results not only indicate that deciding on one's values is a developmental task of emerging adulthood but also suggest that the emphasis on individualism in American culture may be overstated.

Now recall 23-year-old Kate from the chapter case study. In addition to working full-time, Kate is happily married and raising a 3-year-old. Although she and Keith are often stressed out by the many daily tasks of family life, they share parenting, working outside the home, and housework to ease the burden on both partners.

What values or beliefs do you think are the most important to pass on to the next generation?

Concluding Remarks

Some authors have characterized young adults today as members of **generation X** (i.e., coming of age in the 1980s), **generation Y** (i.e., coming of age in the 1990s), or the **millennial generation** (i.e., coming of age in the 2000s) (e.g., Coupland, 1991; Fussell & Furstenberg, 2005; Howe & Strauss, 2000; Ulrich, 2003). Many readers of this text are likely in these age groups, or are themselves the parents of a soon-to-be school-age child, adolescent, or emerging adult. While the media have promoted the view that youth today are disaffected, cynical, and pessimistic about the future, researchers on emerging adulthood disagree (Arnett, 2000b; Wyn & White, 2000).

Interviews with American young adults aged 21 to 28 during the 1990s revealed that they were positive and optimistic about their personal futures despite agreeing with a pessimistic view of the world's future in terms of economic and environmental problems. These emerging adults were likely to think that they would exceed their parents' success—particularly if they were from less privileged backgrounds (Arnett, 2000b). Similarly, studies of young adults in Australia have revealed that they continue to view the transition to adulthood, although increasingly characterized by a lack of employment opportunities, optimistically due to a sense of their own agency in shaping their own developmental pathways (Wyn & White, 2000). This apparent contradiction between personal optimism and social pessimism has been called the "**paradox of youth**" (Wyn & White, 2000; see also Furlong & Cartmel, 1997).

In today's rapidly changing world, the uncertainties of youth are not limited to school-agers, adolescents, or emerging adults. An unemployed parent or spouse, a child or sibling in military service, a relative or grandparent in need of caregiving are human conditions that affect entire families. Our challenge in understanding human development is to view developmental tasks at each stage of the life span in terms of their unique contextual demands and our common life experiences.

How has our developmental-contextual approach provided a roadmap for your future journey on behalf of children, youth, and families?

CHAPTER REVIEW

Defining Emerging Adulthood

- Late adolescence is typically defined as ages 18 to 25 and is often described as the developmental period in which dialectical thinking is possible and socialization into adult society is accomplished.
- Young adulthood is a sociological term commonly used to refer to ages 21 to 30, depending on the age of legal majority in a particular society, and is often used interchangeably with the developmental period of early adulthood.
- Emerging adulthood is a relatively new term that attempts to differentiate the developmental stages of late adolescence and early adulthood while recognizing that the ages from 18 to 25 are simultaneously a *transitional* period.

History of Adulthood

- Although adolescence and adulthood are prevalent social constructions in non-Western cultures, emerging adulthood exists primarily in societies where adult status is not attained until the mid- to late 20s.
- During the first half of the 20th century, marriage was seen as the definitive sign of the transition to adulthood, with the median age of marriage declining steadily for both women and men through the 1950s.
- Since 1960, the concept of "youth" (or emerging adults) has been applied to those in the process of developing the capacities, skills, and qualities of character deemed by their culture as necessary for completing the transition to adulthood.
- "Growing up" in a postmodern society means that emerging adults are often faced with rapid social change, may live in a chaotic, complex, and relativist society, and may face multiple contexts and multiple realities over time.

Developmental Milestones

- In emerging adulthood, physical maturation continues, with continuing growth spurts in neuronal connections, the emergence of wisdom teeth, and an increased health risk of sexually transmitted disease.
- Emerging adulthood is characterized by a qualitative change in cognition involving dialectical reasoning and a new appreciation of complexity and contradiction.
- Emerging adults consolidate their sense of personal identity, experience more intimacy in romantic relationships, and gain competence in the workplace.

- Emerging adults develop intimate, mutual relations with others by establishing households beyond their families of origin, by deepening intimate friendships, and by seeking emergent roles in the adult community.

Theoretical Perspectives

- Research on emerging adulthood has been guided by many theoretical perspectives, including life-span developmental theory, life-course theory, ecological theory, and developmental-contextual theory.
- The focus of applied developmental psychology is on promoting health and welfare across the life span, taking into account culture and ethnic background, economic and social opportunity, physical and cognitive abilities, and family, neighborhood, and community.
- In developmental science, holistic models emphasize the integration of complex processes, continuous bidirectional interactions between persons and environments, and interdisciplinary frameworks.

Contexts of Emerging Adulthood

- Emerging adults are likely to have more independence from their families than adolescents, often living in separate residences.
- Today, most contemporary adolescents leave home at age 18 or 19 and do not marry until age 25 or older.
- Educational and work trajectories are related to workplace networks, mentoring relationships, and the acquisition of work-related skills.
- Deciding on one's personal values and ideology is a developmental task of emerging adulthood.
- Emerging adults are positive and optimistic about their personal futures, despite agreeing with a pessimistic view of the world's future in terms of economic and environmental problems.

TABLE 12–4

Summary of Developmental Theories

In chapter 12, the theoretical perspectives discussed throughout the text are brought together under the interdisciplinary framework of applied developmental science.

Chapter	Theory	Focus
12: Beyond Middle Adolescence: Emerging Adulthood	Applied Developmental Psychology	Health and well-being across the life span, taking into account cultural and ethnic background, economic and social opportunity, physical and cognitive ability, and family, neighborhood, and community
	Developmental Science	Complex interactions between persons and environments using interdisciplinary frameworks, holistic models, and policy applications

KEY TERMS

Adolescere
Adulthood
Adultus
Applied developmental psychology
Autonomy
Community
Developmental science
Dialectical
Divinity
Early adulthood
Emerging adulthood
Generation X
Generation Y
Home
House
Household
Intimacy vs. isolation
Late adolescence
Life structure
Millennial generation
Novice
Paradox of youth
Young adulthood
Youth

SUGGESTED ACTIVITIES

1. Interview your parents or grandparents about their experiences of emerging adulthood. When did they call themselves "adult"? What social, economic, family, or cultural influences were present when their generation was "coming of age"? How do you think these factors affected their experiences of adolescence and emerging adulthood?
2. Watch one of the many primetime television dramas or daytime soap operas that have young adult characters. How does the program portray the transition to adulthood? What factors seem to be most important (e.g., independence, sexual initiation, committed relationships, marriage, parenthood, work, economic independence)? What effect do you think the media have on adolescent expectations of adulthood?
3. Draw a "roadmap" to your own adulthood, beginning with middle childhood. Include important milestones along the way, such as performances, sports competitions, academic awards, school graduations, family events, religious occasions, jobs, and travel. Name the highways less traveled as well as your hoped-for destination. Be creative!

RECOMMENDED RESOURCES

Suggested Readings

Arnett, J. J., & Galambos, N. L. (2003). *Exploring cultural conceptions of the transition to adulthood: New directions for child and adolescent development, no. 100.* San Francisco, CA: Jossey-Bass.

Côté, J. E. (2000). *Arrested development: The changing nature of maturity and identity.* New York: New York University Press.

Coupland, D. (1991). *Generation X: Tales for an accelerated culture.* New York: St. Martin's.

Epstein, J. (1998). *Youth culture: Identity in a postmodern world.* Malden, MA: Blackwell.

Modell, J. (1989). *Into one's own: From youth to adulthood in the United States, 1920–1975.* Berkeley, CA: University of California Press.

Suggested Online Resources

Brown, B. V., Moore, K. A., & Bzostek, S. (2004). *A statistical portrait of well-being in early adulthood.* http://www.childtrendsdatabank.org/PDF/Young%20Adults%20Brief.pdf

Furstenberg, F. F., Jr., Kennedy, S., McLoyd, V. C., Rumbaut, R. R., & Settersten, Jr., R. A. (2003). *Between adolescence and adulthood: Expectations about the timing of adulthood, working paper no. 1,* Network on Transitions to Adulthood.
http://www.pop.upenn.edu/ transad/news/ between.pdf

Halperin, S. (1998). *The forgotten half revisited: American youth and young families 1988–2008.* Washington, DC: American Youth Policy Forum.
http://www.ncwdyouth.info/resources_&_Publications/publications_browse.php?display=35

Rumbaut, R. G. (2004). *Young adults in the United States: A profile, working paper no. 4,* Network on Transition to Adulthood.
http://www.pop.upenn.edu/transad/news/index.htm

Suggested Web Sites

Emerging Adulthood Special Interest Group of the Society for Research on Adolescence
http://www.s-r-a.org/easig.html

Independent Research Group on the Demography of Early Adulthood
http://www.demogr.mpg.de/general/structure/division2/irg-ea/

Monitoring the Future: A Continuing Study of American Youth
http://www.monitoringthefuture.org/

Network on Transitions to Adulthood
http://www.transad.pop.upenn.edu/about/index.htm

Research Committee on Sociology of Youth RC34 of the International Sociological Association
http://www.ucm.es/info/isa/rc34.htm

Suggested Films and Videos

Amelie (2001). Buena Vista Entertainment (122 minutes)

Crashing hard into adulthood: resiliency and at-risk teens (2003). Insight Media, Inc. (30 minutes)

Decisions, decisions (2003). Insight Media, Inc. (30 minutes)

Early adulthood: Parenthood (1999). Magna Systems, Inc. (29 minutes)

Early adulthood: The world of work (1999). Magna Systems, Inc. (29 minutes)

Waking life (2002). Fox Searchlight (99 minutes, R-rated)

APPENDIX

A Primer in Research Design

After you have asked a research question and formed a hypothesis, your next step is to develop the research design, or overall plan for your study. Research designs differ in the number of persons studied, the length of time needed for completion, and the applicability of their conclusions. The best research design will be determined by what you want to know. In this primer, we will describe some of the most common research designs used in developmental research, the types of questions each design best answers, and the strengths and limitations of each.

EXPERIMENTAL DESIGNS

If your research question were "to what extent does watching violence on television *cause* children to behave more aggressively," you might answer this question empirically using an experimental research design. Experimental designs are used to examine cause-and-effect relationships. Experimental studies typically include more than one group (e.g., an experimental and a control group) in which a variable is manipulated (i.e., the independent variable) and the effects of that manipulation are measured (i.e., the dependent variable). The specific components and procedural issues of designing an experiment are presented in Figure A.1.

An experimental design allows inferences about causation to be made because of the strict control it exercises over other variables that could influence the results. If an experiment is well designed and executed, much can be learned about causal influences on human development. However, results from a single experiment rarely define developmental phenomena. Rather, they initiate a systematic study of the phenomena over many trials, manipulating many different variables, under many different settings until we begin to have some understanding of how violence on television influences *some* children under certain circumstances.

Not all developmental phenomena can be manipulated in an experimental setting. This is a limitation of the experimental design. In fact, some researchers think that when children are studied in a laboratory setting rather than in their homes, classrooms, or neighborhoods, the ecological validity, or authenticity of the setting, has been threatened (Bronfenbrenner, 1979; Bronfenbrenner & Morris, 1998). The importance of studying the developmental dynamics of a child within multiple contexts was emphasized in chapter 2 and is not translated easily into a laboratory experiment. In addition, there are interesting and important research questions that

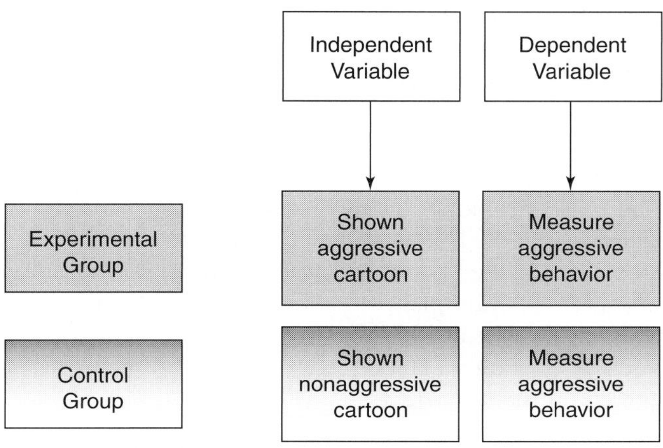

FIGURE A.1 Sample Experimental Design
This figure shows how two groups of participants are exposed to the independent variable and how the outcome of the manipulation is measured in the dependent variable.

practically, or ethically, cannot be fitted into an experimental design. Many psychologists, educators, and practitioners who read this textbook may not find the use of an experimental design feasible in their current or future work environment, but there are several alternative designs that are much more likely to be seen in a classroom, day care center, or after-school program.

Alternative Experimental Designs

In some circumstances not all of the control features in an experiment are possible to institute, most notably the random assignment of participants. For example, a teacher may be interested in trying a new pedagogical technique for teaching science to a fourth-grade class and would like to know if the students learn more using the new teaching technique. According to the procedural rules of a laboratory experiment, students should be randomly assigned to either the experimental or control group. But due to logistical constraints, such as time and space, the teacher cannot feasibly separate the class for the purposes of the experiment. To answer this research question, a pretest-posttest design could be used instead, where the researcher would test the participants *before* and *after* the manipulation or treatment. In this example, the teacher could establish a baseline measure of science knowledge by administering a pretest, introduce the new pedagogy, and then retest the students. The difference in performance between the pre- and posttest scores would be an indication of the success or failure of the new teaching technique.

A time-series design allows the researcher to administer two or more treatments or manipulations to the same participants at different times and then measure their behavior after each treatment or manipulation. Using the same class of science students, the teacher could present a lesson on the planet Neptune using a pedagogical technique that involves small-group projects and assess the learning after that session. This assessment would then be followed by the presentation of material on the planet Uranus, using a pedagogical technique that involves more experiential learning, such as creating a planet out of material that mimics the composition, weight, and density of the planet. This learning would be assessed and the overall amount of learning could be compared between the two pedagogical techniques.

Both the pretest-posttest and time-series designs allow for the use of a single group of research participants, thereby keeping intellectual, personality, and behavioral characteristics constant throughout the study and providing us with information about children's behaviors in their natural settings. These designs, however, do not rule out all factors that may be causing the change in students' science performance, such as motivation or illness or a difference in the level of enthusiasm or competency the teacher offered when teaching similar material in two different ways. Also, they do not allow for a comparison to a similar group of students who have not been exposed to the new pedagogical techniques.

In natural experiments, researchers take advantage of different treatments or manipulations that already exist, such as different parenting styles, neighborhood resources, or after-school programs, and compare them. Bush and Simmons (1987), in a classic study of pubertal timing and school transitions, compared similar groups of girls who were either early, on-time, or later maturers and then compared the self-esteem of those who transitioned to a new school in sixth or seventh grade. They found that those girls who matured early and made a school transition *simultaneously* (sixth grade) exhibited the lowest self-esteem scores compared to those who transitioned later (seventh grade) and began their pubertal change at the same time or later than the other girls. This study illustrates how a natural experiment does not *assign* participants to a group, but rather capitalizes on conditions that exist in the societal structure. They include only groups of participants who are very similar in characteristics that could potentially influence the results. If differences were found between groups, then we could conclude that the differences were more likely the result of the program or, in this case, the interaction of puberty and transition, rather than differences among the participants.

Field experiments allow the researchers to manipulate an independent variable within the child's natural environment. These alternative designs have the advantage of working with participants in their natural environments but the disadvantage of not allowing the elimination of other explanations for the differences between groups or changes in behavior.

Correlational Designs

A correlational study examines the relationship between two variables. If your research question were to ask the extent to which peer rejection and aggression are related, a correlational research design would be the appropriate organizational scheme. It would allow you to take two pieces of information and assess the strength of their relationship. For example, you could assess peer acceptance or rejection by asking a group of boys to list three boys whom they like most and least and then correlate these peer nominations with your observational data of aggressive play behavior on the playground. If there were a relationship between peer rejection and aggression, then a statistical technique called a correlational analysis would yield a significant correlation coefficient, which is a numerical value between +1.0 and −1.0, indicating a relationship between the two variables. More information about coefficient values and the meaning of correlational findings is presented in Figure A.2.

Correlational designs should be used when you are trying to establish a relationship between two or more phenomena and you have a large group of research participants. It is also a useful design to employ when conducting an experiment that would be unethical. For example, a researcher interested in studying the relationship between glue sniffing and later cognitive deficits cannot force a group of middle-schoolers to sniff inhalants in order to compare them to children who were *not* exposed to inhalants. Many interesting research questions exist that cannot be experimentally manipulated, and therefore we must rely on correlational analyses to measure the possible connections between related variables. The major disadvantage associated with using a correlational design is that you *cannot imply causation*. For example, if you found that peer rejection and aggressive behavior were strongly correlated, you could not conclude that aggressive behavior *causes* peer rejection; it may be that peer rejection causes a child to respond more aggressively towards those by whom he is rejected. It is

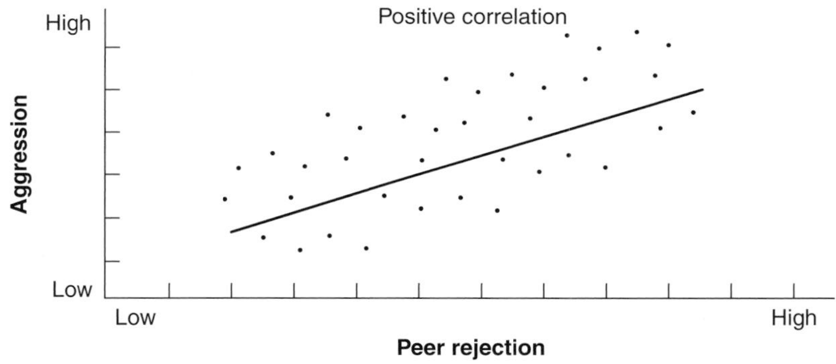

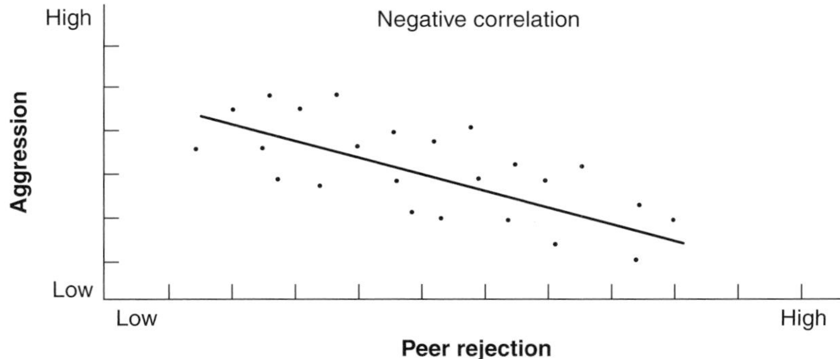

FIGURE A.2 Scatterplots of Positive and Negative Correlations
The top panel shows how an increase in aggressive behaviors is related to an increase in peer rejection. The bottom panel illustrates how an increase in peer rejection is related to a decrease in aggressive behavior.

TABLE A–1

A Summary of Select Research Designs with Their Strengths and Limitations

Design	Strengths	Limitations
Experimental designs	• Causal relationships can be inferred	• Not all phenomena can be treated within this strictly controlled design
Alternative designs		
• Pretest/posttest	• One sample • Compares behavior before and after intervention	• Less control of variables that may influence results
• Time series	• One sample • Administration of two or more interventions to the same participants • Observe behavior after each intervention	• Less control of variables that may influence results
• Natural experiments	• Studying participants in their natural conditions	• Unable to match participants in groups on critical variables
• Field experiments	• Studying participants in their natural environment, but the researcher manipulates the independent variable	• Cannot control for other variables that may influence results
Correlational designs	• Can be used with large participant groups to understand the relationship between two variables	• Cannot infer cause and effect • Cannot determine the causal direction between two variables

Different types of research designs provide the researcher with different tools by which to answer a question about development.

impossible to establish the direction of causality using a correlational design. It also may be that a third variable, such as a developmental disability, is having a causal effect on both peer rejection and aggression. Therefore, you cannot conclude that aggression causes peer rejection, acknowledging that the variables may or may not be significantly related to one another.

REFERENCES

Aalsma, M. C., & Lapsley, D. K. (1999). Religiosity and adolescent narcissism: Implications for values counseling. *Counseling & Values, 44*(1), 17–30.

Aarnio, M., Winter, T., Kujala, U. M., & Kaprio, J. (1997). Familial aggregation of leisure-time physical activity—a three generation study. *International Journal of Sports Medicine, 18*, 549–556.

Aarons, S. J., & Jenkins, R. R. (2002). Sex, pregnancy, and contraception-related motivators and barriers among Latino and African-American youth in Washington, DC. *Sex Education, 2*, 5–30.

Abe, J. A., & Izard, C. E. (1999). Compliance, noncompliance strategies, and the correlates of compliance in 5-year-old Japanese and American children. *Social Development, 8*, 1–20.

Aber, J. L., Brown, J. L., & Jones, S. M. (2003). Developmental trajectories toward violence in middle childhood: Course, demographic differences, and response to school-based intervention. *Developmental Psychology, 39*(2), 324–348.

Abrams, D., Rutland, A., & Cameron, L. (2003). The development of subjective group dynamics: Children's judgments of normative and deviant in-group and out-group individuals. *Child Development, 74*, 1840–1856.

Adair, L. S., & Gordon-Larsen, P. (2001). Maturational timing and overweight prevalence in U.S. adolescent girls. *American Journal of Public Health, 91*, 642–644.

Adams, G. R., Bennion, L., & Kuh, K. (1989). *Objective Measure of Ego Identity Status: A reference manual.* Unpublished manuscript, University of Guelph, Canada.

Adams, G. R., & Marshall, S. K. (1996). A developmental social psychology of identity: Understanding the person in context. *Journal of Adolescence, 19*, 429–442.

Adams, R., & Laursen, B. (2001). The organization and dynamics of adolescent conflict with parents and friends. *Journal of Marriage and Family, 63*, 97–110.

Adler, P. A., & Adler, P. (1998). *Peer power: Preadolescent culture and identity.* Brunswick, NJ: Rutgers University Press.

Agnew, R. (1991). The interactive effects of peer variables on delinquency. *Criminology, 29*, 47–72.

Ainsworth, M. D. S., Bell, S., & Stayton, D. J. (1971). Individual differences in the development of some attachment behaviors. *Merrill-Palmer Quarterly, 18*, 123–143.

Ainsworth, M. D. S., Blehar, M. C., Waters, E., & Wall, S. (1978). *Patterns of attachment: A psychological study of the strange situation.* Hillsdale, NJ: Erlbaum.

Alan Guttmacher Institute. (1998). *Sex and America's teenagers.* New York: Author.

Alan Guttmacher Institute. (1999). *Analyses of data from the 1988 and 1995 national survey of family growth.* New York: Author.

Alexander, C., Piazza, M., Mekos, D., & Valente, T. (2001). Peers, schools, and cigarette smoking. *Journal of Adolescent Health, 29*, 22–30.

Allen, J. P., Hauser, S. T., Eickholt, C., & Bell, K. L. (1994). Autonomy and relatedness in family interactions as predictors of expressions of negative adolescent affect. *Journal of Research on Adolescence, 4*(4), 535–552.

Allington, R. L., & Johnston, P. H. (Eds.). (2002). *Reading to learn: Lessons from exemplary fourth-grade classrooms.* New York: Guilford Press.

Allison, K. W., Burton, L., Marshall, S., Perez-Febles, A., Yarrington, J., Kirsch, L. B., & Merriwether-DeVries, C. (1999). Life experiences among urban adolescents: Examining the role of context. *Child Development, 70*, 1017–1029.

Aloise-Young, P. A., Hennigan, K. M., & Leong, C. W. (2001). Possible selves and negative health behaviors during early adolescence. *Journal of Early Adolescence, 21*(2), 158–181.

Alsaker, F. D. (1992). Pubertal timing, overweight, and psychological adjustment. *Journal of Early Adolescence, 12*(4), 396–419.

Altheide, D. L., & Johnson, J. M. (1994). Criteria for assessing interpretive validity in qualitative research. In N. K. Densin & Y. S. Lincoln (Eds.), *Handbook of qualitative research* (pp. 485–499). Thousand Oaks, CA: Sage.

Alvarez, J. M., Ruble, D. N., & Bolger, N. (2001). Trait understanding or evaluative reasoning? An analysis of children's behavioral predispositions. *Child Development, 72*, 1409–1425.

Amato, P. R. (2000). The consequences of divorce for adults and children. *Journal of Marriage and Family, 62*(4), 1269–1287.

Amato, P. R., & Booth, A. (1996). A prospective study of divorce and parent-child relationships. *Journal of Marriage and Family, 58*, 356–365.

Amato, P. R., & Fowler, F. (2002). Parenting practices, child adjustment, and family diversity. *Journal of Marriage and Family, 64*, 703–716.

Amato, P. R., & Gilbreth, J. (1999). Nonresident fathers and children's well-being: A meta-analysis. *Journal of Marriage and Family, 61*, 557–573.

Amato, P. R., & Keith, B. (1991). Parental divorce and the well-being of children: A meta-analysis. *Psychological Bulletin, 110*, 26–46.

American Academy of Pediatrics. (1983). Weight training and weight lifting: Information for the pediatrician. *Physician and Sportsmedicine, 11*(3), 157–161.

American Association of University Women. (1992). *The AAUW report: How schools shortchange girls*. Washington, DC: The AAUW Educational Foundation and National Education Association.

American College Testing Program. (1995). *The ACT assessment program*. Iowa City, IA: Author.

American Medical Association. (2002). *Fact Sheet: Underage drinking is a D.U.M.B. decision (Drinking underage maims the brain)*. Retrieved December 13, 2002, from http://www.edc.org.hec.thisweek

American Psychiatric Association. (2000). *Diagnostic and statistical manual of mental disorders: DSM-IV-TR* (4th ed.). Washington, DC: Author.

Amundson, N. E., & Penner, K. (1998). Practical techniques: Parent involved career exploration. *Career Development Quarterly, 47*, 135–144.

Andersen, S. L. (2003). Trajectories of brain development: Point of vulnerability or window of opportunity? *Neuroscience and Biobehavioral Reviews, 27*, 3–18.

Anderson, E. R., Hetherington, E. M., Reiss, D., & Howe, G. (1994). Parents' nonshared treatment of siblings and the development of social competence during adolescence. *Journal of Family Psychology, 8*, 303–320.

Anderson, K. M. (1992). Self-complexity and self-esteem in middle childhood. In R. P. Lipka & T. M. Brinthaupt (Eds.), *Self-perspectives across the life span* (pp. 11–51). Albany: State University of New York.

Anderson, R. E. (2002). Youth and information technology. In J. T. Mortimer & R. W. Larson (Eds.), *The changing adolescent experience: Societal trends and the transition to adulthood* (pp. 175–207). New York: Cambridge University Press.

Anderson-Butcher, D., Newsome, W. S., & Ferrari, T. M. (2003). Participation in boys and girls clubs and relationships to youth outcomes. *Journal of Community Psychology, 31*, 39–55.

Andrade, M. M. M., & Menna-Barreto, L. (2002). Sleep patterns of high school students living in Sao Paulo, Brazil. In M. A. Carskadon (Ed.), *Adolescent sleep patterns: Biological, social, and psychological influences* (pp. 118–131). New York: Cambridge University Press.

Andre, T., Whigham, M., Hendrickson, A., & Chambers, S. (1999). Competency beliefs, positive affect, and gender stereotypes of elementary students and their parents about science versus other school subjects. *Journal of Research in Science Teaching, 36*, 719–747.

Anfara, V. A., Jr. (2001). *Handbook of research in middle level education*. Greenwich, CT: Information Age Publishing.

Annett, M. (1999). Left-handedness as a function of sex, maternal versus paternal inheritance, and report bias. *Behavior Genetics, 29*, 103–114.

Anyan, S. E., & Pryor, J. (2002). What is in a family? Adolescent perceptions. *Children & Society, 16*, 306–317.

Archer, S. L. (1982). The lower age boundaries of identity development. *Child Development, 55*, 1551–1556.

Archer, S. L. (1989). Gender differences in identity development: Issues of process, domain and timing. *Journal of Adolescence, 12*, 117–138.

Archer, S. L. (1993). Identity status in early and middle adolescents: Scoring criteria. In J. Marcia, A. Waterman, D. Matteson, S. Archer, & J. Orlofsky (Eds.), *Ego identity* (pp. 177–204). New York: Springer-Verlag.

Aries, P. (1962). *Centuries of childhood: A social history of family life*. (R. Baldick, Trans.). New York: Random House. (Original work published 1960).

Arnett, J. J. (1997). Young people's conceptions of the transition to adulthood. *Youth & Society, 29*, 1–23.

Arnett, J. J. (1998). Learning to stand alone: The contemporary American transition to adulthood in cultural and historical context. *Human Development, 41*, 295–315.

Arnett, J. J. (2000a). Emerging adulthood: A theory of development from the late teens through the 20s. *American Psychologist, 55*, 469–480.

Arnett, J. J. (2000b). High hopes in a grim world: Emerging adults' views of their futures and "Generation X." *Youth & Society, 31*, 267–286.

Arnett, J. J. (2001a). *Adolescence and emerging adulthood: A cultural approach*. Upper Saddle River, NJ: Prentice Hall.

Arnett, J. J. (2001b). Conceptions of the transition to adulthood: Perspectives from adolescence through midlife. *Journal of Adult Development, 8*, 133–143.

Arnett, J. J. (2002). The psychology of globalization. *American Psychologist, 57*, 774–783.

Arnett, J. J. (2003). Conceptions of the transition to adulthood among emerging adults in American ethnic groups. In J. J. Arnett & N. L. Galambos (Eds.), *Exploring cultural conceptions of the transition to adulthood* (pp. 63–76). *New Directions for Child and Adolescent Development,* No. 100. San Francisco: Jossey-Bass.

Arnett, J. J., & Galambos, N. L. (2003). Exploring cultural conceptions of the transition to adulthood (pp. 1–4). *New Directions for Child and Adolescent Development,* No. 100. San Francisco: Jossey-Bass.

Arnett, J. J., Ramos, K. D., & Jensen, L. A. (2001). Ideological views in emerging adulthood: Balancing autonomy and community. *Journal of Adult Development, 8*(2), 69–79.

Arnett, J. J., & Taber, S. (1994). Adolescence terminable and interminable: When does adolescence end? *Journal of Youth & Adolescence, 23*, 517–537.

Arrington, E. G., & Wilson, M. N. (2000). A re-examination of risk and resilience during adolescence: Incorporating culture and diversity. *Journal of Child and Family Studies, 9*, 221–230.

Arsenio, W. F., & Lemerise, E. A. (2001). Varieties of childhood bullying: Values, emotion processes, and social competence. *Social Development, 10*(1), 59–73.

Asher, S. R., Parker, J. G., & Walker, D. L. (1996). Distinguishing friendship from acceptance: Implications for intervention and assessment. In W. M. Bukowski &

A. F. Newcomb (Eds.), *The company they keep: Friendship in childhood and adolescence* (pp. 366–405). New York: Cambridge University Press.

Atkins v. Virginia, 122 S. Ct. 2242 (2002).

Averett, S. L., Rees, D. I., & Argys, L. M. (2002). The impact of government policies and neighborhood characteristics on teenage sexual activity and contraceptive use. *American Journal of Public Health, 92*, 1773–1778.

Avery, P. G. (1992). Political tolerance: How adolescents deal with dissenting groups. In H. Haste & J. Torney-Purta (Eds.), *The development of political understanding: A new perspective* (pp. 39–51). *New Directions for Child Development*, No. 56. San Francisco: Jossey-Bass.

Azmitia, M., Kamprath, N. A., & Linnet, J. (1998). Intimacy and conflict: The dynamics of boys' and girls' friendships during middle childhood and early adolescence. In L. H. Meyer & H. Park (Eds.), *Making friends: The influences of culture and development: Vol. 3. Children, youth, and change: Sociocultural perspectives* (pp. 171–187). Baltimore, MD: Paul H. Brooks.

Bachman, J. G., & Van Duinen, E. (1971). *Youth look at national problems: A special report from the youth in transition project.* Ann Arbor, MI: Institute for Social Research.

Baenen, J. (2002). *Exploring the 'cusp culture' helps adolescents navigate the way to adulthood.* Retrieved July 7, 2002, from http://www.nmsa.org

Bailey, D. A., McKay, H. A., Mirwald, R. L., Crocker, P. R., & Faulkner, R. A. (1999). A six-year longitudinal study of the relationship of physical activity to bone mineral accrual in growing children: The University of Saskatchewan Bone Mineral Accrual Study. *Journal of Bone Mineral Research, 14*, 1672–1679.

Bailey, J. M. (1996). Gender identity. In R. C. Savin-Williams & K. M. Cohen (Eds.), *The lives of lesbians, gays, and bisexuals: Children to adults* (pp. 71–93). Belmont, CA: Thomson.

Bailey, J. M., & Zucker, K. L. (1995). Childhood sex-typed behavior and sexual orientation: A conceptual analysis and quantitative review. *Developmental Psychology, 31*, 43–55.

Baillie, L., Lovato, C. Y., Johnson, J. L., & Kalaw, C. (2005). Smoking decisions from a teen perspective: A narrative study. *Journal of Health Behavior, 29*, 99–106.

Baird, A. A., Gruber, S. A., Cohen, B. M., Renshaw, R. J., & Yureglun-Todd, D. A. (1999). FMRI of the amygdala in children and adolescents. *American Academy of Child and Adolescent Psychiatry, 38*, 195–199.

Baker, D., & Leary, R. (1995). Letting girls speak out about science. *Journal of Research in Science Teaching, 32*, 3–27.

Baker, L. (1996). Social influences on metacognitive development in reading. In C. Cornoldi & J. Oakley (Eds.), *Reading comprehension difficulties: Processes and intervention* (pp. 331–351). Mahwah, NJ: Erlbaum.

Baldwin, S., & Hoffman, J. P. (2002). The dynamics of self-esteem: A growth-curve analysis. *Journal of Youth and Adolescence, 13*, 101–113.

Baltes, P. B. (1968). Longitudinal and cross sectional sequences in the study of age and generational effects. *Human Development, 11*, 145–171.

Baltes, P. B. (1987). Theoretical propositions of life-span developmental psychology: On the dynamics between growth and decline. *Developmental Psychology, 23*, 611–626.

Baltes, P. B. (1997). On the incomplete architecture of human ontogeny: Selection, optimization, and compensation as foundation of developmental theory. *American Psychologist, 57*, 366–380.

Baltes, P. B., Lindenberger, U., & Staudinger, U. M. (1998). Life-span theory in developmental psychology. In W. Damon (Series Ed.) & R. M. Lerner (Vol. Ed.), *Handbook of child psychology: Vol. 1. Theoretical models of human development* (5th ed., pp. 1029–1143). New York: Wiley.

Baltes, P. B., Reese, H. W., & Lipsett, L. P. (1980). Life-span developmental psychology. *Annual Review of Psychology, 31*, 65–110.

Bandura, A. (1971). *Social learning theory.* Englewood Cliffs, NJ: Prentice Hall.

Bandura, A. (1981). Self-referent thought: A developmental analysis of self-efficacy. In J. H. Flavell & L. Ross (Eds.), *Social cognitive development: Frontiers and possible futures* (pp. 200–239). Cambridge, UK: Cambridge University Press.

Bandura, A. (1987). *Social foundations of thought and action: A social cognitive theory.* Englewood Cliffs, NJ: Prentice Hall.

Bandura, A. (1990). Conclusion: Reflections on nonability determinants of competence. In R. J. Sternberg & J. Kolligian (Eds.), *Competence considered* (pp. 315–362). New Haven, CT: Yale University Press.

Bandura, A. (1994). *Self-efficacy: The exercise of control.* New York: Freeman.

Bandura, A. (2001). Social cognitive theory: An agentic perspective. *Annual Review of Psychology, 52*, 1–26.

Banister, P., Burman, E., Parker, I., Taylor, M., & Tindall, C. (1994). *Qualitative methods in psychology.* Bristol, PA: Open University.

Bank, L., Burraston, B., & Snyder, J. (2004). Sibling conflict and ineffective parenting as predictors of adolescent boys' antisocial behavior and peer difficulties: Additive and interactive effects. *Journal of Research on Adolescence, 14*, 99–125.

Barber, B., & Eccles, J. (2003). The joy of romance: Healthy adolescent relationships as an educational agenda. In P. Florsheim (Ed.), *Adolescent romantic relations and sexual behavior: Theory, research, and practical implications* (pp. 355–370). Mahwah, NJ: Erlbaum.

Barber, B. K., & Olsen, J. A. (2004). Assessing the transitions to middle and high school. *Journal of Adolescent Research, 9*, 3–30.

Barbour, A. C. (1999). The impact of playground design on the play behaviors of children with differing levels of physical competence. *Early Childhood Research Quarterly, 14*, 75–98.

Barker, E. T., & Galambos, N. L. (2003). Body dissatisfaction of adolescent girls and boys: Risk and resource factors. *Journal of Early Adolescence, 23*, 141–165.

Barkley, R. A. (1998). *Attention-deficit/hyperactivity disorder: A handbook for diagnosis and treatment* (2nd ed.). New York: Guilford Press.

Barkley, R. A. (2000). *Taking charge of ADHD: The complete, authoritative guide for parents.* New York: Guilford Press.

Barnes, H. L., & Olsen, D. H. (1985). Parent-adolescent communication and the Circumplex model. *Child Development, 56*, 438–447.

Barnes, H. V. (1975). Physical growth and development during puberty. *Medical Clinics of North America, 59*, 1305–1317.

Barr, S., & McKay, H. (1998). Nutrition, exercise and bone status in youth. *International Journal of Sport and Nutrition, 8*, 124–142.

Barrows, H., & Kelson, A. C. (1995). *Problem-based learning in secondary education and the Problem-Based Learning Institute* (Monograph 1). Springfield, IL: Problem-Based Learning Institute.

Barry, C. M., & Nelson, L. J. (2005). The role of religion in the transition to adulthood for young emerging adults. *Journal of Youth and Adolescence, 34*, 245–255.

Bartholomew, K., & Horowitz, L. M. (1991). Attachment styles among young adults: Test of a four-category model. *Journal of Personality and Social Psychology, 61*, 226–244.

Bass, S., Pearce, G., Bradney, M., Hendrich, E., Delmas, P. D., Harding, A., et al. (1998). Exercise before puberty may confer residual benefits in bone density in adulthood: Studies in active prepubertal and retired female gymnasts. *Journal of Bone Mineral Research, 13*, 500–507.

Basseches, M. (1984). *Dialectical thinking and adult development.* Norwood, NJ: Ablex.

Bates, J. E. (2000). Temperament as an emotion construct: Theoretical and practical issues. In M. Lewis & J. M. Haviland-Jones (Eds.), *Handbook of emotions* (2nd ed., pp. 382–396). New York: Guilford Press.

Bauer, K. W., Yang, Y. W., & Austin, S. B. (2004). "How can we stay healthy when you're throwing all of this in front of us?" Findings from focus groups and interviews in middle schools on environmental influences on nutrition and physical activity. *Health Education & Behavior, 31*, 34–46.

Baumann, J. F., Font, G., Edwards, E. C., & Boland, E. (2005). Strategies for teaching middle-grade students to use word-part and context clues to expand reading vocabulary. In E. H. Hiebert & M. L. Kamil (Eds.), *Teaching and learning vocabulary: Bringing research to practice* (pp. 179–205). Mahwah, NJ: Erlbaum.

Baumeister, R. F., & Muraven, M. (1996). Identity as adaptation to social, cultural, and historical context. *Journal of Adolescence, 19*, 405–416.

Baumrind, D. (1971). Current patterns of parental authority. *Developmental Psychology Monographs, 4*(1, Pt. 2).

Baumrind, D. (1978). Parental disciplinary patterns and social competence in children. *Youth and Society, 9*, 239–276.

Beale, A. V. (2001). Emerging career development theories: A test for school counselors. *Professional School Counseling, 5*, 1–5.

Beatty, A. S., Reese, C. M., Perksy, H. R., & Carr, P. (1996). *The NAEP 1994 U.S. History Report Card for the nation and the states.* Washington, DC: U.S. Department of Education, Office of Educational Research and Improvement, National Center for Educational Statistics.

Beaumont, S. (2000). Conversational styles of mothers and their preadolescent and middle adolescent daughters. *Merrill-Palmer Quarterly, 46*, 119–139.

Becker, H. S. (1996). The epistemology of qualitative research. In R. Jessor, A. Colby, & R. A. Shweder (Eds.), *Ethnography and human development* (pp. 53–71). Chicago: University of Chicago Press.

Becker, J. (2000). Distinguishing necessary and contingent knowledge. In M. Laupa (Ed.), *Rights and wrongs: How children and young adults evaluate the world* (pp. 63–76). *New Directions for Child and Adolescent Development*, No. 89. San Francisco: Jossey-Bass.

Beers, K. (2003). *When kids can't read: What teachers can do: A guide for teachers 6–12.* Portsmouth, NH: Heinemann.

Bell, N. J., Wieling, E., & Watson, W. (2004). Self-reflecting in developmental context: Variations in level and patterning during the first 2 university years. *Journal of Genetic Psychology, 165*, 451–465.

Belsky, J., Steinberg, L., & Draper, P. (1991). Childhood experience, interpersonal development, and reproductive strategy: An evolutionary theory of socialization. *Child Development, 62*, 647–670.

Bem, S. L. (1974). The measurement of psychological androgyny. *Journal of Consulting and Clinical Psychology, 42*, 155–162.

Bem, S. L. (1981). Gender schema theory: A cognitive account of sex typing. *Psychological Review, 88*(4), 354–364.

Bem, S. L. (1993). *The lenses of gender: Transforming the debate on sexual inequality.* New Haven, CT: Yale University Press.

Ben-Amos, I. K. (1994). *Adolescence and youth in early modern England.* New Haven, CT: Yale University Press.

Benson, P. L. (2002). Adolescent development in social and community context: A program of research. *New Directions for Youth Development, 95*, 123–147.

Benson, P. L. (2004). Emerging themes in research on adolescent spiritual and religious development. *Applied Developmental Science, 8*(1), 47–50.

Benson, P. L., Espeland, P., & Galbraith, J. (1998). *What teens need to succeed: Proven, practical ways to shape your own future.* Minneapolis: Free Spirit.

Benson, P. L., Scales, P. C., & Mannes, M. (2003). Developmental strengths and their sources: Implications for the study and practice of community building. In R. M. Lerner, F. Jacobs, & D. Wertleib (Eds.), *Handbook of applied developmental science: Vol. 1. Applying developmental science for youth and families: Historical and theoretical foundations* (pp. 369–406). Thousand Oaks, CA: Sage.

Berenbaum, S. A., Korman, K., & Leveroni, C. (1995). Early hormones and sex differences in cognitive abilities. *Learning and Individual Differences, 7*, 303–321.

Bergen, D., & Mauer, D. (2000). Symbolic play, phonological awareness, and literacy skills at three age levels. In K. A. Roskos & J. F. Christie (Eds.), *Play and literacy in early childhood: Research from multiple perspectives* (pp. 45–62). Mahwah, NJ: Erlbaum.

Berger, R. (2001). Gay stepfamilies: A triple-stigmatized group. In J. M. Lehmann (Ed.), *The gay and lesbian marriage & family reader: Analyses of problems and prospects for the 21st century* (pp. 171–194). New York: Gordian Knot/Altschuler.

Berk, L. (2003). *Child development* (6th ed.). New York: Pearson Education.

Berk, L. E., & Spuhl, S. T. (1995). Maternal interaction, private speech, and task performance in preschool children. *Early Childhood Research Quarterly, 10*, 145–169.

Berkey, C. S., Gardner, J. D., Frazier, A. L., & Colditz, G. A. (2000). Relation of childhood diet and body size to menarche and adolescent growth in girls. *American Journal of Epidemiology, 152*, 446–452.

Berndt, T. J. (1989). Obtaining support from friends during childhood and adolescence. In D. Belle (Ed.), *Children's social networks and social supports* (pp. 173–188). New York: Wiley.

Berndt, T. J. (2002). Friendship quality and social development. *Current Directions in Psychological Science, 11*(1), 7–10.

Berscheid, E., Snyder, M., & Omoto, A. M. (1989). The Relationship Closeness Inventory: Assessing the closeness of personal relationships. *Journal of Personality and Social Psychology, 57*, 792–807.

Berzonsky, M. D. (2003). Identity style and well-being: Does commitment matter? *Identity: An International Journal of Theory and Research, 3*, 131–142.

Berzonsky, M. D. (2004). Identity style, parental authority, and identity commitment. *Journal of Youth and Adolescence, 33*, 213–220.

Berzonsky, M. D., & Adams, G. R. (1999). Reevaluating the identity status paradigm: Still useful after 35 years. *Developmental Review, 19*, 557–590.

Berzonsky, M. D., & Sullivan, C. (1992). Social-cognitive aspects of identity style: Need for cognition, experiential openness, and introspection. *Journal of Adolescent Research, 7*, 140–155.

Betancur, C., Leboyer, M., & Gillberg, C. (2002). Increased rate of twins among affected sibling pairs with autism. *American Journal of Human Genetics, 70*, 1381–1383.

Beunen, G., & Malina, R. M. (1988). Growth and physical performance relative to the timing of the adolescent spurt. In K. B. Pandolf (Ed.), *Exercise and sport sciences reviews, Vol. 16* (pp. 503–540). New York: Macmillan.

Bharat, S. (1997). Family socialization of the Indian child. *Trends in Social Science Research, 4*(1), 201–216.

Bigelow, B. J. (1977). Children's friendship expectations: A cognitive-developmental study. *Child Development, 48*, 246–253.

Biro, F. M., McMahon, R. P., Striegel-Moore, R., Crawford, P. B., Obarzanek, E., & Morrison, J. A. (2001). Impact of timing of pubertal maturation on growth in black and white female adolescents: The National Heart, Lung, and Blood Institute Growth and Health Study. *Journal of Pediatrics, 138*, 636–643.

Bjorklund, D. A., & Schneider, W. (1996). The interaction of knowledge, aptitudes, and strategies in children's memory performance. In H. W. Reese (Ed.), *Advances in child development and behavior* (Vol. 26, pp. 59–89). San Diego, CA: Academic Press.

Bjorklund, D. F. (1997). The role of immaturity in human development. *Psychological Bulletin, 122*, 153–169.

Bjorklund, D. F. (2000). *Children's thinking: Developmental function and individual differences* (3rd ed.). Belmont, CA: Wadsworth.

Bjorklund, D. F., & de Marchena, M. R. (1984). Developmental shifts in the basis of organization in memory: The role of associative versus categorical relatedness in children's free-recall. *Child Development, 55*, 952–962.

Black, C., & DeBlassie, R. (1985). Adolescent pregnancy: Contributing factors, consequences, treatment, and plausible solutions. *Adolescence, 20*, 281–290.

Blank, M. J., Shah, B., Johnson, S., Blackwell, W., & Ganley, M. (2003). Reforming education: Developing twenty-first century community schools. In R. M. Lerner, F. Jacobs, & D. Wertleib (Eds.), *Handbook of applied developmental science: Vol. 2. Enhancing the life chances of youth and families: Contributions of programs, policies, and service systems* (pp. 291–310). Thousand Oaks, CA: Sage.

Blasi, A., & Hoeffel, E. C. (1974). Adolescence and formal operations. *Human Development, 17*, 344–363.

Block, J., & Robins, R. W. (1993). A longitudinal study of consistency and change in self-esteem from early adolescence to early adulthood. *Child Development, 64*, 909–923.

Bloom, L. (1998). Language acquisition in its developmental context. In W. Damon (Series Ed.) & D. Kuhn & R. S. Siegler (Vol. Eds.), *Handbook of child psychology: Vol. 2. Cognition, perception, and language* (5th ed., pp. 309–370). New York: Wiley.

Blos, P. (1962). *On adolescence: A psychoanalytic interpretation*. New York: The Free Press.

Blume, L. B. (2001, August). *Body, self, creativity, and identity in adolescent female dancers*. Paper presented at the annual meetings of the American Psychological Association, San Francisco, CA.

Blume, L. B., & Blume, T. W. (1997). Negotiating identity in parent-adolescent relationships. *Theory Construction and Research Methodology, Vol. 27.* Available from the National Council on Family Relations, 5989 Central Avenue, NE, Suite 550, Minneapolis, MN, 55421.

Blume, L. B., & Blume, T. W. (2003). Toward a dialectical model of family gender discourse: Body, identity, and sexuality. *Journal of Marriage and Family, 65*(4), 785–794.

Blume, T. W. (2006). *Becoming a family counselor: A bridge to family therapy, theory, and practice.* New York: Wiley.

Blustein, D. L. (1994). "Who am I?": The question of self and identity in career development. In M. L. Savickas & R. W. Lent (Eds.), *Convergence in career development theories: Implications for science and practice* (pp. 139–154). Palo Alto, CA: Consulting Psychologists Press.

Blustein, D. L. (1997). The role of work in adolescent development. *Career Development Quarterly, 45*, 381–389.

Blyth, D. A., & Leffert, N. (1995). Communities as contexts for adolescent development: An empirical analysis. *Journal of Adolescent Research, 10*, 64–87.

Blythe, J., & Rosenthal, S. L. (2000). Female adolescent sexuality: Promoting healthy sexual development. *Obstetrics and Gynecology in Clinics of North America, 27*, 125–141.

Bohlin, G., Hagekull, B., & Rydell, A. (2000). Attachment and social functioning: A longitudinal study from infancy to middle childhood. *Social Development, 9*, 24–39.

Bolger, K. E., & Patterson, C. (2001). Developmental pathways from child maltreatment to peer rejection. *Child Development, 72*, 549–568.

Bonino, S., & Cattelino, E. (1999). The relationship between cognitive abilities and social abilities in childhood: A research on flexibility in thinking and co-operation with peers. *International Journal of Behavioral Development, 23*(1), 19–36.

Bonnie, R. (1992). The competence of criminal defendants: A theoretical reformulation. *Behavioral Sciences and the Law, 10*, 291–316.

Bonnie, R. (1993). The competence of criminal defendants: Beyond Dusky and Drope. *Miami Law Review, 47*, 539–501.

Boomer, L. (Executive Producer). (2000). *Malcolm in the middle* [Television series]. Beverly Hills, CA: Fox Broadcasting.

Borden, L. M., Donnemeyer, J. F., & Scheer, S. D. (2001). Extracurricular activities and peer influence on substance use. *Journal of Adolescent and Family Health, 2*, 12–19.

Borkowski, J. G., Ramey, S. L., & Bristol-Power, M. (2002). *Parenting and the child's world: Influences on academic, intellectual, and social-emotional development.* Mahwah, NJ: Erlbaum.

Bouchey, H. A., & Furman, W. (2003) Dating and romantic experiences in adolescence. In G. R. Adams & M. D. Berzonsky (Eds.), *Blackwell handbook of adolescence* (pp. 313–329). Malden, MA: Blackwell.

Bowlby, J. (1969). *Attachment and loss, Vol. 1.* New York: Basic.

Bowlby, J. (1973). *Attachment and loss, Vol. 2.* New York: Basic.

Bowlby, J. (1988). *A secure base: Parent-child attachment and healthy human development.* New York: Basic.

Bowlby, S., Evans, S. L., & Mohammad, R. (1998). In T. Skelton & G. Valentine (Eds.), *Cool places: Geographies of youth cultures* (pp. 229–248). London: Routledge.

Boyer, E. L. (1983). *High school: A report on secondary education in America of the Carnegie Foundation for the Advancement of Teaching.* New York: Harper & Row.

Bracey, J. R., Bámaca, M. Y., & Umaña-Taylor, A. J. (2004). Examining ethnic identity and self-esteem among biracial and monoracial adolescents. *Journal of Youth and Adolescence, 33*(2), 123–133.

Bransford, J. D., Brown, A. L., & Cocking, R. (2000). *How people learn.* Washington, DC: National Academy Press.

Brecelj, J., Strucl, M. M., Zidar, I., & Tekavcic-Pompe, M. (2002). Pattern ERG and VEP maturation in schoolchildren. *Clinical Neurophysiology, 113*, 1764–1770.

Brendgen, M., Vitaro, F., & Doyle, A. (2002). Same-sex peer relations and romantic relationships during early adolescence: Interactive links to emotional, behavioral, and academic adjustment. *Merrill-Palmer Quarterly, 48*, 77–103.

Brenner, M. E., Herman, S., Hsui-Zu, H., & Zimmer, J. M. (1999). Cross-national comparison of representational competence. *Journal for Research in Mathematics Education, 30*, 541–557.

Brien, M. J., & Willis, R. J. (1997). Costs and consequences for the fathers. In R. A. Maynard (Ed.), *Kids having kids: Economic costs and social consequences of teen pregnancy* (pp. 95–143). Washington, DC: Urban Institute Press.

Brody, G., Stoneman, Z., & McCoy, J. (1994). Contributions of family relationships and child temperaments to longitudinal variations in sibling relationship quality and sibling relationship styles. *Journal of Family Psychology, 8*, 274–286.

Bronfenbrenner, U. (1979). *The ecology of human development: Experiments by nature and design.* Cambridge, MA: Harvard University Press.

Bronfenbrenner, U., & Ceci, S. J. (1994). Nature-nurture reconceptualized in developmental perspective: A bioecological model. *Psychological Review, 101*, 568–586.

Bronfenbrenner, U., & Crouter, A. C. (1983). The evolution of environmental models in developmental research. In W. Kessen (Series Ed.) & P. H. Mussen (Vol. Ed.), *Handbook of child psychology: Vol. 1. History, theory, and methods* (4th ed., pp. 357–414). New York: Wiley.

Bronfenbrenner, U., & Morris, P. A. (1998). The ecology of developmental process. In W. Damon (Series Ed.) & R. M. Lerner (Vol. Ed.), *Handbook of child psychology: Vol. 1. Theoretical models of human development* (5th ed., pp. 993–1028). New York: Wiley.

Brooks-Gunn, J., Duncan, G., & Aber, J. L. (Eds.). (1997). *Neighborhood poverty: Vol. 1. Context and consequences for children. Vol. 2. Policy implications in studying neighborhoods.* New York: Russell Sage Foundation.

Brooks-Gunn, J., Graber, J., & Paikoff, R. L. (1994). Studying links between hormones and negative affect: Models and measures. *Journal of Research on Adolescence, 4*, 469–486.

Brooks-Gunn, J., Klebanov, P. K., & Liaw, F. (1995). The learning, physical, and emotional environment of the home in the context of poverty: The Infant Health and Development Program. *Children and Youth Services Review, 17*, 251–276.

Brooks-Gunn, J., Petersen, A. C., & Eichorn, D. (1985). The study of maturational timing effects in adolescence. *Journal of Youth and Adolescence, 14*(3), 149–161.

Brooks-Gunn, J., & Reiter, E. O. (1990). The role of pubertal processes. In S. S. Feldman & G. R. Elliot (Eds.), *At the threshold: The developing adolescent* (pp. 16–53). Cambridge, MA: Harvard University Press.

Brooks-Gunn, J., & Warren, M. P. (1989). Biological and social contributions to negative affect in young adolescent girls. *Child Development, 60*, 40–55.

Broude, G. J. (1994). *Marriage, family, and relationships: A cross-cultural encyclopedia.* Santa Barbara, CA: ABC-CLIO.

Broude, G. J. (1995). *Growing up: A cross-cultural encyclopedia.* Santa Barbara, CA: ABC-CLIO.

Broughton, J. M., & Zahaykevich, M. K. (1988). Ego and ideology: A critical review of Loevinger's theory. In D. K. Lapsey & F. C. Power (Eds.), *Self, ego, and identity: Integrative approaches* (pp. 179–207). New York: Springer-Verlag.

Brown, B. B., Eicher, S. A., & Petrie, S. (1986). The importance of peer group ("crowd") affiliation in adolescence. *Journal of Adolescence, 9*, 73–96.

Brown, B. B., Feiring, C., & Furman, W. (1999). Missing the love boat: Why researchers have shied away from adolescent romance. In W. Furman, B. B. Brown, & C. Feiring (Eds.), *The development of romantic relationships in adolescence* (pp. 1–16). Cambridge, UK: Cambridge University Press.

Brown, B. B., Mory, M. S., & Kinney, D. (1994). Casting adolescent crowds in a relational perspective: Caricature, channel, and context. In R. Montemayor, G. R. Adams, & T. P. Gulotta (Eds.), *Personal relationships during adolescence: Advances in adolescent development* (Vol. 3, pp. 125–167). Thousand Oaks, CA: Sage.

Brown, J. L., & Pollitt, E. (1996, November). Malnutrition, poverty and intellectual development. *Scientific American, 274*, 38–43.

Brown, L. M., & Gilligan, C. (1992). *Meeting at the crossroads.* New York: Ballantine.

Brown, S. A., Tapert, S. F., Granholm, E., & Delis, D. C. (2000). Neurocognitive functioning of adolescents: Effects of protracted alcohol use. *Alcoholism: Clinical and Experimental Research, 24*(2), 164–171.

Brownwell, M. D., & Yogendran, M. S. (2002). Attention-deficit hyperactivity disorder in Manitoba children: Medical diagnosis and psychostimulant treatment rates. *Canadian Journal of Psychiatry, 46*, 264–272.

Bryant, A. L., Schulenberg, J. E., Bachman, J. G., O'Malley, P. M., & Johnston, L. D. (2000). Understanding the links among school misbehavior, academic achievement and cigarette use during adolescence: A national panel study of adolescents. *Prevention Science, 1*, 71–87.

Bryant, A. L., Schulenberg, J. E., O'Malley, P. M., Bachman, J. G., & Johnston, L. D. (2003). How academic achievement, attitudes, and behaviors relate to the course of substance use during adolescence: A 6-year, multiwave national longitudinal study. *Journal of Research on Adolescence, 13*, 361–397.

Brydon-Miller, M. (1997). Participatory action research: Psychology and social change. *Journal of Social Issues, 53*, 657–666.

Brydon-Miller, M. (2001). Education, research, and action: Theory and methods of participatory action research. In D. L. Tolman & M. Brydon-Miller (Eds.), *From subjects to subjectivities: A handbook of interpretive and participatory methods* (pp. 76–94). New York: New York University Press.

Buehler, C., & Gerard, J. (2002). Marital conflict, ineffective parenting, and children's and adolescents' maladjustment. *Journal of Marriage and Family, 64*, 78–92.

Buhrmester, D. (1990). Intimacy of friendship, interpersonal competence, and adjustment during preadolescence and adolescence. *Child Development, 61*, 1101–1111.

Buhrmester, D. (1996). Need fulfillment, interpersonal competence, and the developmental contexts of early adolescent friendship. In W. M. Bukowski & A. F. Newcomb (Eds.), *The company they keep: Friendship in childhood and adolescence* (pp. 158–185). New York: Cambridge University Press.

Bukowski, W. M., Sippola, L. K., & Newcomb, A. F. (2000). Variations in patterns of attraction to same- and other-sex peers during early adolescence. *Developmental Psychology, 36*(2), 147–154.

Bulik, C. M. (2002). Eating disorders in adolescents and young adults. *Child and Adolescent Psychiatric Clinics of North America, 11*, 201–218.

Burns, M. S., Griffin, P., & Snow, C. E. (Eds.). (1999). *Starting out right: A guide to promoting children's reading success.* Washington, DC: National Academy Press.

Burton, L. (2002, May). *Adultification in childhood and adolescence: A matter of risk and resilience.* Paper presented at the Center for the Development of Peace and Well-being, University of California. Berkeley, CA.

Bush, D. & Simmons, R. (1987). Gender and coping with the entry into early adolescence. In R. Barnett, L. Biener, & G. Baruch (Eds.), *Gender and stress* (pp. 185–217). New York: The Free Press.

Byrnes, J. P. (2001a). *Cognitive development and learning in instructional contexts* (2nd ed.). Needham Heights, MA: Allyn and Bacon.

Byrnes, J. P. (2001b). *Minds, brains, and education: Understanding the psychological and educational relevance of neuroscientific research*. New York: Guilford Press.

Byrnes, J. P., Miller, D. C., & Reynolds, M. (1999). Learning to make good decisions: A self-regulation perspective. *Child Development, 70*, 1121–1140.

Cain, K., Oakhill, J. V., & Carsten, E. (2003). The ability to learn new word meanings from context by school-age children with and without language comprehension difficulties. *Journal of Child Language, 30*, 681–694.

Cairns, R. B. (1979). *Social development: The origins and plasticity of interchanges*. Oxford, UK: Freeman.

Cairns, R. B. (2000). Developmental science: Three audacious implications. In L. R. Bergman, R. B. Cairns, L. Nilsson, & L. Nystedt (Eds.), *Developmental science and the holistic approach* (pp. 49–62). Mahwah, NJ: Erlbaum.

Call, K. T., & Mortimer, J. T. (2001). *Arenas of comfort in adolescence: A study of adjustment in context*. Mahwah, NJ: Erlbaum.

Camarena, P. M., Stemmler, M., & Petersen, A. C. (1994). The gender-differential significance of work and family: An exploration of adolescent experience and expectation. In. R. K. Silbereisen & E. Todt (Eds.), *Adolescence in context: The interplay of family, school, peers, and work in adjustment* (pp. 201–221). New York: Springer-Verlag.

Camic, P. M., Rhodes, J. E., & Yardley, L. (2003). Naming the stars: Integrating qualitative methods into psychological research. *Qualitative research in psychology: Expanding perspectives in methodology and design* (pp. 3–15). Washington, DC: American Psychological Association.

Campbell, J. R., Hombo, C. M., & Mazzeo, J. (2000). *NAEP 1999: Trends in academic progress*. Washington, DC: Department of Education.

Campos, J. J., Mumme, D. L., Kermoian, R., & Campos, R. G. (1994). A functionalist perspective on the nature of emotion. In N. A. Fox (Ed.), *Monographs of the Society for Research in Child Development, 59*(2–3, Serial No. 240), 284–303.

Capaldi, D. M., & Rothbart, M. K. (1992). Development and validation of an early adolescent temperament measure. *Journal of Early Adolescence, 12*, 153–173.

Capelli, C. A., Nakagawa, N., & Madden, C. M. (1990). How children understand sarcasm: The role of context and intonation. *Child Development, 61*, 1824–1841.

Caprara, G. V., Barbaranelli, C., Pastorelli, C., Bandura, A., & Zimbardo, P. G. (2000). Prosocial foundations of children's academic achievement. *Psychological Science, 11*, 302–306.

Carlo, G., Hausmann, A., Christiansen, S., & Randall, B. A. (2003). Sociocognitive and behavioral correlates of a measure of prosocial tendencies for adolescents. *Journal of Early Adolescence, 23*(1), 107–134.

Carnegie Council on Adolescent Development. (1989). *Turning points: Preparing American youth for the 21st century*. New York: Carnegie Corporation of New York.

Carnegie Council on Adolescent Development. (1995). *Great transitions: Preparing adolescents for a new century*. New York: Carnegie Corporation of New York.

Carpendale, J. I. M. (2000). Kohlberg and Piaget on stages and moral reasoning. *Developmental Review, 20*, 181–205.

Carr, M., & Schneider, W. (1991). Long-term maintenance of organizational strategies in kindergarten children. *Contemporary Educational Psychology, 16*, 61–72.

Carskadon, M. A. (Ed.). (2002). *Adolescent sleep patterns: Biological, social and psychological influences*. New York: Cambridge University Press.

Carskadon, M. A., Wolfson, A. R., Acebo, C., Tzischinsky, O., & Seifer, R. (1998). Adolescent sleep patterns, circadian timing, and sleepiness at a transition to early school days. *Sleep, 21*, 871–881.

Carson, C., Uppal, S., & Prosser, E. C. (2000). Ethnic differences in processes contributing to the self-esteem of early adolescent girls. *Journal of Early Adolescence, 20*, 44–67.

Carver, K., Joyner, K., & Udry, J. R. (2003). National estimates of adolescent romantic relationships. In P. Florsheim (Ed.), *Adolescent romantic relations and sexual behavior: Theory, research, and practical implications* (pp. 23–56). Mahwah, NJ: Erlbaum.

Carver, P. R., Egan, S. K., & Perry, D. G. (2004). Children who question their heterosexuality. *Developmental Psychology, 40*, 43–53.

Carver, P. R., Yunger, J. L., & Perry, D. G. (2003). Gender identity and adjustment in middle childhood. *Sex Roles, 49*(3/4), 95–109.

Case, R. (1991). Stages in the development of the young child's first sense of self. *Developmental Review, 11*, 210–230.

Case, R. (1992). *The mind's staircase: Exploring the conceptual underpinnings of children's thought and knowledge*. Hillsdale, NJ: Erlbaum.

Case, R., Kurland, M., & Goldberg, J. (1982). Operational efficiency and the growth of short-term memory span. *Journal of Experimental Child Psychology, 33*, 386–404.

Casella, R., & Burstyn, J. (2002). Linking academics and social learning: Perceptions of school staff to a violence prevention program at an alternative school. *Journal of School Violence, 1*(1), 83–102.

Casey, B. J., Giedd, J. N., & Thomas, K. M. (2000). Structural and functional brain development and its relation to cognitive development. *Biological Psychiatry, 54*, 241–257.

Casey, B. M., Nuttall, R. L., & Pezaris, E. (2001). Spatial-mechanical reasoning skills versus mathematical self-confidence as mediators of gender differences on mathematics subtests using cross-national gender-based items. *Journal for Research in Mathematics Education, 32*, 28–57.

Caspi, A., & Moffitt, T. E. (1991). Individual differences are accentuated during periods of social change: The sample case of girls at puberty. *Journal of Personality and Social Psychology, 61*, 157–168.

Cass, V. (1984). Homosexual identity: A concept in need of a definition. *Journal of Homosexuality, 4*, 105–126.

Castro-Vazquez, G., & Kishi, I. (2002). "Nemureru ko wo okosu mono dearu": Learning about sex at a top ranking Japanese senior high school. *Sexualities, 5*(4), 465–486.

Ceballo, R., McLoyd, V. C., & Toyokawa, T. (2004). The influence of neighborhood quality on adolescents' educational values and school effort. *Journal of Adolescent Research, 19*, 716–739.

Ceci, S. J., & Roazzi, A. (1994). The effects of context on cognition: Postcards from Brazil. In R. Sternberg & R. K. Wagner (Eds.), *Mind in context: Interactionist perspectives on human intelligence* (pp. 74–101). New York: Cambridge University Press.

Ceci, S. J., Rosenblum, T. B., & Kumpf, M. (1998). The shrinking gap between high- and low-scoring groups: Current trends and possible causes. In U. Neisser (Ed.), *The rising curve* (pp. 287–302). Washington, DC: American Psychological Association.

Centers for Disease Control and Prevention. (1999). *Youth Risk Behavior Survey* [On-line]. Available at http://www.cdc.gov/epo/mmwr/preview/mmwr.html/ss4905a.htm

Centers for Disease Control and Prevention. (2003a). *Press release archive: More American children and teens are overweight*. Retrieved April 22, 2003 from Wysiwyg://30/http://www.cdc.gov/nccdphp/dnpa/press/archive/overweight.htm

Centers for Disease Control and Prevention. (2003b). *Results from the Youth Risk Behavior Survey on drinking alcohol*. Retrieved May 17, 2004, from http://apps.nccd.cdc.gov/yrbss/QuestYearTable.asp

Centers for Disease Control and Prevention. (2003c). *Results from the Youth Risk Behavior Survey on tobacco use*. Retrieved May 17, 2004, from http://apps.nccd.dcd.gov/yrbss/QuestYearTable.asp

Centers for Disease Control and Prevention. (2003d). *Results from the Youth Risk Behavior Survey on sexual activity*. Retrieved May 17, 2004, from http://apps.nccd.dcd.gov/yrbss/QuestYearTable.asp

Centers for Disease Control and Prevention. (2003e). *Results from the Youth Risk Behavior Survey on contraceptive use*. Retrieved May 17, 2004, from http://apps.nccd.dcd.gov/yrbss/QuestYearTable.asp

Chall, J. S. (1983). *Stages of reading development*. New York: McGraw-Hill.

Champion, K., Vernberg, E., & Shipman, K. (2003). Nonbullying victims of bullies: Aggression, social skills, and friendship characteristics. *Journal of Applied Developmental Psychology, 24*, 535–551.

Chan, D., Ramey, S., Ramey, C., & Schmitt, N. (2000). Modeling intraindividual change in children's social skills at home and at school: A multivariate latent growth approach to understanding between-settings differences in children's social skill development. *Multivariate Behavioral Research, 35*, 365–396.

Changeux, J-P., & Dehaene, S. (1989). Neuronal models of cognitive functions. *Cognition, 33*, 63–109.

Chao, R. K. (2001). Extending research on the consequences of parenting style for Chinese Americans and European Americans. *Child Development, 72*, 1832–1843.

Chapin, J. R. (2000). Adolescent sex and mass media: A developmental approach. *Adolescence, 35*, 799–811.

Chassin, L., Presson, C. C., Pitts, S. C., & Sherman, S. J. (2000). The natural history of cigarette smoking from adolescence to adulthood in a midwestern community sample: Multiple trajectories and their psychosocial correlates. *Health Psychology, 19*, 223–231.

Chatterjee, P., Bailey, D., & Aronoff, N. (2001). Adolescence and old age in twelve communities. *Journal of Sociology and Social Welfare, 28*(4), 121–159.

Cheek, D. B., Grumbach, M. M., & Grave, G. D., et al. (1974). *Control of onset of puberty*. New York: Wiley.

Chen, C., Lee, S. Y., & Stevenson, H. W. (1996). Long-term prediction of academic achievement of American, Chinese, and Japanese adolescents. *Journal of Educational Psychology, 18*, 750–759.

Chen, C., & Stevenson, H. W. (1988). Cross-linguistic differences in digit span of preschool children. *Journal of Experimental Child Psychology, 46*, 150–158.

Chen, C., & Tonegawa, S. (1997). Molecular genetic analysis of synaptic plasticity, activity-dependent neural development, learning, and memory in the mammalian brain. *Annual Review of Neuroscience, 20*, 157–184.

Chen, H. (2005). *Practical program evaluation: Assessing and improving planning, implementation, and effectiveness*. Thousand Oaks, CA: Sage.

Chen, H., Mechanic, D., & Hansell, S. (1998). A longitudinal study of self-awareness and depressed mood in adolescence. *Journal of Youth and Adolescence, 27*, 719–734.

Chi, M. T. H. (1978). Knowledge structure and memory development. In R. Siegler (Ed.), *Children's thinking: What develops?* (pp. 73–96). Hillsdale, NJ: Erlbaum.

Chicago Department of Transportation (1999). *The walking school bus training manual*. Chicago: Department of Transportation.

Child Trends. (2005). Racial and ethnic composition of the child population. Retrieved July 16, 2005, from http://www.childtrendsdatabank.org/figures/60-Figure-2.gif

Children's Bureau, Administration of Children and Families, U.S. Department of Health and Human Services (2005). *Child maltreatment 2003*. Washington, DC: U.S. Government Printing Office.

Chira, S. (1994, September 5). Parents take less of a role as pupils age. *New York Times*. Sec. 1, p. 6.

Chodorow, N. J. (1999). *The reproduction of mothering: Psychoanalysis and the sociology of gender*. Berkeley, CA: University of California Press.

Chugani, H. T. (1994). Development of regional brain glucose metabolism in relation to behavior and plasticity. In G. Dawson & K. Fischer (Eds.), *Human behavior and the developing brain* (pp. 153–175). New York: Guilford Press.

Cicchetti, D., & Toth, S. L. (1998). The development of depression in children and adolescents. *American Psychologist, 53*, 221–241.

Cillessen, A. H. N., & Bellmore, A. B. (2002). Social skills and interpersonal perception in early and middle childhood. In P. K. Smith & C. H. Hart (Eds.), *Handbook of childhood social development* (pp. 356–374). Malden, MA: Blackwell.

Civil Rights Project and the Southern Poverty Law Center. (2002). Positive interracial outcomes in the classroom. Retrieved July 11, 2005, from http://www.civilrightsproject.harvard.edu/convenings/splc/synopsis.php

Clayton, P. E., & Trueman, J. A. (2000). Leptin and puberty. *Archives of Disease in Childhood, 83*, 1–4.

Coatsworth, J. D., Pantin, H., & Szapocznik, J. (2002). Familias Unidas: A family-centered ecodevelopmental intervention to reduce risk for problem behavior among Hispanic adolescents. *Clinical Child and Family Psychology Review, 5*(2), 113–132.

Cohane, G. H., & Pope, H. G., Jr. (2001). Body image in boys: A review of the literature. *International Journal of Eating Disorders, 29*, 373–379.

Cohen, S. (2005). Liberations, clients, activists: Queer youth organizing, 1966–2003. *Journal of Gay and Lesbian Issues in Education, 2*(3), 67–86.

Cohen-Kettenis, P. T., & Pfäfflin, F. (2003). *Transgenderism and intersexuality in childhood and adolescence*. Thousand Oaks, CA: Sage.

Coie, J. D., & Dodge, K. A. (1998). Aggression and antisocial behavior. In W. Damon (Series Ed.) & N. Eisenberg (Vol. Ed.), *Handbook of child psychology: Vol. 3. Social, emotional, and personality development* (5th ed., pp. 779–862). New York: Wiley.

Colby, A., & Kohlberg, L. (1987a). *The measurement of moral judgment: Vol. 1. Theoretical foundations and research validation*. New York: Cambridge University Press.

Colby, A., & Kohlberg, L. (1987b). *The measurement of moral judgment: Vol. 2. Standard issue scoring manual*. New York: Cambridge University Press.

Colby, A., Kohlberg, L., & Gibbs, J. (1983). A longitudinal study of moral judgment. *Monographs of the Society for Research in Child Development, 48* (Serial No. 1–2).

Colby, S. M., Tiffany, S. T., Shiffman, S., & Niaura, R. S. (2000). Are adolescent smokers dependent on nicotine? A review of the evidence. *Drug & Alcohol Dependence, 59*, S83–S95.

Cole, A., & Kerns, K. (2001). Perceptions of sibling qualities and activities of early adolescents. *Journal of Early Adolescence, 21*, 204–226.

Cole, D. A., Maxwell, S. E., Martin, J. M., Peeke, L. G., Tram, J. M., Hoffman, K. B., Ruiz, M. D., Jacquez, F., & Maschman, T. (2001). The development of multiple domains of child and adolescent self-concept: A cohort sequential longitudinal design. *Child Development, 72*, 1723–1746.

Cole, J. I. (2004). *The digital future report: Surveying the digital future, year four: Ten years, ten trends*. Los Angeles, CA: University of Southern California Annenberg School Center for the Digital Future. Retrieved July 23, 2005, from http://www.digitalcenter.org/downloads/DigitalFutureReport-Year4-2004.pdf

Cole, M. (1990). Cognitive development and formal schooling: The evidence from cross-cultural research. In L. C. Moll (Ed.), *Vygotsky and education*. Cambridge, UK: Cambridge University Press.

Cole, M. (1996). *Cultural psychology: A once and future discipline*. Cambridge, MA: Harvard University Press.

Coleman Dixon, A., Schoonmaker, C. T., & Philliber, W. W. (2000). A journey toward womanhood: Effects of an Afrocentric approach to pregnancy prevention among African-American adolescent females. *Adolescence, 35*, 425–429.

Coleman, P. K. (2003). Perceptions of parent-child attachment, social self-efficacy, and peer relationships in middle childhood. *Infant & Child Development, 12*, 351–368.

Coleman, P. K., & Karraker, K. H. (2000). Parenting self-efficacy among mothers of school-age children: Conceptualization, measurement, and correlates. *Family Relations, 49*, 13–24.

Coles, R., & Stokes, G. (1985). *Sex and the American teenager*. New York: Harper & Row.

Collings, J. N. (1994). Some fundamental questions about scientific thinking. *Research in Science and Technological Education, 12*, 161–173.

Collins, J. F. (2000). Biracial-bisexual individuals: Identity coming of age. *International Journal of Sexuality and Gender Studies, 5*, 221–253.

Collins, M. A., & Amabile, T. M. (1999). Motivation and creativity. In R. J. Sternberg (Ed.), *Handbook of creativity* (pp. 297–312). Cambridge, UK: Cambridge University Press.

Collins, P. H. (1991). *Black feminist thought: Knowledge, consciousness, and the politics of empowerment*. London: Routledge.

Collins, W. A. (1984). *Development during middle childhood: The years from six to twelve*. Washington, DC: National Academy Press.

Collins, W. A. (1990). Parent-child relationships in the transition to adolescence: Continuity and change in interaction, affect, and cognition. In R. Montemayor, G. R. Adams, & T. P. Gullotta (Eds.), *From childhood to adolescence: A transitional period?* Newbury Park, CA: Sage.

Collins, W. A. (2003). More than myth: The developmental significance of romantic relationships during adolescence. *Journal of Research on Adolescence, 13*, 1–24.

Collins, W. A., Gleason, T., & Sesma, A., Jr. (1997). Internalization, autonomy, and relationships: Development during adolescence. In J. E. Grusec & L. Kuczynski (Eds.), *Parenting and children's internalization of values: A handbook of contemporary theory* (pp. 78–99). New York: Wiley.

Collins, W. A., Maccoby, E. E., Steinberg, L., Hetherington, E. M., & Bornstein, M. H. (2000). Contemporary research on parenting: The case for nature and nurture. *American Psychologist, 55*, 218–232.

Collins, W. A., & Repinski, D. J. (1994). Relationships during adolescence: Continuity and change in developmental perspective. In R. Montemayor, G. R. Adams, & T. P. Gulotta (Eds.), *Personal relationships during adolescence: Advances in adolescent development* (Vol. 3, pp. 7–36). Thousand Oaks, CA: Sage.

Collins, W. A., & Sroufe, L. A. (1999). Capacity for intimate relationships: A developmental construction. In W. Furman, B. B. Brown, & C. Feiring (Eds.), *The development of romantic relationships in adolescence* (pp. 125–145). Cambridge, UK: Cambridge University Press.

Comings, D. E., Muhleman, D., Johnson, J. P., & MacMurray, J. P. (2002). Parent-daughter transmission of the androgen receptor gene as an explanation of the effect of father absence on age of menarche. *Child Development, 73*, 1046–1051.

Committee on the Prevention of Reading Difficulties in Young Children. (1998). *Preventing reading difficulties in young children*. Washington, DC: National Academy Press.

Community programs to promote youth development. (2002). Washington, DC: National Academy Press. Retrieved March 21, 2005, from http://books.nap.edu/books/0309072751/html/index.html

Conant, J. B. (1959/1967). *The American high school today: A first report to interested citizens*. New York: McGraw-Hill.

Condon, R. G. (1987). *Inuit youth: Growth and change in the Canadian Arctic*. New Brunswick, NJ: Rutgers University Press.

Conger, K. J., & Conger, R. D. (1994). Differential parenting and change in sibling differences in delinquency. *Journal of Family Psychology, 8*, 287–302.

Connell, R. (1996). Teaching the boys: New research on masculinity and gender strategies for schools. *Teachers College Record, 98*, 206–235.

Conner, D. B., Knight, D. K., & Cross, D. R. (1997). Mothers' and fathers' scaffolding of their 2-year-olds during problem-solving and literacy interactions. *British Journal of Developmental Psychology, 15*, 323–338.

Connolly, J., Craig, W., Goldberg, A., & Pepler, D. (2004). Mixed-gender groups, dating, and romantic relationships in early adolescence. *Journal of Research on Adolescence, 14*, 185–207.

Connolly, J., Furman, W., & Konarski, R. (2000). The role of peers in the emergence of heterosexual romantic relationships in adolescence. *Child Development, 71*, 1395–1408.

Connolly, J., & Goldberg, A. (1999). Romantic relationships in adolescence: The role of friends and peers in their emergence and development. In W. Furman, B. B. Brown, & C. Feiring (Eds.), *The development of romantic relationships in adolescence* (pp. 266–290). Cambridge, UK: Cambridge University Press.

Constantine, M. G., Erickson, C. D., Banks, R. W., & Timberlake, T. L. (1998). Challenges to the career development of urban racial and ethnic minority youth: Implications for vocational intervention. *Journal of Multicultural Counseling & Development, 26*(2), 82–95.

Conturo, T., Lori, N., Cull, T., Akbudak, E., Snyder, A., & Shimony, J., et al. (1999). Tracking neuronal fiber pathways in the living human brain. *Proceedings of the National Academy of Sciences of the United States of America, 96*, 10422–10427.

Cooley, C. H. (1902). *Human nature and the social order*. New York: Charles Scribner and Sons.

Cooper, C. R. (1999). Multiple selves, multiple worlds: Cultural perspectives on individuality and connectedness in adolescent development. In A. S. Masten (Ed.), *Cultural processes in child development* (pp. 25–57). Mahwah, NJ: Erlbaum.

Cooper, C. R., Grotevant, H. D., & Condon, S. M. (1983). Individuality and connectedness in the family as a context for adolescent identity formation and role-taking skill. *New Directions for Child Development, 22*, 43–59.

Cooper, C. R., Jackson, J. F., Azmitia, M., & Lopez, E. M. (1998). Multiple selves, multiple worlds: Three useful strategies for research with ethnic minority youth on identity relationships, and opportunity structures. In V. C. McLoyd & L. Steinberg (Eds.), *Studying minority adolescents: Conceptual, methodological, and theoretical issues* (pp. 111–125). Mahwah, NJ: Erlbaum.

Cooper, H. M., Jackson, K., & Nye, B. A. (2001). A model of homework's influence on the performance evaluations of elementary school students. *Journal of Experimental Education, 69*, 181–199.

Cooper, H. M., Lindsay, J. J., & Nye, B. (2000). Homework in the home: How student, family, and parenting-style differences relate to the homework process. *Contemporary Educational Psychology, 25*, 464–487.

Coopersmith, S. (1967). *The antecedents of self-esteem*. San Francisco: Freeman.

Corbin, C. B., & Pangrazi, R. (2000). *Physical activity for children: A statement of guidelines* (pp. 1–21). Reston, VA: Council for Physical Education for Children (COPEC) of the National Association for Sport and Physical Education (NASPE).

Cota-Robles, S., Neiss, M., & Rowe, D. C. (2002). The role of puberty in violent and nonviolent delinquency among Anglo American, Mexican American, and African American boys. *Journal of Adolescent Research, 17*, 364–376.

Côté, J. E. (2000a). The Mead-Freeman controversy in review. *Journal of Youth and Adolescence, 29*, 525–538.

Côté, J. E. (2000b). *Arrested development: The changing nature of maturity and identity.* New York: New York University Press.

Côté, J. E., & Allahar, A. L. (1996). *Generation on hold: Coming of age in the late twentieth century.* New York: New York University Press.

Côté, J. E., & Levine, C. G. (2002). *Identity formation, agency, and culture: A social psychological synthesis.* Mahwah, NJ: Erlbaum.

Coupland, D. (1991). *Generation X: Tales for an accelerated culture.* New York: St. Martin's Press.

Cowan, N., Nugent, L. D., Elliott, E. M., Ponomarev, I., & Saults, J. S. (1999). The role of attention in the development of short-term memory: Age differences in the verbal span of apprehension. *Child Development, 70*, 1082–1097.

Cowan, P. A., Powell, D., & Cowan, C. P. (1998). Parenting interventions: A family systems perspective. In W. Damon (Series Ed.) & N. Eisenberg (Vol. Ed.), *Handbook of child psychology: Vol. 3. Social emotional and personality development* (5th ed., pp. 3–72). New York: Wiley.

Coyle, K. K., Basen-Enquist, K. M., Kirby, D. B., Parcel, G. S., Banspach, S. W., Harrist, R. B., et al. (1999). Short-term impact safer choices: A multi-component school-based HIV, other STD, and pregnancy prevention program. *Journal of School Health, 69*, 181–188.

Crain, W. (2000). *Theories of development: Concepts and applications* (4th ed.) Upper Saddle River, NJ: Prentice Hall.

Cratty, B. J. (1986). *Perceptual and motor development in infants and children* (3rd ed.). Englewood Cliffs, NJ: Prentice Hall.

Creswell, J. W., & Maietta, R. C. (2002). Qualitative research. In D. C. Miller & N. J. Salkind (Eds.), *Handbook of research design and social measurement* (6th ed., pp. 145–194). Thousand Oaks, CA: Sage.

Creusere, M. A. (2000). A developmental test of theoretical perspectives on the understanding of verbal irony: Children's recognition of allusion and pragmatic insincerity. *Metaphor & Symbol, 15*, 29–45.

Crews, F. T., Braun, C. J., Hoplight, B., Switzer, R. C., & Knapp, D. J. (2000). Binge ethanol consumption causes differential brain damage in young adolescent rats compared with adult rats. *Alcoholism: Clinical and Experimental Research, 24*, 1712–1723.

Crick, N. R. (1996). The role of overt aggression, relational aggression, and prosocial behavior in the prediction of children's future social adjustment. *Child Development*, 67, 2317–2327.

Crick, N. R., & Dodge, K. A. (1994). A review and reformulation of social information-processing mechanisms in children's social adjustment. *Psychological Bulletin, 115*(1), 74–101.

Crick, N. R., & Dodge, K. A. (1999). "Superiority" is in the eye of the beholder: A comment on Sutton, Smith and Swettenham. *Social Development, 8*, 128–131.

Crick, N. R., & Grotpeter, J. K. (1995). Relational aggression, gender, and social-psychological adjustment. *Child Development, 66*, 710–722.

Criss, M. M., Shaw, D. S., & Ingoldsby, E. M. (2003). Mother-son positive synchrony in middle childhood: Relation to antisocial behavior. *Social Development, 12*, 379–400.

Crockett, L. J., & Crouter, A. C. (1995). *Pathways through adolescence: Individual development in relation to social contexts.* Mahwah, NJ: Erlbaum.

Crockett, L. J., Shanahan, M. J., & Jackson-Newsom, J. (2000). Rural youth: Ecological and life course perspectives. In R. Montemayor, G. R. Adams & T. P. Gulotta (Eds.), *Adolescent diversity in ethnic, economic, and cultural contexts* (pp. 43–74). Thousand Oaks, CA: Sage.

Croll, J., Neumark-Sztainer, D., Story, M., & Ireland, M. (2002). Prevalence and risk and protective factors related to disordered eating behaviors among adolescents: Relationship to gender and ethnicity. *Journal of Adolescent Health, 31*, 166–175.

Crosby, R. A., & Miller, K. S. (2002). Family influences on adolescent females' sexual health. *Handbook of women's sexual and reproductive health* (pp. 113–127). New York: Kluwer Academic/Plenum.

Crosnoe, R. (2000). Friendships in childhood and adolescence: The life course and new directions. *Social Psychology Quarterly, 63*, 377–391.

Crosnoe, R., & Needham, B. (2004). Holism, contextual variability, and the study of friendships in adolescent development. *Child Development, 75*, 265–279.

Crouter, A. C., Helms-Erikson, H., Updegraff, K., & McHale, S. M. (1999). Conditions underlying parents' knowledge about children's daily lives in middle childhood: Between- and within-family comparisons. *Child Development, 70*, 246–259.

Csikszentmihalyi, M. (1990). *Flow: The psychology of optimal experience.* New York: Harper & Row.

Csikszentmihalyi, M., & Rathunde, K. (1992). The measurement of flow in everyday life: Toward a theory of emergent motivation. In S. Harter, J. S. Eccles, & L. L. Carstensen (Eds.), *Developmental perspectives on motivation* (pp. 57–97). Lincoln, NB: University of Nebraska Press.

Cui, M., Conger, R., Bryant, C. M., & Elder, G. H. (2002). Parental behavior and the quality of adolescent friendships: A social-contextual perspective. *Journal of Marriage and Family, 64*, 676–689.

Cummings, E. M., Braungart-Rieker, J. M., & du Rocher-Scudlich, T. (2003). Emotion and personality development in childhood. In R. M. Lerner & M. A. Easterbrook (Eds.), *Handbook of psychology: Vol. 6. Developmental psychology* (pp. 211–239). New York: Wiley.

Cunningham, M. (1999). African-American adolescent males' perceptions of their community resources and constraints: A longitudinal analysis. *Journal of Community Psychology, 27*, 569–588.

Cunningham, M., & Spencer, M. B. (2000). Conceptual and methodological issues in studying minority adolescents. In R. Montemayor, G. R. Adams, & T. R. Gulotta (Eds.), *Adolescent diversity in ethnic, economic, and cultural contexts* (pp. 235–257). Thousand Oaks, CA: Sage.

Curry, C., & Trew, K. (1994). The effect of life domains on girls' possible selves. *Adolescence, 113*, 133–151.

Curtis, W. J., & Nelson, C. A. (2003). Toward building a better brain: Neurobehavioral outcomes, mechanisms, and processes of environmental enrichment. In S. S. Luthar (Ed.), *Resilience and vulnerability: Adaptation in the context of childhood adversities* (pp. 463–488). London: Cambridge University Press.

Dadisman, K., Vandell, D. L., & Pierce, K. (2002). *Experience sampling provides a window into after-school program experiences.* Paper presented at the Biennial Meeting of the Society for Research on Adolescence, New Orleans, April 14, 2002.

Dahl, R. E. (2001). Affect regulation, brain development, and behavioral/emotional health in adolescence. *CNS Spectrums, 6*, 60–72.

Dahl, R. E., & Lewin, D. S. (2002). Pathways to adolescent health, sleep regulation, and behavior. *Journal of Adolescent Health, 31*, 175–184.

Damon, W. (1975). Early conceptions of positive justice as related to the development of logical operations. *Child Development, 46*, 301–312.

Damon, W. (1983a). *Social and personality development.* New York: Norton.

Damon, W. (1983b). Adolescent identity and the consolidation of self. *Social and personality development: Infancy through adolescence* (pp. 307–347). New York: Norton.

Damon, W., & Hart, D. (1988). *Self-understanding in childhood and adolescence.* New York: Cambridge University Press.

Damon, W., Menon, J., & Bronk, K. C. (2003). The development of purpose during adolescence. *Applied Developmental Science, 7*, 119–128.

Darling, N., & Steinberg, L. (1993). Parenting style as context: An integrative model. *Psychological Bulletin, 113*, 487–496.

D'Augelli, A. R. (1996). Enhancing the development of lesbian, gay, and bisexual youths. In E. D. Rothblum & L. A. Bond (Eds.), *Preventing heterosexism and homophobia* (pp. 124–150). Thousand Oaks, CA: Sage.

D'Augelli, A. R., & Herschberger, S. (1993). Lesbian, gay, and bisexual youths in community settings: Personal challenges and mental health problems. *American Journal of Community Psychology, 21*, 421–448.

D'Augelli, A. R., & Patterson, C. J. (Eds.) (2001). *Lesbian, gay, and bisexual identities and youth: Psychological perspectives.* New York: Oxford University Press.

Darwin, C. (1859). *On the origin of species by means of natural selection.* London: John Murray.

Davey, M., Eaker, D. G., Fish, L. S., & Klock, K. (2003). Ethnic identity in an American White minority group. *Identity: An International Journal of Theory and Research, 3*(2), 143–158.

Davis, E. A. (2003). Prompting middle school science students for productive reflection: Generic and directed prompts. *The Journal of the Learning Sciences, 12*, 91–142.

Davis, G. A. (2001). Point to point: Turning points to Turning Points 2000. In V. A. Anfara (Ed.), *The handbook of research in middle level education* (pp. 215–239). Greenwich, CT: IAP.

Davis, N. J. (1999). *Youth crisis: Growing up in the high-risk society.* Westport, CT: Praeger.

Davis, S. S., & Davis, D. A. (1989). *Adolescence in a Moroccan town.* New Brunswick, NJ: Rutgers University Press.

Davis-Kean, P. E., & Sandler, H. M. (2001). A meta-analysis of measures of self-esteem for young children: A framework for future measures. *Child Development, 72*(3), 887–906.

De Bellis, M. D., Clark, D. B., Beers, S. R., Soloff, P. H., Boring, A. M., Hall, J., et al. (2000). Hippocampal volume in adolescent-onset alcohol use disorders. *American Journal of Psychiatry, 157*, 737–744.

De Bellis, M. D., & Keshavan, M. S. (2003). Sex differences in brain maturation in maltreatment-related pediatric posttraumatic stress disorder. *Neuroscience and Biobehavioral Reviews, 27*, 103–117.

De Bellis, M. D., Keshavan, M. S., Clark, D. B., Casey, B. J., Giedd, J. N., Boring, A. M., Frustaci, K., & Ryan, N. D. (1999). Developmental traumatology part II: Brain development. *Biological Psychiatry, 45*, 1271–1284.

De Bellis, M. D., Keshaven, M. S., & Harenski, K. A. (2001). Anterior cingulated *N*-acetylaspartate/creatine ratios during clonidine treatment in a maltreated child with post-traumatic stress disorder. *Journal of Child and Adolescent Psychopharmacology, 11*, 311–316.

Deci, E. L., & Ryan, R. M. (1985). *Intrinsic motivation and self-determination in human behavior.* New York: Plenum.

Delaney, C. H. (1995). Rites of passage in adolescence. *Adolescence, 30*, 891–897.

Demaray, M. K., Ruffalo, S. L., Carlson, J., & Busse, R. T. (1995). Social skills assessment: A comparative evaluation of six published rating scales. *School Psychology Review, 24*, 648–671.

deMause, L. (1995). *The history of childhood.* Northville, NJ: Jason Aronson.

Demo, D. H., & Savin-Williams, R. C. (1992). Self-concept stability and change during adolescence. In R. P. Lipka & T. M. Brinthaupt (Eds.), *Self-perspectives across the life span* (pp. 116–148). Albany, NY: State University of New York.

Dempster, F. N. (1981). Memory span: Sources of individual and developmental differences. *Psychological Bulletin, 89*, 63–100.

Dempster, F. N. (1995). Interference and inhibition in cognition: An historical perspective. In F. N. Dempster & C. J. Brainerd (Eds.), *Interference and inhibition in cognition* (pp. 3–26). San Diego, CA: Academic Press.

Denizet-Lewis, B. (2004, May 30). Friends, friends with benefits, and the benefits of the local mall. *The New York Times Magazine*, 30–35, 54, 56–58.

Denzin, N. K., & Lincoln, Y. S. (Eds.). (2000). *Handbook of qualitative research* (2nd ed.). Thousand Oaks, CA: Sage.

DeReus, L. A., Few, A. M., & Blume, L. B. (2005). Multicultural and critical race feminisms: Theorizing families in the third wave. In A. Acock, K. Allen, V. Bengtson, D. Klein, & P. Dilworth-Anderson (Eds.), *Sourcebook of family theory and research* (pp. 447–468). Thousand Oaks, CA: Sage.

Diamond, L. M. (1998). The development of sexual orientation among adolescent and young adult women. *Developmental Psychology, 34*, 1085–1095.

Diamond, L. M. (2003). Love matters: Romantic relationships among sexual-minority adolescents. In P. Florsheim (Ed.), *Adolescent romantic relations and sexual behavior: Theory, research, and practical implications* (pp. 85–108). Mahwah, NJ: Erlbaum.

Diamond, L. M., & Savin-Williams, R. C. (2000). Explaining diversity in the development of same-sex sexuality among young women. *Journal of Social Issues, 56*, 297–313.

Diamond, L. M., & Savin-Williams, R. C. (2003a). The intimate relationships of sexual-minority youths. In G. R. Adams & M. D. Berzonsky (Eds.), *Blackwell handbook of adolescence* (pp. 393–412). Malden, MA: Blackwell.

Diamond, L. M., & Savin-Williams, R. C. (2003b). Gender and sexual identity. In R. M. Lerner, F. Jacobs, & D. Wertlieb (Eds.), *Handbook of applied developmental science: Vol. 1. Applying developmental sciences for youth and families: Historical and theoretical foundations* (pp. 101–121). Thousand Oaks, CA: Sage.

Diamond, M. C., & Hopson, J. (1998). *Magic trees of the mind: How to nurture your child's intelligence, creativity, and healthy emotions from birth through adolescence*. New York: Dutton.

Diamond, M. C., Krech, D., & Rosenzweig, M. R. (1964). The effects of an enriched environment on the histology of the rat cerebral cortex. *Journal of Comparative Neurology, 123*, 111–120.

Dick, D. M., Rose, R. J., Pulkkinen, L., & Kaprio, J. (2001). Measuring puberty and understanding its impact: A longitudinal study of adolescent twins. *Journal of Youth and Adolescence, 30*, 385–399.

Dinkmeyer, D., & McKay, G. (1989). *The parents' handbook*. Circle Pines, MN: American Guidance Service.

Diorio, J. A., & Munro, J. (2003). What does puberty mean to adolescents? Teaching and learning about bodily functions. *Sex Education, 3*, 119–131.

Dishion, T. J., Andrews, D. W., & Crosby, L. (1995). Antisocial boys and their friends in early adolescence: Relationship characteristics, quality, and friendship processes. *Child Development, 66*, 139–151.

Dishion, T. J., & Bullock, B. M. (2002). Parenting and adolescent problem behavior: An ecological analysis of the nurturance hypothesis. In J. G. Borkowski, S. L. Ramey, & M. Bristol-Power (Eds.), *Parenting and the child's world: Influences on academic, intellectual, and social-emotional development* (pp. 231–249). Mahwah, NJ: Erlbaum.

Dishion, T. J., McCord, J., & Poulin, F. (1999). When interventions harm: Peer groups and problem behavior. *American Psychologist, 54*, 755–764.

Dishion, T. J., & McMahon, R. J. (1998). Parental monitoring and the prevention of child and adolescent problem behavior: A conceptual and empirical foundation. *Clinical Child and Family Psychology Review, 1*, 61–75.

Dobkin, P. L., Tremblay, R. E., Masse, L. C., & Vitaro, F. (1995). Individual and peer characteristics in predicting boys' early onset of substance abuse: A seven-year longitudinal study. *Child Development, 66*, 1198–1214.

Dodge, K. A., & Petit, G. S. (2003). A biopsychosocial model of the development of chronic behavior conduct problems in adolescence. *Developmental Psychology, 39*, 349–371.

Donovan, P. (1995). *Politics of blame—family planning and the poor*. New York: Alan Guttmacher Institute.

Dowdney, L., Skuse, D., Morris, K., & Pickles, A. (1998). Short normal children and environmental disadvantage: A longitudinal study of growth and cognitive development from 4 to 11 years. *Journal of Child Psychology & Psychiatry, 39*, 1017–1029.

Dowling, E. M., Getsdottic, S., Anderson, P. M., von Eye, A., & Lerner, R. M. (2004). Structural relations among spirituality, religiosity, and thriving in adolescence. *Applied Developmental Science, 8*(1), 7–16.

Doyle, A. B., Brendgen, M., Markiewicz, D., & Kamkar, K. (2003). Family relationships as moderators of the association between romantic relationships and adjustment in early adolescence. *Journal of Early Adolescence, 23*, 316–340.

Drewnowski, A. (2004). Obesity and the food environment: Dietary energy density and diet costs. *American Journal of Preventive Medicine, 27*, 154–162.

Dryfoos, J. D. (1990). *Adolescents at risk: Prevalence and prevention*. New York: Oxford University Press.

Dryfoos, J. D. (1997). The prevalence of problem behaviors: Implications for programs. In R. P. Weissberg & T. P. Gulotta (Eds.), *Healthy children 2010: Enhancing children's wellness*. Thousand Oaks, CA: Sage.

Dryfoos, J. D. (2000). *Evaluation of community schools: Findings to date*. Washington, DC: Coalition for Community Schools. Retrieved December 19, 2002, from http://www.communityschools.org

Dubas, J. S., & Peterson, A. C. (1996). Geographical distance from parents and adjustment during adolescence and young adulthood. In J. A. Graber & J. S. Dubas (Eds.), *Leaving home: Understanding the transition to adulthood. New Directions for Child and Adolescent Development*, No. 71 (pp. 3–20). San Francisco: Jossey-Bass.

Dubé, E. M., & Savin-Williams, R. C. (1999). Sexual identity development among ethnic sexual-minority male youths. *Developmental Psychology, 35*(6), 1389–1398.

DuBois, D. L., Feiner, R. D., Brand, S., Adin, A. M., & Evans, E. G. (1992). A prospective study of life stress, social support, and adaptation in early adolescence. *Child Development, 63*, 542–57.

DuBois, D. L., Lockerd, E. M., Reach, K., & Parra, G. R. (2003). Effective strategies for esteem-enhancement: What do young adolescents have to say? *Journal of Early Adolescence, 23*, 405–434.

Ducharme, J., Doyle, A. B., & Markiewicz, D. (2002). Attachment security with mother and father: Associations with adolescents' reports of interpersonal behavior with parents and peers. *Journal of Social and Personal Relationships, 19*(2), 203–313.

Duncan, G. J., & Brooks-Gunn, J. (2000). Family poverty, welfare reform, and child development. *Child Development, 71*, 188–196.

Dunkel, C. S., & Anthis, K. S. (2001). The role of possible selves in identity formation: A short-term longitudinal study. *Journal of Adolescence, 24*, 765–776.

Dunlop, S. A., Archer, M. A., Quinlivan, J. A., Beazley, L. D., & Newnham, J. P. (1997). Repeated prenatal corticosteroids delay myelination in the ovine contral nervous system. *Journal of Maternal-Fetal Medicine, 6*, 309–313.

Dunn, M. S., Eddy, J. M., Wang, M. Q., Nagy, S., Perko, M. A., & Bartee, R. T. (2001). The influence of significant others on attitudes, subjective norms and intentions regarding dietary supplement use among adolescent athletes. *Adolescence, 36*, 583–591.

Dunphy, D. C. (1963). The social structure of urban adolescent peer groups. *Sociometry, 26*, 230–246.

Durham, M. G. (1998). Dilemmas of desire: Representations of adolescent sexuality in two teen magazines. *Youth and Society, 29*, 369–389.

Durham, M. G. (2003). Girls, media, and the negotiation of sexuality: A study of race, class, and gender in adolescent peer groups. In J. M. Henslin (Ed.), *Down to earth sociology: Introductory readings* (pp. 332–348). New York: Free Press.

Durkin, K. (1995). *Developmental social psychology: From infancy to old age*. London: Blackwell.

Dusek, J. B., & McIntyre, J. G. (2003). Self-concept and self-esteem development. In G. R. Adams & M. D. Berzonsky (Eds.), *Blackwell handbook of adolescence* (pp. 290–309). Malden, MA: Blackwell.

Duvall, E. (1957). *Family development*. Philadelphia: Lippincott.

Dwairy, M. (2004). Internal-structural validity of the *Objective Measure of Ego Identity Status* among Arab adolescents. *Identity: An International Journal of Theory and Research, 4*, 133–144.

Eaton, W. O., McKeen, N. A., & Campbell, D. W. (2001). The waxing and waning of movement: Implications for psychological development. *Developmental Review, 21*, 205–223.

Eccles, J. S. (1987). Adolescence: Gateway to gender-role transcendence. In D. B. Carter (Ed.), *Current conceptions of sex roles and sex typing: Theory and research* (pp. 225–241). New York: Praeger.

Eccles, J. S. (1992). School and family effects on the ontogeny of children's interests, self-perceptions, and activity choices. In S. Harter, J. S. Eccles, & L. L. Carstensen (Eds.), *Developmental perspectives on motivation* (pp. 145–208). Lincoln, NE: University of Nebraska Press.

Eccles, J., Barber, B., Jozefowicz, D., Malenchuk, O., & Vida, M. (1999). Self-evaluations of competence, task values, and self-esteem. In N. G. Johnson, M. C. Roberts, & J. Worell (Eds.), *Beyond appearance: A new look at adolescent girls* (pp. 53–83). Washington, DC: American Psychological Association.

Eccles, J., & Bryan, J. (1994). Adolescence: Critical crossroad in the path of gender-role development. In M. R. Stevenson (Ed.), *Gender roles through the lifespan: A multidisciplinary perspective* (pp. 11–147). Muncie, IN: Ball State University Press.

Eccles, J. S., & Buchanan, C. M. (1996). School transitions in early adolescence: What are we doing to our young people? In J. Graber, J. Brooks-Gunn, & A. Petersen (Eds.), *Transitions through adolescence: Interpersonal domains and context* (pp. 251–284). Mahwah, NJ: Erlbaum.

Eccles, J. S., & Harold, R. D. (1993). Parent-school involvement during the early adolescent years. *Teachers College Record, 94*, 560–587.

Eccles, J. S., Midgley, C., Wigfield, A., Miller Buchanan, C., Rueman, D., Flanagan, C., et al. (1997). Development during adolescence: The impact of stage-environment fit on young adolescents' experiences in schools and in families. *American Psychologist, 48*, 90–101.

Eccles, J. S., & Wigfield, A. (2002). Motivational beliefs, values, and goals. *Annual Review of Psychology, 53*, 109–132.

Eccles, J. S., Wigfield, A., & Byrnes, J. (2003). Cognitive development in adolescence. In R. M. Lerner, M. A. Easterbrook, & J. Mistry (Eds.), *Handbook of psychology*: Vol. 6. *Developmental psychology* (pp. 325–350). New York: Wiley.

Eccles, J. S., Wigfield, A., & Schiefele, U. (1998). Motivation to succeed. In N. Eisenberg (Ed.), *Handbook of child psychology: Vol. 3. Social, emotional, and personality development* (5th ed., pp. 1017–1095). New York: Wiley.

Eccles-Parsons, J., Adler, T. F., Futterman, R., Goff, S. B., Kaczala, C. M., Meece, J. L., & Midgley, C. (1983). Expectancies, values, and academic behaviors. In J. T. Spence (Ed.), *Achievement and achievement motivation* (pp. 75–146). San Francisco: Freeman.

Economos, C. D. (2001). Less exercise now, more disease later? The critical role of childhood exercise interventions in reducing chronic disease burden. *Nutrition in Clinical Care, 4*, 306–313.

Eder, D. (1995). *School talk: Gender and adolescent culture.* Rutgers, NJ: Rutgers University Press.

Egan, S. K., & Perry, D. G. (2001). Gender identity: A multidimensional analysis with implications for psychosocial adjustment. *Developmental Psychology, 37,* 451–463.

Eichhorn, D. H. (1966). *The middle school.* New York: Center for Applied Research in Education.

Eichhorn, D. H. (1980). The school. In M. Johnson (Ed.), *Toward adolescence: The middle school years, 79th yearbook of the National Society for the Study of Education.* Chicago: National Society for the Study of Education.

Eisenberg, N., & Fabes, R. A. (1998). Prosocial development. In W. Damon & N. Eisenberg (Eds.), *Handbook of child psychology: Vol. 3. Social emotional and personality development* (5th ed., pp. 701–778). New York: Wiley.

Eisenberg, N., Fabes, R. A., Karbon, M., Murphy, B. C., Wosinski, M., Polazzi, L., Carlo, G., & Juhnke, C. (1996). The relations of children's dispositional prosocial behavior to emotionality, regulation, and social functioning. *Child Development, 67,* 974–992.

Eisenberg, N., Guthrie, I. K., Murphy, B. C., Shepard, S. A., Cumberland, A., & Carlo, G. (1999). Consistency and development of prosocial dispositions: A longitudinal study. *Child Development, 70,* 1360–1372.

Elder, G. H., Jr. (1998). The life course and human development. In W. Damon (Series Ed.) & R. M. Lerner (Vol. Ed.), *Handbook of child psychology: Vol. 1. Theoretical models of human development* (5th ed., pp. 939–991). New York: Wiley.

Elder, G. H., Jr., & Conger, R. D. (2000). *Children of the land: Adversity and success in rural America.* Chicago: University of Chicago Press.

Elicker, J., Englund, M., & Sroufe, A. L. (1992). Predicting peer competence and peer relationships in childhood from early parent-child relationships. In R. D. Parke & G. W. Ladd (Eds.), *Family-peer relationships: Models of linkage* (pp. 71–106). Hillsdale, NJ: Erlbaum.

Elkind, D. (1967). Egocentrism in adolescence. *Child Development, 38,* 1025–1034.

Elkind, D. (1978). *The child's reality: Three developmental themes.* Hillsdale, NJ: Erlbaum.

Elkind, D. (1985). Egocentrism, redux. *Developmental Review, 5,* 218–226.

Elkind, D. (1997). *All grown up and no place to go: Teenagers in crisis* (Rev. ed.). New York: Perseus.

Ellis, B. J. (2005). Determinants of pubertal timing: An evolutionary developmental approach. In *Origins of the social mind: Evolutionary psychology and child development* (pp. 164–188). New York: Guilford Press.

Ellis, B. J., Bates, J. E., Dodge, K. A., Fergusson, D. M., Horwood, J. L., et al. (2003). Does father absence place daughters at special risk for early sexual activity and teenage pregnancy? *Child Development, 74,* 801–821.

Ellis, B. J., & Garber, J. (2000). Psychosocial antecedents of variation in girls' pubertal timing: Maternal depression, stepfather presence, and marital and family stress. *Child Development, 71,* 485–501.

Ellis, B. J., McFayden-Ketchum, S., Dodge, K. A., Pettit, G. S., & Bates, J. E. (1999). Quality of early family relationships and individual differences in the timing of pubertal maturation in girls: A longitudinal test of an evolutionary model. *Journal of Personality and Social Psychology, 77,* 387–401.

Engels, R., Finkenauer, C., Meeus, W., & Deloic, M. (2001). Parental attachment and adolescents' emotional adjustment: The association with social skills and relational competence. *Journal of Counseling Psychology, 48,* 428–439.

Erikson, E. H. (1950). *Childhood and society.* New York: W. W. Norton.

Erikson, E. H. (1968). *Identity, youth, and crisis.* New York: W. W. Norton.

Erkut, S., Marx, F., Fields, J. P., & Sing, R. (1999). Raising confident and competent girls: One size does not fit all. In L. A. Peplau, S. C. DeBro, R. C. Veniegas, & P. L. Taylor (Eds.), *Gender, culture, and ethnicity: Current research about women and men* (pp. 83–101). Mountain View, CA: Mayfield.

Erkut, S., Szalacha, L. A., García Coll, C., & Alarcón, O. (2000). Puerto Rican early adolescents' self-esteem patterns. *Journal of Research on Adolescence, 10*(3), 339–364.

Ernest, P. (2000). Teaching and learning mathematics. In V. Koshy, P. Ernest, & R. Casey (Eds.), *Mathematics for primary teachers.* New York: Routledge.

Espelage, D. L., & Asidao, C. S. (2002). Conversations with middle school students about bullying and victimization: Should we be concerned? In R. A. Geffner, M. Loring, & C. Young (Eds.), *Bullying behavior: Current issues, research, and interventions* (pp. 49–62). New York: Haworth.

Evans, M. A., Whigham, M., & Wang, M. C. (1995). The effect of a role model project upon the attitudes of ninth-grade science students. *Journal of Research in Science Teaching, 32,* 195–204.

Ewing, M. E., Gano-Overway, L. A., Branta, C. F., & Seefeldt, V. D. (2002). The role of sports in youth development. In M. Gatz & M. A. Messner (Eds.), *Paradoxes of youth and sport* (pp. 31–47). Albany, NY: State University of New York Press.

Fagan, J., & Zimring, F. (Eds.). (2000). *The changing borders of juvenile justice: Transfer of adolescents to the criminal court.* Chicago: University of Chicago Press.

Fahrmeier, E. D. (1978). The development of concrete operations among the Hausa. *Journal of Cross-Cultural Psychology, 9,* 23–44.

Faigenbaum, A., Westcott, W., Michell, L., Outerbridge, A., Long, C., LaRosa Loud, R., & Zaichkowsky, L. (1996). The effects of strength training and detraining on children. *Journal of Strength and Conditioning Research, 10*(2), 109–114.

Faircloth, B. S., & Hamm, J. V. (2005). Sense of belonging among high school students representing 4 ethnic groups. *Journal of Youth and Adolescence, 34,* 293–309.

Farkas, G., & Beron, K. (2004). The detailed age trajectory of oral vocabulary knowledge: Differences by class and race. *Social Science Research, 33*, 464–497.

Fashola, O. S. (1998). *Review of extended-day and after-school programs and their effectiveness.* Report No. 24, Center for Research on the Education of Students Placed At-Risk, Johns Hopkins University.

Fassler, A. L. C., & Bonjour, J. P. (1995). Osteoporosis as a pediatric problem. *Pediatric Clinics of North America, 42*, 811–824.

Fauth, R. C., Leventhal, T., & Brooks-Gunn, J. (2005). Early impacts of moving from poor to middle-class neighborhoods on low-income youth. *Journal of Applied Developmental Psychology, 26*, 415–439.

Federal Interagency Forum on Child and Family Statistics (2003). *America's children: Key national indicators on well-being, 2003.* Federal Interagency Forum on Child and Family Statistics, Washington, DC: U.S. Government Printing Office.

Feeney, J. A., Noller, P., & Roberts, N. (2001). Attachment and close relationships. In C. Hendrick & S. S. Hendrick (Eds.), *Close relationships: A sourcebook* (pp. 185–201). Thousand Oaks, CA: Sage.

Feiring, C. (1993, March). Developing concepts of romance from 13 to 18 years. In W. Furman (Chair), *Adolescent romantic relationships: A new look.* Symposium conducted at the biennial meetings of the Society for Research in Child Development, New Orleans, LA.

Feiring, C. (1999a). Gender identity and the development of romantic relationships in adolescence. In W. Furman, B. B. Brown, & C. Feiring (Eds.), *The development of romantic relationships in adolescence* (pp. 211–232). Cambridge, UK: Cambridge University Press.

Feiring, C. (1999b). Other-sex friendship networks and the development of romantic relationships in adolescence. *Journal of Youth and Adolescence, 28*, 495–512.

Feldman, D. H. (2003). Cognitive development in childhood. In R. M. Lerner, M. A. Easterbooks, & J. Mistry (Eds.), *Handbook of psychology*: Vol. 6. *Developmental psychology* (pp. 195–210). New York: Wiley.

Feldman, S. S., & Elliott, G. R. (1990). *At the threshold: The developing adolescent.* Cambridge, MA: Harvard University Press.

Fennema, E., Sowder, J., & Carpenter, T. P. (1999). Creating classrooms that promote understanding. In E. Fennema & T. A. Romberg (Eds.), *Mathematics classrooms that promote understanding* (pp. 185–199). Mahwah, NJ: Erlbaum.

Fenzel, L. M. (2000). Prospective study of changes in global self-worth and strain during the transition to middle school. *Journal of Early Adolescence, 20*, 93–116.

Ferrer-Wreder, L., Lorente, C. C., Kurtines, W., Briones, E., Bussell, J., Berman, S & Arrufat, O. (2002). Promoting identity development in marginalized youth. *Journal of Adolescent Research, 17*, 168–187.

Feshbach, N. D., & Feshbach, S. (1982). Empathy training and the regulation of aggression: Potentialities and limitations. *Academic Psychology Bulletin, 4*, 399–413.

Feshbach, N. D., & Feshbach, S. (1983). *Learning to care: Classroom activities for social and affective development.* Glenview, IL: Scott, Foresman.

Field, A., Camargo, C., Taylor, C. B., Berkey, C., Frazier, L., Gillman, M., et al. (1999). Overweight, weight concerns, and bulimic behaviors among girls and boys. *Journal of the American Academy of Adolescent Psychiatry, 38*, 754–760.

Fine, M. (1997). Sexuality, schooling, and adolescent females: The missing discourse of desire. In M. M. Gergen & S. N. Davis (Eds.), *Toward a new psychology of gender: A reader.* New York: Routledge.

Fingerson, L. (1999). Active viewing: Girls' interpretations of family television programs. *Journal of Contemporary Ethnography, 28*(4), 389–418.

Finkelstein, J. (1998). Methods, models, and measures of health-related quality of life for children and adolescents. In D. Drotar (Ed.), *Measuring health-related quality of life in children and adolescents: Implications for research and practice* (pp. 39–52). Mahwah, NJ: Erlbaum.

Finkelstein, J., Susman, E., Chinchilli, V., Kunselman, S., D'arcangelo, R., & Schwab, J. (1997). Estrogen or testosterone increases self-reported aggressive behaviors in hypogonadal adolescents. *Journal of Clinical Endocrinology and Metabolism, 82*, 2433–2438.

Finn, J. D. (1989). Withdrawing from school. *Review of Educational Research, 59*, 117–142.

Finnegan, R. A., Hodges, E. V. E., & Perry, D. C. (1996). Preoccupied and avoidant coping during middle childhood. *Child Development, 67*, 1318–1328.

Fischer, K. W., & Rose, S. P. (1994). Dynamic development of coordination of components in brain and behavior. In G. Dawson & K. Fischer (Eds.), *Human behavior and the developing brain* (pp. 3–66). New York: Guilford.

Fischer, K. W., Shaver, P., & Carnochan, P. (1990). How emotions develop and how they organize development. *Cognition and Emotion, 4*, 81–127.

Fisher, C. B., & Lerner, R. L. (1994). Foundations of applied developmental psychology. In C. B. Fisher & R. M. Lerner (Eds.), *Applied developmental psychology* (pp. 3–20). New York: McGraw-Hill.

Flavell, J. H. (2000). Development of children's knowledge about the mental world. *International Journal of Behavioral Development, 24*, 15–23.

Flavell, J. H., & Miller, P. H. (1998). Social cognition. In W. Damon (Series Ed.) & D. Kuhn & R. S. Siegler (Vol. Eds.), *Handbook of child psychology, Vol. 2. Cognition, perception, and language* (5th ed., pp. 851–898). New York: Wiley.

Flavell, J. H., Miller, P. H., & Miller, S. A. (2002). *Cognitive development* (4th ed.). Upper Saddle River, NJ: Prentice Hall.

Fletcher, A. C., Darling, N. E., Steinberg, L., & Dornbusch, S. L. (1995). The company they keep: Relation of adolescents' adjustment and behavior to their friends' perceptions of authoritative parenting in the social network. *Developmental Psychology, 31*, 300–310.

Flick, U. (2002). *An introduction to qualitative research* (2nd ed.). Thousand Oaks, CA: Sage.

Flory, R. W., & Miller, D. E. (Eds.) (2000). *Gen-X religion*. New York: Routledge.

Flouri, E., & Buchanan, A. (2002). The role of work-related skills and career role models in adolescent career maturity. *Career Development Quarterly, 51*, 36–43.

Floyd, F. J., & Stein, T. S. (2002). Sexual orientation identity formation among gay, lesbian, and bisexual youths: Multiple patterns of milestone experiences. *Journal of Research on Adolescence, 12*, 167–191.

Flum, H., & Lavi-Yudelevitch, M. (2002). Adolescents' relatedness and identity formation: A narrative study. *Journal of Social and Personal Relationships, 19*(4), 527–548.

Fonagy, P. (1999). Psychoanalytic theory from the viewpoint of attachment theory and research. In J. Cassidy & P. R. Shaver (Eds.), *Handbook of attachment: Theory, research, and clinical applications* (pp. 595–624). New York: Guilford.

Ford, D. H., & Lerner, R. M. (1992). *Developmental systems theory: An integrative approach*. Newbury Park, CA: Sage.

Foucault, M. (1978). *The history of sexuality: An introduction: Vol. 1.* (R. Hurley, Trans.). New York: Vintage. (Original work published 1976).

Fowler, J. W. (1981). *Stages of faith: The psychology of human development and the quest for meaning*. San Francisco: Harper & Row.

Fowler, J. W. (1991). Stages in faith consciousness. In F. K. Oser & W. G. Scarlett (Eds.), *Religious development in childhood and adolescence* (pp. 27–45). *New Directions for Child Development*, No. 52. San Francisco: Jossey-Bass.

Fox, C., Porter, R., & Wokler, R. (Eds.) (1995). *Inventing human science*. Berkeley, CA: University of California Press.

Fox, N. A. (Ed.) (1994). The development of emotion regulation: Biological and behavioral considerations. *Monographs of the Society for Research in Child Development, 59*(2–3, Serial No. 240).

Frank, N. C., & Kendall, S. J. (2001). Religion, risk prevention and health promotion in adolescents: A community-based approach. *Mental Health, Religion, & Culture, 4*(2), 133–148.

Franke, M. L. (2003). Fostering young children's mathematical understanding. In C. Howes (Ed.), *Teaching 4- to 8-year-olds: Literacy, math, multiculturalism, and classroom community* (pp. 93–112). Baltimore, MD: Paul H. Brooks.

Frankenberger, K. D. (2000). Adolescent egocentrism: A comparison among adolescents and adults. *Journal of Adolescence, 23*, 343–354.

Frankenberger, K. D. (2004). Adolescent egocentrism, risk perceptions, and sensation seeking among smoking and nonsmoking youth. *Journal of Adolescent Research, 19*, 576–590.

Fredriks, A. M., Van Buuren, S., Burgmeijer, R. J. F., Muelmeester, J. F., Roelien, J., Brugman, E. et al., (2000). Continuing positive secular growth change in the Netherlands 1955–1997. *Pediatric Research, 47*, 316–323.

Freedman, D. S., Kettel Khan, L., Serdula, M. K., Srinivasan, S. R., & Berenson, G. S. (2000). Secular trends in height among children during 2 decades. *Archives of Pediatrics and Adolescent Medicine, 154*, 155–161.

Freeman, H. S., & Newland, L. A. (2002). Family transitions during the adolescent transition: Implications for parenting. *Adolescence, 37*, 457–475.

Freeman, M., Csikzsentmihalyi, M., & Larson, R. (1986). Adolescence and its recollection: Towards an interpretive model of development. *Merrill-Palmer Quarterly, 52*, 167–185.

Freitag, M. K., Belsky, J., Grossmann, K., Grossmann, K. E., & Scheuerer-Englisch, H. (1996). Continuity in parent-child relationships from infancy to middle childhood and relations with friendship competence. *Child Development, 67*, 1437–1454.

French, S. A., Fulkerson, J. A., & Story, M. (2000). Increasing weight-bearing physical activity and calcium intake for bone mass growth in children and adolescents: A review of intervention trials. *Preventative Medicine, 31*, 722–731.

Frenn, M., & Malin, S. (2003). Diet and exercise in low-income culturally diverse middle school students. *Public Health Nursing, 20*, 361–368.

Freud, S. (1959). *The collected works of Sigmund Freud*. London: Hogarth Press and the Institute of Psycho-Analysis.

Frey, K. S., & Ruble, D. N. (1990). Strategies for comparative evaluation: Maintaining a sense of competence across the life span. In R. J. Sternberg & J. Kolligian (Eds.), *Competence considered* (pp. 167–189). New Haven, CT: Yale University Press.

Frey, M. C., & Detterman, D. K. (2004). Scholastic assessment or *g*?: The relationship between the Scholastic Assessment Test and general cognitive ability. *Psychological Science, 15*, 373–378.

Friedman, M. S., Silvestre, A. J., Gold, M. A., Markovic, N., Savin-Williams, R. C., Huggins, J., & Sell, R. L. (2004). Adolescents define sexual orientation and suggest ways to measure it. *Journal of Adolescence, 27*, 307–317.

Fuligni, A. J., Eccles, J. S., Barber, B. L., & Clements, P. (2001). Early adolescent peer orientation and adjustment during high school. *Developmental Psychology, 37*(1), 28–36.

Furlong, A., & Cartmel, F. (1997). *Young people and social change*. Buckingham, UK: Open University Press.

Furman, W. (2001). Working models of friendship. *Journal of Social and Personal Relationships*, 18, 583–602.

Furman, W., & Shaffer, L. (2003). The role of romantic relationships in adolescent development. In P. Florsheim (Ed.), *Adolescent romantic relations and sexual behavior: Theory, research, and practical implications* (pp. 3–22). Mahwah, NJ: Erlbaum.

Furman, W., & Simon, V. A. (1999). Cognitive representations of adolescent romantic relationships. In W. Furman, B. B. Brown, & C. Feiring (Eds.), *The development of romantic relationships in adolescence* (pp. 75–98). Cambridge, UK: Cambridge University Press.

Furman, W., Simon, V. A., Shaffer, L., & Bouchey, H. A. (2002). Adolescents' working models and styles for relationships with parents, friends, and romantic partners. *Child Development, 73*, 241–266.

Furman, W., & Wehner, E. A. (1994). Romantic views: Toward a theory of adolescent romantic relationships. In R. Montemayor, G. R. Adams, & T. P. Gulotta (Eds.), *Personal relationships during adolescence: Advances in adolescent development* (Vol. 3, pp. 168–195). Thousand Oaks, CA: Sage.

Furman, W., & Wehner, E. A. (1997). Adolescent romantic relationships: A developmental perspective. In S. Shulman & W. A. Collins (Eds.), *Romantic relationships in adolescence: Developmental perspectives* (pp. 21–36). *New Directions for Child and Adolescent Development*, No. 78. San Francisco: Jossey-Bass.

Furrow, J. L., King, P. E., & White, K. (2004). Religion and positive youth development: Identity, meaning, and prosocial concerns. *Applied Developmental Science, 8*, 17–26.

Furstenberg, F. F., Jr. (1976). *Unplanned parenthood: The social consequences of unplanned parenthood*. New York: Free Press.

Furstenberg, F. F., Jr. (2001). The sociology of adolescence and youth in the 1990s: A critical commentary. In R. M. Milardo (Ed.), *Understanding families into the new millennium: A decade in review*. Minneapolis, MN: National Council on Family Relations.

Furstenberg, F. F., Jr., Kennedy, S., McLoyd, V. C., Rumbaut, R. R., & Settersten, R. A. Jr. (2003). *Between adolescence and adulthood: Expectations about the timing of adulthood, Working Paper No. 1*, Network on Transitions to Adulthood. Retrieved August 2, 2004, from http://www.pop.upenn.edu/transad/news/between.pdf

Fury, G., Carlson. E. A., & Sroufe, L. A. (1997). Children's representations of attachment relationships in family drawings. *Child Development, 68*, 1154–1164.

Fussell, E., & Furstenberg, F. F., Jr. (2005). The transition to adulthood during the twentieth century: Race, nativity, and gender. In R. A. Settersten, Jr., F. F. Furstenberg, Jr., & R. G. Rumbaut (Eds.), *On the frontier of adulthood: Theory, research, and public policy* (pp. 29–75). Chicago: University of Chicago Press.

Gable, S., & Lutz, S. (2000). Household, parent, and child contributions to childhood obesity. *Family Relations, 49*, 293–300.

Galambos, N. L., Almeida, D. M., & Petersen, A. C. (1990). Masculinity, femininity, and sex role attitudes in early adolescence: Exploring gender identification. *Child Development, 61*, 1905–1914.

Galambos, N. L., & Costigan, C. L. (2003). Emotion and personality development in adolescence. In R. M. Lerner & M. A. Easterbrook (Eds.), *Handbook of psychology: Vol. 6. Developmental psychology* (pp. 351–372). New York: Wiley.

Galambos, N. L., & Tilton-Weaver, L. C. (2000). Adolescents' psychosocial maturity, problem behavior, and subjective age: In search of the adultoid. *Applied Developmental Science, 4*, 178–192.

Ganzel, A. K. (1999). Adolescent decision making: The influence of mood, age, and gender on the consideration of information. *Journal of Adolescent Research, 14*, 289–318.

Garbarino, J., Hammond, W. R., Mercy, J., & Yung, B. R. (2004). Community violence and children: Preventing exposure and reducing harm. In K. I. Maton & C. J. Schellenbach (Eds.), *Investing in children, youth, families, and communities: Strengths-based research and policy* (pp. 303–320). Washington, DC: American Psychological Association.

Garber, J., & Little, S. A. (2001). Emotional autonomy and adolescent adjustment. *Journal of Adolescent Research, 16*, 355–371.

García Coll, C., Lamberty, G., Jenkins, R., McAdoo, H. P., Crnic, K., Wasik, B. H., & Vasquez García, H. (1996). An integrative model for the study of developmental competencies in minority children. *Child Development, 67*, 1891–1914.

García Coll, C., & Szalacha, L. A. (2004). The multiple contexts of middle childhood. *Future of Children, 14*(2), 81–97.

Gardner, H. (1983). *Frames of mind: The theory of multiple intelligences*. New York: Basic Books.

Gardner, H. (1999). *Intelligence reframed*. New York: Basic Books.

Gardner, H., Kornhaber, M., & Wake, W. (1996). *Intelligence: Multiple perspectives*. Fort Worth, TX: Harcourt Brace.

Gardner, W., & Herman, J. (1990). Adolescents' AIDS risk taking: A rational choice perspective. In W. Gardner, S. Millstein, & B. Wilcox (Eds.), *Adolescent in the AIDS epidemic* (pp. 17–34). San Francisco: Jossey-Bass.

Garlick, D. (2002). Understanding the nature of the general factor of intelligence: The role of individual differences in neural plasticity as an explanatory mechanism. *Psychological Review, 109*, 116–136.

Garofalo, R., & Katz, E. (2001). Health care issues of gay and lesbian youth. *Journal of the American Academy of Child and Adolescent Psychiatry, 41*, 449–451.

Garrity, C., Jens, K., Porter, W., Sager, N., & Short-Camilli, C. (1995). *Bully-proofing your school: A comprehensive approach for elementary schools*. Longmount, CO: Sopris West.

Garry, J. P., Morrissey, S. L., & Whetstone, L. M. (2003). Substance use and weight loss tactics among middle school youth. *International Journal of Eating Disorders, 33*, 55–63.

Gaskins, S. (1999). Children's daily lives in a Mayan village: A case study of culturally constructed roles and activities. In A. Goncu (Ed.), *Children's engagement in the world: Sociocultural perspectives* (pp. 25–60). New York: Cambridge University Press.

Gates, G. J., & Sonenstein, F. L. (2000). Heterosexual genital sexual activity among adolescent males: 1988 and 1995. *Family Planning Perspectives, 32*, 295–297.

Gathercole, S. E. (1998). The development of memory. *Journal of Child Psychology and Psychiatry, 39*, 3–27.

Gau, S. F., & Soong, W. T. (1995). Sleep problems of junior high school students in Taipei. *Sleep, 18*, 667–673.

Gauvain, M. (2000). Reading at home and at school in the primary grades: Cultural and social influences. *Early Education and Development, 11*, 447–463.

Gavadini, C., Siega-riz, A. M., & Popkin, B. M. (2000). U.S. adolescent food intake trends from 1965 to 1996. *Archives of Diseases in Childhood, 83*, 18–24.

Ge, X., Conger, R. D., & Elder, G. H., Jr. (1996). Coming of age too early: Pubertal influences on girls' vulnerability to psychological distress. *Child Development, 67*, 3386–3400.

Ge, X., Conger, R. D., & Elder, G. H., Jr. (2001). The relation between puberty and psychological distress in adolescent boys. *Journal of Research on Adolescence, 11*, 49–70.

Ge, X., Kim, I. J., Brody, G. H., Conger, R. D., Simons, R. L., Gibbons, F. X., et al. (2003). It's about timing and change: Pubertal transition effects on symptoms of major depression among African American youths. *Developmental Psychology, 39*, 430–439.

Geary, D. C. (1998). *Male, female: The evolution of human sex differences.* Washington, DC: American Psychological Association.

Geary, D. C. (2000). Attachment, caregiving, and parental investment. *Psychological Inquiry, 11*(2), 84–86.

Geary, D. C., & Bjorkland, D. F. (2000). Evolutionary developmental psychology. *Child Development, 71*(1), 57–65.

Gergen, K. J. (1991). *The saturated self: Dilemmas of identity in contemporary life.* New York: Basic Books.

Gershoff, E. T., & Aber, J. L. (2004a) (Eds.). Special issue: Part 1: Assessing the impact of September 11th, 2001 on children, youth, and parents in the United States: Lessons from applied developmental science. *Applied Developmental Science, 8*, 106–169.

Gershoff, E. T., & Aber, J. L. (2004b) (Eds.). Special issue: Part 2: Assessing the impact of September 11th, 2001 on children, youth, and parents in the United States: Lessons from applied developmental science. *Applied Developmental Science, 8*, 172–225.

Gesell, A., & Ilg, F. L. (1943). *Infant and child in the culture of today.* New York: Harper & Row.

Gesell, A., & Ilg, F. L. (1946). *The child from five to ten.* New York: Harper & Row.

Gesell, A., Ilg, F. L., & Ames, L. B. (1956). *Youth: The years from ten to sixteen.* New York: Harper & Row.

Giannotti, F., & Cortesi, F. (2002). Sleep patterns and daytime function in adolescence: An epidemiological survey of an Italian high school student sample. In M. A. Carskadon (Ed.), *Adolescent sleep patterns: Biological, social, and psychological influences* (pp. 132–147). New York: Cambridge University Press.

Gibbons, J. L. (2000). Gender development in cross-cultural perspective. In T. S. Eckes & H. N. Trautner (Eds.), *The developmental social psychology of gender* (pp. 389–415). Mahwah, NJ: Erlbaum.

Giedd, J. N., Blumenthal, J., Jeffries, N. O., Rajapakse, J. C., Vaituzis, C., Liu, H., et al. (1999). Development of the human corpus callosum during childhood and adolescence: A longitudinal MRI study. *Progress in Neuropsychopharmacology and Biological Psychiatry, 23*, 571–588.

Giles, H. C. (2005). Three narratives of parent-educator relationships: Toward counselor *repertoires* for bridging the urban parent-school divide. *Professional School Counseling*, 8, *228–235*.

Gilliam, F. D., Jr., & Bales, S. N. (2001). Strategic frame analysis: Reframing America's youth. *Social Policy Report, Vol. 15, No. 3.* Retrieved March 21, 2005, from http://www.srcd.org/spr.html

Gilliam, J. (2002). Respecting the rights of GLBTQ youth, a responsibility of youth-serving professionals. *Transitions, 14*(4), 1–2.

Gilligan, C. (1977). In a different voice: Women's conceptions of the self and of morality. *Harvard Educational Review, 47*, 481–517.

Gilligan, C. (1982). *In a different voice: Psychological theory and women's development.* Cambridge, MA: Harvard University Press.

Gilligan, C., & Brown, L. M. (1992). *Meeting at the crossroads: Women's psychology and girls' development.* Cambridge, MA: Harvard University Press.

Gilligan, C., Lyons, N. P., & Hanmer, T. J. (1990). *Making connections: The relational worlds of adolescent girls at Emma Willard School.* Cambridge, MA: Harvard University Press.

Gilpin, E. A., Choi, W. S., Berry, C., & Pierce, J. P. (1999). How many adolescents start smoking each day in the United States? *Journal of Adolescent Health, 25*, 248–255.

Gjerde, P. F., & Onishi, M. (2000). In search of theory: The study of "ethnic groups" in developmental psychology. *Journal of Research on Adolescence, 10*, 289–298.

Glaser, D. (2000). Child abuse and neglect and the brain: A review. *Journal of Child Psychology and Psychiatry, 41*, 97–116.

Gogate, N., Giedd, J., Janson, K., & Rapoport, J. L. (2001). Brain imaging in normal and abnormal brain development: New perspectives for child psychiatry. *Clinical Neuroscience Research, 1*, 283–290.

Goldberg, J. H., Halpern-Felsher, B. L., & Millstein, S. G. (2002). Beyond invulnerability: The importance of benefits in adolescents' decision to drink alcohol. *Health Psychology, 21*, 477–484.

Goldsmith, H. H. (1993). Temperament: Variability in developing emotion systems. In M. Lewis & J. M. Haviland (Eds.), *Handbook of emotions* (pp. 353–364). New York: Guilford.

Goldstein, S. (Ed.). (1995). *Understanding and managing children's classroom behavior*. New York: Wiley.

Gollwitzer, P. N., Bayer, U., Scherer, M., & Seifert, A. E. (1999). A motivational-volitional perspective on identity development. In J. Brandtstadler & R. M. Lerner (Eds.), *Action & self-development: Theory and research through the life span* (pp. 283–314). Thousand Oaks, CA: Sage.

Gonzalez, V. (2005). Cultural, linguistic, and socioeconomic factors influencing monolingual and bilingual children's cognitive development. In V. Gonzalez and J. Tinajero (Eds.), *Review of research and practice* (Vol.3, pp. 67–104). Mahwah, NJ: Erlbaum.

Goossens, L., Beyers, W., Emmen, M., & van Aken, M. A. G. (2002). The imaginary audience and personal fable: Factor analyses and concurrent validity of the "new look" measures. *Journal of Research on Adolescence, 12*, 193–215.

Goossens, L., & Phinney, J. S. (1996). Commentary: Identity, context, and development. *Journal of Adolescence, 19*, 491–496.

Gootman, J. A. (Ed.). (2000). *After-school programs that promote child and adolescent development: Summary of a workshop*. Washington, DC: National Academy Press. Retrieved March 21, 2005, from http://books.nap.edu/books/0309071798/html/index.html

Goran, M. I., Gower, B. A., Nagy, T. R., Johnson, R. (1998). Developmental changes in energy expenditure and physical activity in children: Evidence for a decline in physical activity prior to puberty. *Pediatrics, 101*, 887–891.

Gordon, D. E. (1988). Formal operations and interpersonal and affective disturbances in adolescents. In E. D. Nannis & P. A. Cowan (Eds.), *Developmental psychopathology and its treatment* (pp. 51–72). *New Directions for Child Development*, No. 39. San Francisco: Jossey-Bass.

Gorman, R. M. (1972). *Discovering Piaget: A guide for teachers*. Oxford, UK: Merrill.

Gottfredson, L. S. (1997). Why *g* matters: The complexity of everyday life. *Intelligence, 24*, 79–132.

Gottfried, A. E., Fleming, J. S., & Gottfried, A. W. (2001). Continuity of academic intrinsic motivation from childhood through late adolescence: A longitudinal study. *Journal of Educational Psychology, 93*, 3–13.

Graber, J. A., & Brooks-Gunn, J. (2002). Adolescent girls' sexual development. In G. W. Wingood & R. J. DiClemente (Eds.), *Handbook of women's sexual and reproductive health* (pp. 21–42). New York: Kluwer Academic/Plenum.

Graber, J., Brooks-Gunn, J., & Petersen, A. (1996). Adolescent transitions in context. *Transitions through adolescence: Interpersonal domains and context* (pp. 369–383). Mahwah, NJ: Erlbaum.

Graber, J. A., Brooks-Gunn, J., & Warren, M. P. (1995). The antecedents of menarcheal age: Heredity, family environment, and stressful life events. *Child Development, 66*, 346–359.

Graber, J. A., Lewisohn, P. M., Seeley, J. R., & Brooks-Gunn, J. (1997). Is psychopathology associated with the timing of pubertal development? *Journal of the American Academy of Child and Adolescent Psychiatry, 36*, 1768–1776.

Graham, S., & Taylor, A. Z. (2002). Ethnicity, gender, and the development of achievement values. In A. Wigfield & J. S. Eccles (Eds.), *The development of achievement motivation* (pp. 121–146). San Diego, CA: Academic.

Granic, I., Dishion, T. J., & Hollenstein, T. (2003). The family ecology of adolescence: A dynamic systems perspective on normative development. In G. R. Adams & M. D. Berzonsky (Eds.), *Blackwell handbook of adolescence* (pp. 60–91). Malden, MA: Blackwell.

Granot, D., & Mayseless, O. (2001). Attachment security and adjustment to school in middle childhood. *International Journal of Behavioral Development, 25*(6), 530–541.

Grant, C. A., & Gomez, M. L. (2001). *Campus and classroom: Making schooling multicultural* (2nd ed.). Upper Saddle River, NJ: Merrill/Prentice Hall.

Grantham-McGregor, S., Ani, C., & Fernald, L. (2001). The role of nutrition in intellectual development. In R. J. Sternberg & E. L. Grigorenko (Eds.), *Environmental effects on cognitive abilities* (pp. 119–155). Mahwah, NJ: Erlbaum.

Graue, M. E., & Walsh, D. J. (1998). *Studying children in context*. Thousand Oaks, CA: Sage.

Gray, M. R., & Steinberg, L. (1999a). Unpacking authoritative parenting: Reassessing a multidimensional construct. *Journal of Marriage and the Family, 61*, 574–587.

Gray, M. R., & Steinberg, L. (1999b). Adolescent romance and the parent-child relationship: A contextual perspective. In W. Furman, B. B. Brown, & C. Feiring (Eds.), *The development of romantic relationships in adolescence* (pp. 235–265). Cambridge, UK: Cambridge University Press.

Great transitions: Preparing adolescents for a new century (1995). New York: Carnegie Corporation of New York. Retrieved March 21, 2005, from http://www.carnegie.org/sub/pubs/reports/great_transitions/gr_intro.html

Green, R. C. (1985). Potholes on the research road to sexual identity development. *Journal of Sex Research, 21*, 96–101.

Greenberg, M. T., Weissberg, R. P., O'Brien, M. U., Zins, J. E., Fredericks, L., Resnik, H., et al. (2003). Enhancing school-based prevention and youth development through coordinated social, emotional, and academic learning. *American Psychologist, 58*, 466–474.

Greenberger, E., & Steinberg, L. (1986). *When teenagers work: The psychological and social costs of adolescent employment*. New York: Basic Books.

Greene, M. L., & Way, N. (2005). Self-esteem trajectories among ethnic minority adolescents: A growth curve analysis of the patterns and predictors of change. *Journal of Research on Adolescence, 15*, 151–178.

Greener, S., & Crick, N. R. (1999). Normative beliefs about prosocial behavior in middle childhood: What does it mean to be nice? *Social Development, 8*(3), 349–363.

Greeno, J. G., Collins, A., & Resnick, L. B. (1996). Cognition and learning. In D. C. Berliner & R. C. Calfee (Eds.), *Handbook of educational psychology* (pp. 15–46). New York: Macmillan.

Greenough, W., & Black, J. (1992). Induction of brain structure by experience: Substrate for cognitive development. In M. R. Gummar & C. A. Nelson (Eds.), *Minnesota symposia on child psychology: Vol. 24. Developmental behavioral neuroscience* (pp. 155–200). Hillsdale, NJ: Erlbaum.

Greenwood, D. J., & Levin, M. (Eds.). (1998). *Introduction to action research: Social research for social change*. Thousand Oaks, CA: Sage.

Greer, B., & Mulhern, G. (2002). *Making sense of data and statistics in psychology*. New York: Palgrave.

Gregory, A., & Weinstein, R. S. (2004). Connection and regulation at home and in school: Predicting growth in achievement for adolescents. *Journal of Adolescent Research, 19*, 404–427.

Gresham, F. M., & Elliott, S. N. (1990). *Social Skills Rating System manual*. Circle Pines, MN: American Guidance Service.

Griffin, R. S. (1998). *Sports in the lives of children and adolescents*. Westport, CT: Praeger.

Grigorenko, E. L., Jarvin, L., & Sternberg, R. J. (2002). School-based tests of the triarchic theory of intelligence: Three settings, three samples, three syllabi. *Contemporary Educational Psychology, 27*, 167–208.

Grigorenko, E. L., Meier, E., Lipka, J., Mohatt, G. Yanez, E., & Sternberg, R. J. (2004). Academic and practical intelligence: A case study of the Yup'ik in Alaska. *Learning and Individual Differences, 14*, 183–207.

Grissmer, D. W., Williamson, S., Kirby, S. N., & Berends, M. (1998). Exploring the rapid rise in black achievement scores in the United States (1970–1990). In U. Neisser (Ed.), *The rising curve: Long-term gains in IQ and related measures* (pp. 251–285). Washington, DC: American Psychological Association.

Grisso, T., & Schwartz, B. (2000). (Eds.). *Youth on trial: A developmental perspective on juvenile justice*. Chicago: University of Chicago Press.

Grisso, T., Steinberg, L., Woolard, J., Cauffman, E., Scott, E., Graham, S., et al. (2003). Juveniles' competence to stand trial: A comparison of adolescents' and adults' capacities as trial defendants. *Law and Human Behavior, 27*, 333–363.

Grogger, J. (1997). Incarceration-related costs of early childbearing. In R. A. Maynard (Ed.), *Kids having kids: Economic costs and social consequences of teen pregnancy* (pp. 231–256). Washington, DC: Urban Institute Press.

Grolnick, W. S., Gurland, S. T., Jacob, K. F., & Decourcey, W. (2002). The development of self-determination in middle childhood and adolescence. In A. Wigfield & J. S. Eccles (Eds.), *The development of achievement motivation* (pp. 147–171). San Diego, CA: Academic Press.

Grolnick, W., & Slowiaczek, M. (1994). Parents' involvement in children's schooling: A multidimensional conceptualization and motivational model. *Child Development, 64*, 237–252.

Grotevant, H. D., & Cooper, C. R. (1985). Patterns of interaction in family relationships and the development of identity exploration in adolescence. *Child Development, 56*, 405–428.

Growing up: W. K. Kellogg Foundation 2001 annual report. Retrieved August 1, 2002, from http://www.wkkf.org/pubs/Pub3363.pdf

Grueneich, R. (1982). The development of children's integration rules for making moral judgments. *Child Development, 53*, 887–894.

Grumbach, M. M., & Styne, D. M. (1998). Puberty: Ontogeny, neuroendocrinology, physiology, and disorders. In J. D. Wilson, D. W. Foster, & H. M. Kronenberg (Eds.), *Williams textbook of endocrinology* (pp. 1509–1625). Philadelphia: W. B. Saunders.

Grusec, J., Goodnow, J. J., & Kuczynski, L. (2000). New directions in analyses of parenting contributions to children's acquisition of values. *Child Development, 71*, 205–211.

Grusec, J. E., & Mammone, N. (1995). Features and sources of parents' attributions about themselves and their children. In N. Eisenberg (Ed.), *Social development* (pp. 49–73). Thousand Oaks, CA: Sage.

Guberman, S. R. (1999). Supportive environments for cognitive development: Illustrations from children's mathematical activities outside of school. In A. Goncu (Ed.), *Children's engagement in the world: Sociocultural perspectives* (pp. 202–227). Cambridge, UK: Cambridge University Press.

Guillame, M., Lapidus, L., Beckers, F., Lambert, A., & Bjorntop, P. (1995). Familial trends of obesity through three generations: The Belgian-Luxembourg child study. *International Journal of Obesity Related to Metabolic Disorders*, (Suppl.), *3*, S5–S9.

Guillaume, M., Lapidus, L., Bjorntorp, P., & Lambert, A. (1997). Physical activity, obesity, and cardiovascular risk factors in children: The Belgian-Luxembourg child study II. *Obesity Research, 5*, 549–556.

Gunnoe, M. L., Hetherington, E. M., & Reiss, D. (1999). Parental religiosity, parenting style, and adolescent social responsibility. *Journal of Early Adolescence, 19*, 199–225.

Guttentag, R. E. (1995). Children's associative learning: Automatic and deliberate encoding of meaningful associations. *American Journal of Psychology, 108*, 99–114.

Guttentag, R. E., Ornstein, P. A., & Siemens, L. (1987). Children's spontaneous rehearsal: Transitions in strategy acquisition. *Cognitive Development, 2*, 307–326.

Guy, J. A., & Michell, L. J. (2001). Strength training for children and adolescents. *Journal of the American Academy of Orthopaedic Surgeons. 9*(1), 29–36.

Hains, A., & Ryan, E. (1983). The development of social cognitive processes among juvenile delinquents and nondelinquent peers. *Child Development, 54*, 1536–1544.

Halberstadt, A. G., Dunsmore, J. C., Denham, S. A. (2001) Spinning the pinwheel, together: More thoughts on affective social competence. *Social Development, 10*, 130–136.

Hall, G. S. (1904). *Adolescence: Psychology and its relation to physiology, anthropology, sociology, sex, crime, and education*. New York: Appleton.

Halperin, S. (Ed.). (1998). *The forgotten half revisited: American youth and young families 1988–2008*. Washington, DC: American Youth Policy Forum.

Halpern, C. T., Udry, J. R., Campbell, B., & Suchindran, C. (1993). Testosterone and pubertal development as predictors of sexual activity: A panel analysis of adolescent males. *Psychosomatic Medicine, 55*, 436–447.

Halpern, C. T., Udry, J. R., & Suchindran, C. (1997). Testosterone predicts initiation of coitus in adolescent females. *Psychosomatic Medicine, 59*, 161–171.

Halpern, C. T., Udry, J. R., Suchindran, C., & Campbell, B. (2000). Adolescent males' willingness to report masturbation. *The Journal of Sex Research, 37*, 327–332.

Halpern, D. (2004). A cognitive-process taxonomy for sex differences in cognitive abilities. *Current Directions in Psychological Science, 13*, 135–139.

Halpern-Felsher, B., & Cauffman, E. (2001). Costs and benefits of a decision: Decision-making competence in adolescents and adults. *Developmental Psychology, 22*, 257–273.

Halpern-Felsher, B., Millstein, S., Ellen, J., Adler, N., Tschann, J., & Biehl, M. (2001). The role of behavioral experience in judging risks. *Health Psychology, 20*, 120–126.

Halverson, L. E., Roberton, M. A., & Langendorfer, S. (1982). Development of the overarm throw: Movement and ball velocity changes by seventh grade. *Research Quarterly for Exercise and Sport, 53*, 198–205.

Hammersley, M. (1992). *What's wrong with ethnography?* New York: Routledge.

Hancox, R. J., Milne, B. J., & Poulton, R. (2004). Association between child and adolescent television viewing and adult health: A longitudinal birth cohort study. *Lancet, 364*, 257–262.

Hardy, C. L., Bukowski, W. M., & Sippola, L. K. (2002). Stability and change in peer relationships during the transition to middle-level school. *Journal of Early Adolescence, 22*(2), 117–142.

Harlow, H. F., & Harlow, M. K. (1962). Social deprivation in monkeys. *Scientific American, 207*(5), 136.

Harris, J. R. (1998). *The nurture assumption: Why children turn out the way they do*. New York: Touchstone.

Harter, S. (1982). The Perceived Competence Scale for Children. *Child Development, 53*, 87–97.

Harter, S. (1985). *The Self-Perception Profile for Children*. Unpublished manual. Denver, CO: University of Denver.

Harter, S. (1987). The determinants and mediational role of global self-worth in children. In N. Eisenberg (Ed.), *Contemporary topics in developmental psychology* (pp. 219–242). New York: Wiley.

Harter, S. (1990). Self and identity development. In S. S. Feldman & G. R. Elliott (Eds.), *At the threshold: The developing adolescent* (pp. 352–387). Cambridge, MA: Harvard University Press.

Harter, S. (1992). Visions of self: Beyond the me in the mirror. In S. Harter, J. S. Eccles, & L. L. Carstensen (Eds.), *Developmental perspectives on motivation* (pp. 99–144). Lincoln, NB: University of Nebraska Press.

Harter, S. (1996a). Developmental changes in self-understanding across the 5 to 7 shift. In A. J. Sameroff & M. M. Haith (Eds.), *The five to seven year shift* (pp. 207–236). Chicago: University of Chicago Press.

Harter, S. (1996b). Historical roots of contemporary issues involving self-concept. In B. A. Bracken (Ed.), *Handbook of self-concept: Developmental, social, and clinical considerations* (pp. 1–37). New York: Wiley.

Harter, S. (1998). The development of self-representations. In W. Damon (Series Ed.) & N. Eisenberg (Vol. Ed.), *Handbook of child psychology: Vol. 3. Social, emotional, and personality development* (5th ed., pp. 553–617). New York: Wiley.

Harter, S. (1999). Symbolic interactionism revisited: Potential liabilities for the self constructed in the crucible of interpersonal relationships. *Merrill-Palmer Quarterly, 45*, 677–701.

Harter, S., Bresnick, S., Bouchey, H. A., & Whitesell, N. R. (1997). The development of multiple role-related selves during adolescence. *Development and Psychopathology, 9*, 835–853.

Harter, S., & Jackson, B. K. (1993). Young adolescents' perceptions of the link between low self-worth and depressed affect. *Journal of Early Adolescence, 13*(4), 383–407.

Harter, S., & Pike, R. (1984). The pictorial scale of perceived competence and social acceptance for young children. *Child Development, 55*, 1969–1982.

Harter, S., Stocker, C., & Robinson, N. S. (1996). The perceived directionality of the link between approval and self-worth: The liabilities of a looking glass self-orientation among young adolescents. *Journal of Research on Adolescence, 6*, 285–308.

Harter, S., Waters, P., & Whitesell, N. R. (1998). Relational self-worth: Differences in perceived worth as a person across interpersonal contexts among adolescents. *Child Development, 69*, 756–766.

Harter, S., & Whitesell, N. R. (1989). Developmental changes in children's understanding of single, multiple, and blended emotion concepts. In C. Saarni & P. Harris (Eds.), *Children's understanding of emotion* (pp. 81–116). Cambridge, UK: Cambridge University Press.

Harter, S., Whitesell, N. R., & Kowalski, P. (1992). Individual differences in the effects of educational transitions on young adolescents' perceptions of competence and motivational orientation. *American Educational Research Journal, 29*, 777–807.

Hartup, W. W. (1996). The company they keep: Friendships and their developmental significance. *Child Development, 67*, 1–13.

Hashey, J. M., & Connor, D. J. (2003). Learn from our journey: Reciprocal teaching action research. *The Reading Teacher, 57*, 224–232.

Haste, H., & Torney-Purta, J. (Eds.) (1992). *The development of political understanding: A new perspective. New Directions for Child Development*, No. 56. San Francisco: Jossey-Bass.

Haveman, R., Wolfe, B., & Peterson, E. (1997). Children of early childbearers as young adults. In R. A. Maynard (Ed.), *Kids having kids: Economic costs and social consequences of teen pregnancy* (pp. 257–284). Washington, DC: Urban Institute Press.

Haviland, J. M., Davidson, R. B., & Ruetsch, C. (1994). The place of emotion in identity. *Journal of Research on Adolescence, 4*, 503–518.

Haviland-Jones, J. M., & Kahlbaugh, P. (2000). Emotion and identity. In M. Lewis & J. M. Haviland-Jones (Eds.), *Handbook of emotion* (2nd ed., pp. 293–305). New York: Guilford Press.

Hawkins, D. L., Pepler, D. J., & Craig, W. M. (2001). Naturalistic observations of peer interventions in bullying. *Social Development, 10*(4), 512–527.

Hayes, N. (2000). *Doing psychological research: Gathering and analyzing data*. Buckingham, UK: Open University Press.

Haynes, N. M., Emmons, C. L., & Woodruff, D. W. (1998). School development program effects: Linking implementation to outcomes. *Journal of Education for Students Placed at Risk, 3*, 71–85.

Haywood, K. M., & Getchell, N. (2001). *Life span motor development* (3rd ed.). Champaign, IL: Human Kinetics.

Hazan, C., & Shaver, P. R. (1987). Romantic love conceptualized as an attachment process. *Journal of Personality and Social Psychology, 52*, 511–524.

Heary, C. M., & Hennessy, E. (2002). The use of focus group interviews in pediatric health care research. *Journal of Pediatric Psychology, 27*, 47–57.

Hedges, L. V., & Nowell, A. (1995). Sex differences I mental test scores: Variability and numbers of high-scoring individuals. *Science, 269*, 41–45.

Heelan, K. A., Donnelly, J. E., Jacobsen, D. J., Mayo, M. S., Washburn, R., & Greene, L. (2005). Active commuting to and from school and BMI in elementary school children—Preliminary data. *Child: Care, Health & Development, 31*, 341–349.

Hegarty, P. (2002). "More feminine than 999 men out of 1000": Measuring sex roles and gender nonconformity in psychology. In T. Lester (Ed.), *Gender nonconformity, race, and sexuality: Charting the connections* (pp. 62–83). Madison, WI: University of Wisconsin Press.

Heinberg, L. J. (1996). Theories of body image disturbance: Perceptual, developmental and sociocultural factors. In J. K. Thompson (Ed.), *Body image, eating disorders, and obesity: An integrative guide for assessment and treatment* (pp. 27–47). Washington, DC: American Psychological Association.

Heinberg, L. J., Thompson, J. K., & Matson, J. L. (2001). Body image dissatisfaction as a motivator for healthy lifestyle change: Is some distress beneficial? In R. Striegel-Moore & L. Smolak (Eds.), *Eating disorders: Innovative directions for research and practice* (pp. 215–232). Washington, DC: American Psychological Association.

Helms, J. E. (2003). Racial identity and racial socialization as aspects of adolescents' identity development. In R. M. Lerner, F. Jacobs, & D. Wertleib (Eds.), *Handbook of applied developmental science: Promoting positive child, adolescent, and family development through research, policies, and programs*: Vol. 1. *Applying developmental science for youth and families: Historical and theoretical foundations* (pp. 143–163). Thousand Oaks, CA: Sage.

Henderson, V. L., & Dweck, C. S. (1990). Motivation and achievement. In S. Feldman & G. R. Elliott (Eds.), *At the threshold: The developing adolescent* (pp. 308–329). Cambridge, MA: Harvard University Press.

Hendrick, C., & Hendrick, S. S. (2001). Romantic love. In C. Hendrick & S. S. Hendrick (Eds.), *Close relationships: A sourcebook* (pp. 203–216). Thousand Oaks, CA: Sage.

Henry, B., Moffitt, T. E., Caspi, A., Langley, J., & Silva, P. A. (1994). On the "remembrance of things past": A longitudinal evaluation of the retrospective method. *Psychological Assessment, 6*, 92–101.

Herman, M. (2004). Forced to choose: Some determinants of racial identification in multiracial adolescents. *Child Development, 75*, 730–748.

Herman-Giddens, M. E., Slora, E. J., Wasserman, R. C., Bourdony, C. J., Bhapkar, M. V., Koch, G. G., et al. (1997). Secondary sexual characteristics and menses in young girls seen in office practice: A study from the Pediatric Research in Office Settings Network. *Pediatrics, 99*, 505–512.

Herman-Giddens, M. E., Wang, L., & Koch, G. (2001). Secondary sexual characteristics and menses in boys: Estimates from the National Health and Nutrition Examination Survey III, 1988–1994. *Archives of Pediatrics and Adolescent Medicine, 155*, 1022–1028.

Hersch, P. (1998). *A tribe apart: A journey into the heart of American adolescence*. New York: Ballantine.

Herschberger, S. L., & D'Augelli, A. R. (1995). The impact of victimization on the mental health and suicidality of gay, lesbian, and bisexual youth. *Developmental Psychology, 31*, 65–74.

Hetherington, E. M. (1994). Siblings, family relationships, and child development. *Journal of Family Psychology, 8*, 251–253.

Hewitt, J. P. (1998). *The myth of self-esteem: Finding happiness and solving problems in America*. New York: St. Martin's Press.

Hickling, A. K., & Wellman, H. M. (2001). The emergence of children's causal explanations and theories: Evidence from everyday conversation. *Developmental Psychology, 37*, 668–683.

Higgins, E. T. (1991). Development of self-regulatory and self-evaluative processes: Costs, benefits, and trade-offs. In M. R. Gunnar & L. A. Sroufe (Eds.), *Self processes in development. Twenty-third Minnesota Symposium on Child Psychology*. Hillsdale, NJ: Erlbaum.

High achieving students see much prejudice. (1994, November 25). *Washington Blade*, 16.

Hildebrand, D. K., & Ledbetter, M. F. (2001). Assessing children's intelligence and memory: The Wechsler Intelligence Scale for Children—Third Edition and and the Children's Memory Scale. In J. J. C. Andrews, D. H. Saklofske, & H. L. Janzen (Eds.), *Handbook of psychoeducational assessment* (pp. 13–32). San Diego, CA: Academic Press.

Hill, J. P., & Lynch, M. E. (1983). The intensification of gender-related role expectations during early adolescence. In J. Brooks-Gunn & A. C. Petersen (Eds.), *Girls at puberty: Biological and psychological perspectives* (pp. 201–228). New York: Plenum.

Hill, K., & Pomeroy, C. (2001). Assessment of physical status of children and adolescents with eating disorders and obesity. In J. K. Thompson & L. Smolak (Eds.), *Body image, eating disorders, and obesity in youth: Assessment, prevention, and treatment* (pp. 171–191). Washington, DC: American Psychological Association.

Hillier, L., Warr, D., & Haste, B. (1996). *The rural mural: Sexuality and diversity in rural youth*. Carlton, Australia: National Centre in HIV Social Research, La Trobe University.

Hine, T. (1999). *Rise and fall of the American teenager*. New York: Avon.

Hines, A. N. (1997). Divorce-related transitions, adolescent development, and the role of the parent-child relationship: A review of the literature. *Journal of Marriage and the Family, 59*, 375–388.

Hitch, G. J., & Towse, J. (1995). Working memory: What develops? In F. E. Weinert & W. Schneider (Eds.), *Research on memory development: State-of-the-art and future directions* (pp. 3–21). Hillsdale, NJ: Erlbaum.

Hmelo, C. E., Holton, D., & Kolodner, J. L. (2000). Designing to learn about complex systems. *Journal of Learning Science, 9*, 247–298.

Hmelo-Silver, C. E. (2004). Problem-based learning: What and how do students learn? *Educational Psychology Review, 16*, 253–266.

Ho, E., & Willms, J. D. (1996). Effects of parental involvement on eighth-grade achievement. *Sociological Quarterly, 69*, 126–141.

Hoff, E., & Tian, C. (2005). Socioeconomic status and cultural influences on language. *Journal of Communication Disorders, 38*, 271–278.

Hofferth, S. L., & Sandberg, J. F. (2001). How American children spend their time. *Journal of Marriage and Family, 63*, 295–308.

Hoge, D. R., Smit, E. K., & Hanson, S. K. (1990). School experiences predicted changes in self-esteem of sixth- and seventh-grade students. *Journal of Educational Psychology, 82*, 117–127.

Hollingshead, A. B. (1949). *Elmtown's youth: The impact social classes on adolescents*. New York: Wiley.

Hoover, H. D., Dunbar, S. B., & Frisbie, D. A. (2001). *Iowa Tests of Basic Skills*. Boston: Riverside.

Hoover-Dempsey, K. V., Walker, J. M. T., Jones, P., & Reed, R. P. (2002). Teachers Involving Parents (TIP): Results from an in-service teacher education program for enhancing parental involvement. *Teaching & Teacher Education, 18*, 843–867.

Horn, M. (1993). Childhood and children. In M. K. Cayton, E. J. Gorn, & P. W. Williams (Eds.), *Encyclopedia of American social history* (*Vol. 3*, pp. 2023–2036). New York: Scribner.

Horner, S. D. (1999). Asthma self-care: Just another piece of school work. *Pediatric Nursing, 25*, 597.

Horner, S. D. (2000). Using focus group methods with middle school children. *Research in Nursing & Health, 23*, 510–517.

Horowitz, F. D. (2000). Child development and the PITS: Simple questions, complex answers, and developmental theory. *Child Development, 71*(1), 1–20.

Hotz, V. J., McElroy, S. W., & Sanders, S. G. (1997). The impacts of teenage childbearing on the mothers and the consequences of those impacts for government. In R. A. Maynard (Ed.), *Kids having kids: Economic costs and social consequences of teen pregnancy* (pp. 55–94). Washington, DC: The Urban Institute Press.

Howe, N., & Strauss, W. (2000). *Millennials rising: The next great generation*. New York: Vintage.

Howes, C. (Ed.). (2003). *Teaching 4- to 8-year olds: Literacy, math, multiculturalism, and classroom community*. Baltimore, MD: Paul H. Brooks.

Huddleston, J., & Ge, X. (2003). Boys at puberty: Psychosocial implications. In C. Hayward (Ed.), *Gender differences at puberty* (pp. 113–134). New York: Cambridge University Press.

Hudson, L. M., & Gray, W. M. (1986). Formal operations, the imaginary audience and the personal fable. *Adolescence, 21*, 211–219.

Hudspeth, W. J., & Pribram, K. H. (1992). Psychophysiological indices of cognitive maturation. *International Journal of Psychophysiology, 12*, 19–29.

Huffman, H. A. (1994). *A character education program: One school district's experience*. Alexandria, VA: Association for Supervision and Curriculum Development.

Hughes, D., & Chen, L. (1997). When and what parents tell children about race: An examiniation of race-related socialization among African American families. *Applied Developmental Science, 1*(4), 200–214.

Humphreys, L. G., & Davey, T. C. (1988). Continuity in intellectual growth from 12 months to 9 years. *Intelligence, 12*, 183–197.

Hurks, P. P. M., Hendriksen, J. G. M., Vles, J. S. H., Kalff, A. C., Feron, F. J. M., Kroes, M., et al. (2004). Verbal fluency over time as a measure of automatic and controlled processing in children with ADHD. *Brain and Cognition, 55*, 535–544.

Huttenlocher, P. R. (1979). Synaptic density in the human frontal cortex: Developmental changes and effects of aging. *Brain Research, 163*, 195–205.

Huttenlocher, P. R., & Dabholkar, J. C. (1997). Developmental anatomy of the prefrontal cortex. In N. A. Krasnegor, G. R. Lyon, & P. S. Goldman-Rakic (Eds.), *Development of the prefrontal cortex: Evolution, neurobiology, and behavior* (pp. 69–84). Baltimore, MD: Paul H. Brooks.

Huttenlocher, P. R., & Dabholkar, A. S. (1997). Regional differences in synaptogenesis in the human cerebral cortex. *Journal of Comparative Neurology, 387*, 167–178.

Hyde, J. S. (1984). How large are gender differences in aggression? A developmental meta-analysis. *Developmental Psychology, 20*, 722–736.

Hyde, J. S., & Jaffee, S. R. (2000). Becoming a heterosexual adult: The experiences of young women. *Journal of Social Issues, 56*, 283–296.

Hyde, J. S., & Linn, M. C. (1990). Gender differences in self-esteem: A meta-analysis. *Psychological Bulletin, 104*, 53–69.

Hyde, J. S., & Plant, E. A. (1995). Magnitude of psychological gender differences. *American Psychologist, 50*(3), 159–161.

Inhelder, B., & Piaget, J. (1958). *The growth of logical thinking from childhood to adolescence: An essay on the construction of formal operational structures* (A. Parsons & S. Milgram, Trans.). London: Routledge and Kegan Paul.

Ireh, M. (2000). Career development theories and their implications for high school career guidance and counseling. *The High School Journal, Dec/Jan*, 28–40.

Isaacs, D. (2001). *Character building: A guide for parents and teachers*. Dublin, Ireland: Four Courts Press.

Isen, A. M. (2000). Positive affect and decision making. In M. Lewis & J. M. Haviland-Jones (Eds.), *Handbook of emotions* (2nd ed., pp. 417–435). New York: Guilford Press.

Izard, M. K. (1990). Social influences on the reproductive success and reproductive endocrinology of prosimian primates. In T. E. Ziegler & F. B. Bercovitch (Eds.), *Socioendocrinology of primate reproduction* (pp. 159–186). New York: Wiley-Liss.

Jackson, A. W., & Davis, G. A. (2000). *Turning points 2000: Educating adolescents in the 21st century*. New York: Teachers College Press.

Jackson, D. R. (2004). Eighty years of Indian voting: A call to protect Indian voting rights. *Montana Law Review, 65*, 269–288.

Jacobs, J. E., Chhin, C. S., & Shaver, K. (2005). Longitudinal links between perceptions of adolescence and the social beliefs of adolescents: Are parents' stereotypes related to beliefs held about and by their children? *Journal of Youth and Adolescence, 34*, 61–72.

Jacobs, J. E., Bleeker, M. M., & Constantino, M. J. (2003). The self-system during childhood and adolescence: Development, influences, and implications. *Journal of Psychotherapy Integration, 13*, 33–65.

Jahnke, H. C., & Blanchard-Fields, F. (1993). Two models of adolescent egocentrism. *Journal of Youth and Adolescence, 22*, 313–326.

James, W. (1890). *Principles of psychology*. New York: Henry Holt.

Jankowski, S. M. (1992) Ethnic identity and political consciousness in different social orders. In H. Haste & J. Torney-Purta (Eds.), *The development of political understanding: A new perspective* (pp. 79–93). *New Directions for Child Development*, No. 56. San Francisco: Jossey-Bass.

Janz, K. Physical activity and bone development during childhood and adolescence: Implications for the prevention of osteoporosis. *Minerva Pediatrics, 54*, 93–104.

Jemmott, J. B., Jemmott, L. S., & Gong, G. T. (1998). Abstinence and safe sex HIV risk-reduction interventions for African-American adolescents. *Journal of the American Medical Association, 279*, 1529–1536.

Jenkins, D., & Reaburn, P. (2000). *Guiding the young athlete: All you need to know*. St Leonards, NSW: Allen & Unwin.

Jensen, A. R. (1998). *The g factor: The science of mental ability*. Westport, CT: Praeger.

Jensen, A. R. (2001). Spearman's hypothesis. In J. M. Collis & S. Messick (Eds.), *Intelligence and personality: Bridging the gap in theory and measurement* (pp. 3–24). Mahwah, NJ: Erlbaum.

Jensen, A. R., & Reynolds, C. R. (1982). Race, social class and ability patterns on the WISC-R. *Personality and Individual Differences, 3*, 423–438.

Jensen, L. A. (1997). Culture wars: American moral divisions across the adult lifespan. *Journal of Adult Development, 4*, 107–121.

Jepsen, D. A., & Dickson, G. L. (2003). Continuity in lifespan career development: Career exploration as a precursor to career establishment. *Career Development Quarterly, 51*, 217–233.

Jessor, R., Turbin, M. S., & Costa, F. M. (1998). Risk and protection in successful outcomes among disadvantaged adolescents. *Applied Developmental Science, 2*(4), 194–208.

Johnson, C. M., & Johnson, S. (2002). Construct stability of the Cognitive Abilities Scale—Second Edition for infants and toddlers. *Journal of Psychoeducational Assessment, 20*, 144–151.

Johnson, M. (1980). *Toward adolescence: The middle school years, 79th yearbook of the National Society for the Study of Education*. Chicago: National Society for the Study of Education.

Johnson, M. H. (2003). Development of human brain functions. *Biological Psychiatry, 54*, 1312–1316.

Johnson, M. H. (2005). Sensitive periods in functional brain development: Problems and prospects. *Developmental Psychobiology, 46*, 287–292.

Johnson, L. D., Terry-McElrath, Y. M., O'Malley, P. M., & Wakefield, M. (2005). Trends in recall and appraisal of antismoking advertising among American youth: National survey results, 1997–2001. *Prevention Science, 6*, 1–19.

Johnson, R. (2002). Pathways to adolescent health: Early intervention. *Journal of Adolescent Health, 31*, 240–250.

Jones, D. C., Vigfusdottir, F. H., & Lee, Y. (2004). Body image and the appearance culture among adolescent girls and boys: An examination of friend conversations, peer criticism, appearance magazine, and the internalization of appearance ideals. *Journal of Adolescent Research, 19*(3), 323–339.

Jones, E. F., & Forest, J. D. (1992). Under reporting of abortion in surveys of U.S. women: 1976 to 1988. *Demography, 29*, 113–126.

Jones, M. C., & Bayley, N. (1950). Physical maturing among boys as related to behavior. *Journal of Educational Psychology, 41*, 129–148.

Joshi, A., & Ferris, J. C. (2002). Causal attributions regarding conflicts between friends in middle childhood. *Social Behavior and Personality, 30*, 65–74.

Josselson, R. (1987). *Finding herself: Pathways to identity development in women*. San Francisco: Jossey-Bass.

Josselson, R. (1988). The embedded self: I and thou revisited. In D. K. Lapsley & F. C. Power (Eds.), *Self, ego, and identity: Integrative approaches* (pp. 91–106). New York: Springer-Verlag.

Kagan, J. (1980). Perspectives on continuity. In O. G. Brim, Jr. & J. Kagan (Eds.), *Constancy and change in human development* (pp. 26–74). Cambridge, MA: Harvard University Press.

Kagan, J. (1983). Developmental categories and the premise of connectivity. In R. M. Lerner (Ed.), *Developmental psychology: Historical and philosophical perspectives*. Hillsdale, NJ: Erlbaum.

Kagan, J., & Saudino, K. (2001). Behavioral inhibition and related temperaments. In R. M. Emde & J. K. Hewitt (Eds.), *Infancy to early childhood: Genetic and environmental influences on developmental change* (pp. 111–119). London: Oxford University Press.

Kahle, J. B., & Lakes, M. K. (2003). The myth of equality in science classrooms. *Journal of Research in Science Teaching, 40*, S58–S67.

Kail, R. (1991). Development of processing speed in childhood and adolescence. In H. W. Reese (Ed.), *Advances in child development and behavior*, Vol. 23 (pp. 151–185). San Diego: Academic Press.

Kail, R. (2000). Speed of information processing: Developmental change and links to intelligence. *Journal of School Psychology, 38*, 51–61.

Kanemura, H., Aihara, M., Aoki, S., Araki, T., & Nakazawa, S. (2003). Development of the prefrontal lobe in infants and children: A three-dimensional magnetic resonance volumetric study. *Brain & Development, 25*, 195–199.

Kanemura, H., Aihara, M., & Nakazawa, S. (2002). Measurement of the frontal and prefrontal lobe volumes in children with malnutrition by three dimensional magnetic resonance imaging scan. *Brain and development, 34*, 398–403.

Kaplan, S. J., Pelcovitz, D., & Labruna, V. (1999). Child and adolescent abuse and neglect research: A review of the past 10 years. Part I: Physical and emotional abuse and neglect. *Journal of the American Academy of Child & Adolescent Psychiatry, 38*, 1214–1222.

Karcher, M. J. (2002). The cycle of violence and disconnection among middle school students: Teacher disconnection as a consequence of violence. *Journal of School Violence, 1*(1), 35–51.

Karofsky, P. S., Zeng, L., & Kosorock, M. R. (2001). Relationship between adolescent-parental communication and initiation of first intercourse by adolescents. *Journal of Adolescent Health, 28*, 41–45.

Katchadourian, H. (1990). Sexuality. In S. S. Feldman & G. R. Elliot (Eds.), *At the threshold: The developing adolescent* (pp. 330–351). Cambridge, MA: Harvard University Press.

Katz, C. (1998). Disintegrating developments: Global economic restructuring and the eroding ecologies of youth. In T. Skelton & G. Valentine (Eds.), *Cool places: Geographies of youth cultures*. London: Routledge.

Keller, M., & Edelstein, W. (1991). The development of socio-moral meaning-making: Domains, categories, and perspective-taking. In W. M. Kurtines & J. L. Gewirtz (Eds.), *Handbook of moral behavior and development: Vol. 1. Theory* (pp. 89–114). Hillsdale, NJ: Erlbaum.

Kelley, H. H., Berscheid, E., Christiensen, A., Harvey, J. H., Huston, T. L., Levinger, G., McClintock, E., Peplau, L. A., & Peterson, D. R. (1983). *Close relationships*. New York: Freeman.

Kelly, J. B., & Emery, R. E. (2003). Children's adjustment following divorce: Risk and resilience perspectives. *Family Relations, 52*, 352–362.

Keniston, K. (1971). *Youth and dissent: The rise of a new opposition*. New York: Harcourt Brace Jovanovitch.

Kennedy, C., Kools, S., & Krueger, R. (2001). Methodological considerations in children's focus groups. *Nursing Research, 50*, 184–187.

Kennedy, S. G., Washburn, G., & Martinez, M. (1998, January 13). Volunteer shield stands up for Taylor Homes' children. *Chicago Tribune*, 1.

Kerchoff, A. C. (2002). The transition from school to work. In J. T. Mortimer & R. Larson (Eds.), *The changing adolescent experience: Societal trends and the transition to adulthood* (pp. 52–87). Cambridge, UK: Cambridge University Press.

Kerestes, M., & Youniss, J. E. (2003). Rediscovering the importance of religion in adolescent development. In R. M. Lerner, F. Jacobs, & D. Wertlieb (Eds.), *Handbook of applied developmental science: Vol. 1. Applied developmental sciences for youth and families: Historical and theoretical foundations* (pp. 165–184). Thousand Oaks, CA: Sage.

Kerestes, M., Youniss, J. E., & Metz, E. (2004). Longitudinal patterns of religious perspective and civic engagement. *Applied Developmental Science, 8*(1), 39–46.

Kerns, K. A., Klepac, L., & Cole, A. K. (1996). Peer relationships and preadolescents' perceptions of security in the mother-child relationship. *Developmental Psychology, 32*, 457–466.

Kerns, K. A., Tomich, P. L., Aspelmeier, J. E., & Contreras, J. M. (2000). Attachment-based assessment of parent-child relationships in middle childhood. *Developmental Psychology, 36*, 614–626.

Kerns, S. E. U., & Prinz, R. J. (2002). Critical issues in the prevention of violence-related behavior in youth. *Clinical Child and Family Psychology Review, 5*(2), 133–160.

Kerr, M., Stattin, H., Biesecker, G., & Ferrer-Wreder, L. (2003). Relationships with parents and peers in adolescence. Emotion and personality development in childhood. In R. M. Lerner & M. A. Easterbrook (Eds.), *Handbook of psychology: Vol. 6. Developmental psychology* (pp. 395–419). New York: Wiley.

Kester, K., & Marshall, S. K. (2003). Intergenerational similitude of ethnic identification and ethnic identity: A brief report on immigrant Chinese mother-adolescent dyads in Canada. *Identity: An International Journal of Theory and Research, 3*, 367–373.

Killen, J., Taylor, C., Hayward, C., Haydel, K., Wilson, D., Hammer, L., et al. (1996). Weight concerns influence the development of eating disorders: A four year prospective study. *Journal of Consulting and Clinical Psychology, 64*, 936–940.

Kim, S. (2000). Creating campus communities: Second-generation Korean-American ministries at UCLA. In R. W. Flory & D. C. Miller (Eds.), *GenX religion* (pp. 92–112). New York: Routledge.

Kim, S., Brody, G. H., & Murry, V. M. (2003). Factor structure of the Early Adolescent Temperament Questionnaire and measurement invariance across gender. *Journal of Early Adolescence, 23*, 268–294.

King, C. M., & Johnson, L. M. Parent (1999). Constructing meaning via reciprocal teaching. *Reading Research & Instruction, 38*, 169–186.

King, P. E. (2003). Religion and identity: The role of ideological, social, and spiritual contexts. *Applied Developmental Science, 7*, 197–204.

King, P. E., & Boyatzis, C. J., (2004). Exploring adolescent spiritual and religious development: Current and future theoretical and empirical perspectives. *Applied Developmental Science, 8*, 2–6.

King, P. E., Furrow, J. L., & Roth, N. (2002). The influence of family and peers on adolescent religiousness. *Journal of Psychology & Christianity, 21*, 109–120.

Kirby, D. (2001). *Emerging answers: Research findings on programs to reduce teen pregnancy*. Washington, DC: National Campaign to Prevent Teen Pregnancy.

Kirby, D. (2002a). Antecedents of adolescent initiation of sex, contraceptive use, and pregnancy. *American Journal of Health Behavior, 26*, 473–485.

Kirby, D. (2002b). Effective approaches to reducing adolescent unprotected sex, pregnancy, and childbearing. *The Journal of Sex Research, 39*, 51–57.

Kirkpatrick, J. (1987). *Taure' are' a*: A liminal category and passage to Marquesan adulthood. *Ethos, 15*, 382–405.

Kitchener, K. S., Lynch, C. L., Fischer, K. W., & Wood, P. K. (1993). Developmental range of reflective judgment: A six-year longitudinal study. *Journal of Applied Developmental Psychology, 10*, 73–95.

Klaczynski, P. A. (2000). Motivated scientific reasoning biases, epistemological beliefs, and theory polarization: A two-process approach to adolescent cognition. *Child Development, 71*, 1347–1366.

Klaczynski, P. A., & Gordon, D. H. (1996). Self-serving influences on adolescents' evaluations of belief-relevant evidence. *Journal of Experimental Child Psychology, 62*, 317–339.

Klevens, J., & Roca, J. (1999). Nonviolent youth in a violent society: Resilience and vulnerability in the country of Columbia. *Violence and Victims, 14*(3), 311–322.

Kling, K. C., Hyde, J. S., Showers, C., & Buswell, B. (1999). Gender differences in self-esteem: A meta-analysis. *Psychological Bulletin, 125*, 470–500.

Klintsova, A. Y., & Greenough, W. T. (1999). Synaptic plasticity in cortical systems. *Current Opinion in Neurobiology, 9*, 203–208.

Knox, M., Funk, J., Elliott, R., & Bush, E. G. (2000). Gender differences in adolescents' possible selves. *Youth & Society, 31*, 287–309.

Koerner, S. S., Wallace, S., Lehman, S. J., Lee, S., & Escalante, K. A. (2004). Sensitive mother-to-adolescent disclosures after divorce: Is the experience of sons different from that of daughters? *Journal of Family Psychology, 18*, 46–57.

Kokis, J. V., Macpherson, R., Toplak, M. E., West, R. F., & Stanovich, K. E. (2002). Heuristic and analytical processing: Age trends and associations with cognitive ability and cognitive styles. *Journal of Experimental Child Psychology, 83*, 26–52.

Kolb, B. (1989). Brain development, plasticity, and behavior. *American Psychologist, 44*, 1203–1212.

Kolb, B., & Wishaw, I. Q. (1998). Brain plasticity and behavior. *Annual Review of Psychology, 49*, 43–64.

Koniak-Griffin, D., Lesser, J., Uman, G., & Nyamathi, A. (2003). Teen pregnancy, motherhood, and unprotected sexual activity. *Research in Nursing & Health, 26*, 4–19.

Kontula, O., & Haavio-Mannila, E. (2002). Masturbation in a generational perspective. *Journal of Psychology and Human Sexuality, 14*, 49–83.

Kracke, B. (1997). Parental behaviors and adolescents' career exploration. *Career Development Quarterly, 45*, 341–350.

Krettenauer, T. (2005). The role of epistemic stance in adolescent identity formation: Further evidence. *Journal of Youth and Adolescence, 34*, 185–198.

Kreutzer, M. A., Leonard, C., & Flavell, J. H. (1975). An interview study of children's knowledge about memory. *Monographs of the Society for Research in Child Development, 40*(1, Serial No. 159).

Kroger, J. (1997). Gender and identity: The intersection of structure, content, and context. *Sex Roles, 36*(11/12), 747–770.

Kroger, J. (2000). Ego identity status research in the new millennium. *International Journal of Behavioral Development, 24*(3), 197–220.

Kroger, J. (2003). Identity development during adolescence. In G. R. Adams & M. D. Berzonsky (Eds.), *Blackwell handbook of adolescence* (pp. 205–226). Malden, MA: Blackwell.

Krogman, W. M. (1972). *Child growth*. Ann Arbor, MI: The University of Michigan Press.

Krueger, R. A., & Casey, M. A. (2000). *Focus groups: A practical guide for applied research* (3rd ed.). Thousand Oaks, CA: Sage.

Kuhn, D. (2000). Does memory development belong on an endangered topic list? *Child Development, 71*, 21–25.

Kuhn, D., Cheney, R., & Weinstock, M. (2000). The development of epistemological understanding. *Cognitive Development, 15*, 309–328.

Kuhn, D., Langer, J., Kohlberg, L., & Haan, N. (1977). The development of formal operations in logical moral judgment. *Genetic Psychology Monographs, 95*, 97–188.

Kuttler, A. F., Parker, J. G., & La Greca, A. M. (2002). Developmental and gender differences in preadolescents' judgments of the veracity of gossip. *Merrill-Palmer Quarterly, 48*, 105–132.

Ladd, G. W. (1999). Peer relationships and social competence during early and middle childhood. *Annual Review of Psychology, 50*, 333–359.

Ladd, G. W., & Kochenderfer, B. J. (1996). Linkages between friendship and adjustment during early school transitions. In W. M. Bukowski & A. F. Newcomb (Eds.), *The company they keep: Friendship in childhood and adolescence* (pp. 322–345). New York: Cambridge University Press.

Lagana, L. (1999). Psychosocial correlates of contraceptive practices during late adolescence. *Adolescence, 34*, 463–482.

Laitinen-Krispijn, S., Van der Ende, J., Hazebroek-Kampschreur, A. A. J. M., & Verhulst, F. C. (1999). Pubertal maturation and the development of behavioural and emotional problems in early adolescence. *Acta Psychiatrica Scandinavica, 99*, 16–25.

Lam, T. H., Shi, H. J., Ho, L. M., Stewart, S. M., & Fan, S. (2002). Timing of pubertal maturation and heterosexual behavior among Hong Kong Chinese adolescents. *Archives of Sexual Behavior, 31*, 359–366.

Lam, T. H., Stewart, S. M., Leung, G., Ho, S. Y., Fan, A. H., & Ma, A. L. T. (2002). Sex differences in body satisfaction, feeling fat and pressure to diet among Chinese adolescents in Hong Kong. *European Eating Disorders Review, 10*, 347–358.

Lamborn, S. D., & Steinberg, L. (1993). Emotional autonomy redux: Revisiting Ryan and Lynch. *Child Development, 64*, 483–499.

Landau, M. (2000, April 21). Deciphering the adolescent brain. *Focus: News from Harvard, Medical, Dental & Public Health Schools*. Retrieved December 30, 2002, from http://focus.hms.harvard.edu/2000/Apr21_2000/psychiatry.html

Landrine, H. (1995). *Bringing cultural diversity to feminist psychology: Theory, research, and practice*. Washington, DC: American Psychological Association.

Lapsley, D. K. (1993). Toward an integrated theory of adolescent ego development: The "new look" at adolescent egocentrism. *American Journal of Orthopsychiatry, 63*, 562–571.

Lapsley, D. K. (1996). *Moral psychology*. Boulder, CO: Westview.

Lapsley, D. K., Flannery, D. J., Gottschalk, H., & Raney, M. (1996, March). Sources of risk and resilience in adolescent mental health. Poster at the Sixth Biennial Meetings of the Society for Research on Adolescence, Boston, MA.

Lapsley, D. K., & Rice, K. (1988). The "new look" at the imaginary audience and the personal fable: Toward a general model of adolescent ego development. In D. K. Lapsley & F. C. Power (Eds.), *Self, ego, identity: Integrative approaches* (pp. 109–129). New York: Springer.

Lareau, A. (2000). Social class and the daily lives of children: A study from the United States. *Childhood: A Global Journal of Child Research, 7*(2), 155–171.

Larson, R. W. (1994). Youth organizations, hobbies, and sports as developmental contexts. In R. K. Silbereisen & E. Todt (Eds.), *Adolescence in context: The interplay of family, school, peers, and work in adjustment* (pp. 46–65). New York: Springer-Verlag.

Larson, R. W. (2000). Toward a psychology of positive youth development. *American Psychologist, 55*, 170–183.

Larson, R. W. (2002). Globalization, societal change, and new technologies. What they mean for the future of adolescence. *Journal of Research on Adolescence, 12*, 1–30.

Larson, R. W., Brown, B. B., & Mortimer, J. T. (2002a). *Adolescents' preparation for the future: Perils and promise*. Malden, MA: Blackwell.

Larson, R. W., Brown, B. B., & Mortimer, J. T. (2002b). *Adolescents' preparation for the future: Perils and promise*. Preface to the report of the Study Group on Adolescence in the Twenty-first Century. *Journal of Research on Adolescence, 12*, iii–v.

Larson, R., Csikszentmihalyi, M., & Graef, R. (1980). Mood variability and the psychosocial adjustment of adolescents. *Journal of Youth and Adolescence, 9*, 469–490.

Larson, R., & Ham, M. (1993). Stress and "storm and stress" in early adolescence: The relationship of negative events with dysphoric affect. *Developmental Psychology, 29*(1), 130–140.

Larson, R., & Lampman-Petraitis, C. (1989). Daily emotional states reported by children and adolescents. *Child Development, 60*, 1250–1260.

Larson, R., Moneta, G., Richards, M. H., & Wilson, S. (2002). Continuity, stability, and change in daily emotional experience across adolescence. *Child Development, 73*, 1151–1165.

Larson, R., Verma, S., & Dworkin, J. (2000). *Adolescents' family relationships in India: The daily lives of Indian middle-class teenagers*. Paper presented at the biennial meeting of the Society for Research on Adolescence, Chicago.

Larson, R. W., Wilson, S., Brown, B. B., Furstenberg, F. F., Jr., & Verma, S. (2002). Changes in adolescents' interpersonal experiences: Are they being prepared for adult relationships in the twenty-first century? *Journal of Research on Adolescence, 12*, 31–68.

Latendresse, C. (2004). Literature circles: Meeting reading standards, making personal connections, and appreciating other interpretations. *Middle School Journal, 35*, 13–20.

Lather, P. (1993). Fertile obsession: Validity after poststructuralism. *Sociological Quarterly, 34*, 673–693.

Laursen, B. (1996). Closeness and conflict in adolescent peer relationships: Interdependence with friends and romantic partners. In W. M. Bukowski & A. F. Newcomb (Eds.), *The company they keep: Friendship in childhood and adolescence* (pp. 186–210). New York: Cambridge University Press.

Laursen, B., Coy, K. C., & Collins, W. A. (1998) Reconsidering changes in parent-adolescent conflict across adolescence: A meta-analysis. *Child Development, 69*, 817–832.

Leaper, C. (1994). Exploring the consequences of gender segregation on social relationships. In C. Leaper (Ed.), *Childhood gender segregation: Causes and consequences* (pp. 67–86). *New Directions for Child Development*, No. 65. San Francisco: Jossey-Bass.

Leaper, C., & Anderson, K. J. (1997). Gender development and heterosexual romantic relationships during adolescence. In S. Shulman & W. A. Collins (Eds.), *Romantic relationships in adolescence: Developmental perspectives* (pp. 85–103). San Francisco: Jossey-Bass.

Lease, A. M., & Axelrod, J. J. (2001). Position in the peer group's perceived organizational structure: Relation to social status and friendship. *Journal of Early Adolescence, 21*, 377–404.

Lease, A. M., McFall, R. M., & Viken, R. J. (2003). Distance from peers in the group's perceived organizational structure: Relation to individual characteristics. *Journal of Early Adolescence, 23*(2), 194–217.

Lederer, J. M. (2000). Reciprocal teaching of social studies in inclusive elementary classrooms. *Journal of Learning Disabilities, 33*, 91–106.

Lee, R. E., & Cubbin, C. (2002). Neighborhood context and youth cardiovascular health behaviors. *American Journal of Public Health, 92*, 428–436.

Lefebvre, C., & Reid, G. (1998). Prediction in ball catching by children with and without a developmental coordination disorder. *Adapted Physical Activity Quarterly, 15*, 299–315.

L'Engle, K. L., Brown, J. D., & Kenneavy, K. (2006). The mass media are important context for adolescents' sexual behavior. *Journal of Adolescent Health, 38*, 186–192.

Lengua, L. J. (2003). Associations among emotionality, self-regulation, adjustment problems, and positive adjustment in middle childhood. *Journal of Applied Developmental Psychology, 24*, 595–618.

Lengua, L. J., & Long, A. C. (2002). The role of emotionality and self-regulation in the appraisal-coping process: Tests of direct and moderating effects. *Journal of Applied Developmental Psychology, 23*, 471–493.

Leone, C. M., & Richards, M. H. (1989). Classwork and homework in early adolescence: The ecology of achievement. *Journal of Youth and Adolescence, 18*, 531–547.

Lerner, R. M. (1985). Individual and context in developmental psychology: Conceptual and theoretical issues. In J. R. Nesselroade & A. von Eye (Eds.), *Individual development and social change: Explanatory analysis* (pp. 155–187). New York: Academic Press.

Lerner, R. M. (1996). Relative plasticity, integration, temporality, and diversity in human development: A developmental contextual perspective about theory, process, and method. *Developmental Psychology, 32*, 781–786.

Lerner, R. M. (1998). Theories of human development: Contemporary perspectives. In W. Damon (Series Ed.) & R. M. Lerner (Vol. Ed.), *Handbook of child psychology: Vol. 1. Theoretical models of human development* (pp. 1–24). New York: Wiley.

Lerner, R. M. (2002a). *Adolescence: Development, diversity, context, and application*. Upper Saddle River, NJ: Prentice Hall.

Lerner, R. M. (2002b). *Concepts and theories of human development* (3rd ed.). Mahwah, NJ: Erlbaum.

Lerner, R. M., Brentano, C., Dowling, E. M., & Anderson, P. M. (2002). Positive youth development: Thriving as the basis of personhood and civil society. *New Directions for Youth Development, 95*, 11–33.

Lerner, R. M., Fisher, C. B., & Weinberg, R. A. (2000). Toward a science for and of the people: Promoting civil society through the application of developmental science. *Child Development, 71*, 11–20.

Lerner, R. M., & Knapp, J. R. (1975). Actual and perceived intrafamilial attitudes of late adolescents and their parents. *Journal of Youth and Adolescence, 4*, 17–36.

Lerner, R. M., Taylor, C. S., & von Eye, A. (Eds.). (2002). *Pathways to positive development among diverse youth. New Directions for Youth Development* No. 95. New York: Jossey-Bass.

Leventhal, T., & Brooks-Gunn, J. (2003). Children and youth in neighborhood contexts. *Current Directions in Psychological Science, 12*, 27–31.

Leventhal, T., Graber, J. A., & Brooks-Gunn, J. (2001). Adolescent transitions to young adulthood: Antecedents, correlates, and consequences of adolescent employment. *Journal of Research on Adolescence, 11*, 297–323.

Levin, I., Siegler, R. S., & Druyan, S. (1990). Misconceptions about motion: Development and training effects. *Child Development, 61*, 1544–1557.

Levine, M., Smolak, L., Moodey, A., Shuman, M., & Hessen, L. (1994). Normative developmental challenges and dieting and eating disturbances in middle school girls. *International Journal of Eating Disorders, 15*, 11–20.

Levinson, D. (1978). *The seasons of a man's life*. New York: Ballantine.

Levinson, D. (1986). A conception of adult development. *American Psychologist, 41*, 3–13.

Levinson, S. C. (1997). Language and cognition: The cognitive consequences of spatial description in Guugu Yimithirr. *Journal of Linguistic Anthropology, 7*, 98–131.

Lewis, C. C. (1995). *Educating hearts and minds: Reflections on Japanese preschool and elementary education*. Cambridge, UK: Cambridge University Press.

Lewis, M., Feiring, C., & Rosenthal, S. (2000). Attachment over time. *Child Development, 71*, 707–720.

Lewis, M. D. (2000). The promise of dynamic systems approaches for an integrated account of human development. *Child Development, 71*(1), 36–43.

Lewis, T. L. & Maurer, D. (2005). Multiple sensitive periods in human visual development: Evidence from visually deprived children. *Developmental Psychobiology, 46*, 163–183.

Li, S., Chen, W., Srinivasan, S. R., Bond, M. G., Tang, R., Urbina, E. M., et al. (2003). Childhood cardiovascular risk factors and carotid vascular changes in adulthood: The Bogalusa heart study. *JAMA: Journal of the American Medical Association, 290*, 2271–2275.

Li, T., & Noseworthy, M. D. (2002). Mapping the development of white matter tracts with diffusion tensor imaging. *Developmental Science, 5*, 293–300.

Liben, L. S., & Bigler, R. S. (2002). The developmental course of gender differentiation. *Monographs of the Society for Research in Child Development, 67*(2, Serial No. 269).

Liberman, I. Y. (1973). Segmentation of the spoken word and reading acquisition. *Bulletin of the Orton Society, 23*, 65–77.

Lickona, T. (1991). *Educating for character: How our schools can teach respect and responsibility*. New York: Bantam.

Liddell, C. (2002). Emic perspectives on risk in African childhood. *Developmental Review, 22*, 97–116.

Lightfoot, C. (1997). *The culture of adolescent risk-taking*. New York: Guilford Press.

Lightfoot, C. (2001a). Breathing lessons: Self as genre and aesthetic. In T. Brown & L. Smith (Eds.), *Reductionism and the development of knowledge* (pp. 177–198). Mahwah, NJ: Erlbaum.

Lightfoot, C. (2001b, May). *The self imagined: An analysis of adolescents' fiction writing*. Poster session presented at the meeting of the Society for Research on Identity Formation, London, Ontario, Canada.

Lightfoot, C., & Bullock, M. (1990). Interpreting contradictory communications: Age and context effects. *Developmental Psychology, 26*, 830–836.

Lim, L., & Renshaw, P. (2001). The relevance of sociocultural theory to culturally diverse partnerships and communities. *Journal of Child and Family Studies, 10*, 9–21.

Lin, C. H., Hsiao, C. K., & Chen, W. J. (1999). Development of sustained attention assessed using the Continuous Performance Test among children 6–15 years of age. *Journal of Abnormal Child Psychology, 27*, 403–412.

Lincoln, Y. S., & Guba, E. G. (2000). Paradigmatic controversies, contradictions, and emerging confluences. In N. K. Densin & Y. S. Lincoln (Eds.), *The handbook of qualitative research* (2nd ed., pp. 163–188). Beverly Hills, CA: Sage.

Lips, H. M. (2004). The gender gap in possible selves: Divergence of academic self-views among high-school and university students. *Sex Roles, 50*, 357–371.

Lipsitz, J. S. (1980). In M. Johnson (Ed.), *Toward adolescence: The middle school years, 79th yearbook of the National Society for the Study of Education* (pp. 7–31). Chicago: National Society for the Study of Education.

Little, B. R. (1987). Personal projects and fuzzy selves: Aspects of self-identity in adolescence. In T. Honess & K. Yardley (Eds.), *Self and identity: Perspectives across the lifespan* (pp. 230–245). New York: Routledge.

Little, B. R. (1999). Personal projects and social ecology: Themes and variations across the life span. In J. Brandtstadler & R. M. Lerner (Eds.), *Action & self-development: Theory and research through the life span* (pp. 197–221). Thousand Oaks, CA: Sage.

Livesly, W. L., & Bromley, D. B. (1973). *Person perception in childhood and adolescence*. Chichester, UK: Wiley.

Livingstone, M. B. E., Robson, P. J., Wallace, J. M. W., & McKinley, M. C. (2003). How active are we? Levels of routine physical activity in children and adults. *Proceedings of the Nutrition Society, 62*, 681–701.

Loevinger, J. (1976). *Ego development*. San Francisco: Jossey-Bass.

Loevinger, J. (1990). Ego development in adolescence. In R. E. Muuss (Ed.), *Adolescent development: A book of readings* (4th ed., pp. 111–117). New York: McGraw-Hill.

Loevinger, J., & Knoll, J. (1983). Personality: Stages, traits, and the self. *Annual Review of Psychology, 34*, 195–222.

Longmore, M. A., Manning, W., & Giordano, P. C. (2001). Preadolescent parenting strategies and teen's dating and sexual initiation: A longitudinal analysis. *Journal of Marriage and Family, 63*, 322–335.

Loovis, E. M., & Butterfield, S. A. (2000). Influence of age, sex and balance on mature skipping by children in grades K–8. *Perceptual & Motor Skills, 90*, 974–978.

Lorch, E. P., Diener, M. B., Sanchez, R. P., Milich, R., Welsh, R., & van den Broek, P. (1999). The effects of story structure on the recall of stories in children with attention deficit hyperactivity disorder. *Journal of Educational Psychology, 92*, 273–283.

Lorch, E. P., Eastman, D., Milich, R., & Lemberger, C. C. (2004). Difficulties in comprehending causal relations among children with ADHD: The role of cognitive engagement. *Journal of Abnormal Psychology, 113*, 1–8.

Lorch, E. P., Milich, R., & Sanchez, R. P. (1998). Story comprehension in children with ADHD. *Clinical Child and Family Psychology Review, 1*, 163–178.

Lorch, E. P., O'Neil, K., Berthiaume, K. S., Milich, R., Eastham, D., & Brooks, T. (2004). Story comprehension and the impact of studying on recall in children with attention deficit hyperactivity disorder. *Journal of Clinical Child and Adolescent Psychology, 33*, 506–515.

Lorenz, K. (1970). *Studies in animal and human behaviour: Vol. 1* (R. Martin, Trans.). Oxford, UK: Harvard University Press.

Lozoff, B., Jimenez, E., Hagen, J., Mollen, E., & Wolf, A. W. (2000). Poorer behavioral and developmental outcome more than 10 years after treatment for iron deficiency in infancy. *Pediatrics, 105*, E51.

Lubart, T. I. (1999). Creativity across cultures. In R. J. Sternberg (Ed.), *Handbook of creativity* (pp. 339–350). Cambridge, UK: Cambridge University Press.

Luke, C. (1999). Cyborg pedagogy in cyborg culture. *Teaching Education, 10*, 69–72.

Lunner, K., Werthem, E. H., Thompson, J. K., Paxton, S. J., McDonald, F., & Halverson, K. S. (2000). A cross-cultural examination of weight-related teasing, body image, and eating disturbance in Swedish and Australian samples. *International Journal of Eating Disorders, 28*, 430–435.

Luthar, S. S., Cicchetti, D., & Becker, B. (2000). Research on resilience: Response to commentaries. *Child Development, 71*, 573–575.

Luthar, S. S., & Latendresse, S. J. (2002). Adolescent risk: The costs of affluence. *New Directions for Youth Development, 95*, 101–121.

Lyon, R. (1999). *Testimony to the Committee on Education and the Workforce, U.S. House of Representatives: Hearing on Title I of the Elementary and Secondary Education Act.* Retrieved from http://156.40.88.3/about/crmc/cdb

Lypaczewski, G., Lappe, J., & Stubby, J. (2002). "Mom & me" and healthy bones: An innovative approach to teaching bone health. *Orthopedic Nursing, 21*, 35–42.

Ma, X., Stewin, L. L., & Mah, D. L. (2001). Bullying in school: Nature, effects, and remedies. *Research Papers in Education, 16*(3), 247–270.

MacArthur Network on Successful Pathways Through Middle Childhood research initiatives. (1997). Retrieved October 21, 2002, from http://midchild.soe.umich.edu/research/

MacArthur Network on Successful Pathways Through Middle Childhood. (2002). Retrieved October 22, 2002, from http://www.macfound.org/research/hcd/hcd_15.htm

Maccoby, E. E. (1990). Gender and relationships: A developmental account. *American Psychologist, 45*, 513–520.

Maccoby, E. E. (1998). *The two sexes: Growing up apart, coming together.* Cambridge, MA: Harvard University Press.

Maccoby, E. E. (2000). Parenting and its effects on children: On reading and misreading behavior genetics. *Annual Review of Psychology, 51*, 1–27.

MacDonald, R., & Marsh, J. (2002). Crossing the Rubicon: Youth transitions, poverty, drugs and social exclusion. *International Journal of Drug Policy, 13*, 27–38.

MacKinnon, C., Volling, B. L., & Lamb, M. (1994). A cross-contextual analysis of boys' social competence: From family to school. *Developmental Psychology, 30*, 325–333.

Magee, V. (2002, January). Perspective and balance: Considering qualitative research methods in psychology. Review essay: M. Kopala & L. A. Suzuki (Eds.) (1999). Using qualitative methods in psychology [40 paragraphs]. *Forum Qualitative Sozialforschung/Forum: Qualitative Social Research* [On-line Journal], *3*(1). Retrieved March 21, 2005, from http://www.qualitative-research.net/fqs-eng.htm

Magnusson, D. (1995). Individual development: A holistic, integrated model. In P. Moen, G. H. Elder, & K. Lusher (Eds.), *Examining lives in context: Perspectives on the ecology of human development* (pp. 19–60). Washington, DC: American Psychological Association.

Magnusson, D. (2000). The individual as the organizing principle in psychological inquiry: A holistic approach. In L. R. Bergman, R. B. Cairns, L. Nilsson, & L. Nystedt (Eds.), *Developmental science and the holistic approach* (pp. 33–48). Mahwah, NJ: Erlbaum.

Magnusson, D., & Stattin, H. (1998). Person-context interaction theories. In W. Damon (Series Ed.) & R. M. Lerner (Vol. Ed.), *Handbook of child psychology: Vol. 1. Theoretical models of human development* (5th ed., pp. 685–759). New York: Wiley.

Magnusson, D., Stattin, H., & Allen, V. (1985). Biological maturation and social development: A longitudinal study of some adjustment processes from mid-adolescence to adulthood. *Journal of Youth and Adolescence, 14*, 267–283.

Maguen, S., Floyd, F. J., Bakeman, R., & Armistead, L. (2002). Developmental milestones and disclosure of sexual orientation among gay, lesbian, and bisexual youths. *Journal of Applied Developmental Psychology, 23*, 219–233.

Mahler, M. S., Pine, F., & Bergman, A. (1975). *The psychological birth of the human infant: Symbiosis and individuation.* New York: Basic Books.

Mahoney, J. L. (2000). School extracurricular activity participation as a moderator in the development of antisocial patterns. *Child Development, 71*, 502–516.

Main, M., Kaplan, K., & Cassidy, J. (1985). Security in infancy, childhood and adulthood: A move to the level of representation. In I. Bretherton & E. Waters (Eds.), *Growing points in attachment theory and research* (pp. 66–104). *Monographs of the Society for Research in Child Development, 50*(1–2, Serial No. 209).

Main, M., & Solomon, J. (1990). Procedures for identifying infants as disorganized/disoriented during the Ainsworth strange situation. In M. T. Greenberg, D. Cicchetti, & E. M. Cummings (Eds.), *Attachment in the preschool years* (pp. 121–160). Chicago: University of Chicago Press.

Maine, M. (2000). *Body wars: Making peace with women's bodies: An activist's guide.* Carlsbad, CA: Gurze.

Mainess, K. J., Champion, T. B., & McCabe, A. (2002). Telling the unknown story: Complex and explicit narration by African American preadolescents—preliminary examination of gender and socioeconomic issues. *Linguistics and Education, 13*, 151–173.

Maira, S., & Soep, E. (2004). United States of adolescence? Reconsidering U.S. youth culture studies. *Youth: Nordic Journal of Youth Studies, 12*, 245–269.

Makros, J., & McCabe, M. P. (2001). Relationships between identity and self-representations during adolescence. *Journal of Youth and Adolescence, 30*, 623–639.

Mancini, J. A., & Huebner, A. J. (2004). Adolescent risk behavior patterns: Effects of structured time-use, interpersonal connections, self-system characteristics, and socio-demographic influences. *Child and Adolescent Social Work Journal, 21*, 647–668.

Manning, M. L., & Bucher, K. T. (2000). Middle schools should be both learner-centered and subject-centered. *Childhood Education, 77*, 41–42.

Manning, W. D. (2002). The implications of cohabitation for children's well-being. In A. Booth & A. C. Crouter (Eds.), *Just living together: Implications of cohabitation on families, children, and social policy* (pp. 121–152). Mahwah, NJ: Erlbaum.

Marcia, J. E. (1966). Development and validation of ego-identity status. *Journal of Personality and Social Psychology, 3*, 551–558.

Margolin, G., & Gordis, E. B. (2000). The effects of family and community violence on children. *Annual Review of Psychology, 51*, 445–479.

Marion, M. (1999). *Guidance of young children*. Columbus, OH: Merrill.

Markstrom, C. A. (1999). Religious involvement and adolescent psychosocial development. *Journal of Adolescence, 22*, 205–221.

Markstrom, C. A., & Iborra, A. (2003). Adolescent identity formation and rites of passage: The Navaho Kinaaldá ceremony for girls. *Journal of Research on Adolescence, 13*, 399–425.

Markstrom-Adams, C. (1992). A consideration of intervening factors in adolescent identity formation. In G. R. Adams, T. P. Gullotta, & R. Montemayor (Eds.), *Adolescent identity formation* (pp. 173–192). Newbury Park, CA: Sage.

Markstrom-Adams, C., Hofstra, G., & Dougher, K. (1994). The ego-virtue of fidelity: A case for the study of religion and identity formation in adolescence. *Journal of Youth & Adolescence, 23*, 453–469.

Markus, H., & Nurius, P. (1986). Possible selves. *American Psychologist, 41*, 954–969.

Marsh, H. W. (1989). Age and sex effects in multiple dimensions of self-concept: Preadolescence to early adulthood. *Journal of Educational Psychology, 81*, 417–430.

Marsh, H. W., & Hattie, J. (1996). Theoretical perspectives on the structure of self-concept. In B. A. Bracken (Ed.), *Handbook of self-concept: Developmental, social, and clinical considerations* (pp. 38–90). New York: Wiley.

Marshall, S. K. (2001). Do I matter? Construct validation of adolescents' perceived mattering to parents and friends. *Journal of Adolescence, 24*, 473–490.

Marshall, W. A., & Tanner, J. M. (1969). Variations in patterns of pubertal change in girls. *Archives of Disease in Childhood, 44*, 291–303.

Martin, C. L., Ruble, D. N., & Szkrybalo, J. (2002). Cognitive theories of early gender development. *Psychological Bulletin, 128*(6), 903–933.

Martin, T. F., White, J. M., & Perlman, D. (2003). Religious socialization: A test of the channeling hypothesis of parental influence on adolescent faith maturity. *Journal of Adolescent Research, 18*(2), 169–187.

Mascarenhas, M. R., Zemel, B. S., Tershakovec, A. M., & Stallings, V. A. (2001). Adolescence. In B. A. Bowman & R. M. Russell (Eds.), *Present knowledge in nutrition* (8th ed., pp. 426–438). Washington, DC: ILSI Press.

Maslow, A. H. (1962). Some basic propositions of a growth and self-actualizing psychology. In *Perceiving, behaving, becoming: A new focus for education*. Washington, DC: Association for Supervision and Curriculum Development.

Maslow, A. H. (1971). *The farther reaches of human nature*. New York: Viking.

Maslow, A. H. (1987). *Motivation and personality* (3rd ed.). New York: Harper & Row.

Masten, A. S., & Coatsworth, J. D. (1998). The development of competence in favorable and unfavorable environments: Lessons from research on successful children. *American Psychologist, 56*, 205–220.

Masten, A. S., & Curtis, W. J. (2000). Integrating competence and psychopathology: Pathways toward a comprehensive science of adaptation in development. *Development and Psychopathology, 12*, 529–550.

Mathematics Achievement. (1996). *Mathematics achievement in the middle school years: IEA's third international mathematics and science report*. Chestnut Hill, MA: Boston College, Center for the Study of Testing, Evaluation, and Educational Policy.

Maurer, D. (2005). Introduction to the special issue on critical periods reexamined: Evidence from human sensory development. *Developmental Psychobiology, 46*, [np].

Mayer, R. E., Sims, V., & Tajika, H. (1995). A comparison of how textbooks teach mathematical problem solving in Japan and the United States. *American Educational Research Journal, 32*, 443–460.

Maynard, R. A. (1997). The costs of adolescent childbearing. In R. A. Maynard (Ed.), *Kids having kids: Economic costs and social consequences of teen pregnancy* (pp. 285–337). Washington, DC: Urban Institute Press.

McAdoo, H. P. (1999). *Family ethnicity: Strength in diversity* (2nd ed.). Thousand Oaks, CA: Sage.

McBride, C. K., Paikoff, R. L., & Holmbeck, G. N. (2003). Individual and familial influences on the onset of sexual intercourse among urban African American adolescents. *Journal of Consulting & Clinical Psychology, 71*, 159–167.

McCabe, M. P., & Ricciardelli, L. A. (2003). A longitudinal study of body change strategies among adolescent males. *Journal of Youth and Adolescence, 32*, 105–113.

McCall, R. B., Evahn, C., & Kratzer, L. (1992). *High school underachievers: What do they achieve as adults?* Newbury Park, CA: Sage.

McCall, R. B., & Groark, C. J. (2000). The future of applied child development research and public policy. *Child Development, 71*, 197–204.

McCarthy, R. J. (1972). *The ungraded middle school.* West Nyack, NJ: Parker.

McCurdy, D. W., Spradley, J. P., & Shandy, D. J. (2005). *The cultural experience: Ethnography in complex society* (2nd ed.). Long Grove, IL: Waveland Press.

McGhee, P. E. (1976). Children's appreciation of humor: A test of the cognitive congruency principle. *Child Development, 47*, 420–426.

McGill, H. C., & McMahan, C. A. (2003). Starting earlier to prevent heart disease. *JAMA: Journal of the American Medical Association, 290*, 2320–2322.

McGuire, S., Manke, B., Saudino, K. J., Reiss, D., Hetherington, E. M., & Plomin, R. (1999). Perceived competence and self-worth during adolescence: A longitudinal behavioral genetic study. *Child Development, 70*, 1283–1296.

McHale, S. M., Crouter, A. C., & Tucker, C. J. (1999). Family context and gender role socialization in middle childhood: Comparing girls to boys and sisters to brothers. *Child Development, 70*, 990–1004.

McHale, S. M., Crouter, A. C., & Tucker, C. J. (2001). Freetime activities in middle childhood: Links with adjustment in early adolescence. *Child Development, 72*(6), 1764–1778.

McHale, S. M., Dariotis, J. K., & Kauh, T. J. (2003). Social development and social relationships in middle childhood. In R. M. Lerner & M. A. Easterbrook (Eds.), *Handbook of psychology:* Vol. 6. *Developmental psychology* (pp. 241–265). New York: Wiley.

McHale, S. M., Updegraff, K. A., Helms-Erikson, H., & Crouter, A. C. (2001). Sibling influences on gender development in middle childhood and early adolescence: A longitudinal study. *Developmental Psychology, 37*, 115–125.

McHale, S. M., Updegraff, K. A., Tucker, C. J., & Crouter, A. C. (2000). Step in or stay out? Parents' roles in adolescent siblings' relationships. *Journal of Marriage and Family, 62*, 746–760.

McKay, A. (2004). Oral sex among teenagers: Research, discourse, and education. *The Canadian Journal of Human Sexuality, 13*, 3–4.

McKay, H. A., Bailey, D. A., Mirwald, R. L., Davison, K. S., & Faulkner, R. A. (1998). Peak bone mineral accrual and age at menarche in adolescent girls: A 6-year longitudinal study. *The Journal of Pediatrics, 133*, 682–687.

McKown, C. (2004). Age and ethnic variation in children's thinking about the nature of racism. *Applied Developmental Psychology, 25*, 597–617.

McKown, C., & Weinstein, R. S. (2003). The development and consequences of stereotype consciousness in middle childhood. *Child Development, 74*, 498–515.

McLelland, J. A., & Youniss, J. (2003). Two systems of youth service: Determinants of voluntary and required youth community service. *Journal of Youth & Adolescence, 32*, 47–58.

McLoyd, V. C. (1998). Socioeconomic disadvantage and child development. *American Psychologist, 53*, 185–204.

McNamara, C. A. (1998). *Basic guide to program evaluation.* Retrieved July 16, 2005 from http://www.mapnp.org/library/evaluatn/fnl_eval.htm

McNeely, C., Shew, M. L., Beuhring, T., Sieving, R., Miller, B. C., & Blum, R. W. (2002). Mothers' influence on the timing of first sex among 14- and 15-year-olds. *Journal of Adolescent Health, 31*, 256–265.

Mead, G. H. (1934). *Mind, self, and society from the standpoint of a social behaviorist.* Chicago: University of Chicago Press.

Mead, M. (1973/1928). *Coming of age in Samoa: A psychological study of primitive youth for Western civilization.* New York: Morrow.

Meerum Terwogt, M., & Olthuf, T. (1989). Awareness and self-regulation of emotion in young children. In C. Saarni & P. Harris (Eds.), *Children's understanding of emotion* (pp. 209–237). Cambridge, UK: Cambridge University Press.

Meeus, W., Iedema, J., Helsen, M., & Vollebergh, W. (1999). Patterns of adolescent identity development: Review of literature and longitudinal analysis. *Developmental Review, 19*, 419–461.

Meeus, W., Iedema, J., Maassen, G., & Engels, R. (2005). Separation-individuation revisited: On the interplay of parent-adolescent relations, identity and emotional adjustment in adolescence. *Journal of Adolescence, 28*, 89–106.

Meininger, E., Cohen, E., Neinstein, L., & Remafedi, G. (2002). Gay, lesbian and bisexual adolescents. In L. S. Neinstein (Ed.), *Adolescent health care: A practical guide* (4th ed., pp. 793–809). New York: Lippincott, Williams & Wilkins.

Melaville, A. (1998). *Learning together: The developing field of community-school initiatives.* Washington, DC: Charles Stewart Mott Foundation.

Menzulis, A. H., Hyde, J, S., & Abramson, L. Y. (2003, June). *Can temperament provide protection against risk for depression? Relationships between temperament and cognitive style in middle childhood.* Poster presented at the MacArthur Conference on Successful Pathways through Adolescence, Washington, DC.

Merriam-Webster's collegiate dictionary (10th ed.) (2002). Springfield, MA: Merriam-Webster.

Merrick, E. (1999). An exploration of quality in qualitative research: Are "reliability" and "validity" relevant? In M. Kopala & L. Suzuki (Eds.), *Using qualitative methods in psychology* (pp. 25–36). Thousand Oaks, CA: Sage.

Merser, C. (1987). *Grownups: A generation in search of adulthood.* New York: Putnam.

Middle Start Initiative. (2002). *Starting again in the middle.* Available from the Michigan League for Human Services, 300 N. Washington Square, Suite 401, Lansing, MI, 48933.

Mikulincer, M., & Selinger, M. (2001). The interplay between attachment and affiliation systems in adolescents' same-sex friendships: The role of attachment style. *Journal of Social and Personal Relationships, 18*, 81–106.

Miles, M. B., & Huberman, A. M. (1994). *Qualitative data analysis*. Thousand Oaks, CA: Sage.

Miller, A. L., Notaro, P. C., & Zimmerman, M. A. (2002). Stability and change in internal working models of friendship: Associations with multiple domains of urban adolescent functioning. *Journal of Social and Personal Relationships, 119*(2), 233–259.

Miller, B. C., Benson, B., & Galbraith, K. A. (2001). Family relationships and adolescent pregnancy risk: A research synthesis. *Developmental Review, 21*, 1–38.

Miller, C. T., & Downey, K. T. (1999). A meta-analysis of heavyweight and self-esteem. *Personality & Social Psychology Review, 3*, 68–84.

Miller, P. H. (2002). *Theories of developmental psychology* (4th ed.). New York: Worth.

Millstein, S. G., & Halpern-Felsher, B. L. (2002). Judgments about risk and perceived invulnerability in adolescents and young adults. *Journal of Research on Adolescence, 12*(4), 399–422.

Mintz, S. (1993). Life stages. In M. K. Cayton, E. J. Gorn, & P. W. Williams (Eds.), *Encyclopedia of American social history* (Vol. 3, pp. 2011–2022). New York: Scribner.

Mistry, J., & Saraswathi, T. S. (2003). The cultural context of child development. In R. M. Lerner, M. A. Easterbrooks, & J. Mistry (Vol. Eds.), *Handbook of psychology: Vol. 6. Developmental psychology* (pp. 267–291). New York: Wiley.

Mitic, W., & Greschner, J. (2002). Alcohol's role in the deaths of BC children and youth. *Canadian Journal of Public Health, 93*, 173–175.

Modell, J. (1989). *Into one's own: From youth to adulthood in the United States, 1920–1975*. Berkeley, CA: University of California Press.

Modell, J., & Elder, G. H. (2002). Children develop in history: So what's new? In W. W. Hartup & R. A. Weinberg (Eds.), *Child psychology in retrospect and prospect: Vol. 32. The Minnesota symposia on child psychology*. Mahwah, NJ: Erlbaum.

Moely, B. E., Hart, S. S., Leal, L., Santulli, K. A., Rao, N., & Johnson, T., et al., (1992). The teacher's role in facilitating memory and study strategy development in the elementary school classroom. *Child Development, 63*, 653–672.

Mohn, J. K., Tingle, L. R., & Finger, R. (2003). An analysis of the causes of the decline in non-marital birth and pregnancy rates for teens from 1991 to 1995. *Adolescent and Family Health, 3*, 39–47.

Moilanen, D. (1993). Depressive experiences of nonreferred adolescents and young adults: A cognitive-developmental perspective. *Journal of Adolescent Research, 8*, 311–325.

Moneta, G. B., Schneider, B., & Csikszentmihalyi, M. (2001). A longitudinal study of the self-concept and experiential components of self-worth and affect across adolescence. *Applied Developmental Psychology, 5*(3), 125–142.

Montemayor, R. (2000). The variety of adolescent experiences. In R. Montemayor, G. R. Adams, & T. R. Gulotta (Eds.), *Adolescent diversity in ethnic, economic, and cultural contexts* (pp. 256–271). Thousand Oaks, CA: Sage.

Montemayor, R., Adams, G. R., & Gullotta, T. P. (1990). *From childhood to adolescence: A transitional period?* Newbury Park, CA: Sage.

Montemayor, R., & Flannery, D. J. (1990). Making the transition from childhood to early adolescence. In R. Montemayor, G. R. Adams, & T. P. Gullotta. *From childhood to adolescence: A transitional period?* (pp. 291–301). Newbury Park, CA: Sage.

Moore, K. A., Morrison, D. R., & Greene, A. D. (1997). Effects on the children born to adolescent mothers. In R. A. Maynard (Ed.), *Kids having kids: Economic costs and social consequences of teen pregnancy* (pp. 145–180). Washington, DC: Urban Institute Press.

Moore, K. A., Papillo, A. R., Williams, S., Jager, J., & Jones, F. (1999). *Teen birthrates for 1998: Facts at a glance*. Washington, DC: Child Trends.

Moore, S., & Rosenthal, D. (1991). Adolescent invulnerability and perceptions of AIDS risk. *Journal of Adolescent Research, 6*, 164–180.

Moore, S., & Rosenthal, D. (1993). *Sexuality in adolescence*. London: Routledge.

Morgan, D. L. (1996). Focus groups. *Annual Review of Sociology, 22*, 129–153.

Morgan, D. L. (1997). *Focus groups as qualitative research* (2nd ed.). Thousand Oaks, CA: Sage.

Morgan, M., Gibbs, S., Maxwell, K., & Britten, N. (2002). Methodological issues in conducting focus groups with children ages 7–11 years. *Qualitative Research, 2*, 5–20.

Morrison, F. J., McMahon Griffith, E., & Frazier, J. A. (1996). Schooling and the 5 to 7 shift: A natural experiment. In A. J. Sameroff & M. M. Haith (Eds.), *The five to seven year shift: The age of reason and responsibility*. Chicago: The University of Chicago Press.

Morrow, S. L. (2005). Quality and trustworthiness in qualitative research in counseling psychology. *Journal of Counseling Psychology, 52*, 250–260.

Mortimer, J. T., & Finch, M. D. (1996). Work, family, and adolescent development. In J. T. Mortimer & M. D. Finch (Eds.), *Adolescents, work and family: An intergenerational developmental analysis* (pp. 1–24). Thousand Oaks, CA: Sage.

Mortimer, J. T., & Larson, R. (2002). Macrostructural trends and the reshaping of adolescence. In J. T. Mortimer & R. Larson (Eds.), *The changing adolescent experience: Societal trends and the transition to adulthood* (pp. 1–17). Cambridge, UK: Cambridge University Press.

Moving an out-of-school agenda: Lessons and challenges across cities (Executive summary). Retrieved September 8,

2002, from http://www.forumforyouthinvestment.org/grasp/execsumm.htm

Mruk, C. (1995). *Self-esteem: Research, theory, practice.* New York: Springer.

Muir, S. L., Wertheim, E. H., & Paxton, S. J. (1999). Adolescent girls' first diets: Triggers and the role of multiple dimensions of self-concept. *Eating Disorders: The Journal of Treatment and Prevention, 7,* 259–270.

Mukherjee, P., Miller, J., Shimony, J., Philip, J., Nehra, D., & Snyder, A., et al. (2002). Diffusion-tensor MR imaging of gray and white matter development during normal human brain maturation. *American Journal of Neuroradiology, 23,* 1445–1456.

Muller, C., & Kerbow, D. (1993). Parent involvement in the home, school, and community. In B. Schneider & J. S. Coleman (Eds.), *Parents, their children, and schools* (pp. 13–42). Boulder, CO: Westview.

Muller, J. (1999). Narrative approaches to qualitative research in primary care. In B. Crabtree & W. Miller (Eds.), *Doing qualitative research* (2nd ed., pp. 221–238). Thousand Oaks, CA: Sage.

Murphy, K. R., & Davidshofer, C. O. (2001). *Psychological testing: Principles and applications.* Upper Saddle River, NJ: Prentice Hall.

Murphy, M. M. (2002). *Character education in America's blue ribbon schools: Best practices for meeting the challenge* (2nd ed.). Lanham, MD: Scarecrow Press.

Mussen, P., & Eisenberg, N. (2001). Prosocial development in context. In A. C. Bohart & D. J. Stipek (Eds.), *Constructive & destructive behavior: Implications for family, school, & society* (pp. 103–126). Washington, DC: American Psychological Association.

Mussen, P. H., & Jones, M. C. (1957). Self-conceptions, motivations, and interpersonal attitudes of late- and early-maturing boys. *Child Development, 28,* 243–256.

Muuss, R. E. (1982). Social cognition: David Elkind's theory of adolescent egocentrism. *Adolescence, 17,* 249–265.

Muuss, R. E. (1996). *Theories of adolescence* (6th ed.). New York: McGraw-Hill.

Mwamwenda, T. S. (1999). Undergraduate and graduate students' combinatorial reasoning and formal operations. *Journal of Genetic Psychology, 160,* 503–506.

Mwamwenda, T. S., & Mwamwenda, B. B. (1991). Africans' cognitive development and schooling. *International Journal of Educational Development, 11,* 129–134.

Myers, M. G., & MacPherson, L. (2004). Smoking cessation efforts among substance abusing adolescents. *Drug & Alcohol Dependence, 73,* 209–213.

Nagin, D., & Tremblay, R. E. (1999). Trajectories of boys' physical aggression, opposition, and hyperactivity on the path to physically violent and nonviolent juvenile delinquency. *Child Development, 70,* 1181–1196.

Naimi, T. S., Brewer, R. D., Mokdad, A., Denny, C., Serdula, M. K., & Marks, J. S. (2003). Binge drinking among U. S. adults. *Journal of the American Medical Association, 289,* 70–75.

Nakkula, M. J., & Nikitopoulos, C. E. (2001). Negotiation training and interpersonal development: An exploratory study of early adolescents in Argentina. *Adolescence, 36,* 1–20.

Närvänen, A., & Näsman, E. (2004). Childhood as generation or life phase? *Young: Nordic Journal of Youth Research, 12*(1), 71–91.

National Association for Sport and Physical Education (NASPE) (1998). *Physical activity for children: A statement of guidelines.* Reston, VA: NASPE Publications.

National Center for Health Statistics (2001). *Prevalence of overweight among children and adolescents: United States, 1999.* Centers for Disease Control and Prevention, Health E-Stats.

National Education Association (1969). *Report of the Committee on Secondary School Studies.* New York: Arno/New York Times.

National Institute on Alcohol Abuse and Alcoholism (1998). *Alcohol Alert, No. 41: Alcohol and sleep.* Washington, DC: Author.

National Science Board (1998). Science and engineering indicators—1998. (NSB 98-1). Arlington, VA: National Science Foundation.

Neisser, U., Boodoo, G., Bouchard, T. J., Jr., Boykin, A. W., Brody, N., Ceci, S. J., et al. (1996). Intelligence: Knowns and unknowns. *American Psychologist, 51,* 77–101.

Nelson, L. J., & Barry, C. M. (2005). Distinguishing features of emerging adulthood: The role of self-classification as an adult. *Journal of Adolescent Research, 20,* 242–262.

Nesselroade, J. R., & Baltes, P. B. (1974). Adolescent personality development and historical changes: 1970–1972. *Monographs of the Society for Research in Child Development, 39*(1, Serial No. 154).

Neumark-Sztainer, D., Story, M., Falkner, N. H., Beuhring, T., & Resnick, M. D. (1999). Sociodemographic and personal characteristics of adolescents engaged in weight loss and weight/muscle gain behaviors: Who is doing what? *Preventive Medicine, 28,* 40–50.

Newcomb, A. E., Bukowski, W., & Pattee, L. (1993). Children's peer relations: A meta-analytic review of popular, rejected, neglected, controversial, and average sociometric status. *Psychological Bulletin, 113,* 99–128.

Newman, B. M., Myers, M. C., Newman, P. R., Lohman, B. J., & Smith, V. L. (2000). The transition to high school for academically promising, urban, low-income African American youth. *Adolescence, 35,* 45–66.

Newman, B. M., & Newman, P. R. (2001). Group identity and alienation: Giving the we its due. *Journal of Youth and Adolescence, 30,* 515–538.

Newman, D. L. (2005). Ego development and ethnic identity formation in rural American Indian adolescents. *Child Development, 76,* 734–746.

Newman, R. S. (2002). What do I need to do to succeed. . . when I don't understand what I'm doing!?: Developmental influences on students' adaptive help-seeking. In A. Wigfield & J. S. Eccles (Eds.), *The development of achievement motivation* (pp. 285–305). San Diego, CA: Academic Press.

Nickerson, A. B., & Nagle, R. J. (2005). Parent and peer attachment in late childhood and early adolescence. *Journal of Early Adolescence, 25*(2), 225–249.

Ninio, A., & Snow, C. E. (1996). *Pragmatic development.* Boulder, CO: Westview Press.

Nippold, M. A., Taylor, C. L., & Baker, J. M. (1996). Idiom understanding in Australian youth: A cross-cultural comparison. *Journal of Speech and Hearing Research, 39*, 442–447.

Niu, W., & Sternberg, R. J. (2003). Societal and school influences on student creativity: The case of China. *Psychology in the Schools, 40*, 103–114.

Noom, M. J., Dekovic, M., & Meeus, W. (2001). Conceptual analysis and measurement of adolescent identity. *Journal of Youth and Adolescence, 30*, 577–595.

Novick, N., Cauce, A. M., & Grove, K. (1998). Competence self-concept. In B. A. Bracken (Ed.), *Handbook of self-concept: Developmental, social, and clinical considerations* (pp. 210–258). New York: Wiley.

Nucci, L. P. (2001). *Education in the moral domain.* New York: Cambridge University Press.

Nussbaum, M. C. (2000). Emotions and social norms. In L. P. Nucci, G. B. Saxe, & E. Turiel (Eds.), *Culture, thought, and development* (pp. 41–63). Mahwah, NJ: Erlbaum.

Nyborg, H., & Jensen, A. R., (2001). Occupation and income related to psychometric *g*. *Intelligence, 29*, 45–56.

O'Brien, M. (1992). Gender identity and sex roles. In V. B. Van Hasselt & M. Hersen (Eds.), *Handbook of social development: A lifespan perspective* (pp. 325–345). New York: Plenum.

Oden, S. (1995). Studying youth programs to assess influences on youth development: New roles for researchers. *Journal of Adolescent Research, 10*(1), 174–186.

Offer, D. (1969). *The psychological world of the teenager.* New York: Basic Books.

Offer, D., Ostrow, E., & Howard, K. I. (1981). *The adolescent: A psychological self-portrait.* New York: Basic Books.

O'Grady, W. (1997). *Syntactic development.* Chicago: University of Chicago Press.

Okin, S. M. (1989). *Justice, gender, and the family.* New York: Basic Books.

Oliver, M. B., & Hyde, J. S. (1993). Gender differences in sexuality: A meta-analysis. *Psychological Bulletin, 114*, 29–51.

Olweus, D., Mattsson, A., Schalling, D., & Low, H. (1988). Circulating testosterone levels and aggression in adolescent males: A causal analysis. *Psychosomatic Medicine, 3*, 261–272.

O'Malley, P. M., & Bachman, J. G. (1983). Self-esteem: Change and stability between ages 13 and 23. *Developmental Psychology, 19*, 257–268.

O'Moore, M., & Kirkham, C. (2001). Self-esteem and its relationship to bullying behaviour. *Aggressive Behavior, 27*, 269–283.

O'Neil, M. L. (2002). Youth curfews in the United States: The creation of public spheres for some young people. *Journal of Youth Studies, 5*, 49–67.

O'Neil, R., Parke, R. D., & McDowell, D. J. (2001). Objective and subjective features of children's neighborhoods: Relations to parental regulatory strategies and children's social competence. *Journal of Applied Developmental Psychology, 22*, 135–155.

Oppenheim, D., & Waters, H. S. (1995). Narrative processes and attachment representations: Issues of development and assessment. In E. Waters, B. E. Vaughn, G. Posada, & K. Kondo-Ikemura (Eds.), *Caregiving, cultural, and cognitive perspectives on secure-base behavior and working models: New growing points of attachment theory and research* (pp. 197–214). *Monographs of the Society for Research in Child Development, 60*(2–3, Serial No. 244).

Orenstein, P. (1994). *Young women, self-esteem, and the confidence gap.* New York: Anchor.

Ornstein, P. A., & Naus, M. J. (1985). Effects of the knowledge base on children's memory strategies. In H. W. Reese (Ed.), *Advances in child development and behavior: Vol. 19.* New York: Academic Press.

Ornstein, P. A., Naus, M. J., & Liberty, C. (1975). Rehearsal and organizational processes in children's memory. *Child Development, 46*, 818–830.

Osgood, D. W., Ruth, G., Eccles, J. S., Jacobs, J. E., & Barber, B. L. (2005). Six paths to adulthood: Fast starters, parents without careers, educated partners, educated singles, working singles, and slow starters. In R. A. Settersten, Jr., F. F. Furstenberg, Jr., & R. G. Rumbaut (Eds.), *On the frontier of adulthood: Theory, research, and public policy* (pp. 320–355). Chicago: University of Chicago Press.

O'Sullivan, J. T. (1996). Children's metamemory about the influence of conceptual relations on recall. *Journal of Experimental Child Psychology, 62*, 1–29.

Oswald, R. F., Blume, L. B., & Marks, S. (2005). Decentering heteronormativity: A model for family studies. In A. Acock, K. Allen, V. Bengtson, D. Klein, & P. Dilworth-Anderson (Eds.), *Sourcebook of family theory and research* (pp. 447–468). Thousand Oaks, CA: Sage.

Overton, W. F. (1998). Developmental psychology: Philosophy, concepts, and methodology. In W. Damon (Series Ed.) & N. Eisenberg (Vol. Ed.), *Handbook of child psychology: Vol. 3. Social, emotional, and personality development* (5th ed., pp. 107–188). New York: Wiley.

Owens, R. E., Jr. (1998). *Queer kids: The challenges and promises for lesbian, gay, and bisexual youth.* Binghamton, NY: Haworth.

Oyserman, D., Bybee, D., Terry, K., & Hart-Johnson, T. (2004). Possible selves as roadmaps. *Journal of Research in Personality, 38*(2), 130–149.

Oyserman, D., & Markus, H. (1990). Possible selves and delinquency. *Journal of Personality and Social Psychology, 59*, 112–125.

Oyserman, D., & Saltz, E. (1993). Competence, delinquency, and attempts to attain possible selves. *Journal of Personality and Social Psychology, 65*, 360–374.

Oyserman, D., Terry, K., & Bybee, D. (2002). A possible selves intervention to enhance school involvement. *Journal of Adolescence, 25*, 313–326.

Ozturk, C., Durmazlar, N., Ural, B., Karaagaoglu, E., Yalaz, K., & Anlar, B. (1999). Hand and eye preference in normal preschool children. *Clinical Pediatrics, 38*, 677–680.

Palinscar, A. S., & Brown, A. L. (1984). Reciprocal teaching of comprehension-fostering and comprehension monitoring activities. *Cognition and Instruction, 1*, 117–175.

Park, Y. M., Matsumoto, K., Seo, Y. J., Kang, M. J., & Nagashima, H. (2002). Changes of sleep or waking habits by age and sex in Japanese. *Perceptual and Motor Skills, 94*, 1199–1213.

Parke, R. D., & Buriel, R. (1998). Socialization in the family: Ethnic and ecological perspectives. In W. Damon (Series Ed.) & N. Eisenberg (Vol. Ed.), *Handbook of child psychology: Vol. 3. Social, emotional, and personality development* (5th ed., pp. 463–552). New York: Wiley.

Parker, J. G., & Asher, S. R. (1993). Friendship and friendship quality in middle childhood: Links with peer group acceptance and feelings of loneliness and social dissatisfaction. *Developmental Psychology, 29*, 611–621.

Parker, J. G., & Seal, J. (1996). Forming, losing, renewing, and replacing friendships: Applying temporal parameters to the assessment of children's friendship experiences. *Child Development, 67*, 2248–2268.

Parrish, M. (2004). Urban poverty and homelessness as hidden demographic variables relevant to academic achievement. In D. Boothe and J. C. Stanley (Eds.), *In the eyes of the beholder: Critical issues for diversity in gifted education* (pp. 203–211). Waco, TX: Prufrock Press.

Passarotti, A. M., Paus, B. M., Bussiere, J. R., Buxton, R. B., Wong, E. C., & Stiles, J. (2003). The development of face and location processing: An MRI study. *Developmental Science, 6*, 100–117.

Patton, M. Q. (2002). *Qualitative evaluation and research methods* (3rd ed.). Thousand Oaks, CA: Sage.

Paus, T., Zijdenbos, A., Worsley, K., Collins, D. L., Blumenthal, J., Giedd, J. N., et al. (1999). Structural maturation of neural pathways in children and adolescents: In vivo study. *Science, 283*, 1908–1911.

Pechman, C. (1997). Does anti-smoking advertising combat underage smoking? A review of past practices and research. In M. E. Goldberg, M. Fishbein, & S. E. Middlestadt (Eds.), *Social marketing: Theoretical and practical perspectives* (pp. 189–216). Mahwah, NJ: Erlbaum.

Pedersen, S. (2005). Urban adolescents' out-of-school activity profiles: Associations with youth, family, and school transition characteristics. *Applied Developmental Science, 9*, 107–124.

Peevers, B. H., & Secord, P. F. (1973). Developmental changes in attribution of descriptive concepts to persons. *Journal of Personality and Social Psychology, 27*, 120–128.

Pellegrini, A. D. (2001). A longitudinal study of heterosexual relationships, aggression, and sexual harassment during the transition from primary school through middle school. *Journal of Applied Developmental Psychology, 22*(2), 119–133.

Pellegrini, A. D., & Bjorklund, D. F. (1997). The role of recess in children's cognitive performance. *Educational Psychologist, 32*, 35–40.

Pellegrini, A. D., & Bohn, C. M. (2005). The role of recess in children's cognitive performance and school adjustment. *Educational Researcher, 34*, 13–19.

Pellegrini, A. D., & Smith, P. K. (1998). Physical activity play: The nature and function of a neglected aspect of play. *Child Development, 69*, 577–598.

Penza-Clyve, S. M., Mansell, C., & McQuaid, E. L. (2004). Why don't children take their asthma medications? A qualitative analysis of children's perspectives of adherence. *Journal of Asthma, 41*, 189–197.

Perkins, D. F., & Borden, L. M. (2003). Positive behaviors, problem behaviors, and resiliency in adolescence. In I. B. Weiner (Series Ed.) & R. M. Lerner, M. A. Easterbrooks, & J. Mistry (Vol. Eds.), *Handbook of psychology: Vol. 6. Developmental psychology* (pp. 373–394). New York: Wiley.

Perkins, D. F., Jacobs, J. E., Barber, B. L., & Eccles, J. S. (2004). Childhood and adolescent sports participation as predictors of participation in sports and physical fitness activities during young adulthood. *Youth & Society, 35*, 495–520.

Perry, P. (2001). White means never having to say you're ethnic: White youth and the construction of "cultureless" identities. *Journal of Contemporary Ethnography, 30*, 56–91.

Perry, W. G. (1970/1999). *Forms of ethical and intellectual development in the college years.* San Francisco, CA: Jossey-Bass.

Perugini, E. M., Harvey, E. A., Lovejoy, D. W., Sandstrom, K., & Webb, A. H. (2000). The predictive power of combined neuropsychological measures for attention-deficit/hyperactivity disorder in children. *Child Neuropsychology, 6*, 101–114.

Petersen, A. C. (1984). The early adolescence study: An overview. *Journal of Early Adolescence, 4*, 103–106.

Petersen, A. C., & Taylor, B. (1980). The biological approach to adolescence: Biological change and psychological adaptation. In J. Adelson (Ed.), *Handbook of adolescent psychology* (pp. 117–155). New York: Wiley.

Peterson, K. L., & Roscoe, B. (1991). Imaginary audience behavior in older adolescent females. *Adolescence, 26*, 195–200.

Phelan, P., Davidson, A. L., & Yu, H. C. (1991). Students' multiple worlds: Navigating the borders of family, peer, and school cultures. In P. Phelan & A. L. Davidson (Eds.), *Cultural diversity: Implications for education* (pp. 52–88). New York: Teachers College Press.

Phillips, D. A., & Zimmerman, M. D. (1990). The developmental course of perceived competence and incompetence among competent children. In R. J. Sternberg & J. Kolligian (Eds.), *Competence considered* (pp. 41–66). New Haven, CT: Yale University Press.

Phinney, J. S. (1989). Stages of ethnic identity development in minority group adolescents. *Journal of Early Adolescence, 9*, 34–49.

Phinney, J. S. (1992). The Multigroup Identity Measure: A new scale for use with diverse groups. *Journal of Adolescent Research, 7*, 156–176.

Phinney, J. S., & Alipuria, L. L. (1996). At the interface of cultures: Multiethnic/multiracial high school and college students. *Journal of Social Psychology, 136*, 139–158.

Phinney, J. S., Cantu, C. L., & Kurtz, D. A. (1997). Ethnic and American identity as predictors of self-esteem among African American, Latino, and White adolescents. *Journal of Youth and Adolescence, 26*, 165–185.

Phinney, J. S., & Rosenthal, D. A. (1992). Ethnic identity in adolescence: Process, context, and outcome. In G. R. Adams, T. P. Gullotta, & R. Montemayor (Eds.), *Adolescent identity formation* (pp. 145–172). Newbury Park, CA: Sage.

Piaget, J. (1963). *The origins of intelligence in children* (M. Cook, Trans.). New York: W. W. Norton. (Original work published 1953).

Piaget, J. (1965). *The moral judgment of the child* (M. Gabain, Trans.). New York: W. W. Norton. (Original work published 1932).

Piaget, J. (1972). Intellectual evolution from adolescence to adulthood. *Human Development, 15*, 1–12.

Piaget, J. (1977). *Piaget on Piaget* [Motion Picture]. New Haven, CT: Yale University Press. (Distributed by Yale University Media Design Studio, New Haven, CT, 06520).

Piaget, J., & Inhelder, B. (1967). *The child's conception of space* (F. J. Langdon & J. L. Lunzer, Trans.). New York: W. W. Norton.

Piaget, J., & Inhelder, B. (1969). *The psychology of the child* (H. Weaver, Trans.). New York: Basic Books.

Pianta, R. C., Stuhlman, M. W., & Hamre, B. K. (2002). How schools can do better: Fostering stronger connections between teachers and students. In J. E. Rhodes (Ed.), *A critical view of youth mentoring* (pp. 91–107). San Francisco: Jossey-Bass.

Pike, A. (2002). Behavioral genetics, shared and nonshared environment. In P. K. Smith & C. H. Hart (Eds.), *Blackwell handbook of childhood social development* (pp. 27–43). Malden, MA: Blackwell.

Pike, A., Manke, B., Reiss, D., & Plomin, R. (2000). A genetic analysis of differential experiences of adolescent siblings across three years. *Social Development, 9*, 96–114.

Pipher, M. B. (1994). *Reviving Ophelia: Saving the selves of adolescent girls.* New York: Putnam.

Pittman, K., Diversi, M., & Ferber, T. (2002). Social policy supports for adolescence in the twenty-first century: Framing questions. *Journal of Research on Adolescence, 12*, 149–158.

Pleck, J. H., & Sonenstein, F. L., & Ku, L. C. (1993). Masculinity ideology: Its impact on adolescent males' heterosexual relationships. *Journal of Social Issues, 49*(3), 11–29.

Plomin, R. (2000). Behavioural genetics in the 21st century. *International Journal of Behavioral Development, 24*, 30–34.

Plomin, R., Chipuer, H. M., & Neiderhiser, J. M. (1994). Behavioral genetic evidence for the importance of nonshared environment. In E. M. Hetherington, D. Reiss, & R. Plomin (Eds.), *Separate social worlds of siblings: The impact of non-shared environment on development* (pp. 1–31). Hillsdale, NJ: Erlbaum.

Plomin, R., & Petrill, S. A. (1997). Genetics and intelligence: What's new? *Intelligence, 24*, 53–77.

Polakow Suransky, V. (1982). *The erosion of childhood.* Chicago: University of Chicago Press.

Pomerantz, E. M., & Ruble, D. N. (1997). Distinguishing multiple dimensions of conceptions of ability: Implication for self-evaluation. *Child Development, 68*, 1165–1180.

Pomerantz, E. M., Ruble, D. N., Frey, K. S., & Greulich, F. (1995). Meeting goals and confronting conflict: Children's changing perceptions of social comparison. *Child Development, 66*, 723–738.

Pomerantz, E. M., & Saxon, J. L. (2001). Conceptions of ability as stable and self-evaluative processes: A longitudinal evaluation. *Child Development, 72*, 152–173.

Ponterotto, J. G. (2005). Qualitative research in counseling psychology: A primer on research paradigms and philosophy of science. *Journal of Counseling Psychology, 52*, 126–136.

Posner, J. K., & Vandell, D. L. (1999). After-school activities and the development of low-income urban children: A longitudinal study. *Developmental Psychology, 35*, 868–879.

Poythress, N., Nicholson, R., Otto, R., Edens, J., Bonnie, R., Monahan, J., & Hoge, S. (1999). *The MacArthur Competence Assessment Tool—Criminal adjudication: Professional manual.* Odessa, FL: Psychological Assessment Resources.

Pratt, S., & George, R. (2005). Transferring friendship: Girls' and boys' friendships in the transition from primary to secondary school. *Children & Society, 19*, 16–26.

Pressley, M., Forrest-Pressley, D. J., Elliott-Faust, D. J., & Miller, G. E. (1985). Children's use of cognitive strategies, how to teach strategies, and what to do if they can't be taught. In M. Pressley & C. Brainerd (Eds.), *Cognitive learning and memory in children.* New York: Springer.

Price-Williams, D. R., Gordon, W., & Ramirez, M., III. (1969). Skill and conservation: A study of pottery-making children. *Developmental Psychology, 1*, 769.

Prieto, L. (2000). An urban mosaic in shangri-la. In R. W. Flory & D. C. Miller, (Eds.), *GenX religion* (pp. 57–73). New York: Routledge.

Prinstein, M. J., & La Greca, A. M. (2002). Peer crowd affiliation and internalizing distress in childhood and adolescence: A follow-back study. *Journal of Research on Adolescence, 12*, 325–351.

Prochaska, J. O., & Norcross, J. C. (2002). *Systems of psychotherapy: A transtheoretical analysis* (5th ed.). Pacific Grove, CA: Wadsworth.

Provins, K. A. (1997). The specificity of motor skill and manual asymmetry: A review of the evidence and its implications. *Journal of Motor Behavior, 29*, 183–192.

Puckett, M. B., & Black, J. K. (2001). *The young child: Development from prebirth through age eight* (3rd edition). Upper Saddle River, NJ: Merrill/Prentice Hall.

Pugh, S., Wolff, R., DeFrancesco, C., Gilley, W., & Heitman, R. (2000). A case study of elite male youth baseball athletes' perception of the youth sports experience. *Education, 120*, 773–781.

Pyapali, G. K., Turner, D. A., Wilson, W. A., & Swartzwelder, S. H. (1999). Age and dose-dependent effects of ethanol on the induction of hippocampal long-term potentiation. *Alcohol, 19(2)*, 107–111.

Quadrel, M. J., Fischoff, B., & Davis, W. (1993). Adolescent (in)vulnerability. *American Psychologist, 48*, 102–116.

Quinn, W., Newfield, N. A., & Protinsky, H. O. (1985). Rites of passage in families with adolescents. *Family Process, 24*, 101–111.

Raffaelli, M., & Duckett, E. (1989). "We were just talking. . . ": Conversations in early adolescence. *Journal of Youth and Adolescence, 18*, 567–581.

Rathunde, K. (2001). Family context and the development of undivided interest: A longitudinal study of family support and challenge and adolescents' quality of experience. *Applied Developmental Science, 5*, 158–171.

Raymond, D. (1994). Homophobia, identity, and the meaning of desire: Reflections on the cultural construction of gay and lesbian adolescent sexuality. In J. M. Irvine (Ed.), *Sexual cultures and the construction of adolescent identities* (pp. 115–150). Philadelphia, PA: Temple University Press.

Ream, G. J., & Savin-Williams, R. C. (2003). Religious development in adolescence. In G. R. Adams & M. D. Berzonsky (Eds.), *Blackwell handbook of adolescence* (pp. 51–59). Malden, MA: Blackwell.

Rebecca, M., Hefner, R., & Oleshansky, B. (1976). A model of sex-role transcendence. *Journal of Social Issues*, 32(3), 197–207.

Ree, M. J., & Earles, J. A. (1992). Intelligence is the best predictor of job performance. *Current Directions in Psychological Science, 1*, 86–89.

Reid, P. T. (2002). Multicultural psychology: Bringing together gender and ethnicity. *Cultural Diversity and Ethnic Minority Psychology, 8*(2), 103–114.

Reiss, D., Neiderhiser, J. M., Hetherington, E. M., & Plomin, R. (2000). *The relationship code: Deciphering genetic and social influences on adolescent development.* Cambridge, MA: Harvard University Press.

Remafedi, G. (1987). Adolescent homosexuality: Psychosocial and medical implications. *Pediatrics, 79*, 331–337.

Remafedi, G. (1994). Predictors of unprotected intercourse among gay and bisexual youth: Knowledge, beliefs, and behavior. *Pediatrics, 94*, 163–168.

Resnick, M. D., et al. (1997). Protecting adolescents from harm: Findings from the National Longitudinal Study on Adolescent Health. *Journal of the American Medical Association, 278*, 823–832.

Rest, J., Narvaez, D., Bebeau, M. J., & Thoma, S. J. (1999). *Postconventional moral thinking: A neo-Kohlbergian approach*. Mahwah, NJ: Erlbaum.

Rich, A. (1980). Compulsory heterosexuality and lesbian existence. *Signs, 5*, 198–210.

Richards, M., Crowe, P., Larson, R., & Swarr, A. (1998). Developmental patterns and gender differences in the experience of peer companionship during adolescence. *Child Development, 69*, 154–163.

Richards, M. H., & Larson, R. (1993). Pubertal development and the daily subjective states of young adolescents. *Journal of Research on Adolescence, 3*, 145–169.

Richman, J. M., & Cook, P. G. (2004). A framework for teaching family development for the changing family. *Journal of Teaching in Social Work, 24*, 1–18.

Riegel, K. F. (1976). The dialectics of human development. *American Psychologist, 31*, 689–700.

Riessman, C. K. (1993). *Narrative analysis* (Qualitative Research Methods Series, Vol. 30). Newbury Park, CA: Sage.

Ringel, B. A., & Springer, C. J. (1980). On knowing how well one is remembering: The persistence of strategy use during transfer. *Journal of Experimental Child Psychology, 29*, 322–333.

Risman, B. J. (1998). *Gender vertigo: American families in transition*. New Haven, CT: Yale University Press.

Risman, B. J., & Johnson-Sumerford, D. (1998). Doing it fairly: A study of postgender marriages. *Journal of Marriage and the Family, 60*, 23–40.

Risman, B. J., & Myers, K. (1997). As the twig is bent: Children reared in feminist households. *Qualitative Sociology, 20*, 229–252.

Rivers, I., & Carragher, D. J. (2003). Social-developmental factors affecting lesbian and gay youth: A review of cross-national research findings. *Children & Society, 17*, 374–385.

Roberton, M. A., & Konczak, J. (2001). Predicting children's overarm throw ball velocities from their developmental levels in throwing. *Research Quarterly for Exercise & Sport, 72*, 91–103.

Robinson, L. A., Klesges, R. C., Zbikowski, S. M., & Glaser, R. (1997). Predictors of risk for different stages of adolescent smoking in a biracial sample. *Journal of Consulting & Clinical Psychology, 65*, 653–662.

Rodkin, P. C., Farmer, T. W., Pearl, R., & Van Acker, R. (2000). Heterogeneity of popular boys: Antisocial and prosocial configurations. *Developmental Psychology, 36*(1), 14–24.

Roesner, R. W., Eccles, J. S., & Sameroff, A. J. (2000). School as a context of early adolescents' academic and social-emotional development: A summary of research findings. *The Elementary School Journal, 100*, 443.

Roffman, J. G., Pagano, M. E., & Hirsch, B. J. (2001). Youth functioning and experiences in inner-city after-school programs among age, gender, and race groups. *Journal of Child and Family Studies, 10*, 85–100.

Rogers, C. R. (1961). *On becoming a person*. Boston: Houghton Mifflin.

Rogers, C. R. (1969). *Freedom to learn*. Columbus, OH: Merrill.

Rogers, C. R. (1980). *A way of being*. Boston: Houghton Mifflin.

Rogoff, B. (1990). *Apprenticeship in thinking: Cognitive development in social context*. New York: Oxford University Press.

Rogoff, B. (1996). Developmental transitions in children's participation in sociocultural activities. In A. J. Sameroff & M. M. Haith (Eds.), *The five to seven year shift: The age of reason and responsibility*. Chicago: University of Chicago Press.

Rogoff, B. (2003). *The cultural nature of human development*. New York: Oxford University Press.

Rogoff, B., & Waddell, K. J. (1982). Memory for information organized in a scene by children from two cultures. *Child Development, 53*, 1224–1228.

Rogol, A. D., Roemmich, J. N., & Clark, P. A. (2002). Growth at puberty. *Journal of Adolescent Health, 31*, 192–200.

Roid, G. H. (2003). *Stanford-Binet Intelligence Scales* (5th ed.). Itasca, IL: Riverside.

Rosario, M., Schrimshaw, E. W., & Hunter, J. (2004). Ethnic/racial differences in the coming-out process of lesbian, gay, and bisexual youths: A comparison of sexual identity development over time. *Cultural Diversity and Mental Health, 10*(3), 215–288.

Rosenblum, G. D., & Lewis M. (2003). Emotional development in adolescence. In G. R. Adams & M. D. Berzonsky (Eds.), *Blackwell handbook of adolescence* (pp. 269–289). Malden, MA: Blackwell.

Rosenshine, B., & Meister, C. (1994). Reciprocal teaching: A review of the research. *Review of Educational Research, 64*, 479–530.

Rosenshine, B., & Meister, C. (1997). Cognitive strategy instruction in reading. In S. A. Stahl & D. A. Hayes (Eds.), *Instructional models in reading* (pp. 85–107). Hillsdale, NJ: Erlbaum.

Rosenthal, D., & Hrynevich, C. (1985). Ethnicity and ethnic identity: A comparative study of Greek-, Italian-, and Anglo-Australian adolescents. *International Journal of Psychology, 20*, 723–724.

Roth, J., & Brooks-Gunn, J. (2000). What do adolescents need for healthy development? Implications for youth policy. *Social Policy Report, Vol. 14, No. 1*. Retrieved March 21, 2005, from http://www.srcd.org/spr.html

Roth, J., & Brooks-Gunn, J. (2003). What is a youth development program? Identification of defining principles. In R. M. Lerner, F. Jacobs, & D. Wertleib (Eds.), *Handbook of applied developmental science: Vol. 2. Enhancing the life chances of youth and families: Contributions of programs, policies, and service systems* (pp. 197–223). Thousand Oaks, CA: Sage.

Roth, J., Brooks-Gunn, J., Murray, L., & Foster, W. (1998). Promoting healthy adolescence: Synthesis of youth development program evaluations. *Journal of Research on Adolescence, 8*, 432–459.

Roth, S. (1993). Speaking the unspoken: A work-group consultation to reopen dialogue. In E. Imber-Black (Ed.), *Secrets in families and family therapy* (pp. 268–291). New York: Norton.

Rothbart, M. K., & Bates, J. E. (1998). Temperament. In W. Damon (Series Ed.) & N. Eisenberg (Vol. Ed.), *Handbook of child psychology: Vol. 3. Social, emotional, and personality development* (5th ed., pp. 105–176). New York: Wiley.

Rotheram, M. J., & Phinney, J. S. (1987). Definitions and perspectives in the study of children's ethnic socialization. In. J. S. Phinney & M. J. Rotheram (Eds.), *Children's ethnic socialization: Pluralism and development* (pp. 10–31). Newbury Park, CA: Sage.

Rotheram-Borus, M. J., & Langabeer, K. A. (2001). Developmental trajectories of gay, lesbian, and bisexual youths. In A. R. D'Augelli & C. J. Patterson (Eds.), *Lesbian, gay, and bisexual identities and youth: Psychological perspectives*. New York: Oxford University Press.

Rotheram-Borus, M. J., Meyer-Bahlburg, H., Rosario, M., Koopman, C., Haignere, C., Exner, T., et al. (1992). Lifetime sexual behaviors among predominantly minority male runaways and gay/bisexual adolescents in New York City. *AIDS Education and Prevention, 4*(Suppl.), 34–42.

Rousseau, J. J. (1970). *The Emile* (W. Boyd, Trans.). New York: Teacher's College Press. (Original work published 1762)

Roy, R., Benenson, J. F., & Lilly, F. (2000). Beyond intimacy: Conceptualizing differences in same-sex friendships. *The Journal of Psychology, 134*, 93–101.

Royse, D., Thyer, B. A., Padgett, D. K., & Logan, T. K. (2006). *Program evaluation: An introduction*. Belmont, CA: Thomson Brooks/Cole.

Rubin, K. H. (1998). Social and emotional development from a cultural perspective. *Developmental Psychology, 34*, 611–615.

Rubin, K. H., Bukowski, W., & Parker, J. G. (1998). Peer interactions, relationships, and groups. In W. Damon (Series Ed.) & N. Eisenberg (Vol Ed.), *Handbook of child psychology*: Vol. 3. *Social, emotional, and personality development* (5th ed., pp. 619–695). New York: Wiley.

Rubin, K. H., Dwyer, K. M., Booth-LaForce, C., Kim, A. H., Burgess, K. B., & Rose-Krasnor, L. (2004). Attachment, friendship, and psychosocial functioning in early adolescence. *Journal of Early Adolescence, 24*, 326–356.

Ruble, D. N. (1987). The acquisition of self-knowledge: A self-socialization perspective. In N. Eisenberg (Ed.), *Contemporary topics in developmental psychology* (pp. 243–270). New York: Wiley.

Ruble, D. N. & Dweck, C. S. (1995). Self-conceptions, person conceptions, and their development. In N. Eisenberg (Ed.), *Social development* (pp. 109–139). Thousand Oaks, CA: Sage.

Ruble, D. N., Eisenberg, R., & Higgins, E. T. (1994). Developmental changes in achievement motivation: Motivational implications of self-other differences. *Child Development, 65*, 1095–1110.

Ruble, D. N., & Martin, C. L. (1998). Gender development. In W. Damon (Series Ed.) & N. Eisenberg (Vol. Ed.), *Handbook of child psychology: Vol. 3. Social, emotional, and personality development* (5th ed., pp. 993–1016). New York: Wiley.

Ruiselova, Z. (1998). Relationships with parents and teachers in connection with pubertal maturation timing in girls. *Studia Psychologica, 40*, 277–281.

Rumbaut, R. G. (2004). *Young adults in the United States: A profile*. The Network on Transitions to Adulthood. Retrieved August 2, 2004, from http://www.pop.upenn.edu/transad/news/index.htm

Runion, B. P., Langendorfer, S. J., & Roberton, M. A. (2003). Forceful overarm throwing: A comparison of two cohorts measured 20 years apart. *Research Quarterly for Exercise & Sport, 74*, 324–330.

Russell, S. T. (2005). Beyond risk: Resilience in the lives of sexual-minority youth. *Journal of GLBT Issues in Education, 2*(3), 5–18.

Russell, S. T., Seif, H., & Truong, N. L. (2001). School outcomes of sexual minority youth in the United States: Evidence from a national study. *Journal of Adolescence, 24*, 111–127.

Saarni, C. (1990). Emotional competence: How emotions and relationships become integrated. In R. A. Thompson (Ed.), *Nebraska symposium on motivation: Vol. 36. Socioemotional development* (pp. 115–182). Lincoln, NB: University of Nebraska Press.

Saarni, C. (1998). Issues of cultural meaningfulness in emotional development. *Developmental Psychology, 34*, 647–652.

Saarni, C. (2000). The social context of emotional development. In M. Lewis & J. M. Haviland-Jones (Eds.), *Handbook of emotions* (2nd ed., pp. 306–322). New York: Guilford Press.

Saarni, C. (2001a). Epilogue: Emotion communication and relationship context. *International Journal of Behavioral Development, 25*, 354–356.

Saarni, C. (2001b). Cognition, context, and goals: Significant components in social-emotional effectiveness. *Social Development, 10*, 125–129.

Saarni, C., Mumme, D. L., & Campos, J. L. (1998). Emotional development: Action, communication, and understanding. In W. Damon (Series Ed.) & N. Eisenberg (Vol. Ed.), *Handbook of child psychology: Vol. 3. Social, emotional, and personality development* (5th ed., pp. 237–309). New York: Wiley.

Sabatelli, R., & Mazor, A. (1985). Differentiation, individuation, and identity formation: The integration of family system and individual developmental perspectives. *Adolescence, 20*, 619–633.

Sadker, M., & Sadker, D. (1994). *Failing at fairness: How America's schools cheat girls*. New York: Charles Scribner's Sons.

Salasuo, M., & Seppala, P. (2004). Drug use within the Finnish club culture as marks of distinction. *Contemporary Drug Problems, 31*, 213–229.

Sallis, J. F., Woodruff, S. I., Vargas, R., Deosaransingh, K., Laniado-Laborin, R., Moreno, C., & Elder, J. P. (1997). Reliability and validity of a cigarette refusal skills test for Latino youth. *American Journal of Health Behavior, 21*, 345–355.

Salovey, P., Bedell, B. T., Detweiler, J. B., & Mayer, J. D. (2000). Current directions in emotional intelligence research. In M. Lewis & J. M. Haviland-Jones (Eds.), *Handbook of emotions* (2nd ed., pp. 504–520). New York: Guilford Press.

Sameroff, A. J. (1983). Developmental systems: Contexts and evolution. In P. H. Mussen (Series Ed.) & W. Kessen (Vol. Ed.), *Handbook of child psychology: Vol. 1. History, theory, and methods* (4th ed., pp. 237–294). New York: Wiley.

Sameroff, A. J., & Haith, M. M. (1996). *The five to seven year shift: The age of reason and responsibility*. Chicago: University of Chicago Press.

Sampson, R. J., & Morenoff, J. (1997). Ecological perspectives on the neighborhood context of urban poverty: Past and present. In J. Brooks-Gunn, G. J. Duncan, & J. L. Aber (Eds.), *Neighborhood poverty: Vol. 2. Policy implications in studying neighborhoods* (pp. 1–22). New York: Russell Sage Foundation.

Sandberg, D. E., Bukowski, W. M., Fung, C. M., & Noll, R. B. (2004). Height and social adjustment: Are extremes a cause for concern and action? *Pediatrics, 114*, 744–750.

Sandberg, D. E., Kranzler, J., Bukowski, W. M., & Rosenbloom, A. L. (1999). Psychosocial aspects of short stature and growth hormone therapy. *The Journal of Pediatrics, 135*, 133–134.

Sandberg, D. E., Ognibene, T. C., Brook, A. E., Barrick, C., Shine, B., & Grundner, W. (1998). Academic outcomes among children and adolescents receiving growth hormone therapy. *Children's Health Care, 27*, 265–282.

Sarampote, N. C., Bassett, H. H., & Winsler, A. (2004). After-school care: Child outcomes and recommendations for research and policy. *Child and Youth Care Forum, 33*, 329–348.

Sarigiani, P. A., Heath, P. A., & Camarena, P. M. (2003). The significance of parental depressed mood for young adolescents' emotional and family experiences. *Journal of Early Adolescence, 23*(3), 241–267.

Saris, W. H. M. (1986). Habitual physical activity in children: Methodology and findings in health and disease. *Medicine Science Sports Exercise, 18*, 253–263.

Saudi Arabia Information Resource. (2005). Riyadh population by age groups. Retrieved June 26, 2005, from http://www.saudinf.com/main/y7938.htm

Savickas, M. L. (1994). Vocational psychology in the postmodern era: Comment on Richardson (1993). *Journal of Counseling Psychology, 41*, 1–5.

Savickas, M. L. (1999). The transition from school to work: A developmental perspective. *Career Development Quarterly, 47*, 326–336.

Savin-Williams, R. C. (1994a). Dating those you can't love and loving those you can't date. In R. Montemayor, G. R. Adams, & T. P. Gulotta (Eds.), *Personal relationships during adolescence: Advances in adolescent development* (Vol. 3, pp. 196–215). Thousand Oaks, CA: Sage.

Savin-Williams, R. C. (1994b). Verbal and physical abuse as stressors in the lives of lesbian, gay male and bisexual youths: Associations with school problems, running away, substance abuse, prostitution, and suicide. *Journal of Consulting and Clinical Psychology, 62*, 261–269.

Savin-Williams, R. C. (1995). An exploratory study of pubertal maturation timing and self-esteem among gay and bisexual male youths. *Developmental Psychology, 31*, 56–64.

Savin-Williams, R. C. (1996). Memories of childhood and early adolescent sexual feelings among gay and bisexual boys: A narrative approach. In R. C. Savin-Williams & K. M. Cohen (Eds.), *The lives of lesbians, gays, and bisexuals: Children to adults* (pp. 94–109). Belmont, CA: Thomson.

Savin-Williams, R. C. (2001a). *Mom, dad. I'm gay: How families negotiate coming out.* Washington, DC: American Psychological Association.

Savin-Williams, R. C. (2001b). A critique of research on sexual-minority youths. *Journal of Adolescence, 24*, 5–13.

Savin-Williams, R. C. (2003). Are adolescent same-sex romantic relationships on our radar screen? In P. Florsheim (Ed.), *Adolescent romantic relations and sexual behavior: Theory, research, and practical implications* (pp. 325–336). Mahwah, NJ: Erlbaum.

Savin-Williams, R. C., & Berndt, T. J. (1990). Friendship and peer relations. In S. S. Feldman & G. R. Elliott (Eds.), *At the threshold: The developing adolescent* (pp. 277–307). Cambridge, MA: Harvard University Press.

Savin-Williams, R. C., & Diamond, L. M. (2000). Sexual-identity trajectories among sexual-minority youth: Gender comparisons. *Archives of Sexual Behavior, 29*, 607–627.

Savin-Williams, R. C., & Rodriguez, R. G. (1993). A developmental clinical perspective on lesbian, gay male, and bisexual youths. In T. P. Gullotta, G. R. Adams, & R. Montemayor (Eds.), *Adolescent sexuality* (pp. 77–101). Newbury Park, CA: Sage.

Saxe, G. B. (1988b). The mathematics of street vendors. *Child Development, 59*, 1415–1425.

Scales, P. C., Benson, P. L., Leffert, N., & Blyth, D. A. (2000). Contribution of developmental assets to the prediction of thriving among adolescents. *Applied Developmental Science, 4*, 27–46.

Scarborough, H. S. (1998). Early identification of children at risk for reading disabilities: Phonological awareness and some other promising predictors. In B. K. Shapiro, P. J. Accardo, & A. J. Capute (Eds.), *Specific reading disability: A view of the spectrum* (pp. 75–119). Timonium, MD: York Press.

Scarr, S. (1997). Behavior-genetic and socialization theories of intelligence: Truce and reconciliation. In R. J. Sternberg & E. L. Grigorenko (Eds.), *Intelligence, heredity, and environment* (pp. 3–41). New York: Cambridge University Press.

Scarr, S., & McCartney, K. (1983). How people make their own environments: A theory of genotype-environment effects. *Child Development, 54*, 424–435.

Schachter, E. P. (2004). Identity configurations: A new perspective on identity formation in contemporary society. *Journal of Personality, 72*, 167–199.

Schachter, E. P. (2005). Context and identity formation: A theoretical analysis and a case study. *Journal of Adolescent Research, 20*, 375–395.

Schaie, K. W. (1994). The course of intellectual development in adulthood. *American Psychologist, 49*, 304–313.

Schaie, K. W., & Willis, S. L. (2000). A stage theory model of adult cognitive development revisited. In R. L. Rubenstein, M. Moss, & M. H. Kleban (Eds.), *The many dimensions of aging*. New York: Springer.

Schalet, A., Hunt, G., & Joe-Laidler, K. (2003). Respectability and autonomy: The articulation and meaning of sexuality among the girls in the gang. *Journal of Contemporary Ethnography, 32*(1), 108–143.

Schneider, W. (1998). Performance prediction in young children: Effects of skill, metacognition, and wishful thinking. *Developmental Science, 1*, 291–297.

Schneider, W., & Bjorklund, D. (2003). Memory and knowledge development. In J. Valsiner & K. J. Connolly (Eds.), *Handbook of developmental psychology* (pp. 370–403). Thousand Oaks, CA: Sage.

Schneider, W., Bjorklund, D. A., & Maier-Bruckner, W. (1996). The effects of expertise and IQ on children's memory: When knowledge is, and when it is not enough. *International Journal of Behavioral Development, 19*, 773–796.

Schneider, W., & Pressley, M. (1997). *Memory development between 2 and 20* (2nd ed.). Mahwah, NJ: Erlbaum.

Schulenberg, J., O'Malley, P. M., Bachman, J. F., Wadsworth, K. N., & Johnston, L. D. (1996). Getting drunk and growing up: Trajectories of frequent binge drinking during the transition to young adulthood. *Journal of Studies on Alcohol, 57*, 289–304.

Schultz, R., & Curnow, C. (1988). Peak performance and age among superathletes: Track and field, swimming, baseball, tennis, and golf. *Journal of Gerontology, 43*, 113–120.

Schunk, D. H., & Pajares, F. (2002). The development of academic self-efficacy. In A. Wigfield & J. S. Eccles

(Eds.), *The development of achievement motivation* (pp. 15–31). San Diego, CA: Academic Press.

Schuster, M. A., Bell, R. M., Berry, S. H., & Kanouse, D. E. (1998). Impact of a high school condom availability program on sexual attitudes and behaviors. *Family Planning Perspectives, 30*, 67–72.

Schwartz, P., & Rutter, P. (2000). *The gender of sexuality.* Walnut Creek, CA: AltaMira.

Schwartz, S. J. (2002). In search of mechanisms of change in identity development: Integrating the constructivist and discovery perspectives on identity. *Identity: An International Journal of Theory and Research, 2*, 317–339.

Schwebel, D. C., Plumert, J. M., & Pick, H. L. (2000). Integrating basic and applied research: A new model for the twenty-first century. *Child Development, 71*(1), 220–230.

Sebold, H. (1968). *Adolescence: A sociological analysis.* Englewood Cliffs, NJ: Prentice Hall.

SEICUS Report (1998). Volume 26, Number 6—August/September.

Sellers, D. E., McGraw, S. A., & McKinlay, J. B. (1994). Does the promotion and distribution of condoms increase teen sexual activity? Evidence from an HIV prevention program for Latino youth. *American Journal of Public Health, 84*, 1952–1959.

Selman, R. L. (1980). Four domains, five stages: A summary portrait of interpersonal understanding. In *The growth of interpersonal understanding: Developmental and clinical implications* (pp. 131–155). New York: Academic Press.

Selman, R. L. (2003). *The promotion of social awareness.* New York: Russell Sage Foundation.

Seppa, K., & Sillanaukee, P. (1999). Binge drinking and ambulatory blood pressure. *Hypertension, 33*, 79–82.

Serafini, T. E., & Adams, G. R. (2002). Functions of identity: Scale construction and validation. *Identity: An International Journal of Theory and Research, 2*, 361–389.

Serbin, L. A., Marchessault, K., McAffer, V., Peters, P., & Schwartzman, A. E. (1993). Patterns of social behavior on the playground in 9- to 11-year-olds girls and boys: Relation to teacher perceptions and to peer ratings of aggression, withdrawal, and likeability. In C. H. Hart (Ed.), *Children on playgrounds: Research perspectives and applications* (pp. 162–183). Albany, NY: State University of New York Press.

Serpell, R. (1979). How specific are perceptual skills? A cross-cultural study of pattern reproduction. *British Journal of Psychology, 70*, 365–380.

Shanahan, M. J., Porfeli, E. J., Mortimer, J. T., & Erickson, L. D. (2005). Subjective age identity and the transition to adulthood: When do adolescents become adults? In R. A. Settersten, Jr., F. F. Furstenberg, Jr., & R. G. Rumbaut (Eds.), *On the frontier of adulthood: Theory, research, and public policy* (pp. 225–255). Chicago: University of Chicago Press.

Shantz, C. U. (1983). Social cognition. In P. H. Mussen (Series Ed.) & J. H. Flavell & E. M. Markman (Vol. Eds.), *Handbook of child psychology: Vol. 3. Cognitive development* (4th ed. pp. 495–555). New York: Wiley.

Sharp, S., & Smith, P. K. (1994). *Tackling bullying in your school: A practical handbook for teachers.* London: Routledge.

Shayer, M. (1980). Piaget and science education. In S. Modgil & C. Modgil (Eds.), *Towards a theory of psychological development.* Windsor, Ontario, Canada: National Foundation for Educational Research.

Sheehan, G., & Noller, P. (2002). Adolescents' perceptions of differential parenting: Links with attachment style and adolescent adjustment. *Personal Relationships, 9*, 173–190.

Sheldon, S. B. (2002). Parents' social networks and beliefs as predictors of parent involvement. *Elementary School Journal, 102*, 301–316.

Sheldon, S. B. (2003). Linking school-family-community partnerships in urban elementary schools to student achievement on state tests. *The Urban Review, 35*, 149–165.

Shemilt, I., Harvey, I., Shepstone, L., Swift, L., Reading, R., Mugford, M., et al. (2004). A national evaluation of school breakfast clubs: Evidence from a cluster randomized controlled trial and an observational analysis. *Child: Care, Health and Development, 30*, 413–427.

Shiffrin, R. M., & Atkinson, R. C. (1969). Storage and retrieval processes in long-term memory. *Psychological Review, 76*, 179–193.

Shirk, S. R., & Renouf, A. G. (1992). The tasks of self-development in middle childhood and early adolescence. In R. P. Lipka & T. M. Brinthaupt (Eds.), *Self-perspectives across the life span* (pp. 53–90). Albany, NY: State University of New York.

Shisslack, C. M., & Crago, M. (2001). Risk and protective factors in the development of eating disorders. In J. K. Thompson & L. Smolak (Eds.), *Body image, eating disorders, and obesity in youth: Assessment, prevention, and treatment* (pp. 103–125). Washington, DC: American Psychological Association.

Shisslack, C. M., Crago, M., & Estes, L. S. (1995). The spectrum of eating disturbances. *International Journal of Eating Disorders, 18*, 209–219.

Shisslack, C. M., Crago, M., McKnight, K., Estes, L., Gray, N., & Parnaby, O. (1998). Potential risk factors associated with weight control behaviors in elementary and middle school girls. *Journal of Psychosomatic Research, 44*, 301–314.

Shulman, S., & Scharf, M. (2000). Adolescent romantic behaviors and perceptions: Age- and gender-related differences, and links with family and peer relationships. *Journal of Research on Adolescence, 10*, 99–118.

Shweder, R. A. (1991). *Thinking through cultures.* Cambridge, MA: Harvard University Press.

Siegel, J. M., Yancey, A. K., Aneshensel, C. S., & Schuler, R. (1999). Body image, perceived pubertal timing, and adolescent mental health. *Journal of Adolescent Health, 25*, 155–165.

Siegler, R. S. (1996). *Emerging minds: The process of change in children's thinking*. New York: Oxford University Press.

Silbereisen, R. K. (2003). Contextual constraints on adolescents' leisure. In S. Verma & R. Larson (Eds.), *Examining adolescent leisure time across cultures: Developmental opportunities and risks* (pp. 95–101). *New Directions for Child and Adolescent Development*, No. 99. San Francisco: Jossey-Bass.

Silbereisen, R. K., & Todt, E. (1994). *Adolescence in context: The interplay of family, school, peers, and work in adjustment*. New York: Springer-Verlag.

Silk, J. S., Steinberg, L., & Morris, A. S. (2003). Adolescents' emotion regulation in daily life: Links to depressive symptoms and problem behavior. *Child Development, 74*, 1869–1880.

Simmons, R. (2003, October 2). Cyberbullying stalks students. *The Detroit News*, 13A, 17A.

Simmons, R. G. (1987). Self-esteem in adolescence. In T. Honess & K. Yardley (Eds.), *Self and identity: Perspectives across the lifespan* (pp. 172–192). New York: Routledge.

Simmons, R. G., & Blyth, D. A. (1987). *Moving into adolescence: The impact of pubertal change and school context*. New York: Aldine de Gruyter.

Simpkins, S. D., & Parke, R. D. (2001). The relations between parental friendships and children's friendships: Self-report and observational analysis. *Child Development, 72*, 569–582.

Sindelar, H. A., Barnett, N. P., & Spirito, A. (2004). Adolescent alcohol use and injury. A summary and critical review of the literature. *Minerva Pediatrica, 56*, 291–309.

Singh, S., & Darroch, J. (2000). Adolescent pregnancy and childbearing: Levels and trends in developed countries. *Family Planning Perspectives, 32*, 14–23.

Sippola, L. K., & Paget, J. (2004, March). Striving for dominance: Understanding relational aggression among adolescent girls. In N. E. Werner & A. Ittel (Chairs), *Advances in the study of social dominance and gender*. Symposium conducted at the biennial meetings of the Society for Research on Adolescence, Baltimore, MD.

Skorikov, V., & Vondracek, F. W. (1998). Vocational identity development: Its relationship to other identity domains and to overall identity development. *Journal of Career Assessment, 6*, 13–35.

Skuse, D., Gilmour, J., Tian, C. S., & Hindmarsh, P. (1994). Psychosocial assessment of children with short stature: A preliminary report. *Acta Paediatrica* (Suppl. 406), 11–16.

Slattery, P. (1999). The excluded middle: Postmodern conceptions of the middle school. In C. W. Walley & W. G. Gerrick (Eds.), *Affirming middle grades education* (pp. 26–37). Boston: Allyn & Bacon.

Small, S. A. (1995). Enhancing contexts of adolescent development: The role of community-based action research. In L. J. Crockett & A. C. Crouter (Eds.), *Pathways through adolescence: Individual development in relation to social contexts* (pp. 211–233). Hillsdale, NJ: Erlbaum.

Small, S. A., & Eastman, G. (1995). Rearing adolescents in contemporary society: A conceptual framework for understanding the responsibilities and needs of parents. In D. H. Demo & A. Ambert (Eds.), *Parents and adolescents in changing families* (pp. 50–61). Minneapolis: National Council on Family Relations.

Smith, C. (2003a). Theorizing religious effects among American adolescents. *Journal for the Scientific Study of Religion, 42*, 17–30.

Smith, C. (2003b). Religious participation and network closure among American adolescents. *Journal for the Scientific Study of Religion, 42*, 259–267.

Smith, C., Denton, L. M., Faris, R., & Regnerus, M. (2002). Mapping American adolescent religious participation. *Journal for the Scientific Study of Religion, 41*, 597–612.

Smith, E. A., & Udry, J. R. (1985). Coital and non-coital sexual behaviors of white and black adolescents. *American Journal of Public Health, 75*, 1200–1203.

Smolak, L., Levine, M., & Thompson, J. K. (2001). Body image in adolescent boys and girls as assessed with the Sociocultural Attitudes Towards Appearance Scale. *International Journal of Eating Disorders, 29*, 216–223.

Snow, C. E., Burns, M. S., & Griffin, P. (1998). *Preventing reading difficulties in young children*. Washington, DC: National Academy Press.

Solomon, J., & George, C. (1999). The measurement of attachment security in infancy and childhood. In J. Cassidy & P. R. Shaver (Eds.), *Handbook of attachment: Theory, research, and clinical applications* (pp. 287–316). New York: Guilford Press.

Sommer, K., Whitman, T. L., Borkowski, J. G., Schellenbach, C. J., Maxwell, S. E., & Keogh, D. (1993). Cognitive readiness and adolescent parenting. *Developmental Psychology, 29*, 389–398.

Soriano, F. I., Rivera, L. M., Williams, K. J., Daley, S. P., & Reznik, V. M. (2004). Navigating between cultures: The role of culture in youth violence. *Journal of Adolescent Health, 34*(3), 169–176.

Spence, J. T., & Helmreich, R. L. (1980). Masculine instrumentality and feminine expressiveness: Their relationships with sex-role attitudes and behaviors. *Psychology of Women Quarterly, 5*, 147–163.

Spencer, M. B. (1995). Old issues and new theorizing about African American youth: A phenomenological variant of ecological systems theory. In R. L. Taylor (Ed.), *Black youth: Perspectives on their status in the United States* (pp. 37–90). Westport, CT: Praeger.

Spencer, M. B., Dupree, D., & Cunningham, M. (2003). Vulnerability to violence: A contextually-sensitive, developmental perspective on African American adolescents. *Journal of Social Issues: Special issue: Youth perspectives on violence and injustice, 59*, 33–49.

Spencer, M. S., Icard, L. D., Harachi, T. W., Catalano, R. F., & Oxford, M. (2000). Ethnic identity among monoracial and biracial early adolescents. *Journal of Early Adolescence, 20*, 365–387.

Spring, B., Rosen, K. H., & Matheson, J. L. (2002). How parents experience a transition to adolescence: A qualitative study. *Journal of Child and Family Studies, 11*, 411–425.

Stacey, J., & Davenport, E. (2002). Queer families quack back. In D. Richardson & S. Seidman (Eds.), *Handbook of gay and lesbian studies* (pp. 355–374). London: Sage.

Stack, C. (1990). Different voices, different visions: Race, gender, and moral reasoning. In R. Ginsberg & A. Tsing (Eds.), *The negotiation of gender in American society* (pp. 19–27). Boston: Beacon Press.

Stanton, B. S., Li, X., Ricardo, I., Galbraith, J., Feigelman, S., & Kaljee, L. (1996). A randomized controlled effectiveness trial of an AIDS prevention program for low-income African-American youths. *Archives of Pediatrics and Adolescent Medicine, 150*, 363–372.

Stattin, H., & Magnusson, D. (1990). *Pubertal maturation in female development*. Hillsdale, NJ: Erlbaum.

Steinberg, K. S. The importance of physical activity in the prevention of overweight and obesity in childhood: A review and opinion. *Obesity Reviews, 2*, 117–130.

Steinberg, L. (1986). Latchkey children and susceptibility to peer pressure: An ecological analysis. *Developmental Psychology, 22*, 433–439.

Steinberg, L. (1995). Commentary: On developmental pathways and social contexts in adolescence. In L. J. Crockett & A. C. Crouter (Eds.), *Pathways through adolescence: Individual development in relation to social contexts* (pp. 245–253). Mahwah, NJ: Erlbaum.

Steinberg, L. (1996). *Beyond the classroom: Why school reform has failed and what parents need to do*. New York: Touchstone.

Steinberg, L. (2001). We know some things: Parent-adolescent relationships in retrospect and prospect. *Journal of Research on Adolescence, 11*, 1–19.

Steinberg, L., & Cauffman, E. (2001). Adolescents as adults in court: A developmental perspective on the transfer of juveniles to criminal court. *Social Policy Report, Vol. 15, No. 4*. Retrieved March 21, 2005, from http://www.srcd.org/spr.html

Steinberg, L., Dornbusch, S. M., & Brown, B. B. (1992). Ethnic differences in adolescent achievement: An ecological perspective. *American Psychologist, 47*, 723–729.

Steinberg, L., Grisso, T., Woolard, J., Cauffman, E., Scott, E., Graham, S., et al. (2003). Juveniles' competence to stand trial as adults. *Social Policy Report, Vol. 17, No. 4*. Ann Arbor, MI: Society for Research in Child Development.

Steinberg, L., & Scott, E. S. (2003). Less guilty by reason of adolescence: Developmental immaturity, diminished responsibility, and the juvenile death penalty. *American Psychologist, 58*, 1009–1018.

Stern, S. (1999). Adolescent girls' expression on Web home pages: Spirited, sombre and self-conscious sites. *Convergence, 5*, 22–41.

Sternberg, R. J. (1985). *Beyond IQ: A triarchic theory of human intelligence*. New York: Cambridge University Press.

Sternberg, R. J. (1999). *Handbook of creativity*. New York: Cambridge University Press.

Sternberg, R. J. (2003a). Our research program validating the triarchic theory of successful intelligence: Reply to Gottfredson. *Intelligence, 31*, 399–413.

Sternberg, R. J. (2003b). Creative thinking in the classroom. *Scandinavian Journal of Educational Research, 47*, 325–338.

Sternberg, R. J., Forsythe, G. B., Hedlund, J., Horvath, J., Snook, S., Williams, W. M., et al. (2000). *Practical intelligence in everyday life*. New York: Cambridge University Press.

Sternberg, R. J., Grigorenko, E. L., Ferrai, M., & Clinkenbeard, P. (1999). A triarchic analysis of an aptitude-treatment interaction. *European Journal of Psychological Assessment, 15*, 1–11.

Sternberg, R. J., Nokes, K., Geissler, P. W., Okatcha, F., Bundy, D. A., et al. (2001). The relationship between academic and practical intelligence: A case study in Kenya. *Intelligence, 29*, 401–418.

Sternberg, R. J., & Williams, W. M. (1996). *How to develop student creativity*. Alexandria, VA: Association for Supervision and Curriculum Development.

Stetsenko, A., Little, T. D., Gordeeva, T., Grasshhof, M., & Oettingen, G. (2000). Gender effects in children's beliefs about school performance: A cross-cultural study. *Child Development, 71*, 517–527.

Stevenson, H. W., & Lee, S. Y. (1990). *Contexts of achievement: A study of American, Chinese, and Japanese children*. Chicago: University of Chicago Press.

Stevenson, H. W., Lee, S. Y., & Stigler, J. W. (1986). Mathematics achievement of Chinese, Japanese, and American children. *Science, 231*, 693–699.

Stice, E., Presnell, K., & Bearman, S. K. (2001). Relation of early menarche to depression, eating disorders, substance abuse, and comorbid psychopathology among adolescent girls. *Developmental Psychology, 37*, 608–619.

Stone, E. J., McKenzie, T. L., Welk, G. J., & Booth, M. L. (1998). Effects of physical activity interventions in youth. Review and synthesis. *American Journal of Prevention Medicine, 15*, 298–315.

Stoneman, Z., & Brody, G. H. (1993). Sibling temperaments, conflict, warmth, and role asymmetry. *Child Development, 64*, 1786–1800.

Story, M., & Alton, I. (1996). Adolescent nutrition: Current trends and critical issues. *Topics in Clinical Nutrition, 11*, 56–69.

Strasberger, V. C., & Wilson, B. J. (2002). *Children, adolescents, and the media*. Thousand Oaks, CA: Sage.

Stratford, R., Mulligan, J., Downey, B., & Voss, L. (1999). Threats to the validity in the longitudinal study of psychological effects: The case of short stature. *Child: Care, Health and Development, 25*, 401–419.

Strauch, L., & Meier, B. (1988). Sleep need in adolescents: A longitudinal approach. *Sleep, 11*, 378–386.

Streib, H. (1999). Off-road religion? A narrative approach to fundamentalist and occult orientations of adolescents. *Journal of Adolescence, 22*, 255–267.

Streib, V. (2002). *The juvenile death penalty today: Death sentences and executions for juvenile crimes, January 1, 1973–November 15, 2002* [Unpublished report]. Retrieved March 21, 2005, from http://www.law.onu.edu/faculty/streib/juvdeath.pdf

Striegel-Moore, R., Schreiber, G. B., Lo, A., Crawford, P., Obarzanek, E., & Rodin, J. (2000). Eating disorder symptoms in a cohort of 11- to 16-year-old Black and White girls: The NHLBI Growth and Health Study. *International Journal of Eating Disorders, 27*, 49–66.

Strohmeyer, H. S., Williams, K., & Schaub-George, D. (1991). Developmental sequences for catching a small ball: A prelongitudinal screening. *Research Quarterly for Exercise and Sport, 62*, 257–266.

Strouse, J. S., Goodwin, M., & Roscoe, B. (1994). Correlates among attitudes toward sexual harassment among early adolescents. *Sex Roles, 31*, 559–578.

Stumpf, H., & Stanley, J. C. (2002). Group data on high school grade point averages and scores on academic aptitude tests as predictors of institutional graduation rates. *Educational and Psychological Measurement, 62*, 1042–1052.

Subrahmanyam, K., Kraut, R. E., Greenfield, P. M., & Gross, E. F. (2000). The impact of home computer use on children's activities and development. *Future of Children, 1*, 123–144.

Substance Abuse and Mental Health Services Administration (1999). *The relationship between mental health and substance abuse among adolescents.* Rockville, MD: Substance Abuse and Mental Health Services Administration.

Sullivan, H. S. (1953/1981). *The interpersonal theory of psychiatry.* New York: Norton.

Sum, A., & Khatiwada, I. (2004). Still young, restless, and jobless: The growing malaise among U.S. teens and young adults. Boston: Center for Labor Market Studies, Northeastern University. Retrieved July 15, 2005, from http://www.aypf.org/pdf/still%20young,%20restless%20and%20jobless%20report.pdf

Sum, A., Khatiwada, I., McLaughlin, J., & Parma, S. (2005). The paradox of rising teen joblessness in an expanding labor market: The absence of teen employment growth in the national jobs recovery of 2003–2004. Boston: Center for Labor Market Studies, Northeastern University. Retrieved July 15, 2005, from http://www.nyec.org/Teen_Employment_jan_2005.pdf

Sun, Y., & Li, Y. (2002). Children's well-being during parents' marital disruption process: A pooled time-series analysis. *Journal of Marriage and Family, 64*, 472–488.

Sussman, S., Lichtman, K., Ritt, A., & Pallonen, U. (1999). Effects of thirty-four adolescent tobacco use cessation and prevention trials on regular users of tobacco products. *Substance Use and Misuse, 34*, 1469–1505.

Suter, E., & Hawes, M. R., (1993). Relationship of physical activity, body fat, diet, and blood lipid profile in youths 10–15 years. *Medicine Science Sports Exercise, 25*, 748–754.

Sutton, J., Smith, P. K., & Swettenham, J. (1999a). Bullying and "theory of mind": A critique of the "social skills deficit" view of anti-social behaviour. *Social Development, 8*, 117–127.

Sutton, J., Smith, P. K., & Swettenham, J. (1999b). Socially undesirable need not be incompetent: A response to Crick and Dodge. *Social Development, 8*, 132–134.

Suzuki, M., Hagino, H., Nohara, S., Zhou, S., Kawasaki, Y., Takahashi, T., et al. (2005). Male-specific volume expansion of the human hippocampus during adolescence. *Cerebral Cortex, 15*, 187–193.

Swaim, R. C., Oetting, E. R., Edwards, R. W., & Beauvais, F. (1989). Links from emotional distress to adolescent drug use: A path model. *Journal of Consulting & Clinical Psychology, 57*, 227–231.

Swanson, D. P., Spencer, M. B., Dell'Angelo, T., Harpalani, V., & Spencer, T. R. (2002). Identity processes and the positive development of African Americans: An explanatory framework. *New Directions for Youth Development, 95*, 73–99.

Swanson, H. L. (1999). What develops in working memory? A life span perspective. *Developmental Psychology, 35*, 986–1000.

Swearer, S. M., & Doll, B. (2002). Bullying in schools: An ecological framework. In R. A. Geffner, M. Loring, & C. Young (Eds.), *Bullying behavior: Current issues, research, and interventions* (pp. 7–23). New York: Haworth.

Tajfel, H. (1981). *Human groups and social categories: Studies in social psychology.* Cambridge, UK: Cambridge University Press.

Tanapat, P., Hastings, N. B., & Gould, E. (2001). Adult neurogenesis in the hippocampal formation. In C. A. Nelson & M. Luciana (Eds.), *Handbook of developmental cognitive neuroscience.* Cambridge, MA: MIT Press.

Tanner, J. M. (1978). *Education and physical growth* (2nd ed.). New York: International Universities Press.

Tanner, J. M. (1990). *Fetus into man: Physical growth from conception to maturity* (2nd ed.). Cambridge, MA: Harvard University Press.

Tapert, S. F., & Brown, S. A. (1999). Neuropsychological correlates of adolescent substance abuse: Four-year outcomes. *Journal of the International Neuropsychological Society, 5*, 481–493.

Tarrant, M. (2002). Adolescent peer groups and social identity. *Social Development, 11*, 110–123.

Tarrant, M., North, A. C., Edridge, M. D., Kirk, L.D., Smith, E. A., & Turner, R. E. (2001). Social identity in adolescence. *Journal of Adolescence, 24*, 597–609.

Tarter, R. E., Mezzrich, A. C., Hsieh, Y. S., & Parker, S. M. (1995). Cognitive capacity in female adolescent subculture abusers. *Drug and Alcohol Dependence, 39*, 15–21.

Tasker, F. L., & Golombek, S. (1997). *Growing up in a lesbian family: Effects on child development.* New York: Guilford Press.

Taylor, C. S., Lerner, R. M., von Eye, A., Balsano, A. B., Dowling, E. M., Anderson, P. M., Bobek, D. L., & Bjelobrk, D. (2002a). Individual and ecological assets and positive developmental trajectories among African American male youth involved in gangs and in community-based organizations serving youth. *New Directions for Youth Development, 95*, 57–72.

Taylor, C. S., Lerner, R. M., von Eye, A., Balsano, A. B., Dowling, E. M., Anderson, P. M., Bobek, D. L., & Bjelobrk, D. (2002b). Stability of attributes of positive functioning and of developmental assets among African American male gang and community-based organization members. *New Directions for Youth Development, 95*, 35–55.

Taylor, M. (1996). A theory of mind perspective on social cognitive development. In R. Gelman & T. Kit-Fong (Eds.), *Perceptual and cognitive development* (pp. 283–329). San Diego, CA: Academic Press.

Teicher, M. H., Andersen, S. L., Polcari, A., Anderson, C. M., Navalta, C. P., & Kim, D. M. (2003). The neurobiological consequences of early stress and childhood maltreatment. *Neuroscience & Biobehavioral Reviews, 27*, 33–44.

Teitelman, A. M. (2004). Adolescent girls' perspectives of family interactions related to menarche and sexual health. *Qualitative Health Research, 14*, 1292–1308.

Tharinger, D., & Wells, G. (2000). An attachment perspective on the developmental challenges of gay and lesbian adolescents: The need for continuity of caregiving from family and schools. *The School Psychology Journal, 29*(2), 158–172.

Third National Health and Nutrition Examination Survey, Phase 1, 1988–1991. (1994). *Advance data from vital and health statistics*, No. 258. U.S. Department of Health and Human Services. Hyattsville, MD: National Center for Health Statistics.

Thomas, S., & Robinson, M. (1981). Development of a measure of androgyny for young adolescents. *Journal of Early Adolescence, 1*, 195–209.

Thompson, A. M., Baxter-Jones, A. D. G., & Mirwald, R. L. (2003). Comparison of physical activity in male and female children: Does maturation matter? *Medicine and Science in Sports and Exercise, 35*, 1684–1690.

Thompson, A. M., Humbert, L. M., & Mirwald, R. L. (2003). A longitudinal study of the impact of childhood and adolescent physical activity experiences on adult physical activity perceptions and behaviors. *Qualitative Health Research, 13*, 358–377.

Thompson, D., Arora, T., & Sharp, S. (2002). *Bullying: Effective strategies for long-term improvement*. London: Routledge Falmer.

Thompson, J. K., & Smolak, L. (2001). Body image, eating disorders, and obesity in youth—the future is now. In J. K. Thompson and L. Smolak (Eds.), *Body image, eating disorders, and obesity in youth: Assessment, prevention, and treatment* (pp. 1–18). Washington, DC: American Psychological Association.

Thompson, N. E., & Gurney, A. G. (2003). "He is everything": Religion's role in the lives of immigrant youth. *New Directions for Youth Development, 100*, 75–90.

Thompson, P. M., Giedd, J. N., Woods, R. P., MacDonald, D., Evans, A. C., & Toga, A. W. (2000). Growth patterns in the developing brain detected by using continuum mechanical tensor maps. *Nature, 404*, 190–193.

Thompson, R. A. (1990). Emotion and self-regulation. In R. A. Thompson (Ed.), *Nebraska symposium on motivation: Vol. 36. Socioemotional development* (pp. 367–467). Lincoln, NE: University of Nebraska Press.

Thompson, R. A. (1998). Early sociopersonality development. In W. Damon (Series Ed.) & N. Eisenberg (Vol. Ed.), *Handbook of child psychology: Vol. 3. Social, emotional, and personality development* (5th ed., pp. 25–104). New York: Wiley.

Thompson, R. A. (1999). Early attachment and later development. In J. Cassidy & P. R. Shaver (Eds.), *Handbook of attachment: Theory, research, and clinical applications* (pp. 265–286). New York: Guilford Press.

Thompson, R. A., & Nelson, C. A. (2001). Developmental science and the media: Early brain development. *American Psychologist, 56*, 5–15.

Thompson, S. H., Rafiroiu, A. C., & Sargent, R. G. (2003). Examining gender, racial, and age differences in weight concern among third, eighth, and eleventh graders. *Eating Behaviors, 3*, 307–323.

Thornberry, T. P., Smith, C. A., & Howard, G. J. (1997). Risk factors for teenage fatherhood. *Journal of Marriage and the Family, 59*, 505–522.

Thornberry, T. P., Wei, E. H., Stouthamer-Loeber, M., & Van Dyke, J. (2000). Teenage fatherhood and delinquent behavior. *Juvenile Justice Bulletin*, January. Washington, DC: Office of Juvenile Justice and Delinquency Prevention.

Thorndike, R. M. (2005). *Measurement and evaluation in psychology and education* (7th ed.). Upper Saddle River, NJ: Pearson Education.

Thorne, A. (1993). On contextualizing Loevinger's stages of ego development. *Psychological Inquiry, 4*(1), 53–55.

Thorne, A. (2004). Putting the person into social identity. *Human Development, 47*, 361–365.

Thorne, B. (1993). *Gender play: Girls and boys in school.* New Brunswick, NJ: Rutgers University Press.

Thorne, B. (1997a). Children and gender: Constructions of difference. In M. M. Gergen & S. N. Davis (Eds.), *Toward a psychology of gender: A reader* (pp. 185–202). New York: Routledge.

Thorne, B. (1997b). Girls and boys together, but mostly apart: Gender arrangements in elementary schools. In W. W. Hartup & Z. Rubin (Eds.), *Relationships and development.* Hillsdale, NJ: Erlbaum.

Thurstone, L. L. (1938). Primary mental abilities. *Psychometric Monographs*, No. 1.

Tobler, N. S., Roona, M. R., Ochshorn, P., Marshall, D. G., Streke, A. V., & Stackpole, K. M. (2000). School-based adolescent drug prevention programs: 1998 meta-analysis. *Journal of Primary Prevention, 20*, 275–336.

Toblin, R. L., Schwartz, D., Gorman, A. H., & Aboudezzeddine, T. (2005). Social-cognitive and behavioral attributes of aggressive victims of bullying. *Journal of Applied Developmental Psychology, 26*, 329–346.

Todd, R. D. (1992). Neural development is regulated by classical neuro-transmitters: Dopamine D receptor stimulation enhances neurite outgrowth. *Biological Psychiatry, 31*, 794–807.

Tolman, D. L. (1994). Daring to desire: Culture and the bodies of adolescent girls. In J. M. Irvine (Ed.), *Sexual cultures and the construction of adolescent identities* (pp. 250–284). Philadelphia, PA: Temple University Press.

Tolman, D. L. (2002). *Dilemmas of desire: Teenage girls talk about sexuality*. Cambridge, MA: Harvard University Press.

Tolman, D. L., & Brown, L. M. (2001). Adolescent girls' voices: Resonating resistance in body and soul. In R. K. Unger (Ed.), *Handbook of the psychology of women and gender* (pp. 133–155). New York: Wiley.

Tolman, D. L., Spencer, R., Rosen-Reynoso, M., & Porche, M. V. (2003). Sowing the seeds of violence in heterosexual relationships: Early adolescents narrate compulsory heterosexuality. *Journal of Social Issues, 59*, 159–178.

Tolman, D. L., & Szalacha, L. A. (1999). Dimensions of desire: Bridging qualitative and quantitative methods in a study of female adolescent sexuality. *Psychology of Women Quarterly, 23*, 7–39.

Tolman, J., Pittman, K., Yohalem, N., Thomases, J., & Trammel, M. (2002). Moving an out-of-school agenda: Lessons and challenges across cities. Takoma Park, MD: The Forum for Youth Investment.

Torney-Purta, J. (1992). Cognitive representations of the political system in adolescents: The continuum from pre-novice to expert. In H. Haste & J. Torney-Purta (Eds.), *The development of political understanding: A new perspective* (pp. 11–26). *New directions for child development*, No. 56. San Francisco: Jossey-Bass.

Trawick-Smith, J. (2003). *Early childhood development: A multicultural perspective* (3rd ed.). Columbus, OH: Merrill/Prentice Hall.

Tremblay, R. E. (2000). The development of aggressive behaviour during childhood: What have we learned in the past century? *International Journal of Behavioral Development, 24*, 129–141.

Troiano, R. P., & Flegal, K. M. (1998). Overweight children and adolescents: Description, epidemiology, and demographics. *Pediatrics, 101*, 497–504.

Tschann, J. M., Adler, N. E., Millstein, S. G., Gurvey, J. E., & Ellen, J. M. (2002). Relative power between sexual partners and condom use among adolescents. *Journal of Adolescent Health, 31*, 17–25.

Tucker, M. S. (1999). How did we get here and where should we be going? In D. D. Marsh & J. B. Codding (Eds.), *The new American high school*. Thousand Oaks, CA: Corwin/Sage.

Turiel, E. (1998). The development of morality. In W. Damon (Series Ed.) & N. Eisenberg (Vol. Ed.), *Handbook of child psychology: Vol. 3. Social, emotional, and personality development* (5th ed., pp. 863–932). New York: Wiley.

Turiel, E., Hildebrandt, & Wainryb, C. (1991). Judging social issues: Difficulties, inconsistencies, and consistencies. *Monographs of the Society for Research in Child Development, 56* (2, Serial No. 224).

Turkheimer, E., Haley, A., Waldron, M., D'Onofrio, B., & Gottesman, I. (2003). Socioeconomic status modifies heritability of IQ in young children. *Psychological Science, 14*, 623–628.

Turner, J. C. (1987). *Rediscovering the social group: A self-categorization theory*. Oxford, UK: Basil Blackwell.

Turner, J. S. (2003). *Dating and sexuality in America: A reference handbook*. Santa Barbara, CA: ABC-CLIO.

Twenge, J. M., & Baumeister, R. F. (2002). Self-control: A limited yet renewable resource. In Y. Kashima, M. Foddy, & M. Platow (Eds.), *Self and identity: Personal, social, and symbolic* (pp. 57–70). Mahwah, NJ: Erlbaum.

U.S. Bureau of the Census. (2000, August 28). *Census bureau facts for features*. Retrieved July 18, 2002, from http://www.census.gov/Press-Release/www/2000/cb00ff09.html

U.S. Bureau of the Census. (2001a). *School enrollment in the United States: Social and economic characteristics of students*. (U.S. Bureau of the Census Publication No. P20-533). Washington, DC: Government Printing Office.

U.S. Bureau of the Census. (2001b). *Age: 2000*. (U.S. Bureau of the Census Publication No. C2KBR/01-12). Washington, DC: Government Printing Office.

U.S. Bureau of the Census. (2001c). *Home computers and Internet use in the United States: August 2000*. (U.S. Bureau of the Census Publication No. P23-207). Washington, DC: Government Printing Office.

U.S. Department of Education and U.S. Department of Justice. (2000). *Working for children and families: Safe and smart after-school programs*. Retrieved July 31, 2002, from http://www.ed.gov/pubs/parents/SafeSmart

U.S. Department of Health and Human Services. (1994). *Preventing tobacco use among young people: A report of the Surgeon General*. Atlanta, GA: U.S. Department of Health and Human Services, Public Health Service, Centers for Disease Control and Prevention, National Center for Chronic Disease Prevention and Health Promotion, Office on Smoking and Health.

U.S. Department of Health and Human Services. (2001). *Vital statistics of the United States*. Washington, DC: U.S. Government Printing Office.

U.S. Department of Health and Human Services. (2005). *Dietary guidelines for Americans*. Washington, DC: U.S. Government Printing Office.

U.S. Department of Transportation (May 21, 2004). *Fatality analysis reporting system (FARS) web-based encyclopedia*. Retrieved June 9, 2004, from http://www-fars.nhtsa.dot.gov

Udry, J. R., & Campbell, B. C. (1994). Getting started on sexual behavior. In A. S. Rossi (Ed.), *Sexuality across the life course. The John D. and Catherine T. MacArthur Foundation series on mental health and development: Studies on successful midlife development* (pp. 187–207). Chicago: University of Chicago Press.

Udry, J. R., Talbert, L., & Morris, N. M. (1986). Biosocial foundations of adolescent female sexuality. *Demography 23*, 217–230.

Ulrich, J. M. (2003). Generation X: A (sub)cultural genealogy. In J. M. Ulrich & A. L. Harris (Eds.), *GenXegesis: Essays on alternative youth (sub)culture* (pp. 3–37). Madison, WI: University of Wisconsin Press.

Umaña-Taylor, A., Diversi, M., & Fine, M. A. (2002). Ethnic identity and self-esteem of Latino adolescents: Distinctions among the Latino population. *Journal of Adolescent Research, 17*(3), 303–327.

Umaña-Taylor, A., Yazedjian, A., & Bámaca-Gomez, M. (2004). Developing the ethnic identity scale using Eriksonian and social identity perspectives. *Identity: An International Journal of Theory and Research, 4*, 9–38.

UNAIDS/WHO. (2002). *AIDS epidemic update: December 2002*. Geneva: UNAIDS.

Underwood, M. K. (2003). *Social aggression among girls*. New York: Guilford Press.

Underwood, M. K., Galen, B. R., & Paquette, J. A. (2001). Top ten challenges for understanding gender and aggression in children: Why can't we all just get along? *Social Development, 10*(2), 248–266.

Underwood, M. K., & Hurley, J. C. (1999). Emotion regulation in peer relationships in middle childhood. In L. Balter & C. S. Tamis-LeMonda (Eds.), *Child psychology: A handbook of contemporary issues* (pp. 237–258). Philadelphia, PA: Psychology Press.

Ungar, M. (2004). A constructionist discourse on resilience: Multiple contexts, multiple realities among at-risk children and youth. *Youth & Society, 35*, 341–365.

United Nations. (1986). *The situation of youth in the 1980s and prospects and challenges for the year 2000*. New York: Author.

Updegraff, K. A., Madden-Derdich, D. A., Estrada, A. U., Sales, L. J., & Leonard, S. A. (2002). Young adolescents' experiences with parents and friends: Exploring the connections. *Family Relations, 51*, 72–80.

Updegraff, K. A., McHale, S. M., & Crouter, A. (2000). Adolescents' sex-typed friendship experiences: Does having a sister versus a brother matter? *Child Development, 71*, 1597–1610.

Useem, E. L. (1992). Middle schools and math groups: Parents' involvement in children's placement. *Sociology of Education, 65*, 263–279.

Vadum, A. C., & Rankin, N. O. (1998). Psychological research: Methods for discovery and validation. New York: McGraw-Hill.

Valk, A. (2000). Ethnic identity, ethnic attitudes, self-esteem, and esteem toward others among Estonian and Russian adolescents. *Journal of Adolescent Research, 15*, 637–651.

Valsiner, J. (1997). *Culture and the development of children's action* (2nd ed.). New York: Wiley.

van Baal, G. C. M., Boomsma, D. I., & deGeus, E. J. C. (2001). Longitudinal genetic analysis of EEG coherence in young twins. *Behavior Genetics, 31*, 637–651.

van Hoof, A., & Raaumakers, Q. A. W. (2002). The spatial integration of adolescent identity: Its relation to age, education, and subjective well-being. *Scandinavian Journal of Psychology, 43*, 201–212.

van Hoof, A., & Raaumakers, Q. A. W. (2003). The search for the structure of identity formation. *Identity, 3*, 271–289.

van Linden, J. A., & Fertman, C. I. (1998). *Youth leadership: A guide to understanding leadership development in adolescents*. San Francisco: Jossey-Bass.

Van Voorhis, F. L. (2000). The effects of interactive (TIPS) homework on family involvement and science achievement of middle grade students. Unpublished doctoral dissertation, University of Florida, Gainesville.

Vander Wal, J. S., & Thelen, M. H. (2001). Predictors of body image dissatisfaction in elementary-age school girls. *Eating Behaviors, 1*, 1–18.

Vandiver, B. J., Cross, W. E., Jr., & Worrell, F. C. (2002). Validating the Cross Racial Identity Scale. *Journal of Counseling Psychology, 49*, 71–85.

Vartanian, L. R. (1997). Separation-individuation, social support, and adolescent egocentrism: An exploratory study. *Journal of Early Adolescence, 17*, 245–270.

Vartanian, L. R. (2000). Revisiting the imaginary audience and personal fable constructs of adolescent egocentrism: A conceptual review. *Adolescence, 35*, 639–661.

Vartanian, L. R., & Powlishta, K. K. (1996). A longitudinal examination of the social-cognitive foundations of adolescent egocentrism. *Journal of Early Adolescence, 16*, 157–178.

Videon, T. M. (2002). The effects of parent-adolescent relationships and parental separation on adolescent well-being. *Journal of Marriage and Family, 64*(2), 489–503.

Vinha, D., Cavalcante, J. A., & Andrade, M. M. M. (2002). Sleep-wake patterns of student workers and non-workers. *Biological Rhythm Research, 33*, 417–426.

Vion, M., & Colas, A. (2004). On the use of the connective 'and' in oral narration: A study of French-speaking elementary school children. *Journal of Child Language, 31*, 399–419.

Visser, J., Geuze, R. H., & Kalverboer, A. F. (1998). The relationship between physical growth, the level of activity and the development of motor skills in adolescence: Differences between children with DCD and controls. *Human Movement Science, 17*, 573–608.

von Busschbach, J. J., Hinten, M., Rikken, B., Grobbee, D. E., De Charro, F. T., et al. (1999). Some patients with an idiopathic short stature see their short stature as a problem, but others do not: Why this difference? In U. Eiholzer, F. Haverkamp, & L. Voss (Eds.),

Growth, stature, and psychosocial well-being (pp. 27–35). Ashland, OH: Hogrefe and Huber.

Vondracek, F. W., & Porfeli, E. J. (2003). The world of work and careers. In G. R. Adams & M. D. Berzonsky (Eds.), *Blackwell handbook of adolescence* (pp. 109–128). Malden, MA: Blackwell.

Vondracek, F. W., & Skorikov, V. B. (1997). Leisure, school, and work activity preferences and their role in vocational identity development. *Career Development Quarterly, 45*, 322–340.

Voss, L. (1999). Short stature: Does it matter? A review of the evidence. In U. Eiholzer, F. Haverkamp, & L. D. Voss (Eds.), *Growth, stature, and psychosocial well-being* (pp.7–14). Ashland, OH: Hogrefe & Huber.

Voyer, D., Voyer, S., & Bryden, M. P. (1995). Magnitude of sex differences in spatial abilities: A meta-analysis and consideration of critical variables. *Psychological Bulletin, 117*, 250–270.

Vygotsky, L. S. (1978). *Mind in society: The development of higher psychological processes*. Cambridge, MA: Harvard University Press.

Wadsworth, B. J. (1996). *Piaget's theory of cognitive and affective development: Foundations of constructivism* (5th ed.). White Plains, NY: Longman.

Wahlstrom, K. L. (2002). Accommodating the sleep patterns of adolescents within current educational structures: An uncharted path. In M. A. Carskadon (Ed.), *Adolescent sleep patterns: Biological, social, and psychological influences* (pp. 172–197). New York: Cambridge University Press.

Walcott, D. D., Pratt, H. D., & Patel, D. R. (2003). Adolescents and eating disorders: Gender, racial, ethnic, sociocultural, and socioeconomic issues. *Journal of Adolescent Research, 18*, 223–243.

Walker, L. J., de Vries, B., & Trevethan, S. D. (1987). Moral stages and moral orientations in real life and hypothetical dilemmas. *Child Development, 58*, 842–858.

Wallace-Broscious, A., Serafica, F. C., & Osipow, S. H. (1994). Adolescent career development: Relationships to self-concept and identity status. *Journal of Research on Adolescence, 4*, 127–149.

Walsh, A. S. (2000). Slipping into darkness: Popular culture and the creation of a Latino evangelical youth culture. In R. W. Flory & D. C. Miller (Eds.), *GenX religion* (pp. 74–91). New York: Routledge.

Ward, L. M. (2003). Understanding the role of entertainment media in the sexual socialization of American youth: A review of empirical research. *Developmental Review, 23*, 347–388.

Ward, L. M., Hansbrough, E., & Walker, E. (2005). Contributions of music video exposure to Black adolescents' gender and sexual schemas. *Journal of Adolescent Research, 20*, 143–166.

Warren, M. P. (1983). Physical and biological aspects of puberty. In J. Brooks-Gunn & A. C. Petersen (Eds.), *Girls at puberty: Biological and psychosocial perspectives* (pp. 3–28). New York: Plenum.

Wartella, E., Caplovitz, A. G. & Lee, J. H. (2004). From Baby Einstein to Leapfrog, from Doom to the Sims, from instant messaging to Internet chat rooms: Public interest in the role of interactive media in children's lives. *Social Policy Report, Vol. 18, No. 4*. Retrieved March 21, 2005, from http://www.srcd.org/spr.html

Waterman, A. S. (1985). Identity in the context of adolescent psychology. In A. S. Waterman (Ed.), *Identity status in adolescence: Processes and contents* (pp. 5–24). *New Directions for Child Development*, No. 30. San Francisco: Jossey-Bass.

Waterman, A. S. (1993). Developmental perspectives on identity formation: From adolescence to adulthood. In J. Marcia, A. Waterman, D. Matteson, S. Archer, & J. Orlofsky (Eds.), *Ego identity* (pp. 42–68). New York: Springer-Verlag.

Waterman, A. S. (1999). Identity, the identity statuses, and identity status development: A contemporary statement. *Developmental Review, 19*, 591–621.

Waters, E., Hamilton, C. E., & Weinfeld, N. S. (2000). The stability of attachment security from infancy to adolescence and early adulthood: General introduction. *Child Development, 71*, 678–683.

Watson, M. W., & Fischer, K. W. (1980). Development of social roles in elicited and spontaneous behavior during the preschool years. *Developmental Psychology, 16*, 483–494.

Wattigney, W. A., Srinivasan, S. R., Chen, W., Greenlund, K. J., & Berenson, G. S. (1999). Secular trend of earlier onset of menarche with increasing obesity in black and white girls: The Bogalusa Heart Study. *Ethnicity and Disease, 9*, 181–189.

Watts, R., Liston, C., Niogi, S., & Ulug, A. M. (2003). Fiber tracking using magnetic resonance diffusion tensor imaging and its applications to human brain development. *Mental Retardation and Developmental Disabilities Research Reviews, 9*, 168–177.

Way, N. (1995). "Can't you see the courage, the strength that I have?": Listening to urban adolescent girls speak about their relationships. *Psychology of Women Quarterly, 19*, 107–128.

Way, N., & Chen, L. (2000). Close and general friendships among African American, Latino, and Asian American adolescents from low-income families. *Journal of Adolescent Research, 15*, 274–301.

Way, N., & Chu, J. (Eds.) (2004). *Adolescent boys: Exploring diverse cultures of boyhood*. New York: New York University Press.

Way, N., & Robinson, M. G. (2003). A longitudinal study of the effects of family, friends, and school experiences on the psychological adjustment of ethnic-minority low-SES adolescents. *Journal of Adolescent Research, 18*, 324–346.

Wechsler, D. (1939). *The measurement of adult intelligence*. Baltimore, MD: Williams and Wilkins.

Wechsler, D. (1991). *Wechsler Intelligence Scale for Children* (3rd ed.). San Antonio, TX: Psychological Corporation.

Wechsler, D. (1997). *Wechsler Adult Intelligence Scale* (3rd ed.). San Antonio, TX: Psychological Corporation.

Wechsler, D. (2002). *WPPSI—III manual.* San Antonio, TX: Psychological Corporation.

Wechsler, D. (2003). *Wechsler Intelligence Scale for Children* (4th ed.). San Antonio, TX: Psychological Corporation.

Weichold, K., Silbereisen, R. K., & Schmitt-Rodermund, E. (2003). Short-term and long-term consequences of early versus late physical maturation in adolescents. In C. Hayward (Ed.), *Gender differences at puberty* (pp. 241–276). New York: Cambridge University Press.

Weigel, D. J., Martin, S. S., & Bennett, K. K. (2005). Ecological influences of the home and the child-care center on preschool-age children's literacy development, *Reading Research Quarterly, 40,* 204–233.

Weinfeld, N. S., Sroufe, L. A., & Egeland, B. (2000). Attachment from infancy to adulthood in a high-risk sample: Continuity, discontinuity, and their correlates. *Child Development, 71,* 695–702.

Weinstein, N. D. (1980). Unrealistic optimism about future life events. *Journal of Personality and Social Psychology, 39,* 806–820.

Weinstein, N. D. (1984). Why it won't happen to me: Perceptions of risk factors and susceptibility. *Health Psychology, 3,* 431–457.

Weisner, T. S. (1996). The 5 to 7 transition as an ecocultural project. In A. J. Sameroff & M. M. Haith (Eds.), *The five to seven year shift: The age of reason and responsibility* (pp. 295–396). Chicago: University of Chicago Press.

Weisner, T. S. (1998). Human development, child well-being, and the cultural project of development. In D. Sharma & K. Fischer (Eds.), *Socio-emotional development across cultures* (pp. 69–85). *New Directions in Child Development,* No. 81. San Francisco: Jossey-Bass.

Weisner, T. S. (2001). Childhood: Anthropological aspects. In D. L. Sills (Ed.), *The international encyclopedia of the social sciences* (pp. 1697–1701). New York: Macmillan.

Weisner, T. S., Gallimore, R., & Jordan, C. (1988). Unpackaging cultural effects on classroom learning: Native Hawaiian peer assistance and child-generated activity. *Anthropology and Education Quarterly, 19,* 327–351.

Weisner, T. S., & Wilson-Mitchell, J. E. (1990). Nonconventional family lifestyles and sex-typing in six-year-olds. *Child Development, 61,* 1915–1933.

Wentzel, K. R. (2003). Sociometric status and adjustment in middle school: A longitudinal study. *Journal of Early Adolescence, 23*(1), 5–28.

Werner, E. E. (1989). Children of the garden island. *Scientific American, 260*(4), 106–111.

Werner, E. E. (1993). Risk, resilience, and recovery: Perspectives from the Kauai longitudinal study. *Development and Psychopathology, 5,* 503–515.

Werner, E. E., & Smith, R. S. (2001). *Journeys from childhood to midlife: Risk, resilience, and recovery.* Ithaca, NY: Cornell University Press.

Westenberg, P. M., van Strien, S. D., & Drewes, M. J. (2001). Revised description and measurement of ego development in early adolescence: An artifact of the written procedure? *Journal of Early Adolescence, 21*(4), 470–493.

White, J. M. (1991). *Dynamics of family development: The theory of family development.* New York: Guilford Press.

White, J. M., & Klein, D. M. (2002). *Family theories* (2nd ed.). Thousand Oaks, CA: Sage.

White, N. R. (2002). "Not under my roof!": Young people's experience of home. *Youth & Society, 34,* 214–231.

White, R. W. (1959). Motivation reconsidered: The concept of competence. *Psychological Review, 66,* 233–297.

White, S. H. (1996). The child's entry into the "age of reason." In A. J. Sameroff & M. M. Haith (Eds.), *The five to seven year shift: The age of reason and responsibility* (pp. 17–30). Chicago: University of Chicago Press.

Whitesell, N. R., & Harter, S. (1989). Children's reports of conflict between simultaneous opposite-valence emotions. *Child Development, 60,* 673–682.

Whiting, B. B., & Edwards, C. P. (1992). *Children of different worlds.* Cambridge, MA: Harvard University Press.

Whitman, T. L., Borkowski, J. G., Keogh, D. A., & Weed, K. (2001). *Interwoven lives: Adolescent mothers and their children.* Mahwah, NJ: Erlbaum.

Wiesner, M., & Ittel, A. (2002). Relations of pubertal timing and depressive symptoms to substance use in early adolescence. *Journal of Early Adolescence, 22,* 5–23.

Wigfield, A., Battle, A., Keller, L. B., & Eccles, J. S. (2002). Sex differences in motivation, self-concept, career aspiration, and career choice: Implications for cognitive development. In A. McGillicuddy-De Lisi & R. De Lisi (Eds.), *Biology, society, and behavior: The development of sex differences in cognition* (pp. 93–124). Westport, CT: Ablex Publishing.

Wigfield, A., & Eccles, J. S. (2002). The development of competence beliefs, expectancies for success, and achievement values from childhood to adolescence. In A. Wigfield & J. S. Eccles (Eds.), *The development of achievement motivation* (pp. 91–121). San Diego, CA: Academic Press.

Wigfield, A., Eccles, J. S., & Rogriguez, D. (1998). The development of children's motivation in school contexts. *Review of Research in Education, 23,* 73–118.

Wiles, J., & Bondi, J. (2001). *The new American middle school: Educating preadolescents in an era of change* (3rd ed.). Upper Saddle River, NJ: Merrill/Prentice Hall.

Williams, J. M., & Currie, C. (2000). Self-esteem and physical development in early adolescence: Pubertal timing and body image. *Journal of Early Adolescence, 20,* 129–149.

Williams, O. A. (2003). Effects of faith and church on African American adolescents. *Michigan Family Review, 8,* 1–9.

Williams, W. M., Blythe, T., White, N., Li, J., Gardner, H., & Sternberg, R. J. (2002). Practical intelligence for school: Developing metacognitive sources of achievement in adolescence. *Developmental Review, 22,* 162–210.

Wills, T. A., Yaeger, A. M., & Sandy, J. M. (2003). Buffering effect of religiosity for adolescent substance abuse. *Psychology of Addictive Behaviors, 17,* 24–31.

Wilson, D. M., Killen, J. D., Hayward, C., Robinson, T. N., Hammer, L. D., Kraemer, H. C., et al. (1994). Timing and rate of sexual maturation and the onset of cigarette and alcohol use among teenage girls. *Archives of Pediatrics and Adolescent Medicine, 148,* 789–795.

Wilson, J. F. (2003). *Biological foundations of human behavior.* Belmont, CA: Wadsworth/Thomson Learning.

Windle, M. (1992). Revised Dimensions of Temperament Survey (DOTS-R): Simultaneous group confirmatory factor analysis for adolescent gender groups. *Psychological Assessment, 4,* 1–21.

Windle, M., Hooker, K., Lenerz, K., East, P. L., Lerner, J. V., & Lerner, R. M. (1986). Temperament, perceived competence, and depression in early and late adolescents. *Developmental Psychology, 22,* 384–392.

Wolfe, B., & Perozek, M. (1997). Teen children's health and health care use. In R. A. Maynard (Ed.), *Kids having kids: Economic costs and social consequences of teen pregnancy* (pp. 181–203). Washington, DC: Urban Institute Press.

Wolfson, A. R., & Carskadon, M. A. (1998). Sleep schedules and daytime functioning in adolescents. *Child Development, 69,* 875–887.

Wolfson, A. R., Tzischinsky, O., Brown, C., Darley, C., Acebo, C., & Carskadon, M. (1995). Sleep, behavior, and stress at the transition to senior high school. *Sleep Research, 24,* 115.

Wood, E., Senn, C. Y., Desmarais, S., Park, L., & Verberg, N. (2002). Sources of information about dating and their perceived influence on adolescents. *Journal of Adolescent Research, 17,* 401–417.

Wood, K. C., Becker, J. A., & Thompson, J. K. (2001). Body image dissatisfaction in preadolescent children. *Journal of Applied Developmental Psychology, 17,* 85–100.

Woodson, S. E. (1999). Mapping the cultural geography of childhood or, performing monstrous children. *Journal of American Culture, 22*(4), 31–43.

Woodward, L. & Fergusson, D. (2002). Parent, child and contextual predictors of childhood physical punishment. *Infant and Child Development, 11,* 213–236.

Wyn, J., & White, R. (1997). *Rethinking youth.* London: Sage.

Wyn, J., & White, R. (2000). Negotiating social change: The paradox of youth. *Youth & Society, 32*(2), 165–183.

Xue, Y, Leventhal, T., Brooks-Gunn, J., & Earls, F. (2005). Neighborhood residence and mental health problems of 5- to 11-year-olds. *Archives of General Psychiatry, 62,* 554–563.

Yan, J. H., & Jevas, S. (2004). Young girls' developmental skills in underarm throwing. *Perceptual & Motor Skills, 99,* 39–47.

Yan, Z. (2005). Age differences in children's understanding of the complexity of the Internet. *Journal of Applied Developmental Psychology, 26,* 385–396.

Yates, M., & Youniss, J. (1998). Community service and political identity. *Journal of Social Issues, 54,* 495–512.

Yeh, C. (2002). Sexual risk taking among Taiwanese youth. *Public Health Nursing, 19*(1), 68–75.

Young, R. A., Paseluikho, M. A., & Valach, L. (1997). The role of emotion in the construction of career in parent-adolescent conversations. *Journal of Counseling & Development, 76,* 36–44.

Young, R. A., Valach, L., Ball, J., Paseluikho, M. A., Wong, Y. S., DeVries, R. J., McLean, H., & Turkel, H. (2001). Career development in adolescence as a family project. *Journal of Counseling Psychology, 48,* 190–202.

Youniss, J. (1980). *Parents and peers in social development: A Sullivan-Piaget perspective.* Chicago: University of Chicago Press.

Youniss, J., Bales, S., Christmas-Best, V., Diversi, M., McLaughlin, M., & Silbereisen, R. (2002). Youth civic engagement in the twenty-first century. *Journal of Research on Adolescence, 12,* 121–148.

Youniss, J., McClelland, J. A., & Yates, M. (1999). Religion, community service, and identity in American youth. *Journal of Adolescence, 22,* 243–253.

Youniss, J., & Ruth, A. J. (2002). Approaching policy for adolescents in the 21st century. In J. T. Mortimer & R. Larson (Eds.), *The changing adolescent experience: Societal trends and the transition to adulthood* (pp. 250–271). Cambridge, UK: Cambridge University Press.

Youth and America's Future. (1988). *The forgotten half: Pathways to success for America's youth and young families.* Washington, DC: William T. Grant Foundation Commission on Work, Family and Citizenship.

Yowell, C. M. (2000). Possible selves and future orientation: Exploring hopes and fears of Latino boys and girls. *Journal of Early Adolescence, 20,* 245–280.

Yowell, C. M. (2002). Dreams of the future: The pursuit of education and career possible selves among ninth grade Latino youth. *Applied Developmental Science, 6,* 62–72.

Zald, D. H., & Iacono, W. G. (1998). The development of spatial working memory abilities. *Developmental Neuropsychology, 14,* 563–578.

Zarbatany, L., Hartmann, D. P., & Rankin, D. B. (1990). The psychological functions of preadolescent peer activities. *Child Development, 61,* 1067–1080.

Zauszniewki, J. A., Chung, C., Chang, C., & Krafcik, K. (2002). Predictors of resourcefulness in school-aged children. *Journal of Mental Health Nursing, 23,* 385–401.

Zeller, M., Vanatta, K., Schaffer, J., & Noll, R. B. (2003). Behavioral reputation: A cross-age perspective. *Developmental Psychology, 39,* 129–139.

Zimet, G. D., Cutler, M., Litvene, M., Dahms, W., et al. (1995). Psychological adjustment of children evaluated for short stature: A preliminary report. *Journal of Developmental & Behavioral Pediatrics, 16*, 264–270.

Zimmer-Gembeck, M. J., & Collins, W. A. (2003). Autonomy development during adolescence. In G. R. Adams & M. D. Berzonsky (Eds.), *Blackwell handbook of adolescence* (pp. 175–204). Malden, MA: Blackwell.

Zimmer-Gembeck, M. J., Siebenbruner, J., & Collins, W. A. (2004). A prospective study of intraindividual and peer influences on adolescents' heterosexual romantic and sexual behavior. *Archives of Sexual Behavior, 33*, 381–394.

Zimmerman, P., & Becker-Stoll, F. (2002). Stability of attachment representations during adolescence: The influence of ego-identity status. *Journal of Adolescence, 25*, 105–124.

Zinnbauer, B. J., Pargament, K. I., & Cole, B. (1997). Spirituality and religion: Unfuzzying the fuzzy. *Journal for the Scientific Study of Religion, 36*, 549–564.

AUTHOR INDEX

Information in tables, figures, or boxes is indicated by t, f *or* b *following the page number.*

Aalsma, M. C., 277, 317
Aarnio, M., 83
Aarons, S. J., 260, 264
Abe, J. A., 126
Aber, J. L., 42, 90, 195
Abma, J., 262
Aboudezzeddine, T., 188
Abrams, D., 188
Abramson, L. Y., 155
Adair, L. S., 239
Adams, G. R., 38, 308, 308t, 309, 309b, 311f, 355f
Adams, R., 362
Adin, A. M., 332
Adler, P. A., 181, 260
Agnew, R., 185
Aihara, M., 245
Ainsworth, M. D. S., 338, 339
Akbudak, E., 245
Alaimo, K., 249
Alarcón, O., 328
Alexander, C., 255
Alipuria, L. L., 314
Allahar, A. L., 207
Allen, J. P., 326, 332
Allen, V., 241
Allington, R. L., 120
Allison, K. W., 366
Almeida, D. M., 343
Aloise-Young, P. A., 329
Alsaker, F. D., 242t
Altheide, D. L., 23
Alton, I., 250
Alvarez, J. M., 138
Amabile, T. M., 148
Amato, P. R., 193, 364, 365
Ames, L. B., 37, 207
Amundson, N. E., 321
Andersen, S. L., 73
Anderson, E. R., 364
Anderson, K. J., 346
Anderson, P. M., 219
Anderson, R. E., 297t
Anderson-Butcher, D., 53
Andrade, M. M. M., 250
Andre, T., 294
Andrews, D. W., 185, 187
Aneshensel, C. S., 241
Anfara, V. A., Jr., 36
Ani, C., 85
Annett, M., 81
Anthis, K. S., 329
Anyan, S. E., 368
Aoki, S., 245
Araki, T., 245
Archer, S. L., 309, 310
Argys, L. M., 265, 266
Aries, P., 36
Armistead, L., 350
Arnett, J. J., 209, 374, 375, 375f, 376t, 377, 378, 379, 383, 384f, 389, 390, 390f, 390t, 393, 394
Aronoff, N., 41, 208
Arora, T., 185, 188, 189, 190b
Arrington, E. G., 221
Arsenio, W. F., 188, 189
Asher, S. R., 179
Asidao, C. S., 188
Aspelmeier, J. E., 339
Atkinson, R. C., 110, 112f
Austin, S. B., 90
Averett, S. L., 265, 266
Avery, P. G., 324
Axelrod, J. J., 181
Azmitia, M., 179, 180, 188, 333, 377

Bachman, F. F., 254
Bachman, J. G., 207, 255, 327
Baenen, J., 51
Bailey, D., 41, 68, 69, 208
Bailey, J. M., 341, 343, 346
Baillie, L., 21
Baird, A. A., 245
Bakeman, R., 350
Baker, D., 19
Baker, J. M., 102b
Baldwin, S., 328
Bales, S. N., 228
Balter, L., 189b
Baltes, P. B., 9, 212, 213, 213f
Bámaca, M. Y., 310
Bámaca-Gomez, M., 307, 314
Bandura, A., 144, 164, 185, 188
Banister, P., 23
Bank, L., 194, 364
Banks, R. W., 323, 323b
Barbaranelli, C., 185, 188
Barber, B. K., 206, 294, 367
Barber, B. L., 84, 90b, 185, 375
Barbour, A. C., 90
Barker, E. T., 348
Barkley, R. A., 116b
Barnes, H. L., 207, 238
Barnett, N. P., 252
Barr, S., 69
Barrows, H., 278
Barry, C. M., 377
Bartholomew, K., 338, 339, 387
Bass, S., 69
Basseches, M., 385
Bassett, H. H., 50
Bates, J. E., 154, 155f, 156, 235
Battle, A., 294
Bauer, K. W., 90
Bauer, U., 329
Baumann, J. F., 119
Baumeister, R. F., 156, 319
Baumrind, D., 35, 157
Baxter-Jones, A. D. G., 83
Bayley, N., 241
Beale, A. V., 320
Bearman, S. K., 241
Beatty, A. S., 279
Beaumont, S., 13
Bebeau, M. J., 171
Becker, B., 217
Becker, H. S., 22
Becker, J. A., 88, 296
Beckers, F., 70
Becker-Stoll, F., 340
Bedell, B. T., 151
Beers, S. R., 254
Bell, K. L., 326, 332
Bell, N. J., 386
Bell, R. M., 260
Bell, S., 338, 339
Bellmore, A. B., 167, 183
Belsky, J., 235, 340
Bem, S. L., 343
Ben-Amos, I. K., 378
Benenson, J. F., 353
Bennett, K. K., 119
Bennion, L., 309, 309b
Benson, P. L., 202, 217, 219, 221, 221t, 223, 227, 228, 316, 317
Berenbaum, S. A., 294
Berends, M., 289
Berenson, G. S., 239
Bergen, D., 90b
Berger, R., 366
Bergman, A., 339
Berk, L., 5f, 10f, 101t, 102b, 108
Berkey, C. S., 238
Berkowitz, M. W., 177
Berndt, T. J., 181, 184, 185, 352, 357
Beron, K., 119
Berry, C., 255
Berry, S. H., 260
Berscheid, E., 352
Berthiaume, K. S., 116b
Berzonsky, M. D., 308, 310, 311f, 332
Betancur, C., 60
Beuhring, T., 250, 385
Beunen, G., 85, 248

Beyers, W., 305
Biekert, E., 347
Biesecker, G., 193, 341, 342f
Bigelow, B. J., 179
Bigler, R. S., 344
Birom, F. M., 238
Bjorklund, D. A., 112, 113, 114t, 115, 279
Bjorklund, D. F., 83, 114, 213, 234
Bjorntorp, P., 70, 83
Black, C., 276
Black, J., 77b, 121, 134f, 306
Blackwell, W., 226
Blanchard-Fields, F., 277
Blank, M. J., 226
Bleeker, M. M., 136, 140, 143
Blehar, M. C., 339
Block, J., 327, 328
Bloom, L., 119
Blos, P., 305
Blume, L. B., 51, 53, 307, 323b, 346
Blume, T. W., 51, 307, 323b
Blustein, D. L., 320, 321
Blyth, D. A., 39, 143, 223, 265, 327
Blythe, J., 239
Blythe, T., 291b
Bohlin, G., 340
Bohn, C. M., 83
Boland, E., 119
Bolger, K. E., 78b
Bolger, N., 138
Bondi, J., 38
Bonds, L. A., 368t
Bonino, S., 99
Bonjour, J. P., 69
Boomer, L., 40
Boomsma, D. I., 75
Booth, A., 364
Booth, M. L., 61
Borden, L. M., 217, 253
Boring, A. M., 78b, 254
Borkowski, J. G., 263
Bornstein, M. H., 361
Bouchard, C., 70f
Bouchey, H. A., 303, 328, 358, 359
Boulton, M., 192b
Bowlby, J., 226, 338, 339, 340
Boyatzis, C. J., 316, 317
Boyer, E. L., 203, 204, 205b
Bracey, J. R., 310, 314
Bracken, B. A., 143
Brand, S., 332
Bransford, J. D., 278
Branta, C. F., 84
Braun, C. J., 254
Braungart-Rieker, J. M., 326
Brecelj, J., 244
Brendgen, M., 355, 364
Brenner, M. E., 126
Brentano, C., 219
Bresnick, S., 303, 328
Brewer, R. D., 253
Brieifel, R. R., 249
Brien, M. J., 263
Britten, N., 20
Brody, G. H., 154, 363
Bromley, D. B., 138
Bronfenbrenner, U., 5, 13, 45, 46, 47, 49b, 397
Brooks-Gunn, J., 5, 35, 36, 39, 90, 206, 223, 224, 224t, 225, 226, 236, 240, 241, 257, 326, 391, 392, 392f, 393
Broude, G. J., 41
Brown, A. L., 108b, 278
Brown, B. B., 157, 182, 351, 355, 355f, 359, 359f, 389
Brown, J. D., 348
Brown, J. L., 85, 195
Brown, L. M., 21, 173, 349
Brown, M. M., 184f
Brown, S. A., 254
Brownwell, M. D., 83
Brunk, K. C., 325
Bryan, J., 344, 345, 345t, 346
Bryant, A. L., 255, 265, 367
Bryant, C. M., 193
Bryant, R., 366
Bryden, M. P., 294
Brydon-Miller, M., 23
Buchanan, A., 320
Buchanan, C. M., 36
Bucher, K. T., 38
Buehler, C., 365
Buhrmester, D., 178, 179, 182, 352
Bukowski, W. M., 66b, 178, 179, 180, 181, 188
Bullock, B. M., 368
Bullock, M., 153
Buriel, R., 182, 193, 195
Burman, E., 23
Burns, M. S., 120
Burraston, B., 194, 364
Burstyn, J., 191
Burton, L., 205
Bush, E. G., 330
Busse, R. T., 183
Buswell, B., 328
Butterfield, S. A., 81
Bybee, D., 329, 330
Byrnes, J. P., 279, 281, 282

Cain, K., 119
Cairns, R. B., 10, 44, 387
Call, K. T., 265
Camarena, P. M., 226, 332
Cameron, L., 188
Camic, P. M., 18
Campbell, B. C., 257
Campbell, D. W., 82, 82f
Campbell, J. R., 295
Campos, J. J., 151, 152, 153, 154, 155
Cantu, C. L., 307
Capaldi, D. M., 154
Caplovitz, A. G., 43
Cappelli, C. A., 102b
Caprara, G. V., 185, 188
Carlo, G., 185
Carlson, E. A., 340
Carlson, J., 183
Carnochan, P., 140
Carpendale, J. I. M., 172
Carpenter, T. P., 294
Carr, M., 113
Carr, P., 279
Carragher, D. J., 367
Carskadon, M. A., 250, 252
Carson, C., 314
Carsten, E., 119
Carstensen, L. L., 142f, 144f
Cartmel, F., 394
Carver, K., 357
Carver, P. R., 328, 343, 346
Case, R., 114, 140
Casella, R., 191
Casey, B. J., 75, 78b
Casey, B. M., 294
Casey, M. A., 20b
Caspi, A., 15, 240
Cass, V., 258
Cassidy, J., 338, 340
Castro-Vazquez, G., 264
Cattelino, E., 100
Cauce, A. M., 140
Cauffman, E., 34, 282, 284b
Cavalcante, J. A., 250
Ceballo, R., 157
Ceci, S. J., 5, 47, 106, 288
Chambers, S., 294
Champion, K., 191
Champion, T. B., 21
Chan, D., 183
Chang, C., 156
Changeux, J-P., 75
Chao, R. K., 157
Chapin, J. R., 346
Chassin, L., 253
Chatterjee, P., 41, 208
Cheek, D. B., 239
Chen, C., 75, 118, 126
Chen, H., 25, 327
Chen, L., 313, 353
Chen, W. J., 113, 239
Cheney, R., 279
Chi, M. T. H., 115
Chin, C. S., 226
Chipuer, H. M., 61
Chira, S., 293
Chodorow, N. J., 133
Choi, W. S., 255
Christiansen, S., 185
Chugani, H. T., 75

Chung, C., 156
Cicchetti, D., 78b, 217
Cillessen, A. H. N., 167, 183
Clark, D. B., 78b, 254
Clark, P. A., 237
Clayton, P. E., 239
Clements, P., 185
Clinkenbear, P., 291b
Coatsworth, J. D., 221, 222f, 223, 253
Cocking, R., 278
Cohane, G. H., 252
Cohen, E., 259, 356
Cohen, R. J., 286f
Cohen-Kettenis, P. T., 346
Coie, J. D., 185, 187f
Colas, A., 119
Colby, A., 170, 171
Colby, S. M., 255
Colditz, G. A., 238
Cole, A. K., 340, 363, 364
Cole, B., 316
Cole, D. A., 138, 139
Cole, J. I., 296
Cole, M., 41, 105, 275
Coleman, P. K., 264, 340
Collings, J. N., 275
Collins, A., 278
Collins, J. F., 314
Collins, M. A., 148
Collins, P. H., 307
Collins, W. A., 34, 38, 50, 51, 207, 304, 305, 338, 356, 357, 358, 359, 361, 362
Comings, D. E., 235
Conant, J. B., 204
Condon, R. G., 378
Condon, S. M., 305, 332
Conger, K. J., 361, 367
Conger, R., 193, 226, 241, 242t, 361, 366
Connell, R., 343
Conner, D. B., 108
Connolly, J., 353, 353f, 355, 356, 357t
Connolly, K., 114t
Connors, D. J., 108b
Constantine, M. G., 323, 323b
Constantino, M. J., 136, 140, 143
Contreras, J. J., 194f, 339
Conturo, T., 245
Cook, P. G., 216, 216f
Cooley, C., 137–138
Cooper, C. R., 304, 305, 332, 333, 377
Cooper, H. M., 15, 124
Coopersmith, S., 157
Corbin, C. B., 84
Cortesi, F., 250
Costa, F. M., 217, 218, 219
Costigan, C. L., 326
Cota-Robles, S., 241, 242t
Côté, J. E., 3–8, 41, 205, 207, 209, 307, 378, 382
Cowan, C. P., 194, 360
Cowan, N., 277
Cowan, P. A., 194, 360
Coy, K. C., 207, 362
Coyle, K. K., 266
Crago, M., 250, 252
Craig, W. M., 188, 191, 353, 355, 356, 357
Crain, W., 164
Cratty, B. J., 81
Crawford, P., 252
Creswell, J. W., 22
Creusere, M. A., 102b
Crews, F. T., 254
Crick, N. R., 17, 165, 166, 166f, 185, 187, 188, 189
Criss, M. M., 157
Crockett, L. J., 50, 51, 206, 320
Crosby, L., 185, 187
Crosby, R. A., 265
Crosnoe, R., 62, 182, 194, 195, 195f, 196
Cross, D. R., 108
Cross, W. E., Jr., 312
Crouter, A. C., 34, 45, 49b, 50, 50b, 51, 52, 53, 206, 364
Crowe, P., 16b
Csikzentmihalyi, M., 148, 148b, 149b, 326, 327
Cubbin, C., 266
Cui, M., 193, 366, 367
Cummings, E. M., 326
Cunningham, M., 41, 383
Curnow, C., 385
Currie, C., 242t
Curry, C., 330
Curtis, W. J., 217, 219, 245, 247f
Cutler, M., 66b

Dabholkar, J. C., 78, 244
Dadisman, K., 53
Dahl, R., 102b
Dahl, R. E., 245, 250
Dahms, W., 66b
Damon, W., 140, 168, 173, 174, 187f, 213f, 302f, 310, 325
Dariotis, J. K., 180, 193, 195, 196
Darling, N. E., 361
Darwin, C., 234
D'Augelli, A. R., 258, 328, 362, 367, 368t
Davenport, E., 366
Davey, M., 314
Davidshofer, C. O., 17
Davidson, A. L., 333
Davidson, R. B., 326
Davis, D. A., 378
Davis, E. A., 280
Davis, G. A., 52
Davis, N. J., 202
Davis, S. N., 349b
Davis, S. S., 378
Davis, W., 277
Davis-Kean, P. E., 34, 141
Davison, K. S., 68
De Bellis, M. D., 77b, 78b, 254
DeBlassie, R., 276
Deci, E. L., 148
DeFrancesco, C., 84
de Geus, E. J. C., 75
Dehaene, S., 75
Dekovic, M., 304, 340
Delaney, C. H., 206
Delis, D. C., 254
Dell'Angelo, T., 307, 312
Demaray, M. K., 183
de Marchena, M. R., 113
deMause, L., 36
Demo, D. H., 327
Dempster, F. N., 113
Denham, S. A., 151
Denizet-Lewis, B., 356
Denny, C., 253
Denton, L. M., 317, 318b, 319
Denzin, N. K., 19
DeReus, L. A., 307
Desmarais, S., 351
Detweiler, J. B., 151
de Vries, B., 173
Diamond, L. M., 245, 246b, 349, 350, 356
Diaz, M., 383b
Dick, D. M., 242t
Dickinson, D. K., 120b, 121b
Dickson, G. L., 321
Diener, M. B., 116b
Dinkmeyer, D., 137b
Diorio, J. A., 367
Dishion, T. J., 185, 187, 193, 367, 368
Diversi, M., 224, 228, 310, 314
Dixon, A., 264
Dobkin, P. L., 253
Dodge, K. A., 165, 166, 184f, 185, 187f, 188, 189, 235
Doll, B., 191
Donnermeyer, J. F., 253
D'Onofrio, B., 288
Donovan, P., 262
Dornbusch, S. M., 157, 361
Dougher, K., 319
Dowling, E. M., 219, 317
Downey, K. T., 88
Doyle, A., 355
Doyle, A. B., 362, 364
Draper, P., 235
Drewes, M. J., 304
Drewnowski, A., 85
Druyan, S., 281
Dryfoos, J. D., 218, 219, 227
Dubas, J. S., 389, 390

Dubé, E. M., 350, 350t, 351, 351f
DuBois, D. L., 144, 332
Ducharme, J., 362
Duckett, E., 193
Duncan, G., 90
Dunkel, C. S., 329
Dunlop, S. A., 77b
Dunn, M. S., 252
Dunphy, D. C., 355
Dunsmore, J. C., 151
Dupree, D., 383
Durham, M. G., 346, 347, 348
Durkin, K., 167, 168
Durocher-Scudlich, T., 326
Dusek, J. B., 332
Duvall, E., 215, 215f
Dweck, C. S., 138, 146, 146t
Dworkin, J., 16b, 16f

Eaker, D. G., 314
Earles, J. A., 288
Earls, F., 90
Easterbrook, M. A., 342
Eastham, D., 116b
Eastman, G., 226
Eaton, W. O., 82, 82f, 83
Eccles, J. S., 36, 52, 84, 125, 126, 142f, 143, 144, 144f, 147, 147f, 148, 149, 157, 185, 194, 227, 282, 294, 332, 343, 344, 345, 345t, 346, 367, 375
Eccles-Parsons, J., 141
Economos, C. D., 90
Edridge, M. D., 307
Edwards, C. P., 41
Edwards, E. C., 119
Egan, S. K., 341, 346, 350
Egeland, B., 338, 340
Eicher, S. A., 182
Eichorn, D. H., 38, 39, 240
Eickholt, C., 326, 332
Eisenberg, N., 185, 186t, 187f, 196
Eisenberg, R., 145, 184, 185
Elder, G. H., Jr., 41, 43, 193, 214, 214f, 226, 241, 242t, 366, 367
Elicker, J., 338, 340
Elkind, D., 207, 275, 305
Ellen, J. M., 260
Elliott, E. M., 277
Elliott, G. R., 206
Elliott, R., 330
Elliott, S. N., 183
Elliott-Faust, D. J., 279
Ellis, B. J., 235
Emery, R. E., 365, 365b
Emmen, M., 305
Emmons, C. L., 125
Engels, R., 305, 340
Englund, M., 338
Epstein, P., 111b
Erickson, C. D., 323, 323b
Erikson, E., 133, 136, 207, 305, 306, 310, 311, 387
Erkut, S., 126, 328
Ernst, P., 123
Espelage, D. L., 188
Espeland, P., 202
Estes, L. S., 250
Evahn, C., 287
Evans, E. G., 332
Evans, G., 35f, 203f, 374f
Evans, M. A., 295
Evans, S. L., 226
Ewing, M. E., 84, 85

Fabes, R. A., 184
Fagan, J., 283b
Fahrmeier, E. D., 105
Faigenbaum, A., 70
Faircloth, B. S., 332
Falkner, N. H., 250, 385
Fan, S., 242t
Faris, R., 317, 318b, 319
Farkas, G., 119
Farmer, T. W., 188
Fashola, O. S., 53
Fassler, A. L. C., 69
Faulkner, R. A., 68
Fauth, R. C., 225
Feigelman, S., 264
Feiner, R. D., 332
Feiring, C., 338, 340, 341, 351, 352, 355, 359, 359f, 364
Feldman, D. H., 106
Feldman, S. S., 206
Fennema, E., 294
Fenzel, L. M., 143
Ferber, T., 224, 228
Fergusson, D., 235, 263
Fernald, L., 85
Feron, F. J. M., 116b
Ferrari, M., 291b
Ferrari, T. M., 53
Ferrer-Wreder, L., 193, 311, 312, 341, 342f
Ferris, J. C., 183
Feshbach, N. D., 185
Feshbach, S., 185
Few, A. M., 307
Field, A., 88
Fields, J. P., 126
Finch, M. D., 226
Fine, M. A., 310, 314, 349, 349b
Finger, R., 262
Fingerson, L., 346
Finkenauer, C., 340
Finn, J. D., 124
Finnegan, R. A., 340
Fischer, K. W., 133, 140, 244, 245, 385
Fischhoff, B., 277
Fish, L. S., 314
Fisher, C. B., 228, 387
Flanagan, C., 332
Flannery, D. J., 39, 305
Flavell, J. H., 115, 166, 167
Flegal, K. M., 85
Fleming, J. S., 146, 147
Fletcher, A. C., 361
Flory, R. W., 319
Flouri, E., 320
Floyd, F. J., 349, 350
Flum, H., 353
Fonagy, P., 338
Font, G., 119
Ford, D. H., 47, 48f
Forrest-Pressley, D. J., 279
Foster, W., 35
Foucault, M., 40
Fowler, F., 193
Fowler, J. W., 316, 317
Fox, N. A., 151
Frank, N. C., 317
Franke, M. L., 123
Frankenberger, K. D., 277, 305
Frazier, A. L., 238
Frazier, J. A., 105
Fredriks, A. M., 239
Freedman, D. S., 239
Freeman, M., 326
Freitag, M. K., 340
French, S. A., 69
Frenn, M., 83
Freud, S., 132, 133
Frey, K. S., 140
Friedman, M. S., 350
Frustaci, K., 78b
Fuligni, A., 185
Fulkerson, J. A., 69
Fung, C. M., 66b
Funk, J., 330
Furlong, A., 394
Furman, W., 351, 352, 352t, 353f, 355, 358, 359, 359f
Furrow, J. L., 315, 317, 319, 332
Furstenberg, F. F., Jr., 221, 225, 226, 227, 389
Fury, G., 340

Gable, S., 89
Galambos, N. L., 206, 326, 343, 348, 374
Galbraith, J., 202, 264
Galen, B. R., 187, 188
Gallimore, R., 333
Ganley, M., 226
Gano-Overway, L. A., 84
Ganzel, A. K., 326, 327
Garbarino, J., 90
Garber, J., 235, 332
García Coll, C., 42, 221, 328
Gardner, H., 99, 238, 290, 291b

Gardner, W., 275
Garofalo, R., 259
Garrity, C., 191
Garry, J. P., 252
Gaskins, S., 109
Gates, G. J., 258
Gathercole, S. E., 113
Gau, S. F., 250
Gauvain, M., 124
Gavadini, C., 249
Ge, X., 241, 242t
Geary, D. C., 213, 234
George, C., 339
George, R., 181
Gerard, J., 365
Gergen, K. J., 307
Gergen, M. M., 349b
Gershoff, E. T., 42
Gesell, A., 37, 38, 207
Getchell, N., 80, 247
Geuze, R. H., 248
Giannotti, F., 250
Gibbons, J. L., 347b
Gibbs, J., 171
Gibbs, S., 20
Giedd, J., 73, 74, 75, 78b, 245
Gilbreth, J., 365
Giles, H. C., 125
Gillberg, C., 60
Gilley, W., 84
Gilliam, F. D., Jr., 228, 367
Gilligan, C., 21, 172, 173, 173t, 305, 310
Gilmour, J., 66b
Gilpin, E. A., 255
Giordano, P. C., 357
Gjerde, P. F., 41
Glaser, D., 77b
Glaser, R., 255
Gleason, T., 305
Gogate, N., 73
Goldberg, A., 353, 355, 356, 357
Goldberg, J., 114
Goldberg, J. H., 277
Goldsmith, H. H., 154
Gollwitzer, P. N., 329
Golombek, S., 366
Gomez, M. L., 119
Gong, G. T., 264
Gonzalez, V., 119
Gooden, S., 383b
Goodnow, J. J., 194
Goodwin, M., 348
Goossens, L., 305, 331
Gootman, J. A., 51
Goran, M. I., 83
Gordan, W., 106
Gordeeva, T., 158
Gordon, D. E., 275
Gordon, D. H., 282
Gordon-Larsen, P., 239
Gorman, A. H., 188
Gottesman, I., 288
Gottfredson, L. S., 288
Gottfried, A. E., 146, 147
Gottfried, A. W., 146, 147
Gottschalk, H., 305
Gould, E., 78
Gower, B. A., 83
Graber, J. A., 5, 39, 206, 241, 257, 326, 391, 392, 392f, 393
Graef, R., 326
Graham, S., 157
Granholm, E., 254
Granic, I., 367, 368
Granot, D., 340
Grant, C. A., 119
Grantham-McGregor, S., 85
Grasshof, M., 158
Graue, M. E., 20
Graves, G. D., 239
Gray, M. R., 157, 361, 364
Gray, W. M., 275
Green, R. C., 341
Greenberger, E., 205, 226
Greene, A. D., 263
Greene, M. L., 327, 328
Greener, S., 185
Greenfield, P. M., 296
Greenlund, K. J., 239
Greeno, J. G., 278
Greenough, W. T., 73, 76, 77b
Greenwood, D. J., 24
Greer, B., 18
Gregory, A., 293
Greschner, J., 253
Gresham, F. M., 183
Greulich, F., 140
Griffin, P., 120
Griffin, R. S., 84
Griffith, E., 105
Grigorenko, E. L., 290, 291b
Grissmer, D. W., 289
Grisso, T., 283b, 284b
Groark, C. J., 36
Grodin, D., 384b
Grolnick, W., 148, 293
Gross, E. F., 296
Grossman, K., 340
Grotevant, H. D., 304, 305, 332
Grotpeter, J. K., 188
Grove, K., 140
Grueneich, R., 171
Grumbach, M. M., 238, 239
Grusec, J. E., 156, 194
Guba, E. G., 23
Guberman, S. R., 110
Guillaume, M., 70, 83
Gulotta, T. P., 38, 355f
Gunnoe, M. L., 331
Gurney, A. G., 319
Gurvey, J. E., 260
Guttentag, R. E., 113, 115
Guy, J. A., 70

Haan, N., 276
Haavio-Mannila, E., 257
Hagekull, B., 340
Hagen, J., 85
Hagino, H., 245
Hah, D. L., 188
Hains, A., 276
Halberstadt, A. G., 151
Haley, A., 288
Hall, G. S., 37, 202, 207, 209, 315
Halperin, S., 380, 380f
Halpern, C. T., 257
Halpern, D. F., 294, 294t
Halpern-Felsher, B., 219, 275, 277, 282
Halverson, L. E., 248
Ham, M., 326
Hamilton, C. E., 340
Hamm, J. V., 332
Hammersley, M., 22
Hammond, W. R., 90
Hamre, B. K., 126
Hancox, R. J., 83
Hanmer, T. J., 173, 173t
Hansbrough, E., 346
Hansell, S., 327
Hanson, S. K., 332
Hardy, C. L., 181
Harlow, H. F., 339
Harlow, M. K., 339
Harold, R. D., 52
Harpalani, V., 307, 312
Harris, J. R., 51, 193
Hart, D., 140, 143
Hart, F., 302f
Harter, S., 136, 137, 138, 139t, 140, 141, 142f, 144f, 149, 152, 153, 157, 302, 303, 303f, 328
Hart-Johnson, T., 329
Hartmann, D. P., 192, 194
Hartup, W. W., 178, 182, 184
Harvey, E. A., 116b
Hashey, J. M., 108b
Haste, B., 259
Haste, H., 324
Hastings, N. B., 78
Hattie, J., 141, 143f
Hauser, S. T., 326, 332
Hausmann, A., 185
Haveman, R., 263
Haviland, J. M., 326
Haviland-Jones, J. M., 155f, 326
Hawes, M. R., 83
Hawkins, D. L., 188, 191
Hayes, N., 18
Haynes, N. M., 125
Haywood, K. M., 80, 247
Hazan, C., 338, 338t, 364, 387

Hazebroek-Kampschreur, A. A. J. M., 242t
Heary, C. M., 20b
Hedges, L. V., 293
Heelan, K. A., 83
Hefner, R., 344
Hegarty, P., 343
Heinberg, L. J., 85, 88
Heitman, R., 84
Helmreich, R. L., 343
Helms, J. E., 312, 313, 313t
Helms-Erikson, H., 52
Henderson, V. L., 146, 146t
Hendrickson, A., 294
Hendriksen, J. G. M., 116b
Hennessy, E., 20b
Hennigan, K. M., 329
Henry, B., 15
Henshaw, S., 262
Herman, J., 275
Herman, M., 328
Herman, S., 126
Herman-Giddens, M. E., 66, 236, 239
Herschberger, S. L., 328, 362
Hessen, L., 249
Hetherington, E. M., 331, 361, 362, 364
Hewitt, J. P., 158
Hickling, A. K., 281
Higgins, E. T., 145
Hildebrand, D. K., 286
Hill, J. P., 343
Hill, K., 88
Hillier, L., 259
Hindmarsh, P., 66
Hine, T., 202, 203, 204, 207
Hines, A. N., 365
Hinten, M., 66b
Hirsch, B. J., 53
Hitch, G. J., 113
Hmelo, C. E., 278
Hmelo-Silver, C. E., 278
Ho, E., 124
Ho, L. M., 242t
Hodges, E. V. E., 340
Hoff, E., 119
Hofferth, S. L., 51, 84, 89
Hoffman, J. P., 328
Hofstra, G., 319
Hoge, D. R., 332
Hollenstein, T., 367, 368
Hollingshead, A. E., 204b
Holmbeck, G. N., 264
Holton, D., 278
Hombo, C. M., 295
Honess, T., 331t
Hoover-Dempsey, K. V., 125
Hoplight, B., 254
Hopson, J., 245, 246b
Horn, M., 36
Horner, S. D., 20
Horowitz, L. M., 338, 339, 387
Horwood, J. L., 235
Hotz, V. J., 263
Howard, G. J., 263
Howard, K. I., 205, 207
Howe, G., 364
Howe, N., 43
Howes, C., 120
Hrynevich, C., 314
Hsiao, C. K., 113
Hsieh, Y. S., 245
Hsiu-Zu, H., 126
Huberman, A. M., 19
Huddleston, J., 241
Hudson, L. M., 275
Hudspeth, W. J., 385
Huebner, A. J., 221
Huffman, H. A., 175
Hughes, D., 313
Huh, K., 309, 309b
Humbert, L. M., 84
Hunt, G., 349
Hurks, P. P. M., 116b
Hurley, J. C., 189b
Huttenlocher, P. R., 78, 244
Hyde, J. S., 155, 328, 343, 346, 349, 350

Iacono, W. G., 277
Iborra, A., 206
Iedema, J., 305
Ilg, F. L., 37, 38
Ingoldsby, E. M., 157
Inhelder, B., 99, 104, 272, 281
Ireh, M., 320, 321t
Isaacs, D., 175
Isen, A. M., 149
Ittel, A., 242t
Izard, C. E., 126

Jackson, A. W., 52
Jackson, B. K., 328
Jackson, J. F., 333, 377
Jackson, K., 124
Jackson-Newsom, J., 320
Jacobs, F., 313t
Jacobs, J. E., 84, 136, 140, 143, 226, 375
Jaffee, S. R., 346, 349
Jager, J., 262
Jahnke, H. C., 277
James, W., 136
Jankowski, S. M., 325
Janson, K., 73
Janz, K., 69
Jemmott, J. B., 264
Jemmott, L. S., 264
Jenkins, D., 69, 85b, 238, 264
Jenkins, R. R., 260
Jensen, A. R., 288, 289
Jensen, L. A., 393
Jepsen, D. A., 321
Jessor, R., 22, 217, 218b, 219
Jimenez, E., 85
Joe-Laidler, K., 349
Johnson, C. M., 12, 17
Johnson, J. L., 21
Johnson, J. M., 23
Johnson, J. P., 235
Johnson, L. D., 254
Johnson, M., 38
Johnson, M. H., 79
Johnson, R., 83, 261
Johnson, S., 12, 17, 226
Johnson-Sumerford, D., 346
Johnston, F. E., 70f
Johnston, L. D., 254, 255
Johnston, P. H., 120
Jones, D. C., 347
Jones, F., 262
Jones, M. C., 241
Jones, P., 125
Jones, S. M., 195
Jordan, C., 333
Joshi, A., 183
Josselson, R., 305, 310, 385
Joyner, K., 357
Jozefowicz, D., 294

Kagan, J., 4, 9
Kahlbaugh, P., 326
Kahle, J. B., 294
Kail, R., 113, 278
Kajala, U. M., 83
Kalaw, C., 21
Kalff, A. C., 116b
Kaljee, L., 264
Kalverboer, A. F., 248
Kamkar, K., 364
Kamprath, N. A., 179, 180, 188
Kanemura, H., 245
Kang, M. J., 250
Kanouse, D. E., 260
Kaplan, K., 338, 340
Kaplan, S. J., 78b
Kaprio, J., 83, 242t
Karcher, M. J., 195
Karofsky, P. S., 265
Katz, C., 209
Katz, E., 259
Kauh, T. J., 180, 193, 195, 196
Keith, B., 365
Keller, L. B., 294
Kelley, H. H., 338
Kelly, J. B., 365, 365b
Kelson, A. C., 278
Kendall, S. J., 317
Keniston, K., 379
Kenneavey, K., 348
Kennedy, C., 20b
Kennedy, S. G., 90
Keogh, D., 263

Kerbow, D., 124
Kerestes, M., 316, 317
Kerns, K. A., 194f, 339, 340, 363, 364
Kerns, S. E. U., 191
Kerr, M., 193, 341, 342f
Keshavan, M. S., 77b, 78b
Kester, K., 315
Kettel Khan, L., 239
Khatiwada, I., 393
Killen, J., 250
Kim, S., 154
King, P. E., 315, 316, 317, 319, 332
Kinney, D., 355, 355f
Kirby, D., 258, 260, 263
Kirby, S. N., 289
Kirk, L. D., 307
Kirkham, C., 188
Kirkpatrick, J., 378
Kishi, I., 264
Kitchener, K. S., 385
Klaczynski, P. A., 282
Klebanov, P. K., 90
Klein, D. M., 215, 341
Klepac, L., 340
Klesges, R. C., 255
Klevens, J., 383
Kling, K. C., 328
Klintsova, A. Y., 73, 76
Klock, K., 314
Knapp, J. R., 207, 254
Knight, D. K., 108
Knoll, J., 304
Knox, M., 330
Koch, G., 239
Kochenderfer, B. J., 180, 184
Kohlberg, L., 170, 171, 171t, 276
Kokis, J. V., 282
Kolb, B., 73, 78
Kolodner, J. L., 278
Konarski, R., 353, 355
Konczak, J., 80
Koniak-Griffin, D., 261
Kontula, O., 257
Kools, S., 20b
Korman, K., 294
Kornhaber, M., 99
Kosorock, M. R., 265
Kowalski, P., 143, 149
Krafcik, K., 156
Kratzer, L., 287
Kraut, R. E., 296
Krettenauer, T., 310
Kreutzer, M. A., 115
Kroger, J., 305, 310
Krogman, W. M., 67
Krueger, R., 20b
Ku, L. C., 343
Kuczynski, L., 194
Kuhn, D., 276, 279
Kumpf, M., 288
Kurland, M., 114
Kurtz, D. A., 307
Kuttler, A. F., 188

Labruna, V., 78b
Ladd, G. W., 167, 180, 181, 182, 184
Lagana, L., 259
La Greca, A. M., 182, 188, 189
Lakes, M. K., 294
Lam, T. H., 242t, 250
Lamb, M., 52
Lambert, A., 70, 83
Lamborn, S. D., 305, 332
Lampman-Petraitis, C., 327
Landau, M., 244
Landrine, H., 108
Langabeer, K. A., 259
Langendorfer, S. J., 80, 248
Langer, J., 276
Lapidus, L., 70, 83
Lappe, J., 69
Lapsley, D. K., 171, 173, 174, 277, 304, 305, 317
Lareau, A., 52
Larson, R., 16b, 16f, 53, 208, 209, 219, 228, 297t, 326, 327, 379, 381, 389
Lather, P., 22
Latinen-Krispijn, S., 242t
Laursen, B., 207, 351, 352, 362
Lavi-Yudelevitch, M., 353
Leaper, C., 346
Leary, R., 19
Lease, A. M., 181
Leboyer, M., 60
Ledbetter, M. F., 286
Lederer, J. M., 108b
Lee, J. H., 43
Lee, R. E., 266
Lee, S. Y., 126
Lee, Y., 347
Lefebvre, C., 81
Leffert, N., 223
Lemberger, C. C., 116b
Lemerise, E. A., 188, 189
L'Engle, K. L., 348
Lengua, L. J., 155, 156
Leonard, C., 115
Leong, C. W., 329
Lerner, R. M., 4, 5, 6, 10, 46f, 47, 48f, 207, 214, 214f, 219, 223, 228, 253, 313t, 342f, 387
Lesser, J., 261
Leventhal, T., 90, 225, 391, 392, 392f, 393
Leveroni, C., 294
Levin, M., 24, 281
Levine, M., 88, 249, 307
Levinson, D., 379, 386
Levinson, S. C., 106
Lewin, D. S., 250
Lewis, C. C., 126
Lewis, M., 327, 338, 340
Lewis, M. D., 47, 155f, 326
Lewis, T. L., 76
Lewisohn, P. M., 241
Li, J., 291b
Li, S., 84
Li, T., 73
Li, X., 264
Liaw, F., 90
Liberty, C., 113, 279
Lickona, T., 175
Liddell, C., 41
Liben, L. S., 344
Lieberman, I. Y., 121b
Lightfoot, C., 153, 217, 219, 330
Lilly, F., 353
Lim, L., 209
Lin, C. H., 113
Lincoln, Y. S., 19, 23
Lindenberger, U., 212, 213f
Lindlof, T. R., 384b
Lindsay, J. J., 15
Linn, M. C., 295f, 328
Linnet, J., 179, 180, 188
Lipka, J., 290
Lips, H. M., 330
Lipsett, L. P., 212
Lipsitz, J. S., 38
Liss, A. R., 70f
Liston, C., 74
Little, B. R., 330, 331t
Little, S. A., 332
Little, T. D., 158
Litvene, M., 66b
Livesly, W. L., 138
Livingstone, M. B. E., 84
Lo, A., 252
Lockerd, E. M., 144
Loevinger, J., 304
Logan, T. K., 25
Lohman, B. J., 23
Long, A. C., 156
Long, C., 70
Longmore, M. A., 357
Loovis, E. M., 81
Lopez, E. M., 333, 377
Lorch, E. P., 116b, 117f
Lorenz, K., 339
Lori, N., 245
Lovato, C. Y., 21
Lovejoy, D. W., 116b
Low, H., 241
Lozoff, B., 85
Lubart, T. I., 292
Luke, C., 43
Lunner, K., 250
Luthar, S. S., 217
Lutz, S., 89
Lynch, C. L., 385
Lynch, M. E., 343
Lyon, R., 120

Lyons, N. P., 173, 173t
Lypaczewski, G., 69

Ma, X., 188
Maassen, G., 305
Maccoby, E. E., 61, 182, 361
MacDonald, R., 252
MacKinnon, C., 52
MacMurray, J. P., 235
MacPherson, L., 254
Macpherson, R., 282
Madden, C. M., 102b
Magee, V., 18
Magnusson, D., 10, 44, 45, 47, 241, 343, 387
Maguen, S., 350
Mahler, M. S., 339
Mahoney, J. L., 10
Maier-Bruckner, W., 115
Maietta, R. C., 22
Main, M., 338, 339, 340
Mainess, J. H., 21
Maira, S., 209
Makros, J., 303, 311
Malenchuk, O., 294
Malin, S., 83
Malina, R., 70f, 248
Mammone, N., 156
Mancini, J. A., 221
Mannes, M., 217, 219, 221, 227, 228
Manning, M. L., 38, 235
Manning, W., 357
Mansell, C., 20b
Marcia, J. E., 309
Marion, M., 137b
Markiewicz, D., 362, 364
Marks, J. S., 253
Marks, S., 346
Markstrom, C. A., 206, 319
Markstrom-Adams, C., 311, 319
Markus, H., 329
Marsh, H. W., 141, 143f, 328
Marsh, J., 252
Marshall, S. K., 308, 315, 353, 354b
Marshall, W. A., 240f
Martin, C. L., 346
Martin, S. S., 119, 343
Martin, T. F., 331
Martinek, T. J., 80
Martinez, M., 90
Marx, F., 126
Mascarenhas, M. R., 249
Maslow, A. H., 134, 148
Massey, D., 210b
Masten, A. S., 217, 219, 253
Mateson, J. L., 85
Matheson, J. L., 362
Matisson, A., 241
Matsumoto, K., 250
Matus-Grossman, L., 383b
Mauer, D., 90b
Maurer, D., 76, 77
Maxwell, K., 20
Maxwell, S. E., 263
Mayer, J. D., 151
Mayer, R. E., 126
Maynard, R. A., 263
Mayseless, O., 340
Mazor, A., 304
Mazzeo, J., 295
McAdoo, H. P., 41
McBride, C. K., 265
McCabe, A., 21
McCabe, M. P., 252, 303, 311
McCall, R. B., 36, 287
McCarthy, R. J., 52
McCartney, K., 62
McClasky, C. I., 184f
McCord, J., 185
McCoy, J., 363
McCurdy, D. W., 22
McDowell, D. J., 52, 221, 249
McElroy, S. W., 263
McFall, R. M., 181
McFayden-Ketchum, S., 235
McGhee, P. E., 102b
McGill, H. C., 84
McGraw, S. A., 260
McHale, S. M., 5, 34, 49b, 50b, 52, 180, 193, 195, 196, 364
McIntyre, J. G., 332
McKay, A., 258
McKay, G., 137b
McKay, H. A., 68, 69
McKeen, N. A., 82, 82f
McKenzie, T. L., 61
McKinlay, J. B., 260
McKinley, M. C., 84
McKown, C., 188, 313
McLaughlin, J., 393
McLelland, J. A., 317, 325
McLoyd, V. C., 90, 157
McMahan, C., 84
McMahon, R. J., 193
McMahon, R. P., 238
McNamara, C. A., 25
McNeely, C., 265
McQuaid, E. L., 20b
Mead, G. H., 138
Mead, M., 41
Mechanic, D., 327
Meece, J. L., 63
Meerum Terwogt, M., 155
Meeus, W., 304, 305, 309, 340
Meier, B., 250
Meier, E., 290
Meininger, E., 259, 356
Meister, C., 279
Melaville, A., 226, 227t
Menna-Barreto, L., 250
Menon, J., 325
Menzulis, A. H., 155
Mercey, J., 90
Meredith, H. V., 67f
Merenoff, J., 36
Merrick, E., 19
Metz, E., 317
Mezzrich, A. C., 245
Michell, L., 70
Midgley, C., 125, 332
Mikulincer, M., 353, 358
Miles, M. B., 19
Milich, R., 116b
Miller, A. L., 362
Miller, B. C., 258
Miller, C. T., 88
Miller, D. C., 282
Miller, D. E., 319
Miller, G. E., 279
Miller, J., 245
Miller, K. S., 265
Miller, P. H., 4, 110, 166, 167
Miller Buchanan, C., 125, 332
Millstein, S. G., 219, 260, 277
Milne, B. J., 83
Mintz, S., 210
Mirwald, R. L., 68, 83, 84
Mistry, J., 106
Mitic, W., 253
Modell, J., 41, 43, 378
Moely, B. E., 114
Moffitt, T. E., 15, 240
Mohammad, R., 226
Mohatt, G., 290
Mohn, J. K., 262
Moilanen, D., 276
Mokdad, A., 253
Moneta, G., 326, 327, 328
Montemayor, R., 38, 39, 41, 355f
Montessori, M., 111b
Moodey, A., 249
Moore, K. A., 262, 263
Moore, S., 275
Morgan, D. L., 20
Morgan, M., 20
Morris, A. S., 327
Morris, N. M., 257
Morris, P. A., 5, 46, 47
Morrison, D. R., 263
Morrison, F. J., 105
Morrissey, S. L., 252
Morrow, S. L., 23
Mortimer, J. T., 226, 265, 297t, 379, 381
Mory, M. S., 355, 355f
Mosher, W., 262
Mounts, N. S., 194f
Mruk, C., 143
Muhleman, D., 235
Muir, S. L., 88
Mukherjee, P., 245
Mulhern, G., 18
Muller, C., 124

Mumme, D. L., 152, 153, 154, 155
Munro, J., 367
Muraven, M., 319
Murphy, K. R., 17
Murphy, M. M., 175, 175f, 176f
Murray, L., 35
Murry, V. M., 154
Mussen, P., 185, 196
Muuss, R. E., 164, 275, 304
Mwamwenda, B. B., 275
Mwamwenda, T. S., 275
Myers, K., 346
Myers, M. C., 23
Myers, M. G., 254

Nagashima, H., 250
Nagin, D., 84
Nagle, R. J., 339
Nagy, T. R., 83
Naimi, T. S., 253
Nakagawa, N., 102b
Nakazawa, S., 245
Nakkula, M. J., 169, 170b
Narvaez, D., 171
Närvänen, A., 42
Näsman, E., 42
Naus, M. J., 113, 279
Neal-Barnett, A. M., 194f
Needham, B., 194, 195, 195f
Nehra, D., 245
Neiderhiser, J. M., 61, 360, 361
Neinstein, L., 259, 356
Neiss, M., 241, 242t
Neisser, U., 288
Nelson, C. A., 77, 245, 247f
Nelson, L. J., 377
Nesselroade, J. R., 9
Neuman, S. B., 120b, 121b
Neumark-Sztainer, D., 249, 250, 385
Newcomb, A. E., 179, 180, 181
Newfield, N. A., 206, 207
Newman, B. M., 23, 307
Newman, D. L., 314
Newman, P. R., 23, 307
Newman, R. S., 145b, 158
Newsome, W. S., 53
Niamura, R. S., 255
Nickerson, A. B., 339
Nikitopoulos, C. E., 169, 170b
Ninio, A., 119
Niogi, S., 74
Nippold, M. A., 102b, 119
Niu, W., 292
Nohara, S., 245
Noll, R. B., 66b, 178, 181b
Noller, P., 362
Noom, M. J., 304
Norcross, J. C., 134, 136
North, A. C., 307
Noseworthy, M. D., 73
Notaro, P. C., 362
Novick, N., 140
Nowell, A., 293
Nucci, L. P., 174, 174t, 175, 177b, 178
Nugent, L. D., 277
Nurius, P., 329
Nussbaum, M. C., 158
Nuttall, R. L., 294
Nyamanthi, A., 261
Nyborg, H., 288
Nye, B., 15, 124

Obarzanek, E., 252
O'Brien, M., 341, 344
Oden, S., 223
Oettingen, G., 158
Offer, D., 205, 207
Okin, S. M., 173
Oleshansky, B., 344
Oliver, M. B., 350
Olsen, D. H., 207
Olsen, J. A., 206
Olthof, T., 155
Olweus, D., 241
O'Malley, P. M., 254, 255, 327
O'Moore, M., 188
Omoto, A. M., 352
O'Neil, K., 116b
O'Neil, M. L., 40
O'Neil, R., 52, 221
Onishi, M., 41
Openheim, D., 340
Orenstein, P., 158
Ornstein, P. A., 113, 279
Osgood, D. W., 375
Osipow, S. H., 321
Ostrow, E., 205, 207
O'Sullivan, J. T., 115
Oswald, R. F., 346
Outerbridge, A., 70
Owens, R. E., Jr., 119, 346, 367
Oyserman, D., 329, 330
Ozturk, C., 81

Padgett, D. K., 25
Pagano, M. E., 53
Paikoff, R. L., 264, 326
Pajares, F., 144, 148, 157
Palinscar, A. S., 108b
Palma, S., 393
Pangrazi, R., 84
Pantin, H., 221, 222f, 223
Papillo, A. R., 262
Paquette, J. A., 187, 188
Pargament, K. I., 316
Park, L., 351
Park, Y. M., 250
Parke, R. D., 52, 182, 193, 195, 221
Parker, I., 23
Parker, J. G., 178, 179, 188
Parker, S. M., 245
Parra, G. R., 144
Parrish, M., 89
Paseluikho, M. A., 321
Passarotti, A. M., 244
Pastorelli, C., 185, 188
Patel, D. R., 252
Pattee, L., 179, 180
Patterson, C., 78b, 258
Patton, M. Q., 23
Paus, T., 75, 245
Paxton, S. J., 88
Pearl, R., 188
Pederson, S., 53
Peevers, B. H., 138
Pelcovitz, D., 78b
Pellegrini, A. D., 82, 83, 183, 185
Penner, K., 321
Penza-Clyve, S. M., 20b
Pepler, D. J., 188, 191, 353, 355, 356, 357
Perkins, D. F., 84, 217, 253
Perlman, D., 331
Perozek, M., 263
Perry, D. C., 340
Perry, D. G., 328, 341, 343, 346, 350
Perry, P., 314
Perry, W. G., 385
Persky, H. R., 279
Perugini, E. M., 116b
Petersen, A., 39, 206, 240
Petersen, A. C., 226, 241, 243f, 295, 343, 389
Peterson, E., 263
Peterson, K. L., 275
Petit, G. S., 184f
Petrie, S., 182
Petrill, S. A., 60
Pettit, G. S., 235
Pezaris, E., 294
Pfafflin, F., 346
Phelan, P., 333
Philip, J., 245
Philliber, W. W., 264
Phillips, D. A., 140
Phinney, J. S., 307, 312, 313, 314, 315t, 331
Piaget, J., 98–99, 99, 104, 170–171, 272, 281
Pianta, R. C., 126
Pick, H. L., 6
Pierce, J. P., 255
Pierce, K., 53
Pike, A., 61
Pike, R., 141
Pine, F., 339
Pipher, M. B., 173
Pittman, K., 55f, 224, 228
Pitts, S. C., 253
Pleck, J. H., 343
Plomin, R., 60, 61, 294, 361
Plumert, J. M., 6

Pollitt, E., 85
Pomerantz, E. M., 140, 144, 145, 146
Pomeroy, C., 88
Ponomarev, I., 277
Ponterotto, J. G., 19
Pope, H. G., Jr., 252
Popkin, B. M., 249
Porche, M. V., 341
Porfeli, E. J., 319, 320
Posner, J. K., 52
Poulin, F., 185
Poulton, R., 83
Powell, D., 194, 360
Powlishta, K. K., 277, 305
Pratt, H. D., 252
Pratt, S., 180
Presnell, K., 241
Pressley, M., 115, 279
Presson, C. C., 253
Pribram, K. H., 385
Price-Williams, D. R., 106
Prieto, L., 319
Prinstein, M. J., 182
Prinz, R. J., 191
Prochaska, J. O., 134, 136
Prosser, E. C., 314
Protinsky, H. O., 206, 207
Provins, K. A., 81
Pryor, J., 368
Puckett, M. B., 121, 134f, 306
Pugh, S., 84
Pulkkinen, L., 242t
Pyapali, G. K., 254

Quadrel, M. J., 277
Quinn, W., 206, 207

Raaumakers, Q. A. W., 328
Raffaelli, M., 193
Rafiroiu, A. C., 250
Ramey, C., 183
Ramey, S., 183
Ramierez, M., 106
Ramos, K. D., 393
Randall, B. A., 185
Raney, M., 305
Rankin, D. B., 192, 194
Rankin, N. O., 18
Rapoport, J. L., 73
Rathunde, K., 148, 332
Reaburn, P., 69, 85b, 238
Reach, K., 144
Ream, G. J., 315, 319
Rebecca, M., 344
Ree, M. J., 288
Reed, R. P., 125
Rees, D. I., 265, 266
Reese, C. M., 279
Reese, H. W., 212
Regerus, M., 317, 318b, 319
Reid, G., 82
Reid, P. T., 315
Reiss, D., 331, 360, 361, 364
Reiter, E. O., 236
Remafedi, G., 258, 259, 356
Renouf, A. G., 140, 141
Renshaw, P., 209
Repinski, D. J., 338
Resnick, L. B., 278, 385
Resnick, M. D., 219, 250
Rest, J., 171
Reynolds, C. R., 289
Reynolds, M., 282
Rhodes, J. E., 18
Ricardo, I., 264
Ricciardelli, L. A., 252
Rice, K., 305
Rich, A., 346
Richards, M. H., 16b, 326
Richman, J. M., 216, 216f
Riessman, C. K., 22
Rikken, B., 66b
Ringel, B. A., 115
Risman, B. J., 346
Rivers, I., 367
Roazzi, A., 106
Roberton, M. A., 80, 248
Robins, R. W., 327, 328
Robinson, L. A., 255
Robinson, M., 343, 344b
Robinson, M. G., 332
Robinson, N. S., 138, 141
Robson, P. J., 84
Roca, J., 383
Rodin, J., 252
Rodkin, P. C., 188
Rodriguez, D., 227, 349
Roemmich, J. N., 237
Roesner, R. W., 194
Roffman, J. G., 53
Rogers, C., 135, 136b, 148
Rogoff, B., 105, 107, 109, 110, 118
Rogol, A. D., 237, 239
Roscoe, B., 275, 348
Rose, R. J., 242t
Rose, S. P., 244, 245
Rosen, K. H., 362
Rosenblum, G. D., 326, 327
Rosenblum, T. B., 288
Rosen-Reynoso, M., 341
Rosenshine, B., 279
Rosenthal, D., 275, 312, 313, 314
Rosenthal, S. L., 239, 338, 340
Roth, J., 35, 36, 223, 224, 224t, 226
Roth, N., 332
Roth, S., 21
Rothbart, M. K., 154, 156
Rothblum, E. D., 368t
Rotheram-Borus, M. J., 259
Rowe, D. C., 241, 242
Roy, R., 353
Royse, D., 25
Rubin, K. H., 158, 178, 179, 188
Ruble, D. N., 138, 140, 144, 145, 146, 149b, 343, 346
Rueman, D., 125, 332
Ruetsch, C., 326
Ruffalo, S. L., 183
Ruiselova, Z., 242t
Rumbaut, R., 389
Runion, B. P., 80
Russell, S. T., 219, 367, 383
Ruth, G., 375
Rutland, A., 188
Rutter, P., 349
Ryan, E., 276
Ryan, N. D., 78b
Ryan, R. M., 148
Rydell, A., 340

Saarni, C., 151, 152, 153, 153b, 154, 155
Sabatelli, R., 304
Sadker, D., 294, 295
Sadker, M., 294, 295
Salasuo, M., 252
Sallis, J. F., 84
Salovey, P., 151, 152t
Saltz, E., 329
Sameroff, A. J., 5, 194
Sampson, R. J., 36
Sanchez, R. P., 116b
Sandberg, D. E., 66b
Sandberg, J. F., 51, 84, 89
Sanders, S. G., 263
Sandler, H. M., 34, 141
Sandstrom, K., 116b
Sandy, J. M., 317
Sarampote, N. C., 50
Saraswathi, T. S., 106
Sargent, R. G., 250
Saris, W. H. M., 83
Saudino, K., 9
Saults, J. S., 277
Savin-Williams, R. C., 258, 259, 315, 319, 327, 346, 349, 350, 350t, 351f, 352, 353, 356, 357, 362, 363b
Saxon, J. L., 144, 145, 146
Scales, P. C., 217, 219, 221, 223, 227, 228
Scarr, S., 60, 62
Schachter, E. P., 307
Schaffer, J., 178, 181b
Schaie, K. W., 385
Schalet, A., 349
Schalling, D., 241
Scharf, M., 359
Schaub-George, D., 248
Scheer, S. D., 253
Schellenbach, C. J., 263
Schere, M., 329

Scheuerer-Englisch, H., 340
Schiefele, U., 144, 147, 147f, 148, 149
Schmitt, N., 183
Schneider, B., 327
Schneider, W., 112, 113, 114t, 115, 279
Schoonmaker, C. T., 264
Schreiber, G. B., 252
Schulenberg, J., 254, 255
Schuler, R., 241
Schultz, R., 385
Schunk, D. H., 144, 148, 157
Schuster, M. A., 260
Schwartz, B., 283b
Schwartz, D., 188
Schwartz, S. J., 311, 349
Schwebel, D. C., 6
Scott, E. S., 282, 283b, 284b
Seal, J., 178
Secord, P. P., 138
Seefeldt, V. D., 84, 85
Seeley, J. R., 241
Seif, H., 367
Seifert, A. E., 329
Seldin, T., 111b
Selinger, M., 353, 358
Sellers, D. E., 260
Selman, R. L., 167, 168, 168t, 169, 169t, 170b, 179, 179t, 277
Senn, C. Y., 351
Seo, Y. J., 250
Seppa, K., 254
Seppala, P., 252
Serafica, F. C., 321
Serafini, T. E., 308, 308t
Serbin, L. A., 188
Serdula, M. K., 239, 253
Serpell, R., 106
Sesma, A., Jr., 305
Seupersad, R., 383
Shaffer, L., 352, 358, 359
Shah, B., 226
Shanahan, M. J., 320
Shandy, D. J., 22
Shantz, C. U., 166
Sharp, S., 185, 188, 189, 190b, 191, 192b
Shaver, K., 226
Shaver, P., 140
Shaver, P. R., 338, 364, 387
Shaw, D. S., 157
Sheehan, G., 362
Sheldon, S. B., 125
Shemilt, I., 85
Shepard, R. J., 71f
Sherman, S. J., 253
Shi, H. J., 242t
Shiffman, S., 255
Shiffrin, R. M., 110, 112f
Shimony, J., 245
Shipman, K., 191
Shirk, S. R., 140, 141
Shisslak, C. M., 250, 252
Showers, C., 328
Shulman, S., 359
Shuman, M., 249
Shweder, R. A., 172
Siebenbruner, J., 356
Siega-Riz, A. M., 249
Siegel, J. M., 241
Siegler, R. S., 114, 124, 281
Siemens, L., 113
Silbereisen, R. K., 50, 225
Silk, J. S., 327
Sillanaukee, P., 254
Silva, P. A., 15
Simmons, R. G., 39, 143, 188, 265, 327
Simon, V. A., 358, 359, 359f
Simpkins, S. D., 193
Sims, V., 126
Sindelar, H. A., 252
Sing, R., 126
Sippola, L. K., 181, 188
Skelton, T., 210b
Skorikov, V., 321, 323
Skuse, D., 66b
Slattery, P., 43
Slora, E. J., 236
Slowiaczek, M., 293
Small, S. A., 23, 226
Smit, E. K., 332
Smith, C. A., 263, 317, 318b, 319
Smith, E. A., 307
Smith, P. K., 82, 188, 189, 191, 192b
Smith, R. S., 7, 8b
Smith, V. L., 23
Smolak, L., 88, 249
Snow, C. E., 119, 120
Snyder, J., 194, 364
Snyder, M., 352
Soep, E., 209
Soloff, P. H., 254
Solomon, J., 339
Sommer, K., 263
Sonenstein, F. L., 258, 343
Soong, W. T., 250
Sowder, J., 294
Spearman, C., 284–285
Spence, J. T., 343
Spencer, M. B., 41, 307, 312, 383
Spencer, M. S., 314
Spencer, R., 341
Spencer, T. R., 307, 312
Spirito, A., 252
Spradley, J. P., 22
Spring, B., 362
Springer, C. J., 115
Spuhl, S. T., 108
Srinivasan, S. R., 239
Sroufe, L. A., 338, 340, 357
Stacey, J., 366
Stack, C., 173
Stallings, V. A., 249
Stanovich, K. E., 282
Stanton, B. S., 264
Stattin, H., 10, 47, 193, 241, 341, 342f, 343
Staudinger, U. M., 212, 213f
Stayton, D. J., 339
Stein, T. S., 349
Steinberg, L., 34, 39, 157, 194, 205, 226, 235, 282, 283b, 284b, 293, 305, 327, 332, 361, 364
Stemmler, M., 226
Stern, S., 306
Sternberg, R. J., 290, 291, 291b, 292
Stetsenko, A., 158
Stevenson, H. W., 118, 126
Stewart, S. M., 242t
Stewin, L. L., 188
Stice, E., 241
Stigler, J. W., 126
Stiles, D. A., 347b
Stocker, C., 138, 141
Stone, E. J., 61
Stoneman, Z., 363
Story, M., 69, 249, 250, 385
Strasburger, V. C., 133
Strauch, L., 250
Strauss, W., 43
Striegel-Moore, R., 238, 252
Strohmeyer, H. S., 248
Strouse, J. S., 348
Strucl, M. M., 244
Stubby, J., 69
Stuhlman, M. W., 126
Styne, D. M., 238
Subrahmanyam, K., 296
Suchindran, C., 257
Sullivan, C., 310
Sullivan, H. S., 178
Sum, A., 393
Susman, S., 239
Suter, E., 83
Sutton, J., 188, 189
Suzuki, M., 245
Swanson, D. P., 228, 307, 312
Swanson, H. L., 277
Swarr, A., 16b
Swartzenwelder, S. H., 254
Swearer, S. M., 191
Swerdik, M. E., 286f
Swettenham, J., 188, 189
Switzer, R. C., 254
Szalacha, L. A., 42, 328, 349
Szapocznik, J., 221, 222f, 223
Szkrybalo, J., 343

Tajfel, H., 307
Tajika, H., 126
Talbert, L., 257
Tamis-LaMonda, C. S., 189b

Tanapat, P., 78
Tanner, J. M., 65, 68, 238, 240f
Tapert, S. F., 254
Tarrant, M., 307
Tarter, R. E., 245
Tasker, F. L., 366
Taylor, A. Z., 157
Taylor, B., 241, 243
Taylor, C. L., 102b
Taylor, C. S., 223, 228
Taylor, M., 23, 124
Teicher, M. H., 76, 77b
Tekavcic-Pompe, M., 244
Terry, K., 329, 330
Terry-McElrath, Y. M., 254
Tershakovec, A. M., 249
Tharinger, D., 328, 367
Thelen, M. H., 88, 252
Thoma, S. J., 171
Thomas, K. M., 75
Thomas, S., 343, 344b
Thomases, J., 55f
Thompson, A. M., 83, 84, 88
Thompson, D., 185, 188, 189, 190b
Thompson, J. K., 85, 88
Thompson, N. E., 319
Thompson, P. M., 244
Thompson, R. A., 77, 151, 153, 158, 338, 340
Thompson, S. H., 250
Thornberry, T. P., 263
Thorndike, E. L., 285
Thorne, A., 305, 307, 343
Thorne, B., 183
Thurstone, L. L., 285
Thyer, B. A., 25
Tian, C. S., 66b, 119
Tiffany, S. T., 255
Tilton-Weaver, L. C., 206
Timberlake, T. L., 323, 323b
Tindall, C., 23
Tingle, L. R., 262
Toblin, R. L., 188
Todd, R. D., 77b
Todt, E., 50, 225
Tolman, D. L., 341, 349
Tolman, J., 55f
Tomich, P. L., 339
Tonegawa, S., 75
Toplak, M. E., 282
Torney-Purta, J., 324
Toth, S. L., 78b
Towse, J., 113
Toyokawa, T., 157
Trammel, M., 55f
Trawick-Smith, J., 36
Tremblay, R. E., 17, 84
Trevethan, S. D., 173
Trew, K., 330
Troiano, R. P., 85
Trueman, J. A., 239
Truong, N. L., 367
Tschann, J. M., 242t, 260
Tucker, C. J., 34, 49b, 50b, 53, 364
Tucker, M. S., 204, 205
Turbin, M. S., 217, 218b, 219
Turiel, E., 173, 317
Turkheimer, E., 60, 288
Turkle, S., 384b
Turner, D. A., 254
Turner, J. C., 307
Turner, J. S., 343, 347, 356
Turner, R. E., 307
Twenge, J. M., 156

Udry, J. R., 257, 357
Ulug, A. M., 74
Uman, G., 261
Umaña-Taylor, A., 307, 310, 314
Underwood, M. K., 187, 188, 188b
Ungar, M., 382, 383
Updegraff, K., 52, 360, 364
Uppal, S., 314
Useem, E. L., 125

Vadum, A. C., 18
Valach, L., 321
Valentine, G., 210b
Valsiner, J., 114t, 211
Van Acker, R., 188
van Aken, M. A., 305
van Baal, G. C. M., 75
Van de Ende, J., 242t
Vandell, D. L., 52, 53
van den Broek, P., 116b
Vander Wal, J. S., 88, 252
Vandiver, B. J., 312
Van Duinen, E., 207
van Hoof, A., 328
Vannatta, K., 178, 181b
van Strien, S. D., 304
Van Voorhis, F. L., 124, 125
Vartanian, L. R., 277, 305, 332
Ventura, S., 262f
Verberg, N., 351
Verhulst, F. C., 242t
Verma, S., 16b, 16f, 389
Vernberg, E., 191
Vida, M., 294
Videon, T. M., 89, 365
Vigfusdottir, F. H., 347
Viken, R. J., 181
Vinha, D., 250
Vion, M., 119
Visser, J., 248
Vitaro, F., 355
Vles, J. S. H., 116b
Volling, B. L., 52
von Busschbach, J. J., 66b
Vondracek, F. W., 319, 320, 321, 323
von Eye, A., 223, 228
Voss, L., 66b
Voyer, D., 294
Voyer, S., 294
Vygotsky, L., 107, 108, 109, 110

Wadell, K. J., 118
Wadsworth, B. J., 104
Wadsworth, K. N., 254
Wahlstrom, K. L., 252
Wainryb, C., 317
Wake, W., 99
Wakefield, M., 254
Walcott, D. D., 252
Waldron, M., 288
Walker, E., 346
Walker, J. M. T., 125
Walker, L. J., 173
Wall, S., 339
Wallace, J. M. W., 84
Wallace-Broscious, A., 321
Walsh, A. S., 319
Walsh, D. J., 20
Wang, L., 239
Wang, M. C., 295
Ward, L. M., 346
Warr, D., 259
Warren, M. P., 5, 39, 241
Wartella, E., 43
Washburn, G., 90
Wasserman, R. C., 236
Waterman, A. S., 309, 385
Waters, E., 339, 340
Waters, P., 303
Watson, M. W., 133
Watson, W., 386
Wattigney, W. A., 239
Watts, R., 74
Wavelet, M., 383b
Way, N., 327, 328, 332, 353, 362
Webb, A. H., 116b
Weed, K., 263
Wehner, E. A., 355, 358
Weigel, D. J., 119
Weinberg, R. A., 228
Weinfeld, N. S., 338, 340
Weinstein, R. S., 188, 275, 293
Weinstock, M., 279
Weisner, T. S., 41, 43, 195, 333, 346
Welk, G. J., 61
Wellman, H. M., 281
Wells, G., 328, 367
Welsh, R., 116b
Wentzel, K. R., 181
Werner, E. E., 7, 8b, 9
Wertheim, E. H., 88
Wertleib, D., 313t
Weschsler, D., 285
West, R. F., 282
Westcott, W., 70
Westenberg, P. M., 304
Whetstone, L. M., 252

Whigham, M., 294, 295
Whishaw, I. Q., 78
White, J. M., 215, 331, 341
White, K., 315, 317, 319
White, N. R., 291b, 390, 391
White, R., 34, 39, 40, 41, 42, 144, 394
Whitesell, N. R., 143, 149, 152, 153, 303, 303f, 328
Whiting, B. B., 41
Whitman, T. L., 263
Wieling, E., 386
Wiesner, M., 242t
Wigfield, A., 125, 144, 147, 147f, 148, 149, 157, 227, 282, 294, 332
Wiles, J., 38
Williams, J. M., 242t
Williams, K., 248
Williams, O. A., 319
Williams, S., 262
Williams, W. M., 291b, 292
Williamson, S., 289
Willis, R. J., 263
Willis, S. L., 385
Willms, J. D., 124
Wills, T. A., 317
Wilson, B. J., 133
Wilson, D. M., 241
Wilson, J. F., 236
Wilson, M. N., 221
Wilson, S., 326, 389
Wilson, W. A., 254
Wilson-Mitchell, J. E., 346
Windle, M., 154, 154f
Winsler, A., 50
Winter, T., 83
Wolf, A. W., 85
Wolfe, B., 263
Wolff, R., 84
Wolfson, A. R., 250
Wollard, J., 284b
Wood, E., 351
Wood, K. C., 88
Wood, P. K., 385
Wood, Y., 347b
Woodruff, D. W., 125
Woodson, S. E., 41
Woodward, L., 263
Wormeli, R., 105b, 122, 125b
Worrell, F. C., 312
Wyn, J., 34, 39, 40, 41, 42, 394

Xue, Y., 90

Yaeger, A. M., 317
Yancey, A. K., 241
Yanez, E., 290
Yang, Y. W., 90
Yardley, L., 18
Yates, M., 319, 324, 325
Yazedijian, A., 307, 314
Yeh, C., 264
Yogendran, M. S., 83
Young, R. A., 321
Youniss, J., 171, 228, 316, 317, 319, 324, 325
Yowell, C. M., 329, 329t, 330
Yu, H. C., 333
Yung, B. R., 90
Yunger, J. L., 328, 343, 346

Zaichkowsky, L. B., 80f
Zaichkowsky, L. D., 80f
Zald, D. H., 277
Zarbatany, L., 192, 194
Zausneiwski, J. A., 156
Zbikowski, S. M., 255
Zeifman, D., 338t
Zeller, M., 178, 181b
Zemel, B. S., 249
Zeng, L., 265
Zidar, I., 244
Zimbardo, P. G., 185, 188
Zimet, G. D., 66b
Zimmer, J. M., 126
Zimmer-Gembeck, M. J., 304, 356
Zimmerman, M. A., 362
Zimmerman, M. D., 140
Zimmerman, P., 340
Zimring, F., 283b
Zinnbauer, B. J., 316
Zucker, K. L., 346

SUBJECT INDEX

Information in tables, figures, or boxes is indicated by t, f *or* b *following the page number.*

A Nation at Risk, 227
Abortion
  induced, 262, 262f
  spontaneous, 262, 262f
Abstract concepts, in Piaget's formal operational stage, 272–273
Abuse
  alcohol, in middle adolescence, 252–253, 253f, 254b
  child, brain development effects of, 77b–78b, 78f
  drug, in middle adolescence, 256, 256t
  substance, in middle adolescence, 252–256, 253f, 254b, 255t, 256t
Academic achievement, intelligence and, relationship between, 288–289, 288b, 289f
Acceptance
  group, sociometric classification of, 180, 180f
  moving toward, 363b
  peer, 180–181, 180f
Accommodation, 99
Acculturation, 314
Achieved, example of, 309, 309b, 310t
Achievement motivation, 146–149, 148b–150b
Achievement tests, 12
  for adolescents, 288b
Action research, 24–25, 25f
Active learning, in Montessori approach, 111b
Active rehearsal, defined, 113
Activity(ies)
  self-motivated, in Montessori approach, 111b
  spontaneous, in Montessori approach, 111b
Adaptation, 98
Adaptive environments, 42
Add-Health, 357
Adequacy, referential, 23
ADHD. *See* Attention deficit hyperactivity disorder (ADHD)
Adipose tissue, 69
Adiposity rebound, 69
Adolescence. *See also* Adolescent(s); Middle adolescence
  affective development in, described, 302–303, 302f, 303f
  construction of, modern contributions to, 203–207, 203f, 204b, 205b
  defined, 205
  developmental assets in, 220t–221t
  developmental domains of, 211–212, 211f
  developmental milestones in, 211–212, 211f
  diverse ecological contexts related to, 208–209, 210b
  globalization effects on, 209
  high-risk involvement among, characteristics predicting, 218–219
  history of, 202–207, 203f, 204b, 205b, 208b
  late, defined, 374
  middle. *See* Middle adolescence
  multiple selves in, 303, 303f
  "new," 208
  opposing attributes during, 328, 328f
  positive youth development despite presence of risks in environment among, elements predicting, 219
  in postmodern societies, meanings of, 208–209, 210b
  poststructural ideas on, 209
  risk and opportunity in, research on, 217–225
    social policy implications, 223–226
    study of risk and protection in successful outcomes among disadvantaged adolescents, 218b
  romantic activities in, participation in, 356, 357t
  social development in, described, 338
  as stage, 206–207
  as structural period, 206
  structural view of, 209
  studying of, 2–31
  as transition, 205–206
Adolescent(s). *See also* Adolescence
  adjustment to divorce by, intervention programs for, 365b
  aptitude and achievement tests for, 288b
  bisexual, 258–259
  development of, youth programs for, characteristics of, 224t
  disadvantaged, risk and protection in successful outcomes among, 218b
  early, depression described by, 153
  gay, 258–259
    lesbian, and bisexual, 258–259
  information processing in
    advanced metacognitive skills due to, 279–281, 280b
    capacity increases due to, 277–278
    effective use of mneumonic strategies due to, 279
    increase in knowledge base due to, 278–279
    theoretical viewpoints on, 277–281, 278b, 280b
  lesbian, 258–259
  in middle adolescence, efficiency increase due to, 278
  pregnancy among, 261–263, 262f, 263f, 264b
  with romantic relationships, percent of, 355, 356f
  sexual-minority, unique risk factors for, 219
  term derivation, 202
  tried as adults, developmental competency of, 283b–284b, 283f, 285f
Adolescent crowds, developmental changes in, 355, 355f
Adolescent egocentrism, in middle adolescence, 305
Adolescent employment, theoretical model of, 392, 392f
Adolescent sex-role inventory, 343, 344b
Adolescere, defined, 378
Adrenarche, 234
Adult(s), emerging, 374, 374f
Adult transitions, completing of, in 1960 and 2000, 382f
Adulthood
  construction of, modern contributions to, 379–381, 379f, 380f, 381b, 382f
  criteria for, 375, 376t

Adulthood (*Continued*)
early, defined, 374
emerging, 372–400. *See also* Emerging adulthood
history of, 378–381, 379f, 380f, 381b, 382f
early history, 378–379
in postmodern societies, meaning of, 382–383, 383b, 384b, 385f
transitions to, 377t
timing of, factors affecting, 380–381, 382f
young, defined, 374
Adultification, 205
Adultoid, 205
Adultus, defined, 378
Affective autonomy, 304
Affective development
in adolescence, described, 302–303, 302f, 303f
in emerging adulthood, 386–387, 386f
in middle adolescence, 211f, 212, 300–335
adolescent egocentrism in, 305
biracial/multiethnic identity in, 314–315
contexts of, 331–333
community contexts, 332–333
family contexts, 332
school contexts, 332
described, 302–303, 302f, 303f
ego development in, 304–305, 304t
emotion and self-esteem in, 326–330, 328f, 329t, 330b–331b, 331t
faith development in, 317
identity in, 307–325. *See also* Identity, in middle adolescence
postmodern identities in, 307
theoretical viewpoints on, 303–307, 304t, 306f
psychoanalytic perspectives, 304–306, 304t, 306f
social-identity theory, 307
social-psychological perspectives, 306–307
symbolic interaction theory, 307
in middle childhood, 44, 45f, 130–161
contexts of, 156–159
community contexts, 158–159
family contexts, 156–157
school contexts, 157–158
described, 132
emotional development in, 151–156, 152f, 152t, 153b, 154b, 155f, 156b
emotional intelligence in, 151–153, 152f, 152t, 153b
self-understanding in, development of, 136–150. *See also* Self-understanding, development of, in middle childhood
temperament in, 154–156, 155f, 156b
theoretical viewpoints on, 132–136, 132f, 134f, 135f, 136b, 137b
humanistic perspectives, 133–136, 135f, 136b, 137b, 138f
personality perspectives, 132–133, 132f, 134f
person-centered theory, 135–136, 137b
psychosocial theory, 133, 134f
self-actualization theory, 134–135, 135f, 136b
Piaget's formal operational stage implications for, 276b
Affective experiences, self-esteem and, 328
Affilitative interchanges, 355
After-school programs, in children's development, 51–53, 51b, 52f
Agape, defined, 360t
Age
as factor in binge drinking, 13- to 30-year-olds, 383, 384f
as indication for high-risk involvement among adolescents, 218
residential change by, 389, 390f
Age grading, 41
Age trends, marriage-related, 390, 390t, 391f
Agency, described, 165
Agentic needs, 178
Aggression
antisocial behavior and, 187–188
physical, 187
proactive, 189
reactive, 189
relational, 187
types of, 187
verbal, 187
Aggressive behaviors, 185, 187f
AIDS, in middle adolescence, 261, 261f
Alan Guttmacher Institute, 262
Alcohol, use and abuse of, in middle adolescence, 252–253, 253f, 254b
Altruism, 184
AMA. *See* American Medical Association (AMA)
Amelia Bedelia, 102b
Amenorrheic, 239
American College Testing (ACT) Assessment Program, 288b
American Medical Association (AMA), 254b
American Psychological Association, 387
American Revolution, 378
Amygdala, 245
Analysis(es), narrative, 21–22, 24t
Analytical reasoning, 282
Anorexia nervosa, 251b
Antibullying programs, 191
Antisocial behavior
defined, 185
in middle childhood, 185, 187–191, 187f, 189b, 190b, 190t, 191f
aggression and, 187–188
bullying and, 188–191, 189b, 190b, 190t, 191b, 192b
dimensions of, 185, 187f
Anxious attachment, 339
Anxious-avoidant attachment, 339
Anxious-resistant attachment, 339
Appearance, cultural effects on, in middle adolescence, 348, 348f
Applied developmental psychology, focus of, 387
Applied research, in middle childhood development, 6
Aptitude tests, 12
for adolescents, 288b
Arenas of comfort, 265
Asset(s)
developmental, in adolescent development, 219–221, 220t–221t
ecological, 221
Assimilation, 98
Associative memory, 285
Asynchrony, 275
At the Threshold, 206
Atkins v. Virginia, 283b
Attachment
advantages of, 359
anxious, 339
anxious-avoidant, 339
anxious-resistant, 339
categories of, 339–340, 340f
disorganized, 339
goals of, 339, 339t
phases of, 338–339, 338t
secure, 339
stages of, 338–339, 338t, 339t
working models of, 340

Attachment perspectives, of social development in middle adolescence, 338–340, 338t, 339t, 340f
Attention
in information-processing theory of cognitive development in middle childhood, 113
selective, 113
in social learning, 164
Attention deficit hyperactivity disorder (ADHD), symptoms of, 83–84
reading comprehension and, 116b, 117b, 117f
school performance and, 116b, 117b, 117f
Attribute(s), opposing, during adolescence, 328, 328f
Attribution(s), 156
Attrition, defined, 9
Audience, imaginary, 275
Authoritarian parenting, 361
Authoritative parenting, 156–157, 361
Automaticity, defined, 115
Autonomy, 133, 393
affective, 304
behavioral, 304
sexual, 349
types of, 304
Awareness, lateral, 81

Balancing, motor skills involved in, 80–81, 81f
Bandura's social learning theory, 164–165
Bar Mitzvah, 206
Basic research, in middle childhood development, 6
Basic trust, 133
Bat Mitzvah, 206
Behavior(s)
aggressive, 185, 187f
antisocial, in middle childhood, 185, 187–191, 187f, 189b, 190b, 190t, 191f. *See also* Antisocial behavior, in middle childhood
delinquent, differential-association hypothesis of, 185
dietary, in middle adolescence, 249
in distributive justice reasoning, 174
eating, disordered, in middle adolescence, 249–250, 251b–252b
general, as indication for high-risk involvement among adolescents, 218
health, physical development in adolescents and, 234
health-related, physical development in adolescents and, 234
play-related, playground design effects on, 91b–92b, 91f
prosocial, in middle childhood, 184–185, 186t
sexual, noncoital, in middle adolescence, 257–258
social, in middle childhood, 183–191. *See also* Social behavior, in middle childhood
in social learning, 165, 165f
Behavior enactment, in social information processing, 165, 166f
Behavioral autonomy, 304
Behavioral functioning, myelinated brain structures and, 75, 76t
Behavioral genetics, in physical development in middle childhood, 60
Behavioral neuroscience, 62
Behaviorism, 98
Betweenager(s), 34, 35f
Bias(es)
cohort, 7
honesty, 15
intergroup, in gender identity, 343
memory, 15
social desirability, 15
Bicultural, 314
Binge drinking, 252
from ages 13 to 30, rates of, 383, 384f
Binge-eating disorder, 251b
Bioecological model, 47
Biological development, in middle childhood, 60
Biological maturation, in middle adolescence, 234–243
body weight and composition, 238–239, 238f
direct-effects model, 241
factors influencing, 239–240, 240f
indirect-effects model, 241
linear growth, 237–238, 238f
psychological development and, relationship between, 243, 243f
pubertal process, 234–236, 236f
puberty-function relationships, 241–243, 242t, 243f
secondary sex characteristics, 234, 236–237, 237t
skeletal size, 239
somatic growth, 237–239, 238f
status of, outcomes in diverse populations, 242t
timing of, psychosocial consequences of, 240–241, 242t
Biology
in brain development, 75–79, 77b–78b, 79f
in physical development in middle childhood, 70–71
Biracial/multiethnic identity, in middle adolescence, 314–315
Bisexual adolescents, 258–259
"Blogs," 306
"Blue Ribbon Schools," 175–176, 176f
BMI. *See* Body mass index (BMI)
Bodily-kinesthetic intelligence, 290
Body awareness, perception of, development of, in middle childhood, 81
Body fat levels, in physical development in middle childhood, 69, 70f
Body image
cultural effects on, in middle adolescence, 348, 348f
increased awareness of, in middle adolescence, 249
Body mass index (BMI), 69
Body proportions, changes in, in physical development in middle childhood, 67–68, 67f
Body satisfaction, in middle childhood, 85, 88
Body size, changes in, in physical development in middle childhood, 63–66, 64f–65f, 65b
Body status, in middle childhood, 85–89, 87f, 87t, 88f
Body weight and composition, in middle adolescence, 238–239, 238f
Bone growth, 68–69, 68f
Bone mineralization, threats to, 69
Boundaries, in adolescent development, 220t
Boys and Girls Clubs, 53
Brain
functioning of, alcohol use effects on, 254b
lobes of, 73, 73f
traumatic stress effects on, 77b, 78f
Brain development, 71–79
alcohol use effects on, 254b
biology in, 75–79, 79f
child abuse and neglect effects on, 77b–78b, 78f

Brain development (*Continued*)
course of, 78, 79f
environment in, 75–79, 79f
fiber tracts in, 74–75
genetics in, 75–79, 79f
in middle adolescence, 243–245, 244f, 246b, 247f
role of environment in, 245, 246b, 247f
structural and functional change, 243–245, 244f
myelination in, 73–74, 74f, 75f
neuronal development, 72–75, 72f–75f
related changes in function, 75, 76t
synaptogenesis in, 73, 74f
"Brokering," 333
Bronfenbrenner's ecological model, 45–46, 46f, 222f
Brown v. Board of Education, 204
"Buddy system," 177b
Bulimia nervosa, 251b
Bullying
antisocial behavior and, 188–191, 189b, 190b, 190t, 191b, 192b
homophobic, 188
naturalistic study of, in grades 1–6, 191
prevention of, 192b
Bullying index, scoring of, 191f

Calcium, for bone growth, 69
Care
advantages of, 359
ethics of, in moral development, 172–173, 173t
Career(s), family, 215
Career counseling, with ethnic-minority youth, 323b
Career development, in middle adolescence, 320–324, 321t, 322b–323b
Carnegie Commission, 204
Carnegie Corporation, 206
Carnegie Council on Adolescent Development, 126, 206
Carnegie Foundation for the Advancement of Teaching, 204
Case studies, described, 23
Casual dating, 355
Catecholamine(s), 77b
Causality, in concrete operational period, 103–104
CDC. *See* Centers for Disease Control
Cell(s), glial, 73
Centers for Disease Control and Prevention (CDC), 84
online Youth Risk Behavior Survey of, 254, 255t
Cephalocaudal development, 67
Cerebral cortex, 73, 74f
Change
intraindividual, 212
over time, studying of, 6–11, 7f, 8b, 10f, 10t
temporality of, in early adulthood, 387
within-person, in early adulthood, 387
Changing demographics, as factor in transition to adulthood, 380
Character, moral, 171
Character education
in moral development, 175–176, 175f, 176f, 177b, 177t
model for, 175, 176f
types of, 177t
Charles Stewart Mott Foundation, 54b
Charlie and the Chocolate Factory, 102b
Child abuse, brain development effects of, 77b–78b, 78f
Child care subsidies, 383b
Child-centered environment, in Montessori approach, 111b
Childhood
cultural ecology of, 41–42, 42f
middle, studying of, 2–31. *See also* Middle childhood, studying of
in postmodern societies, meanings of, 40–44, 42f, 43f, 44b
social construction of, 40–41
stages of, 36
Children. *See also School-age children; specific age-related groupings, e.g.,* Middle childhood
maltreated, brain development in, 77b–78b, 78f
neglected, described, 179, 180
overweight, race and gender and, 85, 87f, 88
popular, described, 179, 180
in U.S., ethnic population of, 42f
Chums, 178
Cigarette smoking, in middle adolescence, 253–256, 255t
Circadian cycle, 250
Citizenship Act of 1924, 378
Civic engagement, 324
Class inclusion task, 103, 103f
"Class Play," 181, 181b
Classical conditioning, 98
Classification
in concrete operational period, 100, 102–103, 103f
hierarchical, 102
Classification task, 103, 103f
Classroom strategies, supporting self-competence and self-worth, 145b
Climate, school, defined, 332
Clinical interview method, 19
Clique(s), 355
defined, 181, 182f
Close relationships, in middle adolescence, 351–366
family relationships, 360–366. *See also* Family relationships, in middle adolescence
friendships, 351–359, 352t, 353f, 354b, 355f–359f, 357t, 360t. *See also* Friendship, in middle adolescence
Closeness, defined, 3, 52
Coaching, as parental reaction to sibling conflicts, 364
Cocaine, use and abuse of, in middle adolescence, 256t
Cognition, in middle childhood, 98
Cognitive autonomy, 304
Cognitive development
in emerging adulthood, 385–386, 386f
in middle adolescence, 211f, 212, 270–299
contexts of, 293–296, 294t, 295f, 296f, 297t
community contexts, 296
family contexts, 293
school contexts, 293–296, 294t, 295f, 296f
decision making in, 282
psychometric approach to intelligence in, 282–292. *See also* Psychometric approach to intelligence, in middle adolescence
scientific reasoning in, 281–282, 283b–284b, 283f, 284f
theoretical viewpoints on, 272–281, 274f, 276b, 278b, 280b
information processing in adolescents, 277–281, 278b, 280b
Piaget's formal operational stage, 272–275, 274f. *See also* Piaget's formal operational stage, in middle adolescence
thinking about possibilities in, 273
in middle childhood, 44, 45f, 96–129
basis of, 104
concrete operational period in, 99–104, 101t, 102b, 103f,

104f, 105b. *See also* Concrete operational period
in context, 124–127, 125b, 127f
community context, 126–127
family context, 124–125
school context, 125–126, 125b
culture in, 105–106
information-processing perspective on, 110, 112–118. *See also* Information-processing theory, in middle childhood
language development, 118–123, 121b–122b
mathematical operations in, 123–124
Piaget's cognitive developmental theory, 98–99
sociocultural perspective on, 107–110, 107f, 108b, 109f. *See also* Sociocultural perspective, on cognitive development in middle childhood
theoretical viewpoints on, 98–106
Vygotsky's theory on, 107–108
Piaget's stages of, 99
Cognitive disequilibrium, 99
Cognitive efficiency, in information-processing theory of cognitive development in middle childhood, 115
Cognitive functioning, myelinated brain structures and, 75, 76t
Cognitive inhibition, 113
Cognitive tasks, gender differences in, 294, 294t
Cohort, 42
Cohort bias, 7
Cold War, 204
Cold weather, exercise effects on children in, 84, 86b
Combinatorial system, 274
Comfort, arenas of, 265
Coming of Age in Samoa, 41
Coming out, as indication for high-risk involvement among adolescents, 219
Commission on Work, Family, and Citizenship, 204, 379
Commitment, 308
Commitment to learning, in adolescent development, 220t
Committed relationships, 355
"Committee of Ten," 203
Committee on Secondary School Studies, 203
Communal needs, 178
Communication
family, systems model of, 341, 342f
intrasensory, increase in, in middle childhood, 81
Communities That Care, 224
Community(ies), 393
developmentally attentive, 227–228
Community contexts
in emerging adulthood, 393
in middle adolescence, 227–228
affective development-related, 332–333
cognitive development-related, 296
physical development and maturation-related, 266
social development-related, 227, 228, 367–368
in middle childhood, 53, 54b–55b, 54f
affective development-related, 158–159
cognitive development-related, 126–127
developmentally attentive, 227–228
development-related, 90
global, role in transition to adulthood, 381
social development-related, 195–196
Community schools, strategies of, 227t
Community-based human development, 228
Companionship, advantages of, 359
Compensation, 213
Competence
cultural, defined, 158–159
emotional, 151, 326
as indicator of positive youth development despite presence of risks in environment among adolescents, 219
ratings of, as predictors of self-esteem, 141, 142f
social
in adolescent development, 220t–221t
defined, 164, 183
model of, 183, 184f
teachers' support for, 144, 145b
Competence, Confidence, Character, Connection, and Caring, 219
Competence-performance distinction, 172
Complex processes, integration of, in early adulthood, 388
Comprehension
reading
ADHD and, 116b, 117b, 117f
enhancement of, reciprocal teaching in, 108b
verbal, 285
Conceptual knowledge, 278
Concrete operational period
causality, 103–104
classification, 100, 102–103, 103f
conservation in, 99–100, 101t, 102b
in middle childhood, 99–104, 101t, 102b, 103f, 104f, 105b
seriation, 103, 104f
Concrete operational stage, of cognitive development, 99
Conditioning
classical, 98
operant, 98
Conditions of worth, 136
Conflict(s)
among friends, in middle childhood, causes of, 183
parent-adolescent, 362
Conflicted interaction, among siblings, in middle adolescence, 363
Confusion, identity, *vs.* identity, 306, 306f
Connectedness, as indicator of positive youth development despite presence of risks in environment among adolescents, 219
Conservation
in concrete operational period, 99–100, 101t, 102b
defined, 99–100
Conservation tasks, Piagetian, 101t
Constructive use of time, in adolescent development, 220t
Constructivist view, of cognitive development, 98
Context(s). *See School contexts; specific type, e.g.* Community contexts
centrality of, in early adulthood, 388
Continuity
defined, 4
in human development, 4–5, 5f
Continuous bidirectional interactions, between persons and environments, in emerging adulthood, 389
Continuous development, 4–5, 5f
Contraceptive use, in middle adolescence, 259–261
Controversial children, described, 179, 180
Conventional moral reasoning, 171t, 172
Convergent thinking, 292

Conversion, 315
Cooperative play, 92b
Corpus callosum, 74, 75f
Cortex, frontal, 74, 75f
Cortisol, 77b
Counseling, career, with ethnic-minority youth, 323b
Counting, rote, 123
Creative flow, 149f
Creativity, 291–292
Credibility, of qualitative data, 23
Criterion-referenced tests, 12
"Critical periods," 77
Cross-cultural drawings of ideal woman and man in nontraditional role, 346, 347b
Cross-sectional research designs, 6–7, 7f, 10t
  limitations of, 7
Cross-sectional studies, 6–7, 7f, 10t
Crowd(s), 355
  defined, 182
Cue(s)
  internal and external, encoding of, in social information processing, 165, 166f
  interpretation and mental representation of, in social information processing, 165, 166f
Cultural competence, defined, 158–159
Cultural ecology of childhood, 41–42, 42f
Cultural globalization, 209
Cultural influences, in middle childhood, 41–42, 42f
Culture(s)
  in cognitive development in middle childhood, 105–106, 109–110, 111b
  effects on family relationships, self-report reflections of, 16b, 16f
  in information-processing theory of cognitive development in middle childhood, 118
  Mayan, 210b
  youth, construction of, 210b
Cumulative rehearsal, defined, 113
"Cyberbullying," 188

Data
  qualitative, evaluation of, 22–23
  quantitative, collection of, 11–17, 12f, 14f, 15f, 16b, 18t. *See also* Quantitative data collection
Data collection techniques, 11–23, 12f, 14f, 15f, 16b, 18t, 20b, 20f, 27
  qualitative data collection, 18–22, 20b, 20f, 24t
  quantitative data collection, 11–17, 12f, 14f, 15f, 16b, 18t
Dating
  casual, 355
  heterosexual, stages of, 355
  in middle adolescence, 353, 353f, 355–358, 356f–358f, 357t
Decentration, defined, 100
Decision, response, in social information processing, 165, 166f
Decision making, in middle adolescence, 282
Declarative knowledge, 278
Deconstruct, 40
Deductive reasoning, 6
Delinquent behavior, differential-association hypothesis of, 185
Demineralization, 69
Demographics
  changing, as factor in transition to adulthood, 380
  influences of, in middle childhood, 42–43
Dendrite(s), 72, 74f
Dendritic branching, 244
Dependability, of qualitative data, 23
Depression, as described by early adolescents, 153
Determinism, reciprocal, 164–165, 165f
Developing sense of humor, 102b
Development,
  affective. *See* Affective development
  biological, in middle childhood, 60
  career, in middle adolescence, 320–324, 321t, 322b–323b
  cephalocaudal, 67
  change over time in, 6–11, 7f, 8b, 10f, 10t
  cognitive
    in emerging adulthood, 385–386, 386f
    in middle adolescence, 211f, 212
  community-based human, 228
  continuous, 4–5, 5f
  discontinuous, 4–5, 5f
  ego, in middle adolescence, 304–305, 304t
  emotional, in middle childhood, 151–156, 152f, 152t, 153b, 154bg, 155f, 156b
  faith, in middle adolescence, 317
  family, framework for, new, 216, 216f
  holistic approach to, 44–45
  human. *See* Human development
  identity, 303
  individual progress and, in Montessori approach, 111b
  interpersonal, Piaget's formal operational stage implications for, 276b
  language, in middle childhood, 118–123, 121b–122b. *See also* Language development, in middle childhood
  life-course
    in middle adolescence, 211f, 212
    theoretical model of, 214, 214f
  life-span, theoretical model of, 213, 213f
  longitudinal research designs in, 7–9, 7f, 8b, 10t
  longitudinal-sequential research designs in, 9, 10f
  in middle childhood. *See* Middle childhood, development in
  neuronal, 72–75, 72f–75f
  physical
    in emerging adulthood, 384f, 385, 386f
    in middle adolescence, 211, 211f, 232–269. *See also* Physical development and maturation, in middle adolescence
    in middle childhood, 58–95. *See also* Physical development, in middle childhood
  political. *See* Political development
  proximodistal, 67, 67f
  psychological, pubertal maturation and, relationship between, 243, 243f
  semantic, 119
  skeletal, 68–69, 68f
  social
    in emerging adulthood, 386f, 387
    in middle adolescence, 211f, 212, 336–371. *See also* Social development, in middle adolescence
    in middle childhood, 162–198. *See also* Social development, in middle childhood
  syntax, 119
  variable-centered *vs.* person-centered approaches in, 9, 11
  of youth of color, factors affecting, 221
Developmental assets, 219–221, 220t, 221t
Developmental domain, 44

Developmental research, 27
focus groups in, 20b
Developmental science, 388
Developmental strengths, 219
Developmental theory, 4
Developmental time, 214, 214f
Developmental traumatology, 77b
Developmental-contextual theory, of human development, 47, 48b–50b, 48f
Developmentally attentive community, 227–228
Dialectical, 385
Dietary behavior, in middle adolescence, 249
Dieting, in middle childhood, 88–89
Differential-association hypothesis of delinquent behavior, 185
Diffuse/avoidant identity style, 310
Diffused, example of, 309, 309b, 310t
Digit span task, 112–113
Direct-effects model, 241
Discontinuity
defined, 4
in human development, 4–5, 5f
Discontinuous development, 4–5, 5f
Disequilibrium, cognitive, 99
Disordered eating behavior, in middle adolescence, 249–250, 251b–252b
Disorganized attachment, 339
Dissatisfaction, marital, gender-stereotypical patterns in adolescence due to, 364–365, 365b
Distance curves, for height and weight, 63, 64f–65f
Distributive justice reasoning, 173–174, 173t
Divergent thinking, 292
Diverse youth, friendships among, in middle adolescence, 353, 354b
Diversity, ethnic, as factor in transition to adulthood, 380
Diversity issues, integration into sex education and pregnancy prevention programs, 264b
Divinity, 393
Divorce, adolescent's adjustment to parent's, intervention programs for, 365b
Domain, developmental, 44
Dominance, lateral, 81
Dominant sensory system, shift in, in middle childhood, 81
Dress, in identity, in middle adolescence, 308f
Drinking, binge, from ages 13 to 30, rates of, 383, 384f
Drug use and abuse, in middle adolescence, 256, 256t
DSM-IV diagnostic criteria
for anorexia nervosa, 251b
for bulimia nervosa, 251b

Early adolescents, depression described by, 153
Early adulthood, defined, 374
Earned Income Credits, 383b
Eating behaviors, disordered, in middle adolescence, 249–250, 251b–252b
Eating disorders, symptomology and health consequences of, 251b–252b
Ecocultural perspective, 333
Ecological assets, 221
Ecological theory, of human development, 45
Economic globalization, 209
Economy, work and, as factor in transition to adulthood, 380
Ecstasy, use and abuse of, in middle adolescence, 256t
Generalizability, of quantitative data, 17–18
Education, character, in moral development, 175–176, 175f, 176f, 177b, 177t. *See also* Character education
Education in the Moral Domain, 177b
Education-related expectations, as indication for high-risk involvement among adolescents, 218
Effectance motivation, 144
Effective human enrichment, model of, 247f
Ego, 132
Ego development, in middle adolescence, 304–305, 304t
Ego ideal, 132
Ego identity, 305
Ego identity status, revised objective measure of, 309b
Egocentric, defined, 120, 167
Egocentrism, adolescent, in middle adolescence, 305
Elaboration, 279
Electra complex, 133
Elementary and Secondary Education Act, Title X, Part 1 of, 51b
Elementary School Recognition Program, of U.S. Department of Education, 175–176, 176f
Elmtown's youth, 204b
Embodiment, 348
Emerging adulthood, 372–400
bidirectional relationship between knowledge generation and knowledge application in, 388
centrality of context in, 388
continuous bidirectional interactions between persons and environments in, 389
defined, 374–377, 374f, 375f, 376t, 377t
developmental domains of, 386–387, 386f
developmental milestones in, 385–387, 386f
affective development, 386–387, 386f
cognitive development, 385–386, 386f
physical development, 384f, 385, 386f
social development, 386f, 387
diverse contexts of, 389–393, 390f–392f
community context, 393
family contexts, 389–391, 390f, 390t, 391f
school/workplace context, 391–393, 392f
individual differences and within-person change in, 387
integration of complex processes in, 388
integration of theoretical viewpoints in, 387–389, 388f
normative developmental processes in, 388
temporality of change in, 387
Emerging adults, 374, 374f
Emic approach, 41
Emotion(s)
defined, 151
functionalist approach to, 151
in middle adolescence, 326–330, 328f, 329t, 330b–331b, 331t
mood and, 326–327
regulation of, study of, 189b
self-regulation and, relationship between, 185, 186t
semantic differential of, 137t
temperament and, 154, 155f
Emotional competence, 151, 326
Emotional development, in middle childhood, 151–156, 152f, 152t, 153b, 154b, 155f, 156b
Emotional intelligence, in middle childhood, 151–153, 152f, 152t, 153b

Emotional intelligence framework, 151, 152t
Emotional reaction, altering of, in middle childhood, 151
Emotionality, 154
Empathic, defined, 185
Empathy skills, in middle childhood, 185
Employment, adolescent, theoretical model of, 392, 392f
Empowerment, in adolescent development, 220t
Encoded, defined, 110
Environment(s)
 adaptive, 42
 in brain development, 245, 246b, 247f
 child-centered, in Montessori approach, 111b
 nonshared, 61
 persons and, continuous bidirectional interactions between, in emerging adulthood, 389
 in physical development in middle childhood, 70–71
 responsive prepared, in Montessori approach, 111b
 shared, 61
 in social learning, 165, 165f
Environment, in brain development, 75–79, 77b–78b, 79f
Epigenesis, probabilistic, 47
Epiphyses, 68, 68f
Epistemological understanding, 279–280
Equality, in distributive justice reasoning, 173
Equilibration, 99
Equity, in distributive justice reasoning, 174
Eriksonian theory, 314
Erikson's lifespan theory, 305–306, 306f
Erikson's psychosocial stages, 133, 134f
Erikson's psychosocial theory, 141
Eros, defined, 360t
Ethic(s), role in transition to adulthood, 381
Ethical relativism, 172
Ethical standards, for research, 26–27, 26t
Ethics of care, in moral development, 172–173, 173t
Ethnic differences, in middle adolescence, 350–351, 351f
Ethnic diversity, as factor in transition to adulthood, 380
Ethnic identity, in middle adolescence, 313–314, 315t
Ethnicity, 41
 intelligence scores effects of, 289–290
 of U.S. children, 42f
Ethnic-minority youth, career counseling with, 323b
Ethnography, 22, 24t
Ethology, 339
Etic approach, 41
Evaluation, program, 25
Event sampling, 14, 15f
Evolutionary developmental theory
 application to pubertal timing, 235b
 in physical development and maturation in middle adolescence, 234, 235b
Evolutionary psychology, 213
Exaggerated masculinity, 383
Excitement, advantages of, 359
Exercise, in middle childhood, 84, 86b
Existential intelligence, 290
Exosystem, 45–46, 46f
Expectation(s)
 in adolescent development, 220t
 for education and school grades, as indication for high-risk involvement among adolescents, 218
Experience(s)
 flow, 148
 peak, 148
 self-, 148
Experience Sampling Method (ESM), 16b
Experience-expectant processes, 77b
Exploration, 308
Extrinsic motivation, 146

Fable(s), personal, 275
Factor analysis, 285
Fairness
 justice reasoning *vs.*, 174, 174t
 in moral development, 173–175, 174t
Faith
 defined, 316
 individual-reflective, 317
 mythic-literal, 317
 spirituality, religion and, interrelationships between, 315–316
 synthetic-conventional, 317
Faith development, in middle adolescence, 317
Familias Unidas, 221, 222b, 222f
Family careers, 215
Family communication, systems model of, 341, 342f
Family contexts
 in emerging adulthood, 389–391, 390f, 390t, 391f
 in middle adolescence, 225–226
  affective development-related, 332
  cognitive development-related, 293
  social development-related, 366–367
 in middle childhood, 50–51
  affective development-related, 156–157
  cognitive development-related, 124–125
  development-related, 89–90
  social development-related, 193–194, 193f, 194f
 in physical development and maturation in middle adolescents, 265
Family development
 framework for, new, 216, 216f
 traditional model of, 215, 215f
Family development theory, 215
Family income, median, by education, in 1989 and 1996, 380, 380f
Family life cycle, 215
Family relationships
 cultural influences on, self-report reflections of, 16b
 in middle adolescence, 360–366
  parent-adolescent conflict, 362
  parental relationships, 364–366, 365b
  person characteristics in, 360–361
  quality of parenting in, 361–362
  sibling interaction, 362–364, 363b
Family systems, 341
Family systems perspectives, of social development in middle adolescence, 341, 342f
Family time, 214, 214f
Fantasy, in middle adolescence, 257
Female(s), strength in, *vs.* strength in males, 69, 71f
Fiber tracts, in brain development, 74–75
Fine motor skills, 81
First-World cities of United States, 209
Flow, 148
 creative, 149f
 psychology of, 148b–149b, 149f
Flow experiences, 148
Fluency, word, 285
Focus groups, in developmental research, 20b
Food Stamps, 383b
Foreclosed, example of, 309, 309b, 310t

Formal operational stage, of cognitive development, 99
Formal religion, 319
Forum for Youth Investment, 54b
Forum on Adolescence, 51b
4H, 53
Free Time Activities in Middle Childhood: Links with Adjustment in Early Adolescence, 49b
Freedom to Learn, 135, 136b
Freedom within limits, in Montessori approach, 111b
Free-time activities, in middle childhood, 49b–50b
Freud's psychosexual stages, 132, 132f
Friend(s), conflicts among, in middle childhood, causes of, 183
Friendship
  in middle adolescence, 351–359
    among diverse youth, 353, 354b
    dating, 353, 353f, 355–358, 356f–358f, 357t
    romantic love, 359, 360t
    romantic relationships, 358–359, 359f
    working models of, 352t
  in middle childhood, 178–183, 179t, 180f, 181b, 182f, 183b
    peer networks, 181–183, 182f, 183b
    popularity, 179–181, 180f, 181b
    stages of, 178–179, 179t
  peer relations *vs.,* 179, 179t
From Childhood to Adolescence: A Transitional Period, 38
Frontal cortex, 74, 75f
Function(s)
  behavioral, myelinated brain structures and, 75, 76t
  cognitive, myelinated brain structures and, 75, 76t

Gatekeeping, 333
Gay, lesbian, bisexual, or transgender (GLBT) youth, 367, 368t
Gay adolescents, 258–259
Gay-Straight Alliances, 367, 368t
Gender
  as factor in cognitive tasks, 294, 294t
  as factor in percentage of children who are overweight, 87f
Gender conformity, pressure for, in gender identity, 343
Gender contentedness, in gender identity, 341
Gender development, stages of, in middle adolescence, 343–345, 344t
Gender differences, in middle adolescence, 350
Gender identity
  components of, 341–342
  in middle adolescence, 341, 343–346, 344b, 345t, 347b
    gender development in, 343–345, 344t
    gender-role orientation in, 343–344, 344b
Gender intensification hypothesis, 343
Gender nonconforming, 346
Gender roles, in middle adolescence, 341
Gender schemas, 343
Gender typicality, in gender identity, 341
Gender-role orientation, in middle adolescence, 343–344, 344b
Gender-stereotypical patterns, in adolescence, marital dissatisfaction of parents and, 364–365, 365b
General behavior, as indication for high-risk involvement among adolescents, 218
Generalized other role-taking, 168
Generation X, 394
Generation Y, 394
Genetic(s)
  behavioral, in physical development in middle childhood, 60
  in brain development, 75–79, 77b–78b, 79f
  in physical development in middle childhood, 70–71
Genetic predisposition, 76
Genetic theories, in physical development in middle childhood, 60–61, 61f
Gen-X Religion, 319
Gerontological Association of America, 387
GLBT youth. *See* Gay, lesbian, bisexual, or transgender (GLBT) youth
Glial cells, 73
Global community, role in transition to adulthood, 381
Global knowledge economy, demands of, implications for youth in terms of required skills and learning strategies, 297t
Globalization
  cultural, 209
  defined, 209
  economic, 209
  effects on adolescence, 209
Goal(s), clarification of, in social information processing, 165, 166f
Gonadarche, 235
Gonadotropin(s), 235–236
Government resources, role in transition to adulthood, 381
GRASP Project, 54b–55b
Greater Resources for After-School Programming (GRASP), 54b–55b
Gross motor skills, 71f, 80–81
Group acceptance, sociometric classification of, 180, 180f
Grownups: A Generation in Search of Adulthood, 206
Growth
  defined, 63
  secular trend in, 65
Growth plates, 68, 68f
Guided participation, 109
Guidelines for School and Community Programs to Promote Lifelong Physical Activity Among Young People, 84

Hands-on learning, in Montessori approach, 111b
Harassment, in bullying behavior, 188
Harmonious interaction, among siblings, in middle adolescence, 363
Harvard Law School, *Program on Negotiation* at, 170b
Health and well-being, in middle childhood, 82–89
  body status and, 85–89, 87f, 87t, 88f
  exercise and, 84, 86b
  nutrition and, 85–89, 87f, 87t, 88f
  physical activity and, functions of, 82–84
  sports participation and, 84–85, 86b
Health behaviors, physical development in adolescents and, 234
Health issues, in middle adolescence, physical development and maturation effects on, 248–256
  cigarette smoking, 253–256, 255t
  dietary behavior, 249
  disordered eating behavior, 249–250, 251b–252b
  nutritional needs, 249, 249t
  sleep, 250, 252
  substance use and abuse, 252–256, 253f, 254b, 255t, 256t

Healthy Communities—Healthy Youth Initiative, 224
Hegemonic masculinity, 343
Height, distance curves for, 63, 64f–65f
Heritability estimate, 60
Heteronomous morality, 171, 171t
Heteronormality, 346
Heterosexual dating, stages of, 355
Heuristic reasoning, 282
Hierarchical classification, 102
Hierarchy of needs, 134, 135f
"High School: An Agenda for Action," 205b
Hispanic origin, as factor in percentage of children who are overweight, 87f
Historical time, 214, 214f
HIV infection. *See* Human immunodeficiency virus (HIV) infection
Holistic approach to human development, 44–45
Home, defined, 391
Homework, help for, for students and parents, 124–125, 125b
Homophobic bullying, 188
Honesty bias, 15
Hot weather, exercise effects on children in, 84, 86b
House, defined, 391
Household, defined, 391
Human development
  ecology of, 45–47, 46f
  holistic approach to, 44–45
  theoretical questions about, 4–6, 5f
  theories of, 45–47, 46f, 48b–50b, 48f
    developmental-contextual theory, 47, 48b–50b, 48f
Human immunodeficiency virus (HIV) infection, in middle adolescence, 261, 261f
Humanistic perspectives, in affective development in middle childhood, 133–136, 135f, 136b, 137b, 138f
Humor, developing sense of, 102b
Hypertrophy, 69
Hypokalemia, 251b
Hypothesis(es)
  defined, 6
  generating and evaluating of, in Piaget's formal operational stage, 273–274
Hypotheticodeductive reasoning, 273

"I," defined, 136, 137
Id, 132
Ideal, ego, 132
Ideal self, 144
Identity
  ego, 305
  ethnic, in middle adolescence, 313–314, 315t
  exploration of, possible selves in, 330b
  functions of, 308t
  gender, in middle adolescence, 341, 343–346, 344b, 345t, 347b. *See also* Gender identity, in middle adolescence
  identity confusion *vs.,* 306, 306f
  ideological, 309, 309b
  interpersonal, 309, 309b
  in middle adolescence
    formation of, 305–306, 306f
    identity processes, 310–312, 311f, 312b
    identity status, 308t, 308–312, 309b, 308f, 311f, 312b
    postmodern identities, 307
    racial/ethnic identity, 312–315, 313t, 315t
    research on, 307–325
    spiritual/religious identity, 315–319, 316f, 318f
    vocational/political identity, 319–325, 321t, 322b–323b, 324f
  in parent-adolescent relationships, negotiating of, 322b–323b
  positive, in adolescent development, 221t
  racial, in middle adolescence, 312–315, 313t
  social-cognitive model of, 310, 311f
  spiritual/religious, in middle adolescence, 315–319, 316f, 318f
Identity: Youth and Crisis, 305
Identity confusion, identity *vs.,* 306, 306f
Identity crisis, 306
Identity development, 303
Identity formation, in middle adolescence, 305–306, 306f
Identity processes, in middle adolescence, 310–312, 311f, 312b
Identity status
  categories of, 309, 309b, 310t
  ego, revised objective measures of, 309b
  in middle adolescence, 308t, 308–312, 309b, 308f, 311f, 312b
Identity styles, 310
Ideological identity, 309, 309b
Ideology, masculinity, 343
Imaginary audience, 275
Income, family, median, by education, in 1989 and 1996, 380, 380f
Indirect-effects model, 241
Individual differences, in early adulthood, 387
Individual progress and development, in Montessori approach, 111b
Individual-reflective faith, 317
Individuation, 304
Induced abortion, 262, 262f
Inductive reasoning, 6
Industry, sense of, 133
Infant and Child in the Culture of Today, 37
Inferencing, 120
Influence(s), peer-related, as indication for high-risk involvement among adolescents, 218
Information processing, in adolescents, theoretical viewpoints on, 277–281, 278b, 280b
Information seeking, self-evaluative, laboratory study of, 150b
Information-oriented identity style, 310
Information-processing theory, in middle childhood, 110, 112–118
  attention in, 113
  bases of, 116, 116b–117b, 117f
  cognitive efficiency in, 115
  culture in, 118
  developmental components of, 112–115, 112f, 114t
  knowledge base in, 114–115
  metacognition in, 115
  mneumonic strategies in, 113–114, 114t
  speed of processing in, 113
Inhalant(s), use and abuse of, in middle adolescence, 256t
Inhibition, cognitive, 113
Initiative, 133, 219
Instability, in human development, 5–6
Institute for Educational Leadership, 226
Instrumental morality, 171t, 172
Integration
  social, 53, 54b–55b, 195
  spatial-temporal, 328
Intelligence
  alternative views of, 290–292, 291b, 292f
  bodily-kinesthetic, 290

emotional, in middle childhood, 151–153, 152f, 152t, 153b
forms of, 290
interpersonal, 290
intrapersonal, 290
linguistic, 290
logical-mathematical, 290
measures of, in psychometric approach to intelligence, 285–287, 286f, 287f
multiple, 290
musical, 290
naturalist, 290
practical, 292f
psychometric approach to, in middle adolescence, 282–292. *See also* Psychometric approach to intelligence, in middle adolescence
relationship to academic achievement and occupation, in psychometric approach to intelligence, 288–289, 288b, 289f
spatial, 290
successful, 290
theories of, in psychometric approach to intelligence, 284–285
triarchic model of, 290–291, 291b
types of, 290
Intelligence quotient (IQ), 286–287, 286f, 287f
interpretation of, 286–287, 286f, 287f
stability of, 287
Intelligence scores, factors influencing, 289–290
Interaction(s)
conflicted, among siblings, in middle adolescence, 363
continuous bidirectional, between persons and environments, in emerging adulthood, 389
harmonious, among siblings, in middle adolescence, 363
sibling. *See* Sibling interactions
symbolic, 306–307
typical, among siblings, in middle adolescence, 363
Interchange(s), affiliative, 355
Intergroup bias, in gender identity, 343
Interindividual differences, 212
Internal working model, 340
Internet, 384b
bullying behavior on, 188
Interpersonal, 304
Interpersonal action, stages of, 168, 169t
Interpersonal action framework, 168
Interpersonal development, Piaget's formal operational stage implications for, 276b
Interpersonal identity, 309, 309b
Interpersonal intelligence, 290
Interpersonal morality, 171t, 172
Interpersonal negotiation, 168–169, 168f, 169t
Interpersonal orientation, 169
Interpersonal understanding, in middle childhood, 167–169, 168f, 168t, 169t, 170b
Interrater reliability, 17
Intersectionality, 307
Intervention, as parental reaction to sibling conflicts, 364
Intervention programs, for adolescents' adjustment to divorce, 365b
Interview(s)
clinical, 19
structured, 19–21, 20b, 20f
Interview questions, semistructured, 20b
Interview studies, 19–21, 20b, 20f, 24t
Intimacy, advantages of, 359
Intimacy *vs.* isolation stage, 387
Intraindividual change, 212
Intrapersonal intelligence, 290
Intrapsychic, 304
Intrinsic motivation, 146
Intuitive-projective stage, 317
IOWA Test for Basic Skills, 12
IQ. *See* Intelligence quotient (IQ)
Iraq, war in, 207
"I-self," 137

Journey Toward Womanhood, 264b
Judgment, moral, 171
stages of, 171–172, 171t
Jumping, motor skills involved in, 80
"Just say no to drugs," 196
Justice reasoning, fairness reasoning *vs.,* 174, 174t

Kauai Longitudinal Study, 8b, 217
Knowledge
conceptual, 278
declarative, 278
membership, in gender identity, 341
types of, 278
Knowledge base, in information-processing theory of cognitive development in middle childhood, 114–115
Knowledge economy, global, demands of, implications for youth in terms of required skills and learning strategies, 297t
Kohlberg's stages of moral reasoning, 171–172, 174, 174t

Language, pragmatics of, 119
Language development, in middle childhood, 118–123, 121b–122b
reading, 120, 121b–122b, 121f
syntax, 119
writing, 120, 122–123
Lanugo, 251b
Late adolescence, defined, 374
Latency stage, 133
Lateral awareness, 81
Lateral dominance, 81
Laterality, 81
Learning
active, in Montessori approach, 111b
commitment to, in adolescent development, 220t
hands-on, in Montessori approach, 111b
lifelong, as factor in transition to adulthood, 380
problem-based, from sociocultural perspective, 278b
self-disciplined, in Montessori approach, 111b
service, moral action through, 177b
social, 164–165
Learning Together, 226
Leptin, 239
Lerner's developmental-contextual model of human development, 47, 48f
Lesbian adolescents, 258–259
Life Choices, 311, 312b
Life cycle, family, 215
Life events, 214
Life histories, 214
Life in School Checklist, 190b, 190t
Life-course development
in middle adolescence, 211f, 212
theoretical model of, 214, 214f
Life-course theory, for middle adolescence, 213–216, 214f–216f
Lifelong learning, as factor in transition to adulthood, 380
Life-span development, theoretical model of, 213, 213f
Life-span theory, for middle adolescence, 212–213, 213f
Limbic system, 74, 75f
Linear growth (height), in middle adolescence, 237–238, 238f
Linguistic intelligence, 290

Little League, 53
Loevinger's ego development theory, 304, 304t, 305
Logical positivism, 40
Logical-mathematical intelligence, 290
Longitudinal research, limitations of, 9
Longitudinal research designs, 7–9, 7f, 8b, 10t
Longitudinal study, described, 7–9, 7f, 8b, 10t
Longitudinal-sequential research designs, 9, 10f
Long-term store (LTS), 112
Love
  romantic, in middle adolescence, 348–349, 349b, 359, 360t
  styles of, 359, 360t
LTS. *See* Long-term store (LTS)
Ludus, defined, 360t

MacArthur Foundation, 39
  Reproductive Transition Group of, 206
  Research Network on Adolescent Development and Juvenile Justice of, 283b, 284b
MacArthur Network on Successful Pathways through Middle Childhood, 39, 40t
MacArthur Network on Transitions to Adulthood and Public Policy, 380, 381b
MacCat-CA, 283b
Machismo, 383
Macrosystem, 45–46, 46f
Macrotime, 46
Magic Trees of the Mind, 246b
Making Life Choices Program (MLCP), 312b
Malcolm in the Middle, 40
Male(s)
  ideal, cross-cultural drawings of, in nontraditional role, 346, 347b
  strength in, *vs.* strength in females, 69, 71f
Maltreated children, brain development in, 77b–78b, 78f
Mania, defined, 360t
Marijuana, use and abuse of, in middle adolescence, 256t
Marital dissatisfaction, gender-stereotypical patterns in adolescence due to, 364–365, 365b
Marriage, age trends in, 390, 390t, 391f
Masculinity
  exaggerated, 383
  hegemonic, 343
Masculinity ideology, 343
Maslow's hierarchy of needs, 134, 135f
Masturbation, in middle adolescence, 257
Math performance, expectations for, in middle childhood, 143, 144f
Mathematical operations, in middle childhood, 123–124
Mattering, in middle adolescence friendships, 353, 354b
Maturation
  biological, in middle adolescence, 234–243. *See also* Biological maturation, in middle adolescence
  physical development and
    in middle adolescence, 232–269. *See also* Physical development and maturation, in middle adolescence
    in middle childhood, 62
Maturational-deviance hypothesis, 241
Mayan culture, 210b
MDMA, use and abuse of, in middle adolescence, 256t
"Me," defined, 136, 137
Media, new, 43–44, 43f
Median family income, by education, in 1989 and 1996, 380, 380f
Medicaid, 383b
Melatonin, 250
Membership knowledge, in gender identity, 341
Memory
  associative, 285
  short-term, 110
Memory bias, 15
Menarche, 237, 237t
Mental abilities, primary, 285
Merit, in distributive justice reasoning, 173
Mesosystem, 45–46, 46f
Mesotime, 46
Meta-analysis, 343
Metacognition, in information-processing theory of cognitive development in middle childhood, 115
Metacognitive skills, 115
Metamemory, 115, 279
Metatheoretical paradigm, 213
Michigan Study of Middle Childhood, 157
Microsystem, 45–46, 46f
Microtime, 46
Middle adolescence. *See also* Adolescence
  affective development in, 211f, 212, 300–335. *See also* Affective development, in middle adolescence
  beyond, 372–400. *See also* Emerging adulthood
  close relationships in, 351–366. *See also* Close relationships, in middle adolescence
  cognitive development in, 211f, 212, 270–299. *See also* Cognitive development, in middle adolescence
  contexts of, 225–228
    community contexts, 227–228
    family contexts, 225–226
    school contexts, 226–227, 227t
  defined, 202
  described, 202
  emotion and self-esteem in, 326–330, 328f, 329t, 330b–331b, 331t
  identity in, research on, 307–325. *See also* Identity, in middle adolescence
  life-course development in, 211f, 212
  personal projects during, examples of, 331b, 331t
  perspectives on, 200–231
  physical development and maturation in, 211, 211f, 232–269. *See also* Physical development and maturation, in middle adolescence
  social development in, 211f, 212, 336–371. *See also* Social development, in middle adolescence
  theoretical viewpoints on, 212–216, 213f–216f
    life-course theory, 213–216, 214f–216f
    life-span theory, 212–213, 213f
Middle childhood
  affective development in, 130–161. *See also* Affective development, in middle childhood
  biological development in, 60
  brain development in, 71–79. *See also* Brain development
  cognitive development in, 96–129. *See also* Cognitive development, in middle childhood
  contexts of, 50–53, 51b, 52f, 54b–55b, 54f, 56

community contexts, 53, 54b–55b, 54f
family contexts, 50–51
school contexts, 51–53, 51b, 52f
cultural definition of, 34
defined, 34–35, 35f
development in, 44–45, 45f
affective, 44, 45f
after-school programs in, 51–53, 51b, 52f
assumptions about, 34–35
cognitive, 44, 45f
in context, 89–90, 91b–92b, 91f
continuity in, 4–5, 5f
cultural influences on, 41–42, 42f
demographic influences on, 42–43
discontinuity in, 4–5, 5f
linking and practice in, 6
nature *vs.* nurture in, 5
physical development, 44, 45f
social development, 44, 45f
stability *vs.* instability in, 5–6
studies of, 34
technological influences on, 43, 43f
theoretical questions about, 4–6, 5f
theoretical viewpoints of, 45–47, 46f, 48b–50b, 48f
theory and research in, linking of, 6
understanding of, 4–6, 5f
developmental definition of, 34
developmental milestones in, 44–45, 45f
as developmental period, 37–38
developmental perspectives on, 56
developments in, contexts of, 89–90, 91b–92b, 91f
community contexts, 90
family contexts, 89–90
school contexts, 90
free-time activities in, 49b–50b
health and well-being in, 82–89. *See also* Health and well-being, in middle childhood
historical views of, 36–39, 37t, 39b, 40t
history of, 56
modern contributions to understanding, 37–39, 39b, 40t
motor skill development in, 80–82, 80f, 81f, 82b
nature of, 34
perspectives on, 32–57
physical development in, 58–95. *See also* Physical development, in middle childhood
research initiatives on, 39, 40t
self-understanding in, development of, 136–150. *See also* Self-understanding, development of, in middle childhood
social development in, 162–198. *See also* Social development, in middle childhood
studying of, 2–31
change over time, 6–11, 7f, 8b, 10f, 10t
data collection techniques, 11–23, 12f, 14f, 15f, 16b, 18t, 20b, 20f
development, 4–6, 5f. *See also* Development,
reasons for, 35–36
theoretical perspectives on, 56
as transition, 38–39, 40t
"Millennial" generation, 42, 394
Mineral(s), sources of, 85, 87t
Minority(ies), sexual, 350, 350f
Miscarriage, 262
MLCP. *See Making Life Choices Program* (MLCP)
Mnemonic strategies
effective use of, in middle adolescence, 279
in information-processing theory of cognitive development in middle childhood, 113–114, 114t
Mom, Dad, I'm Gay, 362, 363b
Monitoring the Future, 316
Montessori approach, 111b
Mood, emotion and, 326–327
Moral action, through service learning, 177b
Moral character, 171
Moral development, in middle childhood, 169–172
character education in, 175–176, 175f, 176f, 177b, 177t
ethics of care in, 172–173, 173t
fairness in, 173–175, 174t
stages of moral judgment in, 171–172
Moral judgment, 171
stages of, in moral development, 171–172, 171t
Moral motivation, 171
Moral orientations, comparison of, 172–173, 173t
Moral realists, 171
Moral reasoning, 171–172, 171t
Moral relativists, 171
Moral sensitivity, 171
Moral values, 175, 175f
Morality
heteronomous, 171, 171t
instrumental, 171t, 172
interpersonal, 171t, 172
principled, 171t, 172
social system, 171t, 172
social welfare, 171t, 172
Moratorium, 207, 306
example of, 309, 309b, 310t
Motivation
achievement, 146–149, 148b–150b
effectance, 144
extrinsic, 146
intrinsic, 146
moral, 171
student, instructional strategies and, 147, 147f
Motivational process model, 146t
Motor activity, maturation and improvements in, in middle adolescence, 248, 248t
Motor reproduction, in social learning, 164
Motor skills
development of, in middle childhood, 80–82, 80f, 81f, 82b
fine, 81
gross, 80–81, 81f
perceptual-motor skills, 81–82
performance and, in middle adolescence, 247–248, 248t
phases of, 80, 80f
Moving an Out-of-School Agenda, 54b–55b
MUDs. *See* Multiuser domains (MUDs)
Multidisciplinarity, role in transition to adulthood, 381
Multigroup Ethnic Identity Measure, 314
Multiple selves, in adolescence, 303, 303f
Multiple worlds model, 333
Multiuser domains (MUDs), 384b
Muscle mass, in physical development in middle childhood, 69–70, 71f
Musical intelligence, 290
Mutual role-taking, 167–168
Mutual socialization, in peer and friendship networks, 182
Myelin, 73
Myelination, in brain development, 73–74, 74f, 75f
Mythic-literal faith, 317

NAEPs. *See* National Assessments of Educational Progress (NAEPs)
Narrative analysis, 21–22, 24t
NASPE. *See* National Association for Sport and Physical Education (NASPE)

National Assessments of Educational Progress (NAEPs), 279
National Association for Sport and Physical Education (NASPE), 84
National Commission on Excellence in Education, 227
National Council on Family Relations, 387
National Education Association, 203
National Research Council, 38, 51b
National Research Council Board for Children, Youth, and Families, 51b
National Society for the Study of Education, Committee on the Middle School Years of, 38
National Survey of Adolescent Health (Add-Health), 357
National Task Force on Applied Developmental Science, 387
Natural selection, 234
Naturalist intelligence, 290
Naturalistic observational techniques, 13–14, 14f, 18t
"Naturally occurring sex," 264b
Nature
  in human development, 5
  nurture and, interaction of, in physical development in middle childhood, 62, 63f
Nature *vs.* nurture controversy, 60
Need(s)
  agentic, 178
  communal, 178
  hierarchy of, 134, 135f
  survival, 178
Neglect, brain development effects of, 77b–78b, 78f
Neglected children, described, 179, 180
Negotiation, interpersonal, 168–169, 168f, 169t
Negotiator(s), young, program for, 170b
Neighborhood quality, as indication for high-risk involvement among adolescents, 219
"Nemureru ko wo okosu mono dearu," 264b
Neo-Piagetians, 140
Network(s), peer, 181–183, 182f, 183b
Neuron(s), 72
Neuronal development, 72–75, 72f–75f
Neuroscience, behavioral, 62
Neurotransmitter(s), 72, 72f
"New adolescences," 208
New media, 43–44, 43f
Niche(s), 195–196
Niche-picking, in physical development in middle childhood, 62
Noncoital sexual behavior, in middle adolescence, 257–258
Nonconforming, gender, 346
Noninvolvement, as parental reaction to sibling conflicts, 364
Nonshared environments, 61
Norm(s), 12
Normative developmental processes, in emerging adulthood, 388
Normative identity style, 310
Normative risks, 219
Norm-referenced tests, 12
Notre Dame Parenting Project, 263
Novice, defined, 379
Number, 285
Nurture, in human development, 5
Nutrition, in middle childhood, 85–89, 87f, 87t, 88f
Nutritional needs, in middle adolescence, 249, 249t

Obesity, 85–88, 87f, 88f
  defined, 85
Observation
  participant, 22
  structured, 13
  systematic, 13–14, 14f, 18t
Observational techniques, 13–14, 14f, 18t
Occupation, intelligence and, relationship between, 288–289, 288b, 289f
Oedipal complex, 133
On Adolescence, 304
Ontogenesis, 212
Ontogenetic time, 213
Ontogeny, 207
Opening Doors: Students' Perspectives on Juggling Work, Family, and College, 383b
Operant conditioning, 98
Operation, defined, 99
Opportunity(ies)
  in adolescence, research on, 217, 219–223. *See also* Adolescence, risk and opportunity in, research on
  teen, perspectives on, 218b, 219–223. *See also under* Adolescence
Optimization, selective, 213
Oral sex, in middle adolescence, 257–258
Organization, defined, 113
Orientation, interpersonal, 169
Ossification, 68
Overweight children, race and gender and, 85, 87f, 88
Oxford English Dictionary, 378

Paired-association task, 279
"Paradox of youth," 394
Parallel lives, 384b
Parent(s)
  homework help for, 124–125, 125b
  role in transition to adulthood, 381
Parent Effectiveness Training (PET), 137b
Parent-adolescent conflict, in family relationships, 362
Parent-adolescent relationships, identity in, negotiating of, 322b–323b
Parental relationships, in family relationships, 364–366, 365b
Parental role, as indication for high-risk involvement among adolescents, 218
Parenting
  authoritarian, 361
  authoritative, 156–157, 361
  permissive, 361
  quality of, in family relationships, 361–362
Parenting strategies, in social development in middle childhood, 193–194, 194f
Parenting styles, 361
Participant observation, 22
Participation, guided, 109
Passive rehearsal, defined, 113
Pathways through Adolescence, 206
PBL. *See* Problem-based learning (PBL)
Peak experiences, 134, 148
Peer acceptance, 180–181, 180f
Peer influence, as indication for high-risk involvement among adolescents, 218
Peer networks, in middle childhood, 181–183, 182f, 183b
Peer relations, in middle childhood, 178–183
  friendship, 178–183, 179t, 180f, 181b, 182f, 183b
  peer networks, 181–183, 182f, 183b
  popularity, 179–181, 180f, 181b
Perceived mattering scale, 353, 354b
Perceptual speed, 285
Perceptual-motor skills, in middle childhood, 81–82
Performance, motor skills and, in middle adolescence, 247–248, 248t
Performance measures, 12–13

Periods of vulnerability, 77
Permissive parenting, 361
Person(s)
characteristics of, in family relationships in middle adolescence, 360–361
environments and, continuous bidirectional interactions between, in emerging adulthood, 389
in social learning, 165, 165f
Personal fables, 275
Personal projects, adolescent, 331b, 331t
Personality perspectives, in affective development in middle childhood, 132–133, 132f, 134f
Personality psychology, origin of, 132
Personality traits, 140
Person-centered approach, 11
Person-centered theory, in affective development in middle childhood, 135–136, 137b
Perspective(s)
ecocultural, 333
personality, in affective development in middle childhood, 132–133, 132f, 134f
PET. *See* Parent Effectiveness Training (PET)
Petting, in middle adolescence, 257–258
Phenomenological, defined, 135
Pheromone(s), 235b
Phoneme, 121b
Phylogeny, 207
Physical activity
defined, 82
development domains and, relationship between, 83
functions of, 82–84
implications for parents, educators, and practitioners, 83–84
levels of, factors influencing, 83
Physical aggression, defined, 187
Physical development
described, 63
in emerging adulthood, 384f, 385, 386f
maturation and, 232–269. *See also* Physical development and maturation
in middle childhood, 44, 45f, 58–95
biological perspectives on, 62
biology in, 70–71
body fat levels, 69, 70f
brain development, 71–79. *See also* Brain development
changes in body proportions, 67–68, 67f
changes in body size, 63–66, 64f–65f, 65b
environment in, 70–71
genetic perspectives on, 60–61, 61f
genetics in, 70–71
maturation in, 62
muscle mass and, 69–70, 71f
nature and nurture interaction in, 62, 63f
niche-picking in, 62
reaction ranges in, 62, 63f
skeletal development, 68–69, 68f
theoretical viewpoints on, 60–62, 61f, 63f
Physical development and maturation, in middle adolescence, 211, 211f, 232–269
biological maturation, 234–243. *See also* Biological maturation, in middle adolescence
brain development, 243–245, 244f, 246b, 247f. *See also* Brain development, in middle adolescence
contexts of, 265–266
community context, 266
family context, 265
school context, 265–266
health behaviors and, 234
health issues and, 248–256. *See also* Health issues, in middle adolescence, physical development and maturation effects on
motor skills and performance, 247–248, 248t
sexuality, 257–263, 258t, 261f–263f, 264b. *See also* Sexuality, adolescent
theoretical viewpoint on, 234, 235b
timing of, application of evolutionary developmental theory to, 235b
Physical factors, in distributive justice reasoning, 174
Physical theories, in physical development in middle childhood, 62
Piaget's cognitive developmental theory, 98–99
Piaget's formal operational stage
implications for affective and interpersonal development, 276b
in middle adolescence, 272–275, 274f
abstract concepts in, 272–273
generating and evaluating hypotheses in, 273–274
limitations of, 275–277, 276b
thinking about possibilities in, 273
thinking about thought in, 274–275
Piaget's four-stage structural sequence, 385
Plasticity, defined, 78
Play
cooperative, 92b
rough-and-tumble, 83
sociodramatic, 92b
Play behavior, playground design effects on, 91b–92b, 91f
Playground(s), design of, children's play behavior related to, 91b–92b, 91f
Policy, Research, and Intervention for Development in Early Adolescence (PRIDE) project, 206
Politic(s), learning about, by middle adolescents, methods of, 324–325
Political development
defined, 324
in middle adolescence, 324–325, 324f
stages of, 324
Popular children, described, 179, 180
Popularity, in middle childhood, 179–181, 180f, 181b
Positive identity, in adolescent development, 221t
Positive self-regard, 136
Positive values, in adolescent development, 220t
Positivism, logical, 40
Possibility(ies), thinking about, in Piaget's formal operational stage, 273
Possible selves
enhancing identity exploration with, 330b–331b, 331t
in middle adolescence, 328–330, 329t, 330b–331b, 331t
self-esteem and, 328–330, 329t, 330b–331b, 331t
Postconventional moral reasoning, 171t, 172
Postmodern identities, in middle adolescence, 307
Postmodern societies
adolescence in, meanings of, 208–209, 210b
meaning of adulthood in, 382–383, 383b, 384b, 385f

Postmodern spirituality, in middle adolescence, 319
Postmodernism, 40
Postmodernity, 40
Poststructuralism, 209
Practical intelligence, 292f
Pragma, defined, 360t
Pragmatics of language, 119
Preconventional moral reasoning, 171t, 172
Predictive validity, 17
Prefrontal cortex, with prefrontal lobes, 244, 244f
Prefrontal lobes, 244f, 245
Pregnancy, adolescent, 261–263, 262f, 263f, 264b
Pregnancy prevention programs, integrating diversity issues into, 264b
Preoperational stage, of cognitive development, 99
PRIDE project. *See* Policy, Research, and Intervention for Development in Early Adolescence (PRIDE) project
Primary mental abilities, 285
Principled morality, 171t, 172
Private speech, 108
Proactive aggression, 189
Probabilistic, defined, 47
Probabilistic epigenesis, 47
Problem-based learning (PBL), from sociocultural perspective, 278b
Procedural knowledge, 278
Proficient, defined, 247
Program evaluation, 25
Program on Negotiation, at Harvard Law School, 170b
Prompting, in promotion of productive thinking and learning, 280b
Propositional thought, 272
Prosocial behavior, in middle childhood, 184–185, 186t
Protective factors, 217, 218b
  as indicator of positive youth development despite presence of risks in environment among adolescents, 219
Proximal processes, 47
Proximodistal development, 67, 67f
Psychoanalytic theories, in affective development in middle adolescence, 304–306, 304t, 306f
Psychological development, pubertal maturation and, relationship between, 243, 243f
Psychology
  applied developmental, focus of, 387
  evolutionary, 213
  life-span, 212
  personality, origin of, 132
Psychology of flow, 148b–149b, 149f
Psychometric approach to intelligence, in middle adolescence, 282–292
  alternative views of intelligence, 290–292, 291b, 292f
  factors that influence intelligence scores, 289–290
  measures of intelligence, 285–287, 286f, 287f
  relationship of intelligence to academic achievement and occupation, 288–289, 288b, 289f
  theories of intelligence, 284–285
Psychosexual stages, Freud's, 132, 132f
Psychosocial consequences of pubertal timing, 240–241, 242t
Psychosocial stages, Erikson's, 133, 134f
Psychosocial theory, in affective development in middle childhood, 133, 134f
Pubertal growth, factors influencing, 239–240, 240f
Pubertal maturation, secular trend in, 239, 240f
Pubertal process, 234–236, 236f
Pubertal timing
  application of evolutionary developmental theory to, 235b
  psychosocial consequences of, 240–241, 242t
Puberty, 234
  functioning during, 241–243, 242t, 243f
  onset of, 39
  sexuality and, 257
Purpose
  defined, 325
  sense of, 325

Qualitative data
  credibility of, 23
  dependability of, 23
  evaluation of, 22–23
  transferability of, 23
Qualitative data collection, 18–22, 20b, 20f, 24t
  ethnography in, 22, 24t
  interview studies in, 19–21, 20b, 20f, 24t
  narrative studies in, 21–22, 24t
Quality of neighborhood, as indication for high-risk involvement among adolescents, 219
Quantitative data
  evaluation of, 17–18, 18t
  generalizability of, 17–18
  reliability of, 17
  validity of, 17
Quantitative data collection, 11–17, 12f, 14f, 15f, 16b, 18t
  evaluation of, 17–18, 18t
  self-report techniques in, 14–17, 16b, 16f, 18t
  standardized measures in, 12–13, 12f, 18t
  systematic observation in, 13–14, 14f, 18t
Quinceañera, 206

Race, as factor in percentage of children who are overweight, 87f
Racial harassment, in bullying behavior, 188
Racial identity, in middle adolescence, 312–315, 313t
Racial socialization, in middle adolescence, 313
Racial/ethnic identity, in middle adolescence, 312–315, 313t, 315t
Ramona and Her Father, 153b
Reaction range, in physical development in middle childhood, 62, 63f
Reactive aggression, 189
Readiness, 211
Reading, in language development in middle childhood, 120, 121b–122b, 121f
Reading comprehension
  ADHD and, 116b, 117b, 117f
  enhancement of, reciprocal teaching in, 108b
Real self, 144
Reasoning, 285
  analytical, 282
  deductive, 6
  distributive justice, 173–174, 173t
  heuristic, 282
  hypotheticodeductive, 273
  inductive, 6
  justice, *vs.* fairness reasoning, 174, 174t
  moral, 171–172, 171t
  scientific, in middle adolescence, 281–282, 283b–284b, 283f, 284f
Recapitulation theory, 207
Reciprocal determinism, 164–165, 165f
Reciprocal role-taking, 167

Reciprocal teaching, in reading comprehension enhancement, 108b
Redefining of situation, in middle childhood, 151
Referential adequacy, 23
Rehearsal
cumulative, defined, 113
defined, 113
Reinforcement
in social learning, 164
vicarious, 164
Rejected children, described, 179, 180
Relational aggression, defined, 187
Relationship(s)
cognitive model of, 358, 359f
committed, 355
parent-adolescent, identity in, negotiating of, 322b–323b
parental, in family relationships, 364–366, 365b
romantic
adolescents with, percent of, 355, 356f
in middle adolescence, 358–359, 359f
sibling, in social development in middle childhood, 193
stable, 355
Relativism, 385
ethical, 172
Reliability, 12
interrater, 17
of quantitative data, 17
test-retest, 17
Religion
formal, 319
participation in, among adolescents, mapping of, 318b
spirituality, faith and, interrelationships between, 315–316
Religiosity
defined, 316
in middle adolescence, 317, 319
Reproduction, motor, in social learning, 164
Reproductive Transition Group, of MacArthur Foundation, 206
Research
action, 24–25, 25f
applied, in middle childhood development, 6
basic, in middle childhood development, 6
conducting your own, 23–27, 24t, 25f, 26t, 27
developmental, 27
focus groups in, 20b
ethical standards for, 26–27, 26t
longitudinal. *See under* Longitudinal research
practice and, 6
theory and, linking of, 6
Research design
alternative experimental designs, 398, 400t
correlational designs, 398–400, 399f, 400t
experimental designs, 397–398, 397f, 400t
primer in, 397–399, 397f, 399f, 400t
Resilience, 221
defined, 383
Resource(s), government, role in transition to adulthood, 381
Respectability, sexual, 349
Response, construction of, in social information processing, 165, 166f
Response decision, in social information processing, 165, 166f
Responsive prepared environment, in Montessori approach, 111b
Retention, in social learning, 164
Reversibility, 100
Revised Class Play, 181, 181b
Risk(s)
in adolescence, research on, 217–225. *See also* Adolescence, risk and opportunity in, research on
teen, perspectives on, 217–219, 218b
Risk factors, 217, 218b
Rites of passage, 206
Rogerian(s), 137b
Rogerian techniques, 136, 137b, 137t
Role-taking, types of, 167–168
Romance, love and, in middle adolescence, 348–349, 349b
Romantic activities, in adolescence, participation in, 356, 357t
Romantic love, in middle adolescence, 359, 360t
Romantic relationships
adolescents with, percent of, 355, 356f
in middle adolescence, 358–359, 359f
Romantic views, 358, 359f
Rote counting, 123
Rough-and-tumble play, 83
Running, motor skills involved in, 80
Safe Schools/Healthy Students Initiative, 51b
SAT, 288b
Scaffolding, in cognitive development in middle childhood, 108–109, 108b
Schema, 98
School(s)
community, strategies of, 227t
discourses of
sexuality in, 349, 349b
in middle childhood, 51–53, 51b, 52f
School assignments, making more concrete, 105b
School climate, defined, 332
School contexts
in middle adolescence, 226–227, 227t
affective development-related, 332
cognitive development-related, 293–296, 294t, 295f, 296f
physical development and maturation-related, 265–266
social development-related, 367
in middle childhood
affective development-related, 157–158
cognitive development-related, 125–126, 125b
development-related, 90
social development-related, 194–195, 197f
School grades, expectations related to, as indication for high-risk involvement among adolescents, 218
School performance, ADHD and, 116b, 117b, 117f
School-age children, defined, 42, 43f
Schoolnotes.com, 125b
School/workplace context, in emerging adulthood, 391–393, 392f
Science, developmental, 388
Scientific reasoning, in middle adolescence, 281–282, 283b–284b, 283f, 284f
Scouts, 53
Search Institute, 224
Secondary sex characteristics, development of, in middle adolescence, 234, 236–237, 237t
Section 8 housing vouchers, 383b
Secular trends, 38
in growth, 65
Secure attachment, 339
Selective attention, 113

Selective optimization, 213
Self(ves)
  ideal, 144
  multiple, in adolescence, 303, 303f
  possible
    enhancing identity exploration with, 330b–331b, 331t
    in middle adolescence, 328–330, 329t, 330b–331b, 331t
    self-esteem and, 328–330, 329t, 330b–331b, 331t
  real, 144
Self-actualization, defined, 134
Self-actualization theory, in affective development in middle childhood, 134–135, 135f, 136b
Self-competence, 136, 138–140, 139t, 145b
Self-completion, 329, 329t
Self-concept, 136, 138–140, 139t
Self-determination, 148
Self-disciplined learning, in Montessori approach, 111b
Self-discrepancy, 311
Self-efficacy, 136, 144–149, 146t, 147f, 148b–150b
Self-esteem, 136, 140–144, 141b, 142f–144f, 145b
  affective experiences and, 328
  defined, 327
  in middle adolescence, 327–330, 328f, 329t, 330b–331b, 331t
  possible selves and, 328–330, 329t, 330b–331b, 331t
  ratings of competence as predictors of, 141, 142f
Self-esteem matrix, 138, 138f
Self-evaluative information seeking, laboratory study of, 150b
Self-experiences, 148
Self-guiding speech, 108
Self-interest, in distributive justice reasoning, 174
Self-monitoring, 115
Self-motivated activity, in Montessori approach, 111b
Self-prototypical, 330b
Self-regard, positive, 136
Self-regulation
  emotion and, relationship between, 185, 186t
  temperament and, 155–156
Self-report techniques, 14–17, 16b, 16f, 18t
Self-transcendence, 134
Self-understanding
  development of, in middle childhood, 136–150
    approaches to, 136–138, 138f
    ideal self in, 144, 145b
    self-competence in, 136, 138–140, 139t, 145b
    self-concept in, 136, 138–140, 139t
    self-efficacy, 136, 144–149, 146t, 147f, 148b–150b
    self-esteem in, 136, 140–144, 141b, 142f–144f, 145b
    self-worth in, 136, 141–144, 142f–144f, 145b
  developmental model of, 302, 302f
Self-worth, 136, 141–144, 142f–144f, 145b
  hierarchy of, 141, 143f
Semantic development, 119
Semantic differential of emotions, 137t
Semenarche, 237
Semistructured interview questions, 20b
Sense(s), discrimination among, improvement in, 81
Sense of industry, 133
Sense of purpose, 325
Sensitive periods, 78–79, 79f
Sensitivity, moral, 171
Sensorimotor stage, of cognitive development, 99
Sensory register, 110
Seriation, in concrete operational period, 103, 104f
Seriation task, 104f
Service learning, moral action through, 177b
SES. *See* Socioeconomic status (SES)
Sex
  advantages of, 359
  oral, in middle adolesence, 257–258
Sex education programs, integrating diversity issues into, 264b
Sex-role inventory, adolescent, 343, 344b
Sexual autonomy, 349
Sexual behavior, noncoital, in middle adolescence, 257–258
Sexual debut, 258
Sexual disclosure, in middle adolescence, 349–350, 350t
Sexual harassment, in bullying behavior, 188
Sexual identification, predicted sequence of, 350, 350t
Sexual identity, 258
Sexual intercourse, in middle adolescence, 258, 258t
Sexual minority, 350, 350f
Sexual orientation, 258
Sexual respectability, 349
Sexuality
  adolescent, 257–263, 258t, 261f–263f, 264b
    AIDS, 261, 261f
    contraceptive use, 259–261
    gay, lesbian, and bisexual orientations, 258–259
    HIV infection, 261, 261f
    noncoital sexual behavior, 257–258
    pregnancy, 261–263, 262f, 263f, 264b
    sexual intercourse, 258, 258t
    STDs, 261
  discourses of, in schools, 349, 349b
  puberty and, 257
  social constructions of, in middle adolescence, 346–351, 348f, 349b, 350t, 351f
    bodies and appearance, 348, 348f
    ethnic differences, 350–351, 351f
    love and romance, 348–349, 349b
    sexual disclosure in, 349–350, 350t
Sexuality Information and Education Council of the United States (SIECUS), 367
Sexually transmitted diseases (STDs), in middle adolescence, 261
Sexual-minority adolescents, unique risk factors for, 219
Shading, 119
Shared environments, 61
Short of stature (SS), psychosocial and cognitive consequences of, 66
Short-term memory, 110
Short-term store (STS) capacity, 112–113
Sibling interactions
  in family relationships, 362–364, 363b
    parental involvement in, 364
  styles of, 363
Sibling relationships, in social development in middle childhood, 193
SIECUS. *See* Sexuality Information and Education Council of the United States (SIECUS)
"Single parasites," 208
Situation(s), redefining of, in middle childhood, 151
Skeletal development, 68–69, 68f
Skeletal size, in middle adolescence, 239
Skinfold(s), 69
Skinfold caliper, 69
Sleep, in middle adolescence, 250, 252

Smoking, cigarette, in middle adolescence, 253–256, 255t
Social address variables, 195
Social and moral understanding, in middle childhood, 167–176. *See also specific area, e.g.,* Moral development, in middle childhood
  interpersonal understanding, 167–169, 168f, 168t, 169t, 170b
  moral understanding, 169–172
Social behavior, in middle childhood, 183–191
  antisocial behavior, 185, 187–191, 187f, 189b, 190b, 190t, 191f
  prosocial behavior, 184–185, 186t
Social cognitive theory, 164–165, 165f
Social comparison, 140
Social competence
  defined, 164, 183
  model of, 183, 184f
Social competencies, in adolescent development, 220t–221t
Social construction, 40
  of childhood, 40–41
Social conventions, 171
Social desirability bias, 15
Social development
  in adolescence, described, 338
  in emerging adulthood, 386f, 387
  in middle adolescence, 211f, 212, 336–371
    contexts of, 366–368, 368t
      community contexts, 367–368
      family contexts, 366–367
      school contexts, 367
    gender identity in, 341, 343–346, 344b, 345t, 347b
    gender in. *See also* Gender identity, in middle adolescence
    sexuality in, social constructions of, 346–351, 348f, 349b, 350t, 351f.
    theoretical viewpoints on, 338–341, 338t, 339f, 340f, 342f
      attachment perspectives, 338–340, 338t, 339t, 340f
      family systems perspectives, 341, 342f
  in middle childhood, 44, 45f, 162–198. *See also specific topics, e.g.,* Peer relations, in middle childhood
    contexts of, 192–196
      community contexts, 195–196
      family contexts, 193–194, 193f, 194f
      school contexts, 194–195, 197f
    described, 164
    peer relations, 178–183
    social and moral understanding in, 167–176. *See also* Social and moral understanding, in middle childhood
    social behavior, 183–191
    social information processing, 165–166, 166f
    social learning in, 164–165
    social skills, 183–191
    social theories of mind in, 166–167
    theoretical viewpoints on, 164–167, 165f, 166f
Social Development Research Group, 224
Social information processing, in middle childhood, 165–166, 166f
Social informational role-taking, 167
Social integration, 53, 54b–55b, 195
Social learning, 164–165
Social learning theory, 164–165
Social norms, 172
Social perspective-taking, stages of, 168, 168t
Social policy implications, of research on risk and opportunity in adolescence, 223–226
Social provisions, 178
Social reproduction, 209
Social selection, in peer and friendship networks, 182
Social skills, in middle childhood, 183–191
Social status, in middle childhood, 179–181, 180f, 181b
Social system morality, 171t, 172
Social theories of mind, in middle childhood, 166–167
Social welfare morality, 171t, 172
Social-identity theory, in affective development in middle adolescence, 307
Socialization
  mutual, in peer and friendship networks, 182
  racial, in middle adolescence, 313
Social-psychological theory, 306–307
Society(ies), postmodern
  meaning of adolescence in, 208–209, 210b
  meaning of adulthood in, 382–383, 383b, 384b, 385f
Society for Research in Child Development, 26, 387
Society for Research on Adolescence, 208, 387
Sociocultural perspective
  on cognitive development in middle childhood, 107–110, 107f, 108b, 109f
    basis of, 109
    culture in, 109–110, 111b
    scaffolding in, 108–109, 108b
    ZPD in, 107–108
  problem-based learning from, 278b
Sociodemographics, in peer and friendship networks, 182
Sociodramatic play, 92b
Socioeconomic status (SES), intelligence scores effects of, 289
Sociogram, 180, 180f
Sociometric classification of group acceptance, 180, 180f
Soma, 72
Somatic growth, in middle adolescence, 237–239, 238f
Space, 285
Spatial intelligence, 290
Spatial tasks, types of, 295f
Spatial-temporal integration, 328
Specimen record, 13
Speech
  private, 108
  self-guiding, 108
Speed, perceptual, 285
Speed of processing, in information-processing theory of cognitive development in middle childhood, 113
Spirituality
  defined, 316
  faith, religion and, interrelationships between, 315–316
  postmodern, in middle adolescence, 319
Spiritual/religious identity, in middle adolescence, 315–319, 316f, 318f
Spontaneous abortion, 262, 262f
Spontaneous activity, in Montessori approach, 111b
Sports participation, in middle childhood, 84–85, 86b
SS. *See* Short of stature (SS)
Stability, in human development, 5–6
Stable relationships, 355
Standard deviation, 287
Standardized tests, 12–13, 12f, 18t
Stanford-Binet Intelligence Scale, Fifth Edition, 285
Stature, described, 67, 67f
Status, advantages of, 359
STDs. *See* Sexually transmitted diseases (STDs)

STEP. *See* Systematic Training for Effective Parenting (STEP)
Storge, defined, 360t
"Storm and stress," 202
Strange Situation, 339
Strength(s)
  developmental, 219
  differences between males and females, 69, 71f
Stress, defined, 77b
Structuralism, 209
Structured interview, 19–21, 20b, 20f
Structured observation, 13
STS capacity. *See* Short-term store (STS) capacity
Student(s), homework help for, 124–125, 125b
Student motivation, instructional strategies and, 147, 147f
Study Group on Adolescence in the 21st Century, 208
Sturm und drang, 202
Substance use and abuse, in middle adolescence, 252–256, 253f, 254b, 255t, 256t
Successful intelligence, 290
Superego, 132
Support, in adolescent development, 220t
Supreme Court, 283b
Survival needs, 178
Symbolic interaction, 306–307
Symbolic interaction theory, in affective development in middle adolescence, 307
Synapse, 72
Synaptic pruning, 73
Synaptic transmission, 72, 72f
Synaptogenesis, in brain development, 73, 74f
Syntax development, in language development in middle childhood, 119
Synthetic-conventional faith, 317
Systematic observation, 13–14, 14f, 18t
Systematic Training for Effective Parenting (STEP), 137b
Systems theory, 341

Task Force on Middle Childhood, 39
Task Force on the Education of Young Adolescents, 53
Taure'are, 378
Teacher(s), support for competence by, 144, 145b
Teacher Effectiveness Training (TET), 137b
Teaching, reciprocal, in reading comprehension enhancement, 108b
Technological influences, in middle childhood, 43, 43f
Teen opportunities, perspectives on, 218b, 219–223, 220t–221t, 222b, 222f, 223f, 224t. *See also under* Adolescence
Teen risks, research on, 217–219, 218b. *See also under* Adolescence
Temperament
  defined, 154
  dimensions of, 154, 155f
  emotions and, 154, 155f
  in middle childhood, 154–156, 155f, 156b
  self-regulation and, 155–156
Teratogen(s), 78b
Test-retest reliability, 17
TET. *See* Teacher Effectiveness Training (TET)
The American High School Today, 204
The Black Child Development Institute, 387
The Cardinal Principles of Secondary Education, 203
The Child from Five to Ten, 37
The Forgotten Half: Non–College-Bound Youth in America, 204, 379
The Forgotten Half Revisited, 379, 380
The Heritage of Latin America, 291b
The International Society for Infant Studies, 387
The Interpersonal Theory of Psychiatry, 178
The Network on Transitions to Adulthood, 380, 381b
The Relationship Code, 361
The Rise and Fall of the American Teenager, 207
Theoretical issues, 27
Theory, research and, linking of, 6
Thinking
  convergent, 292
  divergent, 292
Thought
  propositional, 272
  thinking about, in Piaget's formal operational stage, 274–275
Throwing, motor skills involved in, 80
Time sampling, 13–14, 14f
Tissue(s), adipose, 69
Tooth (teeth), wisdom, 385
Toward a Psychology of Being, 134
Trait(s), personality, 140
Transescence, 39
Transferability, of qualitative data, 23
Transformation, 100
Transformation task, 103f
Transgender, defined, 346
Transition, middle childhood as part of, 38–39, 40t
Transition through Adolescence, 206
Traumatic stress, brain effects of, 77b, 78f
Traumatology, developmental, 77b
Triangulation, 23
Triarchic model of intelligence, 290–291, 291b
Trust, basic, 133
Turning Points: Preparing American Youth for the Twenty-First Century, 126
Turning Points 2000, 53
21st Century Community Learning Center Program, 51b
21st Century Learning Centers, 226
Typical interaction, among siblings, in middle adolescence, 363

Understanding
  epistemological, 279–280
  interpersonal, in middle childhood, 167–169, 168f, 168t, 169t, 170b
  social and moral, in middle childhood, 167–176. *See also* Social and moral understanding, in middle childhood
Understanding and Reasoning subscales of *MacCat-CA,* 283b–284b, 283f
United Nations, 41, 209
University of California, 288b
U.S. Bureau of Education, 203
U.S. Commission on Behavioral and Social Sciences and Education, 38
U.S. Committee on Child Development Research and Public Policy, 38
U.S. Constitution, 378
U.S. Department of Education, 51b
  Elementary School Recognition Program of, 175–176, 176f
U.S. Supreme Court, 204

Validity, 12
  predictive, 17
  of quantitative data, 17
Value(s)
  moral, 175, 175f
  positive, in adolescent development, 220t
Variable(s), defined, 9
Variable-centered approach, 9, 11
Verbal aggression, defined, 187
Verbal comprehension, 285

Vicarious reinforcement, 164
Vietnam, military involvement in, 207
Vitamin(s), sources of, 85, 87t
Vocational/political identity
  defined, 320
  in middle adolescence, 319–325, 321t, 322b–323b, 324f
    career development, 320–324, 321t, 322b–323b
    political development in, 324–325, 324f
Voting Rights Act of 1965, 378
Vulnerability, periods of, 77
Vygotsky's theory, 278b

"War on Poverty," 204
Weather, exercise effects on children in, 84, 86b
Wechsler Scale of Intelligence for Children, Fourth Edition, 12
Wechsler Scales, 285
Weight, distance curves for, 63, 64f–65f
Weight gain, in middle adolescence, 238–239, 238f
"What I am Like" scale, sample items from, 138, 139t
What Teens Need to Succeed: Prove, Practical Ways to Shape Your Own Future, 202
William T. Grant Foundation, 204, 379
Wisdom teeth, 385
Within-person change, in early adulthood, 387
Woman, ideal, cross-cultural drawings of, in nontraditional role, 346, 347b
Word fluency, 285
Work, economy and, as factor in transition to adulthood, 380
Workplace/school context, in emerging adulthood, 391–393, 392f
Worth, conditions of, 136
Writing, in language development in middle childhood, 120, 122–123

Yale Child Study Center, 37
Yale University, 204
YMCA, 53
Young adulthood, defined, 374
Young Negotiators, 170b
Youth
  of color, factors affecting development of, 221
  described, 379
  ethnic-minority, career counseling with, 323b
Youth: The Years from Ten to Sixteen, 37
Youth and Dissent: The Rise of a New Opposition, 379
Youth Crisis: Growing Up in a High Risk Society, 202
Youth cultures, construction of, 210b
Youth development programs, characteristics of, 224t
Youth Risk Behavior Survey, 259
  online, of CDC, 254, 255t
YWCA, 53

Zone of proximal development (ZPD), 107–108
ZPD. *See* Zone of proximal development (ZPD)